THE
COMPLETE OXFORD
SHAKESPEARE

VOLUME III · TRAGEDIES

General Editors
STANLEY WELLS AND GARY TAYLOR

Editors
STANLEY WELLS, GARY TAYLOR
JOHN JOWETT, AND WILLIAM MONTGOMERY

With Introductions by
STANLEY WELLS

OXFORD UNIVERSITY PRESS

Oxford University Press, Walton Street, Oxford OX2 6DP

Oxford New York Toronto
Delhi Bombay Calcutta Madras Karachi
Kuala Lumpur Singapore Hong Kong Tokyo
Nairobi Dar es Salaam Cape Town
Melbourne Auckland Madrid
and associated companies in
Berlin Ibadan

Oxford is a trade mark of Oxford University Press

Published in the United States
by Oxford University Press Inc., New York

© Oxford University Press 1987

First published 1987
Reprinted 1988, 1989 (twice), 1990
First published in paperback 1994

British Library Cataloguing in Publication Data
Shakespeare, William
[Works]. The Oxford library: the complete
works of William Shakespeare.
I. Title   II. Wells, Stanley, 1930–
III. Taylor, Gary   IV. William Shakespeare, the complete works
822.3'3   PR2754
ISBN 0–19–818274–0 (Pbk)

Library of Congress Cataloging in Publication Data
Shakespeare, William, 1564–1616.
The complete Oxford Shakespeare.
Contents: v. 1. The histories—v. 2. The comedies—v. 3. The tragedies.
I. Wells, Stanley, W., 1930–   .   II. Taylor, Gary.
III. Title   IV. Series.
PR2754.W45 1987   822.3'3   87–7850
ISBN 0–19–818274–0 (Pbk)

Printed in Spain
by Printer Industria Gráfica SA

CONTENTS

TITUS ANDRONICUS

SHAKESPEARE'S first, most sensation-packed tragedy appeared in print in 1594, and a performance record dating from January of that year appears to indicate that it was then a new play. But according to its title-page it had been acted by three companies, one of which was bankrupt by the summer of 1593; and the play's style, too, suggests that it was written earlier. Shakespeare seems to have added a scene after the play's earliest performances, for Act 3, Scene 2 was first printed in the 1623 Folio. The 1594 performance record may refer to the revised play, not the original, or to the play's first London performance after plague had closed the theatres from June 1592.

By convention, Elizabethan tragedies treated historical subjects, and *Titus Andronicus* is set in Rome during the fourth century AD; but its story (like that of Shakespeare's other early tragedy, *Romeo and Juliet*) is fictitious. Whether Shakespeare invented it is an open question: the same tale is told in both a ballad and a chap-book which survive only in eighteenth-century versions but which could derive from pre-Shakespearian originals. Even if Shakespeare knew these works, they could have supplied only a skeletal narrative. His play's spirit and style owe much to Ovid's *Metamorphoses*, one of his favourite works of classical literature, which he actually brings on stage in Act 4, Scene 1. Ovid's tale of the rape of Philomela was certainly in Shakespeare's mind as he wrote, and the play's more horrific elements owe something to the Roman dramatist Seneca.

In its time, *Titus Andronicus* was popular, perhaps because it combines sensational incident with high-flown rhetoric of a kind that was fashionable around 1590. It tells a story of double revenge. Tamora, Queen of the Goths, seeks revenge on her captor, Titus, for the ritual slaughter of her son Alarbus; she achieves it when her other sons, Chiron and Demetrius, rape and mutilate Titus' daughter, Lavinia. Later, Titus himself seeks revenge on Tamora and her husband, Saturninus, after Tamora's black lover, Aaron, has falsely led him to believe that he can save his sons' lives by allowing his own hand to be chopped off. Though he is driven to madness, Titus, with his brother Marcus and his last surviving son, Lucius, achieves a spectacular sequence of vengeance in which he cuts Tamora's sons' throats, serves their flesh baked in a pie to their mother, kills Lavinia to save her from her shame, and stabs Tamora to death. Then, in rapid succession, Saturninus kills Titus and is himself killed by Lucius, who, as the new Emperor, is left with Marcus to bury the dead, to punish Aaron, and 'To heal Rome's harms and wipe away her woe'.

In *Titus Andronicus*, as in his early history plays, Shakespeare is at his most successful in the expression of grief and the portrayal of vigorously energetic evil. The play's piling of horror upon horror can seem ludicrous, and the reader may be surprised by the apparent disjunction between terrifying events and the measured verse in which characters react; but a few remarkable modern productions have revealed that the play may still arouse pity as well as terror in its audiences.

THE PERSONS OF THE PLAY

SATURNINUS, eldest son of the late Emperor of Rome; later Emperor

BASSIANUS, his brother

TITUS ANDRONICUS, a Roman nobleman, general against the Goths

LUCIUS
QUINTUS
MARTIUS } sons of Titus
MUTIUS

LAVINIA, daughter of Titus

YOUNG LUCIUS, a boy, son of Lucius

MARCUS ANDRONICUS, a tribune of the people, Titus' brother

PUBLIUS, his son

SEMPRONIUS
CAIUS } kinsmen of Titus
VALENTINE

A CAPTAIN

AEMILIUS

TAMORA, Queen of the Goths, later wife of Saturninus

ALARBUS
DEMETRIUS } her sons
CHIRON

AARON, a Moor, her lover

A NURSE

A CLOWN

Senators, tribunes, Romans, Goths, soldiers, and attendants

The Most Lamentable Roman Tragedy of
Titus Andronicus

1.1 ⌈*Flourish.*⌉ *Enter the Tribunes and Senators aloft,*
and then enter below Saturninus and his followers
at one door and Bassianus and his followers ⌈*at the*
other, with drummer and colours⌉

SATURNINUS
Noble patricians, patrons of my right,
Defend the justice of my cause with arms.
And countrymen, my loving followers,
Plead my successive title with your swords.
I am his first-born son that was the last   5
That ware the imperial diadem of Rome.
Then let my father's honours live in me,
Nor wrong mine age with this indignity.

BASSIANUS
Romans, friends, followers, favourers of my right,
If ever Bassianus, Caesar's son,   10
Were gracious in the eyes of royal Rome,
Keep then this passage to the Capitol,
And suffer not dishonour to approach
The imperial seat, to virtue consecrate,
To justice, continence, and nobility;   15
But let desert in pure election shine,
And, Romans, fight for freedom in your choice.

⌈*Enter*⌉ *Marcus Andronicus* ⌈*aloft*⌉ *with the crown*

MARCUS
Princes that strive by factions and by friends
Ambitiously for rule and empery,
Know that the people of Rome, for whom we stand   20
A special party, have by common voice
In election for the Roman empery
Chosen Andronicus, surnamèd *Pius*
For many good and great deserts to Rome.
A nobler man, a braver warrior,   25
Lives not this day within the city walls.
He by the Senate is accited home
From weary wars against the barbarous Goths,
That with his sons, a terror to our foes,
Hath yoked a nation strong, trained up in arms.   30
Ten years are spent since first he undertook
This cause of Rome, and chastisèd with arms
Our enemies' pride. Five times he hath returned
Bleeding to Rome, bearing his valiant sons
In coffins from the field.   35
And now at last, laden with honour's spoils,
Returns the good Andronicus to Rome,
Renownèd Titus, flourishing in arms.
Let us entreat by honour of his name
Whom worthily you would have now succeeded,   40
And in the Capitol and Senate's right,
Whom you pretend to honour and adore,
That you withdraw you and abate your strength,

Dismiss your followers, and, as suitors should,
Plead your deserts in peace and humbleness.   45

SATURNINUS
How fair the Tribune speaks to calm my thoughts.

BASSIANUS
Marcus Andronicus, so I do affy
In thy uprightness and integrity,
And so I love and honour thee and thine,
Thy noble brother Titus and his sons,   50
And her to whom my thoughts are humbled all,
Gracious Lavinia, Rome's rich ornament,
That I will here dismiss my loving friends
And to my fortunes and the people's favour
Commit my cause in balance to be weighed.   55

⌈*Exeunt his soldiers and followers*⌉

SATURNINUS
Friends that have been thus forward in my right,
I thank you all, and here dismiss you all,
And to the love and favour of my country
Commit myself, my person, and the cause.

⌈*Exeunt his soldiers and followers*⌉

(*To the Tribunes and Senators*)
Rome, be as just and gracious unto me   60
As I am confident and kind to thee.
Open the gates and let me in.

BASSIANUS
Tribunes, and me, a poor competitor.

⌈*Flourish.*⌉ *They go up into the Senate House.*
Enter a Captain

CAPTAIN
Romans, make way. The good Andronicus,
Patron of virtue, Rome's best champion,   65
Successful in the battles that he fights,
With honour and with fortune is returned
From where he circumscribèd with his sword
And brought to yoke the enemies of Rome.

Sound drums and trumpets, and then enter Martius
and Mutius, two of Titus' sons, and then ⌈*men*
bearing coffins⌉ *covered with black, then Lucius and*
Quintus, two other sons; then Titus Andronicus ⌈*in*
his chariot⌉ *and then Tamora the Queen of Goths*
and her sons Alarbus, Chiron, and Demetrius, with
Aaron the Moor and others as many as can be.
Then set down the ⌈*coffins*⌉, *and Titus speaks*

TITUS
Hail, Rome, victorious in thy mourning weeds!   70
Lo, as the bark that hath discharged his freight
Returns with precious lading to the bay
From whence at first she weighed her anchorage,
Cometh Andronicus, bound with laurel bows,
To re-salute his country with his tears,   75

Tears of true joy for his return to Rome.
Thou great defender of this Capitol,
Stand gracious to the rites that we intend.
Romans, of five-and-twenty valiant sons,
Half of the number that King Priam had,   80
Behold the poor remains, alive and dead.
These that survive let Rome reward with love;
These that I bring unto their latest home,
With burial amongst their ancestors.
Here Goths have given me leave to sheathe my sword.
Titus unkind, and careless of thine own,   86
Why suffer'st thou thy sons unburied yet
To hover on the dreadful shore of Styx?
Make way to lay them by their brethren.
    They open the tomb
There greet in silence as the dead are wont,   90
And sleep in peace, slain in your country's wars.
O sacred receptacle of my joys,
Sweet cell of virtue and nobility,
How many sons hast thou of mine in store
That thou wilt never render to me more!   95
LUCIUS
Give us the proudest prisoner of the Goths,
That we may hew his limbs and on a pile
Ad manes fratrum sacrifice his flesh
Before this earthy prison of their bones,
That so the shadows be not unappeased,   100
Nor we disturbed with prodigies on earth.
TITUS
I give him you, the noblest that survives,
The eldest son of this distressèd Queen.
TAMORA ⌈*kneeling*⌉
Stay, Roman brethren! Gracious conqueror,
Victorious Titus, rue the tears I shed—   105
A mother's tears in passion for her son—
And if thy sons were ever dear to thee,
O, think my son to be as dear to me!
Sufficeth not that we are brought to Rome
To beautify thy triumphs, and return   110
Captive to thee and to thy Roman yoke;
But must my sons be slaughtered in the streets
For valiant doings in their country's cause?
O, if to fight for king and commonweal
Were piety in thine, it is in these.   115
Andronicus, stain not thy tomb with blood.
Wilt thou draw near the nature of the gods?
Draw near them then in being merciful.
Sweet mercy is nobility's true badge.
Thrice-noble Titus, spare my first-born son.   120
TITUS
Patient yourself, madam, and pardon me.
These are their brethren whom your Goths beheld
Alive and dead, and for their brethren slain
Religiously they ask a sacrifice.
To this your son is marked, and die he must   125
T'appease their groaning shadows that are gone.
LUCIUS
Away with him, and make a fire straight,

And with our swords upon a pile of wood
Let's hew his limbs till they be clean consumed.
    Exeunt Titus' sons with Alarbus
TAMORA ⌈*rising*⌉
O cruel irreligious piety!   130
CHIRON
Was never Scythia half so barbarous.
DEMETRIUS
Oppose not Scythia to ambitious Rome.
Alarbus goes to rest, and we survive
To tremble under Titus' threat'ning look.
Then, madam, stand resolved; but hope withal   135
The selfsame gods that armed the Queen of Troy
With opportunity of sharp revenge
Upon the Thracian tyrant in his tent
May favour Tamora, the Queen of Goths—
When Goths were Goths and Tamora was queen—   140
To quit her bloody wrongs upon her foes.
    Enter Quintus, Marcus, Mutius, and Lucius, the
    sons of Andronicus, again, with bloody swords
LUCIUS
See, lord and father, how we have performed
Our Roman rites. Alarbus' limbs are lopped
And entrails feed the sacrificing fire,
Whose smoke like incense doth perfume the sky.   145
Remaineth naught but to inter our brethren
And with loud 'larums welcome them to Rome.
TITUS
Let it be so, and let Andronicus
Make this his latest farewell to their souls.
    ⌈*Flourish.*⌉ *Then sound trumpets and lay the*
    ⌈*coffins*⌉ *in the tomb*
In peace and honour rest you here, my sons;   150
Rome's readiest champions, repose you here in rest,
Secure from worldly chances and mishaps.
Here lurks no treason, here no envy swells,
Here grow no damnèd drugs, here are no storms,
No noise, but silence and eternal sleep.   155
In peace and honour rest you here, my sons.
    Enter Lavinia
LAVINIA
In peace and honour live Lord Titus long,
My noble lord and father, live in fame.
Lo, at this tomb my tributary tears
I render for my brethren's obsequies,   160
(*Kneeling*) And at thy feet I kneel with tears of joy
Shed on this earth for thy return to Rome.
O, bless me here with thy victorious hand,
Whose fortunes Rome's best citizens applaud.
TITUS
Kind Rome, that hast thus lovingly reserved   165
The cordial of mine age to glad my heart!
Lavinia, live; outlive thy father's days
And fame's eternal date, for virtue's praise.
    ⌈*Lavinia rises*⌉
MARCUS ⌈*aloft*⌉
Long live Lord Titus, my belovèd brother,
Gracious triumpher in the eyes of Rome!   170

TITUS
Thanks, gentle Tribune, noble brother Marcus.
MARCUS
And welcome, nephews, from successful wars,
You that survive and you that sleep in fame.
Fair lords, your fortunes are alike in all,
That in your country's service drew your swords,   175
But safer triumph is this funeral pomp
That hath aspired to Solon's happiness
And triumphs over chance in honour's bed.
Titus Andronicus, the people of Rome,
Whose friend in justice thou hast ever been,   180
Send thee by me, their tribune and their trust,
This palliament of white and spotless hue,
And name thee in election for the empire
With these our late-deceasèd emperor's sons.
Be *candidatus* then, and put it on,   185
And help to set a head on headless Rome.
TITUS
A better head her glorious body fits
Than his that shakes for age and feebleness.
What should I don this robe and trouble you?—
Be chosen with proclamations today,   190
Tomorrow yield up rule, resign my life,
And set abroad new business for you all.
Rome, I have been thy soldier forty years,
And led my country's strength successfully,
And buried one-and-twenty valiant sons,   195
Knighted in field, slain manfully in arms
In right and service of their noble country.
Give me a staff of honour for mine age,
But not a sceptre to control the world.
Upright he held it, lords, that held it last.   200
MARCUS
Titus, thou shalt obtain and ask the empery.
SATURNINUS
Proud and ambitious Tribune, canst thou tell?
TITUS
Patience, Prince Saturninus.
SATURNINUS   Romans, do me right.
Patricians, draw your swords, and sheathe them not
Till Saturninus be Rome's emperor.   205
Andronicus, would thou were shipped to hell
Rather than rob me of the people's hearts!
LUCIUS
Proud Saturnine, interrupter of the good
That noble-minded Titus means to thee.
TITUS
Content thee, Prince. I will restore to thee   210
The people's hearts, and wean them from themselves.
BASSIANUS
Andronicus, I do not flatter thee
But honour thee, and will do till I die.
My faction if thou strengthen with thy friends
I will most thankful be; and thanks to men   215
Of noble minds is honourable meed.
TITUS
People of Rome, and people's tribunes here,
I ask your voices and your suffrages.
Will ye bestow them friendly on Andronicus?
TRIBUNES
To gratify the good Andronicus   220
And gratulate his safe return to Rome
The people will accept whom he admits.
TITUS
Tribunes, I thank you, and this suit I make:
That you create our emperor's eldest son
Lord Saturnine, whose virtues will, I hope,   225
Reflect on Rome as Titan's rays on earth,
And ripen justice in this commonweal.
Then if you will elect by my advice,
Crown him and say, 'Long live our Emperor!'
MARCUS
With voices and applause of every sort,   230
Patricians and plebeians, we create
Lord Saturninus Rome's great emperor,
And say, 'Long live our Emperor Saturnine!'
⌈*A long flourish while Marcus and the other
Tribunes, with Saturninus and Bassianus,
come down.*
*Marcus invests Saturninus in the white
palliament and hands him a sceptre*⌉
SATURNINUS
Titus Andronicus, for thy favours done
To us in our election this day   235
I give thee thanks in part of thy deserts,
And will with deeds requite thy gentleness.
And for an onset, Titus, to advance
Thy name and honourable family,
Lavinia will I make my empress,   240
Rome's royal mistress, mistress of my heart,
And in the sacred Pantheon her espouse.
Tell me, Andronicus, doth this motion please thee?
TITUS
It doth, my worthy lord, and in this match
I hold me highly honoured of your grace,   245
And here in sight of Rome to Saturnine,
King and commander of our commonweal,
The wide world's emperor, do I consecrate
My sword, my chariot, and my prisoners—
Presents well worthy Rome's imperious lord.   250
Receive them, then, the tribute that I owe,
Mine honour's ensigns humbled at thy feet.
SATURNINUS
Thanks, noble Titus, father of my life.
How proud I am of thee and of thy gifts
Rome shall record; and when I do forget   255
The least of these unspeakable deserts,
Romans, forget your fealty to me.
TITUS (*to Tamora*)
Now, madam, are you prisoner to an emperor,
To him that for your honour and your state
Will use you nobly, and your followers.   260
SATURNINUS
A goodly lady, trust me, of the hue
That I would choose were I to choose anew.

Clear up, fair queen, that cloudy countenance.
Though chance of war hath wrought this change of
　　cheer,
Thou com'st not to be made a scorn in Rome.　　265
Princely shall be thy usage every way.
Rest on my word, and let not discontent
Daunt all your hopes. Madam, he comforts you
Can make you greater than the Queen of Goths.
Lavinia, you are not displeased with this?　　270

LAVINIA
Not I, my lord, sith true nobility
Warrants these words in princely courtesy.

SATURNINUS
Thanks, sweet Lavinia. Romans, let us go.
Ransomless here we set our prisoners free.　　274
Proclaim our honours, lords, with trump and drum.
　　　　　⌈Flourish. Exeunt Saturninus, Tamora,
　　　　　Demetrius, Chiron, and Aaron the Moor⌉

BASSIANUS
Lord Titus, by your leave, this maid is mine.

TITUS
How, sir, are you in earnest then, my lord?

BASSIANUS
Ay, noble Titus, and resolved withal
To do myself this reason and this right.

MARCUS
Suum cuique is our Roman justice.　　280
This prince in justice seizeth but his own.

LUCIUS
And that he will and shall, if Lucius live.

TITUS
Traitors, avaunt! Where is the Emperor's guard?

MUTIUS
Brothers, help to convey her hence away,
And with my sword I'll keep this door safe.　　285
　　　　　Exeunt Bassianus, Marcus, Quintus, and
　　　　　Martius, with Lavinia
(*To Titus*) My lord, you pass not here.

TITUS　　　　　　　What, villain boy,
Barr'st me my way in Rome?
　　　He attacks Mutius

MUTIUS　　　　　　Help, Lucius, help!
　　　Titus kills him

LUCIUS (*to Titus*)
My lord, you are unjust; and more than so,
In wrongful quarrel you have slain your son.

TITUS
Nor thou nor he are any sons of mine.　　290
My sons would never so dishonour me.
Traitor, restore Lavinia to the Emperor.

LUCIUS
Dead, if you will, but not to be his wife
That is another's lawful promised love.
　　　　　Exit with Mutius' body
　　　Enter aloft Saturninus the Emperor with Tamora
　　　and Chiron and Demetrius, her two sons, and
　　　Aaron the Moor

TITUS
Follow, my lord, and I'll soon bring her back.　　295

SATURNINUS
No, Titus, no. The Emperor needs her not,
Nor her, nor thee, nor any of thy stock.
I'll trust by leisure him that mocks me once,
Thee never, nor thy traitorous haughty sons,
Confederates all thus to dishonour me.　　300
Was none in Rome to make a stale
But Saturnine? Full well, Andronicus,
Agree these deeds with that proud brag of thine
That saidst I begged the empire at thy hands.

TITUS
O monstrous, what reproachful words are these?　　305

SATURNINUS
But go thy ways, go give that changing piece
To him that flourished for her with his sword.
A valiant son-in-law thou shalt enjoy,
One fit to bandy with thy lawless sons,
To ruffle in the commonwealth of Rome.　　310

TITUS
These words are razors to my wounded heart.

SATURNINUS
And therefore, lovely Tamora, Queen of Goths,
That like the stately Phoebe 'mongst her nymphs
Dost overshine the gallant'st dames of Rome,
If thou be pleased with this my sudden choice,　　315
Behold, I choose thee, Tamora, for my bride,
And will create thee Empress of Rome.
Speak, Queen of Goths, dost thou applaud my choice?
And here I swear by all the Roman gods,
Sith priest and holy water are so near,　　320
And tapers burn so bright, and everything
In readiness for Hymenaeus stand,
I will not re-salute the streets of Rome,
Or climb my palace, till from forth this place
I lead espoused my bride along with me.　　325

TAMORA
And here, in sight of heaven, to Rome I swear
If Saturnine advance the Queen of Goths
She will a handmaid be to his desires,
A loving nurse, a mother to his youth.

SATURNINUS
Ascend, fair Queen, Pantheon. Lords, accompany　　330
Your noble emperor and his lovely bride,
Sent by the heavens for Prince Saturnine,
Whose wisdom hath her fortune conquerèd.
There shall we consummate our spousal rites.
　　　　　　　Exeunt all but Titus

TITUS
I am not bid to wait upon this bride.　　335
Titus, when wert thou wont to walk alone,
Dishonoured thus and challengèd of wrongs?
　　　Enter Marcus and Titus' sons Lucius, Quintus, and
　　　Martius, ⌈carrying Mutius' body⌉

MARCUS
O Titus, see, O see what thou hast done—
In a bad quarrel slain a virtuous son.

TITUS
No, foolish Tribune, no; no son of mine,　　340
Nor thou, nor these, confederates in the deed

That hath dishonoured all our family;
Unworthy brother and unworthy sons!
LUCIUS
But let us give him burial as becomes,
Give Mutius burial with our brethren.   345
TITUS
Traitors, away, he rests not in this tomb.
This monument five hundred years hath stood,
Which I have sumptuously re-edified.
Here none but soldiers and Rome's servitors
Repose in fame, none basely slain in brawls.   350
Bury him where you can; he comes not here.
MARCUS
My lord, this is impiety in you.
My nephew Mutius' deeds do plead for him.
He must be buried with his brethren.
⌜QUINTUS and MARTIUS⌝
And shall, or him we will accompany.   355
TITUS
'And shall'? What villain was it spake that word?
⌜QUINTUS⌝
He that would vouch it in any place but here.
TITUS
What, would you bury him in my despite?
MARCUS
No, noble Titus, but entreat of thee
To pardon Mutius and to bury him.   360
TITUS
Marcus, even thou hast struck upon my crest,
And with these boys mine honour thou hast
        wounded.
My foes I do repute you every one,
So trouble me no more, but get you gone.
⌜MARTIUS⌝
He is not with himself, let us withdraw.   365
⌜QUINTUS⌝
Not I, till Mutius' bones be burièd.
        Marcus, Lucius, Quintus, and Martius kneel
MARCUS
Brother, for in that name doth nature plead—
⌜QUINTUS⌝
Father, and in that name doth nature speak—
TITUS
Speak thou no more, if all the rest will speed.
MARCUS
Renownèd Titus, more than half my soul—   370
LUCIUS
Dear father, soul and substance of us all—
MARCUS
Suffer thy brother Marcus to inter
His noble nephew here in virtue's nest,
That died in honour and Lavinia's cause.
Thou art a Roman; be not barbarous.   375
The Greeks upon advice did bury Ajax,
That slew himself; and wise Laertes' son
Did graciously plead for his funerals.
Let not young Mutius then, that was thy joy,
Be barred his entrance here.
TITUS   Rise, Marcus, rise.   380

The dismall'st day is this that e'er I saw,
To be dishonoured by my sons in Rome.
Well, bury him, and bury me the next.
        They put Mutius in the tomb
LUCIUS
There lie thy bones, sweet Mutius, with thy friends',
Till we with trophies do adorn thy tomb.   385
ALL ⌜BUT TITUS⌝ (kneeling)
No man shed tears for noble Mutius;
He lives in fame, that died in virtue's cause.
        Exeunt ⌜all but Marcus and Titus⌝
MARCUS
My lord—to step out of these dreary dumps—
How comes it that the subtle Queen of Goths
Is of a sudden thus advanced in Rome?   390
TITUS
I know not, Marcus, but I know it is—
Whether by device or no, the heavens can tell.
Is she not then beholden to the man
That brought her for this high good turn so far?
⌜MARCUS⌝
Yes, and will nobly him remunerate.   395
        ⌜Flourish.⌝ Enter the Emperor Saturninus, Tamora,
        and her two sons (Chiron and Demetrius), with
        Aaron the Moor at one door.
        Enter at the other door Bassianus and Lavinia with
        ⌜Lucius, Quintus, and Martius⌝
SATURNINUS
So, Bassianus, you have played your prize.
God give you joy, sir, of your gallant bride.
BASSIANUS
And you of yours, my lord. I say no more,
Nor wish no less; and so I take my leave.
SATURNINUS
Traitor, if Rome have law or we have power,   400
Thou and thy faction shall repent this rape.
BASSIANUS
'Rape' call you it, my lord, to seize my own—
My true betrothèd love, and now my wife?
But let the laws of Rome determine all;
Meanwhile am I possessed of that is mine.   405
SATURNINUS
'Tis good, sir; you are very short with us.
But if we live we'll be as sharp with you.
BASSIANUS
My lord, what I have done, as best I may
Answer I must, and shall do with my life.
Only thus much I give your grace to know: 410
By all the duties that I owe to Rome,
This noble gentleman, Lord Titus here,
Is in opinion and in honour wronged,
That, in the rescue of Lavinia,
With his own hand did slay his youngest son   415
In zeal to you, and highly moved to wrath
To be controlled in that he frankly gave.
Receive him then to favour, Saturnine,
That hath expressed himself in all his deeds
A father and a friend to thee and Rome.   420

TITUS
Prince Bassianus, leave to plead my deeds.
'Tis thou and those that have dishonoured me.
⌐He kneels⌐
Rome and the righteous heavens be my judge
How I have loved and honoured Saturnine!
TAMORA (*to Saturninus*)
My worthy lord, if ever Tamora   425
Were gracious in those princely eyes of thine,
Then hear me speak indifferently for all;
And at my suit, sweet, pardon what is past.
SATURNINUS
What, madam—be dishonoured openly
And basely put it up without revenge?   430
TAMORA
Not so, my lord. The gods of Rome forfend
I should be author to dishonour you.
But on mine honour dare I undertake
For good lord Titus' innocence in all,
Whose fury not dissembled speaks his griefs.   435
Then at my suit look graciously on him.
Lose not so noble a friend on vain suppose,
Nor with sour looks afflict his gentle heart.
(*Aside to Saturninus*)
My lord, be ruled by me, be won at last,
Dissemble all your griefs and discontents.   440
You are but newly planted in your throne;
Lest then the people, and patricians too,
Upon a just survey take Titus' part,
And so supplant you for ingratitude,
Which Rome reputes to be a heinous sin,   445
Yield at entreats; and then let me alone:
I'll find a day to massacre them all,
And raze their faction and their family,
The cruel father and his traitorous sons
To whom I sued for my dear son's life,   450
And make them know what 'tis to let a queen
Kneel in the streets and beg for grace in vain.
(*Aloud*) Come, come, sweet Emperor; come,
    Andronicus,
Take up this good old man, and cheer the heart
That dies in tempest of thy angry frown.   455
SATURNINUS
Rise, Titus, rise; my empress hath prevailed.
TITUS (*rising*)
I thank your majesty and her, my lord,
These words, these looks, infuse new life in me.
TAMORA
Titus, I am incorporate in Rome,
A Roman now adopted happily,   460
And must advise the Emperor for his good.
This day all quarrels die, Andronicus;
And let it be mine honour, good my lord,
That I have reconciled your friends and you.
For you, Prince Bassianus, I have passed   465
My word and promise to the Emperor
That you will be more mild and tractable.
And fear not, lords, and you, Lavinia;

By my advice, all humbled on your knees,
You shall ask pardon of his majesty.   470
    ⌐*Bassianus*⌐, *Lavinia, Lucius, Quintus, and*
    Martius kneel
⌐LUCIUS⌐
We do, and vow to heaven and to his highness
That what we did was mildly as we might,
Tend'ring our sister's honour and our own.
MARCUS ⌐*kneeling*⌐
That on mine honour here do I protest.
SATURNINUS
Away, and talk not, trouble us no more.   475
TAMORA
Nay, nay, sweet Emperor, we must all be friends.
The Tribune and his nephews kneel for grace.
I will not be denied; sweetheart, look back.
SATURNINUS
Marcus, for thy sake and thy brother's here,
And at my lovely Tamora's entreats,   480
I do remit these young men's heinous faults.
Stand up!
    Marcus, Bassianus, Lavinia, and Titus' sons stand
        Lavinia, though you left me like a churl,
I found a friend, and sure as death I swore
I would not part a bachelor from the priest.
Come, if the Emperor's court can feast two brides   485
You are my guest, Lavinia, and your friends.
This day shall be a love-day, Tamora.
TITUS
Tomorrow an it please your majesty
To hunt the panther and the hart with me,   489
With horn and hound we'll give your grace *bonjour*.
SATURNINUS
Be it so, Titus, and gramercy, too.   ⌐*Flourish. Exeunt*⌐

❀

2.1   ⌐*Enter Aaron alone*⌐
AARON
Now climbeth Tamora Olympus' top,
Safe out of fortune's shot, and sits aloft,
Secure of thunder's crack or lightning flash,
Advanced above pale envy's threat'ning reach.
As when the golden sun salutes the morn   5
And, having gilt the ocean with his beams,
Gallops the zodiac in his glistering coach
And overlooks the highest-peering hills,
So Tamora.
Upon her wit doth earthly honour wait,   10
And virtue stoops and trembles at her frown.
Then, Aaron, arm thy heart and fit thy thoughts
To mount aloft with thy imperial mistress,
And mount her pitch whom thou in triumph long
Hast prisoner held fettered in amorous chains,   15
And faster bound to Aaron's charming eyes
Than is Prometheus tied to Caucasus.
Away with slavish weeds and servile thoughts!
I will be bright, and shine in pearl and gold
To wait upon this new-made empress.   20

To wait, said I?—to wanton with this queen,
This goddess, this Semiramis, this nymph,
This siren that will charm Rome's Saturnine
And see his shipwreck and his commonweal's.
Hollo, what storm is this?   25
   Enter Chiron and Demetrius, braving
DEMETRIUS
Chiron, thy years wants wit, thy wits wants edge
And manners to intrude where I am graced
And may, for aught thou knowest, affected be.
CHIRON
Demetrius, thou dost overween in all,
And so in this, to bear me down with braves.   30
'Tis not the difference of a year or two
Makes me less gracious, or thee more fortunate.
I am as able and as fit as thou
To serve, and to deserve my mistress' grace,
And that my sword upon thee shall approve,   35
And plead my passions for Lavinia's love.
AARON (*aside*)
Clubs, clubs! These lovers will not keep the peace.
DEMETRIUS
Why, boy, although our mother, unadvised,
Gave you a dancing-rapier by your side,
Are you so desperate grown to threat your friends?   40
Go to, have your lath glued within your sheath
Till you know better how to handle it.
CHIRON
Meanwhile, sir, with the little skill I have
Full well shalt thou perceive how much I dare.
DEMETRIUS
Ay, boy, grow ye so brave?
   They draw
AARON   Why, how now, lords?   45
So near the Emperor's palace dare ye draw
And maintain such a quarrel openly?
Full well I wot the ground of all this grudge.
I would not for a million of gold
The cause were known to them it most concerns,   50
Nor would your noble mother for much more
Be so dishonoured in the court of Rome.
For shame, put up.
DEMETRIUS   Not I, till I have sheathed
My rapier in his bosom, and withal
Thrust those reproachful speeches down his throat   55
That he hath breathed in my dishonour here.
CHIRON
For that I am prepared and full resolved,
Foul-spoken coward, that thund'rest with thy tongue,
And with thy weapon nothing dar'st perform.
AARON   Away, I say.   60
Now, by the gods that warlike Goths adore,
This petty brabble will undo us all.
Why, lords, and think you not how dangerous
It is to jet upon a prince's right?
What, is Lavinia then become so loose,   65
Or Bassianus so degenerate,
That for her love such quarrels may be broached

Without controlment, justice, or revenge?
Young lords, beware; and should the Empress know
This discord's ground, the music would not please.   70
CHIRON
I care not, I, knew she and all the world,
I love Lavinia more than all the world.
DEMETRIUS
Youngling, learn thou to make some meaner choice.
Lavinia is thine elder brother's hope.
AARON
Why, are ye mad? Or know ye not in Rome   75
How furious and impatient they be,
And cannot brook competitors in love?
I tell you, lords, you do but plot your deaths
By this device.
CHIRON   Aaron, a thousand deaths
Would I propose to achieve her whom I love.   80
AARON
To achieve her how?
DEMETRIUS   Why makes thou it so strange?
She is a woman, therefore may be wooed;
She is a woman, therefore may be won;
She is Lavinia, therefore must be loved.
What, man, more water glideth by the mill   85
Than wots the miller of, and easy it is
Of a cut loaf to steal a shive, we know.
Though Bassianus be the Emperor's brother,
Better than he have worn Vulcan's badge.
AARON (*aside*)
Ay, and as good as Saturninus may.   90
DEMETRIUS
Then why should he despair that knows to court it
With words, fair looks, and liberality?
What, hast not thou full often struck a doe
And borne her cleanly by the keeper's nose?
AARON
Why then, it seems some certain snatch or so   95
Would serve your turns.
CHIRON   Ay, so the turn were served.
DEMETRIUS
Aaron, thou hast hit it.
AARON   Would you had hit it too,
Then should not we be tired with this ado.
Why, hark ye, hark ye, and are you such fools
To square for this? Would it offend you then   100
That both should speed?
CHIRON   Faith, not me.
DEMETRIUS   Nor me, so I were one.
AARON
For shame, be friends, and join for that you jar.
'Tis policy and stratagem must do   105
That you affect, and so must you resolve
That what you cannot as you would achieve,
You must perforce accomplish as you may.
Take this of me: Lucrece was not more chaste
Than this Lavinia, Bassianus' love.   110
A speedier course than ling'ring languishment
Must we pursue, and I have found the path.

My lords, a solemn hunting is in hand;
There will the lovely Roman ladies troop.
The forest walks are wide and spacious,   115
And many unfrequented plots there are,
Fitted by kind for rape and villainy.
Single you thither then this dainty doe,
And strike her home by force, if not by words,
This way or not at all stand you in hope.   120
Come, come; our Empress, with her sacred wit
To villainy and vengeance consecrate,
Will we acquaint with all what we intend,
And she shall file our engines with advice
That will not suffer you to square yourselves,   125
But to your wishes' height advance you both.
The Emperor's court is like the house of Fame,
The palace full of tongues, of eyes and ears,
The woods are ruthless, dreadful, deaf, and dull.
There speak and strike, brave boys, and take your
    turns.   130
There serve your lust, shadowed from heaven's eye,
And revel in Lavinia's treasury.
CHIRON
Thy counsel, lad, smells of no cowardice.
DEMETRIUS
Sit fas aut nefas, till I find the stream
To cool this heat, a charm to calm these fits,   135
Per Styga, per manes vehor.   *Exeunt*

2.2   *Enter Titus Andronicus and his three sons (Quintus,*
         Lucius, and Martius), and Marcus, making a noise
         with hounds and horns
TITUS
The hunt is up, the morn is bright and grey,
The fields are fragrant and the woods are green.
Uncouple here, and let us make a bay
And wake the Emperor and his lovely bride,
And rouse the Prince, and ring a hunter's peal,   5
That all the court may echo with the noise.
Sons, let it be your charge, as it is ours,
To attend the Emperor's person carefully.
I have been troubled in my sleep this night,
But dawning day new comfort hath inspired.   10
   Here a cry of hounds, and wind horns in a peal;
   then enter Saturninus, Tamora, Bassianus, Lavinia,
   Chiron, Demetrius, and their attendants
Many good-morrows to your majesty.
Madam, to you as many, and as good.
I promisèd your grace a hunter's peal.
SATURNINUS
And you have rung it lustily, my lords,
Somewhat too early for new-married ladies.   15
BASSIANUS
Lavinia, how say you?
LAVINIA   I say no.
I have been broad awake two hours and more.
SATURNINUS
Come on then, horse and chariots let us have,

And to our sport. (*To Tamora*) Madam, now shall ye
    see
Our Roman hunting.
MARCUS   I have dogs, my lord,   20
Will rouse the proudest panther in the chase,
And climb the highest promontory top.
TITUS
And I have horse will follow where the game
Makes way, and run like swallows o'er the plain.
DEMETRIUS (*aside*)
Chiron, we hunt not, we, with horse nor hound,   25
But hope to pluck a dainty doe to ground.   *Exeunt*

2.3   *Enter Aaron alone, with gold*
AARON
He that had wit would think that I had none,
To bury so much gold under a tree
And never after to inherit it.
Let him that thinks of me so abjectly
Know that this gold must coin a stratagem   5
Which, cunningly effected, will beget
A very excellent piece of villainy.
And so repose, sweet gold, for their unrest
That have their alms out of the Empress' chest.
   He hides the gold.
   Enter Tamora alone to the Moor
TAMORA
My lovely Aaron, wherefore look'st thou sad   10
When everything doth make a gleeful boast?
The birds chant melody on every bush,
The snakes lies rollèd in the cheerful sun,
The green leaves quiver with the cooling wind
And make a chequered shadow on the ground.   15
Under their sweet shade, Aaron, let us sit,
And whilst the babbling echo mocks the hounds,
Replying shrilly to the well-tuned horns,
As if a double hunt were heard at once,
Let us sit down and mark their yellowing noise,   20
And after conflict such as was supposed
The wand'ring prince and Dido once enjoyed
When with a happy storm they were surprised,
And curtained with a counsel-keeping cave,
We may, each wreathèd in the other's arms,   25
Our pastimes done, possess a golden slumber
Whiles hounds and horns and sweet melodious birds
Be unto us as is a nurse's song
Of lullaby to bring her babe asleep.
AARON
Madam, though Venus govern your desires,   30
Saturn is dominator over mine.
What signifies my deadly-standing eye,
My silence, and my cloudy melancholy,
My fleece of woolly hair that now uncurls
Even as an adder when she doth unroll   35
To do some fatal execution?
No, madam, these are no venereal signs.
Vengeance is in my heart, death in my hand,

Blood and revenge are hammering in my head.
Hark, Tamora, the empress of my soul,   40
Which never hopes more heaven than rests in thee,
This is the day of doom for Bassianus.
His Philomel must lose her tongue today,
Thy sons make pillage of her chastity
And wash their hands in Bassianus' blood.   45
Seest thou this letter? (*Giving a letter*) Take it up, I
      pray thee,
And give the King this fatal-plotted scroll.
Now question me no more. We are espied.
Here comes a parcel of our hopeful booty,
Which dreads not yet their lives' destruction.   50
      Enter Bassianus and Lavinia
TAMORA (*aside to Aaron*)
Ah, my sweet Moor, sweeter to me than life!
AARON (*aside to Tamora*)
No more, great Empress; Bassianus comes.
Be cross with him, and I'll go fetch thy sons
To back thy quarrels, whatsoe'er they be.   *Exit*
BASSIANUS
Who have we here? Rome's royal empress   55
Unfurnished of her well-beseeming troop?
Or is it Dian, habited like her
Who hath abandonèd her holy groves
To see the general hunting in this forest?
TAMORA
Saucy controller of my private steps,   60
Had I the power that some say Dian had,
Thy temples should be planted presently
With horns, as was Actaeon's, and the hounds
Should drive upon thy new-transformèd limbs,
Unmannerly intruder as thou art!   65
LAVINIA
Under your patience, gentle Empress,
'Tis thought you have a goodly gift in horning,
And to be doubted that your Moor and you
Are singled forth to try experiments.
Jove shield your husband from his hounds today—   70
'Tis pity they should take him for a stag.
BASSIANUS
Believe me, Queen, your swart Cimmerian
Doth make your honour of his body's hue,
Spotted, detested, and abominable.
Why are you sequestered from all your train,   75
Dismounted from your snow-white goodly steed,
And wandered hither to an obscure plot,
Accompanied but with a barbarous Moor,
If foul desire had not conducted you?
LAVINIA
And being intercepted in your sport,   80
Great reason that my noble lord be rated
For sauciness. (*To Bassianus*) I pray you, let us hence,
And let her joy her raven-coloured love.
This valley fits the purpose passing well.
BASSIANUS
The King my brother shall have note of this.   85

LAVINIA
Ay, for these slips have made him noted long.
Good King, to be so mightily abused!
TAMORA
Why have I patience to endure all this?
      Enter Chiron and Demetrius
DEMETRIUS
How now, dear sovereign and our gracious mother,
Why doth your highness look so pale and wan?   90
TAMORA
Have I not reason, think you, to look pale?
These two have 'ticed me hither to this place.
A barren detested vale you see it is;
The trees, though summer, yet forlorn and lean,
Overcome with moss and baleful mistletoe.   95
Here never shines the sun, here nothing breeds
Unless the nightly owl or fatal raven,
And when they showed me this abhorrèd pit
They told me here at dead time of the night
A thousand fiends, a thousand hissing snakes,   100
Ten thousand swelling toads, as many urchins
Would make such fearful and confusèd cries
As any mortal body hearing it
Should straight fall mad or else die suddenly.
No sooner had they told this hellish tale   105
But straight they told me they would bind me here
Unto the body of a dismal yew
And leave me to this miserable death.
And then they called me foul adulteress,
Lascivious Goth, and all the bitterest terms   110
That ever ear did hear to such effect.
And had you not by wondrous fortune come,
This vengeance on me had they executed.
Revenge it as you love your mother's life,
Or be ye not henceforward called my children.   115
DEMETRIUS
This is a witness that I am thy son.
      He stabs Bassianus
CHIRON
And this for me, struck home to show my strength.
      He stabs Bassianus, who dies.
      ⌈*Tamora turns to Lavinia*⌉
LAVINIA
Ay, come, Semiramis—nay, barbarous Tamora,
For no name fits thy nature but thy own.
TAMORA (*to Chiron*)
Give me the poniard. You shall know, my boys,   120
Your mother's hand shall right your mother's wrong.
DEMETRIUS
Stay, madam, here is more belongs to her.
First thresh the corn, then after burn the straw.
This minion stood upon her chastity,
Upon her nuptial vow, her loyalty,   125
And with that quaint hope braves your mightiness.
And shall she carry this unto her grave?
CHIRON
An if she do I would I were an eunuch.

Drag hence her husband to some secret hole,
And make his dead trunk pillow to our lust.   130
TAMORA
But when ye have the honey ye desire
Let not this wasp outlive, us both to sting.
CHIRON
I warrant you, madam, we will make that sure.
Come, mistress, now perforce we will enjoy
That nice-preservèd honesty of yours.   135
LAVINIA
O Tamora, thou bearest a woman's face—
TAMORA
I will not hear her speak. Away with her!
LAVINIA
Sweet lords, entreat her hear me but a word.
DEMETRIUS (to Tamora)
Listen, fair madam, let it be your glory
To see her tears, but be your heart to them   140
As unrelenting flint to drops of rain.
LAVINIA
When did the tiger's young ones teach the dam?
O, do not learn her wrath! She taught it thee.
The milk thou sucked'st from her did turn to marble,
Even at thy teat thou hadst thy tyranny.   145
Yet every mother breeds not sons alike.
(To Chiron) Do thou entreat her show a woman's pity.
CHIRON
What, wouldst thou have me prove myself a bastard?
LAVINIA
'Tis true, the raven doth not hatch a lark.
Yet have I heard—O, could I find it now!—   150
The lion, moved with pity, did endure
To have his princely paws pared all away.
Some say that ravens foster forlorn children
The whilst their own birds famish in their nests.
O, be to me, though thy hard heart say no,   155
Nothing so kind, but something pitiful.
TAMORA
I know not what it means. Away with her!
LAVINIA
O, let me teach thee for my father's sake,
That gave thee life when well he might have slain
thee.
Be not obdurate, open thy deaf ears.   160
TAMORA
Hadst thou in person ne'er offended me
Even for his sake am I pitiless.
Remember, boys, I poured forth tears in vain
To save your brother from the sacrifice,
But fierce Andronicus would not relent.   165
Therefore away with her, and use her as you will—
The worse to her, the better loved of me.
LAVINIA
O Tamora, be called a gentle queen,
And with thine own hands kill me in this place;
For 'tis not life that I have begged so long;   170
Poor I was slain when Bassianus died.
TAMORA
What begg'st thou then, fond woman? Let me go.

LAVINIA
'Tis present death I beg, and one thing more
That womanhood denies my tongue to tell.
O, keep me from their worse-than-killing lust,   175
And tumble me into some loathsome pit
Where never man's eye may behold my body.
Do this, and be a charitable murderer.
TAMORA
So should I rob my sweet sons of their fee.
No, let them satisfy their lust on thee.   180
DEMETRIUS (to Lavinia)
Away, for thou hast stayed us here too long.
LAVINIA
No grace, no womanhood—ah, beastly creature,
The blot and enemy to our general name,
Confusion fall—
CHIRON
Nay then, I'll stop your mouth. (To Demetrius) Bring
thou her husband.   185
This is the hole where Aaron bid us hide him.
      Demetrius and Chiron cast Bassianus' body into the
      pit ⌈and cover the mouth of it with branches⌉, then
      exeunt dragging Lavinia
TAMORA
Farewell, my sons. See that you make her sure.
Ne'er let my heart know merry cheer indeed
Till all the Andronici be made away.
Now will I hence to seek my lovely Moor,   190
And let my spleenful sons this trull deflower.   Exit
      Enter Aaron with Quintus and Martius, two of
      Titus' sons
AARON
Come on, my lords, the better foot before.
Straight will I bring you to the loathsome pit
Where I espied the panther fast asleep.
QUINTUS
My sight is very dull, whate'er it bodes.   195
MARTIUS
And mine, I promise you. Were it not for shame,
Well could I leave our sport to sleep awhile.
      He falls into the pit
QUINTUS
What, art thou fallen? What subtle hole is this,
Whose mouth is covered with rude-growing briers,
Upon whose leaves are drops of new-shed blood   200
As fresh as morning dew distilled on flowers?
A very fatal place it seems to me.
Speak, brother. Hast thou hurt thee with the fall?
MARTIUS
O brother, with the dismall'st object hurt
That ever eye with sight made heart lament.   205
AARON (aside)
Now will I fetch the King to find them here,
That he thereby may have a likely guess
How these were they that made away his brother.
                                             Exit
MARTIUS
Why dost not comfort me and help me out
From this unhallowed and bloodstainèd hole?   210

QUINTUS
I am surprisèd with an uncouth fear.
A chilling sweat o'erruns my trembling joints;
My heart suspects more than mine eye can see.
MARTIUS
To prove thou hast a true-divining heart,
Aaron and thou look down into this den,   215
And see a fearful sight of blood and death.
QUINTUS
Aaron is gone, and my compassionate heart
Will not permit mine eyes once to behold
The thing whereat it trembles by surmise.
O, tell me who it is, for ne'er till now   220
Was I a child to fear I know not what.
MARTIUS
Lord Bassianus lies berayed in blood
All on a heap, like to a slaughtered lamb,
In this detested, dark, blood-drinking pit.
QUINTUS
If it be dark how dost thou know 'tis he?   225
MARTIUS
Upon his bloody finger he doth wear
A precious ring that lightens all this hole,
Which like a taper in some monument
Doth shine upon the dead man's earthy cheeks
And shows the ragged entrails of this pit.   230
So pale did shine the moon on Pyramus
When he by night lay bathed in maiden blood.
O brother, help me with thy fainting hand—
If fear hath made thee faint, as me it hath—
Out of this fell devouring receptacle,   235
As hateful as Cocytus' misty mouth.
QUINTUS
Reach me thy hand, that I may help thee out,
Or, wanting strength to do thee so much good,
I may be plucked into the swallowing womb
Of this deep pit, poor Bassianus' grave.   240
I have no strength to pluck thee to the brink,
MARTIUS
Nor I no strength to climb without thy help.
QUINTUS
Thy hand once more, I will not loose again
Till thou art here aloft or I below.
Thou canst not come to me; I come to thee.   245
    He falls into the pit.
    Enter Saturninus the Emperor ⌈with attendants⌉,
    and Aaron the Moor
SATURNINUS
Along with me! I'll see what hole is here,
And what he is that now is leapt into it.
    He speaks into the pit
Say, who art thou that lately didst descend
Into this gaping hollow of the earth?
MARTIUS
The unhappy sons of old Andronicus,   250
Brought hither in a most unlucky hour
To find thy brother Bassianus dead.
SATURNINUS
My brother dead! I know thou dost but jest.

He and his lady both are at the lodge
Upon the north side of this pleasant chase.   255
'Tis not an hour since I left them there.
MARTIUS
We know not where you left them all alive,
But, out alas, here have we found him dead!
    Enter Tamora, Titus Andronicus, and Lucius
TAMORA Where is my lord the King?
SATURNINUS
Here, Tamora, though gripped with killing grief.   260
TAMORA
Where is thy brother Bassianus?
SATURNINUS
Now to the bottom dost thou search my wound.
Poor Bassianus here lies murderèd.
TAMORA
Then all too late I bring this fatal writ,
The complot of this timeless tragedy,   265
And wonder greatly that man's face can fold
In pleasing smiles such murderous tyranny.
    She giveth Saturnine a letter
SATURNINUS (*reads*)
'An if we miss to meet him handsomely,
Sweet huntsman—Bassianus 'tis we mean—
Do thou so much as dig the grave for him.   270
Thou know'st our meaning. Look for thy reward
Among the nettles at the elder tree
Which overshades the mouth of that same pit
Where we decreed to bury Bassianus.
Do this, and purchase us thy lasting friends.'   275
O Tamora, was ever heard the like!
This is the pit, and this the elder tree.
Look, sirs, if you can find the huntsman out
That should have murdered Bassianus here.
AARON
My gracious lord, here is the bag of gold.   280
SATURNINUS (*to Titus*)
Two of thy whelps, fell curs of bloody kind,
Have here bereft my brother of his life.
Sirs, drag them from the pit unto the prison.
There let them bide until we have devised
Some never-heard-of torturing pain for them.   285
TAMORA
What, are they in this pit? O wondrous thing!
How easily murder is discoverèd!
    Attendants drag Quintus, Martius, and Bassianus'
    body from the pit
TITUS (*kneeling*)
High Emperor, upon my feeble knee
I beg this boon with tears not lightly shed:
That this fell fault of my accursèd sons—   290
Accursèd if the fault be proved in them—
SATURNINUS
If it be proved? You see it is apparent.
Who found this letter? Tamora, was it you?
TAMORA
Andronicus himself did take it up.
TITUS
I did, my lord, yet let me be their bail,   295

For by my father's reverend tomb I vow
They shall be ready at your highness' will
To answer their suspicion with their lives.　298
SATURNINUS
Thou shalt not bail them. See thou follow me.
Some bring the murdered body, some the murderers.
Let them not speak a word—the guilt is plain;
For by my soul, were there worse end than death
That end upon them should be executed.　⌜Exit⌝
TAMORA
Andronicus, I will entreat the King.
Fear not thy sons, they shall do well enough.　305
TITUS ⌜rising⌝
Come, Lucius, come, stay not to talk with them.
　　　　　　　　　　　　　　　Exeunt

2.4　Enter the Empress' sons, Chiron and Demetrius,
　　with Lavinia, her hands cut off and her tongue cut
　　out, and ravished
DEMETRIUS
So, now go tell, an if thy tongue can speak,
Who 'twas that cut thy tongue and ravished thee.
CHIRON
Write down thy mind, bewray thy meaning so,
An if thy stumps will let thee play the scribe.
DEMETRIUS
See how with signs and tokens she can scrawl.　5
CHIRON (to Lavinia)
Go home, call for sweet water, wash thy hands.
DEMETRIUS
She hath no tongue to call nor hands to wash,
And so let's leave her to her silent walks.
CHIRON
An 'twere my cause I should go hang myself.
DEMETRIUS
If thou hadst hands to help thee knit the cord.　10
　　　　　　　　Exeunt Chiron and Demetrius
　　⌜Wind horns.⌝ Enter Marcus from hunting to
　　Lavinia
MARCUS
Who is this—my niece that flies away so fast?
Cousin, a word. Where is your husband?
If I do dream, would all my wealth would wake me.
If I do wake, some planet strike me down
That I may slumber an eternal sleep.　15
Speak, gentle niece, what stern ungentle hands
Hath lopped and hewed and made thy body bare
Of her two branches, those sweet ornaments
Whose circling shadows kings have sought to sleep in,
And might not gain so great a happiness　20
As half thy love. Why dost not speak to me?
Alas, a crimson river of warm blood,
Like to a bubbling fountain stirred with wind,
Doth rise and fall between thy rosèd lips,
Coming and going with thy honey breath.　25
But sure some Tereus hath deflowered thee
And, lest thou shouldst detect him, cut thy tongue.
Ah, now thou turn'st away thy face for shame,
And notwithstanding all this loss of blood,

As from a conduit with three issuing spouts,　30
Yet do thy cheeks look red as Titan's face
Blushing to be encountered with a cloud.
Shall I speak for thee? Shall I say 'tis so?
O that I knew thy heart, and knew the beast,
That I might rail at him to ease my mind!　35
Sorrow concealèd, like an oven stopped,
Doth burn the heart to cinders where it is.
Fair Philomel, why she but lost her tongue
And in a tedious sampler sewed her mind.
But, lovely niece, that mean is cut from thee.　40
A craftier Tereus, cousin, hast thou met,
And he hath cut those pretty fingers off
That could have better sewed than Philomel.
O, had the monster seen those lily hands
Tremble like aspen leaves upon a lute　45
And make the silken strings delight to kiss them,
He would not then have touched them for his life.
Or had he heard the heavenly harmony
Which that sweet tongue hath made,
He would have dropped his knife and fell asleep,　50
As Cerberus at the Thracian poet's feet.
Come, let us go and make thy father blind,
For such a sight will blind a father's eye.
One hour's storm will drown the fragrant meads:
What will whole months of tears thy father's eyes?　55
Do not draw back, for we will mourn with thee.
O, could our mourning ease thy misery!　Exeunt

3.1　Enter the Judges, Tribunes, and Senators with Titus'
　　two sons, Martius and Quintus, bound, passing
　　⌜over⌝ the stage to the place of execution, and Titus
　　going before, pleading
TITUS
Hear me, grave fathers; noble Tribunes, stay.
For pity of mine age, whose youth was spent
In dangerous wars whilst you securely slept;
For all my blood in Rome's great quarrel shed;
For all the frosty nights that I have watched,　5
And for these bitter tears which now you see
Filling the agèd wrinkles in my cheeks,
Be pitiful to my condemnèd sons,
Whose souls is not corrupted as 'tis thought.
For two-and-twenty sons I never wept,　10
Because they died in honour's lofty bed.
　　Andronicus lieth down, and the Judges pass by him
For these two, Tribunes, in the dust I write
My heart's deep languor and my soul's sad tears.
Let my tears stanch the earth's dry appetite;
My sons' sweet blood will make it shame and blush.　15
　　　　　　　　　　　⌜Exeunt all but Titus⌝
O earth, I will befriend thee more with rain
That shall distil from these two ancient ruins
Than youthful April shall with all his showers.
In summer's drought I'll drop upon thee still.
In winter with warm tears I'll melt the snow　20
And keep eternal springtime on thy face,
So thou refuse to drink my dear sons' blood.

Enter Lucius with his weapon drawn
O reverend Tribunes, O gentle, agèd men,
Unbind my sons, reverse the doom of death,
And let me say, that never wept before,   25
My tears are now prevailing orators!
LUCIUS
O noble father, you lament in vain.
The Tribunes hear you not. No man is by,
And you recount your sorrows to a stone.
TITUS
Ah Lucius, for thy brothers let me plead.   30
Grave Tribunes, once more I entreat of you—
LUCIUS
My gracious lord, no tribune hears you speak.
TITUS
Why, 'tis no matter, man. If they did hear,
They would not mark me; if they did mark,
They would not pity me; yet plead I must.   35
Therefore I tell my sorrows to the stones,
Who, though they cannot answer my distress,
Yet in some sort they are better than the Tribunes
For that they will not intercept my tale.
When I do weep they humbly at my feet   40
Receive my tears and seem to weep with me,
And were they but attirèd in grave weeds
Rome could afford no tribunes like to these.
A stone is soft as wax, tribunes more hard than
    stones.
A stone is silent and offendeth not,   45
And tribunes with their tongues doom men to death.
But wherefore stand'st thou with thy weapon drawn?
LUCIUS
To rescue my two brothers from their death,
For which attempt the Judges have pronounced
My everlasting doom of banishment.   50
TITUS [*rising*]
O happy man, they have befriended thee!
Why, foolish Lucius, dost thou not perceive
That Rome is but a wilderness of tigers?
Tigers must prey, and Rome affords no prey
But me and mine. How happy art thou then   55
From these devourers to be banishèd!
But who comes with our brother Marcus here?
Enter Marcus with Lavinia
MARCUS
Titus, prepare thy agèd eyes to weep,
Or if not so, thy noble heart to break.
I bring consuming sorrow to thine age.   60
TITUS
Will it consume me? Let me see it then.
MARCUS This was thy daughter.
TITUS Why, Marcus, so she is.
LUCIUS (*falling on his knees*) Ay me, this object kills me.
TITUS
Faint-hearted boy, arise and look upon her.   65
    [*Lucius rises*]
Speak, Lavinia, what accursèd hand
Hath made thee handless in thy father's sight?

What fool hath added water to the sea,
Or brought a faggot to bright-burning Troy?
My grief was at the height before thou cam'st,   70
And now like Nilus it disdaineth bounds.
Give me a sword, I'll chop off my hands too,
For they have fought for Rome, and all in vain;
And they have nursed this woe in feeding life;
In bootless prayer have they been held up,   75
And they have served me to effectless use.
Now all the service I require of them
Is that the one will help to cut the other.
'Tis well, Lavinia, that thou hast no hands,
For hands to do Rome service is but vain.   80
LUCIUS
Speak, gentle sister, who hath martyred thee.
MARCUS
O, that delightful engine of her thoughts,
That blabbed them with such pleasing eloquence,
Is torn from forth that pretty hollow cage
Where, like a sweet melodious bird, it sung   85
Sweet varied notes, enchanting every ear.
LUCIUS
O, say thou for her, who hath done this deed?
MARCUS
O, thus I found her, straying in the park,
Seeking to hide herself, as doth the deer
That hath received some unrecuring wound.   90
TITUS
It was my dear, and he that wounded her
Hath hurt me more than had he killed me dead;
For now I stand as one upon a rock
Environed with a wilderness of sea,
Who marks the waxing tide grow wave by wave,   95
Expecting ever when some envious surge
Will in his brinish bowels swallow him.
This way to death my wretched sons are gone.
Here stands my other son, a banished man,
And here my brother, weeping at my woes.   100
But that which gives my soul the greatest spurn
Is dear Lavinia, dearer than my soul.
Had I but seen thy picture in this plight
It would have madded me. What shall I do
Now I behold thy lively body so?   105
Thou hast no hands to wipe away thy tears,
Nor tongue to tell me who hath martyred thee.
Thy husband he is dead, and for his death
Thy brothers are condemned and dead by this.
Look, Marcus, ah, son Lucius, look on her!   110
When I did name her brothers, then fresh tears
Stood on her cheeks, as doth the honey-dew
Upon a gathered lily almost witherèd.
MARCUS
Perchance she weeps because they killed her
    husband;
Perchance because she knows them innocent.   115
TITUS
If they did kill thy husband, then be joyful,
Because the law hath ta'en revenge on them.

No, no, they would not do so foul a deed;
Witness the sorrow that their sister makes.
Gentle Lavinia, let me kiss thy lips;   120
Or make some sign how I may do thee ease.
Shall thy good uncle, and thy brother Lucius,
And thou, and I, sit round about some fountain,
Looking all downwards to behold our cheeks
How they are stained, like meadows yet not dry   125
With miry slime left on them by a flood?
And in the fountain shall we gaze so long
Till the fresh taste be taken from that clearness,
And made a brine pit with our bitter tears?
Or shall we cut away our hands like thine?   130
Or shall we bite our tongues, and in dumb shows
Pass the remainder of our hateful days?
What shall we do? Let us that have our tongues
Plot some device of further misery,
To make us wondered at in time to come.   135

LUCIUS
Sweet father, cease your tears, for at your grief
See how my wretched sister sobs and weeps.

MARCUS
Patience, dear niece. Good Titus, dry thine eyes.

TITUS
Ah, Marcus, Marcus, brother, well I wot
Thy napkin cannot drink a tear of mine,   140
For thou, poor man, hast drowned it with thine own.

LUCIUS
Ah, my Lavinia, I will wipe thy cheeks.

TITUS
Mark, Marcus, mark. I understand her signs.
Had she a tongue to speak, now would she say
That to her brother which I said to thee.   145
His napkin with his true tears all bewet
Can do no service on her sorrowful cheeks.
O, what a sympathy of woe is this—
As far from help as limbo is from bliss.
        Enter Aaron the Moor, alone

AARON
Titus Andronicus, my lord the Emperor   150
Sends thee this word: that, if thou love thy sons,
Let Marcus, Lucius or thyself, old Titus,
Or any one of you, chop off your hand
And send it to the King. He for the same
Will send thee hither both thy sons alive,   155
And that shall be the ransom for their fault.

TITUS
O gracious Emperor! O gentle Aaron,
Did ever raven sing so like a lark
That gives sweet tidings of the sun's uprise?
With all my heart I'll send the Emperor my hand. 160
Good Aaron, wilt thou help to chop it off?

LUCIUS
Stay, father, for that noble hand of thine,
That hath thrown down so many enemies,
Shall not be sent. My hand will serve the turn.
My youth can better spare my blood than you,   165
And therefore mine shall save my brothers' lives.

MARCUS
Which of your hands hath not defended Rome
And reared aloft the bloody battleaxe,
Writing destruction on the enemy's castle?
O, none of both but are of high desert.   170
My hand hath been but idle; let it serve
To ransom my two nephews from their death,
Then have I kept it to a worthy end.

AARON
Nay, come, agree whose hand shall go along,
For fear they die before their pardon come.   175

MARCUS
My hand shall go.

LUCIUS   By heaven it shall not go.

TITUS
Sirs, strive no more. Such withered herbs as these
Are meet for plucking up, and therefore mine.

LUCIUS
Sweet father, if I shall be thought thy son,
Let me redeem my brothers both from death.   180

MARCUS
And for our father's sake and mother's care,
Now let me show a brother's love to thee.

TITUS
Agree between you. I will spare my hand.

LUCIUS
Then I'll go fetch an axe.

MARCUS   But I will use the axe.
                        Exeunt Lucius and Marcus

TITUS
Come hither, Aaron. I'll deceive them both.   185
Lend me thy hand, and I will give thee mine.

AARON *(aside)*
If that be called deceit, I will be honest
And never whilst I live deceive men so.
But I'll deceive you in another sort,
And that you'll say ere half an hour pass.   190
        He cuts off Titus' hand.
        Enter Lucius and Marcus again

TITUS
Now stay your strife. What shall be is dispatched.
Good Aaron, give his majesty my hand.
Tell him it was a hand that warded him
From thousand dangers; bid him bury it.
More hath it merited; that let it have.   195
As for my sons, say I account of them
As jewels purchased at an easy price,
And yet dear too, because I bought mine own.

AARON
I go, Andronicus; and for thy hand
Look by and by to have thy sons with thee.   200
(Aside) Their heads, I mean. O, how this villainy
Doth fat me with the very thoughts of it!
Let fools do good, and fair men call for grace:
Aaron will have his soul black like his face.   *Exit*

TITUS
O, here I lift this one hand up to heaven   205
And bow this feeble ruin to the earth.

He kneels
If any power pities wretched tears,
To that I call. (*To Lavinia, who kneels*) What, wouldst
  thou kneel with me?
Do then, dear heart; for heaven shall hear our prayers,
Or with our sighs we'll breathe the welkin dim   210
And stain the sun with fog, as sometime clouds
When they do hug him in their melting bosoms.
MARCUS
O brother, speak with possibility,
And do not break into these deep extremes.
TITUS
Is not my sorrows deep, having no bottom?   215
Then be my passions bottomless with them.
MARCUS
But yet let reason govern thy lament.
TITUS
If there were reason for these miseries,
Then into limits could I bind my woes.
When heaven doth weep, doth not the earth
  o'erflow?   220
If the winds rage, doth not the sea wax mad,
Threat'ning the welkin with his big-swoll'n face?
And wilt thou have a reason for this coil?
I am the sea. Hark how her sighs doth blow.
She is the weeping welkin, I the earth.   225
Then must my sea be movèd with her sighs,
Then must my earth with her continual tears
Become a deluge overflowed and drowned,
Forwhy my bowels cannot hide her woes,
But like a drunkard must I vomit them.   230
Then give me leave, for losers will have leave
To ease their stomachs with their bitter tongues.
    Enter a Messenger with two heads and a hand
MESSENGER
Worthy Andronicus, ill art thou repaid
For that good hand thou sent'st the Emperor.
Here are the heads of thy two noble sons,   235
And here's thy hand in scorn to thee sent back—
Thy grief their sports, thy resolution mocked,
That woe is me to think upon thy woes
More than remembrance of my father's death.
    ⌈*He sets down the heads and hand. Exit*⌉
MARCUS
Now let hot Etna cool in Sicily,   240
And be my heart an ever-burning hell.
These miseries are more than may be borne.
To weep with them that weep doth ease some deal,
But sorrow flouted at is double death.
LUCIUS
Ah, that this sight should make so deep a wound   245
And yet detested life not shrink thereat—
That ever death should let life bear his name
Where life hath no more interest but to breathe!
    Lavinia kisses Titus
MARCUS
Alas, poor heart, that kiss is comfortless
As frozen water to a starvèd snake.   250

TITUS
When will this fearful slumber have an end?
MARCUS
Now farewell, flatt'ry; die, Andronicus.
Thou dost not slumber. See thy two sons' heads,
Thy warlike hand, thy mangled daughter here,
Thy other banished son with this dear sight   255
Struck pale and bloodless, and thy brother, I,
Even like a stony image, cold and numb.
Ah, now no more will I control thy griefs.
Rend off thy silver hair, thy other hand
Gnawing with thy teeth, and be this dismal sight   260
The closing up of our most wretched eyes.
Now is a time to storm. Why art thou still?
TITUS Ha, ha, ha!
MARCUS
Why dost thou laugh? It fits not with this hour.
TITUS
Why, I have not another tear to shed.   265
Besides, this sorrow is an enemy,
And would usurp upon my wat'ry eyes
And make them blind with tributary tears.
Then which way shall I find Revenge's cave?—
For these two heads do seem to speak to me   270
And threat me I shall never come to bliss
Till all these mischiefs be returned again
Even in their throats that hath committed them.
Come, let me see what task I have to do.
    ⌈*He and Lavinia rise*⌉
You heavy people, circle me about,   275
That I may turn me to each one of you
And swear unto my soul to right your wrongs.
    Marcus, Lucius, and Lavinia circle Titus. He
    pledges them
The vow is made. Come, brother, take a head,
And in this hand the other will I bear.
And Lavinia, thou shalt be employed.   280
Bear thou my hand, sweet wench, between thine arms.
As for thee, boy, go get thee from my sight.
Thou art an exile and thou must not stay.
Hie to the Goths, and raise an army there,
And if ye love me, as I think you do,   285
Let's kiss and part, for we have much to do.
    They kiss. Exeunt all but Lucius
LUCIUS
Farewell, Andronicus, my noble father,
The woefull'st man that ever lived in Rome.
Farewell, proud Rome, till Lucius come again;
He loves his pledges dearer than his life.   290
Farewell, Lavinia, my noble sister:
O, would thou wert as thou tofore hast been!
But now nor Lucius nor Lavinia lives
But in oblivion and hateful griefs.
If Lucius live he will requite your wrongs   295
And make proud Saturnine and his empress
Beg at the gates like Tarquin and his queen.
Now will I to the Goths and raise a power,
To be revenged on Rome and Saturnine.   *Exit*

3.2   *A banquet. Enter Titus Andronicus, Marcus,*
      Lavinia, and the boy (young Lucius)
TITUS
  So, so, now sit, and look you eat no more
  Than will preserve just so much strength in us
  As will revenge these bitter woes of ours.
    ⌈*They sit*⌉
  Marcus, unknit that sorrow-wreathen knot.
  Thy niece and I, poor creatures, want our hands,   5
  And cannot passionate our tenfold grief
  With folded arms. This poor right hand of mine
  Is left to tyrannize upon my breast,
  Who, when my heart, all mad with misery,
  Beats in this hollow prison of my flesh,   10
  Then thus I thump it down.
    He beats his breast
  (*To Lavinia*) Thou map of woe, that thus dost talk in
    signs,
  When thy poor heart beats with outrageous beating
  Thou canst not strike it thus to make it still!
  Wound it with sighing, girl; kill it with groans,   15
  Or get some little knife between thy teeth
  And just against thy heart make thou a hole,
  That all the tears that thy poor eyes let fall
  May run into that sink and, soaking in,
  Drown the lamenting fool in sea-salt tears.   20
MARCUS
  Fie, brother, fie! Teach her not thus to lay
  Such violent hands upon her tender life.
TITUS
  How now! Has sorrow made thee dote already?
  Why, Marcus, no man should be mad but I.
  What violent hands can she lay on her life?   25
  Ah, wherefore dost thou urge the name of hands
  To bid Aeneas tell the tale twice o'er
  How Troy was burnt and he made miserable?
  O, handle not the theme, to talk of hands,
  Lest we remember still that we have none.   30
  Fie, fie, how franticly I square my talk,
  As if we should forget we had no hands
  If Marcus did not name the word of hands!
  Come, let's fall to; and, gentle girl, eat this.
  Here is no drink! Hark, Marcus, what she says.   35
  I can interpret all her martyred signs.
  She says she drinks no other drink but tears,
  Brewed with her sorrow, mashed upon her cheeks.
  Speechless complainer, I will learn thy thought.
  In thy dumb action will I be as perfect   40
  As begging hermits in their holy prayers.
  Thou shalt not sigh, nor hold thy stumps to heaven,
  Nor wink, nor nod, nor kneel, nor make a sign,
  But I of these will wrest an alphabet,
  And by still practice learn to know thy meaning.   45
YOUNG LUCIUS
  Good grandsire, leave these bitter deep laments.
  Make my aunt merry with some pleasing tale.
MARCUS
  Alas, the tender boy in passion moved
  Doth weep to see his grandsire's heaviness.

TITUS
  Peace, tender sapling, thou art made of tears,   50
  And tears will quickly melt thy life away.
    Marcus strikes the dish with a knife
  What dost thou strike at, Marcus, with thy knife?
MARCUS
  At that that I have killed, my lord—a fly.
TITUS
  Out on thee, murderer! Thou kill'st my heart.
  Mine eyes are cloyed with view of tyranny.   55
  A deed of death done on the innocent
  Becomes not Titus' brother. Get thee gone.
  I see thou art not for my company.
MARCUS
  Alas, my lord, I have but killed a fly.
TITUS
  'But'? How if that fly had a father, brother?   60
  How would he hang his slender gilded wings
  And buzz lamenting dirges in the air!
  Poor harmless fly,
  That with his pretty buzzing melody
  Came here to make us merry—and thou hast killed
    him!   65
MARCUS
  Pardon me, sir, it was a black ill-favoured fly,
  Like to the Empress' Moor. Therefore I killed him.
TITUS O, O, O!
  Then pardon me for reprehending thee,
  For thou hast done a charitable deed.   70
  Give me thy knife. I will insult on him,
  Flattering myself as if it were the Moor
  Come hither purposely to poison me.
    He takes a knife and strikes
  There's for thyself, and that's for Tamora. Ah, sirrah!
  Yet I think we are not brought so low   75
  But that between us we can kill a fly
  That comes in likeness of a coal-black Moor.
MARCUS
  Alas, poor man! Grief has so wrought on him
  He takes false shadows for true substances.
TITUS
  Come, take away. Lavinia, go with me.   80
  I'll to thy closet and go read with thee
  Sad stories chancèd in the times of old.
  Come, boy, and go with me. Thy sight is young,
  And thou shalt read when mine begin to dazzle.
                              Exeunt

❧

4.1   *Enter Lucius' son and Lavinia running after him,*
      and the boy flies from her with his books under his
      arm. Enter Titus and Marcus
YOUNG LUCIUS
  Help, grandsire, help! My aunt Lavinia
  Follows me everywhere, I know not why.
  Good uncle Marcus, see how swift she comes.
  Alas, sweet aunt, I know not what you mean.
    ⌈*He drops his books*⌉

MARCUS
Stand by me, Lucius. Do not fear thine aunt.   5
TITUS
She loves thee, boy, too well to do thee harm.
YOUNG LUCIUS
Ay, when my father was in Rome she did.
MARCUS
What means my niece Lavinia by these signs?
TITUS
Fear her not, Lucius; somewhat doth she mean.
⌜MARCUS⌝
See, Lucius, see how much she makes of thee.   10
Somewhither would she have thee go with her.
Ah, boy, Cornelia never with more care
Read to her sons than she hath read to thee
Sweet poetry and Tully's *Orator*.
Canst thou not guess wherefore she plies thee thus? 15
YOUNG LUCIUS
My lord, I know not, I, nor can I guess,
Unless some fit or frenzy do possess her;
For I have heard my grandsire say full oft
Extremity of griefs would make men mad,
And I have read that Hecuba of Troy   20
Ran mad for sorrow. That made me to fear,
Although, my lord, I know my noble aunt
Loves me as dear as e'er my mother did,
And would not but in fury fright my youth,
Which made me down to throw my books and fly,   25
Causeless, perhaps. But pardon me, sweet aunt;
And, madam, if my uncle Marcus go
I will most willingly attend your ladyship.
MARCUS Lucius, I will.
Lavinia turns the books over with her stumps
TITUS
How now, Lavinia? Marcus, what means this?   30
Some book there is that she desires to see.
Which is it, girl, of these?—Open them, boy.
(*To Lavinia*) But thou art deeper read and better
        skilled.
Come and take choice of all my library,
And so beguile thy sorrow till the heavens   35
Reveal the damned contriver of this deed.—
Why lifts she up her arms in sequence thus?
MARCUS
I think she means that there were more than one
Confederate in the fact. Ay, more there was,
Or else to heaven she heaves them for revenge.   40
TITUS
Lucius, what book is that she tosseth so?
YOUNG LUCIUS
Grandsire, 'tis Ovid's *Metamorphoses*.
My mother gave it me.
MARCUS   For love of her that's gone,
Perhaps, she culled it from among the rest.
TITUS
Soft, so busily she turns the leaves.   45
Help her. What would she find? Lavinia, shall I read?
This is the tragic tale of Philomel,

And treats of Tereus' treason and his rape,
And rape, I fear, was root of thy annoy.
MARCUS
See, brother, see. Note how she quotes the leaves.   50
TITUS
Lavinia, wert *thou* thus surprised, sweet girl,
Ravished and wronged as Philomela was,
Forced in the ruthless, vast, and gloomy woods?
See, see. Ay, such a place there is where we did hunt—
O, had we never, never hunted there!—   55
Patterned by that the poet here describes,
By nature made for murders and for rapes.
MARCUS
O, why should nature build so foul a den,
Unless the gods delight in tragedies?
TITUS
Give signs, sweet girl, for here are none but friends, 60
What Roman lord it was durst do the deed.
Or slunk not Saturnine, as Tarquin erst,
That left the camp to sin in Lucrece' bed?
MARCUS
Sit down, sweet niece. Brother, sit down by me.
        They sit
Apollo, Pallas, Jove, or Mercury   65
Inspire me, that I may this treason find.
My lord, look here. Look here, Lavinia.
This sandy plot is plain. Guide if thou canst
This after me.
        He writes his name with his staff, and guides it
        with feet and mouth
                I here have writ my name
Without the help of any hand at all.   70
Cursed be that heart that forced us to this shift!
Write thou, good niece, and here display at last
What God will have discovered for revenge.
Heaven guide thy pen to print thy sorrows plain,
That we may know the traitors and the truth.   75
        She takes the staff in her mouth, and guides it with
        her stumps, and writes
O, do ye read, my lord, what she hath writ?
⌜TITUS⌝ 'Stuprum—Chiron—Demetrius.'
MARCUS
What, what!—The lustful sons of Tamora
Performers of this heinous bloody deed?
TITUS
Magni dominator poli,   80
Tam lentus audis scelera, tam lentus vides?
MARCUS
O, calm thee, gentle lord, although I know
There is enough written upon this earth
To stir a mutiny in the mildest thoughts,
And arm the minds of infants to exclaims.   85
My lord, kneel down with me; Lavinia, kneel;
And kneel, sweet boy, the Roman Hector's hope,
        All kneel
And swear with me—as, with the woeful fere
And father of that chaste dishonoured dame
Lord Junius Brutus sware for Lucrece' rape—   90

That we will prosecute by good advice
Mortal revenge upon these traitorous Goths,
And see their blood, or die with this reproach.
   They rise
TITUS
'Tis sure enough an you knew how,
But if you hunt these bear-whelps, then beware.   95
The dam will wake, and if she wind ye once
She's with the lion deeply still in league,
And lulls him whilst she playeth on her back,
And when he sleeps will she do what she list.
You are a young huntsman, Marcus. Let alone,   100
And come, I will go get a leaf of brass
And with a gad of steel will write these words,
And lay it by. The angry northern wind
Will blow these sands like Sibyl's leaves abroad,
And where's our lesson then? Boy, what say you? 105
YOUNG LUCIUS
I say, my lord, that if I were a man
Their mother's bedchamber should not be safe
For these base bondmen to the yoke of Rome.
MARCUS
Ay, that's my boy! Thy father hath full oft
For his ungrateful country done the like.   110
YOUNG LUCIUS
And, uncle, so will I, an if I live.
TITUS
Come go with me into mine armoury.
Lucius, I'll fit thee; and withal, my boy,
Shall carry from me to the Empress' sons
Presents that I intend to send them both.   115
Come, come, thou'lt do my message, wilt thou not?
YOUNG LUCIUS
Ay, with my dagger in their bosoms, grandsire.
TITUS
No, boy, not so. I'll teach thee another course.
Lavinia, come. Marcus, look to my house.
Lucius and I'll go brave it at the court.   120
Ay, marry, will we, sir, and we'll be waited on.
   Exeunt all but Marcus
MARCUS
O heavens, can you hear a good man groan
And not relent, or not compassion him?
Marcus, attend him in his ecstasy,
That hath more scars of sorrow in his heart   125
Than foemen's marks upon his battered shield,
But yet so just that he will not revenge.
Revenge the heavens for old Andronicus!   *Exit*

4.2   *Enter Aaron, Chiron, and Demetrius at one door,*
   and at the other door young Lucius and another
   with a bundle of weapons, and verses writ upon
   them
CHIRON
Demetrius, here's the son of Lucius.
He hath some message to deliver us.
AARON
Ay, some mad message from his mad grandfather.

YOUNG LUCIUS
My lords, with all the humbleness I may
I greet your honours from Andronicus   5
(Aside) And pray the Roman gods confound you both.
DEMETRIUS
Gramercy, lovely Lucius. What's the news?
YOUNG LUCIUS *(aside)*
That you are both deciphered, that's the news,
For villains marked with rape. *(Aloud)* May it please
   you,
My grandsire, well advised, hath sent by me   10
The goodliest weapons of his armoury
To gratify your honourable youth,
The hope of Rome, for so he bid me say;
   His attendant gives the weapons
And so I do, and with his gifts present
Your lordships that, whenever you have need,   15
You may be armèd and appointed well;
And so I leave you both *(aside)* like bloody villains.
   Exit with attendant
DEMETRIUS
What's here—a scroll, and written round about?
Let's see.
'*Integer vitae, scelerisque purus,*   20
Non eget Mauri iaculis, nec arcu.'
CHIRON
O, 'tis a verse in Horace, I know it well.
I read it in the grammar long ago.
AARON
Ay, just, a verse in Horace; right, you have it.
(Aside) Now what a thing it is to be an ass!   25
Here's no sound jest. The old man hath found their
   guilt,
And sends them weapons wrapped about with lines
That wound beyond their feeling to the quick.
But were our witty Empress well afoot
She would applaud Andronicus' conceit.   30
But let her rest in her unrest a while.
(To Chiron and Demetrius)
And now, young lords, was't not a happy star
Led us to Rome, strangers and, more than so,
Captives, to be advancèd to this height?
It did me good before the palace gate   35
To brave the Tribune in his brother's hearing.
DEMETRIUS
But me more good to see so great a lord
Basely insinuate and send us gifts.
AARON
Had he not reason, Lord Demetrius?
Did you not use his daughter very friendly?   40
DEMETRIUS
I would we had a thousand Roman dames
At such a bay, by turn to serve our lust.
CHIRON
A charitable wish, and full of love.
AARON
Here lacks but your mother for to say amen.
CHIRON
And that would she, for twenty thousand more.   45

DEMETRIUS
Come, let us go and pray to all the gods
For our belovèd mother in her pains.   .

AARON
Pray to the devils; the gods have given us over.
Trumpets sound

DEMETRIUS
Why do the Emperor's trumpets flourish thus?

CHIRON
Belike for joy the Emperor hath a son.   50

DEMETRIUS
Soft, who comes here?
Enter Nurse with a blackamoor child

NURSE   Good morrow, lords.
O tell me, did you see Aaron the Moor?

AARON
Well, more or less, or ne'er a whit at all,
Here Aaron is; and what with Aaron now?

NURSE
O gentle Aaron, we are all undone.   55
Now help, or woe betide thee evermore!

AARON
Why, what a caterwauling dost thou keep!
What dost thou wrap and fumble in thy arms?

NURSE
O, that which I would hide from heaven's eye,
Our Empress' shame and stately Rome's disgrace.   60
She is delivered, lords, she is delivered.

AARON
To whom?

NURSE   I mean she is brought abed.

AARON
Well, God give her good rest. What hath he sent her?

NURSE
A devil.

AARON   Why then, she is the devil's dam.
A joyful issue!   65

NURSE
A joyless, dismal, black, and sorrowful issue.
Here is the babe, as loathsome as a toad
Amongst the fair-faced breeders of our clime.
The Empress sends it thee, thy stamp, thy seal,
And bids thee christen it with thy dagger's point.   70

AARON
Zounds, ye whore, is black so base a hue?
Sweet blowze, you are a beauteous blossom, sure.

DEMETRIUS Villain, what hast thou done?

AARON That which thou canst not undo.

CHIRON Thou hast undone our mother.   75

AARON Villain, I have done thy mother.

DEMETRIUS
And therein, hellish dog, thou hast undone her.
Woe to her chance, and damned her loathèd choice,
Accursed the offspring of so foul a fiend.

CHIRON
It shall not live.

AARON   It shall not die.   80

NURSE
Aaron, it must; the mother wills it so.

AARON
What, must it, nurse? Then let no man but I
Do execution on my flesh and blood.

DEMETRIUS
I'll broach the tadpole on my rapier's point.
Nurse, give it me. My sword shall soon dispatch it.   85

AARON
Sooner this sword shall plough thy bowels up.
He takes the child and draws his sword
Stay, murderous villains, will you kill your brother?
Now, by the burning tapers of the sky
That shone so brightly when this boy was got,
He dies upon my scimitar's sharp point   90
That touches this, my first-born son and heir.
I tell you, younglings, not Enceladus
With all his threat'ning band of Typhon's brood,
Nor great Alcides, nor the god of war
Shall seize this prey out of his father's hands.   95
What, what, ye sanguine, shallow-hearted boys,
Ye whitelimed walls, ye alehouse painted signs,
Coal-black is better than another hue
In that it scorns to bear another hue;
For all the water in the ocean   100
Can never turn the swan's black legs to white,
Although she lave them hourly in the flood.
Tell the Empress from me I am of age
To keep mine own, excuse it how she can.

DEMETRIUS
Wilt thou betray thy noble mistress thus?   105

AARON
My mistress is my mistress, this myself,
The figure and the picture of my youth.
This before all the world do I prefer;
This maugre all the world will I keep safe,
Or some of you shall smoke for it in Rome.   110

DEMETRIUS
By this our mother is forever shamed.

CHIRON
Rome will despise her for this foul escape.

NURSE
The Emperor in his rage will doom her death.

CHIRON
I blush to think upon this ignomy.

AARON
Why, there's the privilege your beauty bears.   115
Fie, treacherous hue, that will betray with blushing
The close enacts and counsels of thy heart.
Here's a young lad framed of another leer.
Look how the black slave smiles upon the father,
As who should say 'Old lad, I am thine own.'   120
He is your brother, lords, sensibly fed
Of that self blood that first gave life to you,
And from that womb where you imprisoned were
He is enfranchisèd and come to light.
Nay, he is your brother by the surer side,   125
Although my seal be stampèd in his face.

NURSE
Aaron, what shall I say unto the Empress?

DEMETRIUS
Advise thee, Aaron, what is to be done,
And we will all subscribe to thy advice.
Save thou the child, so we may all be safe.   130
AARON
Then sit we down, and let us all consult.
My son and I will have the wind of you.
Keep there; now talk at pleasure of your safety.
    They sit
DEMETRIUS (*to the Nurse*)
How many women saw this child of his?
AARON
Why, so, brave lords, when we do join in league   135
I am a lamb; but if you brave the Moor,
The chafèd boar, the mountain lioness,
The ocean swells not so as Aaron storms.
(*To the Nurse*) But say again, how many saw the
    child?
NURSE
Cornelia the midwife, and myself,   140
And no one else but the delivered Empress.
AARON
The Empress, the midwife, and yourself.
Two may keep counsel when the third's away.
Go to the Empress, tell her this I said.   144
    He kills her
'Wheak, wheak'—so cries a pig preparèd to the spit.
DEMETRIUS
What mean'st thou, Aaron? Wherefore didst thou this?
AARON
O Lord, sir, 'tis a deed of policy.
Shall she live to betray this guilt of ours—
A long-tongued, babbling gossip? No, lords, no.
And now be it known to you my full intent.   150
Not far, one Muliteus my countryman
His wife but yesternight was brought to bed.
His child is like to her, fair as you are.
Go pack with him, and give the mother gold,
And tell them both the circumstance of all,   155
And how by this their child shall be advanced
And be receivèd for the Emperor's heir,
And substituted in the place of mine,
To calm this tempest whirling in the court;
And let the Emperor dandle him for his own.   160
Hark ye, lords, you see I have given her physic,
And you must needs bestow her funeral.
The fields are near, and you are gallant grooms.
This done, see that you take no longer days,
But send the midwife presently to me.   165
The midwife and the nurse well made away,
Then let the ladies tattle what they please.
CHIRON
Aaron, I see thou wilt not trust the air
With secrets.
DEMETRIUS   For this care of Tamora,
Herself and hers are highly bound to thee.   170
    Exeunt Chiron and Demetrius with
    the Nurse's body

AARON
Now to the Goths, as swift as swallow flies,
There to dispose this treasure in mine arms
And secretly to greet the Empress' friends.
Come on, you thick-lipped slave, I'll bear you hence,
For it is you that puts us to our shifts.   175
I'll make you feed on berries and on roots,
And fat on curds and whey, and suck the goat,
And cabin in a cave, and bring you up
To be a warrior and command a camp.
    Exit with the child

4.3   *Enter Titus, old Marcus, his son Publius, young*
       Lucius, and other gentlemen (Sempronius, Caius)
       with bows; and Titus bears the arrows with letters
       on the ends of them
TITUS
Come, Marcus, come; kinsmen, this is the way.
Sir boy, let me see your archery.
Look ye draw home enough, and 'tis there straight.
Terras Astraea reliquit.
Be you remembered, Marcus: she's gone, she's fled. 5
Sirs, take you to your tools. You, cousins, shall
Go sound the ocean and cast your nets.
Happily you may catch her in the sea;
Yet there's as little justice as at land.
No, Publius and Sempronius, you must do it.   10
'Tis you must dig with mattock and with spade
And pierce the inmost centre of the earth.
Then, when you come to Pluto's region,
I pray you deliver him this petition.
Tell him it is for justice and for aid,   15
And that it comes from old Andronicus,
Shaken with sorrows in ungrateful Rome.
Ah, Rome! Well, well, I made thee miserable
What time I threw the people's suffrages
On him that thus doth tyrannize o'er me.   20
Go, get you gone, and pray be careful all,
And leave you not a man-of-war unsearched.
This wicked Emperor may have shipped her hence,
And, kinsmen, then we may go pipe for justice.
MARCUS
O, Publius, is not this a heavy case,   25
To see thy noble uncle thus distraught?
PUBLIUS
Therefore, my lords, it highly us concerns
By day and night t'attend him carefully
And feed his humour kindly as we may,
Till time beget some careful remedy.   30
MARCUS
Kinsmen, his sorrows are past remedy,
But ⌉
Join with the Goths, and with revengeful war
Take wreak on Rome for this ingratitude,
And vengeance on the traitor Saturnine.   35
TITUS
Publius, how now? How now, my masters?
What, have you met with her?

PUBLIUS
No, my good lord, but Pluto sends you word
If you will have Revenge from hell, you shall.
Marry, for Justice, she is now employed,   40
He thinks, with Jove, in heaven or somewhere else,
So that perforce you must needs stay a time.

TITUS
He doth me wrong to feed me with delays.
I'll dive into the burning lake below
And pull her out of Acheron by the heels.   45
Marcus, we are but shrubs, no cedars we,
No big-boned men framed of the Cyclops' size,
But metal, Marcus, steel to the very back,
Yet wrung with wrongs more than our backs can
    bear;
And sith there's no justice in earth nor hell,   50
We will solicit heaven and move the gods
To send down Justice for to wreak our wrongs.
Come, to this gear. You are a good archer, Marcus.
    He gives them the arrows
'Ad Iovem', that's for you. Here, 'ad Apollinem'.
'Ad Martem', that's for myself.   55
Here, boy, 'to Pallas'. Here 'to Mercury'.
'To Saturn', Caius—not 'to Saturnine'!
You were as good to shoot against the wind.
To it, boy! Marcus, loose when I bid.
Of my word, I have written to effect.   60
There's not a god left unsolicited.

MARCUS
Kinsmen, shoot all your shafts into the court.
We will afflict the Emperor in his pride.

TITUS
Now, masters, draw.
    They shoot
           O, well said, Lucius!
Good boy, in Virgo's lap! Give it Pallas.   65

MARCUS
My lord, I aim a mile beyond the moon.
Your letter is with Jupiter by this.

TITUS
Ha, ha! Publius, Publius, what hast thou done?
See, see, thou hast shot off one of Taurus' horns.

MARCUS
This was the sport, my lord. When Publius shot,   70
The Bull, being galled, gave Aries such a knock
That down fell both the Ram's horns in the court,
And who should find them but the Empress' villain!
She laughed, and told the Moor he should not choose
But give them to his master for a present.   75

TITUS
Why, there it goes. God give his lordship joy.
    Enter the Clown with a basket and two pigeons in it
News, news from heaven! Marcus, the post is come.
Sirrah, what tidings? Have you any letters?
Shall I have justice? What says Jupiter?   79

CLOWN Ho, the gibbet-maker? He says that he hath taken
them down again, for the man must not be hanged till
the next week.

TITUS
But what says Jupiter, I ask thee?

CLOWN Alas, sir, I know not 'Jupiter'. I never drank with
him in all my life.   85

TITUS
Why, villain, art not thou the carrier?

CLOWN Ay, of my pigeons, sir; nothing else.

TITUS Why, didst thou not come from heaven?   88

CLOWN From heaven? Alas, sir, I never came there. God
forbid I should be so bold to press to heaven in my
young days. Why, I am going with my pigeons to the
tribunal plebs to take up a matter of brawl betwixt my
uncle and one of the Emperal's men.

TITUS
Sirrah, come hither. Make no more ado,
But give your pigeons to the Emperor.   95
By me thou shalt have justice at his hands.
Hold, hold—(*giving money*) meanwhile, here's money
    for thy charges.
Give me pen and ink. Sirrah, can you with a grace
Deliver up a supplication?

CLOWN Ay, sir.   100

TITUS (*writing and giving the Clown a paper*) Then here is
a supplication for you, and when you come to him, at
the first approach you must kneel, then kiss his foot,
then deliver up your pigeons, and then look for your
reward. I'll be at hand, sir; see you do it bravely.   105

CLOWN I warrant you, sir. Let me alone.

TITUS
Sirrah, hast thou a knife? Come, let me see it.
Here, Marcus, fold it in the oration,
For thou hast made it like an humble suppliant.
And when thou hast given it to the Emperor,   110
Knock at my door and tell me what he says.

CLOWN God be with you, sir. I will.   *Exit*

TITUS
Come, Marcus, let us go. Publius, follow me.   *Exeunt*

4.4   *Enter Saturninus, the Emperor, and Tamora, the*
        Empress, and Chiron and Demetrius, her two sons,
        and others. The Emperor brings the arrows in his
        hand that Titus shot at him

SATURNINUS
Why, lords, what wrongs are these! Was ever seen
An emperor in Rome thus overborne,
Troubled, confronted thus, and for the extent
Of egall justice used in such contempt?
My lords, you know, as know the mightful gods,   5
However these disturbers of our peace
Buzz in the people's ears, there naught hath passed
But even with law against the wilful sons
Of old Andronicus. And what an if
His sorrows have so overwhelmed his wits?   10
Shall we be thus afflicted in his wreaks,
His fits, his frenzy, and his bitterness?
And now he writes to heaven for his redress.
See, here's 'to Jove' and this 'to Mercury',
This 'to Apollo', this 'to the god of war'—   15

Sweet scrolls to fly about the streets of Rome!
What's this but libelling against the Senate
And blazoning our unjustice everywhere?
A goodly humour, is it not, my lords?—
As who would say, in Rome no justice were. 20
But, if I live, his feignèd ecstasies
Shall be no shelter to these outrages,
But he and his shall know that justice lives
In Saturninus' health, whom if he sleep
He'll so awake as he in fury shall 25
Cut off the proud'st conspirator that lives.

TAMORA
My gracious lord, my lovely Saturnine,
Lord of my life, commander of my thoughts,
Calm thee, and bear the faults of Titus' age,
Th'effects of sorrow for his valiant sons 30
Whose loss hath pierced him deep and scarred his
   heart;
And rather comfort his distressèd plight
Than prosecute the meanest or the best
For these contempts. (Aside) Why, thus it shall become
High-witted Tamora to gloze with all. 35
But, Titus, I have touched thee to the quick.
Thy life blood out if Aaron now be wise,
Then is all safe, the anchor in the port.
   Enter Clown
How now, good fellow, wouldst thou speak with us?

CLOWN Yea, forsooth, an your mistress-ship be Emperial.

TAMORA Empress I am, but yonder sits the Emperor. 41

CLOWN 'Tis he. God and Saint Stephen give you goode-
e'en. I have brought you a letter and a couple of
pigeons here.
   Saturninus reads the letter

SATURNINUS (to an attendant)
Go, take him away, and hang him presently. 45

CLOWN How much money must I have?

TAMORA Come, sirrah, you must be hanged.

CLOWN Hanged, by' Lady? Then I have brought up a
neck to a fair end.   Exit ⌈with attendant⌉

SATURNINUS
Despiteful and intolerable wrongs! 50
Shall I endure this monstrous villainy?
I know from whence this same device proceeds.
May this be borne?—As if his traitorous sons,
That died by law for murder of our brother,
Have by my means been butchered wrongfully! 55
Go, drag the villain hither by the hair.
Nor age nor honour shall shape privilege.
For this proud mock I'll be thy slaughterman,
Sly frantic wretch, that holp'st to make me great
In hope thyself should govern Rome and me. 60
   Enter Aemilius, a messenger

SATURNINUS
What news with thee, Aemilius?

AEMILIUS
Arm, my lords! Rome never had more cause.
The Goths have gathered head, and with a power
Of high-resolvèd men bent to the spoil

They hither march amain under conduct 65
Of Lucius, son to old Andronicus,
Who threats in course of this revenge to do
As much as ever Coriolanus did.

SATURNINUS
Is warlike Lucius general of the Goths?
These tidings nip me, and I hang the head, 70
As flowers with frost, or grass beat down with storms.
Ay, now begins our sorrows to approach.
'Tis he the common people love so much.
Myself hath often heard them say,
When I have walkèd like a private man, 75
That Lucius' banishment was wrongfully,
And they have wished that Lucius were their
   emperor.

TAMORA
Why should you fear? Is not your city strong?

SATURNINUS
Ay, but the citizens favour Lucius,
And will revolt from me to succour him. 80

TAMORA
King, be thy thoughts imperious like thy name.
Is the sun dimmed, that gnats do fly in it?
The eagle suffers little birds to sing,
And is not careful what they mean thereby,
Knowing that with the shadow of his wings 85
He can at pleasure stint their melody.
Even so mayst thou the giddy men of Rome.
Then cheer thy spirit; for know thou, Emperor,
I will enchant the old Andronicus
With words more sweet and yet more dangerous 90
Than baits to fish or honey-stalks to sheep
Whenas the one is wounded with the bait,
The other rotted with delicious feed.

SATURNINUS
But he will not entreat his son for us.

TAMORA
If Tamora entreat him, then he will, 95
For I can smooth and fill his agèd ears
With golden promises that, were his heart
Almost impregnable, his old ears deaf,
Yet should both ear and heart obey my tongue.
(To Aemilius) Go thou before to be our ambassador. 100
Say that the Emperor requests a parley
Of warlike Lucius, and appoint the meeting
Even at his father's house, the old Andronicus.

SATURNINUS
Aemilius, do this message honourably,
And if he stand on hostage for his safety, 105
Bid him demand what pledge will please him best.

AEMILIUS
Your bidding shall I do effectually.   Exit

TAMORA
Now will I to that old Andronicus,
And temper him with all the art I have
To pluck proud Lucius from the warlike Goths. 110
And now, sweet Emperor, be blithe again,
And bury all thy fear in my devices.

SATURNINUS
Then go incessantly, and plead to him.
                                        Exeunt severally

5.1 ⌈*Flourish.*⌉ *Enter Lucius with an army of Goths,*
      with drums and soldiers
LUCIUS
Approvèd warriors and my faithful friends,
I have receivèd letters from great Rome
Which signifies what hate they bear their emperor
And how desirous of our sight they are.
Therefore, great lords, be as your titles witness,   5
Imperious, and impatient of your wrongs,
And wherein Rome hath done you any scath
Let him make treble satisfaction.
A GOTH
Brave slip sprung from the great Andronicus,
Whose name was once our terror, now our comfort, 10
Whose high exploits and honourable deeds
Ingrateful Rome requites with foul contempt,
Be bold in us. We'll follow where thou lead'st,
Like stinging bees in hottest summer's day
Led by their master to the flowered fields,   15
And be avenged on cursèd Tamora.
GOTHS
And as he saith, so say we all with him.
LUCIUS
I humbly thank him, and I thank you all.
But who comes here, led by a lusty Goth?
      Enter a Goth, leading of Aaron with his child in his
      arms
GOTH
Renownèd Lucius, from our troops I strayed   20
To gaze upon a ruinous monastery,
And as I earnestly did fix mine eye
Upon the wasted building, suddenly
I heard a child cry underneath a wall.
I made unto the noise, when soon I heard   25
The crying babe controlled with this discourse:
'Peace, tawny slave, half me and half thy dam!
Did not thy hue bewray whose brat thou art,
Had nature lent thee but thy mother's look,
Villain, thou mightst have been an emperor.   30
But where the bull and cow are both milk-white
They never do beget a coal-black calf.
Peace, villain, peace!'—even thus he rates the babe—
'For I must bear thee to a trusty Goth
Who, when he knows thou art the Empress' babe,   35
Will hold thee dearly for thy mother's sake.'
With this, my weapon drawn, I rushed upon him,
Surprised him suddenly, and brought him hither
To use as you think needful of the man.
LUCIUS
O worthy Goth, this is the incarnate devil   40
That robbed Andronicus of his good hand.
This is the pearl that pleased your Empress' eye,
And here's the base fruit of her burning lust.
(*To Aaron*) Say, wall-eyed slave, whither wouldst thou
   convey
This growing image of thy fiendlike face?   45
Why dost not speak? What, deaf? What, not a word?
A halter, soldiers! Hang him on this tree,
And by his side his fruit of bastardy.
AARON
Touch not the boy; he is of royal blood.
LUCIUS
Too like the sire for ever being good.   50
First hang the child, that he may see it sprawl—
A sight to vex the father's soul withal.
Get me a ladder.
      ⌈*A Goth brings a ladder which Aaron climbs*⌉
AARON   Lucius, save the child,
And bear it from me to the Empress.
If thou do this, I'll show thee wondrous things   55
That highly may advantage thee to hear.
If thou wilt not, befall what may befall,
I'll speak no more but 'Vengeance rot you all!'
LUCIUS
Say on, and if it please me which thou speak'st
Thy child shall live, and I will see it nourished.   60
AARON
And if it please thee? Why, assure thee, Lucius,
'Twill vex thy soul to hear what I shall speak;
For I must talk of murders, rapes, and massacres,
Acts of black night, abominable deeds,
Complots of mischief, treason, villainies   65
Ruthful to hear yet piteously performed,
And this shall all be buried in my death
Unless thou swear to me my child shall live.
LUCIUS
Tell on thy mind. I say thy child shall live.
AARON
Swear that he shall, and then I will begin.   70
LUCIUS
Who should I swear by? Thou believest no god.
That granted, how canst thou believe an oath?
AARON
What if I do not?—as indeed I do not—
Yet for I know thou art religious
And hast a thing within thee callèd conscience,   75
With twenty popish tricks and ceremonies
Which I have seen thee careful to observe,
Therefore I urge thy oath; for that I know
An idiot holds his bauble for a god,
And keeps the oath which by that god he swears,   80
To that I'll urge him, therefore thou shalt vow
By that same god, what god soe'er it be,
That thou adorest and hast in reverence,
To save my boy, to nurse and bring him up,
Or else I will discover naught to thee.   85
LUCIUS
Even by my god I swear to thee I will.
AARON
First know thou I begot him on the Empress.

LUCIUS
O most insatiate and luxurious woman!
AARON
Tut, Lucius, this was but a deed of charity
To that which thou shalt hear of me anon.   90
'Twas her two sons that murdered Bassianus.
They cut thy sister's tongue, and ravished her,
And cut her hands, and trimmed her as thou sawest.
LUCIUS
O detestable villain! Call'st thou that trimming?
AARON
Why, she was washed and cut and trimmed, and 'twas
Trim sport for them which had the doing of it.   96
LUCIUS
O barbarous beastly villains, like thyself!
AARON
Indeed, I was their tutor to instruct them.
That codding spirit had they from their mother,
As sure a card as ever won the set.   100
That bloody mind I think they learned of me,
As true a dog as ever fought at head.
Well, let my deeds be witness of my worth.
I trained thy brethren to that guileful hole
Where the dead corpse of Bassianus lay.   105
I wrote the letter that thy father found,
And hid the gold within that letter mentioned,
Confederate with the Queen and her two sons;
And what not done that thou hast cause to rue
Wherein I had no stroke of mischief in it?   110
I played the cheater for thy father's hand,
And when I had it drew myself apart,
And almost broke my heart with extreme laughter.
I pried me through the crevice of a wall
When for his hand he had his two sons' heads,   115
Beheld his tears, and laughed so heartily
That both mine eyes were rainy like to his;
And when I told the Empress of this sport
She swooonèd almost at my pleasing tale,
And for my tidings gave me twenty kisses.   120
A GOTH
What, canst thou say all this and never blush?
AARON
Ay, like a black dog, as the saying is.
LUCIUS
Art thou not sorry for these heinous deeds?
AARON
Ay, that I had not done a thousand more.
Even now I curse the day—and yet I think   125
Few come within the compass of my curse—
Wherein I did not some notorious ill,
As kill a man, or else devise his death;
Ravish a maid, or plot the way to do it;
Accuse some innocent and forswear myself;   130
Set deadly enmity between two friends;
Make poor men's cattle break their necks;
Set fire on barns and haystacks in the night,
And bid the owners quench them with their tears.
Oft have I digged up dead men from their graves   135

And set them upright at their dear friends' door,
Even when their sorrows almost was forgot,
And on their skins, as on the bark of trees,
Have with my knife carvèd in Roman letters
'Let not your sorrow die though I am dead.'   140
But I have done a thousand dreadful things
As willingly as one would kill a fly,
And nothing grieves me heartily indeed
But that I cannot do ten thousand more.
LUCIUS
Bring down the devil, for he must not die   145
So sweet a death as hanging presently.
      Goths bring Aaron down the ladder
AARON
If there be devils, would I were a devil,
To live and burn in everlasting fire,
So I might have your company in hell
But to torment you with my bitter tongue.   150
LUCIUS
Sirs, stop his mouth, and let him speak no more.
      Goths gag Aaron.
      Enter Aemilius
A GOTH
My lord, there is a messenger from Rome
Desires to be admitted to your presence.
LUCIUS Let him come near.
Welcome, Aemilius. What's the news from Rome?   155
AEMILIUS
Lord Lucius, and you princes of the Goths,
The Roman Emperor greets you all by me,
And for he understands you are in arms,
He craves a parley at your father's house,
Willing you to demand your hostages,   160
And they shall be immediately delivered.
A GOTH What says our general?
LUCIUS
Aemilius, let the Emperor give his pledges
Unto my father and my uncle Marcus,
And we will come. Away!   165
      ⌐Flourish.⌐ Exeunt ⌐marching⌐

5.2   *Enter Tamora and Chiron and Demetrius, her two*
      sons, disguised
TAMORA
Thus, in this strange and sad habiliment,
I will encounter with Andronicus
And say I am Revenge, sent from below
To join with him and right his heinous wrongs.
Knock at his study, where they say he keeps   5
To ruminate strange plots of dire revenge.
Tell him Revenge is come to join with him
And work confusion on his enemies.
      They knock, and Titus ⌐aloft⌐ opens his study door
TITUS
Who doth molest my contemplation?
Is it your trick to make me ope the door,   10
That so my sad decrees may fly away
And all my study be to no effect?

You are deceived; for what I mean to do,
See here, in bloody lines I have set down,
And what is written shall be executed.   15

TAMORA
Titus, I am come to talk with thee.

TITUS
No, not a word. How can I grace my talk,
Wanting a hand to give it action?
Thou hast the odds of me, therefore no more.

TAMORA
If thou didst know me thou wouldst talk with me.   20

TITUS
I am not mad, I know thee well enough;
Witness this wretched stump, witness these crimson
          lines,
Witness these trenches made by grief and care,
Witness the tiring day and heavy night,
Witness all sorrow that I know thee well   25
For our proud empress, mighty Tamora.
Is not thy coming for my other hand?

TAMORA
Know, thou sad man, I am not Tamora.
She is thy enemy, and I thy friend.
I am Revenge, sent from th'infernal kingdom   30
To ease the gnawing vulture of thy mind
By working wreakful vengeance on thy foes.
Come down, and welcome me to this world's light.
Confer with me of murder and of death.
There's not a hollow cave or lurking-place,   35
No vast obscurity or misty vale
Where bloody murder or detested rape
Can couch for fear, but I will find them out,
And in their ears tell them my dreadful name,
Revenge, which makes the foul offender quake.   40

TITUS
Art thou Revenge, and art thou sent to me
To be a torment to mine enemies?

TAMORA
I am; therefore come down, and welcome me.

TITUS
Do me some service ere I come to thee.
Lo by thy side where Rape and Murder stands.   45
Now give some surance that thou art Revenge,
Stab them, or tear them on thy chariot wheels,
And then I'll come and be thy wagoner,
And whirl along with thee about the globe,
Provide two proper palfreys, black as jet,   50
To hale thy vengeful wagon swift away
And find out murderers in their guilty caves.
And when thy car is loaden with their heads
I will dismount, and by thy wagon wheel
Trot like a servile footman all day long,   55
Even from Hyperion's rising in the east
Until his very downfall in the sea;
And day by day I'll do this heavy task,
So thou destroy Rapine and Murder there.

TAMORA
These are my ministers, and come with me.   60

TITUS
Are they thy ministers? What are they called?

TAMORA
Rape and Murder, therefore callèd so
'Cause they take vengeance of such kind of men.

TITUS
Good Lord, how like the Empress' sons they are,
And you the Empress! But we worldly men   65
Have miserable, mad, mistaking eyes.
O sweet Revenge, now do I come to thee,
And if one arm's embracement will content thee,
I will embrace thee in it by and by.   *Exit* ⌈*aloft*⌉

TAMORA
This closing with him fits his lunacy.   70
Whate'er I forge to feed his brainsick humours
Do you uphold and maintain in your speeches,
For now he firmly takes me for Revenge,
And being credulous in this mad thought
I'll make him send for Lucius his son,   75
And whilst I at a banquet hold him sure
I'll find some cunning practice out of hand
To scatter and disperse the giddy Goths,
Or at the least make them his enemies.
See, here he comes, and I must ply my theme.   80
          Enter Titus, below

TITUS
Long have I been forlorn, and all for thee.
Welcome, dread Fury, to my woeful house.
Rapine and Murder, you are welcome, too.
How like the Empress and her sons you are!
Well are you fitted, had you but a Moor.   85
Could not all hell afford you such a devil?—
For well I wot the Empress never wags
But in her company there is a Moor,
And would you represent our Queen aright
It were convenient you had such a devil.   90
But welcome as you are. What shall we do?

TAMORA
What wouldst thou have us do, Andronicus?

DEMETRIUS
Show me a murderer, I'll deal with him.

CHIRON
Show me a villain that hath done a rape,
And I am sent to be revenged on him.   95

TAMORA
Show me a thousand that hath done thee wrong,
And I will be revengèd on them all.

TITUS (*to Demetrius*)
Look round about the wicked streets of Rome,
And when thou find'st a man that's like thyself,
Good Murder, stab him; he's a murderer.   100
(*To Chiron*) Go thou with him, and when it is thy hap
To find another that is like to thee,
Good Rapine, stab him; he is a ravisher.
(*To Tamora*) Go thou with them, and in the Emperor's
          court
There is a queen attended by a Moor.   105
Well shalt thou know her by thine own proportion,

For up and down she doth resemble thee.
I pray thee, do on them some violent death;
They have been violent to me and mine.
TAMORA
Well hast thou lessoned us. This shall we do;   110
But would it please thee, good Andronicus,
To send for Lucius, thy thrice-valiant son,
Who leads towards Rome a band of warlike Goths,
And bid him come and banquet at thy house—
When he is here, even at thy solemn feast,   115
I will bring in the Empress and her sons,
The Emperor himself, and all thy foes,
And at thy mercy shall they stoop and kneel,
And on them shalt thou ease thy angry heart.
What says Andronicus to this device?   120
TITUS
Marcus, my brother! 'Tis sad Titus calls.
    Enter Marcus
Go, gentle Marcus, to thy nephew Lucius.
Thou shalt enquire him out among the Goths.
Bid him repair to me, and bring with him
Some of the chiefest princes of the Goths.   125
Bid him encamp his soldiers where they are.
Tell him the Emperor and the Empress too
Feast at my house, and he shall feast with them.
This do thou for my love, and so let him,
As he regards his agèd father's life.   130
MARCUS
This will I do, and soon return again.   *Exit*
TAMORA
Now will I hence about thy business,
And take my ministers along with me.
TITUS
Nay, nay, let Rape and Murder stay with me,
Or else I'll call my brother back again,   135
And cleave to no revenge but Lucius.
TAMORA (*aside to her sons*)
What say you, boys, will you abide with him
Whiles I go tell my lord the Emperor
How I have governed our determined jest?
Yield to his humour, smooth and speak him fair,   140
And tarry with him till I turn again.
TITUS (*aside*)
I knew them all, though they supposed me mad,
And will o'erreach them in their own devices—
A pair of cursèd hell-hounds and their dam.
DEMETRIUS
Madam, depart at pleasure. Leave us here.   145
TAMORA
Farewell, Andronicus. Revenge now goes
To lay a complot to betray thy foes.
TITUS
I know thou dost, and sweet Revenge, farewell.
                                    Exit Tamora
CHIRON
Tell us, old man, how shall we be employed?
TITUS
Tut, I have work enough for you to do.   150
Publius, come hither; Caius and Valentine.

    Enter Publius, Caius, and Valentine
PUBLIUS
What is your will?
TITUS   Know you these two?
PUBLIUS
The Empress' sons I take them—Chiron, Demetrius.
TITUS
Fie, Publius, fie! Thou art too much deceived.
The one is Murder, and Rape is the other's name. 155
And therefore bind them, gentle Publius;
Caius and Valentine, lay hands on them.
Oft have you heard me wish for such an hour,
And now I find it. Therefore bind them sure,
And stop their mouths if they begin to cry.   *Exit*
CHIRON
Villains, forbear! We are the Empress' sons.   161
PUBLIUS
And therefore do we what we are commanded.
    *Publius, Caius, and Valentine bind and gag Chiron
    and Demetrius*
Stop close their mouths. Let them not speak a word.
Is he sure bound? Look that you bind them fast.
    *Enter Titus Andronicus with a knife, and Lavinia
    with a basin*
TITUS
Come, come, Lavinia. Look, thy foes are bound.   165
Sirs, stop their mouths. Let them not speak to me,
But let them hear what fearful words I utter.
O villains, Chiron and Demetrius!
Here stands the spring whom you have stained with
    mud,
This goodly summer with your winter mixed.   170
You killed her husband, and for that vile fault
Two of her brothers were condemned to death,
My hand cut off and made a merry jest,
Both her sweet hands, her tongue, and that more
    dear
Than hands or tongue, her spotless chastity,   175
Inhuman traitors, you constrained and forced.
What would you say if I should let you speak?
Villains, for shame. You could not beg for grace.
Hark, wretches, how I mean to martyr you.
This one hand yet is left to cut your throats,   180
Whiles that Lavinia 'tween her stumps doth hold
The basin that receives your guilty blood.
You know your mother means to feast with me,
And calls herself Revenge, and thinks me mad.
Hark, villains, I will grind your bones to dust, 185
And with your blood and it I'll make a paste,
And of the paste a coffin I will rear,
And make two pasties of your shameful heads,
And bid that strumpet, your unhallowed dam,
Like to the earth swallow her own increase.   190
This is the feast that I have bid her to,
And this the banquet she shall surfeit on;
For worse than Philomel you used my daughter,
And worse than Progne I will be revenged.
And now, prepare your throats. Lavinia, come.   195
Receive the blood, and when that they are dead

Let me go grind their bones to powder small,
And with this hateful liquor temper it,
And in that paste let their vile heads be baked.
Come, come, be everyone officious   200
To make this banquet, which I wish may prove
More stern and bloody than the Centaurs' feast.
    He cuts their throats
So, now bring them in, for I'll play the cook
And see them ready against their mother comes.
                    Exeunt carrying the bodies

5.3   *Enter Lucius, Marcus, and the Goths, with Aaron,*
    prisoner, ⌈and an attendant with his child⌉
LUCIUS
Uncle Marcus, since 'tis my father's mind
That I repair to Rome, I am content.
A GOTH
And ours with thine, befall what fortune will.
LUCIUS
Good uncle, take you in this barbarous Moor,
This ravenous tiger, this accursèd devil.   5
Let him receive no sust'nance, fetter him
Till he be brought unto the Empress' face
For testimony of her foul proceedings,
And see the ambush of our friends be strong.
I fear the Emperor means no good to us.   10
AARON
Some devil whisper curses in my ear
And prompt me, that my tongue may utter forth
The venomous malice of my swelling heart.
LUCIUS
Away, inhuman dog, unhallowed slave!
Sirs, help our uncle to convey him in.   15
        ⌈*Exeunt Goths with Aaron and his child*⌉
  Flourish
The trumpets show the Emperor is at hand.
  Enter Saturninus the Emperor, and Tamora the
  Empress, with Aemilius, Tribunes, Senators, and
  others
SATURNINUS
What, hath the firmament more suns than one?
LUCIUS
What boots it thee to call thyself a sun?
MARCUS
Rome's emperor and nephew, break the parle.
These quarrels must be quietly debated.   20
The feast is ready which the careful Titus
Hath ordained to an honourable end,
For peace, for love, for league, and good to Rome.
Please you therefore draw nigh, and take your places.
SATURNINUS Marcus, we will.   25
    ⌈*Hautboys. A table brought in.*⌉ *They sit.*
  Enter Titus like a cook, placing the dishes, and
  Lavinia with a veil over her face; ⌈young Lucius,
  and others⌉
TITUS
Welcome, my gracious lord; welcome, dread Queen;
Welcome, ye warlike Goths; welcome, Lucius;

And welcome, all. Although the cheer be poor,
'Twill fill your stomachs. Please you, eat of it.
SATURNINUS
Why art thou thus attired, Andronicus?   30
TITUS
Because I would be sure to have all well
To entertain your highness and your Empress.
TAMORA
We are beholden to you, good Andronicus.
TITUS
An if your highness knew my heart, you were.
My lord the Emperor, resolve me this: 35
Was it well done of rash Virginius
To slay his daughter with his own right hand
Because she was enforced, stained, and deflowered?
SATURNINUS
It was, Andronicus.
TITUS   Your reason, mighty lord?
SATURNINUS
Because the girl should not survive her shame,   40
And by her presence still renew his sorrows.
TITUS
A reason mighty, strong, effectual;
A pattern, precedent, and lively warrant
For me, most wretched, to perform the like.
Die, die, Lavinia, and thy shame with thee,   45
And with thy shame thy father's sorrow die.
    ⌈*He kills her*⌉
SATURNINUS
What hast thou done, unnatural and unkind?
TITUS
Killed her for whom my tears have made me blind.
I am as woeful as Virginius was,
And have a thousand times more cause than he   50
To do this outrage, and it now is done.
SATURNINUS
What, was she ravished? Tell who did the deed.
TITUS
Will't please you eat? Will't please your highness
    feed?
TAMORA
Why hast thou slain thine only daughter thus?
TITUS
Not I, 'twas Chiron and Demetrius.   55
They ravished her, and cut away her tongue,
And they, 'twas they, that did her all this wrong.
SATURNINUS
Go, fetch them hither to us presently.
TITUS ⌈*revealing the heads*⌉
Why, there they are, both bakèd in this pie,
Whereof their mother daintily hath fed,   60
Eating the flesh that she herself hath bred.
'Tis true, 'tis true, witness my knife's sharp point.
    He stabs the Empress
SATURNINUS
Die, frantic wretch, for this accursèd deed.
    He kills Titus

LUCIUS
Can the son's eye behold his father bleed?
There's meed for meed, death for a deadly deed.　65
　　He kills Saturninus. Confusion follows.
　　⌈*Enter Goths. Lucius, Marcus and others go aloft*⌉
MARCUS
You sad-faced men, people and sons of Rome,
By uproars severed, as a flight of fowl
Scattered by winds and high tempestuous gusts,
O, let me teach you how to knit again
This scattered corn into one mutual sheaf,　70
These broken limbs again into one body.
A ROMAN LORD
Let Rome herself be bane unto herself,
And she whom mighty kingdoms curtsy to,
Like a forlorn and desperate castaway,
Do shameful execution on herself　75
But if my frosty signs and chaps of age,
Grave witnesses of true experience,
Cannot induce you to attend my words.
　(*To Lucius*) Speak, Rome's dear friend, as erst our
　　　ancestor
When with his solemn tongue he did discourse　80
To lovesick Dido's sad-attending ear
The story of that baleful-burning night
When subtle Greeks surprised King Priam's Troy.
Tell us what Sinon hath bewitched our ears,
Or who hath brought the fatal engine in　85
That gives our Troy, our Rome, the civil wound.
My heart is not compact of flint nor steel,
Nor can I utter all our bitter grief,
But floods of tears will drown my oratory
And break my utt'rance even in the time　90
When it should move ye to attend me most,
And force you to commiseration.
Here's Rome's young captain. Let him tell the tale,
While I stand by and weep to hear him speak.
LUCIUS
Then, gracious auditory, be it known to you　95
That Chiron and the damned Demetrius
Were they that murderèd our Emperor's brother,
And they it were that ravishèd our sister.
For their fell faults our brothers were beheaded,
Our father's tears despised, and basely cozened　100
Of that true hand that fought Rome's quarrel out
And sent her enemies unto the grave.
Lastly myself, unkindly banishèd,
The gates shut on me, and turned weeping out
To beg relief among Rome's enemies,　105
Who drowned their enmity in my true tears
And oped their arms to embrace me as a friend.
I am the turned-forth, be it known to you,
That have preserved her welfare in my blood,
And from her bosom took the enemy's point,　110
Sheathing the steel in my advent'rous body.
Alas, you know I am no vaunter, I.
My scars can witness, dumb although they are,
That my report is just and full of truth.

But soft, methinks I do digress too much,　115
Citing my worthless praise. O, pardon me,
For when no friends are by, men praise themselves.
MARCUS
Now is my turn to speak. Behold the child.
Of this was Tamora deliverèd,
The issue of an irreligious Moor,　120
Chief architect and plotter of these woes.
The villain is alive in Titus' house,
And as he is to witness, this is true.
Now judge what cause had Titus to revenge
These wrongs unspeakable, past patience,　125
Or more than any living man could bear.
Now have you heard the truth. What say you,
　　Romans?
Have we done aught amiss, show us wherein,
And from the place where you behold us pleading
The poor remainder of Andronici　130
Will hand in hand all headlong hurl ourselves
And on the ragged stones beat forth our souls
And make a mutual closure of our house.
Speak, Romans, speak, and if you say we shall,
Lo, hand in hand Lucius and I will fall.　135
AEMILIUS
Come, come, thou reverend man of Rome,
And bring our emperor gently in thy hand,
Lucius, our emperor—for well I know
The common voice do cry it shall be so.
ROMANS
Lucius, all hail, Rome's royal emperor!　140
MARCUS (*to attendants*)
Go, go into old Titus' sorrowful house
And hither hale that misbelieving Moor
To be adjudged some direful slaught'ring death
As punishment for his most wicked life.　*Exeunt some*
　　⌈*Lucius, Marcus, and the others come down*⌉
⌈ROMANS⌉
Lucius, all hail, Rome's gracious governor!　145
LUCIUS
Thanks, gentle Romans. May I govern so
To heal Rome's harms and wipe away her woe.
But, gentle people, give me aim awhile,
For nature puts me to a heavy task.
Stand all aloof, but, uncle, draw you near　150
To shed obsequious tears upon this trunk.
　(*Kissing Titus*) O, take this warm kiss on thy pale cold
　　lips,
These sorrowful drops upon thy bloodstained face,
The last true duties of thy noble son.
MARCUS (*kissing Titus*)
Tear for tear, and loving kiss for kiss,　155
Thy brother Marcus tenders on thy lips.
O, were the sum of these that I should pay
Countless and infinite, yet would I pay them.
LUCIUS (*to young Lucius*)
Come hither, boy, come, come, and learn of us
To melt in showers. Thy grandsire loved thee well.　160
Many a time he danced thee on his knee,

Sung thee asleep, his loving breast thy pillow.
Many a story hath he told to thee,
And bid thee bear his pretty tales in mind,
And talk of them when he was dead and gone.   165
MARCUS
How many thousand times hath these poor lips,
When they were living, warmed themselves on thine!
O now, sweet boy, give them their latest kiss.
Bid him farewell. Commit him to the grave.
Do them that kindness, and take leave of them.   170
YOUNG LUCIUS (*kissing Titus*)
O grandsire, grandsire, ev'n with all my heart
Would I were dead, so you did live again.
O Lord, I cannot speak to him for weeping.
My tears will choke me if I ope my mouth.
    Enter some with Aaron
A ROMAN
You sad Andronici, have done with woes.   175
Give sentence on this execrable wretch
That hath been breeder of these dire events.
LUCIUS
Set him breast-deep in earth and famish him.
There let him stand, and rave, and cry for food.

If anyone relieves or pities him,   180
For the offence he dies. This is our doom.
Some stay to see him fastened in the earth.
AARON
Ah, why should wrath be mute and fury dumb?
I am no baby, I, that with base prayers
I should repent the evils I have done.   185
Ten thousand worse than ever yet I did
Would I perform if I might have my will.
If one good deed in all my life I did
I do repent it from my very soul.
LUCIUS
Some loving friends convey the Emperor hence,   190
And give him burial in his father's grave.
My father and Lavinia shall forthwith
Be closèd in our household's monument.
As for that ravenous tiger, Tamora,
No funeral rite nor man in mourning weed,   195
No mournful bell shall ring her burial;
But throw her forth to beasts and birds to prey.
Her life was beastly and devoid of pity,
And being dead, let birds on her take pity.
    Exeunt with the bodies

ADDITIONAL PASSAGES

A. AFTER 1.1.35

The following passage, found in the First Quarto following
a comma after 'field' but not included in the Second or
Third Quartos or the Folio, conflicts with the subsequent
action and presumably should have been deleted. (In the
second line, Q1 reads 'of that' for 'of the'.)

              and at this day
To the monument of the Andronici
Done sacrifice of expiation,
And slain the noblest prisoner of the Goths.

B. AFTER 1.1.283

The following passage found in the quartos and the Folio
is difficult to reconcile with the apparent need for
Saturninus and his party to leave the stage at 275.1–2
before entering 'above' at 294.2–4. It is omitted from our
text in the belief that Shakespeare intended it to be deleted
after adding the episode of Mutius' killing to his original
draft, and that the printers of Q1 included it by accident.

[TITUS]
  Treason, my lord! Lavinia is surprised.
SATURNINUS
  Surprised, by whom?
BASSIANUS   By him that justly may
  Bear his betrothed from all the world away.

C. AFTER 4.3.93

The following lines, found in the early texts, appear to be
a draft of the subsequent six lines.

MARCUS (*to Titus*) Why, sir, that is as fit as can be to serve
  for your oration, and let him deliver the pigeons to the
  Emperor from you.
TITUS (*to the Clown*) Tell me, can you deliver an oration to
  the Emperor with a grace?   5
CLOWN Nay, truly, sir, I could never say grace in all my
  life.

ROMEO AND JULIET

ON its first appearance in print, in 1597, *Romeo and Juliet* was described as 'An excellent conceited tragedy' that had 'been often (with great applause) played publicly'; its popularity is witnessed by the fact that this is a pirated version, put together from actors' memories as a way of cashing in on its success. A second printing, two years later, offered a greatly superior text apparently printed from Shakespeare's working papers. Probably he wrote it in 1594 or 1595.

The story was already well known, in Italian, French, and English. Shakespeare owes most to Arthur Brooke's long poem *The Tragical History of Romeus and Juliet* (1562), which had already supplied hints for *The Two Gentlemen of Verona*; he may also have looked at some of the other versions. In his address 'To the Reader', Brooke says that he has seen 'the same argument lately set forth on stage with more commendation than I can look for', but no earlier play survives.

Shakespeare's Prologue neatly sketches the plot of the two star-crossed lovers born of feuding families whose deaths 'bury their parents' strife'; and the formal verse structure of the Prologue—a sonnet—is matched by the carefully patterned layout of the action. At the climax of the first scene, Prince Escalus stills a brawl between representatives of the houses of Montague (Romeo's family) and Capulet (Juliet's); at the end of Act 3, Scene 1, he passes judgement on another, more serious brawl, banishing Romeo for killing Juliet's cousin Tybalt after Tybalt had killed Romeo's friend and the Prince's kinsman, Mercutio; and at the end of Act 5, the Prince presides over the reconciliation of Montagues and Capulets. Within this framework of public life Romeo and Juliet act out their brief tragedy: in the first act they meet and declare their love—in another sonnet; in the second they arrange to marry in secret; in the third, after Romeo's banishment, they consummate their marriage and part; in the fourth, Juliet drinks a sleeping draught prepared by Friar Laurence so that she may escape marriage to Paris and, after waking in the family tomb, run off with Romeo; in the fifth, after Romeo, believing her to be dead, has taken poison, she stabs herself to death.

The play's structural formality is offset by an astonishing fertility of linguistic invention, showing itself no less in the comic bawdiness of the servants, the Nurse, and (on a more sophisticated level) Mercutio than in the rapt and impassioned poetry of the lovers. Shakespeare's mastery over a wide range of verbal styles combines with his psychological perceptiveness to create a richer gallery of memorable characters than in any of his earlier plays; and his theatrical imagination compresses Brooke's leisurely narrative into a dramatic masterpiece.

THE PERSONS OF THE PLAY

CHORUS

ROMEO

MONTAGUE, his father

MONTAGUE'S WIFE

BENVOLIO, Montague's nephew

ABRAHAM, Montague's servingman

BALTHASAR, Romeo's man

JULIET

CAPULET, her father

CAPULET'S WIFE

TYBALT, her nephew

His page

PETRUCCIO

CAPULET'S COUSIN

Juliet's NURSE

PETER
SAMSON } servingmen of the Capulets
GREGORY

Other SERVINGMEN

MUSICIANS

Escalus, PRINCE of Verona

MERCUTIO
County PARIS } his kinsmen

PAGE to Paris

FRIAR LAURENCE

FRIAR JOHN

An APOTHECARY

CHIEF WATCHMAN

Other CITIZENS OF THE WATCH

Masquers, guests, gentlewomen, followers of the Montague and
Capulet factions

The Most Excellent and Lamentable
Tragedy of Romeo and Juliet

Prologue   *Enter Chorus*
CHORUS
Two households, both alike in dignity
   In fair Verona, where we lay our scene,
From ancient grudge break to new mutiny,
   Where civil blood makes civil hands unclean.
From forth the fatal loins of these two foes   5
   A pair of star-crossed lovers take their life,
Whose misadventured piteous overthrows
   Doth with their death bury their parents' strife.
The fearful passage of their death-marked love
   And the continuance of their parents' rage—   10
Which but their children's end, naught could remove—
   Is now the two-hours' traffic of our stage;
The which if you with patient ears attend,
What here shall miss, our toil shall strive to mend.
                              Exit

1.1   *Enter Samson and Gregory, of the house of Capulet,*
   with swords and bucklers
SAMSON Gregory, on my word, we'll not carry coals.
GREGORY No, for then we should be colliers.
SAMSON I mean an we be in choler, we'll draw.
GREGORY Ay, while you live, draw your neck out of collar.
SAMSON I strike quickly, being moved.   5
GREGORY But thou art not quickly moved to strike.
SAMSON A dog of the house of Montague moves me.
GREGORY To move is to stir, and to be valiant is to stand,
   therefore if thou art moved, thou runn'st away.   9
SAMSON A dog of that house shall move me to stand. I
   will take the wall of any man or maid of Montague's.
GREGORY That shows thee a weak slave, for the weakest
   goes to the wall.
SAMSON 'Tis true, and therefore women, being the weaker
   vessels, are ever thrust to the wall; therefore I will
   push Montague's men from the wall, and thrust his
   maids to the wall.
GREGORY The quarrel is between our masters and us their
   men.   19
SAMSON 'Tis all one. I will show myself a tyrant: when I
   have fought with the men I will be civil with the
   maids—I will cut off their heads.
GREGORY The heads of the maids?
SAMSON Ay, the heads of the maids, or their maidenheads,
   take it in what sense thou wilt.   25
GREGORY They must take it in sense that feel it.
SAMSON Me they shall feel while I am able to stand, and
   'tis known I am a pretty piece of flesh.
GREGORY 'Tis well thou art not fish. If thou hadst, thou
   hadst been poor-john.   30

Enter Abraham and another servingman of the
Montagues
Draw thy tool. Here comes of the house of Montagues.
SAMSON My naked weapon is out. Quarrel, I will back
   thee.
GREGORY How—turn thy back and run?
SAMSON Fear me not.   35
GREGORY No, marry—I fear thee!
SAMSON Let us take the law of our side. Let them begin.
GREGORY I will frown as I pass by, and let them take it
   as they list.
SAMSON Nay, as they dare. I will bite my thumb at them,
   which is disgrace to them if they bear it.   41
He bites his thumb
ABRAHAM Do you bite your thumb at us, sir?
SAMSON I do bite my thumb, sir.
ABRAHAM Do you bite your thumb at us, sir?
SAMSON (*to Gregory*) Is the law of our side if I say 'Ay'? 45
GREGORY No.
SAMSON (*to Abraham*) No, sir, I do not bite my thumb at
   you, sir, but I bite my thumb, sir.
GREGORY (*to Abraham*) Do you quarrel, sir?
ABRAHAM Quarrel, sir? No, sir.   50
SAMSON But if you do, sir, I am for you. I serve as good
   a man as you.
ABRAHAM No better.
SAMSON Well, sir.
Enter Benvolio
GREGORY Say 'better'. Here comes one of my master's
   kinsmen.   56
SAMSON (*to Abraham*) Yes, better, sir.
ABRAHAM You lie.
SAMSON Draw, if you be men. Gregory, remember thy
   washing blow.   60
They draw and fight
BENVOLIO (*drawing*) Part, fools. Put up your swords. You
   know not what you do.
Enter Tybalt
TYBALT (*drawing*)
What, art thou drawn among these heartless hinds?
Turn thee, Benvolio. Look upon thy death.
BENVOLIO
I do but keep the peace. Put up thy sword,   65
Or manage it to part these men with me.
TYBALT
What, drawn and talk of peace? I hate the word
As I hate hell, all Montagues, and thee.
Have at thee, coward.
They fight. Enter three or four Citizens ⌜of the
watch⌝, with clubs or partisans

⌈CITIZENS OF THE WATCH⌉
Clubs, bills and partisans! Strike! Beat them down! 70
Down with the Capulets. Down with the Montagues.
Enter Capulet in his gown, and his Wife
CAPULET
What noise is this? Give me my long sword, ho!
CAPULET'S WIFE
A crutch, a crutch—why call you for a sword?
Enter Montague ⌈with his sword drawn⌉, and his
Wife
CAPULET
My sword, I say. Old Montague is come,
And flourishes his blade in spite of me. 75
MONTAGUE
Thou villain Capulet!
⌈*His Wife holds him back*⌉
           Hold me not, let me go.
MONTAGUE'S WIFE
Thou shalt not stir one foot to seek a foe.
⌈*The Citizens of the watch attempt to part*
the factions.⌉
Enter Prince Escalus with his train
PRINCE
Rebellious subjects, enemies to peace,
Profaners of this neighbour-stainèd steel—
Will they not hear? What ho, you men, you beasts, 80
That quench the fire of your pernicious rage
With purple fountains issuing from your veins:
On pain of torture, from those bloody hands
Throw your mistempered weapons to the ground,
And hear the sentence of your movèd Prince. 85
⌈*Montague, Capulet, and their followers throw down*
their weapons⌉
Three civil brawls bred of an airy word
By thee, old Capulet, and Montague,
Have thrice disturbed the quiet of our streets
And made Verona's ancient citizens
Cast by their grave-beseeming ornaments 90
To wield old partisans in hands as old,
Cankered with peace, to part your cankered hate.
If ever you disturb our streets again
Your lives shall pay the forfeit of the peace.
For this time all the rest depart away. 95
You, Capulet, shall go along with me;
And Montague, come you this afternoon
To know our farther pleasure in this case
To old Freetown, our common judgement-place.
Once more, on pain of death, all men depart. 100
         Exeunt all but Montague,
         his Wife, and Benvolio
MONTAGUE
Who set this ancient quarrel new abroach?
Speak, nephew: were you by when it began?
BENVOLIO
Here were the servants of your adversary
And yours, close fighting ere I did approach.
I drew to part them. In the instant came 105
The fiery Tybalt with his sword prepared,

Which, as he breathed defiance to my ears,
He swung about his head and cut the winds
Who, nothing hurt withal, hissed him in scorn.
While we were interchanging thrusts and blows, 110
Came more and more, and fought on part and part
Till the Prince came, who parted either part.
MONTAGUE'S WIFE
O where is Romeo—saw you him today?
Right glad I am he was not at this fray.
BENVOLIO
Madam, an hour before the worshipped sun 115
Peered forth the golden window of the east,
A troubled mind drive me to walk abroad,
Where, underneath the grove of sycamore
That westward rooteth from this city side,
So early walking did I see your son. 120
Towards him I made, but he was ware of me,
And stole into the covert of the wood.
I, measuring his affections by my own—
Which then most sought where most might not be
found,
Being one too many by my weary self— 125
Pursued my humour not pursuing his,
And gladly shunned who gladly fled from me.
MONTAGUE
Many a morning hath he there been seen,
With tears augmenting the fresh morning's dew,
Adding to clouds more clouds with his deep sighs. 130
But all so soon as the all-cheering sun
Should in the farthest east begin to draw
The shady curtains from Aurora's bed,
Away from light steals home my heavy son,
And private in his chamber pens himself, 135
Shuts up his windows, locks fair daylight out,
And makes himself an artificial night.
Black and portentous must this humour prove,
Unless good counsel may the cause remove.
BENVOLIO
My noble uncle, do you know the cause? 140
MONTAGUE
I neither know it nor can learn of him.
BENVOLIO
Have you importuned him by any means?
MONTAGUE
Both by myself and many other friends,
But he, his own affection's counsellor,
Is to himself—I will not say how true, 145
But to himself so secret and so close,
So far from sounding and discovery,
As is the bud bit with an envious worm
Ere he can spread his sweet leaves to the air
Or dedicate his beauty to the sun. 150
Could we but learn from whence his sorrows grow
We would as willingly give cure as know.
Enter Romeo
BENVOLIO
See where he comes. So please you step aside,
I'll know his grievance or be much denied.

MONTAGUE

I would thou wert so happy by thy stay   155
To hear true shrift. Come, madam, let's away.
                    Exeunt Montague and his Wife

BENVOLIO

Good morrow, cousin.

ROMEO   Is the day so young?

BENVOLIO

But new struck nine.

ROMEO   Ay me, sad hours seem long.
Was that my father that went hence so fast?

BENVOLIO

It was. What sadness lengthens Romeo's hours?   160

ROMEO

Not having that which, having, makes them short.

BENVOLIO In love.

ROMEO Out.

BENVOLIO Of love?

ROMEO

Out of her favour where I am in love.   165

BENVOLIO

Alas that love, so gentle in his view,
Should be so tyrannous and rough in proof.

ROMEO

Alas that love, whose view is muffled still,
Should without eyes see pathways to his will.
Where shall we dine? ⌈*Seeing blood*⌉ O me! What fray
    was here?   170
Yet tell me not, for I have heard it all.
Here's much to do with hate, but more with love.
Why then, O brawling love, O loving hate,
O anything of nothing first create;
O heavy lightness, serious vanity,   175
Misshapen chaos of well-seeming forms,
Feather of lead, bright smoke, cold fire, sick health,
Still-waking sleep, that is not what it is!
This love feel I, that feel no love in this.
Dost thou not laugh?

BENVOLIO   No, coz, I rather weep.   180

ROMEO

Good heart, at what?

BENVOLIO   At thy good heart's oppression.

ROMEO Why, such is love's transgression.
Griefs of mine own lie heavy in my breast,
Which thou wilt propagate to have it pressed
With more of thine. This love that thou hast shown
Doth add more grief to too much of mine own.   186
Love is a smoke made with the fume of sighs,
Being purged, a fire sparkling in lovers' eyes,
Being vexed, a sea nourished with lovers' tears.
What is it else? A madness most discreet,   190
A choking gall and a preserving sweet.
Farewell, my coz.

BENVOLIO   Soft, I will go along;
An if you leave me so, you do me wrong.

ROMEO

Tut, I have lost myself. I am not here.
This is not Romeo; he's some other where.   195

BENVOLIO

Tell me in sadness, who is that you love?

ROMEO What, shall I groan and tell thee?

BENVOLIO

Groan? Why no; but sadly tell me who.

ROMEO

Bid a sick man in sadness make his will,
A word ill urged to one that is so ill.   200
In sadness, cousin, I do love a woman.

BENVOLIO

I aimed so near when I supposed you loved.

ROMEO

A right good markman; and she's fair I love.

BENVOLIO

A right fair mark, fair coz, is soonest hit.

ROMEO

Well, in that hit you miss. She'll not be hit   205
With Cupid's arrow; she hath Dian's wit,
And, in strong proof of chastity well armed,
From love's weak childish bow she lives unharmed.
She will not stay the siege of loving terms,
Nor bide th'encounter of assailing eyes,   210
Nor ope her lap to saint-seducing gold.
O, she is rich in beauty, only poor
That when she dies, with beauty dies her store.

BENVOLIO

Then she hath sworn that she will still live chaste?

ROMEO

She hath, and in that sparing makes huge waste; 215
For beauty starved with her severity
Cuts beauty off from all posterity.
She is too fair, too wise, wisely too fair,
To merit bliss by making me despair.
She hath forsworn to love, and in that vow   220
Do I live dead, that live to tell it now.

BENVOLIO

Be ruled by me; forget to think of her.

ROMEO

O, teach me how I should forget to think!

BENVOLIO

By giving liberty unto thine eyes.
Examine other beauties.

ROMEO   'Tis the way   225
To call hers, exquisite, in question more.
These happy masks that kiss fair ladies' brows,
Being black, puts us in mind they hide the fair.
He that is strucken blind cannot forget
The precious treasure of his eyesight lost.   230
Show me a mistress that is passing fair,
What doth her beauty serve but as a note
Where I may read who passed that passing fair?
Farewell, thou canst not teach me to forget.

BENVOLIO

I'll pay that doctrine, or else die in debt.   *Exeunt*

1.2   *Enter Capulet, Paris, and* ⌈*Peter,*⌉ *a servingman*

CAPULET

But Montague is bound as well as I,

In penalty alike, and 'tis not hard, I think,
For men so old as we to keep the peace.
PARIS
Of honourable reckoning are you both,
And pity 'tis you lived at odds so long.   5
But now, my lord: what say you to my suit?
CAPULET
But saying o'er what I have said before.
My child is yet a stranger in the world;
She hath not seen the change of fourteen years,
Let two more summers wither in their pride   10
Ere we may think her ripe to be a bride.
PARIS
Younger than she are happy mothers made.
CAPULET
And too soon marred are those so early made.
But woo her, gentle Paris, get her heart;
My will to her consent is but a part,   15
And, she agreed, within her scope of choice
Lies my consent and fair-according voice.
This night I hold an old-accustomed feast
Whereto I have invited many a guest
Such as I love, and you among the store,   20
One more most welcome, makes my number more.
At my poor house look to behold this night
Earth-treading stars that make dark heaven light.
Such comfort as do lusty young men feel
When well-apparelled April on the heel   25
Of limping winter treads—even such delight
Among fresh female buds shall you this night
Inherit at my house; hear all, all see,
And like her most whose merit most shall be,
Which on more view of many, mine, being one,   30
May stand in number, though in reck'ning none.
Come, go with me. (*Giving ⌈Peter⌉ a paper*) Go, sirrah,
    trudge about;
Through fair Verona find those persons out
Whose names are written there, and to them say
My house and welcome on their pleasure stay.   35
                              Exeunt Capulet and Paris
⌈PETER⌉ Find them out whose names are written here? It
is written that the shoemaker should meddle with his
yard and the tailor with his last, the fisher with his
pencil and the painter with his nets; but I am sent to
find those persons whose names are here writ, and can
never find what names the writing person hath here
writ. I must to the learned.
    Enter Benvolio and Romeo
In good time.
BENVOLIO (*to Romeo*)
Tut, man, one fire burns out another's burning,
    One pain is lessened by another's anguish.   45
Turn giddy, and be holp by backward turning.
    One desperate grief cures with another's languish.
Take thou some new infection to thy eye,
And the rank poison of the old will die.
ROMEO
Your plantain leaf is excellent for that.   50

BENVOLIO For what, I pray thee?
ROMEO For your broken shin.
BENVOLIO Why, Romeo, art thou mad?
ROMEO
Not mad, but bound more than a madman is;
Shut up in prison, kept without my food,   55
Whipped and tormented and— (*to ⌈Peter⌉*) Good e'en,
    good fellow.
⌈PETER⌉
God gi'good e'en. I pray, sir, can you read?
ROMEO
Ay, mine own fortune in my misery.
⌈PETER⌉ Perhaps you have learned it without book. But I
pray, can you read anything you see?   60
ROMEO
Ay, if I know the letters and the language.
⌈PETER⌉ Ye say honestly. Rest you merry.
ROMEO Stay, fellow, I can read.
    He reads the letter
'Signor Martino and his wife and daughters,
County Anselme and his beauteous sisters,   65
The lady widow of Vitruvio,
Signor Placentio and his lovely nieces,
Mercutio and his brother Valentine,
Mine uncle Capulet, his wife and daughters,
My fair niece Rosaline and Livia,   70
Signor Valentio and his cousin Tybalt,
Lucio and the lively Helena.'
A fair assembly. Whither should they come?
⌈PETER⌉ Up.
ROMEO Whither?   75
⌈PETER⌉ To supper to our house.
ROMEO Whose house?
⌈PETER⌉ My master's.
ROMEO
Indeed, I should have asked thee that before.   79
⌈PETER⌉ Now I'll tell you without asking. My master is
the great rich Capulet, and if you be not of the house
of Montagues, I pray come and crush a cup of wine.
Rest you merry.   *Exit*
BENVOLIO
At this same ancient feast of Capulet's
Sups the fair Rosaline, whom thou so loves,   85
With all the admirèd beauties of Verona.
Go thither, and with unattainted eye
Compare her face with some that I shall show,
And I will make thee think thy swan a crow.
ROMEO
When the devout religion of mine eye   90
    Maintains such falsehood, then turn tears to fires;
And these who, often drowned, could never die,
    Transparent heretics, be burnt for liars.
One fairer than my love!—the all-seeing sun
Ne'er saw her match since first the world begun.   95
BENVOLIO
Tut, you saw her fair, none else being by,
Herself poised with herself in either eye;

But in that crystal scales let there be weighed
Your lady's love against some other maid
That I will show you shining at this feast,   100
And she shall scant show well that now seems best.

ROMEO
I'll go along, no such sight to be shown,
But to rejoice in splendour of mine own.   *Exeunt*

1.3   *Enter Capulet's Wife and the Nurse*

CAPULET'S WIFE
Nurse, where's my daughter? Call her forth to me.

NURSE
Now, by my maidenhead at twelve year old,
I bade her come. What, lamb, what, ladybird—
God forbid—where is this girl? What, Juliet!
        Enter Juliet

JULIET How now, who calls?   5

NURSE Your mother.

JULIET
Madam, I am here. What is your will?

CAPULET'S WIFE
This is the matter.—Nurse, give leave a while.
We must talk in secret.—Nurse, come back again.
I have remembered me, thou s' hear our counsel.   10
Thou knowest my daughter's of a pretty age.

NURSE
Faith, I can tell her age unto an hour.

CAPULET'S WIFE She's not fourteen.

NURSE I'll lay fourteen of my teeth—and yet, to my teen
be it spoken, I have but four—she's not fourteen. How
long is it now to Lammastide?   16

CAPULET'S WIFE A fortnight and odd days.

NURSE
Even or odd, of all days in the year
Come Lammas Eve at night shall she be fourteen.
Susan and she—God rest all Christian souls!—   20
Were of an age. Well, Susan is with God;
She was too good for me. But, as I said,
On Lammas Eve at night shall she be fourteen,
That shall she, marry, I remember it well.
'Tis since the earthquake now eleven years,   25
And she was weaned—I never shall forget it—
Of all the days of the year upon that day,
For I had then laid wormwood to my dug,
Sitting in the sun under the dovehouse wall.
My lord and you were then at Mantua.   30
Nay, I do bear a brain! But, as I said,
When it did taste the wormwood on the nipple
Of my dug and felt it bitter, pretty fool,
To see it tetchy and fall out wi'th' dug!
'Shake', quoth the dove-house! 'Twas no need, I trow,
To bid me trudge;   36
And since that time it is eleven years,
For then she could stand high-lone. Nay, by th' rood,
She could have run and waddled all about,
For even the day before, she broke her brow,   40
And then my husband—God be with his soul,
A was a merry man!—took up the child.

'Yea,' quoth he, 'dost thou fall upon thy face?
Thou wilt fall backward when thou hast more wit,
Wilt thou not, Jule?' And, by my holidam,   45
The pretty wretch left crying and said 'Ay'.
To see now how a jest shall come about!
I warrant an I should live a thousand years
I never should forget it. 'Wilt thou not, Jule?' quoth he,
And, pretty fool, it stinted and said 'Ay'.   50

CAPULET'S WIFE
Enough of this. I pray thee hold thy peace.

NURSE
Yes, madam. Yet I cannot choose but laugh
To think it should leave crying and say 'Ay'.
And yet, I warrant, it had upon it brow
A bump as big as a young cock'rel's stone.   55
A perilous knock, and it cried bitterly.
'Yea,' quoth my husband, 'fall'st upon thy face?
Thou wilt fall backward when thou com'st to age,
Wilt thou not, Jule?' It stinted and said 'Ay'.

JULIET
And stint thou too, I pray thee, Nurse, say I.   60

NURSE
Peace, I have done. God mark thee to his grace,
Thou wast the prettiest babe that e'er I nursed.
An I might live to see thee married once,
I have my wish.

CAPULET'S WIFE
Marry, that 'marry' is the very theme   65
I came to talk of. Tell me, daughter Juliet,
How stands your dispositions to be married?

JULIET
It is an honour that I dream not of.

NURSE
'An honour'! Were not I thine only nurse,
I would say thou hadst sucked wisdom from thy teat. 70

CAPULET'S WIFE
Well, think of marriage now. Younger than you
Here in Verona, ladies of esteem,
Are made already mothers. By my count
I was your mother much upon these years
That you are now a maid. Thus then, in brief: 75
The valiant Paris seeks you for his love.

NURSE
A man, young lady, lady, such a man
As all the world—why, he's a man of wax.

CAPULET'S WIFE
Verona's summer hath not such a flower.

NURSE
Nay, he's a flower, in faith, a very flower.   80

CAPULET'S WIFE *(to Juliet)*
What say you? Can you love the gentleman?
This night you shall behold him at our feast.
Read o'er the volume of young Paris' face,
And find delight writ there with beauty's pen.
Examine every married lineament,   85
And see how one another lends content;
And what obscured in this fair volume lies
Find written in the margin of his eyes.

This precious book of love, this unbound lover,
To beautify him only lacks a cover.   90
The fish lives in the sea, and 'tis much pride
For fair without the fair within to hide.
That book in many's eyes doth share the glory
That in gold clasps locks in the golden story.
So shall you share all that he doth possess   95
By having him, making yourself no less.
NURSE
    No less, nay, bigger. Women grow by men.
CAPULET'S WIFE (*to Juliet*)
    Speak briefly: can you like of Paris' love?
JULIET
    I'll look to like, if looking liking move;
But no more deep will I endart mine eye   100
Than your consent gives strength to make it fly.
            Enter ⸢Peter⸣
⸢PETER⸣ Madam, the guests are come, supper served up,
    you called, my young lady asked for, the Nurse cursed
    in the pantry, and everything in extremity. I must hence
    to wait. I beseech you follow straight.   105
CAPULET'S WIFE
    We follow thee.   *Exit* ⸢Peter⸣
            Juliet, the County stays.
NURSE
    Go, girl; seek happy nights to happy days.   *Exeunt*

1.4   *Enter Romeo, Mercutio, and Benvolio, as masquers,*
        with five or six other masquers, ⸢*bearing a drum and*⸣
        torches⸣
ROMEO
    What, shall this speech be spoke for our excuse,
    Or shall we on without apology?
BENVOLIO
    The date is out of such prolixity.
    We'll have no Cupid hoodwinked with a scarf,
    Bearing a Tartar's painted bow of lath,   5
    Scaring the ladies like a crowkeeper,
    Nor no without-book Prologue faintly spoke
    After the prompter for our entrance.
    But let them measure us by what they will,
    We'll measure them a measure, and be gone.   10
ROMEO
    Give me a torch. I am not for this ambling;
    Being but heavy, I will bear the light.
MERCUTIO
    Nay, gentle Romeo, we must have you dance.
ROMEO
    Not I, believe me. You have dancing shoes
    With nimble soles; I have a soul of lead   15
    So stakes me to the ground I cannot move.
MERCUTIO
    You are a lover; borrow Cupid's wings,
    And soar with them above a common bound.
ROMEO
    I am too sore empiercèd with his shaft
    To soar with his light feathers, and so bound   20
    I cannot bound a pitch above dull woe;
    Under love's heavy burden do I sink.

MERCUTIO
    And to sink in it should you burden love—
    Too great oppression for a tender thing.
ROMEO
    Is love a tender thing? It is too rough,   25
    Too rude, too boist'rous, and it pricks like thorn.
MERCUTIO
    If love be rough with you, be rough with love.
    Prick love for pricking, and you beat love down.
    Give me a case to put my visage in,
    A visor for a visor. What care I   30
    What curious eye doth quote deformity?
    Here are the beetle brows shall blush for me.
            ⸢*They put on visors*⸣
BENVOLIO
    Come, knock and enter, and no sooner in
    But every man betake him to his legs.
ROMEO
    A torch for me. Let wantons light of heart   35
    Tickle the sense-less rushes with their heels,
    For I am proverbed with a grandsire phrase,
    I'll be a candle-holder and look on.
    The game was ne'er so fair, and I am done.
            ⸢*He takes a torch*⸣
MERCUTIO
    Tut, dun's the mouse, the constable's own word.   40
    If thou art dun we'll draw thee from the mire
    Of—save your reverence—love, wherein thou stickest
    Up to the ears. Come, we burn daylight, ho!
ROMEO
    Nay, that's not so.
MERCUTIO   I mean, sir, in delay
    We waste our lights in vain, like lights by day.   45
    Take our good meaning, for our judgement sits
    Five times in that ere once in our five wits.
ROMEO
    And we mean well in going to this masque,
    But 'tis no wit to go.
MERCUTIO   Why, may one ask?
ROMEO
    I dreamt a dream tonight.
MERCUTIO   And so did I.   50
ROMEO
    Well, what was yours?
MERCUTIO   That dreamers often lie.
ROMEO
    In bed asleep while they do dream things true.
MERCUTIO
    O, then I see Queen Mab hath been with you.
BENVOLIO Queen Mab, what's she?
MERCUTIO
    She is the fairies' midwife, and she comes   55
    In shape no bigger than an agate stone
    On the forefinger of an alderman,
    Drawn with a team of little atomi
    Athwart men's noses as they lie asleep.
    Her wagon spokes made of long spinners' legs;   60
    The cover, of the wings of grasshoppers;

Her traces, of the moonshine's wat'ry beams;
Her collars, of the smallest spider web;
Her whip, of cricket's bone, the lash of film;
Her wagoner, a small grey-coated gnat   65
Not half so big as a round little worm
Pricked from the lazy finger of a maid.   .
Her chariot is an empty hazelnut
Made by the joiner squirrel or old grub,
Time out o' mind the fairies' coachmakers.   70
And in this state she gallops night by night
Through lovers' brains, and then they dream of love;
O'er courtiers' knees, that dream on curtsies straight;
O'er ladies' lips, who straight on kisses dream,
Which oft the angry Mab with blisters plagues   75
Because their breaths with sweetmeats tainted are.
Sometime she gallops o'er a lawyer's lip,
And then dreams he of smelling out a suit;
And sometime comes she with a tithe-pig's tail
Tickling a parson's nose as a lies asleep;   80
Then dreams he of another benefice.
Sometime she driveth o'er a soldier's neck,
And then dreams he of cutting foreign throats,
Of breaches, ambuscados, Spanish blades,
Of healths five fathom deep; and then anon   85
Drums in his ear, at which he starts and wakes,
And being thus frighted, swears a prayer or two,
And sleeps again. This is that very Mab
That plaits the manes of horses in the night,
And bakes the elf-locks in foul sluttish hairs,   90
Which once untangled much misfortune bodes.
This is the hag, when maids lie on their backs,
That presses them and learns them first to bear,
Making them women of good carriage.
This is she—
ROMEO   Peace, peace, Mercutio, peace!   95
Thou talk'st of nothing.
MERCUTIO   True. I talk of dreams,
Which are the children of an idle brain,
Begot of nothing but vain fantasy,
Which is as thin of substance as the air,
And more inconstant than the wind, who woos   100
Even now the frozen bosom of the north,
And, being angered, puffs away from thence,
Turning his face to the dew-dropping south.
BENVOLIO
This wind you talk of blows us from ourselves.
Supper is done, and we shall come too late.   105
ROMEO
I fear too early, for my mind misgives
Some consequence yet hanging in the stars
Shall bitterly begin his fearful date
With this night's revels, and expire the term
Of a despisèd life, closed in my breast,   110
By some vile forfeit of untimely death.
But he that hath the steerage of my course
Direct my sail! On, lusty gentlemen.
BENVOLIO Strike, drum.
They march about the stage and ⌈exeunt⌉

1.5   ⌈*Peter*⌉ *and other Servingmen come forth with napkins*
⌈PETER⌉ Where's Potpan, that he helps not to take away?
He shift a trencher, he scrape a trencher!
FIRST SERVINGMAN When good manners shall lie all in one
or two men's hands, and they unwashed too, 'tis a foul
thing.   5
⌈PETER⌉ Away with the joint-stools, remove the court-
cupboard, look to the plate. Good thou, save me a piece
of marzipan, and, as thou loves me, let the porter let in
Susan Grindstone and Nell. Anthony and Potpan!
SECOND SERVINGMAN Ay, boy, ready.   10
⌈PETER⌉ You are looked for and called for, asked for and
sought for, in the great chamber.
⌈FIRST⌉ SERVINGMAN We cannot be here and there too.
Cheerly, boys! Be brisk a while, and the longest liver
take all.   15
    ⌈*They come and go, setting forth tables and chairs*⌉
    Enter ⌈*Musicians, then*⌉ *at one door Capulet,* ⌈*his*
    Wife,⌉ *his Cousin, Juliet,* ⌈*the Nurse,*⌉ *Tybalt, his*
    page, Petruccio, and all the guests and gentlewomen;
    at another door, the masquers: ⌈*Romeo, Benvolio and*
    Mercutio⌉
CAPULET (*to the masquers*)   85
Welcome, gentlemen. Ladies that have their toes
Unplagued with corns will walk a bout with you.
Aha, my mistresses, which of you all
Will now deny to dance? She that makes dainty,
She, I'll swear, hath corns. Am I come near ye now? 20
Welcome, gentlemen. I have seen the day
That I have worn a visor, and could tell
A whispering tale in a fair lady's ear
Such as would please. 'Tis gone, 'tis gone, 'tis gone.
You are welcome, gentlemen. Come, musicians, play. 25
    Music plays, and the masquers, guests, and
    gentlewomen dance. ⌈*Romeo stands apart*⌉
A hall, a hall! Give room, and foot it, girls.
(*To Servingmen*) More light, you knaves, and turn the
    tables up,
And quench the fire, the room is grown too hot.
(*To his Cousin*) Ah sirrah, this unlooked-for sport comes
    well.
Nay, sit, nay, sit, good cousin Capulet,   30
For you and I are past our dancing days.
    ⌈*Capulet and his Cousin sit*⌉
How long is't now since last yourself and I
Were in a masque?
CAPULET'S COUSIN   By'r Lady, thirty years.
CAPULET
What, man, 'tis not so much, 'tis not so much.
'Tis since the nuptial of Lucentio,   35
Come Pentecost as quickly as it will,
Some five-and-twenty years; and then we masqued.
CAPULET'S COUSIN
'Tis more, 'tis more. His son is elder, sir.
His son is thirty.
CAPULET   Will you tell me that?
His son was but a ward two years ago.   40

ROMEO (*to a Servingman*)
  What lady's that which doth enrich the hand
  Of yonder knight?
SERVINGMAN   I know not, sir.
ROMEO
  O, she doth teach the torches to burn bright!
  It seems she hangs upon the cheek of night
  As a rich jewel in an Ethiope's ear—   45
  Beauty too rich for use, for earth too dear.
  So shows a snowy dove trooping with crows
  As yonder lady o'er her fellows shows.
  The measure done, I'll watch her place of stand,
  And, touching hers, make blessèd my rude hand.   50
  Did my heart love till now? Forswear it, sight,
  For I ne'er saw true beauty till this night.
TYBALT
  This, by his voice, should be a Montague.
  Fetch me my rapier, boy.   ⌜*Exit page*⌝
                    What, dares the slave
  Come hither, covered with an antic face,   55
  To fleer and scorn at our solemnity?
  Now, by the stock and honour of my kin,
  To strike him dead I hold it not a sin.
CAPULET ⌜*standing*⌝
  Why, how now, kinsman? Wherefore storm you so?
TYBALT
  Uncle, this is a Montague, our foe,   60
  A villain that is hither come in spite
  To scorn at our solemnity this night.
CAPULET
  Young Romeo, is it?
TYBALT   'Tis he, that villain Romeo.
CAPULET
  Content thee, gentle coz, let him alone.
  A bears him like a portly gentleman,   65
  And, to say truth, Verona brags of him
  To be a virtuous and well-governed youth.
  I would not for the wealth of all this town
  Here in my house do him disparagement.
  Therefore be patient, take no note of him.   70
  It is my will, the which if thou respect,
  Show a fair presence and put off these frowns,
  An ill-beseeming semblance for a feast.
TYBALT
  It fits when such a villain is a guest.
  I'll not endure him.
CAPULET   He shall be endured.   75
  What, goodman boy, I say he shall. Go to,
  Am I the master here or you? Go to—
  You'll not endure him! God shall mend my soul.
  You'll make a mutiny among my guests,
  You will set cock-a-hoop! You'll be the man!   80
TYBALT
  Why, uncle, 'tis a shame.
CAPULET   Go to, go to,
  You are a saucy boy. Is't so, indeed?
  This trick may chance to scathe you. I know what,
  You must contrary me. Marry, 'tis time—

⌜*A dance ends. Juliet retires to her place of stand,*
  where Romeo awaits her⌝
  (*To the guests*) Well said, my hearts! (*To Tybalt*) You are
    a princox, go.   85
  Be quiet, or— (*to Servingmen*) more light, more light!—
    (*to Tybalt*) for shame,
  I'll make you quiet. (*To the guests*) What, cheerly, my
    hearts!
  ⌜*The music plays again, and the guests dance*⌝
TYBALT
  Patience perforce with wilful choler meeting
  Makes my flesh tremble in their different greeting.
  I will withdraw, but this intrusion shall,   90
  Now seeming sweet, convert to bitt'rest gall.   *Exit*
ROMEO (*to Juliet, touching her hand*)
  If I profane with my unworthiest hand
    This holy shrine, the gentler sin is this:
  My lips, two blushing pilgrims, ready stand
    To smooth that rough touch with a tender kiss.   95
JULIET
  Good pilgrim, you do wrong your hand too much,
    Which mannerly devotion shows in this.
  For saints have hands that pilgrims' hands do touch,
    And palm to palm is holy palmers' kiss.
ROMEO
  Have not saints lips, and holy palmers, too?   100
JULIET
  Ay, pilgrim, lips that they must use in prayer.
ROMEO
  O then, dear saint, let lips do what hands do:
    They pray; grant thou, lest faith turn to despair.
JULIET
  Saints do not move, though grant for prayers' sake.
ROMEO
  Then move not while my prayer's effect I take.   105
    He kisses her
  Thus from my lips, by thine my sin is purged.
JULIET
  Then have my lips the sin that they have took.
ROMEO
  Sin from my lips? O trespass sweetly urged!
    Give me my sin again.
    He kisses her
JULIET   You kiss by th' book.
NURSE
  Madam, your mother craves a word with you.   110
    ⌜*Juliet departs to her mother*⌝
ROMEO
  What is her mother?
NURSE   Marry, bachelor,
  Her mother is the lady of the house,
  And a good lady, and a wise and virtuous.
  I nursed her daughter that you talked withal.
  I tell you, he that can lay hold of her   115
  Shall have the chinks.
ROMEO (*aside*)   Is she a Capulet?
  O dear account! My life is my foe's debt.

BENVOLIO

Away, be gone, the sport is at the best.

ROMEO

Ay, so I fear, the more is my unrest.

CAPULET

Nay, gentlemen, prepare not to be gone.   120

We have a trifling foolish banquet towards.

⌈*They whisper in his ear*⌉

Is it e'en so? Why then, I thank you all.

I thank you, honest gentlemen. Good night.

More torches here! Come on then, let's to bed.

(*To his Cousin*) Ah, sirrah, by my fay, it waxes late.   125

I'll to my rest.

Exeunt Capulet, ⌈his Wife,⌉ and his Cousin. The

guests, gentlewomen, masquers, musicians, and

servingmen begin to leave

JULIET

Come hither, Nurse. What is yon gentleman?

NURSE

The son and heir of old Tiberio.

JULIET

What's he that now is going out of door?

NURSE

Marry, that, I think, be young Petruccio.   130

JULIET

What's he that follows here, that would not dance?

NURSE I know not.

JULIET

Go ask his name.

The Nurse goes

If he be marrièd,

My grave is like to be my wedding bed.

NURSE (*returning*)

His name is Romeo, and a Montague,   135

The only son of your great enemy.

JULIET ⌈*aside*⌉

My only love sprung from my only hate!

Too early seen unknown, and known too late!

Prodigious birth of love it is to me

That I must love a loathèd enemy.   140

NURSE

What's tis? what's tis?

JULIET   A rhyme I learnt even now

Of one I danced withal.

One calls within 'Juliet!'

NURSE   Anon, anon.

Come, let's away. The strangers all are gone.   *Exeunt*

2.0   *Enter Chorus*

CHORUS

Now old desire doth in his deathbed lie,

And young affection gapes to be his heir.

That fair for which love groaned for and would die,

With tender Juliet matched, is now not fair.

Now Romeo is beloved and loves again,   5

Alike bewitchèd by the charm of looks;

But to his foe supposed he must complain,

And she steal love's sweet bait from fearful hooks.

Being held a foe, he may not have access

To breathe such vows as lovers use to swear,   10

And she as much in love, her means much less

To meet her new belovèd anywhere.

But passion lends them power, time means, to meet,

Temp'ring extremities with extreme sweet.   *Exit*

2.1   *Enter Romeo*

ROMEO

Can I go forward when my heart is here?

Turn back, dull earth, and find thy centre out.

⌈*He turns back and withdraws.*⌉

Enter Benvolio with Mercutio

BENVOLIO (*calling*)

Romeo, my cousin Romeo, Romeo!

MERCUTIO

He is wise, and, on my life, hath stol'n him home to

bed.

BENVOLIO

He ran this way, and leapt this orchard wall.   5

Call, good Mercutio.

⌈MERCUTIO⌉   Nay, I'll conjure too.

Romeo! Humours! Madman! Passion! Lover!

Appear thou in the likeness of a sigh.

Speak but one rhyme and I am satisfied.

Cry but 'Ay me!' Pronounce but 'love' and 'dove'.   10

Speak to my gossip Venus one fair word,

One nickname for her purblind son and heir,

Young Adam Cupid, he that shot so trim

When King Cophetua loved the beggar maid.—

He heareth not, he stirreth not, he moveth not.   15

The ape is dead, and I must conjure him.—

I conjure thee by Rosaline's bright eyes,

By her high forehead and her scarlet lip,

By her fine foot, straight leg, and quivering thigh,

And the demesnes that there adjacent lie,   20

That in thy likeness thou appear to us.

BENVOLIO

An if he hear thee, thou wilt anger him.

MERCUTIO

This cannot anger him. 'Twould anger him

To raise a spirit in his mistress' circle

Of some strange nature, letting it there stand   25

Till she had laid it and conjured it down.

That were some spite. My invocation

Is fair and honest. In his mistress' name,

I conjure only but to raise up him.

BENVOLIO

Come, he hath hid himself among these trees   30

To be consorted with the humorous night.

Blind is his love, and best befits the dark.

MERCUTIO

If love be blind, love cannot hit the mark.

Now will he sit under a medlar tree

And wish his mistress were that kind of fruit   35

As maids call medlars when they laugh alone.

O Romeo, that she were, O that she were

An open-arse, and thou a popp'rin' pear.

Romeo, good night. I'll to my truckle-bed.
This field-bed is too cold for me to sleep.   40
Come, shall we go?
BENVOLIO   Go then, for 'tis in vain
To seek him here that means not to be found.
          Exeunt Benvolio and Mercutio
ROMEO ⌈*coming forward*⌉
He jests at scars that never felt a wound.
But soft, what light through yonder window breaks?
It is the east, and Juliet is the sun.   45
Arise, fair sun, and kill the envious moon,
Who is already sick and pale with grief
That thou, her maid, art far more fair than she.
Be not her maid, since she is envious.
Her vestal livery is but sick and green,   50
And none but fools do wear it; cast it off.
          ⌈*Enter Juliet aloft*⌉
It is my lady, O, it is my love.
O that she knew she were!
She speaks, yet she says nothing. What of that?
Her eye discourses; I will answer it.   55
I am too bold. 'Tis not to me she speaks.
Two of the fairest stars in all the heaven,
Having some business, do entreat her eyes
To twinkle in their spheres till they return.
What if her eyes were there, they in her head?—   60
The brightness of her cheek would shame those stars
As daylight doth a lamp; her eye in heaven
Would through the airy region stream so bright
That birds would sing and think it were not night.
See how she leans her cheek upon her hand.   65
O, that I were a glove upon that hand,
That I might touch that cheek!
JULIET   Ay me.
ROMEO (*aside*)   She speaks.
O, speak again, bright angel; for thou art
As glorious to this night, being o'er my head,
As is a wingèd messenger of heaven   70
Unto the white upturnèd wond'ring eyes
Of mortals that fall back to gaze on him
When he bestrides the lazy-passing clouds
And sails upon the bosom of the air.
JULIET (*not knowing Romeo hears her*)
O Romeo, Romeo, wherefore art thou Romeo?   75
Deny thy father and refuse thy name,
Or if thou wilt not, be but sworn my love,
And I'll no longer be a Capulet.
ROMEO (*aside*)
Shall I hear more, or shall I speak at this?
JULIET
'Tis but thy name that is my enemy.   80
Thou art thyself, though not a Montague.
What's Montague? It is nor hand, nor foot,
Nor arm, nor face, nor any other part
Belonging to a man. O, be some other name!
What's in a name? That which we call a rose   85
By any other word would smell as sweet.
So Romeo would, were he not Romeo called,

Retain that dear perfection which he owes
Without that title. Romeo, doff thy name,
And for thy name—which is no part of thee—   90
Take all myself.
ROMEO (*to Juliet*)   I take thee at thy word.
Call me but love and I'll be new baptized.
Henceforth I never will be Romeo.
JULIET
What man art thou that, thus bescreened in night,
So stumblest on my counsel?
ROMEO   By a name   95
I know not how to tell thee who I am.
My name, dear saint, is hateful to myself
Because it is an enemy to thee.
Had I it written, I would tear the word.
JULIET
My ears have yet not drunk a hundred words   100
Of thy tongue's uttering, yet I know the sound.
Art thou not Romeo, and a Montague?
ROMEO
Neither, fair maid, if either thee dislike.
JULIET
How cam'st thou hither, tell me, and wherefore?
The orchard walls are high and hard to climb,   105
And the place death, considering who thou art,
If any of my kinsmen find thee here.
ROMEO
With love's light wings did I o'erperch these walls,
For stony limits cannot hold love out,
And what love can do, that dares love attempt.   110
Therefore thy kinsmen are no stop to me.
JULIET
If they do see thee, they will murder thee.
ROMEO
Alack, there lies more peril in thine eye
Than twenty of their swords. Look thou but sweet,
And I am proof against their enmity.   115
JULIET
I would not for the world they saw thee here.
ROMEO
I have night's cloak to hide me from their eyes,
And but thou love me, let them find me here.
My life were better ended by their hate
Than death proroguèd, wanting of thy love.   120
JULIET
By whose direction found'st thou out this place?
ROMEO
By love, that first did prompt me to enquire.
He lent me counsel, and I lent him eyes.
I am no pilot, yet wert thou as far
As that vast shore washed with the farthest sea,   125
I should adventure for such merchandise.
JULIET
Thou knowest the mask of night is on my face,
Else would a maiden blush bepaint my cheek
For that which thou hast heard me speak tonight.
Fain would I dwell on form, fain, fain deny   130
What I have spoke; but farewell, compliment.

Dost thou love me? I know thou wilt say 'Ay',
And I will take thy word. Yet if thou swear'st
Thou mayst prove false. At lovers' perjuries,
They say, Jove laughs. O gentle Romeo,   135
If thou dost love, pronounce it faithfully;
Or if thou think'st I am too quickly won,
I'll frown, and be perverse, and say thee nay,
So thou wilt woo; but else, not for the world.
In truth, fair Montague, I am too fond,   140
And therefore thou mayst think my 'haviour light.
But trust me, gentleman, I'll prove more true
Than those that have more cunning to be strange.
I should have been more strange, I must confess,
But that thou overheard'st, ere I was ware,   145
My true-love passion. Therefore pardon me,
And not impute this yielding to light love,
Which the dark night hath so discoverèd.

ROMEO
Lady, by yonder blessèd moon I vow,
That tips with silver all these fruit-tree tops—   150
JULIET
O swear not by the moon, th'inconstant moon
That monthly changes in her circled orb,
Lest that thy love prove likewise variable.
ROMEO
What shall I swear by?
JULiET   Do not swear at all,
Or if thou wilt, swear by thy gracious self,   155
Which is the god of my idolatry,
And I'll believe thee.
ROMEO   If my heart's dear love—
JULIET
Well, do not swear. Although I joy in thee,
I have no joy of this contract tonight.
It is too rash, too unadvised, too sudden,   160
Too like the lightning which doth cease to be
Ere one can say it lightens. Sweet, good night.
This bud of love by summer's ripening breath
May prove a beauteous flower when next we meet.
Good night, good night. As sweet repose and rest   165
Come to thy heart as that within my breast.
ROMEO
O, wilt thou leave me so unsatisfied?
JULIET
What satisfaction canst thou have tonight?
ROMEO
Th'exchange of thy love's faithful vow for mine.
JULIET
I gave thee mine before thou didst request it,   170
And yet I would it were to give again.
ROMEO
Wouldst thou withdraw it? For what purpose, love?
JULIET
But to be frank and give it thee again.
And yet I wish but for the thing I have.
My bounty is as boundless as the sea,   175
My love as deep. The more I give to thee
The more I have, for both are infinite.

Nurse calls within
I hear some noise within. Dear love, adieu.—
Anon, good Nurse!—Sweet Montague, be true.
Stay but a little; I will come again.   *Exit*
ROMEO
O blessèd, blessèd night! I am afeard,   181
Being in night, all this is but a dream,
Too flattering-sweet to be substantial.
Enter Juliet aloft
JULIET
Three words, dear Romeo, and good night indeed.
If that thy bent of love be honourable,   185
Thy purpose marriage, send me word tomorrow,
By one that I'll procure to come to thee,
Where and what time thou wilt perform the rite,
And all my fortunes at thy foot I'll lay,
And follow thee, my lord, throughout the world.   190
⌜NURSE⌝ (*within*)
Madam!
JULIET
I come, anon. (*To Romeo*) But if thou mean'st not well,
I do beseech thee—
⌜NURSE⌝ (*within*) Madam!
JULIET By and by I come.—   195
To cease thy strife and leave me to my grief.
Tomorrow will I send.
ROMEO So thrive my soul—
JULIET A thousand times good night.   *Exit*
ROMEO
A thousand times the worse to want thy light.   200
Love goes toward love as schoolboys from their books,
But love from love, toward school with heavy looks.
⌜*He is going.*⌝
Enter Juliet aloft again
JULIET
Hist, Romeo! Hist! O for a falconer's voice
To lure this tassel-gentle back again.
Bondage is hoarse, and may not speak aloud,   205
Else would I tear the cave where Echo lies,
And make her airy tongue more hoarse than mine
With repetition of my Romeo's name. Romeo!
ROMEO
It is my soul that calls upon my name.
How silver-sweet sound lovers' tongues by night,   210
Like softest music to attending ears!
JULIET
Romeo!
ROMEO   My nyas?
JULIET   What o'clock tomorrow
Shall I send to thee?
ROMEO   By the hour of nine.
JULIET
I will not fail; 'tis twenty year till then.
I have forgot why I did call thee back.   215
ROMEO
Let me stand here till thou remember it.
JULIET
I shall forget, to have thee still stand there,
Rememb'ring how I love thy company.

ROMEO
　And I'll still stay, to have thee still forget,
　Forgetting any other home but this.　　　　220
JULIET
　'Tis almost morning. I would have thee gone—
　And yet no farther than a wanton's bird,
　That lets it hop a little from his hand,
　Like a poor prisoner in his twisted gyves,
　And with a silk thread plucks it back again,　　225
　So loving-jealous of his liberty.
ROMEO
　I would I were thy bird.
JULIET　　　　　　　　Sweet, so would I.
　Yet I should kill thee with much cherishing.
　Good night, good night. Parting is such sweet sorrow
　That I shall say good night till it be morrow.　　230
⌜ROMEO⌝
　Sleep dwell upon thine eyes, peace in thy breast.

　　　　　　　　　　　　　　　　　　　Exit Juliet
　Would I were sleep and peace, so sweet to rest.
　Hence will I to my ghostly sire's close cell,
　His help to crave, and my dear hap to tell.　　Exit

2.2　　Enter Friar Laurence, with a basket
FRIAR LAURENCE
　The grey-eyed morn smiles on the frowning night,
　Chequ'ring the eastern clouds with streaks of light,
　And fleckled darkness like a drunkard reels
　From forth day's path and Titan's fiery wheels.
　Now, ere the sun advance his burning eye　　5
　The day to cheer and night's dank dew to dry,
　I must up-fill this osier cage of ours
　With baleful weeds and precious-juicèd flowers.
　The earth, that's nature's mother, is her tomb.
　What is her burying grave, that is her womb,　　10
　And from her womb children of divers kind
　We sucking on her natural bosom find,
　Many for many virtues excellent,
　None but for some, and yet all different.
　O mickle is the powerful grace that lies　　15
　In plants, herbs, stones, and their true qualities,
　For naught so vile that on the earth doth live
　But to the earth some special good doth give;
　Nor aught so good but, strained from that fair use,
　Revolts from true birth, stumbling on abuse.　　20
　Virtue itself turns vice being misapplied,
　And vice sometime's by action dignified.
　　　Enter Romeo
　Within the infant rind of this weak flower
　Poison hath residence, and medicine power,
　For this, being smelt, with that part cheers each part;
　Being tasted, slays all senses with the heart.　　26
　Two such opposèd kings encamp them still
　In man as well as herbs—grace and rude will;
　And where the worser is predominant,
　Full soon the canker death eats up that plant.　　30
ROMEO
　Good morrow, father.
FRIAR LAURENCE　　　　Benedicite.

What early tongue so sweet saluteth me?
Young son, it argues a distempered head
So soon to bid good morrow to thy bed.
Care keeps his watch in every old man's eye,　　35
And where care lodges, sleep will never lie,
But where unbruisèd youth with unstuffed brain
Doth couch his limbs, there golden sleep doth reign.
Therefore thy earliness doth me assure
Thou art uproused with some distemp'rature;　　40
Or if not so, then here I hit it right:
Our Romeo hath not been in bed tonight.
ROMEO
That last is true; the sweeter rest was mine.
FRIAR LAURENCE
God pardon sin!—Wast thou with Rosaline?
ROMEO
With Rosaline, my ghostly father? No,　　45
I have forgot that name and that name's woe.
FRIAR LAURENCE
That's my good son; but where hast thou been then?
ROMEO
I'll tell thee ere thou ask it me again.
I have been feasting with mine enemy,
Where on a sudden one hath wounded me　　50
That's by me wounded. Both our remedies
Within thy help and holy physic lies.
I bear no hatred, blessèd man, for lo,
My intercession likewise steads my foe.
FRIAR LAURENCE
Be plain, good son, and homely in thy drift.　　55
Riddling confession finds but riddling shrift.
ROMEO
Then plainly know my heart's dear love is set
On the fair daughter of rich Capulet.
As mine on hers, so hers is set on mine,
And all combined save what thou must combine　　60
By holy marriage. When and where and how
We met, we wooed, and made exchange of vow
I'll tell thee as we pass; but this I pray,
That thou consent to marry us today.
FRIAR LAURENCE
Holy Saint Francis, what a change is here!　　65
Is Rosaline, that thou didst love so dear,
So soon forsaken? Young men's love then lies
Not truly in their hearts, but in their eyes.
Jesu Maria, what a deal of brine
Hath washed thy sallow cheeks for Rosaline!　　70
How much salt water thrown away in waste
To season love, that of it doth not taste!
The sun not yet thy sighs from heaven clears.
Thy old groans yet ring in mine ancient ears.
Lo, here upon thy cheek the stain doth sit　　75
Of an old tear that is not washed off yet.
If e'er thou wast thyself, and these woes thine,
Thou and these woes were all for Rosaline.
And art thou changed? Pronounce this sentence then:
Women may fall when there's no strength in men.　　80
ROMEO
Thou chidd'st me oft for loving Rosaline.

FRIAR LAURENCE
For doting, not for loving, pupil mine.
ROMEO
And bad'st me bury love.
FRIAR LAURENCE   Not in a grave
To lay one in, another out to have.
ROMEO
I pray thee, chide me not. Her I love now   85
Doth grace for grace and love for love allow.
The other did not so.
FRIAR LAURENCE   O, she knew well
Thy love did read by rote, that could not spell.
But come, young waverer, come, go with me.
In one respect I'll thy assistant be;   90
For this alliance may so happy prove
To turn your households' rancour to pure love.
ROMEO
O, let us hence! I stand on sudden haste.
FRIAR LAURENCE
Wisely and slow. They stumble that run fast.   *Exeunt*

2.3   *Enter Benvolio and Mercutio*
MERCUTIO Where the devil should this Romeo be? Came
he not home tonight?
BENVOLIO
Not to his father's. I spoke with his man.
MERCUTIO
Why, that same pale hard-hearted wench, that Rosaline,
Torments him so that he will sure run mad.   5
BENVOLIO
Tybalt, the kinsman to old Capulet,
Hath sent a letter to his father's house.
MERCUTIO
A challenge, on my life.
BENVOLIO   Romeo will answer it.
MERCUTIO Any man that can write may answer a letter.
BENVOLIO Nay, he will answer the letter's master, how he
dares, being dared.   11
MERCUTIO Alas, poor Romeo, he is already dead—stabbed
with a white wench's black eye, run through the ear
with a love song, the very pin of his heart cleft with the
blind bow-boy's butt-shaft; and is he a man to encounter
Tybalt?   16
⌈BENVOLIO⌉ Why, what is Tybalt?
MERCUTIO More than Prince of Cats. O, he's the courageous
captain of compliments. He fights as you sing pricksong:
keeps time, distance, and proportion. He rests his minim
rests: one, two, and the third in your bosom; the very
butcher of a silk button. A duellist, a duellist; a gentleman
of the very first house of the first and second cause. Ah,
the immortal *passado*, the *punto reverso*, the *hai*.
BENVOLIO The what?   25
MERCUTIO The pox of such antic, lisping, affecting
phantasims, these new tuners of accent! 'By Jesu, a very
good blade, a very tall man, a very good whore.' Why
is not this a lamentable thing, grandsire, that we should
be thus afflicted with these strange flies, these fashion-

mongers, these 'pardon-me's', who stand so much on
the new form that they cannot sit at ease on the old
bench? O, their bones, their bones!
    Enter Romeo
BENVOLIO Here comes Romeo, here comes Romeo!   34
MERCUTIO Without his roe, like a dried herring. O flesh,
flesh, how art thou fishified! Now is he for the numbers
that Petrarch flowed in. Laura to his lady was a kitchen
wench—marry, she had a better love to berhyme her—
Dido a dowdy, Cleopatra a gypsy, Helen and Hero
hildings and harlots, Thisbe a grey eye or so, but not to
the purpose. Signor Romeo, *bonjour*. There's a French
salutation to your French slop. You gave us the
counterfeit fairly last night.
ROMEO Good morrow to you both. What counterfeit did I
give you?   45
MERCUTIO The slip, sir, the slip. Can you not conceive?
ROMEO Pardon, good Mercutio. My business was great, and
in such a case as mine a man may strain courtesy.
MERCUTIO That's as much as to say such a case as yours
constrains a man to bow in the hams.   50
ROMEO Meaning to curtsy.
MERCUTIO Thou hast most kindly hit it.
ROMEO A most courteous exposition.
MERCUTIO Nay, I am the very pink of courtesy.
ROMEO Pink for flower.   55
MERCUTIO Right.
ROMEO Why, then is my pump well flowered.
MERCUTIO Sure wit, follow me this jest now till thou hast
worn out thy pump, that when the single sole of it is
worn, the jest may remain, after the wearing, solely
singular.   61
ROMEO O single-soled jest, solely singular for the singleness!
MERCUTIO Come between us, good Benvolio. My wits faints.
ROMEO Switch and spurs, switch and spurs, or I'll cry a
match.   65
MERCUTIO Nay, if our wits run the wild-goose chase, I am
done, for thou hast more of the wild goose in one of thy
wits than I am sure I have in my whole five. Was I with
you there for the goose?
ROMEO Thou wast never with me for anything when thou
wast not there for the goose.   71
MERCUTIO I will bite thee by the ear for that jest.
ROMEO Nay, good goose, bite not.
MERCUTIO Thy wit is very bitter sweeting, it is a most sharp
sauce.   75
ROMEO And is it not then well served in to a sweet goose?
MERCUTIO O, here's a wit of cheveril, that stretches from
an inch narrow to an ell broad.
ROMEO I stretch it out for that word 'broad', which, added
to the goose, proves thee far and wide a broad goose. 80
MERCUTIO Why, is not this better now than groaning for
love? Now art thou sociable, now art thou Romeo, now
art thou what thou art by art as well as by nature, for
this drivelling love is like a great natural that runs lolling
up and down to hide his bauble in a hole.   85
BENVOLIO Stop there, stop there.

MERCUTIO Thou desirest me to stop in my tale against the hair.

BENVOLIO Thou wouldst else have made thy tale large. 89

MERCUTIO O, thou art deceived, I would have made it short, for I was come to the whole depth of my tale, and meant indeed to occupy the argument no longer.

Enter the Nurse, and Peter, her man

ROMEO Here's goodly gear.

⌈BENVOLIO⌉ A sail, a sail!

MERCUTIO Two, two—a shirt and a smock. 95

NURSE Peter.

PETER Anon.

NURSE My fan, Peter.

MERCUTIO Good Peter, to hide her face, for her fan's the fairer face. 100

NURSE God ye good morrow, gentlemen.

MERCUTIO God ye good e'en, fair gentlewoman.

NURSE Is it good e'en?

MERCUTIO 'Tis no less, I tell ye: for the bawdy hand of the dial is now upon the prick of noon. 105

NURSE Out upon you, what a man are you!

ROMEO One, gentlewoman, that God hath made for himself to mar.

NURSE By my troth, it is well said. 'For himself to mar', quoth a? Gentlemen, can any of you tell me where I may find the young Romeo? 111

ROMEO I can tell you, but young Romeo will be older when you have found him than he was when you sought him. I am the youngest of that name, for fault of a worse.

NURSE You say well. 115

MERCUTIO Yea, is the worst well? Very well took, i'faith, wisely, wisely.

NURSE (*to Romeo*) If you be he, sir, I desire some confidence with you.

BENVOLIO She will endite him to some supper. 120

MERCUTIO A bawd, a bawd, a bawd. So ho!

ROMEO What hast thou found?

MERCUTIO No hare, sir, unless a hare, sir, in a lenten pie, that is something stale and hoar ere it be spent.

⌈*He walks by them and*⌉ *sings*

    An old hare hoar 125

    And an old hare hoar

      Is very good meat in Lent.

    But a hare that is hoar

    Is too much for a score

      When it hoars ere it be spent. 130

Romeo, will you come to your father's? We'll to dinner thither.

ROMEO I will follow you.

MERCUTIO Farewell, ancient lady. Farewell, ⌈*sings*⌉ 'lady, lady, lady'. *Exeunt Mercutio and Benvolio*

NURSE I pray you, sir, what saucy merchant was this that was so full of his ropery?

ROMEO A gentleman, Nurse, that loves to hear himself talk, and will speak more in a minute than he will stand to in a month. 140

NURSE An a speak anything against me, I'll take him down

an a were lustier than he is, and twenty such jacks; an if I cannot, I'll find those that shall. Scurvy knave! I am none of his flirt-jills, I am none of his skeans-mates. (*To Peter*) And thou must stand by, too, and suffer every knave to use me at his pleasure. 146

PETER I saw no man use you at his pleasure. If I had, my weapon should quickly have been out; I warrant you, I dare draw as soon as another man if I see occasion in a good quarrel, and the law on my side. 150

NURSE Now, afore God, I am so vexed that every part about me quivers. Scurvy knave! (*To Romeo*) Pray you, sir, a word; and, as I told you, my young lady bid me enquire you out. What she bid me say I will keep to myself, but first let me tell ye if ye should lead her in a fool's paradise, as they say, it were a very gross kind of behaviour, as they say, for the gentlewoman is young; and therefore if you should deal double with her, truly it were an ill thing to be offered to any gentlewoman, and very weak dealing. 160

ROMEO Nurse, commend me to thy lady and mistress. I protest unto thee—

NURSE Good heart, and i'faith I will tell her as much. Lord, Lord, she will be a joyful woman.

ROMEO What wilt thou tell her, Nurse? Thou dost not mark me. 166

NURSE I will tell her, sir, that you do protest; which as I take it is a gentlemanlike offer.

ROMEO Bid her devise

Some means to come to shrift this afternoon, 170

And there she shall at Friar Laurence' cell

Be shrived and married. (*Offering money*) Here is for thy pains.

NURSE No, truly, sir, not a penny.

ROMEO Go to, I say, you shall.

NURSE ⌈*taking the money*⌉

This afternoon, sir. Well, she shall be there. 175

ROMEO

And stay, good Nurse, behind the abbey wall.

Within this hour my man shall be with thee

And bring thee cords made like a tackled stair,

Which to the high topgallant of my joy

Must be my convoy in the secret night. 180

Farewell. Be trusty, and I'll quit thy pains.

Farewell. Commend me to thy mistress.

NURSE

Now God in heaven bless thee! Hark you, sir.

ROMEO What sayst thou, my dear Nurse?

NURSE

Is your man secret? Did you ne'er hear say 185

'Two may keep counsel, putting one away'?

ROMEO

I warrant thee my man's as true as steel.

NURSE

Well, sir, my mistress is the sweetest lady.

Lord, Lord, when 'twas a little prating thing—

O, there is a nobleman in town, one Paris, 190

That would fain lay knife aboard; but she, good soul,

Had as lief see a toad, a very toad,

As see him. I anger her sometimes,
And tell her that Paris is the properer man;
But I'll warrant you, when I say so she looks   195
As pale as any clout in the versal world.
Doth not rosemary and Romeo begin
Both with a letter?

ROMEO
Ay, Nurse, what of that? Both with an 'R'.   199

NURSE Ah, mocker—that's the dog's name. 'R' is for the—
no, I know it begins with some other letter, and she
hath the prettiest sententious of it, of you and rosemary,
that it would do you good to hear it.

ROMEO Commend me to thy lady.

NURSE Ay, a thousand times. Peter!   205

PETER Anon.

NURSE ⌈*giving Peter her fan*⌉ Before, and apace.

                    Exeunt ⌈*Peter and Nurse at one door,*
                              Romeo at another door⌉

2.4   *Enter Juliet*

JULIET
The clock struck nine when I did send the Nurse.
In half an hour she promised to return.
Perchance she cannot meet him. That's not so.
O, she is lame! Love's heralds should be thoughts,
Which ten times faster glides than the sun's beams   5
Driving back shadows over louring hills.
Therefore do nimble-pinioned doves draw Love,
And therefore hath the wind-swift Cupid wings.
Now is the sun upon the highmost hill
Of this day's journey, and from nine till twelve   10
Is three long hours, yet she is not come.
Had she affections and warm youthful blood
She would be as swift in motion as a ball.
My words would bandy her to my sweet love,
And his to me.   15
But old folks, many feign as they were dead—
Unwieldy, slow, heavy, and pale as lead.

Enter the Nurse and Peter

O God, she comes! O honey Nurse, what news?
Hast thou met with him? Send thy man away.   19

NURSE Peter, stay at the gate.   *Exit Peter*

JULIET
Now, good sweet Nurse—O Lord, why look'st thou sad?
Though news be sad, yet tell them merrily;
If good, thou sham'st the music of sweet news
By playing it to me with so sour a face.

NURSE
I am a-weary. Give me leave a while.   25
Fie, how my bones ache. What a jaunce have I!

JULIET
I would thou hadst my bones and I thy news.
Nay, come, I pray thee speak, good, good Nurse, speak.

NURSE
Jesu, what haste! Can you not stay a while?
Do you not see that I am out of breath?   30

JULIET
How art thou out of breath when thou hast breath
To say to me that thou art out of breath?
The excuse that thou dost make in this delay
Is longer than the tale thou dost excuse.
Is thy news good or bad? Answer to that.   35
Say either, and I'll stay the circumstance.
Let me be satisfied: is't good or bad?

NURSE Well, you have made a simple choice. You know
not how to choose a man. Romeo? No, not he; though
his face be better than any man's, yet his leg excels all
men's, and for a hand and a foot and a body, though
they be not to be talked on, yet they are past compare.
He is not the flower of courtesy, but, I'll warrant him,
as gentle as a lamb. Go thy ways, wench. Serve God.
What, have you dined at home?   45

JULIET
No, no. But all this did I know before.
What says he of our marriage—what of that?

NURSE
Lord, how my head aches! What a head have I!
It beats as it would fall in twenty pieces.
My back—
          ⌈*Juliet rubs her back*⌉
                    a' t'other side—ah, my back, my back!   50
Beshrew your heart for sending me about
To catch my death with jauncing up and down.

JULIET
I'faith, I am sorry that thou art not well.
Sweet, sweet, sweet Nurse, tell me, what says my love?

NURSE Your love says, like an honest gentleman, and a
courteous, and a kind, and a handsome, and, I warrant,
a virtuous—where is your mother?

JULIET
Where is my mother? Why, she is within.
Where should she be? How oddly thou repliest!
'Your love says like an honest gentleman   60
"Where is your mother?"'

NURSE   O, God's Lady dear!
Are you so hot? Marry come up, I trow.
Is this the poultice for my aching bones?
Henceforward do your messages yourself.

JULIET
Here's such a coil! Come, what says Romeo?   65

NURSE
Have you got leave to go to shrift today?

JULIET I have.

NURSE
Then hie you hence to Friar Laurence' cell.
There stays a husband to make you a wife.
Now comes the wanton blood up in your cheeks.   70
They'll be in scarlet straight at any news.
Hie you to church. I must another way,
To fetch a ladder by the which your love
Must climb a bird's nest soon, when it is dark.
I am the drudge, and toil in your delight,   75
But you shall bear the burden soon at night.
Go, I'll to dinner. Hie you to the cell.

JULIET
Hie to high fortune! Honest Nurse, farewell.

                              Exeunt ⌈*severally*⌉

2.5   *Enter Friar Laurence and Romeo*

FRIAR LAURENCE
So smile the heavens upon this holy act
That after-hours with sorrow chide us not!

ROMEO
Amen, amen. But come what sorrow can,
It cannot countervail the exchange of joy
That one short minute gives me in her sight.   5
Do thou but close our hands with holy words,
Then love-devouring death do what he dare—
It is enough I may but call her mine.

FRIAR LAURENCE
These violent delights have violent ends,
And in their triumph die like fire and powder,   10
Which as they kiss consume. The sweetest honey
Is loathsome in his own deliciousness,
And in the taste confounds the appetite.
Therefore love moderately. Long love doth so.
Too swift arrives as tardy as too slow.   15
          Enter Juliet ⌐somewhat fast, and embraceth Romeo⌐
Here comes the lady. O, so light a foot
Will ne'er wear out the everlasting flint.
A lover may bestride the gossamers
That idles in the wanton summer air,
And yet not fall, so light is vanity.   20

JULIET
Good even to my ghostly confessor.

FRIAR LAURENCE
Romeo shall thank thee, daughter, for us both.

JULIET
As much to him, else is his thanks too much.

ROMEO
Ah, Juliet, if the measure of thy joy
Be heaped like mine, and that thy skill be more   25
To blazon it, then sweeten with thy breath
This neighbour air, and let rich music's tongue
Unfold the imagined happiness that both
Receive in either by this dear encounter.

JULIET
Conceit, more rich in matter than in words,   30
Brags of his substance, not of ornament.
They are but beggars that can count their worth,
But my true love is grown to such excess
I cannot sum up some of half my wealth.

FRIAR LAURENCE
Come, come with me, and we will make short work,   35
For, by your leaves, you shall not stay alone
Till Holy Church incorporate two in one.   *Exeunt*

3.1   *Enter Mercutio with his page, Benvolio, and men*

BENVOLIO
I pray thee, good Mercutio, let's retire.
The day is hot, the Capels are abroad,
And if we meet we shall not scape a brawl,
For now, these hot days, is the mad blood stirring.   4

MERCUTIO Thou art like one of these fellows that, when he
enters the confines of a tavern, claps me his sword upon
the table and says 'God send me no need of thee', and
by the operation of the second cup, draws him on the
drawer when indeed there is no need.

BENVOLIO Am I like such a fellow?   10

MERCUTIO Come, come, thou art as hot a jack in thy mood
as any in Italy, and as soon moved to be moody, and
as soon moody to be moved.

BENVOLIO And what to?   14

MERCUTIO Nay, an there were two such, we should have
none shortly, for one would kill the other. Thou—why,
thou wilt quarrel with a man that hath a hair more or
a hair less in his beard than thou hast. Thou wilt quarrel
with a man for cracking nuts, having no other reason
but because thou hast hazel eyes. What eye but such
an eye would spy out such a quarrel? Thy head is as
full of quarrels as an egg is full of meat, and yet thy
head hath been beaten as addle as an egg for quarrelling.
Thou hast quarrelled with a man for coughing in the
street because he hath wakened thy dog that hath lain
asleep in the sun. Didst thou not fall out with a tailor
for wearing his new doublet before Easter; with another
for tying his new shoes with old ribbon? And yet thou
wilt tutor me from quarrelling!   29

BENVOLIO An I were so apt to quarrel as thou art, any
man should buy the fee-simple of my life for an hour
and a quarter.

MERCUTIO The fee simple? O, simple!
          Enter Tybalt, Petruccio, and others

BENVOLIO By my head, here comes the Capulets.

MERCUTIO By my heel, I care not.   35

TYBALT (*to Petruccio and the others*)
Follow me close, for I will speak to them.
          (*To the Montagues*) Gentlemen, good e'en. A word with
          one of you.

MERCUTIO And but one word with one of us? Couple it
with something: make it a word and a blow.

TYBALT You shall find me apt enough to that, sir, an you
will give me occasion.   41

MERCUTIO Could you not take some occasion without
giving?

TYBALT
Mercutio, thou consort'st with Romeo.   44

MERCUTIO 'Consort'? What, dost thou make us minstrels?
An thou make minstrels of us, look to hear nothing but
discords. ⌐*Touching his rapier*⌐ Here's my fiddlestick; here's
that shall make you dance. Zounds—'Consort'!

BENVOLIO
We talk here in the public haunt of men.
Either withdraw unto some private place,   50
Or reason coldly of your grievances,
Or else depart. Here all eyes gaze on us.

MERCUTIO
Men's eyes were made to look, and let them gaze.
I will not budge for no man's pleasure, I.
          Enter Romeo

TYBALT
Well, peace be with you, sir. Here comes my man.   55

MERCUTIO
But I'll be hanged, sir, if he wear your livery.
Marry, go before to field, he'll be your follower.
Your worship in that sense may call him 'man'.

TYBALT
Romeo, the love I bear thee can afford
No better term than this: thou art a villain.   60

ROMEO
Tybalt, the reason that I have to love thee
Doth much excuse the appertaining rage
To such a greeting. Villain am I none.
Therefore, farewell. I see thou knowest me not.

TYBALT
Boy, this shall not excuse the injuries   65
That thou hast done me. Therefore turn and draw.

ROMEO
I do protest I never injured thee,
But love thee better than thou canst devise
Till thou shalt know the reason of my love.
And so, good Capulet—which name I tender   70
As dearly as mine own—be satisfied.

MERCUTIO ⌈drawing⌉
O calm, dishonourable, vile submission!
Alla stoccado carries it away.
Tybalt, you ratcatcher, come, will you walk?

TYBALT What wouldst thou have with me?   75

MERCUTIO Good King of Cats, nothing but one of your nine
lives. That I mean to make bold withal, and, as you
shall use me hereafter, dry-beat the rest of the eight.
Will you pluck your sword out of his pilcher by the ears?
Make haste, lest mine be about your ears ere it be out.

TYBALT (drawing) I am for you.   81

ROMEO
Gentle Mercutio, put thy rapier up.

MERCUTIO (to Tybalt) Come, sir, your passado.
        They fight

ROMEO ⌈drawing⌉
Draw, Benvolio. Beat down their weapons.
Gentlemen, for shame forbear this outrage.   85
Tybalt, Mercutio, the Prince expressly hath
Forbid this bandying in Verona streets.
Hold, Tybalt, good Mercutio.
        ⌈Romeo beats down their points and rushes between
        them. Tybalt under Romeo's arm thrusts Mercutio in⌉
⌈PETRUCCIO⌉ Away, Tybalt!
        Exeunt Tybalt, Petruccio, and their followers

MERCUTIO I am hurt.   90
A plague o' both your houses. I am sped.
Is he gone, and hath nothing?

BENVOLIO   What, art thou hurt?

MERCUTIO
Ay, ay, a scratch, a scratch; marry, 'tis enough.
Where is my page? Go, villain. Fetch a surgeon.
        Exit page

ROMEO
Courage, man. The hurt cannot be much.   95

MERCUTIO No, 'tis not so deep as a well, nor so wide as a
church door, but 'tis enough. 'Twill serve. Ask for me
tomorrow, and you shall find me a grave man. I am
peppered, I warrant, for this world. A plague o' both
your houses! Zounds, a dog, a rat, a mouse, a cat, to
scratch a man to death! A braggart, a rogue, a villain,
that fights by the book of arithmetic! Why the devil
came you between us? I was hurt under your arm.

ROMEO I thought all for the best.

MERCUTIO
Help me into some house, Benvolio,   105
Or I shall faint. A plague o' both your houses.
They have made worms' meat of me.
I have it, and soundly, too. Your houses!
        Exeunt all but Romeo

ROMEO
This gentleman, the Prince's near ally,
My very friend, hath got this mortal hurt   110
In my behalf, my reputation stained
With Tybalt's slander—Tybalt, that an hour
Hath been my cousin! O sweet Juliet,
Thy beauty hath made me effeminate,
And in my temper softened valour's steel.   115
        Enter Benvolio

BENVOLIO
O Romeo, Romeo, brave Mercutio is dead!
That gallant spirit hath aspired the clouds,
Which too untimely here did scorn the earth.

ROMEO
This day's black fate on more days doth depend.
This but begins the woe others must end.   120
        Enter Tybalt

BENVOLIO
Here comes the furious Tybalt back again.

ROMEO
He gad in triumph, and Mercutio slain?
Away to heaven, respective lenity,
And fire-eyed fury be my conduct now.
Now, Tybalt, take the 'villain' back again   125
That late thou gav'st me, for Mercutio's soul
Is but a little way above our heads,
Staying for thine to keep him company.
Either thou, or I, or both must go with him.

TYBALT
Thou, wretched boy, that didst consort him here,   130
Shalt with him hence.

ROMEO   This shall determine that.
        They fight. Tybalt is wounded. He falls and dies

BENVOLIO Romeo, away, be gone.
The citizens are up, and Tybalt slain.
Stand not amazed. The Prince will doom thee death
If thou art taken. Hence, be gone, away.   135

ROMEO
O, I am fortune's fool!

BENVOLIO   Why dost thou stay?
        Exit Romeo

Enter Citizens ⌈of the watch⌉

CITIZEN ⌈OF THE WATCH⌉
Which way ran he that killed Mercutio?
Tybalt, that murderer, which way ran he?

BENVOLIO
There lies that Tybalt.

CITIZEN ⌈OF THE WATCH⌉ *(to Tybalt)* Up, sir, go with me.
I charge thee in the Prince's name, obey.   140
*Enter the Prince, old Montague, Capulet, their
Wives, and all*

PRINCE
Where are the vile beginners of this fray?

BENVOLIO
O noble Prince, I can discover all
The unlucky manage of this fatal brawl.
There lies the man, slain by young Romeo,
That slew thy kinsman, brave Mercutio.   145

CAPULET'S WIFE
Tybalt, my cousin, O, my brother's child!
O Prince, O cousin, husband! O, the blood is spilled
Of my dear kinsman! Prince, as thou art true,
For blood of ours shed blood of Montague!
O cousin, cousin!

PRINCE   Benvolio, who began this fray?   150

BENVOLIO
Tybalt, here slain, whom Romeo's hand did slay.
Romeo, that spoke him fair, bid him bethink
How nice the quarrel was, and urged withal
Your high displeasure. All this—uttered
With gentle breath, calm look, knees humbly bowed—
Could not take truce with the unruly spleen   156
Of Tybalt deaf to peace, but that he tilts
With piercing steel at bold Mercutio's breast,
Who, all as hot, turns deadly point to point,
And, with a martial scorn, with one hand beats   160
Cold death aside, and with the other sends
It back to Tybalt, whose dexterity
Retorts it. Romeo, he cries aloud,
'Hold, friends, friends, part!' and swifter than his
tongue
His agent arm beats down their fatal points,   165
And 'twixt them rushes, underneath whose arm
An envious thrust from Tybalt hit the life
Of stout Mercutio, and then Tybalt fled,
But by and by comes back to Romeo,
Who had but newly entertained revenge,   170
And to't they go like lightning; for ere I
Could draw to part them was stout Tybalt slain,
And as he fell did Romeo turn and fly.
This is the truth, or let Benvolio die.

CAPULET'S WIFE
He is a kinsman to the Montague.   175
Affection makes him false; he speaks not true.
Some twenty of them fought in this black strife,
And all those twenty could but kill one life.
I beg for justice, which thou, Prince, must give.
Romeo slew Tybalt; Romeo must not live.   180

PRINCE
Romeo slew him, he slew Mercutio.
Who now the price of his dear blood doth owe?

⌈MONTAGUE⌉
Not Romeo, Prince. He was Mercutio's friend.
His fault concludes but what the law should end,
The life of Tybalt.

PRINCE   And for that offence   185
Immediately we do exile him hence.
I have an interest in your hate's proceeding;
My blood for your rude brawls doth lie a-bleeding.
But I'll amerce you with so strong a fine
That you shall all repent the loss of mine.   190
I will be deaf to pleading and excuses.
Nor tears nor prayers shall purchase out abuses.
Therefore use none. Let Romeo hence in haste,
Else, when he is found, that hour is his last.
Bear hence this body, and attend our will.   195
Mercy but murders, pardoning those that kill.
Exeunt with the body

3.2   *Enter Juliet*

JULIET
Gallop apace, you fiery-footed steeds,
Towards Phoebus' lodging. Such a waggoner
As Phaëton would whip you to the west
And bring in cloudy night immediately.
Spread thy close curtain, love-performing night,   5
That runaways' eyes may wink, and Romeo
Leap to these arms untalked of and unseen.
Lovers can see to do their amorous rites
By their own beauties; or, if love be blind,
It best agrees with night. Come, civil night,   10
Thou sober-suited matron all in black,
And learn me how to lose a winning match
Played for a pair of stainless maidenhoods.
Hood my unmanned blood, bating in my cheeks,
With thy black mantle till strange love grown bold   15
Think true love acted simple modesty.
Come night, come Romeo; come, thou day in night,
For thou wilt lie upon the wings of night
Whiter than new snow on a raven's back.
Come, gentle night; come, loving, black-browed night,
Give me my Romeo, and when I shall die   21
Take him and cut him out in little stars,
And he will make the face of heaven so fine
That all the world will be in love with night
And pay no worship to the garish sun.   25
O, I have bought the mansion of a love
But not possessed it, and though I am sold,
Not yet enjoyed. So tedious is this day
As is the night before some festival
To an impatient child that hath new robes   30
And may not wear them.
*Enter the Nurse, ⌈wringing her hands,⌉ with the
ladder of cords ⌈in her lap⌉*
O, here comes my Nurse,

And she brings news, and every tongue that speaks
But Romeo's name speaks heavenly eloquence.
Now, Nurse, what news? What, hast thou there   34
The cords that Romeo bid thee fetch?
NURSE *[putting down the cords]*   Ay, ay, the cords.
JULIET
Ay me, what news? Why dost thou wring thy hands?
NURSE
Ah, welladay! He's dead, he's dead, he's dead!
We are undone, lady, we are undone.
Alack the day, he's gone, he's killed, he's dead!
JULIET
Can heaven be so envious?
NURSE   Romeo can,   40
Though heaven cannot. O Romeo, Romeo,
Who ever would have thought it Romeo?
JULIET
What devil art thou that dost torment me thus?
This torture should be roared in dismal hell.
Hath Romeo slain himself? Say thou but 'Ay',   45
And that bare vowel 'I' shall poison more
Than the death-darting eye of cockatrice.
I am not I if there be such an 'Ay',
Or those eyes shut that makes thee answer 'Ay'.
If he be slain, say 'Ay'; or if not, 'No'.   50
Brief sounds determine of my weal or woe.
NURSE
I saw the wound, I saw it with mine eyes,
God save the mark, here on his manly breast—
A piteous corpse, a bloody, piteous corpse—
Pale, pale as ashes, all bedaubed in blood,   55
All in gore blood; I swooned at the sight.
JULIET
O, break, my heart, poor bankrupt, break at once!
To prison, eyes; ne'er look on liberty.
Vile earth, to earth resign; end motion here,
And thou and Romeo press one heavy bier!   60
NURSE
O Tybalt, Tybalt, the best friend I had!
O courteous Tybalt, honest gentleman,
That ever I should live to see thee dead!
JULIET
What storm is this that blows so contrary?
Is Romeo slaughtered, and is Tybalt dead?   65
My dearest cousin, and my dearer lord?
Then, dreadful trumpet, sound the general doom,
For who is living if those two are gone?
NURSE
Tybalt is gone and Romeo banishèd.
Romeo that killed him—he is banishèd.   70
JULIET
O God, did Romeo's hand shed Tybalt's blood?
[NURSE]
It did, it did, alas the day, it did.
[JULIET]
O serpent heart hid with a flow'ring face!
Did ever dragon keep so fair a cave?

Beautiful tyrant, fiend angelical!   75
Dove-feathered raven, wolvish-ravening lamb!
Despisèd substance of divinest show!
Just opposite to what thou justly seem'st—
A damnèd saint, an honourable villain.
O nature, what hadst thou to do in hell   80
When thou didst bower the spirit of a fiend
In mortal paradise of such sweet flesh?
Was ever book containing such vile matter
So fairly bound? O, that deceit should dwell
In such a gorgeous palace!   85
NURSE
There's no trust, no faith, no honesty in men;
All perjured, all forsworn, all naught, dissemblers all.
Ah, where's my man? Give me some aqua vitae.
These griefs, these woes, these sorrows make me old.
Shame come to Romeo!
JULIET   Blistered be thy tongue   90
For such a wish! He was not born to shame.
Upon his brow shame is ashamed to sit,
For 'tis a throne where honour may be crowned
Sole monarch of the universal earth.
O, what a beast was I to chide at him!   95
NURSE
Will you speak well of him that killed your cousin?
JULIET
Shall I speak ill of him that is my husband?
Ah, poor my lord, what tongue shall smooth thy name
When I, thy three-hours wife, have mangled it?
But wherefore, villain, didst thou kill my cousin?   100
That villain cousin would have killed my husband.
Back, foolish tears, back to your native spring!
Your tributary drops belong to woe,
Which you, mistaking, offer up to joy.
My husband lives, that Tybalt would have slain;   105
And Tybalt's dead, that would have slain my husband.
All this is comfort. Wherefore weep I then?
Some word there was, worser than Tybalt's death,
That murdered me. I would forget it fain,
But O, it presses to my memory   110
Like damnèd guilty deeds to sinners' minds!
'Tybalt is dead, and Romeo banishèd.'
That 'banishèd', that one word 'banishèd'
Hath slain ten thousand Tybalts. Tybalt's death
Was woe enough, if it had ended there;   115
Or, if sour woe delights in fellowship
And needly will be ranked with other griefs,
Why followed not, when she said 'Tybalt's dead',
'Thy father', or 'thy mother', nay, or both,
Which modern lamentation might have moved?   120
But with a rearward following Tybalt's death,
'Romeo is banishèd'—to speak that word
Is father, mother, Tybalt, Romeo, Juliet,
All slain, all dead. 'Romeo is banishèd'—
There is no end, no limit, measure, bound,   125
In that word's death. No words can that woe sound.
Where is my father and my mother, Nurse?

NURSE
Weeping and wailing over Tybalt's corpse.
Will you go to them? I will bring you thither.   129
JULIET
Wash they his wounds with tears; mine shall be spent
When theirs are dry, for Romeo's banishment.
Take up those cords. Poor ropes, you are beguiled,
Both you and I, for Romeo is exiled.
He made you for a highway to my bed,
But I, a maid, die maiden-widowèd.   135
Come, cords; come, Nurse; I'll to my wedding bed,
And death, not Romeo, take my maidenhead!
NURSE (*taking up the cords*)
Hie to your chamber. I'll find Romeo
To comfort you. I wot well where he is.
Hark ye, your Romeo will be here at night.   140
I'll to him. He is hid at Laurence' cell.
JULIET (*giving her a ring*)
O, find him! Give this ring to my true knight,
And bid him come to take his last farewell.
                                        Exeunt ⌈severally⌉

3.3   *Enter Friar Laurence*
FRIAR LAURENCE
Romeo, come forth, come forth, thou fear-full man.
Affliction is enamoured of thy parts,
And thou art wedded to calamity.
         Enter Romeo
ROMEO
Father, what news? What is the Prince's doom?
What sorrow craves acquaintance at my hand   5
That I yet know not?
FRIAR LAURENCE   Too familiar
Is my dear son with such sour company.
I bring thee tidings of the Prince's doom.
ROMEO
What less than doomsday is the Prince's doom?
FRIAR LAURENCE
A gentler judgement vanished from his lips: 10
Not body's death, but body's banishment.
ROMEO
Ha, banishment? Be merciful, say 'death',
For exile hath more terror in his look,
Much more than death. Do not say 'banishment'.
FRIAR LAURENCE
Hence from Verona art thou banishèd.   15
Be patient, for the world is broad and wide.
ROMEO
There is no world without Verona walls
But purgatory, torture, hell itself.
Hence banishèd is banished from the world,
And world's exile is death. Then 'banishèd'   20
Is death mistermed. Calling death 'banishèd'
Thou cutt'st my head off with a golden axe,
And smil'st upon the stroke that murders me.
FRIAR LAURENCE
O deadly sin, O rude unthankfulness!
Thy fault our law calls death, but the kind Prince,   25
Taking thy part, hath rushed aside the law

And turned that black word 'death' to banishment.
This is dear mercy, and thou seest it not.
ROMEO
'Tis torture, and not mercy. Heaven is here
Where Juliet lives, and every cat and dog   30
And little mouse, every unworthy thing,
Live here in heaven and may look on her,
But Romeo may not. More validity,
More honourable state, more courtship lives
In carrion flies than Romeo. They may seize   35
On the white wonder of dear Juliet's hand,
And steal immortal blessing from her lips,
Who, even in pure and vestal modesty,
Still blush, as thinking their own kisses sin.
But Romeo may not, he is banishèd.   40
Flies may do this, but I from this must fly.
They are free men, but I am banishèd.
And sayst thou yet that exile is not death?
Hadst thou no poison mixed, no sharp-ground knife,
No sudden mean of death, though ne'er so mean,   45
But 'banishèd' to kill me—'banishèd'?
O friar, the damnèd use that word in hell.
Howling attends it. How hast thou the heart,
Being a divine, a ghostly confessor,
A sin-absolver and my friend professed,   50
To mangle me with that word 'banishèd'?
FRIAR LAURENCE
Thou fond mad man, hear me a little speak.
ROMEO
O, thou wilt speak again of banishment.
FRIAR LAURENCE
I'll give thee armour to keep off that word—
Adversity's sweet milk, philosophy,   55
To comfort thee though thou art banishèd.
ROMEO
Yet 'banishèd'? Hang up philosophy!
Unless philosophy can make a Juliet,
Displant a town, reverse a prince's doom,
It helps not, it prevails not. Talk no more.   60
FRIAR LAURENCE
O, then I see that madmen have no ears.
ROMEO
How should they, when that wise men have no eyes?
FRIAR LAURENCE
Let me dispute with thee of thy estate.
ROMEO
Thou canst not speak of that thou dost not feel.
Wert thou as young as I, Juliet thy love,   65
An hour but married, Tybalt murderèd,
Doting like me, and like me banishèd,
Then mightst thou speak, then mightst thou tear thy
         hair,
And fall upon the ground, as I do now,
         He falls upon the ground
Taking the measure of an unmade grave.   70
         Knock within
FRIAR LAURENCE
Arise, one knocks. Good Romeo, hide thyself.

ROMEO
Not I, unless the breath of heartsick groans
Mist-like enfold me from the search of eyes.
          Knocking within
FRIAR LAURENCE
Hark, how they knock!—Who's there?—Romeo, arise.
Thou wilt be taken.—Stay a while.—Stand up.   75
          Still knock within
Run to my study.—By and by!—God's will,
What simpleness is this?
          Knock within
                    I come, I come.
Who knocks so hard? Whence come you? What's your
          will?
NURSE (*within*)
Let me come in, and you shall know my errand.
I come from Lady Juliet.
FRIAR LAURENCE ⌜*opening the door*⌝ Welcome then.   80
          Enter the Nurse
NURSE
O holy friar, O tell me, holy friar,
Where is my lady's lord? Where's Romeo?
FRIAR LAURENCE
There on the ground, with his own tears made drunk.
NURSE
O, he is even in my mistress' case,
Just in her case! O woeful sympathy,   85
Piteous predicament! Even so lies she,
Blubb'ring and weeping, weeping and blubb'ring.
(*To Romeo*) Stand up, stand up, stand an you be a man,
For Juliet's sake, for her sake, rise and stand.
Why should you fall into so deep an O?   90
ROMEO (*rising*)
Nurse.
NURSE   Ah sir, ah sir, death's the end of all.
ROMEO
Spak'st thou of Juliet? How is it with her?
Doth not she think me an old murderer,
Now I have stained the childhood of our joy
With blood removed but little from her own?   95
Where is she, and how doth she, and what says
My concealed lady to our cancelled love?
NURSE
O, she says nothing, sir, but weeps and weeps,
And now falls on her bed, and then starts up,
And 'Tybalt' calls, and then on Romeo cries,   100
And then down falls again.
ROMEO   As if that name
Shot from the deadly level of a gun
Did murder her as that name's cursèd hand
Murdered her kinsman. O tell me, friar, tell me,
In what vile part of this anatomy   105
Doth my name lodge? Tell me, that I may sack
The hateful mansion.
          ⌜*He offers to stab himself, and the Nurse snatches the
          dagger away*⌝
FRIAR LAURENCE   Hold thy desperate hand.
Art thou a man? Thy form cries out thou art.

Thy tears are womanish, thy wild acts denote
The unreasonable fury of a beast.   110
Unseemly woman in a seeming man,
And ill-beseeming beast in seeming both!
Thou hast amazed me. By my holy order,
I thought thy disposition better tempered.
Hast thou slain Tybalt? Wilt thou slay thyself,   115
And slay thy lady that in thy life lives
By doing damnèd hate upon thyself?
Why rail'st thou on thy birth, the heaven, and earth,
Since birth and heaven and earth, all three, do meet
In thee at once, which thou at once wouldst lose?   120
Fie, fie, thou sham'st thy shape, thy love, thy wit,
Which like a usurer abound'st in all,
And usest none in that true use indeed
Which should bedeck thy shape, thy love, thy wit.
Thy noble shape is but a form of wax,   125
Digressing from the valour of a man;
Thy dear love sworn but hollow perjury,
Killing that love which thou hast vowed to cherish;
Thy wit, that ornament to shape and love,
Misshapen in the conduct of them both,   130
Like powder in a skilless soldier's flask
Is set afire by thine own ignorance,
And thou dismembered with thine own defence.
What, rouse thee, man! Thy Juliet is alive,
For whose dear sake thou wast but lately dead: 135
There art thou happy. Tybalt would kill thee,
But thou slewest Tybalt: there art thou happy.
The law that threatened death becomes thy friend,
And turns it to exile: there art thou happy.
A pack of blessings light upon thy back,   140
Happiness courts thee in her best array,
But, like a mishavèd and sullen wench,
Thou pout'st upon thy fortune and thy love.
Take heed, take heed, for such die miserable.
Go, get thee to thy love, as was decreed.   145
Ascend her chamber; hence and comfort her.
But look thou stay not till the watch be set,
For then thou canst not pass to Mantua,
Where thou shalt live till we can find a time
To blaze your marriage, reconcile your friends,   150
Beg pardon of the Prince, and call thee back
With twenty hundred thousand times more joy
Than thou went'st forth in lamentation.
Go before, Nurse. Commend me to thy lady,
And bid her hasten all the house to bed,   155
Which heavy sorrow makes them apt unto.
Romeo is coming.
NURSE
O Lord, I could have stayed here all the night
To hear good counsel! O, what learning is!
My lord, I'll tell my lady you will come.   160
ROMEO
Do so, and bid my sweet prepare to chide.
          ⌜*Nurse offers to go in, and turns again*⌝
NURSE (*giving the ring*)
Here, sir, a ring she bid me give you, sir.
Hie you, make haste, for it grows very late.

ROMEO
How well my comfort is revived by this.   *Exit Nurse*
FRIAR LAURENCE
Go hence, good night, and here stands all your state.
Either be gone before the watch be set,   166
Or by the break of day disguised from hence.
Sojourn in Mantua. I'll find out your man,
And he shall signify from time to time
Every good hap to you that chances here.   170
Give me thy hand. 'Tis late. Farewell. Good night.
ROMEO
But that a joy past joy calls out on me,
It were a grief so brief to part with thee.
Farewell.   *Exeunt ⌈severally⌉*

3.4   *Enter Capulet, his Wife, and Paris*
CAPULET
Things have fall'n out, sir, so unluckily
That we have had no time to move our daughter.
Look you, she loved her kinsman Tybalt dearly,
And so did I. Well, we were born to die.
'Tis very late. She'll not come down tonight.   5
I promise you, but for your company
I would have been abed an hour ago.
PARIS
These times of woe afford no times to woo.
Madam, good night. Commend me to your daughter.
CAPULET'S WIFE
I will, and know her mind early tomorrow.   10
Tonight she's mewed up to her heaviness.
        ⌈Paris offers to go in, and Capulet calls him again⌉
CAPULET
Sir Paris, I will make a desperate tender
Of my child's love. I think she will be ruled
In all respects by me. Nay, more, I doubt it not.
Wife, go you to her ere you go to bed.   15
Acquaint her here of my son Paris' love,
And bid her—mark you me?—on Wednesday next—
But soft—what day is this?
PARIS   Monday, my lord.
CAPULET
Monday. Ha, ha! Well, Wednesday is too soon.
O' Thursday let it be. O' Thursday, tell her,   20
She shall be married to this noble earl.
Will you be ready? Do you like this haste?
We'll keep no great ado—a friend or two.
For hark you, Tybalt being slain so late,
It may be thought we held him carelessly,   25
Being our kinsman, if we revel much.
Therefore we'll have some half a dozen friends,
And there an end. But what say you to Thursday?
PARIS
My lord, I would that Thursday were tomorrow.
CAPULET
Well, get you gone. O' Thursday be it, then.   30
(*To his Wife*) Go you to Juliet ere you go to bed.
Prepare her, wife, against this wedding day.—
Farewell, my lord.—Light to my chamber, ho!—

Afore me, it is so very late that we
May call it early by and by. Good night.   35
        *Exeunt ⌈Capulet and his wife at
        one door, Paris at another door⌉*

3.5   *Enter Romeo and Juliet aloft ⌈with the ladder of cords⌉*
JULIET
Wilt thou be gone? It is not yet near day.
It was the nightingale, and not the lark,
That pierced the fear-full hollow of thine ear.
Nightly she sings on yon pom'granate tree.
Believe me, love, it was the nightingale.   5
ROMEO
It was the lark, the herald of the morn,
No nightingale. Look, love, what envious streaks
Do lace the severing clouds in yonder east.
Night's candles are burnt out, and jocund day
Stands tiptoe on the misty mountain tops.   10
I must be gone and live, or stay and die.
JULIET
Yon light is not daylight; I know it, I.
It is some meteor that the sun exhaled
To be to thee this night a torchbearer
And light thee on thy way to Mantua.   15
Therefore stay yet. Thou need'st not to be gone.
ROMEO
Let me be ta'en, let me be put to death.
I am content, so thou wilt have it so.
I'll say yon grey is not the morning's eye,
'Tis but the pale reflex of Cynthia's brow;   20
Nor that is not the lark whose notes do beat
The vaulty heaven so high above our heads.
I have more care to stay than will to go.
Come, death, and welcome; Juliet wills it so.
How is't, my soul? Let's talk. It is not day.   25
JULIET
It is, it is. Hie hence, be gone, away.
It is the lark that sings so out of tune,
Straining harsh discords and unpleasing sharps.
Some say the lark makes sweet division;
This doth not so, for she divideth us.   30
Some say the lark and loathèd toad changed eyes.
O, now I would they had changed voices, too,
Since arm from arm that voice doth us affray,
Hunting thee hence with hunt's-up to the day.
O, now be gone! More light and light it grows.   35
ROMEO
More light and light, more dark and dark our woes.
        Enter the Nurse ⌈hastily⌉
NURSE Madam.
JULIET Nurse.
NURSE
Your lady mother is coming to your chamber.
The day is broke; be wary, look about.   *Exit*
JULIET
Then, window, let day in, and let life out.   41
ROMEO
Farewell, farewell! One kiss, and I'll descend.

[He lets down the ladder of cords and goes down]
JULIET
  Art thou gone so, love, lord, my husband, friend?
  I must hear from thee every day in the hour,
  For in a minute there are many days.   45
  O, by this count I shall be much in years
  Ere I again behold my Romeo.
ROMEO Farewell.
  I will omit no opportunity
  That may convey my greetings, love, to thee.   50
JULIET
  O, think'st thou we shall ever meet again?
ROMEO
  I doubt it not, and all these woes shall serve
  For sweet discourses in our times to come.
[JULIET]
  O God, I have an ill-divining soul!
  Methinks I see thee, now thou art so low,   55
  As one dead in the bottom of a tomb.
  Either my eyesight fails, or thou look'st pale.
ROMEO
  And trust me, love, in my eye so do you.
  Dry sorrow drinks our blood. Adieu, adieu.   *Exit*
JULIET *[pulling up the ladder and weeping]*
  O fortune, fortune, all men call thee fickle.   60
  If thou art fickle, what dost thou with him
  That is renowned for faith? Be fickle, fortune,
  For then I hope thou wilt not keep him long,
  But send him back.
      Enter Capulet's Wife [below]
CAPULET'S WIFE   Ho, daughter, are you up?
JULIET
  Who is't that calls? It is my lady mother.   65
  Is she not down so late, or up so early?
  What unaccustomed cause procures her hither?
      [She goes down and enters below]
CAPULET'S WIFE
  Why, how now, Juliet?
JULIET   Madam, I am not well.
CAPULET'S WIFE
  Evermore weeping for your cousin's death?
  What, wilt thou wash him from his grave with tears? 70
  An if thou couldst, thou couldst not make him live,
  Therefore have done. Some grief shows much of love,
  But much of grief shows still some want of wit.
JULIET
  Yet let me weep for such a feeling loss.
CAPULET'S WIFE
  So shall you feel the loss, but not the friend   75
  Which you so weep for.
JULIET   Feeling so the loss,
  I cannot choose but ever weep the friend.
CAPULET'S WIFE
  Well, girl, thou weep'st not so much for his death
  As that the villain lives which slaughtered him.
JULIET
  What villain, madam?
CAPULET'S WIFE   That same villain Romeo.   80

JULIET *(aside)*
  Villain and he be many miles asunder.
  (To her mother) God pardon him—I do, with all my
      heart,
  And yet no man like he doth grieve my heart.
CAPULET'S WIFE
  That is because the traitor murderer lives.
JULIET
  Ay, madam, from the reach of these my hands.   85
  Would none but I might venge my cousin's death.
CAPULET'S WIFE
  We will have vengeance for it, fear thou not.
  Then weep no more. I'll send to one in Mantua,
  Where that same banished runagate doth live,
  Shall give him such an unaccustomed dram   90
  That he shall soon keep Tybalt company;
  And then I hope thou wilt be satisfied.
JULIET
  Indeed, I never shall be satisfied
  With Romeo till I behold him, dead,
  Is my poor heart so for a kinsman vexed.   95
  Madam, if you could find out but a man
  To bear a poison, I would temper it
  That Romeo should, upon receipt thereof,
  Soon sleep in quiet. O, how my heart abhors
  To hear him named and cannot come to him   100
  To wreak the love I bore my cousin
  Upon his body that hath slaughtered him!
CAPULET'S WIFE
  Find thou the means, and I'll find such a man.
  But now I'll tell thee joyful tidings, girl.
JULIET
  And joy comes well in such a needy time.   105
  What are they, I beseech your ladyship?
CAPULET'S WIFE
  Well, well, thou hast a careful father, child;
  One who, to put thee from thy heaviness,
  Hath sorted out a sudden day of joy
  That thou expect'st not, nor I looked for.   110
JULIET
  Madam, in happy time. What day is that?
CAPULET'S WIFE
  Marry, my child, early next Thursday morn
  The gallant, young, and noble gentleman
  The County Paris at Saint Peter's Church
  Shall happily make thee there a joyful bride.   115
JULIET
  Now, by Saint Peter's Church, and Peter too,
  He shall not make me there a joyful bride.
  I wonder at this haste, that I must wed
  Ere he that should be husband comes to woo.
  I pray you, tell my lord and father, madam,   120
  I will not marry yet; and when I do, I swear
  It shall be Romeo—whom you know I hate—
  Rather than Paris. These are news indeed.
      Enter Capulet and the Nurse
CAPULET'S WIFE
  Here comes your father. Tell him so yourself,
  And see how he will take it at your hands.   125

CAPULET
When the sun sets, the earth doth drizzle dew,
But for the sunset of my brother's son
It rains downright.
How now, a conduit, girl? What, still in tears?
Evermore show'ring? In one little body   130
Thou counterfeit'st a barque, a sea, a wind,
For still thy eyes—which I may call the sea—
Do ebb and flow with tears. The barque thy body is,
Sailing in this salt flood; the winds thy sighs,
Who, raging with thy tears and they with them,   135
Without a sudden calm will overset
Thy tempest-tossèd body.—How now, wife?
Have you delivered to her our decree?

CAPULET'S WIFE
Ay, sir, but she will none, she gives you thanks.
I would the fool were married to her grave.   140

CAPULET
Soft, take me with you, take me with you, wife.
How, will she none? Doth she not give us thanks?
Is she not proud? Doth she not count her blest,
Unworthy as she is, that we have wrought
So worthy a gentleman to be her bride?   145

JULIET
Not proud you have, but thankful that you have.
Proud can I never be of what I hate,
But thankful even for hate that is meant love.

CAPULET
How, how, how, how—chopped logic? What is this?
'Proud', and 'I thank you', and 'I thank you not',   150
And yet 'not proud'? Mistress minion, you,
Thank me no thankings, nor proud me no prouds,
But fettle your fine joints 'gainst Thursday next
To go with Paris to Saint Peter's Church,
Or I will drag thee on a hurdle thither.   155
Out, you green-sickness carrion! Out, you baggage,
You tallow-face!

CAPULET'S WIFE   Fie, fie, what, are you mad?

JULIET (kneeling)
Good father, I beseech you on my knees,
Hear me with patience but to speak a word.

CAPULET
Hang thee, young baggage, disobedient wretch!   160
I tell thee what: get thee to church o' Thursday,
Or never after look me in the face.
Speak not, reply not, do not answer me.
        ⌜Juliet rises⌝
My fingers itch. Wife, we scarce thought us blest
That God had lent us but this only child,   165
But now I see this one is one too much,
And that we have a curse in having her.
Out on her, hilding!

NURSE   God in heaven bless her!
You are to blame, my lord, to rate her so.

CAPULET
And why, my lady Wisdom? Hold your tongue,   170
Good Prudence. Smatter with your gossips, go!

NURSE
I speak no treason.

⌜CAPULET⌝   O, God-i'-good-e'en!

⌜NURSE⌝
May not one speak?

CAPULET   Peace, you mumbling fool,
Utter your gravity o'er a gossip's bowl,
For here we need it not.

CAPULET'S WIFE   You are too hot.   175

CAPULET
God's bread, it makes me mad. Day, night; work, play;
Alone, in company, still my care hath been
To have her matched; and having now provided
A gentleman of noble parentage,
Of fair demesnes, youthful, and nobly lined,   180
Stuffed, as they say, with honourable parts,
Proportioned as one's thought would wish a man—
And then to have a wretched puling fool,
A whining maumet, in her fortune's tender,
To answer 'I'll not wed, I cannot love;   185
I am too young, I pray you pardon me'!
But an you will not wed, I'll pardon you!
Graze where you will, you shall not house with me.
Look to't, think on't. I do not use to jest.
Thursday is near. Lay hand on heart. Advise.   190
An you be mine, I'll give you to my friend.
An you be not, hang, beg, starve, die in the streets,
For, by my soul, I'll ne'er acknowledge thee,
Nor what is mine shall never do thee good.
Trust to't. Bethink you. I'll not be forsworn.   Exit

JULIET
Is there no pity sitting in the clouds   196
That sees into the bottom of my grief?
O sweet my mother, cast me not away!
Delay this marriage for a month, a week;
Or if you do not, make the bridal bed   200
In that dim monument where Tybalt lies.

CAPULET'S WIFE
Talk not to me, for I'll not speak a word.
Do as thou wilt, for I have done with thee.   Exit

JULIET
O, God—O Nurse, how shall this be prevented?
My husband is on earth, my faith in heaven.   205
How shall that faith return again to earth
Unless that husband send it me from heaven
By leaving earth? Comfort me, counsel me.
Alack, alack, that heaven should practise stratagems
Upon so soft a subject as myself!   210
What sayst thou? Hast thou not a word of joy?
Some comfort, Nurse.

NURSE   Faith, here it is: Romeo
Is banishèd, and all the world to nothing
That he dares ne'er come back to challenge you,
Or if he do, it needs must be by stealth.   215
Then, since the case so stands as now it doth,
I think it best you married with the County.
O, he's a lovely gentleman!

Romeo's a dishclout to him. An eagle, madam,
Hath not so green, so quick, so fair an eye   220
As Paris hath. Beshrew my very heart,
I think you are happy in this second match,
For it excels your first; or if it did not,
Your first is dead, or 'twere as good he were
As living hence and you no use of him.   225

JULIET Speak'st thou from thy heart?

NURSE
And from my soul, too, else beshrew them both.

JULIET Amen.

NURSE What?

JULIET
Well, thou hast comforted me marvellous much.   230
Go in; and tell my lady I am gone,
Having displeased my father, to Laurence' cell
To make confession and to be absolved.

NURSE
Marry, I will; and this is wisely done.   ⌈Exit⌉

JULIET (watching her go)
Ancient damnation! O most wicked fiend!   235
Is it more sin to wish me thus forsworn,
Or to dispraise my lord with that same tongue
Which she hath praised him with above compare
So many thousand times? Go, counsellor!
Thou and my bosom henceforth shall be twain.   240
I'll to the friar, to know his remedy.
If all else fail, myself have power to die.   Exit

4.1   *Enter Friar Laurence and Paris*

FRIAR LAURENCE
On Thursday, sir? The time is very short.

PARIS
My father Capulet will have it so,
And I am nothing slow to slack his haste.

FRIAR LAURENCE
You say you do not know the lady's mind?
Uneven is the course. I like it not.   5

PARIS
Immoderately she weeps for Tybalt's death,
And therefore have I little talked of love,
For Venus smiles not in a house of tears.
Now, sir, her father counts it dangerous
That she do give her sorrow so much sway,   10
And in his wisdom hastes our marriage
To stop the inundation of her tears,
Which, too much minded by herself alone,
May be put from her by society.
Now do you know the reason of this haste.   15

FRIAR LAURENCE (aside)
I would I knew not why it should be slowed.—
        Enter Juliet
Look, sir, here comes the lady toward my cell.

PARIS
Happily met, my lady and my wife.

JULIET
That may be, sir, when I may be a wife.

PARIS
That 'may be' must be, love, on Thursday next.   20

JULIET
What must be shall be.

FRIAR LAURENCE   That's a certain text.

PARIS
Come you to make confession to this father?

JULIET
To answer that, I should confess to you.

PARIS
Do not deny to him that you love me.

JULIET
I will confess to you that I love him.   25

PARIS
So will ye, I am sure, that you love me.

JULIET
If I do so, it will be of more price,
Being spoke behind your back, than to your face.

PARIS
Poor soul, thy face is much abused with tears.

JULIET
The tears have got small victory by that,   30
For it was bad enough before their spite.

PARIS
Thou wrong'st it more than tears with that report.

JULIET
That is no slander, sir, which is a truth,
And what I spake, I spake it to my face.

PARIS
Thy face is mine, and thou hast slandered it.   35

JULIET
It may be so, for it is not mine own.—
Are you at leisure, holy father, now,
Or shall I come to you at evening mass?

FRIAR LAURENCE
My leisure serves me, pensive daughter, now.
My lord, we must entreat the time alone.   40

PARIS
God shield I should disturb devotion!—
Juliet, on Thursday early will I rouse ye.
(*Kissing her*) Till then, adieu, and keep this holy kiss.
                                                     Exit

JULIET
O, shut the door, and when thou hast done so,
Come weep with me, past hope, past cure, past help! 45

FRIAR LAURENCE
O Juliet, I already know thy grief.
It strains me past the compass of my wits.
I hear thou must, and nothing may prorogue it,
On Thursday next be married to this County.

JULIET
Tell me not, friar, that thou hear'st of this,   50
Unless thou tell me how I may prevent it.
If in thy wisdom thou canst give no help,
Do thou but call my resolution wise,
        She draws a knife
And with this knife I'll help it presently.

God joined my heart and Romeo's, thou our hands,   55
And ere this hand, by thee to Romeo's sealed,
Shall be the label to another deed,
Or my true heart with treacherous revolt
Turn to another, this shall slay them both.
Therefore, out of thy long-experienced time,   60
Give me some present counsel; or, behold,
'Twixt my extremes and me this bloody knife
Shall play the umpire, arbitrating that
Which the commission of thy years and art
Could to no issue of true honour bring.   65
Be not so long to speak. I long to die
If what thou speak'st speak not of remedy.
FRIAR LAURENCE
Hold, daughter, I do spy a kind of hope
Which craves as desperate an execution
As that is desperate which we would prevent.   70
If, rather than to marry County Paris,
Thou hast the strength of will to slay thyself,
Then is it likely thou wilt undertake
A thing like death to chide away this shame,
That cop'st with death himself to scape from it;   75
And, if thou dar'st, I'll give thee remedy.
JULIET
O, bid me leap, rather than marry Paris,
From off the battlements of any tower,
Or walk in thievish ways, or bid me lurk
Where serpents are. Chain me with roaring bears,   80
Or hide me nightly in a charnel house,
O'ercovered quite with dead men's rattling bones,
With reeky shanks and yellow chapless skulls;
Or bid me go into a new-made grave
And hide me with a dead man in his tomb—   85
Things that, to hear them told, have made me
    tremble—
And I will do it without fear or doubt,
To live an unstained wife to my sweet love.
FRIAR LAURENCE
Hold, then; go home, be merry, give consent
To marry Paris. Wednesday is tomorrow.   90
Tomorrow night look that thou lie alone.
Let not the Nurse lie with thee in thy chamber.
Take thou this vial, being then in bed,
And this distilling liquor drink thou off,
When presently through all thy veins shall run   95
A cold and drowsy humour; for no pulse
Shall keep his native progress, but surcease.
No warmth, no breath shall testify thou livest.
The roses in thy lips and cheeks shall fade
To wanny ashes, thy eyes' windows fall   100
Like death when he shuts up the day of life.
Each part, deprived of supple government,
Shall, stiff and stark and cold, appear like death;
And in this borrowed likeness of shrunk death
Thou shalt continue two-and-forty hours,   105
And then awake as from a pleasant sleep.
Now, when the bridegroom in the morning comes

To rouse thee from thy bed, there art thou dead.
Then, as the manner of our country is,
In thy best robes, uncovered on the bier   110
Thou shalt be borne to that same ancient vault
Where all the kindred of the Capulets lie.
In the meantime, against thou shalt awake,
Shall Romeo by my letters know our drift,
And hither shall he come, and he and I   115
Will watch thy waking, and that very night
Shall Romeo bear thee hence to Mantua.
And this shall free thee from this present shame,
If no inconstant toy nor womanish fear
Abate thy valour in the acting it.   120
JULIET
Give me, give me! O, tell not me of fear!
FRIAR LAURENCE (giving her the vial)
Hold, get you gone. Be strong and prosperous
In this resolve. I'll send a friar with speed
To Mantua with my letters to thy lord.   124
JULIET
Love give me strength, and strength shall help afford.
Farewell, dear father.   Exeunt ⌐severally⌐

4.2   Enter Capulet, his Wife, the Nurse, and ⌐two⌐
        Servingmen
CAPULET (giving a Servingman a paper)
So many guests invite as here are writ.
                                ⌐Exit Servingman⌐
(To the other Servingman) Sirrah, go hire me twenty
    cunning cooks.
SERVINGMAN You shall have none ill, sir, for I'll try if they
    can lick their fingers.
CAPULET How canst thou try them so?   5
SERVINGMAN Marry, sir, 'tis an ill cook that cannot lick his
    own fingers, therefore he that cannot lick his fingers
    goes not with me.
CAPULET Go, be gone.   ⌐Exit Servingman⌐
We shall be much unfurnished for this time.   10
(To the Nurse) What, is my daughter gone to Friar
    Laurence?
NURSE Ay, forsooth.
CAPULET
Well, he may chance to do some good on her.
A peevish, self-willed harlotry it is.
        Enter Juliet
NURSE
See where she comes from shrift with merry look.   15
CAPULET (to Juliet)
How now, my headstrong, where have you been
    gadding?
JULIET
Where I have learned me to repent the sin
Of disobedient opposition
To you and your behests, and am enjoined
By holy Laurence to fall prostrate here   20
To beg your pardon. (Kneeling) Pardon, I beseech you.
Henceforward I am ever ruled by you.

CAPULET ⌈*to the Nurse*⌉
Send for the County; go tell him of this.
I'll have this knot knit up tomorrow morning.
JULIET
I met the youthful lord at Laurence' cell,   25
And gave him what becoming love I might,
Not stepping o'er the bounds of modesty.
CAPULET
Why, I am glad on't. This is well. Stand up.
     Juliet rises
This is as't should be. Let me see the County.
⌈*To Nurse*⌉ Ay, marry, go, I say, and fetch him hither. 30
Now, afore God, this reverend holy friar,
All our whole city is much bound to him.
JULIET
Nurse, will you go with me into my closet
To help me sort such needful ornaments
As you think fit to furnish me tomorrow?   35
CAPULET'S WIFE
No, not till Thursday. There is time enough.
CAPULET
Go, Nurse, go with her. We'll to church tomorrow.
                         Exeunt Juliet and Nurse
CAPULET'S WIFE
We shall be short in our provision.
'Tis now near night.
CAPULET   Tush, I will stir about,
And all things shall be well, I warrant thee, wife.   40
Go thou to Juliet, help to deck up her.
I'll not to bed tonight. Let me alone.
I'll play the housewife for this once. What, ho!
They are all forth. Well, I will walk myself
To County Paris to prepare up him   45
Against tomorrow. My heart is wondrous light,
Since this same wayward girl is so reclaimed.
                         Exeunt ⌈*severally*⌉

4.3   *Enter Juliet and the Nurse* ⌈*with garments*⌉
JULIET
Ay, those attires are best. But, gentle Nurse,
I pray thee leave me to myself tonight,
For I have need of many orisons
To move the heavens to smile upon my state,
Which—well thou knowest—is cross and full of sin.   5
     Enter Capulet's Wife
CAPULET'S WIFE
What, are you busy, ho? Need you my help?
JULIET
No, madam, we have culled such necessaries
As are behoveful for our state tomorrow.
So please you, let me now be left alone,
And let the Nurse this night sit up with you,   10
For I am sure you have your hands full all
In this so sudden business.
CAPULET'S WIFE   Good night.
Get thee to bed, and rest, for thou hast need.
                    Exeunt Capulet's Wife ⌈*and Nurse*⌉

JULIET
Farewell. God knows when we shall meet again.
I have a faint cold fear thrills through my veins   15
That almost freezes up the heat of life.
I'll call them back again to comfort me.
Nurse!—What should she do here?
          ⌈*She opens curtains, behind which is seen her bed*⌉
My dismal scene I needs must act alone.
Come, vial. What if this mixture do not work at all? 20
Shall I be married then tomorrow morning?
No, no, this shall forbid it. Lie thou there.
          She lays down a knife
What if it be a poison which the friar
Subtly hath ministered to have me dead,
Lest in this marriage he should be dishonoured   25
Because he married me before to Romeo?
I fear it is—and yet methinks it should not,
For he hath still been tried a holy man.
How if, when I am laid into the tomb,
I wake before the time that Romeo   30
Come to redeem me? There's a fearful point.
Shall I not then be stifled in the vault,
To whose foul mouth no healthsome air breathes in,
And there die strangled ere my Romeo comes?
Or, if I live, is it not very like   35
The horrible conceit of death and night,
Together with the terror of the place—
As in a vault, an ancient receptacle
Where for this many hundred years the bones
Of all my buried ancestors are packed;   40
Where bloody Tybalt, yet but green in earth,
Lies fest'ring in his shroud; where, as they say,
At some hours in the night spirits resort—
Alack, alack, is it not like that I,
So early waking—what with loathsome smells,   45
And shrieks like mandrakes torn out of the earth,
That living mortals, hearing them, run mad—
O, if I wake, shall I not be distraught,
Environèd with all these hideous fears,
And madly play with my forefathers' joints,   50
And pluck the mangled Tybalt from his shroud,
And, in this rage, with some great kinsman's bone
As with a club dash out my desp'rate brains?
O, look! Methinks I see my cousin's ghost
Seeking out Romeo that did spit his body   55
Upon a rapier's point. Stay, Tybalt, stay!
Romeo, Romeo, Romeo! Here's drink. I drink to thee.
          She drinks from the vial and falls upon the bed,
          ⌈*pulling closed the curtains*⌉

4.4   *Enter Capulet's Wife, and the Nurse* ⌈*with herbs*⌉
CAPULET'S WIFE
Hold, take these keys, and fetch more spices, Nurse.
NURSE
They call for dates and quinces in the pastry.
     Enter Capulet
CAPULET
Come, stir, stir, stir! The second cock hath crowed.

The curfew bell hath rung. 'Tis three o'clock.
Look to the baked meats, good Angelica.   5
Spare not for cost.
NURSE   Go, you cot-quean, go.
Get you to bed. Faith, you'll be sick tomorrow
For this night's watching.
CAPULET
No, not a whit. What, I have watched ere now
All night for lesser cause, and ne'er been sick.   10
CAPULET'S WIFE
Ay, you have been a mouse-hunt in your time,
But I will watch you from such watching now.
    Exeunt Capulet's Wife and Nurse
CAPULET
A jealous-hood, a jealous-hood!
    Enter three or four Servingmen, with spits and
    logs and baskets
                        Now, fellow, what is there?
FIRST SERVINGMAN
Things for the cook, sir, but I know not what.
CAPULET
Make haste, make haste.
    Exit First Servingman ⌜*and one or two others*⌝
                        Sirrah, fetch drier logs.   15
Call Peter. He will show thee where they are.
SECOND SERVINGMAN
I have a head, sir, that will find out logs
And never trouble Peter for the matter.
CAPULET
Mass, and well said! A merry whoreson, ha!
Thou shalt be loggerhead.   *Exit Second Servingman*
                        Good faith, 'tis day.   20
The County will be here with music straight,
For so he said he would.
    Music plays within
                        I hear him near.
Nurse! Wife! What ho, what, Nurse, I say!
    Enter the Nurse
Go waken Juliet. Go and trim her up.
I'll go and chat with Paris. Hie, make haste,   25
Make haste, the bridegroom he is come already.
Make haste, I say.   *Exit*
NURSE
Mistress, what, mistress! Juliet! Fast, I warrant her, she.
Why, lamb, why, lady! Fie, you slug-abed!
Why, love, I say, madam, sweetheart, why, bride!   30
What, not a word? You take your pennyworths now.
Sleep for a week, for the next night, I warrant,
The County Paris hath set up his rest
That you shall rest but little. God forgive me!
Marry, and amen. How sound is she asleep!   35
I needs must wake her. Madam, madam, madam!
Ay, let the County take you in your bed.
He'll fright you up, i'faith. Will it not be?
    ⌜*She draws back the curtains*⌝
What, dressed and in your clothes, and down again?
I must needs wake you. Lady, lady, lady!   40

Alas, alas! Help, help! My lady's dead.
O welladay, that ever I was born!
Some aqua-vitae, ho! My lord, my lady!
    Enter Capulet's Wife
CAPULET'S WIFE
What noise is here?
NURSE   O lamentable day!
CAPULET'S WIFE
What is the matter?
NURSE   Look, look. O heavy day!   45
CAPULET'S WIFE
O me, O me, my child, my only life!
Revive, look up, or I will die with thee.
Help, help, call help!
    Enter Capulet
CAPULET
For shame, bring Juliet forth. Her lord is come.
NURSE
She's dead, deceased. She's dead, alack the day!   50
CAPULET'S WIFE
Alack the day, she's dead, she's dead, she's dead!
CAPULET
Ha, let me see her! Out, alas, she's cold.
Her blood is settled, and her joints are stiff.
Life and these lips have long been separated.
Death lies on her like an untimely frost   55
Upon the sweetest flower of all the field.
NURSE
O lamentable day!
CAPULET'S WIFE   O woeful time!
CAPULET
Death, that hath ta'en her hence to make me wail,
Ties up my tongue, and will not let me speak.
    Enter Friar Laurence and Paris, with Musicians
FRIAR LAURENCE
Come, is the bride ready to go to church?   60
CAPULET
Ready to go, but never to return.
(*To Paris*) O son, the night before thy wedding day
Hath death lain with thy wife. See, there she lies,
Flower as she was, deflowerèd by him.
Death is my son-in-law, death is my heir.   65
My daughter he hath wedded. I will die,
And leave him all. Life, living, all is death's.
    ⌜*Paris, Capulet and his Wife, and the Nurse all at*
    once wring their hands and cry out together:⌝
PARIS
Have I thought long to see this morning's face,
And doth it give me such a sight as this?
Beguiled, divorcèd, wrongèd, spited, slain!   70
Most detestable death, by thee beguiled,
By cruel, cruel thee quite overthrown.
O love, O life: not life, but love in death.
CAPULET'S WIFE
Accursed, unhappy, wretched, hateful day!
Most miserable hour that e'er time saw   75
In lasting labour of his pilgrimage!
But one, poor one, one poor and loving child,

But one thing to rejoice and solace in,
And cruel death hath catched it from my sight!

NURSE
O woe! O woeful, woeful, woeful day!   80
Most lamentable day! Most woeful day
That ever, ever, I did yet behold!
O day, O day, O day, O hateful day,
Never was seen so black a day as this!
O woeful day, O woeful day!   85

CAPULET
Despisèd, distressèd, hated, martyred, killed!
Uncomfortable time, why cam'st thou now
To murder, murder our solemnity?
O child, O child, my soul and not my child!
Dead art thou, alack, my child is dead,   90
And with my child my joys are buried.

FRIAR LAURENCE
Peace, ho, for shame! Confusion's cure lives not
In these confusions. Heaven and yourself
Had part in this fair maid. Now heaven hath all,
And all the better is it for the maid.   95
Your part in her you could not keep from death,
But heaven keeps his part in eternal life.
The most you sought was her promotion,
For 'twas your heaven she should be advanced,
And weep ye now, seeing she is advanced   100
Above the clouds as high as heaven itself?
O, in this love you love your child so ill
That you run mad, seeing that she is well.
She's not well married that lives married long,
But she's best married that dies married young.   105
Dry up your tears, and stick your rosemary
On this fair corpse, and, as the custom is,
All in her best array bear her to church;
For though fond nature bids us all lament,
Yet nature's tears are reason's merriment.   110

CAPULET
All things that we ordainèd festival
Turn from their office to black funeral.
Our instruments to melancholy bells,
Our wedding cheer to a sad burial feast,
Our solemn hymns to sullen dirges change;   115
Our bridal flowers serve for a buried corpse,
And all things change them to the contrary.

FRIAR LAURENCE
Sir, go you in; and madam, go with him,
And go, Sir Paris. Everyone prepare
To follow this fair corpse unto her grave.   120
The heavens do lour upon you for some ill.
Move them no more by crossing their high will.
    ⌈*They cast rosemary on Juliet, and shut the curtains.*⌉
    Exeunt all but the Nurse and Musicians

⌈FIRST⌉ MUSICIAN Faith, we may put up our pipes and be
gone.

NURSE
Honest good fellows, ah, put up, put up,   125
For well you know this is a pitiful case.

⌈FIRST⌉ MUSICIAN
Ay, by my troth, the case may be amended.
                            Exit Nurse
    Enter Peter
PETER Musicians, O, musicians! 'Heart's ease', 'Heart's
ease'; O, an you will have me live, play 'Heart's ease'.
⌈FIRST⌉ MUSICIAN Why 'Heart's ease'?   130
PETER O, musicians, because my heart itself plays 'My heart
is full of woe'. O, play me some merry dump to comfort
me.
⌈FIRST⌉ MUSICIAN Not a dump, we. 'Tis no time to play
now.   135
PETER You will not then?
FIRST MUSICIAN No.
PETER I will then give it you soundly.
FIRST MUSICIAN What will you give us?
PETER No money, on my faith, but the gleek. I will give
you the minstrel.   141
FIRST MUSICIAN Then will I give you the serving-creature.
PETER (*drawing his dagger*) Then will I lay the serving-
creature's dagger on your pate. I will carry no crochets.
I'll re you, I'll fa you. Do you note me?   145
FIRST MUSICIAN An you re us and fa us, you note us.
SECOND MUSICIAN Pray you, put up your dagger and put
out your wit.
⌈PETER⌉ Then have at you with my wit. I will dry-beat you
with an iron wit, and put up my iron dagger. Answer
me like men.   151
⌈*Sings*⌉
    When griping grief the heart doth wound,
      And doleful dumps the mind oppress,
    Then music with her silver sound—
Why 'silver sound', why 'music with her silver sound'?
What say you, Matthew Minikin?   156
FIRST MUSICIAN Marry, sir, because silver hath a sweet
sound.
PETER Prates! What say you, Hugh Rebec?
SECOND MUSICIAN I say 'silver sound' because musicians
sound for silver.   161
PETER Prates too! What say you, Simon Soundpost?
THIRD MUSICIAN Faith, I know not what to say.
PETER O, I cry you mercy, you are the singer. I will say
for you. It is 'music with her silver sound' because
musicians have no gold for sounding.   166
⌈*Sings*⌉
    Then music with her silver sound
      With speedy help doth lend redress.   *Exit*
FIRST MUSICIAN What a pestilent knave is this same!
SECOND MUSICIAN Hang him, jack! Come, we'll in here,
tarry for the mourners, and stay dinner.   *Exeunt*

5.1   *Enter Romeo*
ROMEO
If I may trust the flattering truth of sleep,
My dreams presage some joyful news at hand.
My bosom's lord sits lightly in his throne,
And all this day an unaccustomed spirit

Lifts me above the ground with cheerful thoughts.   5
I dreamt my lady came and found me dead—
Strange dream, that gives a dead man leave to
      think!—
And breathed such life with kisses in my lips
That I revived and was an emperor.
Ah me, how sweet is love itself possessed   10
When but love's shadows are so rich in joy!
      Enter Balthasar, Romeo's man, ⌈booted⌉
News from Verona! How now, Balthasar?
Dost thou not bring me letters from the friar?
How doth my lady? Is my father well?
How fares my Juliet? That I ask again,   15
For nothing can be ill if she be well.
BALTHASAR
Then she is well, and nothing can be ill.
Her body sleeps in Capel's monument,
And her immortal part with angels lives.
I saw her laid low in her kindred's vault,   20
And presently took post to tell it you.
O, pardon me for bringing these ill news,
Since you did leave it for my office, sir.
ROMEO
Is it e'en so? Then I defy you, stars.
Thou knowest my lodging. Get me ink and paper,   25
And hire posthorses. I will hence tonight.
BALTHASAR
I do beseech you, sir, have patience.
Your looks are pale and wild, and do import
Some misadventure.
ROMEO   Tush, thou art deceived.
Leave me, and do the thing I bid thee do.   30
Hast thou no letters to me from the friar?
BALTHASAR
No, my good lord.
ROMEO   No matter. Get thee gone,
And hire those horses. I'll be with thee straight.
      Exit Balthasar
Well, Juliet, I will lie with thee tonight.
Let's see for means. O mischief, thou art swift   35
To enter in the thoughts of desperate men!
I do remember an apothecary,
And hereabouts a dwells, which late I noted,
In tattered weeds, with overwhelming brows,
Culling of simples. Meagre were his looks.   40
Sharp misery had worn him to the bones,
And in his needy shop a tortoise hung,
An alligator stuffed, and other skins
Of ill-shaped fishes; and about his shelves
A beggarly account of empty boxes,   45
Green earthen pots, bladders, and musty seeds,
Remnants of packthread, and old cakes of roses
Were thinly scattered to make up a show.
Noting this penury, to myself I said
'An if a man did need a poison now,   50
Whose sale is present death in Mantua,
Here lives a caitiff wretch would sell it him.'
O, this same thought did but forerun my need,
And this same needy man must sell it me.

As I remember, this should be the house.   55
Being holiday, the beggar's shop is shut.
What ho, apothecary!
      Enter Apothecary
APOTHECARY   Who calls so loud?
ROMEO
Come hither, man. I see that thou art poor.
      He offers money
Hold, there is forty ducats. Let me have
A dram of poison—such soon-speeding gear   60
As will disperse itself through all the veins,
That the life-weary taker may fall dead,
And that the trunk may be discharged of breath
As violently as hasty powder fired
Doth hurry from the fatal cannon's womb.   65
APOTHECARY
Such mortal drugs I have, but Mantua's law
Is death to any he that utters them.
ROMEO
Art thou so bare and full of wretchedness,
And fear'st to die? Famine is in thy cheeks,
Need and oppression starveth in thy eyes,   70
Contempt and beggary hangs upon thy back.
The world is not thy friend, nor the world's law.
The world affords no law to make thee rich.
Then be not poor, but break it, and take this.
APOTHECARY
My poverty but not my will consents.   75
ROMEO
I pay thy poverty and not thy will.
APOTHECARY (*handing Romeo poison*)
Put this in any liquid thing you will
And drink it off, and if you had the strength
Of twenty men it would dispatch you straight.
ROMEO (*giving money*)
There is thy gold—worse poison to men's souls,   80
Doing more murder in this loathsome world,
Than these poor compounds that thou mayst not sell.
I sell thee poison; thou hast sold me none.
Farewell, buy food, and get thyself in flesh.
      ⌈*Exit Apothecary*⌉
Come, cordial and not poison, go with me   85
To Juliet's grave, for there must I use thee.   *Exit*

5.2   *Enter Friar John at one door*
FRIAR JOHN
Holy Franciscan friar, brother, ho!
      Enter Friar Laurence at another door
FRIAR LAURENCE
This same should be the voice of Friar John.
Welcome from Mantua! What says Romeo?
Or if his mind be writ, give me his letter.
FRIAR JOHN
Going to find a barefoot brother out—   5
One of our order—to associate me
Here in this city visiting the sick,
And finding him, the searchers of the town,
Suspecting that we both were in a house
Where the infectious pestilence did reign,   10

Sealed up the doors, and would not let us forth,
So that my speed to Mantua there was stayed.

FRIAR LAURENCE
Who bare my letter then to Romeo?

FRIAR JOHN
I could not send it—here it is again—
Nor get a messenger to bring it thee,   15
So fearful were they of infection.

FRIAR LAURENCE
Unhappy fortune! By my brotherhood,
The letter was not nice, but full of charge,
Of dear import, and the neglecting it
May do much danger. Friar John, go hence.   20
Get me an iron crow, and bring it straight
Unto my cell.

FRIAR JOHN   Brother, I'll go and bring it thee.   *Exit*

FRIAR LAURENCE
Now must I to the monument alone.
Within this three hours will fair Juliet wake.
She will beshrew me much that Romeo   25
Hath had no notice of these accidents.
But I will write again to Mantua,
And keep her at my cell till Romeo come.
Poor living corpse, closed in a dead man's tomb!   *Exit*

5.3   *Enter Paris and his Page, with flowers, sweet water,
and a torch*

PARIS
Give me thy torch, boy. Hence, and stand aloof.
Yet put it out, for I would not be seen.
    ⌐His Page puts out the torch⌐
Under yon yew trees lay thee all along,
Holding thy ear close to the hollow ground.
So shall no foot upon the churchyard tread,   5
Being loose, unfirm, with digging up of graves,
But thou shalt hear it. Whistle then to me
As signal that thou hear'st something approach.
Give me those flowers. Do as I bid thee. Go.

PAGE ⌐aside⌐
I am almost afraid to stand alone   10
Here in the churchyard, yet I will adventure.
    He hides himself at a distance from Paris

PARIS (*strewing flowers*)
Sweet flower, with flowers thy bridal bed I strew.
    He sprinkles water
O woe! Thy canopy is dust and stones,
Which with sweet water nightly I will dew,
Or, wanting that, with tears distilled by moans.   15
The obsequies that I for thee will keep
Nightly shall be to strew thy grave and weep.
    The Page whistles
The boy gives warning. Something doth approach.
What cursèd foot wanders this way tonight
To cross my obsequies and true love's rite?   20
    *Enter Romeo and ⌐Balthasar⌐ his man, with a torch,
    a mattock, and a crow of iron*
What, with a torch? Muffle me, night, a while.
    He stands aside

ROMEO
Give me that mattock and the wrenching iron.
Hold, take this letter. Early in the morning
See thou deliver it to my lord and father.
Give me the light. Upon thy life I charge thee,   25
Whate'er thou hear'st or seest, stand all aloof,
And do not interrupt me in my course.
Why I descend into this bed of death
Is partly to behold my lady's face,
But chiefly to take thence from her dead finger   30
A precious ring, a ring that I must use
In dear employment. Therefore hence, be gone.
But if thou, jealous, dost return to pry
In what I farther shall intend to do,
By heaven, I will tear thee joint by joint,   35
And strew this hungry churchyard with thy limbs.
The time and my intents are savage-wild,
More fierce and more inexorable far
Than empty tigers or the roaring sea.

⌐BALTHASAR⌐
I will be gone, sir, and not trouble ye.   40

ROMEO
So shalt thou show me friendship. Take thou that.
    He gives money
Live and be prosperous, and farewell, good fellow.

⌐BALTHASAR⌐ (*aside*)
For all this same, I'll hide me hereabout.
His looks I fear, and his intents I doubt.
    He hides himself at a distance from Romeo.
    ⌐Romeo begins to force open the tomb⌐

ROMEO
Thou detestable maw, thou womb of death,   45
Gorged with the dearest morsel of the earth,
Thus I enforce thy rotten jaws to open,
And in despite I'll cram thee with more food.

PARIS (*aside*)
This is that banished haughty Montague
That murdered my love's cousin, with which grief   50
It is supposèd the fair creature died;
And here is come to do some villainous shame
To the dead bodies. I will apprehend him.
    ⌐Drawing⌐ Stop thy unhallowed toil, vile Montague!
Can vengeance be pursued further than death?   55
Condemnèd villain, I do apprehend thee.
Obey and go with me, for thou must die.

ROMEO
I must indeed, and therefore came I hither.
Good gentle youth, tempt not a desp'rate man.
Fly hence, and leave me. Think upon these gone.   60
Let them affright thee. I beseech thee, youth,
Put not another sin upon my head
By urging me to fury. O, be gone.
By heaven, I love thee better than myself,
For I come hither armed against myself.   65
Stay not, be gone. Live, and hereafter say
A madman's mercy bid thee run away.

PARIS
I do defy thy conjuration,
And apprehend thee for a felon here.

ROMEO (*drawing*)

  Wilt thou provoke me? Then have at thee, boy.   70

    They fight

⌈PAGE⌉

  O Lord, they fight! I will go call the watch.   *Exit*

PARIS

  O, I am slain! If thou be merciful,

  Open the tomb, lay me with Juliet.

ROMEO

  In faith, I will.   *Paris dies*

          Let me peruse this face.

  Mercutio's kinsman, noble County Paris!   75

  What said my man when my betossèd soul

  Did not attend him as we rode? I think

  He told me Paris should have married Juliet.

  Said he not so? Or did I dream it so?

  Or am I mad, hearing him talk of Juliet,   80

  To think it was so? O, give me thy hand,

  One writ with me in sour misfortune's book.

  I'll bury thee in a triumphant grave.

    ⌈*He opens the tomb, revealing Juliet*⌉

  A grave—O no, a lantern, slaughtered youth,

  For here lies Juliet, and her beauty makes   85

  This vault a feasting presence full of light.

    ⌈*He bears the body of Paris to the tomb*⌉

  Death, lie thou there, by a dead man interred.

  How oft, when men are at the point of death,

  Have they been merry, which their keepers call

  A lightning before death! O, how may I   90

  Call this a lightning? O my love, my wife!

  Death, that hath sucked the honey of thy breath,

  Hath had no power yet upon thy beauty.

  Thou art not conquered. Beauty's ensign yet

  Is crimson in thy lips and in thy cheeks,   95

  And death's pale flag is not advancèd there.

  Tybalt, liest thou there in thy bloody sheet?

  O, what more favour can I do to thee

  Than with that hand that cut thy youth in twain

  To sunder his that was thine enemy?   100

  Forgive me, cousin. Ah, dear Juliet,

  Why art thou yet so fair? Shall I believe

  That unsubstantial death is amorous,

  And that the lean abhorrèd monster keeps

  Thee here in dark to be his paramour?   105

  For fear of that I still will stay with thee,

  And never from this pallet of dim night

  Depart again. Here, here will I remain

  With worms that are thy chambermaids. O, here

  Will I set up my everlasting rest,   110

  And shake the yoke of inauspicious stars

  From this world-wearied flesh. Eyes, look your last.

  Arms, take your last embrace, and lips, O you

  The doors of breath, seal with a righteous kiss

  A dateless bargain to engrossing death.   115

    ⌈*He kisses Juliet, then pours poison into the cup*⌉

  Come, bitter conduct, come, unsavoury guide,

  Thou desperate pilot, now at once run on

  The dashing rocks thy seasick weary barque!

  Here's to my love.

    He drinks the poison

              O true apothecary,

  Thy drugs are quick! Thus with a kiss I die.   120

    He kisses Juliet, falls, and dies.

    Enter Friar Laurence with lantern, crow, and spade

FRIAR LAURENCE

  Saint Francis be my speed! How oft tonight

  Have my old feet stumbled at graves? Who's there?

BALTHASAR

  Here's one, a friend, and one that knows you well.

FRIAR LAURENCE

  Bliss be upon you. Tell me, good my friend,

  What torch is yon that vainly lends his light   125

  To grubs and eyeless skulls? As I discern,

  It burneth in the Capels' monument.

BALTHASAR

  It doth so, holy sir, and there's my master,

  One that you love.

FRIAR LAURENCE   Who is it?

BALTHASAR   Romeo.

FRIAR LAURENCE

  How long hath he been there?

BALTHASAR   Full half an hour.   130

FRIAR LAURENCE

  Go with me to the vault.

BALTHASAR   I dare not, sir.

  My master knows not but I am gone hence,

  And fearfully did menace me with death

  If I did stay to look on his intents.

FRIAR LAURENCE

  Stay then, I'll go alone. Fear comes upon me.   135

  O, much I fear some ill unthrifty thing.

BALTHASAR

  As I did sleep under this yew tree here

  I dreamt my master and another fought,

  And that my master slew him.

FRIAR LAURENCE   Romeo!

    He ⌈stoops and⌉ looks on the blood and weapons

  Alack, alack, what blood is this which stains   140

  The stony entrance of this sepulchre?

  What mean these masterless and gory swords

  To lie discoloured by this place of peace?

  Romeo! O, pale! Who else? What, Paris, too,

  And steeped in blood? Ah, what an unkind hour   145

  Is guilty of this lamentable chance!

    Juliet awakes ⌈and rises⌉

  The lady stirs.

JULIET

  O comfortable friar, where is my lord?

  I do remember well where I should be,

  And there I am. Where is my Romeo?   150

FRIAR LAURENCE

  I hear some noise. Lady, come from that nest

  Of death, contagion, and unnatural sleep.

  A greater power than we can contradict

  Hath thwarted our intents. Come, come away.

  Thy husband in thy bosom there lies dead,   155

And Paris, too. Come, I'll dispose of thee
Among a sisterhood of holy nuns.
Stay not to question, for the watch is coming.
Come, go, good Juliet. I dare no longer stay.   *Exit*
JULIET
Go, get thee hence, for I will not away.   160
What's here? A cup closed in my true love's hand?
Poison, I see, hath been his timeless end.
O churl!—drunk all, and left no friendly drop
To help me after? I will kiss thy lips.
Haply some poison yet doth hang on them,   165
To make me die with a restorative.
            She kisses Romeo's lips
Thy lips are warm.
CHIEF WATCHMAN ⌈*within*⌉ Lead, boy. Which way?
JULIET
Yea, noise? Then I'll be brief.
            She takes Romeo's dagger
                        O happy dagger,
This is thy sheath! There rust, and let me die.
            She stabs herself, falls, and dies.
            Enter the Page and Watchmen
⌈PAGE⌉
This is the place, there where the torch doth burn.   170
CHIEF WATCHMAN
The ground is bloody. Search about the churchyard.
Go, some of you. Whoe'er you find, attach.
                        Exeunt some Watchmen
Pitiful sight! Here lies the County slain,
And Juliet bleeding, warm, and newly dead,
Who here hath lain this two days buried.   175
Go tell the Prince. Run to the Capulets,
Raise up the Montagues. Some others search.
                        Exeunt other Watchmen ⌈*severally*⌉
We see the ground whereon these woes do lie,
But the true ground of all these piteous woes
We cannot without circumstance descry.   180
            Enter ⌈*Watchmen*⌉ *with Balthasar*
⌈SECOND⌉ WATCHMAN
Here's Romeo's man. We found him in the
            churchyard.
CHIEF WATCHMAN
Hold him in safety till the Prince come hither.
            Enter another Watchman with Friar Laurence
THIRD WATCHMAN
Here is a friar that trembles, sighs, and weeps.
We took this mattock and this spade from him
As he was coming from this churchyard's side.   185
CHIEF WATCHMAN
A great suspicion. Stay the friar, too.
            Enter the Prince ⌈*with others*⌉
PRINCE
What misadventure is so early up,
That calls our person from our morning rest?
            Enter Capulet and his Wife
CAPULET
What should it be that is so shrieked abroad?

CAPULET'S WIFE
O, the people in the street cry 'Romeo',   190
Some 'Juliet', and some 'Paris', and all run
With open outcry toward our monument.
PRINCE
What fear is this which startles in our ears?
CHIEF WATCHMAN
Sovereign, here lies the County Paris slain,
And Romeo dead, and Juliet, dead before,   195
Warm, and new killed.
PRINCE
Search, seek, and know how this foul murder comes.
CHIEF WATCHMAN
Here is a friar, and slaughtered Romeo's man,
With instruments upon them fit to open
These dead men's tombs.   200
CAPULET
O heavens! O wife, look how our daughter bleeds!
This dagger hath mista'en, for lo, his house
Is empty on the back of Montague,
And it mis-sheathèd in my daughter's bosom.
CAPULET'S WIFE
O me, this sight of death is as a bell   205
That warns my old age to a sepulchre.
            Enter Montague
PRINCE
Come, Montague, for thou art early up
To see thy son and heir more early down.
MONTAGUE
Alas, my liege, my wife is dead tonight.
Grief of my son's exile hath stopped her breath.   210
What further woe conspires against mine age?
PRINCE Look, and thou shalt see.
MONTAGUE (*seeing Romeo's body*)
O thou untaught! What manners is in this,
To press before thy father to a grave?
PRINCE
Seal up the mouth of outrage for a while,   215
Till we can clear these ambiguities
And know their spring, their head, their true descent;
And then will I be general of your woes,
And lead you even to death. Meantime, forbear,
And let mischance be slave to patience.   220
Bring forth the parties of suspicion.
FRIAR LAURENCE
I am the greatest, able to do least,
Yet most suspected, as the time and place
Doth make against me, of this direful murder;
And here I stand, both to impeach and purge   225
Myself condemnèd and myself excused.
PRINCE
Then say at once what thou dost know in this.
FRIAR LAURENCE
I will be brief, for my short date of breath
Is not so long as is a tedious tale.
Romeo, there dead, was husband to that Juliet,   230
And she, there dead, that Romeo's faithful wife.
I married them, and their stol'n marriage day

Was Tybalt's doomsday, whose untimely death
Banished the new-made bridegroom from this city,
For whom, and not for Tybalt, Juliet pined.   235
You, to remove that siege of grief from her,
Betrothed and would have married her perforce
To County Paris. Then comes she to me,
And with wild looks bid me devise some mean
To rid her from this second marriage,   240
Or in my cell there would she kill herself.
Then gave I her—so tutored by my art—
A sleeping potion, which so took effect
As I intended, for it wrought on her
The form of death. Meantime I writ to Romeo   245
That he should hither come as this dire night
To help to take her from her borrowed grave,
Being the time the potion's force should cease.
But he which bore my letter, Friar John,
Was stayed by accident, and yesternight   250
Returned my letter back. Then all alone,
At the prefixèd hour of her waking,
Came I to take her from her kindred's vault,
Meaning to keep her closely at my cell
Till I conveniently could send to Romeo.   255
But when I came, some minute ere the time
Of her awakening, here untimely lay
The noble Paris and true Romeo dead.
She wakes, and I entreated her come forth
And bear this work of heaven with patience.   260
But then a noise did scare me from the tomb,
And she, too desperate, would not go with me,
But, as it seems, did violence on herself.
All this I know, and to the marriage
Her nurse is privy; and if aught in this   265
Miscarried by my fault, let my old life
Be sacrificed, some hour before his time,
Unto the rigour of severest law.

PRINCE
We still have known thee for a holy man.
Where's Romeo's man? What can he say to this?   270

BALTHASAR
I brought my master news of Juliet's death,
And then in post he came from Mantua
To this same place, to this same monument.
This letter he early bid me give his father,

And threatened me with death, going in the vault,   275
If I departed not and left him there.

PRINCE
Give me the letter. I will look on it.
        He takes the letter
Where is the County's page that raised the watch?
Sirrah, what made your master in this place?

PAGE
He came with flowers to strew his lady's grave,   280
And bid me stand aloof, and so I did.
Anon comes one with light to ope the tomb,
And by and by my master drew on him,
And then I ran away to call the watch.

PRINCE
This letter doth make good the friar's words,   285
Their course of love, the tidings of her death;
And here he writes that he did buy a poison
Of a poor 'pothecary, and therewithal
Came to this vault to die, and lie with Juliet.
Where be these enemies? Capulet, Montague,   290
See what a scourge is laid upon your hate,
That heaven finds means to kill your joys with love.
And I, for winking at your discords, too
Have lost a brace of kinsmen. All are punishèd.

CAPULET
O brother Montague, give me thy hand.   295
This is my daughter's jointure, for no more
Can I demand.

MONTAGUE   But I can give thee more,
For I will raise her statue in pure gold,
That whiles Verona by that name is known
There shall no figure at such rate be set   300
As that of true and faithful Juliet.

CAPULET
As rich shall Romeo's by his lady's lie,
Poor sacrifices of our enmity.

PRINCE
A glooming peace this morning with it brings.
The sun for sorrow will not show his head.   305
Go hence, to have more talk of these sad things.
Some shall be pardoned, and some punishèd;
For never was a story of more woe
Than this of Juliet and her Romeo.
                        ⌈*The tomb is closed.*⌉ *Exeunt*

JULIUS CAESAR

ON 21 September 1599 a Swiss doctor, Thomas Platter, saw what can only have been Shakespeare's *Julius Caesar* 'very pleasingly performed' in the newly built Globe Theatre— 'the straw-thatched house'—on the south side of the Thames. Francis Meres does not mention the play in *Palladis Tamia* of 1598, and minor resemblances with works printed in the early part of 1599 suggest that Shakespeare wrote it during that year. It was first printed in the 1623 Folio.

Julius Caesar shows Shakespeare turning from English to Roman history, which he had last used in *Titus Andronicus* and *The Rape of Lucrece*. Caesar was regarded as perhaps the greatest ruler in the history of the world, and his murder by Brutus as one of the foulest crimes: but it was also recognized that Caesar had faults and Brutus virtues. Other plays, some now lost, had been written about Caesar and may have influenced Shakespeare; but there is no question that he made extensive use (for the first time in this play) of Sir Thomas North's great translation (based on Jacques Amyot's French version and published in 1579) of *Lives of the Noble Grecians and Romans* by the Greek historian Plutarch, who lived from about AD 50 to 130.

Shakespeare was interested in the aftermath of Caesar's death as well as in the events leading up to it, and in the public and private motives of those responsible for it. So, although the Folio calls the play *The Tragedy of Julius Caesar*, Caesar is dead before the play is half over; Brutus, Cassius, and Antony have considerably longer roles, and Brutus is portrayed with a degree of introspection which links him more closely to Shakespeare's other tragic heroes. Shakespeare draws mainly on the last quarter of Plutarch's Life of Caesar, showing his fall; he also uses the Lives of Antony and Brutus for the play's first sweep of action, showing the rise of the conspiracy against Caesar, its leaders' efforts to persuade Brutus to join them, the assassination itself, and its immediate aftermath as Antony incites the citizens to revenge. The second part, showing the formation of the triumvirate of Antony, Lepidus, and Octavius Caesar, the uneasy alliance of Brutus and Cassius, and the battles in which Caesar's spirit revenges itself, depends mainly on the Life of Brutus. Facts are often altered and rearranged in the interests of dramatic economy and effectiveness.

Although Shakespeare wrote the play at a point in his career at which he was tending to use a high proportion of prose, *Julius Caesar* is written mainly in verse; as if to suit the subject matter, the style is classical in its lucidity and eloquence, reaching a climax of rhetorical effectiveness in the speeches over Caesar's body (3.2). The play's stageworthiness has been repeatedly demonstrated; it offers excellent opportunities in all its main roles, and the quarrel between Brutus and Cassius (4.2) has been admired ever since Leonard Digges, a contemporary of Shakespeare, praised it at the expense of Ben Jonson:

> So have I seen, when Caesar would appear,
> And on the stage at half-sword parley were
> Brutus and Cassius; O, how the audience
> Were ravished, with what wonder they went thence,
> When some new day they would not brook a line
> Of tedious though well-laboured *Catiline*.

THE PERSONS OF THE PLAY

Julius CAESAR

CALPURNIA, his wife

Marcus BRUTUS, a noble Roman, opposed to Caesar

PORTIA, his wife

LUCIUS, his servant

Caius CASSIUS ⎫
CASCA ⎪
TREBONIUS ⎪
DECIUS Brutus ⎬ opposed to Caesar
METELLUS Cimber ⎪
CINNA ⎪
Caius LIGARIUS ⎭

Mark ANTONY ⎫
OCTAVIUS Caesar ⎬ rulers of Rome after Caesar's death
LEPIDUS ⎭

FLAVIUS ⎫
⎬ tribunes of the people
MURELLUS ⎭

CICERO ⎫
PUBLIUS ⎬ senators
POPILLIUS Laena ⎭

A SOOTHSAYER

ARTEMIDORUS

CINNA the Poet

PINDARUS, Cassius' bondman

TITINIUS, an officer in Cassius' army

LUCILLIUS ⎫
MESSALA ⎪
VARRUS ⎪
CLAUDIO ⎪
YOUNG CATO ⎬ officers and soldiers in Brutus' army
STRATO ⎪
VOLUMNIUS ⎪
FLAVIUS ⎪
DARDANIUS ⎪
CLITUS ⎭

A POET

GHOST of Caesar

A COBBLER

A CARPENTER

Other PLEBEIANS

A MESSENGER

SERVANTS

Senators, soldiers, and attendants

The Tragedy of Julius Caesar

1.1 *Enter Flavius, Murellus, and certain commoners*
over the stage

FLAVIUS

Hence, home, you idle creatures, get you home!
Is this a holiday? What, know you not,
Being mechanical, you ought not walk
Upon a labouring day without the sign
Of your profession?—Speak, what trade art thou?   5

CARPENTER Why, sir, a carpenter.

MURELLUS

Where is thy leather apron and thy rule?
What dost thou with thy best apparel on?—
You, sir, what trade are you?

COBBLER Truly, sir, in respect of a fine workman I am
but, as you would say, a cobbler.   11

MURELLUS

But what trade art thou? Answer me directly.

COBBLER A trade, sir, that I hope I may use with a safe
conscience, which is indeed, sir, a mender of bad soles.

FLAVIUS

What trade, thou knave? Thou naughty knave, what
trade?   15

COBBLER Nay, I beseech you, sir, be not out with me. Yet
if you be out, sir, I can mend you.

MURELLUS

What mean'st thou by that? Mend me, thou saucy
fellow?

COBBLER Why, sir, cobble you.

FLAVIUS Thou art a cobbler, art thou?   20

COBBLER Truly, sir, all that I live by is with the awl. I
meddle with no tradesman's matters, nor women's
matters, but withal I am indeed, sir, a surgeon to old
shoes: when they are in great danger I recover them.
As proper men as ever trod upon neat's leather have
gone upon my handiwork.   26

FLAVIUS ·

But wherefore art not in thy shop today?
Why dost thou lead these men about the streets?

COBBLER Truly, sir, to wear out their shoes to get myself
into more work. But indeed, sir, we make holiday to
see Caesar, and to rejoice in his triumph.   31

MURELLUS

Wherefore rejoice? What conquest brings he home?
What tributaries follow him to Rome
To grace in captive bonds his chariot wheels?
You blocks, you stones, you worse than senseless
things!   35
O, you hard hearts, you cruel men of Rome,
Knew you not Pompey? Many a time and oft
Have you climbed up to walls and battlements,
To towers and windows, yea to chimney-tops,
Your infants in your arms, and there have sat   40
The livelong day with patient expectation

To see great Pompey pass the streets of Rome.
And when you saw his chariot but appear,
Have you not made an universal shout,
That Tiber trembled underneath her banks   45
To hear the replication of your sounds
Made in her concave shores?
And do you now put on your best attire?
And do you now cull out a holiday?
And do you now strew flowers in his way   50
That comes in triumph over Pompey's blood?
Be gone!
Run to your houses, fall upon your knees,
Pray to the gods to intermit the plague
That needs must light on this ingratitude.   55

FLAVIUS

Go, go, good countrymen, and for this fault
Assemble all the poor men of your sort;
Draw them to Tiber banks, and weep your tears
Into the channel, till the lowest stream
Do kiss the most exalted shores of all.   60
                    Exeunt all the commoners
See whe'er their basest mettle be not moved.
They vanish tongue-tied in their guiltiness.
Go you down that way towards the Capitol;
This way will I. Disrobe the images
If you do find them decked with ceremonies.   65

MURELLUS May we do so?
You know it is the Feast of Lupercal.

FLAVIUS

It is no matter. Let no images
Be hung with Caesar's trophies. I'll about,
And drive away the vulgar from the streets;   70
So do you too where you perceive them thick.
These growing feathers plucked from Caesar's wing
Will make him fly an ordinary pitch,
Who else would soar above the view of men
And keep us all in servile fearfulness.   *Exeunt*

1.2 ⌐*Loud music.*⌐ *Enter Caesar, Antony stripped for the*
course, Calpurnia, Portia, Decius, Cicero, Brutus,
Cassius, Casca, a Soothsayer, ⌐a throng of citizens⌐;
after them, Murellus and Flavius

CAESAR Calpurnia.

CASCA Peace, ho! Caesar speaks.
                    ⌐*Music ceases*⌐

CAESAR Calpurnia.

CALPURNIA Here, my lord.

CAESAR

Stand you directly in Antonio's way   5
When he doth run his course.—Antonio.

ANTONY Caesar, my lord.

CAESAR

Forget not in your speed, Antonio,

To touch Calpurnia, for our elders say
The barren, touchèd in this holy chase, 10
Shake off their sterile curse.

ANTONY   I shall remember:
When Caesar says 'Do this', it is performed.

CAESAR
Set on, and leave no ceremony out.
      ⌈*Music*⌉

SOOTHSAYER Caesar!

CAESAR Ha! Who calls? 15

CASCA
Bid every noise be still. Peace yet again.
      ⌈*Music ceases*⌉

CAESAR
Who is it in the press that calls on me?
I hear a tongue shriller than all the music
Cry 'Caesar!' Speak. Caesar is turned to hear.

SOOTHSAYER
Beware the ides of March.

CAESAR   What man is that? 20

BRUTUS
A soothsayer bids you beware the ides of March.

CAESAR
Set him before me; let me see his face.

CASSIUS
Fellow, come from the throng; look upon Caesar.
     The Soothsayer comes forward

CAESAR
What sayst thou to me now? Speak once again.

SOOTHSAYER Beware the ides of March. 25

CAESAR
He is a dreamer. Let us leave him. Pass!
     Sennet. Exeunt all but Brutus and Cassius

CASSIUS
Will you go see the order of the course?

BRUTUS Not I.

CASSIUS I pray you, do.

BRUTUS
I am not gamesome; I do lack some part 30
Of that quick spirit that is in Antony.
Let me not hinder, Cassius, your desires.
I'll leave you.

CASSIUS
Brutus, I do observe you now of late.
I have not from your eyes that gentleness 35
And show of love as I was wont to have.
You bear too stubborn and too strange a hand
Over your friend that loves you.

BRUTUS   Cassius,
Be not deceived. If I have veiled my look,
I turn the trouble of my countenance 40
Merely upon myself. Vexèd I am
Of late with passions of some difference,
Conceptions only proper to myself,
Which give some soil, perhaps, to my behaviours.
But let not therefore my good friends be grieved— 45
Among which number, Cassius, be you one—
Nor construe any further my neglect

Than that poor Brutus, with himself at war,
Forgets the shows of love to other men.

CASSIUS
Then, Brutus, I have much mistook your passion, 50
By means whereof this breast of mine hath buried
Thoughts of great value, worthy cogitations.
Tell me, good Brutus, can you see your face?

BRUTUS
No, Cassius, for the eye sees not itself
But by reflection, by some other things. 55

CASSIUS 'Tis just;
And it is very much lamented, Brutus,
That you have no such mirrors as will turn
Your hidden worthiness into your eye,
That you might see your shadow. I have heard 60
Where many of the best respect in Rome—
Except immortal Caesar—speaking of Brutus,
And groaning underneath this age's yoke,
Have wished that noble Brutus had his eyes.

BRUTUS
Into what dangers would you lead me, Cassius, 65
That you would have me seek into myself
For that which is not in me?

CASSIUS
Therefor, good Brutus, be prepared to hear.
And since you know you cannot see yourself
So well as by reflection, I, your glass, 70
Will modestly discover to yourself
That of yourself which you yet know not of.
And be not jealous on me, gentle Brutus.
Were I a common laughter, or did use
To stale with ordinary oaths my love 75
To every new protester; if you know
That I do fawn on men and hug them hard,
And after scandal them; or if you know
That I profess myself in banqueting
To all the rout: then hold me dangerous. 80
     Flourish and shout within

BRUTUS
What means this shouting? I do fear the people
Choose Caesar for their king.

CASSIUS   Ay, do you fear it?
Then must I think you would not have it so.

BRUTUS
I would not, Cassius; yet I love him well.
But wherefore do you hold me here so long? 85
What is it that you would impart to me?
If it be aught toward the general good,
Set honour in one eye and death i'th' other,
And I will look on both indifferently;
For let the gods so speed me as I love 90
The name of honour more than I fear death.

CASSIUS
I know that virtue to be in you, Brutus,
As well as I do know your outward favour.
Well, honour is the subject of my story.
I cannot tell what you and other men 95
Think of this life; but for my single self,

I had as lief not be, as live to be
In awe of such a thing as I myself.
I was born free as Caesar, so were you.
We both have fed as well, and we can both 100
Endure the winter's cold as well as he.
For once upon a raw and gusty day,
The troubled Tiber chafing with her shores,
Said Caesar to me 'Dar'st thou, Cassius, now
Leap in with me into this angry flood, 105
And swim to yonder point?' Upon the word,
Accoutred as I was I plungèd in,
And bade him follow. So indeed he did.
The torrent roared, and we did buffet it
With lusty sinews, throwing it aside, 110
And stemming it with hearts of controversy.
But ere we could arrive the point proposed,
Caesar cried 'Help me, Cassius, or I sink!'
Ay, as Aeneas our great ancestor
Did from the flames of Troy upon his shoulder 115
The old Anchises bear, so from the waves of Tiber
Did I the tirèd Caesar. And this man
Is now become a god, and Cassius is
A wretched creature, and must bend his body
If Caesar carelessly but nod on him. 120
He had a fever when he was in Spain,
And when the fit was on him, I did mark
How he did shake. 'Tis true, this god did shake.
His coward lips did from their colour fly;
And that same eye whose bend doth awe the world 125
Did lose his lustre. I did hear him groan,
Ay, and that tongue of his that bade the Romans
Mark him and write his speeches in their books,
'Alas!' it cried, 'Give me some drink, Titinius',
As a sick girl. Ye gods, it doth amaze me 130
A man of such a feeble temper should
So get the start of the majestic world,
And bear the palm alone!
     Flourish and shout within
BRUTUS   Another general shout!
I do believe that these applauses are
For some new honours that are heaped on Caesar. 135
CASSIUS
Why, man, he doth bestride the narrow world
Like a Colossus, and we petty men
Walk under his huge legs, and peep about
To find ourselves dishonourable graves.
Men at sometime were masters of their fates. 140
The fault, dear Brutus, is not in our stars,
But in ourselves, that we are underlings.
Brutus and Caesar: what should be in that 'Caesar'?
Why should that name be sounded more than yours?
Write them together: yours is as fair a name. 145
Sound them: it doth become the mouth as well.
Weigh them: it is as heavy. Conjure with 'em:
'Brutus' will start a spirit as soon as 'Caesar'.
Now in the names of all the gods at once,
Upon what meat doth this our Caesar feed 150
That he is grown so great? Age, thou art shamed.

Rome, thou hast lost the breed of noble bloods.
When went there by an age since the great flood,
But it was famed with more than with one man?
When could they say till now, that talked of Rome, 155
That her wide walls encompassed but one man?
Now is it Rome indeed, and room enough
When there is in it but one only man.
O, you and I have heard our fathers say
There was a Brutus once that would have brooked 160
Th'eternal devil to keep his state in Rome
As easily as a king.
BRUTUS
That you do love me I am nothing jealous.
What you would work me to I have some aim.
How I have thought of this and of these times 165
I shall recount hereafter. For this present,
I would not, so with love I might entreat you,
Be any further moved. What you have said
I will consider. What you have to say
I will with patience hear, and find a time 170
Both meet to hear and answer such high things.
Till then, my noble friend, chew upon this:
Brutus had rather be a villager
Than to repute himself a son of Rome
Under these hard conditions as this time 175
Is like to lay upon us.
CASSIUS   I am glad
That my weak words have struck but thus much show
Of fire from Brutus.
    ⌈*Music.*⌉ *Enter Caesar and his train*
BRUTUS
The games are done, and Caesar is returning.
CASSIUS
As they pass by, pluck Casca by the sleeve, 180
And he will, after his sour fashion, tell you
What hath proceeded worthy note today.
BRUTUS
I will do so. But look you, Cassius,
The angry spot doth glow on Caesar's brow,
And all the rest look like a chidden train. 185
Calpurnia's cheek is pale, and Cicero
Looks with such ferret and such fiery eyes
As we have seen him in the Capitol
Being crossed in conference by some senators.
CASSIUS
Casca will tell us what the matter is. 190
CAESAR Antonio.
ANTONY Caesar.
CAESAR
Let me have men about me that are fat,
Sleek-headed men, and such as sleep a-nights.
Yon Cassius has a lean and hungry look. 195
He thinks too much. Such men are dangerous.
ANTONY
Fear him not, Caesar, he's not dangerous.
He is a noble Roman, and well given.
CAESAR
Would he were fatter! But I fear him not.

Yet if my name were liable to fear,   200
I do not know the man I should avoid
So soon as that spare Cassius. He reads much,
He is a great observer, and he looks
Quite through the deeds of men. He loves no plays,
As thou dost, Antony; he hears no music.   205
Seldom he smiles, and smiles in such a sort
As if he mocked himself, and scorned his spirit
That could be moved to smile at anything.
Such men as he be never at heart's ease
Whiles they behold a greater than themselves,   210
And therefore are they very dangerous.
I rather tell thee what is to be feared
Than what I fear, for always I am Caesar.
Come on my right hand, for this ear is deaf,
And tell me truly what thou think'st of him.   215
          Sennet. Exeunt Caesar and his train. Brutus,
                          Cassius, and Casca remain
CASCA (*to Brutus*) You pulled me by the cloak. Would you
   speak with me?
BRUTUS
   Ay, Casca. Tell us what hath chanced today,
   That Caesar looks so sad.
CASCA Why, you were with him, were you not?   220
BRUTUS
   I should not then ask Casca what had chanced.
CASCA Why, there was a crown offered him; and being
   offered him, he put it by with the back of his hand,
   thus; and then the people fell a-shouting.
BRUTUS What was the second noise for?   225
CASCA Why, for that too.
CASSIUS
   They shouted thrice. What was the last cry for?
CASCA Why, for that too.
BRUTUS Was the crown offered him thrice?   229
CASCA Ay, marry, was't; and he put it by thrice, every
   time gentler than other; and at every putting by, mine
   honest neighbours shouted.
CASSIUS
   Who offered him the crown?
CASCA   Why, Antony.
BRUTUS
   Tell us the manner of it, gentle Casca.   234
CASCA I can as well be hanged as tell the manner of it.
   It was mere foolery, I did not mark it. I saw Mark
   Antony offer him a crown—yet 'twas not a crown
   neither, 'twas one of these coronets—and as I told you
   he put it by once; but for all that, to my thinking he
   would fain have had it. Then he offered it to him again;
   then he put it by again—but to my thinking he was
   very loath to lay his fingers off it. And then he offered
   it the third time; he put it the third time by. And still
   as he refused it, the rabblement hooted, and clapped
   their chapped hands, and threw up their sweaty
   nightcaps, and uttered such a deal of stinking breath
   because Caesar refused the crown that it had almost
   choked Caesar; for he swooned and fell down at it.
   And for mine own part, I durst not laugh for fear of
   opening my lips and receiving the bad air.   250

CASSIUS
   But soft, I pray you. What, did Caesar swoon?
CASCA He fell down in the market-place, and foamed at
   mouth, and was speechless.
BRUTUS
   'Tis very like: he hath the falling sickness.
CASSIUS
   No, Caesar hath it not; but you and I   255
   And honest Casca, we have the falling sickness.
CASCA I know not what you mean by that, but I am sure
   Caesar fell down. If the tag-rag people did not clap him
   and hiss him, according as he pleased and displeased
   them, as they use to do the players in the theatre, I
   am no true man.   261
BRUTUS
   What said he when he came unto himself?
CASCA Marry, before he fell down, when he perceived the
   common herd was glad he refused the crown, he
   plucked me ope his doublet and offered them his throat
   to cut. An I had been a man of any occupation, if I
   would not have taken him at a word, I would I might
   go to hell among the rogues. And so he fell. When he
   came to himself again, he said, if he had done or said
   anything amiss, he desired their worships to think it
   was his infirmity. Three or four wenches where I stood
   cried 'Alas, good soul!' and forgave him with all their
   hearts. But there's no heed to be taken of them: if
   Caesar had stabbed their mothers they would have
   done no less.   275
BRUTUS
   And after that he came thus sad away?
CASCA Ay.
CASSIUS Did Cicero say anything?
CASCA Ay, he spoke Greek.
CASSIUS To what effect?   280
CASCA Nay, an I tell you that, I'll ne'er look you i'th'
   face again. But those that understood him smiled at
   one another, and shook their heads. But for mine own
   part, it was Greek to me. I could tell you more news,
   too. Murellus and Flavius, for pulling scarves off
   Caesar's images, are put to silence. Fare you well. There
   was more foolery yet, if I could remember it.
CASSIUS Will you sup with me tonight, Casca?
CASCA No, I am promised forth.
CASSIUS Will you dine with me tomorrow?   290
CASCA Ay, if I be alive, and your mind hold, and your
   dinner worth the eating.
CASSIUS Good; I will expect you.
CASCA Do so. Farewell both.   *Exit*
BRUTUS
   What a blunt fellow is this grown to be!   295
   He was quick mettle when he went to school.
CASSIUS
   So is he now, in execution
   Of any bold or noble enterprise,
   However he puts on this tardy form.
   This rudeness is a sauce to his good wit,   300
   Which gives men stomach to digest his words
   With better appetite.

BRUTUS
And so it is. For this time I will leave you.
Tomorrow, if you please to speak with me,
I will come home to you; or if you will,   305
Come home to me and I will wait for you.
CASSIUS
I will do so. Till then, think of the world.   *Exit Brutus*
Well, Brutus, thou art noble; yet I see
Thy honourable mettle may be wrought
From that it is disposed. Therefore it is meet   310
That noble minds keep ever with their likes;
For who so firm that cannot be seduced?
Caesar doth bear me hard, but he loves Brutus.
If I were Brutus now, and he were Cassius,
He should not humour me. I will this night   315
In several hands in at his windows throw—
As if they came from several citizens—
Writings, all tending to the great opinion
That Rome holds of his name, wherein obscurely
Caesar's ambition shall be glancèd at.   320
And after this, let Caesar seat him sure,
For we will shake him, or worse days endure.   *Exit*

1.3   *Thunder and lightning. Enter Casca ⌜at one door,*
       with his sword drawn⌝, and Cicero ⌜at another⌝
CICERO
Good even, Casca. Brought you Caesar home?
Why are you breathless, and why stare you so?
CASCA
Are not you moved, when all the sway of earth
Shakes like a thing unfirm? O Cicero,
I have seen tempests when the scolding winds   5
Have rived the knotty oaks, and I have seen
Th'ambitious ocean swell and rage and foam
To be exalted with the threat'ning clouds;
But never till tonight, never till now,
Did I go through a tempest dropping fire.   10
Either there is a civil strife in heaven,
Or else the world, too saucy with the gods,
Incenses them to send destruction.
CICERO
Why, saw you anything more wonderful?
CASCA
A common slave—you know him well by sight—   15
Held up his left hand, which did flame and burn
Like twenty torches joined; and yet his hand,
Not sensible of fire, remained unscorched.
Besides—I ha' not since put up my sword—
Against the Capitol I met a lion   20
Who glazed upon me, and went surly by
Without annoying me. And there were drawn
Upon a heap a hundred ghastly women,
Transformèd with their fear, who swore they saw
Men all in fire walk up and down the streets.   25
And yesterday the bird of night did sit
Even at noonday upon the market-place,
Hooting and shrieking. When these prodigies
Do so conjointly meet, let not men say

'These are their reasons', 'they are natural',   30
For I believe they are portentous things
Unto the climate that they point upon.
CICERO
Indeed it is a strange-disposèd time;
But men may construe things after their fashion,
Clean from the purpose of the things themselves.   35
Comes Caesar to the Capitol tomorrow?
CASCA
He doth, for he did bid Antonio
Send word to you he would be there tomorrow.
CICERO
Good night then, Casca. This disturbèd sky
Is not to walk in.
CASCA   Farewell, Cicero.   *Exit Cicero*
            Enter Cassius, ⌜unbraced⌝
CASSIUS
Who's there?
CASCA   A Roman.
CASSIUS   Casca, by your voice.   41
CASCA
Your ear is good. Cassius, what night is this?
CASSIUS
A very pleasing night to honest men.
CASCA
Who ever knew the heavens menace so?
CASSIUS
Those that have known the earth so full of faults.   45
For my part, I have walked about the streets,
Submitting me unto the perilous night;
And thus unbracèd, Casca, as you see,
Have bared my bosom to the thunder-stone;
And when the cross blue lightning seemed to open   50
The breast of heaven, I did present myself
Even in the aim and very flash of it.
CASCA
But wherefore did you so much tempt the heavens?
It is the part of men to fear and tremble
When the most mighty gods by tokens send   55
Such dreadful heralds to astonish us.
CASSIUS
You are dull, Casca, and those sparks of life
That should be in a Roman you do want,
Or else you use not. You look pale, and gaze,
And put on fear, and cast yourself in wonder,   60
To see the strange impatience of the heavens;
But if you would consider the true cause
Why all these fires, why all these gliding ghosts,
Why birds and beasts from quality and kind—
Why old men, fools, and children calculate—   65
Why all these things change from their ordinance,
Their natures, and preformèd faculties,
To monstrous quality—why, you shall find
That heaven hath infused them with these spirits
To make them instruments of fear and warning   70
Unto some monstrous state. Now could I, Casca,
Name to thee a man most like this dreadful night,
That thunders, lightens, opens graves, and roars

As doth the lion in the Capitol;
A man no mightier than thyself or me   75
In personal action, yet prodigious grown,
And fearful, as these strange eruptions are.

CASCA
'Tis Caesar that you mean, is it not, Cassius?

CASSIUS
Let it be who it is; for Romans now
Have thews and limbs like to their ancestors.   80
But woe the while! Our fathers' minds are dead,
And we are governed with our mothers' spirits.
Our yoke and sufferance show us womanish.

CASCA
Indeed they say the senators tomorrow
Mean to establish Caesar as a king,   85
And he shall wear his crown by sea and land
In every place save here in Italy.

CASSIUS (drawing his dagger)
I know where I will wear this dagger then:
Cassius from bondage will deliver Cassius.
Therein, ye gods, you make the weak most strong;   90
Therein, ye gods, you tyrants do defeat.
Nor stony tower, nor walls of beaten brass,
Nor airless dungeon, nor strong links of iron,
Can be retentive to the strength of spirit;
But life, being weary of these worldly bars,   95
Never lacks power to dismiss itself.
If I know this, know all the world besides,
That part of tyranny that I do bear
I can shake off at pleasure.
          Thunder still

CASCA   So can I.
So every bondman in his own hand bears   100
The power to cancel his captivity.

CASSIUS
And why should Caesar be a tyrant then?
Poor man, I know he would not be a wolf
But that he sees the Romans are but sheep.
He were no lion, were not Romans hinds.   105
Those that with haste will make a mighty fire
Begin it with weak straws. What trash is Rome,
What rubbish, and what offal, when it serves
For the base matter to illuminate
So vile a thing as Caesar! But, O grief,   110
Where hast thou led me? I perhaps speak this
Before a willing bondman; then I know
My answer must be made. But I am armed,
And dangers are to me indifferent.

CASCA
You speak to Casca, and to such a man   115
That is no fleering tell-tale. Hold. My hand.
Be factious for redress of all these griefs,
And I will set this foot of mine as far
As who goes farthest.
          They join hands

CASSIUS   There's a bargain made.
Now know you, Casca, I have moved already   120
Some certain of the noblest-minded Romans

To undergo with me an enterprise
Of honourable-dangerous consequence.
And I do know by this they stay for me
In Pompey's Porch; for now, this fearful night,   125
There is no stir or walking in the streets,
And the complexion of the element
In favour's like the work we have in hand,
Most bloody, fiery, and most terrible.
          Enter Cinna

CASCA
Stand close a while, for here comes one in haste.   130

CASSIUS
'Tis Cinna; I do know him by his gait.
He is a friend.—Cinna, where haste you so?

CINNA
To find out you. Who's that? Metellus Cimber?

CASSIUS
No, it is Casca, one incorporate
To our attempts. Am I not stayed for, Cinna?   135

CINNA
I am glad on't. What a fearful night is this!
There's two or three of us have seen strange sights.

CASSIUS Am I not stayed for? Tell me.

CINNA Yes, you are.
O Cassius, if you could   140
But win the noble Brutus to our party—

CASSIUS
Be you content. Good Cinna, take this paper,
          He gives Cinna letters
And look you lay it in the Praetor's Chair,
Where Brutus may but find it; and throw this
In at his window. Set this up with wax   145
Upon old Brutus' statue. All this done,
Repair to Pompey's Porch where you shall find us.
Is Decius Brutus and Trebonius there?

CINNA
All but Metellus Cimber, and he's gone
To seek you at your house. Well, I will hie,   150
And so bestow these papers as you bade me.

CASSIUS
That done, repair to Pompey's Theatre.   Exit Cinna
Come, Casca, you and I will yet ere day
See Brutus at his house. Three parts of him
Is ours already, and the man entire   155
Upon the next encounter yields him ours.

CASCA
O, he sits high in all the people's hearts,
And that which would appear offence in us
His countenance, like richest alchemy,
Will change to virtue and to worthiness.   160

CASSIUS
Him and his worth, and our great need of him,
You have right well conceited. Let us go,
For it is after midnight, and ere day
We will awake him and be sure of him.   Exeunt

2.1   Enter Brutus in his orchard   120
BRUTUS What, Lucius, ho!—

I cannot by the progress of the stars
Give guess how near to day.—Lucius, I say!—
I would it were my fault to sleep so soundly.—
When, Lucius, when? Awake, I say! What, Lucius! 5
    Enter Lucius
LUCIUS Called you, my lord?
BRUTUS
Get me a taper in my study, Lucius.
When it is lighted, come and call me here.
LUCIUS I will, my lord.   *Exit*
BRUTUS
It must be by his death. And for my part   10
I know no personal cause to spurn at him,
But for the general. He would be crowned.
How that might change his nature, there's the
    question.
It is the bright day that brings forth the adder,
And that craves wary walking. Crown him: that! 15
And then I grant we put a sting in him
That at his will he may do danger with.
Th'abuse of greatness is when it disjoins
Remorse from power. And to speak truth of Caesar,
I have not known when his affections swayed   20
More than his reason. But 'tis a common proof
That lowliness is young ambition's ladder,
Whereto the climber-upward turns his face;
But when he once attains the upmost round,
He then unto the ladder turns his back,   25
Looks in the clouds, scorning the base degrees
By which he did ascend. So Caesar may.
Then lest he may, prevent. And since the quarrel
Will bear no colour for the thing he is,
Fashion it thus: that what he is, augmented,   30
Would run to these and these extremities;
And therefore think him as a serpent's egg,
Which, hatched, would as his kind grow mischievous,
And kill him in the shell.
    Enter Lucius, with a letter
LUCIUS
The taper burneth in your closet, sir.   35
Searching the window for a flint, I found
This paper, thus sealed up, and I am sure
It did not lie there when I went to bed.
    He gives him the letter
BRUTUS
Get you to bed again; it is not day.
Is not tomorrow, boy, the ides of March?   40
LUCIUS I know not, sir.
BRUTUS
Look in the calendar and bring me word.
LUCIUS I will, sir.   *Exit*
BRUTUS
The exhalations whizzing in the air
Give so much light that I may read by them.   45
    He opens the letter and reads
'Brutus, thou sleep'st. Awake, and see thyself.
Shall Rome, et cetera? Speak, strike, redress.'-
'Brutus, thou sleep'st. Awake.'

Such instigations have been often dropped
Where I have took them up.   50
'Shall Rome, et cetera?' Thus must I piece it out:
Shall Rome stand under one man's awe? What,
    Rome?
My ancestors did from the streets of Rome
The Tarquin drive when he was called a king.
'Speak, strike, redress.' Am I entreated   55
To speak and strike? O Rome, I make thee promise,
If the redress will follow, thou receivest
Thy full petition at the hand of Brutus.
    Enter Lucius
LUCIUS
Sir, March is wasted fifteen days.
    Knock within
BRUTUS
'Tis good. Go to the gate; somebody knocks.   60
                 Exit Lucius
Since Cassius first did whet me against Caesar
I have not slept.
Between the acting of a dreadful thing
And the first motion, all the interim is
Like a phantasma or a hideous dream.   65
The genius and the mortal instruments
Are then in counsel, and the state of man,
Like to a little kingdom, suffers then
The nature of an insurrection.
    Enter Lucius
LUCIUS
Sir, 'tis your brother Cassius at the door,   70
Who doth desire to see you.
BRUTUS   Is he alone?
LUCIUS
No, sir, there are more with him.
BRUTUS   Do you know them?
LUCIUS
No, sir; their hats are plucked about their ears,
And half their faces buried in their cloaks,
That by no means I may discover them   75
By any mark of favour.
BRUTUS   Let 'em enter.   *Exit Lucius*
They are the faction. O conspiracy,
Sham'st thou to show thy dang'rous brow by night,
When evils are most free? O then by day
Where wilt thou find a cavern dark enough   80
To mask thy monstrous visage? Seek none, conspiracy.
Hide it in smiles and affability;
For if thou put thy native semblance on,
Not Erebus itself were dim enough
To hide thee from prevention.   85
    Enter the conspirators, muffled: Cassius, Casca,
    Decius, Cinna, Metellus, and Trebonius
CASSIUS
I think we are too bold upon your rest.
Good morrow, Brutus. Do we trouble you?
BRUTUS
I have been up this hour, awake all night.
Know I these men that come along with you?

CASSIUS
Yes, every man of them; and no man here   90
But honours you; and every one doth wish
You had but that opinion of yourself
Which every noble Roman bears of you.
This is Trebonius.
BRUTUS   He is welcome hither.
CASSIUS
This, Decius Brutus.
BRUTUS   He is welcome too.   95
CASSIUS
This, Casca; Cinna, this; and this, Metellus Cimber.
BRUTUS They are all welcome.
What watchful cares do interpose themselves
Betwixt your eyes and night?
CASSIUS   Shall I entreat a word?
Cassius and Brutus ⌈stand aside and⌉ whisper
DECIUS
Here lies the east. Doth not the day break here?   100
CASCA No.
CINNA
O pardon, sir, it doth; and yon grey lines
That fret the clouds are messengers of day.
CASCA
You shall confess that you are both deceived.
He points his sword
Here, as I point my sword, the sun arises,   105
Which is a great way growing on the south,
Weighing the youthful season of the year.
Some two months hence up higher toward the north
He first presents his fire, and the high east
Stands, as the Capitol, directly here.   110
He points his sword
⌈*Brutus and Cassius join the other conspirators*⌉
BRUTUS
Give me your hands all over, one by one.
He shakes their hands
CASSIUS
And let us swear our resolution.
BRUTUS
No, not an oath. If not the face of men,
The sufferance of our souls, the time's abuse—
If these be motives weak, break off betimes,   115
And every man hence to his idle bed.
So let high-sighted tyranny range on
Till each man drop by lottery. But if these,
As I am sure they do, bear fire enough
To kindle cowards and to steel with valour   120
The melting spirits of women, then, countrymen,
What need we any spur but our own cause
To prick us to redress? What other bond
Than secret Romans, that have spoke the word
And will not palter? And what other oath   125
Than honesty to honesty engaged
That this shall be or we will fall for it?
Swear priests and cowards and men cautelous,
Old feeble carrions, and such suffering souls
That welcome wrongs; unto bad causes swear   130

Such creatures as men doubt; but do not stain
The even virtue of our enterprise,
Nor th'insuppressive mettle of our spirits,
To think that or our cause or our performance
Did need an oath, when every drop of blood   135
That every Roman bears, and nobly bears,
Is guilty of a several bastardy
If he do break the smallest particle
Of any promise that hath passed from him.
CASSIUS
But what of Cicero? Shall we sound him?   140
I think he will stand very strong with us.
CASCA
Let us not leave him out.
CINNA   No, by no means.
METELLUS
O, let us have him, for his silver hairs
Will purchase us a good opinion,
And buy men's voices to commend our deeds.   145
It shall be said his judgement ruled our hands.
Our youths and wildness shall no whit appear,
But all be buried in his gravity.
BRUTUS
O, name him not! Let us not break with him,
For he will never follow anything   150
That other men begin.
CASSIUS Then leave him out.
CASCA Indeed he is not fit.
DECIUS
Shall no man else be touched, but only Caesar?
CASSIUS
Decius, well urged. I think it is not meet   155
Mark Antony, so well beloved of Caesar,
Should outlive Caesar. We shall find of him
A shrewd contriver. And you know his means,
If he improve them, may well stretch so far
As to annoy us all; which to prevent,   160
Let Antony and Caesar fall together.
BRUTUS
Our course will seem too bloody, Caius Cassius,
To cut the head off and then hack the limbs,
Like wrath in death and envy afterwards—
For Antony is but a limb of Caesar.   165
Let's be sacrificers, but not butchers, Caius.
We all stand up against the spirit of Caesar,
And in the spirit of men there is no blood.
O, that we then could come by Caesar's spirit,
And not dismember Caesar! But, alas,   170
Caesar must bleed for it. And, gentle friends,
Let's kill him boldly, but not wrathfully.
Let's carve him as a dish fit for the gods,
Not hew him as a carcass fit for hounds.
And let our hearts, as subtle masters do,   175
Stir up their servants to an act of rage,
And after seem to chide 'em. This shall make
Our purpose necessary, and not envious;
Which so appearing to the common eyes,
We shall be called purgers, not murderers.   180

And for Mark Antony, think not of him,
For he can do no more than Caesar's arm
When Caesar's head is off.
CASSIUS   Yet I fear him;
For in the engrafted love he bears to Caesar—
BRUTUS
Alas, good Cassius, do not think of him.   185
If he love Caesar, all that he can do
Is to himself: take thought, and die for Caesar.
And that were much he should, for he is given
To sports, to wildness, and much company.
TREBONIUS
There is no fear in him. Let him not die;   190
For he will live, and laugh at this hereafter.
    Clock strikes
BRUTUS
Peace, count the clock.
CASSIUS   The clock hath stricken three.
TREBONIUS
'Tis time to part.
CASSIUS   But it is doubtful yet
Whether Caesar will come forth today or no;
For he is superstitious grown of late,   195
Quite from the main opinion he held once
Of fantasy, of dreams and ceremonies.
It may be these apparent prodigies,
The unaccustomed terror of this night,
And the persuasion of his augurers,   200
May hold him from the Capitol today.
DECIUS
Never fear that. If he be so resolved
I can o'ersway him; for he loves to hear
That unicorns may be betrayed with trees,
And bears with glasses, elephants with holes,   205
Lions with toils, and men with flatterers;
But when I tell him he hates flatterers;
He says he does, being then most flattered. Let me
    work,
For I can give his humour the true bent,
And I will bring him to the Capitol.   210
CASSIUS
Nay, we will all of us be there to fetch him.
BRUTUS
By the eighth hour. Is that the uttermost?
CINNA
Be that the uttermost, and fail not then.
METELLUS
Caius Ligarius doth bear Caesar hard,
Who rated him for speaking well of Pompey.   215
I wonder none of you have thought of him.
BRUTUS
Now good Metellus, go along by him.
He loves me well, and I have given him reasons.
Send him but hither, and I'll fashion him.
CASSIUS
The morning comes upon's. We'll leave you, Brutus.
And, friends, disperse yourselves; but all remember 221
What you have said, and show yourselves true Romans.

BRUTUS
Good gentlemen, look fresh and merrily.
Let not our looks put on our purposes;
But bear it as our Roman actors do,   225
With untired spirits and formal constancy.
And so good morrow to you every one.
                        Exeunt all but Brutus
Boy, Lucius!—Fast asleep? It is no matter.
Enjoy the honey-heavy dew of slumber.
Thou hast no figures nor no fantasies   230
Which busy care draws in the brains of men;
Therefore thou sleep'st so sound.
    Enter Portia
PORTIA   Brutus, my lord.
BRUTUS
Portia, what mean you? Wherefore rise you now?
It is not for your health thus to commit
Your weak condition to the raw cold morning.   235
PORTIA
Nor for yours neither. You've ungently, Brutus,
Stole from my bed; and yesternight at supper
You suddenly arose, and walked about
Musing and sighing, with your arms across;
And when I asked you what the matter was,   240
You stared upon me with ungentle looks.
I urged you further; then you scratched your head,
And too impatiently stamped with your foot.
Yet I insisted; yet you answered not,
But with an angry wafture of your hand   245
Gave sign for me to leave you. So I did,
Fearing to strengthen that impatience
Which seemed too much enkindled, and withal
Hoping it was but an effect of humour,
Which sometime hath his hour with every man.   250
It will not let you eat, nor talk, nor sleep;
And could it work so much upon your shape
As it hath much prevailed on your condition,
I should not know you Brutus. Dear my lord,
Make me acquainted with your cause of grief.   255
BRUTUS
I am not well in health, and that is all.
PORTIA
Brutus is wise, and were he not in health
He would embrace the means to come by it.
BRUTUS
Why, so I do. Good Portia, go to bed.
PORTIA
Is Brutus sick? And is it physical   260
To walk unbracèd and suck up the humours
Of the dank morning? What, is Brutus sick?
And will he steal out of his wholesome bed
To dare the vile contagion of the night,
And tempt the rheumy and unpurgèd air   265
To add unto his sickness? No, my Brutus,
You have some sick offence within your mind,
Which by the right and virtue of my place
I ought to know of. (*Kneeling*) And upon my knees,

I charm you by my once-commended beauty,   270
By all your vows of love, and that great vow
Which did incorporate and make us one,
That you unfold to me, your self, your half,
Why you are heavy, and what men tonight
Have had resort to you—for here have been   275
Some six or seven, who did hide their faces
Even from darkness.
BRUTUS   Kneel not, gentle Portia.
PORTIA ⌐rising⌐
I should not need if you were gentle Brutus.
Within the bond of marriage, tell me, Brutus,
Is it excepted I should know no secrets   280
That appertain to you? Am I your self
But as it were in sort or limitation?
To keep with you at meals, comfort your bed,
And talk to you sometimes? Dwell I but in the
      suburbs
Of your good pleasure? If it be no more,   285
Portia is Brutus' harlot, not his wife.
BRUTUS
You are my true and honourable wife,
As dear to me as are the ruddy drops
That visit my sad heart.
PORTIA
If this were true, then should I know this secret.   290
I grant I am a woman, but withal
A woman that Lord Brutus took to wife.
I grant I am a woman, but withal
A woman well reputed, Cato's daughter.
Think you I am no stronger than my sex,   295
Being so fathered and so husbanded?
Tell me your counsels; I will not disclose 'em.
I have made strong proof of my constancy,
Giving myself a voluntary wound
Here in the thigh. Can I bear that with patience,   300
And not my husband's secrets?
BRUTUS   O ye gods,
Render me worthy of this noble wife!
      Knocking within
Hark, hark, one knocks. Portia, go in a while,
And by and by thy bosom shall partake
The secrets of my heart.   305
All my engagements I will construe to thee,
All the charactery of my sad brows.
Leave me with haste.   *Exit Portia*
                  Lucius, who's that knocks?
*Enter Lucius, and Ligarius, with a kerchief ⌐round
his head⌐*
LUCIUS
Here is a sick man that would speak with you.
BRUTUS
Caius Ligarius, that Metellus spake of.—   310
Boy, stand aside.   ⌐*Exit*⌐ *Lucius*
                  Caius Ligarius, how?
LIGARIUS
Vouchsafe good morrow from a feeble tongue.

BRUTUS
O, what a time have you chose out, brave Caius,
To wear a kerchief! Would you were not sick!
LIGARIUS
I am not sick if Brutus have in hand   315
Any exploit worthy the name of honour.
BRUTUS
Such an exploit have I in hand, Ligarius,
Had you a healthful ear to hear of it.
LIGARIUS
By all the gods that Romans bow before,
I here discard my sickness.
      He pulls off his kerchief
                              Soul of Rome,   320
Brave son derived from honourable loins,
Thou like an exorcist hast conjured up
My mortifièd spirit. Now bid me run,
And I will strive with things impossible,
Yea, get the better of them. What's to do?   325
BRUTUS
A piece of work that will make sick men whole.
LIGARIUS
But are not some whole that we must make sick?
BRUTUS
That must we also. What it is, my Caius,
I shall unfold to thee as we are going
To whom it must be done.
LIGARIUS   Set on your foot,   330
And with a heart new-fired I follow you
To do I know not what; but it sufficeth
That Brutus leads me on.
BRUTUS   Follow me then.   *Exeunt*

2.2   *Thunder and lightning.*
         Enter Julius Caesar in his nightgown
CAESAR
Nor heaven nor earth have been at peace tonight.
Thrice hath Calpurnia in her sleep cried out
'Help, ho! They murder Caesar!'—Who's within?
      Enter a Servant
SERVANT My lord.
CAESAR
Go bid the priests do present sacrifice,   5
And bring me their opinions of success.
SERVANT I will, my lord.   *Exit*
      Enter Calpurnia
CALPURNIA
What mean you, Caesar? Think you to walk forth?
You shall not stir out of your house today.
CAESAR
Caesar shall forth. The things that threatened me   10
Ne'er looked but on my back; when they shall see
The face of Caesar, they are vanishèd.
CALPURNIA
Caesar, I never stood on ceremonies,
Yet now they fright me. There is one within,
Besides the things that we have heard and seen,   15

Recounts most horrid sights seen by the watch.
A lioness hath whelpèd in the streets,
And graves have yawned and yielded up their dead.
Fierce fiery warriors fight upon the clouds,
In ranks and squadrons and right form of war,   20
Which drizzled blood upon the Capitol.
The noise of battle hurtled in the air.
Horses do neigh, and dying men did groan,
And ghosts did shriek and squeal about the streets.
O Caesar, these things are beyond all use,   25
And I do fear them.

CAESAR   What can be avoided
Whose end is purposed by the mighty gods?
Yet Caesar shall go forth, for these predictions
Are to the world in general as to Caesar.

CALPURNIA
When beggars die there are no comets seen;   30
The heavens themselves blaze forth the death of
    princes.

CAESAR
Cowards die many times before their deaths;
The valiant never taste of death but once.
Of all the wonders that I yet have heard,
It seems to me most strange that men should fear,   35
Seeing that death, a necessary end,
Will come when it will come.

    Enter Servant
                                What say the augurers?

SERVANT
They would not have you to stir forth today.
Plucking the entrails of an offering forth,
They could not find a heart within the beast.   40

CAESAR
The gods do this in shame of cowardice.
Caesar should be a beast without a heart
If he should stay at home today for fear.
No, Caesar shall not. Danger knows full well
That Caesar is more dangerous than he.   45
We are two lions littered in one day,
And I the elder and more terrible.
And Caesar shall go forth.

CALPURNIA   Alas, my lord,
Your wisdom is consumed in confidence.
Do not go forth today. Call it my fear   50
That keeps you in the house, and not your own.
We'll send Mark Antony to the Senate House,
And he shall say you are not well today.
Let me upon my knee prevail in this.

    She kneels

CAESAR
Mark Antony shall say I am not well,   55
And for thy humour I will stay at home.

    Enter Decius
Here's Decius Brutus; he shall tell them so.
    ⌈*Calpurnia rises*⌉

DECIUS
Caesar, all hail! Good morrow, worthy Caesar.
I come to fetch you to the Senate House.

CAESAR
And you are come in very happy time   60
To bear my greeting to the senators
And tell them that I will not come today.
Cannot is false, and that I dare not, falser.
I will not come today; tell them so, Decius.

CALPURNIA
Say he is sick.

CAESAR   Shall Caesar send a lie?   65
Have I in conquest stretched mine arm so far,
To be afeard to tell greybeards the truth?
Decius, go tell them Caesar will not come.

DECIUS
Most mighty Caesar, let me know some cause,
Lest I be laughed at when I tell them so.   70

CAESAR
The cause is in my will; I will not come.
That is enough to satisfy the Senate.
But for your private satisfaction,
Because I love you, I will let you know.
Calpurnia here, my wife, stays me at home.   75
She dreamt tonight she saw my statue,
Which like a fountain with an hundred spouts
Did run pure blood; and many lusty Romans
Came smiling and did bathe their hands in it.
And these does she apply for warnings and portents 80
Of evils imminent, and on her knee
Hath begged that I will stay at home today.

DECIUS
This dream is all amiss interpreted.
It was a vision fair and fortunate.
Your statue spouting blood in many pipes,   85
In which so many smiling Romans bathed,
Signifies that from you great Rome shall suck
Reviving blood, and that great men shall press
For tinctures, stains, relics, and cognizance.
This by Calpurnia's dream is signified.   90

CAESAR
And this way have you well expounded it.

DECIUS
I have, when you have heard what I can say.
And know it now: the Senate have concluded
To give this day a crown to mighty Caesar.
If you shall send them word you will not come,   95
Their minds may change. Besides, it were a mock
Apt to be rendered for someone to say
'Break up the Senate till another time,
When Caesar's wife shall meet with better dreams.'
If Caesar hide himself, shall they not whisper   100
'Lo, Caesar is afraid'?
Pardon me, Caesar; for my dear dear love
To your proceeding bids me tell you this,
And reason to my love is liable.

CAESAR
How foolish do your fears seem now, Calpurnia!   105
I am ashamèd I did yield to them.
Give me my robe, for I will go.

Enter ⌈Cassius,⌉ Brutus, Ligarius, Metellus, Casca,
  Trebonius, and Cinna
And look where Cassius is come to fetch me.
⌈CASSIUS⌉
  Good morrow, Caesar.
CAESAR   Welcome, Cassius.—
  What, Brutus, are you stirred so early too?—   110
  Good morrow, Casca.—Caius Ligarius,
  Caesar was ne'er so much your enemy
  As that same ague which hath made you lean.
  What is't o'clock?
BRUTUS   Caesar, 'tis strucken eight.
CAESAR
  I thank you for your pains and courtesy.   115
      Enter Antony
  See, Antony that revels long a-nights
  Is notwithstanding up. Good morrow, Antony.
ANTONY
  So to most noble Caesar.
CAESAR ⌈*to Calpurnia*⌉   Bid them prepare within.
  I am to blame to be thus waited for.   ⌈*Exit Calpurnia*⌉
  Now, Cinna.—Now, Metellus.—What, Trebonius!   120
  I have an hour's talk in store for you.
  Remember that you call on me today.
  Be near me, that I may remember you.
TREBONIUS
  Caesar, I will, ⌈*aside*⌉ and so near will I be
  That your best friends shall wish I had been further.
CAESAR
  Good friends, go in and taste some wine with me,   126
  And we, like friends, will straightway go together.
BRUTUS (*aside*)
  That every like is not the same, O Caesar,
  The heart of Brutus ernes to think upon.   *Exeunt*

2.3   *Enter Artemidorus, reading a letter*
ARTEMIDORUS 'Caesar, beware of Brutus. Take heed of
  Cassius. Come not near Casca. Have an eye to Cinna.
  Trust not Trebonius. Mark well Metellus Cimber. Decius
  Brutus loves thee not. Thou hast wronged Caius
  Ligarius. There is but one mind in all these men, and
  it is bent against Caesar. If thou beest not immortal,
  look about you. Security gives way to conspiracy.
  The mighty gods defend thee!
                                  Thy lover,
                                  Artemidorus.'
  Here will I stand till Caesar pass along,   11
  And as a suitor will I give him this.
  My heart laments that virtue cannot live
  Out of the teeth of emulation.
  If thou read this, O Caesar, thou mayst live.   15
  If not, the fates with traitors do contrive.   *Exit*

2.4   *Enter Portia and Lucius*
PORTIA
  I prithee, boy, run to the Senate House.
  Stay not to answer me, but get thee gone.—
  Why dost thou stay?
LUCIUS   To know my errand, madam.

PORTIA
  I would have had thee there and here again
  Ere I can tell thee what thou shouldst do there.   5
  (*Aside*) O constancy, be strong upon my side;
  Set a huge mountain 'tween my heart and tongue.
  I have a man's mind, but a woman's might.
  How hard it is for women to keep counsel!
  (*To Lucius*) Art thou here yet?
LUCIUS   Madam, what should I do?
  Run to the Capitol, and nothing else?   11
  And so return to you, and nothing else?
PORTIA
  Yes, bring me word, boy, if thy lord look well,
  For he went sickly forth; and take good note
  What Caesar doth, what suitors press to him.   15
  Hark, boy, what noise is that?
LUCIUS I hear none, madam.
PORTIA Prithee, listen well.
  I heard a bustling rumour, like a fray,
  And the wind brings it from the Capitol.   20
LUCIUS Sooth, madam, I hear nothing.
      Enter the Soothsayer
PORTIA
  Come hither, fellow. Which way hast thou been?
SOOTHSAYER
  At mine own house, good lady.
PORTIA What is't o'clock?
SOOTHSAYER About the ninth hour, lady.   25
PORTIA
  Is Caesar yet gone to the Capitol?
SOOTHSAYER
  Madam, not yet. I go to take my stand
  To see him pass on to the Capitol.
PORTIA
  Thou hast some suit to Caesar, hast thou not?
SOOTHSAYER
  That I have, lady. If it will please Caesar   30
  To be so good to Caesar as to hear me,
  I shall beseech him to befriend himself.
PORTIA
  Why, know'st thou any harms intended towards him?
SOOTHSAYER
  None that I know will be; much that I fear may chance.
  Good morrow to you.
      ⌈*He moves away*⌉
                      Here the street is narrow.   35
  The throng that follows Caesar at the heels,
  Of senators, of praetors, common suitors,
  Will crowd a feeble man almost to death.
  I'll get me to a place more void, and there
  Speak to great Caesar as he comes along.   *Exit*
PORTIA (*aside*)
  I must go in. Ay me! How weak a thing   41
  The heart of woman is! O Brutus,
  The heavens speed thee in thine enterprise!—
  Sure the boy heard me. (*To Lucius*) Brutus hath a suit
  That Caesar will not grant. (*Aside*) O, I grow faint!   45
  (*To Lucius*) Run, Lucius, and commend me to my lord.

Say I am merry. Come to me again,
And bring me word what he doth say to thee.
                              Exeunt ⌈severally⌉

3.1 *Enter ⌈at one door⌉ Artemidorus, the Soothsayer,
and citizens. Flourish. Enter ⌈at another door⌉
Caesar, Brutus, Cassius, Casca, Decius, Metellus,
Trebonius, Cinna, ⌈Ligarius,⌉ Antony, Lepidus,
Publius, Popillius, ⌈and other senators⌉*
CAESAR (*to the Soothsayer*) The ides of March are come.
SOOTHSAYER Ay, Caesar, but not gone.
ARTEMIDORUS Hail, Caesar! Read this schedule.
DECIUS (*to Caesar*)
  Trebonius doth desire you to o'er-read
  At your best leisure this his humble suit.   5
ARTEMIDORUS
  O Caesar, read mine first, for mine's a suit
  That touches Caesar nearer. Read it, great Caesar.
CAESAR
  What touches us ourself shall be last served.
ARTEMIDORUS
  Delay not, Caesar, read it instantly.
CAESAR
  What, is the fellow mad?
PUBLIUS (*to Artemidorus*)   Sirrah, give place.   10
CASSIUS (*to Artemidorus*)
  What, urge you your petitions in the street?
  Come to the Capitol.
      ⌈*They walk about the stage*⌉
POPILLIUS (*aside to Cassius*)
  I wish your enterprise today may thrive.
CASSIUS
  What enterprise, Popillius?
POPILLIUS   Fare you well.
      He leaves Cassius, and makes to Caesar
BRUTUS What said Popillius Laena?   15
CASSIUS
  He wished today our enterprise might thrive.
  I fear our purpose is discoverèd.
BRUTUS
  Look how he makes to Caesar. Mark him.
CASSIUS
  Casca, be sudden, for we fear prevention.—
  Brutus, what shall be done? If this be known,   20
  Cassius or Caesar never shall turn back,
  For I will slay myself.
BRUTUS   Cassius, be constant.
  Popillius Laena speaks not of our purposes,
  For look, he smiles, and Caesar doth not change.
CASSIUS
  Trebonius knows his time, for look you, Brutus,   25
  He draws Mark Antony out of the way.
              Exeunt Trebonius and Antony
DECIUS
  Where is Metellus Cimber? Let him go
  And presently prefer his suit to Caesar.
      ⌈*Caesar sits*⌉
BRUTUS
  He is addressed. Press near, and second him.

CINNA
  Casca, you are the first that rears your hand.   30
      ⌈*The conspirators and the other senators take their
      places*⌉
CAESAR
  Are we all ready? What is now amiss
  That Caesar and his Senate must redress?
METELLUS (*coming forward and kneeling*)
  Most high, most mighty, and most puissant Caesar,
  Metellus Cimber throws before thy seat
  An humble heart.
CAESAR   I must prevent thee, Cimber.   35
  These couchings and these lowly courtesies
  Might fire the blood of ordinary men,
  And turn preordnance and first decree
  Into the law of children. Be not fond
  To think that Caesar bears such rebel blood   40
  That will be thawed from the true quality
  With that which melteth fools: I mean sweet words,
  Low-crookèd curtsies, and base spaniel fawning.
  Thy brother by decree is banishèd.
  If thou dost bend and pray and fawn for him,   45
  I spurn thee like a cur out of my way.
  Know Caesar doth not wrong but with just cause,
  Nor without cause will he be satisfied.
METELLUS
  Is there no voice more worthy than my own
  To sound more sweetly in great Caesar's ear   50
  For the repealing of my banished brother?
BRUTUS (*coming forward and kneeling*)
  I kiss thy hand, but not in flattery, Caesar,
  Desiring thee that Publius Cimber may
  Have an immediate freedom of repeal.
CAESAR
  What, Brutus?
CASSIUS (*coming forward and kneeling*)
          Pardon, Caesar; Caesar, pardon.   55
  As low as to thy foot doth Cassius fall
  To beg enfranchisement for Publius Cimber.
CAESAR
  I could be well moved if I were as you.
  If I could pray to move, prayers would move me.
  But I am constant as the Northern Star,   60
  Of whose true fixed and resting quality
  There is no fellow in the firmament.
  The skies are painted with unnumbered sparks;
  They are all fire, and every one doth shine;
  But there's but one in all doth hold his place.   65
  So in the world: 'tis furnished well with men,
  And men are flesh and blood, and apprehensive;
  Yet in the number I do know but one
  That unassailable holds on his rank,
  Unshaked of motion; and that I am he   70
  Let me a little show it even in this—
  That I was constant Cimber should be banished,
  And constant do remain to keep him so.
CINNA (*coming forward and kneeling*)
  O Caesar!
CAESAR   Hence! Wilt thou lift up Olympus?

DECIUS (*coming forward* ⌈*with Ligarius*⌉ *and kneeling*)
　Great Caesar!
CAESAR　　　*ı*　Doth not Brutus bootless kneel?　　75
CASCA (*coming forward* ⌈*and kneeling*⌉
　Speak hands for me.
　　　They stab Caesar, ⌈*Casca first, Brutus last*⌉
CAESAR　　　　Et tu, Br#té?—Then fall Caesar.
　　　　　　　　　　　　　　　　　　He dies
CINNA
　Liberty! Freedom! Tyranny is dead!
　Run hence, proclaim, cry it about the streets.
CASSIUS
　Some to the common pulpits, and cry out
　'Liberty, freedom, and enfranchisement!'　　80
BRUTUS
　People and senators, be not affrighted.
　　　⌈*Exeunt in a tumult Lepidus, Popillius, other*
　　　　　senators, Artemidorus, Soothsayer, and
　　　　　　　　　　　　　　　　　　citizens⌉

　Fly not! Stand still! Ambition's debt is paid.
CASCA Go to the pulpit, Brutus.
DECIUS And Cassius too.
BRUTUS Where's Publius?　　　　　　　　85
CINNA
　Here, quite confounded with this mutiny.
METELLUS
　Stand fast together, lest some friend of Caesar's
　Should chance—
BRUTUS
　Talk not of standing.—Publius, good cheer!
　There is no harm intended to your person,　　90
　Nor to no Roman else—so tell them, Publius.
CASSIUS
　And leave us, Publius, lest that the people,
　Rushing on us, should do your age some mischief.
BRUTUS
　Do so; and let no man abide this deed
　But we the doers.　　　　　⌈*Exit Publius*⌉
　　　Enter Trebonius
CASSIUS Where is Antony?　　　　　　96
TREBONIUS Fled to his house, amazed.
　Men, wives, and children stare, cry out, and run,
　As it were doomsday.
BRUTUS　　　　　Fates, we will know your pleasures.
　That we shall die, we know; 'tis but the time　100
　And drawing days out that men stand upon.
CASCA
　Why, he that cuts off twenty years of life
　Cuts off so many years of fearing death.
BRUTUS
　Grant that, and then is death a benefit.
　So are we Caesar's friends, that have abridged　105
　His time of fearing death. Stoop, Romans, stoop,
　And let us bathe our hands in Caesar's blood
　Up to the elbows, and besmear our swords;
　Then walk we forth even to the market-place,
　And, waving our red weapons o'er our heads,　110
　Let's all cry 'peace, freedom, and liberty!'

CASSIUS
　Stoop, then, and wash.
　　　They smear their hands with Caesar's blood
　　　　　　　　　How many ages hence
　Shall this our lofty scene be acted over,
　In states unborn and accents yet unknown!
BRUTUS
　How many times shall Caesar bleed in sport,　115
　That now on Pompey's basis lies along,
　No worthier than the dust!
CASSIUS　　　　　　So oft as that shall be,
　So often shall the knot of us be called
　The men that gave their country liberty.
DECIUS
　What, shall we forth?
CASSIUS　　　　Ay, every man away.　　120
　Brutus shall lead, and we will grace his heels
　With the most boldest and best hearts of Rome.
　　　Enter Antony's Servant
BRUTUS
　Soft; who comes here? A friend of Antony's.
SERVANT (*kneeling and falling prostrate*)
　Thus, Brutus, did my master bid me kneel.
　Thus did Mark Antony bid me fall down,　　125
　And, being prostrate, thus he bade me say.
　'Brutus is noble, wise, valiant, and honest.
　Caesar was mighty, bold, royal, and loving.
　Say I love Brutus, and I honour him.
　Say I feared Caesar, honoured him, and loved him. 130
　If Brutus will vouchsafe that Antony
　May safely come to him and be resolved
　How Caesar hath deserved to lie in death,
　Mark Antony shall not love Caesar dead
　So well as Brutus living, but will follow　　135
　The fortunes and affairs of noble Brutus
　Thorough the hazards of this untrod state
　With all true faith.' So says my master Antony.
BRUTUS
　Thy master is a wise and valiant Roman.
　I never thought him worse.　　　　　140
　Tell him, so please him come unto this place,
　He shall be satisfied, and, by my honour,
　Depart untouched.
SERVANT ⌈*rising*⌉　I'll fetch him presently.　*Exit*
BRUTUS
　I know that we shall have him well to friend.
CASSIUS
　I wish we may. But yet have I a mind　　145
　That fears him much; and my misgiving still
　Falls shrewdly to the purpose.
　　　Enter Antony
BRUTUS
　But here comes Antony.—Welcome, Mark Antony.
ANTONY
　O mighty Caesar! Dost thou lie so low?
　Are all thy conquests, glories, triumphs, spoils,　150
　Shrunk to this little measure? Fare thee well.—
　I know not, gentlemen, what you intend—

Who else must be let blood, who else is rank.
If I myself, there is no hour so fit
As Caesar's death's hour, nor no instrument   155
Of half that worth as those your swords, made rich
With the most noble blood of all this world.
I do beseech ye, if you bear me hard,
Now, whilst your purpled hands do reek and smoke,
Fulfil your pleasure. Live a thousand years,   160
I shall not find myself so apt to die.
No place will please me so, no mean of death,
As here by Caesar, and by you cut off,
The choice and master spirits of this age.

BRUTUS
O Antony, beg not your death of us!   165
Though now we must appear bloody and cruel,
As by our hands and this our present act
You see we do, yet see you but our hands,
And this the bleeding business they have done.
Our hearts you see not; they are pitiful;   170
And pity to the general wrong of Rome—
As fire drives out fire, so pity pity—
Hath done this deed on Caesar. For your part,
To you our swords have leaden points, Mark Antony.
Our arms, unstrung of malice, and our hearts   175
Of brothers' temper, do receive you in
With all kind love, good thoughts, and reverence.

CASSIUS
Your voice shall be as strong as any man's
In the disposing of new dignities.

BRUTUS
Only be patient till we have appeased   180
The multitude, beside themselves with fear,
And then we will deliver you the cause
Why I, that did love Caesar when I struck him,
Have thus proceeded.

ANTONY   I doubt not of your wisdom.
Let each man render me his bloody hand.   185
He shakes hands with the conspirators
First, Marcus Brutus, will I shake with you.—
Next, Caius Cassius, do I take your hand.—
Now, Decius Brutus, yours;—now yours, Metellus;—
Yours, Cinna;—and my valiant Casca, yours;—
Though last, not least in love, yours, good Trebonius.
Gentlemen all—alas, what shall I say?   191
My credit now stands on such slippery ground
That one of two bad ways you must conceit me:
Either a coward or a flatterer.
That I did love thee, Caesar, O, 'tis true.   195
If then thy spirit look upon us now,
Shall it not grieve thee dearer than thy death
To see thy Antony making his peace,
Shaking the bloody fingers of thy foes—
Most noble!—in the presence of thy corpse?   200
Had I as many eyes as thou hast wounds,
Weeping as fast as they stream forth thy blood,
It would become me better than to close
In terms of friendship with thine enemies.   204
Pardon me, Julius. Here wast thou bayed, brave hart;

Here didst thou fall, and here thy hunters stand
Signed in thy spoil and crimsoned in thy lethe.
O world, thou wast the forest to this hart;
And this indeed, O world, the heart of thee.
How like a deer strucken by many princes   210
Dost thou here lie!

CASSIUS Mark Antony.

ANTONY Pardon me, Caius Cassius.
The enemies of Caesar shall say this;
Then in a friend it is cold modesty.   215

CASSIUS
I blame you not for praising Caesar so;
But what compact mean you to have with us?
Will you be pricked in number of our friends,
Or shall we on, and not depend on you?

ANTONY
Therefore I took your hands, but was indeed   220
Swayed from the point by looking down on Caesar.
Friends am I with you all, and love you all
Upon this hope: that you shall give me reasons
Why and wherein Caesar was dangerous.

BRUTUS
Or else were this a savage spectacle.   225
Our reasons are so full of good regard,
That were you, Antony, the son of Caesar,
You should be satisfied.

ANTONY   That's all I seek;
And am, moreover, suitor that I may
Produce his body to the market-place,   230
And in the pulpit, as becomes a friend,
Speak in the order of his funeral.

BRUTUS
You shall, Mark Antony.

CASSIUS   Brutus, a word with you.
(Aside to Brutus) You know not what you do. Do not
consent
That Antony speak in his funeral.   235
Know you how much the people may be moved
By that which he will utter?

BRUTUS *(aside to Cassius)*   By your pardon,
I will myself into the pulpit first,
And show the reason of our Caesar's death.
What Antony shall speak I will protest   240
He speaks by leave and by permission;
And that we are contented Caesar shall
Have all true rites and lawful ceremonies,
It shall advantage more than do us wrong.

CASSIUS *(aside to Brutus)*
I know not what may fall. I like it not.   245

BRUTUS
Mark Antony, here, take you Caesar's body.
You shall not in your funeral speech blame us;
But speak all good you can devise of Caesar,
And say you do't by our permission;
Else shall you not have any hand at all   250
About his funeral. And you shall speak
In the same pulpit whereto I am going,
After my speech is ended.

ANTONY Be it so;
I do desire no more.   255
BRUTUS
Prepare the body then, and follow us.
Exeunt all but Antony
ANTONY
O pardon me, thou bleeding piece of earth,
That I am meek and gentle with these butchers.
Thou art the ruins of the noblest man
That ever livèd in the tide of times.   260
Woe to the hand that shed this costly blood!
Over thy wounds now do I prophesy—
Which like dumb mouths do ope their ruby lips
To beg the voice and utterance of my tongue—
A curse shall light upon the limbs of men;   265
Domestic fury and fierce civil strife
Shall cumber all the parts of Italy;
Blood and destruction shall be so in use,
And dreadful objects so familiar,
That mothers shall but smile when they behold   270
Their infants quartered with the hands of war,
All pity choked with custom of fell deeds;
And Caesar's spirit, ranging for revenge,
With Ate by his side come hot from hell,
Shall in these confines with a monarch's voice   275
Cry 'havoc!' and let slip the dogs of war,
That this foul deed shall smell above the earth
With carrion men, groaning for burial.
Enter Octavius' Servant
You serve Octavius Caesar, do you not?
SERVANT I do, Mark Antony.   280
ANTONY
Caesar did write for him to come to Rome.
SERVANT
He did receive his letters, and is coming,
And bid me say to you by word of mouth—
(*Seeing the body*) O Caesar!
ANTONY
Thy heart is big. Get thee apart and weep.   285
Passion, I see, is catching, for mine eyes,
Seeing those beads of sorrow stand in thine,
Began to water. Is thy master coming?
SERVANT
He lies tonight within seven leagues of Rome.
ANTONY
Post back with speed and tell him what hath
    chanced.   290
Here is a mourning Rome, a dangerous Rome,
No Rome of safety for Octavius yet.
Hie hence and tell him so.—Yet stay awhile.
Thou shalt not back till I have borne this corpse
Into the market-place. There shall I try   295
In my oration how the people take
The cruel issue of these bloody men;
According to the which thou shalt discourse
To young Octavius of the state of things.   299
Lend me your hand.   *Exeunt with Caesar's body*

3.2   *Enter Brutus and Cassius, with the Plebeians*
ALL THE PLEBEIANS
We will be satisfied! Let us be satisfied!
BRUTUS
Then follow me, and give me audience, friends.
(*Aside to Cassius*) Cassius, go you into the other street,
And part the numbers.
(*To the Plebeians*)
Those that will hear me speak, let 'em stay here;   5
Those that will follow Cassius, go with him;
And public reasons shall be renderèd
Of Caesar's death.
Brutus ascends to the pulpit
FIRST PLEBEIAN   I will hear Brutus speak.
SECOND PLEBEIAN
I will hear Cassius, and compare their reasons
When severally we hear them renderèd.   10
Exit Cassius, with some Plebeians
⌈*Enter*⌉ *Brutus* ⌈*above*⌉ *in the pulpit*
THIRD PLEBEIAN
The noble Brutus is ascended. Silence.
BRUTUS Be patient till the last.
Romans, countrymen, and lovers, hear me for my
cause, and be silent that you may hear. Believe me for
mine honour, and have respect to mine honour, that
you may believe. Censure me in your wisdom, and
awake your senses, that you may the better judge. If
there be any in this assembly, any dear friend of
Caesar's, to him I say that Brutus' love to Caesar was
no less than his. If then that friend demand why Brutus
rose against Caesar, this is my answer: not that I loved
Caesar less, but that I loved Rome more. Had you
rather Caesar were living, and die all slaves, than that
Caesar were dead, to live all free men? As Caesar loved
me, I weep for him. As he was fortunate, I rejoice at
it. As he was valiant, I honour him. But as he was
ambitious, I slew him. There is tears for his love, joy
for his fortune, honour for his valour, and death for
his ambition. Who is here so base that would be a
bondman? If any, speak, for him have I offended. Who
is here so rude that would not be a Roman? If any,
speak, for him have I offended. Who is here so vile that
will not love his country? If any, speak, for him have
I offended. I pause for a reply.
ALL THE PLEBEIANS None, Brutus, none.   35
BRUTUS Then none have I offended. I have done no more
to Caesar than you shall do to Brutus. The question of
his death is enrolled in the Capitol, his glory not
extenuated wherein he was worthy, nor his offences
enforced for which he suffered death.   40
Enter Mark Antony, with ⌈*others bearing*⌉ *Caesar's*
body ⌈*in a coffin*⌉
Here comes his body, mourned by Mark Antony, who,
though he had no hand in his death, shall receive the
benefit of his dying: a place in the commonwealth—as
which of you shall not? With this I depart: that as I
slew my best lover for the good of Rome, I have the

same dagger for myself when it shall please my country
to need my death.

ALL THE PLEBEIANS Live, Brutus, live, live!

FIRST PLEBEIAN

Bring him with triumph home unto his house.

⌐FOURTH⌐ PLEBEIAN

Give him a statue with his ancestors.   50

THIRD PLEBEIAN

Let him be Caesar.

⌐FIFTH⌐ PLEBEIAN   Caesar's better parts

Shall be crowned in Brutus.

FIRST PLEBEIAN

We'll bring him to his house with shouts and
          clamours.

BRUTUS

My countrymen.

⌐FOURTH⌐ PLEBEIAN Peace, silence. Brutus speaks.

FIRST PLEBEIAN Peace, ho!   55

BRUTUS

Good countrymen, let me depart alone,
And, for my sake, stay here with Antony.
Do grace to Caesar's corpse, and grace his speech
Tending to Caesar's glories, which Mark Antony,
By our permission, is allowed to make.   60
I do entreat you, not a man depart
Save I alone till Antony have spoke.   *Exit*

FIRST PLEBEIAN

Stay, ho, and let us hear Mark Antony.

THIRD PLEBEIAN

Let him go up into the public chair.
We'll hear him. Noble Antony, go up.   65

ANTONY

For Brutus' sake I am beholden to you.

          Antony ascends to the pulpit

⌐FIFTH⌐ PLEBEIAN

What does he say of Brutus?

THIRD PLEBEIAN   He says, for Brutus' sake

He finds himself beholden to us all.

⌐FIFTH⌐ PLEBEIAN

'Twere best he speak no harm of Brutus here!

FIRST PLEBEIAN

This Caesar was a tyrant.

THIRD PLEBEIAN   Nay, that's certain.   70

We are blessed that Rome is rid of him.

          ⌐*Enter*⌐ *Antony in the pulpit*

⌐FOURTH⌐ PLEBEIAN

Peace, let us hear what Antony can say.

ANTONY

You gentle Romans.

ALL THE PLEBEIANS   Peace, ho! Let us hear him.

ANTONY

Friends, Romans, countrymen, lend me your ears.
I come to bury Caesar, not to praise him.   75
The evil that men do lives after them;
The good is oft interrèd with their bones.
So let it be with Caesar. The noble Brutus
Hath told you Caesar was ambitious.

If it were so, it was a grievous fault,   80
And grievously hath Caesar answered it.
Here, under leave of Brutus and the rest—
For Brutus is an honourable man,
So are they all, all honourable men—
Come I to speak in Caesar's funeral.   85
He was my friend, faithful and just to me.
But Brutus says he was ambitious,
And Brutus is an honourable man.
He hath brought many captives home to Rome,
Whose ransoms did the general coffers fill.   90
Did this in Caesar seem ambitious?
When that the poor have cried, Caesar hath wept.
Ambition should be made of sterner stuff.
Yet Brutus says he was ambitious,
And Brutus is an honourable man.   95
You all did see that on the Lupercal
I thrice presented him a kingly crown,
Which he did thrice refuse. Was this ambition?
Yet Brutus says he was ambitious,
And sure he is an honourable man.   100
I speak not to disprove what Brutus spoke,
But here I am to speak what I do know.
You all did love him once, not without cause.
What cause withholds you then to mourn for him?
O judgement, thou art fled to brutish beasts,   105
And men have lost their reason!

          He weeps

                         Bear with me.
My heart is in the coffin there with Caesar,
And I must pause till it come back to me.

FIRST PLEBEIAN

Methinks there is much reason in his sayings.

⌐FOURTH⌐ PLEBEIAN

If thou consider rightly of the matter,   110
Caesar has had great wrong.

THIRD PLEBEIAN   Has he not, masters?

I fear there will a worse come in his place.

⌐FIFTH⌐ PLEBEIAN

Marked ye his words? He would not take the crown,
Therefore 'tis certain he was not ambitious.

FIRST PLEBEIAN

If it be found so, some will dear abide it.   115

⌐FOURTH⌐ PLEBEIAN

Poor soul, his eyes are red as fire with weeping.

THIRD PLEBEIAN

There's not a nobler man in Rome than Antony.

⌐FIFTH⌐ PLEBEIAN

Now mark him; he begins again to speak.

ANTONY

But yesterday the word of Caesar might
Have stood against the world. Now lies he there,   120
And none so poor to do him reverence.
O masters, if I were disposed to stir
Your hearts and minds to mutiny and rage,
I should do Brutus wrong, and Cassius wrong,
Who, you all know, are honourable men.   125
I will not do them wrong. I rather choose

To wrong the dead, to wrong myself and you,
Than I will wrong such honourable men.
But here's a parchment with the seal of Caesar.
I found it in his closet. 'Tis his will.   130
Let but the commons hear this testament—
Which, pardon me, I do not mean to read—
And they would go and kiss dead Caesar's wounds,
And dip their napkins in his sacred blood,
Yea, beg a hair of him for memory,   135
And, dying, mention it within their wills,
Bequeathing it as a rich legacy
Unto their issue.
FIFTH PLEBEIAN
We'll hear the will. Read it, Mark Antony.
ALL THE PLEBEIANS
The will, the will! We will hear Caesar's will.   140
ANTONY
Have patience, gentle friends, I must not read it.
It is not meet you know how Caesar loved you.
You are not wood, you are not stones, but men;
And, being men, hearing the will of Caesar,
It will inflame you, it will make you mad.   145
'Tis good you know not that you are his heirs,
For if you should, O what would come of it?
FIFTH PLEBEIAN
Read the will. We'll hear it, Antony.
You shall read us the will, Caesar's will.
ANTONY
Will you be patient? Will you stay a while?   150
I have o'ershot myself to tell you of it.
I fear I wrong the honourable men
Whose daggers have stabbed Caesar; I do fear it.
FIFTH PLEBEIAN They were traitors. Honourable men?
ALL THE PLEBEIANS The will, the testament!   155
FOURTH PLEBEIAN They were villains, murderers. The
will, read the will!
ANTONY
You will compel me then to read the will?
Then make a ring about the corpse of Caesar,
And let me show you him that made the will.   160
Shall I descend? And will you give me leave?
ALL THE PLEBEIANS
Come down.
FOURTH PLEBEIAN Descend.
THIRD PLEBEIAN   You shall have leave.
Antony descends from the pulpit
FIFTH PLEBEIAN   A ring.
Stand round.
FIRST PLEBEIAN
Stand from the hearse. Stand from the body.
FOURTH PLEBEIAN
Room for Antony, most noble Antony!
Enter Antony below
ANTONY
Nay, press not so upon me. Stand farre off.   165
ALL THE PLEBEIANS Stand back! Room! Bear back!
ANTONY
If you have tears, prepare to shed them now.

You all do know this mantle. I remember
The first time ever Caesar put it on.
'Twas on a summer's evening in his tent,   170
That day he overcame the Nervii.
Look, in this place ran Cassius' dagger through.
See what a rent the envious Casca made.
Through this the well-belovèd Brutus stabbed;
And as he plucked his cursèd steel away,   175
Mark how the blood of Caesar followed it,
As rushing out of doors to be resolved
If Brutus so unkindly knocked or no—
For Brutus, as you know, was Caesar's angel.
Judge, O you gods, how dearly Caesar loved him!   180
This was the most unkindest cut of all.
For when the noble Caesar saw him stab,
Ingratitude, more strong than traitors' arms,
Quite vanquished him. Then burst his mighty heart,
And in his mantle muffling up his face,   185
Even at the base of Pompey's statue,
Which all the while ran blood, great Caesar fell.
O, what a fall was there, my countrymen!
Then I, and you, and all of us fell down,
Whilst bloody treason flourished over us.   190
O now you weep, and I perceive you feel
The dint of pity. These are gracious drops.
Kind souls, what, weep you when you but behold
Our Caesar's vesture wounded? Look you here.
Here is himself, marred, as you see, with traitors.   195
He uncovers Caesar's body
FIRST PLEBEIAN
O piteous spectacle!
FOURTH PLEBEIAN   O noble Caesar!
THIRD PLEBEIAN O woeful day!
FIFTH PLEBEIAN
O traitors, villains!
FIRST PLEBEIAN   O most bloody sight!
FOURTH PLEBEIAN We will be revenged.
ALL THE PLEBEIANS
Revenge! About! Seek! Burn! Fire! Kill! Slay!   200
Let not a traitor live!
ANTONY   Stay, countrymen.
FIRST PLEBEIAN Peace there, hear the noble Antony.
FOURTH PLEBEIAN We'll hear him, we'll follow him, we'll
die with him!
ANTONY
Good friends, sweet friends, let me not stir you up   205
To such a sudden flood of mutiny.
They that have done this deed are honourable.
What private griefs they have, alas, I know not,
That made them do it. They are wise and honourable,
And will no doubt with reasons answer you.   210
I come not, friends, to steal away your hearts.
I am no orator as Brutus is,
But, as you know me all, a plain blunt man
That love my friend; and that they know full well
That gave me public leave to speak of him.   215
For I have neither wit, nor words, nor worth,
Action, nor utterance, nor the power of speech,

To stir men's blood. I only speak right on.
I tell you that which you yourselves do know,
Show you sweet Caesar's wounds, poor poor dumb
    mouths,   220
And bid them speak for me. But were I Brutus,
And Brutus Antony, there were an Antony
Would ruffle up your spirits, and put a tongue
In every wound of Caesar that should move
The stones of Rome to rise and mutiny.   225

ALL THE PLEBEIANS
We'll mutiny.

FIRST PLEBEIAN We'll burn the house of Brutus.

THIRD PLEBEIAN
Away then! Come, seek the conspirators.

ANTONY
Yet hear me, countrymen, yet hear me speak.

ALL THE PLEBEIANS
Peace, ho! Hear Antony, most noble Antony.

ANTONY
Why, friends, you go to do you know not what.   230
Wherein hath Caesar thus deserved your loves?
Alas, you know not. I must tell you then.
You have forgot the will I told you of.

ALL THE PLEBEIANS
Most true. The will. Let's stay and hear the will.

ANTONY
Here is the will, and under Caesar's seal.   235
To every Roman citizen he gives—
To every several man—seventy-five drachmas.

⌈FOURTH⌉ PLEBEIAN
Most noble Caesar! We'll revenge his death.

THIRD PLEBEIAN
O royal Caesar!

ANTONY   Hear me with patience.

ALL THE PLEBEIANS   Peace, ho!

ANTONY
Moreover he hath left you all his walks,   240
His private arbours, and new-planted orchards,
On this side Tiber. He hath left them you,
And to your heirs for ever—common pleasures
To walk abroad and recreate yourselves.
Here was a Caesar. When comes such another?   245

FIRST PLEBEIAN
Never, never! Come, away, away!
We'll burn his body in the holy place,
And with the brands fire the traitors' houses.
Take up the body.

⌈FOURTH⌉ PLEBEIAN Go, fetch fire!   250

THIRD PLEBEIAN Pluck down benches!

⌈FIFTH⌉ PLEBEIAN Pluck down forms, windows, anything!
        Exeunt Plebeians ⌈with Caesar's body⌉

ANTONY
Now let it work. Mischief, thou art afoot.
Take thou what course thou wilt.
    Enter ⌈Octavius'⌉ Servant
                      How now, fellow?

SERVANT
Sir, Octavius is already come to Rome.   255

ANTONY Where is he?

SERVANT
He and Lepidus are at Caesar's house.

ANTONY
And thither will I straight to visit him.
He comes upon a wish. Fortune is merry,
And in this mood will give us anything.   260

SERVANT
I heard him say Brutus and Cassius
Are rid like madmen through the gates of Rome.

ANTONY
Belike they had some notice of the people,
How I had moved them. Bring me to Octavius.
                                Exeunt

3.3   *Enter Cinna the poet*

CINNA
I dreamt tonight that I did feast with Caesar,
And things unlucky charge my fantasy.
I have no will to wander forth of doors,
Yet something leads me forth.
    Enter the Plebeians

FIRST PLEBEIAN What is your name?   5
SECOND PLEBEIAN Whither are you going?
THIRD PLEBEIAN Where do you dwell?
FOURTH PLEBEIAN Are you a married man or a bachelor?
SECOND PLEBEIAN Answer every man directly.
FIRST PLEBEIAN Ay, and briefly.   10
FOURTH PLEBEIAN Ay, and wisely.
THIRD PLEBEIAN Ay, and truly, you were best.
CINNA What is my name? Whither am I going? Where
do I dwell? Am I a married man or a bachelor? Then
to answer every man directly and briefly, wisely and
truly: wisely, I say, I am a bachelor.   16
SECOND PLEBEIAN That's as much as to say they are fools
that marry. You'll bear me a bang for that, I fear.
Proceed directly.
CINNA Directly I am going to Caesar's funeral.   20
FIRST PLEBEIAN As a friend or an enemy?
CINNA As a friend.
SECOND PLEBEIAN That matter is answered directly.
FOURTH PLEBEIAN For your dwelling—briefly.
CINNA Briefly, I dwell by the Capitol.   25
THIRD PLEBEIAN Your name, sir, truly.
CINNA Truly, my name is Cinna.
FIRST PLEBEIAN Tear him to pieces! He's a conspirator.
CINNA I am Cinna the poet, I am Cinna the poet.
FOURTH PLEBEIAN Tear him for his bad verses, tear him
for his bad verses.   31
CINNA I am not Cinna the conspirator.
FOURTH PLEBEIAN It is no matter, his name's Cinna. Pluck
but his name out of his heart, and turn him going.
THIRD PLEBEIAN Tear him, tear him!   35
    ⌈*They set upon Cinna*⌉
Come, brands, ho! Firebrands! To Brutus', to Cassius'!
Burn all! Some to Decius' house, and some to Casca's;
some to Ligarius'. Away, go!
    Exeunt all the Plebeians, with Cinna

4.1　*Enter Antony with papers, Octavius, and Lepidus*

ANTONY
　These many, then, shall die; their names are pricked.

OCTAVIUS (*to Lepidus*)
　Your brother too must die. Consent you, Lepidus?

LEPIDUS
　I do consent.

OCTAVIUS　　　　Prick him down, Antony.

LEPIDUS
　Upon condition Publius shall not live,
　Who is your sister's son, Mark Antony.　　　　5

ANTONY
　He shall not live. Look, with a spot I damn him.
　But Lepidus, go you to Caesar's house;
　Fetch the will hither, and we shall determine
　How to cut off some charge in legacies.

LEPIDUS What, shall I find you here?　　　　10

OCTAVIUS Or here or at the Capitol.　　*Exit Lepidus*

ANTONY
　This is a slight, unmeritable man,
　Meet to be sent on errands. Is it fit,
　The three-fold world divided, he should stand
　One of the three to share it?

OCTAVIUS　　　　So you thought him,　　　　15
　And took his voice who should be pricked to die
　In our black sentence and proscription.

ANTONY
　Octavius, I have seen more days than you,
　And though we lay these honours on this man
　To ease ourselves of divers sland'rous loads,　　　　20
　He shall but bear them as the ass bears gold,
　To groan and sweat under the business,
　Either led or driven as we point the way;
　And having brought our treasure where we will,
　Then take we down his load, and turn him off,　　　　25
　Like to the empty ass, to shake his ears
　And graze in commons.

OCTAVIUS　　　　You may do your will;
　But he's a tried and valiant soldier.

ANTONY
　So is my horse, Octavius, and for that
　I do appoint him store of provender.　　　　30
　It is a creature that I teach to fight,
　To wind, to stop, to run directly on,
　His corporal motion governed by my spirit;
　And in some taste is Lepidus but so.
　He must be taught, and trained, and bid go forth—　　　　35
　A barren-spirited fellow, one that feeds
　On objects, arts, and imitations,
　Which, out of use and staled by other men,
　Begin his fashion. Do not talk of him
　But as a property. And now, Octavius,　　　　40
　Listen great things. Brutus and Cassius
　Are levying powers. We must straight make head.
　Therefore let our alliance be combined,
　Our best friends made, our meinies stretched,
　And let us presently go sit in council,　　　　45

How covert matters may be best disclosed,
And open perils surest answerèd.

OCTAVIUS
　Let us do so, for we are at the stake
　And bayed about with many enemies;
　And some that smile have in their hearts, I fear,　　　　50
　Millions of mischiefs.　　　　*Exeunt*

4.2　*Drum. Enter Brutus, Lucius, and the army.*
　⌈*Lucillius,*⌉ *Titinius, and Pindarus meet them*

BRUTUS Stand, ho!

⌈SOLDIER⌉ Give the word 'ho', and stand.

BRUTUS
　What now, Lucillius: is Cassius near?

LUCILLIUS
　He is at hand, and Pindarus is come
　To do you salutation from his master.　　　　5

BRUTUS
　He greets me well. Your master, Pindarus,
　In his own change or by ill officers,
　Hath given me some worthy cause to wish
　Things done undone. But if he be at hand,
　I shall be satisfied.

PINDARUS　　　　I do not doubt　　　　10
　But that my noble master will appear
　Such as he is, full of regard and honour.

BRUTUS
　He is not doubted.—A word, Lucillius.
　Brutus and Lucillius speak apart
　How he received you let me be resolved.

LUCILLIUS
　With courtesy and with respect enough,　　　　15
　But not with such familiar instances,
　Nor with such free and friendly conference,
　As he hath used of old.

BRUTUS　　　　Thou hast described
　A hot friend cooling. Ever note, Lucillius:
　When love begins to sicken and decay　　　　20
　It useth an enforcèd ceremony.
　There are no tricks in plain and simple faith;
　But hollow men, like horses hot at hand,
　Make gallant show and promise of their mettle;
　Low march within
　But when they should endure the bloody spur,　　　　25
　They fall their crests and, like deceitful jades,
　Sink in the trial. Comes his army on?

LUCILLIUS
　They mean this night in Sardis to be quartered.
　The greater part, the horse in general,
　Are come with Cassius.
　Enter Cassius and his powers

BRUTUS　　　　Hark, he is arrived.　　　　30
　March gently on to meet him.
　The armies march

CASSIUS Stand, ho!

BRUTUS Stand, ho! Speak the word along.

⌈FIRST SOLDIER⌉ Stand!

⌈SECOND SOLDIER⌉ Stand!
⌈THIRD SOLDIER⌉ Stand!
CASSIUS
Most noble brother, you have done me wrong.
BRUTUS
Judge me, you gods: wrong I mine enemies?
And if not so, how should I wrong a brother?
CASSIUS
Brutus, this sober form of yours hides wrongs, 40
And when you do them—
BRUTUS   Cassius, be content.
Speak your griefs softly. I do know you well.
Before the eyes of both our armies here,
Which should perceive nothing but love from us,
Let us not wrangle. Bid them move away, 45
Then in my tent, Cassius, enlarge your griefs,
And I will give you audience.
CASSIUS   Pindarus,
Bid our commanders lead their charges off
A little from this ground.
BRUTUS
Lucillius, do you the like; and let no man 50
Come to our tent till we have done our conference.
Let Lucius and Titinius guard our door.

Exeunt the armies
Brutus and Cassius remain, ⌈with Titinius, and
Lucius guarding the door⌉

CASSIUS
That you have wronged me doth appear in this:
You have condemned and noted Lucius Pella
For taking bribes here of the Sardians, 55
Wherein my letters praying on his side,
Because I knew the man, was slighted off.
BRUTUS
You wronged yourself to write in such a case.
CASSIUS
In such a time as this it is not meet
That every nice offence should bear his comment. 60
BRUTUS
Let me tell you, Cassius, you yourself
Are much condemned to have an itching palm,
To sell and mart your offices for gold
To undeservers.
CASSIUS   I, an itching palm?
You know that you are Brutus that speaks this, 65
Or, by the gods, this speech were else your last.
BRUTUS
The name of Cassius honours this corruption,
And chastisement doth therefore hide his head.
CASSIUS Chastisement?
BRUTUS
Remember March, the ides of March, remember. 70
Did not great Julius bleed for justice' sake?
What villain touched his body, that did stab,
And not for justice? What, shall one of us,
That struck the foremost man of all this world
But for supporting robbers, shall we now 75

Contaminate our fingers with base bribes, 35
And sell the mighty space of our large honours
For so much trash as may be graspèd thus?
I had rather be a dog and bay the moon
Than such a Roman.
CASSIUS   Brutus, bay not me. 80
I'll not endure it. You forget yourself
To hedge me in. I am a soldier, I,
Older in practice, abler than yourself
To make conditions.
BRUTUS Go to, you are not, Cassius. 85
CASSIUS I am.
BRUTUS I say you are not.
CASSIUS
Urge me no more, I shall forget myself.
Have mind upon your health. Tempt me no farther.
BRUTUS Away, slight man. 90
CASSIUS Is't possible?
BRUTUS Hear me, for I will speak.
Must I give way and room to your rash choler?
Shall I be frighted when a madman stares?
CASSIUS
O ye gods, ye gods! Must I endure all this? 95
BRUTUS
All this? Ay, more. Fret till your proud heart break.
Go show your slaves how choleric you are,
And make your bondmen tremble. Must I budge?
Must I observe you? Must I stand and crouch
Under your testy humour? By the gods, 100
You shall digest the venom of your spleen,
Though it do split you. For from this day forth
I'll use you for my mirth, yea for my laughter,
When you are waspish.
CASSIUS   Is it come to this?
BRUTUS
You say you are a better soldier. 105
Let it appear so, make your vaunting true,
And it shall please me well. For mine own part,
I shall be glad to learn of noble men.
CASSIUS
You wrong me every way, you wrong me, Brutus.
I said an elder soldier, not a better. 110
Did I say better?
BRUTUS   If you did, I care not.
CASSIUS
When Caesar lived he durst not thus have moved me.
BRUTUS
Peace, peace; you durst not so have tempted him.
CASSIUS I durst not?
BRUTUS No. 115
CASSIUS What, durst not tempt him?
BRUTUS For your life you durst not.
CASSIUS
Do not presume too much upon my love.
I may do that I shall be sorry for.
BRUTUS
You have done that you should be sorry for. 120

There is no terror, Cassius, in your threats,
For I am armed so strong in honesty
That they pass by me as the idle wind,
Which I respect not. I did send to you
For certain sums of gold, which you denied me;   125
For I can raise no money by vile means.
By heaven, I had rather coin my heart
And drop my blood for drachmas·than to wring
From the hard hands of peasants their vile trash
By any indirection. I did send   130
To you for gold to pay my legions,
Which you denied me. Was that done like Cassius?
Should I have answered Caius Cassius so?
When Marcus Brutus grows so covetous
To lock such rascal counters from his friends,   135
Be ready, gods, with all your thunderbolts;
Dash him to pieces.

CASSIUS   I denied you not.

BRUTUS
You did.

CASSIUS   I did not. He was but a fool
That brought my answer back. Brutus hath rived my
    heart.
A friend should bear his friend's infirmities,   140
But Brutus makes mine greater than they are.

BRUTUS
I do not, till you practise them on me.

CASSIUS
You love me not.

BRUTUS   I do not like your faults.

CASSIUS
A friendly eye could never see such faults.

BRUTUS
A flatterer's would not, though they do appear   145
As huge as high Olympus.

CASSIUS
Come, Antony and young Octavius, come,
Revenge yourselves alone on Cassius;
For Cassius is aweary of the world,
Hated by one he loves, braved by his brother,   150
Checked like a bondman; all his faults observed,
Set in a notebook, learned and conned by rote,
To cast into my teeth. O, I could weep
My spirit from mine eyes! There is my dagger,
And here my naked breast; within, a heart   155
Dearer than Pluto's mine, richer than gold.
If that thou beest a Roman, take it forth.
I that denied thee gold will give my heart.
Strike as thou didst at Caesar; for I know
When thou didst hate him worst, thou loved'st him
    better   160
Than ever thou loved'st Cassius.

BRUTUS   Sheathe your dagger.
Be angry when you will; it shall have scope.
Do what you will; dishonour shall be humour.
O Cassius, you are yokèd with a lamb
That carries anger as the flint bears fire,   165

Who, much enforcèd, shows a hasty spark
And straight is cold again.

CASSIUS   Hath Cassius lived
To be but mirth and laughter to his Brutus
When grief and blood ill-tempered vexeth him?

BRUTUS
When I spoke that, I was ill-tempered too.   170

CASSIUS
Do you confess so much? Give me your hand.

BRUTUS
And my heart too.
        ⌜They embrace⌝

CASSIUS   O Brutus!

BRUTUS   What's the matter?

CASSIUS
Have not you love enough to bear with me
When that rash humour which my mother gave me
Makes me forgetful?

BRUTUS   Yes, Cassius, and from henceforth,
When you are over-earnest with your Brutus,   176
He'll think your mother chides, and leave you so.
        Enter ⌜Lucillius and⌝ a Poet

POET
Let me go in to see the generals.
There is some grudge between 'em; 'tis not meet
They be alone.

LUCILLIUS   You shall not come to them.   180

POET
Nothing but death shall stay me.

CASSIUS   How now! What's the matter?

POET
For shame, you generals, what do you mean?
Love and be friends, as two such men should be,
For I have seen more years, I'm sure, than ye.

CASSIUS
Ha, ha! How vilely doth this cynic rhyme!   185

BRUTUS (to the Poet)
Get you hence, sirrah; saucy fellow, hence!

CASSIUS
Bear with him, Brutus, 'tis his fashion.

BRUTUS
I'll know his humour when he knows his time.
What should the wars do with these jigging fools?
(To the Poet) Companion, hence!

CASSIUS (to the Poet)   Away, away, be gone!
        Exit Poet

BRUTUS
Lucillius and Titinius, bid the commanders   191
Prepare to lodge their companies tonight.

CASSIUS
And come yourselves, and bring Messala with you
Immediately to us.   Exeunt Lucillius and Titinius

BRUTUS   Lucius, a bowl of wine.
        Exit Lucius

CASSIUS
I did not think you could have been so angry.   195

BRUTUS
O Cassius, I am sick of many griefs.

CASSIUS
Of your philosophy you make no use,
If you give place to accidental evils.
BRUTUS
No man bears sorrow better. Portia is dead.
CASSIUS Ha! Portia?   200
BRUTUS She is dead.
CASSIUS
How scaped I killing when I crossed you so?
O insupportable and touching loss!
Upon what sickness?
BRUTUS   Impatience of my absence,
And grief that young Octavius with Mark Antony   205
Have made themselves so strong—for with her death
That tidings came. With this, she fell distraught,
And, her attendants absent, swallowed fire.
CASSIUS
And died so?
BRUTUS   Even so.
CASSIUS   O ye immortal gods!
Enter Lucius, with wine and tapers
BRUTUS
Speak no more of her. (*To Lucius*) Give me a bowl of
wine.   210
(*To Cassius*) In this I bury all unkindness, Cassius.
He drinks
CASSIUS
My heart is thirsty for that noble pledge.
Fill, Lucius, till the wine o'erswell the cup.
I cannot drink too much of Brutus' love.
He drinks.   ⌈*Exit Lucius*⌉
Enter Titinius and Messala
BRUTUS
Come in, Titinius; welcome, good Messala.   215
Now sit we close about this taper here,
And call in question our necessities.
CASSIUS (*aside*)
Portia, art thou gone?
BRUTUS   No more, I pray you.
⌈*They sit*⌉
Messala, I have here receivèd letters
That young Octavius and Mark Antony   220
Come down upon us with a mighty power,
Bending their expedition toward Philippi.
MESSALA
Myself have letters of the selfsame tenor.
BRUTUS With what addition?
MESSALA
That by proscription and bills of outlawry   225
Octavius, Antony, and Lepidus
Have put to death an hundred senators.
BRUTUS
Therein our letters do not well agree.
Mine speak of seventy senators that died
By their proscriptions, Cicero being one.   230
CASSIUS
Cicero one?
MESSALA   Ay, Cicero is dead,

And by that order of proscription.
(*To Brutus*)
Had you your letters from your wife, my lord?
BRUTUS No, Messala.
MESSALA
Nor nothing in your letters writ of her?   235
BRUTUS
Nothing, Messala.
MESSALA   That methinks is strange.
BRUTUS
Why ask you? Hear you aught of her in yours?
MESSALA No, my lord.
BRUTUS
Now as you are a Roman, tell me true.
MESSALA
Then like a Roman bear the truth I tell;   240
For certain she is dead, and by strange manner.
BRUTUS
Why, farewell, Portia. We must die, Messala.
With meditating that she must die once,
I have the patience to endure it now.
MESSALA
Even so great men great losses should endure.   245
CASSIUS
I have as much of this in art as you,
But yet my nature could not bear it so.
BRUTUS
Well, to our work alive. What do you think
Of marching to Philippi presently?
CASSIUS
I do not think it good.
BRUTUS   Your reason?
CASSIUS   This it is: 250
'Tis better that the enemy seek us;
So shall he waste his means, weary his soldiers,
Doing himself offence; whilst we, lying still,
Are full of rest, defence, and nimbleness.
BRUTUS
Good reasons must of force give place to better.   255
The people 'twixt Philippi and this ground
Do stand but in a forced affection,
For they have grudged us contribution.
The enemy marching along by them
By them shall make a fuller number up,   260
Come on refreshed, new added, and encouraged;
From which advantage shall we cut him off,
If at Philippi we do face him there,
These people at our back.
CASSIUS   Hear me, good brother.
BRUTUS
Under your pardon. You must note beside   265
That we have tried the utmost of our friends;
Our legions are brim-full, our cause is ripe.
The enemy increaseth every day;
We at the height are ready to decline.
There is a tide in the affairs of men   270
Which, taken at the flood, leads on to fortune;
Omitted, all the voyage of their life

Is bound in shallows and in miseries.
On such a full sea are we now afloat,
And we must take the current when it serves,   275
Or lose our ventures.

CASSIUS   Then, with your will, go on.
We'll along ourselves, and meet them at Philippi.

BRUTUS
The deep of night is crept upon our talk,
And nature must obey necessity,
Which we will niggard with a little rest.   280
There is no more to say.

CASSIUS   No more. Good night.
Early tomorrow will we rise and hence.

BRUTUS
Lucius.
    Enter Lucius
            My gown.   *Exit Lucius*
                    Farewell, good Messala.
Good night, Titinius. Noble, noble, Cassius,
Good night and good repose.

CASSIUS   O my dear brother,   285
This was an ill beginning of the night!
Never come such division 'tween our souls.
Let it not, Brutus.
    Enter Lucius with the gown
BRUTUS   Everything is well.
CASSIUS
Good night, my lord.

BRUTUS   Good night, good brother.

TITINIUS *and* MESSALA
Good night, Lord Brutus.

BRUTUS   Farewell, every one.   290
        Exeunt Cassius, Titinius, and Messala
Give me the gown.
    ⌜*He puts on the gown*⌝
                    Where is thy instrument?

LUCIUS
Here in the tent.

BRUTUS   What, thou speak'st drowsily.
Poor knave, I blame thee not; thou art o'erwatched.
Call Claudio and some other of my men.
I'll have them sleep on cushions in my tent.   295

LUCIUS
Varrus and Claudio!
    Enter Varrus and Claudio
VARRUS   Calls my lord?

BRUTUS
I pray you, sirs, lie in my tent and sleep.
It may be I shall raise you by and by
On business to my brother Cassius.

VARRUS
So please you, we will stand and watch your pleasure.

BRUTUS
I will not have it so. Lie down, good sirs.   301
It may be I shall otherwise bethink me.
    Varrus and Claudio lie down to sleep
Look, Lucius, here's the book I sought for so.
I put it in the pocket of my gown.

LUCIUS
I was sure your lordship did not give it me.   305
BRUTUS
Bear with me, good boy, I am much forgetful.
Canst thou hold up thy heavy eyes a while,
And touch thy instrument a strain or two?

LUCIUS
Ay, my lord, an't please you.

BRUTUS   It does, my boy.
I trouble thee too much, but thou art willing.   310

LUCIUS It is my duty, sir.

BRUTUS
I should not urge thy duty past thy might.
I know young bloods look for a time of rest.

LUCIUS I have slept, my lord, already.

BRUTUS
It was well done, and thou shalt sleep again.   315
I will not hold thee long. If I do live,
I will be good to thee.
    Lucius plays music and sings a song, and so falls
    asleep
This is a sleepy tune. O murd'rous slumber,
Lay'st thou thy leaden mace upon my boy
That plays thee music?—Gentle knave, good night.   320
I will not do thee so much wrong to wake thee.
If thou dost nod thou break'st thy instrument;
I'll take it from thee, and, good boy, good night.
    He takes away Lucius' instrument, then opens
    the book
Let me see, let me see, is not the leaf turned down
Where I left reading? Here it is, I think.   325
    Enter the Ghost of Caesar
How ill this taper burns! Ha! Who comes here?
I think it is the weakness of mine eyes
That shapes this monstrous apparition.
It comes upon me. Art thou any thing?
Art thou some god, some angel, or some devil,   330
That mak'st my blood cold and my hair to stare?
Speak to me what thou art.

GHOST Thy evil spirit, Brutus.

BRUTUS Why com'st thou?

GHOST
To tell thee thou shalt see me at Philippi.   335

BRUTUS
Well; then I shall see thee again?

GHOST   Ay, at Philippi.

BRUTUS
Why, I will see thee at Philippi then.   *Exit Ghost*
Now I have taken heart, thou vanishest.
Ill spirit, I would hold more talk with thee.—
Boy, Lucius, Varrus, Claudio, sirs, awake!   340
Claudio!

LUCIUS   The strings, my lord, are false.

BRUTUS
He thinks he still is at his instrument.—
Lucius, awake!

LUCIUS My lord.

BRUTUS
Didst thou dream, Lucius, that thou so cried'st out? 345
LUCIUS
My lord, I do not know that I did cry.
BRUTUS
Yes, that thou didst. Didst thou see anything?
LUCIUS Nothing, my lord.
BRUTUS
Sleep again, Lucius.—Sirrah Claudio!
(*To Varrus*)   Fellow,
Thou, awake!   350
VARRUS My lord.
CLAUDIO My lord.
BRUTUS
Why did you so cry out, sirs, in your sleep?
BOTH
Did we, my lord?
BRUTUS   Ay. Saw you anything?
VARRUS
No, my lord, I saw nothing.
CLAUDIO   Nor I, my lord.   355
BRUTUS
Go and commend me to my brother Cassius.
Bid him set on his powers betimes before,
And we will follow.
BOTH   It shall be done, my lord.
*Exeunt ⸢Varrus and Claudio at one door, Brutus
and Lucius at another door⸣*

5.1   *Enter Octavius, Antony, and their army*
OCTAVIUS
Now, Antony, our hopes are answerèd.
You said the enemy would not come down,
But keep the hills and upper regions.
It proves not so; their battles are at hand.
They mean to warn us at Philippi here,   5
Answering before we do demand of them.
ANTONY
Tut, I am in their bosoms, and I know
Wherefore they do it. They could be content
To visit other places; and come down
With fearful bravery, thinking by this face   10
To fasten in our thoughts that they have courage;
But 'tis not so.
Enter a Messenger
MESSENGER   Prepare you, generals.
The enemy comes on in gallant show.
Their bloody sign of battle is hung out,
And something to be done immediately.   15
ANTONY
Octavius, lead your battle softly on
Upon the left hand of the even field.
OCTAVIUS
Upon the right hand, I; keep thou the left.
ANTONY
Why do you cross me in this exigent?
OCTAVIUS
I do not cross you, but I will do so.   20

*⸢Drum. Antony and Octavius march with their
army.⸣
Drum within. Enter, marching, Brutus, Cassius,
and their army, amongst them Titinius, Lucillius,
and Messala.
Octavius' and Antony's army makes a stand*
BRUTUS They stand, and would have parley.
CASSIUS
Stand fast, Titinius. We must out and talk.
Brutus' and Cassius' army makes a stand
OCTAVIUS
Mark Antony, shall we give sign of battle?
ANTONY
No, Caesar, we will answer on their charge.
Make forth, the generals would have some words. 25
OCTAVIUS (*to his army*)
Stir not until the signal.
Antony and Octavius meet Brutus and Cassius
BRUTUS
Words before blows: is it so, countrymen?
OCTAVIUS
Not that we love words better, as you do.
BRUTUS
Good words are better than bad strokes, Octavius.
ANTONY
In your bad strokes, Brutus, you give good words. 30
Witness the hole you made in Caesar's heart,
Crying 'Long live, hail Caesar'.
CASSIUS   Antony,
The posture of your blows are yet unknown;
But for your words, they rob the Hybla bees,
And leave them honeyless.   35
ANTONY Not stingless too.
BRUTUS O yes, and soundless too,
For you have stolen their buzzing, Antony,
And very wisely threat before you sting.
ANTONY
Villains, you did not so when your vile daggers 40
Hacked one another in the sides of Caesar.
You showed your teeth like apes, and fawned like
      hounds,
And bowed like bondmen, kissing Caesar's feet,
Whilst damnèd Casca, like a cur, behind,
Struck Caesar on the neck. O you flatterers!   45
CASSIUS
Flatterers? Now, Brutus, thank yourself.
This tongue had not offended so today
If Cassius might have ruled.
OCTAVIUS
Come, come, the cause. If arguing make us sweat,
The proof of it will turn to redder drops.   50
He draws
Look, I draw a sword against conspirators.
When think you that the sword goes up again?
Never till Caesar's three and thirty wounds
Be well avenged, or till another Caesar
Have added slaughter to the swords of traitors. 55

BRUTUS
Caesar, thou canst not die by traitors' hands,
Unless thou bring'st them with thee.
OCTAVIUS   So I hope.
I was not born to die on Brutus' sword.
BRUTUS
O, if thou wert the noblest of thy strain,
Young man, thou couldst not die more honourable. 60
CASSIUS
A peevish schoolboy, worthless of such honour,
Joined with a masquer and a reveller!
ANTONY
Old Cassius still.
OCTAVIUS   Come, Antony, away.
Defiance, traitors, hurl we in your teeth.
If you dare fight today, come to the field.   65
If not, when you have stomachs.
                    Exeunt Octavius, Antony, and their army
CASSIUS
Why, now blow wind, swell billow, and swim bark.
The storm is up, and all is on the hazard.
BRUTUS
Ho, Lucillius! Hark, a word with you.
LUCILLIUS   My lord.
       He stands forth, and speaks with Brutus
CASSIUS
Messala.
MESSALA (*standing forth*) What says my general?
CASSIUS   Messala,
This is my birthday; as this very day   71
Was Cassius born. Give me thy hand, Messala.
Be thou my witness that, against my will,
As Pompey was, am I compelled to set
Upon one battle all our liberties.   75
You know that I held Epicurus strong,
And his opinion. Now I change my mind,
And partly credit things that do presage.
Coming from Sardis, on our former ensigns
Two mighty eagles fell, and there they perched, 80
Gorging and feeding from our soldiers' hands,
Who to Philippi here consorted us.
This morning are they fled away and gone,
And in their steads do ravens, crows, and kites
Fly o'er our heads and downward look on us,   85
As we were sickly prey. Their shadows seem
A canopy most fatal, under which
Our army lies ready to give the ghost.
MESSALA
Believe not so.
CASSIUS   I but believe it partly,
For I am fresh of spirit, and resolved   90
To meet all perils very constantly.
BRUTUS
Even so, Lucillius.
CASSIUS (*joining Brutus*) Now, most noble Brutus,
The gods today stand friendly, that we may,
Lovers in peace, lead on our days to age.
But since the affairs of men rest still incertain, 95
Let's reason with the worst that may befall.

If we do lose this battle, then is this
The very last time we shall speak together.
What are you then determinèd to do?
BRUTUS
Even by the rule of that philosophy   100
By which I did blame Cato for the death
Which he did give himself—I know not how,
But I do find it cowardly and vile
For fear of what might fall so to prevent
The time of life—arming myself with patience   105
To stay the providence of some high powers
That govern us below.
CASSIUS   Then if we lose this battle,
You are contented to be led in triumph
Thorough the streets of Rome?
BRUTUS No, Cassius, no.   110
Think not, thou noble Roman,
That ever Brutus will go bound to Rome.
He bears too great a mind. But this same day
Must end that work the ides of March begun;
And whether we shall meet again I know not.   115
Therefore our everlasting farewell take.
For ever and for ever farewell, Cassius.
If we do meet again, why, we shall smile.
If not, why then, this parting was well made.
CASSIUS
For ever and for ever farewell, Brutus.   120
If we do meet again, we'll smile indeed.
If not, 'tis true this parting was well made.
BRUTUS
Why then, lead on. O that a man might know
The end of this day's business ere it come!
But it sufficeth that the day will end,   125
And then the end is known.—Come, ho, away!
                                        Exeunt

5.2   *Alarum. Enter Brutus and Messala*
BRUTUS
Ride, ride, Messala, ride, and give these bills
Unto the legions on the other side.
       Loud alarum
Let them set on at once, for I perceive
But cold demeanour in Octavio's wing,
And sudden push gives them the overthrow.   5
Ride, ride, Messala; let them all come down.
                        Exeunt ⌈severally⌉

5.3   *Alarums. Enter Cassius ⌈with an ensign⌉, and*
       Titinius
CASSIUS
O look, Titinius, look: the villains fly.
Myself have to mine own turned enemy:
This ensign here of mine was turning back;
I slew the coward, and did take it from him.
TITINIUS
O Cassius, Brutus gave the word too early,   5
Who, having some advantage on Octavius,
Took it too eagerly. His soldiers fell to spoil,
Whilst we by Antony are all enclosed.

Enter Pindarus

PINDARUS
Fly further off, my lord, fly further off!
Mark Antony is in your tents, my lord;   10
Fly therefore, noble Cassius, fly farre off.

CASSIUS
This hill is far enough. Look, look, Titinius,
Are those my tents where I perceive the fire?

TITINIUS
They are, my lord.

CASSIUS   Titinius, if thou lovest me,
Mount thou my horse, and hide thy spurs in him   15
Till he have brought thee up to yonder troops
And here again, that I may rest assured
Whether yon troops are friend or enemy.

TITINIUS
I will be here again even with a thought.   *Exit*

CASSIUS
Go, Pindarus, get higher on that hill.   20
My sight was ever thick. Regard, Titinius,
And tell me what thou not'st about the field.
                                        Exit Pindarus
This day I breathèd first. Time is come round,
And where I did begin, there shall I end.
My life is run his compass.
         Enter Pindarus above
                        Sirrah, what news?   25

PINDARUS O my lord!

CASSIUS What news?

PINDARUS
Titinius is enclosèd round about
With horsemen, that make to him on the spur.
Yet he spurs on. Now they are almost on him.   30
Now Titinius. Now some light. O, he lights too.
He's ta'en.
         Shout within
And hark, they shout for joy.

CASSIUS   Come down; behold no more.
                                        Exit Pindarus
O coward that I am, to live so long
To see my best friend ta'en before my face!   35
         Enter Pindarus below
Come hither, sirrah. In Parthia did I take thee prisoner,
And then I swore thee, saving of thy life,
That whatsoever I did bid thee do
Thou shouldst attempt it. Come now, keep thine oath.
Now be a freeman, and, with this good sword   40
That ran through Caesar's bowels, search this bosom.
Stand not to answer. Here, take thou the hilts,
         Pindarus takes the sword
And when my face is covered, as 'tis now,
Guide thou the sword.
         Pindarus stabs him
                        Caesar, thou art revenged,
Even with the sword that killed thee.   *He dies*

PINDARUS
So, I am free, yet would not so have been   46
Durst I have done my will. O Cassius!

Far from this country Pindarus shall run,
Where never Roman shall take note of him.   *Exit*
         Enter Titinius, wearing a wreath of victory, and
         Messala

MESSALA
It is but change, Titinius, for Octavius   50
Is overthrown by noble Brutus' power,
As Cassius' legions are by Antony.

TITINIUS
These tidings will well comfort Cassius.

MESSALA
Where did you leave him?

TITINIUS   All disconsolate,
With Pindarus his bondman, on this hill.   55

MESSALA
Is not that he that lies upon the ground?

TITINIUS
He lies not like the living.—O my heart!

MESSALA
Is not that he?

TITINIUS   No, this was he, Messala;
But Cassius is no more. O setting sun,
As in thy red rays thou dost sink tonight,   60
So in his red blood Cassius' day is set.
The sun of Rome is set. Our day is gone.
Clouds, dews, and dangers come. Our deeds are done.
Mistrust of my success hath done this deed.

MESSALA
Mistrust of good success hath done this deed.   65
O hateful Error, Melancholy's child,
Why dost thou show to the apt thoughts of men
The things that are not? O Error, soon conceived,
Thou never com'st unto a happy birth,
But kill'st the mother that engendered thee.   70

TITINIUS
What, Pindarus! Where art thou, Pindarus?

MESSALA
Seek him, Titinius, whilst I go to meet
The noble Brutus, thrusting this report
Into his ears. I may say 'thrusting' it,
For piercing steel and darts envenomèd   75
Shall be as welcome to the ears of Brutus
As tidings of this sight.

TITINIUS   Hie you, Messala,
And I will seek for Pindarus the while.   *Exit Messala*
Why didst thou send me forth, brave Cassius?
Did I not meet thy friends, and did not they   80
Put on my brows this wreath of victory,
And bid me give it thee? Didst thou not hear their
         shouts?
Alas, thou hast misconstrued everything.
But hold thee, take this garland on thy brow.
Thy Brutus bid me give it thee, and I   85
Will do his bidding. Brutus, come apace
And see how I regarded Caius Cassius.
By your leave, gods, this is a Roman's part:
Come Cassius' sword, and find Titinius' heart.
         He stabs himself, and dies

Alarum. Enter Brutus, Messala, young Cato,
Strato, Volumnius, Lucillius, ⌈Labio, and Flavio⌉

BRUTUS

Where, where, Messala, doth his body lie?   90

MESSALA

Lo yonder, and Titinius mourning it.

BRUTUS

Titinius' face is upward.

CATO   He is slain.

BRUTUS

O Julius Caesar, thou art mighty yet.
Thy spirit walks abroad, and turns our swords
In our own proper entrails.

Low Alarums

CATO   Brave Titinius,   95
Look whe'er he have not crowned dead Cassius.

BRUTUS

Are yet two Romans living such as these?
The last of all the Romans, fare thee well.
It is impossible that ever Rome
Should breed thy fellow. Friends, I owe more tears   100
To this dead man than you shall see me pay.—
I shall find time, Cassius, I shall find time.—
Come, therefore, and to Thasos send his body.
His funerals shall not be in our camp,
Lest it discomfort us. Lucillius, come;   105
And come, young Cato. Let us to the field.
Labio and Flavio, set our battles on.
'Tis three o'clock, and, Romans, yet ere night
We shall try fortune in a second fight.

Exeunt ⌈with the bodies⌉

5.4   *Alarum. Enter Brutus, Messala, young Cato,*
Lucillius, and Flavius

BRUTUS

Yet, countrymen, O yet hold up your heads.

⌈Exit with Messala and Flavius⌉

CATO

What bastard doth not? Who will go with me?
I will proclaim my name about the field.
I am the son of Marcus Cato, ho!
A foe to tyrants, and my country's friend.   5
I am the son of Marcus Cato, ho!

Enter Soldiers, and fight

⌈LUCILLIUS⌉

And I am Brutus, Marcus Brutus, I,
Brutus, my country's friend. Know me for Brutus.

Soldiers kill Cato

O young and noble Cato, art thou down?
Why, now thou diest as bravely as Titinius,   10
And mayst be honoured, being Cato's son.

⌈FIRST⌉ SOLDIER

Yield, or thou diest.

LUCILLIUS   Only I yield to die.
There is so much, that thou wilt kill me straight:
Kill Brutus, and be honoured in his death.

⌈FIRST⌉ SOLDIER

We must not.—A noble prisoner.   15

SECOND SOLDIER

Room, ho! Tell Antony Brutus is ta'en.

Enter Antony

FIRST SOLDIER

I'll tell the news. Here comes the general.—
(*To Antony*) Brutus is ta'en, Brutus is ta'en, my lord.

ANTONY Where is he?

LUCILLIUS

Safe, Antony, Brutus is safe enough.   20
I dare assure thee that no enemy
Shall ever take alive the noble Brutus.
The gods defend him from so great a shame.
When you do find him, or alive or dead,
He will be found like Brutus, like himself.   25

ANTONY (*to First Soldier*)

This is not Brutus, friend, but, I assure you,
A prize no less in worth. Keep this man safe.
Give him all kindness. I had rather have
Such men my friends than enemies.
⌈*To another Soldier*⌉   Go on,
And see whe'er Brutus be alive or dead,   30
And bring us word unto Octavius' tent
How everything is chanced.

Exeunt ⌈the Soldier at one door, Antony,
Lucillius and other Soldiers, some bearing
Cato's body, at another door⌉

5.5   *Enter Brutus, Dardanius, Clitus, Strato, and*
Volumnius

BRUTUS

Come, poor remains of friends, rest on this rock.

⌈He sits. Strato rests and falls asleep⌉

CLITUS

Statillius showed the torchlight, but, my lord,
He came not back. He is or ta'en or slain.

BRUTUS

Sit thee down, Clitus. Slaying is the word:
It is a deed in fashion. Hark thee, Clitus.   5

He whispers

CLITUS

What I, my lord? No, not for all the world.

BRUTUS

Peace, then, no words.

CLITUS   I'll rather kill myself.

He stands apart

BRUTUS

Hark thee, Dardanius.

He whispers

DARDANIUS   Shall I do such a deed?

He joins Clitus

CLITUS O Dardanius!

DARDANIUS O Clitus!   10

CLITUS

What ill request did Brutus make to thee?

DARDANIUS

To kill him, Clitus. Look, he meditates.

CLITUS

Now is that noble vessel full of grief,
That it runs over even at his eyes.

BRUTUS
Come hither, good Volumnius. List a word.   15
VOLUMNIUS
What says my lord?
BRUTUS   Why this, Volumnius.
The ghost of Caesar hath appeared to me
Two several times by night—at Sardis once,
And this last night, here in Philippi fields.
I know my hour is come.
VOLUMNIUS   Not so, my lord.   20
BRUTUS
Nay, I am sure it is, Volumnius.
Thou seest the world, Volumnius, how it goes.
Our enemies have beat us to the pit,
    Low alarums
It is more worthy to leap in ourselves
Than tarry till they push us. Good Volumnius,   25
Thou know'st that we two went to school together.
Even for that, our love of old, I prithee,
Hold thou my sword hilts whilst I run on it.
VOLUMNIUS
That's not an office for a friend, my lord.
    Alarum still
CLITUS
Fly, fly, my lord! There is no tarrying here.   30
BRUTUS
Farewell to you, and you, and you, Volumnius.—
Strato, thou hast been all this while asleep.
    ⌜*Strato wakes*⌝
Farewell to thee too, Strato. Countrymen,
My heart doth joy that yet in all my life
I found no man but he was true to me.   35
I shall have glory by this losing day,
More than Octavius and Mark Antony
By this vile conquest shall attain unto.
So fare you well at once, for Brutus' tongue
Hath almost ended his life's history.   40
Night hangs upon mine eyes. My bones would rest,
That have but laboured to attain this hour.
    Alarum. Cry within: 'Fly, fly, fly!'
CLITUS
Fly, my lord, fly!
BRUTUS   Hence; I will follow.
    Exeunt Clitus, Dardanius, and Volumnius
I prithee, Strato, stay thou by thy lord.
Thou art a fellow of a good respect.   45
Thy life hath had some smatch of honour in it.
Hold then my sword, and turn away thy face
While I do run upon it. Wilt thou, Strato?
STRATO
Give me your hand first. Fare you well, my lord.

BRUTUS
Farewell, good Strato.
    Strato holds the sword, while Brutus runs on it
                              Caesar, now be still.   50
I killed not thee with half so good a will.   *He dies*
    Alarum. Retreat. Enter Antony, Octavius, Messala,
    Lucillius, and the army
OCTAVIUS What man is that?
MESSALA
My master's man. Strato, where is thy master?
STRATO
Free from the bondage you are in, Messala.
The conquerors can but make a fire of him,   55
For Brutus only overcame himself,
And no man else hath honour by his death.
LUCILLIUS
So Brutus should be found. I thank thee, Brutus,
That thou hast proved Lucillius' saying true.
OCTAVIUS
All that served Brutus, I will entertain them.   60
    (*To Strato*)
Fellow, wilt thou bestow thy time with me?
STRATO
Ay, if Messala will prefer me to you.
OCTAVIUS
Do so, good Messala.
MESSALA   How died my master, Strato?
STRATO
I held the sword, and he did run on it.
MESSALA
Octavius, then take him to follow thee,   65
That did the latest service to my master.
ANTONY
This was the noblest Roman of them all.
All the conspirators save only he
Did that they did in envy of great Caesar.
He only in a general honest thought   70
And common good to all made one of them.
His life was gentle, and the elements
So mixed in him that nature might stand up
And say to all the world 'This was a man'.
OCTAVIUS
According to his virtue let us use him,   75
With all respect and rites of burial.
Within my tent his bones tonight shall lie,
Most like a soldier, ordered honourably.
So call the field to rest, and let's away
To part the glories of this happy day.   80
    Exeunt ⌜*with Brutus' body*⌝

HAMLET

SEVERAL references from 1589 onwards witness the existence of a play about Hamlet, but Francis Meres did not attribute a play with this title to Shakespeare in 1598. The first clear reference to Shakespeare's play is its entry in the Stationers' Register on 26 July 1602 as *The Revenge of Hamlet Prince [of] Denmark*, when it was said to have been 'lately acted by the Lord Chamberlain his servants'. It survives in three versions; their relationship is a matter of dispute on which views about when Shakespeare wrote his play, and in what form, depend. In 1603 appeared an inferior text apparently assembled from actors' memories; it has only about 2,200 lines. In the following year, as if to put the record straight, James Roberts (to whom the play had been entered in 1602) published it as 'newly imprinted and enlarged to almost as much again as it was, according to the true and perfect copy'. At about 3,800 lines, this is the longest version. The 1623 Folio offers a still different text, some 230 lines shorter than the 1604 version, differing verbally from that at many points, and including about 70 additional lines. It is our belief that Shakespeare wrote *Hamlet* about 1600, and revised it later; that the 1604 edition was printed from his original papers; that the Folio represents the revised version; and that the 1603 edition represents a very imperfect report of an abridged version of the revision. So our text is based on the Folio; passages present in the 1604 quarto but absent from the Folio are printed as Additional Passages because we believe that, however fine they may be in themselves, Shakespeare decided that the play as a whole would be better without them.

The plot of *Hamlet* originates in a Scandinavian folk-tale told in the twelfth-century *Danish History* written in Latin by the Danish Saxo Grammaticus. François de Belleforest retold it in the fifth volume (1570) of his *Histoires Tragiques*, not translated into English until 1608. Saxo, through Belleforest, provided the basic story of a Prince of Denmark committed to revenge his father's murder by his own brother (Claudius) who has married the dead man's widow (Gertrude). As in Shakespeare, Hamlet pretends to be mad, kills his uncle's counsellor (Polonius) while he is eavesdropping, rebukes his mother, is sent to England under the escort of two retainers (Rosencrantz and Guildenstern) who bear orders that he be put to death on arrival, finds the letter containing the orders and alters it so that it is the retainers who are executed, returns to Denmark, and kills the King.

Belleforest's story differs at some points from Shakespeare's, and Shakespeare elaborates it, adding, for example, the Ghost of Hamlet's father, the coming of the actors to Elsinore, the performance of the play through which Hamlet tests his uncle's guilt, Ophelia's madness and death, Laertes' plot to revenge *his* father's death, the grave-digger, Ophelia's funeral, and the characters of Osric and Fortinbras. How much he owed to the lost Hamlet play we cannot tell; what is certain is that Shakespeare used his mastery of a wide range of diverse styles in both verse and prose, and his genius for dramatic effect, to create from these and other sources the most complex, varied, and exciting drama that had ever been seen on the English stage. Its popularity was instant and enduring. The play has had a profound influence on Western culture, and Shakespeare's Hamlet has himself entered the world of myth.

THE PERSONS OF THE PLAY

GHOST of Hamlet, the late King of Denmark

KING CLAUDIUS, his brother

QUEEN GERTRUDE of Denmark, widow of King Hamlet, now wife of Claudius

Prince HAMLET, son of King Hamlet and Queen Gertrude

POLONIUS, a lord

LAERTES, son of Polonius

OPHELIA, daughter of Polonius

REYNALDO, servant of Polonius

HORATIO
ROSENCRANTZ } friends of Prince Hamlet
GUILDENSTERN

FRANCISCO
BARNARDO } soldiers
MARCELLUS

VALTEMAND
CORNELIUS } courtiers
OSRIC
GENTLEMEN

A SAILOR

Two CLOWNS, a gravedigger and his companion

A PRIEST

FORTINBRAS, Prince of Norway

A CAPTAIN in his army

AMBASSADORS from England

PLAYERS, who play the parts of the Prologue, Player King, Player Queen, and Lucianus, in 'The Mousetrap'

Lords, messengers, attendants, guards, soldiers, followers of Laertes, sailors

The Tragedy of Hamlet, Prince of Denmark

1.1 *Enter Barnardo and Francisco, two sentinels, at several doors*

BARNARDO Who's there?

FRANCISCO
Nay, answer me. Stand and unfold yourself.

BARNARDO
Long live the King!

FRANCISCO   Barnardo?

BARNARDO   He.

FRANCISCO
You come most carefully upon your hour.

BARNARDO
'Tis now struck twelve. Get thee to bed, Francisco.   5

FRANCISCO
For this relief much thanks. 'Tis bitter cold,
And I am sick at heart.

BARNARDO   Have you had quiet guard?

FRANCISCO
Not a mouse stirring.

BARNARDO   Well, good night.
If you do meet Horatio and Marcellus,
The rivals of my watch, bid them make haste.   10
Enter Horatio and Marcellus

FRANCISCO
I think I hear them.—Stand! Who's there?

HORATIO   Friends to this ground.

MARCELLUS
And liegemen to the Dane.

FRANCISCO   Give you good night.

MARCELLUS
O farewell, honest soldier. Who hath relieved you?

FRANCISCO
Barnardo has my place. Give you good night.   *Exit*

MARCELLUS Holla, Barnardo!   15

BARNARDO Say—what, is Horatio there?

HORATIO A piece of him.

BARNARDO
Welcome, Horatio. Welcome, good Marcellus.

MARCELLUS
What, has this thing appeared again tonight?

BARNARDO I have seen nothing.   20

MARCELLUS
Horatio says 'tis but our fantasy,
And will not let belief take hold of him
Touching this dreaded sight twice seen of us.
Therefore I have entreated him along
With us to watch the minutes of this night,   25
That if again this apparition come
He may approve our eyes and speak to it.

HORATIO
Tush, tush, 'twill not appear.

BARNARDO   Sit down a while,
And let us once again assail your ears,

That are so fortified against our story,   30
What we two nights have seen.

HORATIO   Well, sit we down,
And let us hear Barnardo speak of this.

BARNARDO Last night of all,
When yon same star that's westward from the pole
Had made his course t'illume that part of heaven   35
Where now it burns, Marcellus and myself,
The bell then beating one—
Enter the Ghost in complete armour, holding a truncheon, with his beaver up

MARCELLUS
Peace, break thee off. Look where it comes again.

BARNARDO
In the same figure like the King that's dead.

MARCELLUS (*to Horatio*)
Thou art a scholar—speak to it, Horatio.   40

BARNARDO
Looks it not like the King?—Mark it, Horatio.

HORATIO
Most like. It harrows me with fear and wonder.

BARNARDO
It would be spoke to.

MARCELLUS   Question it, Horatio.

HORATIO (*to the Ghost*)
What art thou that usurp'st this time of night,
Together with that fair and warlike form   45
In which the majesty of buried Denmark
Did sometimes march? By heaven, I charge thee speak.

MARCELLUS
It is offended.

BARNARDO   See, it stalks away.

HORATIO (*to the Ghost*)
Stay, speak, speak, I charge thee speak.   *Exit Ghost*

MARCELLUS 'Tis gone, and will not answer.   50

BARNARDO
How now, Horatio? You tremble and look pale.
Is not this something more than fantasy?
What think you on't?

HORATIO
Before my God, I might not this believe
Without the sensible and true avouch   55
Of mine own eyes.

MARCELLUS Is it not like the King?

HORATIO As thou art to thyself.
Such was the very armour he had on
When he th'ambitious Norway combated.   60
So frowned he once when in an angry parley
He smote the sledded Polacks on the ice.
'Tis strange.

MARCELLUS
Thus twice before, and just at this dead hour,
With martial stalk hath he gone by our watch.   65

HORATIO

In what particular thought to work I know not,
But in the gross and scope of my opinion
This bodes some strange eruption to our state.

MARCELLUS

Good now, sit down, and tell me, he that knows,
Why this same strict and most observant watch   70
So nightly toils the subject of the land,
And why such daily cast of brazen cannon,
And foreign mart for implements of war,
Why such impress of shipwrights, whose sore task
Does not divide the Sunday from the week: 75
What might be toward that this sweaty haste
Doth make the night joint-labourer with the day,
Who is't that can inform me?

HORATIO   That can I—

At least the whisper goes so: our last king,
Whose image even but now appeared to us,   80
Was as you know by Fortinbras of Norway,
Thereto pricked on by a most emulate pride,
Dared to the combat; in which our valiant Hamlet—
For so this side of our known world esteemed him—
Did slay this Fortinbras, who by a sealed compact   85
Well ratified by law and heraldry
Did forfeit with his life all those his lands
Which he stood seized on to the conqueror;
Against the which a moiety competent
Was gagèd by our King, which had returned   90
To the inheritance of Fortinbras
Had he been vanquisher, as by the same cov'nant
And carriage of the article designed
His fell to Hamlet. Now sir, young Fortinbras,
Of unimprovèd mettle hot and full,   95
Hath in the skirts of Norway here and there
Sharked up a list of landless resolutes
For food and diet to some enterprise
That hath a stomach in't, which is no other—
And it doth well appear unto our state—   100
But to recover of us by strong hand
And terms compulsative those foresaid lands
So by his father lost. And this, I take it,
Is the main motive of our preparations,
The source of this our watch, and the chief head   105
Of this post-haste and rummage in the land.

     Enter the Ghost, as before

But soft, behold—lo where it comes again!
I'll cross it though it blast me.—Stay, illusion.

     The Ghost spreads his arms

If thou hast any sound or use of voice,
Speak to me.   110
If there be any good thing to be done
That may to thee do ease and grace to me,
Speak to me.
If thou art privy to thy country's fate
Which happily foreknowing may avoid,   115
O speak!
Or if thou hast uphoarded in thy life
Extorted treasure in the womb of earth—

For which, they say, you spirits oft walk in death—

     The cock crows

Speak of it, stay and speak.—Stop it, Marcellus.   120

MARCELLUS

Shall I strike at it with my partisan?

HORATIO

Do, if it will not stand.

BARNARDO   'Tis here.

HORATIO   'Tis here.   *Exit Ghost*

MARCELLUS   'Tis gone.

We do it wrong, being so majestical,
To offer it the show of violence,   125
For it is as the air invulnerable,
And our vain blows malicious mockery.

BARNARDO

It was about to speak when the cock crew.

HORATIO

And then it started like a guilty thing
Upon a fearful summons. I have heard   130
The cock, that is the trumpet to the morn,
Doth with his lofty and shrill-sounding throat
Awake the god of day, and at his warning,
Whether in sea or fire, in earth or air,
Th'extravagant and erring spirit hies   135
To his confine; and of the truth herein
This present object made probation.

MARCELLUS

It faded on the crowing of the cock.
Some say that ever 'gainst that season comes
Wherein our saviour's birth is celebrated   140
The bird of dawning singeth all night long;
And then, they say, no spirit can walk abroad,
The nights are wholesome; then no planets strike,
No fairy takes, nor witch hath power to charm,
So hallowed and so gracious is the time.   145

HORATIO

So have I heard, and do in part believe it.
But look, the morn in russet mantle clad
Walks o'er the dew of yon high eastern hill.
Break we our watch up, and by my advice
Let us impart what we have seen tonight   150
Unto young Hamlet; for upon my life,
This spirit, dumb to us, will speak to him.
Do you consent we shall acquaint him with it,
As needful in our loves, fitting our duty?

MARCELLUS

Let's do't, I pray; and I this morning know   155
Where we shall find him most conveniently.   *Exeunt*

1.2   *Flourish. Enter Claudius, King of Denmark,*
       Gertrude the Queen, members of the Council, such
       as Polonius, his son Laertes and daughter Ophelia,
       Prince Hamlet dressed in black, with others

KING CLAUDIUS

Though yet of Hamlet our dear brother's death
The memory be green, and that it us befitted
To bear our hearts in grief and our whole kingdom
To be contracted in one brow of woe,

Yet so far hath discretion fought with nature
That we with wisest sorrow think on him
Together with remembrance of ourselves.
Therefore our sometime sister, now our queen,
Th'imperial jointress of this warlike state,
Have we as 'twere with a defeated joy,   10
With one auspicious and one dropping eye,
With mirth in funeral and with dirge in marriage,
In equal scale weighing delight and dole,
Taken to wife. Nor have we herein barred
Your better wisdoms, which have freely gone   15
With this affair along. For all, our thanks.
Now follows that you know young Fortinbras,
Holding a weak supposal of our worth,
Or thinking by our late dear brother's death
Our state to be disjoint and out of frame,   20
Co-leaguèd with the dream of his advantage,
He hath not failed to pester us with message
Importing the surrender of those lands
Lost by his father, with all bonds of law,
To our most valiant brother. So much for him.   25
Enter Valtemand and Cornelius
Now for ourself, and for this time of meeting,
Thus much the business is: we have here writ
To Norway, uncle of young Fortinbras—
Who, impotent and bed-rid, scarcely hears
Of this his nephew's purpose—to suppress   30
His further gait herein, in that the levies,
The lists, and full proportions are all made
Out of his subject; and we here dispatch
You, good Cornelius, and you, Valtemand,
For bearers of this greeting to old Norway,   35
Giving to you no further personal power
To business with the King more than the scope
Of these dilated articles allow.
Farewell, and let your haste commend your duty.
VALTEMAND
In that and all things will we show our duty.   40
KING CLAUDIUS
We doubt it nothing, heartily farewell.
            Exeunt Valtemand and Cornelius
And now, Laertes, what's the news with you?
You told us of some suit. What is't, Laertes?
You cannot speak of reason to the Dane
And lose your voice. What wouldst thou beg, Laertes,
That shall not be my offer, not thy asking?   46
The head is not more native to the heart,
The hand more instrumental to the mouth,
Than is the throne of Denmark to thy father.
What wouldst thou have, Laertes?
LAERTES   Dread my lord,   50
Your leave and favour to return to France,
From whence though willingly I came to Denmark
To show my duty in your coronation,
Yet now I must confess, that duty done,
My thoughts and wishes bend again towards France 55
And bow them to your gracious leave and pardon.

KING CLAUDIUS   5
Have you your father's leave? What says Polonius?
POLONIUS
He hath, my lord, wrung from me my slow leave
By laboursome petition, and at last
Upon his will I sealed my hard consent.   60
I do beseech you give him leave to go.
KING CLAUDIUS
Take thy fair hour, Laertes. Time be thine,
And thy best graces spend it at thy will.
But now, my cousin Hamlet, and my son—
HAMLET
A little more than kin and less than kind.   65
KING CLAUDIUS
How is it that the clouds still hang on you?
HAMLET
Not so, my lord, I am too much i'th' sun.
QUEEN GERTRUDE
Good Hamlet, cast thy nightly colour off,
And let thine eye look like a friend on Denmark.
Do not for ever with thy vailèd lids   70
Seek for thy noble father in the dust.
Thou know'st 'tis common—all that lives must die,
Passing through nature to eternity.
HAMLET
Ay, madam, it is common.
QUEEN GERTRUDE   If it be,
Why seems it so particular with thee?   75
HAMLET
Seems, madam? Nay, it *is*. I know not 'seems'.
'Tis not alone my inky cloak, good-mother,
Nor customary suits of solemn black,
Nor windy suspiration of forced breath,
No, nor the fruitful river in the eye,   80
Nor the dejected haviour of the visage,
Together with all forms, moods, shows of grief
That can denote me truly. These indeed 'seem',
For they are actions that a man might play;
But I have that within which passeth show—   85
These but the trappings and the suits of woe.
KING CLAUDIUS
'Tis sweet and commendable in your nature, Hamlet,
To give these mourning duties to your father;
But you must know your father lost a father,
That father lost, lost his; and the survivor bound   90
In filial obligation for some term
To do obsequious sorrow. But to persever
In obstinate condolement is a course
Of impious stubbornness, 'tis unmanly grief,
It shows a will most incorrect to heaven,   95
A heart unfortified, a mind impatient,
An understanding simple and unschooled;
For what we know must be, and is as common
As any the most vulgar thing to sense,
Why should we in our peevish opposition   100
Take it to heart? Fie, 'tis a fault to heaven,
A fault against the dead, a fault to nature,

To reason most absurd, whose common theme
Is death of fathers, and who still hath cried
From the first corpse till he that died today,　105
'This must be so'. We pray you throw to earth
This unprevailing woe, and think of us
As of a father; for let the world take note
You are the most immediate to our throne,
And with no less nobility of love　110
Than that which dearest father bears his son
Do I impart towards you. For your intent
In going back to school in Wittenberg,
It is most retrograde to our desire,
And we beseech you bend you to remain　115
Here in the cheer and comfort of our eye,
Our chiefest courtier, cousin, and our son.

QUEEN GERTRUDE
Let not thy mother lose her prayers, Hamlet.
I pray thee stay with us, go not to Wittenberg.

HAMLET
I shall in all my best obey you, madam.　120

KING CLAUDIUS
Why, 'tis a loving and a fair reply.
Be as ourself in Denmark. (*To Gertrude*) Madam, come.
This gentle and unforced accord of Hamlet
Sits smiling to my heart; in grace whereof,
No jocund health that Denmark drinks today　125
But the great cannon to the clouds shall tell,
And the King's rouse the heavens shall bruit again,
Re-speaking earthly thunder. Come, away.
⌈*Flourish.*⌉ *Exeunt all but Hamlet*

HAMLET
O that this too too solid flesh would melt,
Thaw, and resolve itself into a dew,　130
Or that the Everlasting had not fixed
His canon 'gainst self-slaughter! O God, O God,
How weary, stale, flat, and unprofitable
Seem to me all the uses of this world!
Fie on't, ah fie, fie! 'Tis an unweeded garden　135
That grows to seed; things rank and gross in nature
Possess it merely. That it should come to this—
But two months dead—nay, not so much, not two—
So excellent a king, that was to this
Hyperion to a satyr, so loving to my mother　140
That he might not beteem the winds of heaven
Visit her face too roughly! Heaven and earth,
Must I remember? Why, she would hang on him
As if increase of appetite had grown
By what it fed on, and yet within a month—　145
Let me not think on't; frailty, thy name is woman—
A little month, or ere those shoes were old
With which she followed my poor father's body,
Like Niobe, all tears, why she, even she—
O God, a beast that wants discourse of reason　150
Would have mourned longer!—married with mine
　　uncle,
My father's brother, but no more like my father
Than I to Hercules; within a month,
Ere yet the salt of most unrighteous tears

Had left the flushing of her gallèd eyes,　155
She married. O most wicked speed, to post
With such dexterity to incestuous sheets!
It is not, nor it cannot come to good.
But break, my heart, for I must hold my tongue.
Enter Horatio, Marcellus, and Barnardo

HORATIO
Hail to your lordship.

HAMLET　　　　　　　　I am glad to see you well.　160
Horatio—or I do forget myself.

HORATIO
The same, my lord, and your poor servant ever.

HAMLET
Sir, my good friend; I'll change that name with you.
And what make you from Wittenberg, Horatio?—
Marcellus.

MARCELLUS　My good lord.　165

HAMLET
I am very glad to see you. (*To Barnardo*) Good even,
　　sir.—
But what in faith make you from Wittenberg?

HORATIO
A truant disposition, good my lord.

HAMLET
I would not have your enemy say so,
Nor shall you do mine ear that violence　170
To make it truster of your own report
Against yourself. I know you are no truant.
But what is your affair in Elsinore?
We'll teach you to drink deep ere you depart.

HORATIO
My lord, I came to see your father's funeral.　175

HAMLET
I prithee do not mock me, fellow-student;
I think it was to see my mother's wedding.

HORATIO
Indeed, my lord, it followed hard upon.

HAMLET
Thrift, thrift, Horatio. The funeral baked meats
Did coldly furnish forth the marriage tables.　180
Would I had met my dearest foe in heaven
Ere I had ever seen that day, Horatio.
My father—methinks I see my father.

HORATIO
O where, my lord?

HAMLET　　　　　　　In my mind's eye, Horatio.

HORATIO
I saw him once. A was a goodly king.　185

HAMLET
A was a man. Take him for all in all,
I shall not look upon his like again.

HORATIO
My lord, I think I saw him yesternight.

HAMLET Saw? Who?

HORATIO My lord, the King your father.

HAMLET The King my father?　190

HORATIO
Season your admiration for a while

With an attent ear till I may deliver,
Upon the witness of these gentlemen,
This marvel to you.
HAMLET   For God's love let me hear!   195
HORATIO
Two nights together had these gentlemen,
Marcellus and Barnardo, on their watch,
In the dead waste and middle of the night,
Been thus encountered. A figure like your father,
Armed at all points exactly, cap-à-pie,   200
Appears before them, and with solemn march
Goes slow and stately by them. Thrice he walked
By their oppressed and fear-surprisèd eyes
Within his truncheon's length, whilst they distilled
Almost to jelly with the act of fear   205
Stand dumb and speak not to him. This to me
In dreadful secrecy impart they did,
And I with them the third night kept the watch,
Where, as they had delivered, both in time,
Form of the thing, each word made true and good,   210
The apparition comes. I knew your father;
These hands are not more like.
HAMLET   But where was this?
MARCELLUS
My lord, upon the platform where we watched.
HAMLET
Did you not speak to it?
HORATIO   My lord, I did,
But answer made it none; yet once methought   215
It lifted up it head and did address
Itself to motion like as it would speak,
But even then the morning cock crew loud,
And at the sound it shrunk in haste away
And vanished from our sight.
HAMLET   'Tis very strange.   220
HORATIO
As I do live, my honoured lord, 'tis true,
And we did think it writ down in our duty
To let you know of it.
HAMLET
Indeed, indeed, sirs; but this troubles me.—
Hold you the watch tonight?
BARNARDO and MARCELLUS   We do, my lord.   225
HAMLET
Armed, say you?
BARNARDO and MARCELLUS Armed, my lord.
HAMLET   From top to toe?
BARNARDO and MARCELLUS
My lord, from head to foot.
HAMLET   Then saw you not his face.
HORATIO
O yes, my lord, he wore his beaver up.
HAMLET
What looked he? Frowningly?
HORATIO   A countenance more
In sorrow than in anger.
HAMLET   Pale or red?   230

HORATIO
Nay, very pale.
HAMLET   And fixed his eyes upon you?
HORATIO Most constantly.
HAMLET I would I had been there.
HORATIO It would have much amazed you.
HAMLET
Very like, very like. Stayed it long?   235
HORATIO
While one with moderate haste might tell a hundred.
BARNARDO and MARCELLUS Longer, longer.
HORATIO Not when I saw't.
HAMLET His beard was grizzly, no?
HORATIO
It was as I have seen it in his life,   240
A sable silvered.
HAMLET   I'll watch tonight. Perchance
'Twill walk again.
HORATIO   I warrant you it will.
HAMLET
If it assume my noble father's person
I'll speak to it though hell itself should gape
And bid me hold my peace. I pray you all,   245
If you have hitherto concealed this sight,
Let it be treble in your silence still,
And whatsoever else shall hap tonight,
Give it an understanding but no tongue.
I will requite your loves. So fare ye well.   250
Upon the platform 'twixt eleven and twelve
I'll visit you.
ALL THREE   Our duty to your honour.
HAMLET
Your love, as mine to you. Farewell.
                              Exeunt all but Hamlet
My father's spirit in arms! All is not well.
I doubt some foul play. Would the night were come.
Till then, sit still, my soul. Foul deeds will rise,   256
Though all the earth o'erwhelm them, to men's eyes.
                                                    Exit

1.3   Enter Laertes and Ophelia, his sister
LAERTES
My necessaries are inbarqued. Farewell.
And, sister, as the winds give benefit
And convoy is assistant, do not sleep
But let me hear from you.
OPHELIA   Do you doubt that?
LAERTES
For Hamlet and the trifling of his favour,   5
Hold it a fashion and a toy in blood,
A violet in the youth of primy nature,
Forward not permanent, sweet not lasting,
The perfume and suppliance of a minute,
No more.
OPHELIA   No more but so?
LAERTES   Think it no more.   10
For nature crescent does not grow alone

In thews and bulk, but as his temple waxes
The inward service of the mind and soul
Grows wide withal. Perhaps he loves you now,
And now no soil nor cautel doth besmirch   15
The virtue of his will; but you must fear,
His greatness weighed, his will is not his own,
For he himself is subject to his birth.
He may not, as unvalued persons do,
Carve for himself, for on his choice depends   20
The sanity and health of the whole state;
And therefore must his choice be circumscribed
Unto the voice and yielding of that body
Whereof he is the head. Then if he says he loves you,
It fits your wisdom so far to believe it   25
As he in his peculiar sect and force
May give his saying deed, which is no further
Than the main voice of Denmark goes withal.
Then weigh what loss your honour may sustain
If with too credent ear you list his songs,   30
Or lose your heart, or your chaste treasure open
To his unmastered importunity.
Fear it, Ophelia, fear it, my dear sister,
And keep within the rear of your affection,
Out of the shot and danger of desire.   35
The chariest maid is prodigal enough
If she unmask her beauty to the moon.
Virtue itself scapes not calumnious strokes.
The canker galls the infants of the spring
Too oft before their buttons be disclosed,   40
And in the morn and liquid dew of youth
Contagious blastments are most imminent.
Be wary then; best safety lies in fear;
Youth to itself rebels, though none else near.

OPHELIA
I shall th'effect of this good lesson keep   45
As watchman to my heart; but, good my brother,
Do not, as some ungracious pastors do,
Show me the steep and thorny way to heaven
Whilst like a puffed and reckless libertine
Himself the primrose path of dalliance treads   50
And recks not his own rede.

LAERTES   O fear me not.
Enter Polonius
I stay too long—but here my father comes.
A double blessing is a double grace;
Occasion smiles upon a second leave.

POLONIUS
Yet here, Laertes? Aboard, aboard, for shame!   55
The wind sits in the shoulder of your sail,
And you are stayed for. There—my blessing with
    thee,
And these few precepts in thy memory
See thou character. Give thy thoughts no tongue,
Nor any unproportioned thought his act.   60
Be thou familiar but by no means vulgar.
The friends thou hast, and their adoption tried,
Grapple them to thy soul with hoops of steel,
But do not dull thy palm with entertainment
Of each new-hatched unfledged comrade. Beware   65

Of entrance to a quarrel, but being in,
Bear't that th'opposèd may beware of thee.
Give every man thine ear but few thy voice.
Take each man's censure, but reserve thy judgement.
Costly thy habit as thy purse can buy,   70
But not expressed in fancy; rich not gaudy;
For the apparel oft proclaims the man,
And they in France of the best rank and station
Are of all most select and generous chief in that.
Neither a borrower nor a lender be,   75
For loan oft loses both itself and friend,
And borrowing dulls the edge of husbandry.
This above all—to thine own self be true,
And it must follow, as the night the day,
Thou canst not then be false to any man.   80
Farewell—my blessing season this in thee.

LAERTES
Most humbly do I take my leave, my lord.

POLONIUS
The time invites you. Go; your servants tend.

LAERTES
Farewell, Ophelia, and remember well
What I have said to you.

OPHELIA   'Tis in my memory locked,   85
And you yourself shall keep the key of it.

LAERTES Farewell.   *Exit*

POLONIUS
What is't, Ophelia, he hath said to you?

OPHELIA
So please you, something touching the Lord Hamlet.

POLONIUS Marry, well bethought.   90
'Tis told me he hath very oft of late
Given private time to you, and you yourself
Have of your audience been most free and bounteous.
If it be so—as so 'tis put on me,
And that in way of caution—I must tell you   95
You do not understand yourself so clearly
As it behoves my daughter and your honour.
What is between you? Give me up the truth.

OPHELIA
He hath, my lord, of late made many tenders
Of his affection to me.   100

POLONIUS
Affection, pooh! You speak like a green girl
Unsifted in such perilous circumstance.
Do you believe his 'tenders' as you call them?

OPHELIA
I do not know, my lord, what I should think.

POLONIUS
Marry, I'll teach you: think yourself a baby   105
That you have ta'en his tenders for true pay,
Which are not sterling. Tender yourself more dearly,
Or—not to crack the wind of the poor phrase,
Running it thus—you'll tender me a fool.

OPHELIA
My lord, he hath importuned me with love   110
In honourable fashion—

POLONIUS
Ay, fashion you may call it. Go to, go to.

OPHELIA
And hath given countenance to his speech, my lord,
With all the vows of heaven.
POLONIUS
Ay, springs to catch woodcocks. I do know   115
When the blood burns how prodigal the soul
Lends the tongue vows. These blazes, daughter,
Giving more light than heat, extinct in both
Even in their promise as it is a-making,
You must not take for fire. From this time, daughter,
Be somewhat scanter of your maiden presence.   121
Set your entreatments at a higher rate
Than a command to parley. For Lord Hamlet,
Believe so much in him, that he is young,
And with a larger tether may he walk   125
Than may be given you. In few, Ophelia,
Do not believe his vows, for they are brokers,
Not of the dye which their investments show,
But mere imploratators of unholy suits,
Breathing like sanctified and pious bawds   130
The better to beguile. This is for all—
I would not, in plain terms, from this time forth
Have you so slander any moment leisure
As to give words or talk with the Lord Hamlet.
Look to't, I charge you. Come your ways.   135
OPHELIA I shall obey, my lord.   *Exeunt*

1.4   *Enter Prince Hamlet, Horatio, and Marcellus*
HAMLET
The air bites shrewdly, it is very cold.
HORATIO
It is a nipping and an eager air.
HAMLET What hour now?
HORATIO I think it lacks of twelve.
MARCELLUS No, it is struck.   5
HORATIO
Indeed? I heard it not. Then it draws near the season
Wherein the spirit held his wont to walk.
    *A flourish of trumpets, and two pieces of ordnance
    goes off*
What does this mean, my lord?
HAMLET
The King doth wake tonight and takes his rouse,
Keeps wassail, and the swagg'ring upspring reels,   10
And as he drains his draughts of Rhenish down
The kettle-drum and trumpet thus bray out
The triumph of his pledge.
HORATIO Is it a custom?
HAMLET Ay, marry is't,   15
And to my mind, though I am native here
And to the manner born, it is a custom
More honoured in the breach than the observance.
    Enter the Ghost, as before
HORATIO Look, my lord, it comes.
HAMLET
Angels and ministers of grace defend us!   20
Be thou a spirit of health or goblin damned,
Bring with thee airs from heaven or blasts from hell,

Be thy intents wicked or charitable,
Thou com'st in such a questionable shape
That I will speak to thee. I'll call thee Hamlet,   25
King, father, royal Dane. O answer me!
Let me not burst in ignorance, but tell
Why thy canonized bones, hearsèd in death,
Have burst their cerements, why the sepulchre
Wherein we saw thee quietly enurned   30
Hath oped his ponderous and marble jaws
To cast thee up again. What may this mean,
That thou, dead corpse, again in complete steel,
Revisitst thus the glimpses of the moon,
Making night hideous, and we fools of nature   35
So horridly to shake our disposition
With thoughts beyond the reaches of our souls?
Say, why is this? Wherefore? What should we do?
    The Ghost beckons Hamlet
HORATIO
It beckons you to go away with it
As if it some impartment did desire   40
To you alone.
MARCELLUS (*to Hamlet*) Look with what courteous action
It wafts you to a more removèd ground.
But do not go with it.
HORATIO (*to Hamlet*)   No, by no means.
HAMLET
It will not speak. Then will I follow it.
HORATIO
Do not, my lord.
HAMLET   Why, what should be the fear?   45
I do not set my life at a pin's fee,
And for my soul, what can it do to that,
Being a thing immortal as itself?
    The Ghost beckons Hamlet
It waves me forth again. I'll follow it.
HORATIO
What if it tempt you toward the flood, my lord,   50
Or to the dreadful summit of the cliff
That beetles o'er his base into the sea,
And there assume some other horrible form
Which might deprive your sovereignty of reason
And draw you into madness? Think of it.   55
    The Ghost beckons Hamlet
HAMLET
It wafts me still. (*To the Ghost*) Go on, I'll follow thee.
MARCELLUS
You shall not go, my lord.
HAMLET   Hold off your hand.
HORATIO
Be ruled. You shall not go.
HAMLET   My fate cries out,
And makes each petty artere in this body
As hardy as the Nemean lion's nerve.   60
    The Ghost beckons Hamlet
Still am I called. Unhand me, gentlemen.
By heav'n, I'll make a ghost of him that lets me.
I say, away! (*To the Ghost*) Go on, I'll follow thee.
    Exeunt the Ghost and Hamlet

HORATIO
He waxes desperate with imagination.
MARCELLUS
Let's follow. 'Tis not fit thus to obey him.   65
HORATIO
Have after. To what issue will this come?
MARCELLUS
Something is rotten in the state of Denmark.
HORATIO
Heaven will direct it.
MARCELLUS   Nay, let's follow him.   *Exeunt*

1.5   *Enter the Ghost, and Prince Hamlet following*
HAMLET
Whither wilt thou lead me? Speak. I'll go no further.
GHOST
Mark me.
HAMLET   I will.
GHOST   My hour is almost come
When I to sulph'rous and tormenting flames
Must render up myself.
HAMLET   Alas, poor ghost!
GHOST
Pity me not, but lend thy serious hearing   5
To what I shall unfold.
HAMLET   Speak, I am bound to hear.
GHOST
So art thou to revenge when thou shalt hear.
HAMLET What?
GHOST I am thy father's spirit,
Doomed for a certain term to walk the night,   10
And for the day confined to fast in fires
Till the foul crimes done in my days of nature
Are burnt and purged away. But that I am forbid
To tell the secrets of my prison-house
I could a tale unfold whose lightest word   15
Would harrow up thy soul, freeze thy young blood,
Make thy two eyes like stars start from their spheres,
Thy knotty and combinèd locks to part,
And each particular hair to stand on end
Like quills upon the fretful porcupine.   20
But this eternal blazon must not be
To ears of flesh and blood. List, Hamlet, list, O list!
If thou didst ever thy dear father love—
HAMLET O God!
GHOST
Revenge his foul and most unnatural murder.   25
HAMLET Murder?
GHOST
Murder most foul, as in the best it is,
But this most foul, strange, and unnatural.
HAMLET
Haste, haste me to know it, that with wings as swift
As meditation or the thoughts of love   30
May sweep to my revenge.
GHOST   I find thee apt,
And duller shouldst thou be than the fat weed
That rots itself in ease on Lethe wharf

Wouldst thou not stir in this. Now, Hamlet, hear.
'Tis given out that, sleeping in mine orchard,   35
A serpent stung me. So the whole ear of Denmark
Is by a forgèd process of my death
Rankly abused. But know, thou noble youth,
The serpent that did sting thy father's life
Now wears his crown.   40
HAMLET
O my prophetic soul! Mine uncle?
GHOST
Ay, that incestuous, that adulterate beast,
With witchcraft of his wit, with traitorous gifts—
O wicked wit and gifts, that have the power
So to seduce!—won to his shameful lust   45
The will of my most seeming-virtuous queen.
O Hamlet, what a falling off was there!—
From me, whose love was of that dignity
That it went hand-in-hand even with the vow
I made to her in marriage, and to decline   50
Upon a wretch whose natural gifts were poor
To those of mine.
But virtue, as it never will be moved,
Though lewdness court it in a shape of heaven,
So lust, though to a radiant angel linked,   55
Will sate itself in a celestial bed,
And prey on garbage.
But soft, methinks I scent the morning's air.
Brief let me be. Sleeping within mine orchard,
My custom always in the afternoon,   60
Upon my secure hour thy uncle stole
With juice of cursèd hebenon in a vial,
And in the porches of mine ears did pour
The leperous distilment, whose effect
Holds such an enmity with blood of man   65
That swift as quicksilver it courses through
The natural gates and alleys of the body,
And with a sudden vigour it doth posset
And curd, like eager droppings into milk,
The thin and wholesome blood. So did it mine;   70
And a most instant tetter barked about,
Most lazar-like, with vile and loathsome crust,
All my smooth body.
Thus was I, sleeping, by a brother's hand
Of life, of crown, of queen at once dispatched,   75
Cut off even in the blossoms of my sin,
Unhouseled, dis-appointed, unaneled,
No reck'ning made, but sent to my account
With all my imperfections on my head.
O horrible, O horrible, most horrible!   80
If thou hast nature in thee, bear it not.
Let not the royal bed of Denmark be
A couch for luxury and damnèd incest.
But howsoever thou pursuest this act,
Taint not thy mind, nor let thy soul contrive   85
Against thy mother aught. Leave her to heaven,
And to those thorns that in her bosom lodge
To prick and sting her. Fare thee well at once.
The glow-worm shows the matin to be near,

And gins to pale his uneffectual fire.   90
Adieu, adieu, Hamlet. Remember me.   *Exit*
HAMLET
O all you host of heaven! O earth! What else?
And shall I couple hell? O fie! Hold, hold, my heart,
And you, my sinews, grow not instant old,
But bear me stiffly up. Remember thee?   95
Ay, thou poor ghost, while memory holds a seat
In this distracted globe. Remember thee?
Yea, from the table of my memory
I'll wipe away all trivial fond records,
All saws of books, all forms, all pressures past,   100
That youth and observation copied there,
And thy commandment all alone shall live
Within the book and volume of my brain
Unmixed with baser matter. Yes, yes, by heaven.
O most pernicious woman!   105
O villain, villain, smiling, damnèd villain!
My tables,
My tables—meet it is I set it down
That one may smile and smile and be a villain.
At least I'm sure it may be so in Denmark.   110
     He writes
So, uncle, there you are. Now to my word:
It is 'Adieu, adieu, remember me'.
I have sworn't.
HORATIO *and* MARCELLUS (*within*) My lord, my lord.
     Enter Horatio and Marcellus
MARCELLUS (*calling*) Lord Hamlet!   115
HORATIO Heaven secure him.
HAMLET So be it.
HORATIO (*calling*) Illo, ho, ho, my lord.
HAMLET
Hillo, ho, ho, boy; come, bird, come.
MARCELLUS How is't, my noble lord?   120
HORATIO (*to Hamlet*) What news, my lord?
HAMLET O wonderful!
HORATIO
Good my lord, tell it.
HAMLET   No, you'll reveal it.
HORATIO
Not I, my lord, by heaven.
MARCELLUS   Nor I, my lord.
HAMLET
How say you then, would heart of man once think it?
But you'll be secret?
HORATIO *and* MARCELLUS Ay, by heav'n, my lord.   126
HAMLET
There's ne'er a villain dwelling in all Denmark
But he's an arrant knave.
HORATIO
There needs no ghost, my lord, come from the grave
To tell us this.
HAMLET   Why, right, you are i'th' right,   130
And so without more circumstance at all
I hold it fit that we shake hands and part,
You as your business and desires shall point you—
For every man has business and desire,

Such as it is—and for mine own poor part,   135
Look you, I'll go pray.
HORATIO
These are but wild and whirling words, my lord.
HAMLET
I'm sorry they offend you, heartily,
Yes, faith, heartily.
HORATIO   There's no offence, my lord.
HAMLET
Yes, by Saint Patrick, but there is, Horatio,   140
And much offence, too. Touching this vision here,
It is an honest ghost, that let me tell you.
For your desire to know what is between us,
O'ermaster't as you may. And now, good friends,
As you are friends, scholars, and soldiers,   145
Give me one poor request.
HORATIO   What is't, my lord? We will.
HAMLET
Never make known what you have seen tonight.
HORATIO *and* MARCELLUS
My lord, we will not.
HAMLET   Nay, but swear't.
HORATIO
In faith, my lord, not I.
MARCELLUS   Nor I, my lord, in faith.
HAMLET
Upon my sword.
MARCELLUS   We have sworn, my lord, already.   150
HAMLET
Indeed, upon my sword, indeed.
     The Ghost cries under the stage
GHOST   Swear.
HAMLET
Ah ha, boy, sayst thou so? Art thou there, truepenny?—
Come on. You hear this fellow in the cellarage.
Consent to swear.
HORATIO   Propose the oath, my lord.
HAMLET
Never to speak of this that you have seen,   155
Swear by my sword.
GHOST (*under the stage*) Swear.
     ⌜*They swear*⌝
HAMLET
Hic et ubique? Then we'll shift our ground.—
Come hither, gentlemen,
And lay your hands again upon my sword.   160
Never to speak of this that you have heard,
Swear by my sword.
GHOST (*under the stage*) Swear.
     ⌜*They swear*⌝
HAMLET
Well said, old mole. Canst work i'th' earth so fast?
A worthy pioneer.—Once more remove, good friends.
HORATIO
O day and night, but this is wondrous strange!   166
HAMLET
And therefore as a stranger give it welcome.
There are more things in heaven and earth, Horatio,

Than are dreamt of in our philosophy. But come,
Here as before, never, so help you mercy,   170
How strange or odd soe'er I bear myself—
As I perchance hereafter shall think meet
To put an antic disposition on—
That you at such time seeing me never shall,
With arms encumbered thus, or this headshake,   175
Or by pronouncing of some doubtful phrase
As 'Well, we know' or 'We could an if we would',
Or 'If we list to speak', or 'There be, an if they might',
Or such ambiguous giving out, to note
That you know aught of me—this not to do,   180
So grace and mercy at your most need help you, swear.
GHOST (*under the stage*) Swear.
     ⌈*They swear*⌉
HAMLET
Rest, rest, perturbèd spirit.—So, gentlemen,
With all my love I do commend me to you,
And what so poor a man as Hamlet is   185
May do t'express his love and friending to you,
God willing, shall not lack. Let us go in together,
And still your fingers on your lips, I pray.
The time is out of joint. O cursèd spite
That ever I was born to set it right!   190
Nay, come, let's go together.   *Exeunt*

2.1   *Enter old Polonius with his man Reynaldo*
POLONIUS
Give him this money and these notes, Reynaldo.
REYNALDO I will, my lord.
POLONIUS
You shall do marv'lous wisely, good Reynaldo,
Before you visit him to make enquire
Of his behaviour.
REYNALDO   My lord, I did intend it.   5
POLONIUS
Marry, well said, very well said. Look you, sir,
Enquire me first what Danskers are in Paris,
And how, and who, what means, and where they keep,
What company, at what expense; and finding
By this encompassment and drift of question   10
That they do know my son, come you more nearer
Than your particular demands will touch it.
Take you, as 'twere, some distant knowledge of him,
As thus: 'I know his father and his friends,
And in part him'—do you mark this, Reynaldo?   15
REYNALDO Ay, very well, my lord.
POLONIUS
'And in part him, but', you may say, 'not well,
But if't be he I mean, he's very wild,
Addicted so and so'; and there put on him
What forgeries you please—marry, none so rank   20
As may dishonour him, take heed of that—
But, sir, such wanton, wild, and usual slips
As are companions noted and most known
To youth and liberty.
REYNALDO As gaming, my lord?   25
POLONIUS Ay, or drinking, fencing, swearing,
Quarrelling, drabbing—you may go so far.

REYNALDO
My lord, that would dishonour him.
POLONIUS
Faith, no, as you may season it in the charge.
You must not put another scandal on him,   30
That he is open to incontinency.
That's not my meaning—but breathe his faults so
     quaintly
That they may seem the taints of liberty,
The flash and outbreak of a fiery mind,
A savageness in unreclaimèd blood,   35
Of general assault.
REYNALDO   But, my good lord—
POLONIUS
Wherefore should you do this?
REYNALDO   Ay, my lord.
I would know that.
POLONIUS   Marry, sir, here's my drift,
And I believe it is a fetch of warrant:
You laying these slight sullies on my son,   40
As 'twere a thing a little soiled i'th' working,
Mark you, your party in converse, him you would
     sound,
Having ever seen in the prenominate crimes
The youth you breathe of guilty, be assured
He closes with you in this consequence: 45
'Good sir', or so, or 'friend', or 'gentleman',
According to the phrase and the addition
Of man and country.
REYNALDO   Very good, my lord.
POLONIUS
And then, sir, does a this—a does—
what was I about to say? By the mass, I was about to
say something. Where did I leave?   51
REYNALDO
At 'closes in the consequence', at 'friend,
Or so', and 'gentleman'.
POLONIUS
At 'closes in the consequence'—ay, marry,
He closes with you thus: 'I know the gentleman,   55
I saw him yesterday'—or t'other day,
Or then, or then—'with such and such, and, as you
     say,
There was a gaming, there o'ertook in 's rouse,
There falling out at tennis', or perchance
'I saw him enter such a house of sale',   60
Videlicet, a brothel, or so forth. See you now,
Your bait of falsehood takes this carp of truth;
And thus do we of wisdom and of reach
With windlasses and with assays of bias
By indirections find directions out.   65
So, by my former lecture and advice,
Shall you my son. You have me, have you not?
REYNALDO My lord, I have.
POLONIUS God b'wi' ye. Fare ye well.
REYNALDO Good my lord.   70
POLONIUS
Observe his inclination in yourself.
REYNALDO I shall, my lord.

POLONIUS And let him ply his music.
REYNALDO Well, my lord.
    Enter Ophelia
POLONIUS
    Farewell.   *Exit Reynaldo*
       How now, Ophelia, what's the matter?   75
OPHELIA
    Alas, my lord, I have been so affrighted.
POLONIUS With what, i'th' name of God?
OPHELIA
    My lord, as I was sewing in my chamber,
    Lord Hamlet, with his doublet all unbraced,
    No hat upon his head, his stockings fouled,   80
    Ungartered, and down-gyvèd to his ankle,
    Pale as his shirt, his knees knocking each other,
    And with a look so piteous in purport
    As if he had been loosèd out of hell
    To speak of horrors, he comes before me.   85
POLONIUS
    Mad for thy love?
OPHELIA   My lord, I do not know,
    But truly I do fear it.
POLONIUS   What said he?
OPHELIA
    He took me by the wrist and held me hard,
    Then goes he to the length of all his arm,
    And with his other hand thus o'er his brow   90
    He falls to such perusal of my face
    As a would draw it. Long stayed he so.
    At last, a little shaking of mine arm,
    And thrice his head thus waving up and down,
    He raised a sigh so piteous and profound   95
    That it did seem to shatter all his bulk
    And end his being. That done, he lets me go,
    And, with his head over his shoulder turned,
    He seemed to find his way without his eyes,
    For out o' doors he went without their help,   100
    And to the last bended their light on me.
POLONIUS
    Come, go with me. I will go seek the King.
    This is the very ecstasy of love,
    Whose violent property fordoes itself
    And leads the will to desperate undertakings   105
    As oft as any passion under heaven
    That does afflict our natures. I am sorry—
    What, have you given him any hard words of late?
OPHELIA
    No, my good lord, but as you did command
    I did repel his letters and denied   110
    His access to me.
POLONIUS   That hath made him mad.
    I am sorry that with better speed and judgement
    I had not quoted him. I feared he did but trifle
    And meant to wreck thee. But beshrew my jealousy!
    By heaven, it is as proper to our age   115
    To cast beyond ourselves in our opinions
    As it is common for the younger sort
    To lack discretion. Come, go we to the King.

    This must be known, which, being kept close, might
      move
    More grief to hide than hate to utter love.   *Exeunt*

2.2 ⌈*Flourish.*⌉ *Enter King Claudius and Queen*
    Gertrude, Rosencrantz and Guildenstern, with
    others
KING CLAUDIUS
    Welcome, dear Rosencrantz and Guildenstern.
    Moreover that we much did long to see you,
    The need we have to use you did provoke
    Our hasty sending. Something have you heard
    Of Hamlet's transformation—so I call it,   5
    Since not th'exterior nor the inward man
    Resembles that it was. What it should be,
    More than his father's death, that thus hath put him
    So much from th'understanding of himself,
    I cannot deem of. I entreat you both   10
    That, being of so young days brought up with him,
    And since so neighboured to his youth and humour,
    That you vouchsafe your rest here in our court
    Some little time, so by your companies
    To draw him on to pleasures, and to gather,   15
    So much as from occasions you may glean,
    Whether aught to us unknown afflicts him thus
    That, opened, lies within our remedy.
QUEEN GERTRUDE
    Good gentlemen, he hath much talked of you,
    And sure I am two men there is not living   20
    To whom he more adheres. If it will please you
    To show us so much gentry and good will
    As to expend your time with us a while
    For the supply and profit of our hope,
    Your visitation shall receive such thanks   25
    As fits a king's remembrance.
ROSENCRANTZ   Both your majesties
    Might, by the sovereign power you have of us,
    Put your dread pleasures more into command
    Than to entreaty.
GUILDENSTERN   But we both obey,
    And here give up ourselves in the full bent   30
    To lay our service freely at your feet
    To be commanded.
KING CLAUDIUS
    Thanks, Rosencrantz and gentle Guildenstern.
QUEEN GERTRUDE
    Thanks, Guildenstern and gentle Rosencrantz.
    And I beseech you instantly to visit   35
    My too-much changèd son.—Go, some of ye,
    And bring the gentlemen where Hamlet is.
GUILDENSTERN
    Heavens make our presence and our practices
    Pleasant and helpful to him.
QUEEN GERTRUDE   Ay, amen!
    Exeunt Rosencrantz and Guildenstern ⌈*with others*⌉
    Enter Polonius
POLONIUS
    Th'ambassadors from Norway, my good lord,   40
    Are joyfully returned.

KING CLAUDIUS
Thou still hast been the father of good news.
POLONIUS
Have I, my lord? Assure you, my good liege,
I hold my duty, as I hold my soul,
Both to my God and to my gracious King.   45
And I do think—or else this brain of mine
Hunts not the trail of policy so sure
As it hath used to do—that I have found
The very cause of Hamlet's lunacy.
KING CLAUDIUS
O speak of that, that I do long to hear!   50
POLONIUS
Give first admittance to th'ambassadors.
My news shall be the fruit to that great feast.
KING CLAUDIUS
Thyself do grace to them, and bring them in.
                                  Exit Polonius
He tells me, my sweet queen, that he hath found
The head and source of all your son's distemper.   55
QUEEN GERTRUDE
I doubt it is no other but the main—
His father's death and our o'er-hasty marriage.
KING CLAUDIUS
Well, we shall sift him.
       Enter Polonius, Valtemand, and Cornelius
                      Welcome, my good friends.
Say, Valtemand, what from our brother Norway?
VALTEMAND
Most fair return of greetings and desires.   60
Upon our first he sent out to suppress
His nephew's levies, which to him appeared
To be a preparation 'gainst the Polack;
But better looked into, he truly found
It was against your highness; whereat grieved   65
That so his sickness, age, and impotence
Was falsely borne in hand, sends out arrests
On Fortinbras, which he, in brief, obeys,
Receives rebuke from Norway, and, in fine,
Makes vow before his uncle never more   70
To give th'essay of arms against your majesty;
Whereon old Norway, overcome with joy,
Gives him three thousand crowns in annual fee
And his commission to employ those soldiers
So levied as before, against the Polack,   75
With an entreaty herein further shown,
       He gives a letter to Claudius
That it might please you to give quiet pass
Through your dominions for his enterprise
On such regards of safety and allowance
As therein are set down.
KING CLAUDIUS   It likes us well,   80
And at our more considered time we'll read,
Answer, and think upon this business.
Meantime we thank you for your well-took labour.
Go to your rest; at night we'll feast together.
Most welcome home.   85
       Exeunt Valtemand and Cornelius

POLONIUS
This business is very well ended.
My liege, and madam, to expostulate
What majesty should be, what duty is,
Why day is day, night night, and time is time,
Were nothing but to waste night, day, and time.   90
Therefore, since brevity is the soul of wit,
And tediousness the limbs and outward flourishes,
I will be brief. Your noble son is mad—
'Mad' call I it, for to define true madness,
What is't but to be nothing else but mad?   95
But let that go.
QUEEN GERTRUDE   More matter with less art.
POLONIUS
Madam, I swear I use no art at all.
That he is mad, 'tis true; 'tis true 'tis pity,
And pity 'tis 'tis true—a foolish figure,
But farewell it, for I will use no art.   100
Mad let us grant him, then; and now remains
That we find out the cause of this effect—
Or rather say 'the cause of this *defect*',
For this effect defective comes by cause.
Thus it remains, and the remainder thus.   105
Perpend.
I have a daughter—have whilst she is mine—
Who in her duty and obedience, mark,
Hath given me this. Now gather and surmise.   109
       He reads a letter
'To the celestial and my soul's idol, the most beautified
Ophelia'—that's an ill phrase, a vile phrase, 'beautified'
is a vile phrase. But you shall hear—'these in her
excellent white bosom, these'.
QUEEN GERTRUDE   Came this from Hamlet to her?
POLONIUS
Good madam, stay a while. I will be faithful.   115
    'Doubt thou the stars are fire,
      Doubt that the sun doth move,
      Doubt truth to be a liar,
      But never doubt I love.   119
O dear Ophelia, I am ill at these numbers. I have not
art to reckon my groans. But that I love thee best, O
most best, believe it. Adieu.
    Thine evermore, most dear lady, whilst this
    machine is to him,
                               Hamlet.'
This in obedience hath my daughter showed me,   125
And more above hath his solicitings,
As they fell out by time, by means, and place,
All given to mine ear.
KING CLAUDIUS   But how hath she
Received his love?
POLONIUS   What do you think of me?
KING CLAUDIUS
As of a man faithful and honourable.   130
POLONIUS
I would fain prove so. But what might you think,
When I had seen this hot love on the wing,
As I perceived it—I must tell you that—

Before my daughter told me, what might you,
Or my dear majesty your queen here, think,   135
If I had played the desk or table-book,
Or given my heart a winking mute and dumb,
Or looked upon this love with idle sight—
What might you think? No, I went round to work,
And my young mistress thus I did bespeak: 140
'Lord Hamlet is a prince out of thy star.
This must not be'. And then I precepts gave her,
That she should lock herself from his resort,
Admit no messengers, receive no tokens;
Which done, she took the fruits of my advice,   145
And he, repulsèd—a short tale to make—
Fell into a sadness, then into a fast,
Thence to a watch, thence into a weakness,
Thence to a lightness, and, by this declension,
Into the madness wherein now he raves,   150
And all we wail for.
KING CLAUDIUS (to Gertrude) Do you think 'tis this?
QUEEN GERTRUDE It may be; very likely.
POLONIUS
Hath there been such a time—I'd fain know that—
That I have positively said ' 'Tis so'   155
When it proved otherwise?
KING CLAUDIUS   Not that I know.
POLONIUS (touching his head, then his shoulder)
Take this from this if this be otherwise.
If circumstances lead me I will find
Where truth is hid, though it were hid indeed
Within the centre.
KING CLAUDIUS   How may we try it further?   160
POLONIUS
You know sometimes he walks four hours together
Here in the lobby.
QUEEN GERTRUDE   So he does indeed.
POLONIUS
At such a time I'll loose my daughter to him.
(To Claudius) Be you and I behind an arras then.
Mark the encounter. If he love her not,   165
And be not from his reason fall'n thereon,
Let me be no assistant for a state,
But keep a farm and carters.
KING CLAUDIUS   We will try it.
          Enter Prince Hamlet, madly attired, reading on a book
QUEEN GERTRUDE
But look where sadly the poor wretch comes reading.
POLONIUS
Away, I do beseech you both, away.   170
I'll board him presently. O give me leave.
                    Exeunt Claudius and Gertrude
How does my good Lord Hamlet?
HAMLET Well, God-'a'-mercy.
POLONIUS Do you know me, my lord?
HAMLET Excellent, excellent well. You're a fishmonger.
POLONIUS Not I, my lord.   176
HAMLET Then I would you were so honest a man.
POLONIUS Honest, my lord?

HAMLET Ay, sir. To be honest, as this world goes, is to
be one man picked out of ten thousand.   180
POLONIUS That's very true, my lord.
HAMLET For if the sun breed maggots in a dead dog, being
a good kissing carrion—have you a daughter?
POLONIUS I have, my lord.   184
HAMLET Let her not walk i'th' sun. Conception is a
blessing, but not as your daughter may conceive.
Friend, look to't.
POLONIUS (aside) How say you by that? Still harping on
my daughter. Yet he knew me not at first—a said I
was a fishmonger. A is far gone, far gone, and truly,
in my youth I suffered much extremity for love, very
near this. I'll speak to him again.—What do you read,
my lord?
HAMLET Words, words, words.
POLONIUS What is the matter, my lord?   195
HAMLET Between who?
POLONIUS I mean the matter you read, my lord.
HAMLET Slanders, sir; for the satirical slave says here that
old men have grey beards, that their faces are wrinkled,
their eyes purging thick amber or plum-tree gum, and
that they have a plentiful lack of wit, together with
most weak hams. All which, sir, though I most
powerfully and potently believe, yet I hold it not honesty
to have it thus set down; for you yourself, sir, should
be old as I am—if, like a crab, you could go backward.
POLONIUS (aside) Though this be madness, yet there is
method in't.—Will you walk out of the air, my lord?
HAMLET Into my grave.   208
POLONIUS Indeed, that is out o'th' air. (Aside) How pregnant sometimes his replies are! A happiness that often
madness hits on, which reason and sanity could not
so prosperously be delivered of. I will leave him, and
suddenly contrive the means of meeting between him
and my daughter.—My lord, I will take my leave of
you.   215
HAMLET You cannot, sir, take from me anything that I
will more willingly part withal—except my life, my life,
my life.
POLONIUS (going) Fare you well, my lord.
HAMLET These tedious old fools!   220
          ⌜Enter Guildenstern and Rosencrantz⌝
POLONIUS You go to seek the Lord Hamlet. There he is.
ROSENCRANTZ God save you, sir.
GUILDENSTERN ⌜to Polonius⌝ Mine honoured lord.
                              ⌜Exit Polonius⌝
ROSENCRANTZ (to Hamlet) My most dear lord.   224
HAMLET My ex'llent good friends. How dost thou,
Guildenstern? Ah, Rosencrantz—good lads, how do ye
both?
ROSENCRANTZ
As the indifferent children of the earth.
GUILDENSTERN
Happy in that we are not over-happy,
On Fortune's cap we are not the very button.   230
HAMLET Nor the soles of her shoe?

ROSENCRANTZ Neither, my lord.

HAMLET Then you live about her waist, or in the middle of her favour?

GUILDENSTERN Faith, her privates we.   235

HAMLET In the secret parts of Fortune? O, most true, she is a strumpet. What's the news?

ROSENCRANTZ None, my lord, but that the world's grown honest.   239

HAMLET Then is doomsday near. But your news is not true. Let me question more in particular. What have you, my good friends, deserved at the hands of Fortune that she sends you to prison hither?

GUILDENSTERN Prison, my lord?

HAMLET Denmark's a prison.   245

ROSENCRANTZ Then is the world one.

HAMLET A goodly one, in which there are many confines, wards, and dungeons, Denmark being one o'th' worst.

ROSENCRANTZ We think not so, my lord.   249

HAMLET Why, then 'tis none to you, for there is nothing either good or bad but thinking makes it so. To me it is a prison.

ROSENCRANTZ Why, then your ambition makes it one; 'tis too narrow for your mind.   254

HAMLET O God, I could be bounded in a nutshell and count myself a king of infinite space, were it not that I have bad dreams.

GUILDENSTERN Which dreams indeed are ambition; for the very substance of the ambitious is merely the shadow of a dream.   260

HAMLET A dream itself is but a shadow.

ROSENCRANTZ Truly, and I hold ambition of so airy and light a quality that it is but a shadow's shadow.

HAMLET Then are our beggars bodies, and our monarchs and outstretched heroes the beggars' shadows. Shall we to th' court? For, by my fay, I cannot reason.   266

ROSENCRANTZ and GUILDENSTERN We'll wait upon you.

HAMLET No such matter. I will not sort you with the rest of my servants, for, to speak to you like an honest man, I am most dreadfully attended. But in the beaten way of friendship, what make you at Elsinore?   271

ROSENCRANTZ To visit you, my lord, no other occasion.

HAMLET Beggar that I am, I am even poor in thanks, but I thank you; and sure, dear friends, my thanks are too dear a halfpenny. Were you not sent for? Is it your own inclining? Is it a free visitation? Come, deal justly with me. Come, come. Nay, speak.

GUILDENSTERN What should we say, my lord?   278

HAMLET Why, anything—but to th' purpose. You were sent for, and there is a kind of confession in your looks which your modesties have not craft enough to colour. I know the good King and Queen have sent for you.

ROSENCRANTZ To what end, my lord?   283

HAMLET That you must teach me. But let me conjure you by the rights of our fellowship, by the consonancy of our youth, by the obligation of our ever-preserved love, and by what more dear a better proposer could charge you withal, be even and direct with me whether you were sent for or no.

ROSENCRANTZ (to Guildenstern) What say you?   290

HAMLET Nay then, I have an eye of you—if you love me, hold not off.

GUILDENSTERN My lord, we were sent for.

HAMLET I will tell you why. So shall my anticipation prevent your discovery, and your secrecy to the King and Queen moult no feather. I have of late—but wherefore I know not—lost all my mirth, forgone all custom of exercise; and indeed it goes so heavily with my disposition that this goodly frame, the earth, seems to me a sterile promontory. This most excellent canopy the air, look you, this brave o'erhanging, this majestical roof fretted with golden fire—why, it appears no other thing to me than a foul and pestilent congregation of vapours. What a piece of work is a man! How noble in reason, how infinite in faculty, in form and moving how express and admirable, in action how like an angel, in apprehension how like a god—the beauty of the world, the paragon of animals! And yet to me what is this quintessence of dust? Man delights not me—no, nor woman neither, though by your smiling you seem to say so.   311

ROSENCRANTZ My lord, there was no such stuff in my thoughts.

HAMLET Why did you laugh, then, when I said 'Man delights not me'?   315

ROSENCRANTZ To think, my lord, if you delight not in man what lenten entertainment the players shall receive from you. We coted them on the way, and hither are they coming to offer you service.   319

HAMLET He that plays the King shall be welcome; his majesty shall have tribute of me. The adventurous Knight shall use his foil and target, the Lover shall not sigh gratis, the Humorous Man shall end his part in peace, the Clown shall make those laugh whose lungs are tickled o'th' sear, and the Lady shall say her mind freely, or the blank verse shall halt for't. What players are they?

ROSENCRANTZ Even those you were wont to take delight in, the tragedians of the city.   329

HAMLET How chances it they travel? Their residence both in reputation and profit was better both ways.

ROSENCRANTZ I think their inhibition comes by the means of the late innovation.

HAMLET Do they hold the same estimation they did when I was in the city? Are they so followed?   335

ROSENCRANTZ No, indeed, they are not.

HAMLET How comes it? Do they grow rusty?

ROSENCRANTZ Nay, their endeavour keeps in the wonted pace. But there is, sir, an eyrie of children, little eyases, that cry out on the top of question and are most tyrannically clapped for't. These are now the fashion, and so berattle the common stages—so they call them—that many wearing rapiers are afraid of goose-quills, and dare scarce come thither.   344

HAMLET What, are they children? Who maintains 'em? How are they escoted? Will they pursue the quality no longer than they can sing? Will they not say afterwards,

if they should grow themselves to common players—
as it is like most will, if their means are not better—
their writers do them wrong to make them exclaim
against their own succession? 351

ROSENCRANTZ Faith, there has been much to-do on both
sides, and the nation holds it no sin to tarre them to
controversy. There was for a while no money bid for
argument unless the poet and the player went to cuffs
in the question. 356

HAMLET Is't possible?

GUILDENSTERN O, there has been much throwing about of
brains.

HAMLET Do the boys carry it away? 360

ROSENCRANTZ Ay, that they do, my lord, Hercules and his
load too.

HAMLET It is not strange; for mine uncle is King of
Denmark, and those that would make mows at him
while my father lived give twenty, forty, an hundred
ducats apiece for his picture in little. 'Sblood, there is
something in this more than natural, if philosophy
could find it out.

A flourish for the Players

GUILDENSTERN There are the players. 369

HAMLET Gentlemen, you are welcome to Elsinore. Your
hands, come. Th'appurtenance of welcome is fashion
and ceremony. Let me comply with you in the garb,
lest my extent to the players—which, I tell you, must
show fairly outward—should more appear like
entertainment than yours. 375

⌈*He shakes hands with them*⌉

You are welcome. But my uncle-father and aunt-mother
are deceived.

GUILDENSTERN In what, my dear lord?

HAMLET I am but mad north-north-west; when the wind
is southerly, I know a hawk from a handsaw. 380

Enter Polonius

POLONIUS Well be with you, gentlemen.

HAMLET (*aside*) Hark you, Guildenstern, and you too—at
each ear a hearer—that great baby you see there is
not yet out of his swathing-clouts.

ROSENCRANTZ (*aside*) Haply he's the second time come to
them, for they say an old man is twice a child. 386

HAMLET (*aside*) I will prophesy he comes to tell me of the
players. Mark it.—You say right, sir, for o' Monday
morning, 'twas so indeed.

POLONIUS My lord, I have news to tell you. 390

HAMLET My lord, I have news to tell you. When Roscius
was an actor in Rome—

POLONIUS The actors are come hither, my lord.

HAMLET Buzz, buzz.

POLONIUS Upon mine honour— 395

HAMLET Then came each actor on his ass.

POLONIUS The best actors in the world, either for tragedy,
comedy, history, pastoral, pastorical-comical, historical-
pastoral, tragical-historical, tragical-comical-historical-
pastoral, scene individable or poem unlimited. Seneca
cannot be too heavy, nor Plautus too light. For the law
of writ and the liberty, these are the only men.

HAMLET O Jephthah, judge of Israel, what a treasure hadst
thou!

POLONIUS What a treasure had he, my lord? 405

HAMLET Why,
'One fair daughter and no more,
The which he lovèd passing well'.

POLONIUS (*aside*) Still on my daughter.

HAMLET Am I not i'th' right, old Jephthah? 410

POLONIUS If you call me Jephthah, my lord, I have a
daughter that I love passing well.

HAMLET Nay, that follows not.

POLONIUS What follows then, my lord?

HAMLET Why 415
'As by lot
God wot',
and then you know
'It came to pass
As most like it was'— 420
the first row of the pious chanson will show you more,
for look where my abridgements come.

Enter four or five Players

You're welcome, masters, welcome all.—I am glad to
see thee well.—Welcome, good friends.—O, my old
friend! Thy face is valanced since I saw thee last.
Com'st thou to beard me in Denmark?—What, my
young lady and mistress. By'r Lady, your ladyship is
nearer heaven than when I saw you last by the altitude
of a chopine. Pray God your voice, like a piece of
uncurrent gold, be not cracked within the ring.—
Masters, you are all welcome. We'll e'en to't like French
falc'ners, fly at anything we see. We'll have a speech
straight. Come, give us a taste of your quality. Come,
a passionate speech.

FIRST PLAYER What speech, my good lord? 435

HAMLET I heard thee speak me a speech once, but it was
never acted, or, if it was, not above once; for the play,
I remember, pleased not the million. 'Twas caviare to
the general. But it was—as I received it, and others
whose judgements in such matters cried in the top of
mine—an excellent play, well digested in the scenes,
set down with as much modesty as cunning. I remember
one said there was no sallets in the lines to make the
matter savoury, nor no matter in the phrase that might
indict the author of affectation, but called it an honest
method, as wholesome as sweet, and by very much
more handsome than fine. One speech in it I chiefly
loved, 'twas Aeneas' tale to Dido, and thereabout of it
especially where he speaks of Priam's slaughter. If it
live in your memory, begin at this line—let me see, let
me see: 451
'The rugged Pyrrhus, like th'Hyrcanian beast'—
'tis not so. It begins with Pyrrhus—
'The rugged Pyrrhus, he whose sable arms,
Black as his purpose, did the night resemble 455
When he lay couchèd in the ominous horse,
Hath now this dread and black complexion smeared
With heraldry more dismal. Head to foot
Now is he total gules, horridly tricked

With blood of fathers, mothers, daughters, sons,   460
Baked and impasted with the parching streets,
That lend a tyrranous and damnèd light
To their vile murders. Roasted in wrath and fire,
And thus o'er-sizèd with coagulate gore,
With eyes like carbuncles the hellish Pyrrhus   465
Old grandsire Priam seeks.'
So, proceed you.
POLONIUS Fore God, my lord, well spoken, with good
accent and good discretion.
FIRST PLAYER   'Anon he finds him,   470
Striking too short at Greeks. His antique sword,
Rebellious to his arm, lies where it falls,
Repugnant to command. Unequal match,
Pyrrhus at Priam drives, in rage strikes wide;
But with the whiff and wind of his fell sword   475
Th'unnervèd father falls. Then senseless Ilium,
Seeming to feel his blow, with flaming top
Stoops to his base, and with a hideous crash
Takes prisoner Pyrrhus' ear. For lo, his sword,
Which was declining on the milky head   480
Of reverend Priam, seemed i'th' air to stick.
So, as a painted tyrant, Pyrrhus stood,
And, like a neutral to his will and matter,
Did nothing.
But as we often see against some storm   485
A silence in the heavens, the rack stand still,
The bold winds speechless, and the orb below
As hush as death, anon the dreadful thunder
Doth rend the region: so, after Pyrrhus' pause,
A rousèd vengeance sets him new a-work;   490
And never did the Cyclops' hammers fall
On Mars his armour, forged for proof eterne,
With less remorse than Pyrrhus' bleeding sword
Now falls on Priam.
Out, out, thou strumpet Fortune! All you gods,   495
In general synod, take away her power,
Break all the spokes and fellies from her wheel,
And bowl the round nave down the hill of heaven,
As low as to the fiends!'
POLONIUS This is too long.   500
HAMLET It shall to the barber's, with your beard. (To First
Player) Prithee, say on. He's for a jig or a tale of
bawdry, or he sleeps. Say on, come to Hecuba.
FIRST PLAYER
'But who, O who had seen the mobbled queen'—
HAMLET 'The mobbled queen'?   505
POLONIUS That's good; 'mobbled queen' is good.
FIRST PLAYER
'Run barefoot up and down, threat'ning the flames
With bisson rheum; a clout upon that head
Where late the diadem stood, and for a robe,
About her lank and all o'er-teemèd loins,   510
A blanket in th'alarm of fear caught up—
Who this had seen, with tongue in venom steeped,
'Gainst Fortune's state would treason have pronounced.
But if the gods themselves did see her then,

When she saw Pyrrhus make malicious sport   515
In mincing with his sword her husband's limbs,
The instant burst of clamour that she made—
Unless things mortal move them not at all—
Would have made milch the burning eyes of heaven,
And passion in the gods.'   520
POLONIUS Look whe'er he has not turned his colour, and
has tears in 's eyes. (To First Player) Prithee, no more.
HAMLET (to First Player) 'Tis well. I'll have thee speak out
the rest soon. (To Polonius) Good my lord, will you see
the players well bestowed? Do ye hear?—let them be
well used, for they are the abstracts and brief chronicles
of the time. After your death you were better have a
bad epitaph than their ill report while you live.
POLONIUS My lord, I will use them according to their
desert.   530
HAMLET God's bodykins, man, much better. Use every
man after his desert, and who should scape whipping?
Use them after your own honour and dignity—the less
they deserve, the more merit is in your bounty. Take
them in.   535
POLONIUS (to Players) Come, sirs.   Exit
HAMLET (to Players) Follow him, friends. We'll hear a play
tomorrow. Dost thou hear me, old friend? Can you play
the murder of Gonzago?
⌐PLAYERS⌐ Ay, my lord.   540
HAMLET We'll ha't tomorrow night. You could for a need
study a speech of some dozen or sixteen lines which I
would set down and insert in't, could ye not?
⌐PLAYERS⌐ Ay, my lord.   544
HAMLET Very well. Follow that lord, and look you mock
him not.   ⌐Exeunt Players⌐
My good friends, I'll leave you till night. You are
welcome to Elsinore.
ROSENCRANTZ Good my lord.
HAMLET
Ay, so. God b'wi' ye.   Exeunt all but Hamlet
Now I am alone.   550
O, what a rogue and peasant slave am I!
Is it not monstrous that this player here,
But in a fiction, in a dream of passion,
Could force his soul so to his whole conceit
That from her working all his visage wanned,   555
Tears in his eyes, distraction in 's aspect,
A broken voice, and his whole function suiting
With forms to his conceit? And all for nothing.
For Hecuba!
What's Hecuba to him, or he to Hecuba,   560
That he should weep for her? What would he do
Had he the motive and the cue for passion
That I have? He would drown the stage with tears,
And cleave the general ear with horrid speech,
Make mad the guilty and appal the free,   565
Confound the ignorant, and amaze indeed
The very faculty of eyes and ears. Yet I,
A dull and muddy-mettled rascal, peak
Like John-a-dreams, unpregnant of my cause,

And can say nothing—no, not for a king   570
Upon whose property and most dear life
A damned defeat was made. Am I a coward?
Who calls me villain, breaks my pate across,
Plucks off my beard and blows it in my face,
Tweaks me by th' nose, gives me the lie i'th' throat 575
As deep as to the lungs? Who does me this?
Ha? 'Swounds, I should take it; for it cannot be
But I am pigeon-livered and lack gall
To make oppression bitter, or ere this
I should 'a' fatted all the region kites   580
With this slave's offal. Bloody, bawdy villain!
Remorseless, treacherous, lecherous, kindless villain!
O, vengeance!—
Why, what an ass am I? Ay, sure, this is most brave,
That I, the son of the dear murderèd,   585
Prompted to my revenge by heaven and hell,
Must, like a whore, unpack my heart with words
And fall a-cursing like a very drab,
A scullion! Fie upon't, foh!—About, my brain.
I have heard that guilty creatures sitting at a play 590
Have by the very cunning of the scene
Been struck so to the soul that presently
They have proclaimed their malefactions;
For murder, though it have no tongue, will speak
With most miraculous organ. I'll have these players 595
Play something like the murder of my father
Before mine uncle. I'll observe his looks,
I'll tent him to the quick. If a but blench,
I know my course. The spirit that I have seen
May be the devil, and the devil hath power   600
T'assume a pleasing shape; yea, and perhaps,
Out of my weakness and my melancholy—
As he is very potent with such spirits—
Abuses me to damn me. I'll have grounds
More relative than this. The play's the thing   605
Wherein I'll catch the conscience of the King.   Exit

3.1   *Enter King Claudius, Queen Gertrude, Polonius,*
        Ophelia, Rosencrantz, Guildenstern, and lords
KING CLAUDIUS (*to Rosencrantz and Guildenstern*)
And can you by no drift of circumstance
Get from him why he puts on this confusion,
Grating so harshly all his days of quiet
With turbulent and dangerous lunacy?
ROSENCRANTZ
He does confess he feels himself distracted,   5
But from what cause a will by no means speak.
GUILDENSTERN
Nor do we find him forward to be sounded,
But with a crafty madness keeps aloof
When we would bring him on to some confession
Of his true state.   10
QUEEN GERTRUDE Did he receive you well?
ROSENCRANTZ Most like a gentleman.
GUILDENSTERN
But with much forcing of his disposition.

ROSENCRANTZ
Niggard of question, but of our demands
Most free in his reply.
QUEEN GERTRUDE   Did you assay him   15
To any pastime?
ROSENCRANTZ
Madam, it so fell out that certain players
We o'er-raught on the way. Of these we told him,
And there did seem in him a kind of joy
To hear of it. They are about the court,   20
And, as I think, they have already order
This night to play before him.
POLONIUS   'Tis most true,
And he beseeched me to entreat your majesties
To hear and see the matter.
KING CLAUDIUS
With all my heart; and it doth much content me   25
To hear him so inclined.—Good gentlemen,
Give him a further edge, and drive his purpose on
To these delights.
ROSENCRANTZ We shall, my lord.
              Exeunt Rosencrantz and Guildenstern
KING CLAUDIUS Sweet Gertrude, leave us too,   30
For we have closely sent for Hamlet hither,
That he, as 'twere by accident, may here
Affront Ophelia.
Her father and myself, lawful espials,
Will so bestow ourselves that, seeing unseen,   35
We may of their encounter frankly judge,
And gather by him, as he is behaved,
If't be th'affliction of his love or no
That thus he suffers for.
QUEEN GERTRUDE   I shall obey you.
And for your part, Ophelia, I do wish   40
That your good beauties be the happy cause
Of Hamlet's wildness; so shall I hope your virtues
Will bring him to his wonted way again,
To both your honours.
OPHELIA   Madam, I wish it may.
                                 Exit Gertrude
POLONIUS
Ophelia, walk you here.—Gracious, so please you,   45
We will bestow ourselves.—Read on this book,
That show of such an exercise may colour
Your loneliness. We are oft to blame in this:
'Tis too much proved that with devotion's visage
And pious action we do sugar o'er   50
The devil himself.
KING CLAUDIUS   O, 'tis too true.
(*Aside*) How smart a lash that speech doth give my
            conscience.
The harlot's cheek, beautied with plast'ring art,
Is not more ugly to the thing that helps it
Than is my deed to my most painted word.   55
O heavy burden!
POLONIUS
I hear him coming. Let's withdraw, my lord.
                    Exeunt Claudius and Polonius

Enter Prince Hamlet

HAMLET

To be, or not to be; that is the question:
Whether 'tis nobler in the mind to suffer
The slings and arrows of outrageous fortune,　　60
Or to take arms against a sea of troubles,
And, by opposing, end them. To die, to sleep—
No more, and by a sleep to say we end
The heartache and the thousand natural shocks
That flesh is heir to—'tis a consummation　　65
Devoutly to be wished. To die, to sleep.
To sleep, perchance to dream. Ay, there's the rub,
For in that sleep of death what dreams may come
When we have shuffled off this mortal coil
Must give us pause. There's the respect　　70
That makes calamity of so long life,
For who would bear the whips and scorns of time,
Th'oppressor's wrong, the proud man's contumely,
The pangs of disprized love, the law's delay,
The insolence of office, and the spurns　　75
That patient merit of th'unworthy takes,
When he himself might his quietus make
With a bare bodkin? Who would these fardels bear,
To grunt and sweat under a weary life,
But that the dread of something after death,　　80
The undiscovered country from whose bourn
No traveller returns, puzzles the will,
And makes us rather bear those ills we have
Than fly to others that we know not of?
Thus conscience does make cowards of us all,　　85
And thus the native hue of resolution
Is sicklied o'er with the pale cast of thought,
And enterprises of great pith and moment
With this regard their currents turn awry,
And lose the name of action. Soft you, now,　　90
The fair Ophelia!—Nymph, in thy orisons
Be all my sins remembered.

OPHELIA　　　　　　　　　Good my lord,
How does your honour for this many a day?

HAMLET

I humbly thank you, well, well, well.

OPHELIA

My lord, I have remembrances of yours　　95
That I have longèd long to redeliver.
I pray you now receive them.

HAMLET

No, no, I never gave you aught.

OPHELIA

My honoured lord, you know right well you did,
And with them words of so sweet breath composed　100
As made the things more rich. Their perfume lost,
Take these again; for to the noble mind
Rich gifts wax poor when givers prove unkind.
There, my lord.

HAMLET Ha, ha? Are you honest?　　105
OPHELIA My lord.
HAMLET Are you fair?
OPHELIA What means your lordship?

HAMLET That if you be honest and fair, your honesty
should admit no discourse to your beauty.　　110
OPHELIA Could beauty, my lord, have better commerce
than with honesty?
HAMLET Ay, truly, for the power of beauty will sooner
transform honesty from what it is to a bawd than the
force of honesty can translate beauty into his likeness.
This was sometime a paradox, but now the time gives
it proof. I did love you once.
OPHELIA Indeed, my lord, you made me believe so.　　120
HAMLET You should not have believed me, for virtue
cannot so inoculate our old stock but we shall relish
of it. I loved you not.　　121
OPHELIA I was the more deceived.
HAMLET Get thee to a nunnery. Why wouldst thou be a
breeder of sinners? I am myself indifferent honest, but
yet I could accuse me of such things that it were better
my mother had not borne me. I am very proud,
revengeful, ambitious, with more offences at my beck
than I have thoughts to put them in, imagination to
give them shape, or time to act them in. What should
such fellows as I do crawling between heaven and
earth? We are arrant knaves, all. Believe none of us.
Go thy ways to a nunnery. Where's your father?
OPHELIA At home, my lord.
HAMLET Let the doors be shut upon him, that he may
play the fool nowhere but in 's own house. Farewell.
OPHELIA O help him, you sweet heavens!　　136
HAMLET If thou dost marry, I'll give thee this plague for
thy dowry: be thou as chaste as ice, as pure as snow,
thou shalt not escape calumny. Get thee to a nunnery,
go, farewell. Or if thou wilt needs marry, marry a fool;
for wise men know well enough what monsters you
make of them. To a nunnery, go, and quickly, too.
Farewell.
OPHELIA O heavenly powers, restore him!　　144
HAMLET I have heard of your paintings, too, well enough.
God hath given you one face, and you make yourselves
another. You jig, you amble, and you lisp, and
nickname God's creatures, and make your wantonness
your ignorance. Go to, I'll no more on't. It hath made
me mad. I say we will have no more marriages. Those
that are married already—all but one—shall live. The
rest shall keep as they are. To a nunnery, go.　　*Exit*

OPHELIA

O what a noble mind is here o'erthrown!
The courtier's, soldier's, scholar's eye, tongue, sword,
Th'expectancy and rose of the fair state,　　155
The glass of fashion and the mould of form,
Th'observed of all observers, quite, quite, down!
And I, of ladies most deject and wretched,
That sucked the honey of his music vows,
Now see that noble and most sovereign reason　　160
Like sweet bells jangled out of tune and harsh;
That unmatched form and feature of blown youth
Blasted with ecstasy. O woe is me,
T'have seen what I have seen, see what I see!

Enter King Claudius and Polonius
KING CLAUDIUS
Love? His affections do not that way tend,   165
Nor what he spake, though it lacked form a little,
Was not like madness. There's something in his soul
O'er which his melancholy sits on brood,
And I do doubt the hatch and the disclose
Will be some danger; which to prevent   170
I have in quick determination
Thus set it down: he shall with speed to England
For the demand of our neglected tribute.
Haply the seas and countries different,
With variable objects, shall expel   175
This something-settled matter in his heart,
Whereon his brains still beating puts him thus
From fashion of himself. What think you on't?
POLONIUS
It shall do well. But yet do I believe
The origin and commencement of this grief   180
Sprung from neglected love.—How now, Ophelia?
You need not tell us what Lord Hamlet said;
We heard it all.—My lord, do as you please,
But, if you hold it fit, after the play
Let his queen mother all alone entreat him   185
To show his griefs. Let her be round with him,
And I'll be placed, so please you, in the ear
Of all their conference. If she find him not,
To England send him, or confine him where
Your wisdom best shall think.
KING CLAUDIUS   It shall be so.   190
Madness in great ones must not unwatched go.
                                                Exeunt

3.2   *Enter Prince Hamlet and two or three of the Players*
HAMLET Speak the speech, I pray you, as I pronounced
  it to you—trippingly on the tongue; but if you mouth
  it, as many of your players do, I had as lief the town-
  crier had spoke my lines. Nor do not saw the air too
  much with your hand, thus, but use all gently; for in
  the very torrent, tempest, and as I may say the
  whirlwind of your passion, you must acquire and beget
  a temperance that may give it smoothness. O, it offends
  me to the soul to hear a robustious, periwig-pated
  fellow tear a passion to tatters, to very rags, to split
  the ears of the groundlings, who for the most part are
  capable of nothing but inexplicable dumb shows and
  noise. I would have such a fellow whipped for o'erdoing
  Termagant. It out-Herods Herod. Pray you avoid it.
A PLAYER I warrant your honour.   15
HAMLET Be not too tame, neither; but let your own
  discretion be your tutor. Suit the action to the word,
  the word to the action, with this special observance:
  that you o'erstep not the modesty of nature. For
  anything so overdone is from the purpose of playing,
  whose end, both at the first and now, was and is to
  hold as 'twere the mirror up to nature, to show virtue
  her own feature, scorn her own image, and the very
  age and body of the time his form and pressure. Now

this overdone, or come tardy off, though it make the
unskilful laugh, cannot but make the judicious grieve;
the censure of the which one must in your allowance
o'erweigh a whole theatre of others. O, there be players
that I have seen play, and heard others praise, and
that highly, not to speak it profanely, that neither
having the accent of Christians nor the gait of Christian,
pagan, nor no man, have so strutted and bellowed that
I have thought some of nature's journeymen had made
men, and not made them well, they imitated humanity
so abominably.   35
A PLAYER I hope we have reformed that indifferently with
  us, sir.
HAMLET O, reform it altogether. And let those that play
  your clowns speak no more than is set down for them;
  for there be of them that will themselves laugh to set
  on some quantity of barren spectators to laugh too,
  though in the mean time some necessary question of
  the play be then to be considered. That's villainous,
  and shows a most pitiful ambition in the fool that uses
  it. Go make you ready.   *Exeunt Players*
          Enter Polonius, Guildenstern, and Rosencrantz
  (*To Polonius*) How now, my lord? Will the King hear
  this piece of work?
POLONIUS And the Queen too, and that presently.
HAMLET Bid the players make haste.   *Exit Polonius*
  Will you two help to hasten them?
ROSENCRANTZ *and* GUILDENSTERN   We will, my lord. 50
                                                Exeunt
HAMLET
What ho, Horatio!
          Enter Horatio
HORATIO   Here, sweet lord, at your service.
HAMLET
Horatio, thou art e'en as just a man
As e'er my conversation coped withal.
HORATIO
O my dear lord—
HAMLET   Nay, do not think I flatter;
For what advancement may I hope from thee,   55
That no revenue hast but thy good spirits
To feed and clothe thee? Why should the poor be
          flattered?
No, let the candied tongue lick absurd pomp,
And crook the pregnant hinges of the knee
Where thrift may follow feigning. Dost thou hear?— 60
Since my dear soul was mistress of her choice
And could of men distinguish, her election
Hath sealed thee for herself; for thou hast been
As one in suff'ring all that suffers nothing,
A man that Fortune's buffets and rewards   65
Hath ta'en with equal thanks; and blest are those
Whose blood and judgement are so well commingled
That they are not a pipe for Fortune's finger
To sound what stop she please. Give me that man
That is not passion's slave, and I will wear him   70
In my heart's core, ay, in my heart of heart,
As I do thee. Something too much of this.

There is a play tonight before the King.
One scene of it comes near the circumstance
Which I have told thee of my father's death.   75
I prithee, when thou seest that act afoot,
Even with the very comment of thy soul
Observe mine uncle. If his occulted guilt
Do not itself unkennel in one speech,
It is a damnèd ghost that we have seen,   80
And my imaginations are as foul
As Vulcan's stithy. Give him heedful note,
For I mine eyes will rivet to his face,
And after, we will both our judgements join
To censure of his seeming.

HORATIO   Well, my lord.   85
If a steal aught the whilst this play is playing
And scape detecting, I will pay the theft.
⌈*Sound a flourish*⌉

HAMLET
They are coming to the play. I must be idle.
Get you a place.
⌈*Danish march. Enter King Claudius, Queen
Gertrude, Polonius, Ophelia, Rosencrantz,
Guildenstern, and other lords attendant, with the
King's guard carrying torches*⌉

KING CLAUDIUS   How fares our cousin Hamlet?   89
HAMLET Excellent, i'faith, of the chameleon's dish. I eat
the air, promise-crammed. You cannot feed capons so.
KING CLAUDIUS I have nothing with this answer, Hamlet.
These words are not mine.
HAMLET No, nor mine now. (*To Polonius*) My lord, you
played once i'th' university, you say.   95
POLONIUS That I did, my lord, and was accounted a good
actor.
HAMLET And what did you enact?
POLONIUS I did enact Julius Caesar. I was killed i'th'
Capitol. Brutus killed me.   100
HAMLET It was a brute part of him to kill so capital a calf
there.—Be the players ready?
ROSENCRANTZ Ay, my lord, they stay upon your patience.
QUEEN GERTRUDE
Come hither, my good Hamlet. Sit by me.
HAMLET No, good-mother, here's mettle more attractive.
He sits by Ophelia
POLONIUS (*aside*) O ho, do you mark that?   106
HAMLET (*to Ophelia*) Lady, shall I lie in your lap?
OPHELIA No, my lord.
HAMLET I mean my head upon your lap?
OPHELIA Ay, my lord.   110
HAMLET Do you think I meant country matters?
OPHELIA I think nothing, my lord.
HAMLET That's a fair thought to lie between maids' legs.
OPHELIA What is, my lord?
HAMLET No thing.   115
OPHELIA You are merry, my lord.
HAMLET Who, I?
OPHELIA Ay, my lord.
HAMLET O God, your only jig-maker! What should a man

do but be merry? For look you how cheerfully my
mother looks, and my father died within 's two hours.
OPHELIA Nay, 'tis twice two months, my lord.   122
HAMLET So long? Nay then, let the devil wear black, for
I'll have a suit of sables. O heavens, die two months
ago and not forgotten yet! Then there's hope a great
man's memory may outlive his life half a year. But,
by'r Lady, a must build churches then, or else shall a
suffer not thinking on, with the hobby-horse, whose
epitaph is 'For O, for O, the hobby-horse is forgot.'
*Hautboys play. The dumb show enters. Enter a King
and a Queen very lovingly, the Queen embracing him.
She kneels and makes show of protestation unto him.
He takes her up and declines his head upon her neck.
He lays him down upon a bank of flowers. She, seeing
him asleep, leaves him. Anon comes in a fellow, takes
off his crown, kisses it, and pours poison in the King's
ears, and exits. The Queen returns, finds
the King dead, and makes passionate action. The
poisoner, with some two or three mutes, comes in
again, seeming to lament with her. The dead body is
carried away. The poisoner woos the Queen with
gifts. She seems loath and unwilling a while, but in
the end accepts his love. Exeunt the Players*
OPHELIA What means this, my lord?   130
HAMLET Marry, this is miching *malhecho*. That means
mischief.
OPHELIA Belike this show imports the argument of the play.
Enter Prologue
HAMLET We shall know by this fellow. The players cannot
keep counsel, they'll tell all.   135
OPHELIA Will a tell us what this show meant?
HAMLET Ay, or any show that you'll show him. Be not
you ashamed to show, he'll not shame to tell you what
it means.
OPHELIA You are naught, you are naught. I'll mark the
play.   141
PROLOGUE
For us and for our tragedy
Here stooping to your clemency,
We beg your hearing patiently.   *Exit*
HAMLET Is this a prologue, or the posy of a ring?   145
OPHELIA 'Tis brief, my lord.
HAMLET As woman's love.
Enter the Player King and his Queen
PLAYER KING
Full thirty times hath Phoebus' cart gone round
Neptune's salt wash and Tellus' orbèd ground,
And thirty dozen moons with borrowed sheen   150
About the world have times twelve thirties been
Since love our hearts and Hymen did our hands
Unite commutual in most sacred bands.
PLAYER QUEEN
So many journeys may the sun and moon
Make us again count o'er ere love be done.   155
But woe is me, you are so sick of late,
So far from cheer and from your former state,

That I distrust you. Yet, though I distrust,
Discomfort you my lord it nothing must.
For women's fear and love holds quantity,   160
In neither aught, or in extremity.
Now what my love is, proof hath made you know,
And as my love is sized, my fear is so.

PLAYER KING
Faith, I must leave thee, love, and shortly too.
My operant powers their functions leave to do,   165
And thou shalt live in this fair world behind,
Honoured, beloved; and haply one as kind
For husband shalt thou—

PLAYER QUEEN   O, confound the rest!
Such love must needs be treason in my breast.
In second husband let me be accurst;   170
None wed the second but who killed the first.

HAMLET Wormwood, wormwood.

PLAYER QUEEN
The instances that second marriage move
Are base respects of thrift, but none of love.
A second time I kill my husband dead   175
When second husband kisses me in bed.

PLAYER KING
I do believe you think what now you speak;
But what we do determine oft we break.
Purpose is but the slave to memory,
Of violent birth but poor validity,   180
Which now like fruit unripe sticks on the tree,
But fall unshaken when they mellow be.
Most necessary 'tis that we forget
To pay ourselves what to ourselves is debt.
What to ourselves in passion we propose,   185
The passion ending, doth the purpose lose.
The violence of either grief or joy
Their own enactures with themselves destroy.
Where joy most revels, grief doth most lament;
Grief joys, joy grieves, on slender accident.   190
This world is not for aye, nor 'tis not strange
That even our loves should with our fortunes change;
For 'tis a question left us yet to prove
Whether love lead fortune or else fortune love.
The great man down, you mark his favourite flies; 195
The poor advanced makes friends of enemies.
And hitherto doth love on fortune tend,
For who not needs shall never lack a friend,
And who in want a hollow friend doth try
Directly seasons him his enemy.   200
But orderly to end where I begun,
Our wills and fates do so contrary run
That our devices still are overthrown;
Our thoughts are ours, their ends none of our own.
So think thou wilt no second husband wed;   205
But die thy thoughts when thy first lord is dead.

PLAYER QUEEN
Nor earth to me give food, nor heaven light,
Sport and repose lock from me day and night,
Each opposite that blanks the face of joy

Meet what I would have well and it destroy,   210
Both here and hence pursue me lasting strife
If, once a widow, ever I be wife.

HAMLET If she should break it now!

PLAYER KING (to Player Queen)
'Tis deeply sworn. Sweet, leave me here a while.
My spirits grow dull, and fain I would beguile   215
The tedious day with sleep.

PLAYER QUEEN   Sleep rock thy brain,
And never come mischance between us twain.
                    Player King sleeps. Player Queen exits

HAMLET (to Gertrude) Madam, how like you this play?

QUEEN GERTRUDE The lady protests too much, methinks.

HAMLET O, but she'll keep her word.   220

KING CLAUDIUS Have you heard the argument? Is there
no offence in't?

HAMLET No, no, they do but jest, poison in jest. No offence
i'th' world.

KING CLAUDIUS What do you call the play?   225

HAMLET The Mousetrap. Marry, how? Tropically. This play
is the image of a murder done in Vienna. Gonzago is
the Duke's name, his wife Baptista. You shall see anon.
'Tis a knavish piece of work; but what o' that? Your
majesty, and we that have free souls, it touches us not.
Let the galled jade wince, our withers are unwrung.
                    Enter Player Lucianus
This is one Lucianus, nephew to the King.

OPHELIA You are as good as a chorus, my lord.

HAMLET I could interpret between you and your love if I
could see the puppets dallying.   235

OPHELIA You are keen, my lord, you are keen.

HAMLET It would cost you a groaning to take off mine edge.

OPHELIA Still better, and worse.

HAMLET So you mis-take your husbands. (To Lucianus)
Begin, murderer. Pox, leave thy damnable faces and
begin. Come: 'the croaking raven doth bellow for
revenge'.

PLAYER LUCIANUS
Thoughts black, hands apt, drugs fit, and time
   agreeing,
Confederate season, else no creature seeing;
Thou mixture rank of midnight weeds collected,   245
With Hecate's ban thrice blasted, thrice infected,
Thy natural magic and dire property
On wholesome life usurp immediately.
                    He pours the poison in the Player King's ear

HAMLET A poisons him i'th' garden for 's estate. His
name's Gonzago. The story is extant, and writ in choice
Italian. You shall see anon how the murderer gets the
love of Gonzago's wife.

OPHELIA The King rises.

HAMLET What, frighted with false fire?

QUEEN GERTRUDE (to Claudius) How fares my lord?   255

POLONIUS Give o'er the play.

KING CLAUDIUS Give me some light. Away.

⌈COURTIERS⌉ Lights, lights, lights!
                    Exeunt all but Hamlet and Horatio

HAMLET
    Why, let the stricken deer go weep,
      The hart ungallèd play,   260
    For some must watch, while some must sleep,
      So runs the world away.
    Would not this, sir, and a forest of feathers, if the rest
of my fortunes turn Turk with me, with two Provençal
roses on my razed shoes, get me a fellowship in a cry
of players, sir?   266
HORATIO Half a share.
HAMLET A whole one, I.
    For thou dost know, O Damon dear,
      This realm dismantled was   270
    Of Jove himself, and now reigns here
      A very, very—pajock.
HORATIO You might have rhymed.
HAMLET O good Horatio, I'll take the Ghost's word for a
thousand pound. Didst perceive?   275
HORATIO Very well, my lord.
HAMLET Upon the talk of the pois'ning?
HORATIO I did very well note him.
    Enter Rosencrantz and Guildenstern
HAMLET Ah ha! Come, some music, come, the recorders,
    For if the King like not the comedy,   280
    Why then, belike he likes it not, pardie.
    Come, some music.
GUILDENSTERN Good my lord, vouchsafe me a word with
you.
HAMLET Sir, a whole history.   285
GUILDENSTERN The King, sir—
HAMLET Ay, sir, what of him?
GUILDENSTERN Is in his retirement marvellous distempered.
HAMLET With drink, sir?
GUILDENSTERN No, my lord, rather with choler.   290
HAMLET Your wisdom should show itself more richer to
signify this to his doctor, for for me to put him to his
purgation would perhaps plunge him into far more
choler.
GUILDENSTERN Good my lord, put your discourse into some
frame, and start not so wildly from my affair.   296
HAMLET I am tame, sir. Pronounce.
GUILDENSTERN The Queen your mother, in most great
affliction of spirit, hath sent me to you.
HAMLET You are welcome.   300
GUILDENSTERN Nay, good my lord, this courtesy is not of
the right breed. If it shall please you to make me a
wholesome answer, I will do your mother's
commandment; if not, your pardon and my return
shall be the end of my business.   305
HAMLET Sir, I cannot.
GUILDENSTERN What, my lord?
HAMLET Make you a wholesome answer. My wit's
diseased. But, sir, such answers as I can make, you
shall command; or rather, as you say, my mother.
Therefore no more, but to the matter. My mother, you
say?
ROSENCRANTZ Then thus she says: your behaviour hath
struck her into amazement and admiration.   314

HAMLET O wonderful son, that can so astonish a mother!
But is there no sequel at the heels of this mother's
admiration?
ROSENCRANTZ She desires to speak with you in her closet
ere you go to bed.
HAMLET We shall obey, were she ten times our mother.
Have you any further trade with us?   321
ROSENCRANTZ My lord, you once did love me.
HAMLET So I do still, by these pickers and stealers.
ROSENCRANTZ Good my lord, what is your cause of
distemper? You do freely bar the door of your own
liberty if you deny your griefs to your friend.   326
HAMLET Sir, I lack advancement.
ROSENCRANTZ How can that be when you have the voice
of the King himself for your succession in Denmark?
HAMLET Ay, but 'while the grass grows . . .'—the proverb
is something musty.   331
    Enter one with a recorder
    O, the recorder. Let me see. (*To Rosencrantz and
Guildenstern, taking them aside*) To withdraw with you,
why do you go about to recover the wind of me as if
you would drive me into a toil?   335
GUILDENSTERN O my lord, if my duty be too bold, my love
is too unmannerly.
HAMLET I do not well understand that. Will you play
upon this pipe?
GUILDENSTERN My lord, I cannot.   340
HAMLET I pray you.
GUILDENSTERN Believe me, I cannot.
HAMLET I do beseech you.
GUILDENSTERN I know no touch of it, my lord.   344
HAMLET 'Tis as easy as lying. Govern these ventages with
your fingers and thumb, give it breath with your
mouth, and it will discourse most excellent music. Look
you, these are the stops.
GUILDENSTERN But these cannot I command to any
utterance of harmony. I have not the skill.   350
HAMLET Why, look you now, how unworthy a thing you
make of me! You would play upon me, you would
seem to know my stops, you would pluck out the heart
of my mystery, you would sound me from my lowest
note to the top of my compass; and there is much
music, excellent voice in this little organ, yet cannot
you make it speak. 'Sblood, do you think I am easier
to be played on than a pipe? Call me what instrument
you will, though you can fret me, you cannot play
upon me.   360
    Enter Polonius
    God bless you, sir.
POLONIUS My lord, the Queen would speak with you, and
presently.
HAMLET Do you see yonder cloud that's almost in shape
of a camel?   365
POLONIUS By th' mass, and 'tis: like a camel, indeed.
HAMLET Methinks it is like a weasel.
POLONIUS It is backed like a weasel.
HAMLET Or like a whale.
POLONIUS Very like a whale.   370

HAMLET Then will I come to my mother by and by. (*Aside*)
They fool me to the top of my bent. (*To Polonius*) I will
come by and by.
POLONIUS I will say so.
HAMLET 'By and by' is easily said.   *Exit Polonius*
Leave me, friends.   376
           Exeunt all but Hamlet
'Tis now the very witching time of night,
When churchyards yawn, and hell itself breathes out
Contagion to this world. Now could I drink hot blood,
And do such bitter business as the day   380
Would quake to look on. Soft, now to my mother.
O heart, lose not thy nature! Let not ever
The soul of Nero enter this firm bosom.
Let me be cruel, not unnatural.
I will speak daggers to her, but use none.   385
My tongue and soul in this be hypocrites—
How in my words somever she be shent,
To give them seals never my soul consent.   *Exit*

3.3   *Enter King Claudius, Rosencrantz, and Guildenstern*
KING CLAUDIUS
I like him not, nor stands it safe with us
To let his madness range. Therefore prepare you.
I your commission will forthwith dispatch,
And he to England shall along with you.
The terms of our estate may not endure   5
Hazard so dangerous as doth hourly grow
Out of his lunacies.
GUILDENSTERN   We will ourselves provide.
Most holy and religious fear it is
To keep those many many bodies safe
That live and feed upon your majesty.   10
ROSENCRANTZ
The single and peculiar life is bound
With all the strength and armour of the mind
To keep itself from noyance; but much more
That spirit upon whose weal depends and rests
The lives of many. The cease of majesty   15
Dies not alone, but like a gulf doth draw
What's near it with it. It is a massy wheel
Fixed on the summit of the highest mount,
To whose huge spokes ten thousand lesser things
Are mortised and adjoined, which when it falls   20
Each small annexment, petty consequence,
Attends the boist'rous ruin. Never alone
Did the King sigh, but with a general groan.
KING CLAUDIUS
Arm you, I pray you, to this speedy voyage,
For we will fetters put upon this fear   25
Which now goes too free-footed.
ROSENCRANTZ *and* GUILDENSTERN   We will haste us.
           Exeunt both
   Enter Polonius
POLONIUS
My lord, he's going to his mother's closet.
Behind the arras I'll convey myself

To hear the process. I'll warrant she'll tax him home.
And, as you said—and wisely was it said—   30
'Tis meet that some more audience than a mother,
Since nature makes them partial, should o'erhear
The speech of vantage. Fare you well, my liege.
I'll call upon you ere you go to bed,
And tell you what I know.
KING CLAUDIUS   Thanks, dear my lord.   35
           Exit Polonius
O, my offence is rank! It smells to heaven.
It hath the primal eldest curse upon't,
A brother's murder. Pray can I not.
Though inclination be as sharp as will,
My stronger guilt defeats my strong intent,   40
And like a man to double business bound
I stand in pause where I shall first begin,
And both neglect. What if this cursèd hand
Were thicker than itself with brother's blood,
Is there not rain enough in the sweet heavens   45
To wash it white as snow? Whereto serves mercy
But to confront the visage of offence?
And what's in prayer but this twofold force,
To be forestallèd ere we come to fall,
Or pardoned being down? Then I'll look up.   50
My fault is past—but O, what form of prayer
Can serve my turn? 'Forgive me my foul murder'?
That cannot be, since I am still possessed
Of those effects for which I did the murder—
My crown, mine own ambition, and my queen.   55
May one be pardoned and retain th'offence?
In the corrupted currents of this world
Offence's gilded hand may shove by justice,
And oft 'tis seen the wicked prize itself
Buys out the law. But 'tis not so above.   60
There is no shuffling, there the action lies
In his true nature, and we ourselves compelled
Even to the teeth and forehead of our faults
To give in evidence. What then? What rests?
Try what repentance can. What can it not?   65
Yet what can it when one cannot repent?
O wretched state, O bosom black as death,
O limèd soul that, struggling to be free,
Art more engaged! Help, angels! Make assay.
Bow, stubborn knees; and heart with strings of steel, 70
Be soft as sinews of the new-born babe.
All may be well.
   He kneels.
   Enter Prince Hamlet behind him
HAMLET
Now might I do it pat, now a is praying,
And now I'll do't,
   ⌈*He draws his sword*⌉
           and so a goes to heaven,
And so am I revenged. That would be scanned.   75
A villain kills my father, and for that
I, his sole son, do this same villain send
To heaven.

O, this is hire and salary, not revenge!
A took my father grossly, full of bread,   80
With all his crimes broad blown, as flush as May;
And how his audit stands, who knows save heaven?
But in our circumstance and course of thought
'Tis heavy with him. And am I then revenged
To take him in the purging of his soul,   85
When he is fit and seasoned for his passage?
No.
     He sheathes his sword
Up, sword, and know thou a more horrid hint.
When he is drunk asleep, or in his rage,
Or in th'incestuous pleasure of his bed,   90
At gaming, swearing, or about some act
That has no relish of salvation in't,
Then trip him that his heels may kick at heaven,
And that his soul may be as damned and black
As hell whereto it goes. My mother stays.   95
This physic but prolongs thy sickly days.   *Exit*
KING CLAUDIUS
My words fly up, my thoughts remain below.
Words without thoughts never to heaven go.   *Exit*

3.4   *Enter Queen Gertrude and Polonius*
POLONIUS
A will come straight. Look you lay home to him.
Tell him his pranks have been too broad to bear with,
And that your grace hath screened and stood between
Much heat and him. I'll silence me e'en here.
Pray you be round with him.   5
HAMLET (*within*) Mother, mother, mother!
QUEEN GERTRUDE
I'll warr'nt you. Fear me not. Withdraw; I hear him
    coming.
     Polonius hides behind the arras.
     Enter Prince Hamlet
HAMLET Now, mother, what's the matter?
QUEEN GERTRUDE
Hamlet, thou hast thy father much offended.
HAMLET
Mother, you have my father much offended.   10
QUEEN GERTRUDE
Come, come, you answer with an idle tongue.
HAMLET
Go, go, you question with a wicked tongue.
QUEEN GERTRUDE
Why, how now, Hamlet?
HAMLET   What's the matter now?
QUEEN GERTRUDE
Have you forgot me?
HAMLET   No, by the rood, not so.
You are the Queen, your husband's brother's wife.   15
But—would you were not so—you are my mother.
QUEEN GERTRUDE
Nay, then, I'll set those to you that can speak.
HAMLET
Come, come, and sit you down. You shall not budge.

You go not till I set you up a glass
Where you may see the inmost part of you.   20
QUEEN GERTRUDE
What wilt thou do? Thou wilt not murder me?
Help, help, ho!
POLONIUS (*behind the arras*) What ho! Help, help, help!
HAMLET
How now, a rat? Dead for a ducat, dead.
     He thrusts his sword through the arras
POLONIUS
O, I am slain!
QUEEN GERTRUDE (*to Hamlet*) O me, what hast thou done?
HAMLET
Nay, I know not. Is it the King?   25
QUEEN GERTRUDE
O, what a rash and bloody deed is this!
HAMLET
A bloody deed—almost as bad, good-mother,
As kill a king and marry with his brother.
QUEEN GERTRUDE
As kill a king?
HAMLET   Ay, lady, 'twas my word.
(*To Polonius*) Thou wretched, rash, intruding fool,
    farewell.   30
I took thee for thy better. Take thy fortune.
Thou find'st to be too busy is some danger. —
Leave wringing of your hands. Peace, sit you down,
And let me wring your heart; for so I shall
If it be made of penetrable stuff,   35
If damnèd custom have not brassed it so
That it is proof and bulwark against sense.
QUEEN GERTRUDE
What have I done, that thou dar'st wag thy tongue
In noise so rude against me?
HAMLET   Such an act
That blurs the grace and blush of modesty,   40
Calls virtue hypocrite, takes off the rose
From the fair forehead of an innocent love
And sets a blister there, makes marriage vows
As false as dicers' oaths—O, such a deed
As from the body of contraction plucks   45
The very soul, and sweet religion makes
A rhapsody of words. Heaven's face doth glow,
Yea, this solidity and compound mass
With tristful visage, as against the doom,
Is thought-sick at the act.
QUEEN GERTRUDE   Ay me, what act,   50
That roars so loud and thunders in the index?
HAMLET
Look here upon this picture, and on this,
The counterfeit presentment of two brothers.
See what a grace was seated on this brow—
Hyperion's curls, the front of Jove himself,   55
An eye like Mars, to threaten or command,
A station like the herald Mercury
New lighted on a heaven-kissing hill;
A combination and a form indeed

Where every god did seem to set his seal   60
To give the world assurance of a man.
This *was* your husband. Look you now what follows.
Here *is* your husband, like a mildewed ear
Blasting his wholesome brother. Have you eyes?
Could you on this fair mountain leave to feed,   65
And batten on this moor? Ha, have you eyes?
You cannot call it love, for at your age
The heyday in the blood is tame, it's humble,
And waits upon the judgement; and what judgement
Would step from this to this? What devil was't   70
That thus hath cozened you at hood-man blind?
O shame, where is thy blush? Rebellious hell,
If thou canst mutine in a matron's bones,
To flaming youth let virtue be as wax
And melt in her own fire. Proclaim no shame   75
When the compulsive ardour gives the charge,
Since frost itself as actively doth burn,
And reason panders will.
QUEEN GERTRUDE   O Hamlet, speak no more!
Thou turn'st mine eyes into my very soul,
And there I see such black and grainèd spots   80
As will not leave their tinct.
HAMLET   Nay, but to live
In the rank sweat of an enseamèd bed,
Stewed in corruption, honeying and making love
Over the nasty sty—
QUEEN GERTRUDE   O, speak to me no more!
These words like daggers enter in mine ears.   85
No more, sweet Hamlet.
HAMLET   A murderer and a villain,
A slave that is not twenti'th part the tithe
Of your precedent lord, a vice of kings,
A cutpurse of the empire and the rule,
That from a shelf the precious diadem stole   90
And put it in his pocket—
QUEEN GERTRUDE No more.
HAMLET A king of shreds and patches—
    Enter the Ghost in his nightgown
Save me and hover o'er me with your wings,
You heavenly guards! (*To the Ghost*) What would
    you, gracious figure?   95
QUEEN GERTRUDE Alas, he's mad.
HAMLET (*to the Ghost*)
Do you not come your tardy son to chide,
That, lapsed in time and passion, lets go by
Th'important acting of your dread command?
O, say!
GHOST   Do not forget. This visitation   100
Is but to whet thy almost blunted purpose.
But look, amazement on thy mother sits.
O, step between her and her fighting soul.
Conceit in weakest bodies strongest works.
Speak to her, Hamlet.   105
HAMLET How is it with you, lady?
QUEEN GERTRUDE Alas, how is't with you,
That you do bend your eye on vacancy,

And with th'incorporal air do hold discourse?
Forth at your eyes your spirits wildly peep,   110
And, as the sleeping soldiers in th'alarm,
Your bedded hair, like life in excrements,
Start up and stand on end. O gentle son,
Upon the heat and flame of thy distemper
Sprinkle cool patience! Whereon do you look?   115
HAMLET
On him, on him. Look you how pale he glares.
His form and cause conjoined, preaching to stones,
Would make them capable. (*To the Ghost*) Do not look
    upon me,
Lest with this piteous action you convert
My stern effects. Then what I have to do   120
Will want true colour—tears perchance for blood.
QUEEN GERTRUDE
To whom do you speak this?
HAMLET   Do you see nothing there?
QUEEN GERTRUDE
Nothing at all, yet all that is I see.
HAMLET
Nor did you nothing hear?
QUEEN GERTRUDE   No, nothing but ourselves.
HAMLET
Why, look you there. Look how it steals away.   125
My father, in his habit as he lived.
Look where he goes even now out at the portal.
                                      Exit the Ghost
QUEEN GERTRUDE
This is the very coinage of your brain.
This bodiless creation ecstasy
Is very cunning in.
HAMLET   Ecstasy?   130
My pulse as yours doth temperately keep time,
And makes as healthful music. It is not madness
That I have uttered. Bring me to the test,
And I the matter will reword, which madness
Would gambol from. Mother, for love of grace   135
Lay not a flattering unction to your soul
That not your trespass but my madness speaks.
It will but skin and film the ulcerous place
Whilst rank corruption, mining all within,
Infects unseen. Confess yourself to heaven;   140
Repent what's past, avoid what is to come,
And do not spread the compost o'er the weeds
To make them ranker. Forgive me this my virtue,
For in the fatness of these pursy times
Virtue itself of vice must pardon beg,   145
Yea, curb and woo for leave to do him good.
QUEEN GERTRUDE
O Hamlet, thou hast cleft my heart in twain!
HAMLET
O, throw away the worser part of it,
And live the purer with the other half!
Good night—but go not to mine uncle's bed.   150
Assume a virtue if you have it not.
Refrain tonight,

And that shall lend a kind of easiness
To the next abstinence. Once more, good night;
And when you are desirous to be blest,   155
I'll blessing beg of you. For this same lord,
I do repent. But heaven hath pleased it so
To punish me with this, and this with me,
That I must be their scourge and minister.
I will bestow him, and will answer well   160
The death I gave him. So, again, good night.
I must be cruel only to be kind.
Thus bad begins, and worse remains behind.

QUEEN GERTRUDE What shall I do?

HAMLET
Not this, by no means, that I bid you do: 165
Let the bloat King tempt you again to bed,
Pinch wanton on your cheek, call you his mouse,
And let him for a pair of reechy kisses,
Or paddling in your neck with his damned fingers,
Make you to ravel all this matter out,   170
That I essentially am not in madness,
But mad in craft. 'Twere good you let him know,
For who that's but a queen, fair, sober, wise,
Would from a paddock, from a bat, a gib,
Such dear concernings hide? Who would do so?   175
No, in despite of sense and secrecy,
Unpeg the basket on the house's top,
Let the birds fly, and, like the famous ape,
To try conclusions in the basket creep,
And break your own neck down.   180

QUEEN GERTRUDE
Be thou assured, if words be made of breath,
And breath of life, I have no life to breathe
What thou hast said to me.

HAMLET   I must to England.
You know that?

QUEEN GERTRUDE   Alack, I had forgot.
'Tis so concluded on.

HAMLET   This man shall set me packing. 185
I'll lug the guts into the neighbour room.
Mother, good night indeed. This counsellor
Is now most still, most secret, and most grave,
Who was in life a foolish prating knave.—
Come, sir, to draw toward an end with you.—   190
Good night, mother.   *Exit, tugging in Polonius*

4.1   *Enter King Claudius to Queen Gertrude*

KING CLAUDIUS
There's matter in these sighs, these profound heaves;
You must translate. 'Tis fit we understand them.
Where is your son?

QUEEN GERTRUDE
Ah, my good lord, what have I seen tonight!

KING CLAUDIUS What, Gertrude? How does Hamlet?   5

QUEEN GERTRUDE
Mad as the sea and wind when both contend
Which is the mightier. In his lawless fit,
Behind the arras hearing something stir,

He whips his rapier out and cries 'A rat, a rat!',
And in his brainish apprehension kills   10
The unseen good old man.

KING CLAUDIUS   O heavy deed!
It had been so with us had we been there.
His liberty is full of threats to all—
To you yourself, to us, to everyone.
Alas, how shall this bloody deed be answered?   15
It will be laid to us, whose providence
Should have kept short, restrained, and out of haunt
This mad young man. But so much was our love,
We would not understand what was most fit,
But, like the owner of a foul disease,   20
To keep it from divulging, let it feed
Even on the pith of life. Where is he gone?

QUEEN GERTRUDE
To draw apart the body he hath killed,
O'er whom—his very madness, like some ore
Among a mineral of metals base,   25
Shows itself pure—a weeps for what is done.

KING CLAUDIUS O Gertrude, come away!
The sun no sooner shall the mountains touch
But we will ship him hence; and this vile deed
We must with all our majesty and skill   30
Both countenance and excuse.—Ho, Guildenstern!
    Enter Rosencrantz and Guildenstern
Friends both, go join you with some further aid.
Hamlet in madness hath Polonius slain,
And from his mother's closet hath he dragged him.
Go seek him out, speak fair, and bring the body   35
Into the chapel. I pray you haste in this.
    Exeunt Rosencrantz and Guildenstern
Come, Gertrude, we'll call up our wisest friends
To let them know both what we mean to do
And what's untimely done. O, come away!   39
My soul is full of discord and dismay.   *Exeunt*

4.2   *Enter Prince Hamlet*

HAMLET Safely stowed.

ROSENCRANTZ *and* GUILDENSTERN (*within*)
Hamlet, Lord Hamlet!

HAMLET
What noise? Who calls on Hamlet?
    Enter Rosencrantz and Guildenstern
                    O, here they come.

ROSENCRANTZ
What have you done, my lord, with the dead body?

HAMLET
Compounded it with dust, whereto 'tis kin.   5

ROSENCRANTZ
Tell us where 'tis, that we may take it thence
And bear it to the chapel.

HAMLET Do not believe it.

ROSENCRANTZ Believe what?   9

HAMLET That I can keep your counsel and not mine own.
Besides, to be demanded of a sponge—what replication
should be made by the son of a king?

ROSENCRANTZ Take you me for a sponge, my lord?
HAMLET Ay, sir, that soaks up the King's countenance,
his rewards, his authorities. But such officers do the
King best service in the end. He keeps them, like an
ape an apple in the corner of his jaw, first mouthed to
be last swallowed. When he needs what you have
gleaned, it is but squeezing you, and, sponge, you shall
be dry again.   20
ROSENCRANTZ I understand you not, my lord.
HAMLET I am glad of it. A knavish speech sleeps in a
foolish ear.
ROSENCRANTZ My lord, you must tell us where the body
is, and go with us to the King.   25
HAMLET The body is with the King, but the King is not
with the body. The King is a thing—
GUILDENSTERN A thing, my lord?
HAMLET Of nothing. Bring me to him. Hide fox, and all
after.   *Exit running, pursued by the others*

4.3   *Enter King Claudius*
KING CLAUDIUS
I have sent to seek him, and to find the body.
How dangerous is it that this man goes loose!
Yet must not we put the strong law on him.
He's loved of the distracted multitude,
Who like not in their judgement but their eyes,   5
And where 'tis so, th'offender's scourge is weighed,
But never the offence. To bear all smooth and even,
This sudden sending him away must seem
Deliberate pause. Diseases desperate grown
By desperate appliance are relieved,   10
Or not at all.
         Enter Rosencrantz
                 How now, what hath befall'n?
ROSENCRANTZ
Where the dead body is bestowed, my lord,
We cannot get from him.
KING CLAUDIUS   But where is he?
ROSENCRANTZ
Without, my lord, guarded to know your pleasure.
KING CLAUDIUS Bring him before us.   15
ROSENCRANTZ
Ho, Guildenstern! Bring in my lord.
         Enter Prince Hamlet and Guildenstern
KING CLAUDIUS
Now, Hamlet, where's Polonius?
HAMLET At supper.
KING CLAUDIUS At supper? Where?   19
HAMLET Not where he eats, but where a is eaten. A certain
convocation of politic worms are e'en at him. Your worm
is your only emperor for diet. We fat all creatures else to
fat us, and we fat ourselves for maggots. Your fat king
and your lean beggar is but variable service—two dishes,
but to one table. That's the end.   25
KING CLAUDIUS Alas, alas!
HAMLET A man may fish with the worm that hath eat of
a king, and eat of the fish that hath fed of that worm.
KING CLAUDIUS What dost thou mean by this?

HAMLET Nothing but to show you how a king may go a
progress through the guts of a beggar.   31
KING CLAUDIUS Where is Polonius?
HAMLET In heaven. Send thither to see. If your messenger
find him not there, seek him i'th' other place yourself.
But indeed, if you find him not this month, you shall
nose him as you go up the stairs into the lobby.   36
KING CLAUDIUS ⌜*to Rosencrantz*⌝ Go seek him there.
HAMLET ⌜*to Rosencrantz*⌝ A will stay till ye come.
                                          Exit ⌜*Rosencrantz*⌝
KING CLAUDIUS
Hamlet, this deed of thine, for thine especial safety—
Which we do tender as we dearly grieve   40
For that which thou hast done—must send thee hence
With fiery quickness. Therefore prepare thyself.
The barque is ready, and the wind at help,
Th'associates tend, and everything is bent
For England.   45
HAMLET For England?
KING CLAUDIUS Ay, Hamlet.
HAMLET Good.
KING CLAUDIUS
So is it if thou knew'st our purposes.
HAMLET I see a cherub that sees them. But come, for
England. Farewell, dear mother.   51
KING CLAUDIUS Thy loving father, Hamlet.
HAMLET My mother. Father and mother is man and wife,
man and wife is one flesh, and so my mother. Come,
for England.   *Exit*
KING CLAUDIUS ⌜*to Guildenstern*⌝
Follow him at foot. Tempt him with speed aboard.   56
Delay it not. I'll have him hence tonight.
Away, for everything is sealed and done
That else leans on th'affair. Pray you, make haste.
                                          Exit ⌜*Guildenstern*⌝
And, England, if my love thou hold'st at aught—   60
As my great power thereof may give thee sense,
Since yet thy cicatrice looks raw and red
After the Danish sword, and thy free awe
Pays homage to us—thou mayst not coldly set
Our sovereign process, which imports at full,   65
By letters conjuring to that effect,
The present death of Hamlet. Do it, England,
For like the hectic in my blood he rages,
And thou must cure me. Till I know 'tis done,   69
Howe'er my haps, my joys were ne'er begun.   *Exit*

4.4   *Enter Fortinbras with an army over the stage*
FORTINBRAS
Go, captain, from me greet the Danish king.
Tell him that by his licence Fortinbras
Claims the conveyance of a promised march
Over his kingdom. You know the rendezvous.
If that his majesty would aught with us,   5
We shall express our duty in his eye,
And let him know so.
CAPTAIN I will do't, my lord.   ⌜*Exit*⌝
FORTINBRAS Go safely on.   *Exeunt marching*

4.5 *Enter Queen Gertrude and Horatio*
QUEEN GERTRUDE
I will not speak with her.
HORATIO　　　　　　　　She is importunate,
Indeed distraught. Her mood will needs be pitied.
QUEEN GERTRUDE What would she have?
HORATIO
She speaks much of her father, says she hears
There's tricks i'th' world, and hems, and beats her
heart,　　　　　　　　　　　　　　　　　　5
Spurns enviously at straws, speaks things in doubt
That carry but half sense. Her speech is nothing,
Yet the unshapèd use of it doth move
The hearers to collection. They aim at it,
And botch the words up fit to their own thoughts,　10
Which, as her winks and nods and gestures yield
them,
Indeed would make one think there might be thought,
Though nothing sure, yet much unhappily.
QUEEN GERTRUDE
'Twere good she were spoken with, for she may strew
Dangerous conjectures in ill-breeding minds.　　15
Let her come in.
　　⌈Horatio withdraws to admit Ophelia⌉
To my sick soul, as sin's true nature is,
Each toy seems prologue to some great amiss.
So full of artless jealousy is guilt,
It spills itself in fearing to be spilt.　　　　　　20
　　Enter Ophelia mad, ⌈her hair down, with a lute⌉
OPHELIA
Where is the beauteous majesty of Denmark?
QUEEN GERTRUDE How now, Ophelia?
OPHELIA *(sings)*
　　　How should I your true love know
　　　　From another one?—
　　　By his cockle hat and staff,　　　　　　25
　　　　And his sandal shoon.
QUEEN GERTRUDE
Alas, sweet lady, what imports this song?
OPHELIA Say you? Nay, pray you, mark.
　(Sings)　He is dead and gone, lady,
　　　　　　He is dead and gone.　　　　　　30
　　　　At his head a grass-green turf,
　　　　At his heels a stone.
QUEEN GERTRUDE Nay, but Ophelia—
OPHELIA Pray you, mark.
　(Sings)
　　　White his shroud as the mountain snow—　35
　　　Enter King Claudius
QUEEN GERTRUDE Alas, look here, my lord.
OPHELIA *(sings)*
　　　Larded with sweet flowers,
　　　Which bewept to the grave did—not—go
　　　With true-love showers.
KING CLAUDIUS How do ye, pretty lady?　　　40
OPHELIA Well, God'ield you. They say the owl was a
baker's daughter. Lord, we know what we are, but
know not what we may be. God be at your table!
KING CLAUDIUS *(to Gertrude)* Conceit upon her father.

OPHELIA Pray you, let's have no words of this, but when
they ask you what it means, say you this.　　46
(Sings)
　　　Tomorrow is Saint Valentine's day,
　　　　All in the morning betime,
　　　And I a maid at your window
　　　　To be your Valentine.　　　　　　50

　　　Then up he rose, and donned his clothes,
　　　　And dupped the chamber door;
　　　Let in the maid, that out a maid
　　　　Never departed more.

KING CLAUDIUS Pretty Ophelia—　　　　　　55
OPHELIA Indeed, la? Without an oath, I'll make an end
on't.
(Sings)
　　　By Gis, and by Saint Charity,
　　　　Alack, and fie for shame!
　　　Young men will do't if they come to't,　60
　　　　By Cock, they are to blame.

　　　Quoth she 'Before you tumbled me,
　　　　You promised me to wed.'
　　　So would I 'a' done, by yonder sun,
　　　　An thou hadst not come to my bed.　65

KING CLAUDIUS *(to Gertrude)* How long hath she been thus?
OPHELIA I hope all will be well. We must be patient. But
I cannot choose but weep to think they should lay him
i'th' cold ground. My brother shall know of it. And so
I thank you for your good counsel. Come, my coach!
Good night, ladies, good night, sweet ladies, good night,
good night.　　　　　　　　　　　　　*Exit*
KING CLAUDIUS *(to Horatio)*
Follow her close. Give her good watch, I pray you.
　　　　　　　　　　　　　　　　Exit Horatio
O, this is the poison of deep grief! It springs
All from her father's death. O Gertrude, Gertrude,　75
When sorrows come they come not single spies,
But in battalions. First, her father slain;
Next, your son gone, and he most violent author
Of his own just remove; the people muddied,
Thick and unwholesome in their thoughts and whispers
For good Polonius' death; and we have done but
greenly　　　　　　　　　　　　　　　81
In hugger-mugger to inter him; poor Ophelia
Divided from herself and her fair judgement,
Without the which we are pictures or mere beasts;
Last, and as much containing as all these,　　85
Her brother is in secret come from France,
Feeds on this wonder, keeps himself in clouds,
And wants not buzzers to infect his ear
With pestilent speeches of his father's death;
Wherein necessity, of matter beggared,　　　90
Will nothing stick our persons to arraign
In ear and ear. O my dear Gertrude, this,
Like to a murd'ring-piece, in many places
Gives me superfluous death.
　　A noise within
QUEEN GERTRUDE　　　　　Alack, what noise is this?

KING CLAUDIUS
    Where is my Switzers? Let them guard the door.   95
        Enter a Messenger
    What is the matter?
MESSENGER   Save yourself, my lord.
    The ocean, overpeering of his list,
    Eats not the flats with more impetuous haste
    Than young Laertes, in a riotous head,
    O'erbears your officers. The rabble call him lord,   100
    And, as the world were now but to begin,
    Antiquity forgot, custom not known,
    The ratifiers and props of every word,
    They cry 'Choose we! Laertes shall be king.'
    Caps, hands, and tongues applaud it to the clouds,   105
    'Laertes shall be king, Laertes king.'
QUEEN GERTRUDE
    How cheerfully on the false trail they cry!
        A noise within
    O, this is counter, you false Danish dogs!
KING CLAUDIUS The doors are broke.
        Enter Laertes ⌈with his followers at the door⌉
LAERTES
    Where is the King?—Sirs, stand you all without.   110
ALL HIS FOLLOWERS No, let's come in.
LAERTES I pray you, give me leave.
ALL HIS FOLLOWERS We will, we will.
LAERTES
    I thank you. Keep the door.   *⌈Exeunt followers⌉*
                        O thou vile king,
    Give me my father.
QUEEN GERTRUDE   Calmly, good Laertes.   115
LAERTES
    That drop of blood that's calm proclaims me bastard,
    Cries cuckold to my father, brands the harlot
    Even here between the chaste unsmirchèd brow
    Of my true mother.
KING CLAUDIUS   What is the cause, Laertes,
    That thy rebellion looks so giant-like?—   120
    Let him go, Gertrude. Do not fear our person.
    There's such divinity doth hedge a king
    That treason can but peep to what it would,
    Acts little of his will.—Tell me, Laertes,
    Why thou art thus incensed.—Let him go, Gertrude.—
    Speak, man.
LAERTES   Where is my father?
KING CLAUDIUS   Dead.   126
QUEEN GERTRUDE (*to Laertes*)
    But not by him.
KING CLAUDIUS   Let him demand his fill.
LAERTES
    How came he dead? I'll not be juggled with.
    To hell, allegiance! Vows to the blackest devil!
    Conscience and grace to the profoundest pit!   130
    I dare damnation. To this point I stand,
    That both the worlds I give to negligence,
    Let come what comes. Only I'll be revenged
    Most throughly for my father.
KING CLAUDIUS Who shall stay you?   135

LAERTES My will, not all the world;
    And for my means, I'll husband them so well
    They shall go far with little.
KING CLAUDIUS   Good Laertes,
    If you desire to know the certainty   139
    Of your dear father's death, is't writ in your revenge
    That, sweepstake, you will draw both friend and foe,
    Winner and loser?
LAERTES None but his enemies.
KING CLAUDIUS Will you know them then?
LAERTES
    To his good friends thus wide I'll ope my arms,   145
    And, like the kind life-rend'ring pelican,
    Repast them with my blood.
KING CLAUDIUS   Why, now you speak
    Like a good child and a true gentleman.
    That I am guiltless of your father's death,
    And am most sensibly in grief for it,   150
    It shall as level to your judgement pierce
    As day does to your eye.
        A noise within
VOICES (*within*) Let her come in.
LAERTES How now, what noise is that?
        Enter Ophelia as before
    O heat dry up my brains! Tears seven times salt   155
    Burn out the sense and virtue of mine eye!
    By heaven, thy madness shall be paid by weight
    Till our scale turns the beam. O rose of May,
    Dear maid, kind sister, sweet Ophelia!
    O heavens, is't possible a young maid's wits   160
    Should be as mortal as an old man's life?
    Nature is fine in love, and where 'tis fine
    It sends some precious instance of itself
    After the thing it loves.
OPHELIA (*sings*)
        They bore him barefaced on the bier,   165
            Hey non nony, nony, hey nony,
        And on his grave rained many a tear—
    Fare you well, my dove.
LAERTES
    Hadst thou thy wits and didst persuade revenge,
    It could not move thus.   170
OPHELIA You must sing 'Down, a-down', and you, 'Call
    him a-down-a'. O, how the wheel becomes it! It is the
    false steward that stole his master's daughter.
LAERTES This nothing's more than matter.   174
OPHELIA There's rosemary, that's for remembrance. Pray,
    love, remember. And there is pansies; that's for
    thoughts.
LAERTES
    A document in madness—thoughts and remembrance
    fitted.   178
OPHELIA There's fennel for you, and columbines. There's
    rue for you, and here's some for me. We may call it
    herb-grace o' Sundays. O, you must wear your rue
    with a difference. There's a daisy. I would give you
    some violets, but they withered all when my father

died. They say a made a good end.
(*Sings*) For bonny sweet Robin is all my joy.   185
LAERTES
Thought and affliction, passion, hell itself
She turns to favour and to prettiness.
OPHELIA (*sings*)
        And will a not come again,
        And will a not come again?
         No, no, he is dead,   190
         Go to thy death-bed,
        He never will come again.

        His beard as white as snow,
        All flaxen was his poll.
         He is gone, he is gone,   195
         And we cast away moan.
        God 'a' mercy on his soul.

And of all Christian souls, I pray God. God b'wi' ye.
                ⌈*Exeunt Ophelia and Gertrude*⌉
LAERTES Do you see this, O God?
KING CLAUDIUS
Laertes, I must commune with your grief,   200
Or you deny me right. Go but apart,
Make choice of whom your wisest friends you will,
And they shall hear and judge 'twixt you and me.
If by direct or by collateral hand
They find us touched, we will our kingdom give,   205
Our crown, our life, and all that we call ours,
To you in satisfaction. But if not,
Be you content to lend your patience to us,
And we shall jointly labour with your soul
To give it due content.
LAERTES   Let this be so.   210
His means of death, his obscure burial—
No trophy, sword, nor hatchment o'er his bones,
No noble rite nor formal ostentation—
Cry to be heard, as 'twere from heaven to earth,
That I must call't in question.
KING CLAUDIUS   So you shall;   215
And where th'offence is, let the great axe fall.
I pray you go with me.   *Exeunt*

4.6   *Enter Horatio with a Servant*
HORATIO
What are they that would speak with me?
SERVANT
Sailors, sir. They say they have letters for you.
HORATIO Let them come in.   *Exit Servant*
I do not know from what part of the world
I should be greeted if not from Lord Hamlet.   5
    Enter ⌈*Sailors*⌉
A SAILOR God bless you, sir.
HORATIO Let him bless thee too.
A SAILOR A shall, sir, an't please him. There's a letter for
you, sir. It comes from th'ambassador that was bound
for England—if your name be Horatio, as I am let to
know it is.   11
HORATIO (*reads*) 'Horatio, when thou shalt have overlooked

this, give these fellows some means to the King. They
have letters for him. Ere we were two days old at sea,
a pirate of very warlike appointment gave us chase.
Finding ourselves too slow of sail, we put on a compelled
valour, and in the grapple I boarded them. On the
instant they got clear of our ship, so I alone became
their prisoner. They have dealt with me like thieves of
mercy; but they knew what they did: I am to do a
good turn for them. Let the King have the letters I have
sent, and repair thou to me with as much haste as
thou wouldst fly death. I have words to speak in thine
ear will make thee dumb, yet are they much too light
for the bore of the matter. These good fellows will bring
thee where I am. Rosencrantz and Guildenstern hold
their course for England. Of them I have much to tell
thee. Farewell.
                He that thou knowest thine,
                      Hamlet.'   30
Come, I will give you way for these your letters,
And do't the speedier that you may direct me
To him from whom you brought them.   *Exeunt*

4.7   *Enter King Claudius and Laertes*
KING CLAUDIUS
Now must your conscience my acquittance seal,
And you must put me in your heart for friend,
Sith you have heard, and with a knowing ear,
That he which hath your noble father slain
Pursued my life.
LAERTES   It well appears. But tell me   5
Why you proceeded not against these feats,
So crimeful and so capital in nature,
As by your safety, wisdom, all things else,
You mainly were stirred up.
KING CLAUDIUS   O, for two special reasons,
Which may to you perhaps seem much unsinewed,   10
And yet to me they're strong. The Queen his mother
Lives almost by his looks; and for myself—
My virtue or my plague, be it either which—
She's so conjunctive to my life and soul
That, as the star moves not but in his sphere,   15
I could not but by her. The other motive
Why to a public count I might not go
Is the great love the general gender bear him,
Who, dipping all his faults in their affection,
Would, like the spring that turneth wood to stone,   20
Convert his guilts to graces; so that my arrows,
Too slightly timbered for so loud a wind,
Would have reverted to my bow again,
And not where I had aimed them.
LAERTES
And so have I a noble father lost,   25
A sister driven into desp'rate terms,
Who has, if praises may go back again,
Stood challenger, on mount, of all the age
For her perfections. But my revenge will come.
KING CLAUDIUS
Break not your sleeps for that. You must not think   30

That we are made of stuff so flat and dull
That we can let our beard be shook with danger,
And think it pastime. You shortly shall hear more.
I loved your father, and we love ourself.
And that, I hope, will teach you to imagine—   35
Enter a Messenger with letters
How now? What news?
MESSENGER   Letters, my lord, from Hamlet.
This to your majesty; this to the Queen.
KING CLAUDIUS From Hamlet? Who brought them?
MESSENGER
Sailors, my lord, they say. I saw them not.
They were given me by Claudio. He received them.   40
KING CLAUDIUS
Laertes, you shall hear them.—Leave us.
                                        Exit Messenger
(*Reads*) 'High and mighty, you shall know I am set
naked on your kingdom. Tomorrow shall I beg leave
to see your kingly eyes, when I shall, first asking your
pardon, thereunto recount th'occasions of my sudden
and more strange return.   46
                              Hamlet.'
What should this mean? Are all the rest come back?
Or is it some abuse, and no such thing?
LAERTES
Know you the hand?
KING CLAUDIUS   'Tis Hamlet's character.   50
'Naked'—and in a postscript here he says
'Alone'. Can you advise me?
LAERTES
I'm lost in it, my lord. But let him come.
It warms the very sickness in my heart
That I shall live and tell him to his teeth,   55
'Thus diddest thou'.
KING CLAUDIUS   If it be so, Laertes—
As how should it be so, how otherwise?—
Will you be ruled by me?
LAERTES
If so you'll not o'errule me to a peace.
KING CLAUDIUS
To thine own peace. If he be now returned,   60
As checking at his voyage, and that he means
No more to undertake it, I will work him
To an exploit, now ripe in my device,
Under the which he shall not choose but fall;
And for his death no wind of blame shall breathe;   65
But even his mother shall uncharge the practice
And call it accident. Some two months since
Here was a gentleman of Normandy.
I've seen myself, and served against, the French,
And they can well on horseback; but this gallant   70
Had witchcraft in't. He grew into his seat,
And to such wondrous doing brought his horse
As had he been incorpsed and demi-natured
With the brave beast. So far he passed my thought
That I in forgery of shapes and tricks   75
Come short of what he did.
LAERTES   A Norman was't?

KING CLAUDIUS A Norman.
LAERTES
Upon my life, Lamord.
KING CLAUDIUS   The very same.
LAERTES
I know him well. He is the brooch indeed,
And gem, of all the nation.
KING CLAUDIUS   He made confession of you,
And gave you such a masterly report   81
For art and exercise in your defence,
And for your rapier most especially,
That he cried out 'twould be a sight indeed
If one could match you. Sir, this report of his   85
Did Hamlet so envenom with his envy
That he could nothing do but wish and beg
Your sudden coming o'er to play with him.
Now, out of this—
LAERTES   What out of this, my lord?
KING CLAUDIUS
Laertes, was your father dear to you?   90
Or are you like the painting of a sorrow,
A face without a heart?
LAERTES   Why ask you this?
KING CLAUDIUS
Not that I think you did not love your father,
But that I know love is begun by time,
And that I see, in passages of proof,   95
Time qualifies the spark and fire of it.
Hamlet comes back. What would you undertake
To show yourself your father's son in deed
More than in words?
LAERTES   To cut his throat i'th' church.
KING CLAUDIUS
No place indeed should murder sanctuarize.   100
Revenge should have no bounds. But, good Laertes,
Will you do this?—keep close within your chamber.
Hamlet returned shall know you are come home.
We'll put on those shall praise your excellence,
And set a double varnish on the fame   105
The Frenchman gave you; bring you, in fine, together,
And wager on your heads. He, being remiss,
Most generous, and free from all contriving,
Will not peruse the foils; so that with ease,
Or with a little shuffling, you may choose   110
A sword unbated, and, in a pass of practice,
Requite him for your father.
LAERTES   I will do't,
And for that purpose I'll anoint my sword.
I bought an unction of a mountebank
So mortal that, but dip a knife in it,   115
Where it draws blood no cataplasm so rare,
Collected from all simples that have virtue
Under the moon, can save the thing from death
That is but scratched withal. I'll touch my point
With this contagion, that if I gall him slightly,   120
It may be death.
KING CLAUDIUS   Let's further think of this;
Weigh what convenience both of time and means

May fit us to our shape. If this should fail,
And that our drift look through our bad performance,
'Twere better not essayed. Therefore this project   125
Should have a back or second that might hold
If this should blast in proof. Soft, let me see.
We'll make a solemn wager on your cunnings . . .
I ha't! When in your motion you are hot and dry—
As make your bouts more violent to that end—   130
And that he calls for drink, I'll have prepared him
A chalice for the nonce, whereon but sipping,
If he by chance escape your venomed stuck,
Our purpose may hold there.—

Enter Queen Gertrude

How now, sweet Queen?

QUEEN GERTRUDE
One woe doth tread upon another's heel,   135
So fast they follow. Your sister's drowned, Laertes.

LAERTES Drowned? O, where?

QUEEN GERTRUDE
There is a willow grows aslant a brook
That shows his hoar leaves in the glassy stream.
Therewith fantastic garlands did she make   140
Of crow-flowers, nettles, daisies, and long purples,
That liberal shepherds give a grosser name,
But our cold maids do dead men's fingers call them.
There on the pendent boughs her crownet weeds
Clamb'ring to hang, an envious sliver broke,   145
When down the weedy trophies and herself
Fell in the weeping brook. Her clothes spread wide,
And mermaid-like a while they bore her up;
Which time she chanted snatches of old tunes,
As one incapable of her own distress,   150
Or like a creature native and endued
Unto that element. But long it could not be
Till that her garments, heavy with their drink,
Pulled the poor wretch from her melodious lay
To muddy death.   155

LAERTES Alas, then is she drowned.

QUEEN GERTRUDE Drowned, drowned.

LAERTES
Too much of water hast thou, poor Ophelia,
And therefore I forbid my tears. But yet
It is our trick; nature her custom holds,   160
Let shame say what it will.

He weeps

When these are gone,
The woman will be out. Adieu, my lord.
I have a speech of fire that fain would blaze,
But that this folly douts it.   *Exit*

KING CLAUDIUS   Let's follow, Gertrude.
How much I had to do to calm his rage!   165
Now fear I this will give it start again;
Therefore let's follow.   *Exeunt*

5.1   *Enter two Clowns ⌜carrying a spade and a pickaxe⌝*

FIRST CLOWN Is she to be buried in Christian burial that
wilfully seeks her own salvation?

SECOND CLOWN I tell thee she is, and therefore make her
grave straight. The coroner hath sat on her, and finds
it Christian burial.   5

FIRST CLOWN How can that be unless she drowned herself
in her own defence?

SECOND CLOWN Why, 'tis found so.

FIRST CLOWN It must be *se offendendo*, it cannot be else;
for here lies the point: if I drown myself wittingly, it
argues an act; and an act hath three branches: it is
to act, to do, and to perform. Argal she drowned herself
wittingly.

SECOND CLOWN Nay, but hear you, Goodman Delver.   14

FIRST CLOWN Give me leave. Here lies the water—good.
Here stands the man—good. If the man go to this water
and drown himself, it is, will he nill he, he goes. Mark
you that. But if the water come to him and drown him,
he drowns not himself; argal he that is not guilty of
his own death shortens not his own life.   20

SECOND CLOWN But is this law?

FIRST CLOWN Ay, marry, is't: coroner's quest law.

SECOND CLOWN Will you ha' the truth on't? If this had
not been a gentlewoman, she should have been buried
out o' Christian burial.   25

FIRST CLOWN Why, there thou sayst, and the more pity
that great folk should have count'nance in this world
to drown or hang themselves more than their even
Christian. Come, my spade. There is no ancient
gentlemen but gardeners, ditchers, and gravemakers;
they hold up Adam's profession.   31

⌜*First Clown digs*⌝

SECOND CLOWN Was he a gentleman?

FIRST CLOWN A was the first that ever bore arms.

SECOND CLOWN Why, he had none.   34

FIRST CLOWN What, art a heathen? How dost thou
understand the Scripture? The Scripture says Adam
digged. Could he dig without arms? I'll put another
question to thee. If thou answerest me not to the
purpose, confess thyself—

SECOND CLOWN Go to.   40

FIRST CLOWN What is he that builds stronger than either
the mason, the shipwright, or the carpenter?

SECOND CLOWN The gallows-maker; for that frame outlives
a thousand tenants.   44

FIRST CLOWN I like thy wit well, in good faith. The gallows
does well. But how does it well? It does well to those
that do ill. Now thou dost ill to say the gallows is built
stronger than the church, argal the gallows may do
well to thee. To't again, come.

SECOND CLOWN 'Who builds stronger than a mason, a
shipwright, or a carpenter?'   51

FIRST CLOWN Ay, tell me that, and unyoke.

SECOND CLOWN Marry, now I can tell.

FIRST CLOWN To't.

SECOND CLOWN Mass, I cannot tell.   55

Enter Prince Hamlet and Horatio afar off

FIRST CLOWN Cudgel thy brains no more about it, for your
dull ass will not mend his pace with beating; and when

you are asked this question next, say 'a grave-maker'; the houses that he makes lasts till doomsday. Go, get thee to Johan. Fetch me a stoup of liquor. 60

Exit Second Clown

(*Sings*)

In youth when I did love, did love,
    Methought it was very sweet
To contract-O-the time for-a-my behove,
    O methought there-a-was nothing-a-meet.

HAMLET Has this fellow no feeling of his business that a sings at grave-making? 66

HORATIO Custom hath made it in him a property of easiness.

HAMLET 'Tis e'en so; the hand of little employment hath the daintier sense. 70

FIRST CLOWN (*sings*)

    But age with his stealing steps
        Hath caught me in his clutch,
    And hath shipped me intil the land,
        As if I had never been such. 74

⌈*He throws up a skull*⌉

HAMLET That skull had a tongue in it and could sing once. How the knave jowls it to th' ground as if 'twere Cain's jawbone, that did the first murder! This might be the pate of a politician which this ass o'er-offices, one that would circumvent God, might it not?

HORATIO It might, my lord. 80

HAMLET Or of a courtier, which could say 'Good morrow, sweet lord. How dost thou, good lord?' This might be my lord such a one, that praised my lord such a one's horse when a meant to beg it, might it not?

HORATIO Ay, my lord. 85

HAMLET Why, e'en so, and now my lady Worm's, chapless, and knocked about the mazard with a sexton's spade. Here's fine revolution, an we had the trick to see't. Did these bones cost no more the breeding but to play at loggats with 'em? Mine ache to think on't. 90

FIRST CLOWN (*sings*)

    A pickaxe and a spade, a spade,
        For and a shrouding-sheet;
    O, a pit of clay for to be made
        For such a guest is meet. 94

⌈*He throws up another skull*⌉

HAMLET There's another. Why might not that be the skull of a lawyer? Where be his quiddits now, his quillets, his cases, his tenures, and his tricks? Why does he suffer this rude knave now to knock him about the sconce with a dirty shovel, and will not tell him of his action of battery? H'm! This fellow might be in 's time a great buyer of land, with his statutes, his recognizances, his fines, his double vouchers, his recoveries. Is this the fine of his fines and the recovery of his recoveries, to have his fine pate full of fine dirt? Will his vouchers vouch him no more of his purchases, and double ones too, than the length and breadth of a pair of indentures? The very conveyances of his lands

will hardly lie in this box; and must th'inheritor himself have no more, ha?

HORATIO Not a jot more, my lord. 110

HAMLET Is not parchment made of sheepskins?

HORATIO Ay, my lord, and of calf-skins too.

HAMLET They are sheep and calves that seek out assurance in that. I will speak to this fellow. (*To the First Clown*) Whose grave's this, sirrah? 115

FIRST CLOWN Mine, sir.

(*Sings*)   O, a pit of clay for to be made
            For such a guest is meet.

HAMLET I think it be thine indeed, for thou liest in't. 119

FIRST CLOWN You lie out on't, sir, and therefore it is not yours. For my part, I do not lie in't, and yet it is mine.

HAMLET Thou dost lie in't, to be in't and say 'tis thine. 'Tis for the dead, not for the quick; therefore thou liest.

FIRST CLOWN 'Tis a quick lie, sir, 'twill away again from me to you. 125

HAMLET What man dost thou dig it for?

FIRST CLOWN For no man, sir.

HAMLET What woman, then?

FIRST CLOWN For none, neither.

HAMLET Who is to be buried in't? 130

FIRST CLOWN One that was a woman, sir; but, rest her soul, she's dead.

HAMLET How absolute the knave is! We must speak by the card, or equivocation will undo us. By the Lord, Horatio, these three years I have taken note of it. The age is grown so picked that the toe of the peasant comes so near the heel of the courtier he galls his kibe. (*To the First Clown*) How long hast thou been a grave-maker?

FIRST CLOWN Of all the days i'th' year I came to't that day that our last King Hamlet o'ercame Fortinbras. 141

HAMLET How long is that since?

FIRST CLOWN Cannot you tell that? Every fool can tell that. It was the very day that young Hamlet was born—he that was mad and sent into England. 145

HAMLET Ay, marry, why was he sent into England?

FIRST CLOWN Why, because a was mad. A shall recover his wits there; or if a do not, 'tis no great matter there.

HAMLET Why?

FIRST CLOWN 'Twill not be seen in him there. There the men are as mad as he. 151

HAMLET How came he mad?

FIRST CLOWN Very strangely, they say.

HAMLET How strangely?

FIRST CLOWN Faith, e'en with losing his wits. 155

HAMLET Upon what ground?

FIRST CLOWN Why, here in Denmark. I have been sexton here, man and boy, thirty years.

HAMLET How long will a man lie i'th' earth ere he rot?

FIRST CLOWN I'faith, if a be not rotten before a die—as we have many pocky corpses nowadays, that will scarce hold the laying in—a will last you some eight year or nine year. A tanner will last you nine year.

HAMLET Why he more than another?

FIRST CLOWN Why, sir, his hide is so tanned with his trade that a will keep out water a great while, and your water is a sore decayer of your whoreson dead body. Here's a skull, now. This skull has lain in the earth three and twenty years.

HAMLET Whose was it?   170

FIRST CLOWN A whoreson mad fellow's it was. Whose do you think it was?

HAMLET Nay, I know not.

FIRST CLOWN A pestilence on him for a mad rogue—a poured a flagon of Rhenish on my head once! This same skull, sir, was Yorick's skull, the King's jester. 176

HAMLET This?

FIRST CLOWN E'en that.

HAMLET Let me see.   179

He takes the skull

Alas, poor Yorick. I knew him, Horatio—a fellow of infinite jest, of most excellent fancy. He hath borne me on his back a thousand times; and now, how abhorred my imagination is! My gorge rises at it. Here hung those lips that I have kissed I know not how oft. Where be your gibes now, your gambols, your songs, your flashes of merriment that were wont to set the table on a roar? Not one now to mock your own grinning? Quite chop-fallen? Now get you to my lady's chamber and tell her, let her paint an inch thick, to this favour she must come. Make her laugh at that. Prithee, Horatio, tell me one thing.   191

HORATIO What's that, my lord?

HAMLET Dost thou think Alexander looked o' this fashion i'th' earth?

HORATIO E'en so.   195

HAMLET And smelt so? Pah!

⌈*He throws the skull down*⌉

HORATIO E'en so, my lord.

HAMLET To what base uses we may return, Horatio! Why may not imagination trace the noble dust of Alexander till a find it stopping a bung-hole?   200

HORATIO 'Twere to consider too curiously to consider so.

HAMLET No, faith, not a jot; but to follow him thither with modesty enough, and likelihood to lead it, as thus: Alexander died, Alexander was buried, Alexander returneth into dust, the dust is earth, of earth we make loam, and why of that loam whereto he was converted might they not stop a beer-barrel?
Imperial Caesar, dead and turned to clay,
Might stop a hole to keep the wind away.
O, that that earth which kept the world in awe   210
Should patch a wall t'expel the winter's flaw!
But soft, but soft; aside.

Hamlet and Horatio stand aside. Enter King Claudius, Queen Gertrude, Laertes, and a coffin, with a Priest and lords attendant

                Here comes the King,
The Queen, the courtiers—who is that they follow,
And with such maimèd rites? This doth betoken
The corpse they follow did with desp'rate hand   215

Fordo it own life. 'Twas of some estate.
Couch we a while, and mark.

LAERTES   What ceremony else?

HAMLET (*aside to Horatio*)
That is Laertes, a very noble youth. Mark.

LAERTES What ceremony else?

PRIEST
Her obsequies have been as far enlarged   220
As we have warrantise. Her death was doubtful,
And but that great command o'ersways the order
She should in ground unsanctified have lodged
Till the last trumpet. For charitable prayers,
Shards, flints, and pebbles should be thrown on her,
Yet here she is allowed her virgin rites,   226
Her maiden strewments, and the bringing home
Of bell and burial.

LAERTES Must there no more be done?

PRIEST No more be done.   230
We should profane the service of the dead
To sing sage requiem and such rest to her
As to peace-parted souls.

LAERTES   Lay her i'th' earth,
And from her fair and unpolluted flesh
May violets spring. I tell thee, churlish priest,   235
A minist'ring angel shall my sister be
When thou liest howling.

HAMLET (*aside*) What, the fair Ophelia!

QUEEN GERTRUDE (*scattering flowers*)
Sweets to the sweet. Farewell.
I hoped thou shouldst have been my Hamlet's wife. 240
I thought thy bride-bed to have decked, sweet maid,
And not t'have strewed thy grave.

LAERTES   O, treble woe
Fall ten times treble on that cursèd head
Whose wicked deed thy most ingenious sense
Deprived thee of!—Hold off the earth a while,   245
Till I have caught her once more in mine arms.

He leaps into the grave

Now pile your dust upon the quick and dead
Till of this flat a mountain you have made
To o'ertop old Pelion, or the skyish head
Of blue Olympus.

HAMLET (*coming forward*) What is he whose grief   250
Bears such an emphasis, whose phrase of sorrow
Conjures the wand'ring stars and makes them stand
Like wonder-wounded hearers? This is I,
Hamlet the Dane.

⌈*Hamlet leaps in after Laertes*⌉

LAERTES The devil take thy soul.   255

HAMLET Thou pray'st not well.
I prithee take thy fingers from my throat,
For though I am not splenative and rash,
Yet have I something in me dangerous,
Which let thy wiseness fear. Away thy hand.   260

KING CLAUDIUS (*to Lords*)
Pluck them asunder.

QUEEN GERTRUDE   Hamlet, Hamlet!

ALL ⌈THE LORDS⌉
  Gentlemen!
HORATIO (*to Hamlet*) Good my lord, be quiet.
HAMLET
  Why, I will fight with him upon this theme
  Until my eyelids will no longer wag.
QUEEN GERTRUDE O my son, what theme?   265
HAMLET
  I loved Ophelia. Forty thousand brothers
  Could not, with all their quantity of love,
  Make up my sum.—What wilt thou do for her?
KING CLAUDIUS O, he is mad, Laertes.
QUEEN GERTRUDE (*to Laertes*) For love of God, forbear him. 270
HAMLET (*to Laertes*) 'Swounds, show me what thou'lt do.
  Woot weep, woot fight, woot fast, woot tear thyself,
  Woot drink up eisel, eat a crocodile?
  I'll do't. Dost thou come here to whine,
  To outface me with leaping in her grave?   275
  Be buried quick with her, and so will I.
  And if thou prate of mountains, let them throw
  Millions of acres on us, till our ground,
  Singeing his pate against the burning zone,
  Make Ossa like a wart. Nay, an thou'lt mouth,   280
  I'll rant as well as thou.
KING CLAUDIUS ⌈*to Laertes*⌉ This is mere madness,
  And thus a while the fit will work on him.
  Anon, as patient as the female dove
  When that her golden couplets are disclosed,
  His silence will sit drooping.
HAMLET (*to Laertes*)   Hear you, sir,   285
  What is the reason that you use me thus?
  I loved you ever. But it is no matter.
  Let Hercules himself do what he may,
  The cat will mew, and dog will have his day.   *Exit*
KING CLAUDIUS
  I pray you, good Horatio, wait upon him.   *Exit Horatio*
  (*To Laertes*) Strengthen your patience in our last
    night's speech.   291
  We'll put the matter to the present push.—
  Good Gertrude, set some watch over your son.—
  This grave shall have a living monument.
  An hour of quiet shortly shall we see;   295
  Till then, in patience our proceeding be.   *Exeunt*

5.2   *Enter Prince Hamlet and Horatio*
HAMLET
  So much for this, sir. Now, let me see, the other.
  You do remember all the circumstance?
HORATIO Remember it, my lord!
HAMLET
  Sir, in my heart there was a kind of fighting
  That would not let me sleep. Methought I lay   5
  Worse than the mutines in the bilboes. Rashly—
  And praised be rashness for it: let us know
  Our indiscretion sometime serves us well
  When our dear plots do pall, and that should teach us
  There's a divinity that shapes our ends,   10
  Rough-hew them how we will—

HORATIO That is most certain.
HAMLET Up from my cabin,
  My sea-gown scarfed about me in the dark,
  Groped I to find out them, had my desire,   15
  Fingered their packet, and in fine withdrew
  To mine own room again, making so bold,
  My fears forgetting manners, to unseal
  Their grand commission; where I found, Horatio—
  O royal knavery!—an exact command,   20
  Larded with many several sorts of reasons
  Importing Denmark's health, and England's, too,
  With ho! such bugs and goblins in my life,
  That on the supervise, no leisure bated,
  No, not to stay the grinding of the axe,   25
  My head should be struck off.
HORATIO   Is't possible?
HAMLET (*giving it to him*)
  Here's the commission. Read it at more leisure.
  But wilt thou hear me how I did proceed?
HORATIO I beseech you.
HAMLET
  Being thus benetted round with villainies—   30
  Ere I could make a prologue to my brains,
  They had begun the play—I sat me down,
  Devised a new commission, wrote it fair.
  I once did hold it, as our statists do,
  A baseness to write fair, and laboured much   35
  How to forget that learning; but, sir, now
  It did me yeoman's service. Wilt thou know
  Th'effect of what I wrote?
HORATIO   Ay, good my lord.
HAMLET
  An earnest conjuration from the King,
  As England was his faithful tributary,   40
  As love between them like the palm should flourish,
  As peace should still her wheaten garland wear
  And stand a comma 'tween their amities,
  And many such like 'as'es of great charge,
  That on the view and know of these contents,   45
  Without debatement further more or less,
  He should the bearers put to sudden death,
  Not shriving-time allowed.
HORATIO   How was this sealed?
HAMLET
  Why, even in that was heaven ordinant.
  I had my father's signet in my purse,   50
  Which was the model of that Danish seal;
  Folded the writ up in the form of th'other,
  Subscribed it, gave't th'impression, placed it safely,
  The changeling never known. Now the next day
  Was our sea-fight; and what to this was sequent 55
  Thou know'st already.
HORATIO
  So Guildenstern and Rosencrantz go to't.
HAMLET
  Why, man, they did make love to this employment.
  They are not near my conscience. Their defeat
  Doth by their own insinuation grow.   60
  'Tis dangerous when the baser nature comes

Between the pass and fell incensèd points
Of mighty opposites.

HORATIO   Why, what a king is this!

HAMLET
Does it not, think'st thee, stand me now upon—
He that hath killed my king and whored my mother, 65
Popped in between th'election and my hopes,
Thrown out his angle for my proper life,
And with such coz'nage—is't not perfect conscience
To quit him with this arm? And is't not to be damned
To let this canker of our nature come   70
In further evil?

HORATIO
It must be shortly known to him from England
What is the issue of the business there.

HAMLET
It will be short. The interim's mine,
And a man's life's no more than to say 'one'.   75
But I am very sorry, good Horatio,
That to Laertes I forgot myself;
For by the image of my cause I see
The portraiture of his. I'll court his favours.
But sure, the bravery of his grief did put me   80
Into a tow'ring passion.

HORATIO   Peace, who comes here?

Enter young Osric, a courtier, ⌈taking off his hat⌉

OSRIC
Your lordship is right welcome back to Denmark.

HAMLET I humbly thank you, sir. (*To Horatio*) Dost know
this water-fly?

HORATIO No, my good lord.   85

HAMLET Thy state is the more gracious, for 'tis a vice to
know him. He hath much land, and fertile. Let a beast
be lord of beasts, and his crib shall stand at the king's
mess. 'Tis a chuff, but, as I say, spacious in the
possession of dirt.   90

OSRIC Sweet lord, if your friendship were at leisure I
should impart a thing to you from his majesty.

HAMLET I will receive it, sir, with all diligence of spirit.
Put your bonnet to his right use; 'tis for the head.

OSRIC I thank your lordship, 'tis very hot.   95

HAMLET No, believe me, 'tis very cold. The wind is
northerly.

OSRIC It is indifferent cold, my lord, indeed.

HAMLET Methinks it is very sultry and hot for my
complexion.   100

OSRIC Exceedingly, my lord. It is very sultry, as 'twere—
I cannot tell how. But, my lord, his majesty bade me
signify to you that a has laid a great wager on your
head. Sir, this is the matter.

HAMLET I beseech you, remember.   105

OSRIC Nay, good my lord, for mine ease, in good faith.
Sir, you are not ignorant of what excellence Laertes is
at his weapon.

HAMLET What's his weapon?

OSRIC Rapier and dagger.   110

HAMLET That's two of his weapons. But well.

OSRIC The King, sir, hath wagered with him six Barbary

horses, against the which he imponed, as I take it, six
French rapiers and poniards, with their assigns as
girdle, hanger, or so. Three of the carriages, in faith,
are very dear to fancy, very responsive to the hilts,
most delicate carriages, and of very liberal conceit.

HAMLET What call you the carriages?

OSRIC The carriages, sir, are the hangers.   119

HAMLET The phrase would be more germane to the matter
if we could carry cannon by our sides. I would it might
be hangers till then. But on: six Barbary horses against
six French swords, their assigns, and three liberal-
conceited carriages—that's the French bet against the
Danish. Why is this 'imponed', as you call it?   125

OSRIC The King, sir, hath laid, sir, that in a dozen passes
between you and him he shall not exceed you three
hits. He hath on't twelve for nine, and it would come
to immediate trial if your lordship would vouchsafe the
answer.   130

HAMLET How if I answer no?

OSRIC I mean, my lord, the opposition of your person in
trial.

HAMLET Sir, I will walk here in the hall. If it please his
majesty, 'tis the breathing time of day with me. Let the
foils be brought; the gentleman willing, an the King
hold his purpose, I will win for him an I can. If not,
I'll gain nothing but my shame and the odd hits.

OSRIC Shall I re-deliver you e'en so?

HAMLET To this effect, sir; after what flourish your nature
will.   141

OSRIC I commend my duty to your lordship.

HAMLET Yours, yours.   *Exit Osric*
He does well to commend it himself; there are no
tongues else for 's turn.   145

HORATIO This lapwing runs away with the shell on his
head.

HAMLET A did comply with his dug before a sucked it.
Thus has he—and many more of the same bevy that I
know the drossy age dotes on—only got the tune of
the time and outward habit of encounter, a kind of
yeasty collection which carries them through and
through the most fanned and winnowed opinions; and
do but blow them to their trial, the bubbles are out.

HORATIO You will lose this wager, my lord.   155

HAMLET I do not think so. Since he went into France, I
have been in continual practice. I shall win at the odds.
But thou wouldst not think how all here about my
heart—but it is no matter.

HORATIO Nay, good my lord—   160

HAMLET It is but foolery, but it is such a kind of gain-
giving as would perhaps trouble a woman.

HORATIO If your mind dislike anything, obey it. I will
forestall their repair hither, and say you are not fit.

HAMLET Not a whit. We defy augury. There's a special
providence in the fall of a sparrow. If it be now, 'tis
not to come. If it be not to come, it will be now. If it
be not now, yet it will come. The readiness is all. Since
no man has aught of what he leaves, what is't to leave
betimes?   170

*Enter King Claudius, Queen Gertrude, Laertes, and
lords, with Osric and other attendants with
⌜trumpets, drums, cushions⌝, foils, and gauntlets; a
table, and flagons of wine on it*
KING CLAUDIUS
Come, Hamlet, come, and take this hand from me.
HAMLET (*to Laertes*)
Give me your pardon, sir. I've done you wrong;
But pardon't as you are a gentleman.
This presence knows,
And you must needs have heard, how I am punished
With sore distraction. What I have done   176
That might your nature, honour, and exception
Roughly awake, I here proclaim was madness.
Was't Hamlet wronged Laertes? Never Hamlet.
If Hamlet from himself be ta'en away,   180
And when he's not himself does wrong Laertes,
Then Hamlet does it not, Hamlet denies it.
Who does it then? His madness. If't be so,
Hamlet is of the faction that is wronged.
His madness is poor Hamlet's enemy.   185
Sir, in this audience
Let my disclaiming from a purposed evil
Free me so far in your most generous thoughts
That I have shot mine arrow o'er the house
And hurt my brother.
LAERTES   I am satisfied in nature,   190
Whose motive in this case should stir me most
To my revenge. But in my terms of honour
I stand aloof, and will no reconcilement
Till by some elder masters of known honour
I have a voice and precedent of peace   195
To keep my name ungored; but till that time
I do receive your offered love like love,
And will not wrong it.
HAMLET   I do embrace it freely,
And will this brothers' wager frankly play.—
(*To attendants*) Give us the foils. Come on.
LAERTES (*to attendants*)   Come, one for me.
HAMLET
I'll be your foil, Laertes. In mine ignorance   201
Your skill shall, like a star i'th' darkest night,
Stick fiery off indeed.
LAERTES You mock me, sir.
HAMLET No, by this hand.   205
KING CLAUDIUS
Give them the foils, young Osric. Cousin Hamlet,
You know the wager?
HAMLET   Very well, my lord.
Your grace hath laid the odds o'th' weaker side.
KING CLAUDIUS
I do not fear it; I have seen you both.
But since he is bettered, we have therefore odds. 210
LAERTES (*taking a foil*)
This is too heavy; let me see another.
HAMLET (*taking a foil*)
This likes me well. These foils have all a length?
OSRIC Ay, my good lord.

Hamlet and Laertes prepare to play
KING CLAUDIUS (*to attendants*)
Set me the stoups of wine upon that table.
If Hamlet give the first or second hit,   215
Or quit in answer of the third exchange,
Let all the battlements their ordnance fire.
The King shall drink to Hamlet's better breath,
And in the cup an union shall he throw
Richer than that which four successive kings   220
In Denmark's crown have worn. Give me the cups,
And let the kettle to the trumpet speak,
The trumpet to the cannoneer without,
The cannons to the heavens, the heaven to earth,
'Now the King drinks to Hamlet'.
     Trumpets the while he drinks
                                   Come, begin.   225
And you, the judges, bear a wary eye.
HAMLET (*to Laertes*) Come on, sir.
LAERTES Come, my lord.
     They play
HAMLET One.
LAERTES No.   230
HAMLET (*to Osric*) Judgement.
OSRIC A hit, a very palpable hit.
LAERTES Well, again.
KING CLAUDIUS
Stay. Give me drink. Hamlet, this pearl is thine.
Here's to thy health.—   235
     ⌜*Drum and*⌝ *trumpets sound, and shot goes off*
                                   Give him the cup.
HAMLET
I'll play this bout first. Set it by a while.—
Come.
     They play again
          Another hit. What say you?
LAERTES
A touch, a touch, I do confess.
KING CLAUDIUS
Our son shall win.
QUEEN GERTRUDE   He's fat and scant of breath.— 240
Here, Hamlet, take my napkin. Rub thy brows.
The Queen carouses to thy fortune, Hamlet.
HAMLET
Good madam.
KING CLAUDIUS   Gertrude, do not drink.
QUEEN GERTRUDE
I will, my lord, I pray you pardon me.
     She drinks, then offers the cup to Hamlet
KING CLAUDIUS (*aside*)
It is the poisoned cup; it is too late.   245
HAMLET
I dare not drink yet, madam; by and by.
QUEEN GERTRUDE (*to Hamlet*) Come, let me wipe thy face.
LAERTES (*aside to Claudius*) My lord, I'll hit him now.
KING CLAUDIUS (*aside to Laertes*) I do not think't.
LAERTES (*aside*)
And yet 'tis almost 'gainst my conscience.   250

HAMLET
Come for the third, Laertes, you but dally.
I pray you pass with your best violence.
I am afeard you make a wanton of me.
LAERTES
Say you so? Come on.
They play
OSRIC   Nothing neither way.
LAERTES (*to Hamlet*)
Have at you now!
⌜*Laertes wounds Hamlet.*⌝ *In scuffling, they change*
rapiers, ⌜*and Hamlet wounds Laertes*⌝
KING CLAUDIUS (*to attendants*)
Part them, they are incensed.   255
HAMLET (*to Laertes*)
Nay, come again.
⌜*The Queen falls down*⌝
OSRIC   Look to the Queen there, ho!
HORATIO
They bleed on both sides. (*To Hamlet*) How is't, my lord?
OSRIC How is't, Laertes?
LAERTES
Why, as a woodcock to mine own springe, Osric.
I am justly killed with mine own treachery.   260
HAMLET
How does the Queen?
KING CLAUDIUS   She swoons to see them bleed.
QUEEN GERTRUDE
No, no, the drink, the drink! O my dear Hamlet,
The drink, the drink—I am poisoned.   ⌜*She dies*⌝
HAMLET
O villainy! Ho! Let the door be locked!   ⌜*Exit Osric*⌝
Treachery, seek it out.   265
LAERTES
It is here, Hamlet. Hamlet, thou art slain.
No med'cine in the world can do thee good.
In thee there is not half an hour of life.
The treacherous instrument is in thy hand,
Unbated and envenomed. The foul practice   270
Hath turned itself on me. Lo, here I lie,
Never to rise again. Thy mother's poisoned.
I can no more. The King, the King's to blame.
HAMLET
The point envenomed too? Then, venom, to thy work.
He hurts King Claudius
ALL THE COURTIERS Treason, treason!   275
KING CLAUDIUS
O yet defend me, friends! I am but hurt.
HAMLET
Here, thou incestuous, murd'rous, damnèd Dane,
Drink off this potion. Is thy union here?
Follow my mother.   *King Claudius dies*
LAERTES   He is justly served.
It is a poison tempered by himself.   280
Exchange forgiveness with me, noble Hamlet.
Mine and my father's death come not upon thee,
Nor thine on me.   *He dies*

HAMLET
Heaven make thee free of it! I follow thee.
I am dead, Horatio. Wretched Queen, adieu!   285
You that look pale and tremble at this chance,
That are but mutes or audience to this act,
Had I but time—as this fell sergeant Death
Is strict in his arrest—O, I could tell you—
But let it be. Horatio, I am dead,   290
Thou liv'st. Report me and my cause aright
To the unsatisfied.
HORATIO   Never believe it.
I am more an antique Roman than a Dane.
Here's yet some liquor left.
HAMLET   As thou'rt a man,
Give me the cup. Let go. By heaven, I'll ha't.   295
O God, Horatio, what a wounded name,
Things standing thus unknown, shall live behind me!
If thou didst ever hold me in thy heart,
Absent thee from felicity a while,
And in this harsh world draw thy breath in pain   300
To tell my story.
March afar off, and shout within
What warlike noise is this?
Enter Osric
OSRIC
Young Fortinbras, with conquest come from Poland,
To th'ambassadors of England gives
This warlike volley.
HAMLET   O, I die, Horatio!
The potent poison quite o'ercrows my spirit.   305
I cannot live to hear the news from England,
But I do prophesy th'election lights
On Fortinbras. He has my dying voice.
So tell him, with th'occurrents, more and less,
Which have solicited. The rest is silence.   310
O, O, O, O!   *He dies*
HORATIO
Now cracks a noble heart. Good night, sweet prince,
And flights of angels sing thee to thy rest.—
Why does the drum come hither?
Enter Fortinbras with the English ⌜*Ambassadors*⌝,
with a drummer, colours, and attendants
FORTINBRAS Where is this sight?   315
HORATIO What is it ye would see?
If aught of woe or wonder, cease your search.
FORTINBRAS
This quarry cries on havoc. O proud death,
What feast is toward in thine eternal cell
That thou so many princes at a shot   320
So bloodily hast struck!
AMBASSADOR   The sight is dismal,
And our affairs from England come too late.
The ears are senseless that should give us hearing
To tell him his commandment is fulfilled,
That Rosencrantz and Guildenstern are dead.   325
Where should we have our thanks?
HORATIO   Not from his mouth,
Had it th'ability of life to thank you.

He never gave commandment for their death.
But since so jump upon this bloody question
You from the Polack wars, and you from England, 330
Are here arrived, give order that these bodies
High on a stage be placèd to the view;
And let me speak to th' yet unknowing world
How these things came about. So shall you hear
Of carnal, bloody, and unnatural acts, 335
Of accidental judgements, casual slaughters,
Of deaths put on by cunning and forced cause;
And, in this upshot, purposes mistook
Fall'n on th'inventors' heads. All this can I
Truly deliver.
FORTINBRAS   Let us haste to hear it, 340
And call the noblest to the audience.
For me, with sorrow I embrace my fortune.
I have some rights of memory in this kingdom,
Which now to claim my vantage doth invite me.

HORATIO
Of that I shall have also cause to speak, 345
And from his mouth whose voice will draw on more.
But let this same be presently performed,
Even whiles men's minds are wild, lest more
     mischance
On plots and errors happen.
FORTINBRAS   Let four captains
Bear Hamlet like a soldier to the stage, 350
For he was likely, had he been put on,
To have proved most royally; and for his passage,
The soldiers' music and the rites of war
Speak loudly for him.
Take up the body. Such a sight as this 355
Becomes the field, but here shows much amiss.
Go, bid the soldiers shoot.
          Exeunt, marching, with the bodies; after the
          which, a peal of ordnance are shot off

ADDITIONAL PASSAGES

A. Just before the second entrance of the Ghost in 1.1 (l. 106.1), Q2 has these additional lines:

BARNARDO
I think it be no other but e'en so.
Well may it sort that this portentous figure
Comes armèd through our watch so like the king
That was and is the question of these wars.

HORATIO
A mote it is to trouble the mind's eye. 5
In the most high and palmy state of Rome,
A little ere the mightiest Julius fell,
The graves stood tenantless, and the sheeted dead
Did squeak and gibber in the Roman streets
At stars with trains of fire, and dews of blood, 10
Disasters in the sun; and the moist star,
Upon whose influence Neptune's empire stands,
Was sick almost to doomsday with eclipse.
And even the like precurse of feared events,
As harbingers preceding still the fates, 15
And prologue to the omen coming on,
Have heaven and earth together demonstrated
Unto our climature and countrymen.

B. Just before the entrance of the Ghost in 1.4 (l. 18.1), Q2 has these additional lines continuing Hamlet's speech:

This heavy-headed revel east and west
Makes us traduced and taxed of other nations.
They clepe us drunkards, and with swinish phrase
Soil our addition; and indeed it takes
From our achievements, though performed at height, 5
The pith and marrow of our attribute.
So, oft it chances in particular men

That, for some vicious mole of nature in them—
As in their birth, wherein they are not guilty,
Since nature cannot choose his origin,
By the o'ergrowth of some complexion, 10
Oft breaking down the pales and forts of reason,
Or by some habit that too much o'erleavens
The form of plausive manners—that these men,
Carrying, I say, the stamp of one defect, 15
Being nature's livery or fortune's star,
His virtues else be they as pure as grace,
As infinite as man may undergo,
Shall in the general censure take corruption
From that particular fault. The dram of evil 20
Doth all the noble substance over-daub
To his own scandal.

C. After 1.4.55, Q2 has these additional lines continuing Horatio's speech:

The very place puts toys of desperation,
Without more motive, into every brain
That looks so many fathoms to the sea
And hears it roar beneath.

D. After 3.2.163, Q2 has this additional couplet concluding the Player Queen's speech:

Where love is great, the littlest doubts are fear;
Where little fears grow great, great love grows there.

E. After 3.2.208, Q2 has this additional couplet in the middle of the Player Queen's speech:

To desperation turn my trust and hope;
An anchor's cheer in prison be my scope.

F. After 'this?' in 3.4.70, Q2 has this more expansive version of Hamlet's lines of which F retains only 'what devil . . . blind'):

> Sense sure you have,
> Else could you not have motion; but sure that sense
> Is apoplexed, for madness would not err,
> Nor sense to ecstasy was ne'er so thralled
> But it reserved some quantity of choice   5
> To serve in such a difference. What devil was't
> That thus hath cozened you at hoodman-blind?
> Eyes without feeling, feeling without sight,
> Ears without hands or eyes, smelling sans all,
> Or but a sickly part of one true sense   10
> Could not so mope.

G. After 3.4.151, Q2 has this more expansive version of Hamlet's lines of which F retains only 'refrain . . . abstinence':

> That monster custom, who all sense doth eat,
> Of habits devilish, is angel yet in this:
> That to the use of actions fair and good
> He likewise gives a frock or livery
> That aptly is put on. Refrain tonight,   5
> And that shall lend a kind of easiness
> To the next abstinence, the next more easy—
> For use almost can change the stamp of nature—
> And either in the devil, or throw him out
> With wondrous potency.   10

H. At 3.4.185, Q2 has these additional lines before 'This man . . .':

HAMLET

> There's letters sealed, and my two schoolfellows—
> Whom I will trust as I will adders fanged—
> They bear the mandate, they must sweep my way
> And marshal me to knavery. Let it work,
> For 'tis the sport to have the engineer   5
> Hoised with his own petard; and't shall go hard
> But I will delve one yard below their mines
> And blow them at the moon. O, 'tis most sweet
> When in one line two crafts directly meet.

I. After 'done' in 4.1.39, Q2 has these additional lines continuing the King's speech (the first three words are an editorial conjecture):

> So envious slander,
> Whose whisper o'er the world's diameter,
> As level as the cannon to his blank,
> Transports his poisoned shot, may miss our name
> And hit the woundless air.   5

J. Q2 has this more expansive version of the ending of 4.4:

CAPTAIN   I will do't, my lord.

FORTINBRAS

Go softly on.   *Exit with his army*

Enter Prince Hamlet, Rosencrantz, Guildenstern, etc.

HAMLET (*to the Captain*) Good sir, whose powers are these?

CAPTAIN

They are of Norway, sir.

HAMLET   How purposed, sir, I pray you?

CAPTAIN

Against some part of Poland.

HAMLET   Who commands them, sir?

CAPTAIN

The nephew to old Norway, Fortinbras.   5

HAMLET

Goes it against the main of Poland, sir,
Or for some frontier?

CAPTAIN

Truly to speak, and with no addition,
We go to gain a little patch of ground
That hath in it no profit but the name.   10
To pay five ducats, five, I would not farm it,
Nor will it yield to Norway or the Pole
A ranker rate, should it be sold in fee.

HAMLET

Why then, the Polack never will defend it.

CAPTAIN

Yes, it is already garrisoned.   15

HAMLET

Two thousand souls and twenty thousand ducats
Will now debate the question of this straw.
This is th'imposthume of much wealth and peace,
That inward breaks and shows no cause without
Why the man dies. I humbly thank you, sir.   20

CAPTAIN

God buy you, sir.   *Exit*

ROSENCRANTZ   Will't please you go, my lord?

HAMLET

I'll be with you straight. Go a little before.

                  Exeunt all but Hamlet

How all occasions do inform against me
And spur my dull revenge! What is a man
If his chief good and market of his time   25
Be but to sleep and feed?—a beast, no more.
Sure, he that made us with such large discourse,
Looking before and after, gave us not
That capability and god-like reason
To fust in us unused. Now whether it be   30
Bestial oblivion, or some craven scruple
Of thinking too precisely on th'event—
A thought which, quartered, hath but one part wisdom
And ever three parts coward—I do not know
Why yet I live to say 'This thing's to do',   35
Sith I have cause, and will, and strength, and means,
To do't. Examples gross as earth exhort me,
Witness this army of such mass and charge,
Led by a delicate and tender prince,
Whose spirit with divine ambition puffed   40
Makes mouths at the invisible event,
Exposing what is mortal and unsure
To all that fortune, death, and danger dare,
Even for an eggshell. Rightly to be great

Is not to stir without great argument, 45
But greatly to find quarrel in a straw
When honour's at the stake. How stand I, then,
That have a father killed, a mother stained,
Excitements of my reason and my blood,
And let all sleep while, to my shame, I see 50
The imminent death of twenty thousand men
That, for a fantasy and trick of fame,
Go to their graves like beds, fight for a plot
Whereon the numbers cannot try the cause,
Which is not tomb enough and continent 55
To hide the slain. O, from this time forth
My thoughts be bloody or be nothing worth! *Exit*

K. After 'accident' at 4.7.67, Q2 has these additional
lines:

LAERTES   My lord, I will be ruled,
    The rather if you could devise it so
    That I might be the organ.
KING CLAUDIUS   It falls right.
    You have been talked of, since your travel, much,
    And that in Hamlet's hearing, for a quality   5
    Wherein they say you shine. Your sum of parts
    Did not together pluck such envy from him
    As did that one, and that, in my regard,
    Of the unworthiest siege.
LAERTES   What part is that, my lord?
KING CLAUDIUS
    A very ribbon in the cap of youth,   10
    Yet needful too, for youth no less becomes
    The light and careless livery that it wears
    Than settled age his sables and his weeds
    Importing health and graveness.

L. After 'match you' at 4.7.85, Q2 has these additional
lines continuing the King's speech:

                    Th'escrimers of their nation
    He swore had neither motion, guard, nor eye
    If you opposed them.

M. After 4.7.96, Q2 has these additional lines continuing
the King's speech:

    There lives within the very flame of love
    A kind of wick or snuff that will abate it,
    And nothing is at a like goodness still,
    For goodness, growing to a plurisy,
    Dies in his own too much. That we would do   5
    We should do when we would, for this 'would' changes,
    And hath abatements and delays as many
    As there are tongues, are hands, are accidents;
    And then this 'should' is like a spendthrift's sigh,
    That hurts by easing. But to the quick of th'ulcer— 10

N. After 'Sir' at 5.2.107, Q2 has these lines (in place of
F's 'you are not ignorant of what excellence Laertes is at
his weapon'):

here is newly come to court Laertes, believe me, an
absolute gentleman, full of most excellent differences,
of very soft society and great showing. Indeed, to speak
feelingly of him, he is the card or calendar of gentry,
for you shall find in him the continent of what part a
gentleman would see.   6
HAMLET Sir, his definement suffers no perdition in you,
though I know to divide him inventorially would dizzy
th'arithmetic of memory, and yet but yaw neither in
respect of his quick sail. But in the verity of extolment,
I take him to be a soul of great article, and his infusion
of such dearth and rareness as, to make true diction
of him, his semblable is his mirror, and who else would
trace him his umbrage, nothing more.
OSRIC Your lordship speaks most infallibly of him.   15
HAMLET The concernancy, sir? Why do we wrap the
gentleman in our more rawer breath?
OSRIC Sir?
HORATIO Is't not possible to understand in another
tongue? You will to't, sir, rarely.   20
HAMLET What imports the nomination of this gentleman?
OSRIC Of Laertes?
HORATIO (*aside to Hamlet*) His purse is empty already; all
's golden words are spent.
HAMLET (*to Osric*) Of him, sir.   25
OSRIC I know you are not ignorant—
HAMLET I would you did, sir; yet, in faith, if you did it
would not much approve me. Well, sir?
OSRIC You are not ignorant of what excellence Laertes is.
HAMLET I dare not confess that, lest I should compare
with him in excellence. But to know a man well were
to know himself.
OSRIC I mean, sir, for his weapon. But in the imputation
laid on him by them, in his meed he's unfellowed.

O. After 5.2.118, Q2 has the following additional speech:

HORATIO (*aside to Hamlet*) I knew you must be edified by
the margin ere you had done.

P. After 5.2.154, Q2 has the following (in place of F's
'HORATIO You will lose this wager, my lord'):

        Enter a Lord
LORD (*to Hamlet*) My lord, his majesty commended him to
you by young Osric, who brings back to him that you
attend him in the hall. He sends to know if your
pleasure hold to play with Laertes, or that you will
take longer time.   5
HAMLET I am constant to my purposes; they follow the
King's pleasure. If his fitness speaks, mine is ready,
now or whensoever, provided I be so able as now.
LORD The King and Queen and all are coming down.
HAMLET In happy time.   10
LORD The Queen desires you to use some gentle
entertainment to Laertes before you fall to play.
HAMLET She well instructs me.   *Exit Lord*
HORATIO You will lose, my lord.

OTHELLO

Othello was given before James I in the Banqueting House at Whitehall on 1 November 1604. Information about the Turkish invasion of Cyprus appears to derive from Richard Knolles's *History of the Turks*, published no earlier than 30 September 1603, so Shakespeare probably completed his play some time between that date and the summer of 1604. It first appeared in print in a quarto of 1622; the version printed in the 1623 Folio is about 160 lines longer, and has over a thousand differences in wording. It seems that Shakespeare partially revised his play, adding, for example, Desdemona's willow song (4.3) and building up Emilia's role in the closing scenes. We base our text on the Folio as that seems to represent Shakespeare's second thoughts.

Shakespeare's decision to make a black man a tragic hero was bold and original: by an ancient tradition, blackness was associated with sin and death; and blackamoors in plays before Shakespeare are generally villainous (like Aaron in *Titus Andronicus*). The story of a Moorish commander deluded by his ensign (standard-bearer) into believing that his young wife has been unfaithful to him with another soldier derives from a prose tale by the Italian Giambattista Cinzio Giraldi first published in 1565 in a collection of linked tales, *Gli Ecatommiti* (*The Hundred Tales*). Shakespeare must have read it either in Italian or in a French translation of 1584; he may have looked at both. Giraldi tells the tale in a few pages of compressed, matter-of-fact narrative interspersed with brief conversations. His main characters are a Moor of Venice (Othello), his Venetian wife (Desdemona), his ensign (Iago), his ensign's wife (Emilia), and a corporal (Cassio) 'who was very dear to the Moor'. Only Desdemona is named. Shakespeare's invented characters include Roderigo, a young, disappointed suitor of Desdemona, and Brabanzio, Desdemona's father, who opposes her marriage to Othello. Bianca, Cassio's mistress, is developed from a few hints in the source. Shakespeare also introduces the military action between Turkey and Venice—infidels and Christians—which gives especial importance to Othello's posting to Cyprus, a Venetian protectorate which the Turks attacked in 1570 and conquered in the following year. In the source, Othello and Desdemona are already happily settled into married life when they go to Cyprus; Shakespeare compresses the time-scheme and makes many changes to the narrative.

Othello, a great success in Shakespeare's time, was one of the first plays to be acted after the reopening of the theatres in 1660, and since that time has remained one of the most popular plays on the English stage.

THE PERSONS OF THE PLAY

OTHELLO, the Moor of Venice
DESDEMONA, his wife
Michael CASSIO, his lieutenant
BIANCA, a courtesan, in love with Cassio
IAGO, the Moor's ensign
EMILIA, Iago's wife
A CLOWN, a servant of Othello

The DUKE of Venice
BRABANZIO, Desdemona's father, a Senator of Venice

GRAZIANO, Brabanzio's brother
LODOVICO, kinsman of Brabanzio
SENATORS of Venice
RODERIGO, a Venetian gentleman, in love with Desdemona

MONTANO, Governor of Cyprus
A HERALD

A MESSENGER
Attendants, officers, sailors, gentlemen of Cyprus, musicians

The Tragedy of Othello the Moor of Venice

1.1 *Enter Iago and Roderigo*

RODERIGO
Tush, never tell me! I take it much unkindly
That thou, Iago, who hast had my purse
As if the strings were thine, shouldst know of this.

IAGO 'Sblood, but you'll not hear me!
If ever I did dream of such a matter, abhor me.   5

RODERIGO
Thou told'st me thou didst hold him in thy hate.

IAGO Despise me
If I do not. Three great ones of the city,
In personal suit to make me his lieutenant,
Off-capped to him; and by the faith of man   10
I know my price, I am worth no worse a place.
But he, as loving his own pride and purposes,
Evades them with a bombast circumstance
Horribly stuffed with epithets of war,
Nonsuits my mediators; for 'Certes,' says he,   15
'I have already chose my officer.'
And what was he?
Forsooth, a great arithmetician,
One Michael Cassio, a Florentine,
A fellow almost damned in a fair wife,   20
That never set a squadron in the field
Nor the division of a battle knows
More than a spinster—unless the bookish theoric,
Wherein the togaed consuls can propose
As masterly as he. Mere prattle without practice   25
Is all his soldiership; but he, sir, had th'election,
And I—of whom his eyes had seen the proof
At Rhodes, at Cyprus, and on other grounds
Christened and heathen—must be beleed and calmed
By debitor and creditor. This counter-caster,   30
He in good time must his lieutenant be,
And I—God bless the mark!—his Moorship's ensign.

RODERIGO
By heaven, I rather would have been his hangman.

IAGO
Why, there's no remedy. 'Tis the curse of service.
Preferment goes by letter and affection,   35
And not by old gradation, where each second
Stood heir to th' first. Now, sir, be judge yourself
Whether I in any just term am affined
To love the Moor.

RODERIGO I would not follow him then.   40

IAGO O sir, content you.
I follow him to serve my turn upon him.
We cannot all be masters, nor all masters
Cannot be truly followed. You shall mark
Many a duteous and knee-crooking knave   45
That, doting on his own obsequious bondage,
Wears out his time much like his master's ass
For naught but provender, and when he's old,
    cashiered.

Whip me such honest knaves. Others there are
Who, trimmed in forms and visages of duty,   50
Keep yet their hearts attending on themselves,
And, throwing but shows of service on their lords,
Do well thrive by 'em, and when they have lined their
    coats,
Do themselves homage. These fellows have some soul,
And such a one do I profess myself—for, sir,   55
It is as sure as you are Roderigo,
Were I the Moor I would not be Iago.
In following him I follow but myself.
Heaven is my judge, not I for love and duty,
But seeming so for my peculiar end.   60
For when my outward action doth demonstrate
The native act and figure of my heart
In compliment extern, 'tis not long after
But I will wear my heart upon my sleeve
For daws to peck at. I am not what I am.   65

RODERIGO
What a full fortune does the thick-lips owe
If he can carry't thus!

IAGO   Call up her father,
Rouse him, make after him, poison his delight,
Proclaim him in the streets; incense her kinsmen,
And, though he in a fertile climate dwell,   70
Plague him with flies. Though that his joy be joy,
Yet throw such chances of vexation on't
As it may lose some colour.

RODERIGO
Here is her father's house. I'll call aloud.

IAGO
Do, with like timorous accent and dire yell   75
As when, by night and negligence, the fire
Is spied in populous cities.

RODERIGO *(calling)*
What ho, Brabanzio, Signor Brabanzio, ho!

IAGO *(calling)*
Awake, what ho, Brabanzio, thieves, thieves, thieves!
Look to your house, your daughter, and your bags. 80
Thieves, thieves!
    *Enter Brabanzio in his nightgown at a window
    above*

BRABANZIO
What is the reason of this terrible summons?
What is the matter there?

RODERIGO
Signor, is all your family within?

IAGO
Are your doors locked?

BRABANZIO   Why, wherefore ask you this?

IAGO
'Swounds, sir, you're robbed. For shame, put on your
    gown.
Your heart is burst, you have lost half your soul.   87

1167

Even now, now, very now, an old black ram
Is tupping your white ewe. Arise, arise!
Awake the snorting citizens with the bell,   90
Or else the devil will make a grandsire of you.
Arise, I say.
BRABANZIO   What, have you lost your wits?
RODERIGO
Most reverend signor, do you know my voice?
BRABANZIO Not I. What are you?
RODERIGO My name is Roderigo.   95
BRABANZIO The worser welcome.
I have charged thee not to haunt about my doors.
In honest plainness thou hast heard me say
My daughter is not for thee, and now in madness,
Being full of supper and distempering draughts,   100
Upon malicious bravery dost thou come
To start my quiet.
RODERIGO Sir, sir, sir.
BRABANZIO But thou must needs be sure
My spirits and my place have in their power   105
To make this bitter to thee.
RODERIGO   Patience, good sir.
BRABANZIO
What tell'st thou me of robbing? This is Venice.
My house is not a grange.
RODERIGO   Most grave Brabanzio,
In simple and pure soul I come to you.   109
IAGO (to Brabanzio) 'Swounds, sir, you are one of those
that will not serve God if the devil bid you. Because we
come to do you service and you think we are ruffians,
you'll have your daughter covered with a Barbary
horse, you'll have your nephews neigh to you, you'll
have coursers for cousins and jennets for germans. 115
BRABANZIO What profane wretch art thou?
IAGO I am one, sir, that comes to tell you your daughter
and the Moor are now making the beast with two
backs.
BRABANZIO
Thou art a villain.
IAGO   You are a senator.   120
BRABANZIO
This thou shalt answer. I know thee, Roderigo.
RODERIGO
Sir, I will answer anything. But I beseech you,
If't be your pleasure and most wise consent—
As partly I find it is—that your fair daughter,
At this odd-even and dull watch o'th' night,   125
Transported with no worse nor better guard
But with a knave of common hire, a gondolier,
To the gross clasps of a lascivious Moor—
If this be known to you, and your allowance,
We then have done you bold and saucy wrongs.   130
But if you know not this, my manners tell me
We have your wrong rebuke. Do not believe
That, from the sense of all civility,
I thus would play and trifle with your reverence.
Your daughter, if you have not given her leave,   135
I say again hath made a gross revolt,

Tying her duty, beauty, wit, and fortunes
In an extravagant and wheeling stranger
Of here and everywhere. Straight satisfy yourself.
If she be in her chamber or your house,   140
Let loose on me the justice of the state
For thus deluding you.
BRABANZIO (calling)   Strike on the tinder, ho!
Give me a taper, call up all my people.
This accident is not unlike my dream;
Belief of it oppresses me already.   145
Light, I say, light!   Exit
IAGO   Farewell, for I must leave you.
It seems not meet nor wholesome to my place
To be producted—as, if I stay, I shall—
Against the Moor, for I do know the state,
However this may gall him with some check,   150
Cannot with safety cast him, for he's embarked
With such loud reason to the Cyprus wars,
Which even now stands in act, that, for their souls,
Another of his fathom they have none
To lead their business, in which regard—   155
Though I do hate him as I do hell pains—
Yet for necessity of present life
I must show out a flag and sign of love,
Which is indeed but sign. That you shall surely find
him,
Lead to the Sagittary the raisèd search,   160
And there will I be with him. So farewell.   Exit
     Enter below Brabanzio in his nightgown, and
     servants with torches
BRABANZIO
It is too true an evil. Gone she is,
And what's to come of my despisèd time
Is naught but bitterness. Now, Roderigo,
Where didst thou see her?—O unhappy girl!—   165
With the Moor, sayst thou?—Who would be a
father?—
How didst thou know 'twas she?—O, she deceives me
Past thought!—What said she to you? (To servants)
Get more tapers,
Raise all my kindred.   ⌈Exit one or more⌉
(To Roderigo)   Are they married, think you?
RODERIGO Truly, I think they are.   170
BRABANZIO
O heaven, how got she out? O, treason of the blood!
Fathers, from hence trust not your daughters' minds
By what you see them act. Is there not charms
By which the property of youth and maidhood
May be abused? Have you not read, Roderigo,   175
Of some such thing?
RODERIGO   Yes, sir, I have indeed.
BRABANZIO (to servants)
Call up my brother. (To Roderigo) O, would you had
    had her.
(To servants) Some one way, some another.
                          ⌈Exit one or more⌉
(To Roderigo)   Do you know
Where we may apprehend her and the Moor?

RODERIGO
  I think I can discover him, if you please   180
  To get good guard and go along with me.
BRABANZIO
  Pray you lead on. At every house I'll call;
  I may command at most. (Calling) Get weapons, ho,
  And raise some special officers of night.
  On, good Roderigo. I will deserve your pains.   Exeunt

1.2   Enter Othello, Iago, and attendants with torches
IAGO
  Though in the trade of war I have slain men,
  Yet do I hold it very stuff o'th' conscience
  To do no contrived murder. I lack iniquity,
  Sometime, to do me service. Nine or ten times
  I had thought to've yerked him here, under the ribs.
OTHELLO
  'Tis better as it is.
IAGO   Nay, but he prated,
  And spoke such scurvy and provoking terms
  Against your honour
  That, with the little godliness I have,
  I did full hard forbear him. But I pray you, sir,   10
  Are you fast married? Be assured of this:
  That the magnifico is much beloved,
  And hath in his effect a voice potential
  As double as the Duke's. He will divorce you,
  Or put upon you what restraint or grievance   15
  The law, with all his might to enforce it on,
  Will give him cable.
OTHELLO   Let him do his spite.
  My services which I have done the signory
  Shall out-tongue his complaints. 'Tis yet to know—
  Which, when I know that boasting is an honour,   20
  I shall promulgate—I fetch my life and being
  From men of royal siege, and my demerits
  May speak unbonneted to as proud a fortune
  As this that I have reached. For know, Iago,
  But that I love the gentle Desdemona   25
  I would not my unhousèd free condition
  Put into circumscription and confine
  For the seas' worth.
     Enter Cassio and officers, with torches
              But look, what lights come yond?
IAGO
  Those are the raisèd father and his friends.
  You were best go in.
OTHELLO   Not I. I must be found.   30
  My parts, my title, and my perfect soul
  Shall manifest me rightly. Is it they?
IAGO By Janus, I think no.
OTHELLO
  The servants of the Duke, and my lieutenant!
  The goodness of the night upon you, friends.   35
  What is the news?
CASSIO   The Duke does greet you, general,
  And he requires your haste-post-haste appearance
  Even on the instant.
OTHELLO   What is the matter, think you?

CASSIO
  Something from Cyprus, as I may divine;
  It is a business of some heat. The galleys   40
  Have sent a dozen sequent messengers
  This very night at one another's heels,
  And many of the consuls, raised and met,
  Are at the Duke's already. You have been hotly called
    for,
  When, being not at your lodging to be found,   45
  The senate sent about three several quests
  To search you out.
OTHELLO   'Tis well I am found by you.
  I will but spend a word here in the house
  And go with you.   Exit
CASSIO   Ensign, what makes he here?
IAGO
  Faith, he tonight hath boarded a land-carrack.   50
  If it prove lawful prize, he's made for ever.
CASSIO
  I do not understand.
IAGO   He's married.
CASSIO   To who?
     Enter Brabanzio, Roderigo, and officers, with lights
     and weapons
IAGO
  Marry, to—
     Enter Othello
  (To Othello) Come, captain, will you go?
OTHELLO   Have with you.
CASSIO
  Here comes another troop to seek for you.   55
IAGO
  It is Brabanzio. General, be advised.
  He comes to bad intent.
OTHELLO   Holla, stand, there!
RODERIGO (to Brabanzio)
  Signor, it is the Moor.
BRABANZIO   Down with him, thief!
IAGO (drawing his sword)
  You, Roderigo? Come, sir, I am for you.   59
OTHELLO
  Keep up your bright swords, for the dew will rust 'em.
  (To Brabanzio) Good signor, you shall more command
    with years
  Than with your weapons.
BRABANZIO
  O thou foul thief, where hast thou stowed my
    daughter?
  Damned as thou art, thou hast enchanted her,
  For I'll refer me to all things of sense,   65
  If she in chains of magic were not bound,
  Whether a maid so tender, fair, and happy,
  So opposite to marriage that she shunned
  The wealthy curlèd darlings of our nation,
  Would ever have, t'incur a general mock,   70
  Run from her guardage to the sooty bosom
  Of such a thing as thou—to fear, not to delight.
  Judge me the world if 'tis not gross in sense
  That thou hast practised on her with foul charms,

Abused her delicate youth with drugs or minerals 75
That weakens motion. I'll have't disputed on.
'Tis probable, and palpable to thinking.
I therefore apprehend and do attach thee
For an abuser of the world, a practiser
Of arts inhibited and out of warrant.   80
(*To officers*) Lay hold upon him. If he do resist,
Subdue him at his peril.
OTHELLO   Hold your hands,
Both you of my inclining and the rest.
Were it my cue to fight, I should have known it
Without a prompter. Whither will you that I go   85
To answer this your charge?
BRABANZIO   To prison, till fit time
Of law and course of direct session
Call thee to answer.
OTHELLO   What if I do obey?
How may the Duke be therewith satisfied,
Whose messengers are here about my side   90
Upon some present business of the state
To bring me to him?
OFFICER (*to Brabanzio*) 'Tis true, most worthy signor.
The Duke's in council, and your noble self,
I am sure, is sent for.
BRABANZIO   How, the Duke in council?
In this time of the night? Bring him away.   95
Mine's not an idle cause. The Duke himself,
Or any of my brothers of the state,
Cannot but feel this wrong as 'twere their own;
For if such actions may have passage free,
Bondslaves and pagans shall our statesmen be.   100
                                        Exeunt

1.3   *Enter the Duke and Senators set at a table, with*
       lights and officers
DUKE
There is no composition in these news
That gives them credit.
FIRST SENATOR   Indeed, they are disproportioned.
My letters say a hundred and seven galleys.
DUKE
And mine a hundred-forty.
SECOND SENATOR   And mine two hundred.
But though they jump not on a just account—   5
As, in these cases, where the aim reports
'Tis oft with difference—yet do they all confirm
A Turkish fleet, and bearing up to Cyprus.
DUKE
Nay, it is possible enough to judgement.
I do not so secure me in the error,   10
But the main article I do approve
In fearful sense.
SAILOR (*within*)   What ho, what ho, what ho!
             Enter a Sailor
OFFICER
A messenger from the galleys.
DUKE   Now, what's the business?
SAILOR
The Turkish preparation makes for Rhodes.

So was I bid report here to the state   15
By Signor Angelo.
DUKE (*to Senators*) How say you by this change?
FIRST SENATOR This cannot be,
By no assay of reason—'tis a pageant
To keep us in false gaze. When we consider   20
The importancy of Cyprus to the Turk,
And let ourselves again but understand
That, as it more concerns the Turk than Rhodes,
So may he with more facile question bear it,
For that it stands not in such warlike brace,   25
But altogether lacks th'abilities
That Rhodes is dressed in—if we make thought of this,
We must not think the Turk is so unskilful
To leave that latest which concerns him first,
Neglecting an attempt of ease and gain   30
To wake and wage a danger profitless.
DUKE
Nay, in all confidence, he's not for Rhodes.
OFFICER Here is more news.
             Enter a Messenger
MESSENGER
The Ottomites, reverend and gracious,
Steering with due course toward the Isle of Rhodes, 35
Have there injointed them with an after fleet.
FIRST SENATOR
Ay, so I thought. How many, as you guess?
MESSENGER
Of thirty sail, and now they do restem
Their backward course, bearing with frank appearance
Their purposes toward Cyprus. Signor Montano,   40
Your trusty and most valiant servitor,
With his free duty recommends you thus,
And prays you to believe him.
DUKE   'Tis certain then for Cyprus.
Marcus Luccicos, is not he in town?
FIRST SENATOR He's now in Florence.   45
DUKE
Write from us to him post-post-haste. Dispatch.
             Enter Brabanzio, Othello, Roderigo, Iago, Cassio,
             and officers
FIRST SENATOR
Here comes Brabanzio and the valiant Moor.
DUKE
Valiant Othello, we must straight employ you
Against the general enemy Ottoman.
(*To Brabanzio*) I did not see you. Welcome, gentle
             signor.   50
We lacked your counsel and your help tonight.
BRABANZIO
So did I yours. Good your grace, pardon me.
Neither my place, nor aught I heard of business,
Hath raised me from my bed, nor doth the general
             care
Take hold on me; for my particular grief   55
Is of so floodgate and o'erbearing nature
That it engluts and swallows other sorrows,
And it is still itself.
DUKE   Why, what's the matter?

BRABANZIO
My daughter, O, my daughter!
⌈SENATORS⌉   Dead?
BRABANZIO   Ay, to me.
She is abused, stol'n from me, and corrupted   60
By spells and medicines bought of mountebanks.
For nature so preposterously to err,
Being not deficient, blind, or lame of sense,
Sans witchcraft could not.
DUKE
Whoe'er he be that in this foul proceeding   65
Hath thus beguiled your daughter of herself
And you of her, the bloody book of law
You shall yourself read in the bitter letter
After your own sense, yea, though our proper son
Stood in your action.
BRABANZIO   Humbly I thank your grace.   70
Here is the man, this Moor, whom now it seems
Your special mandate for the state affairs
Hath hither brought.
SENATORS   We are very sorry for't.
DUKE (to Othello)
What in your own part can you say to this?
BRABANZIO Nothing but this is so.   75
OTHELLO
Most potent, grave, and reverend signors,
My very noble and approved good masters,
That I have ta'en away this old man's daughter,
It is most true, true I have married her.
The very head and front of my offending   80
Hath this extent, no more. Rude am I in my speech,
And little blessed with the soft phrase of peace,
For since these arms of mine had seven years' pith
Till now some nine moons wasted, they have used
Their dearest action in the tented field,   85
And little of this great world can I speak
More than pertains to feats of broils and battle.
And therefore little shall I grace my cause
In speaking for myself. Yet, by your gracious patience,
I will a round unvarnished tale deliver   90
Of my whole course of love, what drugs, what charms,
What conjuration and what mighty magic—
For such proceeding I am charged withal—
I won his daughter.
BRABANZIO   A maiden never bold,
Of spirit so still and quiet that her motion   95
Blushed at herself—and she in spite of nature,
Of years, of country, credit, everything,
To fall in love with what she feared to look on!
It is a judgement maimed and most imperfect
That will confess perfection so could err   100
Against all rules of nature, and must be driven
To find out practices of cunning hell
Why this should be. I therefore vouch again
That with some mixtures powerful o'er the blood,
Or with some dram conjured to this effect,   105
He wrought upon her.
DUKE   To vouch this is no proof

Without more wider and more overt test
Than these thin habits and poor likelihoods
Of modern seeming do prefer against him.
A SENATOR But Othello, speak.   110
Did you by indirect and forcèd courses
Subdue and poison this young maid's affections,
Or came it by request and such fair question
As soul to soul affordeth?
OTHELLO   I do beseech you,
Send for the lady to the Sagittary,   115
And let her speak of me before her father.
If you do find me foul in her report,
The trust, the office I do hold of you
Not only take away, but let your sentence
Even fall upon my life.
DUKE (to officers)   Fetch Desdemona hither.   120
OTHELLO
Ensign, conduct them. You best know the place.
                        Exit Iago with two or three officers
And till she come, as truly as to heaven
I do confess the vices of my blood,
So justly to your grave ears I'll present
How I did thrive in this fair lady's love,   125
And she in mine.
DUKE   Say it, Othello.
OTHELLO
Her father loved me, oft invited me,
Still questioned me the story of my life
From year to year, the battles, sieges, fortunes
That I have passed.   130
I ran it through even from my boyish days
To th' very moment that he bade me tell it,
Wherein I spoke of most disastrous chances,
Of moving accidents by flood and field,
Of hair-breadth scapes i'th' imminent deadly breach, 135
Of being taken by the insolent foe   136
And sold to slavery, of my redemption thence,
And portance in my traveller's history,
Wherein of antres vast and deserts idle,
Rough quarries, rocks, and hills whose heads touch
  heaven,   140
It was my hint to speak. Such was my process,
And of the cannibals that each other eat,
The Anthropophagi, and men whose heads
Do grow beneath their shoulders. These things to hear
Would Desdemona seriously incline,   145
But still the house affairs would draw her thence,
Which ever as she could with haste dispatch
She'd come again, and with a greedy ear
Devour up my discourse; which I observing,
Took once a pliant hour, and found good means   150
To draw from her a prayer of earnest heart
That I would all my pilgrimage dilate,
Whereof by parcels she had something heard,
But not intentively. I did consent,
And often did beguile her of her tears   155
When I did speak of some distressful stroke
That my youth suffered. My story being done,

She gave me for my pains a world of kisses.
She swore in faith 'twas strange, 'twas passing strange,
'Twas pitiful, 'twas wondrous pitiful.   160
She wished she had not heard it, yet she wished
That heaven had made her such a man. She thankèd
        me,
And bade me, if I had a friend that loved her,
I should but teach him how to tell my story,
And that would woo her. Upon this hint I spake.   165
She loved me for the dangers I had passed,
And I loved her that she did pity them.
This only is the witchcraft I have used.
        Enter Desdemona, Iago, and attendants
Here comes the lady. Let her witness it.
DUKE
I think this tale would win my daughter, too.—   170
Good Brabanzio,
Take up this mangled matter at the best.
Men do their broken weapons rather use
Than their bare hands.
BRABANZIO   I pray you hear her speak.
If she confess that she was half the wooer,   175
Destruction on my head if my bad blame
Light on the man! Come hither, gentle mistress.
Do you perceive in all this noble company
Where most you owe obedience?
DESDEMONA   My noble father,
I do perceive here a divided duty.   180
To you I am bound for life and education.
My life and education both do learn me
How to respect you. You are the lord of duty,
I am hitherto your daughter. But here's my husband,
And so much duty as my mother showed   185
To you, preferring you before her father,
So much I challenge that I may profess
Due to the Moor my lord.
BRABANZIO   God b'wi'you, I ha' done.
Please it your grace, on to the state affairs.
I had rather to adopt a child than get it.   190
Come hither, Moor.
I here do give thee that with all my heart
Which, but thou hast already, with all my heart
I would keep from thee. (*To Desdemona*) For your sake,
        jewel,
I am glad at soul I have no other child,   195
For thy escape would teach me tyranny,
To hang clogs on 'em. I have done, my lord.
DUKE
Let me speak like yourself, and lay a sentence
Which, as a grece or step, may help these lovers
Into your favour.   200
When remedies are past, the griefs are ended
By seeing the worst which late on hopes depended.
To mourn a mischief that is past and gone
Is the next way to draw new mischief on.
What cannot be preserved when fortune takes,   205
Patience her injury a mockery makes.

The robbed that smiles steals something from the thief;
He robs himself that spends a bootless grief.
BRABANZIO
So let the Turk of Cyprus us beguile,
We lose it not so long as we can smile.   210
He bears the sentence well that nothing bears
But the free comfort which from thence he hears,
But he bears both the sentence and the sorrow
That, to pay grief, must of poor patience borrow.
These sentences, to sugar or to gall,   215
Being strong on both sides, are equivocal.
But words are words. I never yet did hear
That the bruised heart was piercèd through the ear.
I humbly beseech you proceed to th'affairs of state. 219
DUKE The Turk with a most mighty preparation makes
for Cyprus. Othello, the fortitude of the place is best
known to you, and though we have there a substitute
of most allowed sufficiency, yet opinion, a more
sovereign mistress of effects, throws a more safer voice
on you. You must therefore be content to slubber the
gloss of your new fortunes with this more stubborn
and boisterous expedition.
OTHELLO
The tyrant custom, most grave senators,
Hath made the flinty and steel couch of war
My thrice-driven bed of down. I do agnize   230
A natural and prompt alacrity
I find in hardness, and do undertake
This present wars against the Ottomites.
Most humbly therefore bending to your state,
I crave fit disposition for my wife,   235
Due reference of place and exhibition,
With such accommodation and besort
As levels with her breeding.
DUKE Why, at her father's!
BRABANZIO I will not have it so.   240
OTHELLO Nor I.
DESDEMONA Nor would I there reside,
To put my father in impatient thoughts
By being in his eye. Most gracious Duke,
To my unfolding lend your prosperous ear,   245
And let me find a charter in your voice
T'assist my simpleness.
DUKE   What would you, Desdemona?
DESDEMONA
That I did love the Moor to live with him,
My downright violence and storm of fortunes
May trumpet to the world. My heart's subdued   250
Even to the very quality of my lord.
I saw Othello's visage in his mind,
And to his honours and his valiant parts
Did I my soul and fortunes consecrate;
So that, dear lords, if I be left behind,   255
A moth of peace, and he go to the war,
The rites for why I love him are bereft me,
And I a heavy interim shall support
By his dear absence. Let me go with him.

OTHELLO (*to the Duke*) Let her have your voice.   260
  Vouch with me heaven, I therefor beg it not
  To please the palate of my appetite,
  Nor to comply with heat—the young affects
  In me defunct—and proper satisfaction,
  But to be free and bounteous to her mind;   265
  And heaven defend your good souls that you think
  I will your serious and great business scant
  When she is with me. No, when light-winged toys
  Of feathered Cupid seel with wanton dullness
  My speculative and officed instruments,   270
  That my disports corrupt and taint my business,
  Let housewives make a skillet of my helm,
  And all indign and base adversities
  Make head against my estimation.
DUKE
  Be it as you shall privately determine,   275
  Either for her stay or going. Th'affair cries haste,
  And speed must answer it.
A SENATOR (*to Othello*)   You must away tonight.
DESDEMONA
  Tonight, my lord?
DUKE   This night.
OTHELLO   With all my heart.
DUKE
  At nine i'th' morning here we'll meet again.
  Othello, leave some officer behind,   280
  And he shall our commission bring to you,
  And such things else of quality and respect
  As doth import you.
OTHELLO   So please your grace, my ensign.
  A man he is of honesty and trust.
  To his conveyance I assign my wife,   285
  With what else needful your good grace shall think
  To be sent after me.
DUKE   Let it be so.
  Good night to everyone. (*To Brabanzio*) And, noble
    signor,
  If virtue no delighted beauty lack,
  Your son-in-law is far more fair than black.   290
A SENATOR
  Adieu, brave Moor. Use Desdemona well.
BRABANZIO
  Look to her, Moor, if thou hast eyes to see.
  She has deceived her father, and may thee.
        ⌈*Exeunt Duke, Brabanzio, Cassio, Senators, and*
                                            officers⌉
OTHELLO
  My life upon her faith. Honest Iago,
  My Desdemona must I leave to thee.   295
  I prithee let thy wife attend on her,
  And bring them after in the best advantage.
  Come, Desdemona. I have but an hour
  Of love, of worldly matter and direction
  To spend with thee. We must obey the time.   300
                Exeunt Othello and Desdemona
RODERIGO Iago.
IAGO What sayst thou, noble heart?

RODERIGO What will I do, think'st thou?
IAGO Why, go to bed and sleep.
RODERIGO I will incontinently drown myself.   305
IAGO If thou dost, I shall never love thee after. Why, thou
  silly gentleman!
RODERIGO It is silliness to live when to live is torment;
  and then have we a prescription to die when death is
  our physician.   310
IAGO O, villainous! I ha' looked upon the world for four
  times seven years, and since I could distinguish betwixt
  a benefit and an injury I never found man that knew
  how to love himself. Ere I would say I would drown
  myself for the love of a guinea-hen, I would change
  my humanity with a baboon.   316
RODERIGO What should I do? I confess it is my shame to
  be so fond, but it is not in my virtue to amend it.
IAGO Virtue? A fig! 'Tis in ourselves that we are thus or
  thus. Our bodies are our gardens, to the which our
  wills are gardeners; so that if we will plant nettles or
  sow lettuce, set hyssop and weed up thyme, supply it
  with one gender of herbs or distract it with many,
  either to have it sterile with idleness or manured with
  industry, why, the power and corrigible authority of
  this lies in our wills. If the beam of our lives had not
  one scale of reason to peise another of sensuality, the
  blood and baseness of our natures would conduct us
  to most preposterous conclusions. But we have reason
  to cool our raging motions, our carnal stings, our
  unbitted lusts; whereof I take this that you call love to
  be a sect or scion.   332
RODERIGO It cannot be.
IAGO It is merely a lust of the blood and a permission of
  the will. Come, be a man. Drown thyself? Drown cats
  and blind puppies. I have professed me thy friend, and
  I confess me knit to thy deserving with cables of
  perdurable toughness. I could never better stead thee
  than now. Put money in thy purse. Follow thou the
  wars, defeat thy favour with an usurped beard. I say,
  put money in thy purse. It cannot be long that
  Desdemona should continue her love to the Moor—put
  money in thy purse—nor he his to her. It was a violent
  commencement in her, and thou shalt see an
  answerable sequestration—put but money in thy purse.
  These Moors are changeable in their wills—fill thy
  purse with money. The food that to him now is as
  luscious as locusts shall be to him shortly as bitter as
  coloquintida. She must change for youth. When she is
  sated with his body, she will find the error of her
  choice. Therefore put money in thy purse. If thou wilt
  needs damn thyself, do it a more delicate way than
  drowning. Make all the money thou canst. If
  sanctimony and a frail vow betwixt an erring barbarian
  and a super-subtle Venetian be not too hard for my
  wits and all the tribe of hell, thou shalt enjoy her;
  therefore make money. A pox o' drowning thyself—it
  is clean out of the way. Seek thou rather to be hanged
  in compassing thy joy than to be drowned and go
  without her.   360

RODERIGO Wilt thou be fast to my hopes if I depend on
the issue?

IAGO Thou art sure of me. Go, make money. I have told
thee often, and I re-tell thee again and again, I hate
the Moor. My cause is hearted, thine hath no less
reason. Let us be conjunctive in our revenge against
him. If thou canst cuckold him, thou dost thyself a
pleasure, me a sport. There are many events in the
womb of time, which will be delivered. Traverse, go,
provide thy money. We will have more of this
tomorrow. Adieu.　　　　　　　　　　　　　　　　371

RODERIGO
Where shall we meet i'th' morning?

IAGO　　　　　　　　　　　　　　At my lodging.

RODERIGO
I'll be with thee betimes.

IAGO　　　　　　　　Go to, farewell—
Do you hear, Roderigo?

RODERIGO　　　　　I'll sell all my land.　　　Exit

IAGO
Thus do I ever make my fool my purse—　　　375
For I mine own gained knowledge should profane
If I would time expend with such a snipe
But for my sport and profit. I hate the Moor,
And it is thought abroad that 'twixt my sheets
He has done my office. I know not if't be true,　380
But I, for mere suspicion in that kind,
Will do as if for surety. He holds me well:
The better shall my purpose work on him.
Cassio's a proper man. Let me see now,
To get his place, and to plume up my will　　385
In double knavery—how, how? Let's see.
After some time to abuse Othello's ears
That he is too familiar with his wife;
He hath a person and a smooth dispose
To be suspected, framed to make women false.　390
The Moor is of a free and open nature,
That thinks men honest that but seem to be so,
And will as tenderly be led by th' nose
As asses are.
I ha't. It is ingendered. Hell and night　　395
Must bring this monstrous birth to the world's light.
　　　　　　　　　　　　　　　　　　　　　　Exit

2.1 _Enter below Montano, Governor of Cyprus; two
other gentlemen ⌈above⌉_

MONTANO
What from the cape can you discern at sea?

FIRST GENTLEMAN
Nothing at all. It is a high-wrought flood.
I cannot 'twixt the heaven and the main
Descry a sail.

MONTANO
Methinks the wind hath spoke aloud at land.　5
A fuller blast ne'er shook our battlements.
If it ha' ruffianed so upon the sea,
What ribs of oak, when mountains melt on them,
Can hold the mortise? What shall we hear of this?

SECOND GENTLEMAN
A segregation of the Turkish fleet;　　　　　10
For do but stand upon the foaming shore,
The chidden billow seems to pelt the clouds,
The wind-shaked surge with high and monstrous mane
Seems to cast water on the burning Bear
And quench the guards of th'ever-fixèd Pole.　15
I never did like molestation view
On the enchafèd flood.

MONTANO　　　　　　　If that the Turkish fleet
Be not ensheltered and embayed, they are drowned.
It is impossible to bear it out.
　　　　Enter a third Gentleman

THIRD GENTLEMAN News, lads! Our wars are done.　20
The desperate tempest hath so banged the Turks
That their designment halts. A noble ship of Venice
Hath seen a grievous wrack and sufferance
On most part of their fleet.

MONTANO How, is this true?　　　　　　　　25

THIRD GENTLEMAN The ship is here put in,
A Veronessa. Michael Cassio,
Lieutenant to the warlike Moor Othello,
Is come on shore; the Moor himself at sea,
And is in full commission here for Cyprus.　30

MONTANO
I am glad on't; 'tis a worthy governor.

THIRD GENTLEMAN
But this same Cassio, though he speak of comfort
Touching the Turkish loss, yet he looks sadly,
And prays the Moor be safe, for they were parted
With foul and violent tempest.

MONTANO　　　　　　　Pray heavens he be, 35
For I have served him, and the man commands
Like a full soldier. Let's to the sea-side, ho!—
As well to see the vessel that's come in
As to throw out our eyes for brave Othello,
Even till we make the main and th'aerial blue　40
An indistinct regard.

THIRD GENTLEMAN　Come, let's do so,
For every minute is expectancy
Of more arrivance.
　　　　Enter Cassio

CASSIO
Thanks, you the valiant of this warlike isle
That so approve the Moor! O, let the heavens　45
Give him defence against the elements,
For I have lost him on a dangerous sea.

MONTANO Is he well shipped?

CASSIO
His barque is stoutly timbered, and his pilot
Of very expert and approved allowance.　　50
Therefore my hopes, not surfeited to death,
Stand in bold cure.

VOICES (_within_)　　　A sail, a sail, a sail!

CASSIO What noise?

A GENTLEMAN
The town is empty. On the brow o'th' sea
Stand ranks of people, and they cry 'A sail!'　55

CASSIO
My hopes do shape him for the governor.
A shot
A GENTLEMAN
They do discharge their shot of courtesy—
Our friends, at least.
CASSIO   I pray you, sir, go forth,
And give us truth who 'tis that is arrived.
A GENTLEMAN I shall.   *Exit*
MONTANO
But, good lieutenant, is your general wived?   61
CASSIO
Most fortunately. He hath achieved a maid
That paragons description and wild fame,
One that excels the quirks of blazoning pens,
And in th'essential vesture of creation   65
Does tire the engineer.
Enter Gentleman
                          How now, who has put in?
GENTLEMAN
'Tis one Iago, ensign to the general.
CASSIO
He's had most favourable and happy speed.
Tempests themselves, high seas, and howling winds,
The guttered rocks and congregated sands,   70
Traitors ensteeped to enclog the guiltless keel,
As having sense of beauty do omit
Their mortal natures, letting go safely by
The divine Desdemona.
MONTANO   What is she?
CASSIO
She that I spake of, our great captain's captain,   75
Left in the conduct of the bold Iago,
Whose footing here anticipates our thoughts
A sennight's speed. Great Jove, Othello guard,
And swell his sail with thine own powerful breath,
That he may bless this bay with his tall ship,   80
Make love's quick pants in Desdemona's arms,
Give renewed fire to our extincted spirits,
And bring all Cyprus comfort.
Enter Desdemona, Iago, Emilia, and Roderigo
                          O, behold,
The riches of the ship is come on shore!
You men of Cyprus, let her have your knees.   85
Montano and the Gentlemen make curtsy to Desdemona
Hail to thee, lady, and the grace of heaven
Before, behind thee, and on every hand
Enwheel thee round!
DESDEMONA   I thank you, valiant Cassio.
What tidings can you tell me of my lord?
CASSIO
He is not yet arrived, nor know I aught   90
But that he's well and will be shortly here.
DESDEMONA
O, but I fear—how lost you company?
CASSIO
The great contention of the sea and skies
Parted our fellowship.

VOICES (*within*) A sail, a sail!   95
CASSIO But hark, a sail.
A shot
A GENTLEMAN
They give their greeting to the citadel.
This likewise is a friend.
CASSIO   See for the news.
                          Exit Gentleman
Good ensign, you are welcome. (*Kissing Emilia*)
          Welcome, mistress.
Let it not gall your patience, good Iago,   100
That I extend my manners. 'Tis my breeding
That gives me this bold show of courtesy.
IAGO
Sir, would she give you so much of her lips
As of her tongue she oft bestows on me,
You would have enough.   105
DESDEMONA Alas, she has no speech!
IAGO In faith, too much.
I find it still when I ha' leave to sleep.
Marry, before your ladyship, I grant,
She puts her tongue a little in her heart,   110
And chides with thinking.
EMILIA   You ha' little cause to say so.
IAGO
Come on, come on. You are pictures out of door,
Bells in your parlours; wildcats in your kitchens,
Saints in your injuries; devils being offended,
Players in your housewifery, and hussies in your
          beds.   115
DESDEMONA
O, fie upon thee, slanderer!
IAGO
Nay, it is true, or else I am a Turk.
You rise to play and go to bed to work.
EMILIA
You shall not write my praise.
IAGO   No, let me not.
DESDEMONA
What wouldst write of me, if thou shouldst praise me?
IAGO
O, gentle lady, do not put me to't,   121
For I am nothing if not critical.
DESDEMONA
Come on, essay—there's one gone to the harbour?
IAGO Ay, madam.
DESDEMONA
I am not merry, but I do beguile   125
The thing I am by seeming otherwise.
Come, how wouldst thou praise me?
IAGO
I am about it, but indeed my invention
Comes from my pate as birdlime does from frieze—
It plucks out brains and all. But my muse labours,   130
And thus she is delivered:
If she be fair and wise, fairness and wit,
The one's for use, the other useth it.

DESDEMONA Well praised! How if she be black and witty?

IAGO
If she be black and thereto have a wit,   135
She'll find a white that shall her blackness fit.

DESDEMONA
Worse and worse.

EMILIA   How if fair and foolish?

IAGO
She never yet was foolish that was fair,
For even her folly helped her to an heir.

DESDEMONA These are old fond paradoxes, to make fools
laugh i'th' alehouse.   141
What miserable praise hast thou for her
That's foul and foolish?

IAGO
There's none so foul and foolish thereunto,
But does foul pranks which fair and wise ones do.   145

DESDEMONA O heavy ignorance! Thou praisest the worst
best. But what praise couldst thou bestow on a
deserving woman indeed—one that, in the authority
of her merit, did justly put on the vouch of very malice
itself?   150

IAGO
She that was ever fair and never proud,
Had tongue at will and yet was never loud,
Never lacked gold and yet went never gay,
Fled from her wish, and yet said 'Now I may';
She that, being angered, her revenge being nigh,   155
Bade her wrong stay and her displeasure fly;
She that in wisdom never was so frail
To change the cod's head for the salmon's tail;
She that could think and ne'er disclose her mind,
See suitors following, and not look behind—   160
She was a wight, if ever such wights were—

DESDEMONA To do what?

IAGO
To suckle fools, and chronicle small beer.

DESDEMONA O most lame and impotent conclusion! Do
not learn of him, Emilia, though he be thy husband.
How say you, Cassio, is he not a most profane and
liberal counsellor?

CASSIO He speaks home, madam. You may relish him
more in the soldier than in the scholar.   169

Cassio and Desdemona talk apart

IAGO (*aside*) He takes her by the palm. Ay, well said—
whisper. With as little a web as this will I ensnare as
great a fly as Cassio. Ay, smile upon her, do. I will
gyve thee in thine own courtship. You say true, 'tis so
indeed. If such tricks as these strip you out of your
lieutenantry, it had been better you had not kissed
your three fingers so oft, which now again you are
most apt to play the sir in. Very good, well kissed, an
excellent curtsy, 'tis so indeed; yet again your fingers
to your lips? Would they were clyster-pipes for your
sake.   180

Trumpets within

(*Aloud*) The Moor—I know his trumpet.

CASSIO   'Tis truly so.

DESDEMONA
Let's meet him and receive him.

CASSIO   Lo where he comes!

Enter Othello and attendants

OTHELLO (*to Desdemona*)
O my fair warrior!

DESDEMONA   My dear Othello.

OTHELLO
It gives me wonder great as my content
To see you here before me. O my soul's joy,   185
If after every tempest come such calms,
May the winds blow till they have wakened death,
And let the labouring barque climb hills of seas
Olympus-high, and duck again as low
As hell's from heaven. If it were now to die   190
'Twere now to be most happy, for I fear
My soul hath her content so absolute
That not another comfort like to this
Succeeds in unknown fate.

DESDEMONA   The heavens forbid
But that our loves and comforts should increase   195
Even as our days do grow.

OTHELLO   Amen to that, sweet powers!
I cannot speak enough of this content.
It stops me here, it is too much of joy.
And this, (*they kiss*) and this, the greatest discords be
That e'er our hearts shall make.

IAGO (*aside*)   O, you are well tuned now,
But I'll set down the pegs that make this music,   201
As honest as I am.

OTHELLO   Come, let us to the castle.
News, friends: our wars are done, the Turks are
drowned.
How does my old acquaintance of this isle?—
Honey, you shall be well desired in Cyprus,   205
I have found great love amongst them. O my sweet,
I prattle out of fashion, and I dote
In mine own comforts. I prithee, good Iago,
Go to the bay and disembark my coffers.
Bring thou the master to the citadel.   210
He is a good one, and his worthiness
Does challenge much respect. Come, Desdemona.—
Once more, well met at Cyprus!

*Exeunt Othello and Desdemona with all but Iago
and Roderigo*

IAGO (*to an attendant as he goes out*) Do thou meet me
presently at the harbour. (*To Roderigo*) Come hither. If
thou beest valiant—as they say base men being in love
have then a nobility in their natures more than is
native to them—list me. The lieutenant tonight watches
on the court of guard. First, I must tell thee this:
Desdemona is directly in love with him.   220

RODERIGO With him? Why, 'tis not possible!

IAGO Lay thy finger thus, and let thy soul be instructed.
Mark me with what violence she first loved the Moor,
but for bragging and telling her fantastical lies. To love
him still for prating?—let not thy discreet heart think
it. Her eye must be fed, and what delight shall she

have to look on the devil? When the blood is made
dull with the act of sport, there should be again to
inflame it, and to give satiety a fresh appetite, loveliness
in favour, sympathy in years, manners, and beauties,
all which the Moor is defective in. Now, for want of
these required conveniences, her delicate tenderness
will find itself abused, begin to heave the gorge, disrelish
and abhor the Moor. Very nature will instruct her in
it and compel her to some second choice. Now, sir, this
granted—as it is a most pregnant and unforced
position—who stands so eminent in the degree of this
fortune as Cassio does?—a knave very voluble, no
further conscionable than in putting on the mere form
of civil and humane seeming for the better compass of
his salt and most hidden loose affection. Why, none;
why, none—a slipper and subtle knave, a finder of
occasion, that has an eye can stamp and counterfeit
advantages, though true advantage never present itself,
a devilish knave! Besides, the knave is handsome,
young, and hath all those requisites in him that folly
and green minds look after. A pestilent complete knave,
and the woman hath found him already.

RODERIGO I cannot believe that in her. She's full of most
blessed condition.   250

IAGO Blessed fig's end! The wine she drinks is made of
grapes. If she had been blessed, she would never have
loved the Moor. Blessed pudding! Didst thou not see
her paddle with the palm of his hand? Didst not mark
that?   255

RODERIGO Yes, that I did, but that was but courtesy.

IAGO Lechery, by this hand; an index and obscure
prologue to the history of lust and foul thoughts. They
met so near with their lips that their breaths embraced
together. Villainous thoughts, Roderigo! When these
mutualities so marshal the way, hard at hand comes
the master and main exercise, th'incorporate conclusion. Pish! But, sir, be you ruled by me. I have brought
you from Venice. Watch you tonight. For the command,
I'll lay't upon you. Cassio knows you not; I'll not be
far from you. Do you find some occasion to anger
Cassio, either by speaking too loud, or tainting his
discipline, or from what other course you please, which
the time shall more favourably minister.

RODERIGO Well.   270

IAGO Sir, he's rash and very sudden in choler, and haply
may strike at you. Provoke him that he may, for even
out of that will I cause these of Cyprus to mutiny,
whose qualification shall come into no true taste again
but by the displanting of Cassio. So shall you have a
shorter journey to your desires by the means I shall
then have to prefer them, and the impediment most
profitably removed, without the which there were no
expectation of our prosperity.

RODERIGO I will do this, if you can bring it to any
opportunity.   281

IAGO I warrant thee. Meet me by and by at the citadel. I
must fetch his necessaries ashore. Farewell.

RODERIGO Adieu.   *Exit*

IAGO
That Cassio loves her, I do well believe it.   285
That she loves him, 'tis apt and of great credit.
The Moor—howbe't that I endure him not—
Is of a constant, loving, noble nature,
And I dare think he'll prove to Desdemona
A most dear husband. Now I do love her too,   290
Not out of absolute lust—though peradventure
I stand accountant for as great a sin—
But partly led to diet my revenge
For that I do suspect the lusty Moor
Hath leapt into my seat, the thought whereof   295
Doth, like a poisonous mineral, gnaw my inwards;
And nothing can or shall content my soul
Till I am evened with him, wife for wife—
Or failing so, yet that I put the Moor
At least into a jealousy so strong   300
That judgement cannot cure, which thing to do,
If this poor trash of Venice whom I trace
For his quick hunting stand the putting on,
I'll have our Michael Cassio on the hip,
Abuse him to the Moor in the rank garb—   305
For I fear Cassio with my nightcap, too—
Make the Moor thank me, love me, and reward me
For making him egregiously an ass,
And practising upon his peace and quiet
Even to madness. 'Tis here, but yet confused.   310
Knavery's plain face is never seen till used.   *Exit*

2.2   *Enter Othello's Herald reading a proclamation*

HERALD It is Othello's pleasure—our noble and valiant
general—that, upon certain tidings now arrived
importing the mere perdition of the Turkish fleet, every
man put himself into triumph: some to dance, some to
make bonfires, each man to what sport and revels his
addiction leads him; for besides these beneficial news,
it is the celebration of his nuptial. So much was his
pleasure should be proclaimed. All offices are open, and
there is full liberty of feasting from this present hour
of five till the bell have told eleven. Heaven bless the
isle of Cyprus and our noble general, Othello!   *Exit*

2.3   *Enter Othello, Desdemona, Cassio, and attendants*

OTHELLO
Good Michael, look you to the guard tonight.
Let's teach ourselves that honourable stop
Not to outsport discretion.

CASSIO
Iago hath direction what to do,
But notwithstanding, with my personal eye   5
Will I look to't.

OTHELLO   Iago is most honest.
Michael, good night. Tomorrow with your earliest
Let me have speech with you. (*To Desdemona*) Come,
    my dear love,
The purchase made, the fruits are to ensue.
That profit's yet to come 'tween me and you.   10
(*To Cassio*) Good night.
          Exeunt Othello, Desdemona, and attendants

Enter Iago

CASSIO

Welcome, Iago. We must to the watch.

IAGO Not this hour, lieutenant; 'tis not yet ten o'th' clock.
Our general cast us thus early for the love of his
Desdemona, who let us not therefore blame. He hath
not yet made wanton the night with her, and she is
sport for Jove.

CASSIO She's a most exquisite lady.

IAGO And I'll warrant her full of game.   19

CASSIO Indeed, she's a most fresh and delicate creature.

IAGO What an eye she has! Methinks it sounds a parley
to provocation.

CASSIO An inviting eye, and yet, methinks, right modest.

IAGO And when she speaks, is it not an alarum to love?

CASSIO She is indeed perfection.   25

IAGO Well, happiness to their sheets. Come, lieutenant. I
have a stoup of wine, and here without are a brace of
Cyprus gallants that would fain have a measure to the
health of black Othello.   29

CASSIO Not tonight, good Iago. I have very poor and
unhappy brains for drinking. I could well wish courtesy
would invent some other custom of entertainment.

IAGO O, they are our friends! But one cup. I'll drink for
you.   34

CASSIO I ha' drunk but one cup tonight, and that was
craftily qualified, too, and behold what innovation it
makes here! I am infortunate in the infirmity, and dare
not task my weakness with any more.

IAGO What, man, 'tis a night of revels, the gallants desire
it!   40

CASSIO Where are they?

IAGO

Here at the door. I pray you call them in.

CASSIO I'll do't, but it dislikes me.   *Exit*

IAGO

If I can fasten but one cup upon him,
With that which he hath drunk tonight already   45
He'll be as full of quarrel and offence
As my young mistress' dog. Now my sick fool Roderigo,
Whom love hath turned almost the wrong side out,
To Desdemona hath tonight caroused
Potations pottle-deep, and he's to watch.   50
Three else of Cyprus—noble swelling spirits
That hold their honours in a wary distance,
The very elements of this warlike isle—
Have I tonight flustered with flowing cups,
And they watch too. Now 'mongst this flock of
                                         drunkards 55
Am I to put our Cassio in some action
That may offend the isle.
            Enter Montano, Cassio, Gentlemen, ⌈and servants⌉
            with wine
                    But here they come.
If consequence do but approve my dream,
My boat sails freely both with wind and stream.

CASSIO

Fore God, they have given me a rouse already.   60

MONTANO

Good faith, a little one; not past a pint,
As I am a soldier.

IAGO   Some wine, ho!
(*Sings*) And let me the cannikin clink, clink,
          And let me the cannikin clink.
          A soldier's a man,   65
          O, man's life's but a span,
          Why then, let a soldier drink.
Some wine, boys!

CASSIO Fore God, an excellent song.   69

IAGO I learned it in England, where indeed they are most
potent in potting. Your Dane, your German, and your
swag-bellied Hollander—drink, ho!—are nothing to
your English.

CASSIO Is your Englishman so exquisite in his drinking?

IAGO Why, he drinks you with facility your Dane dead
drunk. He sweats not to overthrow your Almain. He
gives your Hollander a vomit ere the next pottle can
be filled.

CASSIO To the health of our general!

MONTANO I am for it, lieutenant, and I'll do you justice.

IAGO O sweet England!   81
(*Sings*) King Stephen was and a worthy peer,
          His breeches cost him but a crown;
          He held them sixpence all too dear,
          With that he called the tailor lown.   85
          He was a wight of high renown,
          And thou art but of low degree.
          'Tis pride that pulls the country down,
          Then take thy auld cloak about thee.
Some wine, ho!   90

CASSIO Fore God, this is a more exquisite song than the
other.

IAGO Will you hear't again?

CASSIO No, for I hold him to be unworthy of his place
that does those things. Well, God's above all, and there
be souls must be saved, and there be souls must not
be saved.

IAGO It's true, good lieutenant.

CASSIO For mine own part—no offence to the general, nor
any man of quality—I hope to be saved.   100

IAGO And so do I too, lieutenant.

CASSIO Ay, but, by your leave, not before me. The
lieutenant is to be saved before the ensign. Let's ha'
no more of this. Let's to our affairs. God forgive us our
sins. Gentlemen, let's look to our business. Do not
think, gentlemen, I am drunk. This is my ensign, this
is my right hand, and this is my left. I am not drunk
now. I can stand well enough, and I speak well enough.

GENTLEMEN Excellent well.   109

CASSIO Why, very well then. You must not think then
that I am drunk.   *Exit*

MONTANO

To th' platform, masters. Come, let's set the watch.
                              Exeunt Gentlemen

IAGO

You see this fellow that is gone before—

He's a soldier fit to stand by Caesar
And give direction; and do but see his vice.   115
'Tis to his virtue a just equinox,
The one as long as th'other. 'Tis pity of him.
I fear the trust Othello puts him in,
On some odd time of his infirmity,
Will shake this island.
MONTANO   But is he often thus?   120
IAGO
'Tis evermore his prologue to his sleep.
He'll watch the horologe a double set
If drink rock not his cradle.
MONTANO   It were well
The general were put in mind of it.
Perhaps he sees it not, or his good nature   125
Prizes the virtue that appears in Cassio,
And looks not on his evils. Is not this true?
     Enter Roderigo
IAGO ⌈aside⌉ How now, Roderigo!
I pray you after the lieutenant, go.   Exit Roderigo
MONTANO
And 'tis great pity that the noble Moor   130
Should hazard such a place as his own second
With one of an engraffed infirmity.
It were an honest action to say so
To the Moor.
IAGO   Not I, for this fair island!
I do love Cassio well, and would do much   135
To cure him of this evil.
VOICES (within) Help, help!
IAGO   But hark, what noise?
     Enter Cassio, driving in Roderigo
CASSIO 'Swounds, you rogue, you rascal!
MONTANO What's the matter, lieutenant?   140
CASSIO A knave teach me my duty?—I'll beat the knave
     into a twiggen bottle.
RODERIGO Beat me?
CASSIO Dost thou prate, rogue?
MONTANO Nay, good lieutenant, I pray you, sir, hold your
     hand.   146
CASSIO Let me go, sir, or I'll knock you o'er the mazard.
MONTANO Come, come, you're drunk.
CASSIO Drunk?
     They fight
IAGO (to Roderigo)
Away, I say. Go out and cry a mutiny.   Exit Roderigo
Nay, good lieutenant. God's will, gentlemen!   151
Help, ho! Lieutenant! Sir! Montano! Sir!
Help, masters. Here's a goodly watch indeed.
     A bell rung
Who's that which rings the bell? Diablo, ho!
The town will rise. God's will, lieutenant, hold.   155
You'll be ashamed for ever.
     Enter Othello and attendants, with weapons
OTHELLO   What is the matter here?
MONTANO
'Swounds, I bleed still. I am hurt to th' death.
     (Attacking Cassio) He dies.

OTHELLO Hold, for your lives!
IAGO
Hold, ho, lieutenant, sir, Montano, gentlemen!
Have you forgot all place of sense and duty?   160
Hold, the general speaks to you. Hold, hold, for shame.
OTHELLO
Why, how now, ho? From whence ariseth this?
Are we turned Turks, and to ourselves do that
Which heaven hath forbid the Ottomites?
For Christian shame, put by this barbarous brawl. 165
He that stirs next to carve for his own rage
Holds his soul light. He dies upon his motion.
Silence that dreadful bell—it frights the isle
From her propriety.
     ⌈Bell stops⌉
                    What is the matter, masters?
Honest Iago, that looks dead with grieving,   170
Speak. Who began this? On thy love I charge thee.
IAGO
I do not know. Friends all but now, even now,
In quarter and in terms like bride and groom
Devesting them for bed; and then but now—
As if some planet had unwitted men—   175
Swords out, and tilting one at others' breasts
In opposition bloody. I cannot speak
Any beginning to this peevish odds,
And would in action glorious I had lost
Those legs that brought me to a part of it.   180
OTHELLO
How comes it, Michael, you are thus forgot?
CASSIO
I pray you pardon me. I cannot speak.
OTHELLO
Worthy Montano, you were wont be civil.
The gravity and stillness of your youth
The world hath noted, and your name is great   185
In mouths of wisest censure. What's the matter,
That you unlace your reputation thus,
And spend your rich opinion for the name
Of a night-brawler? Give me answer to it.
MONTANO
Worthy Othello, I am hurt to danger.   190
Your officer Iago can inform you,
While I spare speech—which something now offends
     me—
Of all that I do know; nor know I aught
By me that's said or done amiss this night,
Unless self-charity be sometimes a vice,   195
And to defend ourselves it be a sin
When violence assails us.
OTHELLO   Now, by heaven,
My blood begins my safer guides to rule,
And passion, having my best judgement collied,
Essays to lead the way. 'Swounds, if I stir,   200
Or do but lift this arm, the best of you
Shall sink in my rebuke. Give me to know
How this foul rout began, who set it on,
And he that is approved in this offence,

Though he had twinned with me, both at a birth, 205
Shall lose me. What, in a town of war
Yet wild, the people's hearts brimful of fear,
To manage private and domestic quarrel
In night, and on the court and guard of safety!
'Tis monstrous. Iago, who began't?   210
MONTANO (to Iago)
  If partially affined or leagued in office
  Thou dost deliver more or less than truth,
  Thou art no soldier.
IAGO   Touch me not so near.
  I had rather ha' this tongue cut from my mouth
  Than it should do offence to Michael Cassio.   215
  Yet I persuade myself to speak the truth
  Shall nothing wrong him. This it is, general.
  Montano and myself being in speech,
  There comes a fellow crying out for help,
  And Cassio following him with determined sword 220
  To execute upon him. Sir, this gentleman
  Steps in to Cassio, and entreats his pause.
  Myself the crying fellow did pursue,
  Lest by his clamour, as it so fell out,
  The town might fall in fright. He, swift of foot, 225
  Outran my purpose, and I returned, the rather
  For that I heard the clink and fall of swords
  And Cassio high in oath, which till tonight
  I ne'er might say before. When I came back—
  For this was brief—I found them close together 230
  At blow and thrust, even as again they were
  When you yourself did part them.
  More of this matter cannot I report,
  But men are men. The best sometimes forget.
  Though Cassio did some little wrong to him,   235
  As men in rage strike those that wish them best,
  Yet surely Cassio, I believe, received
  From him that fled some strange indignity
  Which patience could not pass.
OTHELLO   I know, Iago,
  Thy honesty and love doth mince this matter,   240
  Making it light to Cassio. Cassio, I love thee,
  But never more be officer of mine.
    Enter Desdemona, attended
  Look if my gentle love be not raised up.
  I'll make thee an example.
DESDEMONA What is the matter, dear?   245
OTHELLO All's well now, sweeting.
  Come away to bed. (To Montano) Sir, for your hurts
  Myself will be your surgeon. (To attendants) Lead him
  off.   Exeunt attendants with Montano
  Iago, look with care about the town,
  And silence those whom this vile brawl distracted. 250
  Come, Desdemona. 'Tis the soldier's life
  To have their balmy slumbers waked with strife.
              Exeunt all but Iago and Cassio
IAGO What, are you hurt, lieutenant?
CASSIO Ay, past all surgery.
IAGO Marry, God forbid.   255
CASSIO Reputation, reputation, reputation—O, I ha' lost
my reputation, I ha' lost the immortal part of myself,
and what remains is bestial! My reputation, Iago, my
reputation.   259
IAGO As I am an honest man, I thought you had received
some bodily wound. There is more sense in that than
in reputation. Reputation is an idle and most false
imposition, oft got without merit and lost without
deserving. You have lost no reputation at all unless
you repute yourself such a loser. What, man, there are
more ways to recover the general again. You are but
now cast in his mood—a punishment more in policy
than in malice, even so as one would beat his offenceless
dog to affright an imperious lion. Sue to him again,
and he's yours.   270
CASSIO I will rather sue to be despised than to deceive so
good a commander with so slight, so drunken, and so
indiscreet an officer. Drunk, and speak parrot, and
squabble? Swagger, swear, and discourse fustian with
one's own shadow? O thou invisible spirit of wine, if
thou hast no name to be known by, let us call thee
devil.
IAGO What was he that you followed with your sword?
What had he done to you?
CASSIO I know not.   280
IAGO Is't possible?
CASSIO I remember a mass of things, but nothing distinctly; a quarrel, but nothing wherefore. O God, that
men should put an enemy in their mouths to steal
away their brains! That we should with joy, pleasance,
revel, and applause transform ourselves into beasts!
IAGO Why, but you are now well enough. How came you
thus recovered?
CASSIO It hath pleased the devil drunkenness to give place
to the devil wrath. One unperfectness shows me
another, to make me frankly despise myself.   291
IAGO Come, you are too severe a moraller. As the time,
the place, and the condition of this country stands, I
could heartily wish this had not befallen; but since it
is as it is, mend it for your own good.   295
CASSIO I will ask him for my place again. He shall tell me
I am a drunkard. Had I as many mouths as Hydra,
such an answer would stop them all. To be now a
sensible man, by and by a fool, and presently a beast!
O, strange! Every inordinate cup is unblessed, and the
ingredient is a devil.   301
IAGO Come, come. Good wine is a good familiar creature,
if it be well used. Exclaim no more against it. And,
good lieutenant, I think you think I love you.
CASSIO I have well approved it, sir—I drunk?   305
IAGO You or any man living may be drunk at a time,
man. I'll tell you what you shall do. Our general's wife
is now the general. I may say so in this respect, for
that he hath devoted and given up himself to the
contemplation, mark, and denotement of her parts and
graces. Confess yourself freely to her. Importune her
help to put you in your place again. She is of so free,
so kind, so apt, so blessed a disposition, she holds it a
vice in her goodness not to do more than she is

requested. This broken joint between you and her
husband entreat her to splinter, and, my fortunes
against any lay worth naming, this crack of your love
shall grow stronger than it was before.

CASSIO You advise me well.   319

IAGO I protest, in the sincerity of love and honest kindness.

CASSIO I think it freely, and betimes in the morning I will
beseech the virtuous Desdemona to undertake for me.
I am desperate of my fortunes if they check me here.

IAGO You are in the right. Good night, lieutenant. I must
to the watch.   325

CASSIO Good night, honest Iago.   *Exit*

IAGO
  And what's he then that says I play the villain,
  When this advice is free I give, and honest,
  Probal to thinking, and indeed the course
  To win the Moor again? For 'tis most easy   330
  Th'inclining Desdemona to subdue
  In any honest suit. She's framed as fruitful
  As the free elements; and then for her
  To win the Moor, were't to renounce his baptism,
  All seals and symbols of redeemèd sin,   335
  His soul is so enfettered to her love
  That she may make, unmake, do what she list,
  Even as her appetite shall play the god
  With his weak function. How am I then a villain,
  To counsel Cassio to this parallel course   340
  Directly to his good? Divinity of hell:
  When devils will the blackest sins put on,
  They do suggest at first with heavenly shows,
  As I do now; for whiles this honest fool
  Plies Desdemona to repair his fortune,   345
  And she for him pleads strongly to the Moor,
  I'll pour this pestilence into his ear:
  That she repeals him for her body's lust,
  And by how much she strives to do him good
  She shall undo her credit with the Moor.   350
  So will I turn her virtue into pitch,
  And out of her own goodness make the net
  That shall enmesh them all.
    Enter Roderigo
              · How now, Roderigo?

RODERIGO I do follow here in the chase, not like a hound
that hunts, but one that fills up the cry. My money is
almost spent, I ha' been tonight exceedingly well
cudgelled, and I think the issue will be I shall have so
much experience for my pains: and so, with no money
at all and a little more wit, return again to Venice.

IAGO
  How poor are they that ha' not patience!   360
  What wound did ever heal but by degrees?
  Thou know'st we work by wit and not by witchcraft,
  And wit depends on dilatory time.
  Does't not go well? Cassio hath beaten thee,
  And thou by that small hurt hast cashiered Cassio. 365
  Though other things grow fair against the sun,
  Yet fruits that blossom first will first be ripe.

  Content thyself a while. By the mass, 'tis morning.
  Pleasure and action make the hours seem short.
  Retire thee. Go where thou art billeted.   370
  Away, I say. Thou shalt know more hereafter.
  Nay, get thee gone.   *Exit Roderigo*
             Two things are to be done.
  My wife must move for Cassio to her mistress.
  I'll set her on.
  Myself a while to draw the Moor apart,   375
  And bring him jump when he may Cassio find
  Soliciting his wife. Ay, that's the way.
  Dull not device by coldness and delay.   *Exit*

3.1   *Enter Cassio with Musicians*

CASSIO
  Masters, play here—I will content your pains—
  Something that's brief, and bid 'Good morrow, general'.
    Music. Enter Clown

CLOWN Why, masters, ha' your instruments been in
Naples, that they speak i'th' nose thus?

MUSICIAN How, sir, how?   5

CLOWN Are these, I pray you, wind instruments?

MUSICIAN Ay, marry are they, sir.

CLOWN O, thereby hangs a tail.

MUSICIAN Whereby hangs a tale, sir?   9

CLOWN Marry, sir, by many a wind instrument that I
know. But masters, here's money for you, and the
general so likes your music that he desires you, for
love's sake, to make no more noise with it.

MUSICIAN Well, sir, we will not.   14

CLOWN If you have any music that may not be heard,
to't again; but, as they say, to hear music the general
does not greatly care.

MUSICIAN We ha' none such, sir.

CLOWN Then put up your pipes in your bag, for I'll away.
Go, vanish into air, away.   *Exeunt Musicians*

CASSIO Dost thou hear, my honest friend?   21

CLOWN No, I hear not your honest friend, I hear you.

CASSIO Prithee, keep up thy quillets. There's a poor piece
of gold for thee. If the gentlewoman that attends the
general's wife be stirring, tell her there's one Cassio
entreats her a little favour of speech. Wilt thou do this?

CLOWN She is stirring, sir. If she will stir hither, I shall
seem to notify unto her.

CASSIO
  Do, good my friend.   *Exit Clown*
    Enter Iago
            In happy time, Iago.

IAGO
  You ha' not been abed, then.

CASSIO   Why, no. The day had broke
  Before we parted. I ha' made bold, Iago,   31
  To send in to your wife. My suit to her
  Is that she will to virtuous Desdemona
  Procure me some access.

IAGO
  I'll send her to you presently,   35

And I'll devise a mean to draw the Moor
Out of the way, that your converse and business
May be more free.
CASSIO   I humbly thank you for't.
                                        Exit Iago
I never knew a Florentine more kind and honest.
    Enter Emilia
EMILIA
Good morrow, good lieutenant. I am sorry   40
For your displeasure, but all will sure be well.
The general and his wife are talking of it,
And she speaks for you stoutly. The Moor replies
That he you hurt is of great fame in Cyprus,
And great affinity, and that in wholesome wisdom   45
He might not but refuse you. But he protests he loves
    you,
And needs no other suitor but his likings
To take the saf'st occasion by the front
To bring you in again.
CASSIO   Yet I beseech you,
If you think fit, or that it may be done,   50
Give me advantage of some brief discourse
With Desdemon alone.
EMILIA   Pray you come in.
I will bestow you where you shall have time
To speak your bosom freely.
CASSIO   I am much bound to you.
                                        Exeunt

3.2   *Enter Othello, Iago, and Gentlemen*
OTHELLO
These letters give, Iago, to the pilot,
And by him do my duties to the senate.
That done, I will be walking on the works.
Repair there to me.
IAGO   Well, my good lord, I'll do't.   *Exit*
OTHELLO
This fortification, gentlemen—shall we see't?   5
A GENTLEMAN We'll wait upon your lordship.   *Exeunt*

3.3   *Enter Desdemona, Cassio, and Emilia*
DESDEMONA
Be thou assured, good Cassio, I will do
All my abilities in thy behalf.
EMILIA
Good madam, do. I warrant it grieves my husband
As if the cause were his.
DESDEMONA
O, that's an honest fellow. Do not doubt, Cassio,   5
But I will have my lord and you again
As friendly as you were.
CASSIO   Bounteous madam,
Whatever shall become of Michael Cassio
He's never anything but your true servant.
DESDEMONA
I know't. I thank you. You do love my lord.   10
You have known him long, and be you well assured

He shall in strangeness stand no farther off
Than in a politic distance.
CASSIO   Ay, but, lady,
That policy may either last so long,
Or feed upon such nice and wat'rish diet,   15
Or breed itself so out of circumstance,
That, I being absent and my place supplied,
My general will forget my love and service.
DESDEMONA
Do not doubt that. Before Emilia here
I give thee warrant of thy place. Assure thee,   20
If I do vow a friendship I'll perform it
To the last article. My lord shall never rest.
I'll watch him tame, and talk him out of patience.
His bed shall seem a school, his board a shrift.
I'll intermingle everything he does   25
With Cassio's suit. Therefore be merry, Cassio,
For thy solicitor shall rather die
Than give thy cause away.
    Enter Othello and Iago
EMILIA   Madam, here comes my lord.
CASSIO
Madam, I'll take my leave.
DESDEMONA   Why, stay, and hear me speak.
CASSIO
Madam, not now. I am very ill at ease,   30
Unfit for mine own purposes.
DESDEMONA Well, do your discretion.   *Exit Cassio*
IAGO Ha! I like not that.
OTHELLO What dost thou say?
IAGO
Nothing, my lord. Or if, I know not what.   35
OTHELLO
Was not that Cassio parted from my wife?
IAGO
Cassio, my lord? No, sure, I cannot think it,
That he would steal away so guilty-like
Seeing your coming.
OTHELLO I do believe 'twas he.   40
DESDEMONA How now, my lord?
I have been talking with a suitor here,
A man that languishes in your displeasure.
OTHELLO Who is't you mean?
DESDEMONA
Why, your lieutenant, Cassio; good my lord,   45
If I have any grace or power to move you,
His present reconciliation take;
For if he be not one that truly loves you,
That errs in ignorance and not in cunning,
I have no judgement in an honest face.   50
I prithee call him back.
OTHELLO Went he hence now?
DESDEMONA Yes, faith, so humbled
That he hath left part of his grief with me
To suffer with him. Good love, call him back.   55
OTHELLO
Not now, sweet Desdemon. Some other time.

DESDEMONA
But shall't be shortly?
OTHELLO   The sooner, sweet, for you.
DESDEMONA
Shall't be tonight at supper?
OTHELLO   No, not tonight.
DESDEMONA
Tomorrow dinner, then?
OTHELLO   I shall not dine at home.
I meet the captains at the citadel.   60
DESDEMONA
Why then, tomorrow night, or Tuesday morn,
On Tuesday noon, or night, on Wednesday morn—
I prithee name the time, but let it not
Exceed three days. In faith, he's penitent,
And yet his trespass, in our common reason—   65
Save that, they say, the wars must make example
Out of her best—is not almost a fault
T'incur a private check. When shall he come?
Tell me, Othello. I wonder in my soul
What you would ask me that I should deny,   70
Or stand so mamm'ring on? What, Michael Cassio,
That came a-wooing with you, and so many a time
When I have spoke of you dispraisingly
Hath ta'en your part—to have so much to-do
To bring him in? By'r Lady, I could do much.   75
OTHELLO
Prithee, no more. Let him come when he will.
I will deny thee nothing.
DESDEMONA   Why, this is not a boon.
'Tis as I should entreat you wear your gloves,
Or feed on nourishing dishes, or keep you warm,
Or sue to you to do a peculiar profit   80
To your own person. Nay, when I have a suit
Wherein I mean to touch your love indeed,
It shall be full of poise and difficult weight,
And fearful to be granted.
OTHELLO   I will deny thee nothing,
Whereon I do beseech thee grant me this: 85
To leave me but a little to myself.
DESDEMONA
Shall I deny you? No. Farewell, my lord.
OTHELLO
Farewell, my Desdemona. I'll come to thee straight.
DESDEMONA
Emilia, come. (To Othello) Be as your fancies teach you.
Whate'er you be, I am obedient.   90
                    Exeunt Desdemona and Emilia
OTHELLO
Excellent wretch! Perdition catch my soul
But I do love thee, and when I love thee not,
Chaos is come again.
IAGO My noble lord.
OTHELLO What dost thou say, Iago?   95
IAGO
Did Michael Cassio, when you wooed my lady,
Know of your love?

OTHELLO
He did, from first to last. Why dost thou ask?
IAGO
But for a satisfaction of my thought,
No further harm.
OTHELLO   Why of thy thought, Iago?   100
IAGO
I did not think he had been acquainted with her.
OTHELLO
O yes, and went between us very oft.
IAGO Indeed?
OTHELLO
Indeed? Ay, indeed. Discern'st thou aught in that?
Is he not honest?   105
IAGO Honest, my lord?
OTHELLO Honest? Ay, honest.
IAGO
My lord, for aught I know.
OTHELLO   What dost thou think?
IAGO Think, my lord?
OTHELLO
'Think, my lord?' By heaven, thou echo'st me   110
As if there were some monster in thy thought
Too hideous to be shown! Thou dost mean something.
I heard thee say even now thou liked'st not that,
When Cassio left my wife. What didst not like?
And when I told thee he was of my counsel   115
In my whole course of wooing, thou cried'st 'Indeed?'
And didst contract and purse thy brow together
As if thou then hadst shut up in thy brain
Some horrible conceit. If thou dost love me,
Show me thy thought.   120
IAGO My lord, you know I love you.
OTHELLO I think thou dost,
And for I know thou'rt full of love and honesty,
And weigh'st thy words before thou giv'st them
        breath,
Therefore these stops of thine fright me the more; 125
For such things in a false disloyal knave
Are tricks of custom, but in a man that's just,
They're close dilations, working from the heart
That passion cannot rule.
IAGO   For Michael Cassio,
I dare be sworn I think that he is honest.   130
OTHELLO
I think so too.
IAGO   Men should be what they seem,
Or those that be not, would they might seem none.
OTHELLO
Certain, men should be what they seem.
IAGO
Why then, I think Cassio's an honest man.
OTHELLO Nay, yet there's more in this.   135
I prithee speak to me as to thy thinkings,
As thou dost ruminate, and give thy worst of thoughts
The worst of words.
IAGO   Good my lord, pardon me.

Though I am bound to every act of duty,
I am not bound to that all slaves are free to.   140
Utter my thoughts? Why, say they are vile and false,
As where's that palace whereinto foul things
Sometimes intrude not? Who has that breast so pure
But some uncleanly apprehensions
Keep leets and law-days, and in sessions sit   145
With meditations lawful?

OTHELLO
Thou dost conspire against thy friend, Iago,
If thou but think'st him wronged and mak'st his ear
A stranger to thy thoughts.

IAGO   I do beseech you,
Though I perchance am vicious in my guess—   150
As I confess it is my nature's plague
To spy into abuses, and oft my jealousy
Shapes faults that are not—that your wisdom then,
From one that so imperfectly conceits,
Would take no notice, nor build yourself a trouble   155
Out of his scattering and unsure observance.
It were not for your quiet nor your good,
Nor for my manhood, honesty, and wisdom,
To let you know my thoughts.

OTHELLO   What dost thou mean?

IAGO
Good name in man and woman, dear my lord,   160
Is the immediate jewel of their souls.
Who steals my purse steals trash; 'tis something,
          nothing;
'Twas mine, 'tis his, and has been slave to thousands.
But he that filches from me my good name
Robs me of that which not enriches him   165
And makes me poor indeed.

OTHELLO   By heaven, I'll know thy thoughts.

IAGO
You cannot, if my heart were in your hand;
Nor shall not whilst 'tis in my custody.

OTHELLO
Ha!

IAGO O, beware, my lord, of jealousy.
It is the green-eyed monster which doth mock   170
The meat it feeds on. That cuckold lives in bliss
Who, certain of his fate, loves not his wronger.
But O, what damnèd minutes tells he o'er
Who dotes yet doubts, suspects yet fondly loves!

OTHELLO O misery!   175

IAGO
Poor and content is rich, and rich enough,
But riches fineless is as poor as winter
To him that ever fears he shall be poor.
Good God the souls of all my tribe defend
From jealousy!

OTHELLO   Why, why is this?   180
Think'st thou I'd make a life of jealousy,
To follow still the changes of the moon
With fresh suspicions? No, to be once in doubt
Is once to be resolved. Exchange me for a goat
When I shall turn the business of my soul   185

To such exsufflicate and blowed surmises
Matching thy inference. 'Tis not to make me jealous
To say my wife is fair, feeds well, loves company,
Is free of speech, sings, plays, and dances well.
Where virtue is, these are more virtuous,   190
Nor from mine own weak merits will I draw
The smallest fear or doubt of her revolt,
For she had eyes and chose me. No, Iago,
I'll see before I doubt; when I doubt, prove;
And on the proof, there is no more but this: 195
Away at once with love or jealousy.

IAGO
I am glad of this, for now I shall have reason
To show the love and duty that I bear you
With franker spirit. Therefore, as I am bound,
Receive it from me. I speak not yet of proof.   200
Look to your wife. Observe her well with Cassio.
Wear your eyes thus: not jealous, nor secure.
I would not have your free and noble nature
Out of self-bounty be abused. Look to't.
I know our country disposition well.   205
In Venice they do let God see the pranks
They dare not show their husbands; their best
          conscience
Is not to leave't undone, but keep't unknown.

OTHELLO Dost thou say so?

IAGO
She did deceive her father, marrying you,   210
And when she seemed to shake and fear your looks
She loved them most.

OTHELLO   And so she did.

IAGO   Why, go to, then.
She that so young could give out such a seeming,
To seel her father's eyes up close as oak,
He thought 'twas witchcraft! But I am much to blame.
I humbly do beseech you of your pardon   216
For too much loving you.

OTHELLO   I am bound to thee for ever.

IAGO
I see this hath a little dashed your spirits.

OTHELLO
Not a jot, not a jot.

IAGO   I'faith, I fear it has.
I hope you will consider what is spoke   220
Comes from my love. But I do see you're moved.
I am to pray you not to strain my speech
To grosser issues, nor to larger reach
Than to suspicion.

OTHELLO I will not.   225

IAGO Should you do so, my lord,
My speech should fall into such vile success
Which my thoughts aimed not. Cassio's my worthy
          friend.
My lord, I see you're moved.

OTHELLO   No, not much moved.
I do not think but Desdemona's honest.   230

IAGO
Long live she so, and long live you to think so!

OTHELLO
And yet how nature, erring from itself—
IAGO
Ay, there's the point; as, to be bold with you,
Not to affect many proposèd matches
Of her own clime, complexion, and degree,   235
Whereto we see in all things nature tends.
Foh, one may smell in such a will most rank,
Foul disproportions, thoughts unnatural!
But pardon me. I do not in position
Distinctly speak of her, though I may fear   240
Her will, recoiling to her better judgement,
May fall to match you with her country forms
And happily repent.
OTHELLO   Farewell, farewell.
If more thou dost perceive, let me know more.
Set on thy wife to observe. Leave me, Iago.   245
IAGO (going) My lord, I take my leave.
OTHELLO
Why did I marry? This honest creature doubtless
Sees and knows more, much more, than he únfolds.
IAGO (returning)
My lord, I would I might entreat your honour
To scan this thing no farther. Leave it to time.   250
Although 'tis fit that Cassio have his place—
For sure he fills it up with great ability—
Yet, if you please to hold him off a while,
You shall by that perceive him and his means.
Note if your lady strain his entertainment   255
With any strong or vehement importunity.
Much will be seen in that. In the mean time,
Let me be thought too busy in my fears—
As worthy cause I have to fear I am—
And hold her free, I do beseech your honour.   260
OTHELLO
Fear not my government.
IAGO   I once more take my leave.
                                                Exit
OTHELLO
This fellow's of exceeding honesty,
And knows all qualities with a learned spirit
Of human dealings. If I do prove her haggard,
Though that her jesses were my dear heart-strings 265
I'd whistle her off and let her down the wind
To prey at fortune. Haply for I am black,
And have not those soft parts of conversation
That chamberers have; or for I am declined
Into the vale of years—yet that's not much—   270
She's gone. I am abused, and my relief
Must be to loathe her. O curse of marriage,
That we can call these delicate creatures ours
And not their appetites! I had rather be a toad
And live upon the vapour of a dungeon   275
Than keep a corner in the thing I love
For others' uses. Yet 'tis the plague of great ones;
Prerogatived are they less than the base.
'Tis destiny unshunnable, like death.

Even then this forkèd plague is fated to us   280
When we do quicken.
        Enter Desdemona and Emilia
                        Look where she comes.
If she be false, O then heaven mocks itself!
I'll not believe't.
DESDEMONA   How now, my dear Othello?
Your dinner, and the generous islanders
By you invited, do attend your presence.   285
OTHELLO I am to blame.
DESDEMONA
Why do you speak so faintly? Are you not well?
OTHELLO
I have a pain upon my forehead here.
DESDEMONA
Faith, that's with watching. 'Twill away again.
Let me but bind it hard, within this hour   290
It will be well.
OTHELLO   Your napkin is too little.
        He puts the napkin from him. It drops.
Let it alone. Come, I'll go in with you.
DESDEMONA
I am very sorry that you are not well.
                        Exeunt Othello and Desdemona
EMILIA (taking up the napkin)
I am glad I have found this napkin.
This was her first remembrance from the Moor.   295
My wayward husband hath a hundred times
Wooed me to steal it, but she so loves the token—
For he conjured her she should ever keep it—
That she reserves it evermore about her
To kiss and talk to. I'll ha' the work ta'en out,   300
And give't Iago. What he will do with it,
Heaven knows, not I.
I nothing, but to please his fantasy.
        Enter Iago
IAGO
How now, what do you here alone?
EMILIA
Do not you chide. I have a thing for you.   305
IAGO
You have a thing for me? It is a common thing.
EMILIA Ha?
IAGO To have a foolish wife.
EMILIA
O, is that all? What will you give me now
For that same handkerchief?   310
IAGO What handkerchief?
EMILIA What handkerchief?
Why, that the Moor first gave to Desdemona,
That which so often you did bid me steal.
IAGO Hast stol'n it from her?   315
EMILIA
No, faith, she let it drop by negligence,
And to th'advantage I, being here, took't up.
Look, here 'tis.
IAGO   A good wench! Give it me.

EMILIA
What will you do with it, that you have been so earnest
To have me filch it?
IAGO   Why, what is that to you?   320
      He takes the napkin
EMILIA
If it be not for some purpose of import,
Give't me again. Poor lady, she'll run mad
When she shall lack it.
IAGO
Be not acknown on't. I have use for it. Go, leave me.
      Exit Emilia
I will in Cassio's lodging lose this napkin,   325
And let him find it. Trifles light as air
Are to the jealous confirmations strong
As proofs of holy writ. This may do something.
The Moor already changes with my poison.
Dangerous conceits are in their natures poisons,   330
Which at the first are scarce found to distaste,
But, with a little act upon the blood,
Burn like the mines of sulphur.
      Enter Othello
               I did say so.
Look where he comes. Not poppy nor mandragora
Nor all the drowsy syrups of the world   335
Shall ever medicine thee to that sweet sleep
Which thou owedst yesterday.
OTHELLO Ha, ha, false to me?
IAGO
Why, how now, general? No more of that.
OTHELLO
Avaunt, be gone. Thou hast set me on the rack.   340
I swear 'tis better to be much abused
Than but to know't a little.
IAGO   How now, my lord?
OTHELLO
What sense had I of her stol'n hours of lust?
I saw't not, thought it not; it harmed not me.
I slept the next night well, fed well, was free and merry.   345
I found not Cassio's kisses on her lips.
He that is robbed, not wanting what is stol'n,
Let him not know't and he's not robbed at all.
IAGO I am sorry to hear this.
OTHELLO
I had been happy if the general camp,   350
Pioneers and all, had tasted her sweet body,
So I had nothing known. O, now for ever
Farewell the tranquil mind, farewell content,
Farewell the plumèd troops and the big wars
That makes ambition virtue! O, farewell,   355
Farewell the neighing steed and the shrill trump,
The spirit-stirring drum, th'ear-piercing fife,
The royal banner, and all quality,
Pride, pomp, and circumstance of glorious war!
And O, you mortal engines whose rude throats   360

Th'immortal Jove's dread clamours counterfeit,
Farewell! Othello's occupation's gone.
IAGO Is't possible, my lord?
OTHELLO ⌈*taking Iago by the throat*⌉
Villain, be sure thou prove my love a whore.
Be sure of it. Give me the ocular proof,   365
Or, by the worth of mine eternal soul,
Thou hadst been better have been born a dog
Than answer my waked wrath.
IAGO   Is't come to this?
OTHELLO
Make me to see't, or at the least so prove it
That the probation bear no hinge nor loop   370
To hang a doubt on, or woe upon thy life.
IAGO My noble lord.
OTHELLO
If thou dost slander her and torture me,
Never pray more; abandon all remorse,
On horror's head horrors accumulate,   375
Do deeds to make heaven weep, all earth amazed,
For nothing canst thou to damnation add
Greater than that.
IAGO   O grace, O heaven forgive me!
Are you a man? Have you a soul or sense?
God buy you, take mine office. O wretched fool,   380
That lov'st to make thine honesty a vice!
O monstrous world, take note, take note, O world,
To be direct and honest is not safe!
I thank you for this profit, and from hence
I'll love no friend, sith love breeds such offence.   385
OTHELLO Nay, stay. Thou shouldst be honest.
IAGO
I should be wise, for honesty's a fool,
And loses that it works for.
OTHELLO   By the world,
I think my wife be honest, and think she is not.
I think that thou art just, and think thou art not.   390
I'll have some proof. My name, that was as fresh
As Dian's visage, is now begrimed and black
As mine own face. If there be cords, or knives,
Poison, or fire, or suffocating streams,
I'll not endure it. Would I were satisfied!   395
IAGO
I see, sir, you are eaten up with passion.
I do repent me that I put it to you.
You would be satisfied?
OTHELLO   Would? Nay, and I will.
IAGO
And may. But how, how satisfied, my lord?
Would you, the supervisor, grossly gape on,   400
Behold her topped?
OTHELLO   Death and damnation! O!
IAGO
It were a tedious difficulty, I think,
To bring them to that prospect. Damn them then
If ever mortal eyes do see them bolster
More than their own! What then, how then?   405

What shall I say? Where's satisfaction?
It is impossible you should see this,
Were they as prime as goats, as hot as monkeys,
As salt as wolves in pride, and fools as gross
As ignorance made drunk. But yet I say,   410
If imputation, and strong circumstances
Which lead directly to the door of truth,
Will give you satisfaction, you might ha't.
OTHELLO
Give me a living reason she's disloyal.
IAGO I do not like the office,   415
But sith I am entered in this cause so far,
Pricked to't by foolish honesty and love,
I will go on. I lay with Cassio lately,
And being troubled with a raging tooth,
I could not sleep. There are a kind of men   420
So loose of soul that in their sleeps
Will mutter their affairs. One of this kind is Cassio.
In sleep I heard him say 'Sweet Desdemona,
Let us be wary, let us hide our loves',
And then, sir, would he grip and wring my hand, 425
Cry 'O, sweet creature!', then kiss me hard,
As if he plucked up kisses by the roots,
That grew upon my lips, lay his leg o'er my thigh,
And sigh, and kiss, and then cry 'Cursèd fate,
That gave thee to the Moor!'   430
OTHELLO O, monstrous, monstrous!
IAGO Nay, this was but his dream.
OTHELLO
But this denoted a foregone conclusion.
IAGO
'Tis a shrewd doubt, though it be but a dream,
And this may help to thicken other proofs   435
That do demonstrate thinly.
OTHELLO   I'll tear her all to pieces.
IAGO
Nay, yet be wise; yet we see nothing done.
She may be honest yet. Tell me but this:
Have you not sometimes seen a handkerchief
Spotted with strawberries in your wife's hand?   440
OTHELLO
I gave her such a one. 'Twas my first gift.
IAGO
I know not that, but such a handkerchief—
I am sure it was your wife's—did I today
See Cassio wipe his beard with.
OTHELLO   If it be that—
IAGO
If it be that, or any that was hers,   445
It speaks against her with the other proofs.
OTHELLO
O that the slave had forty thousand lives!
One is too poor, too weak for my revenge.
Now do I see 'tis true. Look here, Iago.
All my fond love thus do I blow to heaven—'tis gone.
Arise, black vengeance, from the hollow hell.   451
Yield up, O love, thy crown and hearted throne

To tyrannous hate! Swell, bosom, with thy freight,
For 'tis of aspics' tongues.
IAGO   Yet be content.
OTHELLO
O, blood, blood, blood!
IAGO   Patience, I say. Your mind may change.
OTHELLO
Never, Iago. Like to the Pontic Sea,   456
Whose icy current and compulsive course
Ne'er knows retiring ebb, but keeps due on
To the Propontic and the Hellespont,
Even so my bloody thoughts with violent pace   460
Shall ne'er look back, ne'er ebb to humble love,
Till that a capable and wide revenge
Swallow them up.
        ⌈He kneels⌉
                        Now, by yon marble heaven,
In the due reverence of a sacred vow
I here engage my words.
IAGO   Do not rise yet.   465
        Iago kneels
Witness you ever-burning lights above,
You elements that clip us round about,
Witness that here Iago doth give up
The execution of his wit, hands, heart
To wronged Othello's service. Let him command,   470
And to obey shall be in me remorse,
What bloody business ever.
        ⌈They rise⌉   I greet thy love,
OTHELLO
Not with vain thanks, but with acceptance bounteous,
And will upon the instant put thee to't.
Within these three days let me hear thee say   475
That Cassio's not alive.
IAGO   My friend is dead.
'Tis done at your request; but let her live.
OTHELLO
Damn her, lewd minx! O, damn her, damn her!
Come, go with me apart. I will withdraw
To furnish me with some swift means of death   480
For the fair devil. Now art thou my lieutenant.
IAGO I am your own for ever.   Exeunt

3.4   *Enter Desdemona, Emilia, and the Clown*
DESDEMONA Do you know, sirrah, where Lieutenant Cassio
lies?
CLOWN I dare not say he lies anywhere.
DESDEMONA Why, man?
CLOWN He's a soldier, and for me to say a soldier lies, 'tis
stabbing.   6
DESDEMONA Go to. Where lodges he?
CLOWN To tell you where he lodges is to tell you where I
lie.
DESDEMONA Can anything be made of this?   10
CLOWN I know not where he lodges, and for me to devise
a lodging and say he lies here, or he lies there, were
to lie in mine own throat.

DESDEMONA Can you enquire him out, and be edified by
report?   15

CLOWN I will catechize the world for him; that is, make
questions, and by them answer.

DESDEMONA Seek him, bid him come hither, tell him I
have moved my lord on his behalf, and hope all will
be well.   20

CLOWN To do this is within the compass of man's wit,
and therefore I will attempt the doing it.   *Exit*

DESDEMONA
Where should I lose the handkerchief, Emilia?

EMILIA I know not, madam.

DESDEMONA
Believe me, I had rather have lost my purse   25
Full of crusadoes, and but my noble Moor
Is true of mind, and made of no such baseness
As jealous creatures are, it were enough
To put him to ill thinking.

EMILIA   Is he not jealous?

DESDEMONA
Who, he? I think the sun where he was born   30
Drew all such humours from him.
     Enter Othello

EMILIA   Look where he comes.

DESDEMONA
I will not leave him now till Cassio
Be called to him. How is't with you, my lord?

OTHELLO
Well, my good lady. (*Aside*) O hardness to dissemble!—
How do you, Desdemona?

DESDEMONA   Well, my good lord.   35

OTHELLO
Give me your hand. This hand is moist, my lady.

DESDEMONA
It hath felt no age, nor known no sorrow.

OTHELLO
This argues fruitfulness and liberal heart.
Hot, hot and moist—this hand of yours requires
A sequester from liberty; fasting, and prayer,   40
Much castigation, exercise devout,
For here's a young and sweating devil here
That commonly rebels. 'Tis a good hand,
A frank one.

DESDEMONA   You may indeed say so,
For 'twas that hand that gave away my heart.   45

OTHELLO
A liberal hand. The hearts of old gave hands,
But our new heraldry is hands, not hearts.

DESDEMONA
I cannot speak of this. Come now, your promise.

OTHELLO What promise, chuck?

DESDEMONA
I have sent to bid Cassio come speak with you.   50

OTHELLO
I have a salt and sorry rheum offends me.
Lend me thy handkerchief.

DESDEMONA (*offering a handkerchief*) Here, my lord.

OTHELLO
That which I gave you.

DESDEMONA   I have it not about me.

OTHELLO Not?

DESDEMONA
No, faith, my lord.

OTHELLO   That's a fault. That handkerchief   55
Did an Egyptian to my mother give.
She was a charmer, and could almost read
The thoughts of people. She told her, while she kept it
'Twould make her amiable, and subdue my father
Entirely to her love; but if she lost it,   60
Or made a gift of it, my father's eye
Should hold her loathèd, and his spirits should hunt
After new fancies. She, dying, gave it me,
And bid me, when my fate would have me wived,
To give it her. I did so, and take heed on't.   65
Make it a darling, like your precious eye.
To lose't or give't away were such perdition
As nothing else could match.

DESDEMONA   Is't possible?

OTHELLO
'Tis true. There's magic in the web of it.
A sibyl that had numbered in the world   70
The sun to course two hundred compasses
In her prophetic fury sewed the work.
The worms were hallowed that did breed the silk,
And it was dyed in mummy, which the skilful
Conserved of maidens' hearts.

DESDEMONA   I'faith, is't true?   75

OTHELLO
Most veritable. Therefore look to't well.

DESDEMONA
Then would to God that I had never seen it!

OTHELLO Ha, wherefore?

DESDEMONA
Why do you speak so startingly and rash?

OTHELLO
Is't lost? Is't gone? Speak, is't out o'th' way?   80

DESDEMONA Heaven bless us!

OTHELLO Say you?

DESDEMONA
It is not lost, but what an if it were?

OTHELLO How?

DESDEMONA
I say it is not lost.

OTHELLO   Fetch't, let me see't.   85

DESDEMONA
Why, so I can, sir, but I will not now.
This is a trick to put me from my suit.
Pray you let Cassio be received again.

OTHELLO
Fetch me the handkerchief. My mind misgives.

DESDEMONA
Come, come, you'll never meet a more sufficient man.

OTHELLO
The handkerchief.

DESDEMONA   I pray, talk me of Cassio.   91

OTHELLO
  The handkerchief.
DESDEMONA   A man that all his time
  Hath founded his good fortunes on your love,
  Shared dangers with you—
OTHELLO The handkerchief.   95
DESDEMONA I'faith, you are to blame.
OTHELLO 'Swounds!   *Exit*
EMILIA
  Is not this man jealous?
DESDEMONA   I ne'er saw this before.
  Sure there's some wonder in this handkerchief.
  I am most unhappy in the loss of it.   100
EMILIA
  'Tis not a year or two shows us a man.
  They are all but stomachs, and we all but food.
  They eat us hungrily, and when they are full,
  They belch us.
      Enter Iago and Cassio
          Look you, Cassio and my husband.
IAGO (*to Cassio*)
  There is no other way. 'Tis she must do't,   105
  And lo, the happiness! Go and importune her.
DESDEMONA
  How now, good Cassio? What's the news with you?
CASSIO
  Madam, my former suit. I do beseech you
  That by your virtuous means I may again
  Exist and be a member of his love   110
  Whom I, with all the office of my heart,
  Entirely honour. I would not be delayed.
  If my offence be of such mortal kind
  That nor my service past, nor present sorrows,
  Nor purposed merit in futurity   115
  Can ransom me into his love again,
  But to know so must be my benefit.
  So shall I clothe me in a forced content,
  And shut myself up in some other course
  To fortune's alms.
DESDEMONA   Alas, thrice-gentle Cassio!   120
  My advocation is not now in tune.
  My lord is not my lord, nor should I know him
  Were he in favour as in humour altered.
  So help me every spirit sanctified
  As I have spoken for you all my best,   125
  And stood within the blank of his displeasure
  For my free speech! You must a while be patient.
  What I can do I will, and more I will
  Than for myself I dare. Let that suffice you.
IAGO
  Is my lord angry?
EMILIA   He went hence but now,   130
  And certainly in strange unquietness.
IAGO
  Can he be angry? I have seen the cannon
  When it hath blown his ranks into the air,
  And, like the devil, from his very arm
  Puffed his own brother; and is he angry?   135

  Something of moment then. I will go meet him.
  There's matter in't indeed, if he be angry.
DESDEMONA
  I prithee do so.   *Exit Iago*
          Something sure of state,
  Either from Venice or some unhatched practice
  Made demonstrable here in Cyprus to him,   140
  Hath puddled his clear spirit; and in such cases
  Men's natures wrangle with inferior things,
  Though great ones are their object. 'Tis even so;
  For let our finger ache and it indues
  Our other, healthful members even to a sense   145
  Of pain. Nay, we must think men are not gods,
  Nor of them look for such observancy
  As fits the bridal. Beshrew me much, Emilia,
  I was—unhandsome warrior as I am—
  Arraigning his unkindness with my soul;   150
  But now I find I had suborned the witness,
  And he's indicted falsely.
EMILIA   Pray heaven it be
  State matters, as you think, and no conception
  Nor no jealous toy concerning you.
DESDEMONA
  Alas the day, I never gave him cause.   155
EMILIA
  But jealous souls will not be answered so.
  They are not ever jealous for the cause,
  But jealous for they're jealous. It is a monster
  Begot upon itself, born on itself.
DESDEMONA
  Heaven keep the monster from Othello's mind.   160
EMILIA Lady, amen.
DESDEMONA
  I will go seek him. Cassio, walk here about.
  If I do find him fit I'll move your suit,
  And seek to effect it to my uttermost.
CASSIO
  I humbly thank your ladyship.   165
      Exeunt Desdemona and Emilia
      Enter Bianca
BIANCA
  Save you, friend Cassio.
CASSIO   What make you from home?
  How is't with you, my most fair Bianca?
  I'faith, sweet love, I was coming to your house.
BIANCA
  And I was going to your lodging, Cassio.
  What, keep a week away? Seven days and nights, 170
  Eightscore-eight hours, and lovers' absent hours
  More tedious than the dial eightscore times!
  O weary reckoning!
CASSIO   Pardon me, Bianca,
  I have this while with leaden thoughts been pressed,
  But I shall in a more continuate time   175
  Strike off this score of absence. Sweet Bianca,
  Take me this work out.
      He gives her Desdemona's napkin
BIANCA   O Cassio, whence came this?

This is some token from a newer friend.
To the felt absence now I feel a cause.
Is't come to this? Well, well.
CASSIO   Go to, woman.   180
Throw your vile guesses in the devil's teeth,
From whence you have them. You are jealous now
That this is from some mistress, some remembrance.
No, by my faith, Bianca.
BIANCA   Why, whose is it?
CASSIO
I know not, neither. I found it in my chamber.   185
I like the work well. Ere it be demanded—
As like enough it will—I would have it copied.
Take it, and do't, and leave me for this time.
BIANCA Leave you? Wherefore?
CASSIO
I do attend here on the general,   190
And think it no addition, nor my wish,
To have him see me womaned.
BIANCA   Why, I pray you?
CASSIO
Not that I love you not.
BIANCA   But that you do not love me.
I pray you bring me on the way a little,
And say if I shall see you soon at night.   195
CASSIO
'Tis but a little way that I can bring you,
For I attend here; but I'll see you soon.
BIANCA
'Tis very good. I must be circumstanced.   *Exeunt*

4.1   *Enter Iago and Othello*
IAGO
Will you think so?
OTHELLO   Think so, Iago?
IAGO
What, to kiss in private?
OTHELLO   An unauthorized kiss.
IAGO
Or to be naked with her friend in bed
An hour or more, not meaning any harm?
OTHELLO
Naked in bed, Iago, and not mean harm?   5
It is hypocrisy against the devil.
They that mean virtuously and yet do so,
The devil their virtue tempts, and they tempt heaven.
IAGO
If they do nothing, 'tis a venial slip.
But if I give my wife a handkerchief—   10
OTHELLO What then?
IAGO
Why then, 'tis hers, my lord, and being hers,
She may, I think, bestow't on any man.
OTHELLO
She is protectress of her honour, too.
May she give that?   15
IAGO
Her honour is an essence that's not seen.

They have it very oft that have it not.
But for the handkerchief—
OTHELLO
By heaven, I would most gladly have forgot it.
Thou said'st—O, it comes o'er my memory   20
As doth the raven o'er the infectious house,
Boding to all!—he had my handkerchief.
IAGO
Ay, what of that?
OTHELLO   That's not so good now.
IAGO
What if I had said I had seen him do you wrong,
Or heard him say—as knaves be such abroad,   25
Who having by their own importunate suit
Or voluntary dotage of some mistress
Convincèd or supplied them, cannot choose
But they must blab—
OTHELLO   Hath he said anything?
IAGO
He hath, my lord. But, be you well assured,   30
No more than he'll unswear.
OTHELLO   What hath he said?
IAGO
Faith, that he did—I know not what he did.
OTHELLO
What, what?
IAGO   Lie—
OTHELLO   With her?
IAGO   With her, on her, what you will.
OTHELLO Lie with her? Lie on her? We say 'lie on her'
when they belie her. Lie with her? 'Swounds, that's
fulsome! Handkerchief—confessions—hankerchief. To
confess and be hanged for his labour. First to be hanged
and then to confess! I tremble at it. Nature would not
invest herself in such shadowing passion without some
instruction. It is not words that shakes me thus. Pish!
Noses, ears, and lips! Is't possible? Confess? Hand-
kerchief? O devil!
      He falls down in a trance
IAGO
Work on; my medicine works. Thus credulous fools
    are caught,
And many worthy and chaste dames even thus,
All guiltless, meet reproach. What ho, my lord!   45
My lord, I say. Othello!
      Enter Cassio
       How now, Cassio?
CASSIO What's the matter?
IAGO
My lord is fall'n into an epilepsy.
This is his second fit. He had one yesterday.
CASSIO
Rub him about the temples.
IAGO   No, forbear.   50
The lethargy must have his quiet course.
If not, he foams at mouth, and by and by
Breaks out to savage madness. Look, he stirs.
Do you withdraw yourself a little while,

He will recover straight. When he is gone   55
I would on great occasion speak with you.
                                        Exit Cassio
How is it, general? Have you not hurt your head?
OTHELLO
Dost thou mock me?
IAGO   I mock you not, by heaven.
Would you would bear your fortune like a man.
OTHELLO
A hornèd man's a monster and a beast.   60
IAGO
There's many a beast then in a populous city,
And many a civil monster.
OTHELLO Did he confess it?
IAGO Good sir, be a man.
Think every bearded fellow that's but yoked   65
May draw with you. There's millions now alive
That nightly lie in those unproper beds
Which they dare swear peculiar. Your case is better.
O, 'tis the spite of hell, the fiend's arch-mock,
To lip a wanton in a secure couch   70
And to suppose her chaste! No, let me know,
And knowing what I am, I know what she shall be.
OTHELLO
O, thou art wise, 'tis certain.
IAGO   Stand you a while apart.
Confine yourself but in a patient list.
Whilst you were here, o'erwhelmèd with your grief—
A passion most unsuiting such a man—   76
Cassio came hither. I shifted him away,
And laid good 'scuse upon your ecstasy,
Bade him anon return and here speak with me,
The which he promised. Do but encave yourself,   80
And mark the fleers, the gibes and notable scorns
That dwell in every region of his face.
For I will make him tell the tale anew,
Where, how, how oft, how long ago, and when
He hath and is again to cope your wife.   85
I say, but mark his gesture. Marry, patience,
Or I shall say you're all-in-all in spleen,
And nothing of a man.
OTHELLO   Dost thou hear, Iago?
I will be found most cunning in my patience,
But—dost thou hear?—most bloody.
IAGO   That's not amiss,
But yet keep time in all. Will you withdraw?   91
    Othello stands apart
Now will I question Cassio of Bianca,
A hussy that by selling her desires
Buys herself bread and cloth. It is a creature
That dotes on Cassio—as 'tis the strumpet's plague   95
To beguile many and be beguiled by one.
He, when he hears of her, cannot restrain
From the excess of laughter.
    Enter Cassio
                        Here he comes.
As he shall smile, Othello shall go mad;

And his unbookish jealousy must conster   100
Poor Cassio's smiles, gestures, and light behaviours
Quite in the wrong. How do you now, lieutenant?
CASSIO
The worser that you give me the addition
Whose want even kills me.
IAGO
Ply Desdemona well and you are sure on't.   105
Now, if this suit lay in Bianca's power,
How quickly should you speed!
CASSIO (*laughing*) Alas, poor caitiff!
OTHELLO (*aside*) Look how he laughs already.
IAGO
I never knew a woman love man so.   110
CASSIO
Alas, poor rogue! I think i'faith she loves me.
OTHELLO (*aside*)
Now he denies it faintly, and laughs it out.
IAGO
Do you hear, Cassio?
OTHELLO (*aside*)   Now he importunes him
To tell it o'er. Go to, well said, well said.
IAGO
She gives it out that you shall marry her.   115
Do you intend it?
CASSIO   Ha, ha, ha!
OTHELLO (*aside*)
Do ye triumph, Roman, do you triumph?
CASSIO I marry! What, a customer? Prithee, bear some
    charity to my wit—do not think it so unwholesome.
    Ha, ha, ha!   120
OTHELLO (*aside*) So, so, so, so. They laugh that wins.
IAGO Faith, the cry goes that you marry her.
CASSIO Prithee, say true.
IAGO I am a very villain else.
OTHELLO (*aside*) Ha' you scored me? Well.   125
CASSIO This is the monkey's own giving out. She is
    persuaded I will marry her out of her own love and
    flattery, not out of my promise.
OTHELLO (*aside*) Iago beckons me. Now he begins the story.
    Othello draws closer
CASSIO She was here even now. She haunts me in every
    place. I was the other day talking on the sea-bank with
    certain Venetians, and thither comes the bauble, and
    falls me thus about my neck.
OTHELLO (*aside*) Crying 'O dear Cassio!' as it were. His
    gesture imports it.   135
CASSIO So hangs and lolls and weeps upon me, so shakes
    and pulls me—ha, ha, ha!
OTHELLO (*aside*) Now he tells how she plucked him to my
    chamber. O, I see that nose of yours, but not that dog
    I shall throw it to!   140
CASSIO Well, I must leave her company.
    Enter Bianca
IAGO Before me, look where she comes.
CASSIO 'Tis such another fitchew! Marry, a perfumed one.
    (*To Bianca*) What do you mean by this haunting of me?

BIANCA Let the devil and his dam haunt you. What did
you mean by that same handkerchief you gave me
even now? I was a fine fool to take it. I must take out
the whole work—a likely piece of work, that you should
find it in your chamber and know not who left it there.
This is some minx's token, and I must take out the
work. There, give it your hobby-horse. (*Giving Cassio
the napkin*) Wheresoever you had it, I'll take out no
work on't.

CASSIO How now, my sweet Bianca, how now, how now?

OTHELLO (*aside*)
By heaven, that should be my handkerchief. 155

BIANCA An you'll come to supper tonight, you may. An
you will not, come when you are next prepared for.
Exit

IAGO After her, after her.

CASSIO Faith, I must, she'll rail in the streets else.

IAGO Will you sup there? 160

CASSIO Faith, I intend so.

IAGO Well, I may chance to see you, for I would very
fain speak with you.

CASSIO Prithee, come, will you?

IAGO Go to, say no more. *Exit Cassio*

OTHELLO How shall I murder him, Iago? 166

IAGO Did you perceive how he laughed at his vice?

OTHELLO O Iago!

IAGO And did you see the handkerchief?

OTHELLO Was that mine? 170

IAGO Yours, by this hand. And to see how he prizes the
foolish woman your wife. She gave it him, and he hath
given it his whore.

OTHELLO I would have him nine years a-killing. A fine
woman, a fair woman, a sweet woman. 175

IAGO Nay, you must forget that.

OTHELLO Ay, let her rot and perish, and be damned
tonight; for she shall not live. No, my heart is turned
to stone; I strike it, and it hurts my hand. O, the world
hath not a sweeter creature! She might lie by an
emperor's side, and command him tasks. 181

IAGO Nay, that's not your way.

OTHELLO Hang her, I do but say what she is—so delicate
with her needle, an admirable musician. O, she will
sing the savageness out of a bear! Of so high and
plenteous wit and invention. 186

IAGO She's the worse for all this.

OTHELLO O, a thousand, a thousand times! And then of
so gentle a condition.

IAGO Ay, too gentle. 190

OTHELLO Nay, that's certain. But yet the pity of it, Iago.
O, Iago, the pity of it, Iago!

IAGO If you are so fond over her iniquity, give her patent
to offend; for if it touch not you, it comes near nobody.

OTHELLO I will chop her into messes. Cuckold me! 195

IAGO O, 'tis foul in her.

OTHELLO With mine officer.

IAGO That's fouler.

OTHELLO Get me some poison, Iago, this night. I'll not

expostulate with her, lest her body and beauty
unprovide my mind again. This night, Iago. 201

IAGO Do it not with poison. Strangle her in her bed, even
the bed she hath contaminated.

OTHELLO Good, good, the justice of it pleases, very good.

IAGO And for Cassio, let me be his undertaker. You shall
hear more by midnight. 206

OTHELLO Excellent good.
A trumpet
What trumpet is that same?

IAGO I warrant, something from Venice.
Enter Lodovico, Desdemona, and attendants
'Tis Lodovico. This comes from the Duke. See, your
wife's with him. 211

LODOVICO God save the worthy general.

OTHELLO With all my heart, sir.

LODOVICO (*giving Othello a letter*) The Duke and the senators
of Venice greet you. 215

OTHELLO I kiss the instrument of their pleasures.
He reads the letter

DESDEMONA
And what's the news, good cousin Lodovico?

IAGO (*to Lodovico*) I am very glad to see you, signor.
Welcome to Cyprus.

LODOVICO I thank you. How does Lieutenant Cassio? 220

IAGO Lives, sir.

DESDEMONA
Cousin, there's fall'n between him and my lord
An unkind breach. But you shall make all well.

OTHELLO Are you sure of that?

DESDEMONA My lord. 225

OTHELLO (*reads*) 'This fail you not to do as you will'—

LODOVICO
He did not call, he's busy in the paper.
Is there division 'twixt my lord and Cassio?

DESDEMONA
A most unhappy one. I would do much
T'atone them, for the love I bear to Cassio. 230

OTHELLO
Fire and brimstone!

DESDEMONA My lord?

OTHELLO Are you wise?

DESDEMONA
What, is he angry?

LODOVICO Maybe the letter moved him,
For, as I think, they do command him home,
Deputing Cassio in his government.

DESDEMONA By my troth, I am glad on't. 235

OTHELLO Indeed!

DESDEMONA My lord?

OTHELLO (*to Desdemona*) I am glad to see you mad.

DESDEMONA Why, sweet Othello!

OTHELLO Devil! 240
He strikes her

DESDEMONA I have not deserved this.

LODOVICO
My lord, this would not be believed in Venice,

Though I should swear I saw't. 'Tis very much.
Make her amends, she weeps.

OTHELLO   O, devil, devil!
If that the earth could teem with woman's tears,   245
Each drop she falls would prove a crocodile.
Out of my sight!

DESDEMONA (*going*) I will not stay to offend you.

LODOVICO
Truly, an obedient lady.
I do beseech your lordship call her back.

OTHELLO Mistress!   250

DESDEMONA (*returning*) My lord?

OTHELLO (*to Lodovico*) What would you with her, sir?

LODOVICO Who, I, my lord?

OTHELLO
Ay, you did wish that I would make her turn.
Sir, she can turn and turn, and yet go on   255
And turn again, and she can weep, sir, weep,
And she's obedient, as you say, obedient,
Very obedient. (*To Desdemona*) Proceed you in your
    tears.
(*To Lodovico*) Concerning this, sir—(*To Desdemona*) O
    well painted passion!
(*To Lodovico*) I am commanded home. (*To Desdemona*)
    Get you away.   260
I'll send for you anon. (*To Lodovico*) Sir, I obey the
    mandate,
And will return to Venice. (*To Desdemona*) Hence,
    avaunt!   *Exit Desdemona*
(*To Lodovico*) Cassio shall have my place, and, sir,
    tonight
I do entreat that we may sup together.
You are welcome, sir, to Cyprus. Goats and monkeys!
                                                 Exit

LODOVICO
Is this the noble Moor whom our full senate   266
Call all-in-all sufficient? Is this the nature
Whom passion could not shake, whose solid virtue
The shot of accident nor dart of chance
Could neither graze nor pierce?

IAGO   He is much changed.

LODOVICO
Are his wits safe? Is he not light of brain?   271

IAGO
He's that he is. I may not breathe my censure
What he might be. If what he might he is not,
I would to heaven he were.

LODOVICO   What, strike his wife!

IAGO
Faith, that was not so well. Yet would I knew   275
That stroke would prove the worst.

LODOVICO   Is it his use,
Or did the letters work upon his blood
And new-create his fault?

IAGO   Alas, alas.
It is not honesty in me to speak
What I have seen and known. You shall observe him,
And his own courses will denote him so   281

That I may save my speech. Do but go after,
And mark how he continues.

LODOVICO
I am sorry that I am deceived in him.   *Exeunt*

4.2   *Enter Othello and Emilia*

OTHELLO You have seen nothing then?

EMILIA
Nor ever heard, nor ever did suspect.

OTHELLO
Yes, you have seen Cassio and she together.

EMILIA
But then I saw no harm, and then I heard
Each syllable that breath made up between 'em.   5

OTHELLO What, did they never whisper?

EMILIA Never, my lord.

OTHELLO Nor send you out o'th' way?

EMILIA Never.

OTHELLO
To fetch her fan, her gloves, her mask, nor nothing?

EMILIA Never, my lord.   11

OTHELLO That's strange.

EMILIA
I durst, my lord, to wager she is honest,
Lay down my soul at stake. If you think other,
Remove your thought; it doth abuse your bosom.   15
If any wretch ha' put this in your head,
Let heaven requite it with the serpent's curse,
For if she be not honest, chaste, and true,
There's no man happy; the purest of their wives
Is foul as slander.

OTHELLO   Bid her come hither. Go.   20
                                        Exit Emilia
She says enough, yet she's a simple bawd
That cannot say as much. This is a subtle whore,
A closet lock and key of villainous secrets,
And yet she'll kneel and pray—I ha' seen her do't.
            Enter Desdemona and Emilia

DESDEMONA
My lord, what is your will?

OTHELLO   Pray you, chuck, come hither.

DESDEMONA
What is your pleasure?

OTHELLO   Let me see your eyes.   26
    Look in my face.

DESDEMONA What horrible fancy's this?

OTHELLO (*to Emilia*) Some of your function, mistress.
Leave procreants alone, and shut the door,   30
Cough or cry 'Hem' if anybody come.
Your mystery, your mystery—nay, dispatch.
                                        Exit Emilia

DESDEMONA
Upon my knees, what doth your speech import?
I understand a fury in your words,
But not the words.

OTHELLO   Why, what art thou?   35

DESDEMONA
Your wife, my lord, your true and loyal wife.

OTHELLO Come, swear it, damn thyself,
  Lest, being like one of heaven, the devils themselves
  Should fear to seize thee. Therefore be double-damned:
  Swear thou art honest.
DESDEMONA   Heaven doth truly know it. 40
OTHELLO
  Heaven truly knows that thou art false as hell.
DESDEMONA
  To whom, my lord? With whom? How am I false?
OTHELLO (weeping)
  Ah, Desdemon, away, away, away!
DESDEMONA
  Alas, the heavy day! Why do you weep?
  Am I the motive of these tears, my lord? 45
  If haply you my father do suspect
  An instrument of this your calling back,
  Lay not your blame on me. If you have lost him,
  I have lost him too.
OTHELLO   Had it pleased God
  To try me with affliction; had He rained 50
  All kind of sores and shames on my bare head,
  Steeped me in poverty to the very lips,
  Given to captivity me and my utmost hopes,
  I should have found in some place of my soul
  A drop of patience. But, alas, to make me 55
  The fixèd figure for the time of scorn
  To point his slow and moving finger at—
  Yet could I bear that too, well, very well.
  But there where I have garnered up my heart,
  Where either I must live or bear no life, 60
  The fountain from the which my current runs
  Or else dries up—to be discarded thence,
  Or keep it as a cistern for foul toads
  To knot and gender in! Turn thy complexion there,
  Patience, thou young and rose-lipped cherubin, 65
  Ay, here look grim as hell.
DESDEMONA
  I hope my noble lord esteems me honest.
OTHELLO
  O, ay—as summer flies are in the shambles,
  That quicken even with blowing. O thou weed,
  Who art so lovely fair, and smell'st so sweet, 70
  That the sense aches at thee—would thou hadst ne'er
      been born!
DESDEMONA
  Alas, what ignorant sin have I committed?
OTHELLO
  Was this fair paper, this most goodly book,
  Made to write 'whore' upon? What committed?
  Committed? O thou public commoner, 75
  I should make very forges of my cheeks,
  That would to cinders burn up modesty,
  Did I but speak thy deeds. What committed?
  Heaven stops the nose at it, and the moon winks;
  The bawdy wind, that kisses all it meets, 80
  Is hushed within the hollow mine of earth
  And will not hear't. What committed?
DESDEMONA By heaven, you do me wrong.

OTHELLO Are not you a strumpet?
DESDEMONA No, as I am a Christian. 85
  If to preserve this vessel for my lord
  From any other foul unlawful touch
  Be not to be a strumpet, I am none.
OTHELLO
  What, not a whore?
DESDEMONA   No, as I shall be saved.
OTHELLO Is't possible? 90
DESDEMONA O heaven forgive us!
OTHELLO I cry you mercy then.
  I took you for that cunning whore of Venice
  That married with Othello. (Calling) You, mistress,
  That have the office opposite to Saint Peter 95
  And keeps the gate of hell,
      Enter Emilia
                you, you, ay, you.
  We ha' done our course. (Giving money) There's
    money for your pains.
  I pray you, turn the key and keep our counsel.   Exit
EMILIA
  Alas, what does this gentleman conceive?
  How do you, madam? How do you, my good lady? 100
DESDEMONA Faith, half asleep.
EMILIA
  Good madam, what's the matter with my lord?
DESDEMONA
  With who?
EMILIA   Why, with my lord, madam.
DESDEMONA
  Who is thy lord?
EMILIA   He that is yours, sweet lady.
DESDEMONA
  I ha' none. Do not talk to me, Emilia. 105
  I cannot weep, nor answers have I none
  But what should go by water. Prithee tonight
  Lay on my bed my wedding sheets, remember.
  And call thy husband hither.
EMILIA   Here's a change indeed.
                      Exit
DESDEMONA
  'Tis meet I should be used so, very meet. 110
  How have I been behaved, that he might stick
  The small'st opinion on my least misuse?
      Enter Iago and Emilia
IAGO
  What is your pleasure, madam? How is't with you?
DESDEMONA
  I cannot tell. Those that do teach young babes
  Do it with gentle means and easy tasks. 115
  He might ha' chid me so, for, in good faith,
  I am a child to chiding.
IAGO   What is the matter, lady?
EMILIA
  Alas, Iago, my lord hath so bewhored her,
  Thrown such despite and heavy terms upon her,
  That true hearts cannot bear it. 120
DESDEMONA Am I that name, Iago?

IAGO What name, fair lady?

DESDEMONA
Such as she said my lord did say I was.

EMILIA
He called her whore. A beggar in his drink
Could not have laid such terms upon his callet.   125

IAGO Why did he so?

DESDEMONA
I do not know. I am sure I am none such.

IAGO
Do not weep, do not weep. Alas the day!

EMILIA
Hath she forsook so many noble matches,
Her father and her country and her friends,   130
To be called whore? Would it not make one weep?

DESDEMONA
It is my wretched fortune.

IAGO   Beshrew him for't.
How comes this trick upon him?

DESDEMONA   Nay, heaven doth know.

EMILIA
I will be hanged if some eternal villain,
Some busy and insinuating rogue,   135
Some cogging, cozening slave, to get some office,
Have not devised this slander. I will be hanged else.

IAGO
Fie, there is no such man. It is impossible.

DESDEMONA
If any such there be, heaven pardon him.

EMILIA
A halter pardon him, and hell gnaw his bones!   140
Why should he call her whore? Who keeps her
    company?
What place, what time, what form, what likelihood?
The Moor's abused by some most villainous knave,
Some base, notorious knave, some scurvy fellow.
O heaven, that such companions thou'dst unfold,   145
And put in every honest hand a whip
To lash the rascals naked through the world,
Even from the east to th' west!

IAGO   Speak within door.

EMILIA
O, fie upon them. Some such squire he was
That turned your wit the seamy side without,   150
And made you to suspect me with the Moor.

IAGO
You are a fool. Go to.

DESDEMONA   O God, Iago,
What shall I do to win my lord again?
Good friend, go to him; for by this light of heaven,
I know not how I lost him.
    She kneels
                              Here I kneel.   155
If e'er my will did trespass 'gainst his love,
Either in discourse of thought or actual deed,
Or that mine eyes, mine ears, or any sense
Delighted them in any other form,
Or that I do not yet, and ever did,   160

And ever will—though he do shake me off
To beggarly divorcement—love him dearly,
Comfort forswear me. Unkindness may do much,
And his unkindness may defeat my life,
But never taint my love.
    ⌈*She rises*⌉
                              I cannot say 'whore'.   165
It does abhor me now I speak the word.
To do the act that might the addition earn,
Not the world's mass of vanity could make me.

IAGO
I pray you, be content. 'Tis but his humour.
The business of the state does him offence,   170
And he does chide with you.

DESDEMONA If 'twere no other!

IAGO It is but so, I warrant.
    Flourish within
Hark how these instruments summon you to supper.
The messengers of Venice stays the meat.   175
Go in, and weep not. All things shall be well.
                              Exeunt Desdemona and Emilia
    Enter Roderigo
How now, Roderigo?

RODERIGO
I do not find that thou deal'st justly with me.

IAGO What in the contrary?   179

RODERIGO Every day thou daff'st me with some device,
Iago, and rather, as it seems to me now, keep'st from
me all conveniency than suppliest me with the least
advantage of hope. I will indeed no longer endure it,
nor am I yet persuaded to put up in peace what already
I have foolishly suffered.   185

IAGO Will you hear me, Roderigo?

RODERIGO Faith, I have heard too much, for your words
and performances are no kin together.

IAGO You charge me most unjustly.   189

RODERIGO With naught but truth. I have wasted myself
out of my means. The jewels you have had from me
to deliver Desdemona would half have corrupted a
votarist. You have told me she hath received 'em, and
returned me expectations and comforts of sudden
respect and acquaintance, but I find none.   195

IAGO Well, go to, very well.

RODERIGO 'Very well', 'go to'! I cannot go to, man, nor
'tis not very well. Nay, I think it is scurvy, and begin
to find myself fopped in it.

IAGO Very well.   200

RODERIGO I tell you 'tis not very well. I will make myself
known to Desdemona. If she will return me my jewels,
I will give over my suit and repent my unlawful
solicitation. If not, assure yourself I will seek satisfaction
of you.   205

IAGO You have said now.

RODERIGO Ay, and said nothing but what I protest
intendment of doing.

IAGO Why, now I see there's mettle in thee, and even
from this instant do build on thee a better opinion than
ever before. Give me thy hand, Roderigo. Thou hast

taken against me a most just exception, but yet I protest
I have dealt most directly in thy affair.

RODERIGO It hath not appeared.   214

IAGO I grant, indeed, it hath not appeared, and your
suspicion is not without wit and judgement. But,
Roderigo, if thou hast that in thee indeed which I have
greater reason to believe now than ever—I mean
purpose, courage, and valour—this night show it. If
thou the next night following enjoy not Desdemona,
take me from this world with treachery, and devise
engines for my life.

RODERIGO Well, what is it? Is it within reason and
compass?

IAGO Sir, there is especial commission come from Venice
to depute Cassio in Othello's place.   226

RODERIGO Is that true? Why then, Othello and Desdemona
return again to Venice.

IAGO O no, he goes into Mauritania, and takes away with
him the fair Desdemona, unless his abode be lingered
here by some accident, wherein none can be so
determinate as the removing of Cassio.

RODERIGO How do you mean 'removing' of him?

IAGO Why, by making him uncapable of Othello's place—
knocking out his brains.   235

RODERIGO And that you would have me to do.

IAGO Ay, if you dare do yourself a profit and a right. He
sups tonight with a harlotry, and thither will I go to
him. He knows not yet of his honourable fortune. If
you will watch his going thence, which I will fashion
to fall out between twelve and one, you may take him
at your pleasure. I will be near, to second your attempt,
and he shall fall between us. Come, stand not amazed
at it, but go along with me. I will show you such a
necessity in his death that you shall think yourself
bound to put it on him. It is now high supper-time,
and the night grows to waste. About it.   247

RODERIGO I will hear further reason for this.

IAGO And you shall be satisfied.   *Exeunt*

4.3   *Enter Othello, Desdemona, Lodovico, Emilia, and
attendants*

LODOVICO
I do beseech you, sir, trouble yourself no further.

OTHELLO
O, pardon me, 'twill do me good to walk.

LODOVICO (*to Desdemona*)
Madam, good night. I humbly thank your ladyship.

DESDEMONA
Your honour is most welcome.

OTHELLO   Will you walk, sir?
O, Desdemona!   5

DESDEMONA My lord?

OTHELLO Get you to bed on th'instant. I will be returned
forthwith. Dismiss your attendant there. Look't be done.

DESDEMONA I will, my lord.   9
            Exeunt Othello, Lodovico, and attendants

EMILIA How goes it now? He looks gentler than he did.

DESDEMONA
He says he will return incontinent.
He hath commanded me to go to bed,
And bid me to dismiss you.

EMILIA   Dismiss me?

DESDEMONA
It was his bidding. Therefore, good Emilia,
Give me my nightly wearing, and adieu.   15
We must not now displease him.

EMILIA I would you had never seen him.

DESDEMONA
So would not I. My love doth so approve him
That even his stubbornness, his checks, his frowns—
Prithee unpin me—have grace and favour in them. 20
            Emilia helps Desdemona to undress

EMILIA
I have laid those sheets you bade me on the bed.

DESDEMONA
All's one. Good faith, how foolish are our minds!
If I do die before thee, prithee shroud me
In one of these same sheets.

EMILIA   Come, come, you talk.

DESDEMONA
My mother had a maid called Barbary.   25
She was in love, and he she loved proved mad
And did forsake her. She had a song of willow.
An old thing 'twas, but it expressed her fortune,
And she died singing it. That song tonight
Will not go from my mind. I have much to do   30
But to go hang my head all at one side
And sing it, like poor Barbary. Prithee, dispatch.

EMILIA
Shall I go fetch your nightgown?

DESDEMONA   No. Unpin me here.
This Lodovico is a proper man.

EMILIA
A very handsome man.

DESDEMONA   He speaks well.   35

EMILIA I know a lady in Venice would have walked
barefoot to Palestine for a touch of his nether lip.

DESDEMONA (*sings*)
'The poor soul sat sighing by a sycamore tree,
    Sing all a green willow.
Her hand on her bosom, her head on her knee,   40
    Sing willow, willow, willow.
The fresh streams ran by her and murmured her
        moans,
    Sing willow, willow, willow.
Her salt tears fell from her and softened the stones,
    Sing willow'—   45
Lay by these.—
            'willow, willow.'
Prithee, hie thee. He'll come anon.
'Sing all a green willow must be my garland.

'Let nobody blame him, his scorn I approve'—   50
Nay, that's not next. Hark, who is't that knocks?

EMILIA It's the wind.

DESDEMONA (*sings*)
'I called my love false love, but what said he then?
  Sing willow, willow, willow.
If I court more women, you'll couch with more men.'
So, get thee gone. Good night. Mine eyes do itch.   56
Doth that bode weeping?

EMILIA   'Tis neither here nor there.

DESDEMONA
I have heard it said so. O, these men, these men!
Dost thou in conscience think—tell me, Emilia—
That there be women do abuse their husbands   60
In such gross kind?

EMILIA   There be some such, no question.

DESDEMONA
Wouldst thou do such a deed for all the world?

EMILIA
Why, would not you?

DESDEMONA   No, by this heavenly light.

EMILIA Nor I neither, by this heavenly light. I might do't
as well i'th' dark.   65

DESDEMONA
Wouldst thou do such a deed for all the world?

EMILIA The world's a huge thing. It is a great price for
a small vice.

DESDEMONA In truth, I think thou wouldst not.   69

EMILIA In truth, I think I should, and undo't when I had
done. Marry, I would not do such a thing for a joint
ring, nor for measures of lawn, nor for gowns,
petticoats, nor caps, nor any petty exhibition; but for
all the whole world? Ud's pity, who would not make
her husband a cuckold to make him a monarch? I
should venture purgatory for't.   76

DESDEMONA
Beshrew me if I would do such a wrong
For the whole world.

EMILIA Why, the wrong is but a wrong i'th' world, and
having the world for your labour, 'tis a wrong in your
own world, and you might quickly make it right.   81

DESDEMONA
I do not think there is any such woman.

EMILIA
Yes, a dozen, and as many
To th' vantage as would store the world they played
for.
But I do think it is their husbands' faults   85
If wives do fall. Say that they slack their duties,
And pour our treasures into foreign laps,
Or else break out in peevish jealousies,
Throwing restraint upon us; or say they strike us,
Or scant our former having in despite: 90
Why, we have galls; and though we have some grace,
Yet have we some revenge. Let husbands know
Their wives have sense like them. They see, and smell,
And have their palates both for sweet and sour,
As husbands have. What is it that they do   95
When they change us for others? Is it sport?
I think it is. And doth affection breed it?

I think it doth. Is't frailty that thus errs?
It is so, too. And have not we affections,
Desires for sport, and frailty, as men have?   100
Then let them use us well, else let them know
The ills we do, their ills instruct us so.

DESDEMONA
Good night, good night. God me such uses send
Not to pick bad from bad, but by bad mend!   *Exeunt*

5.1   *Enter Iago and Roderigo*

IAGO
Here, stand behind this bulk. Straight will he come.
Wear thy good rapier bare, and put it home.
Quick, quick, fear nothing. I'll be at thy elbow.
It makes us or it mars us. Think on that,
And fix most firm thy resolution.   5

RODERIGO
Be near at hand. I may miscarry in't.

IAGO
Here at thy hand. Be bold, and take thy stand.

RODERIGO (*aside*)
I have no great devotion to the deed,
And yet he hath given me satisfying reasons.
'Tis but a man gone. Forth my sword—he dies!   10

IAGO (*aside*)
I have rubbed this young quat almost to the sense,
And he grows angry. Now, whether he kill Cassio
Or Cassio him, or each do kill the other,
Every way makes my gain. Live Roderigo,
He calls me to a restitution large   15
Of gold and jewels that I bobbed from him
As gifts to Desdemona.
It must not be. If Cassio do remain,
He hath a daily beauty in his life
That makes me ugly; and besides, the Moor   20
May unfold me to him—there stand I in much peril.
No, he must die. But so, I hear him coming.
    Enter Cassio

RODERIGO
I know his gait, 'tis he. (*Attacking Cassio*) Villain, thou
diest.

CASSIO
That thrust had been mine enemy indeed,
But that my coat is better than thou know'st.   25
I will make proof of thine.
    He stabs Roderigo, who falls

RODERIGO   O, I am slain!
    Iago wounds Cassio in the leg from behind. Exit Iago

CASSIO (*falling*)
I am maimed for ever. Help, ho, murder, murder!
    Enter Othello ⌈above⌉

OTHELLO
The voice of Cassio. Iago keeps his word.

RODERIGO O, villain that I am!

OTHELLO It is even so.   30

CASSIO O, help, ho! Light, a surgeon!

OTHELLO
'Tis he. O brave Iago, honest and just,

That hast such noble sense of thy friend's wrong—
Thou teachest me. Minion, your dear lies dead,
And your unblessed fate hies. Strumpet, I come.   35
Forth of my heart those charms, thine eyes, are blotted.
Thy bed, lust-stained, shall with lust's blood be spotted.

                                        Exit

     Enter Lodovico and Graziano

CASSIO
What ho, no watch, no passage? Murder, murder!
GRAZIANO
'Tis some mischance. The voice is very direful.
CASSIO O, help!   40
LODOVICO Hark.
RODERIGO O wretched villain!
LODOVICO
Two or three groan. 'Tis heavy night.
These may be counterfeits. Let's think't unsafe
To come into the cry without more help.   45
RODERIGO
Nobody come? Then shall I bleed to death.

     Enter Iago with a light

LODOVICO Hark.
GRAZIANO
Here's one comes in his shirt, with light and weapons.
IAGO
Who's there? Whose noise is this that cries on murder?
LODOVICO
We do not know.
IAGO   Do not you hear a cry?   50
CASSIO
Here, here. For heaven's sake, help me.
IAGO   What's the matter?
GRAZIANO (*to Lodovico*)
This is Othello's ensign, as I take it.
LODOVICO
The same indeed, a very valiant fellow.
IAGO (*to Cassio*)
What are you here that cry so grievously?
CASSIO
Iago—O, I am spoiled, undone by villains.   55
Give me some help.
IAGO
O me, lieutenant, what villains have done this?
CASSIO
I think that one of them is hereabout
And cannot make away.
IAGO   O treacherous villains!
(*To Lodovico and Graziano*)
What are you there? Come in and give some help.   60
RODERIGO O, help me there!
CASSIO That's one of 'em.
IAGO (*stabbing Roderigo*) O murderous slave! O villain!
RODERIGO
O damned Iago! O inhuman dog!
IAGO
Kill men i'th' dark? Where be these bloody thieves? 65
How silent is this town! Ho, murder, murder!
(*To Lodovico and Graziano*)
What may you be? Are you of good or evil?

LODOVICO
As you shall prove us, praise us.
IAGO   Signor Lodovico.
LODOVICO He, sir.
IAGO
I cry you mercy. Here's Cassio hurt by villains.   70
GRAZIANO Cassio?
IAGO How is't, brother?
CASSIO My leg is cut in two.
IAGO Marry, heaven forbid!
Light, gentlemen. I'll bind it with my shirt.   75

     Enter Bianca

BIANCA
What is the matter, ho? Who is't that cried?
IAGO
Who is't that cried?
BIANCA   O my dear Cassio,
My sweet Cassio, O, Cassio, Cassio!
IAGO
O notable strumpet! Cassio, may you suspect
Who they should be that have thus mangled you? 80
CASSIO No.
GRAZIANO
I am sorry to find you thus. I have been to seek you.
IAGO
Lend me a garter. So. O for a chair,
To bear him easily hence!
BIANCA
Alas, he faints. O, Cassio, Cassio, Cassio!   85
IAGO
Gentlemen all, I do suspect this trash
To be a party in this injury.
Patience a while, good Cassio. Come, come,
Lend me a light. (*Going to Roderigo*) Know we this face
or no?
Alas, my friend, and my dear countryman.   90
Roderigo? No—yes, sure—O heaven, Roderigo!
GRAZIANO What, of Venice?
IAGO Even he, sir. Did you know him?
GRAZIANO Know him? Ay.
IAGO
Signor Graziano, I cry your gentle pardon.   95
These bloody accidents must excuse my manners
That so neglected you.
GRAZIANO   I am glad to see you.
IAGO
How do you, Cassio? O, a chair, a chair!
GRAZIANO Roderigo.
IAGO
He, he, 'tis he.

     Enter attendants with a chair

              O, that's well said, the chair!   100
Some good man bear him carefully from hence.
I'll fetch the general's surgeon. (*To Bianca*) For you,
mistress,
Save you your labour. He that lies slain here, Cassio,
Was my dear friend. What malice was between you?
CASSIO
None in the world, nor do I know the man.   105

IAGO (*to Bianca*)
What, look you pale? (*To attendants*) O, bear him out
  o'th' air.
(*To Lodovico and Graziano*)
Stay you, good gentlemen.
           *Exeunt attendants with Cassio in the chair
           ⌈and with Roderigo's body⌉*
(*To Bianca*)   Look you pale, mistress?
(*To Lodovico and Graziano*)
Do you perceive the ghastness of her eye?
(*To Bianca*) Nay, an you stare we shall hear more
  anon.
(*To Lodovico and Graziano*)
Behold her well; I pray you look upon her.   110
Do you see, gentlemen? Nay, guiltiness
Will speak, though tongues were out of use.
  Enter Emilia
EMILIA
Alas, what is the matter? What is the matter,
  husband?
IAGO
Cassio hath here been set on in the dark
By Roderigo and fellows that are scaped.
He's almost slain, and Roderigo dead.   115
EMILIA
Alas, good gentleman! Alas, good Cassio!
IAGO
This is the fruits of whoring. Prithee, Emilia,
Go know of Cassio where he supped tonight.
(*To Bianca*) What, do you shake at that?   120
BIANCA
He supped at my house, but I therefore shake not.
IAGO
O, did he so? I charge you go with me.
EMILIA (*to Bianca*) O, fie upon thee, strumpet!
BIANCA
I am no strumpet, but of life as honest
As you that thus abuse me.
EMILIA   As I? Fough, fie upon thee!
IAGO
Kind gentlemen, let's go see poor Cassio dressed. 126
(*To Bianca*) Come, mistress, you must tell's another
  tale.
Emilia, run you to the citadel
And tell my lord and lady what hath happed.
Will you go on afore?   *Exit Emilia*
(*Aside*)   This is the night   130
That either makes me or fordoes me quite. *Exeunt*

5.2   *Enter Othello with a light. ⌈He draws back a
    curtain, revealing⌉ Desdemona asleep in her bed*
OTHELLO
It is the cause, it is the cause, my soul.
Let me not name it to you, you chaste stars.
It is the cause. Yet I'll not shed her blood,
Nor scar that whiter skin of hers than snow,
And smooth as monumental alabaster.   5
Yet she must die, else she'll betray more men.

Put out the light, and then put out the light.
If I quench thee, thou flaming minister,
I can again thy former light restore
Should I repent me; but once put out thy light, 10
Thou cunning'st pattern of excelling nature,
I know not where is that Promethean heat
That can thy light relume. When I have plucked thy
  rose
I cannot give it vital growth again.
It needs must wither. I'll smell thee on the tree. 15
  ⌈*He kisses her*⌉
O balmy breath, that dost almost persuade
Justice to break her sword! One more, one more.
Be thus when thou art dead, and I will kill thee
And love thee after. One more, and that's the last.
  He kisses her
So sweet was ne'er so fatal. I must weep, 20
But they are cruel tears. This sorrow's heavenly,
It strikes where it doth love. She wakes.
DESDEMONA Who's there? Othello?
OTHELLO Ay, Desdemona.
DESDEMONA Will you come to bed, my lord? 25
OTHELLO Have you prayed tonight, Desdemon?
DESDEMONA Ay, my lord.
OTHELLO
If you bethink yourself of any crime
Unreconciled as yet to heaven and grace,
Solicit for it straight. 30
DESDEMONA
Alack, my lord, what may you mean by that?
OTHELLO
Well, do it, and be brief. I will walk by.
I would not kill thy unprepared spirit.
No, heavens forfend! I would not kill thy soul.
DESDEMONA
Talk you of killing?
OTHELLO   Ay, I do.
DESDEMONA   Then heaven 35
Have mercy on me.
OTHELLO   Amen, with all my heart.
DESDEMONA
If you say so, I hope you will not kill me.
OTHELLO Hum!
DESDEMONA
And yet I fear you, for you're fatal then
When your eyes roll so. Why I should fear I know not,
Since guiltiness I know not, but yet I feel I fear. 41
OTHELLO Think on thy sins.
DESDEMONA They are loves I bear to you.
OTHELLO Ay, and for that thou diest.
DESDEMONA
That death's unnatural that kills for loving. 45
Alas, why gnaw you so your nether lip?
Some bloody passion shakes your very frame.
These are portents, but yet I hope, I hope
They do not point on me.
OTHELLO   Peace, and be still.

DESDEMONA
I will so. What's the matter?

OTHELLO   That handkerchief   50
Which I so loved and gave thee, thou gav'st to Cassio.

DESDEMONA
No, by my life and soul. Send for the man
And ask him.

OTHELLO
Sweet soul, take heed, take heed of perjury.
Thou art on thy deathbed.   55

DESDEMONA Ay, but not yet to die.

OTHELLO Presently.
Therefore confess thee freely of thy sin,
For to deny each article with oath
Cannot remove nor choke the strong conception   60
That I do groan withal. Thou art to die.

DESDEMONA
Then Lord have mercy on me.

OTHELLO   I say amen.

DESDEMONA
And have you mercy, too. I never did
Offend you in my life, never loved Cassio
But with such general warranty of heaven   65
As I might love. I never gave him token.

OTHELLO
By heaven, I saw my handkerchief in's hand.
O perjured woman! Thou dost stone my heart,
And makes me call what I intend to do
A murder, which I thought a sacrifice.   70
I saw the handkerchief.

DESDEMONA   He found it, then.
I never gave it him. Send for him hither.
Let him confess a truth.

OTHELLO   He hath confessed.

DESDEMONA
What, my lord?

OTHELLO   That he hath usèd thee.

DESDEMONA How, unlawfully?   75

OTHELLO Ay.

DESDEMONA He will not say so.

OTHELLO No, his mouth is stopped.
Honest Iago hath ta'en order for't.

DESDEMONA
O, my fear interprets! What, is he dead?   80

OTHELLO
Had all his hairs been lives, my great revenge
Had stomach for 'em all.

DESDEMONA (weeping)
Alas, he is betrayed, and I undone.

OTHELLO
Out, strumpet! Weep'st thou for him to my face?

DESDEMONA
O, banish me, my lord, but kill me not.   85

OTHELLO (attacking her) Down, strumpet.

DESDEMONA
Kill me tomorrow; let me live tonight.

OTHELLO Nay, an you strive—

DESDEMONA But half an hour.

OTHELLO Being done, there is no pause.   90

DESDEMONA But while I say one prayer.

OTHELLO It is too late.
He smothers her

DESDEMONA O Lord, Lord, Lord!
Emilia at the door

EMILIA (*within*)
My lord, my lord, what ho, my lord, my lord!

OTHELLO
What noise is this? Not dead? Not yet quite dead?   95
I that am cruel am yet merciful.
I would not have thee linger in thy pain.
So, so.

EMILIA (*within*) What ho, my lord, my lord!

OTHELLO   Who's there?

EMILIA (*within*)
O, good my lord, I would speak a word with you.

OTHELLO (*calling*)
Yes.—'Tis Emilia. (*Calling*) By and by!—She's dead.   100
'Tis like she comes to speak of Cassio's death.
The noise was high. Ha! No more moving.
Still as the grave. Shall she come in? Were't good?
I think she stirs again. No. What's best to do?
If she come in, she'll sure speak to my wife.   105
My wife, my wife! What wife? I ha' no wife.
O insupportable, O heavy hour!
Methinks it should be now a huge eclipse
Of sun and moon, and that th'affrighted globe
Should yawn at alteration.

EMILIA (*within*)   I do beseech you   110
That I may speak with you. O, good my lord!

OTHELLO
I had forgot thee.—O, come in, Emilia.—
Soft, by and by. Let me the curtains draw.
He closes the bed-curtains
Where art thou?
He opens the door. Enter Emilia
                What's the matter with thee now?

EMILIA
O my good lord, yonder's foul murder's done.   115

OTHELLO What, now?

EMILIA But now, my lord.

OTHELLO
It is the very error of the moon,
She comes more nearer earth than she was wont,
And makes men mad.   120

EMILIA
Cassio, my lord, hath killed a young Venetian
Called Roderigo.

OTHELLO   Roderigo killed
And Cassio killed?

EMILIA   No, Cassio is not killed.

OTHELLO
Not Cassio killed? Then murder's out of tune,
And sweet revenge grows harsh.   125

DESDEMONA O, falsely, falsely murdered!

EMILIA O Lord, what cry is that?

OTHELLO That? What?

EMILIA
Out and alas, that was my lady's voice!
  ⌈*She opens the bed-curtains*⌉
Help, help, ho, help! O lady, speak again!   130
Sweet Desdemona, O sweet mistress, speak!
DESDEMONA
A guiltless death I die.
EMILIA   O, who hath done this deed?
DESDEMONA
Nobody, I myself. Farewell.
Commend me to my kind lord. O, farewell!   *She dies*
OTHELLO
Why, how should she be murdered?
EMILIA   Alas, who knows?
OTHELLO
You heard her say herself it was not I.   136
EMILIA
She said so, I must needs report the truth.
OTHELLO
She's like a liar gone to burning hell.
'Twas I that killed her.
EMILIA
O, the more angel she, and you the blacker devil!   140
OTHELLO
She turned to folly, and she was a whore.
EMILIA
Thou dost belie her, and thou art a devil.
OTHELLO
She was false as water.
EMILIA   Thou art rash as fire
To say that she was false. O, she was heavenly true!
OTHELLO
Cassio did top her. Ask thy husband else.   145
O, I were damned beneath all depth in hell
But that I did proceed upon just grounds
To this extremity! Thy husband knew it all.
EMILIA
My husband?
OTHELLO   Thy husband.
EMILIA   That she was false to wedlock?
OTHELLO
Ay, with Cassio. Had she been true,   150
If heaven would make me such another world
Of one entire and perfect chrysolite
I'd not have sold her for it.
EMILIA   My husband?
OTHELLO
Ay, 'twas he that told me on her first.
An honest man he is, and hates the slime   155
That sticks on filthy deeds.
EMILIA   My husband?
OTHELLO
What needs this iterance? Woman, I say thy husband.
EMILIA
O mistress, villainy hath made mocks with love.
My husband say she was false?
OTHELLO   He, woman.

I say thy husband. Dost understand the word?   160
My friend, thy husband, honest, honest Iago.
EMILIA
If he say so, may his pernicious soul
Rot half a grain a day. He lies to th' heart.
She was too fond of her most filthy bargain.
OTHELLO Ha?   165
EMILIA Do thy worst.
This deed of thine is no more worthy heaven
Than thou wast worthy her.
OTHELLO   Peace, you were best.
EMILIA
Thou hast not half that power to do me harm
As I have to be hurt. O gull, O dolt,   170
As ignorant as dirt! Thou hast done a deed—
I care not for thy sword, I'll make thee known
Though I lost twenty lives. Help, help, ho! Help!
The Moor hath killed my mistress. Murder, murder!
  Enter Montano, Graziano, and Iago
MONTANO
What is the matter? How now, general?   175
EMILIA
O, are you come, Iago? You have done well,
That men must lay their murders on your neck.
GRAZIANO What is the matter?
EMILIA (*to Iago*)
Disprove this villain if thou beest a man.
He says thou told'st him that his wife was false.   180
I know thou didst not. Thou'rt not such a villain.
Speak, for my heart is full.
IAGO
I told him what I thought, and told no more
Than what he found himself was apt and true.
EMILIA
But did you ever tell him she was false?   185
IAGO I did.
EMILIA
You told a lie, an odious, damnèd lie,
Upon my soul a lie, a wicked lie.
She false with Cassio? Did you say with Cassio?
IAGO
With Cassio, mistress. Go to, charm your tongue.   190
EMILIA
I will not charm my tongue. I am bound to speak.
My mistress here lies murdered in her bed.
⌈MONTANO *and* GRAZIANO⌉ O heavens forfend!
EMILIA (*to Iago*)
And your reports have set the murder on.
OTHELLO
Nay, stare not, masters. It is true indeed.   195
GRAZIANO
'Tis a strange truth.
MONTANO   O monstrous act!
EMILIA
Villainy, villainy, villainy!
I think upon't, I think. I smell't. O villainy!
I thought so then. I'll kill myself for grief.
O villainy, villainy!   200

IAGO
What, are you mad? I charge you get you home.
EMILIA
Good gentlemen, let me have leave to speak.
'Tis proper I obey him, but not now.
Perchance, Iago, I will ne'er go home.
OTHELLO
O, O, O!
Othello falls on the bed
EMILIA   Nay, lay thee down and roar,   205
For thou hast killed the sweetest innocent
That e'er did lift up eye.
OTHELLO ⌜*rising*⌝   O, she was foul!
    (*To Graziano*) I scarce did know you, uncle. There lies
      your niece,
Whose breath indeed these hands have newly
      stopped.
I know this act shows horrible and grim.   210
GRAZIANO
Poor Desdemon, I am glad thy father's dead.
Thy match was mortal to him, and pure grief
Shore his old thread in twain. Did he live now
This sight would make him do a desperate turn,
Yea, curse his better angel from his side,   215
And fall to reprobance.
OTHELLO
'Tis pitiful. But yet Iago knows
That she with Cassio hath the act of shame
A thousand times committed. Cassio confessed it,
And she did gratify his amorous works   220
With that recognizance and pledge of love
Which I first gave her. I saw it in his hand.
It was a handkerchief, an antique token
My father gave my mother.
EMILIA   O God! O heavenly God!
IAGO
'Swounds, hold your peace!
EMILIA   'Twill out, 'twill out. I peace?
No, I will speak as liberal as the north.   226
Let heaven, and men, and devils, let 'em all,
All, all cry shame against me, yet I'll speak.
IAGO Be wise and get you home.
EMILIA   I will not.   230
Iago draws his sword
GRAZIANO (*to Iago*) Fie, your sword upon a woman?
EMILIA
O thou dull Moor, that handkerchief thou speak'st of
I found by fortune and did give my husband,
For often, with a solemn earnestness—
More than indeed belonged to such a trifle—   235
He begged of me to steal't.
IAGO   Villainous whore!
EMILIA
She give it Cassio? No, alas, I found it,
And I did give't my husband.
IAGO   Filth, thou liest.
EMILIA
By heaven I do not, I do not, gentlemen.

O murderous coxcomb! What should such a fool   240
Do with so good a wife?
OTHELLO   Are there no stones in heaven
But what serves for the thunder? Precious villain!
    The Moor runs at Iago. Montano disarms Othello.
    Iago wounds his wife
GRAZIANO
The woman falls. Sure he hath killed his wife.
EMILIA
Ay, ay. O, lay me by my mistress' side!   *Exit Iago*
GRAZIANO He's gone, but his wife's killed.   245
MONTANO
'Tis a notorious villain. Take you this weapon
Which I have here recovered from the Moor.
Come, guard the door without. Let him not pass,
But kill him rather. I'll after that same villain,
For 'tis a damnèd slave.
      Exeunt Montano and Graziano
OTHELLO   I am not valiant neither,   250
But every puny whipster gets my sword.
But why should honour outlive honesty?
Let it go all.
EMILIA   What did thy song bode, lady?
Hark, canst thou hear me? I will play the swan,
And die in music. (*Sings*) 'Willow, willow, willow.'—
Moor, she was chaste. She loved thee, cruel Moor.   256
So come my soul to bliss as I speak true.
So, speaking as I think, alas, I die.   *She dies*
OTHELLO
I have another weapon in this chamber.
It was a sword of Spain, the ice-brook's temper.   260
O, here it is. (*Calling*) Uncle, I must come forth.
GRAZIANO (*within*)
If thou attempt it, it will cost thee dear.
Thou hast no weapon, and perforce must suffer.
OTHELLO
Look in upon me then, and speak with me,
Or, naked as I am, I will assault thee.   265
    Enter Graziano
GRAZIANO
What is the matter?
OTHELLO   Behold, I have a weapon;
A better never did itself sustain
Upon a soldier's thigh. I have seen the day
That, with this little arm and this good sword,
I have made my way through more impediments   270
Than twenty times your stop. But O, vain boast!
Who can control his fate? 'Tis not so now.
Be not afraid, though you do see me weaponed.
Here is my journey's end, here is my butt
And very sea-mark of my utmost sail.   275
Do you go back dismayed? 'Tis a lost fear.
Man but a rush against Othello's breast
And he retires. Where should Othello go?
(*To Desdemona*) Now, how dost thou look now? O ill-
      starred wench,
Pale as thy smock! When we shall meet at count   280

This look of thine will hurl my soul from heaven,
And fiends will snatch at it.
⌈*He touches her*⌉
                              Cold, cold, my girl,
Even like thy chastity. O cursèd, cursèd slave!
Whip me, ye devils,
From the possession of this heavenly sight.   285
Blow me about in winds, roast me in sulphur,
Wash me in steep-down gulfs of liquid fire!
O Desdemon! Dead Desdemon! Dead! O! O!
Enter Lodovico, Montano, Iago guarded by officers,
   with Cassio in a chair
LODOVICO
Where is this rash and most unfortunate man?
OTHELLO
That's he that was Othello. Here I am.   290
LODOVICO
Where is that viper? Bring the villain forth.
OTHELLO
I look down towards his feet, but that's a fable.
(*To Iago*) If that thou beest a devil I cannot kill thee.
He wounds Iago
LODOVICO
Wrench his sword from him.
Officers disarm Othello
IAGO   I bleed, sir, but not killed.
OTHELLO
I am not sorry, neither. I'd have thee live,   295
For in my sense 'tis happiness to die.
LODOVICO
O thou Othello, that was once so good,
Fall'n in the practice of a cursèd slave,
What shall be said to thee?
OTHELLO   Why, anything;
An honourable murderer, if you will,   300
For naught I did in hate, but all in honour.
LODOVICO
This wretch hath part confessed his villainy.
Did you and he consent in Cassio's death?
OTHELLO Ay.
CASSIO
Dear general, I never gave you cause.   305
OTHELLO
I do believe it, and I ask your pardon.
Will you, I pray, demand that demi-devil
Why he hath thus ensnared my soul and body?
IAGO
Demand me nothing. What you know, you know.
From this time forth I never will speak word.   310
LODOVICO (*to Iago*) What, not to pray?
GRAZIANO (*to Iago*) Torments will ope your lips.
OTHELLO Well, thou dost best.
LODOVICO
Sir, you shall understand what hath befall'n,
Which as, I think, you know not. Here is a letter,   315
Found in the pocket of the slain Roderigo,
And here another. The one of them imports

The death of Cassio, to be undertook
By Roderigo.
OTHELLO O villain!   320
CASSIO Most heathenish and most gross.
LODOVICO
Now here's another discontented paper
Found in his pocket too, and this it seems
Roderigo meant to've sent this damnèd villain,
But that, belike, Iago in the interim   325
Came in and satisfied him.
OTHELLO (*to Iago*) O thou pernicious caitiff!
How came you, Cassio, by that handkerchief
That was my wife's?
CASSIO   I found it in my chamber,
And he himself confessed it, but even now,   330
That there he dropped it for a special purpose
Which wrought to his desire.
OTHELLO   O fool, fool, fool!
CASSIO
There is besides in Roderigo's letter
How he upbraids Iago, that he made him
Brave me upon the watch, whereon it came   335
That I was cast; and even but now he spake
After long seeming dead, Iago hurt him,
Iago set him on.
LODOVICO (*to Othello*)
You must forsake this room and go with us.
Your power and your command is taken off,   340
And Cassio rules in Cyprus. For this slave,
If there be any cunning cruelty
That can torment him much and hold him long,
It shall be his. You shall close prisoner rest
Till that the nature of your fault be known   345
To the Venetian state. (*To officers*) Come, bring away.
OTHELLO
Soft you, a word or two before you go.
I have done the state some service, and they know't.
No more of that. I pray you, in your letters,
When you shall these unlucky deeds relate,   350
Speak of me as I am. Nothing extenuate,
Nor set down aught in malice. Then must you speak
Of one that loved not wisely but too well,
Of one not easily jealous but, being wrought,
Perplexed in the extreme; of one whose hand,   355
Like the base Indian, threw a pearl away
Richer than all his tribe; of one whose subdued eyes,
Albeit unusèd to the melting mood,
Drops tears as fast as the Arabian trees
Their medicinable gum. Set you down this,   360
And say besides that in Aleppo once,
Where a malignant and a turbaned Turk
Beat a Venetian and traduced the state,
I took by th' throat the circumcisèd dog
And smote him thus.   365
He stabs himself
LODOVICO O bloody period!
GRAZIANO All that is spoke is marred.

OTHELLO (*to Desdemona*)
　I kissed thee ere I killed thee. No way but this:
　Killing myself, to die upon a kiss.

　　　　　　　　　　He kisses Desdemona and dies

CASSIO
　This did I fear, but thought he had no weapon,　370
　For he was great of heart.

LODOVICO (*to Iago*)　　　　　O Spartan dog,
　More fell than anguish, hunger, or the sea,
　Look on the tragic loading of this bed.
　This is thy work. The object poisons sight.

Let it be hid.
　　　⌐They close the bed-curtains⌐
　　　　　　　Graziano, keep the house,　375
And seize upon the fortunes of the Moor,
For they succeed on you. (*To Cassio*) To you, Lord
　Governor,
Remains the censure of this hellish villain.
The time, the place, the torture, O, enforce it!
Myself will straight aboard, and to the state　380
This heavy act with heavy heart relate.

　　　　　　　Exeunt ⌐with Emilia's body⌐

TIMON OF ATHENS

BY WILLIAM SHAKESPEARE AND THOMAS MIDDLETON

WE know no more of *Timon of Athens* than we can deduce from the text printed in the 1623 Folio. Some episodes, such as the emblematic opening dialogue featuring a Poet and a Painter, are elegantly finished, but the play has more unpolished dialogue and loose ends of plot than usual: for example, the episode (3.6) in which Alcibiades pleads for a soldier's life is only tenuously related to the main structure; and the final stretch of action seems imperfectly worked out. Various theories of collaboration and revision have been advanced to explain the play's peculiarities. During the 1970s and 1980s strong linguistic and other evidence has been adduced in support of the belief that it is a product of collaboration between Shakespeare and Thomas Middleton, a dramatist born in 1580 and educated at Queen's College, Oxford, who was writing for the stage by 1602 and was to develop into a great playwright. The major passages for which Middleton seems to have taken prime responsibility are Act 1, Scene 2; all of Act 3 except for parts of Scene 7; and the closing episode (4.3.460–537) of Act 4. The theory of collaboration explains some features of the text—Middleton's verse, for example, was less regular than Shakespeare's. There is no record of early performance; the play is conjecturally assigned to 1604.

The story of Timon was well known and had been told in an anonymous play which seems to have been acted at one of the Inns of Court in 1602 or 1603; Middleton has even been suggested as its author. The classical sources of Timon's story are a brief, anecdotal passage in Plutarch's Life of Mark Antony, and a Greek dialogue by Lucian, who wrote during the second century AD; the former was certainly known to the authors of *Timon of Athens*; the latter influences them directly or indirectly. Plutarch records two epitaphs, one written by Timon himself, which recur, conflated as one epitaph, almost word for word in the play. In Lucian, as in the play, Timon is a misanthrope because his friends flattered and sponged on him in prosperity but abandoned him in poverty. The first part of the play dramatizes this process; in the second part, as in Lucian, Timon finds gold and suddenly becomes attractive again to his old friends.

Timon of Athens is an exceptionally schematic play falling into two sharply contrasting parts, the second a kind of mirror image of the first. Many of the characters are presented two-dimensionally, as if the dramatists were more concerned with the play's pattern of ideas than with psychological realism. The overall tone is harsh and bitter; there are passages of magnificent invective along with some brilliant satire, but there is also tenderness in the portrayal of Timon's servants, especially his 'one honest man', Flavius. In the play's comparatively rare performances some adaptation has usually been found necessary; but the exceptionally long role of Timon offers great opportunities to an actor who can convey his vulnerability as well as his virulence, especially in the strange music of the closing scenes which suggests in him a vision beyond the ordinary.

THE PERSONS OF THE PLAY

TIMON of Athens

A POET
A PAINTER
A JEWELLER
A MERCHANT
A mercer
LUCILIUS, one of Timon's servants
An OLD ATHENIAN

LORDS and SENATORS of Athens
VENTIDIUS, one of Timon's false friends
ALCIBIADES, an Athenian captain
APEMANTUS, a churlish philosopher

One dressed as CUPID in the masque
LADIES dressed as Amazons in the masque

FLAVIUS, Timon's steward
FLAMINIUS ⎱
SERVILIUS ⎰ Timon's servants
Other SERVANTS of Timon

A FOOL
A PAGE

CAPHIS ⎫
ISIDORE'S SERVANT ⎬ servants to Timon's creditors
Two of VARRO'S SERVANTS ⎭

LUCULLUS ⎫
LUCIUS ⎬ flattering lords
SEMPRONIUS ⎭
LUCULLUS' SERVANT
LUCIUS' SERVANT
Three STRANGERS, one called Hostilius

TITUS' SERVANT ⎫
HORTENSIUS' SERVANT ⎬ other servants to Timon's creditors
PHILOTUS' SERVANT ⎭

PHRYNIA ⎱
TIMANDRA ⎰ whores with Alcibiades
The banditti, THIEVES
SOLDIER of Alcibiades' army

Messengers, attendants, soldiers

The Life of Timon of Athens

1.1 *Enter Poet ⌜at one door⌝, Painter carrying a picture*
⌜at another door⌝, ⌜followed by⌝ Jeweller,
Merchant, and Mercer, at several doors

POET
Good day, sir.

PAINTER   I am glad you're well.

POET
I have not seen you long. How goes the world?

PAINTER
It wears, sir, as it grows.

POET   Ay, that's well known.
But what particular rarity, what strange,
Which manifold record not matches?—See,   5
Magic of bounty, all these spirits thy power
Hath conjured to attend.
            ⌜Merchant and Jeweller meet. Mercer passes over
            the stage, and exits⌝
                              I know the merchant.

PAINTER
I know them both. Th'other's a jeweller.

MERCHANT *(to Jeweller)*
O, 'tis a worthy lord!

JEWELLER   Nay, that's most fixed.

MERCHANT
A most incomparable man, breathed, as it were,   10
To an untirable and continuate goodness.
He passes.

JEWELLER *(showing a jewel)* I have a jewel here.

MERCHANT
O, pray, let's see't. For the Lord Timon, sir?

JEWELLER
If he will touch the estimate. But for that—

POET *(to himself)*
'When we for recompense have praised the vile,   15
It stains the glory in that happy verse
Which aptly sings the good.'

MERCHANT *(to Jeweller)*   'Tis a good form.

JEWELLER
And rich. Here is a water, look ye.

PAINTER *(to Poet)*
You are rapt, sir, in some work, some dedication
To the great lord.

POET   A thing slipped idly from me.   20
Our poesy is as a gum which oozes
From whence 'tis nourished. The fire i'th' flint
Shows not till it be struck; our gentle flame
Provokes itself, and like the current flies
Each bound it chafes. What have you there?   25

PAINTER
A picture, sir. When comes your book forth?

POET
Upon the heels of my presentment, sir.
Let's see your piece.

PAINTER *(showing the picture)* 'Tis a good piece.

POET
So 'tis. This comes off well and excellent.

PAINTER
Indifferent.

POET   Admirable. How this grace   30
Speaks his own standing! What a mental power
This eye shoots forth! How big imagination
Moves in this lip! To th' dumbness of the gesture
One might interpret.

PAINTER
It is a pretty mocking of the life.   35
Here is a touch; is't good?

POET   I will say of it,
It tutors nature. Artificial strife
Lives in these touches livelier than life.
            Enter certain Senators

PAINTER How this lord is followed!

POET
The senators of Athens. Happy man!   40

PAINTER Look, more.
            ⌜The Senators pass over the stage, and exeunt⌝

POET
You see this confluence, this great flood of visitors.
I have in this rough work shaped out a man
Whom this beneath world doth embrace and hug
With amplest entertainment. My free drift   45
Halts not particularly, but moves itself
In a wide sea of tax. No levelled malice
Infects one comma in the course I hold,
But flies an eagle flight, bold and forth on,
Leaving no tract behind.   50

PAINTER How shall I understand you?

POET I will unbolt to you.
You see how all conditions, how all minds,
As well of glib and slipp'ry creatures as
Of grave and austere quality, tender down   55
Their service to Lord Timon. His large fortune,
Upon his good and gracious nature hanging,
Subdues and properties to his love and tendance
All sorts of hearts; yea, from the glass-faced flatterer
To Apemantus, that few things loves better   60
Than to abhor himself; even he drops down
The knee before him, and returns in peace,
Most rich in Timon's nod.

PAINTER   I saw them speak together.

POET
Sir, I have upon a high and pleasant hill
Feigned Fortune to be throned. The base o'th' mount
Is ranked with all deserts, all kind of natures   66
That labour on the bosom of this sphere
To propagate their states. Amongst them all
Whose eyes are on this sovereign lady fixed
One do I personate of Lord Timon's frame,   70
Whom Fortune with her ivory hand wafts to her,

Whose present grace to present slaves and servants
Translates his rivals.
PAINTER   'Tis conceived to scope.
This throne, this Fortune, and this hill, methinks,
With one man beckoned from the rest below,   75
Bowing his head against the steepy mount
To climb his happiness, would be well expressed
In our condition.
POET   Nay, sir, but hear me on.
All those which were his fellows but of late,
Some better than his value, on the moment   80
Follow his strides, his lobbies fill with tendance,
Rain sacrificial whisperings in his ear,
Make sacred even his stirrup, and through him
Drink the free air.
PAINTER   Ay, marry, what of these?
POET
When Fortune in her shift and change of mood   85
Spurns down her late belovèd, all his dependants,
Which laboured after him to the mountain's top
Even on their knees and hands, let him fall down,
Not one accompanying his declining foot.
PAINTER 'Tis common.   90
A thousand moral paintings I can show
That shall demonstrate these quick blows of Fortune's
More pregnantly than words. Yet you do well
To show Lord Timon that mean eyes have seen
The foot above the head.   95
          Trumpets sound. Enter Timon ⌐wearing a rich
          jewel⌐, with a Messenger from Ventidius; Lucilius
          ⌐and other Servants⌐ attending. Timon addresses
          himself courteously to every suitor, then speaks to
          the Messenger
TIMON Imprisoned is he, say you?
MESSENGER
Ay, my good lord. Five talents is his debt,
His means most short, his creditors most strait.
Your honourable letter he desires
To those have shut him up, which failing,   100
Periods his comfort.
TIMON   Noble Ventidius! Well,
I am not of that feather to shake off
My friend when he must need me. I do know him
A gentleman that well deserves a help,
Which he shall have. I'll pay the debt and free him. 105
MESSENGER Your lordship ever binds him.
TIMON
Commend me to him. I will send his ransom;
And, being enfranchised, bid him come to me.
'Tis not enough to help the feeble up,
But to support him after. Fare you well.   110
MESSENGER All happiness to your honour.   *Exit*
          Enter an Old Athenian
OLD ATHENIAN
Lord Timon, hear me speak.
TIMON   Freely, good father.
OLD ATHENIAN
Thou hast a servant named Lucilius.

TIMON I have so. What of him?
OLD ATHENIAN
Most noble Timon, call the man before thee.   115
TIMON
Attends he here or no? Lucilius!
LUCILIUS (*coming forward*) Here at your lordship's service.
OLD ATHENIAN
This fellow here, Lord Timon, this thy creature,
By night frequents my house. I am a man
That from my first have been inclined to thrift,   120
And my estate deserves an heir more raised
Than one which holds a trencher.
TIMON   Well, what further?
OLD ATHENIAN
One only daughter have I, no kin else
On whom I may confer what I have got.
The maid is fair, o'th' youngest for a bride,   125
And I have bred her at my dearest cost
In qualities of the best. This man of thine
Attempts her love. I prithee, noble lord,
Join with me to forbid him her resort.
Myself have spoke in vain.   130
TIMON The man is honest.
OLD ATHENIAN Therefore he will be, Timon.
His honesty rewards him in itself;
It must not bear my daughter.
TIMON Does she love him?   135
OLD ATHENIAN She is young and apt.
Our own precedent passions do instruct us
What levity's in youth.
TIMON (*to Lucilius*)   Love you the maid?
LUCILIUS
Ay, my good lord, and she accepts of it.
OLD ATHENIAN
If in her marriage my consent be missing,   140
I call the gods to witness, I will choose
Mine heir from forth the beggars of the world,
And dispossess her all.
TIMON   How shall she be endowed
If she be mated with an equal husband?
OLD ATHENIAN
Three talents on the present; in future, all.   145
TIMON
This gentleman of mine hath served me long.
To build his fortune I will strain a little,
For 'tis a bond in men. Give him thy daughter.
What you bestow in him I'll counterpoise,
And make him weigh with her.
OLD ATHENIAN   Most noble lord,   150
Pawn me to this your honour, she is his.
TIMON
My hand to thee; mine honour on my promise.
LUCILIUS
Humbly I thank your lordship. Never may
That state or fortune fall into my keeping
Which is not owed to you.   155
          Exeunt Lucilius and Old Athenian

POET (*presenting a poem to Timon*)
Vouchsafe my labour, and long live your lordship!
TIMON
I thank you. You shall hear from me anon.
Go not away. (*To Painter*) What have you there, my
    friend?
PAINTER
A piece of painting, which I do beseech
Your lordship to accept.
TIMON   Painting is welcome.   160
The painting is almost the natural man;
For since dishonour traffics with man's nature,
He is but outside; these pencilled figures are
Even such as they give out. I like your work,
And you shall find I like it. Wait attendance   165
Till you hear further from me.
PAINTER   The gods preserve ye!
TIMON
Well fare you, gentleman. Give me your hand.
We must needs dine together. (*To Jeweller*) Sir, your jewel
Hath suffered under praise.
JEWELLER   What, my lord, dispraise?
TIMON
A mere satiety of commendations.   170
If I should pay you for't as 'tis extolled
It would unclew me quite.
JEWELLER   My lord, 'tis rated
As those which sell would give; but you well know
Things of like value differing in the owners
Are prizèd by their masters. Believe't, dear lord,   175
You mend the jewel by the wearing it.
TIMON Well mocked.
MERCHANT
No, my good lord, he speaks the common tongue
Which all men speak with him.
    Enter Apemantus
TIMON   Look who comes here.
Will you be chid?   180
JEWELLER We will bear, with your lordship.
MERCHANT He'll spare none.
TIMON
Good morrow to thee, gentle Apemantus.
APEMANTUS
Till I be gentle, stay thou for thy good morrow—   184
When thou art Timon's dog, and these knaves honest.
TIMON
Why dost thou call them knaves? Thou know'st them
    not.
APEMANTUS Are they not Athenians?
TIMON Yes.
APEMANTUS Then I repent not.
JEWELLER You know me, Apemantus?   190
APEMANTUS
Thou know'st I do. I called thee by thy name.
TIMON Thou art proud, Apemantus!
APEMANTUS Of nothing so much as that I am not like
    Timon.

TIMON Whither art going?   195
APEMANTUS To knock out an honest Athenian's brains.
TIMON That's a deed thou'lt die for.
APEMANTUS Right, if doing nothing be death by th' law.
TIMON
How likest thou this picture, Apemantus?
APEMANTUS The best for the innocence.   200
TIMON
Wrought he not well that painted it?
APEMANTUS He wrought better that made the painter, and
    yet he's but a filthy piece of work.
PAINTER You're a dog.
APEMANTUS Thy mother's of my generation. What's she,
    if I be a dog?   206
TIMON Wilt dine with me, Apemantus?
APEMANTUS No, I eat not lords.
TIMON An thou shouldst, thou'dst anger ladies.
APEMANTUS O, they eat lords. So they come by great bellies.
TIMON
That's a lascivious apprehension.   211
APEMANTUS
So thou apprehend'st it; take it for thy labour.
TIMON
How dost thou like this jewel, Apemantus?
APEMANTUS Not so well as plain dealing, which will not
    cost a man a doit.   215
TIMON
What dost thou think 'tis worth?
APEMANTUS   Not worth my thinking.
How now, poet?
POET How now, philosopher?
APEMANTUS Thou liest.
POET Art not one?   220
APEMANTUS Yes.
POET Then I lie not.
APEMANTUS Art not a poet?
POET Yes.
APEMANTUS Then thou liest. Look in thy last work, where
    thou hast feigned him a worthy fellow.   226
POET That's not feigned, he is so.
APEMANTUS Yes, he is worthy of thee, and to pay thee for
    thy labour. He that loves to be flattered is worthy o'th'
    flatterer. Heavens, that I were a lord!   230
TIMON What wouldst do then, Apemantus?
APEMANTUS E'en as Apemantus does now: hate a lord
    with my heart.
TIMON What, thyself?
APEMANTUS Ay.   235
TIMON Wherefore?
APEMANTUS That I had no augury but to be a lord.—Art
    not thou a merchant?
MERCHANT Ay, Apemantus.
APEMANTUS
Traffic confound thee, if the gods will not!   240
MERCHANT If traffic do it, the gods do it.
APEMANTUS
Traffic's thy god, and thy god confound thee!

Trumpet sounds. Enter a Messenger

TIMON What trumpet's that?

MESSENGER

'Tis Alcibiades, and some twenty horse

All of companionship.   245

TIMON (*to Servants*)

Pray entertain them. Give them guide to us.

⌐*Exit one or more Servants*⌐

⌐*To Jeweller*⌐ You must needs dine with me.

⌐*To Poet*⌐   Go not you hence

Till I have thanked you. ⌐*To Painter*⌐ When dinner's done

Show me this piece. ⌐*To all*⌐ I am joyful of your sights.

Enter Alcibiades with ⌐*his horsemen*⌐

Most welcome, sir!   250

APEMANTUS ⌐*aside*⌐ So, so, there.

Aches contract and starve your supple joints!

That there should be small love 'mongst these sweet

knaves,

And all this courtesy! The strain of man's bred out

Into baboon and monkey.   255

ALCIBIADES (*to Timon*)

Sir, you have saved my longing, and I feed

Most hungrily on your sight.

TIMON   Right welcome, sir!

Ere we depart, we'll share a bounteous time

In different pleasures. Pray you, let us in.

Exeunt all but Apemantus

Enter two Lords

FIRST LORD

What time o' day is't, Apemantus?   260

APEMANTUS

Time to be honest.

FIRST LORD   That time serves still.

APEMANTUS

The most accursèd thou, that still omitt'st it.

SECOND LORD

Thou art going to Lord Timon's feast?

APEMANTUS

Ay, to see meat fill knaves, and wine heat fools.

SECOND LORD Fare thee well, fare thee well.   265

APEMANTUS

Thou art a fool to bid me farewell twice.

SECOND LORD Why, Apemantus?

APEMANTUS Shouldst have kept one to thyself, for I mean

to give thee none.

FIRST LORD Hang thyself!   270

APEMANTUS No, I will do nothing at thy bidding. Make

thy requests to thy friend.

SECOND LORD Away, unpeaceable dog, or I'll spurn thee

hence.

APEMANTUS I will fly, like a dog, the heels o'th' ass.   *Exit*

FIRST LORD

He's opposite to humanity. Come, shall we in,   276

And taste Lord Timon's bounty? He outgoes

The very heart of kindness.

SECOND LORD

He pours it out. Plutus the god of gold

Is but his steward; no meed but he repays   280

Sevenfold above itself; no gift to him

But breeds the giver a return exceeding

All use of quittance.

FIRST LORD   The noblest mind he carries

That ever governed man.

SECOND LORD

Long may he live in fortunes! Shall we in?   285

⌐FIRST LORD⌐ I'll keep you company.   *Exeunt*

1.2   *Hautboys playing loud music. A great banquet*

served in, ⌐*Flavius and Servants attending*⌐*; and*

then enter Timon, Alcibiades, the Senators, the

Athenian Lords, and Ventidius which Timon

redeemed from prison. Then comes, dropping after

all, Apemantus, discontentedly, like himself

VENTIDIUS

Most honoured Timon, it hath pleased the gods to

remember

My father's age and call him to long peace.

He is gone happy, and has left me rich.

Then, as in grateful virtue I am bound

To your free heart, I do return those talents,   5

Doubled with thanks and service, from whose help

I derived liberty.

TIMON   O, by no means,

Honest Ventidius. You mistake my love.

I gave it freely ever, and there's none

Can truly say he gives if he receives.   10

If our betters play at that game, we must not dare

To imitate them. Faults that are rich are fair.

VENTIDIUS

A noble spirit!

⌐*The Lords stand with ceremony*⌐

TIMON   Nay, my lords,

Ceremony was but devised at first

To set a gloss on faint deeds, hollow welcomes,   15

Recanting goodness, sorry ere 'tis shown;

But where there is true friendship, there needs none.

Pray sit. More welcome are ye to my fortunes

Than my fortunes to me.

⌐*They sit*⌐

FIRST LORD

My lord, we always have confessed it.   20

APEMANTUS

Ho, ho, confessed it? Hanged it, have you not?

TIMON

O, Apemantus! You are welcome.

APEMANTUS   No,

You shall not make me welcome.

I come to have thee thrust me out of doors.

TIMON

Fie, thou'rt a churl. Ye've got a humour there   25

Does not become a man; 'tis much to blame.

They say, my lords, *Ira furor brevis est,*

But yon man is ever angry.

Go, let him have a table by himself,

For he does neither affect company 30
Nor is he fit for't, indeed.

APEMANTUS
Let me stay at thine apperil, Timon.
I come to observe, I give thee warning on't.

TIMON
I take no heed of thee; thou'rt an Athenian,
Therefore welcome. I myself would have no power: 35
Prithee, let my meat make thee silent.

APEMANTUS I scorn thy meat. 'Twould choke me, for I
should ne'er flatter thee. O you gods, what a number
of men eats Timon, and he sees 'em not! It grieves me
to see so many dip their meat in one man's blood; and
all the madness is, he cheers them up, too. 41
I wonder men dare trust themselves with men.
Methinks they should invite them without knives:
Good for their meat, and safer for their lives.
There's much example for't. The fellow that sits next
him, now parts bread with him, pledges the breath of
him in a divided draught, is the readiest man to kill
him. 'T'as been proved. If I were a huge man, I should
fear to drink at meals, 49
Lest they should spy my windpipe's dangerous notes.
Great men should drink with harness on their throats.

TIMON (drinking to a Lord)
My lord, in heart; and let the health go round.

SECOND LORD
Let it flow this way, my good lord.

APEMANTUS 'Flow this way'? A brave fellow; he keeps his
tides well. Those healths will make thee and thy state
look ill, Timon. 56
Here's that which is too weak to be a sinner:
Honest water, which ne'er left man i'th' mire.
This and my food are equals; there's no odds.
Feasts are too proud to give thanks to the gods. 60
    Apemantus' grace
    Immortal gods, I crave no pelf.
    I pray for no man but myself.
    Grant I may never prove so fond
    To trust man on his oath or bond,
    Or a harlot for her weeping, 65
    Or a dog that seems a-sleeping,
    Or a keeper with my freedom,
    Or my friends if I should need 'em.
    Amen. So fall to't.
    Rich men sin, and I eat root. 70
    ⌈He eats⌉
Much good dich thy good heart, Apemantus.

TIMON Captain Alcibiades, your heart's in the field now.

ALCIBIADES My heart is ever at your service, my lord.

TIMON You had rather be at a breakfast of enemies than
a dinner of friends. 75

ALCIBIADES So they were bleeding new, my lord; there's
no meat like 'em. I could wish my best friend at such
a feast.

APEMANTUS
Would all those flatterers were thine enemies then,
That thou mightst kill 'em and bid me to 'em. 80

FIRST LORD (to Timon) Might we but have that happiness,
my lord, that you would once use our hearts, whereby
we might express some part of our zeals, we should
think ourselves for ever perfect. 84

TIMON O, no doubt, my good friends, but the gods
themselves have provided that I shall have much help
from you. How had you been my friends else? Why
have you that charitable title from thousands, did not
you chiefly belong to my heart? I have told more of
you to myself than you can with modesty speak in
your own behalf; and thus far I confirm you. 'O you
gods,' think I, 'what need we have any friends if we
should ne'er have need of 'em? They were the most
needless creatures living, should we ne'er have use for
'em, and would most resemble sweet instruments hung
up in cases, that keeps their sounds to themselves.'
Why, I have often wished myself poorer, that I might
come nearer to you. We are born to do benefits; and
what better or properer can we call our own than the
riches of our friends? O, what a precious comfort 'tis
to have so many like brothers commanding one
another's fortunes! O, joy's e'en made away ere't can
be born: mine eyes cannot hold out water, methinks.
To forget their faults, I drink to you.

APEMANTUS Thou weep'st to make them drink, Timon.

SECOND LORD (to Timon)
Joy had the like conception in our eyes, 106
And at that instant like a babe sprung up.

APEMANTUS
Ho, ho, I laugh to think that babe a bastard.

THIRD LORD (to Timon)
I promise you, my lord, you moved me much.

APEMANTUS Much! 110
    A tucket sounds within

TIMON What means that trump?
    Enter a Servant
How now?

SERVANT Please you, my lord, there are certain ladies
most desirous of admittance.

TIMON Ladies? What are their wills? 115

SERVANT There comes with them a forerunner, my lord,
which bears that office to signify their pleasures.

TIMON I pray let them be admitted.
    Enter one as Cupid

CUPID
Hail to thee, worthy Timon, and to all
That of his bounties taste! The five best senses 120
Acknowledge thee their patron, and come freely
To gratulate thy plenteous bosom. Th'ear,
Taste, touch, smell, all, pleased from thy table rise,
They only now come but to feast thine eyes.

TIMON
They're welcome all. Let 'em have kind admittance. 125
Music make their welcome!   Exit Cupid
⌈FIRST LORD⌉
You see, my lord, how ample you're beloved.
    Music. Enter a masque of Ladies as Amazons, with
    lutes in their hands, dancing and playing

APEMANTUS

Hey-day, what a sweep of vanity comes this way!
They dance? They are madwomen.
Like madness is the glory of this life   130
As this pomp shows to a little oil and root.
We make ourselves fools to disport ourselves,
And spend our flatteries to drink those men
Upon whose age we void it up again
With poisonous spite and envy.   135
Who lives that's not depravèd or depraves?
Who dies that bears not one spurn to their graves
Of their friends' gift?
I should fear those that dance before me now
Would one day stamp upon me. 'T'as been done.   140
Men shut their doors against a setting sun.

The Lords rise from table with much adoring of
Timon; and to show their loves each singles out an
Amazon, and all dance, men with women, a lofty
strain or two to the hautboys; and cease

TIMON

You have done our pleasures much grace, fair ladies,
Set a fair fashion on our entertainment,
Which was not half so beautiful and kind.
You have added worth unto't and lustre,   145
And entertained me with mine own device.
I am to thank you for't.

FIRST ⌈LADY⌉

My lord, you take us even at the best.

APEMANTUS Faith; for the worst is filthy, and would not
hold taking, I doubt me.   150

TIMON

Ladies, there is an idle banquet 'tends you.
Please you to dispose yourselves.

ALL LADIES Most thankfully, my lord.   *Exeunt Ladies*

TIMON Flavius.

FLAVIUS My lord.   155

TIMON The little casket bring me hither.

FLAVIUS Yes, my lord. (*Aside*) More jewels yet?
There is no crossing him in's humour,
Else I should tell him well, i'faith I should.
When all's spent, he'd be crossed then, an he could.
'Tis pity bounty had not eyes behind,   161
That man might ne'er be wretched for his mind.   *Exit*

FIRST LORD Where be our men?

SERVANT Here, my lord, in readiness.

SECOND LORD Our horses.   ⌈*Exit Servant*⌉

Enter Flavius with the casket. He gives it to Timon,
⌈*and exits*⌉

TIMON

O my friends, I have one word to say to you.   166
Look you, my good lord,
I must entreat you honour me so much
As to advance this jewel. Accept and wear it,
Kind my lord.   170

FIRST LORD

I am so far already in your gifts.

ALL LORDS So are we all.

⌈*Timon gives them jewels.*⌉

Enter a Servant

FIRST SERVANT My lord, there are certain nobles of the
senate newly alighted and come to visit you.   174

TIMON They are fairly welcome.   *Exit Servant*

Enter Flavius

FLAVIUS I beseech your honour, vouchsafe me a word; it
does concern you near.

TIMON

Near? Why then, another time I'll hear thee.
I prithee, let's be provided to show them entertainment.

FLAVIUS I scarce know how.   180

Enter a Second Servant

SECOND SERVANT

May it please your honour, Lord Lucius
Out of his free love hath presented to you
Four milk-white horses trapped in silver.

TIMON

I shall accept them fairly. Let the presents
Be worthily entertained.   *Exit Servant*

Enter a Third Servant

How now, what news?   185

THIRD SERVANT Please you, my lord, that honourable
gentleman Lord Lucullus entreats your company
tomorrow to hunt with him, and has sent your honour
two brace of greyhounds.

TIMON

I'll hunt with him, and let them be received   190
Not without fair reward.   *Exit Servant*

FLAVIUS (*aside*)   What will this come to?
He commands us to provide and give great gifts,
And all out of an empty coffer;
Nor will he know his purse, or yield me this:
To show him what a beggar his heart is,   195
Being of no power to make his wishes good.
His promises fly so beyond his state
That what he speaks is all in debt, he owes
For every word. He is so kind that he now
Pays interest for't. His land's put to their books.   200
Well, would I were gently put out of office
Before I were forced out.
Happier is he that has no friend to feed
Than such that do e'en enemies exceed.
I bleed inwardly for my lord.   *Exit*

TIMON (*to the Lords*)   You do yourselves   205
Much wrong, you bate too much of your own merits.
(*To Second Lord*) Here, my lord, a trifle of our love.

SECOND LORD

With more than common thanks I will receive it.

THIRD LORD

O, he's the very soul of bounty!   209

TIMON (*to First Lord*) And now I remember, my lord, you
gave good words the other day of a bay courser I rode
on. 'Tis yours, because you liked it.

FIRST LORD

O I beseech you pardon me, my lord, in that.

TIMON

You may take my word, my lord, I know no man
Can justly praise but what he does affect.   215

I weigh my friends' affection with mine own.
I'll tell you true, I'll call to you.
ALL LORDS   O, none so welcome.
TIMON
I take all and your several visitations
So kind to heart, 'tis not enough to give.
Methinks I could deal kingdoms to my friends,   220
And ne'er be weary. Alcibiades,
Thou art a soldier, therefore seldom rich.
⌜Giving a present⌝ It comes in charity to thee, for all
thy living
Is 'mongst the dead, and all the lands thou hast
Lie in a pitched field.
ALCIBIADES   Ay, defiled land, my lord.   225
FIRST LORD We are so virtuously bound—
TIMON And so am I to you.
SECOND LORD So infinitely endeared—
TIMON All to you. Lights, more lights!
FIRST LORD
The best of happiness, honour, and fortunes   230
Keep with you, Lord Timon.
TIMON Ready for his friends.
                    Exeunt all but Timon and Apemantus
APEMANTUS What a coil's here,
Serving of becks and jutting-out of bums!
I doubt whether their legs be worth the sums   235
That are given for 'em. Friendship's full of dregs.
Methinks false hearts should never have sound legs.
Thus honest fools lay out their wealth on curtseys.
TIMON
Now, Apemantus, if thou wert not sullen
I would be good to thee.   240
APEMANTUS No, I'll nothing; for if I should be bribed too,
there would be none left to rail upon thee, and then
thou wouldst sin the faster. Thou giv'st so long, Timon,
I fear me thou wilt give away thyself in paper shortly.
What needs these feasts, pomps, and vainglories?   245
TIMON Nay, an you begin to rail on society once, I am
sworn not to give regard to you.
Farewell, and come with better music.   Exit
APEMANTUS   So.
Thou wilt not hear me now, thou shalt not then.
I'll lock thy heaven from thee. O, that men's ears
should be   250
To counsel deaf, but not to flattery!   Exit

2.1   Enter a Senator ⌜with bonds⌝
SENATOR
And late five thousand. To Varro and to Isidore
He owes nine thousand, besides my former sum,
Which makes it five and twenty. Still in motion
Of raging waste! It cannot hold, it will not.
If I want gold, steal but a beggar's dog   5
And give it Timon, why, the dog coins gold.
If I would sell my horse and buy twenty more
Better than he, why, give my horse to Timon—
Ask nothing, give it him—it foals me straight,
And able horses. No porter at his gate,   10

But rather one that smiles and still invites
All that pass by. It cannot hold. No reason
Can sound his state in safety. Caphis ho!
Caphis, I say!
            Enter Caphis
CAPHIS   Here, sir. What is your pleasure?
SENATOR
Get on your cloak and haste you to Lord Timon.   15
Importune him for my moneys. Be not ceased
With slight denial, nor then silenced when
'Commend me to your master', and the cap
Plays in the right hand, thus; but tell him
My uses cry to me, I must serve my turn   20
Out of mine own, his days and times are past,
And my reliances on his fracted dates
Have smit my credit. I love and honour him,
But must not break my back to heal his finger.
Immediate are my needs, and my relief   25
Must not be tossed and turned to me in words,
But find supply immediate. Get you gone.
Put on a most importunate aspect,
A visage of demand, for I do fear
When every feather sticks in his own wing   30
Lord Timon will be left a naked gull,
Which flashes now a phoenix. Get you gone.
CAPHIS
I go, sir.
SENATOR ⌜giving him bonds⌝
            Take the bonds along with you,
And have the dates in count.
CAPHIS   I will, sir.
SENATOR   Go.
                    Exeunt ⌜severally⌝

2.2   Enter Flavius, with many bills in his hand
FLAVIUS
No care, no stop; so senseless of expense
That he will neither know how to maintain it
Nor cease his flow of riot, takes no account
How things go from him, nor resumes no care
Of what is to continue. Never mind   5
Was to be so unwise to be so kind.
What shall be done? He will not hear till feel.
        ⌜A sound of horns within⌝
I must be round with him, now he comes from hunting.
Fie, fie, fie, fie!
        Enter Caphis ⌜at one door⌝ and Servants of Isidore
        and Varro ⌜at another door⌝
CAPHIS
Good even, Varro. What, you come for money?   10
VARRO'S SERVANT Is't not your business too?
CAPHIS
It is; and yours too, Isidore?
ISIDORE'S SERVANT   It is so.
CAPHIS
Would we were all discharged.
VARRO'S SERVANT   I fear it.
CAPHIS   Here comes the lord.

Enter Timon and his train, amongst them
Alcibiades, ⌈as from hunting⌉

TIMON
So soon as dinner's done we'll forth again,
My Alcibiades.

Caphis meets Timon
                   With me? What is your will?   15

CAPHIS
My lord, here is a note of certain dues.

TIMON Dues? Whence are you?

CAPHIS Of Athens here, my lord.

TIMON Go to my steward.

CAPHIS
Please it your lordship, he hath put me off,   20
To the succession of new days, this month.
My master is awaked by great occasion
To call upon his own, and humbly prays you
That with your other noble parts you'll suit
In giving him his right.

TIMON   Mine honest friend,   25
I prithee but repair to me next morning.

CAPHIS
Nay, good my lord.

TIMON   Contain thyself, good friend.

VARRO'S SERVANT
One Varro's servant, my good lord.

ISIDORE'S SERVANT *(to Timon)*
From Isidore. He humbly prays your speedy payment.

CAPHIS *(to Timon)*
If you did know, my lord, my master's wants—   30

VARRO'S SERVANT *(to Timon)*
'Twas due on forfeiture, my lord, six weeks and past.

ISIDORE'S SERVANT *(to Timon)*
Your steward puts me off, my lord, and I ·
Am sent expressly to your lordship.

TIMON   Give me breath.—
I do beseech you, good my lords, keep on.
I'll wait upon you instantly.

Exeunt Alcibiades and Timon's train
(To Flavius)   Come hither. Pray you,   35
How goes the world, that I am thus encountered
With clamorous demands of broken bonds
And the detention of long-since-due debts,
Against my honour?

FLAVIUS *(to Servants)*   Please you, gentlemen,
The time is unagreeable to this business;   40
Your importunacy cease till after dinner,
That I may make his lordship understand
Wherefore you are not paid.

TIMON *(to Servants)*   Do so, my friends.
(To Flavius) See them well entertained.   *Exit*

FLAVIUS   Pray draw near.
                            Exit

Enter Apemantus and Fool

CAPHIS
Stay, stay, here comes the fool with Apemantus.   45
Let's ha' some sport with 'em.

VARRO'S SERVANT Hang him, he'll abuse us.

ISIDORE'S SERVANT A plague upon him, dog!

VARRO'S SERVANT How dost, fool?

APEMANTUS Dost dialogue with thy shadow?   50

VARRO'S SERVANT I speak not to thee.

APEMANTUS No, 'tis to thyself. *(To Fool)* Come away.

ISIDORE'S SERVANT *(to Varro's Servant)* There's the fool
hangs on your back already.

APEMANTUS No, thou stand'st single: thou'rt not on him
yet.   56

CAPHIS *(to Isidore's Servant)* Where's the fool now?

APEMANTUS He last asked the question. Poor rogues' and
usurers' men, bawds between gold and want.

ALL SERVANTS What are we, Apemantus?   60

APEMANTUS Asses.

ALL SERVANTS Why?

APEMANTUS That you ask me what you are, and do not
know yourselves. Speak to 'em, fool.

FOOL How do you, gentlemen?   65

ALL SERVANTS Gramercies, good fool. How does your
mistress?

FOOL She's e'en setting on water to scald such chickens
as you are. Would we could see you at Corinth.

APEMANTUS Good; gramercy.   70

Enter Page with two letters

FOOL Look you, here comes my mistress' page.

PAGE Why, how now, captain? What do you in this wise
company? How dost thou, Apemantus?

APEMANTUS Would I had a rod in my mouth, that I might
answer thee profitably.   75

PAGE Prithee, Apemantus, read me the superscription of
these letters. I know not which is which.

APEMANTUS Canst not read?

PAGE No.   79

APEMANTUS There will little learning die then that day
thou art hanged. This is to Lord Timon, this to
Alcibiades. Go, thou wast born a bastard, and thou'lt
die a bawd.

PAGE Thou wast whelped a dog, and thou shalt famish a
dog's death. Answer not; I am gone.   *Exit*

APEMANTUS E'en so thou outrunn'st grace. Fool, I will go
with you to Lord Timon's.

FOOL Will you leave me there?

APEMANTUS If Timon stay at home. *(To Servants)* You
three serve three usurers?   90

ALL SERVANTS Ay. Would they served us.

APEMANTUS So would I: as good a trick as ever hangman
served thief.

FOOL Are you three usurers' men?

ALL SERVANTS Ay, fool.   95

FOOL I think no usurer but has a fool to his servant. My
mistress is one, and I am her fool. When men come to
borrow of your masters they approach sadly and go
away merry, but they enter my mistress's house merrily
and go away sadly. The reason of this?   100

VARRO'S SERVANT I could render one.

APEMANTUS Do it then, that we may account thee a
whoremaster and a knave, which notwithstanding thou
shalt be no less esteemed.

VARRO'S SERVANT What is a whoremaster, fool?   105
FOOL A fool in good clothes, and something like thee. 'Tis
a spirit; sometime 't appears like a lord, sometime like
a lawyer, sometime like a philosopher with two stones
more than's artificial one. He is very often like a knight;
and generally in all shapes that man goes up and down
in from fourscore to thirteen, this spirit walks in.   111
VARRO'S SERVANT Thou art not altogether a fool.
FOOL Nor thou altogether a wise man. As much foolery
as I have, so much wit thou lack'st.
APEMANTUS That answer might have become Apemantus.
    Enter Timon and Flavius
ALL SERVANTS Aside, aside, here comes Lord Timon.   116
APEMANTUS Come with me, fool, come.
FOOL I do not always follow lover, elder brother, and
woman: sometime the philosopher.
                        Exeunt Apemantus and Fool
FLAVIUS (*to Servants*)
    Pray you, walk near. I'll speak with you anon.   120
                                Exeunt Servants
TIMON
    You make me marvel wherefore ere this time
    Had you not fully laid my state before me,
    That I might so have rated my expense
    As I had leave of means.
FLAVIUS   You would not hear me.
    At many leisures I proposed—
TIMON   Go to.   125
    Perchance some single vantages you took,
    When my indisposition put you back,
    And that unaptness made your minister
    Thus to excuse yourself.
FLAVIUS   O my good lord,
    At many times I brought in my accounts,   130
    Laid them before you; you would throw them off
    And say you summed them in mine honesty.
    When for some trifling present you have bid me
    Return so much, I have shook my head and wept,
    Yea, 'gainst th'authority of manners prayed you   135
    To hold your hand more close. I did endure
    Not seldom nor no slight checks when I have
    Prompted you in the ebb of your estate
    And your great flow of debts. My lovèd lord—
    Though you hear now too late, yet now's a time—   140
    The greatest of your having lacks a half
    To pay your present debts.
TIMON   Let all my land be sold.
FLAVIUS
    'Tis all engaged, some forfeited and gone,
    And what remains will hardly stop the mouth
    Of present dues. The future comes apace.   145
    What shall defend the interim, and at length
    How goes our reck'ning?
TIMON
    To Lacedaemon did my land extend.
FLAVIUS
    O my good lord, the world is but a word.

Were it all yours to give it in a breath,   150
    How quickly were it gone.
TIMON   You tell me true.
FLAVIUS
    If you suspect my husbandry or falsehood,
    Call me before th'exactest auditors
    And set me on the proof. So the gods bless me,
    When all our offices have been oppressed   155
    With riotous feeders, when our vaults have wept
    With drunken spilth of wine, when every room
    Hath blazed with lights and brayed with minstrelsy,
    I have retired me to a wasteful cock,
    And set mine eyes at flow.
TIMON   Prithee, no more.   160
FLAVIUS
    'Heavens,' have I said, 'the bounty of this lord!
    How many prodigal bits have slaves and peasants
    This night englutted! Who is not Timon's?
    What heart, head, sword, force, means, but is Lord
        Timon's?
    Great Timon, noble, worthy, royal Timon!   165
    Ah, when the means are gone that buy this praise,
    The breath is gone whereof this praise is made.
    Feast won, fast lost; one cloud of winter show'rs,
    These flies are couched.'
TIMON   Come, sermon me no further.
    No villainous bounty yet hath passed my heart.   170
    Unwisely, not ignobly, have I given.
    Why dost thou weep? Canst thou the conscience lack
    To think I shall lack friends? Secure thy heart.
    If I would broach the vessels of my love
    And try the argument of hearts by borrowing,   175
    Men and men's fortunes could I frankly use
    As I can bid thee speak.
FLAVIUS   Assurance bless your thoughts!
TIMON
    And in some sort these wants of mine are crowned
    That I account them blessings, for by these
    Shall I try friends. You shall perceive how you   180
    Mistake my fortunes. I am wealthy in my friends.—
    Within there, Flaminius, Servilius!
        Enter Flaminius, Servilius, and a Third Servant
ALL SERVANTS
    My lord, my lord.
TIMON   I will dispatch you severally,
    (*To Servilius*) You to Lord Lucius,
    (*To Flaminius*)   to Lord Lucullus you—
    I hunted with his honour today—   185
    (*To Third Servant*) You to Sempronius. Commend me
        to their loves,
    And I am proud, say, that my occasions have
    Found time to use 'em toward a supply of money.
    Let the request be fifty talents.
FLAMINIUS As you have said, my lord.   190
                                Exeunt Servants
FLAVIUS
    Lord Lucius and Lucullus? Hmh!

TIMON
Go you, sir, to the senators,
Of whom, even to the state's best health, I have
Deserved this hearing. Bid 'em send o'th' instant
A thousand talents to me.
FLAVIUS   I have been bold, 195
For that I knew it the most general way,
To them, to use your signet and your name;
But they do shake their heads, and I am here
No richer in return.
TIMON   Is't true? Can't be?
FLAVIUS
They answer in a joint and corporate voice 200
That now they are at fall, want treasure, cannot
Do what they would, are sorry, you are honourable,
But yet they could have wished—they know not—
Something hath been amiss—a noble nature
May catch a wrench—would all were well—'tis pity;
And so, intending other serious matters, 206
After distasteful looks and these hard fractions,
With certain half-caps and cold moving nods
They froze me into silence.
TIMON   You gods reward them!
Prithee, man, look cheerly. These old fellows 210
Have their ingratitude in them hereditary.
Their blood is caked, 'tis cold, it seldom flows.
'Tis lack of kindly warmth they are not kind;
And nature as it grows again toward earth
Is fashioned for the journey dull and heavy. 215
Go to Ventidius. Prithee, be not sad.
Thou art true and honest—ingenuously I speak—
No blame belongs to thee. Ventidius lately
Buried his father, by whose death he's stepped
Into a great estate. When he was poor, 220
Imprisoned, and in scarcity of friends,
I cleared him with five talents. Greet him from me.
Bid him suppose some good necessity
Touches his friend, which craves to be remembered
With those five talents. That had, give't these fellows
To whom 'tis instant due. Ne'er speak or think 226
That Timon's fortunes 'mong his friends can sink.
FLAVIUS
I would I could not think it. That thought is bounty's
foe:
Being free itself, it thinks all others so.
        Exeunt ⌈*severally*⌉

3.1 *Enter Flaminius, with a box under his cloak,*
  waiting to speak with Lucullus. From his master,
  enters a Servant to him
LUCULLUS' SERVANT I have told my lord of you. He is
coming down to you.
FLAMINIUS I thank you, sir.
  Enter Lucullus
LUCULLUS' SERVANT Here's my lord. 4
LUCULLUS (*aside*) One of Lord Timon's men? A gift, I
warrant. Why, this hits right; I dreamt of a silver basin
and ewer tonight.—Flaminius, honest Flaminius, you

are very respectively welcome, sir. (*To his Servant*) Fill
me some wine.   *Exit Servant*
And how does that honourable, complete, free-hearted
gentleman of Athens, thy very bountiful good lord and
master? 12
FLAMINIUS His health is well, sir.
LUCULLUS I am right glad that his health is well, sir. And
what hast thou there under thy cloak, pretty Flaminius?
FLAMINIUS Faith, nothing but an empty box, sir, which
in my lord's behalf I come to entreat your honour to
supply, who, having great and instant occasion to use
fifty talents, hath sent to your lordship to furnish him,
nothing doubting your present assistance therein. 20
LUCULLUS La, la, la, la, 'nothing doubting' says he? Alas,
good lord! A noble gentleman 'tis, if he would not keep
so good a house. Many a time and often I ha' dined
with him and told him on't, and come again to supper
to him of purpose to have him spend less; and yet he
would embrace no counsel, take no warning by my
coming. Every man has his fault, and honesty is his. I
ha' told him on't, but I could ne'er get him from't.
  Enter Servant, with wine
SERVANT Please your lordship, here is the wine.
LUCULLUS Flaminius, I have noted thee always wise.
(*Drinking*) Here's to thee! 31
FLAMINIUS Your lordship speaks your pleasure.
LUCULLUS I have observed thee always for a towardly
prompt spirit, give thee thy due, and one that knows
what belongs to reason; and canst use the time well if
the time use thee well. (*Drinking*) Good parts in thee!
(*To his Servant*) Get you gone, sirrah. *Exit Servant*
Draw nearer, honest Flaminius. Thy lord's a bountiful
gentleman; but thou art wise, and thou know'st well
enough, although thou com'st to me, that this is no
time to lend money, especially upon bare friendship
without security. (*Giving coins*) Here's three solidares
for thee. Good boy, wink at me, and say thou saw'st
me not. Fare thee well.
FLAMINIUS
Is't possible the world should so much differ, 45
And we alive that lived?
    He throws the coins at Lucullus
      Fly, damnèd baseness,
To him that worships thee.
LUCULLUS Ha! Now I see thou art a fool, and fit for thy
master. *Exit*
FLAMINIUS
May these add to the number that may scald thee. 50
Let molten coin be thy damnation,
Thou disease of a friend, and not himself.
Has friendship such a faint and milky heart
It turns in less than two nights? O you gods,
I feel my master's passion! This slave 55
Unto this hour has my lord's meat in him.
Why should it thrive and turn to nutriment,
When he is turned to poison?
O, may diseases only work upon't; 59
And when he's sick to death, let not that part of nature

Which my lord paid for be of any power
To expel sickness, but prolong his hour.   *Exit*

3.2   *Enter Lucius, with three Strangers*
LUCIUS Who, the Lord Timon? He is my very good friend,
and an honourable gentleman.
FIRST STRANGER We know him for no less, though we are
but strangers to him. But I can tell you one thing, my
lord, and which I hear from common rumours: now
Lord Timon's happy hours are done and past, and his
estate shrinks from him.
LUCIUS Fie, no, do not believe it. He cannot want for
money.   9
SECOND STRANGER But believe you this, my lord, that not
long ago one of his men was with the Lord Lucullus
to borrow so many talents—nay, urged extremely for't,
and showed what necessity belonged to't, and yet was
denied.
LUCIUS How?   15
SECOND STRANGER I tell you, denied, my lord.
LUCIUS What a strange case was that! Now before the
gods, I am ashamed on't. Denied that honourable man?
There was very little honour showed in't. For my own
part, I must needs confess I have received some small
kindnesses from him, as money, plate, jewels, and
suchlike trifles—nothing comparing to his; yet had he
not mistook him and sent to me, I should ne'er have
denied his occasion so many talents.   24
      Enter Servilius
SERVILIUS (*aside*) See, by good hap yonder's my lord. I
have sweat to see his honour. (*To Lucius*) My honoured
lord!
⌜LUCIUS⌝ Servilius! You are kindly met, sir. Fare thee well.
Commend me to thy honourable virtuous lord, my very
exquisite friend.   30
SERVILIUS May it please your honour, my lord hath sent—
LUCIUS Ha! What has he sent? I am so much endeared
to that lord, he's ever sending. How shall I thank him,
think'st thou? And what has he sent now?   34
SERVILIUS He's only sent his present occasion now, my
lord, requesting your lordship to supply his instant use
with so many talents.
⌜LUCIUS⌝
I know his lordship is but merry with me.
He cannot want fifty-five hundred talents.
SERVILIUS
But in the mean time he wants less, my lord.   40
If his occasion were not virtuous
I should not urge it half so faithfully.
LUCIUS
Dost thou speak seriously, Servilius?
SERVILIUS Upon my soul, 'tis true, sir.   44
LUCIUS What a wicked beast was I to disfurnish myself
against such a good time when I might ha' shown
myself honourable! How unluckily it happened that I
should purchase the day before a little part, and undo
a great deal of honour! Servilius, now before the gods
I am not able to do, the more beast I, I say. I was
sending to use Lord Timon myself—these gentlemen

can witness—but I would not for the wealth of Athens
I had done't now. Commend me bountifully to his good
lordship; and I hope his honour will conceive the fairest
of me because I have no power to be kind. And tell
him this from me: I count it one of my greatest
afflictions, say, that I cannot pleasure such an
honourable gentleman. Good Servilius, will you befriend
me so far as to use mine own words to him?
SERVILIUS Yes, sir, I shall.   60
⌜LUCIUS⌝
I'll look you out a good turn, Servilius.   *Exit Servilius*
True as you said: Timon is shrunk indeed;
And he that's once denied will hardly speed.   *Exit*
FIRST STRANGER
Do you observe this, Hostilius?
SECOND STRANGER   Ay, too well.   64
FIRST STRANGER
Why, this is the world's soul, and just of the same piece
Is every flatterer's spirit. Who can call him his friend
That dips in the same dish? For, in my knowing,
Timon has been this lord's father
And kept his credit with his purse,
Supported his estate; nay, Timon's money   70
Has paid his men their wages. He ne'er drinks,
But Timon's silver treads upon his lip;
And yet—O see the monstrousness of man
When he looks out in an ungrateful shape!—
He does deny him, in respect of his,   75
What charitable men afford to beggars.
THIRD STRANGER
Religion groans at it.
FIRST STRANGER   For mine own part,
I never tasted Timon in my life,
Nor came any of his bounties over me
To mark me for his friend; yet I protest,   80
For his right noble mind, illustrious virtue,
And honourable carriage,
Had his necessity made use of me
I would have put my wealth into donation
And the best half should have returned to him,   85
So much I love his heart. But I perceive
Men must learn now with pity to dispense,
For policy sits above conscience.   *Exeunt*

3.3   *Enter Timon's Third Servant, with Sempronius,*
           another of Timon's friends
SEMPRONIUS
Must he needs trouble me in't? Hmh! 'Bove all others?
He might have tried Lord Lucius or Lucullus;
And now Ventidius is wealthy too,
Whom he redeemed from prison. All these
Owes their estates unto him.
SERVANT   My lord,   5
They have all been touched and found base metal,
For they have all denied him.
SEMPRONIUS   How, have they denied him?
Has Ventidius and Lucullus denied him,
And does he send to me? Three? Hmh!
It shows but little love or judgement in him.   10

Must I be his last refuge? His friends, like physicians,
Thrive, give him over; must I take th' cure upon me?
He's much disgraced me in't. I'm angry at him,
That might have known my place. I see no sense for't
But his occasions might have wooed me first,   15
For, in my conscience, I was the first man
That e'er receivèd gift from him.
And does he think so backwardly of me now
That I'll requite it last? No.
So it may prove an argument of laughter   20
To th' rest, and I 'mongst lords be thought a fool.
I'd rather than the worth of thrice the sum
He'd sent to me first, but for my mind's sake.
I'd such a courage to do him good. But now return,
And with their faint reply this answer join: 25
Who bates mine honour shall not know my coin.   *Exit*
SERVANT Excellent. Your lordship's a goodly villain. The
devil knew not what he did when he made man
politic—he crossed himself by't, and I cannot think but
in the end the villainies of man will set him clear. How
fairly this lord strives to appear foul! Takes virtuous
copies to be wicked, like those that under hot ardent
zeal would set whole realms on fire; of such a nature
is his politic love.
This was my lord's best hope. Now all are fled   35
Save only the gods. Now his friends are dead.
Doors that were ne'er acquainted with their wards
Many a bounteous year must be employed
Now to guard sure their master;
And this is all a liberal course allows: 40
Who cannot keep his wealth must keep his house.
                                                 Exit

3.4   *Enter Varro's two Servants, meeting others, all*
           Servants of Timon's creditors, to wait for his coming
           out. Then enter ⌈Servants of⌉ Lucius, Titus, and
           Hortensius
VARRO'S ⌈FIRST⌉ SERVANT
    Well met; good morrow, Titus and Hortensius.
TITUS' SERVANT The like to you, kind Varro.
HORTENSIUS' SERVANT
    Lucius, what, do we meet together?
LUCIUS' SERVANT
    Ay, and I think one business does command us all,
    For mine is money.
TITUS' SERVANT   So is theirs and ours.   5
           Enter ⌈a Servant of⌉ Philotus
LUCIUS' SERVANT
    And Sir Philotus too!
PHILOTUS' SERVANT   Good day at once.
LUCIUS' SERVANT
    Welcome, good brother. What do you think the hour?
PHILOTUS' SERVANT Labouring for nine.
LUCIUS' SERVANT So much?
PHILOTUS' SERVANT Is not my lord seen yet?   10
LUCIUS' SERVANT Not yet.
PHILOTUS' SERVANT
    I wonder on't; he was wont to shine at seven.

LUCIUS' SERVANT
    Ay, but the days are waxed shorter with him.
    You must consider that a prodigal course
    Is like the sun's,   15
    But not, like his, recoverable. I fear
    'Tis deepest winter in Lord Timon's purse; that is,
    One may reach deep enough, and yet find little.
PHILOTUS' SERVANT I am of your fear for that.
TITUS' SERVANT
    I'll show you how t'observe a strange event.   20
    Your lord sends now for money?
HORTENSIUS' SERVANT   Most true, he does.
TITUS' SERVANT
    And he wears jewels now of Timon's gift,
    For which I wait for money.
HORTENSIUS' SERVANT It is against my heart.
LUCIUS' SERVANT Mark how strange it shows.   25
    Timon in this should pay more than he owes,
    And e'en as if your lord should wear rich jewels
    And send for money for 'em.
HORTENSIUS' SERVANT
    I'm weary of this charge, the gods can witness.
    I know my lord hath spent of Timon's wealth,   30
    And now ingratitude makes it worse than stealth.
VARRO'S FIRST SERVANT
    Yes; mine's three thousand crowns. What's yours?
LUCIUS' SERVANT   Five thousand, mine.
VARRO'S FIRST SERVANT
    'Tis much deep, and it should seem by th' sum
    Your master's confidence was above mine,
    Else surely his had equalled.
           Enter Flaminius
TITUS' SERVANT   One of Lord Timon's men.
LUCIUS' SERVANT
    Flaminius! Sir, a word. Pray, is my lord   36
    Ready to come forth?
FLAMINIUS No, indeed he is not.
TITUS' SERVANT We attend his lordship.
    Pray signify so much.
FLAMINIUS   I need not tell   40
    Him that; he knows you are too diligent.
           Enter Flavius, muffled in a cloak
LUCIUS' SERVANT
    Ha, is not that his steward muffled so?
    He goes away in a cloud. Call him, call him.
TITUS' SERVANT (*to Flavius*) Do you hear, sir?
VARRO'S SECOND SERVANT (*to Flavius*) By your leave, sir. 45
FLAVIUS What do ye ask of me, my friend?
TITUS' SERVANT
    We wait for certain money here, sir.
FLAVIUS   Ay,
    If money were as certain as your waiting,
    'Twere sure enough.
    Why then preferred you not your sums and bills   50
    When your false masters ate of my lord's meat?
    Then they could smile and fawn upon his debts,
    And take down th'int'rest into their glutt'nous maws.
    You do yourselves but wrong to stir me up.

Let me pass quietly. 55
Believe't, my lord and I have made an end.
I have no more to reckon, he to spend.
LUCIUS' SERVANT
Ay, but this answer will not serve.
FLAVIUS
If 'twill not serve 'tis not so base as you, 59
For you serve knaves.   Exit
VARRO'S FIRST SERVANT How? What does his cashiered
worship mutter?
VARRO'S SECOND SERVANT No matter what; he's poor, and
that's revenge enough. Who can speak broader than
he that has no house to put his head in? Such may
rail against great buildings. 66
        Enter Servilius
TITUS' SERVANT O, here's Servilius. Now we shall know
some answer.
SERVILIUS If I might beseech you, gentlemen, to repair
some other hour, I should derive much from't; for,
take't of my soul, my lord leans wondrously to
discontent. His comfortable temper has forsook him.
He's much out of health, and keeps his chamber.
LUCIUS' SERVANT
Many do keep their chambers are not sick,
And if it be so far beyond his health 75
Methinks he should the sooner pay his debts
And make a clear way to the gods.
SERVILIUS   Good gods!
TITUS' SERVANT
We cannot take this for an answer, sir.
FLAMINIUS (within)
Servilius, help! My lord, my lord!
        Enter Timon in a rage
TIMON
What, are my doors opposed against my passage? 80
Have I been ever free, and must my house
Be my retentive enemy, my jail?
The place which I have feasted, does it now,
Like all mankind, show me an iron heart?
LUCIUS' SERVANT
Put in now, Titus.
TITUS' SERVANT   My lord, here is my bill. 85
LUCIUS' SERVANT
Here's mine.
⌈HORTENSIUS' SERVANT⌉ And mine, my lord.
VARRO'S ⌈FIRST and⌉ SECOND SERVANTS And ours, my lord.
PHILOTUS' SERVANT All our bills.
TIMON
Knock me down with 'em, cleave me to the girdle.
LUCIUS' SERVANT Alas, my lord.
TIMON Cut my heart in sums. 90
TITUS' SERVANT Mine fifty talents.
TIMON
Tell out my blood.
LUCIUS' SERVANT   Five thousand crowns, my lord.
TIMON
Five thousand drops pays that. What yours? And
yours?

VARRO'S FIRST SERVANT My lord—
VARRO'S SECOND SERVANT My lord— 95
TIMON
Tear me, take me, and the gods fall upon you.   Exit
HORTENSIUS' SERVANT Faith, I perceive our masters may
throw their caps at their money. These debts may well
be called desperate ones, for a madman owes 'em.
                                        Exeunt

3.5   Enter Timon and Flavius
TIMON
They have e'en put my breath from me, the slaves.
Creditors? Devils!
FLAVIUS My dear lord—
TIMON What if it should be so?
FLAVIUS My lord— 5
TIMON
I'll have it so. My steward!
FLAVIUS   Here, my lord.
TIMON
So fitly? Go bid all my friends again:
Lucius, Lucullus, and Sempronius—all luxors, all.
I'll once more feast the rascals.
FLAVIUS   O my lord,
You only speak from your distracted soul. 10
There is not so much left to furnish out
A moderate table.
TIMON   Be it not in thy care.
Go, I charge thee, invite them all. Let in the tide
Of knaves once more. My cook and I'll provide.
                            Exeunt ⌈severally⌉

3.6   Enter three Senators at one door
FIRST SENATOR
My lords, you have my voice to't. The fault's bloody.
'Tis necessary he should die.
Nothing emboldens sin so much as mercy.
SECOND SENATOR Most true; the law shall bruise 'im.
        ⌈Enter Alcibiades at another door, with attendants⌉
ALCIBIADES
Honour, health, and compassion to the senate! 5
FIRST SENATOR Now, captain.
ALCIBIADES
I am an humble suitor to your virtues;
For pity is the virtue of the law,
And none but tyrants use it cruelly.
It pleases time and fortune to lie heavy 10
Upon a friend of mine, who in hot blood
Hath stepped into the law, which is past depth
To those that without heed do plunge into't.
He is a man, setting his feat aside,
Of comely virtues; 15
Nor did he soil the fact with cowardice—
An honour in him which buys out his fault—
But with a noble fury and fair spirit,
Seeing his reputation touched to death,
He did oppose his foe; 20
And with such sober and unnoted passion

He did behave his anger, ere 'twas spent,
As if he had but proved an argument.
FIRST SENATOR
You undergo too strict a paradox,
Striving to make an ugly deed look fair. 25
Your words have took such pains as if they laboured
To bring manslaughter into form, and set quarrelling
Upon the head of valour—which indeed
Is valour misbegot, and came into the world
When sects and factions were newly born. 30
He's truly valiant that can wisely suffer
The worst that man can breathe, and make his
    wrongs his outsides
To wear them like his raiment carelessly,
And ne'er prefer his injuries to his heart
To bring it into danger. 35
If wrongs be evils and enforce us kill,
What folly 'tis to hazard life for ill!
ALCIBIADES
My lord—
FIRST SENATOR You cannot make gross sins look clear.
To revenge is no valour, but to bear.
ALCIBIADES
My lords, then, under favour, pardon me 40
If I speak like a captain.
Why do fond men expose themselves to battle,
And not endure all threats, sleep upon't,
And let the foes quietly cut their throats
Without repugnancy? If there be 45
Such valour in the bearing, what make we
Abroad? Why then, women are more valiant
That stay at home if bearing carry it,
And the ass more captain than the lion, the felon
Loaden with irons wiser than the judge, 50
If wisdom be in suffering. O my lords,
As you are great, be pitifully good.
Who cannot condemn rashness in cold blood?
To kill, I grant, is sin's extremest gust,
But in defence, by mercy, 'tis most just. 55
To be in anger is impiety,
But who is man that is not angry?
Weigh but the crime with this.
SECOND SENATOR You breathe in vain.
ALCIBIADES In vain?
His service done at Lacedaemon and Byzantium
Were a sufficient briber for his life. 60
FIRST SENATOR
What's that?
ALCIBIADES Why, I say, my lords, he's done fair service,
And slain in fight many of your enemies.
How full of valour did he bear himself
In the last conflict, and made plenteous wounds!
SECOND SENATOR
He has made too much plenty with 'em. 65
He's a sworn rioter; he has a sin
That often drowns him and takes his valour prisoner.
If there were no foes, that were enough
To overcome him. In that beastly fury

He has been known to commit outrages 70
And cherish factions. 'Tis inferred to us
His days are foul and his drink dangerous.
FIRST SENATOR
He dies.
ALCIBIADES Hard fate! He might have died in war.
My lords, if not for any parts in him—
Though his right arm might purchase his own time 75
And be in debt to none—yet more to move you,
Take my deserts to his and join 'em both.
And for I know
Your reverend ages love security,
I'll pawn my victories, all my honour to you 80
Upon his good returns.
If by this crime he owes the law his life,
Why, let the war receive't in valiant gore,
For law is strict, and war is nothing more.
FIRST SENATOR
We are for law; he dies. Urge it no more, 85
On height of our displeasure. Friend or brother,
He forfeits his own blood that spills another.
ALCIBIADES
Must it be so? It must not be.
My lords, I do beseech you know me.
SECOND SENATOR How?
ALCIBIADES
Call me to your remembrances.
THIRD SENATOR What? 90
ALCIBIADES
I cannot think but your age has forgot me.
It could not else be I should prove so base
To sue and be denied such common grace.
My wounds ache at you.
FIRST SENATOR Do you dare our anger?
'Tis in few words, but spacious in effect: 95
We banish thee for ever.
ALCIBIADES Banish me?
Banish your dotage, banish usury
That makes the senate ugly.
FIRST SENATOR If after two days' shine
Athens contain thee, attend our weightier judgement;
And, not to swell your spirit, he shall be 100
Executed presently. *Exeunt Senators [and attendants]*
ALCIBIADES
Now the gods keep you old enough that you may live
Only in bone, that none may look on you!
I'm worse than mad. I have kept back their foes
While they have told their money and let out 105
Their coin upon large interest—I myself,
Rich only in large hurts. All those for this?
Is this the balsam that the usuring senate
Pours into captains' wounds? Banishment!
It comes not ill; I hate not to be banished. 110
It is a cause worthy my spleen and fury,
That I may strike at Athens. I'll cheer up
My discontented troops, and lay for hearts.
'Tis honour with most lands to be at odds. 114
Soldiers should brook as little wrongs as gods. *Exit*

3.7 *Enter divers of Timon's friends, ⌈amongst them*
Lucullus, Lucius, Sempronius, and other Lords and
Senators,⌉ at several doors

FIRST LORD The good time of day to you, sir.

SECOND LORD I also wish it to you. I think this honourable
lord did but try us this other day.

FIRST LORD Upon that were my thoughts tiring when we
encountered. I hope it is not so low with him as he
made it seem in the trial of his several friends.   6

SECOND LORD It should not be, by the persuasion of his
new feasting.

FIRST LORD I should think so. He hath sent me an earnest
inviting, which many my near occasions did urge me
to put off, but he hath conjured me beyond them, and
I must needs appear.

SECOND LORD In like manner was I in debt to my
importunate business, but he would not hear my
excuse. I am sorry when he sent to borrow of me that
my provision was out.   16

FIRST LORD I am sick of that grief too, as I understand
how all things go.

SECOND LORD Every man hears so. What would he have
borrowed of you?   20

FIRST LORD A thousand pieces.

SECOND LORD A thousand pieces?

FIRST LORD What of you?

SECOND LORD He sent to me, sir—
      ⌈*Loud music.*⌉ *Enter Timon and attendants*
Here he comes.   25

TIMON With all my heart, gentlemen both; and how fare
you?

FIRST LORD Ever at the best, hearing well of your lordship.

SECOND LORD The swallow follows not summer more
willing than we your lordship.   30

TIMON (*aside*) Nor more willingly leaves winter, such
summer birds are men.—Gentlemen, our dinner will
not recompense this long stay. Feast your ears with
the music a while, if they will fare so harshly o'th'
trumpets' sound; we shall to't presently.   35

FIRST LORD I hope it remains not unkindly with your
lordship that I returned you an empty messenger.

TIMON O sir, let it not trouble you.

SECOND LORD My noble lord—

TIMON Ah, my good friend, what cheer?   40
      ⌈*A table and stools are⌉ brought in*

SECOND LORD My most honourable lord, I am e'en sick of
shame that when your lordship this other day sent to
me I was so unfortunate a beggar.

TIMON Think not on't, sir.

SECOND LORD If you had sent but two hours before—   45

TIMON Let it not cumber your better remembrance.—
Come, bring in all together.
      ⌈*Enter Servants with covered dishes⌉*

SECOND LORD All covered dishes.

FIRST LORD Royal cheer, I warrant you.

THIRD LORD Doubt not that, if money and the season can
yield it.   51

FIRST LORD How do you? What's the news?

THIRD LORD Alcibiades is banished. Hear you of it?

FIRST *and* SECOND LORDS Alcibiades banished?

THIRD LORD 'Tis so, be sure of it.   55

FIRST LORD How, how?

SECOND LORD I pray you, upon what?

TIMON My worthy friends, will you draw near?

THIRD LORD I'll tell you more anon. Here's a noble feast
toward.   60

SECOND LORD This is the old man still.

THIRD LORD Will't hold, will't hold?

SECOND LORD It does; but time will—and so—

THIRD LORD I do conceive.   64

TIMON Each man to his stool with that spur as he would
to the lip of his mistress. Your diet shall be in all places
alike. Make not a city feast of it, to let the meat cool
ere we can agree upon the first place. Sit, sit. The gods
require our thanks.   69
      They sit
You great benefactors, sprinkle our society with
thankfulness. For your own gifts make yourselves
praised; but reserve still to give, lest your deities be
despised. Lend to each man enough that one need not
lend to another; for were your godheads to borrow of
men, men would forsake the gods. Make the meat be
beloved more than the man that gives it. Let no
assembly of twenty be without a score of villains. If
there sit twelve women at the table, let a dozen of them
be as they are. The rest of your foes, O gods—the
senators of Athens, together with the common tag of
people—what is amiss in them, you gods, make suitable
for destruction. For these my present friends, as they
are to me nothing, so in nothing bless them; and to
nothing are they welcome. —Uncover, dogs, and lap.
      The dishes are uncovered, and seen to be full of
      steaming water ⌈and stones⌉

SOME LORDS What does his lordship mean?   85

OTHER LORDS I know not.

TIMON
May you a better feast never behold,
You knot of mouth-friends. Smoke and lukewarm water
Is your perfection. This is Timon's last,
Who, stuck and spangled with your flattery,   90
Washes it off, and sprinkles in your faces
Your reeking villainy.
      ⌈*He throws water in their faces⌉*
            Live loathed and long,
Most smiling, smooth, detested parasites,
Courteous destroyers, affable wolves, meek bears,
You fools of fortune, trencher-friends, time's flies,   95
Cap-and-knee slaves, vapours, and minute-jacks!
Of man and beast the infinite malady
Crust you quite o'er.
      ⌈*A Lord is going⌉*
            What, dost thou go?
Soft, take thy physic first. Thou too, and thou.
      ⌈*He beats them⌉*
Stay, I will lend thee money, borrow none.   100
      Exeunt Lords, leaving caps and gowns

What, all in motion? Henceforth be no feast
Whereat a villain's not a welcome guest.
Burn house! Sink Athens! Henceforth hated be
Of Timon man and all humanity!   *Exit*
 Enter the Senators and other Lords
FIRST LORD How now, my lords?   105
SECOND LORD
 Know you the quality of Lord Timon's fury?
THIRD LORD
 Push! Did you see my cap?
FOURTH LORD   I have lost my gown.
FIRST LORD He's but a mad lord, and naught but humours
 sways him. He gave me a jewel th'other day, and now
 he has beat it out of my hat.   110
 Did you see my jewel?
⌐THIRD⌐ LORD   Did you see my cap?
⌐SECOND⌐ LORD
 Here 'tis.
FOURTH LORD Here lies my gown.
FIRST LORD   Let's make no stay.
SECOND LORD
 Lord Timon's mad.
THIRD LORD   I feel't upon my bones.
FOURTH LORD
 One day he gives us diamonds, next day stones.
           Exeunt

4.1 *Enter Timon*
TIMON
 Let me look back upon thee. O thou wall
 That girdles in those wolves, dive in the earth,
 And fence not Athens! Matrons, turn incontinent!
 Obedience fail in children! Slaves and fools,
 Pluck the grave wrinkled senate from the bench   5
 And minister in their steads! To general filths
 Convert o'th' instant, green virginity!
 Do't in your parents' eyes. Bankrupts, hold fast!
 Rather than render back, out with your knives,
 And cut your trusters' throats. Bound servants, steal!
 Large-handed robbers your grave masters are,   11
 And pill by law. Maid, to thy master's bed!
 Thy mistress is o'th' brothel. Son of sixteen,
 Pluck the lined crutch from thy old limping sire;
 With it beat out his brains! Piety and fear,   15
 Religion to the gods, peace, justice, truth,
 Domestic awe, night rest, and neighbourhood,
 Instruction, manners, mysteries, and trades,
 Degrees, observances, customs, and laws,
 Decline to your confounding contraries,   20
 And let confusion live! Plagues incident to men,
 Your potent and infectious fevers heap
 On Athens, ripe for stroke! Thou cold sciatica,
 Cripple our senators, that their limbs may halt
 As lamely as their manners! Lust and liberty,   25
 Creep in the minds and marrows of our youth,
 That 'gainst the stream of virtue they may strive
 And drown themselves in riot! Itches, blains,

Sow all th'Athenian bosoms, and their crop
Be general leprosy! Breath infect breath,   30
That their society, as their friendship, may
Be merely poison!
 ⌐*He tears off his clothes*⌐
     Nothing I'll bear from thee
But nakedness, thou detestable town;
Take thou that too, with multiplying bans.
Timon will to the woods, where he shall find   35
Th'unkindest beast more kinder than mankind.
The gods confound—hear me you good gods all—
Th'Athenians, both within and out that wall;
And grant, as Timon grows, his hate may grow
To the whole race of mankind, high and low.   40
Amen.   *Exit*

4.2 *Enter Flavius, with two or three Servants*
FIRST SERVANT
 Hear you, master steward, where's our master?
 Are we undone, cast off, nothing remaining?
FLAVIUS
 Alack, my fellows, what should I say to you?
 Let me be recorded: by the righteous gods,
 I am as poor as you.
FIRST SERVANT   Such a house broke,   5
So noble a master fall'n? All gone, and not
One friend to take his fortune by the arm
And go along with him?
SECOND SERVANT   As we do turn our backs
From our companion thrown into his grave,
So his familiars to his buried fortunes   10
Slink all away, leave their false vows with him
Like empty purses picked; and his poor self,
A dedicated beggar to the air,
With his disease of all-shunned poverty,
Walks like contempt alone.
 Enter other Servants
     More of our fellows.   15
FLAVIUS
 All broken implements of a ruined house.
THIRD SERVANT
 Yet do our hearts wear Timon's livery.
 That see I by our faces. We are fellows still,
 Serving alike in sorrow. Leaked is our barque,
 And we, poor mates, stand on the dying deck   20
 Hearing the surges' threat. We must all part
 Into this sea of air.
FLAVIUS   Good fellows all,
 The latest of my wealth I'll share amongst you.
 Wherever we shall meet, for Timon's sake
 Let's yet be fellows. Let's shake our heads and say,   25
 As 'twere a knell unto our master's fortunes,
 'We have seen better days.'
 He gives them money
     Let each take some.
Nay, put out all your hands. Not one word more.
Thus part we rich in sorrow, parting poor.

They embrace, and the Servants part several ways
O, the fierce wretchedness that glory brings us!   30
Who would not wish to be from wealth exempt,
Since riches point to misery and contempt?
Who would be so mocked with glory, or to live
But in a dream of friendship,
To have his pomp and all what state compounds   35
But only painted like his varnished friends?
Poor honest lord, brought low by his own heart,
Undone by goodness! Strange, unusual blood
When man's worst sin is he does too much good!
Who then dares to be half so kind again?   40
For bounty, that makes gods, does still mar men.
My dearest lord, blessed to be most accursed,
Rich only to be wretched, thy great fortunes
Are made thy chief afflictions. Alas, kind lord!
He's flung in rage from this ingrateful seat   45
Of monstrous friends;
Nor has he with him to supply his life,
Or that which can command it.
I'll follow and enquire him out.
I'll ever serve his mind with my best will.   50
Whilst I have gold I'll be his steward still.   *Exit*

4.3   *Enter Timon [from his cave] in the woods, [half
           naked, and with a spade]*
TIMON
O blessèd breeding sun, draw from the earth
Rotten humidity; below thy sister's orb
Infect the air. Twinned brothers of one womb,
Whose procreation, residence, and birth
Scarce is dividant, touch them with several fortunes,   5
The greater scorns the lesser. Not nature,
To whom all sores lay siege, can bear great fortune
But by contempt of nature.
It is the pasture lards the brother's sides,
The want that makes him lean.   10
Raise me this beggar and demit that lord,
The senator shall bear contempt hereditary,
The beggar native honour. Who dares, who dares
In purity of manhood stand upright
And say 'This man's a flatterer'? If one be,   15
So are they all, for every grece of fortune
Is smoothed by that below. The learnèd pate
Ducks to the golden fool. All's obliquy;
There's nothing level in our cursèd natures
But direct villainy. Therefore be abhorred   20
All feasts, societies, and throngs of men.
His semblable, yea, himself, Timon disdains.
Destruction fang mankind. Earth, yield me roots.
    He digs
Who seeks for better of thee, sauce his palate
With thy most operant poison.
    He finds gold
                        What is here?   25
Gold? Yellow, glittering, precious gold?
No, gods, I am no idle votarist:

Roots, you clear heavens. Thus much of this will
    make
Black white, foul fair, wrong right,
Base noble, old young, coward valiant.   30
Ha, you gods! Why this, what, this, you gods? Why,
    this
Will lug your priests and servants from your sides,
Pluck stout men's pillows from below their heads.
This yellow slave
Will knit and break religions, bless th'accursed,   35
Make the hoar leprosy adored, place thieves,
And give them title, knee, and approbation
With senators on the bench. This is it
That makes the wappered widow wed again.
She whom the spittle house and ulcerous sores   40
Would cast the gorge at, this embalms and spices
To th' April day again. Come, damnèd earth,
Thou common whore of mankind, that puts odds
Among the rout of nations; I will make thee
Do thy right nature.
    March afar off
                    Ha, a drum! Thou'rt quick;   45
But yet I'll bury thee.
    He buries gold
                    Thou'lt go, strong thief,
When gouty keepers of thee cannot stand.
    He keeps some gold
Nay, stay thou out for earnest.
    *Enter Alcibiades, with soldiers playing drum and
    fife, in warlike manner; and Phrynia and Timandra*
ALCIBIADES   What art thou there? Speak.
TIMON
A beast, as thou art. The canker gnaw thy heart
For showing me again the eyes of man.   50
ALCIBIADES
What is thy name? Is man so hateful to thee
That art thyself a man?
TIMON
I am Misanthropos, and hate mankind.
For thy part, I do wish thou wert a dog,
That I might love thee something.
ALCIBIADES   I know thee well,   55
But in thy fortunes am unlearned and strange.
TIMON
I know thee too, and more than that I know thee
I not desire to know. Follow thy drum.
With man's blood paint the ground gules, gules.
Religious canons, civil laws, are cruel;   60
Then what should war be? This fell whore of thine
Hath in her more destruction than thy sword,
For all her cherubin look.
PHRYNIA   Thy lips rot off!
TIMON
I will not kiss thee; then the rot returns
To thine own lips again.   65
ALCIBIADES
How came the noble Timon to this change?

TIMON
  As the moon does, by wanting light to give.
  But then renew I could not like the moon;
  There were no suns to borrow of.
ALCIBIADES
  Noble Timon, what friendship may I do thee?   70
TIMON
  None but to maintain my opinion.
ALCIBIADES What is it, Timon?
TIMON Promise me friendship, but perform none. If thou
  wilt promise, the gods plague thee, for thou art a man. If
  thou dost not perform, confound thee, for thou art a
  man.   76
ALCIBIADES
  I have heard in some sort of thy miseries.
TIMON
  Thou saw'st them when I had prosperity.
ALCIBIADES
  I see them now; then was a blessèd time.
TIMON
  As thine is now, held with a brace of harlots.   80
TIMANDRA
  Is this th'Athenian minion, whom the world
  Voiced so regardfully?
TIMON   Art thou Timandra?
TIMANDRA Yes.
TIMON
  Be a whore still. They love thee not that use thee.
  Give them diseases, leaving with thee their lust.   85
  Make use of thy salt hours: season the slaves
  For tubs and baths, bring down rose-cheeked youth
  To the tub-fast and the diet.
TIMANDRA   Hang thee, monster!
ALCIBIADES
  Pardon him, sweet Timandra, for his wits
  Are drowned and lost in his calamities.   90
  I have but little gold of late, brave Timon,
  The want whereof doth daily make revolt
  In my penurious band. I have heard and grieved
  How cursèd Athens, mindless of thy worth,
  Forgetting thy great deeds, when neighbour states   95
  But for thy sword and fortune trod upon them—
TIMON
  I prithee, beat thy drum and get thee gone.
ALCIBIADES
  I am thy friend, and pity thee, dear Timon.
TIMON
  How dost thou pity him whom thou dost trouble?
  I had rather be alone.
ALCIBIADES   Why, fare thee well.   100
  Here is some gold for thee.
TIMON   Keep it. I cannot eat it.
ALCIBIADES
  When I have laid proud Athens on a heap—
TIMON
  Warr'st thou 'gainst Athens?
ALCIBIADES   Ay, Timon, and have cause.

TIMON
  The gods confound them all in thy conquest,
  And thee after, when thou hast conquerèd.   105
ALCIBIADES
  Why me, Timon?
TIMON   That by killing of villains
  Thou wast born to conquer my country.
  Put up thy gold.
      He gives Alcibiades gold
                    Go on; here's gold; go on.
  Be as a planetary plague when Jove
  Will o'er some high-viced city hang his poison   110
  In the sick air. Let not thy sword skip one.
  Pity not honoured age for his white beard;
  He is an usurer. Strike me the counterfeit matron;
  It is her habit only that is honest,
  Herself's a bawd. Let not the virgin's cheek   115
  Make soft thy trenchant sword; for those milk paps
  That through the window-bars bore at men's eyes
  Are not within the leaf of pity writ;
  But set them down horrible traitors. Spare not the
      babe
  Whose dimpled smiles from fools exhaust their mercy.
  Think it a bastard whom the oracle   121
  Hath doubtfully pronounced thy throat shall cut,
  And mince it sans remorse. Swear against objects.
  Put armour on thine ears and on thine eyes
  Whose proof nor yells of mothers, maids, nor babes,
  Nor sight of priests in holy vestments bleeding,   126
  Shall pierce a jot. There's gold to pay thy soldiers.
  Make large confusion, and, thy fury spent,
  Confounded be thyself. Speak not. Be gone.
ALCIBIADES
  Hast thou gold yet? I'll take the gold thou giv'st me,
  Not all thy counsel.   131
TIMON
  Dost thou or dost thou not, heaven's curse upon thee!
PHRYNIA and TIMANDRA
  Give us some gold, good Timon. Hast thou more?
TIMON
  Enough to make a whore forswear her trade,
  And to make wholesomeness a bawd. Hold up, you
      sluts,   135
  Your aprons mountant.
      ⌈He throws gold into their aprons⌉
                    You are not oathable,
  Although I know you'll swear—terribly swear
  Into strong shudders and to heavenly agues—
  Th'immortal gods that hear you. Spare your oaths;
  I'll trust to your conditions. Be whores still,   140
  And he whose pious breath seeks to convert you,
  Be strong in whore, allure him, burn him up.
  Let your close fire predominate his smoke;
  And be no turncoats. Yet may your pain-sick months
  Be quite contrary, and thatch your poor thin roofs 145
  With burdens of the dead—some that were hanged,
  No matter. Wear them, betray with them; whore still;

Paint till a horse may mire upon your face.
A pox of wrinkles!
PHRYNIA *and* TIMANDRA Well, more gold; what then?
Believe't that we'll do anything for gold.   150
TIMON Consumptions sow
In hollow bones of man, strike their sharp shins,
And mar men's spurring. Crack the lawyer's voice,
That he may never more false title plead
Nor sound his quillets shrilly. Hoar the flamen   155
That scolds against the quality of flesh
And not believes himself. Down with the nose,
Down with it flat; take the bridge quite away
Of him that his particular to foresee
Smells from the general weal. Make curled-pate
    ruffians bald,   160
And let the unscarred braggarts of the war
Derive some pain from you. Plague all,
That your activity may defeat and quell
The source of all erection. There's more gold.
Do you damn others, and let this damn you;   165
And ditches grave you all!
PHRYNIA *and* TIMANDRA
More counsel with more money, bounteous Timon.
TIMON
More whore, more mischief first; I have given you
    earnest.
ALCIBIADES
Strike up the drum towards Athens. Farewell, Timon.
If I thrive well, I'll visit thee again.   170
TIMON
If I hope well, I'll never see thee more.
ALCIBIADES I never did thee harm.
TIMON Yes, thou spok'st well of me.
ALCIBIADES Call'st thou that harm?
TIMON
Men daily find it. Get thee away,   175
And take thy beagles with thee.
ALCIBIADES   We but offend him. Strike!
            Exeunt ⌐to drum and fife⌐ all but Timon
TIMON
That nature, being sick of man's unkindness,
Should yet be hungry!
    He digs the earth
                        Common mother—thou
Whose womb unmeasurable and infinite breast
Teems and feeds all, whose selfsame mettle   180
Whereof thy proud child, arrogant man, is puffed
Engenders the black toad and adder blue,
The gilded newt and eyeless venomed worm,
With all th'abhorrèd births below crisp heaven
Whereon Hyperion's quick'ning fire doth shine—   185
Yield him who all thy human sons do hate
From forth thy plenteous bosom, one poor root.
Ensear thy fertile and conceptious womb;
Let it no more bring out ingrateful man.
Go great with tigers, dragons, wolves, and bears;   190
Teem with new monsters whom thy upward face

Hath to the marbled mansion all above
Never presented.
    He finds a root
                O, a root! Dear thanks.
Dry up thy marrows, vines, and plough-torn leas,
Whereof ingrateful man with liquorish draughts   195
And morsels unctuous greases his pure mind,
That from it all consideration slips!—
    Enter Apemantus
More man? Plague, plague!
APEMANTUS
I was directed hither. Men report
Thou dost affect my manners, and dost use them.   200
TIMON
'Tis then because thou dost not keep a dog
Whom I would imitate. Consumption catch thee!
APEMANTUS
This is in thee a nature but infected,
A poor unmanly melancholy, sprung
From change of fortune. Why this spade, this place,
This slave-like habit, and these looks of care?   206
Thy flatterers yet wear silk, drink wine, lie soft,
Hug their diseased perfumes, and have forgot
That ever Timon was. Shame not these woods
By putting on the cunning of a carper.   210
Be thou a flatterer now, and seek to thrive
By that which has undone thee. Hinge thy knee,
And let his very breath whom thou'lt observe
Blow off thy cap. Praise his most vicious strain,
And call it excellent. Thou wast told thus.   215
Thou gav'st thine ears like tapsters that bade welcome
To knaves and all approachers. 'Tis most just
That thou turn rascal. Hadst thou wealth again,
Rascals should have't. Do not assume my likeness.
TIMON
Were I like thee, I'd throw away myself.   220
APEMANTUS
Thou hast cast away thyself being like thyself—
A madman so long, now a fool. What, think'st
That the bleak air, thy boisterous chamberlain,
Will put thy shirt on warm? Will these mossed trees
That have outlived the eagle page thy heels   225
And skip when thou point'st out? Will the cold brook,
Candied with ice, caudle thy morning taste
To cure thy o'ernight's surfeit? Call the creatures
Whose naked natures live in all the spite
Of wreakful heaven, whose bare unhousèd trunks   230
To the conflicting elements exposed
Answer mere nature; bid them flatter thee.
O, thou shalt find—
TIMON   A fool of thee! Depart.
APEMANTUS
I love thee better now than e'er I did.
TIMON
I hate thee worse.
APEMANTUS   Why?
TIMON   Thou flatter'st misery.   235

APEMANTUS
I flatter not, but say thou art a caitiff.
TIMON
Why dost thou seek me out?
APEMANTUS   To vex thee.
TIMON
Always a villain's office, or a fool's.
Dost please thyself in't?
APEMANTUS   Ay.
TIMON   What, a knave too?
APEMANTUS
If thou didst put this sour cold habit on   240
To castigate thy pride, 'twere well; but thou
Dost it enforcèdly. Thou'dst courtier be again
Wert thou not beggar. Willing misery
Outlives incertain pomp, is crowned before.
The one is filling still, never complete;   245
The other at high wish. Best state, contentless,
Hath a distracted and most wretched being,
Worse than the worst, content.
Thou shouldst desire to die, being miserable.
TIMON
Not by his breath that is more miserable.   250
Thou art a slave whom fortune's tender arm
With favour never clasped, but bred a dog.
Hadst thou like us from our first swathe proceeded
The sweet degrees that this brief world affords
To such as may the passive drudges of it   255
Freely command, thou wouldst have plunged thyself
In general riot, melted down thy youth
In different beds of lust, and never learned
The icy precepts of respect, but followed
The sugared game before thee. But myself,   260
Who had the world as my confectionary,
The mouths, the tongues, the eyes and hearts of men
At duty, more than I could frame employment,
That numberless upon me stuck, as leaves
Do on the oak, have with one winter's brush   265
Fell from their boughs, and left me open, bare
For every storm that blows—I to bear this,
That never knew but better, is some burden.
Thy nature did commence in sufferance, time
Hath made thee hard in't. Why shouldst thou hate men?
They never flattered thee. What hast thou given?   171
If thou wilt curse, thy father, that poor rag,
Must be thy subject, who in spite put stuff
To some she-beggar and compounded thee
Poor rogue hereditary. Hence, be gone.   275
If thou hadst not been born the worst of men
Thou hadst been a knave and flatterer.
APEMANTUS Art thou proud yet?
TIMON Ay, that I am not thee.
APEMANTUS I that I was   280
No prodigal.
TIMON   I that I am one now.
Were all the wealth I have shut up in thee
I'd give thee leave to hang it. Get thee gone.
That the whole life of Athens were in this!
Thus would I eat it.

He bites the root
APEMANTUS ⌈*offering food*⌉   Here, I will mend thy feast.
TIMON
First mend my company: take away thyself.   286
APEMANTUS
So I shall mend mine own by th' lack of thine.
TIMON
'Tis not well mended so, it is but botched;
If not, I would it were.
APEMANTUS   What wouldst thou have to Athens?
TIMON
Thee thither in a whirlwind. If thou wilt,   290
Tell them there I have gold. Look, so I have.
APEMANTUS
Here is no use for gold.
TIMON   The best and truest,
For here it sleeps and does no hirèd harm.
APEMANTUS Where liest a-nights, Timon?   294
TIMON Under that's above me. Where feed'st thou a-days,
    Apemantus?
APEMANTUS Where my stomach finds meat; or rather,
    where I eat it.
TIMON Would poison were obedient, and knew my mind!
APEMANTUS Where wouldst thou send it?   300
TIMON To sauce thy dishes.
APEMANTUS The middle of humanity thou never knewest,
    but the extremity of both ends. When thou wast in thy
    gilt and thy perfume, they mocked thee for too much
    curiosity; in thy rags thou know'st none, but art
    despised for the contrary. There's a medlar for thee;
    eat it.
TIMON On what I hate I feed not.
APEMANTUS Dost hate a medlar?
TIMON Ay, though it look like thee.   310
APEMANTUS An thou'dst hated meddlers sooner, thou
    shouldst have loved thyself better now. What man didst
    thou ever know unthrift that was beloved after his
    means?
TIMON Who, without those means thou talk'st of, didst
    thou ever know beloved?   316
APEMANTUS Myself.
TIMON I understand thee: thou hadst some means to keep
    a dog.
APEMANTUS What things in the world canst thou nearest
    compare to thy flatterers?   321
TIMON Women nearest; but men, men are the things
    themselves. What wouldst thou do with the world,
    Apemantus, if it lay in thy power?
APEMANTUS Give it the beasts, to be rid of the men.   325
TIMON Wouldst thou have thyself fall in the confusion of
    men, and remain a beast with the beasts?
APEMANTUS Ay, Timon.
TIMON A beastly ambition, which the gods grant thee
    t'attain to. If thou wert the lion, the fox would beguile
    thee. If thou wert the lamb, the fox would eat thee. If
    thou wert the fox, the lion would suspect thee when
    peradventure thou wert accused by the ass. If thou
    wert the ass, thy dullness would torment thee, and still
    thou lived'st but as a breakfast to the wolf. If thou wert

the wolf, thy greediness would afflict thee, and oft thou
shouldst hazard thy life for thy dinner. Wert thou the
unicorn, pride and wrath would confound thee, and
make thine own self the conquest of thy fury. Wert
thou a bear, thou wouldst be killed by the horse. Wert
thou a horse, thou wouldst be seized by the leopard.
Wert thou a leopard, thou wert german to the lion,
and the spots of thy kindred were jurors on thy life;
all thy safety were remotion, and thy defence absence.
What beast couldst thou be that were not subject to a
beast? And what a beast art thou already, that seest
not thy loss in transformation!

APEMANTUS If thou couldst please me with speaking to
me, thou mightst have hit upon it here. The commonwealth of Athens is become a forest of beasts.   350

TIMON How, has the ass broke the wall, that thou art out
of the city?

APEMANTUS Yonder comes a poet and a painter. The
plague of company light upon thee! I will fear to catch
it, and give way. When I know not what else to do,
I'll see thee again.   356

TIMON When there is nothing living but thee, thou shalt
be welcome. I had rather be a beggar's dog than
Apemantus.

APEMANTUS
Thou art the cap of all the fools alive.   360

TIMON
Would thou wert clean enough to spit upon.

APEMANTUS
A plague on thee! Thou art too bad to curse.

TIMON
All villains that do stand by thee are pure.

APEMANTUS
There is no leprosy but what thou speak'st.

TIMON If I name thee.   365
I'd beat thee, but I should infect my hands.

APEMANTUS
I would my tongue could rot them off.

TIMON
Away, thou issue of a mangy dog!
Choler does kill me that thou art alive.
I swoon to see thee.   370

APEMANTUS Would thou wouldst burst!

TIMON Away, thou tedious rogue!
⌈He throws a stone at Apemantus⌉
I am sorry I shall lose a stone by thee.

APEMANTUS Beast!

TIMON Slave!   375

APEMANTUS Toad!

TIMON Rogue, rogue, rogue!
I am sick of this false world, and will love naught
But even the mere necessities upon't.
Then, Timon, presently prepare thy grave,   380
Lie where the light foam of the sea may beat
Thy gravestone daily. Make thine epitaph,
That death in me at others' lives may laugh.
        He looks on the gold
O, thou sweet king-killer, and dear divorce

'Twixt natural son and sire; thou bright defiler   385
Of Hymen's purest bed; thou valiant Mars;
Thou ever young, fresh, loved, and delicate wooer,
Whose blush doth thaw the consecrated snow
That lies on Dian's lap; thou visible god,
That sold'rest close impossibilities   390
And mak'st them kiss, that speak'st with every tongue
To every purpose; O thou touch of hearts:
Think thy slave man rebels, and by thy virtue
Set them into confounding odds, that beasts
May have the world in empire.

APEMANTUS   Would 'twere so,   395
But not till I am dead. I'll say thou'st gold.
Thou wilt be thronged to shortly.

TIMON   Thronged to?

APEMANTUS   Ay.

TIMON
Thy back, I prithee.

APEMANTUS   Live, and love thy misery.

TIMON
Long live so, and so die. I am quit.
        Enter the Banditti, thieves

APEMANTUS
More things like men. Eat, Timon, and abhor them. 400
                                              Exit

FIRST THIEF Where should he have this gold? It is some
poor fragment, some slender ort of his remainder. The
mere want of gold and the falling-from of his friends
drove him into this melancholy.

SECOND THIEF It is noised he hath a mass of treasure. 405

THIRD THIEF Let us make the assay upon him. If he care
not for't, he will supply us easily. If he covetously
reserve it, how shall 's get it?

SECOND THIEF True, for he bears it not about him; 'tis hid.

FIRST THIEF Is not this he?   410

OTHER THIEVES Where?

SECOND THIEF 'Tis his description.

THIRD THIEF He, I know him.

ALL THIEVES (coming forward) Save thee, Timon.

TIMON Now, thieves.   415

ALL THIEVES
Soldiers, not thieves.

TIMON   Both, too, and women's sons.

ALL THIEVES
We are not thieves, but men that much do want.

TIMON
Your greatest want is, you want much of meat.
Why should you want? Behold, the earth hath roots.
Within this mile break forth a hundred springs.   420
The oaks bear mast, the briars scarlet hips.
The bounteous housewife nature on each bush
Lays her full mess before you. Want? Why want?

FIRST THIEF
We cannot live on grass, on berries, water,
As beasts and birds and fishes.   425

TIMON
Nor on the beasts themselves, the birds and fishes;
You must eat men. Yet thanks I must you con

That you are thieves professed, that you work not
In holier shapes; for there is boundless theft
In limited professions. (*Giving gold*) Rascal thieves,   430
Here's gold. Go suck the subtle blood o'th' grape
Till the high fever seethe your blood to froth,
And so scape hanging. Trust not the physician;
His antidotes are poison, and he slays
More than you rob. Take wealth and lives together.435
Do villainy; do, since you protest to do't,
Like workmen. I'll example you with thievery.
The sun's a thief, and with his great attraction
Robs the vast sea. The moon's an arrant thief,
And her pale fire she snatches from the sun.   440
The sea's a thief, whose liquid surge resolves
The moon into salt tears. The earth's a thief,
That feeds and breeds by a composture stol'n
From gen'ral excrement. Each thing's a thief.
The laws, your curb and whip, in their rough power
Has unchecked theft. Love not yourselves. Away,   446
Rob one another. There's more gold. Cut throats;
All that you meet are thieves. To Athens go,
Break open shops; nothing can you steal
But thieves do lose it. Steal no less for this I give you,
And gold confound you howsoe'er. Amen.   451
THIRD THIEF He's almost charmed me from my profession
by persuading me to it.
FIRST THIEF 'Tis in the malice of mankind that he thus
advises us, not to have us thrive in our mystery.   455
SECOND THIEF I'll believe him as an enemy, and give over
my trade.
FIRST THIEF Let us first see peace in Athens. There is no
time so miserable but a man may be true.

Exeunt Thieves

Enter Flavius to Timon
FLAVIUS O you gods!   460
Is yon despised and ruinous man my lord,
Full of decay and failing? O monument
And wonder of good deeds evilly bestowed!
What an alteration of honour has desp'rate want made!
What viler thing upon the earth than friends,   465
Who can bring noblest minds to basest ends!
How rarely does it meet with this time's guise,
When man was wished to love his enemies!
Grant I may ever love and rather woo
Those that would mischief me than those that do!   470
Timon sees him
He's caught me in his eye. I will present
My honest grief unto him, and as my lord
Still serve him with my life.—My dearest master.
TIMON
Away! What art thou?
FLAVIUS   Have you forgot me, sir?
TIMON
Why dost ask that? I have forgot all men;   475
Then if thou grant'st thou'rt man, I have forgot thee.
FLAVIUS An honest poor servant of yours.
TIMON
Then I know thee not. I never had

Honest man about me; ay, all I kept were knaves,
To serve in meat to villains.
FLAVIUS   The gods are witness,   480
Ne'er did poor steward wear a truer grief
For his undone lord than mine eyes for you.
TIMON
What, dost thou weep? Come nearer then; I love thee
Because thou art a woman, and disclaim'st
Flinty mankind whose eyes do never give   485
But thorough lust and laughter. Pity's sleeping.
Strange times, that weep with laughing, not with
    weeping!
FLAVIUS
I beg of you to know me, good my lord,
T'accept my grief,
    ⌈*He offers his money*⌉
                    and whilst this poor wealth lasts
To entertain me as your steward still.   490
TIMON Had I a steward
So true, so just, and now so comfortable?
It almost turns my dangerous nature mild.
Let me behold thy face. Surely this man
Was born of woman.   495
Forgive my general and exceptless rashness,
You perpetual sober gods! I do proclaim
One honest man—mistake me not, but one,
No more, I pray—and he's a steward.
How fain would I have hated all mankind,   500
And thou redeem'st thyself! But all save thee
I fell with curses.
Methinks thou art more honest now than wise,
For by oppressing and betraying me
Thou mightst have sooner got another service;   505
For many so arrive at second masters
Upon their first lord's neck. But tell me true—
For I must ever doubt, though ne'er so sure—
Is not thy kindness subtle, covetous,
A usuring kindness, and, as rich men deal gifts,   510
Expecting in return twenty for one?
FLAVIUS
No, my most worthy master, in whose breast
Doubt and suspect, alas, are placed too late.
You should have feared false times when you did feast.
Suspect still comes where an estate is least.   515
That which I show, heaven knows, is merely love,
Duty and zeal to your unmatchèd mind,
Care of your food and living; and, believe it,
My most honoured lord,
For any benefit that points to me,   520
Either in hope or present, I'd exchange
For this one wish: that you had power and wealth
To requite me by making rich yourself.
TIMON
Look thee, 'tis so. Thou singly honest man,
    ⌈*He gives Flavius gold*⌉
Here, take. The gods, out of my misery,   525
Has sent thee treasure. Go, live rich and happy,
But thus conditioned: thou shalt build from men,

Hate all, curse all, show charity to none,
But let the famished flesh slide from the bone
Ere thou relieve the beggar. Give to dogs   530
What thou deniest to men. Let prisons swallow 'em,
Debts wither 'em to nothing; be men like blasted woods,
And may diseases lick up their false bloods.
And so farewell, and thrive.
FLAVIUS   O, let me stay
And comfort you, my master.
TIMON   If thou hat'st curses,   535
Stay not. Fly whilst thou art blest and free.
Ne'er see thou man, and let me ne'er see thee.
          Exeunt ⌈Timon into his cave, Flavius another way⌉

5.1   *Enter Poet and Painter*
PAINTER As I took note of the place, it cannot be far where
he abides.
POET What's to be thought of him? Does the rumour hold
for true that he's so full of gold?   4
PAINTER Certain. Alcibiades reports it. Phrynia and
Timandra had gold of him. He likewise enriched poor
straggling soldiers with great quantity. 'Tis said he gave
unto his steward a mighty sum.
POET Then this breaking of his has been but a try for his
friends?   10
PAINTER Nothing else. You shall see him a palm in Athens
again, and flourish with the highest. Therefore 'tis not
amiss we tender our loves to him in this supposed distress
of his. It will show honestly in us, and is very likely to
load our purposes with what they travail for, if it be a
just and true report that goes of his having.   16
POET What have you now to present unto him?
PAINTER Nothing at this time, but my visitation; only I
will promise him an excellent piece.
POET I must serve him so too, tell him of an intent that's
coming toward him.   21
PAINTER Good as the best.
          ⌈*Enter Timon from his cave, unobserved*⌉
Promising is the very air o'th' time; it opens the eyes of
expectation. Performance is ever the duller for his act,
and but in the plainer and simpler kind of people the
deed of saying is quite out of use. To promise is most
courtly and fashionable. Performance is a kind of will or
testament which argues a great sickness in his judgement
that makes it.
TIMON (*aside*) Excellent workman, thou canst not paint a
man so bad as is thyself.   31
POET (*to Painter*) I am thinking what I shall say I have
provided for him. It must be a personating of himself, a
satire against the softness of prosperity, with a discovery
of the infinite flatteries that follow youth and opulency.
TIMON (*aside*) Must thou needs stand for a villain in thine
own work? Wilt thou whip thine own faults in other
men? Do so; I have gold for thee.
POET (*to Painter*) Nay, let's seek him.
Then do we sin against our own estate   40
When we may profit meet and come too late.
PAINTER True.

When the day serves, before black-cornered night,
Find what thou want'st by free and offered light.
Come.   45
TIMON (*aside*)
I'll meet you at the turn. What a god's gold,
That he is worshipped in a baser temple
Than where swine feed!
'Tis thou that rigg'st the barque and plough'st the foam,
Settlest admirèd reverence in a slave.   50
To thee be worship, and thy saints for aye
Be crowned with plagues, that thee alone obey.
Fit I meet them.
          He comes forward to them
POET
Hail, worthy Timon!
PAINTER   Our late noble master!
TIMON
Have I once lived to see two honest men?   55
POET
Sir, having often of your open bounty tasted,
Hearing you were retired, your friends fall'n off,
Whose thankless natures, O abhorrèd spirits,
Not all the whips of heaven are large enough—
What, to you,   60
Whose star-like nobleness gave life and influence
To their whole being! I am rapt, and cannot cover
The monstrous bulk of this ingratitude
With any size of words.
TIMON
Let it go naked; men may see't the better.   65
You that are honest, by being what you are
Make them best seen and known.
PAINTER   He and myself
Have travelled in the great show'r of your gifts,
And sweetly felt it.
TIMON   Ay, you are honest men.
PAINTER
We are hither come to offer you our service.   70
TIMON
Most honest men. Why, how shall I requite you?
Can you eat roots and drink cold water? No.
POET *and* PAINTER
What we can do we'll do to do you service.
TIMON
You're honest men. You've heard that I have gold,
I am sure you have. Speak truth; you're honest men.
PAINTER
So it is said, my noble lord, but therefor   76
Came not my friend nor I.
TIMON
Good honest men. (*To Painter*) Thou draw'st a
          counterfeit
Best in all Athens; thou'rt indeed the best;
Thou counterfeit'st most lively.
PAINTER   So so, my lord.   80
TIMON
E'en so, sir, as I say. (*To Poet*) And for thy fiction,
Why, thy verse swells with stuff so fine and smooth

That thou art even natural in thine art.
But for all this, my honest-natured friends,
I must needs say you have a little fault.   85
Marry, 'tis not monstrous in you, neither wish I
You take much pains to mend.
POET *and* PAINTER   Beseech your honour
To make it known to us.
TIMON   You'll take it ill.
POET *and* PAINTER Most thankfully, my lord.
TIMON Will you indeed?   90
POET *and* PAINTER Doubt it not, worthy lord.
TIMON
There's never a one of you but trusts a knave
That mightily deceives you.
POET *and* PAINTER   Do we, my lord?
TIMON
Ay, and you hear him cog, see him dissemble,
Know his gross patchery, love him, feed him,   95
Keep in your bosom; yet remain assured
That he's a made-up villain.
PAINTER I know none such, my lord.
POET Nor I.
TIMON
Look you, I love you well. I'll give you gold,   100
Rid me these villains from your companies.
Hang them or stab them, drown them in a draught,
Confound them by some course, and come to me,
I'll give you gold enough.
POET *and* PAINTER
                    Name them, my lord, let's know them.
TIMON
You that way and you this—but two in company—105
Each man apart, all single and alone,
Yet an arch-villain keeps him company.
⌈*To Painter*⌉ If where thou art two villains shall not be,
Come not near him. ⌈*To Poet*⌉ If thou wouldst not
    reside
But where one villain is, then him abandon.   110
Hence; pack! ⌈*Striking him*⌉ There's gold. You came
    for gold, ye slaves.
⌈*Striking Painter*⌉ You have work for me; there's
    payment. Hence!
⌈*Striking Poet*⌉ You are an alchemist; make gold of that.
Out, rascal dogs!   *Exeunt* ⌈*Poet and Painter one way,*
                                        Timon into his cave⌉

5.2   *Enter Flavius and two Senators*
FLAVIUS
It is in vain that you would speak with Timon,
For he is set so only to himself
That nothing but himself which looks like man
Is friendly with him.
FIRST SENATOR   Bring us to his cave.
It is our part and promise to th' Athenians   5
To speak with Timon.
SECOND SENATOR   At all times alike
Men are not still the same. 'Twas time and griefs
That framed him thus. Time with his fairer hand

Offering the fortunes of his former days,
The former man may make him. Bring us to him,   10
And chance it as it may.
FLAVIUS   Here is his cave.
(*Calling*) Peace and content be here! Lord Timon,
    Timon,
Look out and speak to friends. Th'Athenians
By two of their most reverend senate greet thee.
Speak to them, noble Timon.   15
            Enter Timon out of his cave
TIMON
Thou sun that comforts, burn! Speak and be hanged.
For each true word a blister, and each false
Be as a cantherizing to the root o'th' tongue,
Consuming it with speaking.
FIRST SENATOR   Worthy Timon—
TIMON
Of none but such as you, and you of Timon.   20
FIRST SENATOR
The senators of Athens greet thee, Timon.
TIMON
I thank them, and would send them back the plague
Could I but catch it for them.
FIRST SENATOR   O, forget
What we are sorry for, ourselves in thee.
The senators with one consent of love   25
Entreat thee back to Athens, who have thought
On special dignities which vacant lie
For thy best use and wearing.
SECOND SENATOR   They confess
Toward thee forgetfulness too general-gross,
Which now the public body, which doth seldom   30
Play the recanter, feeling in itself
A lack of Timon's aid, hath sense withal
Of it own fail, restraining aid to Timon;
And send forth us to make their sorrowed render,
Together with a recompense more fruitful   35
Than their offence can weigh down by the dram;
Ay, even such heaps and sums of love and wealth
As shall to thee blot out what wrongs were theirs,
And write in thee the figures of their love,
Ever to read them thine.
TIMON   You witch me in it,   40
Surprise me to the very brink of tears.
Lend me a fool's heart and a woman's eyes,
And I'll beweep these comforts, worthy senators.
FIRST SENATOR
Therefore so please thee to return with us,
And of our Athens, thine and ours, to take   45
The captainship, thou shalt be met with thanks,
Allowed with absolute power, and thy good name
Live with authority. So soon we shall drive back
Of Alcibiades th'approaches wild,
Who, like a boar too savage, doth root up   50
His country's peace.
SECOND SENATOR   And shakes his threat'ning sword
Against the walls of Athens.
FIRST SENATOR   Therefore, Timon—

TIMON
Well, sir, I will; therefore I will, sir, thus.
If Alcibiades kill my countrymen,
Let Alcibiades know this of Timon: 55
That Timon cares not. But if he sack fair Athens,
And take our goodly agèd men by th' beards,
Giving our holy virgins to the stain
Of contumelious, beastly, mad-brained war,
Then let him know, and tell him Timon speaks it 60
In pity of our agèd and our youth,
I cannot choose but tell him that I care not;
And—let him take't at worst—for their knives care
not
While you have throats to answer. For myself,
There's not a whittle in th' unruly camp 65
But I do prize it at my love before
The reverend'st throat in Athens. So I leave you
To the protection of the prosperous gods,
As thieves to keepers.
FLAVIUS (*to Senators*)   Stay not; all's in vain.
TIMON
Why, I was writing of my epitaph. 70
It will be seen tomorrow. My long sickness
Of health and living now begins to mend,
And nothing brings me all things. Go; live still.
Be Alcibiades your plague, you his,
And last so long enough.
FIRST SENATOR   We speak in vain. 75
TIMON
But yet I love my country, and am not
One that rejoices in the common wrack
As common bruit doth put it.
FIRST SENATOR   That's well spoke.
TIMON
Commend me to my loving countrymen—
FIRST SENATOR
These words become your lips as they pass through
them. 80
SECOND SENATOR
And enter in our ears like great triumphers
In their applauding gates.
TIMON   Commend me to them,
And tell them that to ease them of their griefs,
Their fears of hostile strokes, their aches, losses,
Their pangs of love, with other incident throes 85
That nature's fragile vessel doth sustain
In life's uncertain voyage, I will some kindness do them.
I'll teach them to prevent wild Alcibiades' wrath.
FIRST SENATOR (*aside*)
I like this well; he will return again.
TIMON
I have a tree which grows here in my close 90
That mine own use invites me to cut down,
And shortly must I fell it. Tell my friends,
Tell Athens, in the sequence of degree
From high to low throughout, that whoso please
To stop affliction, let him take his haste, 95
Come hither ere my tree hath felt the axe,
And hang himself. I pray you do my greeting.

FLAVIUS (*to Senators*)
Trouble him no further. Thus you still shall find him.
TIMON
Come not to me again, but say to Athens,
Timon hath made his everlasting mansion 100
Upon the beachèd verge of the salt flood,
Who once a day with his embossèd froth
The turbulent surge shall cover. Thither come,
And let my gravestone be your oracle.
Lips, let four words go by, and language end. 105
What is amiss, plague and infection mend.
Graves only be men's works, and death their gain.
Sun, hide thy beams. Timon hath done his reign.
                      Exit ⌈*into his cave*⌉
FIRST SENATOR
His discontents are unremovably
Coupled to nature. 110
SECOND SENATOR
Our hope in him is dead. Let us return,
And strain what other means is left unto us
In our dear peril.
FIRST SENATOR   It requires swift foot.   *Exeunt*

5.3   *Enter two other Senators, with a Messenger*
⌈THIRD⌉ SENATOR
Thou hast painfully discovered. Are his files
As full as thy report?
MESSENGER   I have spoke the least.
Besides, his expedition promises
Present approach.
⌈FOURTH⌉ SENATOR
We stand much hazard if they bring not Timon. 5
MESSENGER
I met a courier, one mine ancient friend,
Whom, though in general part we were opposed,
Yet our old love made a particular force
And made us speak like friends. This man was riding
From Alcibiades to Timon's cave 10
With letters of entreaty which imported
His fellowship i'th' cause against your city,
In part for his sake moved.
        Enter the other Senators
⌈THIRD⌉ SENATOR   Here come our brothers.
⌈FIRST⌉ SENATOR
No talk of Timon; nothing of him expect.
The enemy's drum is heard, and fearful scouring 15
Doth choke the air with dust. In, and prepare.
Ours is the fall, I fear, our foe's the snare.   *Exeunt*

5.4   *Enter a Soldier, in the woods, seeking Timon*
SOLDIER
By all description, this should be the place.
Who's here? Speak, ho! No answer?
    ⌈*He discovers a gravestone*⌉
                        What is this?
Dead, sure, and this his grave. What's on this tomb
I cannot read. The character I'll take with wax.
Our captain hath in every figure skill, 5
An aged interpreter, though young in days.

Before proud Athens he's set down by this,
Whose fall the mark of his ambition is.   *Exit*

5.5   *Trumpets sound. Enter Alcibiades with his powers,*
             before Athens
ALCIBIADES
Sound to this coward and lascivious town
Our terrible approach.
             A parley sounds. The Senators appear upon the walls
Till now you have gone on and filled the time
With all licentious measure, making your wills
The scope of justice. Till now myself and such   5
As slept within the shadow of your power
Have wandered with our traversed arms, and breathed
Our sufferance vainly. Now the time is flush
When crouching marrow, in the bearer strong,
Cries of itself 'No more'; now breathless wrong   10
Shall sit and pant in your great chairs of ease,
And pursy insolence shall break his wind
With fear and horrid flight.
FIRST SENATOR   Noble and young,
When thy first griefs were but a mere conceit,
Ere thou hadst power or we had cause of fear,   15
We sent to thee to give thy rages balm,
To wipe out our ingratitude with loves
Above their quantity.
SECOND SENATOR   So did we woo
Transformèd Timon to our city's love
By humble message and by promised means.   20
We were not all unkind, nor all deserve
The common stroke of war.
FIRST SENATOR   These walls of ours
Were not erected by their hands from whom
You have received your grief; nor are they such
That these great tow'rs, trophies, and schools should fall
For private faults in them.
SECOND SENATOR   Nor are they living   26
Who were the motives that you first went out.
Shame that they wanted cunning, in excess,
Hath broke their hearts. March, noble lord,
Into our city with thy banners spread.   30
By decimation and a tithèd death,
If thy revenges hunger for that food
Which nature loathes, take thou the destined tenth,
And by the hazard of the spotted die
Let die the spotted.
FIRST SENATOR   All have not offended.   35
For those that were, it is not square to take,
On those that are, revenges. Crimes like lands
Are not inherited. Then, dear countryman,
Bring in thy ranks, but leave without thy rage.
Spare thy Athenian cradle and those kin   40
Which, in the bluster of thy wrath, must fall
With those that have offended. Like a shepherd
Approach the fold and cull th'infected forth,
But kill not all together.
SECOND SENATOR   What thou wilt,

Thou rather shalt enforce it with thy smile   45
Than hew to't with thy sword.
FIRST SENATOR   Set but thy foot
Against our rampired gates and they shall ope,
So thou wilt send thy gentle heart before
To say thou'lt enter friendly.
SECOND SENATOR   Throw thy glove,
Or any token of thine honour else,   50
That thou wilt use the wars as thy redress,
And not as our confusion. All thy powers
Shall make their harbour in our town till we
Have sealed thy full desire.
ALCIBIADES ⌈*throwing up a glove*⌉ Then there's my glove.
Descend, and open your unchargèd ports.   55
Those enemies of Timon's and mine own
Whom you yourselves shall set out for reproof
Fall, and no more; and to atone your fears
With my more noble meaning, not a man
Shall pass his quarter or offend the stream   60
Of regular justice in your city's bounds
But shall be remedied to your public laws
At heaviest answer.
BOTH SENATORS 'Tis most nobly spoken.
ALCIBIADES Descend, and keep your words.   65
             ⌈*Trumpets sound. Exeunt Senators from the walls.*⌉
             Enter Soldier, with a tablet of wax
SOLDIER
My noble general, Timon is dead,
Entombed upon the very hem o'th' sea;
And on his gravestone this insculpture, which
With wax I brought away, whose soft impression
Interprets for my poor ignorance.   70
             Alcibiades reads the epitaph
ALCIBIADES
'Here lies a wretched corpse,
             Of wretched soul bereft.
Seek not my name. A plague consume
             You wicked caitiffs left!
Here lie I, Timon, who alive   75
             All living men did hate.
Pass by and curse thy fill, but pass
             And stay not here thy gait.'
These well express in thee thy latter spirits.
Though thou abhorred'st in us our human griefs,   80
Scorned'st our brains' flow and those our droplets which
From niggard nature fall, yet rich conceit
Taught thee to make vast Neptune weep for aye
On thy low grave, on faults forgiven. Dead
Is noble Timon, of whose memory   85
Hereafter more.
             ⌈*Enter Senators through the gates*⌉
             Bring me into your city,
And I will use the olive with my sword,
·Make war breed peace, make peace stint war, make each
Prescribe to other as each other's leech.
Let our drums strike.   90
             ⌈*Drums.*⌉ *Exeunt* ⌈*through the gates*⌉

THE HISTORY OF KING LEAR
THE QUARTO TEXT

King Lear first appeared in print in a quarto of 1608. A substantially different text appeared in the 1623 Folio. Until now, editors, assuming that each of these early texts imperfectly represented a single play, have conflated them. But research conducted mainly during the 1970s and 1980s confirms an earlier view that the 1608 quarto represents the play as Shakespeare originally wrote it, and the 1623 Folio as he substantially revised it. He revised other plays, too, but usually by making many small changes in the dialogue and adding or omitting passages, as in *Hamlet, Troilus and Cressida*, and *Othello*. For these plays we print the revised text in so far as it can be ascertained. But in *King Lear* revisions are not simply local but structural, too; conflation, as Harley Granville-Barker wrote, 'may make for redundancy or confusion', so we print an edited version of each text. The first, printed in the following pages, represents the play as Shakespeare first conceived it, probably before it was performed.

The story of a king who, angry with the failure of his virtuous youngest daughter (Cordelia) to respond as he desires in a love-test, divides his kingdom between her two malevolent sisters (Gonoril and Regan), had been often told; Shakespeare would have come upon it in Holinshed's *Chronicles* and in *A Mirror for Magistrates* while reading for his plays on English history. It is told also (though briefly) in Edmund Spenser's *Faerie Queene* (Book 2, canto 10), and had been dramatized in a play of unknown authorship—*The True Chronicle History of King Leir and his three daughters*—published in 1605, but probably written some fifteen years earlier. This play particularly gave Shakespeare much, including suggestions for the characters of Lear's loyal servant, Kent, and of Gonoril's husband, Albany, and her steward, Oswald; for the storm; for Lear's kneeling to Cordelia; and for many details of language. Nevertheless, his play is a highly original creation. Lear's madness and the harrowing series of disasters in *King Lear*'s final stages are of Shakespeare's invention, and he complicates the plot by adding the story (based on an episode of Sir Philip Sidney's *Arcadia*) of Gloucester and his two sons, Edmund and Edgar. Edgar's love and loyalty to the father who, failing to see the truth, has rejected him in favour of the villainous Edmund makes him a counterpart to Cordelia; and the horrific blinding of Gloucester brought about by Edmund creates a physical parallel to Lear's madness which reaches its consummation in the scene (Sc. 20) at Dover Cliff when the mad and the blind old men commune together.

The clear-eyed intensity of Shakespeare's tragic vision in *King Lear* has been too much for some audiences, and Nahum Tate's adaptation, which gave the play a happy ending, held the stage from 1681 to 1843; since then, increased understanding of Shakespeare's stagecraft along with a greater seriousness in theatre audiences has assisted in the rehabilitation of a play that is now recognized as one of the profoundest of all artistic explorations of the human condition.

In the text which follows, the Quarto scene numbers are accompanied by the equivalent Folio act and scene numbers in parentheses. There is no equivalent to Sc.17 in the Folio.

THE PERSONS OF THE PLAY

LEAR, King of Britain

GONORIL, Lear's eldest daughter

Duke of ALBANY, her husband

REGAN, Lear's second daughter

Duke of CORNWALL, her husband

CORDELIA, Lear's youngest daughter

King of FRANCE }
Duke of BURGUNDY } suitors of Cordelia

Earl of KENT, later disguised as Caius

Earl of GLOUCESTER

EDGAR, elder son of Gloucester, later disguised as Tom o' Bedlam

EDMUND, bastard son of Gloucester

OLD MAN, a tenant of Gloucester

CURAN, Gloucester's retainer

Lear's FOOL

OSWALD, Gonoril's steward

Three SERVANTS of Cornwall

DOCTOR, attendant on Cordelia

Three CAPTAINS

A HERALD

A KNIGHT

A MESSENGER

Gentlemen, servants, soldiers, followers, trumpeters, others

The History of King Lear

Sc. 1 *Enter the Earl of Kent, the Duke of Gloucester, and*
Edmund the bastard

KENT I thought the King had more affected the Duke of
Albany than Cornwall.

GLOUCESTER It did always seem so to us, but now in the
division of the kingdoms it appears not which of the
Dukes he values most; for equalities are so weighed
that curiosity in neither can make choice of either's
moiety.

KENT Is not this your son, my lord?

GLOUCESTER His breeding, sir, hath been at my charge. I
have so often blushed to acknowledge him that now I
am brazed to it.   11

KENT I cannot conceive you.

GLOUCESTER Sir, this young fellow's mother could,
whereupon she grew round-wombed and had indeed,
sir, a son for her cradle ere she had a husband for her
bed. Do you smell a fault?   16

KENT I cannot wish the fault undone, the issue of it being
so proper.

GLOUCESTER But I have, sir, a son by order of law, some
year elder than this, who yet is no dearer in my
account. Though this knave came something saucily
into the world before he was sent for, yet was his
mother fair, there was good sport at his making, and
the whoreson must be acknowledged. (*To Edmund*) Do
you know this noble gentleman, Edmund?   25

EDMUND No, my lord.

GLOUCESTER (*to Edmund*) My lord of Kent. Remember him
hereafter as my honourable friend.

EDMUND (*to Kent*) My services to your lordship.

KENT I must love you, and sue to know you better.   30

EDMUND Sir, I shall study deserving.

GLOUCESTER (*to Kent*) He hath been out nine years, and
away he shall again.
Sound a sennet
The King is coming.   34
Enter one bearing a coronet, then King Lear, then
the Dukes of Albany and Cornwall; next Gonoril,
Regan, Cordelia, with followers

LEAR
Attend my lords of France and Burgundy, Gloucester.

GLOUCESTER I shall, my liege.   ⌈*Exit*⌉

LEAR
Meantime we will express our darker purposes.
The map there. Know we have divided
In three our kingdom, and 'tis our first intent
To shake all cares and business off our state,   40
Confirming them on younger years.
The two great princes, France and Burgundy—
Great rivals in our youngest daughter's love—
Long in our court have made their amorous sojourn,
And here are to be answered. Tell me, my daughters,
Which of you shall we say doth love us most,   46

That we our largest bounty may extend
Where merit doth most challenge it?
Gonoril, our eldest born, speak first.

GONORIL
Sir, I do love you more than words can wield the
matter;   50
Dearer than eyesight, space, or liberty;
Beyond what can be valued, rich or rare;
No less than life; with grace, health, beauty, honour;
As much as child e'er loved, or father, friend;
A love that makes breath poor and speech unable.   55
Beyond all manner of so much I love you.

CORDELIA (*aside*)
What shall Cordelia do? Love and be silent.

LEAR (*to Gonoril*)
Of all these bounds even from this line to this,
With shady forests and wide skirted meads,
We make thee lady. To thine and Albany's issue   60
Be this perpetual.—What says our second daughter?
Our dearest Regan, wife to Cornwall, speak.

REGAN Sir, I am made
Of the self-same mettle that my sister is,
And prize me at her worth. In my true heart   65
I find she names my very deed of love—
Only she came short, that I profess
Myself an enemy to all other joys
Which the most precious square of sense possesses,
And find I am alone felicitate   70
In your dear highness' love.

CORDELIA (*aside*)   Then poor Cordelia—
And yet not so, since I am sure my love's
More richer than my tongue.

LEAR (*to Regan*)
To thee and thine hereditary ever
Remain this ample third of our fair kingdom,   75
No less in space, validity, and pleasure
Than that confirmed on Gonoril. (*To Cordelia*) But
now our joy,
Although the last not least in our dear love:
What can you say to win a third more opulent
Than your sisters?   80

CORDELIA Nothing, my lord.

LEAR
How? Nothing can come of nothing. Speak again.

CORDELIA
Unhappy that I am, I cannot heave
My heart into my mouth. I love your majesty
According to my bond, nor more nor less.   85

LEAR
Go to, go to, mend your speech a little
Lest it may mar your fortunes.

CORDELIA   Good my lord,
You have begot me, bred me, loved me.
I return those duties back as are right fit—

Obey you, love you, and most honour you.   90
Why have my sisters husbands if they say
They love you all? Haply when I shall wed
That lord whose hand must take my plight shall carry
Half my love with him, half my care and duty.
Sure, I shall never marry like my sisters,   95
To love my father all.
LEAR But goes this with thy heart?
CORDELIA Ay, good my lord.
LEAR So young and so untender?
CORDELIA So young, my lord, and true.   100
LEAR
Well, let it be so. Thy truth then be thy dower;
For by the sacred radiance of the sun,
The mysteries of Hecate and the night,
By all the operation of the orbs
From whom we do exist and cease to be,   105
Here I disclaim all my paternal care,
Propinquity, and property of blood,
And as a stranger to my heart and me
Hold thee from this for ever. The barbarous Scythian,
Or he that makes his generation   110
Messes to gorge his appetite,
Shall be as well neighboured, pitied, and relieved
As thou, my sometime daughter.
KENT   Good my liege—
LEAR
Peace, Kent. Come not between the dragon and his
     wrath.
I loved her most, and thought to set my rest   115
On her kind nursery. ⌈To Cordelia⌉ Hence, and avoid
     my sight!—
So be my grave my peace as here I give
Her father's heart from her. Call France. Who stirs?
Call Burgundy.   ⌈Exit one or more⌉
                    Cornwall and Albany,
With my two daughters' dowers digest this third.   120
Let pride, which she calls plainness, marry her.
I do invest you jointly in my power,
Pre-eminence, and all the large effects
That troop with majesty. Ourself by monthly course,
With reservation of an hundred knights   125
By you to be sustained, shall our abode
Make with you by due turns. Only we still retain
The name and all the additions to a king.
The sway, revenue, execution of the rest,
Belovèd sons, be yours; which to confirm,   130
This crownet part betwixt you.
KENT   Royal Lear,
Whom I have ever honoured as my king,
Loved as my father, as my master followed,
As my great patron thought on in my prayers—
LEAR
The bow is bent and drawn; make from the shaft.   135
KENT
Let it fall rather, though the fork invade
The region of my heart. Be Kent unmannerly
When Lear is mad. What wilt thou do, old man?
Think'st thou that duty shall have dread to speak

When power to flattery bows? To plainness honour's
     bound   140
When majesty stoops to folly. Reverse thy doom,
And in thy best consideration check
This hideous rashness. Answer my life my judgement,
Thy youngest daughter does not love thee least,
Nor are those empty-hearted whose low sound   145
Reverbs no hollowness.
LEAR   Kent, on thy life, no more!
KENT
My life I never held but as a pawn
To wage against thy enemies, nor fear to lose it,
Thy safety being the motive.
LEAR   Out of my sight!
KENT
See better, Lear, and let me still remain   150
The true blank of thine eye.
LEAR   Now, by Apollo—
KENT
Now, by Apollo, King, thou swear'st thy gods in vain.
LEAR ⌈making to strike him⌉
Vassal, recreant!
KENT   Do, kill thy physician,
And the fee bestow upon the foul disease.
Revoke thy doom, or whilst I can vent clamour   155
From my throat I'll tell thee thou dost evil.
LEAR
Hear me; on thy allegiance hear me!
Since thou hast sought to make us break our vow,
Which we durst never yet, and with strayed pride
To come between our sentence and our power,   160
Which nor our nature nor our place can bear,
Our potency made good take thy reward:
Four days we do allot thee for provision
To shield thee from dis-eases of the world,
And on the fifth to turn thy hated back   165
Upon our kingdom. If on the next day following
Thy banished trunk be found in our dominions,
The moment is thy death. Away! By Jupiter,
This shall not be revoked.
KENT
Why, fare thee well, King; since thus thou wilt
     appear,   170
Friendship lives hence, and banishment is here.
(To Cordelia) The gods to their protection take thee,
     maid,
That rightly thinks, and hast most justly said.
(To Gonoril and Regan)
And your large speeches may your deeds approve,
That good effects may spring from words of love.   175
Thus Kent, O princes, bids you all adieu;
He'll shape his old course in a country new.   Exit
     Enter the King of France and the Duke of
     Burgundy, with the Duke of Gloucester
GLOUCESTER
Here's France and Burgundy, my noble lord.
LEAR My lord of Burgundy,
We first address towards you, who with a king   180
Hath rivalled for our daughter: what in the least

Will you require in present dower with her
Or cease your quest of love?

BURGUNDY   Royal majesty,
I crave no more than what your highness offered;
Nor will you tender less.

LEAR   Right noble Burgundy,   185
When she was dear to us we did hold her so;
But now her price is fallen. Sir, there she stands.
If aught within that little seeming substance,
Or all of it, with our displeasure pieced,
And nothing else, may fitly like your grace,   190
She's there, and she is yours.

BURGUNDY   I know no answer.

LEAR
Sir, will you with those infirmities she owes,
Unfriended, new-adopted to our hate,
Covered with our curse and strangered with our oath,
Take her or leave her?

BURGUNDY   Pardon me, royal sir.   195
Election makes not up on such conditions.

LEAR
Then leave her, sir; for by the power that made me,
I tell you all her wealth. (*To France*) For you, great
    King,
I would not from your love make such a stray
To match you where I hate, therefore beseech you   200
To avert your liking a more worthier way
Than on a wretch whom nature is ashamed
Almost to acknowledge hers.

FRANCE
This is most strange, that she that even but now
Was your best object, the argument of your praise,   205
Balm of your age, most best, most dearest,
Should in this trice of time commit a thing
So monstrous to dismantle
So many folds of favour. Sure, her offence
Must be of such unnatural degree   210
That monsters it, or your fore-vouched affections
Fall'n into taint; which to believe of her
Must be a faith that reason without miracle
Could never plant in me.

CORDELIA (*to Lear*)
I yet beseech your majesty,   215
If for I want that glib and oily art
To speak and purpose not—since what I well intend,
I'll do't before I speak—that you acknow
It is no vicious blot, murder, or foulness,
No unclean action or dishonoured step   220
That hath deprived me of your grace and favour,
But even the want of that for which I am rich—
A still-soliciting eye, and such a tongue
As I am glad I have not, though not to have it
Hath lost me in your liking.

LEAR   Go to, go to.   225
Better thou hadst not been born than not to have
    pleased me better.

FRANCE
Is it no more but this—a tardiness in nature,
That often leaves the history unspoke

That it intends to do?—My lord of Burgundy,
What say you to the lady? Love is not love   230
When it is mingled with respects that stands
Aloof from the entire point. Will you have her?
She is herself a dower.

BURGUNDY   Royal Lear,
Give but that portion which yourself proposed,
And here I take Cordelia by the hand,   235
Duchess of Burgundy—

LEAR   Nothing. I have sworn.

BURGUNDY (*to Cordelia*)
I am sorry, then, you have so lost a father
That you must lose a husband.

CORDELIA
Peace be with Burgundy; since that respects
Of fortune are his love, I shall not be his wife.   240

FRANCE
Fairest Cordelia, that art most rich, being poor;
Most choice, forsaken; and most loved, despised:
Thee and thy virtues here I seize upon.
Be it lawful, I take up what's cast away.
Gods, gods! 'Tis strange that from their cold'st neglect
My love should kindle to inflamed respect.—   246
Thy dowerless daughter, King, thrown to my chance,
Is queen of us, of ours, and our fair France.
Not all the dukes in wat'rish Burgundy
Shall buy this unprized precious maid of me.—   250
Bid them farewell, Cordelia, though unkind.
Thou losest here, a better where to find.

LEAR
Thou hast her, France. Let her be thine, for we
Have no such daughter, nor shall ever see
That face of hers again. Therefore be gone,   255
Without our grace, our love, our benison.—
Come, noble Burgundy.
            ⌜*Flourish.*⌝ *Exeunt Lear and Burgundy, then*
                Albany, Cornwall, Gloucester, ⌜*Edmund,*⌝
                                    and followers

FRANCE (*to Cordelia*)   Bid farewell to your sisters.

CORDELIA
Ye jewels of our father, with washed eyes
Cordelia leaves you. I know you what you are,
And like a sister am most loath to call   260
Your faults as they are named. Use well our father.
To your professèd bosoms I commit him.
But yet, alas, stood I within his grace
I would prefer him to a better place.
So farewell to you both.   265

GONORIL Prescribe not us our duties.

REGAN Let your study
Be to content your lord, who hath received you
At fortune's alms. You have obedience scanted,
And well are worth the worst that you have wanted.

CORDELIA
Time shall unfold what pleated cunning hides.   271
Who covers faults, at last shame them derides.
Well may you prosper.

FRANCE   Come, fair Cordelia.
                    Exeunt France and Cordelia

GONORIL Sister, it is not a little I have to say of what most nearly appertains to us both. I think our father will hence tonight.   276
REGAN That's most certain, and with you. Next month with us.
GONORIL You see how full of changes his age is. The observation we have made of it hath not been little. He always loved our sister most, and with what poor judgement he hath now cast her off appears too gross.
REGAN 'Tis the infirmity of his age; yet he hath ever but slenderly known himself.   284
GONORIL The best and soundest of his time hath been but rash; then must we look to receive from his age not alone the imperfection of long-engrafted condition, but therewithal unruly waywardness that infirm and choleric years bring with them.
REGAN Such unconstant starts are we like to have from him as this of Kent's banishment.   291
GONORIL There is further compliment of leave-taking between France and him. Pray, let's hit together. If our father carry authority with such dispositions as he bears, this last surrender of his will but offend us.   295
REGAN We shall further think on't.
GONORIL We must do something, and i'th' heat.
                                                              Exeunt

Sc. 2   *Enter Edmund the bastard*
EDMUND
   Thou, nature, art my goddess. To thy law
   My services are bound. Wherefore should I
   Stand in the plague of custom and permit
   The curiosity of nations to deprive me
   For that I am some twelve or fourteen moonshines   5
   Lag of a brother? Why 'bastard'? Wherefore 'base',
   When my dimensions are as well compact,
   My mind as generous, and my shape as true
   As honest madam's issue?
   Why brand they us with 'base, base bastardy',   10
   Who in the lusty stealth of nature take
   More composition and fierce quality
   Than doth within a stale, dull-eyed bed go
   To the creating a whole tribe of fops
   Got 'tween a sleep and wake? Well then,   15
   Legitimate Edgar, I must have your land.
   Our father's love is to the bastard Edmund
   As to the legitimate. Well, my legitimate, if
   This letter speed and my invention thrive,
   Edmund the base shall to th' legitimate.   20
   I grow, I prosper. Now gods, stand up for bastards!
   Enter the Duke of Gloucester. Edmund reads
   a letter
GLOUCESTER
   Kent banished thus, and France in choler parted,
   And the King gone tonight, subscribed his power,
   Confined to exhibition—all this done
   Upon the gad?—Edmund, how now? What news?   25
EDMUND So please your lordship, none.
GLOUCESTER Why so earnestly seek you to put up that letter?

EDMUND I know no news, my lord.
GLOUCESTER What paper were you reading?   30
EDMUND Nothing, my lord.
GLOUCESTER No? What needs then that terrible dispatch of it into your pocket? The quality of nothing hath not such need to hide itself. Let's see. Come, if it be nothing I shall not need spectacles.   35
EDMUND I beseech you, sir, pardon me. It is a letter from my brother that I have not all o'er-read; for so much as I have perused, I find it not fit for your liking.
GLOUCESTER Give me the letter, sir.   39
EDMUND I shall offend either to detain or give it. The contents, as in part I understand them, are to blame.
GLOUCESTER Let's see, let's see.
EDMUND I hope for my brother's justification he wrote this but as an assay or taste of my virtue.   44
   He gives Gloucester a letter
GLOUCESTER (*reads*) 'This policy of age makes the world bitter to the best of our times, keeps our fortunes from us till our oldness cannot relish them. I begin to find an idle and fond bondage in the oppression of aged tyranny, who sways not as it hath power but as it is suffered. Come to me, that of this I may speak more. If our father would sleep till I waked him, you should enjoy half his revenue for ever and live the beloved of your brother,
                                        Edgar.'   54
Hum, conspiracy! 'Slept till I waked him, you should enjoy half his revenue'—my son Edgar! Had he a hand to write this, a heart and brain to breed it in? When came this to you? Who brought it?
EDMUND It was not brought me, my lord, there's the cunning of it. I found it thrown in at the casement of my closet.   61
GLOUCESTER You know the character to be your brother's?
EDMUND If the matter were good, my lord, I durst swear it were his; but in respect of that, I would fain think it were not.   65
GLOUCESTER It is his.
EDMUND It is his hand, my lord, but I hope his heart is not in the contents.
GLOUCESTER Hath he never heretofore sounded you in this business?   70
EDMUND Never, my lord; but I have often heard him maintain it to be fit that, sons at perfect age and fathers declining, his father should be as ward to the son, and the son manage the revenue.   74
GLOUCESTER O villain, villain—his very opinion in the letter! Abhorred villain, unnatural, detested, brutish villain—worse than brutish! Go, sir, seek him, ay, apprehend him. Abominable villain! Where is he?
EDMUND I do not well know, my lord. If it shall please you to suspend your indignation against my brother till you can derive from him better testimony of this intent, you should run a certain course; where if you violently proceed against him, mistaking his purpose, it would make a great gap in your own honour and shake in pieces the heart of his obedience. I dare pawn down my life for him he hath wrote this to feel my

affection to your honour, and to no further pretence of danger.

GLOUCESTER Think you so? 89

EDMUND If your honour judge it meet, I will place you where you shall hear us confer of this, and by an auricular assurance have your satisfaction, and that without any further delay than this very evening.

GLOUCESTER He cannot be such a monster.

EDMUND Nor is not, sure. 95

GLOUCESTER To his father, that so tenderly and entirely loves him—heaven and earth! Edmund seek him out, wind me into him. I pray you, frame your business after your own wisdom. I would unstate myself to be in a due resolution. 100

EDMUND I shall seek him, sir, presently, convey the business as I shall see means, and acquaint you withal.

GLOUCESTER These late eclipses in the sun and moon portend no good to us. Though the wisdom of nature can reason thus and thus, yet nature finds itself scourged by the sequent effects. Love cools, friendship falls off, brothers divide; in cities mutinies, in countries discords, palaces treason, the bond cracked between son and father. Find out this villain, Edmund; it shall lose thee nothing. Do it carefully. And the noble and true-hearted Kent banished, his offence honesty! Strange, strange! *Exit*

EDMUND This is the excellent foppery of the world: that when we are sick in fortune—often the surfeit of our own behaviour—we make guilty of our disasters the sun, the moon, and the stars, as if we were villains by necessity, fools by heavenly compulsion, knaves, thieves, and treacherers by spherical predominance, drunkards, liars, and adulterers by an enforced obedience of planetary influence, and all that we are evil in by a divine thrusting on. An admirable evasion of whoremaster man, to lay his goatish disposition to the charge of stars! My father compounded with my mother under the Dragon's tail and my nativity was under Ursa Major, so that it follows I am rough and lecherous. Fut! I should have been that I am had the maidenliest star of the firmament twinkled on my bastardy. Edgar . . . 128

Enter Edgar

and on's cue out he comes, like the catastrophe of the old comedy; mine is villainous melancholy, with a sigh like them of Bedlam.—O, these eclipses do portend these divisions.

EDGAR How now, brother Edmund, what serious contemplation are you in?

EDMUND I am thinking, brother, of a prediction I read this other day, what should follow these eclipses. 136

EDGAR Do you busy yourself about that?

EDMUND I promise you, the effects he writ of succeed unhappily, as of unnaturalness between the child and the parent, death, dearth, dissolutions of ancient amities, divisions in state, menaces and maledictions against king and nobles, needless diffidences, banishment of friends, dissipation of cohorts, nuptial breaches, and I know not what.

EDGAR How long have you been a sectary astronomical?

EDMUND Come, come, when saw you my father last? 146

EDGAR Why, the night gone by.

EDMUND Spake you with him?

EDGAR Two hours together.

EDMUND Parted you in good terms? Found you no displeasure in him by word or countenance? 151

EDGAR None at all.

EDMUND Bethink yourself wherein you may have offended him, and at my entreaty forbear his presence till some little time hath qualified the heat of his displeasure, which at this instant so rageth in him that with the mischief of your person it would scarce allay. 157

EDGAR Some villain hath done me wrong.

EDMUND That's my fear, brother. I advise you to the best. Go armed. I am no honest man if there be any good meaning towards you. I have told you what I have seen and heard but faintly, nothing like the image and horror of it. Pray you, away.

EDGAR Shall I hear from you anon?

EDMUND I do serve you in this business. *Exit Edgar*

A credulous father, and a brother noble, 166
Whose nature is so far from doing harms
That he suspects none; on whose foolish honesty
My practices ride easy. I see the business.
Let me, if not by birth, have lands by wit. 170
All with me's meet that I can fashion fit. *Exit*

Sc. 3 *Enter Gonoril and Oswald, her gentleman*

GONORIL
Did my father strike my gentleman
For chiding of his fool?

OSWALD   Yes, madam.

GONORIL
By day and night he wrongs me. Every hour
He flashes into one gross crime or other
That sets us all at odds. I'll not endure it. 5
His knights grow riotous, and himself upbraids us
On every trifle. When he returns from hunting
I will not speak with him. Say I am sick.
If you come slack of former services
You shall do well; the fault of it I'll answer. 10
    ⌜*Hunting horns within*⌝

OSWALD He's coming, madam. I hear him.

GONORIL
Put on what weary negligence you please,
You and your fellow servants. I'd have it come in question.
If he dislike it, let him to our sister,
Whose mind and mine I know in that are one, 15
Not to be overruled. Idle old man,
That still would manage those authorities
That he hath given away! Now, by my life,
Old fools are babes again, and must be used
With checks as flatteries, when they are seen abused.
Remember what I tell you.

OSWALD   Very well, madam. 21

GONORIL
And let his knights have colder looks among you.

What grows of it, no matter. Advise your fellows so.
I would breed from hence occasions, and I shall,
That I may speak. I'll write straight to my sister   25
To hold my very course. Go prepare for dinner.
                                    Exeunt severally

Sc. 4   *Enter the Earl of Kent, disguised*
KENT
If but as well I other accents borrow
That can my speech diffuse, my good intent
May carry through itself to that full issue
For which I razed my likeness. Now, banished Kent,
If thou canst serve where thou dost stand condemned,
Thy master, whom thou lov'st, shall find thee full of
     labour.   6
     Enter King Lear and servants from hunting
LEAR Let me not stay a jot for dinner. Go get it ready.
                                       ⌈Exit one⌉
(*To Kent*) How now, what art thou?
KENT A man, sir.
LEAR What dost thou profess? What wouldst thou with
     us?   11
KENT I do profess to be no less than I seem, to serve him
     truly that will put me in trust, to love him that is
     honest, to converse with him that is wise and says
     little, to fear judgement, to fight when I cannot choose,
     and to eat no fish.   16
LEAR What art thou?
KENT A very honest-hearted fellow, and as poor as the
     King.
LEAR If thou be as poor for a subject as he is for a king,
     thou'rt poor enough. What wouldst thou?   21
KENT Service.
LEAR Who wouldst thou serve?
KENT You.
LEAR Dost thou know me, fellow?   25
KENT No, sir, but you have that in your countenance
     which I would fain call master.
LEAR What's that?
KENT Authority.
LEAR What services canst do?   30
KENT I can keep honest counsel, ride, run, mar a curious
     tale in telling it, and deliver a plain message bluntly.
     That which ordinary men are fit for I am qualified in;
     and the best of me is diligence.
LEAR How old art thou?   35
KENT Not so young to love a woman for singing, nor so
     old to dote on her for anything. I have years on my
     back forty-eight.
LEAR Follow me. Thou shalt serve me, if I like thee no
     worse after dinner. I will not part from thee yet.—
     Dinner, ho, dinner! Where's my knave, my fool? Go
     you and call my fool hither.   *⌈Exit one⌉*
     Enter Oswald the steward
You, sirrah, where's my daughter?
OSWALD So please you—   *Exit*
LEAR What says the fellow there? Call the clotpoll back.
                              Exeunt Servant ⌈and Kent⌉

Where's my fool? Ho, I think the world's asleep.
     Enter the Earl of Kent ⌈and a Servant⌉
How now, where's that mongrel?
KENT He says, my lord, your daughter is not well.
LEAR Why came not the slave back to me when I called
     him?   50
SERVANT Sir, he answered me in' the roundest manner he
     would not.
LEAR A would not?
SERVANT My lord, I know not what the matter is, but to
     my judgement your highness is not entertained with
     that ceremonious affection as you were wont. There's
     a great abatement appears as well in the general
     dependants as in the Duke himself also, and your
     daughter.
LEAR Ha, sayst thou so?   60
SERVANT I beseech you pardon me, my lord, if I be
     mistaken, for my duty cannot be silent when I think
     your highness wronged.
LEAR Thou but rememberest me of mine own conception.
     I have perceived a most faint neglect of late, which I
     have rather blamed as mine own jealous curiosity than
     as a very pretence and purport of unkindness. I will
     look further into't. But where's this fool? I have not
     seen him these two days.
SERVANT Since my young lady's going into France, sir,
     the fool hath much pined away.   71
LEAR No more of that, I have noted it. Go you and tell
     my daughter I would speak with her.   *⌈Exit one⌉*
     Go you, call hither my fool.   *⌈Exit one⌉*
     Enter Oswald the steward ⌈crossing the stage⌉
O you, sir, you, sir, come you hither. Who am I, sir?
OSWALD My lady's father.   76
LEAR My lady's father? My lord's knave, you whoreson
     dog, you slave, you cur!
OSWALD I am none of this, my lord, I beseech you pardon
     me.   80
LEAR Do you bandy looks with me, you rascal?
     ⌈Lear strikes him⌉
OSWALD I'll not be struck, my lord—
KENT (*tripping him*) Nor tripped neither, you base football
     player.
LEAR (*to Kent*) I thank thee, fellow. Thou serv'st me, and
     I'll love thee.   86
KENT (*to Oswald*) Come, sir, I'll teach you differences.
     Away, away. If you will measure your lubber's length
     again, tarry; but away if you have wisdom.
                                         Exit Oswald
LEAR Now, friendly knave, I thank thee.   90
     Enter Lear's Fool
There's earnest of thy service.
     He gives Kent money
FOOL Let me hire him, too. (*To Kent*) Here's my coxcomb.
LEAR How now, my pretty knave, how dost thou?
FOOL (*to Kent*) Sirrah, you were best take my coxcomb.
KENT Why, fool?   95
FOOL Why, for taking one's part that's out of favour. Nay,
     an thou canst not smile as the wind sits, thou'lt catch

cold shortly. There, take my coxcomb. Why, this fellow hath banished two on's daughters and done the third a blessing against his will. If thou follow him, thou must needs wear my coxcomb. (*To Lear*) How now, nuncle? Would I had two coxcombs and two daughters.

LEAR Why, my boy?

FOOL If I gave them my living I'd keep my coxcombs myself. There's mine; beg another off thy daughters.

LEAR Take heed, sirrah—the whip.   106

FOOL Truth is a dog that must to kennel. He must be whipped out when Lady the brach may stand by the fire and stink.

LEAR A pestilent gall to me!   110

FOOL ⌈*to Kent*⌉ Sirrah, I'll teach thee a speech.

LEAR Do.

FOOL Mark it, uncle.
  Have more than thou showest,
  Speak less than thou knowest,   115
  Lend less than thou owest,
  Ride more than thou goest,
  Learn more than thou trowest,
  Set less than thou throwest,
  Leave thy drink and thy whore,   120
  And keep in-a-door,
  And thou shalt have more
  Than two tens to a score.

LEAR This is nothing, fool.   124

FOOL Then, like the breath of an unfee'd lawyer, you gave me nothing for't. Can you make no use of nothing, uncle?

LEAR Why no, boy. Nothing can be made out of nothing.

FOOL (*to Kent*) Prithee, tell him so much the rent of his land comes to. He will not believe a fool.   130

LEAR A bitter fool.

FOOL Dost know the difference, my boy, between a bitter fool and a sweet fool?

LEAR No, lad. Teach me.

FOOL ⌈*sings*⌉ That lord that counselled thee   135
  To give away thy land,
  Come, place him here by me;
  Do thou for him stand.
  The sweet and bitter fool
  Will presently appear,   140
  The one in motley here,
  The other found out there.

LEAR Dost thou call me fool, boy?

FOOL All thy other titles thou hast given away. That thou wast born with.   145

KENT (*to Lear*) This is not altogether fool, my lord.

FOOL No, faith; lords and great men will not let me. If I had a monopoly out, they would have part on't, and ladies too, they will not let me have all the fool to myself—they'll be snatching. Give me an egg, nuncle, and I'll give thee two crowns.   151

LEAR What two crowns shall they be?

FOOL Why, after I have cut the egg in the middle and eat up the meat, the two crowns of the egg. When thou clovest thy crown i'th' middle and gavest away both parts, thou borest thy ass o'th' back o'er the dirt. Thou hadst little wit in thy bald crown when thou gavest thy golden one away. If I speak like myself in this, let him be whipped that first finds it so.

⌈*Sings*⌉
  Fools had ne'er less wit in a year,   160
   For wise men are grown foppish.
  They know not how their wits do wear,
   Their manners are so apish.

LEAR When were you wont to be so full of songs, sirrah?

FOOL I have used it, nuncle, ever since thou madest thy daughters thy mother; for when thou gavest them the rod and puttest down thine own breeches,

⌈*Sings*⌉ Then they for sudden joy did weep,
   And I for sorrow sung,
  That such a king should play bo-peep   170
   And go the fools among.

Prithee, nuncle, keep a schoolmaster that can teach thy fool to lie. I would fain learn to lie.

LEAR An you lie, we'll have you whipped.   174

FOOL I marvel what kin thou and thy daughters are. They'll have me whipped for speaking true, thou wilt have me whipped for lying, and sometime I am whipped for holding my peace. I had rather be any kind of thing than a fool; and yet I would not be thee, nuncle. Thou hast pared thy wit o' both sides and left nothing in the middle.   181

Enter Gonoril

Here comes one of the parings.

LEAR
How now, daughter, what makes that frontlet on?
Methinks you are too much o' late i'th' frown.   184

FOOL Thou wast a pretty fellow when thou hadst no need to care for her frown. Now thou art an O without a figure. I am better than thou art, now. I am a fool; thou art nothing. ⌈*To Gonoril*⌉ Yes, forsooth, I will hold my tongue; so your face bids me, though you say nothing.   190

⌈*Sings*⌉ Mum, mum.
  He that keeps neither crust nor crumb,
  Weary of all, shall want some.

That's a shelled peascod.

GONORIL (*to Lear*)
Not only, sir, this your all-licensed fool,   195
But other of your insolent retinue .
Do hourly carp and quarrel, breaking forth
In rank and not-to-be-endurèd riots.
Sir, I had thought by making this well known unto
 you
To have found a safe redress, but now grow fearful, 200
By what yourself too late have spoke and done,
That you protect this course, and put it on
By your allowance; which if you should, the fault
Would not scape censure, nor the redress sleep
Which in the tender of a wholesome weal   205
Might in their working do you that offence,
That else were shame, that then necessity
Must call discreet proceedings.

FOOL (*to Lear*) For, you trow, nuncle,
⌐*Sings*⌐
       The hedge-sparrow fed the cuckoo so long   210
       That it had it head bit off by it young;
so out went the candle, and we were left darkling.
LEAR (*to Gonoril*) Are you our daughter?
GONORIL
  Come, sir, I would you would make use of that good
    wisdom
  Whereof I know you are fraught, and put away   215
  These dispositions that of late transform you
  From what you rightly are.
FOOL May not an ass know when the cart draws the
  horse? ⌐*Sings*⌐ 'Whoop, jug, I love thee!'
LEAR
  Doth any here know me? Why, this is not Lear.   220
  Doth Lear walk thus, speak thus? Where are his eyes?
  Either his notion weakens, or his discernings
  Are lethargied. Sleeping or waking, ha?
  Sure, 'tis not so.
  Who is it that can tell me who I am?   225
  Lear's shadow? I would learn that, for by the marks
  Of sovereignty, knowledge, and reason
  I should be false persuaded I had daughters.
FOOL Which they will make an obedient father.
LEAR (*to Gonoril*)
  Your name, fair gentlewoman?
GONORIL   Come, sir,   230
  This admiration is much of the savour
  Of other your new pranks. I do beseech you
  Understand my purposes aright,
  As you are old and reverend, should be wise.
  Here do you keep a hundred knights and squires,   235
  Men so disordered, so debauched and bold
  That this our court, infected with their manners,
  Shows like a riotous inn, epicurism
  And lust make more like to a tavern, or brothel,
  Than a great palace. The shame itself doth speak   240
  For instant remedy. Be thou desired,
  By her that else will take the thing she begs,
  A little to disquantity your train,
  And the remainder that shall still depend
  To be such men as may besort your age,   245
  That know themselves and you.
LEAR   Darkness and devils!
  Saddle my horses, call my train together!—
                 ⌐*Exit one or more*⌐
  Degenerate bastard, I'll not trouble thee.
  Yet have I left a daughter.
GONORIL
  You strike my people, and your disordered rabble   250
  Make servants of their betters.
    Enter the Duke of Albany
LEAR
  We tnat too late repent's—O sir, are you come?
  Is it your will that we—prepare my horses.
                 ⌐*Exit one or more*⌐
  Ingratitude, thou marble-hearted fiend,

More hideous when thou show'st thee in a child   255
Than the sea-monster—(*to Gonoril*) detested kite, thou
  liest.
My train are men of choice and rarest parts,
That all particulars of duty know,
And in the most exact regard support
The worships of their name. O most small fault,   260
How ugly didst thou in Cordelia show,
That, like an engine, wrenched my frame of nature
From the fixed place, drew from my heart all love,
And added to the gall! O Lear, Lear!
Beat at this gate that let thy folly in   265
And thy dear judgement out.—Go, go, my people!
ALBANY
  My lord, I am guiltless as I am ignorant.
LEAR
  It may be so, my lord. Hark, nature, hear:
  Dear goddess, suspend thy purpose if
  Thou didst intend to make this creature fruitful.   270
  Into her womb convey sterility.
  Dry up in her the organs of increase,
  And from her derogate body never spring
  A babe to honour her. If she must teem,
  Create her child of spleen, that it may live   275
  And be a thwart disnatured torment to her.
  Let it stamp wrinkles in her brow of youth,
  With cadent tears fret channels in her cheeks,
  Turn all her mother's pains and benefits
  To laughter and contempt, that she may feel—   280
  That she may feel
  How sharper than a serpent's tooth it is
  To have a thankless child.—Go, go, my people!
      Exeunt Lear, ⌐Kent, Fool, and servants⌐
ALBANY
  Now, gods that we adore, whereof comes this?
GONORIL
  Never afflict yourself to know the cause,   285
  But let his disposition have that scope
  That dotage gives it.
      Enter King Lear ⌐and his Fool⌐
LEAR
  What, fifty of my followers at a clap?
  Within a fortnight?
ALBANY   What is the matter, sir?
LEAR
  I'll tell thee. (*To Gonoril*) Life and death! I am
    ashamed   290
  That thou hast power to shake my manhood thus,
  That these hot tears, that break from me perforce
  And should make thee—worst blasts and fogs upon
    thee!
  Untented woundings of a father's curse
  Pierce every sense about thee! Old fond eyes,   295
  Beweep this cause again I'll pluck you out
  And cast you, with the waters that you make,
  To temper clay. Yea,
  Is't come to this? Yet have I left a daughter
  Whom, I am sure, is kind and comfortable.   300

When she shall hear this of thee, with her nails
She'll flay thy wolvish visage. Thou shalt find
That I'll resume the shape which thou dost think
I have cast off for ever; thou shalt, I warrant thee.
                                                  Exit
GONORIL Do you mark that, my lord?   305
ALBANY
  I cannot be so partial, Gonoril,
  To the great love I bear you—
GONORIL   Come, sir, no more.—
  You, more knave than fool, after your master!
FOOL Nuncle Lear, nuncle Lear, tarry, and take the fool
  with thee.   310
      A fox when one has caught her,
      And such a daughter,
      Should sure to the slaughter,
      If my cap would buy a halter.
      So, the fool follows after.   *Exit*
GONORIL What, Oswald, ho!   316
      Enter Oswald
OSWALD Here, madam.
GONORIL
  What, have you writ this letter to my sister?
OSWALD Yes, madam.
GONORIL
  Take you some company, and away to horse.   320
  Inform her full of my particular fears,
  And thereto add such reasons of your own
  As may compact it more. Get you gone,
  And after, your retinue.   *Exit Oswald*
                    Now, my lord,
  This milky gentleness and course of yours,   325
  Though I dislike not, yet under pardon
  You're much more ataxed for want of wisdom
  Than praised for harmful mildness.
ALBANY
  How far your eyes may pierce I cannot tell.
  Striving to better aught, we mar what's well.   330
GONORIL Nay, then—
ALBANY Well, well, the event.   *Exeunt*

Sc. 5 *Enter King Lear, the Earl of Kent disguised, and*
        Lear's Fool
LEAR ⌈*to Kent*⌉ Go you before to Gloucester with these
  letters. Acquaint my daughter no further with anything
  you know than comes from her demand out of the
  letter. If your diligence be not speedy, I shall be there
  before you.   5
KENT I will not sleep, my lord, till I have delivered your
  letter.   *Exit*
FOOL If a man's brains were in his heels, were't not in
  danger of kibes?
LEAR Ay, boy.   10
FOOL Then, I prithee, be merry: thy wit shall ne'er go
  slipshod.
LEAR Ha, ha, ha!
FOOL Shalt see thy other daughter will use thee kindly,

for though she's as like this as a crab is like an apple,
  yet I con what I can tell.   16
LEAR Why, what canst thou tell, my boy?
FOOL She'll taste as like this as a crab doth to a crab.
  Thou canst not tell why one's nose stands in the middle
  of his face?   20
LEAR No.
FOOL Why, to keep his eyes on either side 's nose, that
  what a man cannot smell out, a may spy into.
LEAR I did her wrong.
FOOL Canst tell how an oyster makes his shell?   25
LEAR No.
FOOL Nor I neither; but I can tell why a snail has a
  house.
LEAR Why?
FOOL Why, to put his head in, not to give it away to his
  daughter and leave his horns without a case.   31
LEAR
  I will forget my nature. So kind a father!
  Be my horses ready?
FOOL Thy asses are gone about them. The reason why
  the seven stars are no more than seven is a pretty
  reason.   36
LEAR Because they are not eight.
FOOL Yes. Thou wouldst make a good fool.
LEAR
  To take't again perforce—monster ingratitude!
FOOL If thou wert my fool, nuncle, I'd have thee beaten
  for being old before thy time.   41
LEAR How's that?
FOOL Thou shouldst not have been old before thou hadst
  been wise.
LEAR
  O, let me not be mad, sweet heaven!   45
  I would not be mad.
  Keep me in temper. I would not be mad.
      Enter a Servant
  Are the horses ready?
SERVANT   Ready, my lord.
LEAR (*to Fool*) Come, boy.   *Exeunt Lear and Servant*
FOOL
  She that is maid now, and laughs at my departure, 50
  Shall not be a maid long, except things be cut shorter.
                                                  Exit

Sc. 6 *Enter Edmund the bastard, and Curan, meeting*
EDMUND Save thee, Curan.
CURAN And you, sir. I have been with your father, and
  given him notice that the Duke of Cornwall and his
  duchess will be here with him tonight.
EDMUND How comes that?   5
CURAN Nay, I know not. You have heard of the news
  abroad?—I mean the whispered ones, for there are yet
  but ear-bussing arguments.
EDMUND Not. I pray you, what are they?
CURAN Have you heard of no likely wars towards twixt
  the two Dukes of Cornwall and Albany?   11

EDMUND Not a word.

CURAN You may then in time. Fare you well, sir.   *Exit*

EDMUND

The Duke be here tonight! The better, best.

This weaves itself perforce into my business.   15

   ⌈*Enter Edgar at a window above*⌉

My father hath set guard to take my brother,

And I have one thing of a queasy question

Which must ask briefness. Wit and fortune help!—

Brother, a word. Descend, brother, I say.

   ⌈*Edgar climbs down*⌉

My father watches. O, fly this place.   20

Intelligence is given where you are hid.

You have now the good advantage of the night.

Have you not spoken 'gainst the Duke of Cornwall

   aught?

He's coming hither now, in the night, i'th' haste,

And Regan with him. Have you nothing said   25

Upon his party against the Duke of Albany?

Advise you—

EDGAR   I am sure on't, not a word.

EDMUND

I hear my father coming. Pardon me.

In cunning I must draw my sword upon you.

Seem to defend yourself. Now, quit you well.   30

(*Calling*) Yield, come before my father. Light here,

   here!

(*To Edgar*) Fly, brother, fly! (*Calling*) Torches, torches!

   (*To Edgar*) So, farewell.   *Exit Edgar*

Some blood drawn on me would beget opinion

Of my more fierce endeavour.

   He wounds his arm

                I have seen

Drunkards do more than this in sport. (*Calling*) Father,

   father!   35

Stop, stop! Ho, help!

   Enter the Duke of Gloucester ⌈*and others*⌉

GLOUCESTER   Now, Edmund, where is the villain?

EDMUND

Here stood he in the dark, his sharp sword out,

Warbling of wicked charms, conjuring the moon

To stand 's auspicious mistress.

GLOUCESTER   But where is he?

EDMUND

Look, sir, I bleed.

GLOUCESTER   Where is the villain, Edmund?   40

EDMUND

Fled this way, sir, when by no means he could—

GLOUCESTER

Pursue him, go after.   *Exeunt others*

           By no means what?

EDMUND

Persuade me to the murder of your lordship,

But that I told him the revengive gods

'Gainst parricides did all their thunders bend,   45

Spoke with how manifold and strong a bond

The child was bound to the father. Sir, in fine,

Seeing how loathly opposite I stood

To his unnatural purpose, with fell motion,

With his preparèd sword he charges home   50

My unprovided body, lanced mine arm;

But when he saw my best alarumed spirits

Bold in the quarrel's rights, roused to the encounter,

Or whether ghasted by the noise I made

Or ⌈   ⌉ I know not,   55

But suddenly he fled.

GLOUCESTER   Let him fly far,

Not in this land shall he remain uncaught,

And found, dispatch. The noble Duke my master,

My worthy arch and patron, comes tonight.

By his authority I will proclaim it   60

That he which finds him shall deserve our thanks,

Bringing the murderous caitiff to the stake;

He that conceals him, death.

EDMUND

When I dissuaded him from his intent

And found him pitched to do it, with curst speech   65

I threatened to discover him. He replied,

'Thou unpossessing bastard, dost thou think

If I would stand against thee, could the reposure

Of any trust, virtue, or worth in thee

Make thy words faithed? No, what I should deny—   70

As this I would, ay, though thou didst produce

My very character—I'd turn it all

To thy suggestion, plot, and damned pretence,

And thou must make a dullard of the world

If they not thought the profits of my death   75

Were very pregnant and potential spurs

To make thee seek it.'

GLOUCESTER   Strong and fastened villain!

Would he deny his letter? I never got him.

   Trumpets within

Hark, the Duke's trumpets. I know not why he

   comes.

All ports I'll bar. The villain shall not scape.   80

The Duke must grant me that; besides, his picture

I will send far and near, that all the kingdom

May have note of him—and of my land,

Loyal and natural boy, I'll work the means

To make thee capable.   85

   Enter the Duke of Cornwall and Regan

CORNWALL

How now, my noble friend? Since I came hither,

Which I can call but now, I have heard strange news.

REGAN

If it be true, all vengeance comes too short

Which can pursue the offender. How dost, my lord?

GLOUCESTER

Madam, my old heart is cracked, is cracked.   90

REGAN

What, did my father's godson seek your life?

He whom my father named, your Edgar?

GLOUCESTER

Ay, lady, lady; shame would have it hid.

REGAN
Was he not companion with the riotous knights
That tend upon my father? 95
GLOUCESTER
I know not, madam. 'Tis too bad, too bad.
EDMUND Yes, madam, he was.
REGAN
No marvel, then, though he were ill affected.
'Tis they have put him on the old man's death,
To have the spoil and waste of his revenues. 100
I have this present evening from my sister
Been well informed of them, and with such cautions
That if they come to sojourn at my house
I'll not be there.
CORNWALL   Nor I, assure thee, Regan.
Edmund, I heard that you have shown your father 105
A childlike office.
EDMUND   'Twas my duty, sir.
GLOUCESTER (to Cornwall)
He did betray his practice, and received
This hurt you see striving to apprehend him.
CORNWALL
Is he pursued?
GLOUCESTER   Ay, my good lord.
CORNWALL
If he be taken, he shall never more 110
Be feared of doing harm. Make your own purpose
How in my strength you please. For you, Edmund,
Whose virtue and obedience doth this instant
So much commend itself, you shall be ours.
Natures of such deep trust we shall much need. 115
You we first seize on.
EDMUND   I shall serve you truly,
However else.
GLOUCESTER (to Cornwall) For him I thank your grace.
CORNWALL
You know not why we came to visit you—
REGAN
This out-of-season threat'ning dark-eyed night—
Occasions, noble Gloucester, of some poise, 120
Wherein we must have use of your advice.
Our father he hath writ, so hath our sister,
Of differences which I least thought it fit
To answer from our home. The several messengers
From hence attend dispatch. Our good old friend, 125
Lay comforts to your bosom, and bestow
Your needful counsel to our business,
Which craves the instant use.
GLOUCESTER I serve you, madam. 129
Your graces are right welcome. *Exeunt*

Sc. 7 *Enter the Earl of Kent, disguised, at one door, and*
      Oswald the steward, at another door
OSWALD Good even to thee, friend. Art of the house?
KENT Ay.
OSWALD Where may we set our horses?
KENT I'th' mire.
OSWALD Prithee, if thou love me, tell me. 5

KENT I love thee not.
OSWALD Why then, I care not for thee.
KENT If I had thee in Lipsbury pinfold I would make thee
care for me.
OSWALD Why dost thou use me thus? I know thee not. 10
KENT Fellow, I know thee.
OSWALD What dost thou know me for?
KENT A knave, a rascal, an eater of broken meats, a base,
proud, shallow, beggarly, three-suited, hundred-pound,
filthy worsted-stocking knave; a lily-livered, action-
taking knave; a whoreson, glass-gazing, superfinical
rogue; one-trunk-inheriting slave; one that wouldst be
a bawd in way of good service, and art nothing but
the composition of a knave, beggar, coward, pander,
and the son and heir of a mongrel bitch, whom I will
beat into clamorous whining if thou deny the least
syllable of the addition. 22
OSWALD What a monstrous fellow art thou, thus to rail
on one that's neither known of thee nor knows thee!
KENT What a brazen-faced varlet art thou, to deny thou
knowest me! Is it two days ago since I beat thee and
tripped up thy heels before the King? Draw, you rogue;
for though it be night, the moon shines.
      ⌈*He draws his sword*⌉
I'll make a sop of the moonshine o' you. Draw, you
whoreson, cullionly barber-monger, draw! 30
OSWALD Away. I have nothing to do with thee.
KENT Draw, you rascal. You bring letters against the
King, and take Vanity the puppet's part against the
royalty of her father. Draw, you rogue, or I'll so
carbonado your shanks—draw, you rascal, come your
ways! 36
OSWALD Help, ho, murder, help!
KENT Strike, you slave! Stand, rogue! Stand, you neat
slave, strike!
OSWALD Help, ho, murder, help! 40
      Enter Edmund the bastard with his rapier drawn,
      ⌈*then*⌉ *the Duke of Gloucester, ⌈then⌉ the Duke of*
      Cornwall and Regan the Duchess
EDMUND ⌈*parting them*⌉ How now, what's the matter?
KENT With you, goodman boy. An you please come, I'll
flesh you. Come on, young master.
GLOUCESTER Weapons? Arms? What's the matter here?
CORNWALL Keep peace, upon your lives. He dies that
strikes again. What's the matter? 46
REGAN The messengers from our sister and the King.
CORNWALL (to Kent and Oswald) What's your difference?
Speak.
OSWALD I am scarce in breath, my lord. 50
KENT No marvel, you have so bestirred your valour, you
cowardly rascal. Nature disclaims in thee; a tailor made
thee.
CORNWALL Thou art a strange fellow—a tailor make a
man? 55
KENT Ay, a tailor, sir. A stone-cutter or a painter could
not have made him so ill though he had been but two
hours at the trade.
GLOUCESTER Speak yet; how grew your quarrel?

OSWALD This ancient ruffian, sir, whose life I have spared
   at suit of his grey beard—   61
KENT Thou whoreson Z, thou unnecessary letter—(to
   Cornwall) my lord, if you'll give me leave I will tread
   this unbolted villain into mortar and daub the walls
   of a jakes with him. (To Oswald) Spare my grey beard,
   you wagtail?   66
CORNWALL
   Peace, sir. You beastly knave, have you no reverence?
KENT
   Yes, sir, but anger has a privilege.
CORNWALL Why art thou angry?
KENT
   That such a slave as this should wear a sword,   70
   That wears no honesty. Such smiling rogues
   As these, like rats, oft bite those cords in twain
   Which are too entrenched to unloose, smooth every
      passion
   That in the natures of their lords rebel,
   Bring oil to fire, snow to their colder moods,   75
   Renege, affirm, and turn their halcyon beaks
   With every gale and vary of their masters,
   Knowing naught, like dogs, but following.
   (To Oswald) A plague upon your epileptic visage!
   Smile you my speeches as I were a fool?   80
   Goose, an I had you upon Sarum Plain
   I'd send you cackling home to Camelot.
CORNWALL
   What, art thou mad, old fellow?
GLOUCESTER ⌈to Kent⌉   How fell you out? Say that.
KENT
   No contraries hold more antipathy
   Than I and such a knave.
CORNWALL   Why dost thou call him knave?
   What's his offence?
KENT   His countenance likes me not.   86
CORNWALL
   No more perchance does mine, or his, or hers.
KENT
   Sir, 'tis my occupation to be plain:
   I have seen better faces in my time
   Than stands on any shoulder that I see   90
   Before me at this instant.
CORNWALL   This is a fellow
   Who, having been praised for bluntness, doth affect
   A saucy roughness, and constrains the garb
   Quite from his nature. He cannot flatter, he.
   He must be plain, he must speak truth.   95
   An they will take't, so; if not, he's plain.
   These kind of knaves I know, which in this plainness
   Harbour more craft and more corrupter ends
   Than twenty silly-ducking observants
   That stretch their duties nicely.   100
KENT
   Sir, in good sooth, or in sincere verity,
   Under the allowance of your grand aspect,
   Whose influence, like the wreath of radiant fire
   In flickering Phoebus' front—
CORNWALL   What mean'st thou by this?

KENT To go out of my dialect, which you discommend so
   much. I know, sir, I am no flatterer. He that beguiled
   you in a plain accent was a plain knave, which for my
   part I will not be, though I should win your displeasure
   to entreat me to't.
CORNWALL (to Oswald)
   What's the offence you gave him?
OSWALD   I never gave him any.
   It pleased the King his master very late   111
   To strike at me upon his misconstruction,
   When he, conjunct, and flattering his displeasure,
   Tripped me behind; being down, insulted, railed,
   And put upon him such a deal of man that   115
   That worthied him, got praises of the King
   For him attempting who was self-subdued,
   And in the fleshment of this dread exploit
   Drew on me here again.
KENT   None of these rogues and cowards
   But Ajax is their fool.
CORNWALL ⌈calling⌉   Bring forth the stocks, ho!—   120
   You stubborn, ancient knave, you reverend braggart,
   We'll teach you.
KENT   I am too old to learn.
   Call not your stocks for me. I serve the King,
   On whose employments I was sent to you.
   You should do small respect, show too bold malice   125
   Against the grace and person of my master,
   Stocking his messenger.
CORNWALL ⌈calling⌉   Fetch forth the stocks!—
   As I have life and honour, there shall he sit till noon.
REGAN
   Till noon?—till night, my lord, and all night too.
KENT
   Why, madam, if I were your father's dog   130
   You could not use me so.
REGAN   Sir, being his knave, I will.
          ⌈Stocks brought out⌉
CORNWALL
   This is a fellow of the selfsame nature
   Our sister speaks of.—Come, bring away the stocks.
GLOUCESTER
   Let me beseech your grace not to do so.
   His fault is much, and the good King his master   135
   Will check him for't. Your purposed low correction
   Is such as basest and contemnèd wretches
   For pilf'rings and most common trespasses
   Are punished with. The King must take it ill
   That he's so slightly valued in his messenger,   140
   Should have him thus restrained.
CORNWALL   I'll answer that.
REGAN
   My sister may receive it much more worse
   To have her gentlemen abused, assaulted,
   For following her affairs. Put in his legs.
          They put Kent in the stocks
   Come, my good lord, away!   145
          Exeunt all but Gloucester and Kent
GLOUCESTER
   I am sorry for thee, friend. 'Tis the Duke's pleasure,

Whose disposition, all the world well knows,
Will not be rubbed nor stopped. I'll entreat for thee.
KENT
Pray you, do not, sir. I have watched and travelled
hard.
Some time I shall sleep out; the rest I'll whistle.   150
A good man's fortune may grow out at heels.
Give you good morrow.
GLOUCESTER
The Duke's to blame in this; 'twill be ill took.   *Exit*
KENT
Good King, that must approve the common say:
Thou out of heaven's benediction com'st   155
To the warm sun.
        ⌈*He takes out a letter*⌉
Approach, thou beacon to this under globe,
That by thy comfortable beams I may
Peruse this letter. Nothing almost sees miracles
But misery. I know 'tis from Cordelia,   160
Who hath now fortunately been informed
Of my obscurèd course, and shall find time
For this enormous state, seeking to give
Losses their remedies. All weary and overwatched,
Take vantage, heavy eyes, not to behold   165
This shameful lodging. Fortune, good night;
Smile; once more turn thy wheel.   *He sleeps*
        Enter Edgar
EDGAR   I heard myself proclaimed,
And by the happy hollow of a tree
Escaped the hunt. No port is free, no place
That guard and most unusual vigilance   170
Does not attend my taking. While I may scape
I will preserve myself, and am bethought
To take the basest and most poorest shape
That ever penury in contempt of man
Brought near to beast. My face I'll grime with filth,   175
Blanket my loins, elf all my hair with knots,
And with presented nakedness outface
The wind and persecution of the sky.
The country gives me proof and precedent
Of Bedlam beggars who with roaring voices   180
Strike in their numbed and mortified bare arms
Pins, wooden pricks, nails, sprigs of rosemary,
And with this horrible object from low farms,
Poor pelting villages, sheep-cotes and mills
Sometime with lunatic bans, sometime with prayers   185
Enforce their charity. 'Poor Tuelygod, Poor Tom!'
That's something yet. Edgar I nothing am.   *Exit*
        Enter King Lear, his Fool, and a Knight
LEAR
'Tis strange that they should so depart from home
And not send back my messenger.
KNIGHT   As I learned,
The night before there was no purpose   190
Of his remove.
KENT (*waking*)   Hail to thee, noble master.
LEAR
How! Mak'st thou this shame thy pastime?

FOOL Ha, ha, look, he wears cruel garters! Horses are
tied by the heads, dogs and bears by th' neck, monkeys
by th' loins, and men by th' legs. When a man's over-
lusty at legs, then he wears wooden nether-stocks.   196
LEAR (*to Kent*)
What's he that hath so much thy place mistook
To set thee here?
KENT   It is both he and she:
Your son and daughter.
LEAR   No.
KENT   Yes.
LEAR   No, I say.
KENT
I say yea.
LEAR   No, no, they would not.
KENT   Yes, they have.   200
LEAR
By Jupiter, I swear no. They durst not do't,
They would not, could not do't. 'Tis worse than murder,
To do upon respect such violent outrage.
Resolve me with all modest haste which way
Thou mayst deserve or they propose this usage,   205
Coming from us.
KENT   My lord, when at their home
I did commend your highness' letters to them,
Ere I was risen from the place that showed
My duty kneeling, came there a reeking post
Stewed in his haste, half breathless, panting forth   210
From Gonoril, his mistress, salutations,
Delivered letters spite of intermission,
Which presently they read, on whose contents
They summoned up their meiny, straight took horse,
Commanded me to follow and attend   215
The leisure of their answer, gave me cold looks;
And meeting here the other messenger,
Whose welcome I perceived had poisoned mine—
Being the very fellow that of late
Displayed so saucily against your highness—   220
Having more man than wit about me, drew.
He raised the house with loud and coward cries.
Your son and daughter found this trespass worth
This shame which here it suffers.
LEAR
O, how this mother swells up toward my heart!   225
Histerica passio, down, thou climbing sorrow;
Thy element's below.—Where is this daughter?
KENT
With the Earl, sir, within.
LEAR   Follow me not; stay there.
                                                        Exit
KNIGHT (*to Kent*)
Made you no more offence than what you speak of?
KENT
No. How chance the King comes with so small a train?
FOOL An thou hadst been set in the stocks for that
question, thou hadst well deserved it.   232
KENT Why, fool?
FOOL We'll set thee to school to an ant, to teach thee

there's no labouring in the winter. All that follow their
noses are led by their eyes but blind men, and there's
not a nose among a hundred but can smell him that's
stinking. Let go thy hold when a great wheel runs
down a hill, lest it break thy neck with following it;
but the great one that goes up the hill, let him draw
thee after. When a wise man gives thee better counsel,
give me mine again. I would have none but knaves
follow it, since a fool gives it.

⌜Sings⌝ That sir that serves for gain
    And follows but for form,   245
    Will pack when it begin to rain,
    And leave thee in the storm.

    But I will tarry, the fool will stay,
    And let the wise man fly.
    The knave turns fool that runs away, 250
    The fool no knave, pardie.

KENT Where learnt you this, fool?
FOOL Not in the stocks.
   Enter King Lear and the Duke of Gloucester
LEAR
Deny to speak with me? They're sick, they're weary?
They travelled hard tonight?—mere insolence, 255
Ay, the images of revolt and flying off.
Fetch me a better answer.
GLOUCESTER   My dear lord,
You know the fiery quality of the Duke,
How unremovable and fixed he is   259
In his own course.
LEAR Vengeance, death, plague, confusion!
What 'fiery quality'? Why, Gloucester, Gloucester, I'd
Speak with the Duke of Cornwall and his wife.
GLOUCESTER Ay, my good lord.
LEAR
The King would speak with Cornwall; the dear father
Would with his daughter speak, commands, tends
  service.   265
'Fiery'? The Duke?—tell the hot Duke that Lear—
No, but not yet. Maybe he is not well.
Infirmity doth still neglect all office
Whereto our health is bound. We are not ourselves
When nature, being oppressed, commands the mind
To suffer with the body. I'll forbear, 271
And am fallen out with my more headier will,
To take the indisposed and sickly fit
For the sound man.—Death on my state,
Wherefore should he sit here? This act persuades me
That this remotion of the Duke and her 276
Is practice only. Give me my servant forth.
Tell the Duke and 's wife I'll speak with them,
Now, presently. Bid them come forth and hear me,
Or at their chamber door I'll beat the drum 280
Till it cry sleep to death.
GLOUCESTER   I would have all well
Betwixt you.   *Exit*
LEAR O, my heart, my heart!
FOOL Cry to it, nuncle, as the cockney did to the eels

when she put 'em i'th' paste alive. She rapped 'em
o'th' coxcombs with a stick, and cried 'Down, wantons,
down!' 'Twas her brother that, in pure kindness to his
horse, buttered his hay.
  Enter the Duke of Cornwall and Regan, the Duke of
   Gloucester, and others
LEAR Good morrow to you both.
CORNWALL Hail to your grace.
  ⌜*Kent here set at liberty*⌝
REGAN I am glad to see your highness. 290
LEAR
Regan, I think you are. I know what reason
I have to think so. If thou shouldst not be glad
I would divorce me from thy mother's shrine,
Sepulchring an adultress. (*To Kent*) Yea, are you free?
Some other time for that.—Belovèd Regan, 295
Thy sister is naught. O, Regan, she hath tied
Sharp-toothed unkindness like a vulture here.
I can scarce speak to thee. Thou'lt not believe
Of how depraved a quality—O, Regan!
REGAN
I pray you, sir, take patience. I have hope 300
You less know how to value her desert
Than she to slack her duty.
LEAR My curses on her.
REGAN O sir, you are old.
Nature in you stands on the very verge 305
Of her confine. You should be ruled and led
By some discretion that discerns your state
Better than you yourself. Therefore I pray
That to our sister you do make return;
Say you have wronged her, sir
LEAR   Ask her forgiveness? 310
Do you mark how this becomes the house?
⌜*Kneeling*⌝ 'Dear daughter, I confess that I am old.
Age is unnecessary. On my knees I beg
That you'll vouchsafe me raiment, bed, and food.'
REGAN
Good sir, no more. These are unsightly tricks. 315
Return you to my sister.
LEAR ⌜*rising*⌝   No, Regan.
She hath abated me of half my train,
Looked black upon me, struck me with her tongue
Most serpent-like upon the very heart.
All the stored vengeances of heaven fall 320
On her ungrateful top! Strike her young bones,
You taking airs, with lameness!
CORNWALL   Fie, fie, sir.
LEAR
You nimble lightnings, dart your blinding flames
Into her scornful eyes. Infect her beauty,
You fen-sucked fogs drawn by the pow'rful sun 325
To fall and blast her pride.
REGAN   O, the blest gods!
So will you wish on me when the rash mood—
LEAR
No, Regan. Thou shalt never have my curse.
Thy tender-hested nature shall not give

Thee o'er to harshness. Her eyes are fierce, but thine
Do comfort and not burn. 'Tis not in thee 331
To grudge my pleasures, to cut off my train,
To bandy hasty words, to scant my sizes,
And, in conclusion, to oppose the bolt
Against my coming in. Thou better know'st 335
The offices of nature, bond of childhood,
Effects of courtesy, dues of gratitude.
Thy half of the kingdom hast thou not forgot,
Wherein I thee endowed.

REGAN   Good sir, to th' purpose.

LEAR

Who put my man i'th' stocks?

⌈Trumpets within⌉

CORNWALL   What trumpet's that?

Enter Oswald the steward

REGAN

I know't, my sister's. This approves her letters 341
That she would soon be here. (*To Oswald*) Is your lady
    come?

LEAR

This is a slave whose easy-borrowed pride
Dwells in the fickle grace of her a follows.

⌈He strikes Oswald⌉

Out, varlet, from my sight!

CORNWALL   What means your grace?

Enter Gonoril

GONORIL

Who struck my servant? Regan, I have good hope 346
Thou didst not know on't.

LEAR   Who comes here? O heavens,
If you do love old men, if your sweet sway
Allow obedience, if yourselves are old,
Make it your cause! Send down and take my part. 350
(*To Gonoril*) Art not ashamed to look upon this beard?
O Regan, wilt thou take her by the hand?

GONORIL

Why not by the hand, sir? How have I offended?
All's not offence that indiscretion finds
And dotage terms so.

LEAR   O sides, you are too tough! 355
Will you yet hold?—How came my man i'th' stocks?

CORNWALL

I set him there, sir; but his own disorders
Deserved much less advancement.

LEAR   You? Did you?

REGAN

I pray you, father, being weak, seem so.
If till the expiration of your month 360
You will return and sojourn with my sister,
Dismissing half your train, come then to me.
I am now from home, and out of that provision
Which shall be needful for your entertainment.

LEAR

Return to her, and fifty men dismissed? 365
No, rather I abjure all roofs, and choose
To be a comrade with the wolf and owl,
To wage against the enmity of the air
Necessity's sharp pinch. Return with her?

Why, the hot-blood in France that dowerless took 370
Our youngest born—I could as well be brought
To knee his throne and, squire-like, pension beg
To keep base life afoot. Return with her?
Persuade me rather to be slave and sumpter
To this detested groom.

GONORIL   At your choice, sir. 375

LEAR

Now I prithee, daughter, do not make me mad.
I will not trouble thee, my child. Farewell.
We'll no more meet, no more see one another.
But yet thou art my flesh, my blood, my daughter—
Or rather a disease that lies within my flesh, 380
Which I must needs call mine. Thou art a boil,
A plague-sore, an embossèd carbuncle
In my corrupted blood. But I'll not chide thee.
Let shame come when it will, I do not call it.
I do not bid the thunder-bearer shoot, 385
Nor tell tales of thee to high-judging Jove.
Mend when thou canst; be better at thy leisure.
I can be patient, I can stay with Regan,
I and my hundred knights.

REGAN   Not altogether so, sir.
I look not for you yet, nor am I provided 390
For your fit welcome. Give ear, sir, to my sister;
For those that mingle reason with your passion
Must be content to think you are old, and so—
But she knows what she does.

LEAR   Is this well spoken now?

REGAN

I dare avouch it, sir. What, fifty followers? 395
Is it not well? What should you need of more,
Yea, or so many, sith that both charge and danger
Speaks 'gainst so great a number? How in a house
Should many people under two commands
Hold amity? 'Tis hard, almost impossible. 400

GONORIL

Why might not you, my lord, receive attendance
From those that she calls servants, or from mine?

REGAN

Why not, my lord? If then they chanced to slack you,
We could control them. If you will come to me—
For now I spy a danger—I entreat you 405
To bring but five-and-twenty; to no more
Will I give place or notice.

LEAR I gave you all.

REGAN And in good time you gave it.

LEAR

Made you my guardians, my depositaries, 410
But kept a reservation to be followed
With such a number. What, must I come to you
With five-and-twenty, Regan? Said you so?

REGAN

And speak't again, my lord. No more with me.

LEAR

Those wicked creatures yet do seem well favoured 415
When others are more wicked. Not being the worst
Stands in some rank of praise. (*To Gonoril*) I'll go with
    thee.

Thy fifty yet doth double five-and-twenty,
And thou art twice her love.
GONORIL   Hear me, my lord.
What need you five-and-twenty, ten, or five,   420
To follow in a house where twice so many
Have a command to tend you?
REGAN   What needs one?
LEAR
O, reason not the need! Our basest beggars
Are in the poorest thing superfluous.
Allow not nature more than nature needs,   425
Man's life is cheap as beast's. Thou art a lady.
If only to go warm were gorgeous,
Why, nature needs not what thou, gorgeous, wearest,
Which scarcely keeps thee warm. But for true need—
You heavens, give me that patience, patience I need.
You see me here, you gods, a poor old fellow,   431
As full of grief as age, wretchèd in both.
If it be you that stirs these daughters' hearts
Against their father, fool me not so much
To bear it tamely. Touch me with noble anger.   435
O, let not women's weapons, water-drops,
Stain my man's cheeks! No, you unnatural hags,
I will have such revenges on you both
That all the world shall—I will do such things—
What they are, yet I know not; but they shall be   440
The terrors of the earth. You think I'll weep.
No, I'll not weep.
            ⌜Storm within⌝
I have full cause of weeping, but this heart
Shall break into a hundred thousand flaws
Or ere I'll weep.—O fool, I shall go mad!   445
        Exeunt Lear, Gloucester, Kent, ⌜Knight,⌝
                              and Fool
CORNWALL
Let us withdraw. 'Twill be a storm.
REGAN
This house is little. The old man and his people
Cannot be well bestowed.
GONORIL   'Tis his own blame;
Hath put himself from rest, and must needs taste his
folly.
REGAN
For his particular I'll receive him gladly,   450
But not one follower.
CORNWALL
So am I purposed. Where is my lord of Gloucester?
REGAN
Followed the old man forth.
    Enter the Duke of Gloucester
                    He is returned.
GLOUCESTER
The King is in high rage, and will I know not whither.
REGAN
'Tis good to give him way. He leads himself.   455
GONORIL (to Gloucester)
My lord, entreat him by no means to stay.
GLOUCESTER
Alack, the night comes on, and the bleak winds

Do sorely rustle. For many miles about
There's not a bush.
REGAN   O sir, to wilful men
The injuries that they themselves procure   460
Must be their schoolmasters. Shut up your doors.
He is attended with a desperate train,
And what they may incense him to, being apt
To have his ear abused, wisdom bids fear.
CORNWALL
Shut up your doors, my lord. 'Tis a wild night.   465
My Regan counsels well. Come out o'th' storm.
                                        Exeunt

Sc. 8   Storm. Enter the Earl of Kent disguised, and First
        Gentleman, at several doors
KENT
What's here, beside foul weather?
FIRST GENTLEMAN   One minded like the weather,
Most unquietly.
KENT   I know you. Where's the King?
FIRST GENTLEMAN
Contending with the fretful element;
Bids the wind blow the earth into the sea
Or swell the curlèd waters 'bove the main,   5
That things might change or cease; tears his white
hair,
Which the impetuous blasts, with eyeless rage,
Catch in their fury and make nothing of;
Strives in his little world of man to outstorm
The to-and-fro-conflicting wind and rain.   10
This night, wherein the cub-drawn bear would couch,
The lion and the belly-pinchèd wolf
Keep their fur dry, unbonneted he runs,
And bids what will take all.
KENT   But who is with him?
FIRST GENTLEMAN
None but the fool, who labours to outjest   15
His heart-struck injuries.
KENT   Sir, I do know you,
And dare upon the warrant of my art
Commend a dear thing to you. There is division,
Although as yet the face of it be covered
With mutual cunning, 'twixt Albany and Cornwall;   20
But true it is. From France there comes a power
Into this scattered kingdom, who already,
Wise in our negligence, have secret feet
In some of our best ports, and are at point
To show their open banner. Now to you: 25
If on my credit you dare build so far
To make your speed to Dover, you shall find
Some that will thank you, making just report
Of how unnatural and bemadding sorrow
The King hath cause to plain.   30
I am a gentleman of blood and breeding,
And from some knowledge and assurance offer
This office to you.
FIRST GENTLEMAN I will talk farther with you.
KENT No, do not.   35
For confirmation that I am much more

Than my out-wall, open this purse, and take
What it contains. If you shall see Cordelia—
As fear not but you shall—show her this ring
And she will tell you who your fellow is,   40
That yet you do not know. Fie on this storm!
I will go seek the King.
FIRST GENTLEMAN   Give me your hand.
Have you no more to say?
KENT   Few words, but to effect
More than all yet: that when we have found the King—
In which endeavour I'll this way, you that—   45
He that first lights on him holla the other.

      Exeunt severally

Sc. 9   *Storm. Enter King Lear and his Fool*
LEAR
Blow, wind, and crack your cheeks! Rage, blow,
You cataracts and hurricanoes, spout
Till you have drenched the steeples, drowned the
    cocks!
You sulphurous and thought-executing fires,
Vaunt-couriers to oak-cleaving thunderbolts,   5
Singe my white head; and thou all-shaking thunder,
Smite flat the thick rotundity of the world,
Crack nature's mould, all germens spill at once
That make ingrateful man.   9
FOOL O nuncle, court holy water in a dry house is better
than this rain-water out o' door. Good nuncle, in, and
ask thy daughters blessing. Here's a night pities neither
wise man nor fool.
LEAR
Rumble thy bellyful; spit, fire; spout, rain.
Nor rain, wind, thunder, fire are my daughters.   15
I tax not you, you elements, with unkindness.
I never gave you kingdom, called you children.
You owe me no subscription. Why then, let fall
Your horrible pleasure. Here I stand your slave,
A poor, infirm, weak and despised old man,   20
But yet I call you servile ministers,
That have with two pernicious daughters joined
Your high engendered battle 'gainst a head
So old and white as this. O, 'tis foul!
FOOL He that has a house to put his head in has a good
headpiece.   26
⌐Sings⌐   The codpiece that will house
      Before the head has any,
    The head and he shall louse,
      So beggars marry many.   30

    The man that makes his toe
      What he his heart should make
    Shall have a corn cry woe,
      And turn his sleep to wake—
for there was never yet fair woman but she made
mouths in a glass.   36
LEAR
No, I will be the pattern of all patience.
    ⌐He sits.⌐ *Enter the Earl of Kent disguised*
I will say nothing.

KENT Who's there?
FOOL Marry, here's grace and a codpiece—that's a wise
man and a fool.   41
KENT (*to Lear*)
Alas, sir, sit you here? Things that love night
Love not such nights as these. The wrathful skies
Gallow the very wanderers of the dark
And makes them keep their caves. Since I was man   45
Such sheets of fire, such bursts of horrid thunder,
Such groans of roaring wind and rain I ne'er
Remember to have heard. Man's nature cannot carry
The affliction nor the force.
LEAR   Let the great gods,
That keep this dreadful pother o'er our heads,   50
Find out their enemies now. Tremble, thou wretch
That hast within thee undivulgèd crimes
Unwhipped of justice; hide thee, thou bloody hand,
Thou perjured and thou simular man of virtue
That art incestuous; caitiff, in pieces shake,   55
That under covert and convenient seeming
Hast practised on man's life;
Close pent-up guilts, rive your concealèd centres
And cry these dreadful summoners grace.
I am a man more sinned against than sinning.   60
KENT Alack, bare-headed?
Gracious my lord, hard by here is a hovel.
Some friendship will it lend you 'gainst the tempest.
Repose you there whilst I to this hard house—
More hard than is the stone whereof 'tis raised,   65
Which even but now, demanding after you,
Denied me to come in—return and force
Their scanted courtesy.
LEAR   My wit begins to turn.
(*To Fool*) Come on, my boy. How dost, my boy? Art
    cold?
I am cold myself.—Where is this straw, my fellow?   70
The art of our necessities is strange,
That can make vile things precious. Come, your
    hovel.—
Poor fool and knave, I have one part of my heart
That sorrows yet for thee.
FOOL ⌐sings⌐
    He that has a little tiny wit,   75
      With heigh-ho, the wind and the rain,
    Must make content with his fortunes fit,
      For the rain it raineth every day.
LEAR
True, my good boy. (*To Kent*) Come, bring us to this
    hovel.   *Exeunt*

Sc. 10   *Enter the Duke of Gloucester and Edmund the*
    bastard, with lights
GLOUCESTER
Alack, alack, Edmund, I like not this
Unnatural dealing. When I desired their leave
That I might pity him, they took from me
The use of mine own house, charged me on pain
Of their displeasure neither to speak of him,   5
Entreat for him, nor any way sustain him.

EDMUND Most savage and unnatural!   7
GLOUCESTER Go to, say you nothing. There's a division
betwixt the Dukes, and a worse matter than that. I
have received a letter this night—'tis dangerous to be
spoken—I have locked the letter in my closet. These
injuries the King now bears will be revenged home.
There's part of a power already landed. We must incline
to the King. I will seek him and privily relieve him. Go
you and maintain talk with the Duke, that my charity
be not of him perceived. If he ask for me, I am ill and
gone to bed. Though I die for't—as no less is threatened
me—the King my old master must be relieved. There
is some strange thing toward. Edmund, pray you be
careful.   *Exit*
EDMUND
This courtesy, forbid thee, shall the Duke
Instantly know, and of that letter too.
This seems a fair deserving, and must draw me
That which my father loses: no less than all.   24
The younger rises when the old do fall.   *Exit*

Sc. 11 *Storm. Enter King Lear, the Earl of Kent disguised,
          and Lear's Fool*
KENT
Here is the place, my lord. Good my lord, enter.
The tyranny of the open night's too rough
For nature to endure.
LEAR   Let me alone.
KENT
Good my lord, enter here.
LEAR   Wilt break my heart?
KENT
I had rather break mine own. Good my lord, enter.   5
LEAR
Thou think'st 'tis much that this contentious storm
Invades us to the skin. So 'tis to thee;
But where the greater malady is fixed,
The lesser is scarce felt. Thou'dst shun a bear,
But if thy flight lay toward the roaring sea   10
Thou'dst meet the bear i'th' mouth. When the mind's
    free,
The body's delicate. This tempest in my mind
Doth from my senses take all feeling else
Save what beats there: filial ingratitude.
Is it not as this mouth should tear this hand   15
For lifting food to't? But I will punish sure.
No, I will weep no more.—
In such a night as this! O Regan, Gonoril,
Your old kind father, whose frank heart gave you all—
O, that way madness lies. Let me shun that.   20
No more of that.
KENT   Good my lord, enter.
LEAR
Prithee, go in thyself. Seek thy own ease.
This tempest will not give me leave to ponder
On things would hurt me more; but I'll go in.
                                        ⌜*Exit Fool*⌝
Poor naked wretches, wheresoe'er you are,   25
That bide the pelting of this pitiless night,

How shall your houseless heads and unfed sides,
Your looped and windowed raggedness, defend you
From seasons such as these? O, I have ta'en
Too little care of this. Take physic, pomp,   30
Expose thyself to feel what wretches feel,
That thou mayst shake the superflux to them
And show the heavens more just.
                Enter Lear's Fool
FOOL Come not in here, nuncle; here's a spirit. Help me,
help me!   35
KENT Give me thy hand. Who's there?
FOOL A spirit. He says his name's Poor Tom.
KENT
What art thou that dost grumble there in the straw?
Come forth.   39
            ⌜*Enter Edgar as a Bedlam beggar*⌝
EDGAR Away, the foul fiend follows me. Through the
sharp hawthorn blows the cold wind. Go to thy cold
bed and warm thee.
LEAR
Hast thou given all to thy two daughters,
And art thou come to this?   44
EDGAR Who gives anything to Poor Tom, whom the foul
fiend hath led through fire and through ford and
whirlpool, o'er bog and quagmire; that has laid knives
under his pillow and halters in his pew, set ratsbane
by his potage, made him proud of heart to ride on a
bay trotting-horse over four-inched bridges, to course
his own shadow for a traitor. Bless thy five wits, Tom's
a-cold! Bless thee from whirlwinds, star-blasting, and
taking. Do Poor Tom some charity, whom the foul fiend
vexes. There could I have him, now, and there, and
there again.   55
LEAR
What, has his daughters brought him to this pass?
(*To Edgar*) Couldst thou save nothing? Didst thou give
          them all?
FOOL Nay, he reserved a blanket, else we had been all
shamed.
LEAR (*to Edgar*)
Now all the plagues that in the pendulous air   60
Hang fated o'er men's faults fall on thy daughters!
KENT He hath no daughters, sir.
LEAR
Death, traitor! Nothing could have subdued nature
To such a lowness but his unkind daughters.
(*To Edgar*) Is it the fashion that discarded fathers 65
Should have thus little mercy on their flesh?
Judicious punishment: 'twas this flesh begot
Those pelican daughters.
EDGAR Pillicock sat on pillicock's hill; a lo, lo, lo.   69
FOOL This cold night will turn us all to fools and madmen.
EDGAR Take heed o'th' foul fiend; obey thy parents; keep
thy word justly; swear not; commit not with man's
sworn spouse: set not thy sweet heart on proud array.
Tom's a-cold.
LEAR What hast thou been?   75
EDGAR A servingman, proud in heart and mind, that
curled my hair, wore gloves in my cap, served the lust

of my mistress' heart, and did the act of darkness with
her; swore as many oaths as I spake words, and broke
them in the sweet face of heaven; one that slept in the
contriving of lust, and waked to do it. Wine loved I
deeply, dice dearly, and in woman out-paramoured the
Turk. False of heart, light of ear, bloody of hand; hog
in sloth, fox in stealth, wolf in greediness, dog in
madness, lion in prey. Let not the creaking of shoes
nor the rustlings of silks betray thy poor heart to
women. Keep thy foot out of brothel, thy hand out of
placket, thy pen from lender's book, and defy the foul
fiend. Still through the hawthorn blows the cold wind.
Heigh no nonny. Dolphin, my boy, my boy! Cease, let
him trot by.   91

LEAR Why, thou wert better in thy grave than to answer
with thy uncovered body this extremity of the skies. Is
man no more but this? Consider him well. Thou owest
the worm no silk, the beast no hide, the sheep no wool,
the cat no perfume. Here's three on 's are sophisticated;
thou art the thing itself. Unaccommodated man is no
more but such a poor, bare, forked animal as thou art.
Off, off, you lendings! Come on, be true.   99

FOOL Prithee, nuncle, be content. This is a naughty night
to swim in. Now a little fire in a wild field were like
an old lecher's heart—a small spark, all the rest on 's
body cold. Look, here comes a walking fire.

Enter the Duke of Gloucester with a ⌜torch⌝

EDGAR This is the foul fiend Flibbertigibbet. He begins at
curfew and walks till the first cock. He gives the web
and the pin, squinies the eye, and makes the harelip;
mildews the white wheat, and hurts the poor creature
of earth.

⌜*Sings*⌝

  Swithin footed thrice the wold,
  A met the night mare and her nine foal;   110
    Bid her alight
    And her troth plight,
  And aroint thee, witch, aroint thee!

KENT (*to Lear*)
  How fares your grace?

LEAR   What's he?   114

KENT (*to Gloucester*) Who's there? What is't you seek?

GLOUCESTER What are you there? Your names?

EDGAR Poor Tom, that eats the swimming frog, the toad,
the tadpole, the wall-newt and the water; that in the
fury of his heart, when the foul fiend rages, eats
cowdung for salads, swallows the old rat and the ditch-
dog, drinks the green mantle of the standing pool; who
is whipped from tithing to tithing, and stock-punished,
and imprisoned; who hath had three suits to his back,
six shirts to his body,
  Horse to ride, and weapon to wear.   125
  But mice and rats and such small deer
  Hath been Tom's food for seven long year—
Beware my follower. Peace, Smolking; peace, thou
fiend!

GLOUCESTER (*to Lear*)
  What, hath your grace no better company?   130

EDGAR
  The Prince of Darkness is a gentleman;
  Modo he's called, and Mahu—

GLOUCESTER (*to Lear*)
  Our flesh and blood is grown so vile, my lord,
  That it doth hate what gets it.

EDGAR   Poor Tom's a-cold.

GLOUCESTER (*to Lear*)
  Go in with me. My duty cannot suffer   135
  To obey in all your daughters' hard commands.
  Though their injunction be to bar my doors
  And let this tyrannous night take hold upon you,
  Yet have I ventured to come seek you out
  And bring you where both food and fire is ready. 140

LEAR
  First let me talk with this philosopher.
  (*To Edgar*) What is the cause of thunder?

KENT   My good lord,
  Take his offer; go into the house.

LEAR
  I'll talk a word with this most learnèd Theban.
  (*To Edgar*) What is your study?   145

EDGAR
  How to prevent the fiend, and to kill vermin.

LEAR
  Let me ask you one word in private.

  They converse apart

KENT (*to Gloucester*)
  Importune him to go, my lord.
  His wits begin to unsettle.

GLOUCESTER   Canst thou blame him?
  His daughters seek his death. O, that good Kent, 150
  He said it would be thus, poor banished man!
  Thou sayst the King grows mad; I'll tell thee, friend,
  I am almost mad myself. I had a son,
  Now outlawed from my blood; a sought my life
  But lately, very late. I loved him, friend;   155
  No father his son dearer. True to tell thee,
  The grief hath crazed my wits. What a night's this!
  (*To Lear*) I do beseech your grace—

LEAR   O, cry you mercy.
  (*To Edgar*) Noble philosopher, your company.

EDGAR   Tom's a-cold.

GLOUCESTER
  In, fellow, there in t'hovel; keep thee warm.   160

LEAR
  Come, let's in all.

KENT   This way, my lord.

LEAR   With him!
  I will keep still with my philosopher.

KENT (*to Gloucester*)
  Good my lord, soothe him; let him take the fellow.

GLOUCESTER Take him you on.

KENT ⌜*to Edgar*⌝
  Sirrah, come on. Go along with us.   165

LEAR (*to Edgar*)
  Come, good Athenian.

GLOUCESTER   No words, no words. Hush.

EDGAR Child Roland to the dark tower come,
His word was still 'Fie, fo, and fum;
I smell the blood of a British man.'   *Exeunt*

Sc. 12 *Enter the Duke of Cornwall and Edmund the bastard*

CORNWALL I will have my revenge ere I depart the house.

EDMUND How, my lord, I may be censured, that nature thus gives way to loyalty, something fears me to think of.   4

CORNWALL I now perceive it was not altogether your brother's evil disposition made him seek his death, but a provoking merit set a-work by a reprovable badness in himself.

EDMUND How malicious is my fortune, that I must repent to be just! This is the letter he spoke of, which approves him an intelligent party to the advantages of France. O heavens, that his treason were not, or not I the detector!

CORNWALL Go with me to the Duchess.

EDMUND If the matter of this paper be certain, you have mighty business in hand.   16

CORNWALL True or false, it hath made thee Earl of Gloucester. Seek out where thy father is, that he may be ready for our apprehension.   19

EDMUND ⌈*aside*⌉ If I find him comforting the King, it will stuff his suspicion more fully. (*To Cornwall*) I will persever in my course of loyalty, though the conflict be sore between that and my blood.

CORNWALL I will lay trust upon thee, and thou shalt find a dearer father in my love.   *Exeunt*

Sc. 13 *Enter the Duke of Gloucester and King Lear, the Earl of Kent disguised, Lear's Fool, and Edgar as a Bedlam beggar*

GLOUCESTER Here is better than the open air; take it thankfully. I will piece out the comfort with what addition I can. I will not be long from you.

KENT All the power of his wits have given way to impatience; the gods discern your kindness!   5
    ⌈*Exit Gloucester*⌉

EDGAR Frateretto calls me, and tells me Nero is an angler in the lake of darkness. Pray, innocent; beware the foul fiend.

FOOL (*to Lear*) Prithee, nuncle, tell me whether a madman be a gentleman or a yeoman.   10

LEAR
A king, a king! To have a thousand
With red burning spits come hissing in upon them!

EDGAR The foul fiend bites my back.

FOOL (*to Lear*) He's mad that trusts in the tameness of a wolf, a horse's health, a boy's love, or a whore's oath.

LEAR
It shall be done. I will arraign them straight.   16
  ⌈*To Edgar*⌉ Come, sit thou here, most learnèd justicer.
  ⌈*To Fool*⌉ Thou sapient sir, sit here.—No, you she-foxes—

EDGAR Look where he stands and glares. Want'st thou eyes at troll-madam?   20
  ⌈*Sings*⌉ Come o'er the burn, Bessy, to me.

FOOL ⌈*sings*⌉
    Her boat hath a leak,
    And she must not speak
    Why she dares not come over to thee.   24

EDGAR The foul fiend haunts Poor Tom in the voice of a nightingale. Hoppedance cries in Tom's belly for two white herring. Croak not, black angel: I have no food for thee.

KENT (*to Lear*)
How do you, sir? Stand you not so amazed.
Will you lie down and rest upon the cushions?   30

LEAR
I'll see their trial first. Bring in the evidence.
  ⌈*To Edgar*⌉ Thou robèd man of justice, take thy place;
  ⌈*To Fool*⌉ And thou, his yokefellow of equity,
Bench by his side. ⌈*To Kent*⌉ You are o'th'
    commission,
Sit you, too.   35

EDGAR Let us deal justly.
  ⌈*Sings*⌉
    Sleepest or wakest thou, jolly shepherd?
      Thy sheep be in the corn,
    And for one blast of thy minikin mouth
      Thy sheep shall take no harm.   40
Purr, the cat is grey.

LEAR Arraign her first. 'Tis Gonoril. I here take my oath before this honourable assembly she kicked the poor King her father.

FOOL Come hither, mistress. Is your name Gonoril?   45

LEAR She cannot deny it.

FOOL Cry you mercy, I took you for a join-stool.

LEAR
And here's another, whose warped looks proclaim
What store her heart is made on. Stop her there.
Arms, arms, sword, fire, corruption in the place!   50
False justicer, why hast thou let her scape?

EDGAR Bless thy five wits.

KENT (*to Lear*)
O pity! Sir, where is the patience now
That you so oft have boasted to retain?

EDGAR (*aside*)
My tears begin to take his part so much   55
They'll mar my counterfeiting.

LEAR   The little dogs and all,
Tray, Blanch, and Sweetheart—see, they bark at me.

EDGAR Tom will throw his head at them.—Avaunt, you curs!
    Be thy mouth or black or white,   60
    Tooth that poisons if it bite,
    Mastiff, greyhound, mongrel grim,
    Hound or spaniel, brach or him,
    Bobtail tyke or trundle-tail,
    Tom will make them weep and wail;   65
    For with throwing thus my head,
    Dogs leap the hatch, and all are fled.
Loudla, doodla! Come, march to wakes and fairs
And market towns. Poor Tom, thy horn is dry.   69

LEAR Then let them anatomize Regan; see what breeds about her heart. Is there any cause in nature that

makes this hardness? (*To Edgar*) You, sir, I entertain
you for one of my hundred, only I do not like the
fashion of your garments. You'll say they are Persian
attire; but let them be changed.   75
KENT
Now, good my lord, lie here a while.
LEAR Make no noise, make no noise. Draw the curtains.
So, so, so. We'll go to supper i'th' morning. So, so, so.
    He sleeps. Enter the Duke of Gloucester
GLOUCESTER (*to Kent*)
Come hither, friend. Where is the King my master?
KENT
Here, sir, but trouble him not; his wits are gone.   80
GLOUCESTER
Good friend, I prithee take him in thy arms.
I have o'erheard a plot of death upon him.
There is a litter ready. Lay him in't
And drive towards Dover, friend, where thou shalt
    meet
Both welcome and protection. Take up thy master.   85
If thou shouldst dally half an hour, his life,
With thine and all that offer to defend him,
Stand in assurèd loss. Take up, take up,
And follow me, that will to some provision
Give thee quick conduct.
KENT (*to Lear*)   Oppressèd nature sleeps.   90
This rest might yet have balmed thy broken sinews
Which, if convenience will not allow,
Stand in hard cure. (*To Fool*) Come, help to bear thy
    master.
Thou must not stay behind.
GLOUCESTER   Come, come away.
                    Exeunt all but Edgar
EDGAR
When we our betters see bearing our woes,   95
We scarcely think our miseries our foes.
Who alone suffers, suffers most i'th' mind,
Leaving free things and happy shows behind.
But then the mind much sufferance doth o'erskip
When grief hath mates, and bearing fellowship.   100
How light and portable my pain seems now,
When that which makes me bend, makes the King
    bow.
He childed as I fathered. Tom, away.
Mark the high noises, and thyself bewray   104
When false opinion, whose wrong thoughts defile thee,
In thy just proof repeals and reconciles thee.
What will hap more tonight, safe scape the King!
Lurk, lurk.   *Exit*

Sc. 14 *Enter the Duke of Cornwall and Regan, and Gonoril
    and Edmund the bastard, and Servants*
CORNWALL (*to Gonoril*)
Post speedily to my lord your husband.
Show him this letter. The army of France is landed.
(*To Servants*) Seek out the villain Gloucester.
                        Exeunt some
REGAN   Hang him instantly.

GONORIL
Pluck out his eyes.
CORNWALL   Leave him to my displeasure.—
Edmund, keep you our sister company.   5
The revenges we are bound to take upon your traitorous
father are not fit for your beholding. Advise the Duke
where you are going, to a most festinate preparation;
we are bound to the like. Our posts shall be swift, and
intelligence betwixt us.—   10
Farewell, dear sister. Farewell, my lord of Gloucester.
    Enter Oswald the steward
How now, where's the King?
OSWALD
My lord of Gloucester hath conveyed him hence.
Some five- or six-and-thirty of his knights,
Hot questants after him, met him at gate,   15
Who, with some other of the lord's dependants,
Are gone with him towards Dover, where they boast
To have well-armèd friends.
CORNWALL Get horses for your mistress.   *Exit Oswald*
GONORIL Farewell, sweet lord, and sister.   20
CORNWALL
Edmund, farewell.   *Exeunt Gonoril and Edmund*
(*To Servants*)   Go seek the traitor Gloucester.
Pinion him like a thief; bring him before us.
                    Exeunt other Servants
Though we may not pass upon his life
Without the form of justice, yet our power
Shall do a curtsy to our wrath, which men   25
May blame but not control. Who's there—the traitor?
    *Enter the Duke of Gloucester brought in by two or
    three*
REGAN
Ingrateful fox, 'tis he.
CORNWALL (*to Servants*) Bind fast his corky arms.
GLOUCESTER
What means your graces? Good my friends, consider
You are my guests. Do me no foul play, friends.
CORNWALL (*to Servants*)
Bind him, I say—
REGAN   Hard, hard! O filthy traitor!   30
GLOUCESTER
Unmerciful lady as you are, I am true.
CORNWALL (*to Servants*)
To this chair bind him. (*To Gloucester*) Villain, thou
    shalt find—
    Regan plucks Gloucester's beard
GLOUCESTER
By the kind gods, 'tis most ignobly done,
To pluck me by the beard.
REGAN So white, and such a traitor!   35
GLOUCESTER Naughty lady,
These hairs which thou dost ravish from my chin
Will quicken and accuse thee. I am your host.
With robbers' hands my hospitable favours
You should not ruffle thus. What will you do?   40
CORNWALL
Come, sir, what letters had you late from France?

REGAN
Be simple, answerer, for we know the truth.
CORNWALL
And what confederacy have you with the traitors
Late footed in the kingdom?
REGAN   To whose hands
You have sent the lunatic King. Speak.   45
GLOUCESTER
I have a letter guessingly set down,
Which came from one that's of a neutral heart,
And not from one opposed.
CORNWALL   Cunning.
REGAN   And false.
CORNWALL
Where hast thou sent the King?
GLOUCESTER   To Dover.
REGAN
Wherefore to Dover? Wast thou not charged at peril—
CORNWALL
Wherefore to Dover? Let him first answer that.   51
GLOUCESTER
I am tied to th' stake, and I must stand the course.
REGAN Wherefore to Dover, sir?
GLOUCESTER
Because I would not see thy cruel nails
Pluck out his poor old eyes, nor thy fierce sister   55
In his anointed flesh rash boarish fangs.
The sea, with such a storm as his bowed head
In hell-black night endured, would have buoyed up
And quenched the stellèd fires. Yet, poor old heart,
He holpt the heavens to rage.   60
If wolves had at thy gate howled that dern time,
Thou shouldst have said 'Good porter, türn the key;
All cruels I'll subscribe.' But I shall see
The wingèd vengeance overtake such children.
CORNWALL
See't shalt thou never.—Fellows, hold the chair.—   65
Upon those eyes of thine I'll set my foot.
GLOUCESTER
He that will think to live till he be old
Give me some help!—O cruel! O ye gods!
⌈Cornwall pulls out one of Gloucester's eyes and
stamps on it⌉
REGAN (to Cornwall)
One side will mock another; t'other, too.
CORNWALL (to Gloucester)
If you see vengeance—
SERVANT   Hold your hand, my lord.   70
I have served you ever since I was a child,
But better service have I never done you
Than now to bid you hold.
REGAN   How now, you dog!
SERVANT
If you did wear a beard upon your chin
I'd shake it on this quarrel. ⌈To Cornwall⌉ What do
you mean?   75
CORNWALL My villein!

SERVANT
Why then, come on, and take the chance of anger.
They draw and fight
REGAN ⌈to another Servant⌉
Give me thy sword. A peasant stand up thus!
She takes a sword and runs ⸝at him behind
SERVANT (to Gloucester)
O, I am slain, my lord! Yet have you one eye left
To see some mischief on him.
⌈Regan stabs him again⌉
O!   He dies
CORNWALL
Lest it see more, prevent it. Out, vile jelly!   81
He ⌈pulls out⌉ Gloucester's other eye
Where is thy lustre now?
GLOUCESTER
All dark and comfortless. Where's my son Edmund?
Edmund, enkindle all the sparks of nature
To quite this horrid act.
REGAN   Out, villain!   85
Thou call'st on him that hates thee. It was he
That made the overture of thy treasons to us,
Who is too good to pity thee.
GLOUCESTER
O, my follies! Then Edgar was abused.
Kind gods, forgive me that, and prosper him!   90
REGAN (to Servants)
Go thrust him out at gates, and let him smell
His way to Dover. (To Cornwall) How is't, my lord?
How look you?
CORNWALL
I have received a hurt. Follow me, lady.
(To Servants) Turn out that eyeless villain. Throw this
slave
Upon the dunghill.   Exit one or more with Gloucester
⌈and the body⌉
Regan, I bleed apace.   95
Untimely comes this hurt. Give me your arm.
Exeunt Cornwall and Regan
SECOND SERVANT
I'll never care what wickedness I do
If this man come to good.
THIRD SERVANT   If she live long
And in the end meet the old course of death,
Women will all turn monsters.   100
SECOND SERVANT
Let's follow the old Earl and get the bedlam
To lead him where he would. His roguish madness
Allows itself to anything.
THIRD SERVANT
Go thou. I'll fetch some flax and whites of eggs   104
To apply to his bleeding face. Now heaven help him!
Exeunt severally

Sc. 15 Enter Edgar as a Bedlam beggar
EDGAR
Yet better thus and known to be contemned

Than still contemned and flattered. To be worst,
The low'st and most dejected thing of fortune,
Stands still in esperance, lives not in fear.
The lamentable change is from the best;   5
The worst returns to laughter.

Enter the Duke of Gloucester led by an Old Man

Who's here? My father, parti-eyed? World, world, O
world!
But that thy strange mutations make us hate thee,
Life would not yield to age.

⌈*Edgar stands aside*⌉

OLD MAN (*to Gloucester*)   O my good lord,
I have been your tenant and your father's tenant   10
This fourscore—

GLOUCESTER
Away, get thee away, good friend, be gone.
Thy comforts can do me no good at all;
Thee they may hurt.

OLD MAN
Alack, sir, you cannot see your way.   15

GLOUCESTER
I have no way, and therefore want no eyes.
I stumbled when I saw. Full oft 'tis seen
Our means secure us, and our mere defects
Prove our commodities. Ah dear son Edgar,
The food of thy abusèd father's wrath—   20
Might I but live to see thee in my touch
I'd say I had eyes again.

OLD MAN   How now? Who's there?

EDGAR (*aside*)
O gods! Who is't can say 'I am at the worst'?
I am worse than e'er I was.

OLD MAN   'Tis poor mad Tom.

EDGAR (*aside*)
And worse I may be yet. The worst is not   25
As long as we can say 'This is the worst.'

OLD MAN (*to Edgar*) Fellow, where goest?

GLOUCESTER Is it a beggarman?

OLD MAN Madman and beggar too.

GLOUCESTER
A has some reason, else he could not beg.   30
In the last night's storm I such a fellow saw,
Which made me think a man a worm. My son
Came then into my mind, and yet my mind
Was then scarce friends with him. I have heard more
since.
As flies to wanton boys are we to th' gods;   35
They kill us for their sport.

EDGAR (*aside*)   How should this be?
Bad is the trade that must play fool to sorrow,
Ang'ring itself and others.

⌈*He comes forward*⌉

            Bless thee, master.

GLOUCESTER
Is that the naked fellow?

OLD MAN   Ay, my lord.

GLOUCESTER
Then prithee, get thee gone. If for my sake   40

Thou wilt o'ertake us hence a mile or twain
I'th' way toward Dover, do it for ancient love,
And bring some covering for this naked soul,
Who I'll entreat to lead me.

OLD MAN   Alack, sir, he is mad.

GLOUCESTER
'Tis the time's plague when madmen lead the blind.   45
Do as I bid thee; or rather do thy pleasure.
Above the rest, be gone.

OLD MAN
I'll bring him the best 'parel that I have,
Come on't what will.   *Exit*

GLOUCESTER   Sirrah, naked fellow!

EDGAR
Poor Tom's a-cold. I cannot dance it farther.   50

GLOUCESTER Come hither, fellow.

EDGAR Bless thy sweet eyes, they bleed.

GLOUCESTER Know'st thou the way to Dover?

EDGAR Both stile and gate, horseway and footpath. Poor
Tom hath been scared out of his good wits. Bless thee,
goodman, from the foul fiend. Five fiends have been in
Poor Tom at once, as Obidicut of lust, Hobbididence
prince of dumbness, Mahu of stealing, Modo of murder,
Flibbertigibbet of mocking and mowing, who since
possesses chambermaids and waiting-women. So bless
thee, master.   61

GLOUCESTER
Here, take this purse, thou whom the heavens' plagues
Have humbled to all strokes. That I am wretched
Makes thee the happier. Heavens deal so still.
Let the superfluous and lust-dieted man   65
That stands your ordinance, that will not see
Because he does not feel, feel your power quickly.
So distribution should undo excess,
And each man have enough. Dost thou know Dover?

EDGAR Ay, master.   70

GLOUCESTER
There is a cliff whose high and bending head
Looks saucily in the confinèd deep.
Bring me but to the very brim of it
And I'll repair the misery thou dost bear
With something rich about me. From that place   75
I shall no leading need.

EDGAR Give me thy arm.
Poor Tom shall lead thee.

            Exit Edgar guiding Gloucester

Sc. 16 *Enter* ⌈*at one door*⌉ *Gonoril and Edmund the bastard*

GONORIL
Welcome, my lord. I marvel our mild husband
Not met us on the way.

            Enter ⌈*at another door*⌉ *Oswald the steward*

            Now, where's your master?

OSWALD
Madam, within; but never man so changed.
I told him of the army that was landed;
He smiled at it. I told him you were coming;   5
His answer was 'The worse.' Of Gloucester's treachery

And of the loyal service of his son
When I informed him, then he called me sot,
And told me I had turned the wrong side out.
What he should most defy seems pleasant to him;   10
What like, offensive.
GONORIL (*to Edmund*)   Then shall you go no further.
It is the cowish terror of his spirit
That dares not undertake. He'll not feel wrongs
Which tie him to an answer. Our wishes on the way
May prove effects. Back, Edmund, to my brother.   15
Hasten his musters and conduct his powers.
I must change arms at home, and give the distaff
Into my husband's hands. This trusty servant
Shall pass between us. Ere long you are like to hear,
If you dare venture in your own behalf,   20
A mistress's command. Wear this. Spare speech.
Decline your head. This kiss, if it durst speak,
Would stretch thy spirits up into the air.
⌐*She kisses him*⌐
Conceive, and fare you well.
EDMUND Yours in the ranks of death.   25
GONORIL My most dear Gloucester.   ⌐*Exit Edmund*⌐
To thee a woman's services are due;
My foot usurps my body.
OSWALD   Madam, here comes my lord.
                                                            Exit
Enter the Duke of Albany
GONORIL
I have been worth the whistling.
ALBANY   O Gonoril,
You are not worth the dust which the rude wind   30
Blows in your face. I fear your disposition.
That nature which contemns it origin
Cannot be bordered certain in itself.
She that herself will sliver and disbranch
From her material sap perforce must wither,   35
And come to deadly use.
GONORIL   No more. The text is foolish.
ALBANY
Wisdom and goodness to the vile seem vile;
Filths savour but themselves. What have you done?
Tigers, not daughters, what have you performed?
A father, and a gracious, agèd man,   40
Whose reverence even the head-lugged bear would
   lick,
Most barbarous, most degenerate, have you madded.
Could my good-brother suffer you to do it—
A man, a prince by him so benefacted?
If that the heavens do not their visible spirits   45
Send quickly down to tame these vile offences,
It will come,
Humanity must perforce prey on itself,
Like monsters of the deep.
GONORIL   Milk-livered man,
That bear'st a cheek for blows, a head for wrongs;   50
Who hast not in thy brows an eye discerning
Thine honour from thy suffering; that not know'st
Fools do those villains pity who are punished
Ere they have done their mischief: where's thy drum?

France spreads his banners in our noiseless land,   55
With plumèd helm thy flaxen biggin threats,
Whiles thou, a moral fool, sits still and cries
'Alack, why does he so?'
ALBANY   See thyself, devil.
Proper deformity shows not in the fiend
So horrid as in woman.
GONORIL   O vain fool!   60
ALBANY
Thou changèd and self-covered thing, for shame
Bemonster not thy feature. Were't my fitness
To let these hands obey my blood,
They are apt enough to dislocate and tear
Thy flesh and bones. Howe'er thou art a fiend,   65
A woman's shape doth shield thee.
GONORIL Marry your manhood, mew—
Enter ⌐*Second*⌐ *Gentleman*
ALBANY What news?
⌐SECOND⌐ GENTLEMAN
O my good lord, the Duke of Cornwall's dead,
Slain by his servant going to put out   70
The other eye of Gloucester.
ALBANY   Gloucester's eyes?
⌐SECOND⌐ GENTLEMAN
A servant that he bred, thralled with remorse,
Opposed against the act, bending his sword
To his great master, who thereat enraged
Flew on him, and amongst them felled him dead,   75
But not without that harmful stroke which since
Hath plucked him after.
ALBANY   This shows you are above,
You justicers, that these our nether crimes
So speedily can venge. But O, poor Gloucester!
Lost he his other eye?
⌐SECOND⌐ GENTLEMAN   Both, both, my lord.   80
(*To Gonoril*) This letter, madam, craves a speedy
   answer.
'Tis from your sister.
GONORIL (*aside*)   One way I like this well;
But being widow, and my Gloucester with her,
May all the building on my fancy pluck
Upon my hateful life. Another way   85
The news is not so took.—I'll read and answer.   *Exit*
ALBANY
Where was his son when they did take his eyes?
⌐SECOND⌐ GENTLEMAN
Come with my lady hither.
ALBANY   He is not here.
⌐SECOND⌐ GENTLEMAN
No, my good lord; I met him back again.
ALBANY Knows he the wickedness?   90
⌐SECOND⌐ GENTLEMAN
Ay, my good lord; 'twas he informed against him,
And quit the house on purpose that their punishment
Might have the freer course.
ALBANY   Gloucester, I live
To thank thee for the love thou showed'st the King,
And to revenge thy eyes.—Come hither, friend.   95
Tell me what more thou knowest.   *Exeunt*

Sc. 17 *Enter the Earl of Kent disguised, and* ⌈*First*⌉
Gentleman

KENT Why the King of France is so suddenly gone back
know you no reason?

⌈FIRST⌉ GENTLEMAN
Something he left imperfect in the state
Which, since his coming forth, is thought of; which
Imports to the kingdom so much fear and danger   5
That his personal return was most required
And necessary.

KENT
Who hath he left behind him general?

⌈FIRST⌉ GENTLEMAN
The Maréchal of France, Monsieur la Far.

KENT Did your letters pierce the Queen to any
demonstration of grief?   11

⌈FIRST⌉ GENTLEMAN
Ay, sir. She took them, read them in my presence,
And now and then an ample tear trilled down
Her delicate cheek. It seemed she was a queen
Over her passion who, most rebel-like,   15
Sought to be king o'er her.

KENT   O, then it moved her.

⌈FIRST⌉ GENTLEMAN
Not to a rage. Patience and sorrow strove
Who should express her goodliest. You have seen
Sunshine and rain at once; her smiles and tears
Were like, a better way. Those happy smilets   20
That played on her ripe lip seemed not to know
What guests were in her eyes, which parted thence
As pearls from diamonds dropped. In brief,
Sorrow would be a rarity most beloved
If all could so become it.

KENT   Made she no verbal question?

⌈FIRST⌉ GENTLEMAN
Faith, once or twice she heaved the name of 'father' 26
Pantingly forth as if it pressed her heart,
Cried 'Sisters, sisters, shame of ladies, sisters,
Kent, father, sisters, what, i'th' storm, i'th' night,
Let piety not be believed!' There she shook   30
The holy water from her heavenly eyes
And clamour ma3tered, then away she started
To deal with grief alone.

KENT   It is the stars,
The stars above us govern our conditions,
Else one self mate and make could not beget   35
Such different issues. You spoke not with her since?

⌈FIRST⌉ GENTLEMAN No.

KENT
Was this before the King returned?

⌈FIRST⌉ GENTLEMAN   No, since.

KENT
Well, sir, the poor distressèd Lear's i'th' town,
Who sometime in his better tune remembers   40
What we are come about, and by no means
Will yield to see his daughter.

⌈FIRST⌉ GENTLEMAN   Why, good sir?

KENT
A sovereign shame so elbows him: his own unkindness,
That stripped her from his benediction, turned her
To foreign casualties, gave her dear rights   45
To his dog-hearted daughters—these things sting
His mind so venomously that burning shame
Detains him from Cordelia.

⌈FIRST⌉ GENTLEMAN   Alack, poor gentleman!

KENT
Of Albany's and Cornwall's powers you heard not?

⌈FIRST⌉ GENTLEMAN 'Tis so; they are afoot.   50

KENT
Well, sir, I'll bring you to our master Lear,
And leave you to attend him. Some dear cause
Will in concealment wrap me up a while.
When I am known aright you shall not grieve
Lending me this acquaintance. I pray you go   55
Along with me.   *Exeunt*

Sc. 18 *Enter Queen Cordelia, a Doctor, and others*

CORDELIA
Alack, 'tis he! Why, he was met even now,
As mad as the racked sea, singing aloud,
Crowned with rank fumitor and furrow-weeds,
With burdocks, hemlock, nettles, cuckoo-flowers,
Darnel, and all the idle weeds that grow   5
In our sustaining corn. The centuries send forth.
Search every acre in the high-grown field,
And bring him to our eye.   ⌈*Exit one or more*⌉
                              What can man's wisdom
In the restoring his bereavèd sense,
He that can help him   10
Take all my outward worth.

DOCTOR There is means, madam.
Our foster-nurse of nature is repose,
The which he lacks. That to provoke in him
Are many simples operative, whose power   15
Will close the eye of anguish.

CORDELIA   All blest secrets,
All you unpublished virtues of the earth,
Spring with my tears, be aidant and remediate
In the good man's distress!—Seek, seek for him,
Lest his ungoverned rage dissolve the life   20
That wants the means to lead it.
                    Enter a Messenger

MESSENGER   News, madam.
The British powers are marching hitherward.

CORDELIA
'Tis known before; our preparation stands
In expectation of them.—O dear father,
It is thy business that I go about;   25
Therefore great France
My mourning and important tears hath pitied.
No blown ambition doth our arms incite,
But love, dear love, and our agèd father's right.
Soon may I hear and see him!   *Exeunt*

Sc. 19 *Enter Regan and Oswald, Gonoril's steward*

REGAN
But are my brother's powers set forth?

OSWALD   Ay, madam.

REGAN
Himself in person?

OSWALD   Madam, with much ado.
Your sister is the better soldier.

REGAN
Lord Edmund spake not with your lord at home?

OSWALD No, madam.   5

REGAN
What might import my sister's letters to him?

OSWALD I know not, lady.

REGAN
Faith, he is posted hence on serious matter.
It was great ignorance, Gloucester's eyes being out,
To let him live. Where he arrives he moves   10
All hearts against us. Edmund, I think, is gone,
In pity of his misery, to dispatch
His 'nighted life, moreover to descry
The strength o'th' army.

OSWALD
I must needs after with my letters, madam.   15

REGAN
Our troop sets forth tomorrow. Stay with us.
The ways are dangerous.

OSWALD   I may not, madam.
My lady charged my duty in this business.

REGAN
Why should she write to Edmund? Might not you
Transport her purposes by word? Belike—   20
Something, I know not what. I'll love thee much:
Let me unseal the letter.

OSWALD   Madam, I'd rather—

REGAN
I know your lady does not love her husband.
I am sure of that, and at her late being here
She gave strange oeillades and most speaking looks 25
To noble Edmund. I know you are of her bosom.

OSWALD I, madam?

REGAN
I speak in understanding, for I know't.
Therefore I do advise you take this note.
My lord is dead. Edmund and I have talked,   30
And more convenient is he for my hand
Than for your lady's. You may gather more.
If you do find him, pray you give him this,
And when your mistress hears thus much from you,
I pray desire her call her wisdom to her.   35
So, farewell.
If you do chance to hear of that blind traitor,
Preferment falls on him that cuts him off.

OSWALD
Would I could meet him, madam. I would show
What lady I do follow.

REGAN   Fare thee well.   40

Exeunt severally

Sc. 20 *Enter Edgar disguised as a peasant, with a staff,
    guiding the blind Duke of Gloucester*

GLOUCESTER
When shall we come to th' top of that same hill?

EDGAR
You do climb up it now. Look how we labour.

GLOUCESTER
Methinks the ground is even.

EDGAR   Horrible steep.
Hark, do you hear the sea?

GLOUCESTER   No, truly.

EDGAR
Why, then your other senses grow imperfect   5
By your eyes' anguish.

GLOUCESTER   So may it be indeed.
Methinks thy voice is altered, and thou speak'st
With better phrase and matter than thou didst.

EDGAR
You're much deceived. In nothing am I changed
But in my garments.

GLOUCESTER   Methinks you're better spoken. 10

EDGAR
Come on, sir, here's the place. Stand still. How fearful
And dizzy 'tis to cast one's eyes so low!
The crows and choughs that wing the midway air
Show scarce so gross as beetles. Halfway down
Hangs one that gathers samphire, dreadful trade!   15
Methinks he seems no bigger than his head.
The fishermen that walk upon the beach
Appear like mice, and yon tall anchoring barque
Diminished to her cock, her cock a buoy
Almost too small for sight. The murmuring surge   20
That on the unnumbered idle pebble chafes
Cannot be heard, it's so high. I'll look no more,
Lest my brain turn and the deficient sight
Topple down headlong.

GLOUCESTER   Set me where you stand.

EDGAR
Give me your hand. You are now within a foot   25
Of th'extreme verge. For all beneath the moon
Would I not leap upright.

GLOUCESTER   Let go my hand.
Here, friend, 's another purse; in it a jewel
Well worth a poor man's taking. Fairies and gods
Prosper it with thee! Go thou farther off.   30
Bid me farewell, and let me hear thee going.

EDGAR
Now fare you well, good sir.
    He stands aside

GLOUCESTER   With all my heart.

EDGAR (*aside*)
Why I do trifle thus with his despair
Is done to cure it.

GLOUCESTER   O you mighty gods,
    He kneels
This world I do renounce, and in your sights   35
Shake patiently my great affliction off!
If I could bear it longer, and not fall
To quarrel with your great opposeless wills,
My snuff and loathèd part of nature should
Burn itself out. If Edgar live, O bless him!—   40
Now, fellow, fare thee well.

EDGAR   Gone, sir. Farewell.

Gloucester falls forward
(*Aside*) And yet I know not how conceit may rob
The treasury of life, when life itself
Yields to the theft. Had he been where he thought,
By this had thought been past.—Alive or dead?   45
(*To Gloucester*) Ho you, sir; hear you, sir? Speak.
(*Aside*) Thus might he pass indeed. Yet he revives.
(*To Gloucester*) What are you, sir?
GLOUCESTER   Away, and let me die.
EDGAR
Hadst thou been aught but goss'mer, feathers, air,
So many fathom down precipitating   50
Thou hadst shivered like an egg. But thou dost breathe,
Hast heavy substance, bleed'st not, speak'st, art sound.
Ten masts a-length make not the altitude
Which thou hast perpendicularly fell.
Thy life's a miracle. Speak yet again.   55
GLOUCESTER But have I fallen, or no?
EDGAR
From the dread summit of this chalky bourn.
Look up a-height. The shrill-gorged lark so far
Cannot be seen or heard. Do but look up.
GLOUCESTER Alack, I have no eyes.   60
Is wretchedness deprived that benefit
To end itself by death? 'Twas yet some comfort
When misery could beguile the tyrant's rage
And frustrate his proud will.
EDGAR   Give me your arm.
Up. So, how now? Feel you your legs? You stand.   65
GLOUCESTER
Too well, too well.
EDGAR   This is above all strangeness.
Upon the crown of the cliff what thing was that
Which parted from you?
GLOUCESTER   A poor unfortunate beggar.
EDGAR
As I stood here below, methoughts his eyes
Were two full moons. A had a thousand noses,   70
Horns whelked and waved like the enridgèd sea.
It was some fiend. Therefore, thou happy father,
Think that the clearest gods, who made their honours
Of men's impossibilities, have preserved thee.
GLOUCESTER
I do remember now. Henceforth I'll bear   75
Affliction till it do cry out itself
'Enough, enough,' and die. That thing you speak of,
I took it for a man. Often would it say
'The fiend, the fiend!' He led me to that place.
EDGAR
Bear free and patient thoughts.
*Enter King Lear mad, ⌈crowned with weeds and
flowers⌉*
                          But who comes here? 80
The safer sense will ne'er accommodate
His master thus.
LEAR No, they cannot touch me for coining. I am the
King himself.
EDGAR O thou side-piercing sight!   85
LEAR Nature is above art in that respect. There's your

press-money. That fellow handles his bow like a crow-
keeper. Draw me a clothier's yard. Look, look, a mouse!
Peace, peace, this toasted cheese will do it. There's my
gauntlet. I'll prove it on a giant. Bring up the brown
bills. O, well flown, bird, in the air. Ha! Give the word.
EDGAR Sweet marjoram.
LEAR Pass.
GLOUCESTER I know that voice.   94
LEAR Ha, Gonoril! Ha, Regan! They flattered me like a
dog, and told me I had white hairs in my beard ere
the black ones were there. To say 'ay' and 'no' to
everything I said 'ay' and 'no' to was no good divinity.
When the rain came to wet me once, and the wind to
make me chatter, when the thunder would not peace
at my bidding, there I found them, there I smelt them
out. Go to, they are not men of their words. They told
me I was everything; 'tis a lie, I am not ague-proof.
GLOUCESTER
The trick of that voice I do well remember.
Is't not the King?
LEAR   Ay, every inch a king.   105
⌈*Gloucester kneels*⌉
When I do stare, see how the subject quakes!
I pardon that man's life. What was thy cause?
Adultery? Thou shalt not die for adultery.
No, the wren goes to't, and the small gilded fly
Does lecher in my sight.   110
Let copulation thrive, for Gloucester's bastard son
Was kinder to his father than my daughters
Got 'tween the lawful sheets. To't, luxury, pell-mell,
For I lack soldiers. Behold yon simp'ring dame,
Whose face between her forks presageth snow,   115
That minces virtue, and does shake the head
To hear of pleasure's name:
The fitchew nor the soilèd horse goes to't
With a more riotous appetite. Down from the waist
They're centaurs, though women all above.   120
But to the girdle do the gods inherit;
Beneath is all the fiend's. There's hell, there's
          darkness,
There's the sulphury pit, burning, scalding,
Stench, consummation. Fie, fie, fie; pah, pah!
Give me an ounce of civet, good apothecary,   125
To sweeten my imagination.
There's money for thee.
GLOUCESTER   O, let me kiss that hand!
LEAR Here, wipe it first; it smells of mortality.
GLOUCESTER
O ruined piece of nature! This great world
Shall so wear out to naught. Do you know me?   130
LEAR I remember thy eyes well enough. Dost thou squiny
on me?
No, do thy worst, blind Cupid, I'll not love.
Read thou that challenge. Mark the penning of't.
GLOUCESTER
Were all the letters suns, I could not see one.   135
EDGAR (*aside*)
I would not take this from report; it is,
And my heart breaks at it.

LEAR (*to Gloucester*) Read.

GLOUCESTER What—with the case of eyes?

LEAR O ho, are you there with me? No eyes in your head, nor no money in your purse? Your eyes are in a heavy case, your purse in a light; yet you see how this world goes.

GLOUCESTER I see it feelingly.   144

LEAR What, art mad? A man may see how the world goes with no eyes; look with thy ears. See how yon justice rails upon yon simple thief. Hark in thy ear: handy-dandy, which is the thief, which is the justice? Thou hast seen a farmer's dog bark at a beggar?

GLOUCESTER Ay, sir.   150

LEAR An the creature run from the cur, there thou mightst behold the great image of authority. A dog's obeyed in office.

Thou rascal beadle, hold thy bloody hand.

Why dost thou lash that whore? Strip thine own back.

Thy blood as hotly lusts to use her in that kind   156

For which thou whip'st her. The usurer hangs the cozener.

Through tattered rags small vices do appear;

Robes and furred gowns hides all. Get thee glass eyes,

And, like a scurvy politician, seem   160

To see the things thou dost not. No tears, now.

Pull off my boots. Harder, harder! So.

EDGAR (*aside*)

O, matter and impertinency mixed—

Reason in madness!

LEAR

If thou wilt weep my fortune, take my eyes.   165

I know thee well enough: thy name is Gloucester.

Thou must be patient. We came crying hither.

Thou know'st the first time that we smell the air

We wail and cry. I will preach to thee. Mark me.

GLOUCESTER Alack, alack, the day!   170

LEAR ⌜*removing his crown of weeds*⌝

When we are born, we cry that we are come

To this great stage of fools. This' a good block.

It were a delicate stratagem to shoe

A troop of horse with felt; and when I have stole upon

These son-in-laws, then kill, kill, kill, kill, kill, kill!   175

Enter three Gentlemen

⌜FIRST⌝ GENTLEMAN

O, here he is. Lay hands upon him, sirs.

(*To Lear*) Your most dear—

LEAR

No rescue? What, a prisoner? I am e'en

The natural fool of fortune. Use me well.

You shall have ransom. Let me have a surgeon;   180

I am cut to the brains.

⌜FIRST⌝ GENTLEMAN You shall have anything.

LEAR No seconds? All myself?

Why, this would make a man a man of salt,

To use his eyes for garden water-pots,   185

Ay, and laying autumn's dust.

⌜FIRST⌝ GENTLEMAN Good sir—

LEAR

I will die bravely, like a bridegroom.

What, I will be jovial. Come, come,

I am a king, my masters, know you that?

⌜FIRST⌝ GENTLEMAN

You are a royal one, and we obey you.   190

LEAR Then there's life in't. Nay, an you get it, you shall get it with running.

Exit running, pursued by two Gentlemen

⌜FIRST⌝ GENTLEMAN

A sight most pitiful in the meanest wretch,

Past speaking in a king. Thou hast one daughter

Who redeems nature from the general curse   195

Which twain hath brought her to.

EDGAR Hail, gentle sir.

⌜FIRST⌝ GENTLEMAN Sir, speed you. What's your will?

EDGAR

Do you hear aught of a battle toward?

⌜FIRST⌝ GENTLEMAN

Most sure and vulgar, everyone hears that   200

That can distinguish sense.

EDGAR But, by your favour,

How near's the other army?

⌜FIRST⌝ GENTLEMAN

Near and on speedy foot, the main; descriers   204

Stands on the hourly thoughts.

EDGAR I thank you, sir. That's all.

⌜FIRST⌝ GENTLEMAN

Though that the Queen on special cause is here,

Her army is moved on.

EDGAR I thank you, sir.

Exit Gentleman

GLOUCESTER

You ever gentle gods, take my breath from me.

Let not my worser spirit tempt me again

To die before you please.   210

EDGAR Well pray you, father.

GLOUCESTER Now, good sir, what are you?

EDGAR

A most poor man, made lame by fortune's blows,

Who by the art of known and feeling sorrows

Am pregnant to good pity. Give me your hand,   215

I'll lead you to some biding.

GLOUCESTER ⌜*rising*⌝ Hearty thanks.

The bounty and the benison of heaven

To send thee boot to boot.

Enter Oswald the steward

OSWALD A proclaimed prize! Most happy!

That eyeless head of thine was first framed flesh

To raise my fortunes. Thou most unhappy traitor,   220

Briefly thyself remember. The sword is out

That must destroy thee.

GLOUCESTER Now let thy friendly hand

Put strength enough to't.

OSWALD (*to Edgar*) Wherefore, bold peasant,

Durst thou support a published traitor? Hence,

Lest the infection of his fortune take   225

Like hold on thee. Let go his arm.

EDGAR 'Chill not let go, sir, without 'cagion.

OSWALD Let go, slave, or thou diest.

EDGAR Good gentleman, go your gate. Let poor volk pass.
An 'chud have been swaggered out of my life, it would
not have been so long by a vortnight. Nay, come not
near the old man. Keep out, 'che vor' ye, or I'll try
whether your costard or my baton be the harder; I'll
be plain with you.

OSWALD Out, dunghill!   235

    They fight

EDGAR 'Chill pick your teeth, sir. Come, no matter for
your foins.

    ⌈*Edgar knocks him down*⌉

OSWALD
Slave, thou hast slain me. Villain, take my purse.
If ever thou wilt thrive, bury my body,
And give the letters which thou find'st about me   240
To Edmund, Earl of Gloucester. Seek him out
Upon the British party. O untimely death! Death!

        He dies

EDGAR
I know thee well—a serviceable villain,
As duteous to the vices of thy mistress
As badness would desire.   245

GLOUCESTER What, is he dead?

EDGAR Sit you down, father. Rest you.

  Gloucester sits

Let's see his pockets. These letters that he speaks of
May be my friends. He's dead; I am only sorrow
He had no other deathsman. Let us see.   250
Leave, gentle wax; and manners, blame us not.
To know our enemies' minds we'd rip their hearts;
Their papers is more lawful.

  He reads a letter

'Let your reciprocal vows be remembered. You have
many opportunities to cut him off. If your will want
not, time and place will be fruitfully offered. There is
nothing done if he return the conqueror; then am I
the prisoner, and his bed my jail, from the loathed
warmth whereof, deliver me, and supply the place for
your labour.   260
  Your—wife, so I would say—your affectionate
  servant, and for you her own for venture,
            Gonoril.'

O indistinguished space of woman's wit—
A plot upon her virtuous husband's life,   265
And the exchange my brother!—Here in the sands
Thee I'll rake up, the post unsanctified
Of murderous lechers, and in the mature time
With this ungracious paper strike the sight
Of the death-practisèd Duke. For him 'tis well   270
That of thy death and business I can tell.

    ⌈*Exit with the body*⌉

GLOUCESTER
The King is mad. How stiff is my vile sense,
That I stand up and have ingenious feeling
Of my huge sorrows! Better I were distraught;
So should my thoughts be fencèd from my griefs,   275

And woes by wrong imaginations lose
The knowledge of themselves.

   A drum afar off. ⌈*Enter Edgar*⌉

EDGAR   Give me your hand.
Far off methinks I hear the beaten drum.
Come, father, I'll bestow you with a friend.

    Exit Edgar guiding Gloucester

Sc. 21 ⌈*Soft music.*⌉ *Enter Queen Cordelia, and the Earl of
   Kent, disguised*

CORDELIA O thou good Kent,
How shall I live and work to match thy goodness?
My life will be too short, and every measure fail me.

KENT
To be acknowledged, madam, is o'erpaid.
All my reports go with the modest truth,   5
Nor more, nor clipped, but so.

CORDELIA   Be better suited.
These weeds are memories of those worser hours.
I prithee put them off.

KENT   Pardon me, dear madam.
Yet to be known shortens my made intent.
My boon I make it that you know me not   10
Till time and I think meet.

CORDELIA   Then be't so, my good lord.

   ⌈*Enter the Doctor and First Gentleman*⌉

How does the King?

DOCTOR   Madam, sleeps still.

CORDELIA   O you kind gods,
Cure this great breach in his abusèd nature;
The untuned and hurrying senses O wind up
Of this child-changèd father!

DOCTOR   So please your majesty   15
That we may wake the King? He hath slept long.

CORDELIA
Be governed by your knowledge, and proceed
I'th' sway of your own will. Is he arrayed?

⌈FIRST GENTLEMAN⌉
Ay, madam. In the heaviness of his sleep
We put fresh garments on him.   20

⌈DOCTOR⌉
Good madam, be by when we do awake him.
I doubt not of his temperance.

CORDELIA   Very well.

DOCTOR
Please you draw near. Louder the music there!

  King Lear is ⌈*discovered*⌉ *asleep*

CORDELIA
O my dear father, restoration hang
Thy medicine on my lips, and let this kiss   25
Repair those violent harms that my two sisters
Have in thy reverence made!

KENT   Kind and dear princess!

CORDELIA
Had you not been their father, these white flakes
Had challenged pity of them. Was this a face
To be exposed against the warring winds,   30
To stand against the deep dread-bolted thunder

In the most terrible and nimble stroke
Of quick cross-lightning, to watch—poor *perdu*—
With this thin helm? Mine injurer's mean'st dog,
Though he had bit me, should have stood that night
Against my fire. And wast thou fain, poor father,   36
To hovel thee with swine and rogues forlorn
In short and musty straw? Alack, alack,
'Tis wonder that thy life and wits at once
Had not concluded all! (*To the Doctor*) He wakes.
          Speak to him.   40
DOCTOR Madam, do you; 'tis fittest.
CORDELIA (*to Lear*)
How does my royal lord? How fares your majesty?
LEAR
You do me wrong to take me out o'th' grave.
Thou art a soul in bliss, but I am bound
Upon a wheel of fire, that mine own tears   45
Do scald like molten lead.
CORDELIA   Sir, know me.
LEAR
You're a spirit, I know. Where did you die?
CORDELIA (*to the Doctor*) Still, still far wide!
DOCTOR
He's scarce awake. Let him alone a while.
LEAR
Where have I been? Where am I? Fair daylight?   50
I am mightily abused. I should e'en die with pity
To see another thus. I know not what to say.
I will not swear these are my hands. Let's see:
I feel this pin prick. Would I were assured
Of my condition.
CORDELIA (*kneeling*) O look upon me, sir,   55
And hold your hands in benediction o'er me.
No, sir, you must not kneel.
LEAR   Pray do not mock.
I am a very foolish, fond old man,
Fourscore and upward, and to deal plainly,
I fear I am not in my perfect mind.   60
Methinks I should know you, and know this man;
Yet I am doubtful, for I am mainly ignorant
What place this is; and all the skill I have
Remembers not these garments; nor I know not
Where I did lodge last night. Do not laugh at me,   65
For as I am a man, I think this lady
To be my child, Cordelia.
CORDELIA   And so I am.
LEAR
Be your tears wet? Yes, faith. I pray, weep not.
If you have poison for me, I will drink it.
I know you do not love me; for your sisters   70
Have, as I do remember, done me wrong.
You have some cause; they have not.
CORDELIA   No cause, no cause.
LEAR Am I in France?
KENT In your own kingdom, sir.
LEAR Do not abuse me.   75
DOCTOR
Be comforted, good madam. The great rage

You see is cured in him, and yet it is danger
To make him even o'er the time he has lost.
Desire him to go in; trouble him no more
Till further settling.   80
CORDELIA (*to Lear*) Will't please your highness walk?
LEAR You must bear with me.
Pray now, forget and forgive. I am old
And foolish.
              Exeunt all but Kent and ⌈First⌉ Gentleman
⌈FIRST⌉ GENTLEMAN Holds it true, sir, that the Duke
Of Cornwall was so slain?
KENT   Most certain, sir.   85
⌈FIRST⌉ GENTLEMAN
Who is conductor of his people?
KENT   As 'tis said,
The bastard son of Gloucester.
⌈FIRST⌉ GENTLEMAN   They say Edgar,
His banished son, is with the Earl of Kent
In Germany.
KENT   Report is changeable.
'Tis time to look about. The powers of the kingdom   90
Approach apace.
⌈FIRST⌉ GENTLEMAN The arbitrement is
Like to be bloody. Fare you well, sir.   *Exit*
KENT
My point and period will be throughly wrought,
Or well or ill, as this day's battle's fought.   *Exit*

Sc. 22 *Enter Edmund, Regan, and their powers*
EDMUND
Know of the Duke if his last purpose hold,
Or whether since he is advised by aught
To change the course. He's full of abdication
And self-reproving. Bring his constant pleasure.
                              Exit one or more
REGAN
Our sister's man is certainly miscarried.   5
EDMUND
'Tis to be doubted, madam.
REGAN   Now, sweet lord,
You know the goodness I intend upon you.
Tell me but truly—but then speak the truth—
Do you not love my sister?
EDMUND   Ay: honoured love.
REGAN
But have you never found my brother's way   10
To the forfended place?
EDMUND That thought abuses you.
REGAN I am doubtful
That you have been conjunct and bosomed with her,
As far as we call hers.
EDMUND   No, by mine honour, madam. 15
REGAN
I never shall endure her. Dear my lord,
Be not familiar with her.
EDMUND Fear me not.
She and the Duke her husband—

Enter the Duke of Albany and Gonoril with troops

GONORIL *(aside)*

I had rather lose the battle than that sister   20
Should loosen him and me.

ALBANY *(to Regan)*

Our very loving sister, well bemet,
For this I hear: the King is come to his daughter,
With others whom the rigour of our state
Forced to cry out. Where I could not be honest   25
I never yet was valiant. For this business,
It touches us as France invades our land;
Yet bold's the King, with others whom I fear.
Most just and heavy causes make oppose.

EDMUND

Sir, you speak nobly.

REGAN   Why is this reasoned?   30

GONORIL

Combine together 'gainst the enemy;
For these domestic poor particulars
Are not to question here.

ALBANY

Let us then determine with the ensign of war
On our proceedings.

EDMUND   I shall attend you   35
Presently at your tent.   ⌈*Exit with his powers*⌉

REGAN   Sister, you'll go with us?

GONORIL No.

REGAN

'Tis most convenient. Pray you go with us.

GONORIL ⌈*aside*⌉

O ho, I know the riddle! *(To Regan)* I will go.

Enter Edgar disguised as a peasant

EDGAR *(to Albany)*

If e'er your grace had speech with man so poor,   40
Hear me one word.

ALBANY *(to the others)* I'll overtake you.

Exeunt all but Albany and Edgar

                    Speak.

EDGAR

Before you fight the battle, ope this letter.
If you have victory, let the trumpet sound
For him that brought it. Wretched though I seem,
I can produce a champion that will prove   45
What is avouchèd there. If you miscarry,
Your business of the world hath so an end.
Fortune love you—

ALBANY Stay till I have read the letter.

EDGAR I was forbid it.   50
When time shall serve, let but the herald cry,
And I'll appear again.

ALBANY Why, fare thee well.
I will o'erlook the paper.   *Exit Edgar*

Enter Edmund

EDMUND

The enemy's in view; draw up your powers.   55

He ⌈offers⌉ Albany a paper

Here is the guess of their great strength and forces

By diligent discovery; but your haste
Is now urged on you.

ALBANY   We will greet the time.   *Exit*

EDMUND

To both these sisters have I sworn my love,
Each jealous of the other as the stung   60
Are of the adder. Which of them shall I take?—
Both?—one?—or neither? Neither can be enjoyed
If both remain alive. To take the widow
Exasperates, makes mad, her sister Gonoril,
And hardly shall I carry out my side,   65
Her husband being alive. Now then, we'll use
His countenance for the battle, which being done,
Let her that would be rid of him devise
His speedy taking off. As for his mercy
Which he intends to Lear and to Cordelia,   70
The battle done, and they within our power,
Shall never see his pardon; for my state
Stands on me to defend, not to debate.   *Exit*

Sc. 23 *Alarum. The powers of France pass over the stage
⌈led by⌉ Queen Cordelia with her father in her hand.
Then enter Edgar disguised as a peasant, guiding the
blind Duke of Gloucester*

EDGAR

Here, father, take the shadow of this bush
For your good host; pray that the right may thrive.
If ever I return to you again
I'll bring you comfort.   *Exit*

GLOUCESTER   Grace go with you, sir.

Alarum and retreat. Enter Edgar

EDGAR

Away, old man. Give me thy hand. Away.   5
King Lear hath lost, he and his daughter ta'en.
Give me thy hand. Come on.

GLOUCESTER

No farther, sir. A man may rot even here.

EDGAR

What, in ill thoughts again? Men must endure
Their going hence even as their coming hither.   10
Ripeness is all. Come on.

Exit Edgar guiding Gloucester

Sc. 24 *Enter Edmund with King Lear and Queen Cordelia
prisoners, a Captain, and soldiers*

EDMUND

Some officers take them away. Good guard
Until their greater pleasures best be known
That are to censure them.

CORDELIA *(to Lear)*   We are not the first
Who with best meaning have incurred the worst.
For thee, oppressèd King, am I cast down,   5
Myself could else outfrown false fortune's frown.
Shall we not see these daughters and these sisters?

LEAR

No, no. Come, let's away to prison.
We two alone will sing like birds i'th' cage.

When thou dost ask me blessing, I'll kneel down   10
And ask of thee forgiveness; so we'll live,
And pray, and sing, and tell old tales, and laugh
At gilded butterflies, and hear poor rogues
Talk of court news, and we'll talk with them too—
Who loses and who wins, who's in, who's out,   15
And take upon 's the mystery of things
As if we were God's spies; and we'll wear out
In a walled prison packs and sects of great ones
That ebb and flow by th' moon.
EDMUND (*to soldiers*)   Take them away.
LEAR (*to Cordelia*)
Upon such sacrifices, my Cordelia,   20
The gods themselves throw incense. Have I caught
     thee?
He that parts us shall bring a brand from heaven
And fire us hence like foxes. Wipe thine eyes.
The goodyear shall devour 'em, flesh and fell,
Ere they shall make us weep. We'll see 'em starve
     first. Come.   *Exeunt all but Edmund and the Captain*
EDMUND Come hither, captain. Hark.   26
Take thou this note. Go follow them to prison.
One step I have advanced thee; if thou dost
As this instructs thee, thou dost make thy way
To noble fortunes. Know thou this: that men   30
Are as the time is. To be tender-minded
Does not become a sword. Thy great employment
Will not bear question. Either say thou'lt do't,
Or thrive by other means.
CAPTAIN   I'll do't, my lord.
EDMUND
About it, and write 'happy' when thou hast done.   35
Mark, I say, instantly, and carry it so
As I have set it down.
CAPTAIN   I cannot draw a cart,
Nor eat dried oats. If it be man's work, I'll do't.   *Exit*
     *Enter the Duke of Albany, the two ladies Gonoril
     and Regan, ⌜another Captain,⌝ and others*
ALBANY (*to Edmund*)
Sir, you have showed today your valiant strain,
And fortune led you well. You have the captives   40
That were the opposites of this day's strife.
We do require then of you, so to use them
As we shall find their merits and our safety
May equally determine.
EDMUND   Sir, I thought it fit
To send the old and miserable King   45
To some retention and appointed guard,
Whose age has charms in it, whose title more,
To pluck the common bosom on his side
And turn our impressed lances in our eyes
Which do command them. With him I sent the Queen,
My reason all the same, and they are ready   51
Tomorrow, or at further space, to appear
Where you shall hold your session. At this time
We sweat and bleed. The friend hath lost his friend,
And the best quarrels in the heat are cursed   55

By those that feel their sharpness.
The question of Cordelia and her father
Requires a fitter place.
ALBANY   Sir, by your patience,
I hold you but a subject of this war,
Not as a brother.
REGAN   That's as we list to grace him.   60
Methinks our pleasure should have been demanded
Ere you had spoke so far. He led our powers,
Bore the commission of my place and person,
The which immediate may well stand up
And call itself your brother.
GONORIL   Not so hot.   65
In his own grace he doth exalt himself
More than in your advancement.
REGAN   In my right
By me invested, he compeers the best.
GONORIL
That were the most if he should husband you.
REGAN
Jesters do oft prove prophets.
GONORIL   Holla, holla—   70
That eye that told you so looked but asquint.
REGAN
Lady, I am not well, else I should answer
From a full-flowing stomach. (*To Edmund*) General,
Take thou my soldiers, prisoners, patrimony.
Witness the world that I create thee here   75
My lord and master.
GONORIL   Mean you to enjoy him, then?
ALBANY
The let-alone lies not in your good will.
EDMUND
Nor in thine, lord.
ALBANY   Half-blooded fellow, yes.
EDMUND
Let the drum strike and prove my title good.
ALBANY
Stay yet, hear reason. Edmund, I arrest thee   80
On capital treason, and in thine attaint
This gilded serpent. (*To Regan*) For your claim, fair
     sister,
I bar it in the interest of my wife.
'Tis she is subcontracted to this lord,
And I, her husband, contradict the banns.   85
If you will marry, make your love to me.
My lady is bespoke.—Thou art armed, Gloucester.
If none appear to prove upon thy head
Thy heinous, manifest, and many treasons,
     ⌜*He throws down a glove*⌝
There is my pledge. I'll prove it on thy heart,   90
Ere I taste bread, thou art in nothing less
Than I have here proclaimed thee.
REGAN Sick, O sick!
GONORIL (*aside*) If not, I'll ne'er trust poison.
EDMUND (*to Albany, ⌜throwing down a glove⌝*)
There's my exchange. What in the world he is   95

That names me traitor, villain-like he lies.
Call by thy trumpet. He that dares, approach;
On him, on you—who not?—I will maintain
My truth and honour firmly.
ALBANY A herald, ho!   100
EDMUND A herald, ho, a herald!
ALBANY
Trust to thy single virtue, for thy soldiers,
All levied in my name, have in my name
Took their discharge.
REGAN   This sickness grows upon me.
ALBANY
She is not well. Convey her to my tent.   105
                          Exit one or more with Regan
               ⌈*Enter a Herald and a trumpeter*⌉
Come hither, herald. Let the trumpet sound,
And read out this.
SECOND CAPTAIN Sound, trumpet!
                    Trumpeter sounds
HERALD (*reads*) 'If any man of quality or degree in the
host of the army will maintain upon Edmund, supposed
Earl of Gloucester, that he's a manifold traitor, let him
appear at the third sound of the trumpet. He is bold in
his defence.'
EDMUND Sound! (*Trumpeter sounds*) Again!
      Enter Edgar, armed, at the third sound, a trumpeter
      before him
ALBANY (*to the Herald*)
Ask him his purposes, why he appears   115
Upon this call o'th' trumpet.
HERALD (*to Edgar*)   What are you?
Your name and quality, and why you answer
This present summons?
EDGAR   O, know my name is lost,
By treason's tooth bare-gnawn and canker-bit.
Yet ere I move't, where is the adversary   120
I come to cope withal?
ALBANY   Which is that adversary?
EDGAR
What's he that speaks for Edmund, Earl of Gloucester?
EDMUND
Himself. What sayst thou to him?
EDGAR   Draw thy sword,
That if my speech offend a noble heart
Thy arm may do thee justice. Here is mine.   125
      He draws his sword
Behold, it is the privilege of my tongue,
My oath, and my profession. I protest,
Maugre thy strength, youth, place, and eminence,
Despite thy victor-sword and fire-new fortune,
Thy valour and thy heart, thou art a traitor,   130
False to thy gods, thy brother, and thy father,
Conspirant 'gainst this high illustrious prince,
And from th'extremest upward of thy head
To the descent and dust beneath thy feet
A most toad-spotted traitor. Say thou no,   135
This sword, this arm, and my best spirits are bent

To prove upon thy heart, whereto I speak,
Thou liest.
EDMUND   In wisdom I should ask thy name,
But since thy outside looks so fair and warlike,
And that thy tongue some say of breeding breathes,140
My right of knighthood I disdain and spurn.
Here do I toss those treasons to thy head,
With the hell-hated lie o'erturn thy heart,
Which, for they yet glance by and scarcely bruise,
This sword of mine shall give them instant way   145
Where they shall rest for ever. Trumpets, speak!
      ⌈*Flourish.*⌉ *They fight. Edmund is vanquished*
⌈ALL⌉
Save him, save him!
GONORIL   This is mere practice, Gloucester.
By the law of arms thou art not bound to answer
An unknown opposite. Thou art not vanquished,
But cozened and beguiled.
ALBANY   Stop your mouth, dame, 150
Or with this paper shall I stopple it.
Thou worse than anything, read thine own evil.
Nay, no tearing, lady. I perceive you know't.
GONORIL
Say if I do, the laws are mine, not thine.
Who shall arraign me for't?
ALBANY   Most monstrous!   155
Know'st thou this paper?
GONORIL   Ask me not what I know.
                                         Exit
ALBANY
Go after her. She's desperate. Govern her.
                                Exit one or more
EDMUND
What you have charged me with, that have I done,
And more, much more. The time will bring it out.
'Tis past, and so am I. (*To Edgar*) But what art thou,
That hast this fortune on me? If thou beest noble, 161
I do forgive thee.
EDGAR   Let's exchange charity.
I am no less in blood than thou art, Edmund.
If more, the more ignobly thou hast wronged me.
      ⌈*He takes off his helmet*⌉
My name is Edgar, and thy father's son.   165
The gods are just, and of our pleasant vices
Make instruments to scourge us.
The dark and vicious place where thee he got
Cost him his eyes.
EDMUND   Thou hast spoken truth.
The wheel is come full circled. I am here.   170
ALBANY (*to Edgar*)
Methought thy very gait did prophesy
A royal nobleness. I must embrace thee.
Let sorrow split my heart if I did ever hate
Thee or thy father.
EDGAR Worthy prince, I know't.   175
ALBANY Where have you hid yourself?
How have you known the miseries of your father?

EDGAR
By nursing them, my lord. List a brief tale,
And when 'tis told, O that my heart would burst!
The bloody proclamation to escape   180
That followed me so near—O, our lives' sweetness,
That with the pain of death would hourly die
Rather than die at once!—taught me to shift
Into a madman's rags, to assume a semblance
That very dogs disdained; and in this habit   185
Met I my father with his bleeding rings,
The precious stones new-lost; became his guide,
Led him, begged for him, saved him from despair;
Never—O father!—revealed myself unto him
Until some half hour past, when I was armed.   190
Not sure, though hoping, of this good success,
I asked his blessing, and from first to last
Told him my pilgrimage; but his flawed heart—
Alack, too weak the conflict to support—
'Twixt two extremes of passion, joy and grief,   195
Burst smilingly.

EDMUND   This speech of yours hath moved me,
And shall perchance do good. But speak you on—
You look as you had something more to say.

ALBANY
If there be more, more woeful, hold it in,
For I am almost ready to dissolve,   200
Hearing of this.

EDGAR   This would have seemed a period
To such as love not sorrow; but another
To amplify, too much would make much more,
And top extremity.
Whilst I was big in clamour came there in a man   205
Who, having seen me in my worst estate,
Shunned my abhorred society; but then, finding
Who 'twas that so endured, with his strong arms
He fastened on my neck and bellowed out
As he'd burst heaven; threw him on my father,   210
Told the most piteous tale of Lear and him
That ever ear received, which in recounting
His grief grew puissant and the strings of life
Began to crack. Twice then the trumpets sounded,
And there I left him tranced.

ALBANY   But who was this?   215

EDGAR
Kent, sir, the banished Kent, who in disguise
Followed his enemy king, and did him service
Improper for a slave.
        Enter ⌈Second⌉ Gentleman with a bloody knife
⌈SECOND⌉ GENTLEMAN   Help, help!

ALBANY   What kind of help?
What means that bloody knife?

⌈SECOND⌉ GENTLEMAN   It's hot, it smokes.
It came even from the heart of—

ALBANY   Who, man? Speak.

⌈SECOND⌉ GENTLEMAN
Your lady, sir, your lady; and her sister   221
By her is poisonèd—she hath confessed it.

EDMUND
I was contracted to them both; all three
Now marry in an instant.

ALBANY
Produce their bodies, be they alive or dead.   225
This justice of the heavens, that makes us tremble,
Touches us not with pity.
        Enter Kent as himself

EDGAR   Here comes Kent, sir.

ALBANY
O, 'tis he; the time will not allow
The compliment that very manners urges.

KENT I am come   230
To bid my king and master aye good night.
Is he not here?

ALBANY   Great thing of us forgot!—
Speak, Edmund; where's the King, and where's
    Cordelia?
        The bodies of Gonoril and Regan are brought in
Seest thou this object, Kent?

KENT Alack, why thus?   235

EDMUND Yet Edmund was beloved.
The one the other poisoned for my sake,
And after slew herself.

ALBANY   Even so.—Cover their faces.

EDMUND
I pant for life. Some good I mean to do,
Despite of my own nature. Quickly send,   240
Be brief in't, to th' castle; for my writ
Is on the life of Lear and on Cordelia.
Nay, send in time.

ALBANY   Run, run, O run!

EDGAR
To who, my lord? Who hath the office? Send
Thy token of reprieve.   245

EDMUND
Well thought on! Take my sword. The captain,
Give it the captain.

ALBANY   Haste thee for thy life.
        Exit ⌈Second Captain⌉

EDMUND
He hath commission from thy wife and me
To hang Cordelia in the prison, and
To lay the blame upon her own despair,   250
That she fordid herself.

ALBANY
The gods defend her!—Bear him hence a while.
        Exeunt some with Edmund
        Enter King Lear with Queen Cordelia in his arms,
        ⌈followed by the Second Captain⌉

LEAR
Howl, howl, howl, howl! O, you are men of stones.
Had I your tongues and eyes, I would use them so
That heaven's vault should crack. She's gone for ever.
I know when one is dead and when one lives.   256
She's dead as earth.
        ⌈He lays her down⌉
                    Lend me a looking-glass.

If that her breath will mist or stain the stone,
Why, then she lives.

KENT   Is this the promised end?

EDGAR

Or image of that horror?

ALBANY   Fall and cease.   260

LEAR

This feather stirs. She lives. If it be so,
It is a chance which does redeem all sorrows
That ever I have felt.

KENT ⌈kneeling⌉   Ah, my good master!

LEAR

Prithee, away.

EDGAR   'Tis noble Kent, your friend.

LEAR

A plague upon you, murderous traitors all.   265
I might have saved her; now she's gone for ever.—
Cordelia, Cordelia: stay a little. Ha?
What is't thou sayst?—Her voice was ever soft,
Gentle, and low, an excellent thing in women.—
I killed the slave that was a-hanging thee.   270

⌈SECOND⌉ CAPTAIN

'Tis true, my lords, he did.

LEAR   Did I not, fellow?

I have seen the day with my good biting falchion
I would have made them skip. I am old now,
And these same crosses spoil me. (To Kent) Who are
    you?

Mine eyes are not o' the best, I'll tell you straight.   275

KENT

If fortune bragged of two she loved or hated,
One of them we behold.

LEAR   Are not you Kent?

KENT

The same, your servant Kent. Where is your servant
    Caius?

LEAR

He's a good fellow, I can tell you that.
He'll strike, and quickly too. He's dead and rotten.   280

KENT

No, my good lord, I am the very man—

LEAR I'll see that straight.

KENT

That from your first of difference and decay
Have followed your sad steps.

LEAR   You're welcome hither.

KENT

Nor no man else. All's cheerless, dark, and deadly.   285
Your eldest daughters have fordone themselves,
And desperately are dead.

LEAR   So think I, too.

ALBANY

He knows not what he sees; and vain it is
That we present us to him.

EDGAR   Very bootless.

    Enter another Captain

⌈THIRD⌉ CAPTAIN (to Albany)

Edmund is dead, my lord.

ALBANY   That's but a trifle here.— 290
You lords and noble friends, know our intent.
What comfort to this great decay may come
Shall be applied; for us, we will resign
During the life of this old majesty
To him our absolute power; (to Edgar and Kent) you
    to your rights,   295
With boot and such addition as your honours
Have more than merited. All friends shall taste
The wages of their virtue, and all foes
The cup of their deservings.—O see, see!

LEAR

And my poor fool is hanged. No, no life.   300
Why should a dog, a horse, a rat have life,
And thou no breath at all? O, thou wilt come no more.
Never, never, never.—Pray you, undo
This button. Thank you, sir. O, O, O, O!

EDGAR He faints. (To Lear) My lord, my lord!   305

LEAR Break, heart, I prithee break.

EDGAR Look up, my lord.

KENT

Vex not his ghost. O, let him pass. He hates him
That would upon the rack of this tough world
Stretch him out longer.

    ⌈Lear dies⌉

EDGAR   O, he is gone indeed.   310

KENT

The wonder is he hath endured so long.
He but usurped his life.

ALBANY (to attendants)

Bear them from hence. Our present business
Is to general woe. (To Kent and Edgar) Friends of my
    soul, you twain
Rule in this kingdom, and the gored state sustain.   315

KENT

I have a journey, sir, shortly to go:
My master calls, and I must not say no.

ALBANY

The weight of this sad time we must obey,
Speak what we feel, not what we ought to say.
The oldest have borne most. We that are young   320
Shall never see so much, nor live so long.

    Exeunt carrying the bodies

THE TRAGEDY OF KING LEAR
THE FOLIO TEXT

THE text of *King Lear* given here represents the revision made probably two or three years after the first version had been written and performed; it is based on the text printed in the 1623 Folio. This is a more obviously theatrical text. It makes a number of significant cuts, amounting to some 300 lines. The most conspicuous ones are the dialogue in which Lear's Fool implicitly calls his master a fool (Quarto Sc. 4, 136–51); Kent's account of the French invasion of England (Quarto Sc. 8, 21–33); Lear's mock-trial, in his madness, of his daughters (Quarto Sc. 13, 13–52); Edgar's generalizing couplets at the end of that scene (Quarto Sc. 13, 97–110); the brief, compassionate dialogue of two of Gloucester's servants after his blinding (Quarto Sc. 14, 97–106); parts of Albany's protest to Goneril about the sisters' treatment of Lear (in Quarto Sc. 16); the entire scene (Quarto Sc. 17) in which a Gentleman tells Kent of Cordelia's grief on hearing of her father's condition; the presence of the Doctor and the musical accompaniment to the reunion of Lear and Cordelia; and Edgar's account of his meeting with Kent in which Kent's 'strings of life | Began to crack' (Quarto Sc. 24, 201–18). The Folio also adds about 100 lines that are not in the Quarto— mostly in short passages, including Kent's statement that Albany and Cornwall have servants who are in the pay of France (3.1.13–20), Merlin's prophecy spoken by the Fool at the end of 3.2, and the last lines of both the Fool and Lear. In addition, several speeches are differently assigned, and there are many variations in wording.

The reasons for these variations, and their effect on the play, are to some extent matters of speculation and of individual interpretation. Certainly they streamline the play's action, removing some reflective passages, particularly at the ends of scenes. They affect the characterization of, especially, Edgar, Albany, and Kent, and there are significant differences in the play's closing passages. Structurally the principal differences lie in the presentation of the military actions in the later part of the play; in the Folio-based text Cordelia is more clearly in charge of the forces that come to Lear's assistance, and they are less clearly a French invasion force. The absence from this text of passages that appeared in the 1608 text implies no criticism of them in themselves. The play's revision may have been dictated in whole or in part by theatrical exigencies, or it may have emerged from Shakespeare's own dissatisfaction with what he had first written. Each version has its own integrity, which is distorted by the practice, traditional since the early eighteenth century, of conflation.

THE PERSONS OF THE PLAY

LEAR, King of Britain

GONERIL, Lear's eldest daughter

Duke of ALBANY, her husband

REGAN, Lear's second daughter

Duke of CORNWALL, her husband

CORDELIA, Lear's youngest daughter

King of FRANCE } suitors of Cordelia
Duke of BURGUNDY

Earl of KENT, later disguised as Caius

Earl of GLOUCESTER

EDGAR, elder son of Gloucester, later disguised as Tom o' Bedlam

EDMOND, bastard son of Gloucester

OLD MAN, Gloucester's tenant

CURAN, Gloucester's retainer

Lear's FOOL

OSWALD, Goneril's steward

A SERVANT of Cornwall

A KNIGHT

A HERALD

A CAPTAIN

Gentlemen, servants, soldiers, attendants, messengers

The Tragedy of King Lear

1.1 *Enter the Earl of Kent, the Duke of Gloucester, and Edmond*

KENT I thought the King had more affected the Duke of Albany than Cornwall.

GLOUCESTER It did always seem so to us, but now in the division of the kingdom it appears not which of the Dukes he values most; for qualities are so weighed that curiosity in neither can make choice of either's moiety.

KENT Is not this your son, my lord?

GLOUCESTER His breeding, sir, hath been at my charge. I have so often blushed to acknowledge him that now I am brazed to't. 10

KENT I cannot conceive you.

GLOUCESTER Sir, this young fellow's mother could, whereupon she grew round-wombed and had indeed, sir, a son for her cradle ere she had a husband for her bed. Do you smell a fault? 15

KENT I cannot wish the fault undone, the issue of it being so proper.

GLOUCESTER But I have a son, sir, by order of law, some year older than this, who yet is no dearer in my account. Though this knave came something saucily to the world before he was sent for, yet was his mother fair, there was good sport at his making, and the whoreson must be acknowledged. (*To Edmond*) Do you know this noble gentleman, Edmond?

EDMOND No, my lord. 25

GLOUCESTER (*to Edmond*) My lord of Kent. Remember him hereafter as my honourable friend.

EDMOND (*to Kent*) My services to your lordship.

KENT I must love you, and sue to know you better.

EDMOND Sir, I shall study deserving. 30

GLOUCESTER (*to Kent*) He hath been out nine years, and away he shall again.

Sennet

The King is coming.

Enter King Lear, the Dukes of Cornwall and Albany, Goneril, Regan, Cordelia, and attendants

LEAR

Attend the lords of France and Burgundy, Gloucester.

GLOUCESTER I shall, my lord. *Exit*

LEAR

Meantime we shall express our darker purpose. 36
Give me the map there. Know that we have divided
In three our kingdom, and 'tis our fast intent
To shake all cares and business from our age,
Conferring them on younger strengths while we 40
Unburdened crawl toward death. Our son of Cornwall,
And you, our no less loving son of Albany,
We have this hour a constant will to publish
Our daughters' several dowers, that future strife
May be prevented now. The princes France and
Burgundy— 45

Great rivals in our youngest daughter's love—
Long in our court have made their amorous sojourn,
And here are to be answered. Tell me, my daughters—
Since now we will divest us both of rule,
Interest of territory, cares of state— 50
Which of you shall we say doth love us most,
That we our largest bounty may extend
Where nature doth with merit challenge? Goneril,
Our eldest born, speak first.

GONERIL

Sir, I love you more than words can wield the matter; 55
Dearer than eyesight, space, and liberty;
Beyond what can be valued, rich or rare,
No less than life; with grace, health, beauty, honour;
As much as child e'er loved or father found;
A love that makes breath poor and speech unable. 60
Beyond all manner of so much I love you.

CORDELIA (*aside*)

What shall Cordelia speak? Love and be silent.

LEAR (*to Goneril*)

Of all these bounds even from this line to this,
With shadowy forests and with champaigns riched,
With plenteous rivers and wide-skirted meads, 65
We make thee lady. To thine and Albany's issues
Be this perpetual.—What says our second daughter?
Our dearest Regan, wife of Cornwall?

REGAN

I am made of that self mettle as my sister,
And prize me at her worth. In my true heart 70
I find she names my very deed of love—
Only she comes too short, that I profess
Myself an enemy to all other joys
Which the most precious square of sense possesses,
And find I am alone felicitate 75
In your dear highness' love.

CORDELIA (*aside*) Then poor Cordelia—
And yet not so, since I am sure my love's
More ponderous than my tongue.

LEAR (*to Regan*)

To thee and thine hereditary ever
Remain this ample third of our fair kingdom, 80
No less in space, validity, and pleasure
Than that conferred on Goneril. (*To Cordelia*) Now our joy,
Although our last and least, to whose young love
The vines of France and milk of Burgundy
Strive to be interessed: what can you say to draw 85
A third more opulent than your sisters? Speak.

CORDELIA Nothing, my lord.

LEAR Nothing?

CORDELIA Nothing.

LEAR

Nothing will come of nothing. Speak again. 90

CORDELIA
　Unhappy that I am, I cannot heave
　My heart into my mouth. I love your majesty
　According to my bond, no more nor less.
LEAR
　How, how, Cordelia? Mend your speech a little
　Lest you may mar your fortunes.
CORDELIA　　　　　　　　　　Good my lord,　　95
　You have begot me, bred me, loved me.
　I return those duties back as are right fit—
　Obey you, love you, and most honour you.
　Why have my sisters husbands if they say
　They love you all? Haply when I shall wed　　100
　That lord whose hand must take my plight shall carry
　Half my love with him, half my care and duty.
　Sure, I shall never marry like my sisters.
LEAR But goes thy heart with this?
CORDELIA Ay, my good lord.　　　　　　　　105
LEAR So young and so untender?
CORDELIA So young, my lord, and true.
LEAR
　Let it be so. Thy truth then be thy dower;
　For by the sacred radiance of the sun,
　The mysteries of Hecate and the night,　　110
　By all the operation of the orbs
　From whom we do exist and cease to be,
　Here I disclaim all my paternal care,
　Propinquity, and property of blood,
　And as a stranger to my heart and me　　115
　Hold thee from this for ever. The barbarous Scythian,
　Or he that makes his generation messes
　To gorge his appetite, shall to my bosom
　Be as well neighboured, pitied, and relieved
　As thou, my sometime daughter.
KENT　　　　　　　　　`Good my liege—　　120
LEAR Peace, Kent.
　Come not between the dragon and his wrath.
　I loved her most, and thought to set my rest
　On her kind nursery. ⌜To Cordelia⌝ Hence, and avoid
　　my sight!—
　So be my grave my peace as here I give　　125
　Her father's heart from her. Call France. Who stirs?
　Call Burgundy.　　　　　　　⌜Exit one or more⌝
　　　　　　　Cornwall and Albany,
　With my two daughters' dowers digest the third.
　Let pride, which she calls plainness, marry her.
　I do invest you jointly with my power,　　130
　Pre-eminence, and all the large effects
　That troop with majesty. Ourself by monthly course,
　With reservation of an hundred knights
　By you to be sustained, shall our abode
　Make with you by due turn. Only we shall retain　135
　The name and all th'addition to a king. The sway,
　Revenue, execution of the rest,
　Belovèd sons, be yours; which to confirm,
　This crownet part between you.
KENT　　　　　　　　　Royal Lear,

Whom I have ever honoured as my king,　　140
Loved as my father, as my master followed,
As my great patron thought on in my prayers—
LEAR
　The bow is bent and drawn; make from the shaft.
KENT
　Let it fall rather, though the fork invade
　The region of my heart. Be Kent unmannerly　145
　When Lear is mad. What wouldst thou do, old man?
　Think'st thou that duty shall have dread to speak
　When power to flattery bows? To plainness honour's
　　bound
　When majesty falls to folly. Reserve thy state,
　And in thy best consideration check　　150
　This hideous rashness. Answer my life my judgement,
　Thy youngest daughter does not love thee least,
　Nor are those empty-hearted whose low sounds
　Reverb no hollowness.
LEAR　　　　　　　Kent, on thy life, no more!
KENT
　My life I never held but as a pawn　　155
　To wage against thine enemies, ne'er feared to lose it,
　Thy safety being motive.
LEAR　　　　　　　Out of my sight!
KENT
　See better, Lear, and let me still remain
　The true blank of thine eye.
LEAR　　　　　　　Now, by Apollo—
KENT
　Now, by Apollo, King, thou swear'st thy gods in vain.
LEAR ⌜making to strike him⌝
　O vassal! Miscreant!　　　　　　　　161
ALBANY and ⌜CORDELIA⌝ Dear sir, forbear.
KENT (to Lear)
　Kill thy physician, and thy·fee bestow
　Upon the foul disease. Revoke thy gift,
　Or whilst I can vent clamour from my throat
　I'll tell thee thou dost evil.　　　　　165
LEAR
　Hear me, recreant; on thine allegiance hear me!
　That thou hast sought to make us break our vows,
　Which we durst never yet, and with strained pride
　To come betwixt our sentence and our power,
　Which nor our nature nor our place can bear,　170
　Our potency made good take thy reward:
　Five days we do allot thee for provision
　To shield thee from disasters of the world,
　And on the sixth to turn thy hated back
　Upon our kingdom. If on the seventh day following　175
　Thy banished trunk be found in our dominions,
　The moment is thy death. Away! By Jupiter,
　This shall not be revoked.
KENT
　Fare thee well, King; sith thus thou wilt appear,
　Freedom lives hence, and banishment is here.　180
　(To Cordelia) The gods to their dear shelter take thee,
　　maid,

That justly think'st, and hast most rightly said.
(*To Goneril and Regan*) And your large speeches may
    your deeds approve,
That good effects may spring from words of love.
Thus Kent, O princes, bids you all adieu;   185
He'll shape his old course in a country new.   *Exit*

    Flourish. Enter the Duke of Gloucester with the
    King of France, the Duke of Burgundy, and attendants
⌈CORDELIA⌉
Here's France and Burgundy, my noble lord.
LEAR My lord of Burgundy,
We first address toward you, who with this King
Hath rivalled for our daughter: what in the least   190
Will you require in present dower with her
Or cease your quest of love?
BURGUNDY   Most royal majesty,
I crave no more than hath your highness offered;
Nor will you tender less.
LEAR   Right noble Burgundy,
When she was dear to us we did hold her so;   195
But now her price is fallen. Sir, there she stands.
If aught within that little seeming substance,
Or all of it, with our displeasure pieced,
And nothing more, may fitly like your grace,
She's there, and she is yours.
BURGUNDY   I know no answer.   200
LEAR
Will you with those infirmities she owes,
Unfriended, new adopted to our hate,
Dowered with our curse and strangered with our oath,
Take her or leave her?
BURGUNDY   Pardon me, royal sir.
Election makes not up in such conditions.   205
LEAR
Then leave her, sir; for by the power that made me,
I tell you all her wealth. (*To France*) For you, great King,
I would not from your love make such a stray
To match you where I hate, therefore beseech you
T'avert your liking a more worthier way   210
Than on a wretch whom nature is ashamed
Almost t'acknowledge hers.
FRANCE   This is most strange,
That she whom even but now was your best object,
The argument of your praise, balm of your age,
The best, the dear'st, should in this trice of time   215
Commit a thing so monstrous to dismantle
So many folds of favour. Sure, her offence
Must be of such unnatural degree
That monsters it, or your fore-vouched affection
Fall into taint; which to believe of her   220
Must be a faith that reason without miracle
Should never plant in me.
CORDELIA (*to Lear*)
I yet beseech your majesty,
If for I want that glib and oily art
To speak and purpose not—since what I well intend,
I'll do't before I speak—that you make known   226
It is no vicious blot, murder, or foulness,

No unchaste action or dishonoured step
That hath deprived me of your grace and favour,
But even the want of that for which I am richer— 230
A still-soliciting eye, and such a tongue
That I am glad I have not, though not to have it
Hath lost me in your liking.
LEAR   Better thou
Hadst not been born than not t'have pleased me better.
FRANCE
Is it but this—a tardiness in nature,   235
Which often leaves the history unspoke
That it intends to do?—My lord of Burgundy,
What say you to the lady? Love's not love
When it is mingled with regards that stands
Aloof from th'entire point. Will you have her?   240
She is herself a dowry.
BURGUNDY (*to Lear*)   Royal King,
Give but that portion which yourself proposed,
And here I take Cordelia by the hand,
Duchess of Burgundy.
LEAR Nothing. I have sworn. I am firm.   245
BURGUNDY (*to Cordelia*)
I am sorry, then, you have so lost a father
That you must lose a husband.
CORDELIA   Peace be with Burgundy;
Since that respect and fortunes are his love,
I shall not be his wife.
FRANCE
Fairest Cordelia, that art most rich, being poor;   250
Most choice, forsaken; and most loved, despised:
Thee and thy virtues here I seize upon.
Be it lawful, I take up what's cast away.
Gods, gods! 'Tis strange that from their cold'st neglect
My love should kindle to inflamed respect.—   255
Thy dowerless daughter, King, thrown to my chance,
Is queen of us, of ours, and our fair France.
Not all the dukes of wat'rish Burgundy
Can buy this unprized precious maid of me.—
Bid them farewell, Cordelia, though unkind.   260
Thou losest here, a better where to find.
LEAR
Thou hast her, France. Let her be thine, for we
Have no such daughter, nor shall ever see
That face of hers again. Therefore be gone,
Without our grace, our love, our benison.—   265
Come, noble Burgundy.
    Flourish. Exeunt all but France
               and the sisters
FRANCE   Bid farewell to your sisters.
CORDELIA
Ye jewels of our father, with washed eyes
Cordelia leaves you. I know you what you are,
And like a sister am most loath to call
Your faults as they are named. Love well our father.
To your professèd bosoms I commit him.   271
But yet, alas, stood I within his grace
I would prefer him to a better place.
So farewell to you both.

REGAN Prescribe not us our duty.   275
GONERIL Let your study
  Be to content your lord, who hath received you
  At fortune's alms. You have obedience scanted,
  And well are worth the want that you have wanted.
CORDELIA
  Time shall unfold what pleated cunning hides,   280
  Who covert faults at last with shame derides.
  Well may you prosper.
FRANCE   Come, my fair Cordelia.
                        Exeunt France and Cordelia
GONERIL Sister, it is not little I have to say of what most
  nearly appertains to us both. I think our father will
  hence tonight.   285
REGAN That's most certain, and with you. Next month
  with us.
GONERIL You see how full of changes his age is. The
  observation we have made of it hath been little. He
  always loved our sister most, and with what poor
  judgement he hath now cast her off appears too grossly.
REGAN 'Tis the infirmity of his age; yet he hath ever but
  slenderly known himself.
GONERIL The best and soundest of his time hath been but
  rash; then must we look from his age to receive not
  alone the imperfections of long-engrafted condition, but
  therewithal the unruly waywardness that infirm and
  choleric years bring with them.
REGAN Such unconstant starts are we like to have from
  him as this of Kent's banishment.   300
GONERIL There is further compliment of leave-taking
  between France and him. Pray you, let us sit together.
  If our father carry authority with such disposition as
  he bears, this last surrender of his will but offend us.
REGAN We shall further think of it.   305
GONERIL We must do something, and i'th' heat.   *Exeunt*

1.2   *Enter Edmond the bastard*
EDMOND
  Thou, nature, art my goddess. To thy law
  My services are bound. Wherefore should I
  Stand in the plague of custom and permit
  The curiosity of nations to deprive me
  For that I am some twelve or fourteen moonshines   5
  Lag of a brother? Why 'bastard'? Wherefore 'base',
  When my dimensions are as well compact,
  My mind as generous, and my shape as true
  As honest madam's issue? Why brand they us
  With 'base', with 'baseness, bastardy—base, base'— 10
  Who in the lusty stealth of nature take
  More composition and fierce quality
  Than doth within a dull, stale, tirèd bed
  Go to th' creating a whole tribe of fops
  Got 'tween a sleep and wake? Well then,   15
  Legitimate Edgar, I must have your land.
  Our father's love is to the bastard Edmond
  As to th' legitimate. Fine word, 'legitimate'.
  Well, my legitimate, if this letter speed
  And my invention thrive, Edmond the base   20

  Shall to th' legitimate. I grow, I prosper.
  Now gods, stand up for bastards!
        *Enter the Duke of Gloucester. Edmond reads a
        letter*
GLOUCESTER
  Kent banished thus, and France in choler parted,
  And the King gone tonight, prescribed his power,
  Confined to exhibition—all this done   25
  Upon the gad?—Edmond, how now? What news?
EDMOND So please your lordship, none.
GLOUCESTER Why so earnestly seek you to put up that
  letter?
EDMOND I know no news, my lord.   30
GLOUCESTER What paper were you reading?
EDMOND Nothing, my lord.
GLOUCESTER No? What needed then that terrible dispatch
  of it into your pocket? The quality of nothing hath not
  such need to hide itself. Let's see. Come, if it be nothing
  I shall not need spectacles.   36
EDMOND I beseech you, sir, pardon me. It is a letter from
  my brother that I have not all o'er-read; and for so
  much as I have perused, I find it not fit for your
  o'erlooking.   40
GLOUCESTER Give me the letter, sir.
EDMOND I shall offend either to detain or give it. The
  contents, as in part I understand them, are to blame.
GLOUCESTER Let's see, let's see.
EDMOND I hope for my brother's justification he wrote
  this but as an assay or taste of my virtue.   46
        He gives Gloucester a letter
GLOUCESTER (*reads*) 'This policy and reverence of age makes
  the world bitter to the best of our times, keeps our
  fortunes from us till our oldness cannot relish them. I
  begin to find an idle and fond bondage in the oppression
  of aged tyranny, who sways not as it hath power but
  as it is suffered. Come to me, that of this I may speak
  more. If our father would sleep till I waked him, you
  should enjoy half his revenue for ever and live the
  beloved of your brother,   55
                                    Edgar.'
  Hum, conspiracy! 'Sleep till I wake him, you should
  enjoy half his revenue'—my son Edgar! Had he a hand
  to write this, a heart and brain to breed it in? When
  came you to this? Who brought it?   60
EDMOND It was not brought me, my lord, there's the
  cunning of it. I found it thrown in at the casement of
  my closet.
GLOUCESTER You know the character to be your brother's?
EDMOND If the matter were good, my lord, I durst swear
  it were his; but in respect of that, I would fain think
  it were not.
GLOUCESTER It is his.
EDMOND It is his hand, my lord, but I hope his heart is
  not in the contents.   70
GLOUCESTER Has he never before sounded you in this
  business?
EDMOND Never, my lord; but I have heard him oft
  maintain it to be fit that, sons at perfect age and fathers

declined, the father should be as ward to the son, and the son manage his revenue.   76
GLOUCESTER O villain, villain—his very opinion in the letter! Abhorred villain, unnatural, detested, brutish villain—worse than brutish! Go, sirrah, seek him. I'll apprehend him. Abominable villain! Where is he?   80
EDMOND I do not well know, my lord. If it shall please you to suspend your indignation against my brother till you can derive from him better testimony of his intent, you should run a certain course; where if you violently proceed against him, mistaking his purpose, it would make a great gap in your own honour and shake in pieces the heart of his obedience. I dare pawn down my life for him that he hath writ this to feel my affection to your honour, and to no other pretence of danger.
GLOUCESTER Think you so?   90
EDMOND If your honour judge it meet, I will place you where you shall hear us confer of this, and by an auricular assurance have your satisfaction, and that without any further delay than this very evening.   94
GLOUCESTER He cannot be such a monster. Edmond, seek him out, wind me into him, I pray you. Frame the business after your own wisdom. I would unstate myself to be in a due resolution.
EDMOND I will seek him, sir, presently, convey the business as I shall find means, and acquaint you withal.   100
GLOUCESTER These late eclipses in the sun and moon portend no good to us. Though the wisdom of nature can reason it thus and thus, yet nature finds itself scourged by the sequent effects. Love cools, friendship falls off, brothers divide; in cities, mutinies; in countries, discord; in palaces, treason; and the bond cracked 'twixt son and father. This villain of mine comes under the prediction: there's son against father. The King falls from bias of nature: there's father against child. We have seen the best of our time. Machinations, hollowness, treachery, and all ruinous disorders follow us disquietly to our graves. Find out this villain, Edmond; it shall lose thee nothing. Do it carefully. And the noble and true-hearted Kent banished, his offence honesty! 'Tis strange.   *Exit*
EDMOND This is the excellent foppery of the world: that when we are sick in fortune—often the surfeits of our own behaviour—we make guilty of our disasters the sun, the moon, and stars, as if we were villains on necessity, fools by heavenly compulsion, knaves, thieves, and treachers by spherical predominance, drunkards, liars, and adulterers by an enforced obedience of planetary influence, and all that we are evil in by a divine thrusting on. An admirable evasion of whore-master man, to lay his goatish disposition on the charge of a star! My father compounded with my mother under the Dragon's tail and my nativity was under Ursa Major, so that it follows I am rough and lecherous. Fut! I should have been that I am had the maidenliest star in the firmament twinkled on my bastardizing.   130
Enter Edgar
Pat he comes, like the catastrophe of the old comedy.

my cue is villainous melancholy, with a sigh like Tom o' Bedlam.
⌈He reads a book⌉
—O, these eclipses do portend these divisions. Fa, so, la, mi.   135
EDGAR How now, brother Edmond, what serious contemplation are you in?
EDMOND I am thinking, brother, of a prediction I read this other day, what should follow these eclipses.
EDGAR Do you busy yourself with that?   140
EDMOND I promise you, the effects he writes of succeed unhappily. When saw you my father last?
EDGAR The night gone by.
EDMOND Spake you with him?
EDGAR Ay, two hours together.   145
EDMOND Parted you in good terms? Found you no displeasure in him by word nor countenance?
EDGAR None at all.
EDMOND Bethink yourself wherein you may have offended him, and at my entreaty forbear his presence until some little time hath qualified the heat of his displeasure, which at this instant so rageth in him that with the mischief of your person it would scarcely allay.
EDGAR Some villain hath done me wrong.   154
EDMOND That's my fear. I pray you have a continent forbearance till the speed of his rage goes slower; and, as I say, retire with me to my lodging, from whence I will fitly bring you to hear my lord speak. Pray ye, go. There's my key. If you do stir abroad, go armed.
EDGAR Armed, brother?   160
EDMOND Brother, I advise you to the best. I am no honest man if there be any good meaning toward you. I have told you what I have seen and heard but faintly, nothing like the image and horror of it. Pray you, away.   165
EDGAR Shall I hear from you anon?
EDMOND I do serve you in this business.   *Exit Edgar*
A credulous father, and a brother noble,
Whose nature is so far from doing harms
That he suspects none; on whose foolish honesty   170
My practices ride easy. I see the business.
Let me, if not by birth, have lands by wit.
All with me's meet that I can fashion fit.   *Exit*

1.3   *Enter Goneril and Oswald, her steward*
GONERIL
Did my father strike my gentleman
For chiding of his fool?
OSWALD   Ay, madam.
GONERIL
By day and night he wrongs me. Every hour
He flashes into one gross crime or other
That sets us all at odds. I'll not endure it.   5
His knights grow riotous, and himself upbraids us
On every trifle. When he returns from hunting
I will not speak with him. Say I am sick.
If you come slack of former services
You shall do well; the fault of it I'll answer.   10

⌜*Horns within*⌝

OSWALD He's coming, madam. I hear him.

GONERIL

Put on what weary negligence you please,
You and your fellows. I'd have it come to question.
If he distaste it, let him to my sister,
Whose mind and mine I know in that are one.   15
Remember what I have said.

OSWALD   Well, madam.

GONERIL

And let his knights have colder looks among you.
What grows of it, no matter. Advise your fellows so.
I'll write straight to my sister to hold my course.   19
Prepare for dinner.   *Exeunt severally*

1.4   *Enter the Earl of Kent, disguised*

KENT

If but as well I other accents borrow
That can my speech diffuse, my good intent
May carry through itself to that full issue
For which I razed my likeness. Now, banished Kent,
If thou canst serve where thou dost stand condemned,
So may it come thy master, whom thou lov'st,   6
Shall find thee full of labours.

Horns within. Enter King Lear and attendants from
hunting

LEAR Let me not stay a jot for dinner. Go get it ready.
                                        ⌜*Exit one*⌝

(*To Kent*) How now, what art thou?

KENT A man, sir.   10

LEAR What dost thou profess? What wouldst thou with
us?

KENT I do profess to be no less than I seem, to serve him
truly that will put me in trust, to love him that is
honest, to converse with him that is wise and says
little, to fear judgement, to fight when I cannot choose,
and to eat no fish.

LEAR What art thou?

KENT A very honest-hearted fellow, and as poor as the
King.   20

LEAR If thou be'st as poor for a subject as he's for a king,
thou'rt poor enough. What wouldst thou?

KENT Service.

LEAR Who wouldst thou serve?

KENT You.   25

LEAR Dost thou know me, fellow?

KENT No, sir, but you have that in your countenance
which I would fain call master.

LEAR What's that?

KENT Authority.   30

LEAR What services canst do?

KENT I can keep honest counsel, ride, run, mar a curious
tale in telling it, and deliver a plain message bluntly.
That which ordinary men are fit for I am qualified in;
and the best of me is diligence.   35

LEAR How old art thou?

KENT Not so young, sir, to love a woman for singing, nor

so old to dote on her for anything. I have years on my
back forty-eight.   39

LEAR Follow me. Thou shalt serve me, if I like thee no
worse after dinner. I will not part from thee yet. Dinner,
ho, dinner! Where's my knave, my fool? Go you and
call my fool hither.   ⌜*Exit one*⌝

Enter Oswald the steward

You, you, sirrah, where's my daughter?   44

OSWALD So please you—   *Exit*

LEAR What says the fellow there? Call the clotpoll back.
                                        Exit a knight

Where's my fool? Ho, I think the world's asleep.

Enter a Knight

How now? Where's that mongrel?

KNIGHT He says, my lord, your daughter is not well.

LEAR Why came not the slave back to me when I called
him?   51

KNIGHT Sir, he answered me in the roundest manner he
would not.

LEAR A would not?   54

KNIGHT My lord, I know not what the matter is, but to
my judgement your highness is not entertained with
that ceremonious affection as you were wont. There's
a great abatement of kindness appears as well in the
general dependants as in the Duke himself also, and
your daughter.   60

LEAR Ha, sayst thou so?

KNIGHT I beseech you pardon me, my lord, if I be
mistaken, for my duty cannot be silent when I think
your highness wronged.   64

LEAR Thou but rememberest me of mine own conception.
I have perceived a most faint neglect of late, which I
have rather blamed as mine own jealous curiosity than
as a very pretence and purpose of unkindness. I will
look further into't. But where's my fool? I have not
seen him these two days.   70

KNIGHT Since my young lady's going into France, sir, the
fool hath much pined away.

LEAR No more of that, I have noted it well. Go you and
tell my daughter I would speak with her.   ⌜*Exit one*⌝
Go you, call hither my fool.   ⌜*Exit one*⌝

Enter Oswald the steward ⌜*crossing the stage*⌝

O you, sir, you, come you hither, sir, who am I, sir?

OSWALD My lady's father.

LEAR My lady's father? My lord's knave, you whoreson
dog, you slave, you cur!

OSWALD I am none of these, my lord, I beseech your
pardon.   81

LEAR Do you bandy looks with me, you rascal?
                            ⌜*Lear strikes him*⌝

OSWALD I'll not be strucken, my lord.

KENT ⌜*tripping him*⌝ Nor tripped neither, you base football
player.   85

LEAR (*to Kent*) I thank thee, fellow. Thou serv'st me, and
I'll love thee.

KENT (*to Oswald*) Come, sir, arise, away. I'll teach you
differences. Away, away. If you will measure your

lubber's length again, tarry; but away, go to. Have
you wisdom? So.   *Exit Oswald*

LEAR Now, my friendly knave, I thank thee.
    Enter Lear's Fool
There's earnest of thy service.
    He gives Kent money

FOOL Let me hire him, too. (*To Kent*) Here's my coxcomb.

LEAR How now, my pretty knave, how dost thou?   95

FOOL (*to Kent*) Sirrah, you were best take my coxcomb.

LEAR Why, my boy?

FOOL Why? For taking one's part that's out of favour. (*To
Kent*) Nay, an thou canst not smile as the wind sits,
thou'lt catch cold shortly. There, take my coxcomb.
Why, this fellow has banished two on's daughters and
did the third a blessing against his will. If thou follow
him, thou must needs wear my coxcomb. (*To Lear*)
How now, nuncle? Would I had two coxcombs and
two daughters.   105

LEAR Why, my boy?

FOOL If I gave them all my living I'd keep my coxcombs
myself. There's mine; beg another off thy daughters.

LEAR Take heed, sirrah—the whip.   109

FOOL Truth's a dog must to kennel. He must be whipped
out when the Lady Brach may stand by th' fire and
stink.

LEAR A pestilent gall to me!

FOOL ⌜*to Kent*⌝ Sirrah, I'll teach thee a speech.

LEAR Do.   115

FOOL Mark it, nuncle:
       Have more than thou showest,
       Speak less than thou knowest,
       Lend less than thou owest,
       Ride more than thou goest,   120
       Learn more than thou trowest,
       Set less than thou throwest,
       Leave thy drink and thy whore,
       And keep in-a-door,
       And thou shalt have more   125
       Than two tens to a score.

KENT This is nothing, fool.

FOOL Then 'tis like the breath of an unfee'd lawyer: you
gave me nothing for't. (*To Lear*) Can you make no use
of nothing, nuncle?   130

LEAR Why no, boy. Nothing can be made out of nothing.

FOOL (*to Kent*) Prithee, tell him so much the rent of his
land comes to. He will not believe a fool.

LEAR A bitter fool.

FOOL Dost know the difference, my boy, between a bitter
fool and a sweet one?   136

LEAR No, lad. Teach me.

FOOL Nuncle, give me an egg, and I'll give thee two
crowns.

LEAR What two crowns shall they be?   140

FOOL Why, after I have cut the egg i'th' middle and eat
up the meat, the two crowns of the egg. When thou
clovest thy crown i'th' middle and gavest away both
parts, thou borest thine ass o'th' back o'er the dirt.
Thou hadst little wit in thy bald crown when thou

gavest thy golden one away. If I speak like myself in
this, let him be whipped that first finds it so.
    ⌜*Sings*⌝ Fools had ne'er less grace in a year,
       For wise men are grown foppish,
       And know not how their wits to wear,   150
       Their manners are so apish.

LEAR When were you wont to be so full of songs, sirrah?

FOOL I have used it, nuncle, e'er since thou madest thy
daughters thy mothers; for when thou gavest them the
rod and puttest down thine own breeches,   155
    ⌜*Sings*⌝ Then they for sudden joy did weep,
       And I for sorrow sung,
       That such a king should play bo-peep
       And go the fools among.
Prithee, nuncle, keep a schoolmaster that can teach
thy fool to lie. I would fain learn to lie.   161

LEAR An you lie, sirrah, we'll have you whipped.

FOOL I marvel what kin thou and thy daughters are.
They'll have me whipped for speaking true, thou'lt
have me whipped for lying, and sometimes I am
whipped for holding my peace. I had rather be any
kind o' thing than a fool; and yet I would not be thee,
nuncle. Thou hast pared thy wit o' both sides and left
nothing i'th' middle.
    Enter Goneril
Here comes one o' the parings.   170

LEAR
How now, daughter? What makes that frontlet on?
You are too much of late i'th' frown.

FOOL Thou wast a pretty fellow when thou hadst no need
to care for her frowning. Now thou art an O without
a figure. I am better than thou art, now. I am a fool;
thou art nothing. ⌜*To Goneril*⌝ Yes, forsooth, I will hold
my tongue; so your face bids me, though you say
nothing.
    ⌜*Sings*⌝ Mum, mum.
       He that keeps nor crust nor crumb,   180
       Weary of all, shall want some.
That's a shelled peascod.

GONERIL (*to Lear*)
Not only, sir, this your all-licensed fool,
But other of your insolent retinue
Do hourly carp and quarrel, breaking forth   185
In rank and not-to-be-endurèd riots. Sir,
I had thought by making this well known unto you
To have found a safe redress, but now grow fearful,
By what yourself too late have spoke and done,
That you protect this course, and put it on   190
By your allowance; which if you should, the fault
Would not scape censure, nor the redresses sleep
Which in the tender of a wholesome weal
Might in their working do you that offence,
Which else were shame, that then necessity   195
Will call discreet proceeding.

FOOL (*to Lear*) For, you know, nuncle,
    ⌜*Sings*⌝ The hedge-sparrow fed the cuckoo so long
       That it's had it head bit off by it young;
so out went the candle, and we were left darkling.   200

LEAR (*to Goneril*) Are you our daughter?
GONERIL
  I would you would make use of your good wisdom,
  Whereof I know you are fraught, and put away
  These dispositions which of late transport you
  From what you rightly are.   205
FOOL May not an ass know when the cart draws the
  horse? ⌈*Sings*⌉ 'Whoop, jug, I love thee!'
LEAR
  Does any here know me? This is not Lear.
  Does Lear walk thus, speak thus? Where are his eyes?
  Either his notion weakens, his discernings   210
  Are lethargied—ha, waking? 'Tis not so.
  Who is it that can tell me who I am?
FOOL Lear's shadow.
LEAR (*to Goneril*) Your name, fair gentlewoman?
GONERIL
  This admiration, sir, is much o'th' savour   215
  Of other your new pranks. I do beseech you
  To understand my purposes aright,
  As you are old and reverend, should be wise.
  Here do you keep a hundred knights and squires,
  Men so disordered, so debauched and bold   220
  That this our court, infected with their manners,
  Shows like a riotous inn. Epicurism and lust
  Makes it more like a tavern or a brothel
  Than a graced palace. The shame itself doth speak
  For instant remedy. Be then desired,   225
  By her that else will take the thing she begs,
  A little to disquantity your train,
  And the remainders that shall still depend
  To be such men as may besort your age,
  Which know themselves and you.
LEAR   Darkness and devils!
  Saddle my horses, call my train together!—
                       ⌈*Exit one or more*⌉
  Degenerate bastard, I'll not trouble thee.   232
  Yet have I left a daughter.
GONERIL
  You strike my people, and your disordered rabble
  Make servants of their betters.
     Enter the Duke of Albany
LEAR   Woe that too late repents!
  Is it your will? Speak, sir.—Prepare my horses.
                       ⌈*Exit one or more*⌉
  Ingratitude, thou marble-hearted fiend,
  More hideous when thou show'st thee in a child
  Than the sea-monster—
ALBANY Pray sir, be patient.   240
LEAR (*to Goneril*) Detested kite, thou liest.
  My train are men of choice and rarest parts,
  That all particulars of duty know,
  And in the most exact regard support
  The worships of their name. O most small fault,   245
  How ugly didst thou in Cordelia show,
  Which, like an engine, wrenched my frame of nature
  From the fixed place, drew from my heart all love,
  And added to the gall! O Lear, Lear, Lear!

  Beat at this gate that let thy folly in   250
  And thy dear judgement out.—Go, go, my people!
ALBANY
  My lord, I am guiltless, as I am ignorant
  Of what hath moved you.
LEAR   It may be so, my lord.
  Hear, nature; hear, dear goddess, hear:
  Suspend thy purpose if thou didst intend   255
  To make this creature fruitful.
  Into her womb convey sterility.
  Dry up in her the organs of increase,
  And from her derogate body never spring
  A babe to honour her. If she must teem,   260
  Create her child of spleen, that it may live
  And be a thwart disnatured torment to her.
  Let it stamp wrinkles in her brow of youth,
  With cadent tears fret channels in her cheeks,
  Turn all her mother's pains and benefits   265
  To laughter and contempt, that she may feel—
  That she may feel
  How sharper than a serpent's tooth it is
  To have a thankless child. Away, away!
             Exeunt Lear, ⌈Kent, and attendants⌉
ALBANY
  Now, gods that we adore, whereof comes this?   270
GONERIL
  Never afflict yourself to know more of it,
  But let his disposition have that scope
  As dotage gives it.
     Enter King Lear
LEAR
  What, fifty of my followers at a clap?
  Within a fortnight?
ALBANY   What's the matter, sir?   275
LEAR
  I'll tell thee. (*To Goneril*) Life and death! I am ashamed
  That thou hast power to shake my manhood thus,
  That these hot tears, which break from me perforce,
  Should make thee worth them. Blasts and fogs upon
    thee!
  Th'untented woundings of a father's curse   280
  Pierce every sense about thee! Old fond eyes,
  Beweep this cause again I'll pluck ye out
  And cast you, with the waters that you loose,
  To temper clay. Ha! Let it be so.
  I have another daughter   285
  Who, I am sure, is kind and comfortable.
  When she shall hear this of thee, with her nails
  She'll flay thy wolvish visage. Thou shalt find
  That I'll resume the shape which thou dost think
  I have cast off for ever.   *Exit*
GONERIL   Do you mark that?   290
ALBANY
  I cannot be so partial, Goneril,
  To the great love I bear you—
GONERIL
  Pray you, content. What, Oswald, ho!—
  You, sir, more knave than fool, after your master.

FOOL
    Nuncle Lear, nuncle Lear,   295
    Tarry, take the fool with thee.
    A fox when one has caught her,
    And such a daughter,
    Should sure to the slaughter,
    If my cap would buy a halter.   300
    So, the fool follows after.   *Exit*
GONERIL
    This man hath had good counsel—a hundred
      knights?
    'Tis politic and safe to let him keep
    At point a hundred knights, yes, that on every dream,
    Each buzz, each fancy, each complaint, dislike,   305
    He may enguard his dotage with their powers
    And hold our lives in mercy.—Oswald, I say!
ALBANY
    Well, you may fear too far.
GONERIL   Safer than trust too far.
    Let me still take away the harms I fear,
    Not fear still to be taken. I know his heart.   310
    What he hath uttered I have writ my sister.
    If she sustain him and his hundred knights
    When I have showed th'unfitness—
      Enter Oswald the steward
                   How now, Oswald?
    What, have you writ that letter to my sister?
OSWALD Ay, madam.   315
GONERIL
    Take you some company, and away to horse.
    Inform her full of my particular fear,
    And thereto add such reasons of your own
    As may compact it more. Get you gone,
    And hasten your return.   *Exit Oswald*
            No, no, my lord,   320
    This milky gentleness and course of yours,
    Though I condemn not, yet under pardon
    You are much more attasked for want of wisdom
    Than praised for harmful mildness.
ALBANY
    How far your eyes may pierce I cannot tell.   325
    Striving to better, oft we mar what's well.
GONERIL Nay, then—
ALBANY Well, well, th'event.   *Exeunt*

1.5   *Enter King Lear, the Earl of Kent disguised, the*
      First Gentleman, and Lear's Fool
LEAR ⌈*to the Gentleman, giving him a letter*⌉ Go you before
  to Gloucester with these letters.   ⌈*Exit Gentleman*⌉
  ⌈*To Kent, giving him a letter*⌉ Acquaint my daughter no
  further with anything you know than comes from her
  demand out of the letter. If your diligence be not speedy,
  I shall be there afore you.   6
KENT I will not sleep, my lord, till I have delivered your
  letter.   *Exit*
FOOL If a man's brains were in 's heels, were't not in
  danger of kibes?   ·10
LEAR Ay, boy.

FOOL Then, I prithee, be merry: thy wit shall not go
  slipshod.
LEAR Ha, ha, ha!   14
FOOL Shalt see thy other daughter will use thee kindly,
  for though she's as like this as a crab's like an apple,
  yet I can tell what I can tell.
LEAR What canst tell, boy?
FOOL She will taste as like this as a crab does to a crab.
  Thou canst tell why one's nose stands i'th' middle
  on 's face?   21
LEAR No.
FOOL Why, to keep one's eyes of either side 's nose, that
  what a man cannot smell out, a may spy into.
LEAR I did her wrong.   25
FOOL Canst tell how an oyster makes his shell?
LEAR No.
FOOL Nor I neither; but I can tell why a snail has a
  house.
LEAR Why?   30
FOOL Why, to put 's head in, not to give it away to his
  daughters and leave his horns without a case.
LEAR
    I will forget my nature. So kind a father!
    Be my horses ready?   34
FOOL Thy asses are gone about 'em. The reason why the
  seven stars are no more than seven is a pretty reason.
LEAR Because they are not eight.
FOOL Yes, indeed, thou wouldst make a good fool.
LEAR
    To take't again perforce—monster ingratitude!
FOOL If thou wert my fool, nuncle, I'd have thee beaten
  for being old before thy time.   41
LEAR How's that?
FOOL Thou shouldst not have been old till thou hadst
  been wise.
LEAR
    O, let me not be mad, not mad, sweet heaven!   45
    Keep me in temper. I would not be mad.
      ⌈*Enter the First Gentleman*⌉
    How now, are the horses ready?
⌈FIRST⌉ GENTLEMAN   Ready, my lord.
LEAR (*to Fool*) Come, boy.
              ⌈*Exeunt Lear and Gentleman*⌉
FOOL
    She that's a maid now, and laughs at my departure,
    Shall not be a maid long, unless things be cut shorter.
                       ⌈*Exit*⌉

2.1   *Enter Edmond the bastard, and Curan, severally*
EDMOND Save thee, Curan.
CURAN And you, sir. I have been with your father, and
  given him notice that the Duke of Cornwall and Regan
  his duchess will be here with him this night.
EDMOND How comes that?   5
CURAN Nay, I know not. You have heard of the news
  abroad?—I mean the whispered ones, for they are yet
  but ear-kissing arguments.
EDMOND Not I. Pray you, what are they?

CURAN Have you heard of no likely wars toward twixt
the Dukes of Cornwall and Albany?   11
EDMOND Not a word.
CURAN You may do then in time. Fare you well, sir.
                                Exit
EDMOND
The Duke be here tonight! The better, best.
This weaves itself perforce into my business.   15
⌜*Enter Edgar at a window above*⌝
My father hath set guard to take my brother,
And I have one thing of a queasy question
Which I must act. Briefness and fortune work!—
Brother, a word, descend. Brother, I say.
    ⌜*Edgar climbs down*⌝
My father watches. O sir, fly this place.   20
Intelligence is given where you are hid.
You have now the good advantage of the night.
Have you not spoken 'gainst the Duke of Cornwall?
He's coming hither, now, i'th' night, i'th' haste,
And Regan with him. Have you nothing said   25
Upon his party 'gainst the Duke of Albany?
Advise yourself.
EDGAR   I am sure on't, not a word.
EDMOND
I hear my father coming. Pardon me.
In cunning I must draw my sword upon you.
Draw. Seem to defend yourself. Now, quit you well.   30
(*Calling*) Yield, come before my father. Light ho, here!
(*To Edgar*) Fly, brother! (*Calling*) Torches, torches!
(*To Edgar*)   So, farewell.
                        Exit Edgar
Some blood drawn on me would beget opinion
Of my more fierce endeavour.
    He wounds his arm
                 I have seen drunkards
Do more than this in sport. (*Calling*) Father, father!   35
Stop, stop! Ho, help!
    Enter the Duke of Gloucester, and servants with
    torches
GLOUCESTER   Now, Edmond, where's the villain?
EDMOND
Here stood he in the dark, his sharp sword out,
Mumbling of wicked charms, conjuring the moon
To stand 's auspicious mistress.
GLOUCESTER   But where is he?
EDMOND
Look, sir, I bleed.
GLOUCESTER   Where is the villain, Edmond?   40
EDMOND
Fled this way, sir, when by no means he could—
GLOUCESTER
Pursue him, ho! Go after.
                      Exeunt servants
              By no means what?
EDMOND
Persuade me to the murder of your lordship,
But that I told him the revenging gods
'Gainst parricides did all the thunder bend,   45
Spoke with how manifold and strong a bond
The child was bound to th' father. Sir, in fine,

Seeing how loathly opposite I stood
To his unnatural purpose, in fell motion
With his preparèd sword he charges home   50
My unprovided body, latched mine arm;
And when he saw my best alarumed spirits
Bold in the quarrel's right, roused to th'encounter,
Or whether ghasted by the noise I made,
Full suddenly he fled.
GLOUCESTER   Let him fly far,   55
Not in this land shall he remain uncaught,
And found, dispatch. The noble Duke my master,
My worthy arch and patron, comes tonight.
By his authority I will proclaim it
That he which finds him shall deserve our thanks,   60
Bringing the murderous coward to the stake;
He that conceals him, death.
EDMOND
When I dissuaded him from his intent
And found him pitched to do it, with curst speech
I threatened to discover him. He replied,   65
'Thou unpossessing bastard, dost thou think
If I would stand against thee, would the reposal
Of any trust, virtue, or worth in thee
Make thy words faithed? No, what I should deny—
As this I would, ay, though thou didst produce   70
My very characteṙ—I'd turn it all
To thy suggestion, plot, and damnèd practice,
And thou must make a dullard of the world
If they not thought the profits of my death
Were very pregnant and potential spirits   75
To make thee seek it.'
GLOUCESTER   O strange and fastened villain!
Would he deny his letter, said he?
    Tucket within
Hark, the Duke's trumpets. I know not why he comes.
All ports I'll bar. The villaiṅ shall not scape.
The Duke must grant me that; besides, his picture   80
I will send far and near, that all the kingdom
May have due note of him—and of my land,
Loyal and natural boy, I'll work the means
To make thee capable.
    Enter the Duke of Cornwall, Regan, and attendants
CORNWALL
How now, my noble friend? Since I came hither,   85
Which I can call but now, I have heard strange news.
REGAN
If it be true, all vengeance comes too short
Which can pursue th'offender. How dost, my lord?
GLOUCESTER
O madam, my old heart is cracked, it's cracked.
REGAN
What, did my father's godson seek your life?   90
He whom my father named, your Edgar?
GLOUCESTER
O lady, lady, shame would have it hid!
REGAN
Was he not companion with the riotous knights
That tend upon my father?

GLOUCESTER
I know not, madam. 'Tis too bad, too bad.   95
EDMOND
Yes, madam, he was of that consort.
REGAN
No marvel, then, though he were ill affected.
'Tis they have put him on the old man's death,
To have th'expense and spoil of his revenues.
I have this present evening from my sister   100
Been well informed of them, and with such cautions
That if they come to sojourn at my house
I'll not be there.
CORNWALL   Nor I, assure thee, Regan.
Edmond, I hear that you have shown your father
A childlike office.
EDMOND   It was my duty, sir.   105
GLOUCESTER (to Cornwall)
He did bewray his practice, and received
This hurt you see striving to apprehend him.
CORNWALL
Is he pursued?
GLOUCESTER   Ay, my good lord.
CORNWALL
If he be taken, he shall never more
Be feared of doing harm. Make your own purpose   110
How in my strength you please. For you, Edmond,
Whose virtue and obedience doth this instant
So much commend itself, you shall be ours.
Natures of such deep trust we shall much need.
You we first seize on.
EDMOND   I shall serve you, sir,   115
Truly, however else.
GLOUCESTER (to Cornwall) For him I thank your grace.
CORNWALL
You know not why we came to visit you—
REGAN
Thus out of season, threading dark-eyed night—
Occasions, noble Gloucester, of some poise,
Wherein we must have use of your advice.   120
Our father he hath writ, so hath our sister,
Of differences which I least thought it fit
To answer from our home. The several messengers
From hence attend dispatch. Our good old friend,
Lay comforts to your bosom, and bestow   125
Your needful counsel to our businesses,
Which craves the instant use.
GLOUCESTER   I serve you, madam.
Your graces are right welcome.   *Flourish. Exeunt*

2.2   *Enter the Earl of Kent, disguised, and Oswald the*
      steward, severally
OSWALD Good dawning to thee, friend. Art of this house?
KENT Ay.
OSWALD Where may we set our horses?
KENT I'th' mire.
OSWALD Prithee, if thou lov'st me, tell me.   5
KENT I love thee not.
OSWALD Why then, I care not for thee.

KENT If I had thee in Lipsbury pinfold I would make thee
care for me.
OSWALD Why dost thou use me thus? I know thee not.   10
KENT Fellow, I know thee.
OSWALD What dost thou know me for?
KENT A knave, a rascal, an eater of broken meats, a base,
proud, shallow, beggarly, three-suited, hundred-pound,
filthy worsted-stocking knave; a lily-livered, action-
taking, whoreson, glass-gazing, super-serviceable,
finical rogue; one-trunk-inheriting slave; one that
wouldst be a bawd in way of good service, and art
nothing but the composition of a knave, beggar,
coward, pander, and the son and heir of a mongrel
bitch, one whom I will beat into clamorous whining if
thou deniest the least syllable of thy addition.
OSWALD Why, what a monstrous fellow art thou, thus to
rail on one that is neither known of thee nor knows
thee!   25
KENT What a brazen-faced varlet art thou, to deny thou
knowest me! Is it two days since I tripped up thy heels
and beat thee before the King? Draw, you rogue; for
though it be night, yet the moon shines.
     ⌈*He draws his sword*⌉
I'll make a sop o'th' moonshine of you, you whoreson,
cullionly barber-monger, draw!   31
OSWALD Away. I have nothing to do with thee.
KENT Draw, you rascal. You come with letters against
the King, and take Vanity the puppet's part against the
royalty of her father. Draw, you rogue, or I'll so
carbonado your shanks—draw, you rascal, come your
ways!
OSWALD Help, ho, murder, help!
KENT Strike, you slave! Stand, rogue! Stand, you neat
slave, strike!   40
OSWALD Help, ho, murder, murder!
     Enter Edmond the bastard, ⌈then⌉ the Duke of
     Cornwall, Regan, the Duke of Gloucester, and
     servants
EDMOND How now, what's the matter? Part.
KENT With you, goodman boy. If you please, come, I'll
flesh ye. Come on, young master.
GLOUCESTER Weapons? Arms? What's the matter here? 45
CORNWALL
Keep peace, upon your lives. He dies that strikes again.
What is the matter?
REGAN The messengers from our sister and the King.
CORNWALL (to Kent and Oswald) What is your difference?
Speak.   50
OSWALD I am scarce in breath, my lord.
KENT No marvel, you have so bestirred your valour, you
cowardly rascal. Nature disclaims in thee; a tailor made
thee.
CORNWALL Thou art a strange fellow—a tailor make a
man?   56
KENT A tailor, sir. A stone-cutter or a painter could not
have made him so ill though they had been but two
years o'th' trade.
CORNWALL Speak yet; how grew your quarrel?   60

OSWALD This ancient ruffian, sir, whose life I have spared
    at suit of his grey beard—
KENT Thou whoreson Z, thou unnecessary letter— (*to*
    Cornwall) my lord, if you'll give me leave I will tread
    this unbolted villain into mortar and daub the wall of
    a jakes with him. (*To Oswald*) Spare my grey beard,
    you wagtail?
CORNWALL Peace, sirrah.
    You beastly knave, know you no reverence?
KENT
    Yes, sir, but anger hath a privilege.   70
CORNWALL Why art thou angry?
KENT
    That such a slave as this should wear a sword,
    Who wears no honesty. Such smiling rogues as these,
    Like rats, oft bite the holy cords a-twain
    Which are too intrince t'unloose, smooth every
            passion   75
    That in the natures of their lords rebel;
    Being oil to fire, snow to the colder moods,
    Renege, affirm, and turn their halcyon beaks
    With every gall and vary of their masters,
    Knowing naught, like dogs, but following.   80
    ⌈*To Oswald*⌉ A plague upon your epileptic visage!
    Smile you my speeches as I were a fool?
    Goose, an I had you upon Sarum Plain
    I'd drive ye cackling home to Camelot.
CORNWALL
    What, art thou mad, old fellow?
GLOUCESTER ⌈*to Kent*⌉   How fell you out? Say that.
KENT
    No contraries hold more antipathy   86
    Than I and such a knave.
CORNWALL   Why dost thou call him knave?
    What is his fault?
KENT   His countenance likes me not.
CORNWALL
    No more perchance does mine, nor his, nor hers.
KENT
    Sir, 'tis my occupation to be plain: 90
    I have seen better faces in my time
    Than stands on any shoulder that I see
    Before me at this instant.
CORNWALL   This is some fellow
    Who, having been praised for bluntness, doth affect
    A saucy roughness, and constrains the garb   95
    Quite from his nature. He cannot flatter, he;
    An honest mind and plain, he must speak truth.
    An they will take't, so; if not, he's plain.
    These kind of knaves I know, which in this plainness
    Harbour more craft and more corrupter ends   100
    Than twenty silly-ducking observants
    That stretch their duties nicely.
KENT
    Sir, in good faith, in sincere verity,
    Under th'allowance of your great aspect,
    Whose influence, like the wreath of radiant fire   105
    On flick'ring Phoebus' front—
CORNWALL   What mean'st by this?

KENT To go out of my dialect, which you discommend so
    much. I know, sir, I am no flatterer. He that beguiled
    you in a plain accent was a plain knave, which for my
    part I will not be, though I should win your displeasure
    to entreat me to't.   111
CORNWALL (*to Oswald*)
    What was th'offence you gave him?
OSWALD   I never gave him any.
    It pleased the King his master very late
    To strike at me upon his misconstruction,
    When he, compact, and flattering his displeasure,   115
    Tripped me behind; being down, insulted, railed,
    And put upon him such a deal of man
    That worthied him, got praises of the King
    For him attempting who was self-subdued,
    And in the fleshment of this dread exploit   120
    Drew on me here again.
KENT   None of these rogues and cowards
    But Ajax is their fool.
CORNWALL   Fetch forth the stocks!
                    ⌈*Exeunt some servants*⌉
    You stubborn, ancient knave, you reverend braggart,
    We'll teach you.
KENT   Sir, I am too old to learn.
    Call not your stocks for me. I serve the King,   125
    On whose employment I was sent to you.
    You shall do small respect, show too bold malice
    Against the grace and person of my master,
    Stocking his messenger.
CORNWALL ⌈*calling*⌉   Fetch forth the stocks!—
    As I have life and honour, there shall he sit till noon.
REGAN
    Till noon?—till night, my lord, and all night too.   131
KENT
    Why, madam, if I were your father's dog
    You should not use me so.
REGAN   Sir, being his knave, I will.
                    Stocks brought out
CORNWALL
    This is a fellow of the selfsame colour
    Our sister speaks of.—Come, bring away the stocks.   135
GLOUCESTER
    Let me beseech your grace not to do so.
    The King his master needs must take it ill
    That he, so slightly valued in his messenger,
    Should have him thus restrained.
CORNWALL   I'll answer that.
                    ⌈*They put Kent in the stocks*⌉
REGAN
    My sister may receive it much more worse   140
    To have her gentlemen abused, assaulted.
CORNWALL Come, my good lord, away!
                    Exeunt all but Gloucester and Kent
GLOUCESTER
    I am sorry for thee, friend. 'Tis the Duke's pleasure,
    Whose disposition, all the world well knows,
    Will not be rubbed nor stopped. I'll entreat for thee. 145
KENT
    Pray do not, sir. I have watched and travelled hard.

Some time I shall sleep out; the rest I'll whistle.
A good man's fortune may grow out at heels.
Give you good morrow.

GLOUCESTER

The Duke's to blame in this; 'twill be ill taken.   *Exit*

KENT

Good King, that must approve the common say: 151
Thou out of heaven's benediction com'st
To the warm sun.
　　　⌈*He takes out a letter*⌉
Approach, thou beacon to this under globe,
That by thy comfortable beams I may   155
Peruse this letter. Nothing almost sees miracles
But misery. I know 'tis from Cordelia,
Who hath now fortunately been informed
Of my obscurèd course, and shall find time
For this enormous state, seeking to give   160
Losses their remedies. All weary and o'erwatched,
Take vantage, heavy eyes, not tò behold
This shameful lodging. Fortune, good night;
Smile once more; turn thy wheel.   *He sleeps*
　　　Enter Edgar

EDGAR   I heard myself proclaimed,
And by the happy hollow of a tree   165
Escaped the hunt. No port is free, no place
That guard and most unusual vigilance
Does not attend my taking. Whiles I may scape
I will preserve myself, and am bethought
To take the basest and most poorest shape   170
That ever penury in contempt of man
Brought near to beast. My face I'll grime with filth,
Blanket my loins, elf all my hairs in knots,
And with presented nakedness outface
The winds and persecutions of the sky.   175
The country gives me proof and precedent
Of Bedlam beggars who with roaring voices
Strike in their numbed and mortifièd arms
Pins, wooden pricks, nails, sprigs of rosemary,
And with this horrible object from low farms,   180
Poor pelting villages, sheep-cotes and mills
Sometime with lunatic bans, sometime with prayers
Enforce their charity. 'Poor Tuelygod, Poor Tom.'
That's something yet. Edgar I nothing am.   *Exit*
　　　Enter King Lear, his Fool, and ⌈*the First*⌉ *Gentleman*

LEAR

'Tis strange that they should so depart from home   185
And not send back my messenger.

⌈FIRST⌉ GENTLEMAN   As I learned,
The night before there was no purpose in them
Of this remove.

KENT (*waking*)   Hail to thee, noble master.

LEAR

Ha! Mak'st thou this shame thy pastime?

KENT   No, my lord.

FOOL Ha, ha, he wears cruel garters! Horses are tied by
the heads, dogs and bears by th' neck, monkeys by th'
loins, and men by th' legs. When a man's overlusty at
legs, then he wears wooden nether-stocks.

LEAR (*to Kent*)
What's he that hath so much thy place mistook
To set thee here?

KENT   It is both he and she: 195
Your son and daughter.

LEAR   No.

KENT   Yes.

LEAR   No, I say.

KENT

I say yea.

LEAR   By Jupiter, I swear no.

KENT

By Juno, I swear ay.

LEAR   They durst not do't,
They could not, would not do't. 'Tis worse than
　　　murder,
To do upon respect such violent outrage.   200
Resolve me with all modest haste which way
Thou mightst deserve or they impose this usage,
Coming from us.

KENT   My lord, when at their home
I did commend your highness' letters to them,
Ere I was risen from the place that showed   205
My duty kneeling, came there a reeking post
Stewed in his haste, half breathless, painting forth
From Goneril, his mistress, salutations,
Delivered letters spite of intermission,
Which presently they read, on whose contents   210
They summoned up their meiny, straight took horse,
Commanded me to follow and attend
The leisure of their answer, gave me cold looks;
And meeting here the other messenger,
Whose welcome I perceived had poisoned mine—   215
Being the very fellow which of late
Displayed so saucily against your highness—
Having more man than wit about me, drew.
He raised the house with loud and coward cries.
Your son and daughter found this trespass worth   220
The shame which here it suffers.

FOOL Winter's not gone yet if the wild geese fly that way.
⌈*Sings*⌉   Fathers that wear rags
　　　　　　Do make their children blind,
　　　　　But fathers that bear bags   225
　　　　　　Shall see their children kind.
　　　　Fortune, that arrant whore,
　　　　　Ne'er turns the key to th' poor.
But for all this thou shalt have as many dolours for
thy daughters as thou canst tell in a year.   230

LEAR

O, how this mother swells up toward my heart!
Histerica passio down, thou climbing sorrow;
Thy element's below.—Where is this daughter?

KENT

With the Earl, sir, here within.

LEAR   Follow me not; stay here.
　　　　　　　　　　　　　Exit

⌈FIRST⌉ GENTLEMAN (*to Kent*)
Made you no more offence but what you speak of?   235

KENT None.

How chance the King comes with so small a number?

FOOL An thou hadst been set i'th' stocks for that question, thou'dst well deserved it.

KENT Why, Fool?   240

FOOL We'll set thee to school to an ant, to teach thee there's no labouring i'th' winter. All that follow their noses are led by their eyes but blind men, and there's not a nose among twenty but can smell him that's stinking. Let go thy hold when a great wheel runs down a hill, lest it break thy neck with following; but the great one that goes upward, let him draw thee after. When a wise man gives thee better counsel, give me mine again. I would have none but knaves follow it, since a fool gives it.   250

⌜Sings⌝

That sir which serves and seeks for gain
And follows but for form,
Will pack when it begin to rain,
And leave thee in the storm.

But I will tarry, the fool will stay,   255
And let the wise man fly.
The knave turns fool that runs away,
The fool no knave, pardie.

KENT Where learned you this, Fool?

FOOL Not i'th' stocks, fool.   260

Enter King Lear and the Duke of Gloucester

LEAR

Deny to speak with me? They are sick, they are weary,
They have travelled all the night?—mere fetches,
The images of revolt and flying off.
Fetch me a better answer.

GLOUCESTER   My dear lord,
You know the fiery quality of the Duke,   265
How unremovable and fixed he is
In his own course.

LEAR   Vengeance, plague, death, confusion!
'Fiery'? What 'quality'? Why, Gloucester, Gloucester,
I'd speak with the Duke of Cornwall and his wife.

GLOUCESTER

Well, my good lord, I have informed them so.   270

LEAR

'Informed them'? Dost thou understand me, man?

GLOUCESTER Ay, my good lord.

LEAR

The King would speak with Cornwall; the dear father
Would with his daughter speak, commands, tends
          service.
Are they 'informed' of this? My breath and blood—   275
'Fiery'? The 'fiery' Duke—tell the hot Duke that—
No, but not yet. Maybe he is not well.
Infirmity doth still neglect all office
Whereto our health is bound. We are not ourselves
When nature, being oppressed, commands the mind
To suffer with the body. I'll forbear,   281
And am fallen out with my more headier will,
To take the indisposed and sickly fit

For the sound man.—Death on my state, wherefore
Should he sit here? This act persuades me   285
That this remotion of the Duke and her
Is practice only. Give me my servant forth.
Go tell the Duke and 's wife I'd speak with them,
Now, presently. Bid them come forth and hear me,
Or at their chamber door I'll beat the drum   290
Till it cry sleep to death.

GLOUCESTER   I would have all well betwixt you.
                                                        Exit

LEAR

O me, my heart! My rising heart! But down.

FOOL Cry to it, nuncle, as the cockney did to the eels when she put 'em i'th' paste alive. She knapped 'em o'th' coxcombs with a stick, and cried 'Down, wantons, down!' 'Twas her brother that, in pure kindness to his horse, buttered his hay.

*Enter the Duke of Cornwall, Regan, the Duke of
Gloucester, and servants*

LEAR Good morrow to you both.

CORNWALL Hail to your grace.

Kent here set at liberty

REGAN I am glad to see your highness.   300

LEAR

Regan, I think you are. I know what reason
I have to think so. If thou shouldst not be glad
I would divorce me from thy mother's shrine,
Sepulchring an adultress. (*To Kent*) O, are you free?
Some other time for that.   ⌜*Exit Kent*⌝
                    Belovèd Regan,   305
Thy sister's naught. O, Regan, she hath tied
Sharp-toothed unkindness like a vulture here.
I can scarce speak to thee. Thou'lt not believe
With how depraved a quality—O, Regan!

REGAN

I pray you, sir, take patience. I have hope   310
You less know how to value her desert
Than she to scant her duty.

LEAR   Say, how is that?

REGAN

I cannot think my sister in the least
Would fail her obligation. If, sir, perchance
She have restrained the riots of your followers,   315
'Tis on such ground and to such wholesome end
As clears her from all blame.

LEAR My curses on her.

REGAN O sir, you are old.
Nature in you stands on the very verge   320
Of his confine. You should be ruled and led
By some discretion that discerns your state
Better than you yourself. Therefore I pray you
That to our sister you do make return;
Say you have wronged her.

LEAR   Ask her forgiveness?   325
Do you but mark how this becomes the house?
⌜*Kneeling*⌝ 'Dear daughter, I confess that I am old.
Age is unnecessary. On my knees I beg
That you'll vouchsafe me raiment, bed, and food.'

REGAN
  Good sir, no more. These are unsightly tricks.   330
  Return you to my sister.
LEAR ⌈*rising*⌉   Never, Regan.
  She hath abated me of half my train,
  Looked black upon me, struck me with her tongue
  Most serpent-like upon the very heart.
  All the stored vengeances of heaven fall   335
  On her ingrateful top! Strike her young bones,
  You taking airs, with lameness!
CORNWALL   Fie, sir, fie.
LEAR
  You nimble lightnings, dart your blinding flames
  Into her scornful eyes. Infect her beauty,
  You fen-sucked fogs drawn by the pow'rful sun   340
  To fall and blister.
REGAN   O, the blest gods!
  So will you wish on me when the rash mood is on.
LEAR
  No, Regan. Thou shalt never have my curse.
  Thy tender-hafted nature shall not give
  Thee o'er to harshness. Her eyes are fierce, but thine
  Do comfort and not burn. 'Tis not in thee   346
  To grudge my pleasures, to cut off my train,
  To bandy hasty words, to scant my sizes,
  And, in conclusion, to oppose the bolt
  Against my coming in. Thou better know'st   350
  The offices of nature, bond of childhood,
  Effects of courtesy, dues of gratitude.
  Thy half o'th' kingdom hast thou not forgot,
  Wherein I thee endowed.
REGAN   Good sir, to th' purpose.
LEAR
  Who put my man i'th' stocks?
    Tucket within
CORNWALL   What trumpet's that?
    Enter Oswald the steward
REGAN
  I know't, my sister's. This approves her letter   356
  That she would soon be here. (*To Oswald*) Is your lady
  come?
LEAR
  This is a slave whose easy-borrowed pride
  Dwells in the sickly grace of her a follows.   359
  (*To Oswald*) Out, varlet, from my sight!
CORNWALL   What means your grace?
    Enter Goneril
LEAR
  Who stocked my servant? Regan, I have good hope
  Thou didst not know on't. Who comes here? O heavens,
  If you do love old men, if your sweet sway
  Allow obedience, if you yourselves are old,
  Make it your cause! Send down and take my part.   365
  (*To Goneril*) Art not ashamed to look upon this beard?
  O Regan, will you take her by the hand?
GONERIL
  Why not by th' hand, sir? How have I offended?

  All's not offence that indiscretion finds
  And dotage terms so.
LEAR   O sides, you are too tough!   370
  Will you yet hold?—How came my man i'th' stocks?
CORNWALL
  I set him there, sir; but his own disorders
  Deserved much less advancement.
LEAR   You? Did you?
REGAN
  I pray you, father, being weak, seem so.
  If till the expiration of your month   375
  You will return and sojourn with my sister,
  Dismissing half your train, come then to me.
  I am now from home, and out of that provision
  Which shall be needful for your entertainment.
LEAR
  Return to her, and fifty men dismissed?   380
  No, rather I abjure all roofs, and choose
  To be a comrade with the wolf and owl,
  To wage against the enmity o'th' air
  Necessity's sharp pinch. Return with her?
  Why, the hot-blooded France, that dowerless took   385
  Our youngest born—I could as well be brought
  To knee his throne and, squire-like, pension beg
  To keep base life afoot. Return with her?
  Persuade me rather to be slave and sumpter
  To this detested groom.
GONERIL   At your choice, sir.   390
LEAR
  I prithee, daughter, do not make me mad.
  I will not trouble thee, my child. Farewell.
  We'll no more meet, no more see one another.
  But yet thou art my flesh, my blood, my daughter—
  Or rather a disease that's in my flesh,   395
  Which I must needs call mine. Thou art a boil,
  A plague-sore or embossèd carbuncle
  In my corrupted blood. But I'll not chide thee.
  Let shame come when it will, I do not call it.
  I do not bid the thunder-bearer shoot,   400
  Nor tell tales of thee to high-judging Jove.
  Mend when thou canst; be better at thy leisure.
  I can be patient, I can stay with Regan,
  I and my hundred knights.
REGAN   Not altogether so.
  I looked not for you yet, nor am provided   405
  For your fit welcome. Give ear, sir, to my sister;
  For those that mingle reason with your passion
  Must be content to think you old, and so—
  But she knows what she does.
LEAR   Is this well spoken?
REGAN
  I dare avouch it, sir. What, fifty followers?   410
  Is it not well? What should you need of more,
  Yea, or so many, sith that both charge and danger
  Speak 'gainst so great a number? How in one house
  Should many people under two commands
  Hold amity? 'Tis hard, almost impossible.   415

GONERIL

Why might not you, my lord, receive attendance
From those that she calls servants, or from mine?

REGAN

Why not, my lord? If then they chanced to slack ye,
We could control them. If you will come to me—
For now I spy a danger—I entreat you   420
To bring but five and twenty; to no more
Will I give place or notice.

LEAR I gave you all.

REGAN And in good time you gave it.

LEAR

Made you my guardians, my depositaries,   425
But kept a reservation to be followed
With such a number. What, must I come to you
With five and twenty? Regan, said you so?

REGAN

And speak't again, my lord. No more with me.

LEAR

Those wicked creatures yet do look well favoured   430
When others are more wicked. Not being the worst
Stands in some rank of praise. (*To Goneril*) I'll go with
    thee.
Thy fifty yet doth double five and twenty,
And thou art twice her love.

GONERIL   Hear me, my lord.
What need you five and twenty, ten, or five,   435
To follow in a house where twice so many
Have a command to tend you?

REGAN   What need one?

LEAR

O, reason not the need! Our basest beggars
Are in the poorest thing superfluous.
Allow not nature more than nature needs,   440
Man's life is cheap as beast's. Thou art a lady.
If only to go warm were gorgeous,
Why, nature needs not what thou, gorgeous, wear'st,
Which scarcely keeps thee warm. But for true need—
You heavens, give me that patience, patience I need.
You see me here, you gods, a poor old man,   446
As full of grief as age, wretchèd in both.
If it be you that stirs these daughters' hearts
Against their father, fool me not so much
To bear it tamely. Touch me with noble anger,   450
And let not women's weapons, water-drops,
Stain my man's cheeks. No, you unnatural hags,
I will have such revenges on you both
That all the world shall—I will do such things—
What they are, yet I know not; but they shall be   455
The terrors of the earth. You think I'll weep.
No, I'll not weep. I have full cause of weeping,
        Storm and tempest
But this heart shall break into a hundred thousand
    flaws
Or ere I'll weep.—O Fool, I shall go mad!
        Exeunt Lear, Fool, Gentleman, and Gloucester

CORNWALL

Let us withdraw. 'Twill be a storm.   460

REGAN

This house is little. The old man and 's people
Cannot be well bestowed.

GONERIL   'Tis his own blame;
Hath put himself from rest, and must needs taste his
    folly.

REGAN

For his particular I'll receive him gladly,
But not one follower.

GONERIL   So am I purposed.   465
Where is my lord of Gloucester?

CORNWALL

Followed the old man forth.
        ⌈*Enter the Duke of Gloucester*⌉
                                He is returned.

GLOUCESTER

The King is in high rage.

CORNWALL   Whither is he going?

GLOUCESTER

He calls to horse, but will I know not whither.

CORNWALL

'Tis best to give him way. He leads himself.   470

GONERIL (*to Gloucester*)

My lord, entreat him by no means to stay.

GLOUCESTER

Alack, the night comes on, and the high winds
Do sorely ruffle. For many miles about
There's scarce a bush.

REGAN   O sir, to wilful men
The injuries that they themselves procure   475
Must be their schoolmasters. Shut up your doors.
He is attended with a desperate train,
And what they may incense him to, being apt
To have his ear abused, wisdom bids fear.

CORNWALL

Shut up your doors, my lord. 'Tis a wild night.   480
My Regan counsels well. Come out o' th' storm. *Exeunt*

3.1 *Storm still. Enter the Earl of Kent disguised and*
        ⌈*the First*⌉ *Gentleman, severally*

KENT

Who's there, besides foul weather?

⌈FIRST⌉ GENTLEMAN   One minded like the weather,
Most unquietly.

KENT   I know you. Where's the King?

⌈FIRST⌉ GENTLEMAN

Contending with the fretful elements;
Bids the wind blow the earth into the sea
Or swell the curlèd waters 'bove the main,   5
That things might change or cease.

KENT   But who is with him?

⌈FIRST⌉ GENTLEMAN

None but the Fool, who labours to outjest
His heart-struck injuries.

KENT   Sir, I do know you,
And dare upon the warrant of my note
Commend a dear thing to you. There is division,   10
Although as yet the face of it is covered

With mutual cunning, 'twixt Albany and Cornwall,
Who have—as who have not that their great stars
Throned and set high—servants, who seem no less,
Which are to France the spies and speculations   15
Intelligent of our state. What hath been seen,
Either in snuffs and packings of the Dukes,
Or the hard rein which both of them hath borne
Against the old kind King; or something deeper,
Whereof perchance these are but furnishings—   20

⌜FIRST⌝ GENTLEMAN
I will talk further with you.

KENT   No, do not.
For confirmation that I am much more
Than my out-wall, open this purse, and take
What it contains. If you shall see Cordelia—
As fear not but you shall—show her this ring   25
And she will tell you who that fellow is
That yet you do not know. Fie on this storm!
I will go seek the King.

⌜FIRST⌝ GENTLEMAN
Give me your hand. Have you no more to say?

KENT
Few words, but to effect more than all yet: 30
That when we have found the King—in which your
    pain
That way, I'll this—he that first lights on him
Holla the other.   *Exeunt severally*

3.2   *Storm still. Enter King Lear and his Fool*

LEAR
Blow, winds, and crack your cheeks! Rage, blow,
You cataracts and hurricanoes, spout
Till you have drenched our steeples, drowned the
    cocks!
You sulph'rous and thought-executing fires,
Vaunt-couriers of oak-cleaving thunderbolts,   5
Singe my white head; and thou all-shaking thunder,
Strike flat the thick rotundity o'th' world,
Crack nature's moulds, all germens spill at once
That makes ingrateful man.   9

FOOL O nuncle, court holy water in a dry house is better
than this rain-water out o' door. Good nuncle, in, ask
thy daughters blessing. Here's a night pities neither
wise men nor fools.

LEAR
Rumble thy bellyful; spit, fire; spout, rain.
Nor rain, wind, thunder, fire are my daughters.   15
I tax not you, you elements, with unkindness.
I never gave you kingdom, called you children.
You owe me no subscription. Then let fall
Your horrible pleasure. Here I stand your slave,
A poor, infirm, weak and despised old man,   20
But yet I call you servile ministers,
That will with two pernicious daughters join
Your high-engendered battles 'gainst a head
So old and white as this. O, ho, 'tis foul!

FOOL He that has a house to put 's head in has a good
head-piece.   26

⌜*Sings*⌝ The codpiece that will house
     Before the head has any,
   The head and he shall louse,
     So beggars marry many.   30
   The man that makes his toe
     What he his heart should make
   Shall of a corn cry woe,
     And turn his sleep to wake—
for there was never yet fair woman but she made
mouths in a glass.   36

       Enter the Earl of Kent disguised

LEAR
No, I will be the pattern of all patience.
I will say nothing.

KENT Who's there?

FOOL Marry, here's grace and a codpiece—that's a wise
man and a fool.   41

KENT (*to Lear*)
Alas, sir, are you here? Things that love night
Love not such nights as these. The wrathful skies
Gallow the very wanderers of the dark
And make them keep their caves. Since I was man   45
Such sheets of fire, such bursts of horrid thunder,
Such groans of roaring wind and rain I never
Remember to have heard. Man's nature cannot carry
Th'affliction nor the fear.

LEAR   Let the great gods,
That keep this dreadful pother o'er our heads,   50
Find out their enemies now. Tremble, thou wretch
That hast within thee undivulgèd crimes
Unwhipped of justice; hide thee, thou bloody hand,
Thou perjured and thou simular of virtue
That art incestuous; caitiff, to pieces shake,   55
That under covert and convenient seeming
Has practised on man's life; close pent-up guilts,
Rive your concealing continents and cry
These dreadful summoners grace. I am a man
More sinned against than sinning.

KENT   Alack, bare-headed?
Gracious my lord, hard by here is a hovel.   61
Some friendship will it lend you 'gainst the tempest.
Repose you there while I to this hard house—
More harder than the stones whereof 'tis raised,
Which even but now, demanding after you,   65
Denied me to come in—return and force
Their scanted courtesy.

LEAR   My wits begin to turn.
(*To Fool*) Come on, my boy. How dost, my boy? Art
    cold?
I am cold myself.—Where is this straw, my fellow?
The art of our necessities is strange,   70
And can make vile things precious. Come, your hovel.—
Poor fool and knave, I have one part in my heart
That's sorry yet for thee.

FOOL ⌜*Sings*⌝
He that has and a little tiny wit,
   With heigh-ho, the wind and the rain,   75
Must make content with his fortunes fit,
   Though the rain it raineth every day.

LEAR
True, boy. (*To Kent*) Come, bring us to this hovel.
                                    Exeunt Lear and Kent
FOOL This is a brave night to cool a courtesan. I'll speak
  a prophecy ere I go: 80
    When priests are more in word than matter;
    When brewers mar their malt with water;
    When nobles are their tailors' tutors,
    No heretics burned, but wenches' suitors,
    Then shall the realm of Albion   85
    Come to great confusion.

    When every case in law is right;
    No squire in debt nor no poor knight;
    When slanders do not live in tongues,
    Nor cutpurses come not to throngs;   90
    When usurers tell their gold i'th' field,
    And bawds and whores do churches build,
    Then comes the time, who lives to see't,
    That going shall be used with feet.   94
  This prophecy Merlin shall make; for I live before his
  time.   *Exit*

3.3 *Enter the Duke of Gloucester and Edmond*
GLOUCESTER Alack, alack, Edmond, I like not this
  unnatural dealing. When I desired their leave that I
  might pity him, they took from me the use of mine
  own house, charged me on pain of perpetual displeasure
  neither to speak of him, entreat for him, or any way
  sustain him.   6
EDMOND Most savage and unnatural!
GLOUCESTER Go to, say you nothing. There is division
  between the Dukes, and a worse matter than that. I
  have received a letter this night—'tis dangerous to be
  spoken—I have locked the letter in my closet. These
  injuries the King now bears will be revenged home.
  There is part of a power already footed. We must incline
  to the King. I will look him and privily relieve him. Go
  you and maintain talk with the Duke, that my charity
  be not of him perceived. If he ask for me, I am ill and
  gone to bed. If I die for't—as no less is threatened me—
  the King my old master must be relieved. There is strange
  things toward, Edmond; pray you be careful.   *Exit*
EDMOND
  This courtesy, forbid thee, shall the Duke   20
  Instantly know, and of that letter too.
  This seems a fair deserving, and must draw me
  That which my father loses: no less than all.
  The younger rises when the old doth fall.   *Exit*

3.4 *Enter King Lear, the Earl of Kent disguised, and
  Lear's Fool*
KENT
  Here is the place, my lord. Good my lord, enter.
  The tyranny of the open night's too rough
  For nature to endure.
      Storm still
LEAR   Let me alone.

KENT
  Good my lord, enter here.
LEAR   Wilt break my heart?
KENT
  I had rather break mine own. Good my lord, enter. 5
LEAR
  Thou think'st 'tis much that this contentious storm
  Invades us to the skin. So 'tis to thee;
  But where the greater malady is fixed,
  The lesser is scarce felt. Thou'dst shun a bear,
  But if thy flight lay toward the roaring sea   10
  Thou'dst meet the bear i'th' mouth. When the mind's
      free,
  The body's delicate. This tempest in my mind
  Doth from my senses take all feeling else
  Save what beats there: filial ingratitude.
  Is it not as this mouth should tear this hand   15
  For lifting food to't? But I will punish home.
  No, I will weep no more.—In such a night
  To shut me out? Pour on, I will endure.
  In such a night as this! O Regan, Goneril,
  Your old kind father, whose frank heart gave all— 20
  O, that way madness lies. Let me shun that.
  No more of that.
KENT   Good my lord, enter here.
LEAR
  Prithee, go in thyself. Seek thine own ease.
  This tempest will not give me leave to ponder
  On things would hurt me more; but I'll go in.   25
  (*To Fool*) In, boy; go first. ⌐Kneeling⌐ You houseless
      poverty—
  Nay, get thee in. I'll pray, and then I'll sleep.
                                    Exit Fool
  Poor naked wretches, wheresoe'er you are,
  That bide the pelting of this pitiless storm,
  How shall your houseless heads and unfed sides,   30
  Your looped and windowed raggedness, defend you
  From seasons such as these? O, I have ta'en
  Too little care of this. Take physic, pomp,
  Expose thyself to feel what wretches feel,
  That thou mayst shake the superflux to them   35
  And show the heavens more just.
      *Enter Lear's Fool, ⌐and Edgar as a Bedlam beggar
      in the hovel⌐*
EDGAR
  Fathom and half! Fathom and half! Poor Tom!
FOOL Come not in here, nuncle. Here's a spirit. Help me,
  help me!
KENT Give my thy hand. Who's there?   40
FOOL A spirit, a spirit. He says his name's Poor Tom.
KENT
  What art thou that dost grumble there i'th' straw?
  Come forth.
      ⌐Edgar comes forth⌐
EDGAR   Away, the foul fiend follows me.
  Thorough the sharp hawthorn blow the winds. Hm!
  Go to thy cold bed and warm thee.   45

LEAR
Didst thou give all to thy two daughters,
And art thou come to this?

EDGAR Who gives anything to Poor Tom, whom the foul fiend hath led through fire and through flame, through ford and whirlpool, o'er bog and quagmire; that hath laid knives under his pillow and halters in his pew, set ratsbane by his porridge, made him proud of heart to ride on a bay trotting-horse over four-inched bridges, to course his own shadow for a traitor. Bless thy five wits, Tom's a-cold! O, do, de, do, de, do de. Bless thee from whirlwinds, star-blasting, and taking. Do Poor Tom some charity, whom the foul fiend vexes. There could I have him now, and there, and there again, and there.

Storm still

LEAR
Has his daughters brought him to this pass?
(*To Edgar*) Couldst thou save nothing? Wouldst thou
give 'em all?   60

FOOL Nay, he reserved a blanket, else we had been all shamed.

LEAR (*to Edgar*)
Now all the plagues that in the pendulous air
Hang fated o'er men's faults light on thy daughters!

KENT He hath no daughters, sir.   65

LEAR
Death, traitor! Nothing could have subdued nature
To such a lowness but his unkind daughters.
(*To Edgar*) Is it the fashion that discarded fathers
Should have thus little mercy on their flesh?
Judicious punishment: 'twas this flesh begot   70
Those pelican daughters.

EDGAR Pillicock sat on Pillicock Hill; alow, alow, loo, loo.

FOOL This cold night will turn us all to fools and madmen.

EDGAR Take heed o'th' foul fiend; obey thy parents; keep thy words' justice; swear not; commit not with man's sworn spouse; set not thy sweet heart on proud array. Tom's a-cold.

LEAR What hast thou been?

EDGAR A servingman, proud in heart and mind, that curled my hair, wore gloves in my cap, served the lust of my mistress' heart, and did the act of darkness with her; swore as many oaths as I spake words, and broke them in the sweet face of heaven; one that slept in the contriving of lust, and waked to do it. Wine loved I deeply, dice dearly, and in woman out-paramoured the Turk. False of heart, light of ear, bloody of hand; hog in sloth, fox in stealth, wolf in greediness, dog in madness, lion in prey. Let not the creaking of shoes nor the rustling of silks betray thy poor heart to woman. Keep thy foot out of brothels, thy hand out of plackets, thy pen from lenders' books, and defy the foul fiend. Still through the hawthorn blows the cold wind, says suum, mun, nonny. Dauphin, my boy! Boy, *cessez*; let him trot by.   94

Storm still

LEAR Thou wert better in a grave than to answer with thy uncovered body this extremity of the skies. Is man no more than this? Consider him well. Thou owest the worm no silk, the beast no hide, the sheep no wool, the cat no perfume. Ha, here's three on 's are sophisticated; thou art the thing itself. Unaccommodated man is no more but such a poor, bare, forked animal as thou art. Off, off, you lendings! Come, unbutton here.

Enter the Duke of Gloucester with a torch

FOOL Prithee, nuncle, be contented. 'Tis a naughty night to swim in. Now a little fire in a wild field were like an old lecher's heart—a small spark, all the rest on 's body cold. Look, here comes a walking fire.

EDGAR This is the foul fiend Flibbertigibbet. He begins at curfew and walks till the first cock. He gives the web and the pin, squints the eye, and makes the harelip; mildews the white wheat, and hurts the poor creature of earth.

⌜*Sings*⌝
          Swithin footed thrice the wold,
          A met the night mare and her nine foal,
               Bid her alight   115
               And her troth plight,
          And aroint thee, witch, aroint thee!

KENT (*to Lear*)
How fares your grace?

LEAR   What's he?

KENT (*to Gloucester*) Who's there? What is't you seek?

GLOUCESTER What are you there? Your names?   120

EDGAR Poor Tom, that eats the swimming frog, the toad, the tadpole, the wall-newt and the water; that in the fury of his heart, when the foul fiend rages, eats cowdung for salads, swallows the old rat and the ditch-dog, drinks the green mantle of the standing pool; who is whipped from tithing to tithing, and stocked, punished, and imprisoned; who hath had three suits to his back, six shirts to his body,
          Horse to ride, and weapon to wear;
          But mice and rats and such small deer   130
          Have been Tom's food for seven long year.
Beware my follower. Peace, Smulkin; peace, thou fiend!

GLOUCESTER (*to Lear*)
What, hath your grace no better company?

EDGAR
The Prince of Darkness is a gentleman.
Modo he's called, and Mahu.   135

GLOUCESTER (*to Lear*)
Our flesh and blood, my lord, is grown so vile
That it doth hate what gets it.

EDGAR   Poor Tom's a-cold.

GLOUCESTER (*to Lear*)
Go in with me. My duty cannot suffer
T'obey in all your daughters' hard commands.
Though their injunction be to bar my doors   140
And let this tyrannous night take hold upon you,
Yet have I ventured to come seek you out
And bring you where both fire and food is ready.

LEAR
First let me talk with this philosopher.
(*To Edgar*) What is the cause of thunder? 145

KENT
Good my lord, take his offer; go into th' house.

LEAR
I'll talk a word with this same learnèd Theban.
(*To Edgar*) What is your study?

EDGAR
How to prevent the fiend, and to kill vermin.

LEAR
Let me ask you one word in private. 150
They converse apart

KENT (*to Gloucester*)
Importune him once more to go, my lord.
His wits begin t'unsettle.

GLOUCESTER   Canst thou blame him?
Storm still
His daughters seek his death. Ah, that good Kent,
He said it would be thus, poor banished man!
Thou sayst the King grows mad; I'll tell thee, friend,
I am almost mad myself. I had a son, 156
Now outlawed from my blood; a sought my life
But lately, very late. I loved him, friend;
No father his son dearer. True to tell thee,
The grief hath crazed my wits. What a night's this!
(*To Lear*) I do beseech your grace—

LEAR   O, cry you mercy, sir!
(*To Edgar*) Noble philosopher, your company.

EDGAR   Tom's a-cold.

GLOUCESTER
In, fellow, there in t'hovel; keep thee warm.

LEAR
Come, let's in all.

KENT   This way, my lord.

LEAR   With him!
I will keep still with my philosopher. 165

KENT (*to Gloucester*)
Good my lord, soothe him; let him take the fellow.

GLOUCESTER Take him you on.

KENT ⌈*to Edgar*⌉
Sirrah, come on. Go along with us.

LEAR (*to Edgar*)
Come, good Athenian.

GLOUCESTER   No words, no words. Hush.

EDGAR
Child Roland to the dark tower came, 170
His word was still 'Fie, fo, and fum;
I smell the blood of a British man.'   *Exeunt*

3.5   *Enter the Duke of Cornwall and Edmond*

CORNWALL I will have my revenge ere I depart his house.

EDMOND How, my lord, I may be censured, that nature
thus gives way to loyalty, something fears me to think
of. 4

CORNWALL I now perceive it was not altogether your
brother's evil disposition made him seek his death, but
a provoking merit set a-work by a reprovable badness
in himself.

EDMOND How malicious is my fortune, that I must repent
to be just! This is the letter which he spoke of, which
approves him an intelligent party to the advantages of
France. O heavens, that this treason were not, or not
I the detector!

CORNWALL Go with me to the Duchess.

EDMOND If the matter of this paper be certain, you have
mighty business in hand. 16

CORNWALL True or false, it hath made thee Earl of
Gloucester. Seek out where thy father is, that he may
be ready for our apprehension. 19

EDMOND ⌈*aside*⌉ If I find him comforting the King, it will
stuff his suspicion more fully. (*To Cornwall*) I will
persever in my course of loyalty, though the conflict
be sore between that and my blood.

CORNWALL I will lay trust upon thee, and thou shalt find
a dearer father in my love.   *Exeunt*

3.6   *Enter the Earl of Kent disguised, and the Duke of
Gloucester*

GLOUCESTER Here is better than the open air; take it
thankfully. I will piece out the comfort with what
addition I can. I will not be long from you.

KENT All the power of his wits have given way to his
impatience; the gods reward your kindness! 5
Exit Gloucester
*Enter King Lear, Edgar as a Bedlam beggar, and
Lear's Fool*

EDGAR Fraterretto calls me, and tells me Nero is an angler
in the lake of darkness. Pray, innocent, and beware
the foul fiend.

FOOL Prithee, nuncle, tell me whether a madman be a
gentleman or a yeoman. 10

LEAR A king, a king!

FOOL No, he's a yeoman that has a gentleman to his son;
for he's a mad yeoman that sees his son a gentleman
before him.

LEAR
To have a thousand with red burning spits 15
Come hissing in upon 'em!

EDGAR   Bless thy five wits.

KENT (*to Lear*)
O, pity! Sir, where is the patience now
That you so oft have boasted to retain?

EDGAR (*aside*)
My tears begin to take his part so much
They mar my counterfeiting.

LEAR   The little dogs and all, 20
Tray, Blanch, and Sweetheart—see, they bark at me.

EDGAR Tom will throw his head at them.—Avaunt, you
curs!
Be thy mouth or black or white,
Tooth that poisons if it bite, 25
Mastiff, greyhound, mongrel grim,
Hound or spaniel, brach or him,
Bobtail tyke or trundle-tail,
Tom will make him weep and wail;
For with throwing thus my head, 30
Dogs leapt the hatch, and all are fled.

Do, de, de, de. Sese! Come, march to wakes and fairs
And market towns. Poor Tom, thy horn is dry.
LEAR Then let them anatomize Regan; see what breeds
about her heart. Is there any cause in nature that
makes these hard-hearts? (*To Edgar*) You, sir, I entertain
for one of my hundred, only I do not like the fashion
of your garments. You will say they are Persian; but
let them be changed.
KENT
Now, good my lord, lie here and rest a while.   40
LEAR Make no noise, make no noise. Draw the curtains.
So, so. We'll go to supper i'th' morning.
          ⌜*He sleeps*⌝
FOOL And I'll go to bed at noon.
          Enter the Duke of Gloucester
GLOUCESTER (*to Kent*)
Come hither, friend. Where is the King my master?
KENT
Here, sir, but trouble him not; his wits are gone.   45
GLOUCESTER
Good friend, I prithee take him in thy arms.
I have o'erheard a plot of death upon him.
There is a litter ready. Lay him in't
And drive toward Dover, friend, where thou shalt meet
Both welcome and protection. Take up thy master.   50
If thou shouldst dally half an hour, his life,
With thine and all that offer to defend him,
Stand in assurèd loss. Take up, take up,
And follow me, that will to some provision
Give thee quick conduct. Come, come away.   55
          Exeunt, ⌜*Kent carrying Lear in his arms*⌝

3.7   *Enter the Duke of Cornwall, Regan, Goneril,*
          Edmond the bastard, and Servants
CORNWALL (*to Goneril*)
Post speedily to my lord your husband.
Show him this letter. The army of France is landed.
(*To Servants*) Seek out the traitor Gloucester.
          Exeunt some
REGAN   Hang him instantly.
GONERIL
Pluck out his eyes.
CORNWALL   Leave him to my displeasure.
Edmond, keep you our sister company.   5
The revenges we are bound to take upon your traitorous
father are not fit for your beholding. Advise the Duke
where you are going, to a most festinate preparation;
we are bound to the like. Our posts shall be swift and
intelligent betwixt us. Farewell, dear sister.
(*To Edmond*) Farewell, my lord of Gloucester.   11
          Enter Oswald the steward
How now, where's the King?
OSWALD
My lord of Gloucester hath conveyed him hence.
Some five or six and thirty of his knights,
Hot questrists after him, met him at gate,   15
Who, with some other of the lord's dependants,
Are gone with him toward Dover, where they boast
To have well-armèd friends.

CORNWALL Get horses for your mistress.   *Exit Oswald*
GONERIL Farewell, sweet lord, and sister.   20
CORNWALL
Edmond, farewell.   *Exeunt Goneril and Edmond*
(*To Servants*)   Go seek the traitor Gloucester.
Pinion him like a thief; bring him before us.
          Exeunt other Servants
Though well we may not pass upon his life
Without the form of justice, yet our power
Shall do a curtsy to our wrath, which men   25
May blame but not control.
          Enter the Duke of Gloucester and Servants
          Who's there—the traitor?
REGAN
Ingrateful fox, 'tis he.
CORNWALL (*to Servants*) Bind fast his corky arms.
GLOUCESTER
What means your graces? Good my friends, consider
You are my guests. Do me no foul play, friends.
CORNWALL (*to Servants*)
Bind him, I say.
REGAN   Hard, hard! O filthy traitor!   30
GLOUCESTER
Unmerciful lady as you are, I'm none.
CORNWALL (*to Servants*)
To this chair bind him. (*To Gloucester*) Villain, thou
          shalt find—
          Regan plucks Gloucester's beard
GLOUCESTER
By the kind gods, 'tis most ignobly done,
To pluck me by the beard.
REGAN So white, and such a traitor?   35
GLOUCESTER Naughty lady,
These hairs which thou dost ravish from my chin
Will quicken and accuse thee. I am your host.
With robbers' hands my hospitable favours
You should not ruffle thus. What will you do?   40
CORNWALL
Come, sir, what letters had you late from France?
REGAN
Be simple-answered, for we know the truth.
CORNWALL
And what confederacy have you with the traitors
Late footed in the kingdom?
REGAN   To whose hands
You have sent the lunatic King. Speak.   45
GLOUCESTER
I have a letter guessingly set down,
Which came from one that's of a neutral heart,
And not from one opposed.
CORNWALL   Cunning.
REGAN   And false.
CORNWALL
Where hast thou sent the King?
GLOUCESTER   To Dover.
REGAN
Wherefore to Dover? Wast thou not charged at peril—   50
CORNWALL
Wherefore to Dover?—Let him answer that.

GLOUCESTER
I am tied to th' stake, and I must stand the course.
REGAN Wherefore to Dover?
GLOUCESTER
Because I would not see thy cruel nails
Pluck out his poor old eyes, nor thy fierce sister   55
In his anointed flesh stick boarish fangs.
The sea, with such a storm as his bare head
In hell-black night endured, would have buoyed up
And quenched the stellèd fires.
Yet, poor old heart, he help the heavens to rain.   60
If wolves had at thy gate howled that stern time,
Thou shouldst have said 'Good porter, turn the key;
All cruels I'll subscribe.' But I shall see
The wingèd vengeance overtake such children.
CORNWALL
See't shalt thou never.—Fellows, hold the chair.—   65
Upon these eyes of thine I'll set my foot.
GLOUCESTER
He that will think to live till he be old
Give me some help!—O cruel! O you gods!
⌜Cornwall pulls out one of Gloucester's eyes and
stamps on it⌝
REGAN (to Cornwall)
One side will mock another; th'other, too.
CORNWALL (to Gloucester)
If you see vengeance—
SERVANT   Hold your hand, my lord.   70
I have served you ever since I was a child,
But better service have I never done you
Than now to bid you hold.
REGAN   How now, you dog!
SERVANT
If you did wear a beard upon your chin
I'd shake it on this quarrel. ⌜To Cornwall⌝ What do
you mean?   75
CORNWALL My villein!
SERVANT
Nay then, come on, and take the chance of anger.
They draw and fight
REGAN (to another Servant)
Give me thy sword. A peasant stand up thus!
⌜She takes a sword and runs at him behind⌝
SERVANT (to Gloucester)
O, I am slain. My lord, you have one eye left
To see some mischief on him.
⌜Regan stabs him again⌝
                   O!   He dies
CORNWALL
Lest it see more, prevent it. Out, vile jelly!   81
He ⌜pulls out⌝ Gloucester's other eye
Where is thy lustre now?
GLOUCESTER
All dark and comfortless. Where's my son Edmond?
Edmond, enkindle all the sparks of nature
To quite this horrid act.
REGAN   Out, treacherous villain!   85
Thou call'st on him that hates thee. It was he

That made the overture of thy treasons to us,
Who is too good to pity thee.
GLOUCESTER
O, my follies! Then Edgar was abused.
Kind gods, forgive me that, and prosper him!   90
REGAN (to Servants)
Go thrust him out at gates, and let him smell
His way to Dover.   Exit one or more with Gloucester
           How is't, my lord? How look you?
CORNWALL
I have received a hurt. Follow me, lady.
(To Servants) Turn out that eyeless villain. Throw this
slave
Upon the dunghill. Regan, I bleed apace.   95
Untimely comes this hurt. Give me your arm.
                      Exeunt ⌜with the body⌝

4.1   Enter Edgar as a Bedlam beggar
EDGAR
Yet better thus and known to be contemned
Than still contemned and flattered. To be worst,
The low'st and most dejected thing of fortune,
Stands still in esperance, lives not in fear.
The lamentable change is from the best;   5
The worst returns to laughter. Welcome, then,
Thou unsubstantial air that I embrace.
The wretch that thou hast blown unto the worst
Owes nothing to thy blasts.
     Enter the Duke of Gloucester led by an Old Man
                 But who comes here?
My father, parti-eyed? World, world, O world!   10
But that thy strange mutations make us hate thee,
Life would not yield to age.
     ⌜Edgar stands aside⌝
OLD MAN (to Gloucester)   O my good lord,
I have been your tenant and your father's tenant
These fourscore years.
GLOUCESTER
Away, get thee away, good friend, be gone.   15
Thy comforts can do me no good at all;
Thee they may hurt.
OLD MAN   You cannot see your way.
GLOUCESTER
I have no way, and therefore want no eyes.
I stumbled when I saw. Full oft 'tis seen
Our means secure us, and our mere defects   20
Prove our commodities. O dear son Edgar,
The food of thy abusèd father's wrath—
Might I but live to see thee in my touch
I'd say I had eyes again.
OLD MAN   How now? Who's there?
EDGAR (aside)
O gods! Who is't can say 'I am at the worst'?   25
I am worse than e'er I was.
OLD MAN (to Gloucester)   'Tis poor mad Tom.
EDGAR (aside)
And worse I may be yet. The worst is not
So long as we can say 'This is the worst.'

OLD MAN (*to Edgar*) Fellow, where goest?
GLOUCESTER Is it a beggarman?   30
OLD MAN Madman and beggar too.
GLOUCESTER
A has some reason, else he could not beg.
I'th' last night's storm I such a fellow saw,
Which made me think a man a worm. My son
Came then into my mind, and yet my mind   35
Was then scarce friends with him. I have heard more
    since.
As flies to wanton boys are we to th' gods;
They kill us for their sport.
EDGAR (*aside*)   How should this be?
Bad is the trade that must play fool to sorrow,
Ang'ring itself and others.
    ⌜*He comes forward*⌝
                            Bless thee, master.   40
GLOUCESTER
Is that the naked fellow?
OLD MAN   Ay, my lord.
GLOUCESTER
Get thee away. If for my sake
Thou wilt o'ertake us hence a mile or twain
I'th' way toward Dover, do it for ancient love,
And bring some covering for this naked soul,   45
Which I'll entreat to lead me.
OLD MAN   Alack, sir, he is mad.
GLOUCESTER
'Tis the time's plague when madmen lead the blind.
Do as I bid thee; or rather do thy pleasure.
Above the rest, be gone.
OLD MAN
I'll bring him the best 'parel that I have,   50
Come on't what will.   *Exit*
GLOUCESTER   Sirrah, naked fellow!
EDGAR
Poor Tom's a-cold. (*Aside*) I cannot daub it further.
GLOUCESTER
Come hither, fellow.
EDGAR (*aside*)   And yet I must.
(*To Gloucester*) Bless thy sweet eyes, they bleed.
GLOUCESTER   Know'st thou the way to Dover?
EDGAR Both stile and gate, horseway and footpath. Poor
Tom hath been scared out of his good wits. Bless thee,
goodman's son, from the foul fiend.
GLOUCESTER
Here, take this purse, thou whom the heavens'
    plagues
Have humbled to all strokes. That I am wretched
Makes thee the happier. Heavens deal so still.   60
Let the superfluous and lust-dieted man
That slaves your ordinance, that will not see
Because he does not feel, feel your power quickly.
So distribution should undo excess,
And each man have enough. Dost thou know Dover?
EDGAR Ay, master.   66
GLOUCESTER
There is a cliff whose high and bending head
Looks fearfully in the confinèd deep.

Bring me but to the very brim of it
And I'll repair the misery thou dost bear   70
With something rich about me. From that place
I shall no leading need.
EDGAR Give me thy arm.
Poor Tom shall lead thee.
                    Exit Edgar guiding Gloucester

4.2   *Enter Goneril and Edmond the bastard* ⌜*at one door*⌝
         and Oswald the steward ⌜*at another*⌝
GONERIL
Welcome, my lord. I marvel our mild husband
Not met us on the way. (*To Oswald*) Now, where's
    your master?
OSWALD
Madam, within; but never man so changed.
I told him of the army that was landed;
He smiled at it. I told him you were coming;   5
His answer was 'The worse'. Of Gloucester's treachery
And of the loyal service of his son
When I informed him, then he called me sot,
And told me I had turned the wrong side out.
What most he should dislike seems pleasant to him; 10
What like, offensive.
GONERIL (*to Edmond*)   Then shall you go no further.
It is the cowish terror of his spirit
That dares not undertake. He'll not feel wrongs
Which tie him to an answer. Our wishes on the way
May prove effects. Back, Edmond, to my brother.   15
Hasten his musters and conduct his powers.
I must change names at home, and give the distaff
Into my husband's hands. This trusty servant
Shall pass between us. Ere long you are like to hear,
If you dare venture in your own behalf,   20
A mistress's command. Wear this. Spare speech.
Decline your head. This kiss, if it durst speak,
Would stretch thy spirits up into the air.
    ⌜*She kisses him*⌝
Conceive, and fare thee well.
EDMOND Yours in the ranks of death.   25
GONERIL My most dear Gloucester.   *Exit Edmond*
O, the difference of man and man!
To thee a woman's services are due;
My fool usurps my body.
OSWALD   Madam, here comes my lord.
    Enter the Duke of Albany
GONERIL
I have been worth the whistling.
ALBANY   O Goneril,   30
You are not worth the dust which the rude wind
Blows in your face.
GONERIL   Milk-livered man,
That bear'st a cheek for blows, a head for wrongs;
Who hast not in thy brows an eye discerning
Thine honour from thy suffering—
ALBANY   See thyself, devil. 35
Proper deformity shows not in the fiend
So horrid as in woman.
GONERIL   O vain fool!

Enter a Messenger

MESSENGER
O my good lord, the Duke of Cornwall's dead,
Slain by his servant going to put out
The other eye of Gloucester.
ALBANY   Gloucester's eyes?   40
MESSENGER
A servant that he bred, thrilled with remorse,
Opposed against the act, bending his sword
To his great master, who thereat enraged
Flew on him, and amongst them felled him dead,
But not without that harmful stroke which since   45
Hath plucked him after.
ALBANY   This shows you are above,
You justicers, that these our nether crimes
So speedily can venge. But O, poor Gloucester!
Lost he his other eye?
MESSENGER   Both, both, my lord.—
This letter, madam, craves a speedy answer.   50
'Tis from your sister.
GONERIL (*aside*)   One way I like this well;
But being widow, and my Gloucester with her,
May all the building in my fancy pluck
Upon my hateful life. Another way
The news is not so tart.—I'll read and answer.   55
                                 ⌈*Exit with Oswald*⌉
ALBANY
Where was his son when they did take his eyes?
MESSENGER
Come with my lady hither.
ALBANY   He is not here.
MESSENGER
No, my good lord; I met him back again.
ALBANY Knows he the wickedness?
MESSENGER
Ay, my good lord; 'twas he informed against him,   60
And quit the house on purpose that their punishment
Might have the freer course.
ALBANY   Gloucester, I live
To thank thee for the love thou showed'st the King,
And to revenge thine eyes.—Come hither, friend.   64
Tell me what more thou know'st.   *Exeunt*

4.3   *Enter with a drummer and colours, Queen*
      Cordelia, Gentlemen, and soldiers

CORDELIA
Alack, 'tis he! Why, he was met even now,
As mad as the vexed sea, singing aloud,
Crowned with rank fumitor and furrow-weeds,
With burdocks, hemlock, nettles, cuckoo-flowers,
Darnel, and all the idle weeds that grow   5
In our sustaining corn. A century send forth.
Search every acre in the high-grown field,
And bring him to our eye.   ⌈*Exit one or more*⌉
                          What can man's wisdom
In the restoring his bereavèd sense,
He that helps him take all my outward worth.   10
⌈FIRST⌉ GENTLEMAN There is means, madam.

Our foster-nurse of nature is repose,
The which he lacks. That to provoke in him
Are many simples operative, whose power
Will close the eye of anguish.
CORDELIA   All blest secrets,   15
All you unpublished virtues of the earth,
Spring with my tears, be aidant and remediate
In the good man's distress!—Seek, seek for him,
Lest his ungoverned rage dissolve the life
That wants the means to lead it.
                Enter a Messenger
MESSENGER   News, madam.   20
The British powers are marching hitherward.
CORDELIA
'Tis known before; our preparation stands
In expectation of them.—O dear father,
It is thy business that I go about;
Therefore great France   25
My mourning and importuned tears hath pitied.
No blown ambition doth our arms incite,
But love, dear love, and our aged father's right.
Soon may I hear and see him!   *Exeunt*

4.4   *Enter Regan and Oswald the steward*
REGAN
But are my brother's powers set forth?
OSWALD   Ay, madam.
REGAN
Himself in person there?
OSWALD   Madam, with much ado.
Your sister is the better soldier.
REGAN
Lord Edmond spake not with your lord at home?
OSWALD No, madam.   5
REGAN
What might import my sister's letters to him?
OSWALD I know not, lady.
REGAN
Faith, he is posted hence on serious matter.
It was great ignorance, Gloucester's eyes being out,
To let him live. Where he arrives he moves   10
All hearts against us. Edmond, I think, is gone,
In pity of his misery, to dispatch
His 'nighted life, moreover to descry
The strength o'th' enemy.
OSWALD
I must needs after, madam, with my letter.   15
REGAN
Our troops set forth tomorrow. Stay with us.
The ways are dangerous.
OSWALD   I may not, madam.
My lady charged my duty in this business.
REGAN
Why should she write to Edmond? Might not you
Transport her purposes by word? Belike—   20
Some things—I know not what. I'll love thee much:
Let me unseal the letter.
OSWALD   Madam, I had rather—

REGAN
I know your lady does not love her husband.
I am sure of that, and at her late being here
She gave strange oeillades and most speaking looks 25
To noble Edmond. I know you are of her bosom.

OSWALD I, madam?

REGAN
I speak in understanding. Y'are, I know't.
Therefore I do advise you take this note.
My lord is dead. Edmond and I have talked, 30
And more convenient is he for my hand
Than for your lady's. You may gather more.
If you do find him, pray you give him this,
And when your mistress hears thus much from you,
I pray desire her call her wisdom to her. 35
So, fare you well.
If you do chance to hear of that blind traitor,
Preferment falls on him that cuts him off.

OSWALD
Would I could meet him, madam. I should show
What party I do follow.

REGAN   Fare thee well. 40
                         Exeunt severally

4.5 *Enter Edgar disguised as a peasant, with a staff,*
       guiding the blind Duke of Gloucester

GLOUCESTER
When shall I come to th' top of that same hill?

EDGAR
You do climb up it now. Look how we labour.

GLOUCESTER
Methinks the ground is even.

EDGAR   Horrible steep.
Hark, do you hear the sea?

GLOUCESTER   No, truly.

EDGAR
Why, then your other senses grow imperfect 5
By your eyes' anguish.

GLOUCESTER   So may it be indeed.
Methinks thy voice is altered, and thou speak'st
In better phrase and matter than thou didst.

EDGAR
You're much deceived. In nothing am I changed
But in my garments.

GLOUCESTER   Methinks you're better spoken. 10

EDGAR
Come on, sir, here's the place. Stand still. How fearful
And dizzy 'tis to cast one's eyes so low!
The crows and choughs that wing the midway air
Show scarce so gross as beetles. Halfway down
Hangs one that gathers samphire, dreadful trade! 15
Methinks he seems no bigger than his head.
The fishermen that walk upon the beach
Appear like mice, and yon tall anchoring barque
Diminished to her cock, her cock a buoy
Almost too small for sight. The murmuring surge 20
That on th'unnumbered idle pebble chafes
Cannot be heard so high. I'll look no more,

Lest my brain turn and the deficient sight
Topple down headlong.

GLOUCESTER   Set me where you stand.

EDGAR
Give me your hand. You are now within a foot 25
Of th'extreme verge. For all beneath the moon
Would I not leap upright.

GLOUCESTER   Let go my hand.
Here, friend, 's another purse; in it a jewel
Well worth a poor man's taking. Fairies and gods
Prosper it with thee! Go thou further off. 30
Bid me farewell, and let me hear thee going.

EDGAR
Now fare ye well, good sir.
       He stands aside

GLOUCESTER   With all my heart.

EDGAR (*aside*)
Why I do trifle thus with his despair
Is done to cure it.

GLOUCESTER (*kneeling*) O you mighty gods,
This world I do renounce, and in your sights 35
Shake patiently my great affliction off!
If I could bear it longer, and not fall
To quarrel with your great opposeless wills,
My snuff and loathèd part of nature should
Burn itself out. If Edgar live, O bless him!— 40
Now, fellow, fare thee well.

EDGAR   Gone, sir. Farewell.
       Gloucester falls forward
(*Aside*) And yet I know not how conceit may rob
The treasury of life, when life itself
Yields to the theft. Had he been where he thought,
By this had thought been past.—Alive or dead? 45
(*To Gloucester*) Ho, you, sir, friend; hear you, sir?
       Speak.
(*Aside*) Thus might he pass indeed. Yet he revives.
(*To Gloucester*) What are you, sir?

GLOUCESTER   Away, and let me die.

EDGAR
Hadst thou been aught but gossamer, feathers, air,
So many fathom down precipitating 50
Thou'dst shivered like an egg. But thou dost breathe,
Hast heavy substance, bleed'st not, speak'st, art sound.
Ten masts a-length make not the altitude
Which thou hast perpendicularly fell.
Thy life's a miracle. Speak yet again. 55

GLOUCESTER But have I fall'n, or no?

EDGAR
From the dread summit of this chalky bourn.
Look up a-height. The shrill-gorged lark so far
Cannot be seen or heard. Do but look up.

GLOUCESTER Alack, I have no eyes. 60
Is wretchedness deprived that benefit
To end itself by death? 'Twas yet some comfort
When misery could beguile the tyrant's rage
And frustrate his proud will.

EDGAR   Give me your arm.
Up, so. How is't? Feel you your legs? You stand. 65

GLOUCESTER
Too well, too well.
EDGAR   This is above all strangeness.
Upon the crown o'th' cliff what thing was that
Which parted from you?
GLOUCESTER   A poor unfortunate beggar.
EDGAR
As I stood here below, methoughts his eyes
Were two full moons. He had a thousand noses,   70
Horns whelked and wavèd like the enragèd sea.
It was some fiend. Therefore, thou happy father,
Think that the clearest gods, who make them honours
Of men's impossibilities, have preserved thee.
GLOUCESTER
I do remember now. Henceforth I'll bear   75
Affliction till it do cry out itself
'Enough, enough,' and die. That thing you speak of,
I took it for a man. Often 'twould say
'The fiend, the fiend!' He led me to that place.
EDGAR
Bear free and patient thoughts.
          Enter King Lear mad, ⌐crowned with weeds and
          flowers⌐
                              But who comes here?
The safer sense will ne'er accommodate   81
His master thus.
LEAR No, they cannot touch me for crying. I am the King
himself.
EDGAR O thou side-piercing sight!   85
LEAR Nature's above art in that respect. There's your
press-money. That fellow handles his bow like a crow-
keeper. Draw me a clothier's yard. Look, look, a mouse!
Peace, peace, this piece of toasted cheese will do't.
There's my gauntlet. I'll prove it on a giant. Bring up
the brown bills. O, well flown, bird, i'th' clout, i'th'
clout! Whew! Give the word.
EDGAR Sweet marjoram.
LEAR Pass.
GLOUCESTER I know that voice.   95
LEAR Ha! Goneril with a white beard? They flattered me
like a dog, and told me I had the white hairs in my
beard ere the black ones were there. To say 'ay' and
'no' to everything that I said 'ay' and 'no' to was no
good divinity. When the rain came to wet me once,
and the wind to make me chatter; when the thunder
would not peace at my bidding, there I found 'em,
there I smelt 'em out. Go to, they are not men o' their
words. They told me I was everything; 'tis a lie, I am
not ague-proof.   105
GLOUCESTER
The trick of that voice I do well remember.
Is't not the King?
LEAR   Ay, every inch a king.
          ⌐*Gloucester kneels*⌐
When I do stare, see how the subject quakes!
I pardon that man's life. What was thy cause?
Adultery? Thou shalt not die. Die for adultery!   110
No, the wren goes to't, and the small gilded fly

Does lecher in my sight. Let copulation thrive,
For Gloucester's bastard son
Was kinder to his father than my daughters
Got 'tween the lawful sheets. To't, luxury, pell-mell,
For I lack soldiers. Behold yon simp'ring dame,   116
Whose face between her forks presages snow,
That minces virtue, and does shake the head
To hear of pleasure's name.
The fitchew nor the soilèd horse goes to't   120
With a more riotous appetite. Down from the waist
They're centaurs, though women all above.
But to the girdle do the gods inherit;
Beneath is all the fiend's. There's hell, there's darkness,
there is the sulphurous pit, burning, scalding, stench,
consumption. Fie, fie, fie; pah, pah! Give me an ounce
of civet, good apothecary, sweeten my imagination.
There's money for thee.
GLOUCESTER   O, let me kiss that hand!
LEAR Let me wipe it first; it smells of mortality.
GLOUCESTER
O ruined piece of nature! This great world   130
Shall so wear out to naught. Dost thou know me?
LEAR I remember thine eyes well enough. Dost thou
squiny at me?
No, do thy worst, blind Cupid, I'll not love.
Read thou this challenge. Mark but the penning of it.
GLOUCESTER
Were all thy letters suns, I could not see.   136
EDGAR (*aside*)
I would not take this from report; it is,
And my heart breaks at it.
LEAR (*to Gloucester*) Read.
GLOUCESTER What—with the case of eyes?   140
LEAR O ho, are you there with me? No eyes in your head,
nor no money in your purse? Your eyes are in a heavy
case, your purse in a light; yet you see how this world
goes.
GLOUCESTER I see it feelingly.   145
LEAR What, art mad? A man may see how this world
goes with no eyes; look with thine ears. See how yon
justice rails upon yon simple thief. Hark in thine ear:
change places, and handy-dandy, which is the justice,
which is the thief? Thou hast seen a farmer's dog bark
at a beggar?   151
GLOUCESTER Ay, sir.
LEAR An the creature run from the cur, there thou
mightst behold the great image of authority. A dog's
obeyed in office.   155
Thou rascal beadle, hold thy bloody hand.
Why dost thou lash that whore? Strip thy own back.
Thou hotly lusts to use her in that kind
For which thou whip'st her. The usurer hangs the
cozener.
Through tattered clothes great vices do appear;   160
Robes and furred gowns hide all. Plate sin with gold,
And the strong lance of justice hurtless breaks;
Arm it in rags, a pygmy's straw does pierce it.
None does offend, none, I say none. I'll able 'em.

Take that of me, my friend, who have the power   165
To seal th'accuser's lips. Get thee glass eyes,
And, like a scurvy politician, seem
To see the things thou dost not. Now, now, now, now!
Pull off my boots. Harder, harder! So.

EDGAR (aside)
O, matter and impertinency mixed—   170
Reason in madness!

LEAR
If thou wilt weep my fortunes, take my eyes.
I know thee well enough: thy name is Gloucester.
Thou must be patient. We came crying hither.
Thou know'st the first time that we smell the air   175
We waul and cry. I will preach to thee. Mark.

GLOUCESTER Alack, alack the day!

LEAR ⌈removing his crown of weeds⌉
When we are born, we cry that we are come
To this great stage of fools. This' a good block.
It were a delicate stratagem to shoe   180
A troop of horse with felt. I'll put't in proof,
And when I have stol'n upon these son-in-laws,
Then kill, kill, kill, kill, kill, kill!

Enter ⌈two⌉ Gentlemen

⌈FIRST⌉ GENTLEMAN
O, here he is. Lay hand upon him. ⌈To Lear⌉ Sir,
Your most dear daughter—   185

LEAR
No rescue? What, a prisoner? I am even
The natural fool of fortune. Use me well.
You shall have ransom. Let me have surgeons;
I am cut to th' brains.

⌈FIRST⌉ GENTLEMAN You shall have anything.   190

LEAR No seconds? All myself?
Why, this would make a man a man of salt,
To use his eyes for garden water-pots.
I will die bravely, like a smug bridegroom. What,
I will be jovial. Come, come, I am a king.   195
Masters, know you that?

⌈FIRST⌉ GENTLEMAN
You are a royal one, and we obey you.

LEAR Then there's life in't. Come, an you get it, you shall
get it by running. Sa, sa, sa, sa!

Exit running ⌈pursued by a Gentleman⌉

⌈FIRST⌉ GENTLEMAN
A sight most pitiful in the meanest wretch,   200
Past speaking in a king. Thou hast a daughter
Who redeems nature from the general curse
Which twain have brought her to.

EDGAR Hail, gentle sir.

⌈FIRST⌉ GENTLEMAN Sir, speed you. What's your will?   205

EDGAR
Do you hear aught, sir, of a battle toward?

⌈FIRST⌉ GENTLEMAN
Most sure and vulgar, everyone hears that
That can distinguish sound.

EDGAR But, by your favour,
How near's the other army?   210

⌈FIRST⌉ GENTLEMAN
Near and on speedy foot. The main descry
Stands in the hourly thought.

EDGAR   I thank you, sir. That's all.

⌈FIRST⌉ GENTLEMAN
Though that the Queen on special cause is here,
Her army is moved on.

EDGAR   I thank you, sir.

Exit Gentleman

GLOUCESTER
You ever gentle gods, take my breath from me.   215
Let not my worser spirit tempt me again
To die before you please.

EDGAR Well pray you, father.

GLOUCESTER Now, good sir, what are you?

EDGAR
A most poor man, made tame to fortune's blows,   220
Who by the art of known and feeling sorrows
Am pregnant to good pity. Give me your hand,
I'll lead you to some biding.

GLOUCESTER ⌈rising⌉   Hearty thanks.
The bounty and the benison of heaven
To boot and boot.

Enter Oswald the steward

OSWALD   A proclaimed prize! Most happy!   225
That eyeless head of thine was first framed flesh
To raise my fortunes. Thou old unhappy traitor,
Briefly thyself remember. The sword is out
That must destroy thee.

GLOUCESTER   Now let thy friendly hand
Put strength enough to't.

OSWALD (to Edgar)   Wherefore, bold peasant,   230
Durst thou support a published traitor? Hence,
Lest that th'infection of his fortune take
Like hold on thee. Let go his arm.

EDGAR 'Chill not let go, sir, without vurther 'cagion.

OSWALD Let go, slave, or thou diest.   235

EDGAR Good gentleman, go your gate, and let poor volk
pass. An 'chud ha' been swaggered out of my life,
'twould not ha' been so long as 'tis by a vortnight.
Nay, come not near th'old man. Keep out, 'che vor'
ye, or I's' try whether your costard or my baton be the
harder; I'll be plain with you.   241

OSWALD Out, dunghill!

EDGAR 'Chill pick your teeth, sir. Come, no matter vor
your foins.

⌈Edgar knocks him down⌉

OSWALD
Slave, thou hast slain me. Villain, take my purse.   245
If ever thou wilt thrive, bury my body,
And give the letters which thou find'st about me
To Edmond, Earl of Gloucester. Seek him out
Upon the English party. O untimely death! Death!

He dies

EDGAR
I know thee well—a serviceable villain,   250
As duteous to the vices of thy mistress
As badness would desire.

GLOUCESTER What, is he dead?

EDGAR Sit you down, father. Rest you.

Gloucester sits

Let's see these pockets. The letters that he speaks of
May be my friends. He's dead; I am only sorrow   256
He had no other deathsman. Let us see.
Leave, gentle wax, and manners; blame us not.
To know our enemies' minds we rip their hearts;
Their papers is more lawful.   260

He reads the letter

'Let our reciprocal vows be remembered. You have
many opportunities to cut him off. If your will want
not, time and place will be fruitfully offered. There is
nothing done if he return the conqueror; then am I
the prisoner, and his bed my jail, from the loathed
warmth whereof, deliver me, and supply the place for
your labour.
          Your—wife, so I would say,—affectionate
          servant, and for you her own for venture,
                                        Goneril.'   270
O indistinguished space of woman's will—
A plot upon her virtuous husband's life,
And the exchange my brother!—Here in the sands
Thee I'll rake up, the post unsanctified
Of murderous lechers, and in the mature time   275
With this ungracious paper strike the sight
Of the death-practised Duke. For him 'tis well
That of thy death and business I can tell.
                              ⌈*Exit with the body*⌉

GLOUCESTER
The King is mad. How stiff is my vile sense,
That I stand up and have ingenious feeling   280
Of my huge sorrows! Better I were distraught,
So should my thoughts be severed from my griefs,
          Drum afar off
And woes by wrong imaginations lose
The knowledge of themselves.
          ⌈*Enter Edgar*⌉

EDGAR   Give me your hand.
Far off methinks I hear the beaten drum.   285
Come, father, I'll bestow you with a friend.
                    Exit Edgar guiding Gloucester

4.6 *Enter Queen Cordelia, the Earl of Kent disguised,*
          and ⌈*the First*⌉ *Gentleman*

CORDELIA
O thou good Kent, how shall I live and work
To match thy goodness? My life will be too short,
And every measure fail me.

KENT
To be acknowledged, madam, is o'erpaid.
All my reports go with the modest truth,   5
Nor more, nor clipped, but so.

CORDELIA   Be better suited.
These weeds are memories of those worser hours.
I prithee put them off.

KENT   Pardon, dear madam.
Yet to be known shortens my made intent.

My boon I make it that you know me not   10
Till time and I think meet.

CORDELIA   Then be't so, my good lord.—
How does the King?

FIRST GENTLEMAN   Madam, sleeps still.

CORDELIA   O you kind gods,
Cure this great breach in his abusèd nature;
Th'untuned and jarring senses O wind up
Of this child-changèd father!

⌈FIRST⌉ GENTLEMAN   So please your majesty 15
That we may wake the King? He hath slept long.

CORDELIA
Be governed by your knowledge, and proceed
I'th' sway of your own will. Is he arrayed?

⌈FIRST⌉ GENTLEMAN
Ay, madam. In the heaviness of sleep
We put fresh garments on him.   20
          Enter King Lear asleep, in a chair carried by servants
Be by, good madam, when we do awake him.
I doubt not of his temperance.

CORDELIA
O my dear father, restoration hang
Thy medicine on my lips, and let this kiss
Repair those violent harms that my two sisters   25
Have in thy reverence made!

KENT   Kind and dear princess!

CORDELIA
Had you not been their father, these white flakes
Did challenge pity of them. Was this a face
To be opposed against the warring winds?
Mine enemy's dog, though he had bit me, should
          have stood   30
That night against my fire. And wast thou fain, poor
          father,
To hovel thee with swine and rogues forlorn
In short and musty straw? Alack, alack,
'Tis wonder that thy life and wits at once
Had not concluded all! (*To the Gentleman*) He wakes.
          Speak to him.   35

⌈FIRST⌉ GENTLEMAN Madam, do you; 'tis fittest.

CORDELIA (*to Lear*)
How does my royal lord? How fares your majesty?

LEAR
You do me wrong to take me out o'th' grave.
Thou art a soul in bliss, but I am bound
Upon a wheel of fire, that mine own tears   40
Do scald like molten lead.

CORDELIA   Sir, do you know me?

LEAR
You are a spirit, I know. Where did you die?

CORDELIA (*to the Gentleman*) Still, still far wide!

⌈FIRST⌉ GENTLEMAN
He's scarce awake. Let him alone a while.

LEAR
Where have I been? Where am I? Fair daylight?   45
I am mightily abused. I should ev'n die with pity
To see another thus. I know not what to say.
I will not swear these are my hands. Let's see:

I feel this pin prick. Would I were assured
Of my condition.
CORDELIA (*kneeling*) O look upon me, sir,   50
And hold your hands in benediction o'er me.
You must not kneel.
LEAR   Pray do not mock.
I am a very foolish, fond old man,
Fourscore and upward,
Not an hour more nor less; and to deal plainly,   55
I fear I am not in my perfect mind.
Methinks I should know you, and know this man;
Yet I am doubtful, for I am mainly ignorant
What place this is; and all the skill I have
Remembers not these garments; nor I know not   60
Where I did lodge last night. Do not laugh at me,
For as I am a man, I think this lady
To be my child, Cordelia.
CORDELIA   And so I am, I am.
LEAR
Be your tears wet? Yes, faith. I pray, weep not.
If you have poison for me, I will drink it.   65
I know you do not love me; for your sisters
Have, as I do remember, done me wrong.
You have some cause; they have not.
CORDELIA   No cause, no cause.
LEAR Am I in France?
KENT In your own kingdom, sir.   70
LEAR Do not abuse me.
⌜FIRST⌝ GENTLEMAN
Be comforted, good madam. The great rage
You see is killed in him. Desire him to go in.
Trouble him no more till further settling.
CORDELIA (*to Lear*) Will't please your highness walk?   75
LEAR
You must bear with me. Pray you now, forget
And forgive. I am old and foolish.   *Exeunt*

5.1   *Enter with a drummer and colours Edmond, Regan,*
       Gentlemen, and soldiers
EDMOND
Know of the Duke if his last purpose hold,
Or whether since he is advised by aught
To change the course. He's full of abdication
And self-reproving. Bring his constant pleasure.
                    Exit one or more
REGAN
Our sister's man is certainly miscarried.   5
EDMOND
'Tis to be doubted, madam.
REGAN   Now, sweet lord,
You know the goodness I intend upon you.
Tell me but truly—but then speak the truth—
Do you not love my sister?
EDMOND   In honoured love.
REGAN
But have you never found my brother's way   10
To the forfended place?
EDMOND   No, by mine honour, madam.

REGAN
I never shall endure her. Dear my lord,
Be not familiar with her.
EDMOND Fear me not.
She and the Duke her husband—   15
          Enter with a drummer and colours the Duke of
          Albany, Goneril, and soldiers
ALBANY (*to Regan*)
Our very loving sister, well bemet.
(*To Edmond*) Sir, this I heard: the King is come to his
          daughter,
With others whom the rigour of our state
Forced to cry out.
REGAN   Why is this reasoned?
GONERIL
Combine together 'gainst the enemy;   20
For these domestic and particular broils
Are not the question here.
ALBANY
Let's then determine with th'ensign of war
On our proceeding.
REGAN   Sister, you'll go with us?
GONERIL No.   25
REGAN
'Tis most convenient. Pray go with us.
GONERIL (*aside*)
O ho, I know the riddle! (*To Regan*) I will go.
          Enter Edgar disguised as a peasant
EDGAR (*to Albany*)
If e'er your grace had speech with man so poor,
Hear me one word.
ALBANY (*to the others*) I'll overtake you.
                    Exeunt both the armies
                    Speak.
EDGAR
Before you fight the battle, ope this letter.   30
If you have victory, let the trumpet sound
For him that brought it. Wretched though I seem,
I can produce a champion that will prove
What is avouchèd there. If you miscarry,
Your business of the world hath so an end,   35
And machination ceases. Fortune love you.
ALBANY
Stay till I have read the letter.
EDGAR   I was forbid it.
When time shall serve, let but the herald cry,
And I'll appear again.
ALBANY Why, fare thee well.   40
I will o'erlook thy paper.   *Exit Edgar*
          Enter Edmond
EDMOND
The enemy's in view; draw up your powers.
          He ⌜offers⌝ Albany a paper
Here is the guess of their true strength and forces
By diligent discovery; but your haste   44
Is now urged on you.
ALBANY   We will greet the time.   *Exit*

EDMOND

To both these sisters have I sworn my love,
Each jealous of the other as the stung
Are of the adder. Which of them shall I take?—
Both?—one?—or neither? Neither can be enjoyed
If both remain alive. To take the widow   50
Exasperates, makes mad, her sister Goneril,
And hardly shall I carry out my side,
Her husband being alive. Now then, we'll use
His countenance for the battle, which being done,
Let her who would be rid of him devise   55
His speedy taking off. As for the mercy
Which he intends to Lear and to Cordelia,
The battle done, and they within our power,
Shall never see his pardon; for my state   59
Stands on me to defend, not to debate.   *Exit*

5.2   *Alarum within. Enter with a drummer and colours*
      King Lear, Queen Cordelia, and soldiers over the
      stage; and exeunt. Enter Edgar disguised as a
      peasant, guiding the blind Duke of Gloucester
EDGAR

Here, father, take the shadow of this tree
For your good host; pray that the right may thrive.
If ever I return to you again
I'll bring you comfort.
GLOUCESTER   Grace go with you, sir.
                              Exit Edgar
      Alarum and retreat within. Enter Edgar
EDGAR

Away, old man. Give me thy hand. Away.   5
King Lear hath lost, he and his daughter ta'en.
Give me thy hand. Come on.
GLOUCESTER

No further, sir. A man may rot even here.
EDGAR

What, in ill thoughts again? Men must endure
Their going hence even as their coming hither.   10
Ripeness is all. Come on.
GLOUCESTER   And that's true, too.
                    Exit Edgar guiding Gloucester

5.3   *Enter in conquest with a drummer and colours*
      Edmond; King Lear and Queen Cordelia as
      prisoners; soldiers; a Captain
EDMOND

Some officers take them away. Good guard
Until their greater pleasures first be known
That are to censure them.
CORDELIA (*to Lear*)   We are not the first
Who with best meaning have incurred the worst.
For thee, oppressèd King, I am cast down,   5
Myself could else outfrown false fortune's frown.
Shall we not see these daughters and these sisters?
LEAR

No, no, no, no. Come, let's away to prison.
We two alone will sing like birds i'th' cage.
When thou dost ask me blessing, I'll kneel down   10

And ask of thee forgiveness; so we'll live,
And pray, and sing, and tell old tales, and laugh
At gilded butterflies, and hear poor rogues
Talk of court news, and we'll talk with them too—
Who loses and who wins, who's in, who's out,   15
And take upon 's the mystery of things
As if we were God's spies; and we'll wear out
In a walled prison packs and sects of great ones
That ebb and flow by th' moon.
EDMOND (*to soldiers*)   Take them away.
LEAR

Upon such sacrifices, my Cordelia,   20
The gods themselves throw incense. Have I caught
  thee?
He that parts us shall bring a brand from heaven
And fire us hence like foxes. Wipe thine eyes.
The goodyear shall devour them, flesh and fell,
Ere they shall make us weep. We'll see 'em starved
  first. Come.   *Exeunt all but Edmond and the Captain*
EDMOND Come hither, captain. Hark.   26
Take thou this note. Go follow them to prison.
One step I have advanced thee; if thou dost
As this instructs thee, thou dost make thy way
To noble fortunes. Know thou this: that men   30
Are as the time is. To be tender-minded
Does not become a sword. Thy great employment
Will not bear question. Either say thou'lt do't,
Or thrive by other means.
CAPTAIN   I'll do't, my lord.
EDMOND

About it, and write 'happy' when thou'st done.   35
Mark, I say, instantly, and carry it so
As I have set it down.   *Exit the Captain*
      Flourish. Enter the Duke of Albany, Goneril, Regan,
      ⌜drummer, trumpeter⌝ and soldiers
ALBANY

Sir, you have showed today your valiant strain,
And fortune led you well. You have the captives
Who were the opposites of this day's strife.   40
I do require them of you, so to use them
As we shall find their merits and our safety
May equally determine.
EDMOND   Sir, I thought it fit
To send the old and miserable King
To some retention and appointed guard,   45
Whose age had charms in it, whose title more,
To pluck the common bosom on his side
And turn our impressed lances in our eyes
Which do command them. With him I sent the Queen,
My reason all the same, and they are ready   50
Tomorrow, or at further space, t'appear
Where you shall hold your session.
ALBANY   Sir, by your patience,
I hold you but a subject of this war,
Not as a brother.
REGAN   That's as we list to grace him.
Methinks our pleasure might have been demanded   55
Ere you had spoke so far. He led our powers,

Bore the commission of my place and person,
The which immediacy may well stand up
And call itself your brother.
GONERIL   Not so hot.
In his own grace he doth exalt himself   60
More than in your addition.
REGAN   In my rights
By me invested, he compeers the best.
ALBANY
That were the most if he should husband you.
REGAN
Jesters do oft prove prophets.
GONERIL   Holla, holla—
That eye that told you so looked but asquint.   65
REGAN
Lady, I am not well, else I should answer
From a full-flowing stomach. (*To Edmond*) General,
Take thou my soldiers, prisoners, patrimony.
Dispose of them, of me. The walls is thine.
Witness the world that I create thee here   70
My lord and master.
GONERIL   Mean you to enjoy him?
ALBANY
The let-alone lies not in your good will.
EDMOND
Nor in thine, lord.
ALBANY   Half-blooded fellow, yes.
REGAN (*to Edmond*)
Let the drum strike and prove my title thine.
ALBANY
Stay yet, hear reason. Edmond, I arrest thee   75
On capital treason, and in thy attaint
This gilded serpent. (*To Regan*) For your claim, fair sister,
I bar it in the interest of my wife.
'Tis she is subcontracted to this lord,
And I, her husband, contradict your banns.   80
If you will marry, make your loves to me.
My lady is bespoke.
GONERIL   An interlude!
ALBANY
Thou art armed, Gloucester. Let the trumpet sound.
If none appear to prove upon thy person
Thy heinous, manifest, and many treasons,   85
There is my pledge.
    ⌈*He throws down a glove*⌉
                    I'll make it on thy heart,
Ere I taste bread, thou art in nothing less
Than I have here proclaimed thee.
REGAN Sick, O sick!
GONERIL (*aside*) If not, I'll ne'er trust medicine.   90
EDMOND (*to Albany, ⌈throwing down a glove⌉*)
There's my exchange. What in the world he is
That names me traitor, villain-like he lies.
Call by the trumpet. He that dares, approach;
On him, on you,—who not?—I will maintain
My truth and honour firmly.
ALBANY   A herald, ho!   95

Enter a Herald
(*To Edmond*) Trust to thy single virtue, for thy soldiers,
All levied in my name, have in my name
Took their discharge.
REGAN   My sickness grows upon me.   60
ALBANY
She is not well. Convey her to my tent.
                    Exit one or more with Regan
Come hither, herald. Let the trumpet sound,   100
And read out this.
    A trumpet sounds
HERALD (*reads*) 'If any man of quality or degree within
    the lists of the army will maintain upon Edmond,
    supposed Earl of Gloucester, that he is a manifold
    traitor, let him appear by the third sound of the trumpet.
    He is bold in his defence.'   106
    First trumpet
Again.
    Second trumpet
Again.
    Third trumpet.
    Trumpet answers within. Enter Edgar, armed
ALBANY (*to the Herald*)
Ask him his purposes, why he appears
Upon this call o'th' trumpet.
HERALD (*to Edgar*)   What are you?   110
Your name, your quality, and why you answer
This present summons?
EDGAR   Know, my name is lost,
By treason's tooth bare-gnawn and canker-bit.
Yet am I noble as the adversary
I come to cope.
ALBANY   Which is that adversary?   115
EDGAR
What's he that speaks for Edmond, Earl of Gloucester?
EDMOND
Himself. What sayst thou to him?
EDGAR   Draw thy sword,
That if my speech offend a noble heart
Thy arm may do thee justice. Here is mine.
    He draws his sword
Behold, it is the privilege of mine honour,   120
My oath, and my profession. I protest,
Maugre thy strength, place, youth, and eminence,
Despite thy victor-sword and fire-new fortune,
Thy valour and thy heart, thou art a traitor,
False to thy gods, thy brother, and thy father,   125
Conspirant 'gainst this high illustrious prince,
And from th'extremest upward of thy head
To the descent and dust below thy foot
A most toad-spotted traitor. Say thou no,
This sword, this arm, and my best spirits are bent   130
To prove upon thy heart, whereto I speak,
Thou liest.
EDMOND   In wisdom I should ask thy name,
But since thy outside looks so fair and warlike,
And that thy tongue some say of breeding breathes,
What safe and nicely I might well demand   135

By rule of knighthood I disdain and spurn.
Back do I toss those treasons to thy head,
With the hell-hated lie o'erwhelm thy heart,
Which, for they yet glance by and scarcely bruise,
This sword of mine shall give them instant way   140
Where they shall rest for ever. Trumpets, speak!
    Alarums. They fight. Edmond is vanquished
⌈ALL⌉
Save him, save him!
GONERIL   This is practice, Gloucester.
By th' law of arms thou wast not bound to answer
An unknown opposite. Thou art not vanquished,
But cozened and beguiled.
ALBANY   Shut your mouth, dame, 145
Or with this paper shall I stopple it.
  ⌈*To Edmond*⌉ Hold, sir, thou worse than any name:
  read thine own evil.
(*To Goneril*) No tearing, lady. I perceive you know it.
GONERIL
Say if I do, the laws are mine, not thine.
Who can arraign me for't?   *Exit*
ALBANY   Most monstrous!—   150
O, know'st thou this paper?
EDMOND   Ask me not what I know.
ALBANY
Go after her. She's desperate. Govern her.
                Exit one or more
EDMOND
What you have charged me with, that have I done,
And more, much more. The time will bring it out.
'Tis past, and so am I. (*To Edgar*) But what art thou,
That hast this fortune on me? If thou'rt noble,   156
I do forgive thee.
EDGAR   Let's exchange charity.
I am no less in blood than thou art, Edmond.
If more, the more thou'st wronged me.
    ⌈*He takes off his helmet*⌉
My name is Edgar, and thy father's son.   160
The gods are just, and of our pleasant vices
Make instruments to plague us.
The dark and vicious place where thee he got
Cost him his eyes.
EDMOND   Thou'st spoken right. 'Tis true.
The wheel is come full circle. I am here.   165
ALBANY (*to Edgar*)
Methought thy very gait did prophesy
A royal nobleness. I must embrace thee.
Let sorrow split my heart if ever I
Did hate thee or thy father.
EDGAR Worthy prince, I know't.   170
ALBANY Where have you hid yourself?
How have you known the miseries of your father?
EDGAR
By nursing them, my lord. List a brief tale,
And when 'tis told, O that my heart would burst!
The bloody proclamation to escape   175
That followed me so near—O, our lives' sweetness,
That we the pain of death would hourly die

Rather than die at once!—taught me to shift
Into a madman's rags, t'assume a semblance
That very dogs disdained; and in this habit   180
Met I my father with his bleeding rings,
Their precious stones new-lost; became his guide,
Led him, begged for him, saved him from despair;
Never—O fault!—revealed myself unto him
Until some half hour past, when I was armed.   185
Not sure, though hoping, of this good success,
I asked his blessing, and from first to last
Told him our pilgrimage; but his flawed heart—
Alack, too weak the conflict to support—
'Twixt two extremes of passion, joy and grief,   190
Burst smilingly.
EDMOND   This speech of yours hath moved me,
And shall perchance do good. But speak you on—
You look as you had something more to say.
ALBANY
If there be more, more woeful, hold it in,
For I am almost ready to dissolve,   195
Hearing of this.
    Enter a Gentleman with a bloody knife
GENTLEMAN
Help, help, O help!
EDGAR   What kind of help?
ALBANY   Speak, man.
EDGAR
What means this bloody knife?
GENTLEMAN   'Tis hot, it smokes.
It came even from the heart of—O, she's dead!
ALBANY Who dead? Speak, man.   200
GENTLEMAN
Your lady, sir, your lady; and her sister
By her is poisoned. She confesses it.
EDMOND
I was contracted to them both; all three
Now marry in an instant.
EDGAR   Here comes Kent.
    Enter the Earl of Kent as himself
ALBANY
Produce the bodies, be they alive or dead.   205
    Goneril's and Regan's bodies brought out
This judgement of the heavens, that makes us tremble,
Touches us not with pity.—O, is this he?
(*To Kent*) The time will not allow the compliment
Which very manners urges.
KENT   I am come
To bid my king and master aye good night.   210
Is he not here?
ALBANY   Great thing of us forgot!—
Speak, Edmond; where's the King, and where's
  Cordelia?—
Seest thou this object, Kent?
KENT Alack, why thus?
EDMOND Yet Edmond was beloved.   215
The one the other poisoned for my sake,
And after slew herself.
ALBANY   Even so.—Cover their faces.

EDMOND
  I pant for life. Some good I mean to do,
  Despite of mine own nature. Quickly send,
  Be brief in it, to th' castle; for my writ   220
  Is on the life of Lear and on Cordelia.
  Nay, send in time.
ALBANY   Run, run, O run!
EDGAR
  To who, my lord?—Who has the office? Send
  Thy token of reprieve.
EDMOND
  Well thought on! Take my sword. The captain,   225
  Give it the captain.
EDGAR   Haste thee for thy life.
                              Exit ⌈the Gentleman⌉
EDMOND (to Albany)
  He hath commission from thy wife and me
  To hang Cordelia in the prison, and
  To lay the blame upon her own despair,
  That she fordid herself.   230
ALBANY
  The gods defend her!—Bear him hence a while.
                              Exeunt some with Edmond
           Enter King Lear with Queen Cordelia in his arms,
           ⌈followed by the Gentleman⌉
LEAR
  Howl, howl, howl, howl! O, you are men of stones.
  Had I your tongues and eyes, I'd use them so
  That heaven's vault should crack. She's gone for ever.
  I know when one is dead and when one lives.   235
  She's dead as earth.
           ⌈He lays her down⌉
                    Lend me a looking-glass.
  If that her breath will mist or stain the stone,
  Why, then she lives.
KENT   Is this the promised end?
EDGAR
  Or image of that horror?
ALBANY   Fall and cease.
LEAR
  This feather stirs. She lives. If it be so,   240
  It is a chance which does redeem all sorrows
  That ever I have felt.
KENT ⌈kneeling⌉   O, my good master!
LEAR
  Prithee, away.
EDGAR   'Tis noble Kent, your friend.
LEAR
  A plague upon you, murderers, traitors all.
  I might have saved her; now she's gone for ever.—   245
  Cordelia, Cordelia: stay a little. Ha?
  What is't thou sayst?—Her voice was ever soft,
  Gentle, and low, an excellent thing in woman.—
  I killed the slave that was a-hanging thee.
GENTLEMAN
  'Tis true, my lords, he did.
LEAR   Did I not, fellow?   250
  I have seen the day with my good biting falchion

  I would have made them skip. I am old now,
  And these same crosses spoil me. (To Kent) Who are
      you?
  Mine eyes are not o'th' best, I'll tell you straight.
KENT
  If fortune brag of two she loved and hated,   255
  One of them we behold.
LEAR   This' a dull sight.
  Are you not Kent?
KENT   The same, your servant Kent.
  Where is your servant Caius?
LEAR
  He's a good fellow, I can tell you that.   260
  He'll strike, and quickly too. He's dead and rotten.
KENT
  No, my good lord, I am the very man—
LEAR   I'll see that straight.
KENT
  That from your first of difference and decay
  Have followed your sad steps.
LEAR   You're welcome hither.
KENT
  Nor no man else. All's cheerless, dark, and deadly. 266
  Your eldest daughters have fordone themselves,
  And desperately are dead.
LEAR   Ay, so think I.
ALBANY
  He knows not what he says; and vain is it
  That we present us to him.
           Enter a Messenger
EDGAR   Very bootless.   270
MESSENGER (to Albany)
  Edmond is dead, my lord.
ALBANY   That's but a trifle here.—
  You lords and noble friends, know our intent.
  What comfort to this great decay may come
  Shall be applied; for us, we will resign
  During the life of this old majesty   275
  To him our absolute power;
  (To Edgar and Kent)   you to your rights,
  With boot and such addition as your honours
  Have more than merited. All friends shall taste
  The wages of their virtue, and all foes
  The cup of their deservings.—O see, see!   280
LEAR
  And my poor fool is hanged. No, no, no life?
  Why should a dog, a horse, a rat have life,
  And thou no breath at all? Thou'lt come no more.
  Never, never, never, never, never.
  ⌈To Kent⌉ Pray you, undo this button. Thank you, sir.
  Do you see this? Look on her. Look, her lips.   286
  Look there, look there.   He dies
EDGAR   He faints. (To Lear) My lord, my lord!
KENT ⌈to Lear⌉
  Break, heart, I prithee break.
EDGAR (to Lear)   Look up, my lord.
KENT
  Vex not his ghost. O, let him pass. He hates him

That would upon the rack of this tough world   290
  Stretch him out longer.
EDGAR   He is gone indeed.
KENT
  The wonder is he hath endured so long.
  He but usurped his life.
ALBANY
  Bear them from hence. Our present business
  Is general woe. (*To Edgar and Kent*) Friends of my
     soul, you twain   295
  Rule in this realm, and the gored state sustain.

KENT
  I have a journey, sir, shortly to go:
  My master calls me; I must not say no.
EDGAR
  The weight of this sad time we must obey,
  Speak what we feel, not what we ought to say.   300
  The oldest hath borne most. We that are young
  Shall never see so much, nor live so long.
            Exeunt with a dead march, carrying the bodies

MACBETH

BY WILLIAM SHAKESPEARE
(ADAPTED BY THOMAS MIDDLETON)

SHORTLY after James VI of Scotland succeeded to the English throne, in 1603, he gave his patronage to Shakespeare's company; the Lord Chamberlain's Men became the King's Men, entering into a special relationship with their sovereign. *Macbeth* is the play of Shakespeare's that most clearly reflects this relationship. James regarded the virtuous and noble Banquo, Macbeth's comrade at the start of the action, as his direct ancestor; eight Stuart kings were said to have preceded James, just as, in the play, Banquo points to 'a show of eight kings' as his descendants (4.1.127.1–140); and in the play the English king (historically Edward the Confessor) is praised for the capacity, on which James also prided himself, to cure 'the king's evil' (scrofula). *Macbeth* is obviously a Jacobean play, composed probably in 1606.

But the first printed text, in the 1623 Folio, shows signs of having been adapted at a later date. It is exceptionally short by comparison with Shakespeare's other tragedies; and it includes episodes which there is good reason to believe are not by Shakespeare. These are Act 3, Scene 5 and parts of Act 4, Scene 1: 38.1–60 and 141–8.1. These episodes feature Hecate, who does not appear elsewhere in the play; they are composed largely in octosyllabic couplets in a style conspicuously different from the rest of the play; and they call for the performance of two songs that are found in *The Witch*, a play of uncertain date by Thomas Middleton. Probably Middleton himself adapted Shakespeare's play some years after its first performance. We do not attempt to excise passages probably not written by Shakespeare, because the adapter's hand may have affected the text at other, in-determinable points. The Folio text of *Macbeth* cites only the opening words of the songs; drawing on *The Witch*, we attempt a reconstruction of their staging in *Macbeth*.

Shakespeare took materials for his story from the account in Raphael Holinshed's *Chronicle* of the reigns of Duncan and Macbeth (AD 1034–57). Occasionally (especially in the English episodes of Act 4, Scene 2) he closely followed Holinshed's wording; but essentially the play's structure is his own. He invented the framework of the three witches who tempted both Macbeth and Banquo with prophecies of greatness. His Macbeth is both more introspective and more intensely evil than the competent warrior-king portrayed by Holinshed; conversely, Shakespeare made Duncan, the king whom Macbeth murders, far more venerable and saintly. Some of the play's features, notably the character of Lady Macbeth, originate in Holinshed's account of the murder of an earlier Scottish king, Duff; he was killed in his castle at Forres by Donwald, who had been 'set on' by his wife.

Macbeth can be enjoyed at many levels. It is an exciting story of witchcraft, murder, and retribution that can also be seen as a study in the philosophy and psychology of evil. The witches are not easily made credible in modern performances, and Shakespeare seems deliberately to have drained colour away from some parts of his composition in order to concentrate attention on Macbeth and his Lady. It is Macbeth's neurotic self-absorption, his fear, his anger, and his despair, along with his wife's steely determination, her invoking of the powers of evil, and her eventual revelation in sleep of her repressed humanity, that have given the play its long-proven power to fascinate readers and to challenge performers.

THE PERSONS OF THE PLAY

KING DUNCAN of Scotland

MALCOLM ⎫
DONALBAIN ⎭ his sons

A CAPTAIN in Duncan's army

MACBETH, Thane of Glamis, later Thane of Cawdor, then King of
Scotland

A PORTER at Macbeth's castle

Three MURDERERS attending on Macbeth

SEYTON, servant of Macbeth

LADY MACBETH, Macbeth's wife

A DOCTOR of Physic ⎫
A Waiting-GENTLEWOMAN ⎭ attending on Lady Macbeth

BANQUO, a Scottish thane

FLEANCE, his son

MACDUFF, Thane of Fife

LADY MACDUFF, his wife

MACDUFF'S SON

LENNOX ⎫
ROSS ⎪
ANGUS ⎬ Scottish Thanes
CAITHNESS ⎪
MENTEITH ⎭

SIWARD, Earl of Northumberland

YOUNG SIWARD, his son

An English DOCTOR

HECATE, Queen of the Witches

Six WITCHES

Three APPARITIONS, one an armed head, one a bloody child,
a child crowned

A SPIRIT LIKE A CAT

Other SPIRITS

An OLD MAN

A MESSENGER

MURDERERS

SERVANTS

A show of eight kings; Lords and Thanes, attendants, soldier
drummers

The Tragedy of Macbeth

1.1 *Thunder and lightning. Enter three Witches*
FIRST WITCH
    When shall we three meet again?
    In thunder, lightning, or in rain?
SECOND WITCH
    When the hurly-burly's done,
    When the battle's lost and won.
THIRD WITCH
    That will be ere the set of sun.   5
FIRST WITCH
    Where the place?
SECOND WITCH   Upon the heath.
THIRD WITCH
    There to meet with Macbeth.
FIRST WITCH
    I come, Grimalkin.
SECOND WITCH
    Paddock calls.
THIRD WITCH   Anon.
ALL
    Fair is foul, and foul is fair,   10
    Hover through the fog and filthy air.   *Exeunt*

1.2 *Alarum within. Enter King Duncan, Malcolm,*
    Donalbain, Lennox, with attendants, meeting a
    bleeding Captain
KING DUNCAN
    What bloody man is that? He can report,
    As seemeth by his plight, of the revolt
    The newest state.
MALCOLM   This is the sergeant
    Who like a good and hardy soldier fought
    'Gainst my captivity. Hail, brave friend.   5
    Say to the King the knowledge of the broil
    As thou didst leave it.
CAPTAIN   Doubtful it stood,
    As two spent swimmers that do cling together
    And choke their art. The merciless Macdonald—
    Worthy to be a rebel, for to that   10
    The multiplying villainies of nature
    Do swarm upon him—from the Western Isles
    Of kerns and galloglasses is supplied,
    And fortune on his damnèd quarry smiling
    Showed like a rebel's whore. But all's too weak,   15
    For brave Macbeth—well he deserves that name!—
    Disdaining fortune, with his brandished steel
    Which smoked with bloody execution,
    Like valour's minion
    Carved out his passage till he faced the slave,   20
    Which ne'er shook hands nor bade farewell to him
    Till he unseamed him from the nave to th' chops,
    And fixed his head upon our battlements.

KING DUNCAN
    O valiant cousin, worthy gentleman!
CAPTAIN
    As whence the sun 'gins his reflection   25
    Shipwrecking storms and direful thunders break,
    So from that spring whence comfort seemed to come
    Discomfort swells. Mark, King of Scotland, mark.
    No sooner justice had, with valour armed,
    Compelled these skipping kerns to trust their heels   30
    But the Norwegian lord, surveying vantage,
    With furbished arms and new supplies of men
    Began a fresh assault.
KING DUNCAN
    Dismayed not this our captains, Macbeth and
        Banquo?
CAPTAIN
    Yes, as sparrows eagles, or the hare the lion!   35
    If I say sooth I must report they were
    As cannons overcharged with double cracks,
    So they doubly redoubled strokes upon the foe.
    Except they meant to bathe in reeking wounds
    Or memorize another Golgotha,   40
    I cannot tell—
    But I am faint. My gashes cry for help.
KING DUNCAN
    So well thy words become thee as thy wounds:
    They smack of honour both.—Go get him surgeons.
        Exit Captain with attendants
        Enter Ross and Angus
    Who comes here?
MALCOLM   The worthy Thane of Ross.   45
LENNOX
    What haste looks through his eyes! So should he look
    That seems to speak things strange.
ROSS   God save the King.
KING DUNCAN
    Whence cam'st thou, worthy thane?
ROSS   From Fife, great King,
    Where the Norwegian banners flout the sky
    And fan our people cold.   50
    Norway himself, with terrible numbers,
    Assisted by that most disloyal traitor
    The Thane of Cawdor, began a dismal conflict,
    Till that Bellona's bridegroom, lapped in proof,
    Confronted him with self-comparisons,   55
    Point against point, rebellious arm 'gainst arm,
    Curbing his lavish spirit; and to conclude,
    The victory fell on us—
KING DUNCAN   Great happiness.
ROSS   That now
    Sweno, the Norways' king, craves composition;
    Nor would we deign him burial of his men   60

Till he disbursèd at Saint Colum's inch
Ten thousand dollars to our general use.
KING DUNCAN
No more that Thane of Cawdor shall deceive
Our bosom interest. Go pronounce his present death,
And with his former title greet Macbeth.   65
ROSS I'll see it done.
KING DUNCAN
What he hath lost, noble Macbeth hath won.
                          Exeunt severally

1.3   *Thunder. Enter the three Witches*
FIRST WITCH
Where hast thou been, sister?
SECOND WITCH
Killing swine.
THIRD WITCH   Sister, where thou?
FIRST WITCH
A sailor's wife had chestnuts in her lap,
And munched, and munched, and munched. 'Give
    me,' quoth I.
'Aroint thee, witch,' the rump-fed runnion cries.   5
Her husband's to Aleppo gone, master o'th' Tiger.
But in a sieve I'll thither sail,
And like a rat without a tail
I'll do, I'll do, and I'll do.
SECOND WITCH
I'll give thee a wind.   10
FIRST WITCH
Thou'rt kind.
THIRD WITCH
And I another.
FIRST WITCH
I myself have all the other,
And the very ports they blow,
All the quarters that they know   15
I'th' shipman's card.
I'll drain him dry as hay.
Sleep shall neither night nor day
Hang upon his penthouse lid.
He shall live a man forbid.   20
Weary sennights nine times nine
Shall he dwindle, peak, and pine.
Though his barque cannot be lost,
Yet it shall be tempest-tossed.
Look what I have.
SECOND WITCH   Show me, show me.   25
FIRST WITCH
Here I have a pilot's thumb,
Wrecked as homeward he did come.
          Drum within
THIRD WITCH
A drum, a drum—
Macbeth doth come.
ALL (*dancing in a ring*)
The weird sisters hand in hand,   30
Posters of the sea and land,

Thus do go about, about,
Thrice to thine, and thrice to mine,
And thrice again to make up nine.
Peace! The charm's wound up.   35
     Enter Macbeth and Banquo
MACBETH
So foul and fair a day I have not seen.
BANQUO
How far is't called to Forres?—What are these,
So withered, and so wild in their attire,
That look not like th'inhabitants o'th' earth
And yet are on't?—Live you, or are you aught   40
That man may question? You seem to understand me
By each at once her choppy finger laying
Upon her skinny lips. You should be women,
And yet your beards forbid me to interpret
That you are so.
MACBETH (*to the Witches*)
                Speak, if you can. What are you?   45
FIRST WITCH
All hail, Macbeth! Hail to thee, Thane of Glamis.
SECOND WITCH
All hail, Macbeth! Hail to thee, Thane of Cawdor.
THIRD WITCH
All hail, Macbeth, that shalt be king hereafter!
BANQUO
Good sir, why do you start and seem to fear
Things that do sound so fair? (*To the Witches*) I'th'
    name of truth,   50
Are ye fantastical or that indeed
Which outwardly ye show? My noble partner
You greet with present grace and great prediction
Of noble having and of royal hope,
That he seems rapt withal. To me you speak not.   55
If you can look into the seeds of time
And say which grain will grow and which will not,
Speak then to me, who neither beg nor fear
Your favours nor your hate.
FIRST WITCH Hail!   60
SECOND WITCH Hail!
THIRD WITCH Hail!
FIRST WITCH
Lesser than Macbeth, and greater.
SECOND WITCH
Not so happy, yet much happier.
THIRD WITCH
Thou shalt get kings, though thou be none.   65
So all hail, Macbeth and Banquo!
FIRST WITCH
Banquo and Macbeth, all hail!
MACBETH
Stay, you imperfect speakers, tell me more.
By Sinel's death I know I am Thane of Glamis,
But how of Cawdor? The Thane of Cawdor lives,   70
A prosperous gentleman, and to be king
Stands not within the prospect of belief,
No more than to be Cawdor. Say from whence

You owe this strange intelligence, or why
Upon this blasted heath you stop our way   75
With such prophetic greeting. Speak, I charge you.
    The Witches vanish

BANQUO
The earth hath bubbles, as the water has,
And these are of them. Whither are they vanished?

MACBETH
Into the air, and what seemed corporal
Melted as breath into the wind. Would they had stayed.

BANQUO
Were such things here as we do speak about,   81
Or have we eaten on the insane root
That takes the reason prisoner?

MACBETH
Your children shall be kings.

BANQUO   You shall be king.

MACBETH
And Thane of Cawdor too. Went it not so?   85

BANQUO
To th' self-same tune and words. Who's here?
    Enter Ross and Angus

ROSS
The King hath happily received, Macbeth,
The news of thy success, and when he reads
Thy personal venture in the rebels' sight
His wonders and his praises do contend   90
Which should be thine or his; silenced with that,
In viewing o'er the rest o'th' self-same day
He finds thee in the stout Norwegian ranks,
Nothing afeard of what thyself didst make,
Strange images of death. As thick as hail   95
Came post with post, and every one did bear
Thy praises in his kingdom's great defence,
And poured them down before him.

ANGUS (*to Macbeth*)   We are sent
To give thee from our royal master thanks;
Only to herald thee into his sight,   100
Not pay thee.

ROSS
And, for an earnest of a greater honour,
He bade me from him call thee Thane of Cawdor,
In which addition, hail, most worthy thane,
For it is thine.

BANQUO   What, can the devil speak true?   105

MACBETH
The Thane of Cawdor lives. Why do you dress me
In borrowed robes?

ANGUS   Who was the thane lives yet,
But under heavy judgement bears that life
Which he deserves to lose. Whether he was combined
With those of Norway, or did line the rebel   110
With hidden help and vantage, or that with both
He laboured in his country's wrack, I know not;
But treasons capital, confessed, and proved
Have overthrown him.

MACBETH (*aside*)   Glamis, and Thane of Cawdor.

The greatest is behind. (*To Ross and Angus*) Thanks for
    your pains.   115
(*To Banquo*) Do you not hope your children shall be kings
When those that gave the thane of Cawdor to me
Promised no less to them?

BANQUO   That, trusted home,
Might yet enkindle you unto the crown,
Besides the thane of Cawdor. But 'tis strange,   120
And oftentimes to win us to our harm
The instruments of darkness tell us truths,
Win us with honest trifles to betray's
In deepest consequence.
    (*To Ross and Angus*) Cousins, a word, I pray you.   125

MACBETH (*aside*) Two truths are told
As happy prologues to the swelling act
Of the imperial theme. (*To Ross and Angus*) I thank
    you, gentlemen.
(*Aside*) This supernatural soliciting
Cannot be ill, cannot be good. If ill,   130
Why hath it given me earnest of success
Commencing in a truth? I am Thane of Cawdor.
If good, why do I yield to that suggestion
Whose horrid image doth unfix my hair
And make my seated heart knock at my ribs   135
Against the use of nature? Present fears
Are less than horrible imaginings.
My thought, whose murder yet is but fantastical,
Shakes so my single state of man that function
Is smothered in surmise, and nothing is   140
But what is not.

BANQUO (*to Ross and Angus*)
    Look how our partner's rapt.

MACBETH (*aside*)
If chance will have me king, why, chance may crown
    me
Without my stir.

BANQUO (*to Ross and Angus*)
    New honours come upon him,
Like our strange garments, cleave not to their mould
But with the aid of use.

MACBETH (*aside*)   Come what come may,   145
Time and the hour runs through the roughest day.

BANQUO
Worthy Macbeth, we stay upon your leisure.

MACBETH
Give me your favour. My dull brain was wrought
With things forgotten. (*To Ross and Angus*) Kind
    gentlemen, your pains
Are registered where every day I turn   150
The leaf to read them. Let us toward the King.
(*Aside to Banquo*) Think upon what hath chanced, and
    at more time,
The interim having weighed it, let us speak
Our free hearts each to other.

BANQUO Very gladly.   155

MACBETH Till then, enough. (*To Ross and Angus*) Come,
    friends.   *Exeunt*

1.4   *Flourish. Enter King Duncan, Lennox, Malcolm,*
Donalbain, and attendants

KING DUNCAN
     Is execution done on Cawdor? Are not
     Those in commission yet returned?

MALCOLM   My liege,
     They are not yet come back. But I have spoke
     With one that saw him die, who did report
     That very frankly he confessed his treasons,   5
     Implored your highness' pardon, and set forth
     A deep repentance. Nothing in his life
     Became him like the leaving it. He died
     As one that had been studied in his death
     To throw away the dearest thing he owed   10
     As 'twere a careless trifle.

KING DUNCAN   There's no art
     To find the mind's construction in the face.
     He was a gentleman on whom I built
     An absolute trust.
     Enter Macbeth, Banquo, Ross, and Angus
     (*To Macbeth*)   O worthiest cousin,
     The sin of my ingratitude even now   15
     Was heavy on me! Thou art so far before
     That swiftest wing of recompense is slow
     To overtake thee. Would thou hadst less deserved,
     That the proportion both of thanks and payment
     Might have been mine. Only I have left to say,   20
     'More is thy due than more than all can pay'.

MACBETH
     The service and the loyalty I owe,
     In doing it, pays itself. Your highness' part
     Is to receive our duties, and our duties
     Are to your throne and state children and servants   25
     Which do but what they should by doing everything
     Safe toward your love and honour.

KING DUNCAN   Welcome hither.
     I have begun to plant thee, and will labour
     To make thee full of growing.—Noble Banquo,
     That hast no less deserved, nor must be known   30
     No less to have done so, let me enfold thee
     And hold thee to my heart.

BANQUO   There if I grow
     The harvest is your own.

KING DUNCAN   My plenteous joys,
     Wanton in fullness, seek to hide themselves
     In drops of sorrow. Sons, kinsmen, thanes,   35
     And you whose places are the nearest, know
     We will establish our estate upon
     Our eldest, Malcolm, whom we name hereafter
     The Prince of Cumberland; which honour must
     Not unaccompanied invest him only,   40
     But signs of nobleness, like stars, shall shine
     On all deservers. (*To Macbeth*) From hence to Inverness,
     And bind us further to you.

MACBETH
     The rest is labour which is not used for you.
     I'll be myself the harbinger, and make joyful   45

     The hearing of my wife with your approach;
     So humbly take my leave.

KING DUNCAN   My worthy Cawdor.

MACBETH (*aside*)
     The Prince of Cumberland—that is a step
     On which I must fall down or else o'erleap,
     For in my way it lies. Stars, hide your fires,   50
     Let not light see my black and deep desires;
     The eye wink at the hand; yet let that be
     Which the eye fears, when it is done, to see.   *Exit*

KING DUNCAN
     True, worthy Banquo, he is full so valiant,
     And in his commendations I am fed.   55
     It is a banquet to me. Let's after him,
     Whose care is gone before to bid us welcome.
     It is a peerless kinsman.   *Flourish. Exeunt*

1.5   *Enter Lady Macbeth, with a letter*

LADY MACBETH (*reading*) 'They met me in the day of success,
and I have learned by the perfect'st report they have
more in them than mortal knowledge. When I burned in
desire to question them further, they made themselves
air, into which they vanished. Whiles I stood rapt in the
wonder of it came missives from the King, who all-hailed
me "Thane of Cawdor", by which title before these weird
sisters saluted me, and referred me to the coming on of
time with "Hail, King that shalt be!" This have I thought
good to deliver thee, my dearest partner of greatness,
that thou mightst not lose the dues of rejoicing by being
ignorant of what greatness is promised thee. Lay it to
thy heart, and farewell.'
     Glamis thou art, and Cawdor, and shalt be
     What thou art promised. Yet do I fear thy nature.   15
     It is too full o'th' milk of human kindness
     To catch the nearest way. Thou wouldst be great,
     Art not without ambition, but without
     The illness should attend it. What thou wouldst highly,
     That wouldst thou holily; wouldst not play false,   20
     And yet wouldst wrongly win. Thou'dst have, great
         Glamis,
     That which cries 'Thus thou must do' if thou have it,
     And that which rather thou dost fear to do
     Than wishest should be undone. Hie thee hither,
     That I may pour my spirits in thine ear   25
     And chastise with the valour of my tongue
     All that impedes thee from the golden round
     Which fate and metaphysical aid doth seem
     To have thee crowned withal.
     Enter a Servant
                    What is your tidings?

SERVANT
     The King comes here tonight.

LADY MACBETH   Thou'rt mad to say it.   30
     Is not thy master with him, who, were't so,
     Would have informed for preparation?

SERVANT
     So please you, it is true. Our thane is coming,

One of my fellows had the speed of him,
Who, almost dead for breath, had scarcely more   35
Than would make up his message.
LADY MACBETH   Give him tending;
He brings great news.   *Exit Servant*
                    The raven himself is hoarse
That croaks the fatal entrance of Duncan
Under my battlements. Come, you spirits
That tend on mortal thoughts, unsex me here,   40
And fill me from the crown to the toe top-full
Of direst cruelty. Make thick my blood,
Stop up th'access and passage to remorse,
That no compunctious visitings of nature
Shake my fell purpose, nor keep peace between   45
Th'effect and it. Come to my woman's breasts,
And take my milk for gall, you murd'ring ministers,
Wherever in your sightless substances
You wait on nature's mischief. Come, thick night,
And pall thee in the dunnest smoke of hell,   50
That my keen knife see not the wound it makes,
Nor heaven peep through the blanket of the dark
To cry 'Hold, hold!'
    Enter Macbeth
                    Great Glamis, worthy Cawdor,
Greater than both by the all-hail hereafter,
Thy letters have transported me beyond   55
This ignorant present, and I feel now
The future in the instant.
MACBETH   My dearest love,
Duncan comes here tonight.
LADY MACBETH   And when goes hence?
MACBETH
Tomorrow, as he purposes.
LADY MACBETH   O never
Shall sun that morrow see.   60
Your face, my thane, is as a book where men
May read strange matters. To beguile the time,
Look like the time; bear welcome in your eye,
Your hand, your tongue; look like the innocent flower,
But be the serpent under't. He that's coming   65
Must be provided for; and you shall put
This night's great business into my dispatch,
Which shall to all our nights and days to come
Give solely sovereign sway and masterdom.
MACBETH
We will speak further.
LADY MACBETH   Only look up clear.   70
To alter favour ever is to fear.
Leave all the rest to me.   *Exeunt*

1.6   *⌈Hautboys and torches.⌉ Enter King Duncan,*
       Malcolm, Donalbain, Banquo, Lennox, Macduff,
       Ross, Angus, and attendants
KING DUNCAN
This castle hath a pleasant seat. The air
Nimbly and sweetly recommends itself
Unto our gentle senses.
BANQUO   This guest of summer,

The temple-haunting martlet, does approve
By his loved mansionry that the heavens' breath   5
Smells wooingly here. No jutty, frieze,
Buttress, nor coign of vantage but this bird
Hath made his pendant bed and procreant cradle;
Where they most breed and haunt I have observed
The air is delicate.
    Enter Lady Macbeth
KING DUNCAN   See, see, our honoured hostess!   10
The love that follows us sometime is our trouble,
Which still we thank as love. Herein I teach you
How you shall bid God 'ield us for your pains,
And thank us for your trouble.
LADY MACBETH   All our service
In every point twice done, and then done double,   15
Were poor and single business to contend
Against those honours deep and broad wherewith
Your majesty loads our house. For those of old,
And the late dignities heaped up to them,
We rest your hermits.
KING DUNCAN   Where's the Thane of Cawdor?
We coursed him at the heels, and had a purpose   21
To be his purveyor; but he rides well,
And his great love, sharp as his spur, hath help him
To his home before us. Fair and noble hostess,
We are your guest tonight.
LADY MACBETH   Your servants ever   25
Have theirs, themselves, and what is theirs in count
To make their audit at your highness' pleasure,
Still to return your own.
KING DUNCAN   Give me your hand.
Conduct me to mine host. We love him highly,
And shall continue our graces towards him.   30
By your leave, hostess.   *Exeunt*

1.7   *Hautboys. Torches. Enter a sewer and divers*
       servants with dishes and service over the stage.
       Then enter Macbeth
MACBETH
If it were done when 'tis done, then 'twere well
It were done quickly. If th'assassination
Could trammel up the consequence, and catch
With his surcease success: that but this blow
Might be the be-all and the end-all, here,   5
But here upon this bank and shoal of time,
We'd jump the life to come. But in these cases
We still have judgement here, that we but teach
Bloody instructions which, being taught, return
To plague th'inventor. This even-handed justice   10
Commends th'ingredience of our poisoned chalice
To our own lips. He's here in double trust:
First, as I am his kinsman and his subject,
Strong both against the deed; then, as his host,
Who should against his murderer shut the door,   15
Not bear the knife myself. Besides, this Duncan
Hath borne his faculties so meek, hath been
So clear in his great office, that his virtues
Will plead like angels, trumpet-tongued against

The deep damnation of his taking-off,   20
And pity, like a naked new-born babe,
Striding the blast, or heaven's cherubin, horsed
Upon the sightless couriers of the air,
Shall blow the horrid deed in every eye
That tears shall drown the wind. I have no spur   25
To prick the sides of my intent, but only
Vaulting ambition which o'erleaps itself
And falls on th'other.
    Enter Lady Macbeth
               How now? What news?

LADY MACBETH
He has almost supped. Why have you left the
    chamber?

MACBETH
Hath he asked for me?

LADY MACBETH   Know you not he has?   30

MACBETH
We will proceed no further in this business.
He hath honoured me of late, and I have bought
Golden opinions from all sorts of people,
Which would be worn now in their newest gloss,
Not cast aside so soon.

LADY MACBETH   Was the hope drunk   35
Wherein you dressed yourself? Hath it slept since?
And wakes it now to look so green and pale
At what it did so freely? From this time
Such I account thy love. Art thou afeard
To be the same in thine own act and valour   40
As thou art in desire? Wouldst thou have that
Which thou esteem'st the ornament of life,
And live a coward in thine own esteem,
Letting 'I dare not' wait upon 'I would',
Like the poor cat i'th' adage?

MACBETH   Prithee, peace.   45
I dare do all that may become a man;
Who dares do more is none.

LADY MACBETH   What beast was't then
That made you break this enterprise to me?
When you durst do it, then you were a man;
And to be more than what you were, you would   50
Be so much more the man. Nor time nor place
Did then adhere, and yet you would make both.
They have made themselves, and that their fitness now
Does unmake you. I have given suck, and know
How tender 'tis to love the babe that milks me.   55
I would, while it was smiling in my face,
Have plucked my nipple from his boneless gums
And dashed the brains out, had I so sworn
As you have done to this.

MACBETH   If we should fail?

LADY MACBETH   We fail!
But screw your courage to the sticking-place   60
And we'll not fail. When Duncan is asleep—
Whereto the rather shall his day's hard journey
Soundly invite him—his two chamberlains
Will I with wine and wassail so convince
That memory, the warder of the brain,   65

Shall be a fume, and the receipt of reason
A limbeck only. When in swinish sleep
Their drenchèd natures lies as in a death,
What cannot you and I perform upon
Th'unguarded Duncan? What not put upon   70
His spongy officers, who shall bear the guilt
Of our great quell?

MACBETH   Bring forth men-children only,
For thy undaunted mettle should compose
Nothing but males. Will it not be received,
When we have marked with blood those sleepy two 75
Of his own chamber and used their very daggers,
That they have done't?

LADY MACBETH   Who dares receive it other,
As we shall make our griefs and clamour roar
Upon his death?

MACBETH   I am settled, and bend up
Each corporal agent to this terrible feat.   80
Away, and mock the time with fairest show.
False face must hide what the false heart doth know.
                        Exeunt

            ❀

2.1   *Enter Banquo and Fleance, with a torch before him*
BANQUO How goes the night, boy?

FLEANCE
The moon is down. I have not heard the clock.

BANQUO
And she goes down at twelve.

FLEANCE   I take't 'tis later, sir.

BANQUO (*giving Fleance his sword*)
Hold, take my sword. There's husbandry in heaven,
Their candles are all out. Take thee that, too.   5
A heavy summons lies like lead upon me,
And yet I would not sleep. Merciful powers,
Restrain in me the cursèd thoughts that nature
Gives way to in repose.
    Enter Macbeth, and a servant with a torch
            Give me my sword. Who's there?

MACBETH A friend.   10

BANQUO
What, sir, not yet at rest? The King's a-bed.
He hath been in unusual pleasure, and
Sent forth great largesse to your offices.
This diamond he greets your wife withal
By the name of most kind hostess, and shut up   15
In measureless content.

MACBETH   Being unprepared
Our will became the servant to defect,
Which else should free have wrought.

BANQUO   All's well.
I dreamt last night of the three weird sisters.
To you they have showed some truth.

MACBETH   I think not of them;
Yet, when we can entreat an hour to serve,   21
We would spend it in some words upon that business
If you would grant the time.

BANQUO   At your kind'st leisure.

MACBETH
If you shall cleave to my consent when 'tis,
It shall make honour for you.
BANQUO   So I lose none   25
In seeking to augment it, but still keep
My bosom franchised and allegiance clear,
I shall be counselled.
MACBETH Good repose the while.
BANQUO Thanks, sir. The like to you.   30
                    Exeunt Banquo and Fleance
MACBETH (*to the Servant*)
Go bid thy mistress, when my drink is ready,
She strike upon the bell. Get thee to bed.   *Exit Servant*
Is this a dagger which I see before me,
The handle toward my hand? Come, let me clutch thee.
I have thee not, and yet I see thee still.   35
Art thou not, fatal vision, sensible
To feeling as to sight? Or art thou but
A dagger of the mind, a false creation
Proceeding from the heat-oppressèd brain?
I see thee yet, in form as palpable   40
As this which now I draw.
Thou marshall'st me the way that I was going,
And such an instrument I was to use.
Mine eyes are made the fools o'th' other senses,
Or else worth all the rest. I see thee still,   45
And on thy blade and dudgeon gouts of blood,
Which was not so before. There's no such thing.
It is the bloody business which informs
Thus to mine eyes. Now o'er the one half-world
Nature seems dead, and wicked dreams abuse   50
The curtained sleep. Witchcraft celebrates
Pale Hecate's offerings, and withered murder,
Alarumed by his sentinel the wolf,
Whose howl's his watch, thus with his stealthy pace,
With Tarquin's ravishing strides, towards his design 55
Moves like a ghost. Thou sure and firm-set earth,
Hear not my steps which way they walk, for fear
Thy very stones prate of my whereabout,
And take the present horror from the time,
Which now suits with it. Whiles I threat, he lives. 60
Words to the heat of deeds too cold breath gives.
           A bell rings
I go, and it is done. The bell invites me.
Hear it not, Duncan; for it is a knell
That summons thee to heaven or to hell.   *Exit*

2.2   *Enter Lady Macbeth*
LADY MACBETH
That which hath made them drunk hath made me bold.
What hath quenched them hath given me fire. Hark,
      peace!—
It was the owl that shrieked, the fatal bellman
Which gives the stern'st good-night. He is about it.
The doors are open, and the surfeited grooms   5
Do mock their charge with snores. I have drugged
      their possets

That death and nature do contend about them
Whether they live or die.
           Enter Macbeth ⌈above⌉
MACBETH   Who's there? What ho?
                                                      Exit
LADY MACBETH
Alack, I am afraid they have awaked,
And 'tis not done. Th'attempt and not the deed   10
Confounds us. Hark!—I laid their daggers ready;
He could not miss 'em. Had he not resembled
My father as he slept, I had done't.
      ⌈*Enter Macbeth below*⌉
                                        My husband!
MACBETH
I have done the deed. Didst thou not hear a noise?
LADY MACBETH
I heard the owl scream and the crickets cry.   15
Did not you speak?
MACBETH   When?
LADY MACBETH   Now.
MACBETH   As I descended?
LADY MACBETH
Ay.
MACBETH Hark!—Who lies i'th' second chamber?
LADY MACBETH
Donalbain.
MACBETH (*looking at his hands*) This is a sorry sight.
LADY MACBETH
A foolish thought, to say a sorry sight.
MACBETH
There's one did laugh in's sleep, and one cried 'Murder!'
That they did wake each other. I stood and heard   21
      them.
But they did say their prayers and addressed them
Again to sleep.
LADY MACBETH   There are two lodged together.
MACBETH
One cried 'God bless us' and 'Amen' the other,
As they had seen me with these hangman's hands. 25
List'ning their fear I could not say 'Amen'
When they did say 'God bless us.'
LADY MACBETH
Consider it not so deeply.
MACBETH
But wherefore could not I pronounce 'Amen'?
I had most need of blessing, and 'Amen'   30
Stuck in my throat.
LADY MACBETH   These deeds must not be thought
After these ways. So, it will make us mad.
MACBETH
Methought I heard a voice cry 'Sleep no more,
Macbeth does murder sleep'—the innocent sleep,
Sleep that knits up the ravelled sleave of care,   35
The death of each day's life, sore labour's bath,
Balm of hurt minds, great nature's second course,
Chief nourisher in life's feast—
LADY MACBETH   What do you mean?

MACBETH
Still it cried 'Sleep no more' to all the house,
'Glamis hath murdered sleep, and therefore Cawdor 40
Shall sleep no more, Macbeth shall sleep no more.'
LADY MACBETH
Who was it that thus cried? Why, worthy thane,
You do unbend your noble strength to think
So brain-sickly of things. Go get some water
And wash this filthy witness from your hand. 45
Why did you bring these daggers from the place?
They must lie there. Go, carry them, and smear
The sleepy grooms with blood.
MACBETH   I'll go no more.
I am afraid to think what I have done,
Look on't again I dare not.
LADY MACBETH   Infirm of purpose! 50
Give me the daggers. The sleeping and the dead
Are but as pictures. 'Tis the eye of childhood
That fears a painted devil. If he do bleed
I'll gild the faces of the grooms withal,
For it must seem their guilt.   *Exit*
     Knock within
MACBETH   Whence is that knocking?—
How is't with me when every noise appals me? 56
What hands are here! Ha, they pluck out mine eyes.
Will all great Neptune's ocean wash this blood
Clean from my hand? No, this my hand will rather
The multitudinous seas incarnadine, 60
Making the green one red.
     Enter Lady Macbeth
LADY MACBETH
My hands are of your colour, but I shame
To wear a heart so white.
     Knock within
               I hear a knocking
At the south entry. Retire we to our chamber.
A little water clears us of this deed. 65
How easy is it then! Your constancy
Hath left you unattended.
     Knock within
               Hark, more knocking.
Get on your nightgown, lest occasion call us
And show us to be watchers. Be not lost
So poorly in your thoughts. 70
MACBETH
To know my deed 'twere best not know myself.
     Knock within
Wake Duncan with thy knocking. I would thou
   couldst.   *Exeunt*

2.3   *Enter a Porter. Knocking within*
PORTER Here's a knocking indeed! If a man were porter
of hell-gate he should have old turning the key.
     Knock within
Knock, knock, knock. Who's there, i'th' name of
Beelzebub? Here's a farmer that hanged himself on
th'expectation of plenty. Come in time! Have napkins
enough about you; here you'll sweat for't. 6

     Knock within
Knock, knock. Who's there, in th'other devil's name?
Faith, here's an equivocator that could swear in both
the scales against either scale, who committed treason
enough for God's sake, yet could not equivocate to
heaven. O, come in, equivocator. 11
     Knock within
Knock, knock, knock. Who's there? 'Faith, here's an
English tailor come hither for stealing out of a French
hose. Come in, tailor. Here you may roast your goose.
     Knock within
Knock, knock. Never at quiet. What are you?—But this
place is too cold for hell. I'll devil-porter it no further.
I had thought to have let in some of all professions
that go the primrose way to th'everlasting bonfire.
     Knock within
Anon, anon!
     He opens the gate
I pray you remember the porter. 20
     Enter Macduff and Lennox
MACDUFF
Was it so late, friend, ere you went to bed
That you do lie so late?
PORTER Faith, sir, we were carousing till the second cock,
and drink, sir, is a great provoker of three things.
MACDUFF What three things does drink especially
provoke? 26
PORTER Marry, sir, nose-painting, sleep, and urine.
Lechery, sir, it provokes and unprovokes: it provokes
the desire but it takes away the performance. Therefore
much drink may be said to be an equivocator with
lechery: it makes him and it mars him; it sets him on
and it takes him off; it persuades him and disheartens
him, makes him stand to and not stand to; in
conclusion, equivocates him in a sleep, and, giving him
the lie, leaves him. 35
MACDUFF I believe drink gave thee the lie last night.
PORTER That it did, sir, i'the very throat on me; but I
requited him for his lie, and, I think, being too strong
for him, though he took up my legs sometime, yet I
made a shift to cast him. 40
MACDUFF Is thy master stirring?
     Enter Macbeth
Our knocking has awaked him: here he comes.
                   ⌜Exit Porter⌝
LENNOX (*to Macbeth*)
Good morrow, noble sir.
MACBETH   Good morrow, both.
MACDUFF
Is the King stirring, worthy thane?
MACBETH   Not yet.
MACDUFF
He did command me to call timely on him. 45
I have almost slipped the hour.
MACBETH   I'll bring you to him.
MACDUFF
I know this is a joyful trouble to you,
But yet 'tis one.

MACBETH
The labour we delight in physics pain.
This is the door.
MACDUFF   I'll make so bold to call,   50
For 'tis my limited service.   *Exit Macduff*
LENNOX
Goes the King hence today?
MACBETH   He does; he did appoint so.
LENNOX
The night has been unruly. Where we lay
Our chimneys were blown down, and, as they say,
Lamentings heard i'th' air, strange screams of death,55
And prophesying with accents terrible
Of dire combustion and confused events
New-hatched to th' woeful time. The obscure bird
Clamoured the livelong night. Some say the earth
Was feverous and did shake.
MACBETH   'Twas a rough night.   60
LENNOX
My young remembrance cannot parallel
A fellow to it.
          Enter Macduff
MACDUFF   O horror, horror, horror!
Tongue nor heart cannot conceive nor name thee.
MACBETH *and* LENNOX What's the matter?
MACDUFF
Confusion now hath made his masterpiece.   65
Most sacrilegious murder hath broke ope
The Lord's anointed temple and stole thence
The life o'th' building.
MACBETH What is't you say—the life?
LENNOX Mean you his majesty?   70
MACDUFF
Approach the chamber and destroy your sight
With a new Gorgon. Do not bid me speak.
See, and then speak yourselves.
          Exeunt Macbeth and Lennox
                    Awake, awake!
Ring the alarum bell. Murder and treason!
Banquo and Donalbain, Malcolm, awake!   75
Shake off this downy sleep, death's counterfeit,
And look on death itself. Up, up, and see
The great doom's image. Malcolm, Banquo,
As from your graves rise up, and walk like sprites
To countenance this horror.
          Bell rings. Enter Lady Macbeth
LADY MACBETH   What's the business,   80
That such a hideous trumpet calls to parley
The sleepers of the house? Speak, speak.
MACDUFF   O gentle lady,
'Tis not for you to hear what I can speak.
The repetition in a woman's ear
Would murder as it fell.
          Enter Banquo
                    O Banquo, Banquo,   85
Our royal master's murdered!
LADY MACBETH   Woe, alas—
What, in our house?
BANQUO   Too cruel anywhere.

Dear Duff, I prithee contradict thyself,
And say it is not so.
          Enter Macbeth, Lennox, ⌈and Ross⌉
MACBETH
Had I but died an hour before this chance   90
I had lived a blessèd time, for from this instant
There's nothing serious in mortality.
All is but toys. Renown and grace is dead.
The wine of life is drawn, and the mere lees
Is left this vault to brag of.   95
          Enter Malcolm and Donalbain
DONALBAIN What is amiss?
MACBETH You are, and do not know't.
The spring, the head, the fountain of your blood
Is stopped, the very source of it is stopped.
MACDUFF
Your royal father's murdered.
MALCOLM   O, by whom?   100
LENNOX
Those of his chamber, as it seemed, had done't.
Their hands and faces were all badged with blood,
So were their daggers, which, unwiped, we found
Upon their pillows. They stared and were distracted.
No man's life was to be trusted with them.   105
MACBETH
O, yet I do repent me of my fury
That I did kill them.
MACDUFF   Wherefore did you so?
MACBETH
Who can be wise, amazed, temp'rate and furious,
Loyal and neutral in a moment? No man.
Th'expedition of my violent love   110
Outran the pauser, reason. Here lay Duncan,
His silver skin laced with his golden blood,
And his gashed stabs looked like a breach in nature
For ruin's wasteful entrance; there the murderers,
Steeped in the colours of their trade, their daggers 115
Unmannerly breeched with gore. Who could refrain,
That had a heart to love, and in that heart
Courage to make 's love known?
LADY MACBETH   Help me hence, ho!
MACDUFF
Look to the lady.
MALCOLM (*aside to Donalbain*)
                    Why do we hold our tongues,
That most may claim this argument for ours?   120
DONALBAIN (*aside to Malcolm*)
What should be spoken here, where our fate,
Hid in an auger-hole, may rush and seize us?
Let's away. Our tears are not yet brewed.
MALCOLM (*aside to Donalbain*)   Nor our strong sorrow
Upon the foot of motion.
BANQUO   Look to the lady;
          Exit Lady Macbeth, attended
And when we have our naked frailties hid,   125
That suffer in exposure, let us meet
And question this most bloody piece of work,
To know it further. Fears and scruples shake us.
In the great hand of God I stand, and thence

Against the undivulged pretence I fight   130
Of treasonous malice.
MACDUFF   And so do I.
ALL   So all.
MACBETH
Let's briefly put on manly readiness,
And meet i'th' hall together.
ALL   Well contented.
            Exeunt all but Malcolm and Donalbain
MALCOLM
What will you do? Let's not consort with them.
To show an unfelt sorrow is an office   135
Which the false man does easy. I'll to England.
DONALBAIN
To Ireland, I. Our separated fortune
Shall keep us both the safer. Where we are
There's daggers in men's smiles. The nea'er in blood,
The nearer bloody.
MALCOLM   This murderous shaft that's shot 140
Hath not yet lighted, and our safest way
Is to avoid the aim. Therefore to horse,
And let us not be dainty of leave-taking,
But shift away. There's warrant in that theft
Which steals itself when there's no mercy left.   145
                                        Exeunt

2.4   *Enter Ross with an Old Man*
OLD MAN
Threescore and ten I can remember well,
Within the volume of which time I have seen
Hours dreadful and things strange, but this sore night
Hath trifled former knowings.
ROSS   Ha, good father,
Thou seest the heavens, as troubled with man's act, 5
Threatens his bloody stage. By th' clock 'tis day,
And yet dark night strangles the travelling lamp.
Is't night's predominance or the day's shame
That darkness does the face of earth entomb
When living light should kiss it?
OLD MAN   'Tis unnatural,   10
Even like the deed that's done. On Tuesday last
A falcon, tow'ring in her pride of place,
Was by a mousing owl hawked at and killed.
ROSS
And Duncan's horses—a thing most strange and
            certain—
Beauteous and swift, the minions of their race,   15
Turned wild in nature, broke their stalls, flung out,
Contending 'gainst obedience, as they would
Make war with mankind.
OLD MAN   'Tis said they ate each other.
ROSS
They did so, to th'amazement of mine eyes
That looked upon't.
            Enter Macduff
                  Here comes the good Macduff.   20
How goes the world, sir, now?
MACDUFF   Why, see you not?

ROSS
Is't known who did this more than bloody deed?
MACDUFF
Those that Macbeth hath slain.
ROSS   Alas the day,
What good could they pretend?
MACDUFF   They were suborned.
Malcolm and Donalbain, the King's two sons,   25
Are stol'n away and fled, which puts upon them
Suspicion of the deed.
ROSS   'Gainst nature still.
Thriftless ambition, that will raven up
Thine own life's means! Then 'tis most like
The sovereignty will fall upon Macbeth.   30
MACDUFF
He is already named and gone to Scone
To be invested.
ROSS Where is Duncan's body?
MACDUFF Carried to Colmekill,
The sacred storehouse of his predecessors,   35
And guardian of their bones.
ROSS   Will you to Scone?
MACDUFF
No, cousin, I'll to Fife.
ROSS   Well, I will thither.
MACDUFF
Well, may you see things well done there. Adieu,
Lest our old robes sit easier than our new.
ROSS Farewell, father.   40
OLD MAN
God's benison go with you, and with those
That would make good of bad, and friends of foes.
                                  Exeunt severally

                        ✦

3.1   *Enter Banquo*
BANQUO
Thou hast it now: King, Cawdor, Glamis, all
As the weird women promised; and I fear
Thou played'st most foully for't. Yet it was said
It should not stand in thy posterity,
But that myself should be the root and father   5
Of many kings. If there come truth from them—
As upon thee, Macbeth, their speeches shine—
Why by the verities on thee made good
May they not be my oracles as well,
And set me up in hope? But hush, no more.   10
      Sennet sounded. Enter Macbeth as King, Lady Macbeth
      as Queen, Lennox, Ross, lords, and attendants
MACBETH
Here's our chief guest.
LADY MACBETH   If he had been forgotten
It had been as a gap in our great feast,
And all-thing unbecoming.
MACBETH (*to Banquo*)
Tonight we hold a solemn supper, sir,
And I'll request your presence.
BANQUO   Let your highness   15

Command upon me, to the which my duties
Are with a most indissoluble tie
For ever knit.
MACBETH Ride you this afternoon?
BANQUO Ay, my good lord.   20
MACBETH
We should have else desired your good advice,
Which still hath been both grave and prosperous,
In this day's council; but we'll talk tomorrow.
Is't far you ride?
BANQUO
As far, my lord, as will fill up the time   25
'Twixt this and supper. Go not my horse the better,
I must become a borrower of the night
For a dark hour or twain.
MACBETH Fail not our feast.
BANQUO My lord, I will not.   30
MACBETH
We hear our bloody cousins are bestowed
In England and in Ireland, not confessing
Their cruel parricide, filling their hearers
With strange invention. But of that tomorrow,
When therewithal we shall have cause of state   35
Craving us jointly. Hie you to horse. Adieu,
Till you return at night. Goes Fleance with you?
BANQUO
Ay, my good lord. Our time does call upon 's.
MACBETH
I wish your horses swift and sure of foot,
And so I do commend you to their backs.   40
Farewell.   Exit Banquo
Let every man be master of his time
Till seven at night. To make society
The sweeter welcome, we will keep ourself
Till supper-time alone. While then, God be with you. 45
             Exeunt all but Macbeth and a Servant
Sirrah, a word with you. Attend those men
Our pleasure?
SERVANT
They are, my lord, without the palace gate.
MACBETH
Bring them before us.   Exit Servant
             To be thus is nothing
But to be safely thus. Our fears in Banquo   50
Stick deep, and in his royalty of nature
Reigns that which would be feared. 'Tis much he dares,
And to that dauntless temper of his mind
He hath a wisdom that doth guide his valour
To act in safety. There is none but he   55
Whose being I do fear, and under him
My genius is rebuked as, it is said,
Mark Antony's was by Caesar. He chid the sisters
When first they put the name of king upon me,
And bade them speak to him. Then, prophet-like,   60
They hailed him father to a line of kings.
Upon my head they placed a fruitless crown,
And put a barren sceptre in my grip,

Thence to be wrenched with an unlineal hand,
No son of mine succeeding. If't be so,   65
For Banquo's issue have I filed my mind,
For them the gracious Duncan have I murdered,
Put rancours in the vessel of my peace
Only for them, and mine eternal jewel
Given to the common enemy of man   70
To make them kings, the seeds of Banquo kings.
Rather than so, come fate into the list
And champion me to th'utterance. Who's there?
             Enter Servant and two Murderers
(To the Servant) Now go to the door, and stay there
  till we call.   Exit Servant
Was it not yesterday we spoke together?   75
MURDERERS
It was, so please your highness.
MACBETH   Well then, now
Have you considered of my speeches? Know
That it was he in the times past which held you
So under fortune, which you thought had been
Our innocent self. This I made good to you   80
In our last conference, passed in probation with you
How you were borne in hand, how crossed, the
  instruments,
Who wrought with them, and all things else that
  might
To half a soul, and to a notion crazed,
Say 'Thus did Banquo'.
FIRST MURDERER   You made it known to us.   85
MACBETH
I did so, and went further, which is now
Our point of second meeting. Do you find
Your patience so predominant in your nature
That you can let this go? Are you so gospelled
To pray for this good man and for his issue,   90
Whose heavy hand hath bowed you to the grave
And beggared yours for ever?
FIRST MURDERER   We are men, my liege.
MACBETH
Ay, in the catalogue ye go for men,
As hounds and greyhounds, mongrels, spaniels, curs,
Shoughs, water-rugs, and demi-wolves are clept   95
All by the name of dogs. The valued file
Distinguishes the swift, the slow, the subtle,
The housekeeper, the hunter, every one
According to the gift which bounteous nature
Hath in him closed; whereby he does receive   100
Particular addition from the bill
That writes them all alike. And so of men.
Now, if you have a station in the file,
Not i'th' worst rank of manhood, say't,
And I will put that business in your bosoms   105
Whose execution takes your enemy off,
Grapples you to the heart and love of us,
Who wear our health but sickly in his life,
Which in his death were perfect.
SECOND MURDERER   I am one, my liege,

Whom the vile blows and buffets of the world   110
Hath so incensed that I am reckless what
I do to spite the world.
FIRST MURDERER   And I another,
So weary with disasters, tugged with fortune,
That I would set my life on any chance
To mend it or be rid on't.
MACBETH   Both of you   115
Know Banquo was your enemy.
MURDERERS   True, my lord.
MACBETH
So is he mine, and in such bloody distance
That every minute of his being thrusts
Against my near'st of life; and though I could
With barefaced power sweep him from my sight   120
And bid my will avouch it, yet I must not,
For certain friends that are both his and mine,
Whose loves I may not drop, but wail his fall
Who I myself struck down. And thence it is
That I to your assistance do make love,   125
Masking the business from the common eye
For sundry weighty reasons.
SECOND MURDERER   We shall, my lord,
Perform what you command us.
FIRST MURDERER   Though our lives—
MACBETH
Your spirits shine through you. Within this hour at most
I will advise you where to plant yourselves,   130
Acquaint you with the perfect spy o'th' time,
The moment on't; for't must be done tonight,
And something from the palace; always thought
That I require a clearness; and with him,
To leave no rubs nor botches in the work,   135
Fleance, his son, that keeps him company—
Whose absence is no less material to me
Than is his father's—must embrace the fate
Of that dark hour. Resolve yourselves apart.
I'll come to you anon.
MURDERERS   We are resolved, my lord.   140
MACBETH
I'll call upon you straight. Abide within.
                                        Exeunt Murderers
It is concluded. Banquo, thy soul's flight,
If it find heaven, must find it out tonight.   *Exit*

3.2   *Enter Lady Macbeth and a Servant*
LADY MACBETH Is Banquo gone from court?
SERVANT
Ay, madam, but returns again tonight.
LADY MACBETH
Say to the King I would attend his leisure
For a few words.
SERVANT Madam, I will.   *Exit*
LADY MACBETH Naught's had, all's spent,   6
Where our desire is got without content.
'Tis safer to be that which we destroy
Than by destruction dwell in doubtful joy.

Enter Macbeth
How now, my lord, why do you keep alone,   10
Of sorriest fancies your companions making,
Using those thoughts which should indeed have died
With them they think on? Things without all remedy
Should be without regard. What's done is done.
MACBETH
We have scorched the snake, not killed it.   15
She'll close and be herself, whilst our poor malice
Remains in danger of her former tooth.
But let the frame of things disjoint, both the worlds
    suffer,
Ere we will eat our meal in fear, and sleep
In the affliction of these terrible dreams   20
That shake us nightly. Better be with the dead,
Whom we to gain our peace have sent to peace,
Than on the torture of the mind to lie
In restless ecstasy. Duncan is in his grave.
After life's fitful fever he sleeps well.   25
Treason has done his worst. Nor steel nor poison,
Malice domestic, foreign levy, nothing
Can touch him further.
LADY MACBETH   Come on, gentle my lord,
Sleek o'er your rugged looks, be bright and jovial
Among your guests tonight.
MACBETH   So shall I, love,   30
And so I pray be you. Let your remembrance
Apply to Banquo. Present him eminence
Both with eye and tongue; unsafe the while that we
Must lave our honours in these flattering streams
And make our faces visors to our hearts,   35
Disguising what they are.
LADY MACBETH   You must leave this.
MACBETH
O, full of scorpions is my mind, dear wife!
Thou know'st that Banquo and his Fleance lives.
LADY MACBETH
But in them nature's copy's not eterne.
MACBETH
There's comfort yet, they are assailable.   40
Then be thou jocund. Ere the bat hath flown
His cloistered flight, ere to black Hecate's summons
The shard-borne beetle with his drowsy hums
Hath rung night's yawning peal, there shall be done
A deed of dreadful note.
LADY MACBETH   What's to be done?   45
MACBETH
Be innocent of the knowledge, dearest chuck,
Till thou applaud the deed.—Come, seeling night,
Scarf up the tender eye of pitiful day,
And with thy bloody and invisible hand
Cancel and tear to pieces that great bond   50
Which keeps me pale. Light thickens, and the crow
Makes wing to th' rooky wood.
Good things of day begin to droop and drowse,
Whiles night's black agents to their preys do rouse.

Thou marvell'st at my words; but hold thee still.   55
Things bad begun make strong themselves by ill.
So prithee go with me.   *Exeunt*

3.3   *Enter three Murderers*
FIRST MURDERER (*to Third Murderer*)
   But who did bid thee join with us?
THIRD MURDERER   Macbeth.
SECOND MURDERER (*to First Murderer*)
   He needs not our mistrust, since he delivers
   Our offices and what we have to do
   To the direction just.
FIRST MURDERER (*to Third Murderer*) Then stand with us.
   The west yet glimmers with some streaks of day.   5
   Now spurs the lated traveller apace
   To gain the timely inn, and near approaches
   The subject of our watch.
THIRD MURDERER   Hark, I hear horses.
BANQUO (*within*)
   Give us a light there, ho!
SECOND MURDERER   Then 'tis he. The rest
   That are within the note of expectation   10
   Already are i'th' court.
FIRST MURDERER   His horses go about.
THIRD MURDERER
   Almost a mile; but he does usually,
   So all men do, from hence to th' palace gate
   Make it their walk.
      Enter Banquo and Fleance with a torch
SECOND MURDERER (*aside*) A light, a light.
THIRD MURDERER (*aside*)   'Tis he.
FIRST MURDERER (*aside*) Stand to't.   15
BANQUO
   It will be rain tonight.
FIRST MURDERER   Let it come down.
      First Murderer strikes out the torch. The others
      attack Banquo
BANQUO
   O, treachery! Fly, good Fleance, fly, fly, fly!
   Thou mayst revenge.—O slave!   *He dies. Exit Fleance*
THIRD MURDERER Who did strike out the light?
FIRST MURDERER Was't not the way?   20
THIRD MURDERER
   There's but one down. The son is fled.
SECOND MURDERER
   We have lost best half of our affair.
FIRST MURDERER
   Well, let's away and say how much is done.
                  Exeunt with Banquo's body

3.4   *Banquet prepared. Enter Macbeth as King, Lady*
      Macbeth as Queen, Ross, Lennox, Lords, and
      attendants. ⌈Lady Macbeth sits⌉
MACBETH
   You know your own degrees; sit down. At first and last
   The hearty welcome.
LORDS   Thanks to your majesty.

      They sit
MACBETH
   Ourself will mingle with society
   And play the humble host. Our hostess keeps her
      state,
   But in best time we will require her welcome.   5
LADY MACBETH
   Pronounce it for me, sir, to all our friends,
   For my heart speaks they are welcome.
         Enter First Murderer ⌈to the door⌉
MACBETH
   See, they encounter thee with their hearts' thanks.
   Both sides are even. Here I'll sit, i'th' midst.
   Be large in mirth. Anon we'll drink a measure   10
   The table round. (*To First Murderer*) There's blood
      upon thy face.
FIRST MURDERER (*aside to Macbeth*) 'Tis Banquo's, then.
MACBETH
   'Tis better thee without than he within.
   Is he dispatched?
FIRST MURDERER
   My lord, his throat is cut. That I did for him.   15
MACBETH
   Thou art the best o'th' cut-throats. Yet he's good
   That did the like for Fleance. If thou didst it,
   Thou art the nonpareil.
FIRST MURDERER   Most royal sir,
   Fleance is scaped.
MACBETH
   Then comes my fit again; I had else been perfect,   20
   Whole as the marble, founded as the rock,
   As broad and general as the casing air,
   But now I am cabined, cribbed, confined, bound in
   To saucy doubts and fears. But Banquo's safe?
FIRST MURDERER
   Ay, my good lord. Safe in a ditch he bides,   25
   With twenty trenchèd gashes on his head,
   The least a death to nature.
MACBETH   Thanks for that.
   There the grown serpent lies. The worm that's fled
   Hath nature that in time will venom breed,
   No teeth for th' present. Get thee gone. Tomorrow   30
   We'll hear ourselves again.   *Exit First Murderer*
LADY MACBETH   My royal lord,
   You do not give the cheer. The feast is sold
   That is not often vouched, while 'tis a-making,
   'Tis given with welcome. To feed were best at home.
   From thence the sauce to meat is ceremony,   35
   Meeting were bare without it.
         Enter the Ghost of Banquo, and sits in Macbeth's
         place
MACBETH   Sweet remembrancer.
   Now good digestion wait on appetite,
   And health on both.
LENNOX   May't please your highness sit?
MACBETH
   Here had we now our country's honour roofed

Were the graced person of our Banquo present,   40
Who may I rather challenge for unkindness
Than pity for mischance.

ROSS   His absence, sir,
Lays blame upon his promise. Please't your highness
To grace us with your royal company?

MACBETH
The table's full.

LENNOX   Here is a place reserved, sir.   45

MACBETH Where?

LENNOX
Here, my good lord. What is't that moves your
   highness?

MACBETH
Which of you have done this?

LORDS   What, my good lord?

MACBETH (to the Ghost)
Thou canst not say I did it. Never shake
Thy gory locks at me.   50

ROSS (rising)
Gentlemen, rise. His highness is not well.

LADY MACBETH (rising)
Sit, worthy friends. My lord is often thus,
And hath been from his youth. Pray you, keep seat.
The fit is momentary. Upon a thought
He will again be well. If much you note him   55
You shall offend him, and extend his passion.
Feed, and regard him not.
      She speaks apart with Macbeth
                        Are you a man?

MACBETH
Ay, and a bold one, that dare look on that
Which might appal the devil.

LADY MACBETH   O proper stuff!
This is the very painting of your fear;   60
This is the air-drawn dagger which you said
Led you to Duncan. O, these flaws and starts,
Impostors to true fear, would well become
A woman's story at a winter's fire
Authorized by her grandam. Shame itself,   65
Why do you make such faces? When all's done
You look but on a stool.

MACBETH
Prithee see there. Behold, look, lo—how say you?
Why, what care I? If thou canst nod, speak, too!
If charnel-houses and our graves must send   70
Those that we bury back, our monuments
Shall be the maws of kites.   Exit Ghost

LADY MACBETH   What, quite unmanned in folly?

MACBETH
If I stand here, I saw him.

LADY MACBETH   Fie, for shame!

MACBETH
Blood hath been shed ere now, i'th' olden time,
Ere human statute purged the gentle weal;   75
Ay, and since, too, murders have been performed
Too terrible for the ear. The time has been
That, when the brains were out, the man would die,

And there an end. But now they rise again
With twenty mortal murders on their crowns,   80
And push us from our stools. This is more strange
Than such a murder is.

LADY MACBETH (aloud)   My worthy lord,
Your noble friends do lack you.

MACBETH   I do forget.
Do not muse at me, my most worthy friends.
I have a strange infirmity which is nothing   85
To those that know me. Come, love and health to all,
Then I'll sit down.
(To an attendant) Give me some wine. Fill full.
      Enter Ghost
I drink to th' general joy of th' whole table,
And to our dear friend Banquo, whom we miss.
Would he were here. To all and him we thirst,   90
And all to all.

LORDS   Our duties, and the pledge.
      They drink

MACBETH (seeing the Ghost)
Avaunt, and quit my sight! Let the earth hide thee.
Thy bones are marrowless, thy blood is cold.
Thou hast no speculation in those eyes
Which thou dost glare with.

LADY MACBETH   Think of this, good peers,
But as a thing of custom. 'Tis no other;   96
Only it spoils the pleasure of the time.

MACBETH What man dare, I dare.
Approach thou like the ruggèd Russian bear,
The armed rhinoceros, or th' Hyrcan tiger;   100
Take any shape but that, and my firm nerves
Shall never tremble. Or be alive again,
And dare me to the desert with thy sword.
If trembling I inhabit then, protest me
The baby of a girl. Hence, horrible shadow,   105
Unreal mock'ry, hence!   Exit Ghost
                        Why so, being gone,
I am a man again. Pray you sit still.

LADY MACBETH
You have displaced the mirth, broke the good meeting
With most admired disorder.

MACBETH   Can such things be
And overcome us like a summer's cloud,   110
Without our special wonder? You make me strange
Even to the disposition that I owe,
When now I think you can behold such sights
And keep the natural ruby of your cheeks
When mine is blanched with fear.

ROSS   What sights, my lord?

LADY MACBETH
I pray you, speak not. He grows worse and worse.   116
Question enrages him. At once, good night.
Stand not upon the order of your going,
But go at once.

LENNOX   Good night, and better health
Attend his majesty.

LADY MACBETH   A kind good-night to all.   120
      Exeunt Lords

MACBETH

It will have blood, they say. Blood will have blood.
Stones have been known to move, and trees to speak,
Augurs and understood relations have
By maggot-pies and choughs and rooks brought forth
The secret'st man of blood. What is the night?   125

LADY MACBETH

Almost at odds with morning, which is which.

MACBETH

How sayst thou that Macduff denies his person
At our great bidding?

LADY MACBETH   Did you send to him, sir?

MACBETH

I hear it by the way, but I will send.
There's not a one of them but in his house   130
I keep a servant fee'd. I will tomorrow,
And betimes I will, to the weird sisters.
More shall they speak, for now I am bent to know
By the worst means the worst. For mine own good
All causes shall give way. I am in blood   135
Stepped in so far that, should I wade no more,
Returning were as tedious as go o'er.
Strange things I have in head that will to hand,
Which must be acted ere they may be scanned.

LADY MACBETH

You lack the season of all natures, sleep.   140

MACBETH

Come, we'll to sleep. My strange and self-abuse
Is the initiate fear that wants hard use.
We are yet but young in deed.   *Exeunt*

3.5   *Thunder. Enter the three Witches meeting Hecate*

FIRST WITCH

Why, how now, Hecate? You look angerly.

HECATE

Have I not reason, beldams as you are?
Saucy and over-bold, how did you dare
To trade and traffic with Macbeth
In riddles and affairs of death,   5
And I, the mistress of your charms,
The close contriver of all harms,
Was never called to bear my part
Or show the glory of our art?—
And, which is worse, all you have done   10
Hath been but for a wayward son,
Spiteful and wrathful, who, as others do,
Loves for his own ends, not for you.
But make amends now. Get you gone,
And at the pit of Acheron   15
Meet me i'th' morning. Thither he
Will come to know his destiny.
Your vessels and your spells provide,
Your charms and everything beside.
I am for th'air. This night I'll spend   20
Unto a dismal and a fatal end.
Great business must be wrought ere noon.
Upon the corner of the moon

There hangs a vap'rous drop profound.
I'll catch it ere it come to ground,   25
And that, distilled by magic sleights,
Shall raise such artificial sprites
As by the strength of their illusion
Shall draw him on to his confusion.
He shall spurn fate, scorn death, and bear   30
His hopes 'bove wisdom, grace, and fear;
And you all know security
Is mortals' chiefest enemy.

SPIRITS (*singing dispersedly within*)

Come away, come away.
Hecate, Hecate, come away.   35

HECATE

Hark, I am called! My little spirit, see,
Sits in a foggy cloud and stays for me.

                    The Song

SPIRITS ⌈*within*⌉

Come away, come away,
Hecate, Hecate, come away.

HECATE

I come, I come, I come, I come,   40
With all the speed I may,
With all the speed I may.
Where's Stadlin?

SPIRIT ⌈*within*⌉   Here.

HECATE   Where's Puckle?

ANOTHER SPIRIT ⌈*within*⌉   Here.

OTHER SPIRITS ⌈*within*⌉

And Hoppo, too, and Hellwain, too,
We lack but you, we lack but you.   45
Come away, make up the count.

HECATE

I will but 'noint, and then I mount.
⌈*Spirits appear above.*⌉ *A Spirit like a Cat descends*

SPIRITS ⌈*above*⌉

There's one comes down to fetch his dues,
A kiss, a coll, a sip of blood,
And why thou stay'st so long I muse, I muse,   50
Since the air's so sweet and good.

HECATE

O, art thou come? What news, what news?

SPIRIT LIKE A CAT

All goes still to our delight.
Either come, or else refuse, refuse.

HECATE   Now I am furnished for the flight.   55

She ascends with the spirit and sings

Now I go, now I fly,
Malkin my sweet spirit and I.

⌈**SPIRITS** *and* **HECATE**⌉

O what a dainty pleasure 'tis
To ride in the air
When the moon shines fair,   60
And sing, and dance, and toy, and kiss.
Over woods, high rocks and mountains,
Over seas and misty fountains,
Over steeples, towers and turrets,
We fly by night 'mongst troops of spirits.   65

No ring of bells to our ears sounds,
No howls of wolves, no yelps of hounds.
No, not the noise of waters-breach
Or cannons' throat our height can reach.

SPIRITS ⌈*above*⌉
No ring of bells to our ears sounds,   70
No howls of wolves, no yelps of hounds.
No, not the noise of waters-breach
Or cannons' throat our height can reach.

Exeunt into the heavens the
Spirit like a Cat and Hecate

FIRST WITCH
Come, let's make haste. She'll soon be back again.

Exeunt

3.6   *Enter Lennox and another Lord*

LENNOX
My former speeches have but hit your thoughts,
Which can interpret farther. Only I say
Things have been strangely borne. The gracious
        Duncan
Was pitied of Macbeth: marry, he was dead;
And the right valiant Banquo walked too late,   5
Whom you may say, if't please you, Fleance killed,
For Fleance fled: men must not walk too late.
Who cannot want the thought how monstrous
It was for Malcolm and for Donalbain
To kill their gracious father? Damnèd fact,   10
How it did grieve Macbeth! Did he not straight
In pious rage the two delinquents tear,
That were the slaves of drink, and thralls of sleep?
Was not that nobly done? Ay, and wisely too,
For 'twould have angered any heart alive   15
To hear the men deny't. So that I say
He has borne all things well, and I do think
That had he Duncan's sons under his key—
As, an't please heaven, he shall not—they should find
What 'twere to kill a father. So should Fleance.   20
But peace, for from broad words, and 'cause he failed
His presence at the tyrant's feast, I hear
Macduff lives in disgrace. Sir, can you tell
Where he bestows himself?

LORD   The son of Duncan
From whom this tyrant holds the due of birth   25
Lives in the English court, and is received
Of the most pious Edward with such grace
That the malevolence of fortune nothing
Takes from his high respect. Thither Macduff
Is gone to pray the holy King upon his aid   30
To wake Northumberland and warlike Siward,
That by the help of these—with Him above
To ratify the work—we may again
Give to our tables meat, sleep to our nights,
Free from our feasts and banquets bloody knives,   35
Do faithful homage, and receive free honours,
All which we pine for now. And this report
Hath so exasperate their king that he
Prepares for some attempt of war.

LENNOX   Sent he to Macduff?   40

LORD
He did, and with an absolute 'Sir, not I,'
The cloudy messenger turns me his back
And hums, as who should say 'You'll rue the time
That clogs me with this answer.'

LENNOX   And that well might
Advise him to a caution t'hold what distance   45
His wisdom can provide. Some holy angel
Fly to the court of England and unfold
His message ere he come, that a swift blessing
May soon return to this our suffering country   49
Under a hand accursed.

LORD   I'll send my prayers with him.

Exeunt

❦

4.1   *A Cauldron. Thunder. Enter the three Witches*

FIRST WITCH
Thrice the brinded cat hath mewed.

SECOND WITCH
Thrice, and once the hedge-pig whined.

THIRD WITCH
Harpier cries ''Tis time, 'tis time.'

FIRST WITCH
Round about the cauldron go,
In the poisoned entrails throw.   5
Toad that under cold stone
Days and nights has thirty-one
Sweltered venom sleeping got,
Boil thou first i'th' charmèd pot.

ALL
Double, double, toil and trouble,   10
Fire burn, and cauldron bubble.

SECOND WITCH
Fillet of a fenny snake,
In the cauldron boil and bake.
Eye of newt and toe of frog,
Wool of bat and tongue of dog,   15
Adder's fork and blind-worm's sting,
Lizard's leg and owlet's wing,
For a charm of powerful trouble,
Like a hell-broth boil and bubble.

ALL
Double, double, toil and trouble,   20
Fire burn, and cauldron bubble.

THIRD WITCH
Scale of dragon, tooth of wolf,
Witches' mummy, maw and gulf
Of the ravined salt-sea shark,
Root of hemlock digged i'th' dark,   25
Liver of blaspheming Jew,
Gall of goat, and slips of yew
Slivered in the moon's eclipse,
Nose of Turk, and Tartar's lips,
Finger of birth-strangled babe   30
Ditch-delivered by a drab,
Make the gruel thick and slab.

Add thereto a tiger's chaudron
For th'ingredience of our cauldron.

ALL

Double, double, toil and trouble,   35
Fire burn, and cauldron bubble.

SECOND WITCH

Cool it with a baboon's blood,
Then the charm is firm and good.

Enter Hecate and the other three Witches

HECATE

O, well done! I commend your pains,
And everyone shall share i'th' gains.   40
And now about the cauldron sing
Like elves and fairies in a ring,
Enchanting all that you put in.

Music and a song

HECATE

Black spirits and white, red spirits and grey,
Mingle, mingle, mingle, you that mingle may.   45

FOURTH WITCH

Titty, Tiffin, keep it stiff in;
Firedrake, Puckey, make it lucky;
Liard, Robin, you must bob in.

ALL   Round, around, around, about, about,
All ill come running in, all good keep out.   50

FOURTH WITCH

Here's the blood of a bat.

HECATE

Put in that, O put in that!

FIFTH WITCH

Here's leopard's bane.

HECATE

Put in a grain.

FOURTH WITCH

The juice of toad, the oil of adder.   55

FIFTH WITCH

Those will make the younker madder.

HECATE

Put in, there's all, and rid the stench.

A WITCH

Nay, here's three ounces of a red-haired wench.

ALL   Round, around, around, about, about,
All ill come running in, all good keep out.   60

SECOND WITCH

By the pricking of my thumbs,
Something wicked this way comes.

⌈*Knock within*⌉

Open, locks, whoever knocks.

Enter Macbeth

MACBETH

How now, you secret, black, and midnight hags,
What is't you do?

ALL THE WITCHES   A deed without a name.   65

MACBETH

I conjure you by that which you profess,
Howe'er you come to know it, answer me.
Though you untie the winds and let them fight
Against the churches, though the yeasty waves

Confound and swallow navigation up,   70
Though bladed corn be lodged and trees blown down,
Though castles topple on their warders' heads,
Though palaces and pyramids do slope
Their heads to their foundations, though the treasure
Of nature's germens tumble all together   75
Even till destruction sicken, answer me
To what I ask you.

FIRST WITCH   Speak.

SECOND WITCH   Demand.

THIRD WITCH   We'll answer.

FIRST WITCH

Say if thou'dst rather hear it from our mouths
Or from our masters.

MACBETH   Call 'em, let me see 'em.

FIRST WITCH

Pour in sow's blood that hath eaten   80
Her nine farrow; grease that's sweaten
From the murderer's gibbet throw
Into the flame.

ALL THE WITCHES   Come high or low,
Thyself and office deftly show.

Thunder. First Apparition: an armed head

MACBETH

Tell me, thou unknown power—

FIRST WITCH   He knows thy thought.
Hear his speech, but say thou naught.   86

FIRST APPARITION

Macbeth, Macbeth, Macbeth, beware Macduff,
Beware the Thane of Fife. Dismiss me. Enough.

Apparition descends

MACBETH

Whate'er thou art, for thy good caution thanks.
Thou hast harped my fear aright. But one word
more—   90

FIRST WITCH

He will not be commanded. Here's another,
More potent than the first.

Thunder. Second Apparition: a bloody child

SECOND APPARITION Macbeth, Macbeth, Macbeth.

MACBETH Had I three ears I'd hear thee.

SECOND APPARITION

Be bloody, bold, and resolute. Laugh to scorn   95
The power of man, for none of woman born
Shall harm Macbeth.

Apparition descends

MACBETH

Then live, Macduff—what need I fear of thee?
But yet I'll make assurance double sure,
And take a bond of fate thou shalt not live,   100
That I may tell pale-hearted fear it lies,
And sleep in spite of thunder.

*Thunder. Third Apparition: a child crowned, with a
tree in his hand*

What is this
That rises like the issue of a king,
And wears upon his baby-brow the round
And top of sovereignty?

ALL THE WITCHES   Listen, but speak not to't. 105

THIRD APPARITION
Be lion-mettled, proud, and take no care
Who chafes, who frets, or where conspirers are.
Macbeth shall never vanquished be until
Great Birnam Wood to high Dunsinane Hill
Shall come against him.
    Apparition descends
MACBETH   That will never be.   110
Who can impress the forest, bid the tree
Unfix his earth-bound root? Sweet bodements, good!
Rebellious dead, rise never till the wood
Of Birnam rise, and on's high place Macbeth
Shall live the lease of nature, pay his breath   115
To time and mortal custom. Yet my heart
Throbs to know one thing. Tell me, if your art
Can tell so much, shall Banquo's issue ever
Reign in this kingdom?
ALL THE WITCHES   Seek to know no more.
MACBETH
I will be satisfied. Deny me this,   120
And an eternal curse fall on you! Let me know.
    The cauldron sinks. Hautboys
Why sinks that cauldron? And what noise is this?
FIRST WITCH Show.
SECOND WITCH Show.
THIRD WITCH Show.   125
ALL THE WITCHES
Show his eyes and grieve his heart,
Come like shadows, so depart.
    A show of eight kings, the last with a glass in his
    hand; and Banquo
MACBETH
Thou art too like the spirit of Banquo. Down!
Thy crown does sear mine eyeballs. And thy hair,
Thou other gold-bound brow, is like the first.   130
A third is like the former. Filthy hags,
Why do you show me this?—A fourth? Start, eyes!
What, will the line stretch out to th' crack of doom?
Another yet? A seventh? I'll see no more—
And yet the eighth appears, who bears a glass   135
Which shows me many more; and some I see
That twofold balls and treble sceptres carry.
Horrible sight! Now I see 'tis true,
For the blood-baltered Banquo smiles upon me,
And points at them for his.
    Exeunt kings and Banquo
        What, is this so?   140
⌈HECATE⌉
Ay, sir, all this is so. But why
Stands Macbeth thus amazedly?
Come, sisters, cheer we up his sprites,
And show the best of our delights.
I'll charm the air to give a sound   145
While you perform your antic round,
That this great king may kindly say
Our duties did his welcome pay.
    Music. The Witches dance, and vanish
MACBETH
Where are they? Gone? Let this pernicious hour

Stand aye accursèd in the calendar.   150
Come in, without there.
    Enter Lennox
LENNOX   What's your grace's will?
MACBETH
Saw you the weird sisters?
LENNOX   No, my lord.
MACBETH
Came they not by you?
LENNOX   No, indeed, my lord.
MACBETH
Infected be the air whereon they ride,
And damned all those that trust them. I did hear   155
The galloping of horse. Who was't came by?
LENNOX
'Tis two or three, my lord, that bring you word
Macduff is fled to England.
MACBETH   Fled to England?
LENNOX Ay, my good lord.
MACBETH *(aside)*
Time, thou anticipat'st my dread exploits.   160
The flighty purpose never is o'ertook
Unless the deed go with it. From this moment
The very firstlings of my heart shall be
The firstlings of my hand. And even now,
To crown my thoughts with acts, be it thought and
    done: 165
The castle of Macduff I will surprise,
Seize upon Fife, give to th'edge o'th' sword
His wife, his babes, and all unfortunate souls
That trace him in his line. No boasting like a fool;
This deed I'll do before this purpose cool.   170
But no more sights! *(To Lennox)* Where are these
    gentlemen?
Come bring me where they are.   *Exeunt*

4.2   *Enter Macduff's Wife, her Son, and Ross*
LADY MACDUFF
What had he done to make him fly the land?
ROSS
You must have patience, madam.
LADY MACDUFF   He had none.
His flight was madness. When our actions do not,
Our fears do make us traitors.
ROSS   You know not
Whether it was his wisdom or his fear.   5
LADY MACDUFF
Wisdom—to leave his wife, to leave his babes,
His mansion, and his titles in a place
From whence himself does fly? He loves us not,
He wants the natural touch, for the poor wren,
The most diminutive of birds, will fight,   10
Her young ones in her nest, against the owl.
All is the fear and nothing is the love;
As little is the wisdom, where the flight
So runs against all reason.
ROSS   My dearest coz,
I pray you school yourself. But for your husband,   15

He is noble, wise, judicious, and best knows
The fits o'th' season. I dare not speak much further,
But cruel are the times when we are traitors
And do not know ourselves; when we hold rumour
From what we fear, yet know not what we fear,   20
But float upon a wild and violent sea
Each way and none. I take my leave of you;
Shall not be long but I'll be here again.
Things at the worst will cease, or else climb upward
To what they were before. My pretty cousin,   25
Blessing upon you!

LADY MACDUFF
Fathered he is, and yet he's fatherless.

ROSS
I am so much a fool, should I stay longer
It would be my disgrace and your discomfort.
I take my leave at once.   *Exit*

LADY MACDUFF   Sirrah, your father's dead,   30
And what will you do now? How will you live?

MACDUFF'S SON
As birds do, mother.

LADY MACDUFF   What, with worms and flies?

MACDUFF'S SON
With what I get, I mean, and so do they.

LADY MACDUFF
Poor bird, thou'dst never fear the net nor lime,
The pitfall nor the gin.   35

MACDUFF'S SON
Why should I, mother? Poor birds they are not set for.
My father is not dead, for all your saying.

LADY MACDUFF Yes, he is dead. How wilt thou do for a
father?

MACDUFF'S SON Nay, how will you do for a husband?   40

LADY MACDUFF Why, I can buy me twenty at any market.

MACDUFF'S SON Then you'll buy 'em to sell again.

LADY MACDUFF Thou speak'st with all thy wit, and yet,
i'faith, with wit enough for thee.

MACDUFF'S SON Was my father a traitor, mother?   45

LADY MACDUFF Ay, that he was.

MACDUFF'S SON What is a traitor?

LADY MACDUFF Why, one that swears and lies.

MACDUFF'S SON And be all traitors that do so?

LADY MACDUFF Everyone that does so is a traitor, and
must be hanged.   51

MACDUFF'S SON And must they all be hanged that swear
and lie?

LADY MACDUFF Every one.

MACDUFF'S SON Who must hang them?   55

LADY MACDUFF Why, the honest men.

MACDUFF'S SON Then the liars and swearers are fools, for
there are liars and swearers enough to beat the honest
men and hang up them.

LADY MACDUFF Now God help thee, poor monkey! But
how wilt thou do for a father?   61

MACDUFF'S SON If he were dead you'd weep for him. If
you would not, it were a good sign that I should quickly
have a new father.

LADY MACDUFF Poor prattler, how thou talk'st!   65

Enter a Messenger

MESSENGER
Bless you, fair dame. I am not to you known,
Though in your state of honour I am perfect.
I doubt some danger does approach you nearly.
If you will take a homely man's advice,
Be not found here. Hence with your little ones!   70
To fright you thus methinks I am too savage,
To do worse to you were fell cruelty,
Which is too nigh your person. Heaven preserve you.
I dare abide no longer.   *Exit Messenger*

LADY MACDUFF   Whither should I fly?
I have done no harm. But I remember now   75
I am in this earthly world, where to do harm
Is often laudable, to do good sometime
Accounted dangerous folly. Why then, alas,
Do I put up that womanly defence
To say I have done no harm?

Enter Murderers
                                   What are these faces? 80

A MURDERER Where is your husband?

LADY MACDUFF
I hope in no place so unsanctified
Where such as thou mayst find him.

A MURDERER   He's a traitor.

MACDUFF'S SON
Thou liest, thou shag-haired villain.

A MURDERER (*stabbing him*)   What, you egg!
Young fry of treachery!

MACDUFF'S SON   He has killed me, mother.   85
Run away, I pray you.
⌜*He dies.*⌝ *Exit Macduff's Wife crying 'Murder!'*
                          followed by Murderers ⌜with the Son's body⌝

4.3   *Enter Malcolm and Macduff*

MALCOLM
Let us seek out some desolate shade, and there
Weep our sad bosoms empty.

MACDUFF   Let us rather
Hold fast the mortal sword, and like good men
Bestride our downfall birthdom. Each new morn
New widows howl, new orphans cry, new sorrows   5
Strike heaven on the face that it resounds
As if it felt with Scotland and yelled out
Like syllable of dolour.

MALCOLM   What I believe I'll wail,
What know believe; and what I can redress,
As I shall find the time to friend, I will.   10
What you have spoke it may be so, perchance.
This tyrant, whose sole name blisters our tongues,
Was once thought honest. You have loved him well.
He hath not touched you yet. I am young, but
something
You may discern of him through me: and wisdom   15
To offer up a weak poor innocent lamb
T'appease an angry god.

MACDUFF I am not treacherous.

MALCOLM But Macbeth is.

A good and virtuous nature may recoil   20
In an imperial charge. But I shall crave your pardon.
That which you are my thoughts cannot transpose.
Angels are bright still, though the brightest fell.
Though all things foul would wear the brows of grace,
Yet grace must still look so.
MACDUFF   I have lost my hopes.   25
MALCOLM
Perchance even there where I did find my doubts.
Why in that rawness left you wife and child,
Those precious motives, those strong knots of love,
Without leave-taking? I pray you,
Let not my jealousies be your dishonours,   30
But mine own safeties. You may be rightly just,
Whatever I shall think.
MACDUFF   Bleed, bleed, poor country!
Great tyranny, lay thou thy basis sure,
For goodness dare not check thee. Wear thou thy
          wrongs;
The title is affeered. Fare thee well, lord.   35
I would not be the villain that thou think'st
For the whole space that's in the tyrant's grasp,
And the rich east to boot.
MALCOLM   Be not offended.
I speak not as in absolute fear of you.
I think our country sinks beneath the yoke.   40
It weeps, it bleeds, and each new day a gash
Is added to her wounds. I think withal
There would be hands uplifted in my right,
And here from gracious England have I offer
Of goodly thousands. But for all this,   45
When I shall tread upon the tyrant's head,
Or wear it on my sword, yet my poor country
Shall have more vices than it had before,
More suffer, and more sundry ways, than ever,
By him that shall succeed.
MACDUFF   What should he be?   50
MALCOLM
It is myself I mean, in whom I know
All the particulars of vice so grafted
That when they shall be opened black Macbeth
Will seem as pure as snow, and the poor state
Esteem him as a lamb, being compared   55
With my confineless harms.
MACDUFF   Not in the legions
Of horrid hell can come a devil more damned
In evils to top Macbeth.
MALCOLM   I grant him bloody,
Luxurious, avaricious, false, deceitful,
Sudden, malicious, smacking of every sin   60
That has a name. But there's no bottom, none,
In my voluptuousness. Your wives, your daughters,
Your matrons, and your maids could not fill up
The cistern of my lust, and my desire
All continent impediments would o'erbear   65
That did oppose my will. Better Macbeth
Than such an one to reign.
MACDUFF   Boundless intemperance
In nature is a tyranny. It hath been

Th'untimely emptying of the happy throne,
And fall of many kings. But fear not yet   70
To take upon you what is yours. You may
Convey your pleasures in a spacious plenty
And yet seem cold. The time you may so hoodwink.
We have willing dames enough. There cannot be
That vulture in you to devour so many   75
As will to greatness dedicate themselves,
Finding it so inclined.
MALCOLM   With this there grows
In my most ill-composed affection such
A staunchless avarice that were I king
I should cut off the nobles for their lands,   80
Desire his jewels and this other's house,
And my more having would be as a sauce
To make me hunger more, that I should forge
Quarrels unjust against the good and loyal,
Destroying them for wealth.
MACDUFF   This avarice   85
Sticks deeper, grows with more pernicious root
Than summer-seeming lust, and it hath been
The sword of our slain kings. Yet do not fear.
Scotland hath foisons to fill up your will
Of your mere own. All these are portable,   90
With other graces weighed.
MALCOLM
But I have none. The king-becoming graces,
As justice, verity, temp'rance, stableness,
Bounty, perseverance, mercy, lowliness,
Devotion, patience, courage, fortitude,   95
I have no relish of them, but abound
In the division of each several crime,
Acting it many ways. Nay, had I power I should
Pour the sweet milk of concord into hell,
Uproar the universal peace, confound   100
All unity on earth.
MACDUFF   O Scotland, Scotland!
MALCOLM
If such a one be fit to govern, speak.
I am as I have spoken.
MACDUFF   Fit to govern?
No, not to live. O nation miserable,
With an untitled tyrant bloody-sceptered,   105
When shalt thou see thy wholesome days again,
Since that the truest issue of thy throne
By his own interdiction stands accursed
And does blaspheme his breed? Thy royal father
Was a most sainted king. The Queen that bore thee,
Oft'ner upon her knees than on her feet,   111
Died every day she lived. Fare thee well.
These evils thou repeat'st upon thyself
Hath banished me from Scotland. O, my breast—
Thy hope ends here!
MALCOLM   Macduff, this noble passion,   115
Child of integrity, hath from my soul
Wiped the black scruples, reconciled my thoughts
To thy good truth and honour. Devilish Macbeth
By many of these trains hath sought to win me
Into his power, and modest wisdom plucks me   120

From over-credulous haste; but God above
Deal between thee and me, for even now
I put myself to thy direction and
Unspeak mine own detraction, here abjure
The taints and blames I laid upon myself   125
For strangers to my nature. I am yet
Unknown to woman, never was forsworn,
Scarcely have coveted what was mine own,
At no time broke my faith, would not betray
The devil to his fellow, and delight   130
No less in truth than life. My first false-speaking
Was this upon myself. What I am truly
Is thine and my poor country's to command,
Whither indeed, before thy here-approach,
Old Siward with ten thousand warlike men,   135
Already at a point, was setting forth.
Now we'll together; and the chance of goodness
Be like our warranted quarrel!—Why are you silent?

MACDUFF
Such welcome and unwelcome things at once
'Tis hard to reconcile.   140

Enter a Doctor

MALCOLM
Well, more anon. (*To the Doctor*) Comes the King
    forth, I pray you?

DOCTOR
Ay, sir. There are a crew of wretched souls
That stay his cure. Their malady convinces
The great essay of art, but at his touch,
Such sanctity hath Heaven given his hand,   145
They presently amend.

MALCOLM   I thank you, doctor.

Exit Doctor

MACDUFF
What's the disease he means?

MALCOLM   'Tis called the evil—
A most miraculous work in this good King,
Which often since my here-remain in England
I have seen him do. How he solicits heaven   150
Himself best knows, but strangely visited people,
All swoll'n and ulcerous, pitiful to the eye,
The mere despair of surgery, he cures,
Hanging a golden stamp about their necks,
Put on with holy prayers; and 'tis spoken,   155
To the succeeding royalty he leaves
The healing benediction. With this strange virtue
He hath a heavenly gift of prophecy,
And sundry blessings hang about his throne
That speak him full of grace.

Enter Ross

MACDUFF   See who comes here.   160

MALCOLM
My countryman, but yet I know him not.

MACDUFF
My ever gentle cousin, welcome hither.

MALCOLM
I know him now. Good God betimes remove
The means that makes us strangers!

ROSS   Sir, amen.

MACDUFF
Stands Scotland where it did?

ROSS   Alas, poor country,   165
Almost afraid to know itself. It cannot
Be called our mother, but our grave, where nothing
But who knows nothing is once seen to smile;
Where sighs and groans and shrieks that rend the air
Are made, not marked; where violent sorrow seems
A modern ecstasy. The dead man's knell   171
Is there scarce asked for who, and good men's lives
Expire before the flowers in their caps,
Dying or ere they sicken.

MACDUFF   O relation
Too nice and yet too true!

MALCOLM   What's the newest grief? 175

ROSS
That of an hour's age doth hiss the speaker;
Each minute teems a new one.

MACDUFF   How does my wife?

ROSS
Why, well.

MACDUFF   And all my children?

ROSS   Well, too.

MACDUFF
The tyrant has not battered at their peace?

ROSS
No, they were well at peace when I did leave 'em.   180

MACDUFF
Be not a niggard of your speech. How goes't?

ROSS
When I came hither to transport the tidings
Which I have heavily borne, there ran a rumour
Of many worthy fellows that were out,
Which was to my belief witnessed the rather   185
For that I saw the tyrant's power afoot.
Now is the time of help. (*To Malcolm*) Your eye in
    Scotland
Would create soldiers, make our women fight
To doff their dire distresses.

MALCOLM   Be't their comfort
We are coming thither. Gracious England hath   190
Lent us good Siward and ten thousand men;
An older and a better soldier none
That Christendom gives out.

ROSS   Would I could answer
This comfort with the like. But I have words
That would be howled out in the desert air   195
Where hearing should not latch them.

MACDUFF   What concern they—
The general cause, or is it a fee-grief
Due to some single breast?

ROSS   No mind that's honest
But in it shares some woe, though the main part
Pertains to you alone.

MACDUFF   If it be mine,   200
Keep it not from me; quickly let me have it.

ROSS
Let not your ears despise my tongue for ever,

Which shall possess them with the heaviest sound
That ever yet they heard.
MACDUFF   H'm, I guess at it.
ROSS
Your castle is surprised, your wife and babes   205
Savagely slaughtered. To relate the manner
Were on the quarry of these murdered deer
To add the death of you.
MALCOLM   Merciful heaven!
(*To Macduff*) What, man, ne'er pull your hat upon
    your brows.
Give sorrow words. The grief that does not speak   210
Whispers the o'erfraught heart and bids it break.
MACDUFF
My children too?
ROSS   . Wife, children, servants, all
That could be found.
MACDUFF   And I must be from thence!
My wife killed too?
ROSS   I have said.
MALCOLM   Be comforted.
Let's make us medicines of our great revenge   215
To cure this deadly grief.
MACDUFF
He has no children. All my pretty ones?
Did you say all? O hell-kite! All?
What, all my pretty chickens and their dam
At one fell swoop?   220
MALCOLM Dispute it like a man.
MACDUFF I shall do so,
But I must also feel it as a man.
I cannot but remember such things were
That were most precious to me. Did heaven look on
And would not take their part? Sinful Macduff,   226
They were all struck for thee. Naught that I am,
Not for their own demerits but for mine
Fell slaughter on their souls. Heaven rest them now.
MALCOLM
Be this the whetstone of your sword. Let grief   230
Convert to anger: blunt not the heart, enrage it.
MACDUFF
O, I could play the woman with mine eyes
And braggart with my tongue! But gentle heavens
Cut short all intermission. Front to front
Bring thou this fiend of Scotland and myself.   235
Within my sword's length set him. If he scape,
Heaven forgive him too.
MALCOLM   This tune goes manly.
Come, go we to the King. Our power is ready;
Our lack is nothing but our leave. Macbeth
Is ripe for shaking, and the powers above   240
Put on their instruments. Receive what cheer you may:
The night is long that never finds the day.   *Exeunt*

❀

5.1   *Enter a Doctor of Physic and a Waiting-*
    Gentlewoman
DOCTOR I have two nights watched with you, but can

perceive no truth in your report. When was it she last
walked?
GENTLEWOMAN Since his majesty went into the field I have
seen her rise from her bed, throw her nightgown upon
her, unlock her closet, take forth paper, fold it, write
upon't, read it, afterwards seal it, and again return to
bed, yet all this while in a most fast sleep.   8
DOCTOR A great perturbation in nature, to receive at once
the benefit of sleep and do the effects of watching. In
this slumbery agitation besides her walking and other
actual performances, what at any time have you heard
her say?
GENTLEWOMAN That, sir, which I will not report after her.
DOCTOR You may to me; and 'tis most meet you should.
GENTLEWOMAN Neither to you nor anyone, having no
witness to confirm my speech.
    Enter Lady Macbeth with a taper
Lo you, here she comes. This is her very guise, and,
upon my life, fast asleep. Observe her. Stand close.
DOCTOR How came she by that light?   20
GENTLEWOMAN Why, it stood by her. She has light by her
continually. 'Tis her command.
DOCTOR You see her eyes are open.
GENTLEWOMAN Ay, but their sense are shut.
DOCTOR What is it she does now? Look how she rubs her
hands.   26
GENTLEWOMAN It is an accustomed action with her, to
seem thus washing her hands. I have known her
continue in this a quarter of an hour.
LADY MACBETH Yet here's a spot.   30
DOCTOR Hark, she speaks. I will set down what comes
from her to satisfy my remembrance the more strongly.
LADY MACBETH Out, damned spot; out, I say. One, two,—
why, then 'tis time to do't. Hell is murky. Fie, my lord,
fie, a soldier and afeard? What need we fear who knows
it when none can call our power to account? Yet who
would have thought the old man to have had so much
blood in him?
DOCTOR Do you mark that?   39
LADY MACBETH The Thane of Fife had a wife. Where is
she now? What, will these hands ne'er be clean? No
more o' that, my lord, no more o' that. You mar all
with this starting.
DOCTOR Go to, go to. You have known what you should
not.   45
GENTLEWOMAN She has spoke what she should not, I am
sure of that. Heaven knows what she has known.
LADY MACBETH Here's the smell of the blood still. All the
perfumes of Arabia will not sweeten this little hand. O,
O, O!   50
DOCTOR What a sigh is there! The heart is sorely charged.
GENTLEWOMAN I would not have such a heart in my
bosom for the dignity of the whole body.
DOCTOR Well, well, well.
GENTLEWOMAN Pray God it be, sir.   55
DOCTOR This disease is beyond my practice. Yet I have
known those which have walked in their sleep who
have died holily in their beds.

LADY MACBETH Wash your hands, put on your nightgown,
    look not so pale. I tell you yet again, Banquo's buried.
    He cannot come out on's grave.   61
DOCTOR Even so?
LADY MACBETH To bed, to bed. There's knocking at the
    gate. Come, come, come, come, give me your hand.
    What's done cannot be undone. To bed, to bed, to bed.
                                 Exit
DOCTOR Will she go now to bed?   66
GENTLEWOMAN Directly.
DOCTOR
    Foul whisp'rings are abroad. Unnatural deeds
    Do breed unnatural troubles; infected minds
    To their deaf pillows will discharge their secrets. 70
    More needs she the divine than the physician.
    God, God forgive us all! Look after her.
    Remove from her the means of all annoyance,
    And still keep eyes upon her. So, good night.
    My mind she has mated, and amazed my sight.   75
    I think, but dare not speak.
GENTLEWOMAN   Good night, good doctor.
                                   Exeunt

5.2   *Enter Menteith, Caithness, Angus, Lennox, soldiers,*
     with a drummer and colours
MENTEITH
    The English power is near, led on by Malcolm,
    His uncle Siward, and the good Macduff.
    Revenges burn in them, for their dear causes
    Would to the bleeding and the grim alarm
    Excite the mortified man.
ANGUS   Near Birnam Wood   5
    Shall we well meet them. That way are they coming.
CAITHNESS
    Who knows if Donalbain be with his brother?
LENNOX
    For certain, sir, he is not. I have a file
    Of all the gentry. There is Siward's son,
    And many unrough youths that even now   10
    Protest their first of manhood.
MENTEITH   What does the tyrant?
CAITHNESS
    Great Dunsinane he strongly fortifies.
    Some say he's mad, others that lesser hate him
    Do call it valiant fury; but for certain
    He cannot buckle his distempered cause   15
    Within the belt of rule.
ANGUS   Now does he feel
    His secret murders sticking on his hands.
    Now minutely revolts upbraid his faith-breach.
    Those he commands move only in command,
    Nothing in love. Now does he feel his title   20
    Hang loose about him, like a giant's robe
    Upon a dwarfish thief.
MENTEITH   Who then shall blame
    His pestered senses to recoil and start
    When all that is within him does condemn
    Itself for being there?
CAITHNESS   Well, march we on   25

To give obedience where 'tis truly owed.
Meet we the medicine of the sickly weal,
And with him pour we in our country's purge,
Each drop of us.
LENNOX   Or so much as it needs
    To dew the sovereign flower and drown the weeds. 30
    Make we our march towards Birnam.
                           Exeunt, marching

5.3   *Enter Macbeth, the Doctor of Physic, and*
     attendants
MACBETH
    Bring me no more reports. Let them fly all.
    Till Birnam Wood remove to Dunsinane
    I cannot taint with fear. What's the boy Malcolm?
    Was he not born of woman? The spirits that know
    All mortal consequences have pronounced me thus: 5
    'Fear not, Macbeth. No man that's born of woman
    Shall e'er have power upon thee.' Then fly, false
       thanes,
    And mingle with the English epicures.
    The mind I sway by and the heart I bear
    Shall never sag with doubt nor shake with fear.   10
    Enter Servant
    The devil damn thee black, thou cream-faced loon!
    Where gott'st thou that goose look?
SERVANT There is ten thousand—
MACBETH Geese, villain?
SERVANT   Soldiers, sir.   15
MACBETH
    Go prick thy face and over-red thy fear,
    Thou lily-livered boy. What soldiers, patch?
    Death of thy soul, those linen cheeks of thine
    Are counsellors to fear. What soldiers, whey-face?
SERVANT The English force, so please you.   20
MACBETH
    Take thy face hence.   *Exit Servant*
             Seyton!—I am sick at heart
    When I behold—Seyton, I say!—This push
    Will cheer me ever or disseat me now.
    I have lived long enough. My way of life
    Is fall'n into the sere, the yellow leaf,   25
    And that which should accompany old age,
    As honour, love, obedience, troops of friends,
    I must not look to have, but in their stead
    Curses, not loud but deep, mouth-honour, breath 29
    Which the poor heart would fain deny and dare not.
    Seyton!
    Enter Seyton
SEYTON What's your gracious pleasure?
MACBETH   What news more?
SEYTON
    All is confirmed, my lord, which was reported.
MACBETH
    I'll fight till from my bones my flesh be hacked.
    Give me my armour.
SEYTON 'Tis not needed yet.   35
MACBETH I'll put it on.

Send out more horses. Skirr the country round.
Hang those that talk of fear. Give me mine armour.
How does your patient, doctor?

DOCTOR   Not so sick, my lord,
As she is troubled with thick-coming fancies   40
That keep her from her rest.

MACBETH   Cure her of that.
Canst thou not minister to a mind diseased,
Pluck from the memory a rooted sorrow,
Raze out the written troubles of the brain,
And with some sweet oblivious antidote   45
Cleanse the fraught bosom of that perilous stuff
Which weighs upon the heart?

DOCTOR   Therein the patient
Must minister to himself.

MACBETH
Throw physic to the dogs; I'll none of it.
(*To an attendant*) Come, put mine armour on. Give me
    my staff.   50
Seyton, send out. Doctor, the thanes fly from me.
(*To an attendant*) Come, sir, dispatch.—If thou couldst,
    doctor, cast
The water of my land, find her disease,
And purge it to a sound and pristine health,
I would applaud thee to the very echo,   55
That should applaud again. (*To an attendant*) Pull't off,
    I say.
(*To the Doctor*) What rhubarb, cyme, or what
    purgative drug
Would scour these English hence? Hear'st thou of
    them?

DOCTOR
Ay, my good lord. Your royal preparation
Makes us hear something.

MACBETH (*To an attendant*)   Bring it after me.   60
I will not be afraid of death and bane
Till Birnam Forest come to Dunsinane.

DOCTOR (*aside*)
Were I from Dunsinane away and clear,
Profit again should hardly draw me here.   *Exeunt*

5.4   *Enter Malcolm, Siward, Macduff, Siward's Son,*
        Menteith, Caithness, Angus, and soldiers,
        marching, with a drummer and colours

MALCOLM
Cousins, I hope the days are near at hand
That chambers will be safe.

MENTEITH   We doubt it nothing.

SIWARD
What wood is this before us?

MENTEITH   The wood of Birnam.

MALCOLM
Let every soldier hew him down a bough
And bear't before him. Thereby shall we shadow   5
The numbers of our host, and make discovery
Err in report of us.

A SOLDIER   It shall be done.

SIWARD
We learn no other but the confident tyrant
Keeps still in Dunsinane, and will endure
Our setting down before't.

MALCOLM   'Tis his main hope,   10
For where there is advantage to be gone,
Both more and less have given him the revolt,
And none serve with him but constrainèd things,
Whose hearts are absent too.

MACDUFF   Let our just censures
Attend the true event, and put we on   15
Industrious soldiership.

SIWARD   The time approaches
That will with due decision make us know
What we shall say we have, and what we owe.
Thoughts speculative their unsure hopes relate,
But certain issue strokes must arbitrate;   20
Towards which, advance the war.   *Exeunt, marching*

5.5   *Enter Macbeth, Seyton, and soldiers, with a*
        drummer and colours

MACBETH
Hang out our banners on the outward walls.
The cry is still 'They come.' Our castle's strength
Will laugh a siege to scorn. Here let them lie
Till famine and the ague eat them up.
Were they not forced with those that should be ours   5
We might have met them dareful, beard to beard,
And beat them backward home.
      A cry within of women
                          What is that noise?

SEYTON
It is the cry of women, my good lord.   ⌈*Exit*⌉

MACBETH
I have almost forgot the taste of fears.
The time has been my senses would have cooled   10
To hear a night-shriek, and my fell of hair
Would at a dismal treatise rouse and stir
As life were in't. I have supped full with horrors.
Direness, familiar to my slaughterous thoughts,
Cannot once start me.
      ⌈*Enter Seyton*⌉
                  Wherefore was that cry?   15

SEYTON
The Queen, my lord, is dead.

MACBETH   She should have died hereafter.
There would have been a time for such a word.
Tomorrow, and tomorrow, and tomorrow
Creeps in this petty pace from day to day
To the last syllable of recorded time,   20
And all our yesterdays have lighted fools
The way to dusty death. Out, out, brief candle.
Life's but a walking shadow, a poor player
That struts and frets his hour upon the stage,
And then is heard no more. It is a tale   25
Told by an idiot, full of sound and fury,
Signifying nothing.

Enter a Messenger
                Thou com'st to use
Thy tongue: thy story quickly.
MESSENGER   Gracious my lord,
  I should report that which I say I saw,
  But know not how to do't.
MACBETH   Well, say, sir.   30
MESSENGER
  As I did stand my watch upon the hill
  I looked toward Birnam, and anon methought
  The wood began to move.
MACBETH   Liar and slave!
MESSENGER
  Let me endure your wrath if't be not so.
  Within this three mile may you see it coming.   35
  I say, a moving grove.
MACBETH   If thou speak'st false
  Upon the next tree shalt thou hang alive
  Till famine cling thee. If thy speech be sooth,
  I care not if thou dost for me as much.
  I pall in resolution, and begin   40
  To doubt th'equivocation of the fiend,
  That lies like truth. 'Fear not till Birnam Wood
  Do come to Dunsinane'—and now a wood
  Comes toward Dunsinane. Arm, arm, and out.
  If this which he avouches does appear   45
  There is nor flying hence nor tarrying here.
  I 'gin to be aweary of the sun,
  And wish th'estate o'th' world were now undone.
  Ring the alarum bell. ⌈*Alarums*⌉ Blow wind, come wrack,
  At least we'll die with harness on our back.   *Exeunt*

5.6 *Enter Malcolm, Siward, Macduff, and their army*
      with boughs, with a drummer and colours
MALCOLM
  Now near enough. Your leafy screens throw down,
  And show like those you are.
      ⌈*They throw down the boughs*⌉
                      You, worthy uncle,
  Shall with my cousin, your right noble son,
  Lead our first battle. Worthy Macduff and we
  Shall take upon's what else remains to do   5
  According to our order.
SIWARD   Fare you well.
  Do we but find the tyrant's power tonight,
  Let us be beaten if we cannot fight.
MACDUFF
  Make all our trumpets speak, give them all breath,
  Those clamorous harbingers of blood and death.   10
                  Exeunt. Alarums continued

5.7 *Enter Macbeth*
MACBETH
  They have tied me to a stake. I cannot fly,
  But bear-like I must fight the course. What's he
  That was not born of woman? Such a one
  Am I to fear, or none.

Enter Young Siward
YOUNG SIWARD What is thy name?   5
MACBETH Thou'lt be afraid to hear it.
YOUNG SIWARD
  No, though thou call'st thyself a hotter name
  Than any is in hell.
MACBETH   My name's Macbeth.
YOUNG SIWARD
  The devil himself could not pronounce a title
  More hateful to mine ear.
MACBETH   No, nor more fearful.   10
YOUNG SIWARD
  Thou liest, abhorrèd tyrant. With my sword
  I'll prove the lie thou speak'st.
      They fight, and Young Siward is slain
MACBETH   Thou wast born of woman,
  But swords I smile at, weapons laugh to scorn,
  Brandished by man that's of a woman born.
                      Exit ⌈*with the body*⌉

5.8 *Alarums. Enter Macduff*
MACDUFF
  That way the noise is. Tyrant, show thy face!
  If thou beest slain and with no stroke of mine,
  My wife and children's ghosts will haunt me still.
  I cannot strike at wretched kerns, whose arms
  Are hired to bear their staves. Either thou, Macbeth, 5
  Or else my sword with an unbattered edge
  I sheathe again undeeded. There thou shouldst be;
  By this great clatter one of greatest note
  Seems bruited. Let me find him, fortune,   9
  And more I beg not.   *Exit. Alarums*

5.9 *Enter Malcolm and Siward*
SIWARD
  This way, my lord. The castle's gently rendered.
  The tyrant's people on both sides do fight.
  The noble thanes do bravely in the war.
  The day almost itself professes yours,
  And little is to do.
MALCOLM   We have met with foes   5
  That strike beside us.
SIWARD   Enter, sir, the castle.
                          Exeunt. Alarum

5.10 *Enter Macbeth*
MACBETH
  Why should I play the Roman fool, and die
  On mine own sword? Whiles I see lives, the gashes
  Do better upon them.
      Enter Macduff
MACDUFF   Turn, hell-hound, turn.
MACBETH
  Of all men else I have avoided thee.
  But get thee back. My soul is too much charged   5
  With blood of thine already.
MACDUFF   I have no words;

My voice is in my sword, thou bloodier villain
Than terms can give thee out.
They fight ; alarum

MACBETH   Thou losest labour.
As easy mayst thou the intrenchant air
With thy keen sword impress as make me bleed.   10
Let fall thy blade on vulnerable crests;
I bear a charmèd life, which must not yield
To one of woman born.

MACDUFF   Despair thy charm,
And let the angel whom thou still hast served
Tell thee Macduff was from his mother's womb   15
Untimely ripped.

MACBETH
Accursèd be that tongue that tells me so,
For it hath cowed my better part of man;
And be these juggling fiends no more believed,
That palter with us in a double sense,   20
That keep the word of promise to our ear
And break it to our hope. I'll not fight with thee.

MACDUFF Then yield thee, coward,
And live to be the show and gaze o'th' time.
We'll have thee as our rarer monsters are,   25
Painted upon a pole, and underwrit
'Here may you see the tyrant.'

MACBETH   I will not yield
To kiss the ground before young Malcolm's feet,
And to be baited with the rabble's curse.
Though Birnam Wood be come to Dunsinane,   30
And thou opposed being of no woman born,
Yet I will try the last. Before my body
I throw my warlike shield. Lay on, Macduff,
And damned be him that first cries 'Hold, enough!'
Exeunt fighting. Alarums

*They enter fighting, and Macbeth is slain. ⌈Exit
Macduff with Macbeth's body⌉*

5.11 *Retreat and flourish. Enter with a drummer and colours
Malcolm, Siward, Ross, thanes, and soldiers*

MALCOLM
I would the friends we miss were safe arrived.

SIWARD
Some must go off; and yet by these I see
So great a day as this is cheaply bought.

MALCOLM
Macduff is missing, and your noble son.

ROSS (*to Siward*)
Your son, my lord, has paid a soldier's debt.   5

He only lived but till he was a man,
The which no sooner had his prowess confirmed
In the unshrinking station where he fought,
But like a man he died.

SIWARD   Then he is dead?

ROSS
Ay, and brought off the field. Your cause of sorrow   10
Must not be measured by his worth, for then
It hath no end.

SIWARD   Had he his hurts before?

ROSS
Ay, on the front.

SIWARD   Why then, God's soldier be he.
Had I as many sons as I have hairs
I would not wish them to a fairer death;   15
And so his knell is knolled.

MALCOLM   He's worth more sorrow,
And that I'll spend for him.

SIWARD   He's worth no more.
They say he parted well and paid his score,
And so God be with him. Here comes newer comfort.
Enter Macduff with Macbeth's head

MACDUFF (*to Malcolm*)
Hail, King, for so thou art. Behold where stands   20
Th'usurper's cursèd head. The time is free.
I see thee compassed with thy kingdom's pearl,
That speak my salutation in their minds,
Whose voices I desire aloud with mine:
Hail, King of Scotland!

ALL BUT MALCOLM   Hail, King of Scotland!   25
Flourish

MALCOLM
We shall not spend a large expense of time
Before we reckon with your several loves
And make us even with you. My thanes and kinsmen,
Henceforth be earls, the first that ever Scotland
In such an honour named. What's more to do   30
Which would be planted newly with the time,
As calling home our exiled friends abroad,
That fled the snares of watchful tyranny,
Producing forth the cruel ministers
Of this dead butcher and his fiend-like queen—   35
Who, as 'tis thought, by self and violent hands
Took off her life—this and what needful else
That calls upon us, by the grace of grace
We will perform in measure, time, and place.
So thanks to all at once, and to each one,   40
Whom we invite to see us crowned at Scone.
Flourish. Exeunt Omnes

ANTONY AND CLEOPATRA

FIRST printed in the 1623 Folio, *Antony and Cleopatra* had been entered on the Stationers' Register on 20 May 1608. Echoes of it in Barnabe Barnes's tragedy *The Devil's Charter*, acted by Shakespeare's company in February 1607, suggest that Shakespeare wrote his play no later than 1606, and stylistic evidence supports that date.

The Life of Marcus Antonius in Sir Thomas North's translation of Plutarch's *Lives of the Noble Grecians and Romans* (1579) was one of the sources for *Julius Caesar*; it also provided Shakespeare with most of his material for *Antony and Cleopatra*, in which he draws upon its language to a remarkable extent even in some of the play's most poetic passages. For example, Enobarbus' famous description of Cleopatra in her barge (2.2.197-224) incorporates phrase after phrase of North's prose. And the play's action stays close to North's account, though with significant adjustments, particularly compressions of the time-scheme. It opens in 40 BC, two years after the end of *Julius Caesar*, and portrays events that took place over a period of ten years. Mark Antony has become an older man, though Octavius is still 'scarce-bearded'. Plutarch, who was a connoisseur of human behaviour, also afforded many hints for the characterization; but some characters, particularly Antony's comrade Domitius Enobarbus and Cleopatra's women, Charmian and Iras, are largely created by Shakespeare.

In the earlier play, Mark Antony had formed a triumvirate with Octavius Caesar and Lepidus. In *Antony and Cleopatra* the triumvirate is in a state of disintegration, partly because Mark Antony—married at the play's opening to Fulvia, who is rebelling against Octavius Caesar—is infatuated with Cleopatra, Queen of Egypt (and the former mistress of Julius Caesar). The play's action swings between Rome and Alexandria as Antony is torn between the claims of Rome—strengthened for a while by his marriage, after Fulvia's death, to Octavius Caesar's sister Octavia—and the temptations of Egypt. Gradually opposition between Antony and Octavius increases, until they engage in a sea-fight near Actium (in Greece), in which Antony follows Cleopatra's navy in ignominious retreat. The closing stages of the double tragedy portray Antony's shame, humiliation, and suicide after Cleopatra falsely causes him to believe that she has killed herself; faced with the threat that Caesar will take her captive to Rome, Cleopatra too commits suicide. According to Plutarch, she was thirty-eight years old; as for Antony, 'some say that he lived three-and-fifty years, and others say, six-and-fifty'.

In *Antony and Cleopatra* the classical restraint of *Julius Caesar* gives way to a fine excess of language, of dramatic action, and of individual behaviour. The style is hyperbolical, overflowing the measure of the iambic pentameter. The action is amazingly fluid, shifting with an ease and rapidity that caused bewilderment to ages unfamiliar with the conventions of Shakespeare's theatre. And the characterization is correspondingly extravagant, delighting in the quirks of individual behaviour, above all in the paradoxes and inconsistencies of the Egyptian queen who contains within herself the capacity for every extreme of feminine behaviour, from vanity, meanness, and frivolity to the sublime self-transcendence with which she faces and embraces death.

THE PERSONS OF THE PLAY

Mark ANTONY (Marcus Antonius), triumvir of Rome

DEMETRIUS ⎫
PHILO
Domitius ENOBARBUS
VENTIDIUS
SILIUS ⎬ friends and followers of Antony
EROS
CAMIDIUS
SCARUS
DECRETAS ⎭

Octavius CAESAR, triumvir of Rome

OCTAVIA, his sister

MAECENAS ⎫
AGRIPPA
TAURUS
DOLABELLA ⎬ friends and followers of Caesar
THIDIAS
GALLUS
PROCULEIUS ⎭

LEPIDUS, triumvir of Rome

Sextus POMPEY (Pompeius)

MENECRATES ⎫
MENAS ⎬ friends of Pompey
VARRIUS ⎭

CLEOPATRA, Queen of Egypt

CHARMIAN ⎫
IRAS
ALEXAS
MARDIAN, a eunuch ⎬ attending on Cleopatra
DIOMED
SELEUCUS ⎭

A SOOTHSAYER

An AMBASSADOR

MESSENGERS

A BOY who sings

A SENTRY and men of his WATCH

Men of the GUARD

An EGYPTIAN

A CLOWN

SERVANTS

SOLDIERS

Eunuchs, attendants, captains, soldiers, servants

The Tragedy of Antony and Cleopatra

1.1 *Enter Demetrius and Philo*

PHILO

Nay, but this dotage of our General's
O'erflows the measure. Those his goodly eyes,
That o'er the files and musters of the war
Have glowed like plated Mars, now bend, now turn
The office and devotion of their view   5
Upon a tawny front. His captain's heart,
Which in the scuffles of great fights hath burst
The buckles on his breast, reneges all temper,
And is become the bellows and the fan
To cool a gipsy's lust.
          Flourish. Enter Antony, Cleopatra, her ladies, the
          train, with eunuchs fanning her
                    Look where they come.   10
Take but good note, and you shall see in him
The triple pillar of the world transformed
Into a strumpet's fool. Behold and see.

CLEOPATRA *(to Antony)*

If it be love indeed, tell me how much.

ANTONY

There's beggary in the love that can be reckoned.   15

CLEOPATRA

I'll set a bourn how far to be beloved.

ANTONY

Then must thou needs find out new heaven, new earth.
          Enter a Messenger

MESSENGER News, my good lord, from Rome.

ANTONY Grates me: the sum.

CLEOPATRA Nay, hear them, Antony.   20
Fulvia perchance is angry; or who knows
If the scarce-bearded Caesar have not sent
His powerful mandate to you: 'Do this, or this,
Take in that kingdom and enfranchise that.
Perform't, or else we damn thee.'

ANTONY How, my love?   25

CLEOPATRA Perchance? Nay, and most like.
You must not stay here longer. Your dismission
Is come from Caesar, therefore hear it, Antony.
Where's Fulvia's process—Caesar's, I would say—
          both?   30
Call in the messengers. As I am Egypt's queen,
Thou blushest, Antony, and that blood of thine
Is Caesar's homager; else so thy cheek pays shame
When shrill-tongued Fulvia scolds. The messengers!

ANTONY

Let Rome in Tiber melt, and the wide arch   35
Of the ranged empire fall. Here is my space.
Kingdoms are clay. Our dungy earth alike
Feeds beast as man. The nobleness of life
Is to do thus; when such a mutual pair
And such a twain can do't—in which I bind   40

On pain of punishment the world to weet—
We stand up peerless.

CLEOPATRA *(aside)*   Excellent falsehood!
Why did he marry Fulvia and not love her?
I'll seem the fool I am not. *(To Antony)* Antony
Will be himself.

ANTONY   But stirred by Cleopatra.   45
Now, for the love of Love and her soft hours
Let's not confound the time with conference harsh.
There's not a minute of our lives should stretch
Without some pleasure now. What sport tonight?

CLEOPATRA

Hear the ambassadors.

ANTONY   Fie, wrangling queen,   50
Whom everything becomes—to chide, to laugh,
To weep; how every passion fully strives
To make itself, in thee, fair and admired!
No messenger but thine; and all alone
Tonight we'll wander through the streets and note   55
The qualities of people. Come, my queen.
Last night you did desire it. *(To the Messenger)* Speak
          not to us.
          Exeunt Antony and Cleopatra with the train,
          ⌐and by another door the Messenger⌐

DEMETRIUS

Is Caesar with Antonius prized so slight?

PHILO

Sir, sometimes when he is not Antony
He comes too short of that great property   60
Which still should go with Antony.

DEMETRIUS   ·   I am full sorry
That he approves the common liar who
Thus speaks of him at Rome; but I will hope
Of better deeds tomorrow. Rest you happy.   *Exeunt*

1.2 *Enter Enobarbus, a Soothsayer, Charmian, Iras,*
          Mardian the eunuch, Alexas, ⌐and attendants⌐

CHARMIAN Lord Alexas, sweet Alexas, most anything
          Alexas, almost most absolute Alexas, where's the
          soothsayer that you praised so to th' Queen?
          O that I knew this husband, which you say
          Must charge his horns with garlands!   5

ALEXAS   Soothsayer!   5

SOOTHSAYER Your will?

CHARMIAN
          Is this the man? Is't you, sir, that know things?

SOOTHSAYER
          In nature's infinite book of secrecy
          A little I can read.

ALEXAS *(to Charmian)* Show him your hand.   10

ENOBARBUS *(calling)* Bring in the banquet quickly,
          Wine enough Cleopatra's health to drink.
          ⌐*Enter servants with food and wine, and exeunt*⌐

CHARMIAN (*to Soothsayer*) Good sir, give me good fortune.

SOOTHSAYER I make not, but foresee.

CHARMIAN
Pray then, foresee me one.

SOOTHSAYER   You shall be yet   15
Far fairer than you are.

CHARMIAN   He means in flesh.

IRAS
No, you shall paint when you are old.

CHARMIAN   Wrinkles forbid!

ALEXAS
Vex not his prescience. Be attentive.

CHARMIAN   Hush!

SOOTHSAYER
You shall be more beloving than beloved.

CHARMIAN I had rather heat my liver with drinking.   20

ALEXAS Nay, hear him.

CHARMIAN Good now, some excellent fortune! Let me be
married to three kings in a forenoon and widow them
all. Let me have a child at fifty to whom Herod of Jewry
may do homage. Find me to marry me with Octavius
Caesar, and companion me with my mistress.   26

SOOTHSAYER
You shall outlive the lady whom you serve.

CHARMIAN O, excellent! I love long life better than figs.

SOOTHSAYER
You have seen and proved a fairer former fortune
Than that which is to approach.   30

CHARMIAN Then belike my children shall have no names.
Prithee, how many boys and wenches must I have?

SOOTHSAYER
If every of your wishes had a womb,
And fertile every wish, a million.

CHARMIAN Out, fool—I forgive thee for a witch.   35

ALEXAS You think none but your sheets are privy to your
wishes.

CHARMIAN (*to the Soothsayer*) Nay, come, tell Iras hers.

ALEXAS We'll know all our fortunes.

ENOBARBUS Mine, and most of our fortunes, tonight shall
be drunk to bed.   41

IRAS (*showing her hand to the Soothsayer*) There's a palm
presages chastity, if nothing else.

CHARMIAN E'en as the o'erflowing Nilus presageth famine.

IRAS Go, you wild bedfellow, you cannot soothsay.   45

CHARMIAN Nay, if an oily palm be not a fruitful prognostication, I cannot scratch mine ear. (*To the Soothsayer*)
Prithee, tell her but a workaday fortune.

SOOTHSAYER Your fortunes are alike.

IRAS
But how, but how? Give me particulars.   50

SOOTHSAYER I have said.

IRAS Am I not an inch of fortune better than she?

CHARMIAN Well, if you were but an inch of fortune better
than I, where would you choose it?

IRAS Not in my husband's nose.   55

CHARMIAN Our worser thoughts heavens mend! Alexas—
come, his fortune, his fortune. O, let him marry a
woman that cannot go, sweet Isis, I beseech thee, and
let her die too, and give him a worse, and let worse
follow worse till the worst of all follow him laughing
to his grave, fiftyfold a cuckold. Good Isis, hear me this
prayer, though thou deny me a matter of more weight;
good Isis, I beseech thee.

IRAS Amen, dear goddess, hear that prayer of the people.
For as it is a heart-breaking to see a handsome man
loose-wived, so it is a deadly sorrow to behold a foul
knave uncuckolded. Therefore, dear Isis, keep decorum,
and fortune him accordingly.   68

CHARMIAN Amen.

ALEXAS Lo now, if it lay in their hands to make me a
cuckold, they would make themselves whores but
they'd do't.

Enter Cleopatra

ENOBARBUS
Hush, here comes Antony.

CHARMIAN   Not he, the Queen.

CLEOPATRA
Saw you my lord?

ENOBARBUS   No, lady.

CLEOPATRA   Was he not here?

CHARMIAN No, madam.   75

CLEOPATRA
He was disposed to mirth, but on the sudden
A Roman thought hath struck him. Enobarbus!

ENOBARBUS Madam?

CLEOPATRA
Seek him, and bring him hither. Where's Alexas?

ALEXAS
Here at your service. My lord approaches.   80

Enter Antony with a Messenger

CLEOPATRA
We will not look upon him. Go with us.

Exeunt all but Antony and the Messenger

MESSENGER
Fulvia thy wife first came into the field.

ANTONY Against my brother Lucius?

MESSENGER
Ay, but soon that war had end, and the time's state
Made friends of them, jointing their force 'gainst
Caesar,   85
Whose better issue in the war from Italy
Upon the first encounter drave them.

ANTONY   Well, what worst?

MESSENGER
The nature of bad news infects the teller.

ANTONY
When it concerns the fool or coward. On.
Things that are past are done. With me 'tis thus: 90
Who tells me true, though in his tale lie death,
I hear him as he flattered.

MESSENGER   Labienus—
This is stiff news—hath with his Parthian force
Extended Asia; from Euphrates   95
His conquering banner shook, from Syria

To Lydia and to Ionia,
Whilst—
ANTONY   Antony, thou wouldst say—
MESSENGER   O, my lord!
ANTONY
Speak to me home. Mince not the general tongue.
Name Cleopatra as she is called in Rome.   100
Rail thou in Fulvia's phrase, and taunt my faults
With such full licence as both truth and malice
Have power to utter. O, then we bring forth weeds
When our quick winds lie still, and our ills told us
Is as our earing. Fare thee well a while.   105
MESSENGER At your noble pleasure.   *Exit Messenger*
          Enter another Messenger
ANTONY
From Sicyon, ho, the news? Speak there.
⌜SECOND MESSENGER⌝
The man from Sicyon—
⌜ANTONY⌝   Is there such a one?
⌜SECOND MESSENGER⌝
He stays upon your will.
ANTONY   Let him appear.
                          Exit Second Messenger
These strong Egyptian fetters I must break,   110
Or lose myself in dotage.
          Enter another Messenger with a letter
                          What are you?
⌜THIRD MESSENGER⌝
Fulvia thy wife is dead.
ANTONY   Where died she?
THIRD MESSENGER In Sicyon.
Her length of sickness, with what else more serious
Importeth thee to know, this bears.
          He gives Antony the letter
ANTONY   Forbear me.   115
                      ⌜*Exit Third Messenger*⌝
There's a great spirit gone. Thus did I desire it.
What our contempts doth often hurl from us
We wish it ours again. The present pleasure,
By revolution low'ring, does become
The opposite of itself. She's good being gone;   120
The hand could pluck her back that shoved her on.
I must from this enchanting queen break off.
Ten thousand harms more than the ills I know
My idleness doth hatch. How now, Enobarbus!   124
          ⌜*Enter Enobarbus*⌝
ENOBARBUS
What's your pleasure, sir?
ANTONY   I must with haste from hence.
ENOBARBUS Why, then we kill all our women. We see
how mortal an unkindness is to them; if they suffer
our departure, death's the word.
ANTONY I must be gone.   129
ENOBARBUS Under a compelling occasion let women die.
It were pity to cast them away for nothing, though
between them and a great cause they should be
esteemed nothing. Cleopatra catching but the least
noise of this dies instantly. I have seen her die twenty

times upon far poorer moment. I do think there is
mettle in death, which commits some loving act upon
her, she hath such a celerity in dying.   137
ANTONY She is cunning past man's thought.
ENOBARBUS Alack, sir, no. Her passions are made of
nothing but the finest part of pure love. We cannot call
her winds and waters sighs and tears; they are greater
storms and tempests than almanacs can report. This
cannot be cunning in her; if it be, she makes a shower
of rain as well as Jove.
ANTONY Would I had never seen her!   145
ENOBARBUS O, sir, you had then left unseen a wonderful
piece of work, which not to have been blessed withal
would have discredited your travel.
ANTONY Fulvia is dead.
ENOBARBUS Sir.   150
ANTONY Fulvia is dead.
ENOBARBUS Fulvia?
ANTONY Dead.
ENOBARBUS Why, sir, give the gods a thankful sacrifice.
When it pleaseth their deities to take the wife of a man
from him, it shows to man the tailors of the earth;
comforting therein that when old robes are worn out
there are members to make new. If there were no more
women but Fulvia, then had you indeed a cut, and the
case to be lamented. This grief is crowned with consola-
tion; your old smock brings forth a new petticoat, and
indeed the tears live in an onion that should water this
sorrow.
ANTONY
The business she hath broachèd in the state
Cannot endure my absence.   165
ENOBARBUS And the business you have broached here
cannot be without you, especially that of Cleopatra's,
which wholly depends on your abode.
ANTONY
No more light answers. Let our officers
Have notice what we purpose. I shall break   170
The cause of our expedience to the Queen,
And get her leave to part; for not alone
The death of Fulvia, with more urgent touches,
Do strongly speak to us, but the letters too
Of many our contriving friends in Rome   175
Petition us at home. Sextus Pompeius
Hath given the dare to Caesar and commands
The empire of the sea. Our slippery people,
Whose love is never linked to the deserver
Till his deserts are past, begin to throw   180
Pompey the Great and all his dignities
Upon his son, who—high in name and power,
Higher than both in blood and life—stands up
For the main soldier; whose quality, going on,   184
The sides o'th' world may danger. Much is breeding
Which, like the courser's hair, hath yet but life,
And not a serpent's poison. Say our pleasure,
To such whose place is under us, requires
Our quick remove from hence.
ENOBARBUS   I shall do't.
                          Exeunt severally

1.3   *Enter Cleopatra, Charmian, Alexas, and Iras*

CLEOPATRA
  Where is he?
CHARMIAN   I did not see him since.
CLEOPATRA ⌈*to Alexas*⌉
  See where he is, who's with him, what he does.
  I did not send you. If you find him sad,
  Say I am dancing; if in mirth, report
  That I am sudden sick. Quick, and return.   5
                                Exit ⌈*Alexas*⌉
CHARMIAN
  Madam, methinks, if you did love him dearly,
  You do not hold the method to enforce
  The like from him.
CLEOPATRA   What should I do I do not?
CHARMIAN
  In each thing give him way; cross him in nothing.
CLEOPATRA
  Thou teachest like a fool, the way to lose him.   10
CHARMIAN
  Tempt him not so too far. Iwis, forbear.
  In time we hate that which we often fear.
        Enter Antony
  But here comes Antony.
CLEOPATRA   I am sick and sullen.
ANTONY
  I am sorry to give breathing to my purpose.
CLEOPATRA
  Help me away, dear Charmian, I shall fall.   15
  It cannot be thus long—the sides of nature
  Will not sustain it.
ANTONY   Now, my dearest queen.
CLEOPATRA
  Pray you, stand farther from me.
ANTONY   What's the matter?
CLEOPATRA
  I know by that same eye there's some good news.
  What says the married woman—you may go?   20
  Would she had never given you leave to come.
  Let her not say 'tis I that keep you here.
  I have no power upon you; hers you are.
ANTONY
  The gods best know—
CLEOPATRA   O, never was there queen
  So mightily betrayed! Yet at the first   25
  I saw the treasons planted.
ANTONY   Cleopatra—
CLEOPATRA
  Why should I think you can be mine and true—
  Though you in swearing shake the thrònèd gods—
  Who have been false to Fulvia? Riotous madness,
  To be entangled with those mouth-made vows   30
  Which break themselves in swearing.
ANTONY   Most sweet queen—
CLEOPATRA
  Nay, pray you, seek no colour for your going,
  But bid farewell and go. When you sued staying,
  Then was the time for words; no going then.

  Eternity was in our lips and eyes,   35
  Bliss in our brow's bent; none our parts so poor
  But was a race of heaven. They are so still,
  Or thou, the greatest soldier of the world,
  Art turned the greatest liar.
ANTONY   How now, lady!
CLEOPATRA
  I would I had thy inches. Thou shouldst know   40
  There were a heart in Egypt.
ANTONY   Hear me, Queen.
  The strong necessity of time commands
  Our services a while, but my full heart
  Remains in use with you. Our Italy
  Shines o'er with civil swords. Sextus Pompeius   45
  Makes his approaches to the port of Rome.
  Equality of two domestic powers
  Breed scrupulous faction. The hated, grown to
        strength,
  Are newly grown to love. The condemned Pompey,
  Rich in his father's honour, creeps apace   50
  Into the hearts of such as have not thrived
  Upon the present state, whose numbers threaten;
  And quietness, grown sick of rest, would purge
  By any desperate change. My more particular,
  And that which most with you should safe my going,
  Is Fulvia's death.   56
CLEOPATRA
  Though age from folly could not give me freedom,
  It does from childishness. Can Fulvia die?
ANTONY She's dead, my queen.
        He offers letters
  Look here, and at thy sovereign leisure read   60
  The garboils she awaked. At the last, best,
  See when and where she died.
CLEOPATRA   O most false love!
  Where be the sacred vials thou shouldst fill
  With sorrowful water? Now I see, I see,
  In Fulvia's death how mine received shall be.   65
ANTONY
  Quarrel no more, but be prepared to know
  The purposes I bear, which are or cease
  As you shall give th'advice. By the fire
  That quickens Nilus' slime, I go from hence
  Thy soldier-servant, making peace or war   70
  As thou affects.
CLEOPATRA   Cut my lace, Charmian, come.
  But let it be. I am quickly ill and well;
  So Antony loves.
ANTONY   My precious queen, forbear,
  And give true evidence to his love, which stands
  An honourable trial.
CLEOPATRA   So Fulvia told me.   75
  I prithee turn aside and weep for her,
  Then bid adieu to me, and say the tears
  Belong to Egypt. Good now, play one scene
  Of excellent dissembling, and let it look
  Like perfect honour.
ANTONY   You'll heat my blood. No more. 80

CLEOPATRA
You can do better yet; but this is meetly.
ANTONY
Now by my sword—
CLEOPATRA   And target. Still he mends.
But this is not the best. Look, prithee, Charmian,
How this Herculean Roman does become
The carriage of his chafe.   85
ANTONY I'll leave you, lady.
CLEOPATRA Courteous lord, one word.
Sir, you and I must part; but that's not it.
Sir, you and I have loved; but there's not it;
That you know well. Something it is I would—   90
O, my oblivion is a very Antony,
And I am all forgotten.
ANTONY   But that your royalty
Holds idleness your subject, I should take you
For idleness itself.
CLEOPATRA   'Tis sweating labour
To bear such idleness so near the heart   95
As Cleopatra this. But sir, forgive me,
Since my becomings kill me when they do not
Eye well to you. Your honour calls you hence,
Therefore be deaf to my unpitied folly,
And all the gods go with you. Upon your sword   100
Sit laurel victory, and smooth success
Be strewed before your feet.
ANTONY   Let us go.
Come. Our separation so abides and flies
That thou residing here goes yet with me,
And I hence fleeting, here remain with thee.   105
Away.   *Exeunt severally*

1.4   *Enter Octavius reading a letter, Lepidus, and their*
          train
CAESAR
You may see, Lepidus, and henceforth know,
It is not Caesar's natural vice to hate
Our great competitor. From Alexandria
This is the news: he fishes, drinks, and wastes
The lamps of night in revel; is not more manlike   5
Than Cleopatra, nor the queen of Ptolemy
More womanly than he; hardly gave audience
Or vouchsafed to think he had partners. You shall find
    there
A man who is the abstract of all faults
That all men follow.
LEPIDUS   I must not think there are   10
Evils enough to darken all his goodness.
His faults in him seem as the spots of heaven,
More fiery by night's blackness; hereditary
Rather than purchased; what he cannot change
Than what he chooses.   15
CAESAR
You are too indulgent. Let's grant it is not
Amiss to tumble on the bed of Ptolemy,
To give a kingdom for a mirth, to sit
And keep the turn of tippling with a slave,

To reel the streets at noon, and stand the buffet   20
With knaves that smells of sweat. Say this becomes
    him—
As his composure must be rare indeed
Whom these things cannot blemish—yet must Antony
No way excuse his foils when we do bear
So great weight in his lightness. If he filled   25
His vacancy with his voluptuousness,
Full surfeits and the dryness of his bones
Call on him for't. But to confound such time
That drums him from his sport, and speaks as loud
As his own state and ours—'tis to be chid   30
As we rate boys who, being mature in knowledge,
Pawn their experience to their present pleasure,
And so rebel to judgement.
          Enter a Messenger
LEPIDUS   Here's more news.
MESSENGER
Thy biddings have been done, and every hour,
Most noble Caesar, shalt thou have report   35
How 'tis abroad. Pompey is strong at sea,
And it appears he is beloved of those
That only have feared Caesar. To the ports
The discontents repair, and men's reports
Give him much wronged.   *⌈Exit⌉*
CAESAR   I should have known no less.
It hath been taught us from the primal state   41
That he which is was wished until he were,
And the ebbed man, ne'er loved till ne'er worth love,
Comes deared by being lacked. This common body,
Like to a vagabond flag upon the stream,   45
Goes to, and back, lackeying the varying tide,
To rot itself with motion.
          ⌈Enter a second Messenger⌉
SECOND MESSENGER   Caesar, I bring thee word
Menecrates and Menas, famous pirates,
Makes the sea serve them, which they ear and wound
With keels of every kind. Many hot inroads   50
They make in Italy. The borders maritime
Lack blood to think on't, and flush youth revolt.
No vessel can peep forth but 'tis as soon
Taken as seen; for Pompey's name strikes more
Than could his war resisted.   *⌈Exit⌉*
CAESAR   Antony,   55
Leave thy lascivious wassails. When thou once
Was beaten from Modena, where thou slew'st
Hirtius and Pansa, consuls, at thy heel
Did famine follow, whom thou fought'st against—
Though daintily brought up—with patience more   60
Than savages could suffer. Thou didst drink
The stale of horses, and the gilded puddle
Which beasts would cough at. Thy palate then did
    deign
The roughest berry on the rudest hedge.
Yea, like the stag when snow the pasture sheets,   65
The barks of trees thou browsed. On the Alps
It is reported thou didst eat strange flesh,
Which some did die to look on; and all this—

It wounds thine honour that I speak it now—
Was borne so like a soldier that thy cheek   70
So much as lanked not.
LEPIDUS 'Tis pity of him.
CAESAR Let his shames quickly
Drive him to Rome. 'Tis time we twain
Did show ourselves i'th' field; and to that end   75
Assemble we immediate council. Pompey
Thrives in our idleness.
LEPIDUS   Tomorrow, Caesar,
I shall be furnished to inform you rightly
Both what by sea and land I can be able
To front this present time.
CAESAR   Till which encounter   80
It is my business, too. Farewell.
LEPIDUS
Farewell, my lord. What you shall know meantime
Of stirs abroad I shall beseech you, sir,
To let me be partaker.   84
CAESAR
Doubt not, sir. I knew it for my bond.   *Exeunt*

1.5   *Enter Cleopatra, Charmian, Iras, and Mardian*
CLEOPATRA Charmian!
CHARMIAN Madam?
CLEOPATRA (*yawning*)
Ha, ha. Give me to drink mandragora.
CHARMIAN Why, madam?
CLEOPATRA
That I might sleep out this great gap of time   5
My Antony is away.
CHARMIAN   You think of him too much.
CLEOPATRA
O, 'tis treason!
CHARMIAN   Madam, I trust not so.
CLEOPATRA
Thou, eunuch Mardian!
MARDIAN   What's your highness' pleasure?
CLEOPATRA
Not now to hear thee sing. I take no pleasure
In aught an eunuch has. 'Tis well for thee   10
That, being unseminared, thy freer thoughts
May not fly forth of Egypt. Hast thou affections?
MARDIAN Yes, gracious madam.
CLEOPATRA Indeed?
MARDIAN
Not in deed, madam, for I can do nothing   15
But what indeed is honest to be done.
Yet have I fierce affections, and think
What Venus did with Mars.
CLEOPATRA   O, Charmian,
Where think'st thou he is now? Stands he or sits he?
Or does he walk? Or is he on his horse?   20
O happy horse, to bear the weight of Antony!
Do bravely, horse, for wot'st thou whom thou
      mov'st?—
The demi-Atlas of this earth, the arm
And burgonet of men. He's speaking now,

Or murmuring 'Where's my serpent of old Nile?'—   25
For so he calls me. Now I feed myself
With most delicious poison. Think on me,
That am with Phoebus' amorous pinches black,
And wrinkled deep in time. Broad-fronted Caesar,
When thou wast here above the ground I was   30
A morsel for a monarch, and great Pompey
Would stand and make his eyes grow in my brow.
There would he anchor his aspect, and die
With looking on his life.
        Enter Alexas
ALEXAS   Sovereign of Egypt, hail!
CLEOPATRA
How much unlike art thou Mark Antony!   35
Yet, coming from him, that great medicine hath
With his tinct gilded thee. How goes it
With my brave Mark Antony?
ALEXAS   Last thing he did, dear Queen,
He kissed—the last of many doubled kisses—
This orient pearl. His speech sticks in my heart.   40
CLEOPATRA
Mine ear must pluck it thence.
ALEXAS   'Good friend,' quoth he,
'Say the firm Roman to great Egypt sends
This treasure of an oyster; at whose foot,
To mend the petty present, I will piece
Her opulent throne with kingdoms. All the East,   45
Say thou, shall call her mistress.' So he nodded,
And soberly did mount an arm-jaunced steed,
Who neighed so high that what I would have spoke
Was beastly dumbed by him.
CLEOPATRA   What, was he sad or merry?
ALEXAS
Like to the time o'th' year between the extremes   50
Of hot and cold, he was nor sad nor merry.
CLEOPATRA
O well divided disposition! Note him,
Note him, good Charmian, 'tis the man; but note him.
He was not sad, for he would shine on those
That make their looks by him; he was not merry,   55
Which seemed to tell them his remembrance lay
In Egypt with his joy; but between both.
O heavenly mingle! Be'st thou sad or merry,
The violence of either thee becomes;
So does it no man else. Met'st thou my posts?   60
ALEXAS
Ay, madam, twenty several messengers.
Why do you send so thick?
CLEOPATRA   Who's born that day
When I forget to send to Antony
Shall die a beggar. Ink and paper, Charmian!
Welcome, my good Alexas. Did I, Charmian,   65
Ever love Caesar so?
CHARMIAN   O, that brave Caesar!
CLEOPATRA
Be choked with such another emphasis!
Say 'the brave Antony'.
CHARMIAN   The valiant Caesar.

CLEOPATRA
  By Isis, I will give thee bloody teeth
  If thou with Caesar paragon again   70
  My man of men.
CHARMIAN   By your most gracious pardon,
  I sing but after you.
CLEOPATRA   My salad days,
  When I was green in judgement, cold in blood,
  To say as I said then. But come, away,
  Get me ink and paper.   75
  He shall have every day a several greeting,
  Or I'll unpeople Egypt.   *Exeunt*

2.1   *Enter Pompey, Menecrates, and Menas, in warlike*
       manner
POMPEY
  If the great gods be just, they shall assist
  The deeds of justest men.
⌈MENECRATES⌉   Know, worthy Pompey,
  That what they do delay they not deny.
POMPEY
  Whiles we are suitors to their throne, decays
  The thing we sue for.
⌈MENECRATES⌉   We, ignorant of ourselves,   5
  Beg often our own harms, which the wise powers
  Deny us for our good; so find we profit
  By losing of our prayers.
POMPEY   I shall do well.
  The people love me, and the sea is mine.
  My powers are crescent, and my auguring hope   10
  Says it will come to th' full. Mark Antony
  In Egypt sits at dinner, and will make
  No wars without doors. Caesar gets money where
  He loses hearts. Lepidus flatters both,
  Of both is flattered; but he neither loves,   15
  Nor either cares for him.
⌈MENAS⌉   Caesar and Lepidus
  Are in the field; a mighty strength they carry.
POMPEY
  Where have you this? 'Tis false.
⌈MENAS⌉   From Silvius, sir.
POMPEY
  He dreams. I know they are in Rome together,
  Looking for Antony. But all the charms of love,   20
  Salt Cleopatra, soften thy waned lip.
  Let witchcraft join with beauty, lust with both
  Tie up the libertine, in a field of feasts
  Keep his brain fuming; Epicurean cooks
  Sharpen with cloyless sauce his appetite,   25
  That sleep and feeding may prorogue his honour
  Even till a Lethe'd dullness—
       Enter Varrius
                How now, Varrius?
VARRIUS
  This is most certain that I shall deliver:
  Mark Antony is every hour in Rome
  Expected. Since he went from Egypt, 'tis   30
  A space for farther travel.
POMPEY   I could have given less matter

A better ear. Menas, I did not think
  This amorous surfeiter would have donned his helm
  For such a petty war. His soldiership
  Is twice the other twain. But let us rear   35
  The higher our opinion, that our stirring
  Can from the lap of Egypt's widow pluck
  The ne'er lust-wearied Antony.
MENAS   I cannot hope
  Caesar and Antony shall well greet together.
  His wife that's dead did trespasses to Caesar,   40
  His brother warred upon him, although, I think,
  Not moved by Antony.
POMPEY   I know not, Menas,
  How lesser enmities may give way to greater.
  Were't not that we stand up against them all,
  'Twere pregnant they should square between
       themselves,   45
  For they have entertainèd cause enough
  To draw their swords. But how the fear of us
  May cement their divisions, and bind up
  The petty difference, we yet not know.
  Be't as our gods will have't; it only stands   50
  Our lives upon to use our strongest hands.
  Come, Menas.   *Exeunt*

2.2   *Enter Enobarbus and Lepidus*
LEPIDUS
  Good Enobarbus, 'tis a worthy deed,
  And shall become you well, to entreat your captain
  To soft and gentle speech.
ENOBARBUS   I shall entreat him
  To answer like himself. If Caesar move him,
  Let Antony look over Caesar's head   5
  And speak as loud as Mars. By Jupiter,
  Were I the wearer of Antonio's beard
  I would not shave't today.
LEPIDUS   'Tis not a time
  For private stomaching.
ENOBARBUS   Every time
  Serves for the matter that is then born in't.   10
LEPIDUS
  But small to greater matters must give way.
ENOBARBUS
  Not if the small come first.
LEPIDUS   Your speech is passion.
  But pray you, stir no embers up. Here comes
  The noble Antony.
       Enter at one door Antony and Ventidius
ENOBARBUS   And yonder Caesar.
       Enter at another door Caesar, Maecenas, and
       Agrippa
ANTONY (*to Ventidius*)
  If we compose well here, to Parthia.   15
  Hark, Ventidius.
CAESAR   I do not know,
  Maecenas; ask Agrippa.
LEPIDUS (*to Caesar and Antony*) Noble friends,
  That which combined us was most great; and let not

A leaner action rend us. What's amiss,
May it be gently heard. When we debate   20
Our trivial difference loud, we do commit
Murder in healing wounds. Then, noble partners,
The rather for I earnestly beseech,
Touch you the sourest points with sweetest terms,
Nor curstness grow to th' matter.
ANTONY   'Tis spoken well.   25
Were we before our armies, and to fight,
I should do thus.
                    ⌜Antony and Caesar embrace.⌝ Flourish
CAESAR Welcome to Rome.
ANTONY Thank you.
CAESAR Sit.   30
ANTONY Sit, sir.
CAESAR Nay then.
                    They sit
ANTONY
I learn you take things ill which are not so,
Or being, concern you not.
CAESAR   I must be laughed at
If or for nothing or a little I   35
Should say myself offended, and with you
Chiefly i'th' world; more laughed at that I should
Once name you derogately, when to sound your name
It not concernèd me.
ANTONY
My being in Egypt, Caesar, what was't to you?   40
CAESAR
No more than my residing here at Rome
Might be to you in Egypt. Yet if you there
Did practise on my state, your being in Egypt
Might be my question.
ANTONY   How intend you 'practised'?
CAESAR
You may be pleased to catch at mine intent   45
By what did here befall me. Your wife and brother
Made wars upon me, and their contestation
Was theme for you. You were the word of war.
ANTONY
You do mistake the business. My brother never
Did urge me in his act. I did enquire it,   50
And have my learning from some true reports
That drew their swords with you. Did he not rather
Discredit my authority with yours,
And make the wars alike against my stomach,
Having alike your cause? Of this, my letters   55
Before did satisfy you. If you'll patch a quarrel,
As matter whole you have to make it with,
It must not be with this.
CAESAR   You praise yourself
By laying defects of judgement to me, but
You patched up your excuses.
ANTONY   Not so, not so.   60
I know you could not lack, I am certain on't,
Very necessity of this thought, that I,
Your partner in the cause 'gainst which he fought,

Could not with graceful eyes attend those wars
Which fronted mine own peace. As for my wife,   65
I would you had her spirit in such another.
The third o'th' world is yours, which with a snaffle
You may pace easy, but not such a wife.
ENOBARBUS Would we had all such wives, that the men
might go to wars with the women.   70
ANTONY
So much uncurbable, her garboils, Caesar,
Made out of her impatience—which not wanted
Shrewdness of policy too—I grieving grant
Did you too much disquiet, for that you must
But say I could not help it.
CAESAR   I wrote to you   75
When, rioting in Alexandria, you
Did pocket up my letters, and with taunts
Did gibe my missive out of audience.
ANTONY
Sir, he fell upon me ere admitted, then.
Three kings I had newly feasted, and did want   80
Of what I was i'th' morning; but next day
I told him of myself, which was as much
As to have asked him pardon. Let this fellow
Be nothing of our strife. If we contend,
Out of our question wipe him.
CAESAR   You have broken   85
The article of your oath, which you shall never
Have tongue to charge me with.
LEPIDUS Soft, Caesar.
ANTONY No, Lepidus, let him speak.
The honour is sacred which he talks on now,   90
Supposing that I lacked it. But on, Caesar:
The article of my oath—
CAESAR
To lend me arms and aid when I required them,
The which you both denied.
ANTONY   Neglected, rather,
And then when poisoned hours had bound me up   95
From mine own knowledge. As nearly as I may
I'll play the penitent to you, but mine honesty
Shall not make poor my greatness, nor my power
Work without it. Truth is that Fulvia,
To have me out of Egypt, made wars here,   100
For which myself, the ignorant motive, do
So far ask pardon as befits mine honour
To stoop in such a case.
LEPIDUS   'Tis noble spoken.
MAECENAS
If it might please you to enforce no further
The griefs between ye; to forget them quite   105
Were to remember that the present need
Speaks to atone you.
LEPIDUS   Worthily spoken, Maecenas.
ENOBARBUS Or if you borrow one another's love for the
instant, you may, when you hear no more words of
Pompey, return it again. You shall have time to wrangle
in when you have nothing else to do.   111

ANTONY
  Thou art a soldier only. Speak no more.
ENOBARBUS That truth should be silent I had almost forgot.
ANTONY
  You wrong this presence, therefore speak no more.
ENOBARBUS Go to, then; your considerate stone.   115
CAESAR
  I do not much dislike the matter, but
  The manner of his speech, for't cannot be
  We shall remain in friendship, our conditions
  So diff'ring in their acts. Yet if I knew
  What hoop should hold us staunch, from edge to edge
  O'th' world I would pursue it.   121
AGRIPPA Give me leave, Caesar.
CAESAR Speak, Agrippa.
AGRIPPA
  Thou hast a sister by the mother's side,
  Admired Octavia. Great Mark Antony   125
  Is now a widower.
CAESAR   Say not so, Agrippa.
  If Cleopatra heard you, your reproof
  Were well deserved of rashness.
ANTONY
  I am not married, Caesar. Let me hear
  Agrippa further speak.   130
AGRIPPA
  To hold you in perpetual amity,
  To make you brothers, and to knit your hearts
  With an unslipping knot, take Antony
  Octavia to his wife; whose beauty claims
  No worse a husband than the best of men;   135
  Whose virtue and whose general graces speak
  That which none else can utter. By this marriage
  All little jealousies which now seem great,
  And all great fears which now import their dangers,
  Would then be nothing. Truths would be tales   140
  Where now half-tales be truths. Her love to both
  Would each to other and all loves to both
  Draw after her. Pardon what I have spoke,
  For 'tis a studied, not a present thought,
  By duty ruminated.
ANTONY   Will Caesar speak?   145
CAESAR
  Not till he hears how Antony is touched
  With what is spoke already.
ANTONY What power is in Agrippa,
  If I would say 'Agrippa, be it so',
  To make this good?
CAESAR   The power of Caesar,   150
  And his power unto Octavia.
ANTONY   May I never
  To this good purpose, that so fairly shows,
  Dream of impediment! Let me have thy hand.
  Further this act of grace, and from this hour
  The heart of brothers govern in our loves   155
  And sway our great designs.
CAESAR   There's my hand.

Antony and Caesar clasp hands
  A sister I bequeath you whom no brother
  Did ever love so dearly. Let her live
  To join our kingdoms and our hearts; and never
  Fly off our loves again.
LEPIDUS   Happily, amen.   160
ANTONY
  I did not think to draw my sword 'gainst Pompey,
  For he hath laid strange courtesies and great
  Of late upon me. I must thank him only,
  Lest my remembrance suffer ill report;
  At heel of that, defy him.
LEPIDUS   Time calls upon's.   165
  Of us must Pompey presently be sought,
  Or else he seeks out us.
ANTONY   Where lies he?
CAESAR
  About the Mount Misena.
ANTONY   What is his strength
  By land?
CAESAR   Great and increasing, but by sea
  He is an absolute master.
ANTONY   So is the fame.   170
  Would we had spoke together. Haste we for it;
  Yet ere we put ourselves in arms, dispatch we
  The business we have talked of.
CAESAR   With most gladness,
  And do invite you to my sister's view,
  Whither straight I'll lead you.
ANTONY   Let us, Lepidus,   175
  Not lack your company.
LEPIDUS   Noble Antony,
  Not sickness should detain me.
          Flourish. Exeunt all but Enobarbus, Agrippa,
          and Maecenas
MAECENAS (*to Enobarbus*) Welcome from Egypt, sir.
ENOBARBUS Half the heart of Caesar, worthy Maecenas!
  My honourable friend, Agrippa!   180
AGRIPPA Good Enobarbus!
MAECENAS We have cause to be glad that matters are so
  well digested. You stayed well by't in Egypt.
ENOBARBUS Ay, sir, we did sleep day out of countenance,
  and made the night light with drinking.   185
MAECENAS Eight wild boars roasted whole at a breakfast
  and but twelve persons there—is this true?
ENOBARBUS This was but as a fly by an eagle. We had
  much more monstrous matter of feast, which worthily
  deserved noting.   190
MAECENAS She's a most triumphant lady, if report be
  square to her.
ENOBARBUS When she first met Mark Antony, she pursed
  up his heart upon the river of Cydnus.
AGRIPPA There she appeared indeed, or my reporter
  devised well for her.   196
ENOBARBUS I will tell you.
  The barge she sat in, like a burnished throne
  Burned on the water. The poop was beaten gold;

Purple the sails, and so perfumèd that   200
The winds were love-sick with them. The oars were
     silver,
Which to the tune of flutes kept stroke, and made
The water which they beat to follow faster,
As amorous of their strokes. For her own person,
It beggared all description. She did lie   205
In her pavilion—cloth of gold, of tissue—
O'er-picturing that Venus where we see
The fancy outwork nature. On each side her
Stood pretty dimpled boys, like smiling Cupids,
With divers-coloured fans whose wind did seem   210
To glow the delicate cheeks which they did cool,
And what they undid did.
AGRIPPA   O, rare for Antony!
ENOBARBUS
Her gentlewomen, like the Nereides,
So many mermaids, tended her i'th' eyes,
And made their bends adornings. At the helm   215
A seeming mermaid steers. The silken tackle
Swell with the touches of those flower-soft hands
That yarely frame the office. From the barge
A strange invisible perfume hits the sense
Of the adjacent wharfs. The city cast   220
Her people out upon her, and Antony,
Enthroned i'th' market-place, did sit alone,
Whistling to th'air, which but for vacancy
Had gone to gaze on Cleopatra too,
And made a gap in nature.
AGRIPPA   Rare Egyptian!   225
ENOBARBUS
Upon her landing Antony sent to her,
Invited her to supper. She replied
It should be better he became her guest,
Which she entreated. Our courteous Antony,
Whom ne'er the word of 'No' woman heard speak,   230
Being barbered ten times o'er, goes to the feast,
And for his ordinary pays his heart
For what his eyes eat only.
AGRIPPA   Royal wench!
She made great Caesar lay his sword to bed.
He ploughed her, and she cropped.
ENOBARBUS   I saw her once   235
Hop forty paces through the public street,
And having lost her breath, she spoke and panted,
That she did make defect perfection,
And breathless, pour breath forth.
MAECENAS   Now Antony
Must leave her utterly.
ENOBARBUS   Never. He will not.   240
Age cannot wither her, nor custom stale
Her infinite variety. Other women cloy
The appetites they feed, but she makes hungry
Where most she satisfies. For vilest things
Become themselves in her, that the holy priests   245
Bless her when she is riggish.
MAECENAS
If beauty, wisdom, modesty can settle

The heart of Antony, Octavia is
A blessèd lottery to him.
AGRIPPA   Let us go.
Good Enobarbus, make yourself my guest   250
Whilst you abide here.
ENOBARBUS   Humbly, sir, I thank you.
                                             Exeunt

2.3   *Enter Antony and Caesar ; Octavia between them*
ANTONY
The world and my great office will sometimes
Divide me from your bosom.
OCTAVIA   All which time,
Before the gods my knee shall bow my prayers
To them for you.
ANTONY   Good night, sir. My Octavia,
Read not my blemishes in the world's report.   5
I have not kept my square, but that to come
Shall all be done by th' rule. Good night, dear lady.
Good night, sir.
CAESAR Good night.   *Exeunt Caesar and Octavia*
          Enter Soothsayer
ANTONY
Now, sirrah. You do wish yourself in Egypt?   10
SOOTHSAYER
Would I had never come from thence, nor you
Gone thither.
ANTONY   If you can, your reason?
SOOTHSAYER
I see it in my motion, have it not in my tongue.
But yet hie you to Egypt again.
ANTONY   Say to me
Whose fortunes shall rise higher: Caesar's or mine? 15
SOOTHSAYER
Caesar's. Therefore, O Antony, stay not by his side.
Thy daemon, that thy spirit which keeps thee, is
Noble, courageous, high, unmatchable,
Where Caesar's is not. But near him thy angel
Becomes afeard, as being o'erpowered. Therefore   20
Make space enough between you.
ANTONY   Speak this no more.
SOOTHSAYER
To none but thee; no more but when to thee.
If thou dost play with him at any game
Thou art sure to lose; and of that natural luck
He beats thee 'gainst the odds. Thy lustre thickens   25
When he shines by. I say again, thy spirit
Is all afraid to govern thee near him;
But he away, 'tis noble.
ANTONY   Get thee gone.
Say to Ventidius I would speak with him.
                                        Exit Soothsayer
He shall to Parthia; be it art or hap,   30
He hath spoken true. The very dice obey him,
And in our sports my better cunning faints
Under his chance. If we draw lots, he speeds.
His cocks do win the battle still of mine
When it is all to nought, and his quails ever   35

Beat mine, inhooped, at odds. I will to Egypt;
And though I make this marriage for my peace,
I'th' East my pleasure lies.
    Enter Ventidius
                      O, come, Ventidius.
You must to Parthia, your commission's ready.   39
Follow me, and receive't.   *Exeunt*

2.4   *Enter Lepidus, Maecenas, and Agrippa*
LEPIDUS
Trouble yourselves no further. Pray you, hasten
Your generals after.
AGRIPPA   Sir, Mark Antony
Will e'en but kiss Octavia, and we'll follow.
LEPIDUS
Till I shall see you in your soldier's dress,
Which will become you both, farewell.
MAECENAS   We shall,   5
As I conceive the journey, be at the Mount
Before you, Lepidus.
LEPIDUS   Your way is shorter.
My purposes do draw me much about.
You'll win two days upon me.
MAECENAS *and* AGRIPPA   Sir, good success.
LEPIDUS Farewell.   10
      Exeunt Maecenas and Agrippa at one door,
                Lepidus at another

2.5   *Enter Cleopatra, Charmian, Iras, and Alexas*
CLEOPATRA
Give me some music—music, moody food
Of us that trade in love.
CHARMIAN, IRAS, *and* ALEXAS The music, ho!
    Enter Mardian, the eunuch
CLEOPATRA
Let it alone. Let's to billiards. Come, Charmian.
CHARMIAN
My arm is sore. Best play with Mardian.
CLEOPATRA
As well a woman with an eunuch played   5
As with a woman. Come, you'll play with me, sir?
MARDIAN As well as I can, madam.
CLEOPATRA
And when good will is showed, though't come too
    short
The actor may plead pardon. I'll none now.
Give me mine angle. We'll to th' river. There,   10
My music playing far off, I will betray
Tawny-finned fishes. My bended hook shall pierce
Their slimy jaws, and as I draw them up
I'll think them every one an Antony,
And say 'Ah ha, you're caught!'
CHARMIAN   'Twas merry when 15
You wagered on your angling, when your diver
Did hang a salt fish on his hook, which he
With fervency drew up.
CLEOPATRA   That time—O times!—
I laughed him out of patience, and that night
I laughed him into patience, and next morn,   20

Ere the ninth hour, I drunk him to his bed,
Then put my tires and mantles on him whilst
I wore his sword Philippan.
    Enter a Messenger
                  O, from Italy.
Ram thou thy fruitful tidings in mine ears,
That long time have been barren.
MESSENGER   Madam, madam! 25
CLEOPATRA
Antonio's dead. If thou say so, villain,
Thou kill'st thy mistress; but well and free,
If thou so yield him, there is gold, and here
My bluest veins to kiss—a hand that kings
Have lipped, and trembled kissing.
MESSENGER   First, madam, he is well.
CLEOPATRA
Why, there's more gold. But, sirrah, mark: we use 31
To say the dead are well. Bring it to that,
The gold I give thee will I melt and pour
Down thy ill-uttering throat.
MESSENGER Good madam, hear me.   35
CLEOPATRA Well, go to, I will.
But there's no goodness in thy face. If Antony
Be free and healthful, so tart a favour
To trumpet such good tidings! If not well,
Thou shouldst come like a Fury crowned with snakes,
Not like a formal man.
MESSENGER   Will't please you hear me?   41
CLEOPATRA
I have a mind to strike thee ere thou speak'st.
Yet if thou say Antony lives, is well,
Or friends with Caesar, or not captive to him,
I'll set thee in a shower of gold, and hail   45
Rich pearls upon thee.
MESSENGER   Madam, he's well.
CLEOPATRA   Well said.
MESSENGER
And friends with Caesar.
CLEOPATRA   Thou'rt an honest man.
MESSENGER
Caesar and he are greater friends than ever.
CLEOPATRA
Make thee a fortune from me.
MESSENGER   But yet, madam—
CLEOPATRA
I do not like 'But yet'; it does allay   50
The good precedence. Fie upon 'But yet'.
'But yet' is as a jailer to bring forth
Some monstrous malefactor. Prithee, friend,
Pour out the pack of matter to mine ear,
The good and bad together. He's friends with Caesar,
In state of health, thou sayst; and, thou sayst, free. 56
MESSENGER
Free, madam? No, I made no such report.
He's bound unto Octavia.
CLEOPATRA   For what good turn?
MESSENGER
For the best turn i'th' bed.
CLEOPATRA   I am pale, Charmian.

MESSENGER
Madam, he's married to Octavia.   60
CLEOPATRA
The most infectious pestilence upon thee!
She strikes him down
MESSENGER
Good madam, patience!'
CLEOPATRA   What say you?
She strikes him
Hence, horrible villain, or I'll spurn thine eyes
Like balls before me. I'll unhair thy head,
She hales him up and down
Thou shalt be whipped with wire and stewed in brine,
Smarting in ling'ring pickle.
MESSENGER   Gracious madam,   66
I that do bring the news made not the match.
CLEOPATRA
Say 'tis not so, a province I will give thee,
And make thy fortunes proud. The blow thou hadst
Shall make thy peace for moving me to rage,   70
And I will boot thee with what gift beside
Thy modesty can beg.
MESSENGER   He's married, madam.
CLEOPATRA
Rogue, thou hast lived too long.
She draws a knife
MESSENGER   Nay then, I'll run.
What mean you, madam? I have made no fault.   *Exit*
CHARMIAN
Good madam, keep yourself within yourself.   75
The man is innocent.
CLEOPATRA
Some innocents 'scape not the thunderbolt.
Melt Egypt into Nile, and kindly creatures
Turn all to serpents! Call the slave again.
Though I am mad I will not bite him. Call!   80
CHARMIAN
He is afeard to come.
CLEOPATRA   I will not hurt him.
                          ⌈*Exit Charmian*⌉
These hands do lack nobility that they strike
A meaner than myself, since I myself
Have given myself the cause.
Enter the Messenger again ⌈with Charmian⌉
                          Come hither, sir.
Though it be honest, it is never good   85
To bring bad news. Give to a gracious message
An host of tongues, but let ill tidings tell
Themselves when they be felt.
MESSENGER I have done my duty.
CLEOPATRA Is he married?   90
I cannot hate thee worser than I do
If thou again say 'Yes'.
MESSENGER   He's married, madam.
CLEOPATRA
The gods confound thee! Dost thou hold there still?
MESSENGER
Should I lie, madam?
CLEOPATRA   O, I would thou didst,

So half my Egypt were submerged and made   95
A cistern for scaled snakes. Go, get thee hence.
Hadst thou Narcissus in thy face, to me
Thou wouldst appear most ugly. He is married?
MESSENGER
I crave your highness' pardon.
CLEOPATRA   He is married?
MESSENGER
Take no offence that I would not offend you.   100
To punish me for what you make me do
Seems much unequal. He's married to Octavia.
CLEOPATRA
O that his fault should make a knave of thee,
That act not what thou'rt sure of! Get thee hence.
The merchandise which thou hast brought from
       Rome   105
Are all too dear for me. Lie they upon thy hand,
And be undone by 'em.   *Exit Messenger*
CHARMIAN   Good your highness, patience.
CLEOPATRA
In praising Antony I have dispraised Caesar.
CHARMIAN Many times, madam.
CLEOPATRA
I am paid for't now. Lead me from hence.   110
I faint. O Iras, Charmian—'tis no matter.
Go to the fellow, good Alexas, bid him
Report the feature of Octavia: her years,
Her inclination; let him not leave out
The colour of her hair. Bring me word quickly.   115
                          Exit Alexas
Let him for ever go—let him not, Charmian;
Though he be painted one way like a Gorgon,
The other way's a Mars. ⌈*To Mardian*⌉ Bid you Alexas
Bring me word how tall she is. Pity me, Charmian,
But do not speak to me. Lead me to my chamber.   120
                          Exeunt

2.6   *Flourish. Enter Pompey and Menas at one door,*
        with a drummer and a trumpeter; at another,
        Caesar, Lepidus, Antony, Enobarbus, Maecenas,
        Agrippa, with soldiers marching
POMPEY
Your hostages I have, so have you mine,
And we shall talk before we fight.
CAESAR   Most meet
That first we come to words, and therefore have we
Our written purposes before us sent,
Which if thou hast considered, let us know   5
If 'twill tie up thy discontented sword
And carry back to Sicily much tall youth
That else must perish here.
POMPEY   To you all three,
The senators alone of this great world,
Chief factors for the gods: I do not know   10
Wherefore my father should revengers want,
Having a son and friends, since Julius Caesar,
Who at Philippi the good Brutus ghosted,
There saw you labouring for him. What was't
That moved pale Cassius to conspire? And what   15

Made the all-honoured, honest Roman Brutus,
With the armed rest, courtiers of beauteous freedom,
To drench the Capitol but that they would
Have one man but a man? And that is it
Hath made me rig my navy, at whose burden   20
The angered ocean foams; with which I meant
To scourge th'ingratitude that despiteful Rome
Cast on my noble father.
CAESAR   Take your time.
ANTONY
Thou canst not fear us, Pompey, with thy sails.
We'll speak with thee at sea. At land thou know'st   25
How much we do o'ercount thee.
POMPEY   At land indeed
Thou dost o'ercount me of my father's house,
But since the cuckoo builds not for himself,
Remain in't as thou mayst.
LEPIDUS   Be pleased to tell us—
For this is from the present—how you take   30
The offers we have sent you.
CAESAR   There's the point.
ANTONY
Which do not be entreated to, but weigh
What it is worth, embraced.
CAESAR   And what may follow,
To try a larger fortune?
POMPEY   You have made me offer
Of Sicily, Sardinia; and I must   35
Rid all the sea of pirates; then to send
Measures of wheat to Rome; this 'greed upon,
To part with unhacked edges, and bear back
Our targes undinted.
CAESAR, ANTONY, *and* LEPIDUS That's our offer.
POMPEY   Know, then,
I came before you here a man prepared   40
To take this offer. But Mark Antony
Put me to some impatience. Though I lose
The praise of it by telling, you must know,
When Caesar and your brother were at blows,
Your mother came to Sicily, and did find   45
Her welcome friendly.
ANTONY   I have heard it, Pompey,
And am well studied for a liberal thanks
Which I do owe you.
POMPEY   Let me have your hand.
Pompey and Antony shake hands
I did not think, sir, to have met you here.
ANTONY
The beds i'th' East are soft; and thanks to you,   50
That called me timelier than my purpose hither;
For I have gained by't.
CAESAR (*to Pompey*)   Since I saw you last
There is a change upon you.
POMPEY   Well, I know not
What counts harsh fortune casts upon my face,
But in my bosom shall she never come   55
To make my heart her vassal.
LEPIDUS   Well met here.

POMPEY
I hope so, Lepidus. Thus we are agreed.
I crave our composition may be written
And sealed between us.
CAESAR   That's the next to do.
POMPEY
We'll feast each other ere we part, and let's   60
Draw lots who shall begin.
ANTONY That will I, Pompey.
POMPEY No, Antony, take the lot.
But, first or last, your fine Egyptian cookery
Shall have the fame. I have heard that Julius Caesar   65
Grew fat with feasting there.
ANTONY   You have heard much.
POMPEY I have fair meanings, sir.
ANTONY And fair words to them.
POMPEY Then so much have I heard,
And I have heard Apollodorus carried—   70
ENOBARBUS
No more o' that, he did so.
POMPEY   What, I pray you?
ENOBARBUS
A certain queen to Caesar in a mattress.
POMPEY
I know thee now. How far'st thou, soldier?
ENOBARBUS
Well, and well am like to do, for I perceive
Four feasts are toward.
POMPEY   Let me shake thy hand.   75
Pompey and Enobarbus shake hands
I never hated thee. I have seen thee fight
When I have envied thy behaviour.
ENOBARBUS
Sir, I never loved you much, but I ha' praised ye
When you have well deserved ten times as much
As I have said you did.   80
POMPEY
Enjoy thy plainness. It nothing ill becomes thee.
Aboard my galley I invite you all.
Will you lead, lords?
CAESAR, ANTONY, *and* LEPIDUS Show's the way, sir.
POMPEY   Come.
Exeunt all but Enobarbus and Menas
MENAS (*aside*)
Thy father, Pompey, would ne'er have made this
    treaty.
(*To Enobarbus*) You and I have known, sir.   85
ENOBARBUS At sea, I think.
MENAS We have, sir.
ENOBARBUS You have done well by water.
MENAS And you by land.   89
ENOBARBUS I will praise any man that will praise me,
    though it cannot be denied what I have done by land.
MENAS Nor what I have done by water.
ENOBARBUS Yes, something you can deny for your own
    safety. You have been a great thief by sea.
MENAS And you by land.   95
ENOBARBUS There I deny my land service; but give me

your hand, Menas. If our eyes had authority, here they
might take two thieves kissing.

They shake hands

MENAS All men's faces are true, whatsome'er their hands
  are.   100
ENOBARBUS But there is never a fair woman has a true
  face.
MENAS No slander; they steal hearts.
ENOBARBUS We came hither to fight with you.
MENAS For my part, I am sorry it is turned to a drinking.
  Pompey doth this day laugh away his fortune.   106
ENOBARBUS If he do, sure he cannot weep't back again.
MENAS You've said, sir. We looked not for Mark Antony
  here. Pray you, is he married to Cleopatra?
ENOBARBUS Caesar's sister is called Octavia.   110
MENAS True, sir. She was the wife of Caius Marcellus.
ENOBARBUS But she is now the wife of Marcus Antonius.
MENAS Pray ye, sir?
ENOBARBUS 'Tis true.
MENAS Then is Caesar and he for ever knit together.   115
ENOBARBUS If I were bound to divine of this unity I would
  not prophesy so.
MENAS I think the policy of that purpose made more in
  the marriage than the love of the parties.   119
ENOBARBUS I think so, too. But you shall find the band
  that seems to tie their friendship together will be the
  very strangler of their amity. Octavia is of a holy, cold,
  and still conversation.
MENAS Who would not have his wife so?   124
ENOBARBUS Not he that himself is not so, which is Mark
  Antony. He will to his Egyptian dish again; then shall
  the sighs of Octavia blow the fire up in Caesar, and, as
  I said before, that which is the strength of their amity
  shall prove the immediate author of their variance.
  Antony will use his affection where it is. He married
  but his occasion here.   131
MENAS And thus it may be. Come, sir, will you aboard?
  I have a health for you.
ENOBARBUS I shall take it, sir. We have used our throats
  in Egypt.   135
MENAS Come, let's away.   *Exeunt*

2.7   *Music plays. Enter two or three Servants with a
     banquet*

FIRST SERVANT Here they'll be, man. Some o' their plants
  are ill rooted already; the least wind i'th' world will
  blow them down.
SECOND SERVANT Lepidus is high-coloured.
FIRST SERVANT They have made him drink alms-drink.   5
SECOND SERVANT As they pinch one another by the
  disposition, he cries out 'No more!'—reconciles them
  to his entreaty and himself to th' drink.
FIRST SERVANT But it raises the greater war between him
  and his discretion.   10
SECOND SERVANT Why, this it is to have a name in great
  men's fellowship. I had as lief have a reed that will do
  me no service as a partisan I could not heave.

FIRST SERVANT To be called into a huge sphere and not
  to be seen to move in't, are the holes where eyes should
  be which pitifully disaster the cheeks.   16

*A sennet sounded. Enter Caesar, Antony, Pompey,
  Lepidus, Agrippa, Maecenas, Enobarbus, and
  Menas, with other captains ⌐and a boy⌐*

ANTONY (*to Caesar*)
Thus do they, sir: they take the flow o'th' Nile
By certain scales i'th' pyramid. They know
By th' height, the lowness, or the mean, if dearth
Or foison follow. The higher Nilus swells   20
The more it promises; as it ebbs, the seedsman
Upon the slime and ooze scatters his grain,
And shortly comes to harvest.
LEPIDUS You've strange serpents there?
ANTONY Ay, Lepidus.   25
LEPIDUS Your serpent of Egypt is bred now of your mud
  by the operation of your sun; so is your crocodile.
ANTONY They are so.
POMPEY
Sit, and some wine. A health to Lepidus!   29
    ⌐*Antony, Pompey, and Lepidus sit*⌐
LEPIDUS I am not so well as I should be, but I'll ne'er out.
ENOBARBUS Not till you have slept—I fear me you'll be in
  till then.
LEPIDUS Nay, certainly, I have heard the Ptolemies'
  pyramises are very goodly things: without contra-
  diction I have heard that.   35
MENAS (*aside to Pompey*)
Pompey, a word.
POMPEY (*aside to Menas*) Say in mine ear; what is't?
MENAS (*aside to Pompey*)
Forsake thy seat, I do beseech thee, captain,
And hear me speak a word.
POMPEY (*aside to Menas*)   Forbear me till anon.
  (*Aloud*) This wine for Lepidus!
    Menas whispers in Pompey's ear
LEPIDUS What manner o' thing is your crocodile?   40
ANTONY It is shaped, sir, like itself, and it is as broad as
  it hath breadth. It is just so high as it is, and moves
  with it own organs. It lives by that which nourisheth
  it, and the elements once out of it, it transmigrates.
LEPIDUS What colour is it of?   45
ANTONY Of it own colour, too.
LEPIDUS 'Tis a strange serpent.
ANTONY 'Tis so, and the tears of it are wet.
CAESAR (*to Antony*)
Will this description satisfy him?
ANTONY With the health that Pompey gives him; else he
  is a very epicure.   51
POMPEY (*aside to Menas*)
Go hang, sir, hang! Tell me of that? Away,
Do as I bid you. (*Aloud*) Where's this cup I called for?
MENAS (*aside to Pompey*)
If for the sake of merit thou wilt hear me,
Rise from thy stool.
POMPEY ⌐*rising*⌐   I think thou'rt mad. The matter? 55

⌈*Menas and Pompey stand apart*⌉

MENAS
I have ever held my cap off to thy fortunes.

POMPEY
Thou hast served me with much faith. What's else to
        say?
Be jolly, lords.

ANTONY   These quicksands, Lepidus,
Keep off them, for you sink.

MENAS
Wilt thou be lord of all the world?

POMPEY   What sayst thou? 60

MENAS
Wilt thou be lord of the whole world? That's twice.

POMPEY
How should that be?

MENAS   But entertain it
And, though thou think me poor, I am the man
Will give thee all the world.

POMPEY   Hast thou drunk well?

MENAS
No, Pompey, I have kept me from the cup.   65
Thou art, if thou dar'st be, the earthly Jove.
Whate'er the ocean pales or sky inclips
Is thine, if thou wilt ha't.

POMPEY   Show me which way!

MENAS
These three world-sharers, these competitors,
Are in thy vessel. Let me cut the cable;   70
And when we are put off, fall to their throats.
All there is thine.

POMPEY   Ah, this thou shouldst have done
And not have spoke on't. In me 'tis villainy,
In thee 't had been good service. Thou must know
'Tis not my profit that does lead mine honour;   75
Mine honour, it. Repent that e'er thy tongue
Hath so betrayed thine act. Being done unknown,
I should have found it afterwards well done,
But must condemn it now. Desist, and drink.
        He returns to the others

MENAS (*aside*)
For this, I'll never follow thy palled fortunes more.   80
Who seeks and will not take when once 'tis offered,
Shall never find it more.

POMPEY   This health to Lepidus!

ANTONY
Bear him ashore.—I'll pledge it for him, Pompey.

ENOBARBUS
Here's to thee, Menas!

MENAS   Enobarbus, welcome.

POMPEY
Fill till the cup be hid.
        One lifts Lepidus, drunk, and carries him off

ENOBARBUS   There's a strong fellow, Menas.

MENAS Why?   86

ENOBARBUS
A bears the third part of the world, man; seest not?

MENAS
The third part then is drunk. Would it were all,
That it might go on wheels.

ENOBARBUS   Drink thou, increase the reels.

MENAS Come.   90

POMPEY
This is not yet an Alexandrian feast.

ANTONY
It ripens towards it. Strike the vessels, ho!
Here's to Caesar!

CAESAR   I could well forbear't.
It's monstrous labour when I wash my brain,
An it grow fouler.   95

ANTONY Be a child o'th' time.

CAESAR Possess it, I'll make answer.
But I had rather fast from all, four days,
Than drink so much in one.

ENOBARBUS (*to Antony*)   Ha, my brave Emperor,
Shall we dance now the Egyptian bacchanals,   100
And celebrate our drink?

POMPEY Let's ha't, good soldier.

ANTONY Come, let's all take hands
Till that the conquering wine hath steeped our sense
In soft and delicate Lethe.

ENOBARBUS   All take hands.   105
Make battery to our ears with the loud music.
The while I'll place you, then the boy shall sing.
The holding every man shall beat as loud
As his strong sides can volley.
        Music plays. Enobarbus places them hand in hand

⌈BOY⌉ (*sings*)
        Come, thou monarch of the vine,   110
        Plumpy Bacchus, with pink eyne!
        In thy vats our cares be drowned,
        With thy grapes our hairs be crowned!
        Cup us till the world go round,
        Cup us till the world go round!   115

CAESAR
What would you more? Pompey, good night.
(*To Antony*)   Good-brother,
Let me request you off. Our graver business
Frowns at this levity. Gentle lords, let's part.
You see we have burnt our cheeks. Strong Enobarb
Is weaker than the wine, and mine own tongue   120
Splits what it speaks. The wild disguise hath almost
Anticked us all. What needs more words? Good night.
Good Antony, your hand.

POMPEY   I'll try you on the shore.

ANTONY
And shall, sir. Give's your hand.

POMPEY   O Antony,
You have my father's house. But what, we are friends!
Come down into the boat.   126
        Exeunt all but Enobarbus and Menas

ENOBARBUS
Take heed you fall not, Menas.

MENAS   I'll not on shore.

No, to my cabin. These drums, these trumpets, flutes,
    what!
Let Neptune hear we bid a loud farewell   129
To these great fellows. Sound and be hanged, sound out!
    Sound a flourish, with drums
ENOBARBUS (*throwing his cap in the air*)
Hoo, says a! There's my cap.
MENAS   Ho, noble captain, come!
                                        Exeunt

3.1   *Enter Ventidius, with Silius and other Roman
        soldiers, as it were in triumph; the dead body of
        Pacorus borne before him*
VENTIDIUS
Now, darting Parthia, art thou struck; and now
Pleased fortune does of Marcus Crassus' death
Make me revenger. Bear the King's son's body
Before our army. Thy Pacorus, Orodes,
Pays this for Marcus Crassus.
SILIUS   Noble Ventidius,   5
Whilst yet with Parthian blood thy sword is warm,
The fugitive Parthians follow. Spur through Media,
Mesopotamia, and the shelters whither
The routed fly. So thy grand captain, Antony,
Shall set thee on triumphant chariots and   10
Put garlands on thy head.
VENTIDIUS   O Silius, Silius,
I have done enough. A lower place, note well,
May make too great an act. For learn this, Silius:
Better to leave undone than by our deed
Acquire too high a fame when him we serve's away.15
Caesar and Antony have ever won
More in their officer than person. Sossius,
One of my place in Syria, his lieutenant,
For quick accumulation of renown,
Which he achieved by th' minute, lost his favour.   20
Who does i'th' wars more than his captain can
Becomes his captain's captain; and ambition,
The soldier's virtue, rather makes choice of loss
Than gain which darkens him.
I could do more to do Antonius good,   25
But 'twould offend him, and in his offence
Should my performance perish.
SILIUS   Thou hast, Ventidius, that
Without the which a soldier and his sword
Grants scarce distinction. Thou wilt write to Antony?
VENTIDIUS
I'll humbly signify what in his name,   30
That magical word of war, we have effected;
How, with his banners and his well-paid ranks,
The ne'er-yet-beaten horse of Parthia
We have jaded out o'th' field.
SILIUS   Where is he now?
VENTIDIUS
He purposeth to Athens; whither, with what haste   35
The weight we must convey with's will permit,
We shall appear before him.—On there; pass along.
                                        Exeunt

3.2   *Enter Agrippa at one door, Enobarbus at another*
AGRIPPA What, are the brothers parted?
ENOBARBUS
They have dispatched with Pompey; he is gone.
The other three are sealing. Octavia weeps
To part from Rome, Caesar is sad, and Lepidus
Since Pompey's feast, as Menas says, is troubled   5
With the green-sickness.
AGRIPPA   'Tis a noble Lepidus.
ENOBARBUS
A very fine one. O, how he loves Caesar!
AGRIPPA
Nay, but how dearly he adores Mark Antony!
ENOBARBUS
Caesar? Why, he's the Jupiter of men.
AGRIPPA
What's Antony—the god of Jupiter?   10
ENOBARBUS
Spake you of Caesar? How, the nonpareil?
AGRIPPA
O Antony, O thou Arabian bird!
ENOBARBUS
Would you praise Caesar, say 'Caesar'; go no further.
AGRIPPA
Indeed, he plied them both with excellent praises.
ENOBARBUS
But he loves Caesar best; yet he loves Antony—   15
Hoo! Hearts, tongues, figures, scribes, bards, poets,
    cannot
Think, speak, cast, write, sing, number—hoo!—
His love to Antony. But as for Caesar—
Kneel down, kneel down, and wonder.
AGRIPPA   Both he loves.
ENOBARBUS
They are his shards, and he their beetle.
    ⌈*Trumpet within*⌉   So,   20
This is to horse. Adieu, noble Agrippa.
AGRIPPA
Good fortune, worthy soldier, and farewell.
    Enter Caesar, Antony, Lepidus, and Octavia
ANTONY (*to Caesar*) No further, sir.
CAESAR
You take from me a great part of myself.
Use me well in't. Sister, prove such a wife   25
As my thoughts make thee, and as my farthest bond
Shall pass on thy approof. Most noble Antony,
Let not the piece of virtue which is set
Betwixt us as the cement of our love
To keep it builded, be the ram to batter   30
The fortress of it; for better might we
Have loved without this mean if on both parts
This be not cherished.
ANTONY   Make me not offended
In your distrust.
CAESAR   I have said.
ANTONY   You shall not find,
Though you be therein curious, the least cause   35
For what you seem to fear. So, the gods keep you,

And make the hearts of Romans serve your ends.
We will here part.

CAESAR
Farewell, my dearest sister, fare thee well.
The elements be kind to thee, and make   40
Thy spirits all of comfort. Fare thee well.

OCTAVIA (*weeping*) My noble brother!

ANTONY
The April's in her eyes; it is love's spring,
And these the showers to bring it on. Be cheerful.

OCTAVIA
Sir, look well to my husband's house, and—   45

CAESAR
What, Octavia?

OCTAVIA   I'll tell you in your ear.
She whispers to Caesar

ANTONY
Her tongue will not obey her heart, nor can
Her heart inform her tongue—the swan's-down
     feather,
That stands upon the swell at full of tide,
And neither way inclines.   50

ENOBARBUS (*aside to Agrippa*) Will Caesar weep?

AGRIPPA (*aside to Enobarbus*) He has a cloud in 's face.

ENOBARBUS (*aside to Agrippa*)
He were the worse for that were he a horse;
So is he, being a man.

AGRIPPA (*aside to Enobarbus*) Why, Enobarbus,
When Antony found Julius Caesar dead   55
He cried almost to roaring, and he wept
When at Philippi he found Brutus slain.

ENOBARBUS (*aside to Agrippa*)
That year indeed he was troubled with a rheum.
What willingly he did confound he wailed,
Believe't, till I wept too.

CAESAR   No, sweet Octavia,   60
You shall hear from me still. The time shall not
Outgo my thinking on you.

ANTONY   Come, sir, come,
I'll wrestle with you in my strength of love.
Look, here I have you (*embracing Caesar*); thus I let
     you go,
And give you to the gods.

CAESAR   Adieu, be happy.   65

LEPIDUS
Let all the number of the stars give light
To thy fair way.

CAESAR   Farewell, farewell.
He kisses Octavia

ANTONY   Farewell.
*Trumpets sound. Exeunt Antony, Octavia, and
Enobarbus at one door, Caesar, Lepidus, and
Agrippa at another*

3.3   *Enter Cleopatra, Charmian, Iras, and Alexas*

CLEOPATRA
Where is the fellow?

ALEXAS   Half afeard to come.

CLEOPATRA
Go to, go to.
Enter the Messenger as before
     Come hither, sir.

ALEXAS   Good majesty,
Herod of Jewry dare not look upon you
But when you are well pleased.

CLEOPATRA   That Herod's head
I'll have; but how, when Antony is gone,   5
Through whom I might command it?
(*To the Messenger*)   Come thou near.

MESSENGER
Most gracious majesty!

CLEOPATRA   Didst thou behold
Octavia?

MESSENGER   Ay, dread Queen.

CLEOPATRA   Where?

MESSENGER   Madam, in Rome.
I looked her in the face, and saw her led
Between her brother and Mark Antony.   10

CLEOPATRA
Is she as tall as me?

MESSENGER   She is not, madam.

CLEOPATRA
Didst hear her speak? Is she shrill-tongued or low?

MESSENGER
Madam, I heard her speak. She is low-voiced.

CLEOPATRA
That's not so good. He cannot like her long.

CHARMIAN
Like her? O Isis, 'tis impossible!   15

CLEOPATRA
I think so, Charmian. Dull of tongue, and dwarfish.
What majesty is in her gait? Remember
If e'er thou looked'st on majesty.

MESSENGER   She creeps.
Her motion and her station are as one.
She shows a body rather than a life,   20
A statue than a breather.

CLEOPATRA   Is this certain?

MESSENGER
Or I have no observance.

CHARMIAN   Three in Egypt
Cannot make better note.

CLEOPATRA   He's very knowing,
I do perceive't. There's nothing in her yet.
The fellow has good judgement.

CHARMIAN   Excellent.   25

CLEOPATRA (*to the Messenger*)
Guess at her years, I prithee.

MESSENGER   Madam,
She was a widow—

CLEOPATRA   Widow? Charmian, hark.

MESSENGER And I do think she's thirty.

CLEOPATRA
Bear'st thou her face in mind? Is't long or round?

MESSENGER Round, even to faultiness.   30

CLEOPATRA
For the most part, too, they are foolish that are so.
Her hair—what colour?
MESSENGER   Brown, madam; and her forehead
As low as she would wish it.
CLEOPATRA (giving money)   There's gold for thee.
Thou must not take my former sharpness ill.
I will employ thee back again. I find thee   35
Most fit for business. Go, make thee ready.
Our letters are prepared.   Exit Messenger
CHARMIAN   A proper man.
CLEOPATRA
Indeed he is so. I repent me much
That so I harried him. Why, methinks, by him,
This creature's no such thing.
CHARMIAN   Nothing, madam.   40
CLEOPATRA
The man hath seen some majesty, and should know.
CHARMIAN
Hath he seen majesty? Isis else defend,
And serving you so long!
CLEOPATRA
I have one thing more to ask him yet, good
     Charmian.
But 'tis no matter. Thou shalt bring him to me   45
Where I will write. All may be well enough.
CHARMIAN I warrant you, madam.   Exeunt

3.4   Enter Antony and Octavia
ANTONY
Nay, nay, Octavia, not only that,
That were excusable, that and thousands more
Of semblable import; but he hath waged
New wars 'gainst Pompey, made his will and read it
To public ear, spoke scantly of me;   5
When perforce he could not
But pay me terms of honour, cold and sickly
He vented them, most narrow measure lent me.
When the best hint was given him, he not took't,
Or did it from his teeth.
OCTAVIA   O my good lord,   10
Believe not all, or if you must believe,
Stomach not all. A more unhappy lady,
If this division chance, ne'er stood between,
Praying for both parts.
The good gods will mock me presently,   15
When I shall pray 'O, bless my lord and husband!',
Undo that prayer by crying out as loud
'O, bless my brother!' Husband win, win brother
Prays and destroys the prayer; no midway
'Twixt these extremes at all.
ANTONY   Gentle Octavia,   20
Let your best love draw to that point which seeks
Best to preserve it. If I lose mine honour,
I lose myself. Better I were not yours
Than yours so branchless. But, as you requested,
Yourself shall go between's. The meantime, lady,   25

I'll raise the preparation of a war
Shall stain your brother. Make your soonest haste;
So your desires are yours.
OCTAVIA   Thanks to my lord.
The Jove of power make me most weak, most weak,
Your reconciler! Wars 'twixt you twain would be   30
As if the world should cleave, and that slain men
Should solder up the rift.
ANTONY
When it appears to you where this begins,
Turn your displeasure that way, for our faults
Can never be so equal that your love   35
Can equally move with them. Provide your going,
Choose your own company, and command what cost
Your heart has mind to.   Exeunt

3.5   Enter Enobarbus and Eros, meeting
ENOBARBUS How now, friend Eros?
EROS There's strange news come, sir.
ENOBARBUS What, man?
EROS Caesar and Lepidus have made wars upon Pompey.
ENOBARBUS This is old. What is the success?   5
EROS Caesar, having made use of him in the wars 'gainst
Pompey, presently denied him rivality, would not let
him partake in the glory of the action, and, not resting
here, accuses him of letters he had formerly wrote to
Pompey; upon his own appeal seizes him; so the poor
third is up, till death enlarge his confine.   11
ENOBARBUS
Then, world, thou hast a pair of chops, no more,
And throw between them all the food thou hast,
They'll grind the one the other. Where's Antony?
EROS
He's walking in the garden, thus, and spurns   15
The rush that lies before him, cries 'Fool Lepidus!'
And threats the throat of that his officer
That murdered Pompey.
ENOBARBUS   Our great navy's rigged.
EROS
For Italy and Caesar. More, Domitius:
My lord desires you presently. My news   20
I might have told hereafter.
ENOBARBUS   'Twill be naught.
But let it be; bring me to Antony.
EROS   Come, sir.   Exeunt

3.6   Enter Agrippa, Maecenas, and Caesar
CAESAR
Contemning Rome, he has done all this and more
In Alexandria. Here's the manner of't:
I'th' market place on a tribunal silvered,
Cleopatra and himself in chairs of gold
Were publicly enthroned. At the feet sat   5
Caesarion, whom they call my father's son,
And all the unlawful issue that their lust
Since then hath made between them. Unto her
He gave the stablishment of Egypt; made her

Of lower Syria, Cyprus, Lydia,   10
Absolute queen.
MAECENAS   This in the public eye?
CAESAR
I'th' common showplace, where they exercise.
His sons he there proclaimed the kings of kings;
Great Media, Parthia, and Armenia
He gave to Aléxander. To Ptolemy he assigned   15
Syria, Cilicia, and Phoenicia. She
In th'habiliments of the goddess Isis
That day appeared, and oft before gave audience,
As 'tis reported, so.
MAECENAS   Let Rome be thus informed.
AGRIPPA
Who, queasy with his insolence already,   20
Will their good thoughts call from him.
CAESAR   The people knows it,
And have now received his accusations.
AGRIPPA Who does he accuse?
CAESAR
Caesar, and that having in Sicily
Sextus Pompeius spoiled, we had not rated him   25
His part o'th' isle. Then does he say he lent me
Some shipping, unrestored. Lastly, he frets
That Lepidus of the triumvirate
Should be deposed; and being, that we detain
All his revenue.
AGRIPPA   Sir, this should be answered.   30
CAESAR
'Tis done already, and the messenger gone:
I have told him Lepidus was grown too cruel,
That he his high authority abused
And did deserve his change. For what I have
    conquered,
I grant him part; but then in his Armenia,   35
And other of his conquered kingdoms,
I demand the like.
MAECENAS   He'll never yield to that.
CAESAR
Nor must not then be yielded to in this.
        Enter Octavia with her train
OCTAVIA
Hail, Caesar, and my lord; hail, most dear Caesar!
CAESAR
That ever I should call thee castaway!   40
OCTAVIA
You have not called me so, nor have you cause.
CAESAR
Why have you stol'n upon us thus? You come not
Like Caesar's sister. The wife of Antony
Should have an army for an usher, and
The neighs of horse to tell of her approach   45
Long ere she did appear. The trees by th' way
Should have borne men, and expectation fainted,
Longing for what it had not. Nay, the dust
Should have ascended to the roof of heaven,
Raised by your populous troops. But you are come   50
A market maid to Rome, and have prevented

The ostentation of our love; which, left unshown,
Is often left unloved. We should have met you
By sea and land, supplying every stage
With an augmented greeting.
OCTAVIA   Good my lord,   55
To come thus was I not constrained, but did it
On my free will. My lord, Mark Antony,
Hearing that you prepared for war, acquainted
My grievèd ear withal, whereon I begged
His pardon for return.
CAESAR   Which soon he granted,   60
Being an obstruct 'tween his lust and him.
OCTAVIA
Do not say so, my lord.
CAESAR   I have eyes upon him,
And his affairs come to me on the wind.
Where is he now?
OCTAVIA   My lord, in Athens.
CAESAR
No, my most wrongèd sister. Cleopatra   65
Hath nodded him to her. He hath given his empire
Up to a whore; who now are levying
The kings o'th' earth for war. He hath assembled
Bocchus, the King of Libya; Archelaus
Of Cappadocia; Philadelphos, King   70
Of Paphlagonia; the Thracian King Adallas;
King Malchus of Arabia; King of Pont;
Herod of Jewry; Mithridates, King
Of Comagene; Polemòn and Amyntas,
The Kings of Mede and Lycaonia;   75
With a more larger list of sceptres.
OCTAVIA   Ay me most wretched,
That have my heart parted betwixt two friends
That does afflict each other!
CAESAR   Welcome hither.
Your letters did withhold our breaking forth
Till we perceived both how you were wrong led   80
And we in negligent danger. Cheer your heart.
Be you not troubled with the time, which drives
O'er your content these strong necessities;
But let determined things to destiny
Hold unbewailed their way. Welcome to Rome;   85
Nothing more dear to me. You are abused
Beyond the mark of thought, and the high gods,
To do you justice, makes their ministers
Of us and those that love you. Best of comfort,
And ever welcome to us.
AGRIPPA   Welcome, lady.   90
MAECENAS Welcome, dear madam.
Each heart in Rome does love and pity you.
Only th'adulterous Antony, most large
In his abominations, turns you off,
And gives his potent regiment to a trull   95
That noises it against us.
OCTAVIA   Is it so, sir?
CAESAR
Most certain. Sister, welcome. Pray you
Be ever known to patience. My dear'st sister!   *Exeunt*

3.7   *Enter Cleopatra and Enobarbus*

CLEOPATRA
I will be even with thee, doubt it not.

ENOBARBUS But why, why, why?

CLEOPATRA
Thou hast forspoke my being in these wars,
And sayst it is not fit.

ENOBARBUS   Well, is it, is it?

CLEOPATRA
Is't not denounced against us? Why should not we   5
Be there in person?

ENOBARBUS ⌜*aside*⌝   Well, I could reply
If we should serve with horse and mares together,
The horse were merely lost; the mares would bear
A soldier and his horse.

CLEOPATRA   What is't you say?

ENOBARBUS
Your presence needs must puzzle Antony,   10
Take from his heart, take from his brain, from's time
What should not then be spared. He is already
Traduced for levity; and 'tis said in Rome
That Photinus, an eunuch, and your maids
Manage this war.

CLEOPATRA   Sink Rome, and their tongues rot   15
That speak against us! A charge we bear i'th' war,
And as the president of my kingdom will
Appear there for a man. Speak not against it.
I will not stay behind.

Enter Antony and Camidius

ENOBARBUS   Nay, I have done.
Here comes the Emperor.

ANTONY   Is it not strange, Camidius,   20
That from Tarentum and Brundisium
He could so quickly cut the Ionian Sea
And take in Toryne?—You have heard on't, sweet?

CLEOPATRA
Celerity is never more admired
Than by the negligent.

ANTONY   A good rebuke,   25
Which might have well becomed the best of men
To taunt at slackness. Camidius, we
Will fight with him by sea.

CLEOPATRA   By sea—what else?

CAMIDIUS
Why will my lord do so?

ANTONY   For that he dares us to't.

ENOBARBUS
So hath my lord dared him to single fight.   30

CAMIDIUS
Ay, and to wage this battle at Pharsalia,
Where Caesar fought with Pompey. But these offers
Which serve not for his vantage, he shakes off,
And so should you.

ENOBARBUS   Your ships are not well manned,
Your mariners are muleters, reapers, people   35
Engrossed by swift impress. In Caesar's fleet
Are those that often have 'gainst Pompey fought.
Their ships are yare, yours heavy. No disgrace

Shall fall you for refusing him at sea,
Being prepared for land.

ANTONY   By sea, by sea.   40

ENOBARBUS
Most worthy sir, you therein throw away
The absolute soldiership you have by land;
Distract your army, which doth most consist
Of war-marked footmen; leave unexecuted
Your own renownèd knowledge; quite forgo   45
The way which promises assurance, and
Give up yourself merely to chance and hazard
From firm security.

ANTONY   I'll fight at sea.

CLEOPATRA
I have sixty sails, Caesar none better.

ANTONY
Our overplus of shipping will we burn,   50
And with the rest full-manned, from th'head of
Actium
Beat th'approaching Caesar. But if we fail,
We then can do't at land.

Enter a Messenger

                Thy business?

MESSENGER
The news is true, my lord. He is descried.
Caesar has taken Toryne.   55

ANTONY
Can he be there in person? 'Tis impossible;
Strange that his power should be. Camidius,
Our nineteen legions thou shalt hold by land,
And our twelve thousand horse. We'll to our ship.
Away, my Thetis!

Enter a Soldier

                How now, worthy soldier?   60

SOLDIER
O noble Emperor, do not fight by sea.
Trust not to rotten planks. Do you misdoubt
This sword and these my wounds? Let th'Egyptians
And the Phoenicians go a-ducking; we
Have used to conquer standing on the earth,   65
And fighting foot to foot.

ANTONY   Well, well; away!

Exeunt Antony, Cleopatra, and Enobarbus

SOLDIER
By Hercules, I think I am i'th' right.

CAMIDIUS
Soldier, thou art; but his whole action grows
Not in the power on't. So our leader's led,
And we are women's men.

SOLDIER   You keep by land   70
The legions and the horse whole, do you not?

CAMIDIUS
Marcus Octavius, Marcus Justeius,
Publicola and Caelius are for sea,
But we keep whole by land. This speed of Caesar's
Carries beyond belief.

SOLDIER   While he was yet in Rome   75

His power went out in such distractions
As beguiled all spies.
CAMIDIUS   Who's his lieutenant, hear you?
SOLDIER
They say, one Taurus.
CAMIDIUS   Well I know the man.
    Enter a Messenger
MESSENGER
The Emperor calls Camidius.
CAMIDIUS
With news the time's in labour, and throws forth   80
Each minute some.   *Exeunt*

3.8   *Enter Caesar with his army, marching, and Taurus*
CAESAR Taurus!
TAURUS My lord?
CAESAR
Strike not by land. Keep whole. Provoke not battle
Till we have done at sea. (*Giving a scroll*) Do not
   exceed
The prescript of this scroll. Our fortune lies   5
Upon this jump.
    Exit Caesar and his army at one door, Taurus at
                               another

3.9   *Enter Antony and Enobarbus*
ANTONY
Set we our squadrons on yon side o'th' hill
In eye of Caesar's battle, from which place
We may the number of the ships behold,
And so proceed accordingly.   *Exeunt*

3.10   *Camidius marcheth with his land army one way*
       over the stage, and Taurus, the lieutenant of
       Caesar, with his army the other way. After their
       going in is heard the noise of a sea-fight. Alarum.
       Enter Enobarbus
ENOBARBUS
Naught, naught, all naught! I can behold no longer.
Th'*Antoniad*, the Egyptian admiral,
With all their sixty, fly and turn the rudder.
To see't mine eyes are blasted.
    Enter Scarus
SCARUS   Gods and goddesses—
All the whole synod of them!
ENOBARBUS   What's thy passion?   5
SCARUS
The greater cantle of the world is lost
With very ignorance; we have kissed away
Kingdoms and provinces.
ENOBARBUS   How appears the fight?
SCARUS   .
On our side like the tokened pestilence,
Where death is sure. Yon riband-red nag of Egypt—   10
Whom leprosy o'ertake!—i'th' midst o'th' fight—
When vantage like a pair of twins appeared,
Both as the same, or rather ours the elder—

The breese upon her, like a cow in June,
Hoists sails and flies.
ENOBARBUS   That I beheld.   15
Mine eyes did sicken at the sight, and could not
Endure a further view.
SCARUS   She once being luffed,
The noble ruin of her magic, Antony,
Claps on his sea-wing and, like a doting mallard,
Leaving the fight in height, flies after her.   20
I never saw an action of such shame.
Experience, manhood, honour, ne'er before
Did violate so itself.
ENOBARBUS   Alack, alack!
    Enter Camidius
CAMIDIUS
Our fortune on the sea is out of breath,
And sinks most lamentably. Had our general   25
Been what he knew himself, it had gone well.
O, he has given example for our flight
Most grossly by his own.
ENOBARBUS
Ay, are you thereabouts? Why then, good night
   indeed!
CAMIDIUS
Toward Peloponnesus are they fled.   30
SCARUS
'Tis easy to't, and there I will attend
What further comes.
CAMIDIUS   To Caesar will I render
My legions and my horse. Six kings already
Show me the way of yielding.
ENOBARBUS   I'll yet follow
The wounded chance of Antony, though my reason   35
Sits in the wind against me.   ⌈*Exeunt severally*⌉

3.11   *Enter Antony with Attendants*
ANTONY
Hark, the land bids me tread no more upon't,
It is ashamed to bear me. Friends, come hither.
I am so lated in the world that I
Have lost my way for ever. I have a ship
Laden with gold. Take that; divide it, fly,   5
And make your peace with Caesar.
ATTENDANTS   Fly? Not we.
ANTONY
I have fled myself, and have instructed cowards
To run and show their shoulders. Friends, be gone.
I have myself resolved upon a course
Which has no need of you. Be gone.   10
My treasure's in the harbour. Take it. O,
I followed that I blush to look upon.
My very hairs do mutiny, for the white
Reprove the brown for rashness, and they them
For fear and doting. Friends, be gone. You shall   15
Have letters from me to some friends that will
Sweep your way for you. Pray you, look not sad,
Nor make replies of loathness. Take the hint

Which my despair proclaims. Let that be left
Which leaves itself. To the seaside straightway!   20
I will possess you of that ship and treasure.
Leave me, I pray, a little. Pray you now,
Nay, do so; for indeed I have lost command.
Therefore I pray you; I'll see you by and by.
                                        Exeunt attendants
  He sits down.
  Enter Cleopatra led by Charmian, Iras, and Eros
EROS
  Nay, gentle madam, to him. Comfort him.   25
IRAS Do, most dear Queen.
CHARMIAN Do. Why, what else?
CLEOPATRA Let me sit down. O Juno!
  She sits down
ANTONY No, no, no, no, no.
EROS (*to Antony*) See you here, sir?   30
ANTONY O fie, fie, fie!
CHARMIAN Madam.
IRAS Madam. O good Empress!
EROS Sir, sir.
ANTONY
  Yes, my lord, yes. He at Philippi kept   35
  His sword e'en like a dancer, while I struck
  The lean and wrinkled Cassius; and 'twas I
  That the mad Brutus ended. He alone
  Dealt on lieutenantry, and no practice had
  In the brave squares of war. Yet now—no matter.   40
CLEOPATRA (⌈*rising,*⌉ *to Charmian and Iras*) Ah, stand by.
EROS The Queen, my lord, the Queen.
IRAS Go to him, madam.
  Speak to him. He's unqualitied
  With very shame.
CLEOPATRA   Well then, sustain me. O!   45
EROS
  Most noble sir, arise. The Queen approaches.
  Her head's declined, and death will seize her but
  Your comfort makes the rescue.
ANTONY
  I have offended reputation;
  A most unnoble swerving.
EROS   Sir, the Queen.   50
ANTONY ⌈*rising*⌉
  O, whither hast thou led me, Egypt? See
  How I convey my shame out of thine eyes
  By looking back what I have left behind
  'Stroyed in dishonour.
CLEOPATRA   O, my lord, my lord,
  Forgive my fearful sails! I little thought   55
  You would have followed.
ANTONY   Egypt, thou knew'st too well
  My heart was to thy rudder tied by th' strings,
  And thou shouldst tow me after. O'er my spirit
  Thy full supremacy thou knew'st, and that
  Thy beck might from the bidding of the gods   60
  Command me.
CLEOPATRA   O, my pardon!
ANTONY   Now I must

To the young man send humble treaties, dodge
And palter in the shifts of lowness, who
With half the bulk o'th' world played as I pleased,
Making and marring fortunes. You did know   65
How much you were my conqueror, and that
My sword, made weak by my affection, would
Obey it on all cause.
CLEOPATRA   Pardon, pardon!
ANTONY
  Fall not a tear, I say. One of them rates
  All that is won and lost. Give me a kiss.   70
  He kisses her
  Even this repays me. (*To an Attendant*) We sent our
  schoolmaster;
  Is a come back? (*To Cleopatra*) Love, I am full of lead.
  (*Calling*) Some wine
  Within there, and our viands! Fortune knows
  We scorn her most when most she offers blows.
                                        Exeunt

3.12 *Enter Caesar,* ⌈*Agrippa,*⌉ *Thidias, and Dollabella,*
        with others
CAESAR
  Let him appear that's come from Antony.
  Know you him?
DOLABELLA   Caesar, 'tis his schoolmaster;
  An argument that he is plucked, when hither
  He sends so poor a pinion of his wing,
  Which had superfluous kings for messengers   5
  Not many moons gone by.
  Enter Ambassador from Antony
CAESAR   Approach and speak.
AMBASSADOR
  Such as I am, I come from Antony.
  I was of late as petty to his ends
  As is the morn-dew on the myrtle leaf
  To his grand sea.
CAESAR   Be't so. Declare thine office.   10
AMBASSADOR
  Lord of his fortunes he salutes thee, and
  Requires to live in Egypt; which not granted,
  He lessens his requests, and to thee sues
  To let him breathe between the heavens and earth,
  A private man in Athens. This for him.   15
  Next, Cleopatra does confess thy greatness,
  Submits her to thy might, and of thee craves
  The circle of the Ptolemies for her heirs,
  Now hazarded to thy grace.
CAESAR   For Antony,
  I have no ears to his request. The Queen   20
  Of audience nor desire shall fail, so she
  From Egypt drive her all-disgracèd friend,
  Or take his life there. This if she perform
  She shall not sue unheard. So to them both.
AMBASSADOR
  Fortune pursue thee!
CAESAR   Bring him through the bands.   25
                                Exit Ambassador, attended

(*To Thidias*) To try thy eloquence now 'tis time.
  Dispatch.
From Antony win Cleopatra. Promise,
And in our name, what she requires. Add more
As thine invention offers. Women are not
In their best fortunes strong, but want will perjure   30
The ne'er-touched vestal. Try thy cunning, Thidias.
Make thine own edict for thy pains, which we
Will answer as a law.
THIDIAS   Caesar, I go.
CAESAR
Observe how Antony becomes his flaw,
And what thou think'st his very action speaks   35
In every power that moves.
THIDIAS   Caesar, I shall.
          Exeunt Caesar and his train at one door, and
                                Thidias at another

3.13 *Enter Cleopatra, Enobarbus, Charmian, and Iras*
CLEOPATRA
What shall we do, Enobarbus?
ENOBARBUS   Think, and die.
CLEOPATRA
Is Antony or we in fault for this?
ENOBARBUS
Antony only, that would make his will
Lord of his reason. What though you fled
From that great face of war, whose several ranges   5
Frighted each other? Why should he follow?
The itch of his affection should not then
Have nicked his captainship, at such a point,
When half to half the world opposed, he being
The mooted question. 'Twas a shame no less   10
Than was his loss, to course your flying flags
And leave his navy gazing.
CLEOPATRA   Prithee, peace.
          Enter the Ambassador with Antony
ANTONY
Is that his answer?
AMBASSADOR   Ay, my lord.
ANTONY
The Queen shall then have courtesy, so she
Will yield us up.
AMBASSADOR   He says so.
ANTONY   Let her know't.   15
(*To Cleopatra*) To the boy Caesar send this grizzled head,
And he will fill thy wishes to the brim
With principalities.
CLEOPATRA   That head, my lord?
ANTONY (*to the Ambassador*)
To him again. Tell him he wears the rose
Of youth upon him, from which the world should note
Something particular. His coin, ships, legions,   21
May be a coward's, whose ministers would prevail
Under the service of a child as soon
As i'th' command of Caesar. I dare him therefore
To lay his gay caparisons apart   25

And answer me declined, sword against sword,
Ourselves alone. I'll write it. Follow me.
                    Exeunt Antony and Ambassador
ENOBARBUS (*aside*)
Yes, like enough, high-battled Caesar will
Unstate his happiness and be staged to th' show
Against a sworder! I see men's judgements are   30
A parcel of their fortunes, and things outward
Do draw the inward quality after them
To suffer all alike. That he should dream,
Knowing all measures, the full Caesar will
Answer his emptiness! Caesar, thou hast subdued   35
His judgement, too.
          Enter a Servant
SERVANT   A messenger from Caesar.
CLEOPATRA
What, no more ceremony? See, my women:
Against the blown rose may they stop their nose,
That kneeled unto the buds. Admit him, sir.
                                        Exit Servant
ENOBARBUS (*aside*)
Mine honesty and I begin to square.   40
The loyalty well held to fools does make
Our faith mere folly; yet he that can endure
To follow with allegiance a fall'n lord
Does conquer him that did his master conquer,
And earns a place i'th' story.
          Enter Thidias
CLEOPATRA   Caesar's will?   45
THIDIAS
Hear it apart.
CLEOPATRA   None but friends; say boldly.
THIDIAS
So haply are they friends to Antony.
ENOBARBUS
He needs as many, sir, as Caesar has,
Or needs not us. If Caesar please, our master
Will leap to be his friend. For us, you know,   50
Whose he is, we are: and that is Caesar's.
THIDIAS
So. (*To Cleopatra*) Thus, then, thou most renowned:
    Caesar entreats
Not to consider in what case thou stand'st
Further than he is Caesar.
CLEOPATRA   Go on; right royal.
THIDIAS
He knows that you embraced not Antony   55
As you did love, but as you feared him.
CLEOPATRA O.
THIDIAS
The scars upon your honour therefore he
Does pity as constrainèd blemishes,
Not as deserved.
CLEOPATRA   He is a god, and knows   60
What is most right. Mine honour was not yielded,
But conquered merely.
ENOBARBUS (*aside*)   To be sure of that
I will ask Antony. Sir, sir, thou art so leaky

That we must leave thee to thy sinking, for
Thy dearest quit thee.   *Exit*
THIDIAS   Shall I say to Caesar   65
What you require of him?—For he partly begs
To be desired to give. It much would please him
That of his fortunes you should make a staff
To lean upon. But it would warm his spirits
To hear from me you had left Antony,   70
And put your self under his shroud,
The universal landlord.
CLEOPATRA   What's your name?
THIDIAS
My name is Thidias.
CLEOPATRA   Most kind messenger,
Say to great Caesar this in deputation:
I kiss his conqu'ring hand. Tell him I am prompt   75
To lay my crown at's feet, and there to kneel
Till from his all-obeying breath I hear
The doom of Egypt.
THIDIAS   'Tis your noblest course.
Wisdom and fortune combating together,
If that the former dare but what it can,   80
No chance may shake it. Give me grace to lay
My duty on your hand.
      He kisses Cleopatra's hand
CLEOPATRA   Your Caesar's father oft,
When he hath mused of taking kingdoms in,
Bestowed his lips on that unworthy place,
As it rained kisses.
      Enter Antony and Enobarbus
ANTONY   Favours, by Jove that thunders!   85
What art thou, fellow?
THIDIAS   One that but performs
The bidding of the fullest man, and worthiest
To have command obeyed.
ENOBARBUS   You will be whipped.
ANTONY (*calling*)
Approach, there!—Ah, you kite! Now, gods and
    devils,
Authority melts from me of late. When I cried 'Ho!', 90
Like boys unto a muss kings would start forth,
And cry 'Your will?'—Have you no ears? I am
Antony yet.
      Enter servants
         Take hence this jack, and whip him.
ENOBARBUS [*aside to Thidias*]
'Tis better playing with a lion's whelp
Than with an old one dying.
ANTONY   Moon and stars!   95
Whip him! Were't twenty of the greatest tributaries
That do acknowledge Caesar, should I find them
So saucy with the hand of she here—what's her name
Since she was Cleopatra? Whip him, fellows,
Till like a boy you see him cringe his face,   100
And whine aloud for mercy. Take him hence.
THIDIAS
Mark Antony—
ANTONY   Tug him away. Being whipped,

Bring him again. This jack of Caesar's shall
Bear us an errand to him.
      Exeunt servants with Thidias
You were half blasted ere I knew you. Ha,   105
Have I my pillow left unpressed in Rome,
Forborne the getting of a lawful race,
And by a gem of women, to be abused
By one that looks on feeders?
CLEOPATRA Good my lord—   110
ANTONY You have been a boggler ever.
But when we in our viciousness grow hard—
O misery on't!—the wise gods seel our eyes,
In our own filth drop our clear judgements, make us
Adore our errors, laugh at's while we strut   115
To our confusion.
CLEOPATRA   O, is't come to this?
ANTONY
I found you as a morsel cold upon
Dead Caesar's trencher; nay, you were a fragment
Of Gnaeus Pompey's, besides what hotter hours
Unregistered in vulgar fame you have   120
Luxuriously picked out. For I am sure,
Though you can guess what temperance should be,
You know not what it is.
CLEOPATRA   Wherefore is this?
ANTONY
To let a fellow that will take rewards
And say 'God quit you' be familiar with   125
My playfellow your hand, this kingly seal
And plighter of high hearts! O that I were
Upon the hill of Basan to outroar
The hornèd herd! For I have savage cause,
And to proclaim it civilly were like   130
A haltered neck which does the hangman thank
For being yare about him.
      Enter a Servant with Thidias
         Is he whipped?
SERVANT Soundly, my lord.
ANTONY Cried he, and begged a pardon?
SERVANT He did ask favour.   135
ANTONY (*to Thidias*)
If that thy father live, let him repent
Thou wast not made his daughter; and be thou sorry
To follow Caesar in his triumph, since
Thou hast been whipped for following him. Henceforth
The white hand of a lady fever thee,   140
Shake thou to look on't. Get thee back to Caesar;
Tell him thy entertainment. Look thou say
He makes me angry with him, for he seems
Proud and disdainful, harping on what I am,
Not what he knew I was. He makes me angry,   145
And at this time most easy 'tis to do't,
When my good stars that were my former guides
Have empty left their orbs, and shot their fires
Into th'abyss of hell. If he mislike
My speech and what is done, tell him he has   150
Hipparchus, my enfranchèd bondman, whom
He may at pleasure whip, or hang, or torture,

As he shall like, to quit me. Urge it thou.
Hence, with thy stripes, be gone!
     Exit ⌈Servant with⌉ Thidias
CLEOPATRA Have you done yet?   155
ANTONY Alack, our terrene moon
 Is now eclipsed, and it portends alone
 The fall of Antony.
CLEOPATRA (*aside*) I must stay his time.
ANTONY
 To flatter Caesar would you mingle eyes
 With one that ties his points?
CLEOPATRA   Not know me yet? 160
ANTONY
 Cold-hearted toward me?
CLEOPATRA   Ah, dear, if I be so,
 From my cold heart let heaven engender hail,
 And poison it in the source, and the first stone
 Drop in my neck: as it determines, so
 Dissolve my life! The next Caesarion smite, 165
 Till by degrees the memory of my womb,
 Together with my brave Egyptians all,
 By the discandying of this pelleted storm
 Lie graveless till the flies and gnats of Nile
 Have buried them for prey!
ANTONY   I am satisfied. 170
 Caesar sits down in Alexandria, where
 I will oppose his fate. Our force by land
 Hath nobly held; our severed navy too
 Have knit again, and fleet, threat'ning most sea-like.
 Where hast thou been, my heart? Dost thou hear,
  lady?   175
 If from the field I shall return once more
 To kiss these lips, I will appear in blood.
 I and my sword will ·earn our chronicle.
 There's hope in 't yet.
CLEOPATRA   That's my brave lord.
ANTONY
 I will be treble-sinewed, hearted, breathed, 180
 And fight maliciously; for when mine hours
 Were nice and lucky, men did ransom lives
 .Of me for jests; but now I'll set my teeth,
 And send to darkness all that stop me. Come,
 Let's have one other gaudy night. Call to me 185
 All my sad captains. Fill our bowls once more.
 Let's mock the midnight bell.
CLEOPATRA   It is my birthday.
 I had thought to've held it poor, but since my lord
 Is Antony again, I will be Cleopatra.
ANTONY We will yet do well.   190
CLEOPATRA
 Call all his noble captains to my lord!
ANTONY
 Do so. We'll speak to them, and tonight I'll force
 The wine peep through their scars. Come on, my queen,
 There's sap in 't yet. The next time I do fight
 I'll make death love me, for I will contend 195
 Even with his pestilent scythe.
    Exeunt all but Enobarbus

ENOBARBUS
 Now he'll outstare the lightning. To be furious
 Is to be frighted out of fear, and in that mood
 The dove will peck the estridge; and I see still
 A diminution in our captain's brain 200
 Restores his heart. When valour preys on reason,
 It eats the sword it fights with. I will seek
 Some way to leave him.   *Exit*

4.1 *Enter Caesar, reading a letter, with Agrippa,*
  Maecenas, and his army
CAESAR
 He calls me boy, and chides as he had power
 To beat me out of Egypt. My messenger
 He hath whipped with rods, dares me to personal
  combat,
 Caesar to Antony. Let the old ruffian know
 I have many other ways to die; meantime, 5
 Laugh at his challenge.
MAECENAS   Caesar must think,
 When one so great begins to rage, he's hunted
 Even to falling. Give him no breath, but now
 Make boot of his distraction. Never anger
 Made good guard for itself.
CAESAR   Let our best heads 10
 Know that tomorrow the last of many battles
 We mean to fight. Within our files there are,
 Of those that served Mark Antony but late,
 Enough to fetch him in. See it done,
 And feast the army. We have store to do 't, 15
 And they have earned the waste. Poor Antony!
    Exeunt

4.2 *Enter Antony, Cleopatra, Enobarbus, Charmian,*
  Iras, Alexas, with others
ANTONY
 He will not fight with me, Domitius?
ENOBARBUS   No.
ANTONY Why should he not?
ENOBARBUS
 He thinks, being twenty times of better fortune,
 He is twenty men to one.
ANTONY   Tomorrow, soldier,
 By sea and land I'll fight. Or I will live 5
 Or bathe my dying honour in the blood
 Shall make it live again. Woot thou fight well?
ENOBARBUS
 I'll strike, and cry 'Take all!'
ANTONY   Well said. Come on!
 Call forth my household servants. Let's tonight
 Be bounteous at our meal.
  Enter Servitors
    Give me thy hand. 10
 Thou hast been rightly honest; so hast thou,
 Thou, and thou, and thou; you have served me well,
 And kings have been your fellows.
CLEOPATRA (*to Enobarbus*) What means this?

ENOBARBUS (*to Cleopatra*)
  'Tis one of those odd tricks which sorrow shoots
  Out of the mind.
ANTONY (*to a Servitor*) And thou art honest too.   15
  I wish I could be made so many men,
  And all of you clapped up together in
  An Antony, that I might do you service
  So good as you have done.
SERVITORS   The gods forbid!
ANTONY
  Well, my good fellows, wait on me tonight.   20
  Scant not my cups, and make as much of me
  As when mine empire was your fellow too,
  And suffered my command.
CLEOPATRA (*aside to Enobarbus*) What does he mean?
ENOBARBUS (*aside to Cleopatra*)
  To make his followers weep.
ANTONY   Tend me tonight.
  Maybe it is the period of your duty.   25
  Haply you shall not see me more; or if,
  A mangled shadow. Perchance tomorrow
  You'll serve another master. I look on you
  As one that takes his leave. Mine honest friends,
  I turn you not away, but, like a master   30
  Married to your good service, stay till death.
  Tend me tonight two hours. I ask no more;
  And the gods yield you for't!
ENOBARBUS   What mean you, sir,
  To give them this discomfort? Look, they weep,
  And I, an ass, am onion-eyed. For shame,   35
  Transform us not to women.
ANTONY   Ho, ho, ho,
  Now the witch take me if I meant it thus!
  Grace grow where those drops fall. My hearty friends,
  You take me in too dolorous a sense;
  For I spake to you for your comfort, did desire you   40
  To burn this night with torches. Know, my hearts,
  I hope well of tomorrow, and will lead you
  Where rather I'll expect victorious life
  Than death and honour. Let's to supper, come,   44
  And drown consideration.   *Exeunt*

4.3 *Enter a company of Soldiers*
FIRST SOLDIER
  Brother, good night. Tomorrow is the day.
SECOND SOLDIER
  It will determine one way. Fare you well.
  Heard you of nothing strange about the streets?
FIRST SOLDIER Nothing. What news?
SECOND SOLDIER
  Belike 'tis but a rumour. Good night to you.   5
FIRST SOLDIER
  Well, sir, good night.
          Enter other Soldiers, meeting them
SECOND SOLDIER   Soldiers, have careful watch.
THIRD SOLDIER
  And you. Good night, good night.
          They place themselves in every corner of the stage
SECOND SOLDIER   Here we; an if tomorrow

  Our navy thrive, I have an absolute hope
  Our landmen will stand up.
FIRST SOLDIER   'Tis a brave army,
  And full of purpose.
          Music of the hautboys is under the stage
SECOND SOLDIER   Peace, what noise?
FIRST SOLDIER   List, list!   10
SECOND SOLDIER
  Hark!
FIRST SOLDIER Music i'th' air.
THIRD SOLDIER   Under the earth.
FOURTH SOLDIER
  It signs well, does it not?
THIRD SOLDIER   No.
FIRST SOLDIER   Peace, I say!
  What should this mean?
SECOND SOLDIER
  'Tis the god Hercules, whom Antony loved,
  Now leaves him.
FIRST SOLDIER   Walk. Let's see if other watchmen   15
  Do hear what we do.
SECOND SOLDIER   How now, masters?
ALL (*speaking together*)   How now?
  How now? Do you hear this?
FIRST SOLDIER   Ay. Is't not strange?
THIRD SOLDIER
  Do you hear, masters? Do you hear?
FIRST SOLDIER
  Follow the noise so far as we have quarter.
  Let's see how it will give off.
ALL   Content. 'Tis strange.   20
                                        Exeunt

4.4 *Enter Antony and Cleopatra, with Charmian and*
          others
ANTONY (*calling*)
  Eros, mine armour, Eros!
CLEOPATRA   Sleep a little.
ANTONY
  No, my chuck. Eros, come, mine armour, Eros!
          Enter Eros with armour
  Come, good fellow, put thine iron on.
  If fortune be not ours today, it is
  Because we brave her. Come.
CLEOPATRA   Nay, I'll help, too.   5
  What's this for?
ANTONY   Ah, let be, let be! Thou art
  The armourer of my heart. False, false! This, this!
CLEOPATRA
  Sooth, la, I'll help. Thus it must be.
          She helps Antony to arm
ANTONY   Well, well,
  We shall thrive now. Seest thou, my good fellow?
  Go put on thy defences.
EROS   Briefly, sir.   10
CLEOPATRA
  Is not this buckled well?
ANTONY   Rarely, rarely.

He that unbuckles this, till we do please
To doff't for our repose, shall hear a storm.
Thou fumblest, Eros, and my queen's a squire
More tight at this than thou. Dispatch. O love,   15
That thou couldst see my wars today, and knew'st
The royal occupation! Thou shouldst see
A workman in't.
            Enter an armed Soldier
                        Good morrow to thee. Welcome.
Thou look'st like him that knows a warlike charge.
To business that we love we rise betime,   20
And go to't with delight.
SOLDIER   A thousand, sir,
Early though 't be, have on their riveted trim,
And at the port expect you.
            Shout within. Trumpets flourish. Enter ⌐Captains⌐
            and Soldiers
CAPTAIN
The morn is fair. Good morrow, General.
SOLDIERS
Good morrow, General.
ANTONY   'Tis well blown, lads.   25
This morning, like the spirit of a youth
That means to be of note, begins betimes.
So, so. Come, give me that. This way. Well said.
Fare thee well, dame. Whate'er becomes of me,
This is a soldier's kiss.
            He kisses Cleopatra
                        Rebukable   30
And worthy shameful check it were to stand
On more mechanic compliment. I'll leave thee
Now like a man of steel. You that will fight,
Follow me close. I'll bring you to't. Adieu.
            Exeunt all but Cleopatra and Charmian
CHARMIAN
Please you retire to your chamber?
CLEOPATRA   Lead me.   35
He goes forth gallantly. That he and Caesar might
Determine this great war in single fight!
Then, Antony—but now! Well, on.   *Exeunt*

4.5 *Trumpets sound. Enter Antony and Eros, meeting a*
        Soldier
SOLDIER
The gods make this a happy day to Antony!
ANTONY
Would thou and those thy scars had once prevailed
To make me fight at land!
SOLDIER   Hadst thou done so,
The kings that have revolted, and the soldier
That has this morning left thee, would have still   5
Followed thy heels.
ANTONY   Who's gone this morning?
SOLDIER
Who? One ever near thee. Call for Enobarbus,
He shall not hear thee, or from Caesar's camp
Say 'I am none of thine'.
ANTONY   What sayest thou?

SOLDIER
Sir, he is with Caesar.
EROS *(to Antony)*   Sir, his chests and treasure   10
He has not with him.
ANTONY   Is he gone?
SOLDIER   Most certain.
ANTONY
Go, Eros, send his treasure after. Do it.
Detain no jot, I charge thee. Write to him—
I will subscribe—gentle adieus and greetings.
Say that I wish he never find more cause   15
To change a master. O, my fortunes have
Corrupted honest men! Dispatch. Enobarbus!   *Exeunt*

4.6 *Flourish. Enter Agrippa, Caesar, with Enobarbus*
        and Dollabella
CAESAR
Go forth, Agrippa, and begin the fight.
Our will is Antony be took alive.
Make it so known.
AGRIPPA   Caesar, I shall.   *Exit*
CAESAR
The time of universal peace is near.
Prove this a prosp'rous day, the three-nooked world   5
Shall bear the olive freely.
            Enter a Messenger
MESSENGER   Antony
Is come into the field.
CAESAR   Go charge Agrippa,
Plant those that have revolted in the van,
That Antony may seem to spend his fury
Upon himself.   10
            Exeunt Messenger ⌐at one door⌐, Caesar and
                            Dolabella ⌐at another⌐
ENOBARBUS
Alexas did revolt, and went to Jewry on
Affairs of Antony; there did dissuade
Great Herod to incline himself to Caesar
And leave his master, Antony. For this pains,
Caesar hath hanged him. Camidius and the rest   15
That fell away have entertainment but
No honourable trust. I have done ill,
Of which I do accuse myself so sorely
That I will joy no more.
            Enter a Soldier of Caesar's
SOLDIER   Enobarbus, Antony
Hath after thee sent all thy treasure, with   20
His bounty overplus. The messenger
Came on my guard, and at thy tent is now
Unloading of his mules.
ENOBARBUS I give it you.
SOLDIER Mock not, Enobarbus,   25
I tell you true. Best you safed the bringer
Out of the host. I must attend mine office,
Or would have done't myself. Your Emperor
Continues still a Jove.   *Exit*
ENOBARBUS
I am alone the villain of the earth,   30

And feel I am so most. O Antony,
Thou mine of bounty, how wouldst thou have paid
My better service, when my turpitude
Thou dost so crown with gold! This blows my heart.
If swift thought break it not, a swifter mean   35
Shall outstrike thought; but thought will do't, I feel.
I fight against thee? No, I will go seek
Some ditch wherein to die. The foul'st best fits
My latter part of life.   *Exit*

4.7   *Alarum. Enter Agrippa ⌈with drummers and*
         trumpeters⌉
AGRIPPA
Retire! We have engaged our selves too far.
Caesar himself has work, and our oppression
Exceeds what we expected.   *Exeunt*

4.8   *Alarums. Enter Antony, and Scarus wounded*
SCARUS
O my brave Emperor, this is fought indeed!
Had we done so at first, we had droven them home
With clouts about their heads.
ANTONY   Thou bleed'st apace.
SCARUS
I had a wound here that was like a T,
But now 'tis made an H.
         Retreat sounded far off
ANTONY   They do retire.   5
SCARUS
We'll beat 'em into bench-holes. I have yet
Room for six scotches more.
         Enter Eros
EROS
They are beaten, sir, and our advantage serves
For a fair victory.
SCARUS   Let us score their backs
And snatch 'em up as we take hares, behind.   10
'Tis sport to maul a runner.
ANTONY (*to Eros*)   I will reward thee
Once for thy sprightly comfort, and tenfold
For thy good valour. Come thee on.
SCARUS   I'll halt after.
                                       Exeunt

4.9   *Alarum. Enter Antony again in a march; drummers*
         and trumpeters; Scarus, with others
ANTONY
We have beat him to his camp. Run one before,
And let the Queen know of our gests.   ⌈*Exit a soldier*⌉
                                       Tomorrow,
Before the sun shall see's, we'll spill the blood
That has today escaped. I thank you all,
For doughty-handed are you, and have fought   5
Not as you served the cause, but as't had been
Each man's like mine. You have shown all Hectors.
Enter the city, clip your wives, your friends,
Tell them your feats whilst they with joyful tears

Wash the congealment from your wounds, and kiss   10
The honoured gashes whole.
         Enter Cleopatra
(*To Scarus*)   Give me thy hand.
To this great fairy I'll commend thy acts,
Make her thanks bless thee.
(*To Cleopatra, embracing her*) O thou day o'th' world,
Chain mine armed neck; leap thou, attire and all,
Through proof of harness to my heart, and there   15
Ride on the pants triumphing.
CLEOPATRA   Lord of lords!
O infinite virtue, com'st thou smiling from
The world's great snare uncaught?
ANTONY   My nightingale,
We have beat them to their beds. What, girl, though
   grey
Do something mingle with our younger brown, yet
   ha' we   20
A brain that nourishes our nerves, and can
Get goal for goal of youth. Behold this man.
Commend unto his lips thy favouring hand;
Kiss it, my warrior.
         Scarus kisses Cleopatra's hand
                      He hath fought today
As if a god, in hate of mankind, had   25
Destroyed in such a shape.
CLEOPATRA   I'll give thee, friend,
An armour all of gold. It was a king's.
ANTONY
He has deserved it, were it carbuncled
Like holy Phoebus' car. Give me thy hand.
Through Alexandria make a jolly march.   30
Bear our hacked targets like the men that owe them.
Had our great palace the capacity
To camp this host, we all would sup together
And drink carouses to the next day's fate,
Which promises royal peril. Trumpeters,   35
With brazen din blast you the city's ear;
Make mingle with our rattling taborins,
That heaven and earth may strike their sounds
   together,
Applauding our approach.   *Trumpets sound. Exeunt*

4.10 *Enter a Sentry and his company; Enobarbus follows*
SENTRY
If we be not relieved within this hour
We must return to th' court of guard. The night
Is shiny, and they say we shall embattle
By th' second hour i'th' morn.
FIRST WATCH   This last day was
A shrewd one to's.
ENOBARBUS   O bear me witness, night—   5
SECOND WATCH
What man is this?
FIRST WATCH   Stand close, and list him.
ENOBARBUS
Be witness to me, O thou blessèd moon,
When men revolted shall upon record

Bear hateful memory, poor Enobarbus did
Before thy face repent.
SENTRY   Enobarbus?
SECOND WATCH   Peace; hark further.
ENOBARBUS
    O sovereign mistress of true melancholy,   11
    The poisonous damp of night disponge upon me,
    That life, a very rebel to my will,
    May hang no longer on me. Throw my heart
    Against the flint and hardness of my fault,   15
    Which, being dried with grief, will break to powder,
    And finish all foul thoughts. O Antony,
    Nobler than my revolt is infamous,
    Forgive me in thine own particular,
    But let the world rank me in register   20
    A master-leaver and a fugitive.
    O Antony! O Antony!   He dies
FIRST WATCH Let's speak to him.
SENTRY
    Let's hear him, for the things he speaks
    May concern Caesar.
SECOND WATCH   Let's do so. But he sleeps.   25
SENTRY
    Swoons, rather; for so bad a prayer as his
    Was never yet for sleep.
FIRST WATCH   Go we to him.
SECOND WATCH
    Awake, sir, awake; speak to us.
FIRST WATCH   Hear you, sir?
SENTRY
    The hand of death hath raught him.
        Drums afar off
                                      Hark, the drums
    Demurely wake the sleepers. Let us bear him   30
    To th' court of guard; he is of note. Our hour
    Is fully out.
SECOND WATCH
    Come on, then. He may recover yet.
                              Exeunt with the body

4.11 *Enter Antony and Scarus with their army*
ANTONY
    Their preparation is today by sea;
    We please them not by land.
SCARUS   For both, my lord.
ANTONY
    I would they'd fight i'th' fire or i'th' air;
    We'd fight there too. But this it is: our foot
    Upon the hills adjoining to the city   5
    Shall stay with us. Order for sea is given.
    They have put forth the haven—
    Where their appointment we may best discover,
    And look on their endeavour.   Exeunt

4.12 *Enter Caesar and his army*
CAESAR
    But being charged, we will be still by land—
    Which, as I take't, we shall, for his best force

Is forth to man his galleys. To the vales,
And hold our best advantage.   Exeunt

4.13 ⌈*Alarum afar off, as at a sea fight.*⌉
        Enter Antony and Scarus
ANTONY
    Yet they are not joined. Where yon pine does stand
    I shall discover all. I'll bring thee word
    Straight how 'tis like to go.   Exit
SCARUS   Swallows have built
    In Cleopatra's sails their nests. The augurs
    Say they know not, they cannot tell, look grimly,   5
    And dare not speak their knowledge. Antony
    Is valiant, and dejected, and by starts
    His fretted fortunes give him hope and fear
    Of what he has and has not.
        Enter Antony
ANTONY   All is lost.
    This foul Egyptian hath betrayèd me.   10
    My fleet hath yielded to the foe, and yonder
    They cast their caps up, and carouse together
    Like friends long lost. Triple-turned whore! 'Tis thou
    Hast sold me to this novice, and my heart
    Makes only wars on thee. Bid them all fly;   15
    For when I am revenged upon my charm,
    I have done all. Bid them all fly. Be gone. ⌈*Exit Scarus*⌉
    O sun, thy uprise shall I see no more.
    Fortune and Antony part here; even here
    Do we shake hands. All come to this? The hearts   20
    That spanieled me at heels, to whom I gave
    Their wishes, do discandy, melt their sweets
    On blossoming Caesar; and this pine is barked
    That overtopped them all. Betrayed I am.
    O this false soul of Egypt! This grave charm,   25
    Whose eye becked forth my wars and called them home,
    Whose bosom was my crownet, my chief end,
    Like a right gipsy hath at fast and loose
    Beguiled me to the very heart of loss.
    What, Eros, Eros!
        Enter Cleopatra
                              Ah, thou spell! Avaunt.   30
CLEOPATRA
    Why is my lord enraged against his love?
ANTONY
    Vanish, or I shall give thee thy deserving
    And blemish Caesar's triumph. Let him take thee
    And hoist thee up to the shouting plebeians;
    Follow his chariot, like the greatest spot   35
    Of all thy sex; most monster-like be shown
    For poor'st diminutives, for dolts, and let
    Patient Octavia plough thy visage up
    With her preparèd nails.   Exit Cleopatra
                              'Tis well thou'rt gone,
    If it be well to live. But better 'twere   40
    Thou fell'st into my fury, for one death
    Might have prevented many. Eros, ho!
    The shirt of Nessus is upon me. Teach me,
    Alcides, thou mine ancestor, thy rage.
    Let me lodge Lichas on the horns o'th' moon,   45

And with those hands that grasped the heaviest club
Subdue my worthiest self. The witch shall die.
To the young Roman boy she hath sold me, and I fall
Under this plot. She dies for't. Eros, ho!   *Exit*

4.14 *Enter Cleopatra, Charmian, Iras, Mardian*
CLEOPATRA
Help me, my women! O, he's more mad
Than Telamon for his shield; the boar of Thessaly
Was never so embossed.
CHARMIAN   To th' monument!
There lock yourself, and send him word you are dead.
The soul and body rive not more in parting   5
Than greatness going off.
CLEOPATRA   To th' monument!
Mardian, go tell him I have slain myself.
Say that the last I spoke was 'Antony',
And word it, prithee, piteously. Hence, Mardian,   9
And bring me how he takes my death. To th'
    monument!   *Exeunt*

4.15 *Enter Antony and Eros*
ANTONY
Eros, thou yet behold'st me?
EROS   Ay, noble lord.
ANTONY
Sometime we see a cloud that's dragonish,
A vapour sometime like a bear or lion,
A towered citadel, a pendent rock,
A forkèd mountain, or blue promontory   5
With trees upon't that nod unto the world
And mock our eyes with air. Thou hast seen these signs;
They are black vesper's pageants.
EROS   Ay, my lord.
ANTONY
That which is now a horse even with a thought
The rack distains, and makes it indistinct   10
As water is in water.
EROS   It does, my lord.
ANTONY
My good knave Eros, now thy captain is
Even such a body. Here I am Antony,
Yet cannot hold this visible shape, my knave.
I made these wars for Egypt, and the Queen—   15
Whose heart I thought I had, for she had mine,
Which whilst it was mine had annexed unto't
A million more, now lost—she, Eros, has
Packed cards with Caesar, and false-played my glory
Unto an enemy's triumph.   20
Nay, weep not, gentle Eros. There is left us
Ourselves to end ourselves.
    Enter Mardian
                          O thy vile lady,
She has robbed me of my sword!
MARDIAN   No, Antony,
My mistress loved thee, and her fortunes mingled
With thine entirely.
ANTONY   Hence, saucy eunuch, peace!   25
She hath betrayed me, and shall die the death.

MARDIAN
Death of one person can be paid but once,
And that she has discharged. What thou wouldst do
Is done unto thy hand. The last she spake
Was 'Antony, most noble Antony!'   30
Then in the midst a tearing groan did break
The name of Antony. It was divided
Between her heart and lips. She rendered life,
Thy name so buried in her.
ANTONY   Dead, then?
MARDIAN   Dead.
ANTONY
Unarm, Eros. The long day's task is done,   35
And we must sleep. (*To Mardian*) That thou depart'st
    hence safe
Does pay thy labour richly. Go.   *Exit Mardian*
                           Off, pluck off.
    Eros helps Antony to unarm
The seven-fold shield of Ajax cannot keep
The battery from my heart. O, cleave, my sides!
Heart, once be stronger than thy continent;   40
Crack thy frail case. Apace, Eros, apace.
No more a soldier. Bruisèd pieces, go;
You have been nobly borne.—From me a while.
                                      Exit Eros
I will o'ertake thee, Cleopatra, and
Weep for my pardon. So it must be, for now   45
All length is torture. Since the torch is out,
Lie down, and stray no farther. Now all labour
Mars what it does; yea, very force entangles
Itself with strength. Seal, then, and all is done.
Eros!—I come, my queen.—Eros!—Stay for me.   50
Where souls do couch on flowers we'll hand in hand,
And with our sprightly port make the ghosts gaze.
Dido and her Aeneas shall want troops,
And all the haunt be ours. Come, Eros, Eros!
    Enter Eros
EROS
What would my lord?
ANTONY   Since Cleopatra died   55
I have lived in such dishonour that the gods
Detest my baseness. I, that with my sword
Quartered the world, and o'er green Neptune's back
With ships made cities, condemn myself to lack
The courage of a woman; less noble mind   60
Than she which by her death our Caesar tells
'I am conqueror of myself.' Thou art sworn, Eros,
That when the exigent should come, which now
Is come indeed—when I should see behind me
Th'inevitable prosecution of   65
Disgrace and horror—that on my command
Thou then wouldst kill me. Do't. The time is come.
Thou strik'st not me; 'tis Caesar thou defeat'st.
Put colour in thy cheek.
EROS   The gods withhold me!
Shall I do that which all the Parthian darts,   70
Though enemy, lost aim and could not?
ANTONY   Eros,
Wouldst thou be windowed in great Rome and see

Thy master thus with pleachèd arms, bending down
His corrigible neck, his face subdued
To penetrative shame, whilst the wheeled seat　75
Of fortunate Caesar, drawn before him, branded
His baseness that ensued?
EROS　　　　　　　　　　　I would not see't.
ANTONY
Come then; for with a wound I must be cured.
Draw that thy honest sword, which thou hast worn
Most useful for thy country.
EROS　　　　　　　　　　O sir, pardon me!　80
ANTONY
When I did make thee free, swor'st thou not then
To do this when I bade thee? Do it at once,
Or thy precedent services are all
But accidents unpurposed. Draw, and come.
EROS
Turn from me then that noble countenance　85
Wherein the worship of the whole world lies.
ANTONY (turning away) Lo thee!
EROS
My sword is drawn.
ANTONY　　　　　　　Then let it do at once
The thing why thou hast drawn it.
EROS　　　　　　　　　　　My dear master,
My captain, and my Emperor: let me say,　90
Before I strike this bloody stroke, farewell.
ANTONY 'Tis said, man; and farewell.
EROS
Farewell, great chief. Shall I strike now?
ANTONY　　　　　　　　　　　　Now, Eros.
⌈Eros stabs himself⌉
EROS
Why, there then, thus I do escape the sorrow
Of Antony's death.　　　　　　　He dies
ANTONY　　　　　Thrice nobler than myself,　95
Thou teachest me, O valiant Eros, what
I should and thou couldst not. My queen and Eros
Have by their brave instruction got upon me
A nobleness in record. But I will be
A bridegroom in my death, and run into't　100
As to a lover's bed. Come then, and, Eros,
Thy master dies thy scholar. To do thus
I learned of thee.
He stabs himself
　　　　　How, not dead? Not dead?
The guard, ho! O, dispatch me!
Enter a guard ⌈and Decretas⌉
FIRST GUARD　　　　　　What's the noise?
ANTONY
I have done my work ill, friends. O, make an end　105
Of what I have begun!
SECOND GUARD　　　　The star is fall'n.
FIRST GUARD
And time is at his period.
ALL THE GUARDS　　　　Alas
And woe!
ANTONY　　Let him that loves me strike me dead.

FIRST GUARD
Not I.
SECOND GUARD　Nor I.
THIRD GUARD　　　　Nor anyone.　Exeunt the guard
DECRETAS
Thy death and fortunes bid thy followers fly.　110
He takes Antony's sword
This sword but shown to Caesar, with this tidings,
Shall enter me with him.
Enter Diomedes
DIOMEDES　　　　　　　Where's Antony?
DECRETAS
There, Diomed, there.
DIOMEDES　　　　Lives he? Wilt thou not answer, man?
Exit Decretas
ANTONY
Art thou there, Diomed? Draw thy sword, and give me
Sufficing strokes for death.
DIOMEDES　　　　　　Most absolute lord,　115
My mistress Cleopatra sent me to thee.
ANTONY
When did she send thee?
DIOMEDES　　　　　　Now, my lord.
ANTONY　　　　　　　　　Where is she?
DIOMEDES
Locked in her monument. She had a prophesying fear
Of what hath come to pass; for when she saw—
Which never shall be found—you did suspect　120
She had disposed with Caesar, and that your rage
Would not be purged, she sent word she was dead;
But fearing since how it might work, hath sent
Me to proclaim the truth; and I am come,
I dread, too late.　　　　　　　　　125
ANTONY
Too late, good Diomed. Call my guard, I prithee.
DIOMEDES
What ho, the Emperor's guard! The guard, what ho!
Come, your lord calls.
Enter four or five of the guard of Antony
ANTONY
Bear me, good friends, where Cleopatra bides.
'Tis the last service that I shall command you.　130
FIRST GUARD
Woe, woe are we, sir, you may not live to wear
All your true followers out.
ALL THE GUARDS　　　　Most heavy day!
ANTONY
Nay, good my fellows, do not please sharp fate
To grace it with your sorrows. Bid that welcome
Which comes to punish us, and we punish it,　135
Seeming to bear it lightly. Take me up.
I have led you oft; carry me now, good friends,
And have my thanks for all.
Exeunt bearing Antony ⌈and Eros⌉

4.16　Enter Cleopatra ⌈and her maids aloft⌉, with
　　　　Charmian and Iras
CLEOPATRA
O Charmian, I will never go from hence.

CHARMIAN
Be comforted, dear madam.
CLEOPATRA   No, I will not.
All strange and terrible events are welcome,
But comforts we despise. Our size of sorrow,
Proportioned to our cause, must be as great   5
As that which makes it.
          Enter Diomedes [below]
                              How now? Is he dead?
DIOMEDES
His death's upon him, but not dead.
Look out o'th' other side your monument.
His guard have brought him thither.
          Enter below Antony, borne by the guard
CLEOPATRA   O sun,
Burn the great sphere thou mov'st in; darkling stand
The varying shore o'th' world! O Antony,   11
Antony, Antony! Help, Charmian,
Help, Iras, help, help, friends below!
Let's draw him hither.
ANTONY   Peace. Not Caesar's valour
Hath o'erthrown Antony, but Antony's   15
Hath triumphed on itself.
CLEOPATRA   So it should be,
That none but Antony should conquer Antony.
But woe 'tis so!
ANTONY
I am dying, Egypt, dying. Only
I here importune death awhile until   20
Of many thousand kisses the poor last
I lay upon thy lips.
CLEOPATRA   I dare not, dear,
Dear, my lord, pardon. I dare not,
Lest I be taken. Nor th'imperious show
Of the full-fortuned Caesar ever shall   25
Be brooched with me, if knife, drugs, serpents, have
Edge, sting, or operation. I am safe.
Your wife, Octavia, with her modest eyes
And still conclusion, shall acquire no honour
Demuring upon me. But come, come, Antony.—   30
Help me, my women.—We must draw thee up.
Assist, good friends.
ANTONY   O quick, or I am gone!
CLEOPATRA
Here's sport indeed. How heavy weighs my lord!
Our strength is all gone into heaviness,
That makes the weight. Had I great Juno's power   35
The strong-winged Mercury should fetch thee up
And set thee by Jove's side. Yet come a little.
Wishers were ever fools. O come, come, come!
          They heave Antony aloft to Cleopatra
And welcome, welcome! Die when thou hast lived,
Quicken with kissing. Had my lips that power,   40
Thus would I wear them out.
          They kiss
ALL THE LOOKERS-ON A heavy sight.
ANTONY I am dying, Egypt, dying.
Give me some wine, and let me speak a little.

CLEOPATRA
No, let me speak, and let me rail so high   45
That the false hussy Fortune break her wheel,
Provoked by my offence.
ANTONY   One word, sweet queen,
Of Caesar seek your honour, with your safety. O!
CLEOPATRA
They do not go together.
ANTONY   Gentle, hear me.
None about Caesar trust but Proculeius.   50
CLEOPATRA
My resolution and my hands I'll trust,
None about Caesar.
ANTONY
The miserable change now at my end
Lament nor sorrow at, but please your thoughts
In feeding them with those my former fortunes,   55
Wherein I lived the greatest prince o'th' world,
The noblest; and do now not basely die,
Not cowardly put off my helmet to
My countryman; a Roman by a Roman
Valiantly vanquished. Now my spirit is going;   60
I can no more.
CLEOPATRA   Noblest of men, woot die?
Hast thou no care of me? Shall I abide
In this dull world, which in thy absence is
No better than a sty?
          Antony dies
                    O see, my women,
The crown o'th' earth doth melt. My lord!   65
O, withered is the garland of the war.
The soldier's pole is fall'n. Young boys and girls
Are level now with men. The odds is gone,
And there is nothing left remarkable
Beneath the visiting moon.   70
          She falls
CHARMIAN O, quietness, lady!
IRAS She's dead, too, our sovereign.
CHARMIAN
          Lady!
IRAS   Madam!
CHARMIAN   O, madam, madam, madam!
IRAS
Royal Egypt, Empress!
CHARMIAN   Peace, peace, Iras!
CLEOPATRA *(recovering)*
No more but e'en a woman, and commanded   75
By such poor passion as the maid that milks
And does the meanest chores. It were for me
To throw my sceptre at the injurious gods,
To tell them that this world did equal theirs
Till they had stol'n our jewel. All's but naught.   80
Patience is sottish, and impatience does
Become a dog that's mad. Then is it sin
To rush into the secret house of death
Ere death dare come to us? How do you, women?
What, what, good cheer! Why, how now, Charmian?
My noble girls! Ah, women, women! Look,   86
Our lamp is spent, it's out. Good sirs, take heart;

We'll bury him, and then what's brave, what's noble,
Let's do it after the high Roman fashion,
And make death proud to take us. Come, away.   90
This case of that huge spirit now is cold.
Ah, women, women! Come. We have no friend
But resolution, and the briefest end.
            Exeunt, those above bearing off Antony's body

5.1 *Enter Caesar with his council of war: Agrippa,*
        Dollabella, Maecenas, Gallus, Proculeius
CAESAR
Go to him, Dollabella, bid him yield.
Being so frustrate, tell him, he but mocks
The pauses that he makes.
DOLABELLA   Caesar, I shall.   *Exit*
        Enter Decretas with the sword of Antony
CAESAR
Wherefore is that? And what art thou that dar'st
Appear thus to us?
DECRETAS   I am called Decretas.   5
Mark Antony I served, who best was worthy
Best to be served. Whilst he stood up and spoke
He was my master, and I wore my life
To spend upon his haters. If thou please
To take me to thee, as I was to him   10
I'll be to Caesar; if thou pleasest not,
I yield thee up my life.
CAESAR   What is't thou sayst?
DECRETAS
I say, O Caesar, Antony is dead.
CAESAR
The breaking of so great a thing should make
A greater crack. The rivèd world   15
Should have shook lions into civil streets,
And citizens to their dens. The death of Antony
Is not a single doom; in that name lay
A moiety of the world.
DECRETAS   He is dead, Caesar,
Not by a public minister of justice,   20
Nor by a hirèd knife; but that self hand
Which writ his honour in the acts it did
Hath, with the courage which the heart did lend it,
Splitted the heart. This is his sword;
I robbed his wound of it. Behold it stained   25
With his most noble blood.
CAESAR (*weeping*)   Look you, sad friends,
The gods rebuke me; but it is a tidings
To wash the eyes of kings.
⌈AGRIPPA⌉   And strange it is
That nature must compel us to lament
Our most persisted deeds.
MAECENAS   His taints and honours   30
Waged equal with him.
⌈AGRIPPA⌉   A rarer spirit never
Did steer humanity; but you gods will give us
Some faults to make us men. Caesar is touched.
MAECENAS
When such a spacious mirror's set before him
He needs must see himself.
CAESAR   O Antony,   35

I have followed thee to this. But we do lance
Diseases in our bodies. I must perforce
Have shown to thee such a declining day,
Or look on thine. We could not stall together
In the whole world. But yet let me lament,   40
With tears as sovereign as the blood of hearts,
That thou, my brother, my competitor
In top of all design, my mate in empire,
Friend and companion in the front of war,
The arm of mine own body, and the heart   45
Where mine his thoughts did kindle—that our stars,
Unreconciliable, should divide
Our equalness to this. Hear me, good friends—
        Enter an Egyptian
But I will tell you at some meeter season.
The business of this man looks out of him;   50
We'll hear him what he says.—Whence are you?
EGYPTIAN
A poor Egyptian, yet the Queen my mistress,
Confined in all she has, her monument,
Of thy intents desires instruction,
That she preparèdly may frame herself   55
To th' way she's forced to.
CAESAR   Bid her have good heart.
She soon shall know of us, by some of ours,
How honourable and how kindly we
Determine for her. For Caesar cannot live
To be ungentle.
EGYPTIAN   So; the gods preserve thee!   *Exit*
CAESAR
Come hither, Proculeius. Go, and say   61
We purpose her no shame. Give her what comforts
The quality of her passion shall require,
Lest in her greatness, by some mortal stroke,
She do defeat us; for her life in Rome   65
Would be eternal in our triumph. Go,
And with your speediest bring us what she says
And how you find of her.
PROCULEIUS   Caesar, I shall.   *Exit*
CAESAR
Gallus, go you along.   *Exit Gallus*
                    Where's Dolabella,
To second Proculeius?
ALL BUT CAESAR   Dolabella!   70
CAESAR
Let him alone; for I remember now
How he's employed. He shall in time be ready.
Go with me to my tent, where you shall see
How hardly I was drawn into this war,
How calm and gentle I proceeded still   75
In all my writings. Go with me, and see
What I can show in this.   *Exeunt*

5.2 *Enter Cleopatra, Charmian, Iras, and Mardian*
CLEOPATRA
My desolation does begin to make
A better life. 'Tis paltry to be Caesar.
Not being Fortune, he's but Fortune's knave,
A minister of her will. And it is great

To do that thing that ends all other deeds,   5
Which shackles accidents and bolts up change,
Which sleeps and never palates more the dung,
The beggar's nurse, and Caesar's.
   Enter Proculeius
PROCULEIUS
Caesar sends greeting to the Queen of Egypt,
And bids thee study on what fair demands   10
Thou mean'st to have him grant thee.
CLEOPATRA   What's thy name?
PROCULEIUS
My name is Proculeius.
CLEOPATRA   Antony
Did tell me of you, bade me trust you; but
I do not greatly care to be deceived,
That have no use for trusting. If your master   15
Would have a queen his beggar, you must tell him
That majesty, to keep decorum, must
No less beg than a kingdom. If he please
To give me conquered Egypt for my son,
He gives me so much of mine own as I   20
Will kneel to him with thanks.
PROCULEIUS   Be of good cheer.
You're fall'n into a princely hand; fear nothing.
Make your full reference freely to my lord,
Who is so full of grace that it flows over
On all that need. Let me report to him   25
Your sweet dependency, and you shall find
A conqueror that will pray in aid for kindness,
Where he for grace is kneeled to.
CLEOPATRA   Pray you, tell him
I am his fortune's vassal, and I send him
The greatness he has got. I hourly learn   30
A doctrine of obedience, and would gladly
Look him i'th' face.
PROCULEIUS   This I'll report, dear lady;
Have comfort, for I know your plight is pitied
Of him that caused it.
   ⌈*Enter Roman soldiers from behind*⌉
PROCULEIUS (*to the soldiers*)
You see how easily she may be surprised.   35
Guard her till Caesar come.
IRAS   Royal Queen—
CHARMIAN
O Cleopatra, thou art taken, Queen!
CLEOPATRA (*drawing a dagger*)
Quick, quick, good hands!
PROCULEIUS (*disarming Cleopatra*)
     Hold, worthy lady, hold!
Do not yourself such wrong, who are in this
Relieved but not betrayed.
CLEOPATRA   What, of death too,   40
That rids our dogs of languish?
PROCULEIUS   Cleopatra,
Do not abuse my master's bounty by
Th'undoing of yourself. Let the world see
His nobleness well acted, which your death
Will never let come forth.
CLEOPATRA   Where art thou, death?   45

Come hither, come. Come, come, and take a queen
Worth many babes and beggars.
PROCULEIUS   O temperance, lady!
CLEOPATRA
Sir, I will eat no meat. I'll not drink, sir.
If idle talk will once be necessary,
I'll not sleep, neither. This mortal house I'll ruin,   50
Do Caesar what he can. Know, sir, that I
Will not wait pinioned at your master's court,
Nor once be chastised with the sober eye
Of dull Octavia. Shall they hoist me up
And show me to the shouting varletry   55
Of censuring Rome? Rather a ditch in Egypt
Be gentle grave unto me; rather on Nilus' mud
Lay me stark naked, and let the waterflies
Blow me into abhorring; rather make
My country's high pyramides my gibbet,   60
And hang me up in chains.
PROCULEIUS   You do extend
These thoughts of horror further than you shall
Find cause in Caesar.
   Enter Dolabella
DOLABELLA   Proculeius,
What thou hast done thy master Caesar knows,
And he hath sent for thee. For the Queen,   65
I'll take her to my guard.
PROCULEIUS   So, Dolabella,
It shall content me best. Be gentle to her.
(*To Cleopatra*) To Caesar I will speak what you shall
  please,
If you'll employ me to him.
CLEOPATRA   Say I would die.
       Exit Proculeius
DOLABELLA
Most noble Empress, you have heard of me.   70
CLEOPATRA
I cannot tell.
DOLABELLA   Assuredly you know me.
CLEOPATRA
No matter, sir, what I have heard or known.
You laugh when boys or women tell their dreams;
Is't not your trick?
DOLABELLA   I understand not, madam.
CLEOPATRA
I dreamt there was an Emperor Antony.   75
O, such another sleep, that I might see
But such another man!
DOLABELLA   If it might please ye—
CLEOPATRA
His face was as the heav'ns, and therein stuck
A sun and moon, which kept their course and lighted
The little O o'th' earth.
DOLABELLA   Most sovereign creature—   80
CLEOPATRA
His legs bestrid the ocean; his reared arm
Crested the world. His voice was propertied
As all the tunèd spheres, and that to friends;
But when he meant to quail and shake the orb,
He was as rattling thunder. For his bounty,   85

There was no winter in't; an autumn 'twas,
That grew the more by reaping. His delights
Were dolphin-like; they showed his back above
The element they lived in. In his livery
Walked crowns and crownets. Realms and islands were
As plates dropped from his pocket.
DOLABELLA   Cleopatra—   91
CLEOPATRA
Think you there was, or might be, such a man
As this I dreamt of?
DOLABELLA   Gentle madam, no.
CLEOPATRA
You lie, up to the hearing of the gods.
But if there be, or ever were one such,   95
It's past the size of dreaming. Nature wants stuff
To vie strange forms with fancy; yet t'imagine
An Antony were nature's piece 'gainst fancy,
Condemning shadows quite.
DOLABELLA   Hear me, good madam:
Your loss is as yourself, great, and you bear it   100
As answering to the weight. Would I might never
O'ertake pursued success but I do feel,
By the rebound of yours, a grief that smites
My very heart at root.
CLEOPATRA   I thank you, sir.
Know you what Caesar means to do with me?   105
DOLABELLA
I am loath to tell you what I would you knew.
CLEOPATRA
Nay, pray you, sir.
DOLABELLA   Though he be honourable—
CLEOPATRA
He'll lead me then in triumph.
DOLABELLA   Madam, he will, I know't.
    Flourish. Enter Caesar, with Proculeius, Gallus,
    Maecenas, and others of his train
ALL
Make way, there! Caesar!
CAESAR   Which is the Queen of Egypt?
DOLABELLA (*to Cleopatra*)
It is the Emperor, madam.
    Cleopatra kneels
CAESAR   Arise! You shall not kneel.
I pray you rise, rise, Egypt.
CLEOPATRA (*rising*)   Sir, the gods   111
Will have it thus. My master and my lord
I must obey.
CAESAR   Take to you no hard thoughts.
The record of what injuries you did us,
Though written in our flesh, we shall remember   115
As things but done by chance.
CLEOPATRA   Sole sir o'th' world,
I cannot project mine own cause so well
To make it clear, but do confess I have
Been laden with like frailties which before
Have often shamed our sex.
CAESAR   Cleopatra, know   120
We will extenuate rather than enforce.

If you apply yourself to our intents,
Which towards you are most gentle, you shall find
A benefit in this change; but if you seek
To lay on me a cruelty by taking   125
Antony's course, you shall bereave yourself
Of my good purposes and put your children
To that destruction which I'll guard them from,
If thereon you rely. I'll take my leave.
CLEOPATRA
And may through all the world! 'Tis yours, and we,
Your scutcheons and your signs of conquest, shall   131
Hang in what place you please. (*Giving a paper*) Here,
    my good lord.
CAESAR
You shall advise me in all for Cleopatra.
CLEOPATRA
This is the brief of money, plate, and jewels
I am possessed of. 'Tis exactly valued,   135
Not petty things admitted. Where's Seleucus?
    Enter Seleucus
SELEUCUS Here, madam.
CLEOPATRA (*to Caesar*)
This is my treasurer. Let him speak, my lord,
Upon his peril, that I have reserved
To myself nothing. Speak the truth, Seleucus.   140
SELEUCUS
Madam, I had rather seal my lips
Than to my peril speak that which is not.
CLEOPATRA What have I kept back?
SELEUCUS
Enough to purchase what you have made known.
CAESAR
Nay, blush not, Cleopatra. I approve   145
Your wisdom in the deed.
CLEOPATRA   See, Caesar! O, behold
How pomp is followed! Mine will now be yours,
And should we shift estates, yours would be mine.
The ingratitude of this Seleucus does
Even make me wild.—O slave, of no more trust   150
Than love that's hired! What, goest thou back? Thou
    shalt
Go back, I warrant thee; but I'll catch thine eyes
Though they had wings. Slave, soulless villain, dog!
O rarely base!
CAESAR   Good Queen, let us entreat you.
CLEOPATRA
O Caesar, what a wounding shame is this,   155
That thou vouchsafing here to visit me,
Doing the honour of thy lordliness
To one so meek—that mine own servant should
Parcel the sum of my disgraces by
Addition of his envy. Say, good Caesar,   160
That I some lady trifles have reserved,
Immoment toys, things of such dignity
As we greet modern friends withal; and say
Some nobler token I have kept apart
For Livia and Octavia, to induce   165

Their mediation—must I be unfolded
With one that I have bred? The gods! It smites me
Beneath the fall I have. (*To Seleucus*) Prithee, go hence,
Or I shall show the cinders of my spirits
Through th'ashes of my chance. Wert thou a man   170
Thou wouldst have mercy on me.

CAESAR   Forbear, Seleucus.
                                        Exit Seleucus

CLEOPATRA
Be it known that we, the greatest, are misthought
For things that others do; and when we fall
We answer others' merits in our name,
Are therefore to be pitied.

CAESAR   Cleopatra,   175
Not what you have reserved nor what acknowledged
Put we i'th' roll of conquest. Still be't yours.
Bestow it at your pleasure, and believe
Caesar's no merchant, to make prize with you
Of things that merchants sold. Therefore be cheered.
Make not your thoughts your prisons. No, dear
    Queen;   181
For we intend so to dispose you as
Yourself shall give us counsel. Feed and sleep.
Our care and pity is so much upon you
That we remain your friend; and so adieu.   185

CLEOPATRA
My master and my lord!

CAESAR   Not so. Adieu.
                Flourish. Exeunt Caesar and his train

CLEOPATRA
He words me, girls, he words me, that I should not
Be noble to myself. But hark thee, Charmian.
                She whispers to Charmian

IRAS
Finish, good lady. The bright day is done,
And we are for the dark.

CLEOPATRA (*to Charmian*) Hie thee again.   190
I have spoke already, and it is provided.
Go put it to the haste.

CHARMIAN   Madam, I will.
                Enter Dolabella

DOLABELLA
Where's the Queen?

CHARMIAN   Behold, sir.   *Exit*

CLEOPATRA   Dolabella!

DOLABELLA
Madam, as thereto sworn by your command—
Which my love makes religion to obey—   195
I tell you this: Caesar through Syria
Intends his journey, and within three days
You with your children will he send before.
Make your best use of this. I have performed
Your pleasure, and my promise.

CLEOPATRA   Dolabella,   200
I shall remain your debtor.

DOLABELLA   I your servant.
Adieu, good Queen. I must attend on Caesar.

CLEOPATRA
Farewell, and thanks.   *Exit Dolabella*
                Now, Iras, what think'st thou?
Thou, an Egyptian puppet shall be shown
In Rome, as well as I. Mechanic slaves   205
With greasy aprons, rules, and hammers shall
Uplift us to the view. In their thick breaths,
Rank of gross diet, shall we be enclouded,
And forced to drink their vapour.

IRAS   The gods forbid!

CLEOPATRA
Nay, 'tis most certain, Iras. Saucy lictors   210
Will catch at us like strumpets, and scald rhymers
Ballad us out o' tune. The quick comedians
Extemporally will stage us, and present
Our Alexandrian revels. Antony
Shall be brought drunken forth, and I shall see   215
Some squeaking Cleopatra boy my greatness
I'th' posture of a whore.

IRAS   O, the good gods!

CLEOPATRA Nay, that's certain.

IRAS
I'll never see't! For I am sure my nails
Are stronger than mine eyes.

CLEOPATRA   Why, that's the way   220
To fool their preparation and to conquer
Their most absurd intents.
                Enter Charmian
                         Now, Charmian!
Show me, my women, like a queen. Go fetch
My best attires. I am again for Cydnus
To meet Mark Antony. Sirrah Iras, go.   225
Now, noble Charmian, we'll dispatch indeed,
And when thou hast done this chore I'll give thee
    leave
To play till doomsday.—Bring our crown and all.
                                    ⌈*Exit Iras*⌉
                A noise within
Wherefore's this noise?
                Enter a Guardsman
GUARDSMAN   Here is a rural fellow
That will not be denied your highness' presence.   230
He brings you figs.

CLEOPATRA
Let him come in.   *Exit Guardsman*
                What poor an instrument
May do a noble deed! He brings me liberty.
My resolution's placed, and I have nothing
Of woman in me. Now from head to foot   235
I am marble-constant. Now the fleeting moon
No planet is of mine.
                Enter Guardsman, and Clown with a basket
GUARDSMAN   This is the man.

CLEOPATRA
Avoid, and leave him.   *Exit Guardsman*
                Hast thou the pretty worm
Of Nilus there, that kills and pains not?   239

CLOWN Truly, I have him; but I would not be the party that should desire you to touch him, for his biting is immortal; those that do die of it do seldom or never recover.

CLEOPATRA Remember'st thou any that have died on't?

CLOWN Very many, men, and women too. I heard of one of them no longer than yesterday, a very honest woman, but something given to lie, as a woman should not do but in the way of honesty, how she died of the biting of it, what pain she felt. Truly, she makes a very good report o'th' worm; but he that will believe all that they say shall never be saved by half that they do; but this is most falliable: the worm's an odd worm.

CLEOPATRA Get thee hence, farewell.

CLOWN I wish you all joy of the worm.   255

CLEOPATRA Farewell.

CLOWN You must think this, look you, that the worm will do his kind.

CLEOPATRA Ay, ay; farewell.   259

CLOWN Look you, the worm is not to be trusted but in the keeping of wise people; for indeed there is no goodness in the worm.

CLEOPATRA Take thou no care; it shall be heeded.

CLOWN Very good. Give it nothing, I pray you, for it is not worth the feeding.   265

CLEOPATRA Will it eat me?

CLOWN You must not think I am so simple but I know the devil himself will not eat a woman; I know that a woman is a dish for the gods, if the devil dress her not. But truly, these same whoreson devils do the gods great harm in their women; for in every ten that they make, the devils mar five.

CLEOPATRA Well, get thee gone, farewell.

CLOWN Yes, forsooth. I wish you joy o'th' worm.

Exit, leaving the basket
Enter ⌈Iras⌉ with a robe, crown, and other jewels

CLEOPATRA

Give me my robe. Put on my crown. I have   275
Immortal longings in me. Now no more
The juice of Egypt's grape shall moist this lip.
Charmian and Iras help her to dress
Yare, yare, good Iras, quick—methinks I hear
Antony call. I see him rouse himself
To praise my noble act. I hear him mock   280
The luck of Caesar, which the gods give men
To excuse their after wrath. Husband, I come.
Now to that name my courage prove my title.
I am fire and air; my other elements
I give to baser life. So, have you done?   285
Come then, and take the last warmth of my lips.
She kisses them
Farewell, kind Charmian. Iras, long farewell.
Iras falls and dies
Have I the aspic in my lips? Dost fall?
If thou and nature can so gently part,
The stroke of death is as a lover's pinch,
Which hurts and is desired. Dost thou lie still? 290

If thus thou vanishest, thou tell'st the world
It is not worth leave-taking.

CHARMIAN
Dissolve, thick cloud, and rain, that I may say
The gods themselves do weep.

CLEOPATRA   This proves me base. 295
If she first meet the curlèd Antony
He'll make demand of her, and spend that kiss
Which is my heaven to have.
She takes an aspic from the basket and puts it to her breast
                    Come, thou mortal wretch,
With thy sharp teeth this knot intrinsicate
Of life at once untie. Poor venomous fool,   300
Be angry, and dispatch. O, couldst thou speak,
That I might hear thee call great Caesar ass
Unpolicied!

CHARMIAN   O eastern star!

CLEOPATRA   Peace, peace.
Dost thou not see my baby at my breast,
That sucks the nurse asleep?

CHARMIAN   O, break! O, break!   305

CLEOPATRA
As sweet as balm, as soft as air, as gentle.
O Antony!
She puts another aspic to her arm
        Nay, I will take thee too.
What should I stay—   *She dies*

CHARMIAN   In this vile world? So, fare thee well.
Now boast thee, death, in thy possession lies
A lass unparalleled. Downy windows, close,   310
And golden Phoebus never be beheld
Of eyes again so royal. Your crown's awry.
I'll mend it, and then play—
Enter the Guard, rustling in

FIRST GUARD Where's the Queen?

CHARMIAN Speak softly. Wake her not.   315

FIRST GUARD
Caesar hath sent—

CHARMIAN   Too slow a messenger.
She applies an aspic
O come apace, dispatch! I partly feel thee.

FIRST GUARD
Approach, ho! All's not well. Caesar's beguiled.

SECOND GUARD
There's Dolabella sent from Caesar. Call him.
⌈Exit a Guardsman⌉

FIRST GUARD
What work is here, Charmian? Is this well done?   320

CHARMIAN
It is well done, and fitting for a princess
Descended of so many royal kings.
Ah, soldier!   *She dies*
Enter Dolabella

DOLABELLA
How goes it here?

SECOND GUARD   All dead.

DOLABELLA   Caesar, thy thoughts

Touch their effects in this. Thyself art coming   325
To see performed the dreaded act which thou
So sought'st to hinder.

ALL   A way there, a way for Caesar!
Enter Caesar and all his train, marching

DOLABELLA (*to Caesar*)
O sir, you are too sure an augurer.
That you did fear is done.

CAESAR   Bravest at the last,
She levelled at our purposes, and, being royal,   330
Took her own way. The manner of their deaths?
I do not see them bleed.

DOLABELLA (*to a Guardsman*) Who was last with them?

FIRST GUARD
A simple countryman that brought her figs.
This was his basket.

CAESAR   Poisoned, then.

FIRST GUARD   O Caesar,
This Charmian lived but now; she stood and spake.   335
I found her trimming up the diadem
On her dead mistress; tremblingly she stood,
And on the sudden dropped.

CAESAR   O, noble weakness!
If they had swallowed poison, 'twould appear
By external swelling; but she looks like sleep,   340

As she would catch another Antony
In her strong toil of grace.

DOLABELLA   Here on her breast
There is a vent of blood, and something blown.
The like is on her arm.

FIRST GUARD   This is an aspic's trail,
And these fig-leaves have slime upon them such   345
As th'aspic leaves upon the caves of Nile.

CAESAR Most probable
That so she died; for her physician tells me
She hath pursued conclusions infinite
Of easy ways to die. Take up her bed,   350
And bear her women from the monument.
She shall be buried by her Antony.
No grave upon the earth shall clip in it
A pair so famous. High events as these
Strike those that make them, and their story is   355
No less in pity than his glory which
Brought them to be lamented. Our army shall
In solemn show attend this funeral,
And then to Rome. Come, Dolabella, see
High order in this great solemnity.   360
Exeunt all, soldiers bearing Cleopatra ⌈on her
bed⌉, Charmian, and Iras

CORIOLANUS

FOR *Coriolanus*, Shakespeare turned once more to Roman history as told by Plutarch and translated by Sir Thomas North in the *Lives of the Noble Grecians and Romans* published in 1579. This time he dramatized early events, not much subsequent to those he had written about many years previously in *The Rape of Lucrece*. Plutarch gave him most of his material, but he also drew on other writings, including William Camden's *Remains of a Greater Work Concerning Britain*, published in 1605, for Menenius' fable of the belly (1.1). Though he needed no source other than Plutarch for the insurrections and corn riots of ancient Rome, similar happenings in England during 1607 and 1608 may have stimulated his interest in the story. The cumulative evidence suggests that *Coriolanus*, first printed in the 1623 Folio, is Shakespeare's last Roman play, written around 1608.

In the fifth century BC, following the expulsion of the Tarquins, Rome was an aristocratically controlled republic in which power was invested primarily in two annually elected magistrates, or consuls. For many years the main issues confronting the republic were the internal class struggle between patricians and plebeians, and the external struggle for domination over neighbouring peoples. Among the republic's early enemies were the Volsci (or Volscians), who inhabited an area to the south and south-east of Rome; their towns included Antium and Corioli. According to ancient historians, Rome's greatest leader in campaigns against the Volsci was the patrician Gnaeus (or Caius) Marcius, who, at a time of famine which caused the plebeians to rebel against the patricians, led an army against the Volsci and captured Corioli; as a reward he was granted the cognomen, or surname, of Coriolanus. After this he is said to have been charged with behaving tyrannically in opposing the distribution of corn to starving plebeians, and as a result to have abandoned Rome, joined the Volsci, and led a Volscian army against his native city.

This is the story of conflict between public and private issues that Shakespeare dramatizes, concentrating on the later part of Plutarch's Life and speeding up its time-scheme, while also alluding retrospectively to earlier incidents. He increases the responsibility of the Tribunes, Sicinius Velutus and Junius Brutus, for Coriolanus' banishment, and greatly develops certain characters, such as the Volscian leader Tullus Aufidius and the patrician Menenius Agrippa. The roles of the womenfolk are almost entirely of Shakespeare's devising up to the scene (5.3) of their embassy; here, as in certain other set speeches, Shakespeare draws heavily on the language of North's translation.

Coriolanus is an austere play, gritty in style, deeply serious in its concern with the relationship between personal characteristics and national destiny, but relieved by flashes of comedy (especially in the scenes in which Coriolanus begs for the plebeians' votes in his election campaign for the consulship) which are more apparent on the stage than on the page. Though Coriolanus is arrogant, choleric, and self-centered, he is also a blazingly successful warrior, conspicuous for integrity, who ultimately yields to a tenderness which, he knows, will destroy him. *Coriolanus* is a deeply human as well as a profoundly political play.

THE PERSONS OF THE PLAY

Caius MARTIUS, later surnamed CORIOLANUS ⎫

MENENIUS Agrippa ⎬ patricians of Rome
Titus LARTIUS ⎫ generals
COMINIUS ⎭

VOLUMNIA, Coriolanus' mother
VIRGILIA, his wife
YOUNG MARTIUS, his son
VALERIA, a chaste lady of Rome

SICINIUS Velutus ⎫ tribunes of the Roman people
Junius BRUTUS ⎭
CITIZENS of Rome
SOLDIERS in the Roman army

Tullus AUFIDIUS, general of the Volscian army
His LIEUTENANT
His SERVINGMEN
CONSPIRATORS with Aufidius
Volscian LORDS
Volscian CITIZENS
SOLDIERS in the Volscian army

ADRIAN, a Volscian
NICANOR, a Roman
A Roman HERALD
MESSENGERS
AEDILES

A gentlewoman, an usher, Roman and Volscian senators and nobles, captains in the Roman army, officers, lictors

The Tragedy of Coriolanus

1.1 *Enter a company of mutinous Citizens with staves, clubs, and other weapons*

FIRST CITIZEN Before we proceed any further, hear me speak.

ALL Speak, speak.

FIRST CITIZEN You are all resolved rather to die than to famish? 5

ALL Resolved, resolved.

FIRST CITIZEN First, you know Caius Martius is chief enemy to the people.

ALL We know't, we know't.

FIRST CITIZEN Let us kill him, and we'll have corn at our own price. Is't a verdict? 11

ALL No more talking on't, let it be done. Away, away.

SECOND CITIZEN One word, good citizens.

FIRST CITIZEN We are accounted poor citizens, the patricians good. What authority surfeits on would relieve us. If they would yield us but the superfluity while it were wholesome we might guess they relieved us humanely, but they think we are too dear. The leanness that afflicts us, the object of our misery, is as an inventory to particularize their abundance; our sufferance is a gain to them. Let us revenge this with our pikes ere we become rakes; for the gods know I speak this in hunger for bread, not in thirst for revenge.

SECOND CITIZEN Would you proceed especially against Caius Martius? 25

⌈THIRD CITIZEN⌉ Against him first.

⌈FOURTH CITIZEN⌉ He's a very dog to the commonalty.

SECOND CITIZEN Consider you what services he has done for his country? 29

FIRST CITIZEN Very well, and could be content to give him good report for't, but that he pays himself with being proud.

⌈FIFTH CITIZEN⌉ Nay, but speak not maliciously.

FIRST CITIZEN I say unto you, what he hath done famously, he did it to that end—though soft-conscienced men can be content to say 'it was for his country', 'he did it to please his mother, and to be partly proud'—which he is even to the altitude of his virtue.

SECOND CITIZEN What he cannot help in his nature you account a vice in him. You must in no way say he is covetous. 41

FIRST CITIZEN If I must not, I need not be barren of accusations. He hath faults, with surplus, to tire in repetition.

Shouts within

What shouts are these? The other side o'th' city is risen. Why stay we prating here? To th' Capitol! 46

ALL Come, come.

Enter Menenius

FIRST CITIZEN Soft, who comes here?

SECOND CITIZEN Worthy Menenius Agrippa, one that hath always loved the people. 50

FIRST CITIZEN He's one honest enough. Would all the rest were so!

MENENIUS

What work's, my countrymen, in hand? Where go you
With bats and clubs? The matter. Speak, I pray you.

⌈FIRST⌉ CITIZEN Our business is not unknown to th' senate. They have had inkling this fortnight what we intend to do, which now we'll show 'em in deeds. They say poor suitors have strong breaths; they shall know we have strong arms, too.

MENENIUS

Why, masters, my good friends, mine honest
neighbours, 60
Will you undo yourselves?

⌈FIRST⌉ CITIZEN

We cannot, sir. We are undone already.

MENENIUS

I tell you, friends, most charitable care
Have the patricians of you. For your wants,
Your suffering in this dearth, you may as well 65
Strike at the heaven with your staves as lift them
Against the Roman state, whose course will on
The way it takes, cracking ten thousand curbs
Of more strong link asunder than can ever
Appear in your impediment. For the dearth, 70
The gods, not the patricians, make it, and
Your knees to them, not arms, must help. Alack,
You are transported by calamity
Thither where more attends you, and you slander
The helms o'th' state, who care for you like fathers, 75
When you curse them as enemies.

⌈FIRST⌉ CITIZEN Care for us? True, indeed! They ne'er cared for us yet: suffer us to famish, and their storehouses crammed with grain; make edicts for usury to support usurers; repeal daily any wholesome act established against the rich; and provide more piercing statutes daily to chain up and restrain the poor. If the wars eat us not up, they will; and there's all the love they bear us.

MENENIUS Either you must 85
Confess yourselves wondrous malicious
Or be accused of folly. I shall tell you
A pretty tale. It may be you have heard it,
But since it serves my purpose, I will venture
To stale't a little more. 90

⌈FIRST⌉ CITIZEN Well, I'll hear it, sir. Yet you must not think to fob off our disgrace with a tale. But an't please you, deliver.

MENENIUS

There was a time when all the body's members,

Rebelled against the belly, thus accused it: 95
That only like a gulf it did remain
I'th' midst o'th' body, idle and unactive,
Still cupboarding the viand, never bearing
Like labour with the rest; where th'other instruments
Did see and hear, devise, instruct, walk, feel,   100
And, mutually participate, did minister
Unto the appetite and affection common
Of the whole body. The belly answered—
⌈FIRST⌉ CITIZEN
Well, sir, what answer made the belly?
MENENIUS
Sir, I shall tell you. With a kind of smile,   105
Which ne'er came from the lungs, but even thus—
For look you, I may make the belly smile
As well as speak—it tauntingly replied
To th' discontented members, the mutinous parts
That envied his receipt; even so most fitly   110
As you malign our senators for that
They are not such as you.
⌈FIRST⌉ CITIZEN   Your belly's answer—what?
The kingly crownèd head, the vigilant eye,
The counsellor heart, the arm our soldier,
Our steed the leg, the tongue our trumpeter,   115
With other muniments and petty helps
In this our fabric, if that they—
MENENIUS   What then?
Fore me, this fellow speaks! What then? What then?
⌈FIRST⌉ CITIZEN
Should by the cormorant belly be restrained,
Who is the sink o'th' body—
MENENIUS   Well, what then?   120
⌈FIRST⌉ CITIZEN
The former agents, if they did complain,
What could the belly answer?
MENENIUS   I will tell you,
If you'll bestow a small of what you have little—
Patience—a while, you'st hear the belly's answer.
⌈FIRST⌉ CITIZEN
You're long about it.
MENENIUS   Note me this, good friend: 125
Your most grave belly was deliberate,
Not rash like his accusers, and thus answered:
'True is it, my incorporate friends,' quoth he,
'That I receive the general food at first
Which you do live upon, and fit it is,   130
Because I am the storehouse and the shop
Of the whole body. But, if you do remember,
I send it through the rivers of your blood
Even to the court, the heart, to th' seat o'th' brain;
And through the cranks and offices of man   135
The strongest nerves and small inferior veins
From me receive that natural competency
Whereby they live. And though that all at once'—
You my good friends, this says the belly, mark me—
⌈FIRST⌉ CITIZEN
Ay, sir, well, well.
MENENIUS   'Though all at once cannot   140

See what I do deliver out to each,
Yet I can make my audit up that all
From me do back receive the flour of all
And leave me but the bran.' What say you to't?
⌈FIRST⌉ CITIZEN
It was an answer. How apply you this?   145
MENENIUS
The senators of Rome are this good belly,
And you the mutinous members. For examine
Their counsels and their cares, digest things rightly
Touching the weal o'th' common, you shall find
No public benefit which you receive   150
But it proceeds or comes from them to you,
And no way from yourselves. What do you think,
You, the great toe of this assembly?
⌈FIRST⌉ CITIZEN
I the great toe? Why the great toe?
MENENIUS
For that, being one o'th' lowest, basest, poorest   155
Of this most wise rebellion, thou goest foremost.
Thou rascal, that art worst in blood to run,
Lead'st first to win some vantage.
But make you ready your stiff bats and clubs.
Rome and her rats are at the point of battle.   160
The one side must have bale.
          Enter Martius
                              Hail, noble Martius!
MARTIUS
Thanks.—What's the matter, you dissentious rogues,
That, rubbing the poor itch of your opinion,
Make yourselves scabs?
⌈FIRST⌉ CITIZEN   We have ever your good word.
MARTIUS
He that will give good words to thee will flatter   165
Beneath abhorring. What would you have, you curs
That like nor peace nor war? The one affrights you,
The other makes you proud. He that trusts to you,
Where he should find you lions finds you hares,
Where foxes, geese. You are no surer, no,   170
Than is the coal of fire upon the ice,
Or hailstone in the sun. Your virtue is
To make him worthy whose offence subdues him,
And curse that justice did it. Who deserves greatness
Deserves your hate, and your affections are   175
A sick man's appetite, who desires most that
Which would increase his evil. He that depends
Upon your favours swims with fins of lead,
And hews down oaks with rushes. Hang ye! Trust
     ye?
With every minute you do change a mind,   180
And call him noble that was now your hate,
Him vile that was your garland. What's the matter,
That in these several places of the city
You cry against the noble senate, who,
Under the gods, keep you in awe, which else   185
Would feed on one another?
(To Menenius)   What's their seeking?

MENENIUS
  For corn at their own rates, whereof they say
  The city is well stored.
MARTIUS   Hang 'em! They say?
  They'll sit by th' fire and presume to know
  What's done i'th' Capitol, who's like to rise,   190
  Who thrives and who declines; side factions and give
      out
  Conjectural marriages, making parties strong
  And feebling such as stand not in their liking
  Below their cobbled shoes. They say there's grain
      enough!
  Would the nobility lay aside their ruth   195
  And let me use my sword, I'd make a quarry
  With thousands of these quartered slaves as high
  As I could pitch my lance.
MENENIUS
  Nay, these are all most thoroughly persuaded,
  For though abundantly they lack discretion,   200
  Yet are they passing cowardly. But I beseech you,
  What says the other troop?
MARTIUS   They are dissolved. Hang 'em.
  They said they were an-hungry, sighed forth
      proverbs—
  That hunger broke stone walls, that dogs must eat,
  That meat was made for mouths, that the gods sent
      not   205
  Corn for the rich men only. With these shreds
  They vented their complainings, which being
      answered,
  And a petition granted them—a strange one,
  To break the heart of generosity   209
  And make bold power look pale—they threw their caps
  As they would hang them on the horns o'th' moon,
  Shouting their emulation.
MENENIUS   What is granted them?
MARTIUS
  Five tribunes to defend their vulgar wisdoms,
  Of their own choice. One's Junius Brutus,
  Sicinius Velutus, and I know not. 'Sdeath,   215
  The rabble should have first unroofed the city
  Ere so prevailed with me! It will in time
  Win upon power and throw forth greater themes
  For insurrection's arguing.
MENENIUS This is strange.   220
MARTIUS (to the Citizens) Go get you home, you fragments.
      Enter a Messenger hastily
MESSENGER Where's Caius Martius?
MARTIUS Here. What's the matter?
MESSENGER
  The news is, sir, the Volsces are in arms.
MARTIUS
  I am glad on't. Then we shall ha' means to vent   225
  Our musty superfluity.
      Enter Sicinius, Brutus, Cominius, Lartius, with
      other Senators
                        See, our best elders.

FIRST SENATOR
  Martius, 'tis true that you have lately told us.
  The Volsces are in arms.
MARTIUS   They have a leader,
  Tullus Aufidius, that will put you to't.
  I sin in envying his nobility,   230
  And were I anything but what I am,
  I would wish me only he.
COMINIUS   You have fought together!
MARTIUS
  Were half to half the world by th' ears and he
  Upon my party, I'd revolt to make
  Only my wars with him. He is a lion   235
  That I am proud to hunt.
FIRST SENATOR   Then, worthy Martius,
  Attend upon Cominius to these wars.
COMINIUS (to Martius)
  It is your former promise.
MARTIUS   Sir, it is,
  And I am constant. Titus Lartius, thou
  Shalt see me once more strike at Tullus' face.   240
  What, art thou stiff? Stand'st out?
LARTIUS   No, Caius Martius.
  I'll lean upon one crutch and fight with th'other
  Ere stay behind this business.
MENENIUS   O true bred!
⌜FIRST⌝ SENATOR
  Your company to th' Capitol, where I know
  Our greatest friends attend us.
LARTIUS (to Cominius)   Lead you on.   245
  (To Martius) Follow Cominius. We must follow you,
  Right worthy your priority.
COMINIUS   Noble Martius.
⌜FIRST⌝ SENATOR (to the Citizens)
  Hence to your homes, be gone.
MARTIUS   Nay, let them follow.
  The Volsces have much corn. Take these rats thither
  To gnaw their garners.   Citizens steal away
                              Worshipful mutineers,   250
  Your valour puts well forth. (To the Senators) Pray
      follow.   Exeunt all but Sicinius and Brutus
SICINIUS
  Was ever man so proud as is this Martius?
BRUTUS He has no equal.
SICINIUS
  When we were chosen tribunes for the people—
BRUTUS
  Marked you his lip and eyes?
SICINIUS   Nay, but his taunts.   255
BRUTUS
  Being moved, he will not spare to gird the gods.
SICINIUS Bemock the modest moon.
BRUTUS
  The present wars devour him! He is grown
  Too proud to be so valiant.
SICINIUS   Such a nature,
  Tickled with good success, disdains the shadow   260

Which he treads on at noon. But I do wonder
His insolence can brook to be commanded
Under Cominius.
BRUTUS   Fame, at the which he aims—
In whom already he's well graced—cannot
Better be held nor more attained than by   265
A place below the first; for what miscarries
Shall be the general's fault, though he perform
To th' utmost of a man, and giddy censure
Will then cry out of Martius 'O, if he
Had borne the business!'
SICINIUS   Besides, if things go well,   270
Opinion, that so sticks on Martius, shall
Of his demerits rob Cominius.
BRUTUS   Come,
Half all Cominius' honours are to Martius,
Though Martius earned them not; and all his faults
To Martius shall be honours, though indeed   275
In aught he merit not.
SICINIUS   Let's hence and hear
How the dispatch is made, and in what fashion,
More than his singularity, he goes
Upon this present action.
BRUTUS   Let's along.   *Exeunt*

1.2   *Enter Aufidius, with Senators of Corioles*
FIRST SENATOR
So, your opinion is, Aufidius,
That they of Rome are entered in our counsels
And know how we proceed.
AUFIDIUS   Is it not yours?
What ever have been thought on in this state
That could be brought to bodily act ere Rome   5
Had circumvention? 'Tis not four days gone
Since I heard thence. These are the words. I think
I have the letter here—yes, here it is.
      ⌜*He reads the letter*⌝
'They have pressed a power, but it is not known
Whether for east or west. The dearth is great,   10
The people mutinous, and it is rumoured
Cominius, Martius your old enemy,
Who is of Rome worse hated than of you,
And Titus Lartius, a most valiant Roman,
These three lead on this preparation   15
Whither 'tis bent. Most likely 'tis for you.
Consider of it.'
FIRST SENATOR   Our army's in the field.
We never yet made doubt but Rome was ready
To answer us.
AUFIDIUS   Nor did you think it folly
To keep your great pretences veiled till when   20
They needs must show themselves, which in the
         hatching,
It seemed, appeared to Rome. By the discovery
We shall be shortened in our aim, which was
To take in many towns ere, almost, Rome
Should know we were afoot.
SECOND SENATOR   Noble Aufidius,   25

Take your commission, hie you to your bands.
Let us alone to guard Corioles.
If they set down before's, for the remove
Bring up your army, but I think you'll find
They've not prepared for us.
AUFIDIUS   O, doubt not that.   30
I speak from certainties. Nay, more,
Some parcels of their power are forth already,
And only hitherward. I leave your honours.
If we and Caius Martius chance to meet,
'Tis sworn between us we shall ever strike   35
Till one can do no more.
ALL THE SENATORS   The gods assist you!
AUFIDIUS
And keep your honours safe.
FIRST SENATOR   Farewell.
SECOND SENATOR   Farewell.
ALL   Farewell.
      Exeunt, ⌜Aufidius at one door,
                     Senators at another door⌝

1.3   *Enter Volumnia and Virgilia, mother and wife to*
         Martius. They set them down on two low stools
         and sew
VOLUMNIA I pray you, daughter, sing, or express yourself
in a more comfortable sort. If my son were my husband,
I should freelier rejoice in that absence wherein he won
honour than in the embracements of his bed where he
would show most love. When yet he was but tender-
bodied and the only son of my womb, when youth
with comeliness plucked all gaze his way, when for a
day of kings' entreaties a mother should not sell him
an hour from her beholding, I, considering how honour
would become such a person—that it was no better
than, picture-like, to hang by th' wall if renown made
it not stir—was pleased to let him seek danger where
he was like to find fame. To a cruel war I sent him,
from whence he returned his brows bound with oak. I
tell thee, daughter, I sprang not more in joy at first
hearing he was a man-child than now in first seeing
he had proved himself a man.
VIRGILIA But had he died in the business, madam, how
then?   19
VOLUMNIA Then his good report should have been my
son. I therein would have found issue. Hear me profess
sincerely: had I a dozen sons, each in my love alike,
and none less dear than thine and my good Martius',
I had rather had eleven die nobly for their country
than one voluptuously surfeit out of action.   25
      Enter a Gentlewoman
GENTLEWOMAN Madam, the Lady Valeria is come to visit
you.
VIRGILIA (*to Volumnia*) Beseech you give me leave to retire
myself.
VOLUMNIA Indeed you shall not.   30
Methinks I hear hither your husband's drum,
See him pluck Aufidius down by th' hair;
As children from a bear, the Volsces shunning him.

Methinks I see him stamp thus, and call thus:
'Come on, you cowards, you were got in fear 35
Though you were born in Rome!' His bloody brow
With his mailed hand then wiping, forth he goes,
Like to a harvest-man that's tasked to mow
Or all or lose his hire.

VIRGILIA
His bloody brow? O Jupiter, no blood! 40

VOLUMNIA
Away, you fool! It more becomes a man
Than gilt his trophy. The breasts of Hecuba
When she did suckle Hector looked not lovelier
Than Hector's forehead when it spit forth blood
At Grecian sword, contemning.
(To the Gentlewoman)   Tell Valeria 45
We are fit to bid her welcome.   *Exit Gentlewoman*

VIRGILIA
Heavens bless my lord from fell Aufidius!

VOLUMNIA
He'll beat Aufidius' head below his knee
And tread upon his neck.
        Enter Valeria, with an usher and the Gentlewoman

VALERIA My ladies both, good day to you. 50

VOLUMNIA Sweet madam.

VIRGILIA I am glad to see your ladyship.

VALERIA How do you both? You are manifest
housekeepers. What are you sewing here? A fine spot,
in good faith. How does your little son? 55

VIRGILIA
I thank your ladyship; well, good madam.

VOLUMNIA He had rather see the swords and hear a drum
than look upon his schoolmaster.

VALERIA O' my word, the father's son! I'll swear 'tis a
very pretty boy. O' my troth, I looked upon him o'
Wednesday half an hour together. He's such a
confirmed countenance! I saw him run after a gilded
butterfly, and when he caught it he let it go again,
and after it again, and over and over he comes, and
up again, catched it again. Or whether his fall enraged
him, or how 'twas, he did so set his teeth and tear it!
O, I warrant, how he mammocked it!

VOLUMNIA One on's father's moods.

VALERIA Indeed, la, 'tis a noble child.

VIRGILIA A crack, madam. 70

VALERIA Come, lay aside your stitchery. I must have you
play the idle housewife with me this afternoon.

VIRGILIA No, good madam, I will not out of doors.

VALERIA Not out of doors?

VOLUMNIA She shall, she shall. 75

VIRGILIA Indeed, no, by your patience. I'll not over the
threshold till my lord return from the wars.

VALERIA Fie, you confine yourself most unreasonably.
Come, you must go visit the good lady that lies in.

VIRGILIA I will wish her speedy strength, and visit her
with my prayers, but I cannot go thither. 81

VOLUMNIA Why, I pray you?

VIRGILIA 'Tis not to save labour, nor that I want love.

VALERIA You would be another Penelope. Yet they say

all the yarn she spun in Ulysses' absence did but fill
Ithaca full of moths. Come, I would your cambric were
sensible as your finger, that you might leave pricking
it for pity. Come, you shall go with us.

VIRGILIA No, good madam, pardon me, indeed I will not
forth. 90

VALERIA In truth, la, go with me, and I'll tell you excellent
news of your husband.

VIRGILIA O, good madam, there can be none yet.

VALERIA Verily, I do not jest with you: there came news
from him last night. 95

VIRGILIA Indeed, madam?

VALERIA In earnest, it's true. I heard a senator speak it.
Thus it is: the Volsces have an army forth, against
whom Cominius the general is gone with one part of
our Roman power. Your lord and Titus Lartius are set
down before their city Corioles. They nothing doubt
prevailing, and to make it brief wars. This is true, on
mine honour; and so, I pray, go with us.

VIRGILIA Give me excuse, good madam, I will obey you
in everything hereafter. 105

VOLUMNIA *(to Valeria)* Let her alone, lady. As she is now
she will but disease our better mirth.

VALERIA In truth, I think she would. Fare you well, then.
Come, good sweet lady. Prithee, Virgilia, turn thy
solemness out o' door and go along with us. 110

VIRGILIA No, at a word, madam. Indeed, I must not. I
wish you much mirth.

VALERIA Well then, farewell.
        *Exeunt ⌈Valeria, Volumnia, and usher at one
        door, Virgilia and Gentlewoman at another door⌉*

1.4   *Enter Martius, Lartius with a drummer, ⌈a
        trumpeter,⌉ and colours, with captains and Soldiers
        ⌈carrying scaling ladders⌉, as before the city
        Corioles; to them a Messenger*

MARTIUS
Yonder comes news. A wager they have met.

LARTIUS
My horse to yours, no.

MARTIUS   'Tis done.

LARTIUS   Agreed.

MARTIUS *(to the Messenger)*
Say, has our general met the enemy?

MESSENGER
They lie in view, but have not spoke as yet.

LARTIUS
So, the good horse is mine.

MARTIUS   I'll buy him of you. 5

LARTIUS
No, L'll nor sell nor give him. Lend you him I will,
For half a hundred years.
(To the trumpeter)   Summon the town.

MARTIUS *(to the Messenger)*
How far off lie these armies?

MESSENGER   Within this mile and half.

MARTIUS
Then shall we hear their 'larum, and they ours.

Now Mars, I prithee, make us quick in work,   10
That we with smoking swords may march from hence
To help our fielded friends.
(To the trumpeter)   Come, blow thy blast.
   They sound a parley. Enter two Senators, with
   others, on the walls of Corioles
(To the Senators) Tullus Aufidius, is he within your walls?
FIRST SENATOR
No, nor a man that fears you less than he:
That's lesser than a little.
   Drum afar off
⌐To the Volscians⌐   Hark, our drums   15
Are bringing forth our youth. We'll break our walls
Rather than they shall pound us up. Our gates,
Which yet seem shut, we have but pinned with rushes.
They'll open of themselves.
   Alarum far off
(To the Romans)   Hark you, far off
There is Aufidius. List what work he makes   20
Amongst your cloven army.
          ⌐*Exeunt Volscians from the walls*⌐
MARTIUS   O, they are at it!
LARTIUS
Their noise be our instruction. Ladders, ho!
   ⌐*They prepare to assault the walls.*⌐
   Enter the army of the Volsces from the gates
MARTIUS
They fear us not, but issue forth their city.
Now put your shields before your hearts, and fight
With hearts more proof than shields. Advance, brave
   Titus.   25
They do disdain us much beyond our thoughts,
Which makes me sweat with wrath. Come on, my
   fellows.
He that retires, I'll take him for a Volsce,
And he shall feel mine edge.
   Alarum. The Romans are beat back ⌐and exeunt⌐ to
   their trenches, ⌐the Volsces following⌐

1.5   *Enter ⌐Roman Soldiers, in retreat, followed by⌐*
   Martius, cursing
MARTIUS
All the contagion of the south light on you,
You shames of Rome! You herd of—boils and plagues
Plaster you o'er, that you may be abhorred
Farther than seen, and one infect another
Against the wind a mile! You souls of geese   5
That bear the shapes of men, how have you run
From slaves that apes would beat! Pluto and hell:
All hurt behind! Backs red, and faces pale
With flight and agued fear! Mend and charge home,
Or by the fires of heaven I'll leave the foe   10
And make my wars on you. Look to't. Come on.
If you'll stand fast, we'll beat them to their wives,
As they us to our trenches. Follow.
   ⌐*The Romans come forward towards the walls.*⌐
   Another alarum, and ⌐enter the army of the Volsces.⌐
   Martius beats them back ⌐through⌐ the gates

So, now the gates are ope. Now prove good seconds.
'Tis for the followers fortune widens them,   15
Not for the fliers. Mark me, and do the like.
   He enters the gates
FIRST SOLDIER
Foolhardiness! Not I.
SECOND SOLDIER   Nor I.
   Alarum continues. The gates close, and Martius is
   shut in
FIRST SOLDIER
See, they have shut him in.
⌐THIRD SOLDIER⌐   To th' pot, I warrant him.
   Enter Lartius
LARTIUS
What is become of Martius?
⌐FOURTH SOLDIER⌐   Slain, sir, doubtless.
FIRST SOLDIER
Following the fliers at the very heels,   20
With them he enters, who upon the sudden
Clapped-to their gates. He is himself alone
To answer all the city.
LARTIUS   O noble fellow,
Who sensibly outdares his senseless sword
And, when it bows, stand'st up! Thou art lost, Martius.
A carbuncle entire, as big as thou art,   26
Were not so rich a jewel. Thou wast a soldier
Even to Cato's wish, not fierce and terrible
Only in strokes, but with thy grim looks and
The thunder-like percussion of thy sounds   30
Thou mad'st thine enemies shake as if the world
Were feverous and did tremble.
   Enter Martius, bleeding, assaulted by the enemy
FIRST SOLDIER   Look, sir.
LARTIUS   O, 'tis Martius!
Let's fetch him off, or make remain alike.
   They fight, and all exeunt into the city

1.6   *Enter certain Romans with spoils*
FIRST ROMAN This will I carry to Rome.
SECOND ROMAN And I this.
THIRD ROMAN A murrain on't, I took this for silver.
   ⌐*He throws it away.*⌐
   Alarum continues still afar off. Enter Martius,
   bleeding, and Lartius with a trumpeter. Exeunt
   Romans with spoils
MARTIUS
See here these movers that do prize their honours
At a cracked drachma! Cushions, leaden spoons,   5
Irons of a doit, doublets that hangmen would
Bury with those that wore them, these base slaves,
Ere yet the fight be done, pack up. Down with them!
And hark what noise the general makes. To him.
There is the man of my soul's hate, Aufidius,   10
Piercing our Romans. Then, valiant Titus, take
Convenient numbers to make good the city,
Whilst I, with those that have the spirit, will haste
To help Cominius.
LARTIUS   Worthy sir, thou bleed'st.

Thy exercise hath been too violent   15
For a second course of fight.
MARTIUS   Sir, praise me not.
My work hath yet not warmed me. Fare you well.
The blood I drop is rather physical
Than dangerous to me. To Aufidius thus
I will appear and fight.
LARTIUS   Now the fair goddess fortune 20
Fall deep in love with thee, and her great charms
Misguide thy opposers' swords! Bold gentleman,
Prosperity be thy page.
MARTIUS   Thy friend no less
Than those she placeth highest. So farewell.
LARTIUS Thou worthiest Martius!   Exit Martius
Go sound thy trumpet in the market-place.   26
Call thither all the officers o'th' town,
Where they shall know our mind. Away.
                                    Exeunt ⌈severally⌉

1.7 *Enter Cominius, as it were in retire, with soldiers*
COMINIUS
Breathe you, my friends. Well fought. We are come off
Like Romans, neither foolish in our stands
Nor cowardly in retire. Believe me, sirs,
We shall be charged again. Whiles we have struck,
By interims and conveying gusts we have heard   5
The charges of our friends. The Roman gods
Lead their successes as we wish our own,
That both our powers, with smiling fronts
        encount'ring,
May give you thankful sacrifice!
    Enter a Messenger
                              Thy news?
MESSENGER
The citizens of Corioles have issued,   10
And given to Lartius and to Martius battle.
I saw our party to their trenches driven,
And then I came away.
COMINIUS   Though thou speak'st truth,
Methinks thou speak'st not well. How long is't since?
MESSENGER Above an hour, my lord.   15
COMINIUS
'Tis not a mile; briefly we heard their drums.
How couldst thou in a mile confound an hour,
And bring thy news so late?
MESSENGER   Spies of the Volsces
Held me in chase, that I was forced to wheel
Three or four miles about; else had I, sir,   20
Half an hour since brought my report.   ⌈*Exit*⌉
    Enter Martius, bloody
COMINIUS   Who's yonder,
That does appear as he were flayed? O gods!
He has the stamp of Martius, and I have
Before-time seen him thus.
MARTIUS   Come I too late?
COMINIUS
The shepherd knows not thunder from a tabor   25

More than I know the sound of Martius' tongue
From every meaner man.
MARTIUS   Come I too late?
COMINIUS
Ay, if you come not in the blood of others,
But mantled in your own.
MARTIUS   O, let me clip ye
In arms as sound as when I wooed, in heart   30
As merry as when our nuptial day was done,
And tapers burnt to bedward!
    ⌈*They embrace*⌉
COMINIUS
Flower of warriors! How is't with Titus Lartius?
MARTIUS
As with a man busied about decrees,
Condemning some to death and some to exile,   35
Ransoming him or pitying, threat'ning th'other;
Holding Corioles in the name of Rome
Even like a fawning greyhound in the leash,
To let him slip at will.
COMINIUS   Where is that slave
Which told me they had beat you to your trenches?   40
Where is he? Call him hither.
MARTIUS   Let him alone.
He did inform the truth. But for our gentlemen,
The common file—a plague—tribunes for them?—
The mouse ne'er shunned the cat as they did budge
From rascals worse than they.
COMINIUS   But how prevailed you?
MARTIUS
Will the time serve to tell? I do not think.   46
Where is the enemy? Are you lords o'th' field?
If not, why cease you till you are so?
COMINIUS
Martius, we have at disadvantage fought,
And did retire to win our purpose.   50
MARTIUS
How lies their battle? Know you on which side
They have placed their men of trust?
COMINIUS   As I guess, Martius,
Their bands i'th' vanguard are the Antiates,
Of their best trust; o'er them Aufidius,
Their very heart of hope.
MARTIUS   I do beseech you   55
By all the battles wherein we have fought,
By th' blood we have shed together, by th' vows we
        have made
To endure friends, that you directly set me
Against Aufidius and his Antiates,
And that you not delay the present, but,   60
Filling the air with swords advanced and darts,
We prove this very hour.
COMINIUS   Though I could wish
You were conducted to a gentle bath
And balms applied to you, yet dare I never
Deny your asking. Take your choice of those   65
That best can aid your action.
MARTIUS   Those are they

That most are willing. If any such be here—
As it were sin to doubt—that love this painting
Wherein you see me smeared; if any fear
Lesser his person than an ill report;   70
If any think brave death outweighs bad life,
And that his country's dearer than himself,
Let him alone, or so many so minded,
 He waves his sword
Wave thus to express his disposition,
And follow Martius.   75
 They all shout and wave their swords, ⌈then some⌉
 take him up in their arms and they cast up their
 caps
O' me alone, make you a sword of me?
If these shows be not outward, which of you
But is four Volsces? None of you but is
Able to bear against the great Aufidius
A shield as hard as his. A certain number—   80
Though thanks to all—must I select from all.
The rest shall bear the business in some other fight
As cause will be obeyed. Please you to march,
And I shall quickly draw out my command,
Which men are best inclined.
COMINIUS   March on, my fellows. 85
Make good this ostentation, and you shall
Divide in all with us.   *Exeunt marching*

1.8 *Enter Lartius ⌈through the gates of Corioles⌉, with*
 a drummer and a trumpeter, a Lieutenant, other
 soldiers, and a scout
LARTIUS (*to the Lieutenant*)
So, let the ports be guarded. Keep your duties
As I have set them down. If I do send, dispatch
Those centuries to our aid. The rest will serve
For a short holding. If we lose the field
We cannot keep the town.   5
LIEUTENANT Fear not our care, sir.
LARTIUS Hence, and shut your gates upon's.
         ⌈*Exit Lieutenant*⌉
(*To the scout*) Our guider, come; to th' Roman camp
 conduct us.
  Exeunt towards Cominius and Caius Martius

1.9 *Alarum, as in battle. Enter Martius, bloody, and*
 Aufidius, at several doors
MARTIUS
I'll fight with none but thee, for I do hate thee
Worse than a promise-breaker.
AUFIDIUS   We hate alike.
Not Afric owns a serpent I abhor
More than thy fame and envy. Fix thy foot.
MARTIUS
Let the first budger die the other's slave,   5
And the gods doom him after.
AUFIDIUS   If I fly, Martius,
Holla me like a hare.
MARTIUS   Within these three hours, Tullus,

Alone I fought in your Corioles' walls,
And made what work I pleased. 'Tis not my blood
Wherein thou seest me masked. For thy revenge,   10
Wrench up thy power to th' highest.
AUFIDIUS   Wert thou the Hector
That was the whip of your bragged progeny,
Thou shouldst not scape me here.
 Here they fight, and certain Volsces come in the aid
 of Aufidius. Martius fights till the Volsces be driven
 in breathless, ⌈Martius following⌉
Officious and not valiant, you have shamed me   14
In your condemnèd seconds.   *Exit*

1.10 *Alarum. A retreat is sounded. ⌈Flourish.⌉ Enter at*
 one door Cominius with the Romans, at another door
 Martius with his arm in a scarf
COMINIUS (*to Martius*)
If I should tell thee o'er this thy day's work
Thou'lt not believe thy deeds. But I'll report it
Where senators shall mingle tears with smiles,
Where great patricians shall attend and shrug,
I'th' end admire; where ladies shall be frighted   5
And, gladly quaked, hear more; where the dull
 tribunes,
That with the fusty plebeians hate thine honours,
Shall say against their hearts 'We thank the gods
Our Rome hath such a soldier.'
Yet cam'st thou to a morsel of this feast,   10
Having fully dined before.
 Enter Lartius, with his power, from the pursuit
LARTIUS   O general,
Here is the steed, we the caparison.
Hadst thou beheld—
MARTIUS   Pray now, no more. My mother,
Who has a charter to extol her blood,
When she does praise me grieves me. I have done   15
As you have done, that's what I can; induced
As you have been, that's for my country.
He that has but effected his good will
Hath overta'en mine act.
COMINIUS   You shall not be
The grave of your deserving. Rome must know   20
The value of her own. 'Twere a concealment
Worse than a theft, no less than a traducement,
To hide your doings and to silence that
Which, to the spire and top of praises vouched,
Would seem but modest. Therefore, I beseech you—   25
In sign of what you are, not to reward
What you have done—before our army hear me.
MARTIUS
I have some wounds upon me, and they smart
To hear themselves remembered.
COMINIUS   Should they not,
Well might they fester 'gainst ingratitude,   30
And tent themselves with death. Of all the horses—
Whereof we have ta'en good, and good store—of all
The treasure in this field achieved and city,
We render you the tenth, to be ta'en forth

Before the common distribution   35
At your only choice.
MARTIUS   I thank you, general,
But cannot make my heart consent to take
A bribe to pay my sword. I do refuse it,
And stand upon my common part with those
That have upheld the doing.   40
    A long flourish. They all cry 'Martius, Martius!',
    casting up their caps and lances. Cominius and
    Lartius stand bare
May these same instruments which you profane
Never sound more. When drums and trumpets shall
I'th' field prove flatterers, let courts and cities be
Made all of false-faced soothing. When steel grows
Soft as the parasite's silk, let him be made   45
An overture for th' wars. No more, I say.
For that I have not washed my nose that bled,
Or foiled some debile wretch, which without note
Here's many else have done, you shout me forth
In acclamations hyperbolical,   50
As if I loved my little should be dieted
In praises sauced with lies.
COMINIUS   Too modest are you,
More cruel to your good report than grateful
To us that give you truly. By your patience,
If 'gainst yourself you be incensed we'll put you,   55
Like one that means his proper harm, in manacles,
Then reason safely with you. Therefore be it known,
As to us, to all the world, that Caius Martius
Wears this war's garland, in token of the which
My noble steed, known to the camp, I give him,   60
With all his trim belonging; and from this time,
For what he did before Corioles, call him,
With all th'applause and clamour of the host,
Martius Caius Coriolanus. Bear th'addition
Nobly ever!   65
    Flourish. Trumpets sound, and drums
ALL Martius Caius Coriolanus!
CORIOLANUS (*to Cominius*) I will go wash,
And when my face is fair you shall perceive
Whether I blush or no. Howbeit, I thank you.
I mean to stride your steed, and at all times   70
To undercrest your good addition
To th' fairness of my power.
COMINIUS   So, to our tent,
Where, ere we do repose us, we will write
To Rome of our success. You, Titus Lartius,
Must to Corioles back. Send us to Rome   75
The best, with whom we may articulate
For their own good and ours.
LARTIUS   I shall, my lord.
CORIOLANUS The gods begin to mock me. I, that now
Refused most princely gifts, am bound to beg
Of my lord general.
COMINIUS   Take't, 'tis yours. What is't?   80
CORIOLANUS
I sometime lay here in Corioles,
And at a poor man's house. He used me kindly.
He cried to me; I saw him prisoner;

But then Aufidius was within my view,
And wrath o'erwhelmed my pity. I request you   85
To give my poor host freedom.
COMINIUS   O, well begged!
Were he the butcher of my son he should
Be free as is the wind. Deliver him, Titus.
LARTIUS
Martius, his name?
CORIOLANUS   By Jupiter, forgot!
I am weary, yea, my memory is tired.   90
Have we no wine here?
COMINIUS   Go we to our tent.
The blood upon your visage dries; 'tis time
It should be looked to. Come.
    ⌜*A flourish of cornetts.*⌝ *Exeunt*

1.11 *Enter Aufidius, bloody, with two or three Soldiers*
AUFIDIUS The town is ta'en.
A SOLDIER
'Twill be delivered back on good condition.
AUFIDIUS Condition?
I would I were a Roman, for I cannot,
Being a Volsce, be that I am. Condition?   5
What good condition can a treaty find
I'th' part that is at mercy? Five times, Martius,
I have fought with thee; so often hast thou beat me,
And wouldst do so, I think, should we encounter
As often as we eat. By th' elements,   10
If e'er again I meet him beard to beard,
He's mine, or I am his! Mine emulation
Hath not that honour in't it had, for where
I thought to crush him in an equal force,
True sword to sword, I'll potch at him some way   15
Or wrath or craft may get him.
A SOLDIER   He's the devil.
AUFIDIUS
Bolder, though not so subtle. My valour, poisoned
With only suff'ring stain by him, for him
Shall fly out of itself. Nor sleep nor sanctuary,
Being naked, sick, nor fane nor Capitol,   20
The prayers of priests nor times of sacrifice—
Embargements all of fury—shall lift up
Their rotten privilege and custom 'gainst
My hate to Martius. Where I find him, were it
At home upon my brother's guard, even there,   25
Against the hospitable canon, would I
Wash my fierce hand in's heart. Go you to th' city.
Learn how 'tis held, and what they are that must
Be hostages for Rome.
A SOLDIER   Will not you go?
AUFIDIUS
I am attended at the cypress grove. I pray you—   30
'Tis south the city mills—bring me word thither
How the world goes, that to the pace of it
I may spur on my journey.
A SOLDIER   I shall, sir.
    Exeunt ⌜*Aufidius at one door, Soldiers at*
                     another door⌝

2.1 *Enter Menenius with the two tribunes of the people,*
Sicinius and Brutus

MENENIUS The augurer tells me we shall have news
tonight.

BRUTUS Good or bad?

MENENIUS Not according to the prayer of the people, for
they love not Martius.   5

SICINIUS Nature teaches beasts to know their friends.

MENENIUS Pray you, who does the wolf love?

SICINIUS The lamb.

MENENIUS Ay, to devour him, as the hungry plebeians
would the noble Martius.   10

BRUTUS He's a lamb indeed that baas like a bear.

MENENIUS He's a bear indeed that lives like a lamb. You
two are old men. Tell me one thing that I shall ask
you.

SICINIUS *and* BRUTUS Well, sir?   15

MENENIUS In what enormity is Martius poor in that you
two have not in abundance?

BRUTUS He's poor in no one fault, but stored with all.

SICINIUS Especially in pride.

BRUTUS And topping all others in boasting.   20

MENENIUS This is strange now. Do you two know how
you are censured here in the city—I mean of us o'th'
right-hand file. Do you?

SICINIUS *and* BRUTUS Why, how are we censured?

MENENIUS Because—you talk of pride now—will you not
be angry?   26

SICINIUS *and* BRUTUS Well, well, sir, well?

MENENIUS Why, 'tis no great matter, for a very little thief
of occasion will rob you of a great deal of patience.
Give your dispositions the reins, and be angry at your
pleasures—at the least, if you take it as a pleasure to
you in being so. You blame Martius for being proud?

BRUTUS We do it not alone, sir.   33

MENENIUS I know you can do very little alone, for your
helps are many, or else your actions would grow
wondrous single. Your abilities are too infant-like for
doing much alone. You talk of pride. O that you could
turn your eyes toward the napes of your necks, and
make but an interior survey of your good selves! O
that you could!   40

SICINIUS *and* BRUTUS What then, sir?

MENENIUS Why, then you should discover a brace of
unmeriting, proud, violent, testy magistrates, alias
fools, as any in Rome.

SICINIUS Menenius, you are known well enough too.   45

MENENIUS I am known to be a humorous patrician, and
one that loves a cup of hot wine with not a drop of
allaying Tiber in't; said to be something imperfect in
favouring the first complaint, hasty and tinder-like
upon too trivial motion; one that converses more with
the buttock of the night than with the forehead of the
morning. What I think, I utter, and spend my malice
in my breath. Meeting two such wealsmen as you are—
I cannot call you Lycurguses—if the drink you give me
touch my palate adversely, I make a crooked face at

it. I cannot say your worships have delivered the matter
well, when I find the ass in compound with the major
part of your syllables. And though I must be content
to bear with those that say you are reverend grave
men, yet they lie deadly that tell you have good faces.
If you see this in the map of my microcosm, follows it
that I am known well enough too? What harm can
your bisson conspectuities glean out of this character,
if I be known well enough too?   64

BRUTUS Come, sir, come, we know you well enough.

MENENIUS You know neither me, yourselves, nor anything
You are ambitious for poor knaves' caps and legs. You
wear out a good wholesome forenoon in hearing a
cause between an orange-wife and a faucet-seller, and
then rejourn the controversy of threepence to a second
day of audience. When you are hearing a matter
between party and party, if you chance to be pinched
with the colic, you make faces like mummers, set up
the bloody flag against all patience, and in roaring for
a chamber-pot, dismiss the controversy bleeding, the
more entangled by your hearing. All the peace you
make in their cause is calling both the parties knaves.
You are a pair of strange ones.

BRUTUS Come, come, you are well understood to be a
perfecter giber for the table than a necessary bencher
in the Capitol.   81

MENENIUS Our very priests must become mockers if they
shall encounter such ridiculous subjects as you are.
When you speak best unto the purpose it is not worth
the wagging of your beards, and your beards deserve
not so honourable a grave as to stuff a botcher's
cushion or to be entombed in an ass's pack-saddle. Yet
you must be saying 'Martius is proud', who, in a cheap
estimation, is worth all your predecessors since
Deucalion, though peradventure some of the best of
'em were hereditary hangmen. Good e'en to your
worships. More of your conversation would infect my
brain, being the herdsmen of the beastly plebeians. I
will be bold to take my leave of you.   94

He leaves Brutus and Sicinius, who stand aside.
Enter in haste Volumnia, Virgilia, and Valeria

How now, my as fair as noble ladies—and the moon,
were she earthly, no nobler—whither do you follow
your eyes so fast?

VOLUMNIA Honourable Menenius, my boy Martius
approaches. For the love of Juno, let's go.

MENENIUS Ha, Martius coming home?   100

VOLUMNIA Ay, worthy Menenius, and with most
prosperous approbation.

MENENIUS ⌈*throwing up his cap*⌉ Take my cap, Jupiter, and
I thank thee! Hoo, Martius coming home?

VIRGILIA *and* VALERIA Nay, 'tis true.   105

VOLUMNIA Look, here's a letter from him. The state hath
another, his wife another, and I think there's one at
home for you.

MENENIUS I will make my very house reel tonight. A letter
for me?   110

VIRGILIA Yes, certain, there's a letter for you; I saw't.

MENENIUS A letter for me? It gives me an estate of seven years' health, in which time I will make a lip at the physician. The most sovereign prescription in Galen is but empiricutic and, to this preservative, of no better report than a horse-drench. Is he not wounded? He was wont to come home wounded.

VIRGILIA O, no, no, no!

VOLUMNIA O, he is wounded, I thank the gods for't!

MENENIUS So do I, too, if it be not too much. Brings a victory in his pocket, the wounds become him. 121

VOLUMNIA On's brows, Menenius. He comes the third time home with the oaken garland.

MENENIUS Has he disciplined Aufidius soundly?

VOLUMNIA Titus Lartius writes they fought together, but Aufidius got off. 126

MENENIUS And 'twas time for him too, I'll warrant him that. An he had stayed by him, I would not have been so fidiussed for all the chests in Corioles and the gold that's in them. Is the senate possessed of this? 130

VOLUMNIA Good ladies, let's go. Yes, yes, yes. The senate has letters from the general, wherein he gives my son the whole name of the war. He hath in this action outdone his former deeds doubly. 134

VALERIA In truth, there's wondrous things spoke of him.

MENENIUS Wondrous, ay, I warrant you; and not without his true purchasing.

VIRGILIA The gods grant them true.

VOLUMNIA True? Pooh-whoo! 139

MENENIUS True? I'll be sworn they are true. Where is he wounded? (To the tribunes) God save your good worships. Martius is coming home. He has more cause to be proud. (To Volumnia) Where is he wounded?

VOLUMNIA I'th' shoulder and i'th' left arm. There will be large cicatrices to show the people when he shall stand for his place. He received in the repulse of Tarquin seven hurts i'th' body.

MENENIUS One i'th' neck and two i'th' thigh—there's nine that I know.

VOLUMNIA He had before this last expedition twenty-five wounds upon him. 151

MENENIUS Now it's twenty-seven. Every gash was an enemy's grave.

A shout and flourish

Hark, the trumpets.

VOLUMNIA These are the ushers of Martius. Before him he carries noise, and behind him he leaves tears. 156
Death, that dark spirit, in's nervy arm doth lie,
Which being advanced, declines; and then men die.

Trumpets sound a sennet. Enter ⌈in state⌉ Cominius the general and Lartius, between them Coriolanus, crowned with an oaken garland, with captains and soldiers and a Herald

HERALD
Know, Rome, that all alone Martius did fight
Within Corioles' gates, where he hath won 160
With fame a name to 'Martius Caius'; these

In honour follows 'Coriolanus'.
Welcome to Rome, renownèd Coriolanus!
A flourish sounds

ALL
Welcome to Rome, renownèd Coriolanus!

CORIOLANUS
No more of this, it does offend my heart. 165
Pray now, no more.

COMINIUS   Look, sir, your mother.

CORIOLANUS (to Volumnia)   O,
You have, I know, petitioned all the gods
For my prosperity!
He kneels

VOLUMNIA   Nay, my good soldier, up,
My gentle Martius, worthy Caius,
⌈He rises⌉
And, by deed-achieving honour newly named— 170
What is it?—'Coriolanus' must I call thee?
But O, thy wife!

CORIOLANUS (to Virgilia) My gracious silence, hail.
Wouldst thou have laughed had I come coffined home,
That weep'st to see me triumph? Ah, my dear,
Such eyes the widows in Corioles wear, 175
And mothers that lack sons.

MENENIUS   Now the gods crown thee!
⌈CORIOLANUS⌉ (to Valeria)
And live you yet? O my sweet lady, pardon.

VOLUMNIA
I know not where to turn. O, welcome home!
And welcome, general, and you're welcome all!

MENENIUS
A hundred thousand welcomes! I could weep 180
And I could laugh, I am light and heavy. Welcome!
A curse begnaw at very root on's heart
That is not glad to see thee. You are three
That Rome should dote on. Yet, by the faith of men,
We have some old crab-trees here at home that will not
Be grafted to your relish. Yet welcome, warriors! 186
We call a nettle but a nettle, and
The faults of fools but folly.

COMINIUS Ever right.

CORIOLANUS Menenius, ever, ever. 190

HERALD
Give way there, and go on.

CORIOLANUS ⌈to Volumnia and Virgilia⌉
     Your hand, and yours.
Ere in our own house I do shade my head
The good patricians must be visited,
From whom I have received not only greetings,
But with them change of honours.

VOLUMNIA   I have lived 195
To see inherited my very wishes,
And the buildings of my fancy. Only
There's one thing wanting, which I doubt not but
Our Rome will cast upon thee.

CORIOLANUS   Know, good mother,

I had rather be their servant in my way   200
Than sway with them in theirs.

COMINIUS   On, to the Capitol.

A flourish of cornetts. Exeunt in state, as before, all
but Brutus and Sicinius, who come forward

BRUTUS
All tongues speak of him, and the blearèd sights
Are spectacled to see him. Your prattling nurse
Into a rapture lets her baby cry
While she chats him; the kitchen malkin pins   205
Her richest lockram 'bout her reechy neck,
Clamb'ring the walls to eye him. Stalls, bulks, windows
Are smothered up, leads filled and ridges horsed
With variable complexions, all agreeing
In earnestness to see him. Seld-shown flamens   210
Do press among the popular throngs, and puff
To win a vulgar station. Our veiled dames
Commit the war of white and damask in
Their nicely guarded cheeks to th' wanton spoil
Of Phoebus' burning kisses. Such a pother   215
As if that whatsoever god who leads him
Were slily crept into his human powers
And gave him graceful posture.

SICINIUS   On the sudden
I warrant him consul.

BRUTUS   Then our office may
During his power go sleep.   220

SICINIUS
He cannot temp'rately transport his honours
From where he should begin and end, but will
Lose those he hath won.

BRUTUS   In that there's comfort.

SICINIUS   Doubt not
The commoners, for whom we stand, but they
Upon their ancient malice will forget   225
With the least cause these his new honours, which
That he will give them make I as little question
As he is proud to do't.

BRUTUS   I heard him swear,
Were he to stand for consul, never would he
Appear i'th' market-place nor on him put   230
The napless vesture of humility,
Nor, showing, as the manner is, his wounds
To th' people, beg their stinking breaths.

SICINIUS   'Tis right.

BRUTUS
It was his word. O, he would miss it rather
Than carry it, but by the suit of the gentry to him, 235
And the desire of the nobles.

SICINIUS   I wish no better
Than have him hold that purpose, and to put it
In execution.

BRUTUS   'Tis most like he will.

SICINIUS
It shall be to him then, as our good wills,
A sure destruction.

BRUTUS   So it must fall out   240

To him, or our authority's for an end.
We must suggest the people in what hatred
He still hath held them; that to's power he would
Have made them mules, silenced their pleaders,
And dispropertied their freedoms, holding them   245
In human action and capacity
Of no more soul nor fitness for the world
Than camels in their war, who have their provand
Only for bearing burdens, and sore blows
For sinking under them.

SICINIUS   This, as you say, suggested 250
At some time when his soaring insolence
Shall touch the people—which time shall not want
If he be put upon't, and that's as easy
As to set dogs on sheep—will be his fire
To kindle their dry stubble, and their blaze   255
Shall darken him for ever.

Enter a Messenger

BRUTUS   What's the matter?

MESSENGER
You are sent for to the Capitol. 'Tis thought
That Martius shall be consul. I have seen
The dumb men throng to see him, and the blind
To hear him speak. Matrons flung gloves,   260
Ladies and maids their scarves and handkerchiefs,
Upon him as he passed. The nobles bended
As to Jove's statue, and the commons made
A shower and thunder with their caps and shouts.
I never saw the like.

BRUTUS   Let's to the Capitol, 265
And carry with us ears and eyes for th' time,
But hearts for the event.

SICINIUS   Have with you.   *Exeunt*

2.2   *Enter two Officers, to lay cushions, as it were in the*
              Capitol

FIRST OFFICER Come, come, they are almost here. How
many stand for consulships?

SECOND OFFICER Three, they say, but 'tis thought of every
one Coriolanus will carry it.

FIRST OFFICER That's a brave fellow, but he's vengeance
proud and loves not the common people.   6

SECOND OFFICER Faith, there hath been many great men
that have flattered the people who ne'er loved them;
and there be many that they have loved they know
not wherefore, so that if they love they know not why,
they hate upon no better a ground. Therefore for
Coriolanus neither to care whether they love or hate
him manifests the true knowledge he has in their
disposition, and out of his noble carelessness lets them
plainly see't.   15

FIRST OFFICER If he did not care whether he had their
love or no he waved indifferently 'twixt doing them
neither good nor harm; but he seeks their hate with
greater devotion than they can render it him, and
leaves nothing undone that may fully discover him
their opposite. Now to seem to affect the malice and

displeasure of the people is as bad as that which he
dislikes, to flatter them for their love.   23
SECOND OFFICER He hath deserved worthily of his country,
and his ascent is not by such easy degrees as those
who, having been supple and courteous to the people,
bonneted, without any further deed to have them at
all into their estimation and report. But he hath so
planted his honours in their eyes and his actions in
their hearts that for their tongues to be silent and not
confess so much were a kind of ingrateful injury. To
report otherwise were a malice that, giving itself the
lie, would pluck reproof and rebuke from every ear that
heard it.
FIRST OFFICER No more of him. He's a worthy man. Make
way, they are coming.   36
    A sennet. Enter the Patricians, and Sicinius and
    Brutus, the tribunes of the people, lictors before
    them; Coriolanus, Menenius, Cominius the consul.
    ⌈*The Patricians take their places and sit.*⌉ *Sicinius*
    and Brutus take their places by themselves.
    Coriolanus stands
MENENIUS
Having determined of the Volsces, and
To send for Titus Lartius, it remains
As the main point of this our after-meeting
To gratify his noble service that   40
Hath thus stood for his country. Therefore please you,
Most reverend and grave elders, to desire
The present consul and last general
In our well-found successes to report
A little of that worthy work performed   45
By Martius Caius Coriolanus, whom
We met here both to thank and to remember
With honours like himself.
    ⌈*Coriolanus sits*⌉
FIRST SENATOR   Speak, good Cominius.
Leave nothing out for length, and make us think
Rather our state's defective for requital   50
Than we to stretch it out.
  (*To the tribunes*)   Masters o'th' people,
We do request your kindest ears and, after,
Your loving motion toward the common body
To yield what passes here.
SICINIUS   We are convented
Upon a pleasing treaty, and have hearts   55
Inclinable to honour and advance
The theme of our assembly.
BRUTUS   Which the rather
We shall be blessed to do if he remember
A kinder value of the people than
He hath hereto prized them at.
MENENIUS   That's off, that's off. 60
I would you rather had been silent. Please you
To hear Cominius speak?
BRUTUS   Most willingly,
But yet my caution was more pertinent
Than the rebuke you give it.
MENENIUS   He loves your people,
But tie him not to be their bedfellow.   65

Worthy Cominius, speak.
    Coriolanus rises and offers to go away
  (*To Coriolanus*)   Nay, keep your place.
⌈FIRST⌉ SENATOR Sit, Coriolanus. Never shame to hear
What you have nobly done.
CORIOLANUS   Your honours' pardon,
I had rather have my wounds to heal again
Than hear say how I got them.
BRUTUS   Sir, I hope   70
My words disbenched you not?
CORIOLANUS   No, sir, yet oft
When blows have made me stay I fled from words.
You soothed not, therefore hurt not; but your people,
I love them as they weigh—
MENENIUS   Pray now, sit down.
CORIOLANUS
I had rather have one scratch my head i'th' sun   75
When the alarum were struck than idly sit
To hear my nothings monstered.   *Exit*
MENENIUS   Masters of the people,
Your multiplying spawn how can he flatter—
That's thousand to one good one—when you now see
He had rather venture all his limbs for honour   80
Than one on's ears to hear it? Proceed, Cominius.
COMINIUS
I shall lack voice; the deeds of Coriolanus
Should not be uttered feebly. It is held
That valour is the chiefest virtue, and
Most dignifies the haver. If it be,   85
The man I speak of cannot in the world
Be singly counterpoised. At sixteen years,
When Tarquin made a head for Rome, he fought
Beyond the mark of others. Our then dictator,
Whom with all praise I point at, saw him fight   90
When with his Amazonian chin he drove
The bristled lips before him. He bestrid
An o'erpressed Roman, and, i'th' consul's view,
Slew three opposers. Tarquin's self he met,
And struck him on his knee. In that day's feats,   95
When he might act the woman in the scene,
He proved best man i'th' field, and for his meed
Was brow-bound with the oak. His pupil age
Man-entered thus, he waxèd like a sea,
And in the brunt of seventeen battles since   100
He lurched all swords of the garland. For this last
Before and in Corioles, let me say
I cannot speak him home. He stopped the fliers,
And by his rare example made the coward
Turn terror into sport. As weeds before   105
A vessel under sail, so men obeyed
And fell below his stem. His sword, death's stamp,
Where it did mark, it took. From face to foot
He was a thing of blood, whose every motion
Was timed with dying cries. Alone he entered   110
The mortal gate of th' city, which he, painted
With shunless destiny, aidless came off,
And with a sudden reinforcement struck
Corioles like a planet. Now all's his.
When by and by the din of war gan pierce   115

His ready sense, then straight his doubled spirit
Requickened what in flesh was fatigate,
And to the battle came he, where he did
Run reeking o'er the lives of men as if
'Twere a perpetual spoil; and till we called   120
Both field and city ours he never stood
To ease his breast with panting.
MENENIUS   Worthy man.
⌈FIRST⌉ SENATOR
He cannot but with measure fit the honours
Which we devise him.
COMINIUS   Our spoils he kicked at,
And looked upon things precious as they were   125
The common muck of the world. He covets less
Than misery itself would give, rewards
His deeds with doing them, and is content
To spend the time to end it.
MENENIUS   He's right noble.
Let him be called for.   130
⌈FIRST⌉ SENATOR Call Coriolanus.
OFFICER He doth appear.
    Enter Coriolanus
MENENIUS
The senate, Coriolanus, are well pleased
To make thee consul.
CORIOLANUS   I do owe them still
My life and services.
MENENIUS   It then remains   135
That you do speak to the people.
CORIOLANUS   I do beseech you,
Let me o'erleap that custom, for I cannot
Put on the gown, stand naked, and entreat them
For my wounds' sake to give their suffrage.
Please you that I may pass this doing.
SICINIUS   Sir, the people
Must have their voices, neither will they bate   141
One jot of ceremony.
MENENIUS (*to Coriolanus*) Put them not to't.
Pray you, go fit you to the custom and
Take to you, as your predecessors have,
Your honour with your form.
CORIOLANUS   It is a part   145
That I shall blush in acting, and might well
Be taken from the people.
BRUTUS (*to Sicinius*)   Mark you that?
CORIOLANUS
To brag unto them 'Thus I did, and thus',
Show them th'unaching scars, which I should hide,
As if I had received them for the hire   150
Of their breath only!
MENENIUS   Do not stand upon't.—
We recommend to you, tribunes of the people,
Our purpose to them; and to our noble consul
Wish we all joy and honour.
SENATORS
To Coriolanus come all joy and honour!   155
    A flourish of cornetts, then exeunt all but
          Sicinius and Brutus

BRUTUS
You see how he intends to use the people.
SICINIUS
May they perceive's intent! He will require them
As if he did contemn what he requested
Should be in them to give.
BRUTUS   Come, we'll inform them
Of our proceedings here. On th' market-place   160
I know they do attend us.   *Exeunt*

2.3   *Enter seven or eight Citizens*
FIRST CITIZEN Once, if he do require our voices we ought
   not to deny him.
SECOND CITIZEN We may, sir, if we will.
THIRD CITIZEN We have power in ourselves to do it, but
   it is a power that we have no power to do. For if he
   show us his wounds and tell us his deeds, we are to
   put our tongues into those wounds and speak for them;
   so if he tell us his noble deeds we must also tell him
   our noble acceptance of them. Ingratitude is monstrous,
   and for the multitude to be ingrateful were to make a
   monster of the multitude, of the which we, being
   members, should bring ourselves to be monstrous
   members.   13
FIRST CITIZEN And to make us no better thought of, a
   little help will serve; for once we stood up about the
   corn, he himself stuck not to call us the many-headed
   multitude.
THIRD CITIZEN We have been called so of many, not that
   our heads are some brown, some black, some abram,
   some bald, but that our wits are so diversely coloured;
   and truly I think if all our wits were to issue out of
   one skull, they would fly east, west, north, south, and
   their consent of one direct way should be at once to
   all the points o'th' compass.
SECOND CITIZEN Think you so? Which way do you judge
   my wit would fly?   26
THIRD CITIZEN Nay, your wit will not so soon out as
   another man's will, 'tis strongly wedged up in a
   blockhead. But if it were at liberty, 'twould sure
   southward.   30
SECOND CITIZEN Why that way?
THIRD CITIZEN To lose itself in a fog where, being three
   parts melted away with rotten dews, the fourth would
   return for conscience' sake, to help to get thee a wife.
SECOND CITIZEN You are never without your tricks. You
   may, you may.   36
THIRD CITIZEN Are you all resolved to give your voices?
   But that's no matter, the greater part carries it. I say,
   if he would incline to the people there was never a
   worthier man.   40
    Enter Coriolanus in a gown of humility, with
      Menenius
Here he comes, and in the gown of humility. Mark his
behaviour. We are not to stay all together, but to come
by him where he stands by ones, by twos, and by
threes. He's to make his requests by particulars, wherein
every one of us has a single honour in giving him our

own voices with our own tongues. Therefore follow
me, and I'll direct you how you shall go by him.
ALL THE CITIZENS Content, content.   *Exeunt Citizens*
MENENIUS
O sir, you are not right. Have you not known
The worthiest men have done't?
CORIOLANUS   What must I say?   50
'I pray, sir'? Plague upon't, I cannot bring
My tongue to such a pace. 'Look, sir, my wounds.
I got them in my country's service, when
Some certain of your brethren roared and ran
From th' noise of our own drums'?
MENENIUS   O me, the gods!   55
You must not speak of that, you must desire them
To think upon you.
CORIOLANUS   Think upon me? Hang 'em.
I would they would forget me like the virtues
Which our divines lose by 'em.
MENENIUS   You'll mar all.
I'll leave you. Pray you, speak to 'em, I pray you,   60
In wholesome manner.
CORIOLANUS   Bid them wash their faces
And keep their teeth clean.   *Exit Menenius*
     Enter three of the Citizens
                    So, here comes a brace.
You know the cause, sir, of my standing here.
THIRD CITIZEN
We do, sir. Tell us what hath brought you to't.
CORIOLANUS Mine own desert.   65
SECOND CITIZEN Your own desert?
CORIOLANUS Ay, but not mine own desire.
THIRD CITIZEN How not your own desire?
CORIOLANUS No, sir, 'twas never my desire yet to trouble
the poor with begging.   70
THIRD CITIZEN You must think if we give you anything
we hope to gain by you.
CORIOLANUS Well then, I pray, your price o'th' consulship?
FIRST CITIZEN The price is to ask it kindly.   74
CORIOLANUS Kindly, sir, I pray let me ha't. I have wounds
to show you which shall be yours in private. (*To Second
Citizen*) Your good voice, sir. What say you?
SECOND CITIZEN You shall ha't, worthy sir.
CORIOLANUS A match, sir. There's in all two worthy voices
begged. I have your alms. Adieu.   80
THIRD CITIZEN (*to the other Citizens*) But this is something
odd.
SECOND CITIZEN An 'twere to give again—but 'tis no
matter.   *Exeunt Citizens*
     Enter two other Citizens
CORIOLANUS Pray you now, if it may stand with the tune
of your voices that I may be consul, I have here the
customary gown.
⌜FOURTH⌝ CITIZEN You have deserved nobly of your
country, and you have not deserved nobly.
CORIOLANUS Your enigma?   90
⌜FOURTH⌝ CITIZEN You have been a scourge to her enemies,
you have been a rod to her friends. You have not,
indeed, loved the common people.

CORIOLANUS You should account me the more virtuous
that I have not been common in my love. I will, sir,
flatter my sworn brother the people to earn a dearer
estimation of them. 'Tis a condition they account gentle.
And since the wisdom of their choice is rather to have
my hat than my heart, I will practise the insinuating
nod and be off to them most counterfeitly; that is, sir,
I will counterfeit the bewitchment of some popular
man, and give it bountiful to the desirers. Therefore,
beseech you I may be consul.
⌜FIFTH⌝ CITIZEN We hope to find you our friend, and
therefore give you our voices heartily.   105
⌜FOURTH⌝ CITIZEN You have received many wounds for
your country.
CORIOLANUS I will not seal your knowledge with showing
them. I will make much of your voices, and so trouble
you no farther.   110
BOTH CITIZENS The gods give you joy, sir, heartily.
CORIOLANUS Most sweet voices.   *Exeunt Citizens*
Better it is to die, better to starve,
Than crave the hire which first we do deserve.
Why in this womanish toge should I stand here   115
To beg of Hob and Dick that does appear
Their needless vouches? Custom calls me to't.
What custom wills, in all things should we do't,
The dust on antique time would lie unswept,
And mountainous error be too highly heaped   120
For truth to o'erpeer. Rather than fool it so,
Let the high office and the honour go
To one that would do thus. I am half through.
The one part suffered, the other will I do.
     Enter three Citizens more
Here come more voices.   125
Your voices! For your voices I have fought,
Watched for your voices, for your voices bear
Of wounds two dozen odd; battles thrice six
I have seen and heard of for your voices, have
Done many things, some less, some more. Your
voices!   130
Indeed I would be consul.
⌜SIXTH⌝ CITIZEN He has done nobly, and cannot go without
any honest man's voice.
⌜SEVENTH⌝ CITIZEN Therefore let him be consul. The gods
give him joy and make him good friend to the people!
ALL THE CITIZENS Amen, Amen. God save thee, noble
consul!
CORIOLANUS Worthy voices.   *Exeunt Citizens*
     Enter Menenius with Brutus and Sicinius
MENENIUS
You have stood your limitation, and the tribunes
Endue you with the people's voice. Remains   140
That in th' official marks invested, you
Anon do meet the senate.
CORIOLANUS   Is this done?
SICINIUS
The custom of request you have discharged.
The people do admit you, and are summoned
To meet anon upon your approbation.   145

CORIOLANUS
 Where, at the senate-house?
SICINIUS   There, Coriolanus.
CORIOLANUS
 May I change these garments?
SICINIUS   You may, sir.
CORIOLANUS
 That I'll straight do, and, knowing myself again,
 Repair to th' senate-house.
MENENIUS
 I'll keep you company. (*To the tribunes*) Will you
  along?   150
BRUTUS
 We stay here for the people.
SICINIUS   Fare you well.
   Exeunt Coriolanus and Menenius
 He has it now, and by his looks methinks
 'Tis warm at's heart.
BRUTUS   With a proud heart he wore
 His humble weeds. Will you dismiss the people?
   Enter the Plebeians
SICINIUS
 How now, my masters, have you chose this man? 155
FIRST CITIZEN He has our voices, sir.
BRUTUS
 We pray the gods he may deserve your loves.
SECOND CITIZEN
 Amen, sir. To my poor unworthy notice
 He mocked us when he begged our voices.
THIRD CITIZEN
 Certainly. He flouted us downright.   160
FIRST CITIZEN
 No, 'tis his kind of speech. He did not mock us.
SECOND CITIZEN
 Not one amongst us save yourself but says
 He used us scornfully. He should have showed us
 His marks of merit, wounds received for's country.
SICINIUS
 Why, so he did, I am sure.
ALL THE CITIZENS   No, no; no man saw 'em.
THIRD CITIZEN
 He said he had wounds which he could show in
  private,   166
 And with his hat, thus waving it in scorn,
 'I would be consul,' says he. 'Agèd custom
 But by your voices will not so permit me.
 Your voices therefore.' When we granted that, 170
 Here was 'I thank you for your voices, thank you.
 Your most sweet voices. Now you have left your voices
 I have no further with you.' Was not this mockery?
SICINIUS
 Why either were you ignorant to see't,
 Or, seeing it, of such childish friendliness 175
 To yield your voices?
BRUTUS (*to the Citizens*) Could you not have told him
 As you were lessoned: when he had no power
 But was a petty servant to the state,

He was your enemy, ever spake against
Your liberties and the charters that you bear 180
I'th' body of the weal; and now arriving
A place of potency and sway o'th' state,
If he should still malignantly remain
Fast foe to th' plebeii, your voices might
Be curses to yourselves. You should have said 185
That as his worthy deeds did claim no less
Than what he stood for, so his gracious nature
Would think upon you for your voices and
Translate his malice towards you into love,
Standing your friendly lord.
SICINIUS (*to the Citizens*) Thus to have said 190
As you were fore-advised had touched his spirit
And tried his inclination, from him plucked
Either his gracious promise which you might,
As cause had called you up, have held him to,
Or else it would have galled his surly nature, 195
Which easily endures not article
Tying him to aught. So putting him to rage,
You should have ta'en th'advantage of his choler
And passed him unelected.
BRUTUS (*to the Citizens*) Did you perceive
He did solicit you in free contempt 200
When he did need your loves, and do you think
That his contempt shall not be bruising to you
When he hath power to crush? Why, had your bodies
No heart among you? Or had you tongues to cry
Against the rectorship of judgement?
SICINIUS (*to the Citizens*)   Have you 205
Ere now denied the asker, and now again,
Of him that did not ask but mock, bestow
Your sued-for tongues?
THIRD CITIZEN
 He's not confirmed, we may deny him yet.
SECOND CITIZEN And will deny him. 210
 I'll have five hundred voices of that sound.
FIRST CITIZEN
 I twice five hundred, and their friends to piece 'em.
BRUTUS
 Get you hence instantly, and tell those friends
 They have chose a consul that will from them take
 Their liberties, make them of no more voice 215
 Than dogs that are as often beat for barking,
 As therefor kept to do so.
SICINIUS (*to the Citizens*) Let them assemble,
 And on a safer judgement all revoke
 Your ignorant election. Enforce his pride
 And his old hate unto you. Besides, forget not 220
 With what contempt he wore the humble weed,
 How in his suit he scorned you; but your loves,
 Thinking upon his services, took from you
 Th'apprehension of his present portance,
 Which most gibingly, ungravely he did fashion 225
 After the inveterate hate he bears you.
BRUTUS (*to the Citizens*) Lay
 A fault on us your tribunes, that we laboured

No impediment between, but that you must
Cast your election on him.
SICINIUS (*to the Citizens*)   Say you chose him
    More after our commandment than as guided   230
    By your own true affections, and that your minds,
    Preoccupied with what you rather must do
    Than what you should, made you against the grain
    To voice him consul. Lay the fault on us.
BRUTUS (*to the Citizens*)
    Ay, spare us not. Say we read lectures to you,   235
    How youngly he began to serve his country,
    How long continued, and what stock he springs of,
    The noble house o'th' Martians, from whence came
    That Ancus Martius, Numa's daughter's son,
    Who after great Hostilius here was king;   240
    Of the same house Publius and Quintus were,
    That our best water brought by conduits hither;
    And Censorinus that was so surnamed,
    And nobly named so, twice being censor,
    Was his great ancestor.
SICINIUS (*to the Citizens*)   One thus descended,   245
    That hath beside well in his person wrought
    To be set high in place, we did commend
    To your remembrances, but you have found,
    Scaling his present bearing with his past,
    That he's your fixèd enemy, and revoke   250
    Your sudden approbation.
BRUTUS (*to the Citizens*)   Say you ne'er had done't—
    Harp on that still—but by our putting on;
    And presently when you have drawn your number,
    Repair to th' Capitol.
⌈A CITIZEN⌉   We will so.
⌈ANOTHER CITIZEN⌉   Almost all
    Repent in their election.   *Exeunt Citizens*
BRUTUS   Let them go on.   255
    This mutiny were better put in hazard
    Than stay, past doubt, for greater.
    If, as his nature is, he fall in rage
    With their refusal, both observe and answer
    The vantage of his anger.
SICINIUS   To th' Capitol, come.   260
    We will be there before the stream o'th' people,
    And this shall seem, as partly 'tis, their own,
    Which we have goaded onward.   *Exeunt*

❀

3.1   *Cornetts. Enter Coriolanus, Menenius, all the*
      gentry; Cominius, Lartius, and other Senators
CORIOLANUS
    Tullus Aufidius then had made new head?
LARTIUS
    He had, my lord, and that it was which caused
    Our swifter composition.
CORIOLANUS
    So then the Volsces stand but as at first,
    Ready when time shall prompt them to make raid   5
    Upon's again.
COMINIUS   They are worn, lord consul, so

That we shall hardly in our ages see
    Their banners wave again.
CORIOLANUS (*to Lartius*)   Saw you Aufidius?
LARTIUS
    On safeguard he came to me, and did curse
    Against the Volsces for they had so vilely   10
    Yielded the town. He is retired to Antium.
CORIOLANUS
    Spoke he of me?
LARTIUS   He did, my lord.
CORIOLANUS   How? What?
LARTIUS
    How often he had met you sword to sword;
    That of all things upon the earth he hated
    Your person most; that he would pawn his fortunes 15
    To hopeless restitution, so he might
    Be called your vanquisher.
CORIOLANUS At Antium lives he?
LARTIUS At Antium.
CORIOLANUS
    I wish I had a cause to seek him there,   20
    To oppose his hatred fully. Welcome home.
        Enter Sicinius and Brutus
    Behold, these are the tribunes of the people,
    The tongues o'th' common mouth. I do despise them,
    For they do prank them in authority
    Against all noble sufferance.   25
SICINIUS Pass no further.
CORIOLANUS Ha, what is that?
BRUTUS
    It will be dangerous to go on. No further.
CORIOLANUS What makes this change?
MENENIUS The matter?   30
COMINIUS
    Hath he not passed the noble and the common?
BRUTUS
    Cominius, no.
CORIOLANUS   Have I had children's voices?
⌈FIRST⌉ SENATOR
    Tribunes, give way. He shall to th' market-place.
BRUTUS
    The people are incensed against him.
SICINIUS   Stop,
    Or all will fall in broil.
CORIOLANUS   Are these your herd?   35
    Must these have voices, that can yield them now
    And straight disclaim their tongues? What are your
        offices?
    You being their mouths, why rule you not their
        teeth?
    Have you not set them on?
MENENIUS   Be calm, be calm.
CORIOLANUS
    It is a purposed thing, and grows by plot   40
    To curb the will of the nobility.
    Suffer't, and live with such as cannot rule
    Nor ever will be ruled.
BRUTUS   Call't not a plot.

The people cry you mocked them, and of late
When corn was given them gratis, you repined,   45
Scandalled the suppliants for the people, called them
Time-pleasers, flatterers, foes to nobleness.
CORIOLANUS
Why, this was known before.
BRUTUS   Not to them all.
CORIOLANUS
Have you informed them sithence?
BRUTUS   How, I inform them?
⌈CORIOLANUS⌉
You are like to do such business.   50
BRUTUS Not unlike
Each way to better yours.
CORIOLANUS
Why then should I be consul? By yon clouds,
Let me deserve so ill as you, and make me
Your fellow tribune.
SICINIUS   You show too much of that   55
For which the people stir. If you will pass
To where you are bound, you must enquire your way,
Which you are out of, with a gentler spirit,
Or never be so noble as a consul,
Nor yoke with him for tribune.
MENENIUS   Let's be calm.   60
COMINIUS
The people are abused, set on. This palt'ring
Becomes not Rome, nor has Coriolanus
Deserved this so dishonoured rub, laid falsely
I'th' plain way of his merit.
CORIOLANUS   Tell me of corn?
This was my speech, and I will speak't again.   65
MENENIUS Not now, not now.
⌈FIRST⌉ SENATOR Not in this heat, sir, now.
CORIOLANUS Now as I live,
I will. My nobler friends, I crave their pardons.
For the mutable rank-scented meinie,   70
Let them regard me, as I do not flatter,
And therein behold themselves. I say again,
In soothing them we nourish 'gainst our Senate
The cockle of rebellion, insolence, sedition,
Which we ourselves have ploughed for, sowed, and
     scattered   75
By mingling them with us, the honoured number
Who lack not virtue, no, nor power, but that
Which they have given to beggars.
MENENIUS   Well, no more.
⌈FIRST⌉ SENATOR
No more words, we beseech you.
CORIOLANUS   How, no more?
As for my country I have shed my blood,   80
Not fearing outward force, so shall my lungs
Coin words till their decay against those measles
Which we disdain should tetter us, yet sought
The very way to catch them.
BRUTUS
You speak o'th' people as if you were a god   85
To punish, not a man of their infirmity.

SICINIUS
'Twere well we let the people know't.
MENENIUS   What, what, his choler?
CORIOLANUS
Choler? Were I as patient as the midnight sleep,
By Jove, 'twould be my mind.
SICINIUS   It is a mind
That shall remain a poison where it is,   90
Not poison any further.
CORIOLANUS   'Shall remain'?
Hear you this Triton of the minnows? Mark you
His absolute 'shall'?
COMINIUS   'Twas from the canon.
CORIOLANUS   'Shall'?
O good but most unwise patricians, why,
You grave but reckless senators, have you thus   95
Given Hydra here to choose an officer
That, with his peremptory 'shall', being but
The horn and noise o'th' monster's, wants not spirit
To say he'll turn your current in a ditch
And make your channel his? If he have power,   100
Then vail your impotence; if none, awake
Your dangerous lenity. If you are learned,
Be not as common fools; if you are not,
Let them have cushions by you. You are plebeians
If they be senators, and they are no less   105
When, both your voices blended, the great'st taste
Most palates theirs. They choose their magistrate,
And such a one as he, who puts his 'shall',
His popular 'shall', against a graver bench
Than ever frowned in Greece. By Jove himself,   110
It makes the consuls base, and my soul aches
To know, when two authorities are up,
Neither supreme, how soon confusion
May enter 'twixt the gap of both and take
The one by th' other.
COMINIUS   Well, on to th' market-place. 115
CORIOLANUS
Whoever gave that counsel to give forth
The corn o'th' storehouse gratis, as 'twas used
Sometime in Greece—
MENENIUS   Well, well, no more of that.
CORIOLANUS
Though there the people had more absolute power—
I say they nourished disobedience, fed   120
The ruin of the state.
BRUTUS   Why shall the people give
One that speaks thus their voice?
CORIOLANUS   I'll give my reasons,
More worthier than their voices. They know the corn
Was not our recompense, resting well assured
They ne'er did service for't. Being pressed to th' war,
Even when the navel of the state was touched,   126
They would not thread the gates. This kind of service
Did not deserve corn gratis. Being i'th' war,
Their mutinies and revolts, wherein they showed
Most valour, spoke not for them. Th'accusation   130
Which they have often made against the senate,

All cause unborn, could never be the native
Of our so frank donation. Well, what then?
How shall this bosom multiplied digest
The senate's courtesy? Let deeds express   135
What's like to be their words: 'We did request it,
We are the greater poll, and in true fear
They gave us our demands.' Thus we debase
The nature of our seats, and make the rabble
Call our cares fears, which will in time   140
Break ope the locks o'th' senate and bring in
The crows to peck the eagles.

MENENIUS   Come, enough.

BRUTUS
Enough with over-measure.

CORIOLANUS   No, take more.
What may be sworn by, both divine and human,
Seal what I end withal! This double worship,   145
Where one part does disdain with cause, the other
Insult without all reason, where gentry, title, wisdom
Cannot conclude but by the yea and no
Of general ignorance, it must omit
Real necessities, and give way the while   150
To unstable slightness. Purpose so barred, it follows
Nothing is done to purpose. Therefore beseech you—
You that will be less fearful than discreet,
That love the fundamental part of state
More than you doubt the change on't, that prefer   155
A noble life before a long, and wish
To jump a body with a dangerous physic
That's sure of death without it—at once pluck out
The multitudinous tongue; let them not lick
The sweet which is their poison. Your dishonour   160
Mangles true judgement, and bereaves the state
Of that integrity which should become't,
Not having the power to do the good it would
For th'ill which doth control't.

BRUTUS   He's said enough.

SICINIUS
He's spoken like a traitor, and shall answer   165
As traitors do.

CORIOLANUS   Thou wretch, despite o'erwhelm thee!
What should the people do with these bald tribunes,
On whom depending, their obedience fails
To th' greater bench? In a rebellion,
When what's not meet but what must be was law,   170
Then were they chosen. In a better hour
Let what is meet be said it must be meet,
And throw their power i'th' dust.

BRUTUS
Manifest treason.

SICINIUS   This a consul? No.

BRUTUS
The aediles, ho!

Enter an Aedile

                    Let him be apprehended.   175

SICINIUS
Go call the people,   ⌐*Exit Aedile*¬
(*To Coriolanus*)   in whose name myself

Attach thee as a traitorous innovator,
A foe to th' public weal. Obey, I charge thee,
And follow to thine answer.

CORIOLANUS   Hence, old goat!

ALL ⌐THE PATRICIANS¬
We'll surety him.

COMINIUS (*to Sicinius*) Aged sir, hands off.   180

CORIOLANUS (*to Sicinius*)
Hence, rotten thing, or I shall shake thy bones
Out of thy garments.

SICINIUS   Help, ye citizens!

Enter a rabble of Plebeians, with the Aediles

MENENIUS
On both sides more respect.

SICINIUS   Here's he
That would take from you all your power.

BRUTUS   Seize him, aediles.

ALL ⌐THE CITIZENS¬
Down with him, down with him!

SECOND SENATOR   Weapons, weapons, weapons!
They all bustle about Coriolanus

⌐CITIZENS *and* PATRICIANS¬ ⌐*in dispersed cries*¬
Tribunes! Patricians! Citizens! What ho!   186
Sicinius! Brutus! Coriolanus! Citizens!

⌐SOME CITIZENS *and* PATRICIANS¬
Peace, peace, peace! Stay! Hold! Peace!

MENENIUS
What is about to be? I am out of breath.
Confusion's near; I cannot speak. You tribunes   190
To th' people, Coriolanus, patience!
Speak, good Sicinius.

SICINIUS   Hear me, people, peace.

ALL ⌐THE CITIZENS¬
Let's hear our tribune! Peace! Speak, speak, speak!

SICINIUS
You are at point to lose your liberties.
Martius would have all from you—Martius   195
Whom late you have named for consul.

MENENIUS   Fie, fie, fie,
This is the way to kindle, not to quench.

⌐FIRST¬ SENATOR
To unbuild the city, and to lay all flat.

SICINIUS
What is the city but the people?

ALL ⌐THE CITIZENS¬   True,
The people are the city.

BRUTUS   By the consent of all   200
We were established the people's magistrates.

ALL ⌐THE CITIZENS¬
You so remain.

MENENIUS   And so are like to do.

⌐CORIOLANUS¬
That is the way to lay the city flat,
To bring the roof to the foundation,
And bury all which yet distinctly ranges   205
In heaps and piles of ruin.

SICINIUS   This deserves death.

BRUTUS
Or let us stand to our authority,
Or let us lose it. We do here pronounce,
Upon the part o'th' people in whose power
We were elected theirs, Martius is worthy   210
Of present death.
SICINIUS   Therefore lay hold of him,
Bear him to th' rock Tarpeian; and from thence
Into destruction cast him.
BRUTUS   Aediles, seize him.
ALL THE CITIZENS
Yield, Martius, yield.
MENENIUS   Hear me one word.
Beseech you, tribunes, hear me but a word.   215
AEDILES Peace, peace!
MENENIUS (to the tribunes)
Be that you seem, truly your country's friend,
And temp'rately proceed to what you would
Thus violently redress.
BRUTUS   Sir, those cold ways
That seem like prudent helps are very poisons   220
Where the disease is violent. Lay hands upon him,
And bear him to the rock.
      Coriolanus draws his sword
CORIOLANUS   No, I'll die here.
There's some among you have beheld me fighting.
Come, try upon yourselves what you have seen me.
MENENIUS
Down with that sword. Tribunes, withdraw a while.
BRUTUS
Lay hands upon him.
MENENIUS   Help Martius, help!   226
You that be noble, help him, young and old.
ALL ⌈THE CITIZENS⌉ Down with him, down with him!
   In this mutiny the tribunes, the Aediles, and the
   people are beat in
MENENIUS (to Coriolanus)
Go get you to your house. Be gone, away!
All will be naught else.
SECOND SENATOR (to Coriolanus) Get you gone.   230
⌈CORIOLANUS⌉
Stand fast; we have as many friends as enemies.
MENENIUS
Shall it be put to that?
⌈FIRST⌉ SENATOR   The gods forbid!
(To Coriolanus) I prithee, noble friend, home to thy
   house.
Leave us to cure this cause.
MENENIUS   For 'tis a sore upon us
You cannot tent yourself. Be gone, beseech you.   235
⌈COMINIUS⌉ Come, sir, along with us.
⌈CORIOLANUS⌉
I would they were barbarians, as they are,
Though in Rome littered; not Romans, as they are
   not,
Though calved i'th' porch o'th' Capitol.
⌈MENENIUS⌉   Be gone.

Put not your worthy rage into your tongue.   240
One time will owe another.
CORIOLANUS   On fair ground
I could beat forty of them.
MENENIUS   I could myself
Take up a brace o'th' best of them, yea, the two
   tribunes.
COMINIUS
But now 'tis odds beyond arithmetic,
And manhood is called foolery when it stands   245
Against a falling fabric.
(To Coriolanus)   Will you hence
Before the tag return, whose rage doth rend
Like interrupted waters, and o'erbear
What they are used to bear?
MENENIUS (to Coriolanus)   Pray you be gone.
I'll try whether my old wit be in request   250
With those that have but little. This must be patched
With cloth of any colour.
COMINIUS Nay, come away.
         Exeunt Coriolanus and Cominius
A PATRICIAN This man has marred his fortune.
MENENIUS
His nature is too noble for the world.   255
He would not flatter Neptune for his trident
Or Jove for's power to thunder. His heart's his mouth.
What his breast forges, that his tongue must vent,
And, being angry, does forget that ever
He heard the name of death.
     A noise within
               Here's goodly work.   260
A PATRICIAN
I would they were abed.
MENENIUS   I would they were in Tiber.
What the vengeance, could he not speak 'em fair?
   Enter Brutus and Sicinius, with the rabble again
SICINIUS Where is this viper
That would depopulate the city and
Be every man himself?
MENENIUS   You worthy tribunes—   265
SICINIUS
He shall be thrown down the Tarpeian rock
With rigorous hands. He hath resisted law,
And therefore law shall scorn him further trial
Than the severity of the public power,
Which he so sets at naught.
FIRST CITIZEN   He shall well know   270
The noble tribunes are the people's mouths,
And we their hands.
ALL ⌈THE CITIZENS⌉   He shall, sure on't.
MENENIUS   Sir, sir.
SICINIUS Peace!
MENENIUS
Do not cry havoc where you should but hunt
With modest warrant.
SICINIUS   Sir, how comes't that you   275
Have help to make this rescue?
MENENIUS   Hear me speak.

As I do know the consul's worthiness,
So can I name his faults.
SICINIUS Consul? What consul?
MENENIUS The consul Coriolanus.   280
BRUTUS He consul?
ALL ⌈THE CITIZENS⌉ No, no, no, no, no!
MENENIUS
If, by the tribunes' leave and yours, good people,
I may be heard, I would crave a word or two,
The which shall turn you to no further harm   285
Than so much loss of time.
SICINIUS   Speak briefly, then,
For we are peremptory to dispatch
This viperous traitor. To eject him hence
Were but our danger, and to keep him here
Our certain death. Therefore it is decreed   290
He dies tonight.
MENENIUS   Now the good gods forbid
That our renownèd Rome, whose gratitude
Towards her deservèd children is enrolled
In Jove's own book, like an unnatural dam
Should now eat up her own!   295
SICINIUS
He's a disease that must be cut away.
MENENIUS
O, he's a limb that has but a disease—
Mortal to cut it off, to cure it easy.
What has he done to Rome that's worthy death?
Killing our enemies, the blood he hath lost—   300
Which I dare vouch is more than that he hath
By many an ounce—he dropped it for his country;
And what is left, to lose it by his country
Were to us all that do't and suffer it
A brand to th' end o'th' world.
SICINIUS   This is clean cam.   305
BRUTUS
Merely awry. When he did love his country
It honoured him.
⌈SICINIUS⌉   The service of the foot,
Being once gangrened, is not then respected
For what before it was.
BRUTUS   We'll hear no more.
Pursue him to his house and pluck him thence,   310
Lest his infection, being of catching nature,
Spread further.
MENENIUS   One word more, one word!
This tiger-footed rage, when it shall find
The harm of unscanned swiftness, will too late
Tie leaden pounds to's heels. Proceed by process,   315
Lest parties—as he is beloved—break out
And sack great Rome with Romans.
BRUTUS If it were so?
SICINIUS (to Menenius) What do ye talk?
Have we not had a taste of his obedience: 320
Our aediles smote, ourselves resisted? Come.
MENENIUS
Consider this: he has been bred i'th' wars

Since a could draw a sword, and is ill-schooled
In bolted language. Meal and bran together
He throws without distinction. Give me leave,   325
I'll go to him and undertake to bring him
Where he shall answer by a lawful form,
In peace, to his utmost peril.
FIRST SENATOR   Noble tribunes,
It is the humane way. The other course
Will prove too bloody, and the end of it   330
Unknown to the beginning.
SICINIUS   Noble Menenius,
Be you then as the people's officer.
(To the Citizens) Masters, lay down your weapons.
BRUTUS   Go not home.
SICINIUS
Meet on the market-place. (To Menenius) We'll attend
  you there,
Where if you bring not Martius, we'll proceed   335
In our first way.
MENENIUS   I'll bring him to you.
(To the Senators) Let me desire your company. He must
  come,
Or what is worst will follow.
⌈FIRST⌉ SENATOR   Pray you, let's to him.
                  Exeunt ⌈tribunes and Citizens at one door,
                                Patricians at another door⌉

3.2   Enter Coriolanus, with Nobles
CORIOLANUS
Let them pull all about mine ears, present me
Death on the wheel or at wild horses' heels,
Or pile ten hills on the Tarpeian rock,
That the precipitation might down stretch
Below the beam of sight, yet will I still   5
Be thus to them.
            Enter Volumnia
A PATRICIAN   You do the nobler.
CORIOLANUS   I muse my mother
Does not approve me further, who was wont
To call them woollen vassals, things created
To buy and sell with groats, to show bare heads
In congregations, to yawn, be still, and wonder,   10
When one but of my ordinance stood up
To speak of peace or war. (To Volumnia) I talk of you.
Why did you wish me milder? Would you have me
False to my nature? Rather say I play
The man I am.
VOLUMNIA   O, sir, sir, sir,   15
I would have had you put your power well on
Before you had worn it out.
CORIOLANUS   Let go.
VOLUMNIA
You might have been enough the man you are
With striving less to be so. Lesser had been
The taxings of your dispositions if   20
You had not showed them how ye were disposed
Ere they lacked power to cross you.
CORIOLANUS   Let them hang.

VOLUMNIA Ay, and burn too.
  Enter Menenius, with the Senators
MENENIUS (*to Coriolanus*)
  Come, come, you have been too rough, something too
    rough.
  You must return and mend it.
⌈FIRST⌉ SENATOR   There's no remedy   25
  Unless, by not so doing, our good city
  Cleave in the midst and perish.
VOLUMNIA (*to Coriolanus*)   Pray be counselled.
  I have a heart as little apt as yours,
  But yet a brain that leads my use of anger
  To better vantage.
MENENIUS   Well said, noble woman.   30
  Before he should thus stoop to th' herd, but that
  The violent fit o'th' time craves it as physic
  For the whole state, I would put mine armour on,
  Which I can scarcely bear.
CORIOLANUS What must I do?   35
MENENIUS Return to th' tribunes.
CORIOLANUS Well, what then, what then?
MENENIUS Repent what you have spoke.
CORIOLANUS
  For them? I cannot do it to the gods.
  Must I then do't to them?
VOLUMNIA   You are too absolute,   40
  Though therein you can never be too noble,
  But when extremities speak. I have heard you say,
  Honour and policy, like unsevered friends,
  I'th' war do grow together. Grant that, and tell me
  In peace what each of them by th' other lose   45
  That they combine not there.
CORIOLANUS   Tush, tush!
MENENIUS   A good demand.
VOLUMNIA
  If it be honour in your wars to seem
  The same you are not, which for your best ends
  You adopt your policy, how is it less or worse
  That it shall hold companionship in peace   50
  With honour, as in war, since that to both
  It stands in like request?
CORIOLANUS   Why force you this?
VOLUMNIA
  Because that now it lies you on to speak to th' people,
  Not by your own instruction, nor by th' matter
  Which your heart prompts you, but with such words
  That are but roted in your tongue, though but   56
  Bastards and syllables of no allowance
  To your bosom's truth. Now this no more
  Dishonours you at all than to take in
  A town with gentle words, which else would put you
  To your fortune and the hazard of much blood.   61
  I would dissemble with my nature where
  My fortunes and my friends at stake required
  I should do so in honour. I am in this
  Your wife, your son, these senators, the nobles;   65
  And you will rather show our general louts
  How you can frown than spend a fawn upon 'em

  For the inheritance of their loves and safeguard
  Of what that want might ruin.
MENENIUS   Noble lady!
  (*To Coriolanus*) Come, go with us, speak fair. You may
    salve so,   70
  Not what is dangerous present, but the loss
  Of what is past.
VOLUMNIA   I prithee now, my son,
  ⌈*She takes his bonnet*⌉
  Go to them with this bonnet in thy hand,
  And thus far having stretched it—here be with
    them—
  Thy knee bussing the stones—for in such business   75
  Action is eloquence, and the eyes of th' ignorant
  More learnèd than the ears—waving thy head,
  With often, thus, correcting thy stout heart,
  Now humble as the ripest mulberry
  That will not hold the handling; or say to them   80
  Thou art their soldier and, being bred in broils,
  Hast not the soft way which, thou dost confess,
  Were fit for thee to use as they to claim,
  In asking their good loves; but thou wilt frame
  Thyself, forsooth, hereafter theirs so far   85
  As thou hast power and person.
MENENIUS (*to Coriolanus*)   This but done
  Even as she speaks, why, their hearts were yours;
  For they have pardons, being asked, as free
  As words to little purpose.
VOLUMNIA (*to Coriolanus*)   Prithee now,
  Go, and be ruled, although I know thou hadst rather
  Follow thine enemy in a fiery gulf   91
  Than flatter him in a bower.
  Enter Cominius
                    Here is Cominius.
COMINIUS
  I have been i'th' market-place; and, sir, 'tis fit
  You make strong party, or defend yourself
  By calmness or by absence. All's in anger.   95
MENENIUS
  Only fair speech.
COMINIUS   I think 'twill serve, if he
  Can thereto frame his spirit.
VOLUMNIA   He must, and will.
  Prithee now, say you will, and go about it.
CORIOLANUS
  Must I go show them my unbarbèd sconce?
  Must I with my base tongue give to my noble heart 100
  A lie that it must bear? Well, I will do't.
  Yet were there but this single plot to lose,
  This mould of Martius they to dust should grind it
  And throw't against the wind. To th' market-place.
  You have put me now to such a part which never 105
  I shall discharge to th' life.
COMINIUS   Come, come, we'll prompt you.
VOLUMNIA
  I prithee now, sweet son, as thou hast said
  My praises made thee first a soldier, so,
  To have my praise for this, perform a part

Thou hast not done before.
CORIOLANUS   Well, I must do't.   110
Away, my disposition; and possess me
Some harlot's spirit! My throat of war be turned,
Which choired with my drum, into a pipe
Small as an eunuch or the virgin voice
That babies lull asleep! The smiles of knaves   115
Tent in my cheeks, and schoolboys' tears take up
The glasses of my sight! A beggar's tongue
Make motion through my lips, and my armed knees,
Who bowed but in my stirrup, bend like his
That hath received an alms! I will not do't,   120
Lest I surcease to honour mine own truth,
And by my body's action teach my mind
A most inherent baseness.
VOLUMNIA   At thy choice, then.
To beg of thee it is my more dishonour
Than thou of them. Come all to ruin. Let   125
Thy mother rather feel thy pride than fear
Thy dangerous stoutness, for I mock at death
With as big heart as thou. Do as thou list.
Thy valiantness was mine, thou sucked'st it from me,
But owe thy pride thyself.
CORIOLANUS   Pray be content.   130
Mother, I am going to the market-place.
Chide me no more. I'll mountebank their loves,
Cog their hearts from them, and come home beloved
Of all the trades in Rome. Look, I am going.
Commend me to my wife. I'll return consul,   135
Or never trust to what my tongue can do
I'th' way of flattery further.
VOLUMNIA   Do your will.
                                    Exit Volumnia
COMINIUS
Away! The tribunes do attend you. Arm yourself
To answer mildly, for they are prepared
With accusations, as I hear, more strong   140
Than are upon you yet.
CORIOLANUS
The word is 'mildly'. Pray you let us go.
Let them accuse me by invention, I
Will answer in mine honour.
MENENIUS Ay, but mildly.   145
CORIOLANUS Well, mildly be it, then—mildly.   *Exeunt*

3.3   *Enter Sicinius and Brutus*
BRUTUS
In this point charge him home: that he affects
Tyrannical power. If he evade us there,
Enforce him with his envy to the people,
And that the spoil got on the Antiats
Was ne'er distributed.
        Enter an Aedile
                        What, will he come?   5
AEDILE
He's coming.
BRUTUS   How accompanied?

AEDILE
With old Menenius, and those senators
That always favoured him.
SICINIUS   Have you a catalogue
Of all the voices that we have procured,
Set down by th' poll?
AEDILE   I have, 'tis ready.   10
SICINIUS
Have you collected them by tribes?
AEDILE   I have.
SICINIUS
Assemble presently the people hither,
And when they hear me say 'It shall be so
I'th' right and strength o'th' commons', be it either
For death, for fine, or banishment, then let them,   15
If I say 'Fine', cry 'Fine!', if 'Death', cry 'Death!',
Insisting on the old prerogative
And power i'th' truth o'th' cause.
AEDILE   I shall inform them.
BRUTUS
And when such time they have begun to cry,
Let them not cease, but with a din confused   20
Enforce the present execution
Of what we chance to sentence.
AEDILE   Very well.
SICINIUS
Make them be strong, and ready for this hint
When we shall hap to give't them.
BRUTUS ⌈*to the Aedile*⌉   Go about it.
                                    ⌈*Exit Aedile*⌉
Put him to choler straight. He hath been used   25
Ever to conquer and to have his worth
Of contradiction. Being once chafed, he cannot
Be reined again to temperance. Then he speaks
What's in his heart, and that is there which looks
With us to break his neck.   30
        *Enter Coriolanus, Menenius, and Cominius, with
        other ⌈Senators and Patricians⌉*
SICINIUS Well, here he comes.
MENENIUS (*to Coriolanus*) Calmly, I do beseech you.
CORIOLANUS
Ay, as an hostler that for th' poorest piece
Will bear the knave by th' volume.—Th'honoured
        gods
Keep Rome in safety and the chairs of justice   35
Supplied with worthy men, plant love among's,
Throng our large temples with the shows of peace,
And not our streets with war!
FIRST SENATOR Amen, amen.
MENENIUS A noble wish.   40
        Enter the Aedile with the Citizens
SICINIUS
Draw near, ye people.
AEDILE   List to your tribunes. Audience!
Peace, I say.
CORIOLANUS   First, hear me speak.
SICINIUS *and* BRUTUS   Well, say.—Peace ho!

CORIOLANUS
    Shall I be charged no further than this present?
    Must all determine here?
SICINIUS   I do demand
    If you submit you to the people's voices,   45
    Allow their officers, and are content
    To suffer lawful censure for such faults
    As shall be proved upon you.
CORIOLANUS   I am content.
MENENIUS
    Lo, citizens, he says he is content.
    The warlike service he has done, consider. Think   50
    Upon the wounds his body bears, which show
    Like graves i'th' holy churchyard.
CORIOLANUS   Scratches with briers,
    Scars to move laughter only.
MENENIUS   Consider further
    That when he speaks not like a citizen,
    You find him like a soldier. Do not take   55
    His rougher accents for malicious sounds,
    But, as I say, such as become a soldier
    Rather than envy you.
COMINIUS Well, well, no more.
CORIOLANUS What is the matter   60
    That, being passed for consul with full voice,
    I am so dishonoured that the very hour
    You take it off again?
SICINIUS Answer to us.
CORIOLANUS Say, then. 'Tis true I ought so.   65
SICINIUS
    We charge you that you have contrived to take
    From Rome all seasoned office, and to wind
    Yourself into a power tyrannical,
    For which you are a traitor to the people.
CORIOLANUS
    How, traitor?
MENENIUS   Nay, temperately—your promise.   70
CORIOLANUS
    The fires i'th' lowest hell fold in the people!
    Call me their traitor, thou injurious tribune?
    Within thine eyes sat twenty thousand deaths,
    In thy hands clutched as many millions, in
    Thy lying tongue both numbers, I would say   75
    'Thou liest' unto thee with a voice as free
    As I do pray the gods.
SICINIUS Mark you this, people?
ALL ⌈THE CITIZENS⌉ To th' rock, to th' rock with him!
SICINIUS Peace!   80
    We need not put new matter to his charge.
    What you have seen him do and heard him speak,
    Beating your officers, cursing yourselves,
    Opposing laws with strokes, and here defying
    Those whose great power must try him—   85
    Even this, so criminal and in such capital kind,
    Deserves th'extremest death.
BRUTUS   But since he hath
    Served well for Rome—
CORIOLANUS   What do you prate of service?

BRUTUS
    I talk of that that know it.
CORIOLANUS   You?
MENENIUS
    Is this the promise that you made your mother?   90
COMINIUS
    Know, I pray you—
CORIOLANUS   I'll know no further.
    Let them pronounce the steep Tarpeian death,
    Vagabond exile, flaying, pent to linger
    But with a grain a day, I would not buy
    Their mercy at the price of one fair word,   95
    Nor check my courage for what they can give
    To have't with saying 'Good morrow'.
SICINIUS   For that he has,
    As much as in him lies, from time to time
    Inveighed against the people, seeking means
    To pluck away their power, as now at last   100
    Given hostile strokes, and that not in the presence
    Of dreaded justice, but on the ministers
    That doth distribute it, in the name o'th' people,
    And in the power of us the tribunes, we
    E'en from this instant banish him our city   105
    In peril of precipitation
    From off the rock Tarpeian, never more
    To enter our Rome gates. I'th' people's name
    I say it shall be so.
ALL ⌈THE CITIZENS⌉ It shall be so,
    It shall be so. Let him away. He's banished,   110
    And it shall be so.
COMINIUS
    Hear me, my masters and my common friends.
SICINIUS
    He's sentenced. No more hearing.
COMINIUS   Let me speak.
    I have been consul, and can show for Rome
    Her enemies' marks upon me. I do love   115
    My country's good with a respect more tender,
    More holy and profound, than mine own life,
    My dear wife's estimate, her womb's increase,
    And treasure of my loins. Then if I would
    Speak that—
SICINIUS   We know your drift. Speak what?   120
BRUTUS
    There's no more to be said, but he is banished,
    As enemy to the people and his country.
    It shall be so.
ALL ⌈THE CITIZENS⌉ It shall be so, it shall be so.
CORIOLANUS
    You common cry of curs, whose breath I hate
    As reek o'th' rotten fens, whose loves I prize   125
    As the dead carcasses of unburied men
    That do corrupt my air: I banish you.
    And here remain with your uncertainty.
    Let every feeble rumour shake your hearts;
    Your enemies, with nodding of their plumes,   130
    Fan you into despair! Have the power still
    To banish your defenders, till at length

Your ignorance—which finds not till it feels—
Making but reservation of yourselves,
Still your own foes, deliver you   135
As most abated captives to some nation
That won you without blows! Despising
For you the city, thus I turn my back.
There is a world elsewhere.
    Exeunt Coriolanus, Cominius, and Menenius,
    with the rest of the Patricians. The Citizens
    all shout, and throw up their caps

AEDILE
The people's enemy is gone, is gone.   140
ALL THE CITIZENS
Our enemy is banished, he is gone. Hoo-oo!
SICINIUS
Go see him out at gates, and follow him
As he hath followed you, with all despite.
Give him deserved vexation. Let a guard
Attend us through the city.   145
ALL THE CITIZENS
Come, come, let's see him out at gates. Come.
The gods preserve our noble tribunes! Come.   *Exeunt*

         ✿

4.1   *Enter Coriolanus, Volumnia, Virgilia, Menenius,*
     and Cominius, with the young nobility of Rome
CORIOLANUS
Come, leave your tears. A brief farewell. The beast
With many heads butts me away. Nay, mother,
Where is your ancient courage? You were used
To say extremities was the trier of spirits,
That common chances common men could bear,   5
That when the sea was calm all boats alike
Showed mastership in floating; fortune's blows
When most struck home, being gentle wounded craves
A noble cunning. You were used to load me
With precepts that would make invincible   10
The heart that conned them.
VIRGILIA O heavens, O heavens!
CORIOLANUS Nay, I prithee, woman—
VOLUMNIA
Now the red pestilence strike all trades in Rome,
And occupations perish!
CORIOLANUS   What, what, what?   15
I shall be loved when I am lacked. Nay, mother,
Resume that spirit when you were wont to say,
If you had been the wife of Hercules
Six of his labours you'd have done, and saved
Your husband so much sweat. Cominius,   20
Droop not. Adieu. Farewell, my wife, my mother.
I'll do well yet. Thou old and true Menenius,
Thy tears are salter than a younger man's,
And venomous to thine eyes. My sometime general,
I have seen thee stern, and thou hast oft beheld   25
Heart-hard'ning spectacles. Tell these sad women
'Tis fond to wail inevitable strokes
As 'tis to laugh at 'em. My mother, you wot well
My hazards still have been your solace, and—

Believe't not lightly—though I go alone,   30
Like to a lonely dragon that his fen
Makes feared and talked of more than seen, your son
Will or exceed the common or be caught
With cautelous baits and practice.
VOLUMNIA   My first son,
Whither will thou go? Take good Cominius   35
With thee a while. Determine on some course
More than a wild exposure to each chance
That starts i'th' way before thee.
⌜VIRGILIA⌝   O the gods!
COMINIUS
I'll follow thee a month, devise with thee
Where thou shalt rest, that thou mayst hear of us   40
And we of thee. So, if the time thrust forth
A cause for thy repeal, we shall not send
O'er the vast world to seek a single man,
And lose advantage, which doth ever cool
I'th' absence of the needer.
CORIOLANUS   Fare ye well.   45
Thou hast years upon thee, and thou art too full
Of the wars' surfeits to go rove with one
That's yet unbruised. Bring me but out at gate.
Come, my sweet wife, my dearest mother, and
My friends of noble touch. When I am forth,   50
Bid me farewell, and smile. I pray you come.
While I remain above the ground you shall
Hear from me still, and never of me aught
But what is like me formerly.
MENENIUS   That's worthily
As any ear can hear. Come, let's not weep.   55
If I could shake off but one seven years
From these old arms and legs, by the good gods,
I'd with thee every foot.
CORIOLANUS   Give me thy hand. Come.
                        Exeunt

4.2   *Enter the two tribunes, Sicinius and Brutus, with*
     the Aedile
SICINIUS (*to the Aedile*)
Bid them all home. He's gone, and we'll no further.
The nobility are vexed, whom we see have sided
In his behalf.
BRUTUS   Now we have shown our power,
Let us seem humbler after it is done
Than when it was a-doing.
SICINIUS (*to the Aedile*)   Bid them home.   5
Say their great enemy is gone, and they
Stand in their ancient strength.
BRUTUS   Dismiss them home.
                       Exit Aedile
   Enter Volumnia, Virgilia, ⌜weeping,⌝ and Menenius
Here comes his mother.
SICINIUS Let's not meet her.
BRUTUS Why?   10
SICINIUS They say she's mad.
BRUTUS
They have ta'en note of us. Keep on your way.

VOLUMNIA
O, you're well met! Th'hoarded plague o'th' gods
Requite your love!
MENENIUS   Peace, peace, be not so loud.
VOLUMNIA (*to the tribunes*)
If that I could for weeping, you should hear—   15
Nay, and you shall hear some. Will you be gone?
VIRGILIA (*to the tribunes*)
You shall stay, too. I would I had the power
To say so to my husband.
SICINIUS (*to Volumnia*)   Are you mankind?
VOLUMNIA
Ay, fool. Is that a shame? Note but this, fool:
Was not a man my father? Hadst thou foxship   20
To banish him that struck more blows for Rome
Than thou hast spoken words?
SICINIUS   O blessèd heavens!
VOLUMNIA
More noble blows than ever thou wise words,
And for Rome's good. I'll tell thee what—yet go.
Nay, but thou shalt stay too. I would my son   25
Were in Arabia, and thy tribe before him,
His good sword in his hand.
SICINIUS   What then?
VIRGILIA   What then?
He'd make an end of thy posterity.
VOLUMNIA Bastards and all.
Good man, the wounds that he does bear for Rome! 30
MENENIUS Come, come, peace.
SICINIUS
I would he had continued to his country
As he began, and not unknit himself
The noble knot he made.
BRUTUS   I would he had.
VOLUMNIA
'I would he had'! 'Twas you incensed the rabble- 35
Cats that can judge as fitly of his worth
As I can of those mysteries which heaven
Will not have earth to know.
BRUTUS (*to Sicinius*) Pray, let's go.
VOLUMNIA Now pray, sir, get you gone.   40
You have done a brave deed. Ere you go, hear this:
As far as doth the Capitol exceed
The meanest house in Rome, so far my son—
This lady's husband here, this, do you see?—
Whom you have banished does exceed you all. 45
BRUTUS
Well, well, we'll leave you.
SICINIUS   Why stay we to be baited
With one that wants her wits?   *Exeunt tribunes*
VOLUMNIA   Take my prayers with you.
I would the gods had nothing else to do
But to confirm my curses. Could I meet 'em
But once a day, it would unclog my heart   50
Of what lies heavy to't.
MENENIUS   You have told them home
And, by my troth, you have cause. You'll sup with me?
VOLUMNIA
Anger's my meat, I sup upon myself,

And so shall starve with feeding.
(*To Virgilia*)   Come, let's go.
Leave this faint puling and lament as I do,   55
In anger, Juno-like. Come, come, come.
          Exeunt Volumnia and Virgilia
MENENIUS   Fie, fie, fie.
          Exit

4.3   *Enter Nicanor, a Roman, and Adrian, a Volscian*
NICANOR I know you well, sir, and you know me. Your
name, I think, is Adrian.
ADRIAN It is so, sir. Truly, I have forgot you.
NICANOR I am a Roman, and my services are, as you are,
against 'em. Know you me yet?   5
ADRIAN Nicanor, no?
NICANOR The same, sir.
ADRIAN You had more beard when I last saw you, but
your favour is well approved by your tongue. What's
the news in Rome? I have a note from the Volscian
state to find you out there. You have well saved me a
day's journey.   12
NICANOR There hath been in Rome strange insurrections,
the people against the senators, patricians, and nobles.
ADRIAN Hath been?—is it ended then? Our state thinks
not so. They are in a most warlike preparation, and
hope to come upon them in the heat of their division.
NICANOR The main blaze of it is past, but a small thing
would make it flame again, for the nobles receive so to
heart the banishment of that worthy Coriolanus that
they are in a ripe aptness to take all power from the
people, and to pluck from them their tribunes for ever.
This lies glowing, I can tell you, and is almost mature
for the violent breaking out.
ADRIAN Coriolanus banished?   25
NICANOR Banished, sir.
ADRIAN You will be welcome with this intelligence,
Nicanor.
NICANOR The day serves well for them now. I have heard
it said the fittest time to corrupt a man's wife is when
she's fallen out with her husband. Your noble Tullus
Aufidius will appear well in these wars, his great
opposer Coriolanus being now in no request of his
country.   34
ADRIAN He cannot choose. I am most fortunate thus
accidentally to encounter you. You have ended my
business, and I will merrily accompany you home.
NICANOR I shall between this and supper tell you most
strange things from Rome, all tending to the good of
their adversaries. Have you an army ready, say you?
ADRIAN A most royal one—the centurions and their
charges distinctly billeted already in th'entertainment,
and to be on foot at an hour's warning.
NICANOR I am joyful to hear of their readiness, and am
the man, I think, that shall set them in present action.
So, sir, heartily well met, and most glad of your
company.
ADRIAN You take my part from me, sir. I have the most
cause to be glad of yours.   49
NICANOR Well, let us go together.   *Exeunt*

4.4 *Enter Coriolanus in mean apparel, disguised and*
muffled
CORIOLANUS
 A goodly city is this Antium. City,
 'Tis I that made thy widows. Many an heir
 Of these fair edifices fore my wars
 Have I heard groan and drop. Then know me not,
 Lest that thy wives with spits and boys with stones   5
 In puny battle slay me.
   Enter a Citizen
                    Save you, sir.
CITIZEN
 And you.
CORIOLANUS Direct me, if it be your will,
 Where great Aufidius lies. Is he in Antium?
CITIZEN
 He is, and feasts the nobles of the state
 At his house this night.
CORIOLANUS   Which is his house, beseech you?
CITIZEN
 This here before you.
CORIOLANUS   Thank you, sir. Farewell.   11
                                    Exit Citizen
 O world, thy slippery turns! Friends now fast sworn,
 Whose double bosoms seem to wear one heart,
 Whose hours, whose bed, whose meal and exercise
 Are still together, who twin as 'twere in love   15
 Unseparable, shall within this hour,
 On a dissension of a doit, break out
 To bitterest enmity. So fellest foes,
 Whose passions and whose plots have broke their
   sleep
 To take the one the other, by some chance,   20
 Some trick not worth an egg, shall grow dear friends
 And interjoin their issues. So with me.
 My birthplace hate I, and my love's upon
 This enemy town. I'll enter. If he slay me,
 He does fair justice; if he give me way,   25
 I'll do his country service.   *Exit*

4.5 *Music plays. Enter a Servingman*
FIRST SERVINGMAN Wine, wine, wine! What service is
 here? I think our fellows are asleep.   ⌈*Exit*⌉
   Enter a Second Servingman
SECOND SERVINGMAN Where's Cotus? My master calls for
 him. Cotus!   *Exit*
   Enter Coriolanus, as before
CORIOLANUS A goodly house. The feast   5
 Smells well, but I appear not like a guest.
   Enter the First Servingman
FIRST SERVINGMAN What would you have, friend? Whence
 are you? Here's no place for you. Pray go to the door.
                                                   Exit
CORIOLANUS
 I have deserved no better entertainment
 In being Coriolanus.   10
   Enter Second Servingman
SECOND SERVINGMAN Whence are you, sir? Has the porter

his eyes in his head, that he gives entrance to such
companions? Pray get you out.
CORIOLANUS Away!
SECOND SERVINGMAN Away? Get you away.   15
CORIOLANUS Now thou'rt troublesome.
SECOND SERVINGMAN Are you so brave? I'll have you
 talked with anon.
   Enter Third Servingman. The First meets him
THIRD SERVINGMAN What fellow's this?   19
FIRST SERVINGMAN A strange one as ever I looked on. I
 cannot get him out o'th' house. Prithee, call my master
 to him.
THIRD SERVINGMAN (*to Coriolanus*) What have you to do
 here, fellow? Pray you, avoid the house.
CORIOLANUS
 Let me but stand. I will not hurt your hearth.   25
THIRD SERVINGMAN What are you?
CORIOLANUS A gentleman.
THIRD SERVINGMAN A marvellous poor one.
CORIOLANUS True, so I am.   29
THIRD SERVINGMAN Pray you, poor gentleman, take up
 some other station. Here's no place for you. Pray you,
 avoid. Come.
CORIOLANUS
 Follow your function. Go and batten on cold bits.
   He pushes him away from him
THIRD SERVINGMAN What, you will not?—Prithee tell my
 master what a strange guest he has here.   35
SECOND SERVINGMAN And I shall.
                              Exit Second Servingman
THIRD SERVINGMAN Where dwell'st thou?
CORIOLANUS Under the canopy.
THIRD SERVINGMAN Under the canopy?
CORIOLANUS Ay.   40
THIRD SERVINGMAN Where's that?
CORIOLANUS I'th' city of kites and crows.
THIRD SERVINGMAN I'th' city of kites and crows? What an
 ass it is! Then thou dwell'st with daws, too?
CORIOLANUS No, I serve not thy master.   45
THIRD SERVINGMAN How, sir? Do you meddle with my
 master?
CORIOLANUS Ay, 'tis an honester service than to meddle
 with thy mistress. Thou prat'st and prat'st. Serve with
 thy trencher. Hence!   50
   He beats him away.
   Enter Aufidius, with the Second Servingman
AUFIDIUS Where is this fellow?
SECOND SERVINGMAN Here, sir. I'd have beaten him like a
 dog but for disturbing the lords within.
   ⌈*The Servingmen stand aside*⌉
AUFIDIUS
 Whence com'st thou? What wouldst thou? Thy name?
 Why speak'st not? Speak, man. What's thy name?
CORIOLANUS ⌈*unmuffling his head*⌉   If, Tullus,
 Not yet thou know'st me, and seeing me dost not   56
 Think me for the man I am, necessity
 Commands me name myself.
AUFIDIUS   What is thy name?

CORIOLANUS
A name unmusical to the Volscians' ears
And harsh in sound to thine.
AUFIDIUS   Say, what's thy name? 60
Thou hast a grim appearance, and thy face
Bears a command in't. Though thy tackle's torn,
Thou show'st a noble vessel. What's thy name?
CORIOLANUS
Prepare thy brow to frown. Know'st thou me yet?
AUFIDIUS I know thee not. Thy name?   65
CORIOLANUS
My name is Caius Martius, who hath done
To thee particularly, and to all the Volsces,
Great hurt and mischief. Thereto witness may
My surname Coriolanus. The painful service,
The extreme dangers, and the drops of blood   70
Shed for my thankless country, are requited
But with that surname—a good memory
And witness of the malice and displeasure
Which thou shouldst bear me. Only that name
    remains.
The cruelty and envy of the people,   75
Permitted by our dastard nobles, who
Have all forsook me, hath devoured the rest,
And suffered me by th' voice of slaves to be
Whooped out of Rome. Now this extremity
Hath brought me to thy hearth. Not out of hope—   80
Mistake me not—to save my life, for if
I had feared death, of all the men i'th' world
I would have 'voided thee, but in mere spite
To be full quit of those my banishers
Stand I before thee here. Then if thou hast   85
A heart of wreak in thee, that wilt revenge
Thine own particular wrongs and stop those maims
Of shame seen through thy country, speed thee
    straight,
And make my misery serve thy turn. So use it
That my revengeful services may prove   90
As benefits to thee; for I will fight
Against my cankered country with the spleen
Of all the under-fiends. But if so be
Thou dar'st not this, and that to prove more fortunes
Thou'rt tired, then, in a word, I also am   95
Longer to live most weary, and present
My throat to thee and to thy ancient malice,
Which not to cut would show thee but a fool,
Since I have ever followed thee with hate,
Drawn tuns of blood out of thy country's breast,   100
And cannot live but to thy shame unless
It be to do thee service.
AUFIDIUS   O Martius, Martius!
Each word thou hast spoke hath weeded from my heart
A root of ancient envy. If Jupiter
Should from yon cloud speak divine things   105
And say ' 'Tis true', I'd not believe them more
Than thee, all-noble Martius. Let me twine
Mine arms about that body whereagainst
My grainèd ash an hundred times hath broke,

And scarred the moon with splinters.
    (He embraces Coriolanus)
                                    Here I clip   110
The anvil of my sword, and do contest
As hotly and as nobly with thy love
As ever in ambitious strength I did
Contend against thy valour. Know thou first,
I loved the maid I married; never man   115
Sighed truer breath. But that I see thee here,
Thou noble thing, more dances my rapt heart
Than when I first my wedded mistress saw
Bestride my threshold. Why, thou Mars, I tell thee
We have a power on foot, and I had purpose   120
Once more to hew thy target from thy brawn,
Or lose mine arm for't. Thou hast beat me out
Twelve several times, and I have nightly since
Dreamt of encounters 'twixt thyself and me—
We have been down together in my sleep,   125
Unbuckling helms, fisting each other's throat—
And waked half dead with nothing. Worthy Martius,
Had we no other quarrel else to Rome but that
Thou art thence banished, we would muster all
From twelve to seventy, and, pouring war   130
Into the bowels of ungrateful Rome,
Like a bold flood o'erbear't. O, come, go in,
And take our friendly senators by th' hands
Who now are here taking their leaves of me,
Who am prepared against your territories,   135
Though not for Rome itself.
CORIOLANUS   You bless me, gods.
AUFIDIUS
Therefore, most absolute sir, if thou wilt have
The leading of thine own revenges, take
Th'one half of my commission and set down—
As best thou art experienced, since thou know'st   140
Thy country's strength and weakness—thine own ways:
Whether to knock against the gates of Rome,
Or rudely visit them in parts remote
To fright them ere destroy. But come in.
Let me commend the first to those that shall   145
Say yea to thy desires. A thousand welcomes!
And more a friend than ere an enemy;
Yet, Martius, that was much. Your hand. Most
    welcome!   Exeunt
    ⌈The two Servingmen come forward⌉
FIRST SERVINGMAN Here's a strange alteration!   149
SECOND SERVINGMAN By my hand, I had thought to have
    strucken him with a cudgel, and yet my mind gave me
    his clothes made a false report of him.
FIRST SERVINGMAN What an arm he has! He turned me
    about with his finger and his thumb as one would set
    up a top.   155
SECOND SERVINGMAN Nay, I knew by his face that there
    was something in him. He had, sir, a kind of face,
    methought—I cannot tell how to term it.
FIRST SERVINGMAN He had so, looking, as it were—would
    I were hanged but I thought there was more in him
    than I could think.   161

SECOND SERVINGMAN So did I, I'll be sworn. He is simply the rarest man i'th' world.

FIRST SERVINGMAN I think he is yet a greater soldier than he you wot on.   165

SECOND SERVINGMAN Who, my master?

FIRST SERVINGMAN Nay, it's no matter for that.

SECOND SERVINGMAN Worth six on him.

FIRST SERVINGMAN Nay, not so, neither; but I take him to be the greater soldier.   170

SECOND SERVINGMAN Faith, look you, one cannot tell how to say that. For the defence of a town our general is excellent.

FIRST SERVINGMAN Ay, and for an assault too.

Enter the Third Servingman

THIRD SERVINGMAN O, slaves, I can tell you news—news, you rascals!   276

FIRST *and* SECOND SERVINGMEN What, what, what? Let's partake.

THIRD SERVINGMAN I would not be a Roman of all nations. I had as lief be a condemned man.   180

FIRST *and* SECOND SERVINGMEN Wherefore? Wherefore?

THIRD SERVINGMAN Why, here's he that was wont to thwack our general, Caius Martius.

FIRST SERVINGMAN Why do you say 'thwack our general'?

THIRD SERVINGMAN I do not say 'thwack our general'; but he was always good enough for him.   186

SECOND SERVINGMAN Come, we are fellows and friends. He was ever too hard for him. I have heard him say so himself.   189

FIRST SERVINGMAN He was too hard for him directly. To say the truth on't, before Corioles he scotched him and notched him like a carbonado.

SECOND SERVINGMAN An he had been cannibally given, he might have broiled and eaten him too.

FIRST SERVINGMAN But more of thy news!   195

THIRD SERVINGMAN Why, he is so made on here within as if he were son and heir to Mars; set at upper end o'th' table, no question asked him by any of the senators but they stand bald before him. Our general himself makes a mistress of him, sanctifies himself with's hand, and turns up the white o'th' eye to his discourse. But the bottom of the news is, our general is cut i'th' middle, and but one half of what he was yesterday, for the other has half by the entreaty and grant of the whole table. He'll go, he says, and sowl the porter of Rome gates by th' ears. He will mow all down before him, and leave his passage polled.

SECOND SERVINGMAN And he's as like to do't as any man I can imagine.   209

THIRD SERVINGMAN Do't? He will do't; for look you, sir, he has as many friends as enemies; which friends, sir, as it were durst not—look you, sir—show themselves, as we term it, his friends whilst he's in dejectitude.

FIRST SERVINGMAN Dejectitude? What's that?   214

THIRD SERVINGMAN But when they shall see, sir, his crest up again and the man in blood, they will out of their burrows like conies after rain, and revel all with him.

FIRST SERVINGMAN But when goes this forward?

THIRD SERVINGMAN Tomorrow, today, presently. You shall have the drum struck up this afternoon. 'Tis as it were a parcel of their feast, and to be executed ere they wipe their lips.

SECOND SERVINGMAN Why, then we shall have a stirring world again. This peace is nothing but to rust iron, increase tailors, and breed ballad-makers.   225

FIRST SERVINGMAN Let me have war, say I. It exceeds peace as far as day does night. It's sprightly walking, audible and full of vent. Peace is a very apoplexy, lethargy; mulled, deaf, sleepy, insensible; a getter of more bastard children than war's a destroyer of men.

SECOND SERVINGMAN 'Tis so, and as war in some sort may be said to be a ravisher, so it cannot be denied but peace is a great maker of cuckolds.

FIRST SERVINGMAN Ay, and it makes men hate one another.   235

THIRD SERVINGMAN Reason; because they then less need one another. The wars for my money. I hope to see Romans as cheap as Volscians.
⌜A sound within⌝
They are rising, they are rising.   239

FIRST *and* SECOND SERVINGMEN In, in, in, in.   *Exeunt*

4.6   *Enter the two tribunes, Sicinius and Brutus*

SICINIUS
We hear not of him, neither need we fear him.
His remedies are tame—the present peace
And quietness of the people, which before
Were in wild hurry. Here do we make his friends
Blush that the world goes well, who rather had,   5
Though they themselves did suffer by't, behold
Dissentious numbers pest'ring streets than see
Our tradesmen singing in their shops and going
About their functions friendly.
Enter Menenius

BRUTUS
We stood to't in good time. Is this Menenius?   10

SICINIUS
'Tis he, 'tis he. O, he is grown most kind of late.
Hail, sir.

MENENIUS Hail to you both.

SICINIUS
Your Coriolanus is not much missed
But with his friends. The commonwealth doth stand, 15
And so would do were he more angry at it.

MENENIUS
All's well, and might have been much better if
He could have temporized.

SICINIUS Where is he, hear you?

MENENIUS Nay, I hear nothing.   20
His mother and his wife hear nothing from him.
Enter three or four Citizens

ALL THE CITIZENS (*to the tribunes*)
The gods preserve you both.

SICINIUS   Good e'en, our neighbours.

BRUTUS
Good e'en to you all, good e'en to you all.

FIRST CITIZEN
Ourselves, our wives and children, on our knees
Are bound to pray for you both.
SICINIUS   Live and thrive.   25
BRUTUS Farewell, kind neighbours.
We wished Coriolanus had loved you as we did.
ALL THE CITIZENS
Now the gods keep you!
SICINIUS *and* BRUTUS   Farewell, farewell.
                       Exeunt Citizens
SICINIUS
This is a happier and more comely time
Than when these fellows ran about the streets   30
Crying confusion.
BRUTUS   Caius Martius was
A worthy officer i'th' war, but insolent,
O'ercome with pride, ambitious past all thinking,
Self-loving—
SICINIUS   And affecting one sole throne
Without assistance.
MENENIUS   I think not so.   35
SICINIUS
We should by this, to all our lamentation,
If he had gone forth consul found it so.
BRUTUS
The gods have well prevented it, and Rome
Sits safe and still without him.
         Enter an Aedile
AEDILE   Worthy tribunes,
There is a slave whom we have put in prison   40
Reports the Volsces, with two several powers,
Are entered in the Roman territories,
And with the deepest malice of the war
Destroy what lies before 'em.
MENENIUS   'Tis Aufidius,
Who, hearing of our Martius' banishment,   45
Thrusts forth his horns again into the world,
Which were inshelled when Martius stood for Rome,
And durst not once peep out.
SICINIUS   Come, what talk you of Martius?
BRUTUS (*to the Aedile*)
Go see this rumourer whipped. It cannot be
The Volsces dare break with us.
MENENIUS   Cannot be?   50
We have record that very well it can,
And three examples of the like hath been
Within my age. But reason with the fellow,
Before you punish him, where he heard this,
Lest you shall chance to whip your information   55
And beat the messenger who bids beware
Of what is to be dreaded.
SICINIUS   Tell not me.
I know this cannot be.
BRUTUS   Not possible.
         Enter a Messenger
MESSENGER
The nobles in great earnestness are going

All to the senate-house. Some news is come   60
That turns their countenances.
SICINIUS   'Tis this slave.
(*To the Aedile*) Go whip him fore the people's eyes.—
His raising,
Nothing but his report.   *Exit Aedile*
MESSENGER   Yes, worthy sir,
The slave's report is seconded, and more,
More fearful, is delivered.
SICINIUS   What more fearful?   65
MESSENGER
It is spoke freely out of many mouths—
How probable I do not know—that Martius,
Joined with Aufidius, leads a power 'gainst Rome,
And vows revenge as spacious as between
The young'st and oldest thing.
SICINIUS   This is most likely!   70
BRUTUS
Raised only that the weaker sort may wish
Good Martius home again.
SICINIUS The very trick on't.
MENENIUS This is unlikely.
He and Aufidius can no more atone   75
Than violent'st contrariety.
         Enter another Messenger
SECOND MESSENGER
You are sent for to the senate.
A fearful army, led by Caius Martius
Associated with Aufidius, rages
Upon our territories, and have already   80
O'erborne their way, consumed with fire and took
What lay before them.
         Enter Cominius
COMINIUS O, you have made good work!
MENENIUS What news? What news?
COMINIUS
You have holp to ravish your own daughters and   85
To melt the city leads upon your pates,
To see your wives dishonoured to your noses.
MENENIUS What's the news? What's the news?
COMINIUS
Your temples burnèd in their cement, and
Your franchises, whereon you stood, confined   90
Into an auger's bore.
MENENIUS   Pray now, your news?
(*To the tribunes*) You have made fair work, I fear me.
(*To Cominius*)   Pray, your news.
If Martius should be joined wi'th' Volscians—
COMINIUS
If? He is their god. He leads them like a thing
Made by some other deity than nature,   95
That shapes man better, and they follow him
Against us brats with no less confidence
Than boys pursuing summer butterflies,
Or butchers killing flies.
MENENIUS (*to the tribunes*) You have made good work,
You and your apron-men, you that stood so much   100

Upon the voice of occupation and
The breath of garlic-eaters!
COMINIUS (*to the tribunes*)
He'll shake your Rome about your ears.
MENENIUS
As Hercules did shake down mellow fruit.
(*To the tribunes*) You have made fair work.   105
BRUTUS But is this true, sir?
COMINIUS Ay, and you'll look pale
Before you find it other. All the regions
Do smilingly revolt, and who resists
Are mocked for valiant ignorance,   110
And perish constant fools. Who is't can blame him?
Your enemies and his find something in him.
MENENIUS We are all undone unless
The noble man have mercy.
COMINIUS   Who shall ask it?
The tribunes cannot do't, for shame; the people   115
Deserve such pity of him as the wolf
Does of the shepherds. For his best friends, if they
Should say 'Be good to Rome', they charged him even
As those should do that had deserved his hate,
And therein showed like enemies.
MENENIUS   'Tis true.   120
If he were putting to my house the brand
That should consume it, I have not the face
To say 'Beseech you, cease.'
(*To the tribunes*)   You have made fair hands,
You and your crafts! You have crafted fair!
COMINIUS (*to the tribunes*)   You have brought
A trembling upon Rome such as was never   125
S'incapable of help.
SICINIUS *and* BRUTUS Say not we brought it.
MENENIUS How? Was't we?
We loved him, but like beasts and cowardly nobles
Gave way unto your clusters, who did hoot   130
Him out o'th' city.
COMINIUS   But I fear
They'll roar him in again. Tullus Aufidius,
The second name of men, obeys his points
As if he were his officer. Desperation
Is all the policy, strength, and defence   135
That Rome can make against them.
Enter a troop of Citizens
MENENIUS   Here come the clusters.
(*To the Citizens*) And is Aufidius with him? You are they
That made the air unwholesome when you cast
Your stinking greasy caps in hooting at
Coriolanus' exile. Now he's coming,   140
And not a hair upon a soldier's head
Which will not prove a whip. As many coxcombs
As you threw caps up will he tumble down,
And pay you for your voices. 'Tis no matter.
If he could burn us all into one coal,   145
We have deserved it.
ALL THE CITIZENS Faith, we hear fearful news.
FIRST CITIZEN For mine own part,
When I said 'banish him' I said 'twas pity.

SECOND CITIZEN And so did I.   150
THIRD CITIZEN And so did I, and to say the truth so did
very many of us. That we did, we did for the best, and
though we willingly consented to his banishment, yet
it was against our will.
COMINIUS
You're goodly things, you voices.
MENENIUS   You have made good work,
You and your cry. Shall's to the Capitol?   156
COMINIUS O, ay, what else?
Exeunt Menenius and Cominius
SICINIUS
Go, masters, get you home. Be not dismayed.
These are a side that would be glad to have
This true which they so seem to fear. Go home,   160
And show no sign of fear.
FIRST CITIZEN The gods be good to us! Come, masters,
let's home. I ever said we were i'th' wrong when we
banished him.
SECOND CITIZEN So did we all. But come, let's home. 165
Exeunt Citizens
BRUTUS
I do not like this news.
SICINIUS   Nor I.
BRUTUS
Let's to the Capitol. Would half my wealth
Would buy this for a lie.
SICINIUS   Pray let's go.   *Exeunt*

4.7   *Enter Aufidius with his Lieutenant*
AUFIDIUS Do they still fly to th' Roman?
LIEUTENANT
I do not know what witchcraft's in him, but
Your soldiers use him as the grace fore meat,
Their talk at table, and their thanks at end,
And you are darkened in this action, sir,   5
Even by your own.
AUFIDIUS   I cannot help it now,
Unless by using means I lame the foot
Of our design. He bears himself more proudlier,
Even to my person, than I thought he would
When first I did embrace him. Yet his nature   10
In that's no changeling, and I must excuse
What cannot be amended.
LIEUTENANT   Yet I wish, sir—
I mean for your particular—you had not
Joined in commission with him, but either
Have borne the action of yourself or else   15
To him had left it solely.
AUFIDIUS
I understand thee well, and be thou sure,
When he shall come to his account, he knows not
What I can urge against him. Although it seems—
And so he thinks, and is no less apparent   20
To th' vulgar eye—that he bears all things fairly
And shows good husbandry for the Volscian state,
Fights dragon-like, and does achieve as soon
As draw his sword, yet he hath left undone

That which shall break his neck or hazard mine   25
Whene'er we come to our account.
LIEUTENANT
　Sir, I beseech you, think you he'll carry Rome?
AUFIDIUS
　All places yields to him ere he sits down,
And the nobility of Rome are his.
The senators and patricians love him too.   30
The tribunes are no soldiers, and their people
Will be as rash in the repeal as hasty
To expel him thence. I think he'll be to Rome
As is the osprey to the fish, who takes it
By sovereignty of nature. First he was   35
A noble servant to them, but he could not
Carry his honours even. Whether 'twas pride,
Which out of daily fortune ever taints
The happy man; whether defect of judgement,
To fail in the disposing of those chances   40
Which he was lord of; or whether nature,
Not to be other than one thing, not moving
From th' casque to th' cushion, but commanding peace
Even with the same austerity and garb
As he controlled the war: but one of these—   45
As he hath spices of them all—not all,
For I dare so far free him—made him feared,
So hated, and so banished. But he has a merit
To choke it in the utt'rance. So our virtues
Lie in th'interpretation of the time,   50
And power, unto itself most commendable,
Hath not a tomb so evident as a chair
T'extol what it hath done.
One fire drives out one fire, one nail one nail;
Rights by rights falter, strengths by strengths do fail.   55
Come, let's away. When, Caius, Rome is thine,
Thou art poor'st of all; then shortly art thou mine.
　　　　　　　　　　　　　　　　　　　　Exeunt

❧

5.1　*Enter Menenius, Cominius, Sicinius and Brutus, the*
　　　two tribunes, with others
MENENIUS
　No, I'll not go. You hear what he hath said
Which was sometime his general, who loved him
In a most dear particular. He called me father,
But what o' that? (*To the tribunes*) Go, you that
　　banished him.
A mile before his tent fall down, and knee   5
The way into his mercy. Nay, if he coyed
To hear Cominius speak, I'll keep at home.
COMINIUS
　He would not seem to know me.
MENENIUS (*to the tribunes*)　　　Do you hear?
COMINIUS
　Yet one time he did call me by my name.
I urged our old acquaintance and the drops   10
That we have bled together. 'Coriolanus'
He would not answer to, forbade all names.

He was a kind of nothing, titleless,
Till he had forged himself a name o'th' fire
Of burning Rome.
MENENIUS (*to the tribunes*)
　　　　　　　　　Why, so! You have made good work.
A pair of tribunes that have wracked fair Rome   16
To make coals cheap—a noble memory!
COMINIUS
　I minded him how royal 'twas to pardon
When it was less expected. He replied
It was a bare petition of a state   20
To one whom they had punished.
MENENIUS　　　　　　　　　Very well.
Could he say less?
COMINIUS
　I offered to awaken his regard
For's private friends. His answer to me was
He could not stay to pick them in a pile   25
Of noisome, musty chaff. He said 'twas folly,
For one poor grain or two, to leave unburnt
And still to nose th'offence.
MENENIUS　　　　　　For one poor grain or two?
I am one of those. His mother, wife, his child,
And this brave fellow too—we are the grains.   30
(*To the tribunes*) You are the musty chaff, and you are
　　smelt
Above the moon. We must be burnt for you.
SICINIUS
　Nay, pray be patient. If you refuse your aid
In this so never-needed help, yet do not
Upbraid's with our distress. But sure, if you   35
Would be your country's pleader, your good tongue,
More than the instant army we can make,
Might stop our countryman.
MENENIUS　　　　　　No, I'll not meddle.
SICINIUS
　Pray you go to him.
MENENIUS　　　What should I do?
BRUTUS
　Only make trial what your love can do   40
For Rome towards Martius.
MENENIUS
　Well, and say that Martius return me,
As Cominius is returned, unheard—what then?
But as a discontented friend, grief-shot   44
With his unkindness? Say't be so?
SICINIUS　　　　　　Yet your good will
Must have that thanks from Rome after the measure
As you intended well.
MENENIUS　　　　I'll undertake't.
I think he'll hear me. Yet to bite his lip
And 'hmh' at good Cominius much unhearts me.
He was not taken well, he had not dined.   50
The veins unfilled, our blood is cold, and then
We pout upon the morning, are unapt
To give or to forgive; but when we have stuffed
These pipes and these conveyances of our blood

With wine and feeding, we have suppler souls   55
Than in our priest-like fasts. Therefore I'll watch him
Till he be dieted to my request,
And then I'll set upon him.
BRUTUS
You know the very road into his kindness,   59
And cannot lose your way.
MENENIUS   Good faith, I'll prove him.
Speed how it will, I shall ere long have knowledge
Of my success.   *Exit*
COMINIUS   He'll never hear him.
SICINIUS   Not?
COMINIUS
I tell you, he does sit in gold, his eye
Red as 'twould burn Rome, and his injury
The jailer to his pity. I kneeled before him;   65
'Twas very faintly he said 'Rise', dismissed me
Thus with his speechless hand. What he would do
He sent in writing after me, what he would not,
Bound with an oath to hold to his conditions.
So that all hope is vain unless his noble mother   70
And his wife, who as I hear mean to solicit him
For mercy to his country. Therefore let's hence,
And with our fair entreaties haste them on.   *Exeunt*

5.2   *Enter Menenius to the Watch or guard*
FIRST WATCHMAN Stay. Whence are you?
SECOND WATCHMAN Stand, and go back.
MENENIUS You guard like men; 'tis well.
    But, by your leave, I am an officer
    Of state, and come to speak with Coriolanus.   5
FIRST WATCHMAN From whence?
MENENIUS
    From Rome.
FIRST WATCHMAN You may not pass, you must return.
    Our general will no more hear from thence.
SECOND WATCHMAN
    You'll see your Rome embraced with fire before
    You'll speak with Coriolanus.
MENENIUS   Good my friends,   10
    If you have heard your general talk of Rome
    And of his friends there, it is lots to blanks
    My name hath touched your ears. It is Menenius.
FIRST WATCHMAN
    Be it so; go back. The virtue of your name
    Is not here passable.
MENENIUS   I tell thee, fellow,   15
    Thy general is my lover. I have been
    The book of his good acts, whence men have read
    His fame unparalleled happily amplified;
    For I have ever verified my friends,
    Of whom he's chief, with all the size that verity 20
    Would without lapsing suffer. Nay, sometimes,
    Like to a bowl upon a subtle ground,
    I have tumbled past the throw, and in his praise
    Have almost stamped the leasing. Therefore, fellow,
    I must have leave to pass.   25

FIRST WATCHMAN Faith, sir, if you had told as many lies
    in his behalf as you have uttered words in your own,
    you should not pass here, no, though it were as virtuous
    to lie as to live chastely. Therefore go back.   29
MENENIUS Prithee, fellow, remember my name is
    Menenius, always factionary on the party of your
    general.
SECOND WATCHMAN Howsoever you have been his liar, as
    you say you have, I am one that, telling true under
    him, must say you cannot pass. Therefore go back. 35
MENENIUS Has he dined, canst thou tell? For I would not
    speak with him till after dinner.
FIRST WATCHMAN You are a Roman, are you?
MENENIUS I am as thy general is.   39
FIRST WATCHMAN Then you should hate Rome as he does.
    Can you, when you have pushed out your gates the
    very defender of them, and in a violent popular
    ignorance given your enemy your shield, think to front
    his revenges with the easy groans of old women, the
    virginal palms of your daughters, or with the palsied
    intercession of such a decayed dotant as you seem to
    be? Can you think to blow out the intended fire your
    city is ready to flame in with such weak breath as this?
    No, you are deceived, therefore back to Rome, and
    prepare for your execution. You are condemned, our
    general has sworn you out of reprieve and pardon. 51
MENENIUS Sirrah, if thy captain knew I were here, he
    would use me with estimation.
FIRST WATCHMAN Come, my captain knows you not.
MENENIUS I mean thy general.   55
FIRST WATCHMAN My general cares not for you. Back, I
    say, go, lest I let forth your half pint of blood. Back.
    That's the utmost of your having. Back.
MENENIUS Nay, but fellow, fellow—
            Enter Coriolanus with Aufidius
CORIOLANUS What's the matter?   60
MENENIUS (*to First Watchman*) Now, you companion, I'll
    say an errand for you. You shall know now that I am
    in estimation. You shall perceive that a jack guardant
    cannot office me from my son Coriolanus. Guess but
    by my entertainment with him if thou stand'st not i'th'
    state of hanging, or of some death more long in
    spectatorship and crueller in suffering. Behold now
    presently, and swoon for what's to come upon thee.
    (*To Coriolanus*) The glorious gods sit in hourly synod
    about thy particular prosperity, and love thee no worse
    than thy old father Menenius does! (*Weeping*) O, my
    son, my son, thou art preparing fire for us. Look thee,
    here's water to quench it. I was hardly moved to come
    to thee, but being assured none but myself could move
    thee, I have been blown out of our gates with sighs,
    and conjure thee to pardon Rome and thy petitionary
    countrymen. The good gods assuage thy wrath and
    turn the dregs of it upon this varlet here, this, who
    like a block hath denied my access to thee!
CORIOLANUS Away!   80
MENENIUS How? Away?

CORIOLANUS
Wife, mother, child, I know not. My affairs
Are servanted to others. Though I owe
My revenge properly, my remission lies
In Volscian breasts. That we have been familiar,   85
Ingrate forgetfulness shall poison rather
Than pity note how much. Therefore be gone.
Mine ears against your suits are stronger than
Your gates against my force. Yet, for I loved thee,
He gives him a letter
Take this along. I writ it for thy sake,   90
And would have sent it. Another word, Menenius,
I will not hear thee speak.—This man, Aufidius,
Was my beloved in Rome; yet thou behold'st.
AUFIDIUS You keep a constant temper.
Exeunt Coriolanus and Aufidius
FIRST WATCHMAN Now, sir, is your name Menenius?   95
SECOND WATCHMAN 'Tis a spell, you see, of much power.
You know the way home again.
FIRST WATCHMAN Do you hear how we are shent for
keeping your greatness back?
SECOND WATCHMAN What cause do you think I have to
swoon?   101
MENENIUS I neither care for th' world nor your general.
For such things as you, I can scarce think there's any,
you're so slight. He that hath a will to die by himself
fears it not from another. Let your general do his worst.
For you, be that you are long, and your misery increase
with your age. I say to you as I was said to, 'Away!'
Exit
FIRST WATCHMAN A noble fellow, I warrant him.
SECOND WATCHMAN The worthy fellow is our general.
He's the rock, the oak, not to be wind-shaken.   110
Exeunt

5.3   *Enter Coriolanus and Aufidius, with Volscian*
soldiers. ⌈Coriolanus and Aufidius sit⌉
CORIOLANUS
We will before the walls of Rome tomorrow
Set down our host. My partner in this action,
You must report to th' Volscian lords how plainly
I have borne this business.
AUFIDIUS   Only their ends
You have respected, stopped your ears against   5
The general suit of Rome, never admitted
A private whisper, no, not with such friends
That thought them sure of you.
CORIOLANUS   This last old man,
Whom with a cracked heart I have sent to Rome,
Loved me above the measure of a father,   10
Nay, godded me indeed. Their latest refuge
Was to send him, for whose old love I have—
Though I showed sourly to him—once more offered
The first conditions, which they did refuse
And cannot now accept, to grace him only   15
That thought he could do more. A very little
I have yielded to. Fresh embassies and suits,

Nor from the state nor private friends, hereafter
Will I lend ear to.
Shout within
                    Ha, what shout is this?
Shall I be tempted to infringe my vow   20
In the same time 'tis made? I will not.
Enter Virgilia, Volumnia, Valeria, Young Martius,
with attendants
My wife comes foremost, then the honoured mould
Wherein this trunk was framed, and in her hand
The grandchild to her blood. But out, affection!
All bond and privilege of nature break;   25
Let it be virtuous to be obstinate.
⌈Virgilia⌉ curtsies
What is that curtsy worth? Or those dove's eyes
Which can make gods forsworn? I melt, and am not
Of stronger earth than others.
Volumnia bows
                    My mother bows,
As if Olympus to a molehill should   30
In supplication nod; and my young boy
Hath an aspect of intercession which
Great nature cries 'Deny not'.—Let the Volsces
Plough Rome and harrow Italy! I'll never
Be such a gosling to obey instinct, but stand   35
As if a man were author of himself
And knew no other kin.
VIRGILIA   My lord and husband.
CORIOLANUS
These eyes are not the same I wore in Rome.
VIRGILIA
The sorrow that delivers us thus changed
Makes you think so.
CORIOLANUS   Like a dull actor now   40
I have forgot my part, and I am out
Even to a full disgrace. ⌈*Rising*⌉ Best of my flesh,
Forgive my tyranny, but do not say
For that 'Forgive our Romans'.
⌈Virgilia kisses him⌉
                    O, a kiss
Long as my exile, sweet as my revenge!   45
Now, by the jealous queen of heaven, that kiss
I carried from thee, dear, and my true lip
Hath virgined it e'er since. You gods, I prate,
And the most noble mother of the world
Leave unsaluted! Sink, my knee, i'th' earth.   50
He kneels
Of thy deep duty more impression show
Than that of common sons.
VOLUMNIA   O, stand up blest,
⌈Coriolanus rises⌉
Whilst with no softer cushion than the flint
I kneel before thee, and unproperly
Show duty as mistaken all this while   55
Between the child and parent.
She kneels
CORIOLANUS   What's this?

Your knees to me? To your corrected son?
[He raises her]
Then let the pebbles on the hungry beach
Fillip the stars; then let the mutinous winds
Strike the proud cedars 'gainst the fiery sun,   60
Murd'ring impossibility to make
What cannot be slight work.
VOLUMNIA   Thou art my warrior.
I help to frame thee. Do you know this lady?
CORIOLANUS
The noble sister of Publicola,
The moon of Rome, chaste as the icicle   65
That's candied by the frost from purest snow
And hangs on Dian's temple—dear Valeria!
VOLUMNIA *(showing Coriolanus his son)*
This is a poor epitome of yours,
Which by th' interpretation of full time
May show like all yourself.
CORIOLANUS *(to Young Martius)* The god of soldiers,   70
With the consent of supreme Jove, inform
Thy thoughts with nobleness, that thou mayst prove
To shame unvulnerable, and stick i'th' wars
Like a great sea-mark standing every flaw
And saving those that eye thee!   75
VOLUMNIA *(to Young Martius)* Your knee, sirrah.
[Young Martius kneels]
CORIOLANUS That's my brave boy.
VOLUMNIA
Even he, your wife, this lady, and myself
Are suitors to you.
CORIOLANUS   I beseech you, peace.
Or if you'd ask, remember this before: 80
The things I have forsworn to grant may never
Be held by you denials. Do not bid me
Dismiss my soldiers, or capitulate
Again with Rome's mechanics. Tell me not
Wherein I seem unnatural. Desire not t'allay   85
My rages and revenges with your colder reasons.
VOLUMNIA O, no more, no more!
You have said you will not grant us anything—
For we have nothing else to ask but that
Which you deny already. Yet we will ask,   90
That, if you fail in our request, the blame
May hang upon your hardness. Therefore hear us.
CORIOLANUS
Aufidius and you Volsces, mark, for we'll
Hear naught from Rome in private.
[He sits]
                Your request?
VOLUMNIA
Should we be silent and not speak, our raiment   95
And state of bodies would bewray what life
We have led since thy exile. Think with thyself
How more unfortunate than all living women
Are we come hither, since that thy sight, which should
Make our eyes flow with joy, hearts dance with
     comforts,   100

Constrains them weep and shake with fear and
     sorrow,
Making the mother, wife, and child to see
The son, the husband, and the father tearing
His country's bowels out; and to poor we
Thine enmity's most capital. Thou barr'st us   105
Our prayers to the gods, which is a comfort
That all but we enjoy. For how can we,
Alas, how can we for our country pray,
Whereto we are bound, together with thy victory,
Whereto we are bound? Alack, or we must lose   110
The country, our dear nurse, or else thy person,
Our comfort in the country. We must find
An evident calamity, though we had
Our wish which side should win. For either thou
Must as a foreign recreant be led   115
With manacles thorough our streets, or else
Triumphantly tread on thy country's ruin,
And bear the palm for having bravely shed
Thy wife and children's blood. For myself, son,
I purpose not to wait on fortune till   120
These wars determine. If I cannot persuade thee
Rather to show a noble grace to both parts
Than seek the end of one, thou shalt no sooner
March to assault thy country than to tread—
Trust to't, thou shalt not—on thy mother's womb   125
That brought thee to this world.
VIRGILIA   Ay, and mine,
That brought you forth this boy to keep your name
Living to time.
YOUNG MARTIUS A shall not tread on me.
I'll run away till I am bigger, but then I'll fight.
CORIOLANUS
Not of a woman's tenderness to be   130
Requires nor child nor woman's face to see.
I have sat too long.
[He rises and turns away]
VOLUMNIA   Nay, go not from us thus.
If it were so that our request did tend
To save the Romans, thereby to destroy
The Volsces whom you serve, you might condemn us
As poisonous of your honour. No, our suit   136
Is that you reconcile them: while the Volsces
May say 'This mercy we have showed', the Romans
'This we received', and each in either side
Give the all-hail to thee and cry 'Be blest   140
For making up this peace!' Thou know'st, great son,
The end of war's uncertain; but this certain,
That if thou conquer Rome, the benefit
Which thou shalt thereby reap is such a name
Whose repetition will be dogged with curses,   145
Whose chronicle thus writ: 'The man was noble,
But with his last attempt he wiped it out,
Destroyed his country, and his name remains
To th' ensuing age abhorred.' Speak to me, son.
Thou hast affected the fine strains of honour,   150
To imitate the graces of the gods,

To tear with thunder the wide cheeks o'th' air,
And yet to charge thy sulphur with a bolt
That should but rive an oak. Why dost not speak?
Think'st thou it honourable for a noble man   155
Still to remember wrongs? Daughter, speak you,
He cares not for your weeping. Speak thou, boy.
Perhaps thy childishness will move him more
Than can our reasons. There's no man in the world
More bound to's mother, yet here he lets me prate   160
Like one i'th' stocks. Thou hast never in thy life
Showed thy dear mother any courtesy,
When she, poor hen, fond of no second brood,
Has clucked thee to the wars and safely home,
Loaden with honour. Say my request's unjust,   165
And spurn me back. But if it be not so,
Thou art not honest, and the gods will plague thee
That thou restrain'st from me the duty which
To a mother's part belongs.—He turns away.
Down, ladies. Let us shame him with our knees.   170
To his surname 'Coriolanus' 'longs more pride
Than pity to our prayers. Down! An end.
This is the last.
              The ladies and Young Martius kneel
                  So we will home to Rome,
And die among our neighbours.—Nay, behold's.
This boy, that cannot tell what he would have,   175
But kneels and holds up hands for fellowship,
Does reason our petition with more strength
Than thou hast to deny't.—Come, let us go.
This fellow had a Volscian to his mother.
His wife is in Corioles, and this child   180
Like him by chance.—Yet give us our dispatch.
I am hushed until our city be afire,
And then I'll speak a little.
              He holds her by the hand, silent
CORIOLANUS   O mother, mother!
What have you done? Behold, the heavens do ope,
The gods look down, and this unnatural scene   185
They laugh at. O my mother, mother, O!
You have won a happy victory to Rome;
But for your son, believe it, O believe it,
Most dangerously you have with him prevailed,
If not most mortal to him. But let it come.   190
              ⌈*The ladies and Young Martius rise*⌉
Aufidius, though I cannot make true wars,
I'll frame convenient peace. Now, good Aufidius,
Were you in my stead would you have heard
A mother less, or granted less, Aufidius?
AUFIDIUS
I was moved withal.
CORIOLANUS   I dare be sworn you were.   195
And, sir, it is no little thing to make
Mine eyes to sweat compassion. But, good sir,
What peace you'll make, advise me. For my part,
I'll not to Rome; I'll back with you, and pray you
Stand to me in this cause.—O mother! Wife!   200
AUFIDIUS (*aside*)
I am glad thou hast set thy mercy and thy honour

At difference in thee. Out of that I'll work
Myself a former fortune.
CORIOLANUS (*to Volumnia and Virgilia*) Ay, by and by.
But we will drink together, and you shall bear
A better witness back than words, which we   205
On like conditions will have counter-sealed.
Come, enter with us. Ladies, you deserve
To have a temple built you. All the swords
In Italy, and her confederate arms,   209
Could not have made this peace.   *Exeunt*

5.4   *Enter Menenius and Sicinius*
MENENIUS See you yon coign o'th' Capitol, yon corner-
stone?
SICINIUS Why, what of that?
MENENIUS If it be possible for you to displace it with your
little finger, there is some hope the ladies of Rome,
especially his mother, may prevail with him. But I say
there is no hope in't, our throats are sentenced and
stay upon execution.
SICINIUS Is't possible that so short a time can alter the
condition of a man?   10
MENENIUS There is differency between a grub and a
butterfly, yet your butterfly was a grub. This Martius
is grown from man to dragon. He has wings, he's more
than a creeping thing.
SICINIUS He loved his mother dearly.   15
MENENIUS So did he me, and he no more remembers his
mother now than an eight-year old horse. The tartness
of his face sours ripe grapes. When he walks, he moves
like an engine, and the ground shrinks before his
treading. He is able to pierce a corslet with his eye,
talks like a knell, and his 'hmh!' is a battery. He sits
in his state as a thing made for Alexander. What he
bids be done is finished with his bidding. He wants
nothing of a god but eternity and a heaven to throne
in.   25
SICINIUS Yes: mercy, if you report him truly.
MENENIUS I paint him in the character. Mark what mercy
his mother shall bring from him. There is no more
mercy in him than there is milk in a male tiger. That
shall our poor city find; and all this is 'long of you.   30
SICINIUS The gods be good unto us!
MENENIUS No, in such a case the gods will not be good
unto us. When we banished him we respected not
them, and, he returning to break our necks, they
respect not us.   35
              Enter a Messenger
MESSENGER (*to Sicinius*)
Sir, if you'd save your life, fly to your house.
The plebeians have got your fellow tribune
And hale him up and down, all swearing if
The Roman ladies bring not comfort home
They'll give him death by inches.
              Enter another Messenger
SICINIUS   What's the news?   40
SECOND MESSENGER
Good news, good news. The ladies have prevailed,

The Volscians are dislodged, and Martius gone.
A merrier day did never yet greet Rome,
No, not th'expulsion of the Tarquins.
SICINIUS   Friend,
Art thou certain this is true? Is't most certain?   45
SECOND MESSENGER
As certain as I know the sun is fire.
Where have you lurked that you make doubt of it?
Ne'er through an arch so hurried the blown tide
As the recomforted through th' gates.
     Trumpets, hautboys, drums, beat all together
                                    Why, hark you,
The trumpets, sackbuts, psalteries, and fifes,   50
Tabors and cymbals and the shouting Romans
Make the sun dance.
     A shout within
                    Hark you!
MENENIUS   This is good news.
I will go meet the ladies. This Volumnia
Is worth of consuls, senators, patricians,
A city full; of tribunes such as you,   55
A sea and land full. You have prayed well today.
This morning for ten thousand of your throats
I'd not have given a doit.
     Music sounds still with the shouts
                    Hark how they joy!
SICINIUS (*to the Messenger*)
First, the gods bless you for your tidings. Next,
⌈*Giving money*⌉ Accept my thankfulness.   60
SECOND MESSENGER
Sir, we have all great cause to give great thanks.
SICINIUS
They are near the city.
SECOND MESSENGER   Almost at point to enter.
SICINIUS We'll meet them, and help the joy.   *Exeunt*

5.5 *Enter* ⌈*at one door*⌉ *Lords* ⌈*and Citizens*⌉, ⌈*at another*
     door⌉ *two Senators with the ladies Volumnia,*
     Virgilia, and Valeria, passing over the stage
A SENATOR
Behold our patroness, the life of Rome!
Call all your tribes together, praise the gods,
And make triumphant fires. Strew flowers before them.
Unshout the noise that banished Martius,
Repeal him with the welcome of his mother.   5
Cry 'Welcome, ladies, welcome!'
ALL   Welcome, ladies, welcome!
     A flourish with drums and trumpets. Exeunt

5.6 *Enter Tullus Aufidius with attendants*
AUFIDIUS
Go tell the lords o'th' city I am here.
Deliver them this paper. Having read it,
Bid them repair to th' market-place, where I,
Even in theirs and in the commons' ears,
Will vouch the truth of it. Him I accuse   5
The city ports by this hath entered, and

Intends t'appear before the people, hoping
To purge himself with words. Dispatch.
     Exeunt attendants
     Enter three or four Conspirators of Aufidius' faction
                              Most welcome.
FIRST CONSPIRATOR
How is it with our general?
AUFIDIUS   Even so
As with a man by his own alms impoisoned,   10
And with his charity slain.
SECOND CONSPIRATOR   Most noble sir,
If you do hold the same intent wherein
You wished us parties, we'll deliver you
Of your great danger.
AUFIDIUS   Sir, I cannot tell.
We must proceed as we do find the people.   15
THIRD CONSPIRATOR
The people will remain uncertain whilst
'Twixt you there's difference, but the fall of either
Makes the survivor heir of all.
AUFIDIUS   I know it,
And my pretext to strike at him admits
A good construction. I raised him, and I pawned   20
Mine honour for his truth; who being so heightened,
He watered his new plants with dews of flattery,
Seducing so my friends; and to this end
He bowed his nature, never known before
But to be rough, unswayable, and free.   25
THIRD CONSPIRATOR Sir, his stoutness
When he did stand for consul, which he lost
By lack of stooping—
AUFIDIUS   That I would have spoke of.
Being banished for't, he came unto my hearth,
Presented to my knife his throat. I took him,   30
Made him joint-servant with me, gave him way
In all his own desires; nay, let him choose
Out of my files, his projects to accomplish,
My best and freshest men; served his designments
In mine own person, holp to reap the fame   35
Which he did end all his, and took some pride
To do myself this wrong, till at the last
I seemed his follower, not partner, and
He waged me with his countenance as if
I had been mercenary.
FIRST CONSPIRATOR   So he did, my lord.   40
The army marvelled at it, and in the last,
When he had carried Rome and that we looked
For no less spoil than glory—
AUFIDIUS   There was it,
For which my sinews shall be stretched upon him.
At a few drops of women's rheum, which are   45
As cheap as lies, he sold the blood and labour
Of our great action; therefore shall he die,
And I'll renew me in his fall.
     Drums and trumpets sound, with great shouts of
     the people
                    But hark.

FIRST CONSPIRATOR
  Your native town you entered like a post,
  And had no welcomes home; but he returns   50
  Splitting the air with noise.
SECOND CONSPIRATOR   And patient fools,
  Whose children he hath slain, their base throats tear
  With giving him glory.
THIRD CONSPIRATOR   Therefore, at your vantage,
  Ere he express himself or move the people
  With what he would say, let him feel your sword,   55
  Which we will second. When he lies along,
  After your way his tale pronounced shall bury
  His reasons with his body.
    Enter the Lords of the city
AUFIDIUS   Say no more.
  Here come the lords.
ALL THE LORDS You are most welcome home.   60
AUFIDIUS I have not deserved it.
  But, worthy lords, have you with heed perused
  What I have written to you?
ALL THE LORDS   We have.
FIRST LORD   And grieve to hear't.
  What faults he made before the last, I think
  Might have found easy fines. But there to end   65
  Where he was to begin, and give away
  The benefit of our levies, answering us
  With our own charge, making a treaty where
  There was a yielding—this admits no excuse.
AUFIDIUS He approaches. You shall hear him.   70
    Enter Coriolanus marching with drum and colours,
    the Commoners being with him
CORIOLANUS
  Hail, lords! I am returned your soldier,
  No more infected with my country's love
  Than when I parted hence, but still subsisting
  Under your great command. You are to know
  That prosperously I have attempted, and   75
  With bloody passage led your wars even to
  The gates of Rome. Our spoils we have brought home
  Doth more than counterpoise a full third part
  The charges of the action. We have made peace
  With no less honour to the Antiates   80
  Than shame to th' Romans. And we here deliver,
  Subscribed by th' consuls and patricians,
  Together with the seal o' th' senate, what
  We have compounded on.
    He gives the Lords a paper
AUFIDIUS   Read it not, noble lords,
  But tell the traitor in the highest degree   85
  He hath abused your powers.
CORIOLANUS Traitor? How now?
AUFIDIUS Ay, traitor, Martius.
CORIOLANUS Martius?
AUFIDIUS
  Ay, Martius, Caius Martius. Dost thou think   90
  I'll grace thee with that robbery, thy stol'n name,
  'Coriolanus', in Corioles?

  You lords and heads o' th' state, perfidiously
  He has betrayed your business, and given up,
  For certain drops of salt, your city, Rome—   95
  I say your city—to his wife and mother,
  Breaking his oath and resolution like
  A twist of rotten silk, never admitting
  Counsel o' th' war. But at his nurse's tears
  He whined and roared away your victory,   100
  That pages blushed at him, and men of heart
  Looked wond'ring each at others.
CORIOLANUS   Hear'st thou, Mars?
AUFIDIUS
  Name not the god, thou boy of tears.
CORIOLANUS   Ha?
AUFIDIUS   No more.
CORIOLANUS
  Measureless liar, thou hast made my heart
  Too great for what contains it. 'Boy'? O slave!—   105
  Pardon me, lords, 'tis the first time that ever
  I was forced to scold. Your judgements, my grave lords,
  Must give this cur the lie, and his own notion—
  Who wears my stripes impressed upon him, that
  Must bear my beating to his grave—shall join   110
  To thrust the lie unto him.
FIRST LORD   Peace both, and hear me speak.
CORIOLANUS
  Cut me to pieces, Volsces. Men and lads,
  Stain all your edges on me. 'Boy'! False hound,
  If you have writ your annals true, 'tis there
  That, like an eagle in a dove-cote, I   115
  Fluttered your Volscians in Corioles.
  Alone I did it. 'Boy'!
AUFIDIUS   Why, noble lords,
  Will you be put in mind of his blind fortune,
  Which was your shame, by this unholy braggart,
  Fore your own eyes and ears?
ALL THE CONSPIRATORS   Let him die for't.   120
ALL THE PEOPLE ⌈*shouting dispersedly*⌉
  Tear him to pieces! Do it presently!
  He killed my son! My daughter! He killed my cousin
  Marcus! He killed my father!
SECOND LORD   Peace, ho! No outrage, peace.
  The man is noble, and his fame folds in
  This orb o' th' earth. His last offences to us   125
  Shall have judicious hearing. Stand, Aufidius,
  And trouble not the peace.
CORIOLANUS ⌈*drawing his sword*⌉
  O that I had him with six Aufidiuses,
  Or more, his tribe, to use my lawful sword!
AUFIDIUS ⌈*drawing his sword*⌉
  Insolent villain!
ALL THE CONSPIRATORS Kill, kill, kill, kill, kill him!   130
    Two Conspirators draw and kill Martius, who falls.
    Aufidius ⌈and Conspirators⌉ stand on him
LORDS
  Hold, hold, hold, hold!
AUFIDIUS   My noble masters, hear me speak.

FIRST LORD
  O Tullus!
SECOND LORD (*to Aufidius*)
              Thou hast done a deed whereat
  Valour will weep.
THIRD LORD ⌈*to Aufidius and the Conspirators*⌉
                Tread not upon him, masters.
  All be quiet. Put up your swords.
AUFIDIUS My lords,   135
  When you shall know—as in this rage
  Provoked by him you cannot—the great danger
  Which this man's life did owe you, you'll rejoice
  That he is thus cut off. Please it your honours
  To call me to your senate, I'll deliver   140
  Myself your loyal servant, or endure
  Your heaviest censure.
FIRST LORD   Bear from hence his body,

And mourn you for him. Let him be regarded
As the most noble corpse that ever herald
Did follow to his urn.
SECOND LORD   His own impatience   145
Takes from Aufidius a great part of blame.
Let's make the best of it.
AUFIDIUS   My rage is gone,
And I am struck with sorrow. Take him up.
Help three o'th' chiefest soldiers; I'll be one.
Beat thou the drum, that it speak mournfully.   150
Trail your steel pikes. Though in this city he
Hath widowed and unchilded many a one,
Which to this hour bewail the injury,
Yet he shall have a noble memory. Assist.
                    A dead march sounded. Exeunt
                    bearing the body of Martius

A SELECT GLOSSARY

a, (as pronoun) familiar, unstressed form of 'he'

abate, to shorten, take from, deprive, except, blunt

abatement, reduction, depreciation

abhor, disgust, protest against

abide, await the issue of, pay the penalty for

able, to vouch for

abode, delay, stay; to foretell

about, irregularly, indirectly; be on the move

abram, auburn

abridgement, reduction, pastime

abroad, away, apart, on foot, current

abrogate, abstain from

abruption, breaking off

absolute, complete, certain, positive, beyond doubt

Absyrtus, see MEDEA

abuse, wrong, ill-usage, deception; to deceive, dishonour

aby, pay the penalty for

accident, occurrence, event, incident

accite, summon

accommodate, equip, adapt itself to

accommodation, comfort, entertainment

accomplish, equip, obtain

accountant, accountable

accoutred, dressed, equipped

acerb, bitter

Acheron, river of the underworld

achieve, make an end, finish, win, obtain

Achilles' spear, a mythical spear: rust scraped from it cured a wound that it had inflicted

acknow, acknowledge

acknown, *be acknown*, confess knowledge

aconitum, poison

acquit, atone for, repay, release

Actaeon. Diana turned him into a stag because he saw her bathing; he was torn to pieces by his dogs.

acture, action

adamant, impenetrably hard stone; magnet

addition, mark of distinction, title

admiration, wonder, astonishment, marvel

admire, wonder, marvel

admittance, fashion, reception

adoptious christendoms, fond nicknames

advantage, opportunity, interest on money; to profit

adventure, chance, hazard, to risk

advertise, inform

advertisement, information, advice

advice, consideration, forethought

advised, cautious, aware, carefully considered

Aeneas, a Trojan prince who carried his father, Anchises, from the blazing city. Dido, Queen of Carthage, received him and his son, Ascanius. She fell in love with him, but he left Carthage at the gods' command, and Dido committed suicide.

Aeolus, god of the winds

Aesculapius, god of medicine

affect, affection, tendency, disposition; love, like, imitate

affected, disposed, in love

affection, passion, desire, disposition, affectation

affeer, confirm

affiance, confidence

affined, related, obliged

affront, meet, confront

affy, trust, betroth

after, according to, at the rate of

against, in expectation of, in preparation for the time when, in time for

Agenor, father of Europa

aglet-baby, tag in shape of a tiny figure

agnize, confess, acknowledge

aim, target, guess

Ajax, a strong, dim-witted Greek hero; mad with anger at not being given the arms of the dead Achilles he slaughtered a flock of sheep as if they were human enemies and killed himself

alarum, call to arms, assault

Alcides, Hercules

alder-liefest, dearest of all

Alecto, one of the three fates; her head was wreathed with serpents

allay, relief; to qualify

All-hallond eve, Halloween, the eve of All Saints' Day

Allhallowmas, All Saints' Day (1 November)

All-hallow summer, fine weather in late autumn

allowance, admission of a claim, reputation

alter, exchange

Althaea. Her son, Meleager, was fated to live until a brand of fire burned away. After he killed her brothers she burned it.

amerce, punish with a fine

ames ace, two aces, lowest possible throw at dice

amort, spiritless, dejected

an, if, though, whether, as if

anatomize, dissect, lay bare

anatomy, skeleton

Anchises, see AENEAS

anchor, hermit

Anna, sister of Dido of Carthage

anon, soon, 'coming'

Anthropophagi, cannibals

antic, grotesque pageant, clown; fantastic

antre, cave

ape, to lead apes in hell, an old maid's function

Apollo, god of the sun, music and poetry. Daphne, escaping from his pursuit, was changed to a laurel.

appaid, contented, satisfied

apparently, openly

appeach, inform against

appeal, accusation; to accuse

apple-john, apple eaten when shrivelled

appliance, service, remedy, treatment

appointment, equipment, instruction

apprehensive, lively, quick-witted

approof, proof, trial, approval

approve, prove, show to be true, confirm, put to the proof, test, convict

apt, willing, impressionable

Aquilon, north wind

Arabian bird, phoenix

argosy, large merchant ship

argue, prove, show

argument, proof, subject of debate, subject-matter, summary

Ariadne, deserted by her lover, Theseus

Arion, a singer carried ashore by a dolphin

arm, reach, take in one's arms

arm-jaunced, jolted by armour

armipotent, powerful in arms

aroint thee, be gone

arras, wall-tapestry

articulate, arrange terms, specify

artificial, made by art, skilled, skilful

artist, scholar, doctor

Ascanius, see AENEAS

asnico, ass

aspect, look, glance, position and influence of a planet, sight

aspersion, sprinkling

assay, trial, attempt

assubjugate, debase

assurance, pledge, deed of conveyance, guarantee

assure, betroth, convey property

Astraea, goddess of justice

Atalanta, maiden huntress who killed the suitors she outraced

Ate, goddess of mischief and destruction

atomy, atom, mote

atone, reconcile, unite, agree

atonement, reconciliation

Atropos, one of the three fates; her duty was to cut the thread of life

attach, arrest, seize

attachment, arrest, stop

attaint, conviction, infection; infect, convict of treason, disgrace

attribute, reputation, credit

attribution, praise

aught, anything
aunt, old woman, bawd, girl friend
austringer, falconer
avoid, get rid of, get out of
awkward, oblique, not straightforward

back friend, pretended friend
baffle, disgrace
bait, set dogs on, worry, persecute, entice with bait, feed, feast
balk, let slip, quibble, heap
ballow, cudgel
ban, to curse
Banbury cheese, proverbially thin
bandog, fierce chained dog
banquet, dessert, light meal of fruit and sweetmeats
bases, skirt-like garment worn by a knight
Basilisco-like, like Basilisco, a braggart knight in the play *Soliman and Perseda*
basilisk, fabulous reptile whose look was fatal, large cannon
basta, enough!
bastard, sweet Spanish wine
bastinado, beating
bate, trouble; beat wings ready for flight, blunt, reduce, grow less, deduct
bateless, not to be blunted
bat-fowling, catching birds at night
batlet, bat used in washing clothes
bauble, jester's stick
bavin, brush-wood
bawd, procurer (male or female)
beadle, parish officer with power to punish
beadsman, one who prays for another
bearherd, bear-keeper
bearing cloth, christening garment
beaver, visor, helmet
bedlam, lunatic hospital, lunatic
beetle, heavy hammer-like tool; overhang
beldam, grandmother, hag
bell-wether, castrated ram with a bell round its neck
be-mete, measure
bemoiled, covered with mud
bench, raise to authority, sit as judge
bench-hole, privy
bend, look, glance; to turn, incline, direct, strain, submit
bent, inclination, direction, tension, force, range, aim
berayed, defiled
bergamask, a rustic dance
besonian, beggar, scoundrel
besort, suitable company; to suit
beteem, pour over, grant
bewray, reveal
bias, in bowls, weight which makes a bowl swerve; natural bent, inclination, compelling influence
bigamy, marriage with widow(er)
biggin, nightcap
bilbo, finely-tempered sword
bilboes, shackles
bill, halberd, pike, note, catalogue, label
birdbolt, blunt-headed arrow for shooting birds
bisson, partly blind, blinding
blank, blank page or charter, white mark in centre of target, aim, range; to make pale

blazon, coat of arms, description, proclamation; to proclaim, praise
blood-baltered, stained with clots of blood
blow, swell, blossom, (of flies) deposit eggs (on), defile
blowse, chubby girl
bluecap, Scotsman
blurt, make light of
board, to address, make advances to, mount sexually
bob, taunt, mock, cheat, get by trickery, pummel
bodkin, dagger, hair-pin or ornament
boll'n, swollen
bolt, broad-headed arrow, shackle; to sieve, fetter
bolter, sieve
bolting-hutch, sifting-bin
bombard, leather jug or bottle
bombast, cotton-wool padding for clothes, bombastic
bona-roba, well dressed prostitute
bone-ache, syphilis
boot, booty, profit, advantage, help, use, avail, addition; to be of use, profit, present in addition
Boreas, north wind
borrow, receive, assume, counterfeit
bosky, wooded
botchy, ulcerous
bots, disease of horses caused by worms
bottom, ship, valley, bobbin; to wind on a bobbin
bounce, bang
brabble, brawl
brace, suit of armour, readiness
brach, hound, bitch
braid, deceitful; to reproach
branched, patterned as with branches
brave, finely dressed, splendid, excellent; bravado or threat; to adorn, challenge, defy, swagger, taunt
bravery, bravado, finery, splendour, ostentation, defiance
brawl, French dance; quarrel
break-neck, ruinous course of action
breast, voice
breathe, speak, exercise, rest
breathed, exercised, valiant, inspired
breese, gadfly
Briareus, hundred-handed giant
brief, letter, summary
broke, bargain
broken, (of music) in parts, scored for different instruments
broker, agent, go-between
Brownist, member of a Puritan sect founded by Robert Browne
bruit, rumour, report; to announce
bubuncle, facial eruption
buck, washing, dirty clothes for washing
buckler, shield
Bucklersbury, street of apothecaries' and druggists' shops off Cheapside
budget, wallet, bag
buff, strong leather used for coats of bailiffs and legal officers
bug, bogey, terror
bugle, bead, hunting-horn
bulk, body, stall in front of a shop
bully, friend, fine fellow

bung, pickpocket
burgonet, helmet
burn, infect with venereal disease
buss, kiss

cabin, den
cabinet, dwelling
cacodemon, evil spirit
caddis, woollen tape
cade, barrel
caduceus, Mercury's magic wand entwined by two serpents
caitiff, wretch, miserable person
caliver, light musket
callet, whore
Cambyses, hero of a bombastic tragedy
can, to know, be skilled in
canary, lively dance, light sweet wine
cantle, segment
canvass, toss (as in a blanket)
capable, able to receive, feel, or understand
cap-à-pie, from head to foot
capitulate, specify terms
captious, capacious
carbonado, meat scored across for cooking
carcanet, necklace
card, playing card, compass card; mix, debase
carl, carlot, peasant
carnation, flesh-colour
carrack, galleon
carriage, ability to bear
carve, cut, shape, invite with look and gesture
case, vagina
cast, throw of dice, tinge, founding; to throw, vomit, reckon, add
casual, accidental, subject to accident
cataplasm, poultice
catastrophe, outcome, end, rear
caterpillar, extortioner, parasite
cates, food, delicacies
catling, catgut string
cautel, trick, deceit
cautelous, deceitful
censure, judgement, blame; judge, estimate
centre, centre of the earth or the universe
Cerberus, three-headed dog of the underworld
cerecloth, cerements, winding-sheet
Ceres, goddess of agriculture
certain, fixed
cess, death; *out of all cess,* beyond all measure
challenge, claim, accuse
chamber-lye, urine
chamblet, light fabric
champaign, open country
changeling, waverer
chape, sheath
chapman, merchant, customer
chaps, jaws
character, writing, hand-writing; to write
charactery, writing
charneco, Portuguese wine
Charon, ferryman of the underworld
chaudron, entrails
cheapen, bargain, bid for
cheater, officer appointed to look after property forfeited to the King

GLOSSARY

cherry-pit, game of throwing cherry stones into a little hole

cheverel, kid leather, pliant and easily stretched

child, baby girl, youth of noble birth

childing, fertile

chopine, shoe with high platform-sole

cicatrice, scar, impression

cinquepace, lively dance

cipher, zero, nought; to express, decipher

cittern, wire-stringed instrument

civil, of the city, well-ordered

clack-dish, begging bowl

clapperclaw, maul, thrash

clepe, call

clerk, scholar

clew, ball of thread

climate, region, dwell

cling, shrivel

clinquant, glittering

clip, embrace

closure, bound, enclosure, conclusion

clown, rustic, jester

clyster, enema

cockney, milksop, squeamish or affected woman

cod, testicle

codpiece, bag-shaped flap on breeches, covering the genitals, tied with laces, often embroidered and padded

coffin, pastry case

cog, cheat, flatter

coign, corner-stone, corner

coil, noisy disturbance, fuss, trouble

Colbrand, legendary Danish giant

collection, inference, understanding

collied, darkened

collop, slice, offspring

colour, pretext, excuse

colours, military ensigns

colt, young fool; to make a fool of; to have sexual intercourse with

co-mart, agreement, bargain

commodity, commercial privileges, expediency, advantage, consignment

companion, knave

comparative, proportionate, full of comparisons; one who assumes equality

competitor, associate, partner

complexion, bodily habit or constitution, temperament, appearance, colour

complot, conspiracy

composition, consistency, agreement

con, learn by heart

conceit, idea, device, apprehension, understanding, opinion, judgement, fancy, imagination, fancy trifle; to think, estimate

conceited, full of imagination, ingenious, having a certain opinion

conclusion, experiment, riddle

condolement, mourning

conference, conversation, talk, discussion

confiner, inhabitant

congree, harmonize

conscience, knowledge, understanding, scruple

conscionable, ruled by conscience

consign, agree, yield up possession

consist, insist

conspectuity, sight

contain, keep

continent, container, sum; restrained, temperate

controller, detractor

convenience, fitness, advantage

convent, convene, summon

conversation, intercourse, behaviour

convert, turn, change

convey, lead away, carry

conveyance, underhand dealing

convince, overcome

convive, feast together

convoy, means of conveyance

cony, rabbit

cony-catch, cheat

copatain, highcrowned

cope, sky; have to do with, encounter, recompense

copped, peaked

copy, original; subject-matter, copyhold-tenure

coranto, a dance

Corinthian, reveller

corky, withered

Cornelia, mother of the Gracchi, model of Roman motherhood

cornett, a brass instrument, capable of great brilliance

cornuto, cuckold, deceived husband

corollary, surplus

costard, an apple; the head

cote, cottage; pass by

cotquean, 'old woman', man who interferes in housekeeping

couch, hide, lie hidden, make crouch

counsel, secret, secret purpose or thought

Counter, debtors' prison

counterpoint, quilt, counterpane

countervail, equal, counter-balance

court-cupboard, sideboard

cousin, nephew, kinsman, relative

cowl-staff, pole on which a 'cowl' (or basket) is carried

coy, scorn, stroke

cozen, cheat

cozier, cobbler

crackhemp, gallows-bird, one born (or deserving) to be hanged

crank, twist; wind

crant, wreath

crare, small trading vessel

craze, break

credent, believing, credible

credit, credibility, reputation, report

cresset, fire-basket, torch

crow-keeper, one employed to drive away crows

crusado, Portuguese coin

cry, pack of hounds; yelp in following scent

cubiculo, bedroom

cullion, testicle (term of abuse)

culverin, large cannon

cunning, knowledge, skill; ingenious

Cupid, god of love, son of Venus and Mars (or Mercury), usually thought of as a boy armed with bow and arrows

curate, parish priest

curiosity, exactness, over-scrupulousness, delicacy

curious, anxious, needing care, fastidious,

difficult to please, delicate, beautifully made; delicately

curst, shrewish, cross, cantankerous, malignant, fierce

curtal, having the tail docked

curtal-axe, cutlass

customer, prostitute

cut, docked or gelded horse; vulva

Cyclops, one of a race of one-eyed giants, workmen for Vulcan the smith.

cyme, medicinal plant

Cynthia, goddess of the moon

cypress, fine lawn fabric

Cytherea, Venus, goddess of love

Daedalus, with his son Icarus, escaped from imprisonment on home-made wings. Icarus flew too high, the sun melted the wax, and he was drowned. Daedalus escaped.

danger, harm, injury, power to harm, range (of a weapon), debt

Daphne, see APOLLO

dare, dazzle

date, time, term, term of life, end

daub, cover with false show; *daub it,* pretend

dear, important, energetic, dire

debile, weak

Deborah, prophetess who inspired Israel to victory

decimation, execution of every tenth man

decoct, heat

defeat, destruction; to ruin, destroy, disfigure, defraud

defeature, disfigurement

defend, forbid

defunction, death

defunctive, funereal

delightsome, delightful, delighted

demerit, merit, sin

denier, copper coin of little value

denunciation, formal declaration

deplore, tell with grief

depose, swear, examine on oath

deprave, defame

deputation, office of deputy

deracinate, uproot

derive, inherit, descend, bring down on, draw

dern, dark, drear

determinate, fix; ended, decisive, intended

determination, ending, decision, intention

determine, end, settle, decide

Deucalion, the Greek Noah

dexter, right

dey-woman, dairy-woman

Diana, goddess of hunting, the moon, and chastity

diaper, table napkin

dich, attach to

Dido, see AENEAS

diffidence, distrust, suspicion

diffused, confused, disordered

dilate, relate, express at length

dildo, penis, phallus; used in ballad refrains

dime, tenth man

Dis, god of the underworld

disable, impair, disparage

disappointed, unprepared

disease, undress

discourse, reasoning, talk, conversational power, familiarity
discover, uncover, reveal, make known, recognize, spy out, reconnoitre
disease, trouble, annoyance; to disturb
disedge, dull the appetite, sate
disgracious, disliked, out of favour
dishabit, dislodge
dishonest, dishonourable, unchaste, immoral
dishonesty, dishonour, immorality
dislike, disagreement, disapproval; to displease
disliken, disguise
dismiss, forgive
dismission, dismissal
dismount, lower, draw from sheath
dispiteous, pitiless
dispose, disposal, control, disposition, temperament, manner; to control, direct, incline, come to terms
disputable, argumentative
distain, stain, defile
distemper, ill humour, illness of mind or body, intoxication; disturb, disorder
distemperature, intemperateness of weather, illness, ailment, disturbance of mind
distinction, discrimination
distinctly, separately, individually
distract, divide, perplex, drive-mad
distrain, seize
distressful, hard-earned
dive-dapper, dabchick, little grebe
division, variation, modulation, disposition
divulge, proclaim
do, copulate (with)
doctrine, lesson, learning
document, lesson
dogged, cruel
doit, coin worth half a farthing, a minute sum
dole, portion, share, grief, sorrow
domineer, feast riotously
dominical, red-printed letter in calendar marking the Sundays
doom, judgement
double, false, deceitful; wraith
doubt, suspicion, fear; to suspect, fear
dout, extinguish
dowlas, coarse linen
dowle, downy feather
doxy, beggar's wench
draff, pigwash
draught, cesspool, privy
draw, withdraw, empty, search for game, track by scent
drawer, tapster
dressing, trimming
dribbling, falling short or wide of the mark
drift, purpose, plot, shower
drollery, puppet-show, comic picture
drumble, move slowly
drybeat, beat soundly
dudgeon, hilt of a dagger
duello, duelling code
dump, mournful tune or song
dun, dark; dun horse
dup, open
durance, durability, strong and durable cloth, imprisonment

eager, sour, bitter
ean, to bring forth (lambs)
eanling, young lamb
ear, plough
ecstasy, excitement, trance, madness
edge, appetite, desire
effectual, pertinent, to the point
eftest, easiest
eftsoons, soon
egg, epitome of worthlessness; *take eggs for money,* accept injury tamely
eisel, vinegar
eld, old age, ancient time
elder gun, pop-gun made from elder wood
element, sky, *pl.* atmospheric powers
elf, tangle
embarquement, embargo, prohibition
emboss, to drive (a hunted animal) to extremity
embossed, swollen, foaming at the mouth
embowel, disembowel
empiric, quack
emulation, ambitious rivalry, grudge, envy
emulator, disparager
encompassment, winding course, 'talking round' a subject
enew, drive into water
engine, artifice, plot, mechanical contrivance, rack
engross, write out in a fair hand; collect, monopolize, fatten
enlarge, set free
enlargement, release, liberty
enormous, disordered, irregular
ensconce, shelter, hide
enseamed, defiled with sweat
ensear, dry up
enshield, concealed, emblazoned
ensteeped, lying under water
entreat, treat, negotiate, intercede
entreatment, entering into negotiation
envy, malice, enmity; show malice towards
Ephesian, boon companion
epicurism, luxury, excess
Erebus, place of darkness, hell
ergo, therefore
eringo, aphrodisiac sweetmeat
erne, grieve
erst, formerly
escot, support financially
espial, spy
estimable, appraising
estimate, valuation, value, repute
estimation, value, thing of value, esteem, reputation, conjecture
estridge, goshawk
Europa, carried away by Jupiter who had taken the form of a bull
event, outcome, issue, result
evitate, avoid
exception, objection, dissatisfaction
exclamation, loud reproach
excrement, growth (of hair)
excursion, rush, passage of arms
exempt, cut off
exhalation, meteor
exhale, draw forth
exhaust, draw out
exhibit, to submit, present
exhibition, allowance of money, gift
expectancy, hope

expedience, speed, expedition
expedient, speedy, direct
experimental, of experience
expiate, end
extend, be lavish in praise, exaggerate the worth of, take by force
extent, seizure of property in execution of a writ, attack
extirp, root out
extracting, distracting
extravagancy, wandering
extravagant, straying, vagrant
eyas, young hawk
eyas-musket, young sparrow-hawk
eye-glass, retina, eye's lens
eyestrings, muscles or nerves of eye

face, appearance, appearance of right; to put on a false appearance, brave, bully, brazen, trim
facinorous, vile
fact, deed, crime
factious, seditious
factor, agent
faculty, disposition, quality
fadge, be suitable, succeed
fading, refrain of a song
fail, failure, fault; to offend, die
fain, glad, obliged
fairing, gift
faithed, believed
faitor, cheat, rogue
falchion, sword, scimitar
falling sickness, epilepsy
falsing, deceptive
fame, rumour, report, reputation; make famous
familiar, attendant spirit
fancy, love, whimsicality; to love, fall in love with
fang, seize
fangled, foppish
fantastic, imaginary, fanciful, extravagant
fantasy, delusion, imagination, fancy, whim
fap, drunk
farce, to cram, stuff
farced, stuffed out
fardel, bundle, burden
farm, lease
farthingale, hooped petticoat
fashions, disease of horses
fault, lack, (in hunting) break in the scent
favour, leniency, something given as a mark of favour, badge, charm, appearance, look, face, feature
feat, dexterous, graceful; show to advantage; deed
feature, shape, form, comeliness
fedary, federary, confederate, accomplice
feed, pasture
feeder, servant, parasite, shepherd
fee-farm, fixed rent for perpetual tenancy
fee-grief, individual sorrow
fee-simple, estate belonging to owner and his heirs for ever, absolute possession
felicitate, happy
fell, fierce, cruel, enraged; skin, covering of hair or wool, fleece
felly, section of rim of wooden wheel
fence, art of fencing, defence; to defend

GLOSSARY

fere, spouse

fern seed, believed to be invisible and to confer invisibility

ferret, worry

festinate, hasty

fetch, stratagem, trick; to draw, derive, strike a blow

fettle, make ready

fig, to insult with a 'figo'

fig of Spain, figo, fico, scornful gesture made by thrusting the thumb between two of the closed fingers or into the mouth.

fight, screen for protection of crew in sea battle

file, catalogue, list, roll, rank, number; to smooth, polish, defile

fill, fulfil

fill-horse, shaft horse

fine, end; to end, pay, fix as sum payable, punish

fire-drake, fiery dragon, meteor

firk, thrash

fitchew, polecat

fitment, fit equipment, fitting office

fives, strangles, a disease of the horse

flap-dragon a raisin in burning brandy; to swallow as a flap-dragon

flapjack, pancake

flatness, completeness

flaw, flake of snow, gust, fragment, fault, outburst; to crack, break

fleckled, dappled

fledge, fledged, covered with down

fleer, mock, sneer; to gibe

flesh, initiate in bloodshed, inflame, gratify

fleshment, excitement resulting from a first success

flewed, having large chaps

flirt-jill, woman of loose character

float, sea

flourish, gloss, embellishment, florid decoration, fanfare of trumpets

flush, full, lusty

flux, discharge, flowing, stream

fob, cheat, trick

foin, thrust

foison, harvest, plentiful crop

fond, foolish, silly, trivial, eager, desirous

fool, professional jester, term of endearment or pity, plaything

foot, see FOUTRE

footcloth, saddle cloth

fop, to dupe, fool

foppery, folly, deceit

foppish, foolish

forage, preying

forbid, cursed

fordo, kill, destroy

fordone, exhausted

forecast, foresight

forehorse, first in team

forespent, previously spent, past

forestall, condemn in advance

forgetive, inventive

fork, forked tongue, barbed arrow-head

forked, horned

formal, traditional, dignified. sane

former, foremost

forsake, refuse, reject, renounce

forslow, delay

forspent, exhausted

fortitude, strength

forwhy, because

foutre, strong expression of contempt, a fuck (French)

fox, kind of sword

fracted, broken

fraction, discord, quarrel, fragment

frame, contriving, structure, plan; to prepare, go, bring to pass, perform

frampold, disagreeable

franchise, freedom, privilege

franchised, free

frank, unrestrained, generous, free; sty; to pen up in a sty

franklin, yeoman

fray, frighten

free, generous, magnanimous, innocent, untroubled; to absolve, banish

French crown, French coin, baldness produced by venereal disease

frequent, addicted, familiar

friend, lover, mistress

frieze, coarse woollen cloth

frippery, old-clothes' shop

front, forehead, face, foremost line of battle, beginning; to confront, oppose

frontlet, band worn on forehead

froward, perverse, wilful, rebellious

frush, smash

fullam, false dice

fulsome, pregnant, loathsome, filthy

furnishings, externals

furniture, equipment, harness

fury, rage, passion, poetic passion, goddess of vengeance

fustian, coarse cloth, bombastic gibberish

gaberdine, loose-fitting coat or cloak

gage, pledge; to stake, bind, engage

gain-giving, misgiving

Galen, famous physician of second century

gall, resentment, bitterness; to rub sore, chafe, graze, wound, harass, scoff

galliard, lively dance

galliass, large, heavy ship

galloglasses, heavily-armed foot-soldiers of Ireland or the Western Isles

gallow, frighten

gallows, gallows-bird, one born (or deserving) to be hanged

gamut, musical scale

garboil, disturbance, quarrel

Gargantua, large-mouthed giant in Rabelais

garland, royal crown, glory

garnish, dress; to adorn, equip

gaskins, breeches

gaud, plaything, showy ornament; to ornament

gear, stuff, talk, matter, business

geck, dupe

gender, kind, sort, offspring

generosity, high birth

generous, high-born

genius, spirit, good or bad angel, embodied spirit

gentle, of noble birth; to ennoble

gentry, rank by birth, good breeding, courtesy

George, jewel bearing figure of the saint, part of insignia of Order of the Garter

germen, seed

gest, deed, time allotted to stage of journey

gesture, bearing

ghasted, frightened

ghastness, terror

ghostly, spiritual

gig, whipping-top

giglet, wanton

gimmaled, jointed, hinged

ging, gang

gird, gibe; taunt, besiege

glance (at), hint at, cast a slight on

glass, mirror, sand-glass

glaze, stare

gleek, gibe; to gibe, jest

glib, castrate

glut, swallow

go, walk

go to! expression of disapproval, protest, or disbelief

goatish, lustful

good, financially sound, rich

good-brother, brother-in-law

goodman, husband, yeoman, master

goose, smoothing iron

goose of Winchester, prostitute

gorbellied, fat-bellied

gore, to defile, wound

gorge, what has been swallowed

gorget, piece of armour for the throat

Gorgon, woman whose look turned the beholder to stone

gossip, god-father or -mother, sponsor; make merry

gourd, kind of false dice

gout, drop

government, control, self-command, evenness of temper

grained, ingrained, showing grain of the wood, lined, forked

gramercy, thank you

grange, outlying farmhouse

gratify, thank, reward, pay, do honour to

gratulate, pleasing; greet, express joy at

greasily, obscenely

grece, step, stair, degree

gree, agree

groat, fourpenny piece

groundlings, those who stood in the cheapest part of the theatre

grow, be or become due

guard, caution, border, trimming; to ornament

guidon, pennant

guiled, treacherous

guinea-hen, prostitute

guise, custom, habit

gules, red (heraldry)

gull, unfledged bird, dupe, fool, trick; to cheat

gummed, stiffened with gum

gust, taste, relish

Guy, Guy of Warwick, slayer of the giant Colbrand

gyve, fetter

habit, dress, appearance

habitude, temperament

hackney, prostitute

haggard, wild hawk

haggle, to hack, gash

hag-seed, child of a witch

hai, home-thrust in fencing

hair, kind, character

halcyon, kingfisher

half, partner

half-blooded, of noble blood by one parent only

half-cheek, profile

half-cheeked, with a piece missing or broken on one side

half-face, thin face

half-faced, showing half the face

half-sword, half a sword's length

halidom, holy relic

Hallowmas, All Saints' Day, 1 November

handfast, firm hold, marriage contract

handy-dandy, choose which you please (in a children's game)

haply, perhaps, by chance

happiness, handsomeness, appropriateness, opportunity

hardiment, bold exploit

hardness, difficult, hardship

harlot, man or woman of promiscuous life

harlotry, harlot, silly wench

hatch, engrave, inlay, lower half of a divided door

hatchment, memorial tablet with coat of arms

hautboy, wood-wind instrument, ancestor of the oboe

havoc, devastation; *cry havoc*, give the signal to an army to plunder

hazard, game at dice, chance, venture

head, headland, topic, army

head borough, parish officer

heap, crowd

heavy, important, dull, sluggish, sleepy, grievous

hectic, wasting fever

Hector, Trojan hero

Hecuba, Queen of Troy, wife of Priam and mother of Hector

hedge-pig, hedgehog

Helen, most beautiful woman of her world, wife of the Greek Menelaus, carried off to Troy by Paris

Helicon, mountain of Greece sacred to the Muses

hemp-seed, gallows-bird, one born (or deserving) to be hanged

Hercules, as a baby strangled two serpents; performed twelve great labours, including the obtaining of the golden apples of the Hesperides and the overcoming of Cerberus, the three-headed dog of the underworld

Hero, see LEANDER

Hesperus, the evening star

hest, command

heyday, excitement

high-lone, quite alone, without support

high-proof, in the highest degree

high-stomached, haughty

hight, called

hilding, contemptible, good-for-nothing, baggage

him, male (dog)

hint, occasion, reason, opportunity

hipped, lame in the hip

hit, succeed, agree

hive, hive-shaped hat

hoar, grow mouldy

hobby-horse, figure of a horse used in morris dances, etc., buffoon, prostitute

holding, consistency, burden of a song

holp, helped

honest, worthy, virtuous, chaste

honesty, honour, decency, chastity

honour, chastity

hoodman-blind, blind man's buff

horn, the mark of a cuckold

horn-book, child's first reader

horn-mad, ready to gore the enemy, enraged at being cuckolded

hose, stockings, breeches

host, lodge

hot-house, brothel

housekeeper, householder, watch-dog, stay-at-home

hox, hamstring

hoy, a small vessel

hugger-mugger, secrecy

hull, float, drift with sails furled

humorous, moist, capricious, moody

humour, moisture; bodily fluid supposedly composed of blood, phlegm, choler, and melancholy, the proportions determining personal temperament; temperament, mood, whim, caprice, inclination

Hungarian, hungry, needy

hunt's-up, morning-song to arouse huntsmen

hurricano, waterspout

hurry, commotion, disorder

husband, one who keeps house; to farm, till

husbandry, management, thrift

Hybla, mountain in Sicily famous for fragrant flowers and honey

Hydra, many-headed snake whose heads grew again as they were cut off

Hymen, god of marriage

Hyperion, sun god

Icarus, see DAEDALUS

idea, image

Ides of March, according to the old Roman calendar, 15 March

idle, empty, trifling, worthless, useless, foolish, out of one's mind

ignis fatuus, will-o'-the-wisp

Ilion, Ilium, citadel of Troy

image, likeness, copy, representation, sign, embodiment, idea

imbecility, weakness

imbrue, pierce, shed blood of

immanity, cruelty

imminence, impending evil

immodest, arrogant, immoderate

immoment, insignificant

imp, young shoot, child; to engraft feathers into a bird's wing

impart, afford, make known

impartment, communication

impeach, accusation, reproach; to accuse, challenge, discredit

impeachment, accusation, detriment, hindrance

impertinency, irrelevancy, ramblings

impertinent, irrelevant

imply, involve

import, involve, imply, express, be important, concern, portend

importance, matter, meaning, importunity

importancy, significance

important, importunate, urgent

importless, meaningless, trivial

imposition, imputation, accusation, command

impostume, abscess

impress, impression, to stamp

imputation, reputation

incapable, unable to receive or realize

inclining, compliant; party, inclination

incomprehensible, boundless

incontinently, immediately

incorpsed, made one body

incorrect, unchastened, rebellious

incredulous, incredible

index, table of contents, preface

indifferency, impartiality, moderate size

indifferent, impartial, ordinary; tolerably, fairly

indigest, unformed, unformed mass

indign, unworthy

indirection, roundabout method, dishonest practice

indirectly, wrongfully, evasively, by suggestion, inattentively

indiscreet, lacking judgement

indiscretion, want of judgement

indisposition, disinclination

indistinguishable, mongrel

indrenched, waterlogged

infect, affect with some feeling

influence, supposed flowing from the heavens of an ethereal fluid acting on human character and destiny, inspiration

inform, take shape, inspire, instruct

infuse, shed, imbue

ingenious, talented, intelligent, discerning, skilfully contrived

ingling, engaging in sexual play

inhabitable, uninhabitable

inherit, possess

inhibit, prohibit

inhibition, prohibition

injurious, insulting, malicious

inkle, linen tape, thread, or yarn

inland, of the central, more cultured, part of a country

innocent, idiot, half-wit

inoculate, engraft by budding

insensible, imperceptible to senses

insinuate, ingratiate, suggest

insinuation, ingratiation, hint

instance, cause, detail, proof, mark, presence

intellect, meaning, content

intelligence, communication, information, news, obtaining of secret information, spy; to pass information

intelligencer, agent

intelligencing, informative

intelligent, giving information, open, informative

intemperature, wildness, intemperance

intenable, unretentive

intendment, purpose, intention
intercept, interrupt
interest, right, title, share
interressed, invested right or share
interlude, entertainment, play
intrenchant, invulnerable
intrinse, intrinsicate, closely entwined
investments, vestments, clothes
irreconciled, unexpiated
irregular, irregulous, lawless
iterance, repetition
iwis, indeed, certainly

Jack, jack, fellow, scoundrel, figure striking the bell on a clock; key of a virginal, smaller bowl aimed at, quarter of a pint
Jack-a-Lent, puppet set up as target during Lent
jade, horse of poor condition or vicious temper, term of contempt; to wear out, make a fool of
jakes, privy
jaunce, prance, trudge up and down
jay, a flashy whore
jealous, suspicious, afraid, apprehensive, doubtful
jealousy, suspicion, apprehension, mistrust
jennet, small Spanish horse
jess, strap attached to the leg of a trained hawk
jet, strut, encroach
jig, quick lively dance, short lively comic entertainment
jointress, dowager
jollity, finery
jolthead, block-head
jordan, chamber-pot
journal, daily
journey-bated, exhausted with travel
Jove, poetic form of JUPITER
jowl, strike, knock
jump, just, precisely; hazard; to hazard, agree, coincide
junket, sweetmeat, delicacy
Juno, queen of the gods and wife of Jupiter; goddess of marriage
Jupiter, ruler of the gods. He was thought to hurl thunderbolts at mortals who displeased him, but otherwise was best known for his many amorous adventures.
just, true, honourable, exact
justicer, judge
justify, maintain the innocence of, vindicate, prove, corroborate
justly, with good reason
jut, encroach

keech, fat of slaughtered animal rolled into a lump
keel, skim
ken, range of sight; to see, recognize, know
kennel, pack, gutter
kern, light-armed Irish foot-soldier
kersey, homely; coarse woollen material
kibe, chilblain
kind, natural, tender, courteous, affectionate; nature, way, race, sort
kindle, bring forth
kindly, naturally, properly, exactly
knack, trifle, knick-knack

knap, nibble, strike
knot, fancifully laid-out flower bed or garden plot

laager, camp
label, slip of paper, strip of paper or parchment by which a seal is attached; to add as a codicil
laboured, worn out, highly finished
laboursome, elaborate
lace, to ornament
lag, last, late
lampass, disease of the horse in which flesh swells behind front teeth
land-damn, damn in this world
lank, become thin
lantern, window-turret
lard, fatten, garnish
large, generous, lavish, free, improper
latch, strike, catch, receive, bewitch
laund, glade
lavolt, lavolta, high-leaping dance
lay, wager
lazar, leper, sick beggar
leading, command, direction, generalship
leaguer, camp
Leander, lover of Hero of Sestos, he swam the Hellespont nightly to visit her in her tower, and was drowned in a storm
learn, teach
leasing, lying
leather-coat, russet apple
lecture, lesson, instruction
leer, appearance, complexion
leese, lose
leet, court held by lord of the manor
leman, sweetheart, lover
lengthen, delay, postpone
lenity, gentleness
leno, pimp, pander
lenten, meagre
let, hindrance; to hinder, forbear, cause
Lethe, river in Hades; to drink its waters gave forgetfulness
level, aim, line of fire, range; to aim, guess
liable, subject, suitable
liberal, accomplished, humane, abundant, free in speech, unrestrained, gross
lie, to lodge, stay, be still, in prison or in defensive posture
lief, dear
liege, sovereign lord
light, frivolous, unchaste, swift, easy, merry, trivial, delirious
like, please, be in good condition
liking, bodily condition
limbeck, distilling vessel
limber, flexible
lime, cement, catch with birdlime
limit, prescribed time, time of rest after childbearing, region; to appoint
limitation, allotted time
line, rank, Equator, cord for taking measurements; copulate with
linger, prolong, defer
link, torch, lamp-black
linsey-woolsey, woven material of wool and flax, hence medley, nonsense
linstock, forked stick holding a gunner's match

list, limit, bound, barriers enclosing tilting ground, desire; to please, choose
lither, yielding
livelihood, liveliness, animation
liver, supposedly the seat of love and strong emotion
lob, bumpkin
lockram, linen cloth
lodge, flatten, beat down
loggats, game of aiming small logs at a fixed stake
long, belong
loose, unattached, negligent; moment of arrow's discharge, last moment
lose, to ruin, forget
lover, friend, mistress
luce, pike as heraldic device
luggage, baggage of an army
lune, fit of temper, of frenzy
lurch, lurk, rob
lure, dummy bird for recalling hawk
lust, pleasure, desire
lustihood, vigour
lusty, merry, lustful
luxurious, lustful, lecherous
luxury, lust

maculate, stained, impure
maculation, stain, impurity
mainly, with force, greatly, perfectly
majority, pre-eminence
make, mate, husband or wife
making, form, appearance
malapert, saucy
malkin, servant wench, slut
mammer, hesitate
mammock, tear to bits
manège, art of horsemanship
mandrake, poisonous plant believed to shriek when pulled up
mankind, resembling a man, violent, ferocious
manner, stolen goods found on a thief
mansionry, dwelling-place
map, picture, embodiment
mappery, map-making
marches, border country next to Scotland or Wales
marry, (as an exclamation) by (the Virgin) Mary
Mars, god of war and patron of soldiers
mate, rival, checkmate, destroy, stupefy
material, important, forming the substance, full of sense
maugre, in spite of
maund, basket
mazzard, head
meacock, coward, weakling
meal, spot, stain
mean, something between or intervening, middle, medium position, tenor, alto; to lament
measurable, suitable
measure, a stately dance; tune; to measure
mechanic, labourer
mechanical, mean, vulgar; labourer
Medea, escaping with Jason she tore to pieces her brother Absyrtus, scattering his limbs in her father's path to delay him; restored the youth of Jason's father, Aeson

medicinable, healing, medicinal

medlar, fruit eaten soft and pulpy; prostitute

meed, reward, gift, merit

meiny, company of retainers, multitude

mell, to meddle

memorize, make memorable

memory, memorial, memento, remembrance

Mercury, messenger of the gods

mere, sure, absolute, unqualified, only

merely, simply, entirely

merit, reward

mess, dish, portion, group originally of four persons eating together, set of four

metaphysical, supernatural

mete, measure, aim

metheglin, spiced mead

methinks, it seems to me

method, table of contents

micher, truant

mickle, great

microcosm, little world, man considered as epitome of the universe

milch, in milk, tearful

mince, to extenuate, moderate, affect

mineral, mine

Minerva, goddess of wisdom

minimus, creature of tiniest size

minion, favourite, darling, harlot, saucy creature

Minotaur, devouring monster dwelling in labyrinth of Crete

mirable, wonderful

mirror, model, pattern

mischief, misfortune, injury, disease

misdread, fear of evil

miser, miserable wretch

misgoverned, unruly

misgovernment, misconduct

misgrafted, badly matched

misprision, contempt, mistake, misunderstanding

misproud, arrogant

missive, messenger

mistake, take, undertake or deliver wrongly, misjudge, blunder, feel misgiving about

misthink, think evil of

mistress, the jack at bowls

mobled, muffled

mockery, imitation, futile action

model, architect's plan, mould, copy

modern, everyday, commonplace

modest, moderate, satisfactory, becoming

modestly, without exaggeration

modesty, moderation, avoidance of exaggeration

moiety, half, share, small part

moldwarp, mole

mome, blockhead

moment, cause

monster, make a monster of, show as monstrous

monument, sepulchre, effigy, portent

monumental, memorial, commemorating

mood, anger, outward appearance, mode

mooncalf, misshapen creature

moonish, changeable

mop, grimace

mope, move blindly and stupidly, be bewildered

moralize, interpret, explain

mort, note on a horn at the death of the deer

mortified, dead to the world, deadened, destroyed

mortifying, mortal

mose in the chine, suffer from glanders

mot, motto

mother, hysteria

motion, motive, puppet show, puppet; to propose

motive, cause, instigator, instrument, moving limb or organ

mould, earth

mouse, tear, bite

mouse-hunt, woman-chaser

mow, grimace

mulled, thick, heavy

mummy, dead flesh, medicinal or magical preparation from this

muniments, furnishings

mure, wall

murrain, plague

muse, wonder

muset, gap

muss, scramble

mutine, mutineer; rebel

mutiny, strife, quarrel

mutual, common, intimate

mutually, in return, together

mystery, trade, profession, skill

naked, unarmed, plain

Naso, family name of the poet Ovid

native, source, origin; natural, kindred, closely related, rightful

natural, that is so by birth, related by blood, kind, tender; half-wit

naturalize, familiarize

naught, wickedness, wicked, ruined, ruin

naughty, bad, wicked, good-for-nothing

nave, nub, navel

neaf, fist

neat, animal of the ox kind, cattle

neb, mouth

Nebuchadnezzar, king of Babylon, driven out to eat grass like cattle

neglect, cause of neglect

nephew, cousin, grandson

Neptune, god of the sea

Nereides, sea-nymphs

Nero, Roman emperor, responsible for the assassination of his mother; believed to have played on the lyre and recited while watching the burning of the city set on fire by his orders

nerve, sinew

nervy, sinewy

Nessus, centaur killed by Hercules for trying to rape Deianira; a tunic dyed with his blood poisoned Hercules

Nestor, oldest and wisest of the Greeks at the siege of Troy

next, nearest, quickest

nice, wanton, delicate, shy, difficult to please, fastidious, scrupulous, subtle, needing precision, delicately balanced, intricate, exact, skilful, trivial

nicely, elegantly, scrupulously, sophistically, exactly

niceness, coyness, fastidiousness

nicety, coyness

Nicholas, patron saint of scholars; *Saint Nicholas' clerks,* highwaymen

nickname, name wrongly

niggard, to act in a miserly way, supply sparingly

night-gown, dressing gown

night-rule, disorder by night

nine-men's morris, cutting in turf for game played with nine pegs or discs

Niobe, overboastful of her children, who were slain; she was herself turned to stone.

noise, rumour, music, band of musicians; clamour, spread by rumour

noll, head

nonsuit, to refuse to listen to or grant the suit of

nook-shotten, having a very uneven outline

notedly, precisely

nothing, vulva

notion, understanding, mind

novum, dice-game in which chief throws are nine and five

noyance, injury, harm

nuncio, messenger

nursery, nursing, care

nut-hook, beadle, constable

oathable, fit to take an oath

ob., abbreviation of 'obolus', halfpenny

objection, charge, accusation

obligation, contract

obliged, pledged

obsequious, dutiful, dutiful in funeral rites

observant, obsequious servant

observe, humour

occasion, opportunity, pretext, cause, course of events

occulted, hidden

occupation, business, handicraft, trade

occupy, have to do with sexually

occurrent, event

oddly, unevenly

oeillade, inviting glance, ogling

o'erblow, blow away

o'ercount, outnumber

o'ercrow, triumph over

o'erdyed, dyed with a second colour

o'ereaten, left after most has been eaten

o'erflourished, decorated on the outside

o'erlook, examine, bewitch, despise

o'ermaster, possess

o'erparted, having too difficult a part

o'er-peer, rise above

o'erpost, get over easily

o'er-raught, overtook

o'er-teemed, worn out by child-bearing

o'er-watch, stay awake too long

o'erwhelm, overhang

o'erwrested, strained

offend, harm, hurt

offer, act on the offensive, venture

office, function, service

offices, parts of a house devoted to household matters

omit, neglect, disregard, lay aside

omittance, postponement
open-arse, medlar
operant, effecting, effective
operation, effect, efficacy
opinion, censure, public judgement, self-conceit, self-confidence
opposeless, irresistible
opposite, antagonist, opponent; hostile, adverse
oppress, suppress, distress
oppression, burden, distress
oppugnancy, conflict
orb, circle, sphere, sphere in which a star moves, heavenly body, earth
ordinance, what is ordained, established rule, decree, rank
ordinary, fixed-price tavern meal, 'ordinary run'
orgulous, proud
orifex, aperture
orison, prayer
ort, fragment, scrap
ostent, appearance, show
ostentation, appearance, show, spectacle
othergates, in another way
otherwhiles, at times
ouch, jewel
ounce, lynx
ouph, elf
ousel, blackbird
outbrave, to surpass in beauty or valour
outlandish, foreign
outlive, survive
outpeer, surpass
outsell, exceed in value
outward, outward appearance
overhear, hear over again
overhold, overestimate
overlook, overtop, look down on from above, read through
overpeer, rise above, look down on
overscutched, made haggard with beating, worn out
overture, disclosure; formal opening, first indication
Ovid, Roman poet who was sent into exile
owe, own, possess

pace, train (a horse) to pace
pack, gang; conspire, shuffle (cards), to cheat, be off
packing, plotting
paddock, toad
pageant, show, spectacle
pain, trouble, punishment
painful, laborious, toilsome
pale, fence, enclosure; enclose, encircle
palisado, staked fence
pall, fail
palliament, white robe of a candidate for the Roman consulship
palmer, pilgrim
palter, equivocate, use trickery
pander, go-between in a love affair, pimp
Pandion, see PHILOMEL
pantaloon, foolish old man
pantler, servant in charge of the pantry
paper, notice specifying offence committed; write down
paragon, compare, excel, show as a model

Parca, one of the three fates who prepared and cut the thread of human life
parcel, part, item, group
parcel-gilt, partly gilded
pard, panther or leopard
pardie, certainly, indeed
Paris ball, tennis ball
paritor, official who summoned offenders to an ecclesiastical court
parlous, perilous, cunning, dreadful
part, action, side
partage, freight, cargo
partake, impart, take sides
partaker, confederate, supporter
parted, divided, gifted
partialize, make partial
particular, detail, individual, personal interest, intimacy; private, personal
partisan, footsoldier's weapon, a long-handled spear with a blade
pash, head; to strike violently, smash
passado, a forward thrust in fencing
passant, heraldic term of beast stepping; surpassing
passenger, traveller on foot
passion, suffering, affliction, fit of disease, overpowering emotion, passionate speech, sorrow; feel deep emotion
passionate, express with passion; compassionate, sorrowful
patch, fool
patchery, trickery
paten, thin circular metal plate
patent, title, privilege, authority
patience, permission, leave
patronage, uphold, defend
pattern, precedent, model; to give an example, be a pattern or precedent for
pax, tablet kissed by priest and congregation in celebration of mass
peach, denounce, turn informer
peat, spoilt girl
peck, pitch
peculiar, individual, private, belonging to one person
pedant, schoolmaster
peeled, tonsured
Pegasus, winged horse
peise, balance, weight, suspend
pelf, property, possessions
pelican, believed to feed its young with its own blood
pelt, rage, scold
pelting, paltry, worthless
pencil, paintbrush
pendulous, impending, suspended
pensioners, royal bodyguard
Penthesilea, Amazon queen
peradventure, by chance, perhaps
perdition, ruin, loss, damnation
perdurable, everlasting
peregrinate, travelled, foreign in style
perfect, fully informed, equipped, ready; accomplish, instruct
perfection, performance, completion
periapt, amulet
period, end, goal, highest point, full pause, full stop; to end
perjure, perjurer; corrupt
perniciously, to destruction
perpend, consider

persistive, steadfast
perspective, optical device for producing fantastic images; picture of figure producing a distorted or unexpected effect
pert, lively
pervert, turn aside
pester, throng, obstruct
pestiferous, pernicious
phantasim, fantastic being
Philomel, Philomela, daughter of Pandion, raped by Tereus (husband of her sister Progne), who cut out her tongue; she wove her story into a tapestry. Progne feasted Tereus on their murdered son; Philomela was changed into a nightingale
Phoebe, Diana, goddess of the moon
Phoebus, Apollo, god of the sun
phoenix, unique Arabian bird which, dying, is recreated from its own ashes
phraseless, inexpressible
phthisic, consumptive cough
physical, beneficial to health
pia mater, brain
picked, refined, fastidious
Pickt-hatch, London district noted for brothels
pie, magpie
piece, cask of liquor, masterpiece; add to, augment
pied, parti-coloured
pike, spike in centre of buckler
pill, plunder, rob, strip (of bark), make bald
pillicock, penis
pin and web, disease of the eye
pinch, bite, pang; to bite, harass, distress
pismire, ant
placket, petticoat, opening, slit
planched, made of boards
plant, sole of the foot
plantage, plants
plash, pool
plausible, pleasing
plausibly, with applause
plausive, deserving of applause
Plautus, Roman writer of comedy
pleached, formed by intertwined over-arched boughs, folded
pleasant, merry, jokey
pleurisy, abundance, excess
plight, pledge
Pluto, ruler of the underworld
Plutus, god of riches
poach, to thrust, stab
point, highest point, conclusion, lace with tags (for attaching hose to doublet, etc.), full stop
poking-stick, rod used for pleating ruffs
polecat, prostitute
policy, government, administration, prudence in managing public or private affairs, cunning, craftiness, trick
politic, dealing with government and administration, crafty
politician, schemer, scheming statesman
pomewater, large juicy kind of apple
pomp, procession, pageant
Pontic sea, Black Sea
poop, swamp, overwhelm
poor-john, salted fish
popular, plebeian, vulgar

popularity, common pledge

porridge, porrage, soup

porringer, basin

port, gate, bearing, style of living

portable, bearable, endurable

portage, portholes

portance, behaviour

posied, inscribed with a motto

possess, inform, acquaint

posset, drink of hot milk curdled with ale or wine; curdle, thicken

post, post set up for notices, etc., doorpost on which tavern reckoning was kept, courier, messenger, post-horse; to hasten, carry swiftly

poster, swift traveller

posy, motto inscribed inside a ring

potable, able to be drunk

potato, sweet potato, supposedly aphrodisiac

potency, power, authority

potent, potentate

potential, powerful

potting, tippling

pouncet-box, small box for perfumes

powder, preserve meat with salt or spice

powdering-tub, pickling-tub, sweating-tub used in cure of venereal disease

power, army

pox, syphilis, venereal disease

practice, trickery, conspiracy, plot

practisant, one who carries out a trick

practise, plot, conspire

praemunire, writ for maintaining papal jurisdiction in England

praetor, Roman magistrate

praise, appraise, value

prank, adorn

precedent, former; original from which a copy is made, sign

precisian, puritan

precurrer, forerunner

precurse, heralding

predicament, situation

prefer, present, advance, introduce, recommend

pregnancy, quickness of wit

pregnant, clear, fertile, compelling, resourceful, receptive

prejudicate, influence beforehand

prejudice, injury; injure

premised, sent before

preparation, accomplishment

preposterous, inverting the natural order of things, monstrous

prerogative, precedence, pre-eminence

presage, omen, prognostication, foreboding

presence, presence-chamber, company, person

present, immediate, instant; ready money, to show, represent, bring a charge against

presently, immediately

presentment, dedication

press, crowd, crowding, printing-press, cupboard, authority to enlist men compulsorily; to crowd, oppress, force into military service

pressure, impression, character impressed

pretence, expressed aim, intention, pretext

prevent, anticipate, escape, avoid

prick, mark made by pricking, dot, point, spot in centre of target, prickle, penis; to mark by making a dot, etc., pierce, fix, point, spur

pricket, buck in its second year

prick-song, music sung from notes

pride, magnificence, splendid adornment, highest state, mettle, sexual desire

prig, thief

prime, first, chief, sexually excited; springtime

primogenitive, first-born's right to inherit

principal, superior, abettor, principal rafter

princox, pert youth

Priscian, Roman grammarian

prithee, please

private, private person

privates, sexual organs

prize, contest; to value, esteem

prizer, prize-fighter, wrestler

probal, to, able to bear the probe or examination of

probation, trial, proof

proceeder, one proceeding to a university degree

procurator, proxy

prodigious, ominous, portentous, monstrous, abnormal

proditor, traitor

proface, 'may it do you good', formula of welcome before a meal

profited, proficient

progeny, lineage, race

project, notion, idea; set forth, exhibit

projection, plan

prolixious, prolonged

prolong, postpone

Prometheus, stole fire from heaven and was chained to Mount Caucasus

prone, ready, eager

proof, test, trial, experience, issue, result

propend, incline

proper, (one's) own, private, peculiar, excellent, handsome

property, identity, particular quality, take possession of, endow with qualities, make a tool of

proportion, portion, division, relative size, proportioning, rhythm

propose, put forward, set before one's mind, suppose, converse

propriety, identity, proper state

propugnation, defence

prorogue, prolong, postpone

prosecution, pursuit

Proserpina, daughter of Ceres, carried away by Pluto to become queen of hell

prosperous, favourable

Proteus, a sea-god, able to assume different shapes

protractive, consisting in delay

proud, elated, giving cause for pride, lofty, splendid, spirited, swollen, overluxuriant, sexually excited

prove, try, test, find by experience, experience

publish, make known, proclaim, denounce

pucelle, virgin, maid, slut

puck, pixy, mischievous spirit

pudding, sausage, stuffing

pudency, modesty

puissance, strength, armed force

puissant, strong, powerful

pumpion, pumpkin

punk, prostitute, harlot

punto reverso, back-handed thrust in fencing

purblind, quite blind, partially blind

purchase, booty, prize, annual rent from land; to strive, gain, acquire otherwise than by inheritance

purgation, clearing from accusation or suspicion

purlieu, tract of land bordering on a forest

purpose, proposal, conversation

pursuivant, junior attendant on heralds, herald, messenger

pursy, short-winded, fat

purveyor, steward going ahead to make provision

putter on, instigator

puttock, bird of prey, kite, buzzard

quail, prostitute; to fail, faint, overpower

quaint, skilful, clever, dainty, fine, beautiful, elaborate

qualification, calm and controlled condition

qualify, moderate, mitigate, appease, control, dilute

quality, accomplishment, rank, profession, party, side, manner, cause

quarry, heap of slaughtered game

quarter, part, watch, relations with and conduct towards another

quat, pimple

quatch, word of unknown meaning

quean, hussy, whore

queasy, hazardous, squeamish

quell, slaughter

quest, jury, inquest, search party

questant, seeker

questionable, inviting question

questrist, seeker

quick, flowing, fresh, impatient

quiddity, subtlety, equivocation

quietus, clearing of accounts

quintain, object or figure to practise tilting at

quirk, quibble, clever expression, peculiarity of behaviour, fit, start

quit, set free, rid, acquit, acquit oneself of, revenge, repay, requite

quittal, requital

quittance, discharge from debt, requital; requite

quoif, close-fitting cap

quondam, former

quote, give marginal references to, set down in writing, note, observe, regard

quoth, said

quotidian, (of an intermittent fever) returning every day

race, root (of ginger), lineage, breed, natural disposition

rack, driving cloud; to torture, extend, stretch, strain

rage, madness, angry disposition, sexual passion; to enrage

ramp, loose woman

rampallian, riotous woman

rampire, barricade

rank, growing too luxuriantly, swollen, grown too fat, rebellious, high, full, lustful, in heat, coarse, festering; closely

rankle, cause a festering wound

rankness, overflowing, insolence

rascal, inferior deer

rate, estimate, value, expense

ravel, become entangled, disentangle

raven, devour greedily

rayed, bespattered, fouled

read, teach, discover the meaning of, expound a riddle

re-answer, compensate for

reason, speech, remark; to talk, discuss, explain

reasonable, needing the use of reason

reave, deprive, take away

rebate, make dull, blunt

rebato, stiff collar

receipt, what is received, receptacle, receiving, capacity, recipe

receiving, understanding, reception

recheat, notes sounded on a horn to call hounds together in stag-hunting

reck, to care (for); mind

reclaim, tame, subdue

recognizance, bond, token

recomfort, console

record, witness, memory; to witness, sing

recordation, memorial, impression on the memory

recourse, access, admission, flowing

recover, reconcile, reach, rescue

recovery, process by which entailed estate was transferred from one party to another

rector, ruler, head

rectorship, rule

recure, restore, heal

reduce, bring, bring back

reechy, smoky, dirty, stinking

reek, smoke, steam

refel, refute

reflect, shine

regiment, authority, rule

region, upper air, air

regreet, greeting, contract

reguerdon, reward

rehearsal, account

rehearse, describe, tell

reins, kidneys

rejoindure, reunion

rejourn, adjourn

relative, able to be related and believed

religion, strict fidelity, religious duty

religious, exact, conscientious, strict

remember, mention, commemorate, remind

remit, pardon, give up

remonstrance, demonstration

remorse, pity, tenderness, moderation, qualification, mitigation

remorseful, compassionate

remotion, departing

removed, remote, secluded, separated by time or space

removedness, absence

remover, one who changes

render, surrender, rendering of an account, statement; to give back, represent, describe as being, declare, state, surrender

rendezvous, refuge, last resort

renege, deny, renounce

repair, restoring, coming; go, come, return

repairing, able to renew the attack

repasture, food

repeal, recall from exile; recall as from banishment, call back into favour

repetition, recital, mention

repine, vexation

replenished, perfect

replication, reply, echo

reprisal, prize

reprobance, damnation, rejection by God

reprobate, depraved

reproof, disgrace, disproof, refutation

reprove, disprove, refute

repugn, oppose

repugnancy, resistance

repugnant, refractory

rescue, freeing from legal custody by force

resemblance, appearance, likelihood

resist, affect with distaste

resolve, dissolve, answer (a question), solve (a problem), convince, inform

resolvedly, answering all questions

respect, relationship, discrimination, consideration, esteem; to regard, care for, esteem

respective, careful, worthy of being cared for, discriminating

respectively, respectfully

respite, delay, date to which something is postponed, limit

responsive, suited

rest, place to rest, restored strength, resolution, stakes kept in reserve

restrain, draw tight, withhold

resty, restive, sluggish

retention, detention, reserve, power to hold or retain

retentive, confining, restraining

retire, return

retort, to reflect (heat), reject (an appeal)

retreat, recall of pursuing force

retrograde, contrary, seeming to move in a backward course

reverb, resound

revolt, revulsion, change; rebel

revolution, alteration, change produced by time

revolve, consider

rhapsody, confused medley

rheum, mucus from nose or throat, cold in the head, rheumatism

riggish, wanton

rigol, ring, circle

rim, belly, membrane lining the abdomen

ring-carrier, go-between

ringlet, little circle

riot, loose living, debauchery

rivage, shore

rival, partner

rive, split

rivelled, wrinkled

road, riding, period of riding, stage (of journey), roadstead, highway

robustious, boisterous

roguing, roaming

roguish, vagrant

roisting, blustering, bullying

rondure, circle

ropery, knavery

Roscius, famous Roman actor

rote, fix by memory

round, plain, plain-spoken, severe; round dance, roundabout way, rung of a ladder; surround, become round

roundel, round dance

rouse, full draught of liquor, drinking bout

royal, gold coin of the value of ten shillings (fifty pence)

royalty, prerogative enjoyed, or granted, by the sovereign

roynish, scurvy

rub, in bowls an obstacle hindering or turning aside the bowl, obstacle, hindrance, roughness, unevenness; to turn aside, hinder

rubious, ruby-red

ruddock, robin

rude, ignorant, barbarous, violent, rough

rudeness, violence, roughness

rudesby, rough unmannerly brute

ruffle, bustle; swagger, bear oneself proudly, bluster, be turbulent

rugged, shaggy, frowning

rug-headed, having shaggy hair

ruinous, brought to ruin

rumour, fame, tumult, uproar

runagate, deserter, vagabond

runnion, wretch (a term of abuse)

russet, homely, simple

sable, black

sack, white wine

sackbut, trumpet resembling a trombone

sad, steadfast, grave, serious, dismal

sadly, gravely, seriously

sadness, seriousness

safe, make safe

safety, custody, safeguard

sain, said

salamander, lizard-like animal supposed to live in fire

sale-work, ready-made goods not of the highest quality

sallet, light helmet, something mixed or savoury

salt, lecherous

salute, touch, affect

sample, example

sanctimony, holiness, sanctity

sanctuarize, give sanctuary to

sand-blind, half-blind

sanguine, red

sans, without

sapient, wise

sarcenet, fine soft silk material

sauce, over-charge, rebuke

saucy, insolent, presumptuous, wanton

savagery, wild growth

savour, smell, perfume, style, character

saw, saying, maxim, proverb

say, finely woven cloth, taste, saying

scab, rascal, scurvy fellow

scald, scabby, mean

scale, weigh

scandalize, disgrace

scantling, specimen, sample

scantly, slightingly

scape, escapade, transgression; escape
scarf, officer's sash, sling, streamer; blindfold, deck with streamers
scathe, harm; to injure
schedule, document
school, university, instruction, learning; reprimand, discipline
science, knowledge
scion, shoot, slip for grafting
sconce, head, small fort or earthwork
scope, object, aim, purpose, theme, liberty
score, notch cut in stock or tally in keeping accounts, account; to notch
scorn, taunt, insult, object of contempt
scotch, cut, gash
scour, hasten
scrimer, fencer
scrip, small bag, piece of paper with writing on
scrippage, contents of scrip
scripture, writing
scrubbed, stunted
scruple, tiny part, doubt, difficulty
scurril, coarsely abusive
scut, deer's tail
scutcheon, shield with coat of arms; tablet showing armorial bearings of a dead man
seam, fat, grease
sectary, dissenter, one who pursues a particular study
secure, free from care, confident, unsuspicious; make confident or overconfident
securely, confidently, without suspicion
security, confidence, overconfidence
seed, mature, run to seed
seedness, sowing
seeing, appearance
seel, make blind, close (a person's eyes)
seely, foolish, innocent, harmless
seen, skilled
seld, seldom
self, one's own, same
semblable, similar, like, equal
semblative, like, resembling
Seneca, Roman tragic dramatist
sennight, week
sense, physical feeling, sensuality, sexual desire, mental apprehension, mind, opinion
senseless, without feeling or perception, free from sensual sin
sensible, perceptible, tangible, substantial, having sensation, sensitive, endowed with feeling
sensibly, having sensation, feelingly
sentence, sententious saying, maxim
septentrion, north
sequel, series
sequent, succeeding, following
sequester, separation; to separate
sequestration, separation, seclusion
sere, dry, withered
serpigo, a skin disease
servanted, subject
service, what is placed on the table for a meal
several, distinct, different, individual, respective, various

severally, separately, at different entrances or exits
sewer, attendant in charge of service at a meal
shadow, shade; to hide, shelter
shame, to be ashamed
shard, piece of broken pottery, patch of cow-dung
shark, gather hastily together
shearman, one who shears woollen cloth
sheaved, made of straw
sheep-biter, sneaking rascal
sheep-biting, sneaking
shent, blamed, rebuked, reproved
shift, expedient, resource, trick; *for (a) shift,* to serve a turn; *make (a) shift,* contrive, manage
ship-tire, kind of head-dress
shive, slice
shoal, shallow, sand-bar
shock, to meet with force
shog, go, shift
shotten, that has spawned, lean
shoulder-shotten, having a dislocated shoulder
shove-groat, shovel-board
shrewd, wicked, mischievous, bad-tempered, dangerous, evil, difficult
shrewdly, sharply, grievously, intensely, very much
shrieve, sheriff
shrift, confession and absolution, penance
shrill-gorged, shrill-throated
shrive, to hear confession and absolve
shroud, protection, sailropes; shelter, hide
shuffle, use trickery, smuggle, shift
siege, seat, rank, turd
sight, visor
sightless, unseen, unsightly
simple, medicinal herb, single ingredient in a compound
simpleness, innocence, simplicity, foolishness
simplicity, ignorance, silliness
simular, pretended, plausible; counterfeiter
sinfully, with sins unatoned for
single, slight, trivial, sincere, simple
singularity, eccentricity, own person
sinister, left (hand), unfavourable, unjust
sink, cause to fall, ruin; sewer, drain
Sinon, a Greek who by guile persuaded the Trojans to take the Grecians' wooden horse into Troy
sirrah, form of address used mainly to inferiors
sith, sithence, since
size, allowance
skill, judgement, reason, ability; to make a difference, matter
skilless, ignorant
skimble-skamble, confused, rubbishy
skipper, flighty youth
skirr, fly, scour
slab, half-solid
slander, ill-repute, disgrace, discredit; bring into disgrace, reproach
slanderous, shameful, disgraceful
slave, enslave, make subservient to oneself
sleave, floss-silk, silk untwisted into fine threads
sleeve-hand, cuff

sleided, (of silk) floss, untwisted into fine threads
sliding, slip
slipper, shifty
slippery, unstable, fickle
slipshod, in slippers
slobbery, sloppy, slovenly
slops, wide breeches
slovenly, nasty, disgusting
slubber, sully, hurry over
smatch, taste
smatter, chatter
smock, woman's undergarment, woman
smooth, flatter, gloss over
smother, suffocating smoke
smug, trim, spruce
sneap, snub, pinch with cold
snuff, resentment
sob, opportunity for a horse to recover his wind, respite
sod, steeped, boiled
soiled, fed with fresh-cut green fodder
soilure, sullying, defilement
sole, unique, mere, alone
solely, alone, entirely
solemnity, ceremony, festivity
solicit, urging, entreaty; move, stir, bring something about
sometime, at some time, sometimes, once, formerly
sonance, sounding, signal
sonties, saints
sooth, truth, flattery
soothe, humour, flatter
soother, flatterer
sop, bread or wafer dipped in wine, etc
sophister, one using false arguments
sore, buck, deer, in its fourth year
sorel, buck, deer, in its third year
sort, lot, rank, company, group, way, state; allot, ordain, come about, turn out, be suitable, correspond, adapt, fit, classify, choose, contrive, go in company
sortance, agreement, suitableness
sound, utter, proclaim, keep sound
souse, swoop on, pickle
span-counter, game in which counters are thrown to lie within a hand's span
spavin, disease of horses consisting of swelling of joints, producing lameness
specialty, special characteristic, possession, special contract under seal
spectacles, organs of sight
speculation, watcher, power of seeing, sight, looking on
speculative, seeing
speed, fortune, outcome, protection, assistance; to fare (well or ill), turn out, be successful, assist, favour
speeding, successful, fruitful; lot, outcome, success
spend, consume, exhaust
sphere, orbit of a planet, one of the concentric globes supposed to revolve round the earth with a harmonious sound
spherical, planetary
spial, spy
spigot, peg in faucet of a barrel
spill, destroy
spilth, spilling
spin, spurt

spinner, spider
spinster, spinner
spital, hospital
spleen, bodily organ regarded as the seat of emotions
spoil, plundering, prey, ruin; plunder, seize, destroy
spot, stain, disgrace, embroidered pattern
spring, fountain, source, shoot of a plant
springe, snare for birds
springhalt, disease of horse characterized by twitching and lameness
spurn, kick, insult, blow; to kick, oppose scornfully
square, fair, just; carpenter's set-square, measure, rule; body of troops in square formation, square of material in bosom of a dress; to regulate, quarrel (among), be at variance
squarer, quarreller
squash, unripe peapod
squiny, look asquint
staff, shaft of lance, lance, stanza
stagger, hesitate, waver
staggers, giddiness
stain, tinge, to eclipse, dim, be obscured
stair-work, furtive love-making
stale, decoy, bait, prostitute, laughing-stock, urine (of horses)
stall, install, keep, dwell, bring (a hunted animal) to a stand
stamp, stamping tool, coin, medal, distinguishing mark, imprint; to impress, mark with an impression, give approval to
stanch, satisfy
stanchless, insatiable
stand, place where one stands in ambush or in hiding; confront, oppose, stand firm; *stand at a guard with,* be fully protected against; *stand on, upon,* insist on, persist in, depend on, rely on, concern, be the duty or interest of; *stand to,* have an erection, support, maintain, be firm in, persist in; *stand to it,* maintain a cause, take a stand
standard, standard-bearer
staniel, kestrel
stare, (of hair) stand on end
start, sudden invasion, sudden flight, impulse; to startle, rush
starting-hole, refuge, loop-hole
starve, die, die of cold, kill or benumb with cold
state, condition, condition of health or prosperity, rank, dignity, chair of state, throne, nobles, ruling body, government
station, way of standing, attitude
statist, statesman
statute, bond, mortgage
statute-cap, woollen cap ordered in 1571 to be worn on Sundays and holy days by all below a certain rank
stay, obstacle; detain, stand, stand firm, wait (for), attend on
stead, to be of use to, help
stell, to fix, portray
stern, rudder
stew, brothel, stewpan
stick, stab, be fastened or fixed, hesitate
stickler-like, like an umpire

stigmatic, deformed person
stigmatical, deformed
still, always, continually
stillitory, apparatus for distillation
stilly, softly
sting, sexual desire
stint, stop
stithy, forge
stoccado, thrust with a rapier
stock, block of wood, person without feeling, stocking, dowry; set in the stocks
stockfish, dried cod or other fish, beaten before cooking
stockish, blockish, unfeeling
stomach, appetite, inclination, temper, courage, pride, anger; resent
stomacher, ornamental front over which the bodice was laced
stone, mirror, thunderbolt, testicle; turn to stone
stone-bow, cross-bow used for shooting stones
stoop, (of a bird of prey) swoop
stop, hole in a wind-instrument, stopped to produce a difference in pitch, fingering of musical chords, fret of a lute; staunch, heal
store, breeding, increase; to populate
stout, bold, strong, proud
stoutness, stubborn pride
stover, fodder for cattle
strain, race, character, kind, class, tune; clasp, force, constrain, urge
strait, narrow, tight-fitting, strict, niggardly; narrow place, difficulty
strange, foreign, new, not knowing, unfriendly, cold, shy
strange-achieved, gained at a distance and for others
strange-disposed, of unusual character
strangely, coldly, without greeting, as a stranger, to an extraordinary degree, in an unusual way
strangeness, behaving as a stranger, aloofness, reserve
strappado, torture in which victim was hoisted up by his arms, which were tied behind his back, then let down halfway with a jerk
stratagem, deed of violence
straw, *wisp of straw,* mark of disgrace for a scolding woman
stray, body of stragglers; lead astray
strength, authority, legal power, body of troops
strewment, strewing of flowers
stricture, strictness
strike, to lower (sail), blast, destroy, tap (a cask)
strossers, trousers
stubborn, inflexible, stiff, rude, harsh, ruthless
stuff, semen
style, title
subduement, conquest
subjection, duty as, or of, a subject
submission, confession of error
subscribe, sign, write down, assent, acknowledge, admit, submit, yield up, answer
subscription, submission

substractor, slanderer
subtle, thin, fine, cunning, treacherous, tricky
subtlety, illusion
success, outcome, result, good or bad fortune, succession
successfully, likely to succeed
succession, following on, successors, success
successive, hereditary, descending by succession
successively, by inheritance
sufferance, suffering, damage, patient endurance
suffice, content, satisfy
sufficient, able, able to meet liabilities, solvent
suggest, tempt, prompt to evil, insinuate to
suggestion, prompting to evil, temptation
sumless, incalculable
summoner, officer who summoned offenders to an ecclesiastical court
sumpter, driver of pack-horse, pack-horse
superflux, superabundance, surplus
supernal, heavenly
superscript, superscription, address or direction on letter
superstitious, idolatrously devoted
supervise, perusal; look over
suppliance, pastime
supply, help, reinforcements
supposal, opinion
suppose, supposition, expectation; believe, imagine, guess
supposition, doubt
surcease, cessation; cease
sure, safe, beyond power of doing harm, reliable, united
surety, confidence of safety, certainty, stability, warrant
sur-reined, overridden
suspect, suspicion
suspire, breathe, draw breath
sutler, one who sells provisions to soldiers
swagger, rant, bluster, quarrel
swaggerer, blusterer, quarreller
swart, dark, swarthy
swasher, blustering ruffian
swashing, swaggering, slashing
sway, direction, control, sovereignty; to rule, move
swayed, curved in
swear, *swear out,* forswear
sweat, sweating sickness, sweating cure; take a sweating cure
sweet, scented; scent
sweeting, sweet variety of apple, term of endearment
swim, float
swinge, thrash
swinge-buckler, roisterer
sworder, cut-throat, gladiator
'Swounds, by God's wounds (a strong oath)
sympathize, to be similarly affected, agree (with), match

table, tablet for an inscription, writing-tablet, flat surface on which a picture is painted, quadrangular space between chief lines on palm of hand
table-book, notebook

tables, backgammon

tabor, small drum

tackled stair, rope ladder

tag, tag-rag, rabble

tailor, ? sex organ

take, strike, strike with disease or enchantment, catch, take effect, reckon, measure, write down, accept as true, catch fire, perceive, understand, esteem, take away, conclude; *take head*, deviate, run off its course; *take in*, capture; *take me with you*, speak so that I can understand you; *take it on*, assume authority; *take on*, rage, show great distress, pretend; *take out*, make a copy of; *take up* lift, enlist, arrest, buy on credit, rebuke, reprimand, oppose, encounter, make up (a quarrel)

taking, blasting; state of great excitement or alarm, malignant influence

tale, numbering one after another, talk, story, falsehood

talent, measure for a large sum of money

tall, long, lofty, goodly, fine, brave

tally, stick marked with notches for keeping accounts

'tame, broach (a cask)

tang, ring out

tardy, delay

targe, light shield

tarre, urge, incite

tarriance, delay, waiting

tarry, wait, await, remain, delay

task, tax, impose a task on, occupy, put a strain on, put to proof

tasking, challenge

tassel-gentle, tercel, male hawk

tawdry-lace, silk lace or ribbon for the neck

tax, accusation; blame, accuse, charge

taxation, claim, demand, slander

teem, conceive, bring forth, bear children, be fruitful

teen, affliction, grief, sorrow

tell, count

temper, disposition, temperament, mental balance, hardness and elasticity imparted to steel; to compound, mix, persuade

temperance, mildness of temperature, calmness, chastity

temperate, chaste, secular

temporary, secular

tempt, test, risk

tenant, vassal

tend, listen, watch over, attend on, wait (for)

tendance, attending to, service, people in attendance

tender, offer, thing offered, care; to exhibit, pay down, care for; sensitive, compassionate

tender-hafted, tender-hested, gently framed

tent, probe; to probe, cure (a wound), lodge

Tereus, see PHILOMEL

Termagant, violent character, supposedly god of the Mohammedans, in old miracle plays

termination, expression, term

termless, indescribable

tertian, fever returning every third day

tester, sixpenny piece

tetter, skin disease

text, capital letter

thane, Scottish title or rank, somewhat lower than earl

thankful, deserving thanks

theoric, theory

therefor, for that

Thetis, a sea-goddess, the sea

thews, bodily parts, strength

thick, rapid, dim

thills, shafts of a cart

thing, sexual organ

think, seem

thought, anxiety, sorrow

thrasonical, boastful

three-farthings, thin silver coin, having a profile of Queen Elizabeth with a rose behind the ear

three-nooked, three-cornered

threne, threnos, dirge

thrift, profit, gain, advantage

thriftless, profitless

thrum, thread left at end of a warp

thunder-stone, thunderbolt

tickle, unstable, precarious; please, provoke

tick-tack, game in which pegs were put into holes; fornication

tide, time, course

tidy, plump

tight, sound, able

tilt, thrust, fight, encounter

timeless, untimely, premature

timely, early, in due season

tinct, colour, elixir of the alchemists

tire, equipment, dress, head-dress; attire, prey (on), feed greedily

tis, this (dialectal)

tisick, consumptive cough

Titan, god of the sun, the sun

tithe, tenth; to take the tenth part

tithing, district

tittle, dot

to, in addition to, against, appropriate to, in comparison with, in respect of, as to

tod, 28 lb. weight of wool; to yield this amount of wool

tofore, previously

toge, Roman toga

toil, net, snare; to cause to work hard, weary with work

token, spot of infection, plague-spot

toll, exact toll or tribute

tool, weapon, penis

top, head, forelock, highest point; to surpass, copulate with

top-gallant, highest mast, summit

topless, supreme

tortive, twisted

toss, impale, toss on a pike

tottering, ragged

touch, touchstone, taint; sound, test, wound

touse, pull out of joint

trace, follow, pass (through)

tract, trace, track, course

trade, coming and going, path, habit, business

traded, practised

trade-fallen, out of work

traditional, bound by tradition

train, tail, troop, bait; draw, entice, lead astray

traject, ferry

trammel, bind with the corpse, entangle

transfix, remove

translate, change, transform

transpose, change

trash, check, hold in leash

traverse, march, move from side to side

treatise, tale, talk

treble-dated, living three times as long as man

trench, cut

trencher, wooden plate

trencher-friend, parasite

trenchering, plates

trencher-knight, hanger-on

tribunal, dais

trick, custom, way, knack, touch (of a disease); toy; to adorn, blazon

tricking, adornment

trill, trickle

triple, third

triple-turned, three times faithless

tristful, sorrowful

triumph, public festivity, tournament, trump card

triumphant, triumphal, celebrating a triumph

triumphantly, in celebration

Trojan, good fellow

troll, sing

troll-my-dames, troll-madams, game resembling bagatelle

trophy, token of victory, memorial, monument

tropically, figuratively

trot, bawd

troth, truth, faith, word of honour

trow, believe, think, know

truepenny, honest fellow

trull, prostitute, wench

truncheon, staff carried as a symbol of office

try, test; purify, refine, prove

tub, sweating-tub used in the treatment of venereal disease

tuck, rapier

tucket, signal, flourish on a trumpet

tun-dish, funnel

turtle, turtle-dove, symbol of chaste and faithful love

tushes, tusks

twire, twinkle

type, distinguishing sign, stamp

tyrannically, vehemently

tyranny, violence, outrage

tyrant, usurper

umbrage, shadow

unaccommodated, unprovided

unacquainted, unfamiliar

unadvised, rash, without consideration or knowledge

unagreeable, unsuited

unaneled, not having received extreme unction

unapproved, unconfirmed by proof

unaptness, disinclination

unattainted, without infection, unprejudiced

unattempted, untempted
unavoided, inevitable
unbarbed, unarmed
unbated, unabated, not blunted (with a button)
unbent, with bow unbent, unprepared, unfrowning
unbid, unexpected
unbitted, unbridled
unbolted, unsifted, coarse
unbookish, unskilled, inexperienced
unbreathed, unpractised
uncase, strip, lay bare
uncharge, acquit of guilt
uncharged, unattacked
unchary, carelessly
unchecked, not contradicted
unclasp, reveal
unclew, undo, ruin
uncomprehensive, unplumbable
unconfirmed, uninstructed, ignorant
uncovered, open, bare-headed
uncrossed, not crossed through because bill still unpaid
unction, salve, ointment
uncurrent, not current, not permisible
undercrest, wear as a device of honour
undergo, undertake, come under, support, carry, bear
underhand, unobtrusive
underskinker, under-tapster, assistant barman
undertake, take charge of, assume, have to do with, venture
undertaker, one who takes on himself another's quarrel, one who settles with
underwrite, subscribe, submit to
uneath, with difficulty, scarcely
unexperient, inexperienced
unexpressive, inexpressible
unfair, rob of beauty
unfashionable, badly formed
unfenced, defenceless
unfold, disclose, display, reveal, release from the fold
unfurnished, unprovided, unprepared
ungalled, uninjured
ungenitured, impotent
ungored, unwounded
unhandsome, unskilled, nasty
unhappily, unfavourably, evilly
unhappiness, evil nature
unhappy, ill-fated, wretched, mischievous
unhouseled, not having received the sacrament
union, pearl
unkind, unnatural
unluckily, with foreboding
unmanned, not trained, not broken in
unowed, having no owner
unpaved, without testicles, castrated
unpitied, unmerciful
unplausive, unapproving
unpregnant, unapt
unprevailing, unavailing
unprizable, without value, invaluable
unprized, not valued, beyond value
unproper, not belonging to one person, indecent
unprovide, make unprepared
unquestionable, not inviting conversation

unraked, not covered with fuel to keep it burning
unrecalling, past recall
unreclaimed, untamed
unrecuring, past cure
unrespective, heedless, held back by no consideration, undiscriminating
unrolled, struck off the register
unscanned, unconsidered
unseasoned, ill-timed, inexperienced
unseminared, without seed
unsifted, untried
unsorted, ill-chosen
unspeakable, indescribable, inexpressible
unspeaking, unable to speak
unsquared, inappropriate
unstanched, unquenchable, freely menstruating
unstate, deprive of rank and state
untainted, unaccused
untempering, unwinning
untented, unable to be treated, incurable
untoward, perverse, unruly
untowardly, unluckily
untraded, not customary
untrimmed, undressed
untrussing, undoing hose, undressing
unwarily, unexpectedly
unweighed, hasty, unconsidered
unwrung, not pinched or rubbed
up, in arms, in rebellion, in prison; *up and down,* completely, exactly
upon, because of, in consequence of
urchin, hedgehog, goblin
urinal, glass to hold urine
usance, interest on money
use, habit, custom, usual experience, advantage, profit, lending at interest, interest on something lent, need; to be accustomed, continue, make a practice of, deal with, treat, go often
usurp, take or hold what belongs to another, supplant, assume
utterance, utmost extremity
uttermost, latest

vail, gratuity, tip, setting (of the sun); lower, let fall, do homage
vain, foolish, silly, unreal
valanced, fringed with hair
validity, strength, value
value, estimate, be worth
valued, denoting the value
vantage, advantage, gain, superiority, vantage-ground, opportunity
varletry, rabble
vastidity, immensity
vaulty, arched, hollow
vaunt, beginning
vaunt-courier, herald, harbinger
vengeance, harm, injury
vent, emission, utterance, outlet for energy; let out, emit, utter, make known
ventage, aperture, finger-hole
ventricle, cavity of the brain
Venus, goddess of love and beauty; wife of Vulcan, the smith-god, but more often associated with her lover Mars
verge, compass, circle
vexation, agitation, torment, grief
via, away

vice, character in a morality play representing a vice, jester, buffoon, gripping tool; to screw
vicegerent, deputy, representative
vicious, blameworthy, blemished
vie, add one to another
villein, peasant, servant
vinewed'st, most mouldy
violent, to rage, storm
virginalling, fingering as on the virginals — a keyed musical instrument
virtue, courage, merit, accomplishment, power, efficacy, essence, essential characteristic
virtuous, powerful, beneficial
visitor, one who visits to offer spiritual comfort
voice, speech, words, common talk, rumour, report, expressed opinion, judgement, vote, approval, authority to be heard; to acclaim, vote
voiding lobby, anteroom
voluntary, volunteer
votaress, woman who has taken a vow
votarist, votary one who has taken a vow
vouch, assertion, testimony; affirm, guarantee, bear witness
Vulcan, the smith-god, whose wife, Venus, was unfaithful
vulgar, of the common people, commonly known, common, public, mean; common people, vernacular

waft, to convey by water, beckon, turn
waftage, passage by water
wafture, wave
wage, to wager, hazard, attempt, carry on war, pay
waist, girdle
wake, remain awake, be up late for revelry or on guard, wear out with lack of sleep, arouse
walk, tract of forest
wall-eyed, white-eyed, having glaring eyes
want, lack, miss
wanton, frolicsome, lawless, capricious, luxurious, luxuriant, lustful, unchaste; spoilt child, pampered darling, roguish, sportful, unruly or lustful creature
wappered, worn out
ward, guard, custody, prison-cell, defensive position in fencing; guard, protect
warden, kind of cooking pear
warp, distort, deviate
war-proof, war-tested, courage
warrant, guarantee, assure
warrantize, surety, authorization
warranty, sanction, authorization
warren, game enclosure
warrener, gamekeeper
wassail, drinking, revelling, feast
waste, spend, consume
watch, wakefulness, sleeplessness, watchfulness; be awake, keep from sleep, catch in the act
watchful, sleepless
water, lustre
water-gall, secondary rainbow
watering, drinking
water-standing, tearful
wave, waver

waxen, increase

weal, welfare, commonwealth

wear, fashion; carry, possess, be fashionable, weary

weather, storm

weed, garment, dress

week, *to be in by the*, be caught, ensnared, deeply in love

ween, expect, hope

weet, know

welkin, sky

well-liking, plump

well-respected, well-considered

well to live, prosperous

wharf, river bank

wheel, spinning wheel, tread-wheel on which a dog was harnessed to turn a roasting-spit

whelk, pimple

where, whereas

whiffler, officer who keeps the way clear for a procession

while, whiles, whilst, till

whipstock, whip-handle

whist, become silent

whiting-time, bleaching time

whitster, bleacher

whittle, small clasp-knife

wide, missing the mark, astray

widgeon, to cheat

wight, creature

wild, reckless, distracted, (of sea) open

wilderness, wildness of character, licentiousness

wildly, without cultivation, naturally

wildness, madness

will, sexual desire, sexual organ (male or female)

wimpled, hooded, blinkered

wince, kick

Winchester goose, sufferer from syphilis, prostitute

windgall, soft tumour on horse's leg

windlass, circuit made to intercept game, crafty device

wink, sleep, close one's eyes

wintered, used in winter

wipe, scar

wistly, intently, closely

wit, mental power, mind, sense, wisdom, imagination, one who has such qualities; know

withal, with this, with it, as well, at the same time, with

without, beyond

wittol, a man aware of and tolerating his wife's adultery

witty, wise, cunning

woman-tired, henpecked

wonder, admiration; admire, marvel

wondered, performing wonders

wondering, admiration

wood, mad

woodcock, dupe

woodman, hunter

woolward, wearing wool next to the skin

world, *to go to the*, marry; *a woman of the*, married woman

worm, serpent, snake

worn, exhausted, past

worship, dignity, honour, authority; to honour

wort, vegetable, unfermented beer

worthy, excellent, valuable, deserved, well-founded, fitting

wot, know

wrack, ruin, destruction

wreak, vengeance, revenge

wrest, tuning-key; take by force

wring, wrest, force, writhe, press painfully on

writ, document, writing, mandate, written command, scripture

writhled, wrinkled

wry, to swerve

Xantippe, scolding wife of the philosopher Socrates

yard, yard measure, penis

yare, ready, quick, moving lightly

yaw, sail out of course, lose direction

yellowness, jealousy

yellows, jaundice

yerk, thrust suddenly

younker, fine young man, novice, greenhorn

zany, comic performer awkwardly imitating a clown or mountebank